WITHDRAWN

ENCYCLOPEDIA OF THE AMERICAN LEFT

GARLAND REFERENCE LIBRARY OF THE SOCIAL SCIENCES 502

Contributing Editors

Jon Bloom, Robin D. G. Kelley, Carol Poore,
Franklin Rosemont, Fred Whitehead

Advisory Board

Blanche Wiesen Cook, Ron Grele,
Jacquelyn Dowd Hall, Jesse Lemisch,
Manning Marable, Ethelbert Miller,
Grace Paley, Richard Peña,
Franklin Rosemont, Nick Salvatore,
Susan Sherman, Meredith Tax,
Rudolph Vecoli, Alan Wald,
Daniel Walkowitz, Alden Whitman,
Howard Zinn

Graphics Advisor

Penelope Rosemont

WITHDRAWN

ENCYCLOPEDIA OF THE AMERICAN LEFT

EDITED BY

MARI JO BUHLE ▪ PAUL BUHLE ▪ DAN GEORGAKAS

GARLAND PUBLISHING, INC. ▪ NEW YORK & LONDON 1990

© 1990 Mari Jo Buhle, Paul Buhle, Dan Georgakas
All Rights Reserved

Library of Congress Cataloging-in-Publication Data

Encyclopedia of the American Left / edited by Mari Jo Buhle, Paul Buhle, Dan Georgakas
p. cm.—(Garland reference library of the social sciences; 502)
Includes bibliographical references.
ISBN 0-8240-4781-8
1. Socialism—United States—Dictionaries. 2. Communism—United States—Dictionaries. 3. New Left—United States—Dictionaries. 4. Socialism—Dictionaries. 5. Communism–Dictionaries 6. Right and left (Political science)—Dictionaries. I. Buhle, Mari Jo, 1943- . II. Buhle, Paul, 1944- . III. Georgakas, Dan. IV. Series: Garland Reference library of social sciences; v. 502.
HX86.E58 1990
335'.00973—dc20 90-30202 CIP

10 9 8 7 6 5 4 3
Book and cover design by
Renata Gomes

Printed on acid-free, 250-year-life paper.
Manufactured in the United States of America.

This work is dedicated to
Jenny and Jimmy Higgins.

Table of Contents

Acknowledgments

For assistance in a variety of ways, such as supplying graphics, suggesting contributors, responding to urgent requests for an entry, criticizing or rewriting drafts, acting as computer consultant, advising with promotions, and contributing entries which did not reach publication, we wish to thank: David Montgomery, Linda Gordon, Allen Hunter, Eric Perkins, Elliot Shore, Philip Altbach, Jay Kinney, Immanuel Wallerstein, Ethelbert Miller, Roger Horowitz, Enzo Traverso, Marvin Gettleman, Richard Ellington, Sue Benson, Rebecca Zurier, Dorothy Healey, Morris U. Schappes, Paul Le Blanc, Kate Monteiro, George Scialabba, Gil Green, Scott Molloy, Chuck Schwartz, Saul Wellman, Max Gordon, Herman Benson, Jack N. Porter, David Roediger, Robert G. Lee, Steve Brier, Barbara Saltz, Michael Smith, Stephanie Ogle, Norma Fain Pratt, Michael Honey, and the late H. L. Mitchell. For technical assistance we thank the staff of the Main Branch of the Brooklyn Public Library, and for help on illustrations we thank the Charles H. Kerr Publishing Company. Special thanks go to Kennie Lyman, who gave us superlative editorial support throughout the long and complex process of bringing this project to completion.

INTRODUCTION

This volume is the first comprehensive reference work on the history of the American Left. Defined as that segment of society which has sought fundamental changes in the economic, political and cultural systems, the subject does not include reformers who believe that change can be accommodated to existing capitalist structures, or who believe that an egalitarian society can be attained ultimately within national borders. By placing a strong emphasis upon radicals—anarchists, socialists, and communists—*The Encyclopedia of the American Left* has been able to delve into many topics otherwise little known, or frequently discussed without relation to their actual Left context.

Histories of the United States have, until the 1960s–70s, generally treated radical movements and radicals unfavorably (save perhaps as eccentric personalities). By contrasting the Left with more acceptable reform movements and reformers, standard treatments suggested an unpleasant fanaticism, or at least a lack of basic patriotism toward American institutions. Aside from a handful of valuable memoirs and a scattering of monographs, few serious accounts of radicals themselves could be found. Not surprisingly, serious gaps existed in basic reference materials relating to Left topics.

Our project would, therefore, have been impossible only a generation ago. Two contemporary intellectual developments changed the picture. Many activists with peak years of involvement before World War II turned to writing memoirs, often donating their personal papers to existing archives. The waning of McCarthyism and its threats of political intimidation encouraged individuals and organizational leaders to be more specific and candid about past events. Concurrently, many scholars who had come of age within the 1960s political movements embarked upon academic careers or began working as filmmakers, curators, archivists, or librarians. Many of these younger scholars selected radical movements of the past, including the controversial and many-sided history of the Communist Party, as their scholarly specialties.

The newer scholars merged, for the first time, techniques such as oral history with the fresh insights available from feminist, ethnic, and racial studies and popular culture analyses. Combined in turn with traditional scholarly approaches, these efforts produced a substantial recovery of a hitherto lost history, in definitive biographies, monographs and popular works of various kinds. The present volume draws heavily upon this current. But it also grows out of the neglected traditions of memoirs and in-house histories of American Left personalities and institutions, written in many languages from the late nineteenth century onward. The volume builds upon and from all the layers of the Left's collective autobiography.

Each entry has been written specifically for this encyclopedia, and most entries are based upon primary sources. References have been designed less for definitive documentation—often inaccessible to most readers in archival obscurity, in oral history accounts, or in non-English languages—than for general research on the subject. The "See also" at the end of each entry leads to discussion of that topic in another context or to an allied subject.

Although we have included numerous biographies, ours is not, properly speaking, a biographical dictionary. The overwhelming majority of important individuals have been placed under other than personal headings, in the larger political context of their significance. Those with separate biographical entries have not been deemed "more important," but are rather treated most effectively in this way to discuss a particular historical event, institution, or movement. Such biographical entries do not dwell on personal details (such as family life) unless related directly to political behavior, a limitation dictated by equity and by space.

Mass movements and organizations wider than the Left, but with substantial Left participation, have been discussed via their particular Left involvements. Unions, civil rights movements, women's issues, environmental currents, and artistic trends—excepting in each case those clearly established and led by the Left—fall under this heading. Similarly, movements and individuals attaining their greatest significance before 1870 have been dealt with only in passing, both because of space limitations and to delineate clearly the modern Left (as opposed to the predominantly religious communitarianism of earlier times).

Ethnic and racial groups have been dealt with most extensively here. Some, very small or only slightly involved in radical activities, have been covered in a single entry under their name. Others, central in a continuing way to radicalism, have been treated in so many places that a main entry has become redundant. In most cases, a main entry is supplemented by many separate references to institutions and individuals. Like the discussion of social and cultural movements, much ethnic or racial material has been drawn from personal interviews, archival collections, and non-English language sources.

We have taken special care with the difficult questions posed by often-confusing Left terminology. Some frequently used terms and concepts are discussed in their own separate entries, or in the glossary (along with acronyms, expressions, and other linguistic shortcuts common to Left literature). We have used upper case to illustrate political distinctions. Thus "Socialism" refers to the Socialist Party of Eugene Debs and his successors; "Communism" refers to the modern Communist Party or its immediate forerunners. In lower case, "socialism" and "communism" refer to general principles rather than organizational names. Readers might find a Communist who supports socialist ends, or a Christian socialist who supports communist principles. In instances where there is some ambiguity involved in whether or not to capitalize, we have not. When a foreign language publication or organizational name is translated, unless the English name was also used, only the first word and proper nouns have been capitalized.

We have adopted Left practices in dealing with racial and sexual identifications. We have preferred African American to indicate Americans of African heritage, but "black," "Afro-American," "Negro," and "person of color" will also be found. The particular term used generally relates to the political era under discussion. The term "gay" is used with two meanings. The general movement for the rights of male and female homosexuals is often referred to as the gay rights movement and reflects what has been the terminology of the 1970s and most of the 1980s. In some contexts there is use of formulations such as "gay and lesbian rights," in which case "gay" refers exclusively to male homosexuals.

Approximately one hundred graphics have been included in this volume, embodying the dominant styles of various Left eras and organizations and providing examples of work by many of the outstanding artists of the Left. For technical reasons, as well as cost, "fine art" and portrait photographs have been minimized in favor of the line drawing.

We have scrupulously avoided favoritism toward any sections of the Left, providing factual and respectful accounts of groups which have sometimes condemned each other as ferociously as they condemned capitalism. Our philosophical view is that although the Left has had its share of fools and scoundrels, most of its adherents have been motivated by lofty ideals. To paraphrase Ralph Chaplin, one of the American Left's most popular poets, we have sought to give a faithful account of those who saw the world's great anguish and dared to act against the causes of the suffering.

MARI JO BUHLE
PAUL BUHLE
DAN GEORGAKAS

Often-Cited Acronyms, Terms, Movements and People

A number of acronyms, terms, movements and people are referred to throughout the body of the *Encyclopedia of the American Left* without always being fully defined. Some have an individual entry, but a great many do not, particularly those coming from a European context. The definitions that follow briefly identify those items that appear with some frequency.

ACLU—American Civil Liberties Union. Founded in 1920. Provides legal aid to citizens whose fundamental constitutional rights are endangered. See: Flynn, E. G.; McCarthyism.

AFL—American Federation of Labor. First organized in 1881 as the Federation of Organized Trades and Labor Unions of the United States and Canada. Became the AFL in 1886. Consistently the most conservative of labor federations, although member unions could be quite radical at given times and locations. Organized on the craft principle and generally dedicated to the philosophy of business unionism.

Alternative Culture—A term popular in the 1960s and 1970s. Indicates cultural trends dissenting from mainstream American culture. Applied to activities as diverse as small press publishing, avant garde filmmaking, use of "recreational" drugs, political dissent, and non-traditional sexual involvements. Often used interchangeably with *counter culture*, but a distinction that could be made is that those who preferred the term *alternative culture* often thought of it as "dropping out from" rather than challenging dominant culture. See: Hoffman, Abbie; New Left; Underground Comix; Underground Press; Yippies.

Althusser, Louis—Algerian-born French theorist (b. 1918) best known for his claims to a rigorously scientific Marxist method free of all Hegelian traces. "Theoretical Practice," the prescribed mode of intellectual activity, greatly popularized structuralism and the renewed theoretical emphasis upon language and ideology. It led indirectly to the heavily psychoanalytic post-structuralist modes popular among avant-garde literary critics of the 1980s. See: Literary Criticism.

Blanquist—A supporter of the views of Louis August Blanqui (1805–1881), the French revolutionary who pioneered the doctrine that workers need a dedicated minority to lead them to revolutionary action and that a workers' revolution would entail a temporary dictatorship to carry out a genuine transformation of society.

Bonus March—The march on Washington, D.C., in 1932 by 15,000 WW I veterans who demanded immediate payment of a bonus due them in 1945. Their request was denied and they were dispersed by a federal force commanded by Gen. Douglas MacArthur.

Cavalry, infantry, tanks, and tear gas were used against the marchers. See: Unemployed Movements, 1930s.

Bukharin, Nicolai Ivanovich—Bolshevik leader (1888–1938) identified with the "Right" view of adaptation to capitalist stability, Bukharin became the inspirer of a worldwide tendency that previewed Popular Front perspectives and struggled (until Bukharin's condemnation at the Moscow Trials) for a more democratic, non-sectarian version of them. See: Lovestoneites, Moscow Trials.

CIO—Congress of Industrial Organizations. Began in 1935 as the Committee for Industrial Organization within the AFL. Suspended from the AFL in 1936. Became an independent national union in 1938. Merged with AFL in 1955 to form the AFL-CIO. Based on principles of industrial unionism. During its first decade enlisted ideological radicals, including Communists, as organizers.

CLP—Communist Labor Party. May refer to the CLP of WW I era. If so, see: Communist Party. May refer to the CLP of 1950s origin. If so, see: Anti-revisionism (Maoism), League of Revolutionary Black Workers.

Comintern—Third International or Communist International. See: Third International.

CORE—Congress of Racial Equality. Founded in 1942 to advance the cause of racial integration and civil rights for African Americans. See: Civil Rights Movement, Pacifism.

Counter Culture—A term originating in the 1960s to indicate dissenting cultural movements that consciously posed themselves as adversaries of mainstream or dominant American culture. Often used interchangeably with *alternative culture*. See: Hoffman, Abbie; New Left; Underground Comix; Underground Press; Yippies.

CP—Communist Party. Also CPUSA. For earlier variations in name and history, see: Communist Party.

Dies Committee—Nickname for the first (1938) House Un-American Activities Committee (HUAC), chaired by Martin Dies (1901–1972). Under Dies, HUAC first investigated the German-American Bund, which was considered pro-Nazi. HUAC then investigated Communists in the Hollywood film industry, the Federal Theater of the Work Progress Administration, and various labor unions. See: House Un-American Activities Committee.

Fabian Socialism—Refers to the views originating in the Fabian Society of Great Britain, established in 1884. Fabians believed that socialism could be achieved through mass education and a series of reforms achieved through capture of Parliament. Fabian ideas became the basis of the British Labour Party. Among prominent Fabians were George Bernard Shaw and H. G. Wells. American women reformers and other intellectuals were influenced by Fabianism during the 1890s. See: British Americans; Willard, Frances.

Ferrer or Modern Schools—Schools based on the ideas of Spanish anarchist Francisco y Guardia Ferrer (1869–1909). Ferrer devised a curriculum based totally on science and rationality and excluding religion, racism, militarism, and the spirit of revenge. He believed individuals educated in such manner would build an anarchist society. His first school was in Barcelona. At least one hundred other schools were based on that model, including some in the United States, most notably at the Stelton Colony in New Jersey. Ferrer's manuals were often used by his ideological adversaries, including the Roman Catholic Church. See: Anarchism, Cuban Americans.

Forty-Eighters—Refers to European immigrants who left their native lands after the democratic revolutions of 1848 failed. Most commonly indicates German immigrants. In other contexts might indicate those who went to California in the Gold Rush of 1848. See: German Americans.

Fourierism—The theories advanced by Charles Fourier (1772–1837), a French revolutionary who believed an ideal society could be centered on small cooperative agricultural and industrial units that he called phalanxes. Fourierist communities were set up in the 1840s at Red Bank, New Jersey, and Brook Farm, Massachusetts, as part of the various American experiments with utopian socialism. See: Utopianism.

Frankfurt School—The style of theory shaped within or influenced by the major theorists around the Institute of Social Research, centered in Frankfurt, Germany, from 1923–1933, relocated to the U.S. during the Nazi era, and returned to Germany in the early 1950s. Max Horkheimer, Herbert Marcuse, Theodor Adorno, Walter Benjamin, and others—nearly all German Jews from comfortable backgrounds—elucidated a cultural theory seeking to explain, by way of philosophy, aesthetics, and related fields, the non-revolutionary quality of the contemporary proletariat and the increasingly crushing hegemony of mass culture. See: Marcuse, Herbert; Philosophy.

Freedom of Information Act—Passed in 1966. Requires that records of U.S. government agencies be available to the public. Numerous restrictions apply. These restrictions were increased by an executive order of 1982 signed by President Ronald Reagan. See: FBI, New Left.

Gramsci, Antonio—A founder of the Italian Communist Party, Gramsci (1891–1937) deepened Marxist theory with his writing on workers' culture and the mechanisms of cultural domination. Widely read by post-1960s American radicals.

George, Henry—A reformer (1839–1897) whose advocacy of the "Single-Tax" (on land) and popularity among workers, Irish workers in particular, made him a central character in American radicalism for a very brief period. Candidate for the New York Mayorality in 1886, he directed a purge of the Left from his own United Labor Party. His influence soon faded. See: Irish Americans, Socialist Labor Party.

Hegel, George Wilhelm Friedrich—Formulator of historical dialectics, the philosophical inspirer of Marx and of countless Marxist intellectuals from Antonio Labriola and Lenin to Georg Lukacs and C. L. R. James. In his lifetime (1770–1831) considered the foremost philosopher of Europe, Hegel explained history as "progress in the consciousness of freedom," albeit (from a Marxist standpoint) conceived of in an idealistic fashion. The Young Hegelians, including Marx himself, radicalized Hegel's doctrines against the philosopher's own ultimately conservative conclusions. See: Dunayevskaya, Raya; James, C. L. R.; Philosophy.

HUAC—House Un-American Activities Committee. See: House Un-American Activities Committee.

ILGWU—International Ladies Garment Workers Union. See: International Ladies Garment Workers Union.

IWO—International Workers Order. See: International Workers Order.

IWW—Industrial Workers of the World. Members may be referred to as wobblies, IWWs, wobs. See: Industrial Workers of the World.

Jewish Bund—The primary organization of Jewish socialism in Eastern Europe from its turn-of-the-century founding until the Bolshevik Revolution, the Bund became a training school for mostly Yiddish-speaking Jewish labor and political radicals in the diaspora as well. Following the Russian Revolution, it represented an anti-communist but also an anti-zionist socialism, a position retained among its remaining fragments in the Socialist International of the 1970s–80s. See: Yiddish Left.

Kropotkin, Prince Peter—Russian anarchist and world philosopher whose life (1842–1921) was widely admired as one of personal sacrifice for the masses. His arguments for cooperation rather than competition as the basis of civilization had a great appeal, even among early Marxists. His *Mutual Aid* (1902) presented a scientifically based argument that cooperation was the chief factor in the evolution and preservation of a species. Notwithstanding his support of WW I, his reputation remained high in anarchist circles, especially among American Jewish anarchists. See: Anarchism, *Freie Arbeter Shtimme*.

Lassalle, Ferdinand—A much-revered founder of German Social Democracy, Lassalle (1825–1864) was more personally charismatic than Marx and, until his dramatic death in a duel, far more popular. His stress upon electoral politics and reform through the broadening of state influence exerted considerable influence in Germany and the U.S. See: Socialist Labor Party.

Lenin, V. I.—Pen name for Vladimir Ilich Ulyanov (1870–1924), foremost leader of the Bolsheviks, strategist of the 1917 October Revolution, and head of the post-revolutionary Russian state. Best known among his American followers for his emphasis on the vanguard party concept, Lenin's reputation shifted thereafter to formulator of Third World revolutions for "self-determination" and as leader of a largely peasant but revolutionary society. See: Vanguard Party.

Lukacs, Georg—For decades considered Marxism's most sophisticated dialectician and literary scholar, Lukacs shaped much of "Western Marxism," the theoretical edifice of an intelligentsia in non-revolutionary society. In a long life (1885–1971) of literary activity in his native Hungary and in Germany, Russia, and elsewhere, he reached the apex of his importance with *History and Class Consciousness* (1923), which sought to restore the Hegelian legacy present in Marx's own early writings to modern Marxist materialism. See: Literary Criticism.

Mao Tse-Tung—Leader of the Chinese Revolution and the post-revolutionary Chinese state, he emerged in the last decades of his life as the chief symbol of Third World revolution. Like Stalin, he was a cult figure in his lifetime (1893–1976). Best remembered for his emphasis upon the peasantry in the world-revolutionary process and his dramatic but unsuccessful effort to overcome post-revolutionary bureaucracy through the Cultural Revolution (1966–67). See: Anti-Revision (Maoism).

Marxist-Leninism—The interpretation of Marxist thought put forward by Lenin. Emphasizes the need for a vanguard party composed of professional revolutionaries, displacing the more eclectic combination of radical ideas with a single, unified doctrine. Under Stalin, the USSR made Marxist-Leninism into a state doctrine. See: Communist Party, Vanguard Party.

McCarran-Walter Act—The Internal Security Act passed in 1950 over the veto of President Harry S Truman. Its chief sponsor was Patrick A. McCarran. Aimed primarily at Communists, it sanctioned the jailing, fining, deporting, preventive detention, and political ostracism of "subversives." Other sections barred foreign communists from entering the United States if they did not agree to major restrictions on their movements, activities, and public speech. Much of the Act has been judged unconstitutional by the Supreme Court. Its main use was in the 1950s, but it remains in effect. See: American Committee for Protection of Foreign Born, McCarthyism.

NAACP—National Association for the Advancement of Colored People. Founded in 1905 by a group headed by W. E. B. DuBois and including a number of socialists. Relatively radical in its early years, it eventually came to focus its efforts on judicial and legislative actions. See: Civil Rights Movement; DuBois, W. E. B.

NLRB—National Labor Relations Board. An independent federal agency that administers the National Labor Relations Act (Wagner Act) of 1935 and its successors. Major responsibilities include supervising recognition elections at the workplace and ruling on the fairness of labor practices. Once a bastion of the New Deal reformers who favored unions, during the Reagan era organized labor charged it was decidedly promanagement. See: Taft-Hartley Loyalty Oath.

Nye Committee—Refers to either of the two major senate committees headed by Gerald Prentice Nye (1892–1971), a Progressive Republican from North Dakota. His 1927 committee investigated the Teapot Dome Scandal and his 1934–37 committee investigated the role of American businessmen and bankers in WW I. See: American League Against War and Fascism, Peace Movements.

Old Left—A term used in the 1960s and thereafter to contrast with the "New Left," it connoted essentially the Marxist movements involved in the sectarian quarrels and state-socialist perspective of Communists, Socialists, Trotskyists of the 1920s–50s. Younger people who joined such groups and some Maoist and Marxist-Leninist groups of like nature were considered the dogmatic "Old Left" still on the scene. See: Communist Party, New Left.

Owenism—The views of Robert Owen (1771–1855), a British utopian socialist who used his personal fortune to create cooperative communities in England and the United States. His son, Robert Dale Owen (1801–1877), assisted in establishing the New Harmony community in Indiana (1826–27). Later he established a settlement for freed slaves, served in Congress, helped found the Smithsonian Institution, and was a foreign diplomat. After 1859 he was increasingly involved with spiritualism. See: Spiritualism, Utopianism.

Palmer Raids—Named after A. Mitchell Palmer (1872–1936), the attorney general in the administration of President Woodrow Wilson. At the conclusion of WW I, Palmer administered mass arrests of alleged subversives, mostly of foreign birth. Thousands were rounded up and hundreds were deported. See: Federal Bureau of Investigation, Red Scare.

Paris Commune—The two-month control of Paris by its inhabitants in 1871 that inspired Karl Marx's *Civil War in France* (1895) and proved crucial for Lenin's *State and Revolution* (1917). Coming amid the defeat of France in the Franco-Prussian conflict, the Commune displaced exhausted bourgeois rule with a government largely of workers, some of them anarchists and socialists. The Commune became central to the mythology and martyrology of revolutionaries worldwide, as well as an incitement to preventative action by ruling groups. See: International Workingmen's Association, Railroad Strike of 1877.

Popular Front—The term given to the political line advanced at the Seventh Congress of the Communist International in 1935. Advocating a unity of all classes in the fight against fascism, it reversed the previous emphasis on class struggle and opened the way for Communist cooperation with liberals, particularly in anti-fascist ethnic and national policies. See: Anti-Fascism, Communist Party, *Daily Worker*.

Port Huron Statement—An influential 1962 declaration of principles by the Students for a Democratic Society. See: New Left, Participatory Democracy, Students for a Democratic Society.

Proudhon, Pierre Joseph—A founding intellectual of the anarchist movement and a formulator of anarcho-syndicalism, the French philosopher (1809–65) stressed the "mutualism" of voluntary, collective labor. See: Anarchism, Anarcho-Syndicalism, International Workingmen's Association.

SCEF—Southern Conference Educational Fund. See: Civil Rights Movement, Southern Conference Educational Fund.

SCLC—Southern Christian Leadership Conference. Organized in January 1957 to pursue the cause of civil rights for African Americans. See: Civil Rights Movement.

Single Tax Movement—A nineteenth century movement based on a plan for the abolition of all forms of taxation except land taxes as advanced in Henry George's *Progress and Poverty* (1880).

SLP—Socialist Labor Party. Also referred to in some areas as *Sozialistiche Arbeiter Partei*. See: DeLeon, Daniel; German Americans; Socialist Labor Party.

Smith Act—Anti-sedition legislation (54 St. 670) passed by Congress in 1940. Its major thrust was to make a crime of advocacy of the forcible or violent overthrow of the government, a limitation on freedom of speech that was upheld by the Supreme Court. Its conspiracy clauses have also been upheld. See: McCarthyism; Smith Act Trial, 1943.

SNCC—Student Nonviolent Coordinating Committee. Acronym pronounced "snick." See: Civil Rights Movement, Student Nonviolent Coordinating Committee.

SP—Socialist Party. See: Debs, Eugene; Socialist Party.

Stalin, Joseph—Pen name for Iosif Vissarionovich Dzhugashvili (1879–1953), the leader of the USSR from the late 1920s until his death and determiner of international Communist policies, which varied enormously from period to period but frequently relied upon great brutality. The only top Bolshevik to emerge from the Russian lower classes, Stalin early followed Lenin and was named General Secretary of the Bolshevik Party in 1922. He forcefully identified Marxism with Leninism and advanced the policy of building socialism in one country. See: Anti-Revisionism (Maoism), Communist Party.

Stalinist—An identification used mainly in the pre-1956 period by self-avowed Trotskyists to identify the supporters of the policies of the USSR. "Stalinoid," a more obscure term, identified those close to but not members of a communist party. After 1956, "Stalinist" mainly signified Communists who supported authoritarian forms of socialism as historically necessary, and who referred—sometimes in historical defense of Maoism or even Enver Hoxha's Albanian leadership—to Stalin having committed "errors" rather than "crimes." See: Anti-Revisionism (Maoism), Communist Party, Trotskyism.

Swedenborgianism—A philosophical system, or more popularly a credulity about the presence of a "spirit world" within the mental reach of humanity, popular as a doctrine in the mid-nineteenth century. Named after Swedish mystic Immanuel Swedenborg, it gained political importance around radical circles in the 1870s–90s. See: International Workingmen's Association, *Woodhull & Claflin's Weekly*.

SWP—Socialist Workers Party. See: Socialist Workers Party, Trotskyism.

Theosophy—The mythical doctrine of all-encompassing material and spiritual unity popularized by Madame Helen Blavatsky, it influenced utopian socialist thought in the 1880s–90s. See: Bellamy, Edward; Spiritualism.

Third Period—A term used mostly by Trotskyists and other opponents of Stalin's consolidation of international influence, it refers to the 1928–1935 era, denoting a Third and revolutionary period after the initial Communist revolution in Russia, followed by failures in Central Europe and the acceptance of "building socialism in one country." In effect, it denotes the "ultra-Left" or confrontational phase of Communist policy from the eclectic era of the middle twenties on one hand and the Popular Front of the later thirties on the other. See: Communist Party, *Daily Worker*.

Trotsky, Leon—Pen name for Lyov Davidvoch Bronstein (1879–1940), a leading orator in the 1905 Russian Revolution, a strategist for the Red Army in the immediate post-1917 era, and foremost figure of the international Left Opposition. Best remembered for his criticisms of Stalinism, his theory of "permanent revolution" (rejecting Stalin's "socialism in one country"), and his *The Russian Revolution*. Those supporting his views have been termed "Trotskyists." "Trotskyite" is considered demeaning and was used primarily by supporters of the CP in the course of ideological and organizational struggles before 1956. See: Trotskyism.

Turners—Members of *Turnvereine* (gymnastic societies) that served as a prime social institution for "free thought" and, later, socialist and anarchist German Americans. Turners organized many political-educational activities from the mid- to late nineteenth century. See: Sozialisticher Turnerbund.

UAW—United Automobile Workers. See: United Automobile Workers.

UE—United Electrical, Radio and Machine Workers of America. See: "UE."

United Front—A term used frequently under varying circumstances and with sometimes ambiguous meanings by the Communist movement. Formulated in the 1920s to address the temporary restabilization of capitalism, it originally signified the unity of socialist and communist organizations for a common goal, often to resist fascism. It was bypassed in the United States by the absence of a popular socialist movement and later by the Popular Front embrace of liberals. See: Communist Party.

Urban League—The National Urban League was founded in 1910 to provide services and seek equal opportunities for African Americans. Focus has been on securing jobs. One of the relatively conservative civil rights groups, it became more activist for a brief period in the 1960s and later in some cities, such as Boston. See: Civil Rights Movement.

Wobblies—Nickname for members of the Industrial Workers of the World taken up by the IWWs in the way the once derogatory Yankee Doodle Dandy was taken up by rebels in the American Revolution. See: Industrial Workers of the World.

Yiddishkeit—Literally "Yiddishness." The quality or logic of expression flowing from the use of the Yiddish language by the impoverished inhabitants of the European Pale and their worldwide diaspora. See: Yiddish Left.

BIBLIOGRAPHICAL NOTE

A Brief Guide to Reference Sources

Scholarly resource works on the U.S. Left such as reference volumes and research guides were few and topically scattered until the 1970s and 1980s. The accelerating acquisitions of archival materials by a large number of libraries and the diversity in content and classification of published books and essays makes any comprehensive listing of available sources highly tentative. Nevertheless, a few guidelines can be usefully offered.

Princeton University professors Donald Drew Egbert and Stow Persons, aided by the Rockefeller Foundation, initiated the first effort to compile a general overview and guide to the American Left. First published in 1952 by Princeton University Press, the two volumes of *Socialism and American Life* brought together more than a dozen scholars to describe and discuss (in nearly six hundred pages) aspects ranging from art, philosophy, psychology, and economics to political history. Much of the material analyzed socialist theory in general, with little connection to the U.S., or applied dubious sociological and psychological generalizations with scant relation to particulars. Published at the height of the Cold War and before the broadening of social-historical methodologies, *Socialism and American Life* conveyed (apart from an essay by Paul Sweezy) an ahistorical approach to communism (which it dealt with as a moral evil rather than a specific social experience) and a narrow reading of political history as a succession of leaderships. Despite these limitations, several of the substantial essays offered valuable insights, and the second volume provided highly useful, if now substantially outdated, bibliographic guides. Individual essays by Paul Sweezy, Donald Drew Egbert, and Daniel Bell have lasting value. Bell's essay was expanded into book form and appeared as *Marxian Socialism in the United States.*

Other popular overviews of Left history and achievement can be found in Lillian Symes and Travers Clement's *Rebel America* and in Sidney Lens's *Radicalism in America.* In the late 1980s Richard Flacks's *Making History: The American Left and the American Mind* and Paul Buhle's *Marxism in the USA* attempted scholarly sytheses that drew on the substantial work done by various scholars in the preceeding two decades.

The appearance of substantial reference works dealing with various separate aspects of radicalism has enriched the research picture by providing considerable accessible research on specific personalities and, to a lesser extent, on available sources. With some exceptions, the works described below must be approached with the understanding that the history of the Left, or even the involvement of personalities in the Left, is of secondary importance to most of the authors and editors of these volumes. To obtain more information on particular subjects the researcher must pursue other avenues.

The Biographical Dictionary of the American Left, edited by Bernard Johnpoll and Harvey Klehr, is certainly the most comprehensive volume appearing before the *Encyclopedia of the American Left*. The dictionary offers several hundred biographical sketches, often rich in detail and almost always with adequate bibliographical information. The volume concentrates heavily on the Socialist Party and offers a detailed treatment of many minor as well as major figures, but it treats anarchists, Trotskyists, New Leftists, Wobblies, and most nineteenth century radicals rather cursorily. The treatment of Communists is marred by severe antipathy and little effort is made to deal with personalities in art and culture. The now outdated *Bibliography of the History of American Socialism*, compiled by Virgil Vogel, shows many of the same leanings and limitations from a purely bibliographical standpoint.

Women and the American Left: A Guide to Sources, by Mari Jo Buhle, offers a very different subject matter and a different model of reference work. Apart from the bibliographical citations, this work's utility can be found in the evaluative notations, varying in length from a few sentences to several paragraphs. Due to the paucity of scholarly work on women's radical subjects, ranging from literary output to political involvement, *Women and the American Left* remains a unique resource.

Such large-scale projects as *American Reformers: An H. W. Wilson Biographical Dictionary*, edited by Alden Whitman, *Notable Women: 1607–1950*, edited by Edward T. James, et al, and *Notable American Women: The Modern Period*, edited by Barbara Sicherman, et al, encapsulate information on prominent and, in some cases, not so prominent activists, with ample bibliographical citations. More narrowly defined projects such as the *Dictionary of American Communal and Utopian History*, edited by Robert S. Fogarty, *A Biographical Dictionary of American Labor*, edited by Gary M. Fink, and *Labor Conflict in the United States: An Encyclopedia*, edited by Ronald L. Fillipelli, supplement information on movements and institutions. *The American Left, 1955–1970: A National Union Catalogue of Pamphlets Published in the U.S. and Canada*, edited by Ned Kehde, offers guidance to an important period but, paradoxically, for an era in which pamphlets had ceased to play their once-central role in Left communication.

At a more abstract level, *A Dictionary of Marxist Thought*, compiled by Tom Bottomore and others, has great value as a compendium of general concepts such as "capitalism," "materialism," and "revisionism." Its nearly six hundred pages have considerably less value, however, as a guide to American personalities and institutions, since the volume focuses largely upon Europe, with lesser attention to Asia and the Third World in general, and still less to the U.S. The substantial bibliography remains useful for its listing of relatively recent works on theory.

Archival holdings of personal papers, various print materials, and oral histories have been little-charted with respect to specific Left concerns. Although the standard bibliographical sources can be useful, they cannot be regarded as comprehensive or up-to-date. Inquiries must be directed to reference librarians for current holdings.

The Union List of Serials in the Libraries of the United States and Canada is a generally reliable source with regard to the name of publications, years of availability, and location of holdings. The State Historical Society of Wisconsin, along with the New York Public Library, maintains the largest list of microfilmed radical publications potentially, if not always actually, available via interlibrary loan. Other more limited but specialized guides include the classic work by Walter Goldwater, *Radical Periodicals in America, 1890 to 1950*, and the more updated *Journals of Dissent and Social Change: A Bibliography of Titles in the California State University, Sacramento, Library*, compiled by John Liberty. Gale Skidmore's and Theodore Jurgen Spahn's *From Radical Left to Extreme Right: A Bibliography of Current Periodicals of Protest, Controversy, Advocacy or Dissent* is yet more current.

The National Union Catalogue of Manuscript Collections is somewhat less comprehensive than periodical guides because of the quickened pace of collecting in recent years and because general descriptions of characteristics (such as size) reveal little of a collection's value to the potential researcher.

Among libraries maintaining substantial collections of radical materials, the Labadie Library in Ann Arbor, Michigan, founded by a noted nineteenth century anarchist, has long been a Left history researcher's mecca, particularly but not only in nineteenth century materials. Second, only in terms of precedent, has been the Tamiment Library, New York University, descendent of the Socialist Party–connected Rand School and heir to many socialistic collections. The Immigration History Research Center, University of Minnesota, has by far the largest collection of immigrant materials and microfilms. Its Slavic, Finnish, and Italian holdings are particularly strong.

No particular logic or pattern determines which archive is likely to have a particular Left collection. The Socialist Labor Party collection is housed at the State Historical Society of Wisconsin and the Socialist Party collection is at Duke University. Both are available on microfilm. The IWW archives have been donated to the Walter Reuther Library at Wayne State University. Other organizations and individuals have placed their papers in diverse repositories too numerous to cite in this volume beyond the bibliographical information following specific entries. Researchers should also bear in mind that Left materials are not always so labeled within larger collections. The Reuther Library, which as noted houses the IWW archives, also holds the archives of the United Auto Workers and the personal papers of many Detroit-area militants. These collections contain considerable information relevant to the Left, a circumstance to be found in many research centers.

The relatively new field of oral history is small enough for a more thorough if still incomplete description. Well over half the available oral histories of the Left can be found in the Oral History of the American Left collection at Tamiment Library, New York University. Brief summaries of the interviews' contents are available in the subject guide to the collection and many interviews are transcribed. Other rich collections are found at Columbia University (especially for prominent personalities), the University of Michigan (especially for the New Left), UCLA (especially for regional personalities and institutions of the Southwest), and the Minnesota Historical Society (especially for personalities and institutions of the Midwest).

—The Editors

Selected Reference Material

Bell, Daniel. *Marxian Socialism in the United States*. Princeton: Princeton University Press, 1967.

Bottomore, Tom, et al, eds. *A Dictionary of Marxist Thought*. London: Basil Blackwell, 1983.

Buhle, Mari Jo. *Women and American Radicalism: A Guide to Sources*. Boston: G. K. Hall, 1983.

Buhle, Paul. *Marxism in the USA*. London: Verso, 1987.

Buhle, Paul, and Robin D. G. Kelley. "The Oral History of the Left in the United States: A Survey and Interpretation." *The Journal of American History*. Vol. 76, no. 2 (September, 1989).

Egbert, Donald Drew, and Stow Persons, eds. *Socialism and American Life*, two volumes. Princeton: Princeton University Press, 1952.

Filippelli, Ronald L., ed. *Labor Conflict in the United States: An Encyclopedia*. New York: Garland, 1990.

Fink, Gary, ed. *A Biographical Dictionary of American Labor*. Rev. ed. Westport: Greenwood, 1984.

Flacks, Richard. *Making History: The American Left and the American Mind*. New York: Columbia University Press, 1988.

Fogerty, Robert S., ed. *A Dictionary of American Communal and Utopian History*. Westport: Greenwood, 1980.

Goldwater, Walter. *Radical Periodicals in America, 1890 to 1950*. New Haven: Yale University Library, 1963.

James, Edward T., et al, eds. *Notable American Women: 1607–1950*. Cambridge: Belknap Press of Harvard University Press, 1971.

Johnpoll, Bernard K., and Harvey Klehr, eds. *Biographical Dictionary of the American Left*. Westport: Greenwood, 1986.

Kehde, Ned, ed. *The American Left, 1955–1970: A National Union Catalogue of Pamphlets Published in the United States and Canada*. Westport: Greenwood, 1976.

Lens, Sidney. *Radicalism in America*. Philadelphia: Crowell, 1966.

Liberty, John, compiler. *Journals of Dissent and Social Change: A Bibliography of Titles in the California State University, Sacramento, Library*. 6th edition. Sacramento: California State University Press, 1986.

Miles, Dione. *Something in Common—An IWW Bibliography*. Detroit: Wayne State University Press, 1986.

National Union Catalogue of Manuscript Collections. Washington: Library of Congress. Annual supplements.

Sicherman, Barbara, et al, eds. *Notable American Women: The Modern Period*. Cambridge: Belknap Press of Harvard University Press, 1980.

Skidmore, Gail, and Theodore Jurgen Spahn. *From Radical Left to Extreme Right: A Bibliography of Current Periodicals of Protest, Controversy, Advocacy or Dissent*. 3rd edition. Metuchen: Scarecrow, 1976.

Swanson, Dorothy, et al, compilers. *Guide to the Manuscript Collection of Tamiment Library*. New York: Garland, 1977.

Symes, Lillian, and Travers Clement. *Rebel America*. 2nd edition. Boston: Beacon, 1972.

Titus, Edna Brown, ed. *The Union List of Serials in the United States and Canada*. New York: H. W. Wilson, 1965.

Vogel, Virgil. *Bibliography of the History of Socialism in America*. Milwaukee: Socialist Party, 1977.

Whitman, Alden, ed. *American Reformers: An H. W. Wilson Biographical Dictionary*. New York: H. W. Wilson, 1985.

Contributors

Mari Jo Buhle teaches American Civilization and History at Brown University. She is author of *Women and American Socialism, 1870–1920* and of *Women and the American Left: A Guide to Sources*. She is an editor of the University of Illinois series, Women in American History.

Paul Buhle is Director of the Oral History of the American Left at Tamiment Library, New York University, and founder of the journal *Radical America*. He has written *Marxism in the USA: Remapping the History of the American Left* and *C. L. R. James: The Artist as Revolutionary*. He has edited, among other works, *Popular Culture in America* and *Working Lives: An Oral History of Rhode Island Labor*.

Dan Georgakas has written extensively on ethnicity in America, film, and labor. He is a long-time editor of *Cineaste* and a succession of Greek-American publications. Among other works, he has written the introduction to and coedited *Solidarity Forever: An Oral History of the IWW* and co-authored *Detroit: I Do Mind Dying*.

Nabeel Abraham teaches anthropology at Henry Ford Community College in Dearborn, Michigan.

Frank Adams is the author of *Unearthing Seeds of Fire: The Idea of Highlander* and the forthcoming *Dombrowski: An American Heretic*.

Muhammad Ahmad (a.k.a. Max Stanford) was a founding member of SNCC, the Black Panther Party, and the Revolutionary Action Movement. He was a protege of Malcolm X and a leading figure in the resurgence of black nationalism during the 1960s. He continues to be active in the new Black Liberation Network.

Ernest Allen, Jr., teaches African-American history at the University of Massachusetts-Amherst.

Anna Maria Alonso teaches anthropology at the University of Texas, Austin.

Philip G. Altbach is Director and Professor of the Comparative Education Center, State University of New York at Buffalo. He served as National Chair of the Student Peace Union between 1959 and 1962.

Robert Armstrong was a member of the NACLA staff from 1980 to 1986.

Carolyn Ashbaugh is author of *Lucy Parsons: American Revolutionary*.

Robert Asher, Professor of History at the University of Connecticut-Storrs, is author of *Connecticut Workers and Technological Change* and co-editor of *Life and Labor: Dimensions of American Working-Class History*.

Barbara Bair is associate editor of the Marcus Garvey Papers, University of California, Los Angeles.

Christina L. Baker is an associate professor of English at the University of Maine.

Rudolf Baranik is a Lithuanian-American painter and arts activist.

James R. Barrett teaches at the University of Illinois at Urbana-Champaign and is the author of *Work and Community in the Jungle* and coauthor of *Steve Nelson, American Radical*.

Françoise Basch, a founder of "Groupe des études feministe," is a professor at Université de Paris.

Rosalyn Fraad Baxandall is an associate professor of American Studies at SUNY-Old Westbury and author of *Words on Fire, the Life and Writings of Elizabeth Gurley Flynn*.

Edward D. Beechert is a professor of labor history at the University of Hawaii.

Bettina Berch taught economics for many years at Columbia University and is author of *The Endless Day: The Political Economy of Women and Work* and *Radical By Design: The Life and Style of Elizabeth Hawes*.

Phillip Berryman, who has worked in Panama (1965–1973) and Guatemala (1976–1980), is a translator and writer in Philadelphia.

Steve Best, a graduate student at the University of Chicago, has co-authored (with Doug Kellner) *Postmodernism As Social Theory*.

Fay M. Blake is the author of *The Strike in the American Novel* and (with H. Morton Newman) *Verbis Non Factis: Words Meant to Influence Political Choice in the United States, 1800–1980*. She is currently working on a study of public housing for the elderly in the First, Second, and Third World.

Martin Blatt received his Ph.D. in American Studies from Boston University in 1983. A labor educator living in Cambridge, Massachusetts, he has written widely on nineteenth and twentieth century United States social history.

Alexander Bloom is an associate professor of American history at Wheaton College and is the author of *Prodigal Sons: The New York Intellectuals and Their World*.

Jon Bloom is a staff member of the Oral History of the American Left.

Joseph Blum is a jazz pianist, ethnomusicologist, and music critic. He lives in New York City and teaches at the School of Visual Arts.

Stephane Booth teaches history at Kent State University.

Tom Bottomore, Emeritus Professor at the University of Sussex, has written or edited many books including *Elites and Society, A Dictionary of Marxist Thought*, and *Theories of Modern Capitalism*.

Herb Boyd is a free lance writer and activist who teaches African and African-American history at the College of New Rochelle, Manhattan.

Marjorie Woodford Bray is the coordinator of Latin American studies at California State University, Los Angeles. She is an editor of *Latin American Perspectives* and has participated in the LUCHA Film Collective.

Einar M. S. Bredland, Ph.D., is a practicing psychologist in Pennsylvania.

Paul Breines teaches modern European intellectual history at Boston College. He is coauthor with Andrew Arato of *The Young Lukacs and the Origins of Western Marxism*.

Eric Breitbart is a filmmaker and the writer/co-producer, with Mary Lance, of the film *Diego Rivera: His Life and Times*.

Ernie Brill is literary editor of *Z Magazine* and author of *I Look Over Jordan and Other Stories*.

Lorraine Brown is director of the WPA Theatre Archives at George Mason University.

Peter Buckingham teaches American history at Linfield College. His books include *International Normalcy* and *America Sees Red*.

Orville Vernon Burton teaches history at the University of Illinois, Urbana-Champaign, and is editor of H. L. Mitchell's *Roll the Union On*.

Annette P. Bus is a research assistant at the Tenement Museum of the Lower East Side, New York City.

Lawrence Bush is a novelist and essayist who edits *Genesis, 2*, a Jewish quarterly, and *Babushkin's Digest*, a wild-eyed humor zine.

Oscar V. Campomanes received his B.A. in Philippine studies from the University of the Philippines in 1984 and his M.A. degree in American Civilization from Brown University in 1987.

George W. Carey, professor, teaches in the Department of Urban Studies, Rutgers University, New Brunswick.

Clayborne Carson is a professor of history at Stanford University.

David Malcolm Carson is a student at Howard University.

Larry Ceplair teaches history at Santa Monica College. His books include *Under the Shadow of War: Fascism, Anti-Fascism and Marxists, 1918–1939*.

Jules Chametsky teaches English at the University of Massachusetts-Amherst and is director of the Institute for Advanced Studies in the Humanities.

Robert W. Cherny is a professor of history at San Francisco State University. He is preparing a biography of Harry Bridges.

Harold Christoffel is a retired labor activist.

John P. Clark is a professor of philosophy at Loyola University. He works with the New Orleans Greens and recently edited *Renewing the Earth: The Promise of Social Ecology*.

David Cochran is a graduate student in history at the University of Missouri-Columbia.

Eva Sperling Cockcroft is a well-known painter and muralist who has written extensively on the subjects of Latin American art and art and society.

Jeanette Bailin Cohen taught Yiddish stenography at the School for Jewish Studies and edited a section of her father's autobiography, I. B. Bailin's *Altz in Ein Leben*.

Robert Cohen is an assistant professor of history at the University of California, Berkeley. He has published articles on the history of American activism in the *International Encyclopedia of Student Activism*, the *OAH Magazine of History* and in *Higher Education*.

Joseph R. Conlin has written extensively on the IWW and related topics such as the American radical press.

John Cort, a former editor of the *Labor Leader*, is author of *Christian Socialism*, among other works.

Richard Criley was a founder of the National Committee Against Repressive Legislation (originally the National Committee to Abolish HUAC), served as its midwest director from 1960 to 1970, and is presently its Northern California director.

Mary Cygan is a scholar of the Polish American community.

Robert D'Attilio has written on many topics of the Italian-American experience, focusing particularly on the Sacco-Vanzetti Case, radicalism, and the photographer and political activist Tina Modotti. He is presently at work on a political history of the Sacco-Vanzetti Case.

Eric Leif Davin is a graduate student in history at the University of Pittsburgh and a veteran civil liberties activist.

John De Graaf is a documentary television producer in Seattle.

Gene DeGruson is the curator of the E. Haldeman-Julius Collection, Pittsburgh State University.

Pele deLappe, a teacher at the California Labor School, was for many years a writer and artist for the *People's World* newspaper.

David DeLeon teaches history at Howard University. His books include *The American As Anarchist*.

Michael Denning teaches American studies at Yale University and is author of *Mechanic*

Accents: Dime Novels and Working-Class Culture in America.

Velma Doby is a Community Programs Assistant at the Immigration History Research Center, University of Minnesota.

Ara Dostourian teaches Western civilization at West Georgia College and is translator of the classic work in Armenian, M. Eddessa's *Chronicle of Armenia and the Crusades.*

Joe Doyle is a graduate student in history at New York University and a veteran oral historian of the Irish-American Left.

Peter Drucker, a gay activist, is a member of Solidarity and is working on a biography of Max Shachtman.

Ellen Carol DuBois is a professor of history at the University of California, Los Angeles.

Alice Echols received her Ph.D. in history from the University of Michigan. She is currently a visiting assistant professor in history at SUNY-Buffalo.

Frank Emspak, who earned a Ph.D. at the University of Wisconsin-Madison, has been a machinist since 1972.

Bret Eynon, Education Director of the American Social History Project—City University of New York, is co-editor of *1968, A Student Generation in Revolt: An International Oral History.*

Bill Falkowski is a history Ph.D. candidate at SUNY-Buffalo.

Dianne Feeley, an editor of *Against the Current,* is a veteran activist in the feminist movement and a member of Solidarity.

Thomas Fiehrer is co-editor of the journal *Plantation Society in the Americas.*

Frederick Vanderbilt Field is a former editor of *Amerasia* and author of *From Right to Left.*

Leon Fink is an associate professor of history at the University of North Carolina at Chapel Hill and co-author, with Brian Greenberg, of *Union Power, Soul Power: The Unquiet History of the Hospital Workers.*

Robert Fisher teaches history at the University of Houston-Downtown.

Don Fitz is the editor of *Workers Democracy.*

Tara Fitzpatrick is a professor of history at Sarah Lawrence College.

Harry Fleischman was national secretary of the Socialist Party and managed Norman Thomas's presidential campaigns in 1944 and 1948. He currently chairs the Workers Defense League.

Philip S. Foner, professor emeritus at Lincoln University, is the author of many works on labor and radical history.

John Bellamy Foster teaches sociology and political economy at the University of Oregon. He is the author of *The Theory of Monopoly Capitalism,* among other works.

Dana Frank teaches history at the University of Missouri-St. Louis and is writing a book on consumer organizing and the Seattle labor movement in the 1920s.

Miriam Frank teaches humanities at New York University and women's labor history at Cornell's New York City Extension. She has published widely on women's trade union activism.

Steven Fraser is a senior editor at Basic Books. He is working on a biography of Sidney Hillman and is co-editor, along with Gary Gerstle, of *The Rise and Fall of the New Deal Order.*

Samuel R. Friedman is a veteran labor activist and author of *Teamster Rank and File.*

Michael Furmanovsky is a graduate student at U.C.L.A.

Christine Ward Gailey teaches anthropology at Northeastern University. Her research focuses on gender in class and state formation.

Mario T. Garcia is a professor of history and Chicano studies at the University of California, Santa Barbara.

Virginia Gardner is a veteran progressive journalist.

Paul Garon is a member of the Surrealist Group and author of several books on the Blues.

Dee Garrison is an associate professor of history at Rutgers University, New Brunswick.

Barbara Garson is the author of the plays *MacBird, The Dinosaur Door,* and *The Department* and of the books *All the Livelong Day: The Meaning and Demeaning of Routine Work* (1977) and *The Electronic Sweatshop* (1989).

Hedda Garza is a veteran political activist.

Mark I. Gelfand is an associate professor of history at Boston College.

Daniel Georgianna is a professor of economics at Southeastern Massachusetts University.

Marv Gettleman teaches history at the Marxist School and at Brooklyn Polytechnical University and is the author or editor of many books. He has written widely on U.S. radicalism, Indochina and Central America.

James Gilbert teaches American history at the University of Maryland. He is the author of *Writers and Partisans* and *A Cycle of Outrage*.

Toni Gilpin is a graduate student at Yale University writing on the Farm Equipment Workers Union.

Ann Fagan Ginger is preparing a biography of Carol Weiss King.

Martin Glaberman retired from teaching at Wayne State's Weekend College. He is the author of *Wartime Strikes*.

Sherna Berger Gluck directs the oral history program at California State University, Long Beach, and teaches in the women's studies program. She is the co-founder of the Feminist History Research Project and has conducted extended interviews with women radicals of the early twentieth century.

David J. Goldberg teaches history at Cleveland State University.

Walter L. Goldfrank is a professor of sociology at the University of California, Santa Cruz.

David Goldway, Director of the Jefferson School from 1940 to 1956, is editor of *Science & Society*.

Steve Golin is the author of *The Fragile Bridge: Paterson Silk Strike, 1913*.

Eric A. Gordon is the author of *Mark the Music: The Life and Work of Marc Blitzstein*. He is collaborating on Earl Robinson's autobiography, *Ballad of an American*.

Linda Gordon is a professor of history at the University of Wisconsin-Madison.

Max Gordon was a communist journalist and organizer until early 1958. He edited a civil rights journal and worked as a medical writer and as a free lance political writer. He died in January 1990.

Van Gosse is a Ph.D. candidate in American working-class and women's history at Rutgers University. He is currently writing a history of the Latin American solidarity movement, 1959–1989, to be published by Verso.

John Graham teaches in the Department of English at the University of Colorado in Boulder.

Robert Greene is owner-manager of Moscow Bookpeople, a bookstore in Moscow, Idaho.

David Hacker has been the indexer for *Jewish Currents* since 1980 and was elected to the magazine's editorial advisory council in 1989. A professional librarian, he is president of PeaceSmith Inc., a political, cultural and educational activist group in Long Island, New York.

Rick Halpern is a labor historian who lives in New York City. He is completing a study of Chicago's packinghouse workers in the CIO era.

Marilyn Halter is an assistant professor of history at Wellesley College.

Benjamin Harris writes on the history of psychology and teaches at the University of Wisconsin-Parkside.

Olufson Hauge, former editor of *Ny Tid*, lives in Norway.

Jeffrey Haydu teaches sociology at Syracuse University.

Ulrike Heider is a scholar of anarchism and a radio journalist in West Germany.

Christine Hess, who teaches at the University of Bologna, Italy, is a scholar of German-American socialism.

Pat Hills, a professor of art history at Boston University, has written widely on 19th and 20th century genre and figure painting and on art and politics from the early 20th century to the present.

S. Carl Hirsch, a free lance writer, was present as a cub reporter at the Memorial Day Massacre and covered subsequent hearings by the subcommittee of the US Senate Committee on Education and Labor, June–July 1937.

Dirk Hoerder directs the labor migration project at the University of Bremen.

Eric Homberger teaches English and American Studies at the University of East Anglica and is author of *American Writers and Radical Politics, 1900–30: Equivocal Commitments.*

Michael Honey, a former SCEF worker, is the author of *Labor and Civil Rights in the South: The Industrial Union Movement and Black Workers in Memphis, Tennessee.*

Gerald Horne teaches history at the University of California, San Diego.

Yuji Ichioka is a research associate at the Asian American Studies Center, University of California, Los Angeles.

Noel Ignatiev, long active in the Sojourner Truth Organization, is a graduate student in education at Harvard University.

Maurice Isserman is the author of *Which Side Were You On? The American Communist Party During the Second World War* and *If I Had a Hammer: The Death of the Old Left and the Birth of the New Left.*

Joseph Jablonski is an active unionist and surrealist who writes on the history of ideas.

Maurice Jackson is the National Legislative Representative of the Communist Party U.S.A. and is based in Washington D.C. He is a member of the National Board and National Committee of the CPUSA.

Jim Jacobs teaches economics at Macomb Community College, Warren, Michigan.

Russell Jacoby is the author of *Social Amnesia, The Repression of Psychoanalysis, The Last Intellectuals,* and other works.

Norma Jenckes teaches theatre at the University of Cincinnati.

John Jentz is the director of the Newberry Library's Family and Community History Center and co-editor of *German Workers in Industrial Chicago, 1850–1910.*

Richard Judd teaches history at the University of Maine, edits the *Maine Historical Society Quarterly,* and has written the forthcoming *Socialist Cities: Municipal Politics and the Grass Roots of American Socialism.*

Temma Kaplan is an associate professor of history at the University of California, Los Angeles.

Michael Karni is editor of *Finnish Americana* and a widely published scholar on the Finnish-American Left.

Michael Kazin teaches history at American University in Washington, D.C. He is the author of *Barons of Labor: The San Francisco Building Trades and Union Power in the Progressive Era* and numerous articles and reviews in *The Nation, The New Republic, Labor History, Socialist Review,* and other periodicals.

Roger Keeran is the chair of the Master of Arts Program in Labor and Policy Studies, Empire State College, SUNY.

Robin D. G. Kelley teaches African-American history at Emory University.

Douglas Kellner teaches philosophy at the University of Texas-Austin.

Mark Kesselman is a political scientist at Columbia University. He is the author of *The*

Politics of Power and *Socialism Without the Workers*.

Matjaz Klemencic is an associate professor of history and chair of the Department of History at the University of Maribor, Slovenia/Yugoslavia.

Irwin Klibaner is an instructor of history and sociology at Madison Area Technical College, Madison, Wisconsin.

Mike Konopacki is a labor cartoonist with *Huck/Konopacki Labor Cartoons*. His latest book, with Gary Huck, is *Bye! American, The Labor Cartoons of Huck and Konopacki*.

David Konstan teaches classics at Brown University.

Joyce L. Kornbluh, a noted authority on labor subjects, is editor of *Rebel Voices—An IWW Anthology* and coauthor of the play *I Just Wanted Someone To Know*.

Robert Korstad is a graduate student at the University of North Carolina and a past editor of *Southern Exposure*.

Joel Kovel, trained as a psychiatrist and psychoanalyst, is currently Alger Hiss Professor of Social Studies at Bard College. His most recent books are *In Nicaragua* and *The Radical Spirit*.

Nancy Krieger is an epidemiologist and member of the Health Coalition of the National Rainbow Coalition.

Peter Kuznick teaches at American University and is author of *Beyond the Laboratory: Scientists as Political Activists in 1930s America*.

Saul Landau is a senior fellow at the Transnational Institute.

Andy Lanset produces reports and documentaries for public radio.

Aaron Lansky is executive director of the National Yiddish Book Center.

Ring Lardner, Jr., has been a film writer and political activist.

Walter J. Lear, a former public health official, is devoting full time to research and writing about the US Health Left, 1875 to 1975. He is also creating an archive for the US Health Left at the Institute of Social Medicine and Community Health, Philadelphia, Pennsylvania.

Paul Le Blanc has been a radical activist since the 1960s and is an editor of the *Bulletin in Defense of Marxism*. He is a Ph.D. candidate in history at the University of Pittsburgh.

Arieh Lebowitz is editor of *Israel Horizons* and program associate of the Jewish Labor Committee.

Jerry Lembcke is the co-author of *One Union In Wood* and teaches sociology at Holy Cross College.

James Lerner, a staff member of the United Electrical Workers Union, was a youth representative to the American League Against War and Fascism.

Michael Lerner is editor of *Tikkun*.

Richard Levy became a member of CCAS in 1971 and served on the editorial board of the *Bulletin of Concerned Asian Scholars* for three years. He has been active in progressive movements for twenty years, has written numerous articles on China, and has taught in Boston's Chinatown for many years.

Rose Lewis is a frequent writer for the *People's Daily World*.

George Lipsitz is an associate professor of American studies at the University of Minnesota and author of *Class and Culture in Cold War America: "A Rainbow at Midnight"* and *A Life in the Struggle: Ivory Perry and the Culture of Opposition*.

Priscilla Long, a veteran activist, was a printer for Red Sun Press for ten years and is author of *Mother Jones: Woman Organizer*.

Robert Macieski is curator at the Slater Mill Historic Site, Pawtucket, Rhode Island.

Mark Maier teaches economics at Glendale College, Glendale, California. He is the author of *City Unions*, a history of New York City's municipal unions.

Patrick Manning is an associate professor of history and African-American studies at Northeastern University, and is author of an economic history of Dahomey, *Francophone Sub-Saharan Africa, 1880–1985,* and of the forthcoming *Slavery and African Life.*

David Marc is the author of *Demographic Vistas: Television in American Culture* and *Comic Visions: Television Comedy and American Culture.*

Gerald Markowitz is a professor of history at John Jay College, CUNY.

Norman Markowitz is an associate professor at Rutgers University, New Brunswick.

Charles H. Martin teaches history at the University of Texas at El Paso.

Al McAloon is a veteran of Irish-American causes and is professor emeritus at Bryant College.

Blaine McKinley is a professor of American thought and language at Michigan State University. His articles on American anarchism have appeared in *American Quarterly, Journal of American Culture,* and *Labor History.*

David McReynolds has been a staff member of the War Resisters League since 1960, and is a long-time member of the Socialist Party.

Michael Meeropol teaches at the University of Western New England and is co-author of *We Are Your Sons.*

Joanne Melish is a doctoral candidate in American civilization at Brown University.

Gerald Meyer is coordinator of social sciences at Hostos College, CUNY, and author of *Vito Marcantonio: American Radical, 1902–1954.*

James Miller is the author of *"Democracy in the Streets": From Port Huron to the Siege of Chicago; Rousseau: Dreamer of Democracy;* and *History of Human Existence: From Marx to Merleau-Ponty.* He is also the editor of *The Rolling Stone Illustrated History of Rock and Roll.*

John A. Miller teaches economics at Wheaton College and is a member of the *Dollars and Sense* collective.

Marc S. Miller was a staff member of the Institute for Southern Studies from 1977 to 1986.

Prairie Miller writes on cultural topics for the *People's Daily World.*

Sally M. Miller, a professor of history at the University of the Pacific, is the author or editor of four books and many articles on American radical history.

Paul C. Mishler has taught extensively on the history of American radicalism, currently at Vassar College.

Scott Molloy teaches labor studies at the University of Rhode Island and is co-editor of *A History of Rhode Island Working People.*

Douglas Monroy is an associate professor at The Colorado College, where he teaches the history of the American West and Southwest. He is the author of *Thrown Among Strangers: Life, Labor, and Acculturation in Spanish and Mexican Southern California, 1769–1900.*

Teresa Murphy teaches U.S. history at the University of Rhode Island.

Mark D. Naison teaches history at Fordham University and is the author of *Communists in Harlem During the Depression.*

Bruce Nelson is the author of *Workers on the Waterfront: Seamen, Longshoremen, and Unionism in the 1930s.* He teaches history at Dartmouth College.

Richard Nickson is author of *Staves* and *Philip Freneau: Poet of the American Revolution.*

Daniel Nugent is a fellow at the Center for Latin American Studies, University of Texas, Austin.

Susan Gushee O'Malley is an associate professor of English at Kingsborough, City University of New York. She is editor of *Radical Teacher* and a political activist.

Leslie F. Orear is president of the Illinois Labor History Society. He was editor of *The Packinghouse Worker*, national organ of the UPWA from 1953 to 1968.

Nell Irvin Painter teaches history at Princeton University.

David Paskin, assistant director of Research & Negotiations, District Council 37, AFSCME, is writing a history of District 65.

Elizabeth Payne is an associate professor of history at the University of Arkansas-Fayetteville and is working on women in the Southern Tenant Farmers Union.

David Peck is a professor of English and American studies at California State University, Long Beach, and the co-compiler, with Chris Bullock, of *Guide to Marxist Literary Criticism*.

Harvey Pekar is the editor of *American Splendor* comics. He writes widely on U.S. and Russian novelists.

William Eric Perkins continues to be active in the black Left, working with the Black Liberation Network. He has published extensively on both past and contemporary black radicalism. He is currently researching the Grenadian Revolution.

Nunzio Pernicone is an assistant professor in the Department of History and Politics at Drexel University. He is writing a history of the Italian anarchist movement in the nineteenth century and a political biography of Carlo Tresca.

Ben Perry is preparing a history of the Socialist Labor Party.

Maxine Phillips worked for DSOC and was executive director of DSA. She is currently the managing editor of *Dissent* magazine.

George Pirinsky was a long-time leader of the Bulgarian-American Left.

Carol Poore is an associate professor of German at Brown University.

Chuck Portz is a founder of the Labor Theater of New York.

George E. Pozzetta is a professor of history at the University of Florida. His principal research has focused on the themes of immigration and ethnicity in American life, particularly as they involve Italians.

Albert Prago is a veteran of the Abraham Lincoln Brigade, a history professor (retired), and writer.

Ruth F. Prago, a veteran political activist and social worker, is a staff member of the Oral History of the American Left.

Richard Quinney teaches sociology at Northern Illinois University. His books include *Critique of Legal Order: Crime Control in Capitalist Society* and *Social Existence: Metaphysics, Marxism and the Social Sciences*.

Peter Rachleff is an associate professor of history at Macalester College, St. Paul, Minnesota. He is the author of *Black Labor in the South: Richmond, Virginia, 1865–1890*.

Thaddeus Radzialowski is an associate professor of history at Southwestern Minnesota University.

Bruno Ramirez, who teaches history at the University of Montreal, is author of *When Workers Fight: The Politics of Industrial Relations in the Progressive Era, 1898–1916*.

Arnold Rampersad teaches black studies at Rutgers University and is author of *The Life of Langston Hughes* (2 volumes).

Jill Raymond is a research librarian for a major news organization in Washington, D.C. She has worked politically on feminist, leftist, gay, third-party, and criminal justice issues.

Renqiu Yu is a graduate student in history at New York University.

Sid Resnick is a veteran political and labor activist and translator of Yiddish.

William A. Reuben, former national public relations director of the ACLU, wrote the first articles and books about both the Rosenberg-Sobell and Hiss cases. He has been studying and writing about Hiss for over 35 years and is currently completing a book about Whittaker Chambers.

Dave Reynold is scholar-in-residence at the Blackstone River Valley National Heritage Corridor.

Edward Rice-Maximin is a French history specialist and author of *Accommodation and Resistance: The French Left, Indochina and the Cold War, 1945–54*.

Paul Richards is the author of *Critical Focus: The Black and White Photographs of Harvey Wilson Richards*.

David Riehle is a member of the United Transportation Union in Minneapolis, a labor historian, and an active socialist who has interviewed many of the participants in the 1934 Teamster strikes.

Leonard Rifas self-published his first underground comic in 1969. His work includes the political-educational comics *All-Atomic Comics, Corporate CRIME Comics, Food Comics, Food First Comics, Energy Comics, AIDS NEWS*, and *itchy PLANET*.

Nancy L. Roberts is an associate professor in the School of Journalism and Mass Communication at the University of Minnesota. Her current project is a history of the peace reform press.

Paul Robeson, Jr., has written widely on the Soviet Union.

David Roediger teaches history at the University of Missouri and is co-editor of *The Haymarket Scrapbook*.

Franklin Rosemont, editor of *Arsenal/Surrealist Subversion* and co-editor of *The Haymarket Scrapbook*, has also edited and introduced works by surrealist Andre Breton, dancer Isadora Duncan, libertarian socialist Mary Marcy, IWW humorist T-Bone Slim and utopian Edward Bellamy.

Penelope Rosemont, welcomed into the surrealist movement by Andre Breton in 1966, has taken part in surrealist exhibitions all over the world. Her book of poems, *Athanor*, is now in its third printing. She has designed books for Black Swan Press and Charles H. Kerr.

Ruth Rosen, a professor of history at University of California, Davis, is the editor of *The Maimie Papers* and author of *The Lost Sisterhood: Prostitution in America*.

Mel Rosenthal teaches at the Metro Center of Empire State College (State University of New York) and is known for his socially oriented photography.

Rob Rosenthal is assistant professor of sociology at Wesleyan University and director of Fuse Music, a music production firm concerned with the cultures of social movements. He is the author of the forthcoming work *Homeless in Paradise* and the composer of the rock opera *Seattle, 1919*.

Roy Rosenzweig teaches history at George Mason University and is the author of *Eight Hours for What We Will: Workers and Leisure in an Industrial City*.

Alex Rosner is a former staff member and manager of the Hungarian-American newspaper *Magyar Szo*.

Steven Rosswurm, author of *Arms, Country, and Class: The Philadelphia Militia and "Lower Sort" During the American Revolution*, teaches history at Lake Forest College. He is researching a book on the FBI and the CIO.

Annette Rubinstein is a veteran activist and literary scholar.

Alan Ruff is the author of *We Called Each Other Comrades: Charles Kerr and the Charles H. Kerr Co., Publishers 1886–1986*.

Kirkpatrick Sale is the author of *SDS* and five other books, including *Human Scale, Power Shift*, and *Dwellers in the Land: The Bioregional Vision*.

Sal Salerno is a professor on the Community Faculty Staff of Metropolitan State University in St. Paul, Minnesota.

John B. Salter, Jr., an organizer for more than thirty years, is presently chair of Indian studies, University of North Dakota, Grand Forks.

Margaret Sandburg is the editor of *The Poet and the Dream Girl: The Love Letters of Lilian Steichen & Carl Sandburg* and a volume of her father's poetry, *Breathing Tokens*

Joel Saxe is a filmmaker specializing in historical documentaries.

Morris U. Schappes is editor of *Jewish Currents.*

Walter Schneir and Miriam Schneir are authors whose writings have appeared in books and periodicals. She is the editor of *Feminism: The Essential Historical Writings.* He is the editor of a 30,000-microfiche collection, *VIETNAM: A Documentary Collection, Westmoreland v. CBS.*

Ellen Schrecker, author of *No Ivory Tower: McCarthyism and the University,* teaches U.S. history at Yeshiva University.

Carlos A. Schwantes is an associate professor of history at the University of Idaho.

Mark Selden, author of *The Political Economy of Chinese Socialism,* teaches at the State University of New York, Binghamton.

William Sennett, publisher and general manager of the *Chicago Star,* has in recent years been the publisher of *In These Times.*

Ralph E. Shaffer teaches U.S. history at California Polytechnic.

Robert Shaffer, a New York City high school teacher, became addicted to *Ramparts* at age twelve and worked there as a summer intern in 1974.

Herbert Shapiro is an associate professor of history at the University of Cincinnati.

Linn Shapiro is a writer, editor, and researcher interested in the history and culture of the American Left.

Steve Sherman is editor of *A Scott Nearing Reader.*

Francis Shor teaches history at Wayne State University's Weekend College.

Elliott Shore is the librarian of the Historical Studies-Social Science Library at the Institute for Advanced Study, Princeton University, and has published several books and articles on the history of the alternative press in the United States.

Paul N. Siegel, professor emeritus, Long Island University, is the author of *The Meek and the Militant: Revolution and the Twentieth-Century Novel* and other books.

John Sillito is an archivist at Weber State College and engaged in a long-term study of socialism in twentieth century Utah.

Sam Sills, a co-producer of *The Good Fight,* is a documentary filmmaker and oral history worker.

Alan Singer is a historian, New York City public high school teacher and editor of *The Link,* a community newspaper published by the United Community Centers in Brooklyn, New York.

Nancy B. Sinkoff is a graduate student in Jewish history at Columbia University.

Kathryn Kish Sklar is a professor of history at the State University of New York, Binghamton.

Paul Smith is a Comanche writer and activist. He was active in the American Indian Movement and the International Indian Treaty Council from 1974–1979, and was the founding editor of the *Treaty Council News.*

Daniel Soyer is a history graduate student and former associate archivist at YIVO Institute.

Evan Stark is a veteran radical sociologist.

Michael Staub teaches English at Rhode Island College.

Taylor Stoehr is Paul Goodman's literary executor.

Gregory M. Stone is completing his dissertation in history at Rutgers University.

Ralph Stone is a professor of history at Sangamon State University.

Margaret Strobel directs the Women's Studies Program at the University of Illinois at Chicago. She has written about African women and about European women in Africa and Asia, and is completing a book about the women's unions.

Sharon Hartman Strom teaches U.S. history at the University of Rhode Island.

Jack Stuart teaches at California State University, Long Beach.

Mary Lou Suhor is editor of *The Witness* magazine, a national ecumenical journal reporting on social justice issues, published by the Episcopal Church Publishing Company.

Dorothy Swanson has been the head of the Tamiment Library, New York University, since 1965.

Amy Swerdlow teaches U.S. women's history at Sarah Lawrence College and has written extensively on the history of women in the peace movement.

Malcolm Sylvers is an associate professor of U.S history at the University of Venice, Italy. He is the author of *Sinistra politica e movimento operaio negli Stati Uniti. Del priono dopogurerra ala repressione liberal-maccartista*.

Richard Taskin teaches history at North Adams State College, North Adams, Massachusetts.

Kenneth Teitelbaum is an associate professor in the School of Education and Human Development, State University of New York, Binghamton. His research interests include current and past critical educational practices.

Richard W. Thomas teaches urban studies at Michigan State University.

Barbara L. Tischler is the associate director of the Labor Education and Advancement Project, Queens College, CUNY.

Ellen Wiley Todd is an assistant professor of art history and American studies at George Mason University.

Michael Topp is a graduate student in American civilization at Brown University.

Enzo Traverso lives in Paris and is finishing a dissertation on the immigrant Left in the United States.

Mark Tushnet, Georgetown University Law Center, is former Secretary of the Conference on Critical Legal Studies, and author of works on American legal history and constitutional law.

Jean Tussey, a veteran union and social movement activist, is writing a biography of Max Hayes.

Joseph R. Urgo teaches in the English and Humanities Department, Bryant College.

Rudolph J. Vecoli is a professor of history at the University of Minnesota and the director of the Immigration History Research Center.

Lise Vogel is an associate professor of sociology at Rider College. She has published widely on feminist theory and women's history, and is completing a book on the dilemma of maternity policy in the United States.

Dave Wagner was editor of the underground paper *Madison Kaleidiscope*.

Nora R. Wainer, a Trotskyist veteran of the late 1950s and early 1960s, is working on a study of her grandfather, Chaim Zhitlovsky.

Alan Wald, professor in the English Literature Department and the Program in American Culture at the University of Michigan, is author of *James T. Farrell: The Revolutionary Socialist Years*; *The Revolutionary Imagination*; and *The New York Intellectuals*.

Alan Wallach, who took courses with Meyer Schapiro in the 1960s, is a historian of nineteenth century American art.

Constance Webb is author of *Richard Wright: A Biography*.

Devra Weber has written on Mexican agricultural workers and their organizations in the United States.

Kathleen Weiler teaches education at Tufts University, Boston, and is editor of *Women Teaching For Change*.

Alice Wexler has taught history at Sonoma State University and at the University of California, Riverside. She is the author of *Emma Goldman in America*.

George Abbott White is keeper of the Matthiessen Room at Harvard University.

Fred Whitehead, a native Kansan, has worked on farms and railroads, published a

book of poetry (*Steel Destiny*) and written widely on Midwestern radical culture.

Stephen Whitfield teaches American studies at Brandeis University and is author of *Scott Nearing: Apostle of American Radicalism,* among other works.

Cecile Whiting is a specialist in American art and author of *The Response to Fascism in American Art.*

Sean Wilentz teaches U.S. history at Princeton University.

Jim Williams, a 1960s student activist, has become a labor activist and writer on Marxist topics.

Tim Wohlforth was active in the American Trotskyist movement from 1953 until 1980. He is currently writing his memoirs, *The Prophet's Children.*

Kent Worcester is a graduate student at Columbia University.

Maria Woroby is a reference librarian at Augsburg College in Minneapolis, Minnesota.

James Wrenn received a B.A. in history from Duke University in 1973. He is active in the Left in North Carolina, and has served as a steward and officer in two unions.

Allen Young is assistant editor of the *Athol Daily News,* Athol, Massachusetts. He worked as a Liberation News Services staff member from 1967–70. He has written several books, including *Gays Under the Cuban Revolution,* which describes the oppression of homosexuals under the Castro Regime.

Howard Zinn teaches political studies at Boston University and is the author of books and plays on American radicalism.

Arthur Zipser was a fulltime aide to William Z. Foster during the McCarthy Era and is author of five books.

Rebecca Zurier received her doctorate in the history of art from Yale University, where she organized the exhibition *Art for the Masses* in 1985–86. She is the author of several books on American art and social history, including *Art for the Masses.*

THE ENCYCLOPEDIA

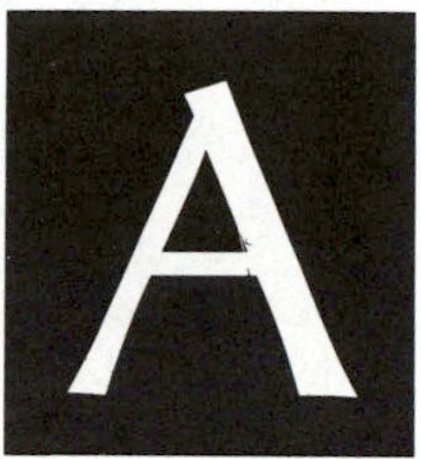

Abortion/Reproductive Rights

Socialist women—in Left groups as well as unaffiliated—played a role in the reproductive rights movement of the late 1960s and 1970s. They (1) supported the right of women to have abortion *on demand,* (2) opposed the use of "population control" arguments, counterposing instead a woman's *right* to control her own body, and (3) explained how genuine control over one's own reproductive life meant knowing one's own body and having the right to be a sexual being (including being a lesbian), the right to decide when and if to have children, and the right to raise one's children in dignity (with access to health care, housing, child care, etc.). It also meant opposition to sterilization abuse. Although there was scant factual evidence of sterilization abuse before the mid-1970s, the Left made the point that while middle-class women found it difficult to be sterilized, poor women—especially black, Chicano, Puerto Rican, and Native American women—were often sterilized without their knowledge or consent.

Socialist women were active in local abortion-rights coalitions, in the National Organization for Women (NOW), and in the Women's National Abortion Action Coalition (WONAAC), a New York–based organization (1971–73) that called nationally and internationally coordinated actions. Speak-outs, where women testified about their own illegal abortions, picketing activities against public figures who opposed abortions, demonstrations, and class-action suits challenging the antiabortion laws were the principal methods of action.

The 1973 Supreme Court decision did not guarantee women's access to abortion, but it did *legalize* abortions. With passage of the Hyde Amendment in 1976, poor women were denied federal funding for most abortions. But hospitals and doctors had never fully implemented the Supreme Court decision. Access to abortion was greatest in urban areas.

Following the 1973 decision, socialist women—particularly through the Committee to End Sterilization Abuse (CESA) in New York City—were instrumental in spotlighting sterilization abuse by publicizing specific cases of abuse and educating the feminist and labor movements about the need to pass federal regulations requiring "informed consent." The thirty-day waiting period (between applying for sterilization and the operation) imposed by the federal government in 1977 as a result of such pressure inhibits doctors from sterilizing women without their knowledge.

The most successful right-wing attacks on abortion have been against the most vulnerable women: poor women, women facing racial oppression, teenage women. Socialist women organized with other women to oppose the passage of the Hyde Amendment, first through local coalitions, then through the Reproductive Rights National Network (R2N2, 1979–84). In fact, R2N2 was modeled on the New York–based Committee for Abortion Rights and Against Sterilization Abuse (CARASA), which was created in 1976 out of the need to oppose the Hyde Amendment. (Although it threw most of its energy into fighting for passage of the Equal Rights Amendment during this period, NOW also opposed the Hyde Amendment.) But demonstrations, speakouts, and a broad-based legal challenge were ultimately unsuccessful in forcing the Supreme Court to rule the amendment unconstitutional.

While today there is no national coalition defending women's reproductive rights, there are still a dozen states where women on Medicaid can obtain abortions. Local women's groups have been instrumental in fighting to keep such funding going. Once again, in explaining why poor women need Medicaid-funded abortions, socialist women assert the right of women to control their own life choices. *See also*: Birth Control, Socialist Feminism, Women's Liberation

—*Dianne Feeley*

REFERENCES

Clarke, Elissa. "R2N2 Collapse: A Defeat for Feminists." *Changes* (May–June 1985).

Committee for Abortion Rights and Against Sterilization Abuse. *Women Under Attack: Abortion, Sterilization Abuse and Reproductive Freedom*. New York: CARASA, 1979.

Fried, Marlene Gerber. "The Politics of the Reproductive Rights National Network." *Changes* (April 1983).

Gordon, Linda. *Woman's Body, Woman's Right*. New York: Penguin, 1977.

Petchesky, Rosalind Pollack. *Abortion & Woman's Choice, The State Sexuality and Reproductive Freedom*. Boston: Northeastern University Press, 1985.

ABRAHAM LINCOLN BRIGADE

During the Spanish Civil War (1936–39), 2,800 American volunteers took up arms to defend the Spanish Republic against a military rebellion led by General Franco and aided by Hitler and Mussolini. To the Abraham Lincoln Brigade, which fought from 1937 through 1938, the defense of the Republic represented the last hope of stopping the spread of international fascism.

The Lincolns fought alongside approximately 35,000 antifascists from fifty-two countries who, like themselves, were organized under the aegis of the Comintern, and who also sought to "make Madrid the tomb of fascism." In keeping with Popular Front culture, the Americans named their units the Abraham Lincoln Battalion, the George Washington Battalion, and the John Brown Battery. Together with the British, Irish, Canadian, and other nationals they formed the Fifteenth International Brigade. ("Lincoln Brigade" is a misnomer originating with an American support organization, Friends of the Abraham Lincoln Brigade.) One hundred twenty-five American men and women also served with the American Medical Bureau as nurses, doctors, technicians, and ambulance drivers.

The conviction that made volunteering for a war against fascism possible was born from the economic calamity and political turmoil of the 1930s. Like many during the Great Depression, the young volunteers had an experience of deprivation and injustice that led them to join the burgeoning student, unemployed, union, and cultural movements that were influenced by the Communist Party and other Left organizations. Involvement in these groups exposed them to a Marxist and internationalist perspective and, with their successes in galvanizing people to conscious, political action, gave rise to a revolutionary élan.

American radicalism was spurred by the appearance of profascist groups like the Liberty League, and the expansion of fascism abroad. With Japan's invasion of Manchuria in 1931, Hitler's ascendance in 1933, and Italy's assault on Ethiopia in 1934—all accomplished without hindrance from the governments of the West—the CP responded with the coalition-building strategy of the Popular Front, attracting thousands of aroused citizens directly into its ranks or into "front" organizations. When four right-wing Spanish generals, with German and Italian support, attacked the legally elected government on July 19, 1936, a desire to confront fascism in Spain swept through the progressive communities in Europe and the Americas. Within weeks, militant German, French, and Italian antifascists were fighting in Madrid. By January 1937, despite a State Department prohibition against travel to Spain, Americans were crossing the Pyrenees.

The Lincolns came from all walks of life, all regions of the country, and included seamen, students, the unemployed, miners, fur workers, lumberjacks, teachers, salesmen, athletes, dancers, and artists. They established the first racially integrated military unit in U.S. history and were the first to be led by a black commander. At least 60 percent were members of the Young Communist League or CP. Wobblies, socialists, and the unaffiliated also joined. The Socialists formed their own Debs Column for Spain, but open recruitment brought on government suppression.

The reaction of Western governments to the war was ambivalent and duplicitous. They agreed to a nonintervention pact and the United States embargoed aid to the Spanish belligerents, policies intended to de-escalate the war but whose selective enforcement undermined the Republic. While Germany and Italy supplied Franco with troops, tanks, submarines, and a modernized air force (the first to bomb open cities, most notably Guernica), the nonintervention policy only prevented arms from reaching the Republic. General Motors, Texaco, and other American corporations further assisted Franco with trucks and fuel. The Soviet Union and Mexico were the only governments to sell armaments to the Republic, although much of them were impounded at the French border. Throughout the war, a vociferous political and cultural movement in America rallied to the Republic by raising money for medical aid and demanding an end to the embargo. Such participants as Albert Einstein, Dorothy Parker, Gene Kelly, Paul Robeson, Helen Keller, A. Philip Randolph, and Gypsy Rose Lee reflected the wide base of support for the Republican cause.

Self-motivated and ideological, the Lincolns attempted to create an egalitarian "people's army"; officers were distinguished only by small bars on their berets and in some cases rank-and-file soldiers elected their own officers. Traditional military protocol was shunned, although not always successfully. A political commissar explained the politics of the war to the volunteers and tended to their needs and morale. The Lincoln Brigade helped ease the pressure on Madrid, giving the Republic time to train and organize its own popular army. The subject of respectful news reports by such writers as Ernest Hemingway, Herbert Matthews, Martha Gellhorn, and Lillian Hellman, the brigade helped strengthen antifascist opinion in the United States. Yet the Lincolns and the Republican military, fighting with inadequate weaponry, could not withstand the forces allied against them. By the end, the Lincolns had lost nearly 750 men and sustained a casualty rate higher than that suffered by Americans in World War II. Few escaped injury. In November 1938, as a last attempt to pressure Hitler and Mussolini into repatriating their troops, Spanish prime minister Juan Negrin ordered the withdrawal of the International Brigades. The Axis coalition refused to follow suit and Madrid fell in March 1939.

The Lincolns returned home as heroes of the antifascist cause but enjoyed no official recognition of their deed. Many Lincolns soon aroused bitterness within sectors of the Left when, with the signing of the Hitler-Stalin nonaggression pact in 1939, they supported the CP's call for the United States to stay out of WW II. Once the United States and the Soviet Union entered the war, however, many of the veterans enlisted in the armed forces or served with the merchant marine. In a foreshadowing of the McCarthy period, the armed forces designated the Lincolns "premature antifascists" and confined them to their bases. Many successfully protested and were allowed to see action. Among the core agents of the Office of Strategic Services were Lincoln veterans whose contacts with the European partisans, forged in Spain, were key to OSS missions.

In the 1950s most veterans, whether Communist or not, were harassed or forced out of their jobs by the FBI. Communist Lincolns in particular were hit hard by the repressive Subversive Activities Control Board, the Smith Act, and state sedition laws, although over time all but a few convictions were overturned. In the 1950s and 1960s the majority of Lincoln veterans quit the CP but continued to be active on the Left. Notwithstanding its exclusion from American textbooks, the Abraham Lincoln Brigade commands attention as a unique example of prescient, radical, and selfless action in the cause of international freedom. *See also:* North America Committee to Aid Spanish Democracy; Spanish Revolution

—*Sam Sills*

REFERENCES

1. Books

Bessie, Alvah. *Men in Battle*. San Francisco: Chandler and Sharp, 1975.

Guttman, Alan. *The Wound in the Heart: America and the Spanish Civil War*. New York: Free Press, 1962.

Jackson, Gabriel. *The Spanish Republic and the Civil War, 1931–1939*. Princeton: Princeton University Press, 1965.

Landis, Arthur, H. *The Abraham Lincoln Brigade*. New York: Citadel Press, 1967.

Rolfe, Edwin. *The Lincoln Battalion*. New York: Veterans of the Abraham Lincoln Brigade, 1974.

Rosenstone, Robert. *Crusade of the Left: The Lincoln Battalion in the Spanish Civil War*. New York: Pegasus, 1969.

2. Films

Buckner, Noel, Mary Dore, and Sam Sills. *The Good Fight: The Abraham Lincoln Brigade in the Spanish Civil War*. New York: 1984. Distributed by First Run Features and Kino International, New York.

L'Adunata dei Refrattari

This Italian-language anarchist journal (the gathering of the incorrigibles) began publication in New York City on April 15, 1922, and ceased fifty years later, April 1971. Its name, literally, "the call of the refractory ones," was a defiant, if rather arcane, reference to words—*refrattario(It.)/refrattaire(Fr.)* —that had been used as a code by European governments before the turn of the century, during the heyday of "the propaganda of the deed," to identify anarchists in laws meant specifically to suppress their movement. The anarchism propagated by *L'Adunata* reflected the exceptional influence of Luigi Galleani, editor of the suppressed anarchist paper *Cronaca Sovversiva* (Barre, Vermont, and Lynn, Massachusetts, 1903–19), who had been deported to Italy in 1919 by the U.S. Government. *L'Adunata*'s mixture of Kropotkinesque anarcho-communism, belief in direct action and revolution, and absolute antiorganizationalism continually involved it in many a passionate polemic within the Left and within the anarchist movement itself. It played a major role in anarchist activities not only in America but throughout the world, especially where concentrations of Italians were to be found. At its peak, during the anti-fascist struggle in the thirties, *L'Adunata* counted between 12,000 and 15,000 militants as its supporters. It always represented the dominant trend within the Italian anarchist movement in America.

L'Adunata appeared in 1922, shortly after the Red Scare had run its course in the United States and when it was clear that social revolution in Italy, whose coming had seemed so imminent after the war, was not going to materialize. It was founded by anarchists who wanted to carry on the legacy of *Cronaca Sovversiva*. *L'Adunata* played a leading role in the abortive struggle to save Sacco and Vanzetti, fellow anarchists who had been caught up in the postwar web of repression and were facing death in Massachusetts. Members of its editorial group were always among the most influential members of the defense committee formed to support the pair, and both Sacco and Vanzetti always considered themselves an integral part of the journal, as they had been part of *Cronaca Sovversiva*. They accepted the militant ideals of *L'Adunata* wholeheartedly and wrote for it, particularly Vanzetti, most of whose political writings were smuggled out from prison article by article and appeared in *L'Adunata* under various noms de guerre —*Il Picconiere*, the man with the pickax, *La Vedetta Solitaria*, the solitary steersman. *L'Adunata* also made several preparations to break the men out of prison, but they never came to fruition. The seizure of power by the fascists in Italy (1922) and the cessation of mass immigration by newly enacted U.S. laws (1924) severely limited the growth of *L'Adunata* in America and in Italy, its two most natural fields of activity. Because of the determined hostility of both the American and Italian governments a significant part of the movement also had to become clandestine. Further energy was dissipated in bitter ideological and personal disputes, but *L'Adunata* managed nonetheless to summon sufficient force to aid political prisoners, to rally *fuorusciti* (Italian antifascist refugees) throughout the world, and to fight fascism on the streets of Little Italies throughout America.

After the tragic close of the Sacco and Vanzetti case—they were executed on August 22, 1927—in order to resolve internal personal and political differences the paper called back one of its most experienced and trusted comrades from Europe to assume the editorship. Raffaele Schiavina (1893–1987), who, as administrator of *Cronaca Sovversiva*, had been deported from the United States in 1919 along with Galleani, was to have one of the most remarkable and least known careers in the story of twentieth-century American radicalism. After his deportation, Schiavina, with Galleani, started to publish *Cronaca Sovversiva* in Torino, Italy, but after the rise of fascism had halted its publication, Schiavina escaped to France. In Paris Schiavina edited several Italian-language journals, *La Difesa per Sacco e Vanzetti* (1923) and *Il Monito* (1925–28), and was deeply involved in many antifascist activities. When in 1927 Luiga Vanzetti passed through Paris on her way to see her brother in Boston just days before his execution, Schiavina helped to organize a massive demonstration on behalf of his two comrades, both of whom he had known well in America. Because of his earlier deportation and the unrelenting search for him by OVRA, the fascist secret police, Schiavina had to reenter the U.S. clandestinely in 1928. Despite his illegal status, Schiavina, under his assumed name, Max Sartin, managed to publish *L'Adunata* week after week for the next forty-three years, until it ceased publication in 1971, and succeeded in eluding all authorities until he died in 1987. He was one of the most incisive, militant, and enduring pens in the service of the anarchist movement; he wrote books, articles, editorials, pamphlets, translations, memorials, obituaries, and maintained a vast correspondence with anarchists throughout the world. His papers contain the fundamental source materials for the as yet unwritten history of the Italian anarchist movement in America. Ironically, for a group with a strong antiorganizational bias, *L'Adunatisti* managed to sustain one of the anarchist movement's longest lasting and most regularly published journals. During critical times they were always among the movement's most dependable elements. *See also*: Anarchism, Italians, Sacco-Vanzetti

—*Robert D'Attilio*

REFERENCES

Berman, Paul. "The Torch and the Axe: The Unknown Aftermath of the Sacco-Vanzetti Affair." *Village Voice*, May 17, 1988.

D'Attilio, Robert. "La Scomparsa di Max Sartin," *L'Internazionale* (Ancona, Italy) 23 (January–February 1988).

D'Attilio, Robert, and Jane Manthorne, eds. *Sacco-Vanzetti: Developments and Reconsiderations—1979*, Conference Proceedings. Boston: Boston Public Library, 1982.

AFRICAN AMERICANS: *see*

American Negro Labor Congress; Armed Struggle; Berry, Abner Winston; Black Nation; Black Panther Party; Civil Rights Congress; Civil Rights Movement; The Crusader; DuBois, W. E. B.; Garveyism; Gray, Eula; Hansberry, Lorraine; Harrison, Hubert H.; Haywood, Harry; Hudson, Hosea; Hughes, Langston; Jones, Claudia; League of Revolutionary Black Workers; McKinney, Edward Britt; McKay, Claude; Moore, Queen Mother; National Negro Congress;

National Negro Labor Council; Ovington, Mary White; Patterson, Louise Thompson; patterson, William L.; Randolph, A. Phillip; Robeson, Paul; Robinson, Earl; Rustin, Bayard; Scottsboro Case; Simkins, Modjeska Monteith; Southern Negro Youth Congress; Student Nonviolent Coordinating Committee; Winston, Henry; Wright, Richard

African Blood Brotherhood: see The Crusader

African Studies

A field of study nourished on international controversy, African studies naturally became an arena of political scholarship. The revolutionary impact of African independence movements, the rise of African socialism, and the continuing influence of imperialism afforded a direct link between revolutionary hopes and intellectual concerns for at least a portion of the Left and of the academy in postwar America.

African studies began in American academia with the work of Columbia-trained anthropologist Melville Herskovits. He published a two-volume study of the kingdom of Dahomey based on his 1931 fieldwork, and went on to establish the first African studies program, at Northwestern. Herskovits's best known work, *The Myth of the Negro Past* (1941), shows his concern for Africa to have been linked to the issue of blacks' status in American society. This link was evident in earlier work by black writers—W. E. B. DuBois's remarkable little 1915 survey of Africa (*The Negro*) makes it clear—and remains a hallmark of African studies in America.

A succession of events from 1950 to 1970 brought African studies from this beginning to a position as an established area of study. The rise of America to world dominance brought government support for area-studies programs in the fifties. Fulbright programs, the National Defense Education and Foreign Language acts, and private foundations supported this expansion. Second, the independence of African countries, beginning with Ghana in 1957 and including Algeria, Kenya, and the Congo (now Zaire), brought greater American attention to Africa. Third, the later stages of the civil rights movement and the black power movement brought wide demands from black and white students for courses on Africa.

Scholarship in African studies was often regarded as radical by those in other areas, more because of its subject matter than because of the approaches of Africanists. In fact the early leaders in the field were liberals rather than radicals. What distinguished American (as opposed to European) Africanists was their greater readiness to criticize colonialism and racism.

The emergence of a clearly radical approach in American studies of Africa took place in 1969 at the ninth annual meeting of the African Studies Association, in Montreal. White radicals brought to the meeting a pamphlet entitled *African Studies: The Extended Family*, which criticized leading scholars for collaborating with American policymakers on Africa. Community black activitists combined with marginalized black scholars to take over some of the sessions. In the end, the Canadians seceded to form their own African studies association, and a dominantly black group seceded to form the African Heritage Studies Association; both these groups thrived.

During the seventies and eighties, many studies appeared relying on Marxism or on Immanuel Wallerstein's world-system approach. The new work by Marxists was particularly important in anthropology, but also in economics, history, and sociology. For instance, the critique of modernization theory and the discussion of modes of production was important in all these disciplines in the 1970s. The Association of Concerned Africanist Scholars formed in the 1970s as a political and lobbying arm of radical scholars: it focused efforts on critique of American policies in South Africa, Angola, Mozambique, and Western Sahara.

By the time of the 1984 Washington meeting of the ASA, hosted by Howard University, the battles between black and white Africanists had subsided, as indeed had the polarization between radical and liberal tendencies. Meanwhile, throughout the 1980s the Social Science Research Council sponsored a series of research overview papers by major scholars. Radicals were prominently featured among them, notably Frederick Cooper, author of studies of African workers, including *From Slaves to Squatters*.

The failure of independent African countries to prosper or to achieve democratic political structures challenged academics to develop a more critical analysis, focusing on internal contradictions in class and gender as well as the critique of imperialism. Radical scholars met this challenge well enough to achieve wide recognition and professional standing, especially as acknowledged in the annual Herskovits Prize for the best book in African studies. *See also*: Wallerstein, Immanuel

—*Patrick Manning*

REFERENCES

Cooper, Frederick. *From Slaves to Squatters: Plantation Labor and Agriculture in Zanzibar and Coastal Kenya, 1890–1925*. New Haven: Yale University Press, 1980.

Du Bois, W. E. B. *The Negro*. New York: Oxford University Press, 1970 [first published 1915].

Herskovits, Melville J. *The Myth of the Negro Past*. New York, 1941.

Cotton Pickers!

STRIKE!

For $1 per 100 lbs

Refuse to pick a boll for less!

Strike on every farm or plantation where cotton is being picked for wages!

Accept No Less Than The Union Prices----
$1 per 100 lbs

Strike Call Effective TODAY
Special Committee
SOUTHERN TENANT FARMERS UNION

See Instructions for local strikes Committees

Please Pass This On

The first strike leaflet of the Southern Tenant Farmers' Union

AGRARIAN RADICALISM

The rural radical movements, rarely outright Marxist or even socialist, have often linked up with the Left by virtue of common enemies and, to a lesser degree, similar aspirations. This ambiguous relationship has hidden a pattern, more usual in labor and reform movements, of agrarian leaders' sophistication in Marxist concepts and has obscured the disproportionately influential role sometimes played by a nucleus of Left activists in rural causes.

The essentially "conservative" character of most agrarian dissent, demanding the preservation of existing small-property relations, could be seen as well in contemporary artisanal movements, both immigrant and (especially) native-born, through most of the nineteenth century. Rural and urban workers alike sought to restrain the destruction being wrought by burgeoning capitalism, not only of economic opportunities, but of republican virtues that seemed to make America a unique site. Irredentist demands for the *return* of stolen lands, by Native Americans and by Mexican Americans, generally followed a different and much less successful course, isolated by a lack of sympathy from the vast majority of white Americans. Yet taken together, the various rural moments of unrest and violent uprisings constitute the most frequent resistance to rising capitalism.

The Civil War accelerated the growth of industrialism enormously, and simultaneously made possible (or politically necessary) the

partial achievement of a long-standing radical demand through the enactment of the 1862 Homestead Act. As envisioned by printer-agitator George Henry Evans and incorporated in early Republican Party platforms, such an act would encourage emigration from the cities, thereby raising wages, and create a formidable small-property democratic stratum. In practice, the granting of huge tracts to railroads along with other speculators and the rapid monopolization of banking and transportation limited the farmer's influence and subjected him to severe exploitation. In the post-Reconstruction "New South," black and white sharecroppers, still landless in any meaningful sense, faced the same problems and worse.

Out of this dilemma emerged a series of agrarian self-help associations, the Grange and the Farmers' Alliance the most prominent. The Grange (or Patrons of Husbandry), founded in 1867, grew rapidly during the 1870s into a honeycomb of social, cultural, and cooperative marketing and supply operations. While its ban on politics and its exclusion of blacks vitiated any militant role, the Grange prepared many individuals for other actions. The Farmers' Alliance developed during the 1880s with a speed unprecedented in U.S. protest movements. It sponsored, at the local and regional level but especially in the South, a "subtreasury" plan whereby every county with sufficient agricultural production of basic grains or commodities such as cotton would have a central warehouse sponsored by the government that would issue receipts for farmers' products at a fair price and with an honest grading of quality. As a few contemporary critics have noted, the arguments of the prolific Alliance press often paralleled Marxian thought in identifying key exploiters if not in advocating any collective resolution.

True to the finest traditions of American radicalism, the Alliance went further in relation to blacks and women than any other contemporary movement, labor or socialist movements included. The "Colored Alliance" appeared in 1888 and spread widely through the South, although probably never near the claimed peak of more than a million members in sixteen states. To a greater degree than among whites, within this movement the effort at economic cooperation predominated, difficult work carried on sub rosa in large part. Its story therefore remains shadowy, and by no means fully explored. Its most dramatic direct action occurred with a strike of black cotton-pickers in September 1891, inciting a wave of repression that ended the Colored Alliance. But the political ramifications went further, surfacing in a variety of political campaigns that promised an end to lynching and, in some cases, embraced full black participation in government. In all, this was the most important movement of black Southerners between Reconstruction and the civil rights era.

Leading Populist women arose, generally from small towns or cities within farming states, to become leading orators and organizers, chapter secretaries, and writer-editors. They argued for the "cooperative household," where, their common oppressions removed, all members of the family would share the work then done by women. They also established a critique of male privilege as a ruinous principle of American capitalism. Establishing their own newspaper, the *Farmer's Wife*, and their own National Women's Alliance in 1891, they viewed their participation as crucial to success ("Put 1,000 women lecturers in the field and the revolution is here," as a *Farmer's Wife* maxim went). Mary Elizabeth Lease (1850–1933), who made her fame calling on Kansas farmers to "raise less corn and more hell," traveled through a variety of movements to become an idol of ordinary Populists and a national leader of their movement. At the end of the 1890s she joined the Socialist Labor Party for a brief period.

Caught between a drought that persisted through most of the 1890s and continuing low prices, the Farmers' Alliance (now increasingly known as the Populists, or People's Party) elected numerous state legislators, along with a few governors and congressional representatives. The Alliance majority favored, although with considerable ambivalence, solidarity not only of women and blacks but also between farmers and workers. By 1892, then, leaders proferred offers of unity to left-leaning urban coalitions and to the waning Knights of Labor, as well as to the fast-growing but politically ambiguous Women's Christian Temperance Union.

This dramatic bid failed due to mutual distrust and deep conflicts of interest. Immigrant socialist activists looked with abhorrence on the temperance movement, many of whose supporters sought the illegalization of alcohol; besides, farmers sought higher prices for commodities, while workers needed lower prices or higher wages. The "Omaha Platform" of 1892 attempted to paper over these differences, calling for the subtreasury, government reclamation of lands held on speculation, government ownership of railroads and telegraph services, support for organized labor, the silver standard, and opposition to "any subsidy or national aid to any private corporation for any purpose." Incidents of racial solidarity in the South, and of material support for labor strikes and movements of the unemployed, encouraged hopes that a grand revolutionary change was close at hand.

But over the following few years, the Populist movement disintegrated with alarming speed and thoroughness. Apparent proximity to power emphasized racial, class, and regional differences. Large farmers in particular sought only minor adjustments in social relations. Even some of the most apparently radical figures ("Sockless Jerry" Simpson, for instance) eagerly supported U.S. overseas military and economic expansion in the name of wider markets. Common cause with blacks, let alone racial egalitarianism, proved difficult to sustain. Western Populists in particular enthused over the "free" minting of silver, ostensibly to increase the circulation of money and ease agrarian debts but also incidentally favoring silver-rich districts. In the 1896 presidential campaign, assembled Populists first turned in the direction of railroad-strike hero Eugene Debs, but closed their major political protest by accepting the Democratic party nominee, reformer William Jennings Bryan. The defeat of Bryan by William McKinley punctured hopes of ordinary Populists and their many radical supporters, rural and urban, of gaining a foothold for change within the political system.

The collapse of Populism and the formation of the Socialist Party in 1901 afforded many former Populists (albeit only a small portion of the Populist movement, mostly in the Southwest and West) an opportunity to cut the Gordian knot that bound them to dreams of merely reforming capitalism. Instrumental in this development was the *Coming Nation*—and its successor, the *Appeal to Reason*—which reached tens and perhaps hundreds of thousands who had passed through agrarian radicalism.

That a vast socialist constituency should be organized through an acerbic, folksy newspaper rather than a political movement was characteristic of American radicalism. In a real sense, the lecturers, conventions, and press of the abolitionist and woman's rights movements a half-century earlier had been the true precursors of southwestern socialism. "One Hoss Philosopher" J. A. Wayland, land speculator and entrepreneurial publisher of the *Coming Nation* and the *Appeal to Reason*, was famous for his sales-talk of socialist ideas to strangers. The two newspapers served as an extension of this logic. He regarded the victims of capitalism as contributing to their own enslavement, and often said so directly in his column; abolishing wage-slavery and its variants, he believed, would complete the task begun with the American Revolution and advanced with the abolition of black slavery. While the *Appeal* supported the SP and urged readers to enlist, it did not focus on inner-party affairs, controversies, or (with a few exceptions such as Eugene Debs, perhaps the most beloved of all living beings to *Appeal* readers) personalities. It raked the muck of capitalist-created misery, and through a chatty style pointed a way out in the promise of a cooperative society.

The area around the *Appeal*'s home territory of Girard, Kansas, offered a striking example of mixed semirural socialist constituencies. Known as the Little Balkans, southeastern Kansas had a major coalfield with half a dozen immigrant nationalities, at least one ethnic socialist periodical, in Italian, and a powerful United Mine Workers socialist contingent. Beyond the coal patches, pastoral and small-town life dominated the scene. Once established, the Appeal Building, "Temple of the Revolution," was the most prominent feature of the town. Here, socialist and middle-American values (with such characteristic tangents as spiritualism and vegetarianism) found a common meeting ground. Too rarely, however, did socialists notice that the most natural proponents of the synthesis were themselves middle-aged, drawing values from a world already disappearing.

The SP developed considerable strength in many rural areas, not only in Kansas, but also in Oklahoma, parts of Texas, Arkansas, the Dakotas, and Minnesota. Typically centered in the small towns, where farmers, coal miners, tradesmen, railroad workers and others shared culture and exchanged information, the SP local upheld education, in the republican spirit, as training ordinary people to attain their own and common interests. Vast encampments modeled upon the revival-tent form drew thousands, sometimes for almost a week at a time, to listen to socialist messages and be entertained by socialist musicians. Contesting local, state, and national political power, while important, was perceived as a means more than a goal of their mass explanatory effort amid crisis-ridden and doomed capitalism.

Ironically, the SP national leaders themselves never resolved what the Germans called the "Agarfrage," whether and how future agrarian production would be state- or private-owned. Farm constituents, especially as they grew toward their political apex in 1910–12, fervently opposed collectivist schemes, eclectically supporting ostensibly "Left" and "Right" positions on various questions within the socialist movement. By and large, the agrarian leaders remained on their own, blessed by a sense of autonomy and the ability to reach formulations acceptable to their constituents.

By 1904, Oklahoma Socialists had scored their first political victory, notably in a mining town of the Choctaw Nation, with the election of a mayor. Many such triumphs followed. By 1910, indeed, Oklahoma had the strongest SP base in the United States, some 5,482 members, 800 more than New York State. Texans, with far fewer members, could boast of a vigorous press, including the Hallettsville *Rebel*, with more than 20,000 circulation. Two years later, at the political flood tide, Oklahoma Socialists polled more than 40,000 votes, 16.6 percent of the state's total. Louisiana added more than 5,000, Arkansas more than 8,000 and Texas more than 25,000.

Socialists were limited by legal disfranchisement of black and white small farmers alike, and were virtually crushed by waves of repression that increased after 1912. Especially in Oklahoma, socialists struggled to resist black disfranchisement as they called for female enfranchisement. Direct action by desperate tenants, whose plight most resembled that of the urban proletariat, both heightened the importance of the socialist movement and threatened it with disaster. Oscar Ameringer and a battalion of other socialist editor-agitators participated widely in such organizations as the Oklahoma Farmers Union, the Texas Land Renters' League, and the Working Class Union, but these could not overcome the enormous power of bankers and landlords. Repression spread, lynchings rose, and vigilantism became the rule in many countries as socialists were publicly identified with banditry and virtually outlawed.

The Green Corn Rebellion of 1917, which pitted radical Oklahoma farmers against the Selective Service System, ended in a military debacle and an open opportunity for government action. Participants received long prison sentences, and the SP in Oklahoma, while retaining selective strengths, never regained its formidable status as threat to the two-party system.

Meanwhile, the war fell hardest upon the rural SP press. The U.S. attorney general's suspension of second-class mailing permits, along with a wave of patriotism upon entry into the war and Woodrow Wilson's liberal declarations, destroyed the vast majority of socialist papers. In another sense, the mostly middle-aged rural socialist population finished out its activism in a bold expression of antiwar sentiments. The next generation, less appalled by the "electric light towns" (a rural socialist phrase for the county seats) than fascinated by sophistication, had abandoned the appeals to republican virtues anyway.

In some regions, the radical agrarian movement gained new strengths, however. To some degree, the war had alienated rural German and Scandinavian stock from the political mainstream. Secondly, more workable forms of reformist radicalism could be created in the absence of a viable socialist movement. In North Dakota the Non-Partisan League, founded by A. C. Townley in 1915, soon took over the state government by political maneuvering, and instituted a state bank and state grain elevator. In Minnesota a Farmer-Labor Party burst forth to answer the severe decline in farm prices and to accommodate militant populations (such as formerly proletarian Finnish workers, removed by blacklist to rural districts). In Wisconsin, the Progressive Party of Robert LaFollette lost the support of the urban middle classes but salvaged its prospects by a shift to rural populations and ethnic workers.

The Farmer-Labor Party ventures of the 1920s afforded Communists important new opportunities, and the SP a last major opportunity, at influencing large rural populations. The Communists gathered pockets of support in Minnesota and such spots as Sheridan County, Montana, where *Producers News* had been a left-wing socialist weekly with a strong local base of support, and its editor, Charles "Red Flag" Taylor (1884–1967) had become both a Communist and a state legislator. Communists, hamstrung by internal party factionalism and by dependence upon their allies in the Chicago Federation of Labor, resolved first to lead an avowedly radical Farmer-Labor Party (with Taylor as chair) and then virtually abandoned the effort as the LaFollette candidacy gathered steam. Opposing LaFollette's Progressive Party run, they lost key contacts and most of the nonethnic support they had gathered. Socialists, on the other hand, threw all their remaining energies into the LaFollette campaign, but emerged with little to show for their effort.

Perhaps the greatest Left triumph and defeat in the entire rural sector was the Cooperative Central Exchange (CCE), centered in the heavily Finnish ironmining region around Superior, Wisconsin, and Duluth, Minnesota. Working outward to the small towns of the region, the "cooperators" established some fifty-six stores by 1921, created their own training school and an educational department that taught Marxism as a facet of the search for a cooperative world. At their peak toward the end of the 1920s the largest single cooperative network in the U.S., the CCE fell into the miasma of Communist factionalism and the larger reality of Party insistence upon ultimate political controls of hitherto largely autonomous efforts. In 1930, after an overwhelming defeat, the Communist cooperators withdrew their eighteen stores and established their own small-scale network, which dissolved itself in Popular Front days.

Communists thus entered the Depression with only a fraction of their former rural influence. Their main asset, Ella Reeve ("Mother") Bloor, had relocated to be with her new husband, a Left farm leader, and immediately set out upon speaking tours of the desperately impoverished rural districts. Joined by young activists Harold Ware and Lem Harris, Bloor and Charlie Taylor revived the United Farmers League, launching new branches in Montana and the Dakotas.

This small Communist contingent existed within a network of newer farm protest leaders and institutions, radical in immediate demands but far from Marxist. Locked in Third Period logic, Communists found the demands of other organizations, let alone the organizations themselves, extremely difficult to endorse—and tempting to attack, however self-isolating the result. The *Farm News Letter*, Lem Harris's cautious alternative to the harsh tones of *Producers News*, took more constructive ground in setting forward a program of farm "holidays" from mortgage payments and federal price supports. Working in a virtual Popular Front manner, Harris and Ware intervened in the series of major conferences farmers themselves held. Their new paper, the *Farmers National Weekly*, had a brief but impressive success.

The failure of a national farm strike and the beginnings of federal payments badly undercut the rural movement by 1934, and the more sectarian Communist wing took control of the apparatus, ironically just as the Popular Front had begun to take hold in Communist strategy generally. A turnaround brought the Farmers National Committee for Action, directed by Harris, into new friendships and alliances, especially with the antiwar sentiments from many non-Marxist rural activists. The *Producers News* folded in 1937, but the *Farmers National Weekly* gained supporters, as Communists battled against Father Coughlin's conservative following (who supported William Lemke in the 1936 election). Communists found a haven in the National Farmers Union, a New Deal–oriented umbrella protest movement. Hard-core support remained concentrated in the upper Midwest, disproportionately Finnish in character. Communist participation in Minnesota's Farmer-Labor Party, severely damaged when Elmer Benson lost his reelection bid as governor in 1938, remained a factor in state politics for a decade.

The SP played a notable role, briefly but poignantly, in support of the Southern Tenant Farmers Union, led by H. L. Mitchell. Reclaiming an abandoned socialist political base and building a unique biracial tenant organization, Mitchell won a few important victories for improvement of conditions. Unlike the southern Communists who participated in a shootout at Reeltown, Alabama, Mitchell (sometimes directly helped by Norman Thomas as visiting speaker) chose a more careful course, by garnering federal support for civil liberties. Even the Trotskyist movement made a contribution to the agrarian struggle, through C. L. R. James's participation in a southeast Missouri tenant farmers' action of 1942.

By wartime, the Left had acquired another ally, the New York State–based Dairy Farmers Union, and its paper, *Farmers Defender*. As in the National Farmers Union, to which the DFU affiliated, the "united front" brought a strong sense of unity, which Roosevelt's death and the emergence of the Cold War thoroughly eclipsed. For a time, the NFU ardently resisted the drift. Identified as Left-linked, it was subject to many attacks, and (to the surprise of Communists as well as others) took no official position of support for the Henry Wallace-Glen Taylor Progressive party ticket in 1948. A modest recovery of Left strength within the NFU fell to pieces with the Korean War.

The Second World War also had another effect. Mobilizing manpower and providing new avenues of economic opportunity, it scattered familiar Left constituencies, drawing many radical farmers and their descendants into the armed forces or into cities from which they did not return to the land.

What remained of Left influence rested largely in the hands of Iowa's Fred Stover, longtime NFU activist and for a time in the 1940s the organization's foremost leader. His opposition to the Korean War was the last of many defeats within the organization. His new National Farm Organization of the mid-1950s contained a handful of now mostly middle-aged radicals, the monthly *Farm News* a final radical outpost. Patterned after the Holiday movement twenty years earlier (an organized refusal to market crops at ruinous prices), NFO found no strategy for the direct, cooperative marketing that it espoused.

The 1960s brought new and different insurgencies to black southern and Chicano western districts. But most later radical agricultural organizations—with a total potential constituency of less than 5 percent of the U.S. population—have experienced only brief success in protests over immediate issues, often for more or different federal aid. As the farm economy worsened again in the later 1980s, a vacuum of power inclined more farmers to lean Right rather than Left, toward the vision of a conspiracy more Jewish than capitalist. New patterns of radicalism, led by such Left-mainstream figures as Texas commissioner of agriculture Jim Hightower and by Jesse Jackson, had only begun by that time to assume political-economic forms sometimes surprisingly similar to the old cooperative schemes of the Farmers' Alliance. *See also*: *Appeal to Reason*; Communist Party; Farmer-Labor Party; Migratory Agricultural Labor; Mitchell, H. L.; Socialist Party; Southern Tenant Farmers Union

—*Mari Jo Buhle*

REFERENCES

Fred Blair Interview. Oral History of the American Left, Tamiment Library, New York University.

Blumberg, Dorothy Rose. "Mary Elizabeth Lease, Popular Orator: A Profile." *Kansas History* 1 (Spring 1978).

Dyson, Lowell K. *Red Harvest: The Communist Party and American Farmers*. Lincoln: University of Nebraska Press, 1982.

Goodwyn, Lawrence. *Democratic Promise: The Populist Movement in America*. New York: Oxford University Press, 1976.

Green, James R. *Grassroots Socialism: Radical Movements in the Southwest, 1895–1943*. Baton Rouge: Louisiana State University Press, 1943.

Harris, Lement. *My Tale in Two Worlds*. New York: International Publishers, 1986.

Hightower, Jim. "'I Do Not Choose to Run,' Raising Hell and Hope." *The Nation* 248 (February 6, 1989).

Shore, Elliott. *Talkin' Socialism: J. A. Wayland and the Role of the Press in American Radicalism, 1890–1912*. Lawrence: University Press of Kansas, 1988.

Agricultural Workers Organization: see Agrarian Radicalism; IWW; Migratory Workers; Neff, Walter

Algren, Nelson (1909–81)

Novelist and essayist of Swedish and German-Jewish ancestry, Algren was born in Detroit, but when he was three his family moved to Chicago, where he remained most of his life. Although he received a degree in journalism (University of Illinois, 1931), the Depression forced him to take odd jobs such as door-to-door salesman, migratory worker, carnival hand, and gas-station attendent. His first published story, "So Help Me," appeared in *Story* in 1933. His first novel, *Somebody in Boots*, was published in 1935 and *Never Come Morning* seven years later.

Most of Algren's fiction is about the despised and desperate subproletariat: "life's other side—men and women who have no alternatives . . . whose lives are nightmares," "backwoodsmen without a backwoods," "hitchhikers alone on the nowhere road," outcasts for whom "everything is hopelessly and forever wrong." His intense realism, sense of foreboding, pessimism, oneiricism, and dark humor always distinguished Algren from the sentimental socialist authors of his generation.

In the 1930s Algren helped Jack Conroy on the *Anvil* and worked on the WPA Writers' Project, helping to complete the *Galena Guide* and writing scripts for a WPA radio series on working-class life. He was close to the Communist Party for some years, but he never became a member, finding in it "a certain kind of rigidity" and an "authoritarian attitude" that repelled him. While his own radicalism did not tend to organizational life, he frequently praised figures such as Eugene Debs and Haymarket martyr Louis Lingg. Algren remained devoted to revolutionary ideals long after more orthodox "reds" of the 1930s had accommodated themselves to the postwar conservative backlash.

Algren warmly supported the civil rights movement as "the only movement that sustains the old American radical tradition," and he was an outspoken critic of the war in Vietnam. In the early 1960s when an interviewer asked him to agree that the U.S. was "more of an open society than Russia," he retorted, "It's as though I were in a flood in Mississippi and the water is up to my waist and you're saying, 'It really isn't serious, because there are people drowning in the Volga.'" In his later years he acknowledged anarchist leanings, and remarked "I would like to think I am basically against government."

The Man with a Golden Arm (1949) and *A Walk on the Wild Side* (1956) brought him a mass audience and movie sales. His stories were collected in *The Neon Wilderness* (1949) and, together with several essays and a few poems, in *The Last Carousel* (1973). Less well known than his fiction are Algren's essays, which are among his finest work and embody some of his most provocative criticism of American society. This category includes the merciless *Chicago: City on the Make* (1951), parts of *Who Lost an American?* (1963), the savagely ironic "The Cortez Gang," his somber reflections on the 1919 "Black Sox" scandal, and his warm evocation of Depression bank-robbers Bonnie and Clyde.

As the 1960s wore on, Algren stated he did not know of any culture that was as hard on its writers as America. His own experiences with publishers and film producers had not been pleasant. Implacably hostile to the literary establishment, he found himself ostracized by major publishers and book reviewers.

In 1975 Algren relocated to New Jersey and then to New York. He was researching the life of black middleweight boxer and political prisoner Rubin "Hurricane" Carter for what would be his last novel, *The Devil's Stocking*. Rejected by mainstream publishers, the novel remained unpublished at the time of Algren's death and only appeared two years later under the imprint of a minor firm. Of this last book Algren said, "I've tried to write about a man's struggle against injustice—that's the only story worth telling." *See also*: Proletarian and Radical Writers

—*Franklin Rosemont*

REFERENCES

Donahue, H. E. *Conversations with Nelson Algren*. New York: Hill and Wang, 1964.

ALINSKY, SAUL DAVID (1909–72)

Born to orthodox Jewish emigrants from Russia, Alinsky was raised and educated in Chicago and came of age amid the radical ferment of the Great Depression. The "Alinsky method" of community organizing, for which he is best known, was shaped in the late 1930s by his involvement with initial efforts to organize the Congress of Industrial Organizations (CIO), his contact with community efforts sponsored by the Communist Party during its Popular Front period, and his social work with the innovative Chicago Area Project (CAP). In the Back of the Yards Neighborhood Council (BYNC), which he oganized with neighborhood resident Joseph Meegan in 1939, Alinsky combined his prior experiences into a blueprint for community organizing: (1) develop a pragmatic "trade union in the social factory" where people at the neighborhood level can bargain, strike, struggle, and advance their interests as they did in the CIO, (2) create a power-oriented community organization willing to use militant, conflict tactics like the Unemployed Councils but without the council's ideology or Party-building orientation, and (3) promote a democratic organization, such as CAP, in which organizers do not lead but rather develop indigenous leaders and in which the process of self-determination—letting the people decide—reveals the progressive nature of grass-roots democracy.

The initial BYNC was a classic project of the Popular Front period. At this time, Alinsky saw himself as a "professional antifascist" and the council as a skillfully organized coalition of all sectors of Back of the Yards—residents, merchants, clergy, and packinghouse union organizers, among whom were Communists. The enemy was outside the neighborhood—factory owners and local officials.

Throughout his life Alinsky was a defender of the downtrodden, a Jeffersonian democrat, a populist antagonist of concentrated power and privilege. Before 1947 this tied him closely with Left efforts. But in the constrained context of Cold War America, the Alinsky method and initial efforts like the BYNC veered Right. The BYNC became a powerful neighborhood organization in Chicago, known as much for its segregationist stands as its progressive victories. Alinsky even sought to assist anticommunist efforts in both France and Italy. By the 1960s, the "professional antifascist" had become an "urban populist," committed to empowering those at the bottom of society with an organizing method and a set of tactics. This "nonideological" organizing, advanced through his Industrial Areas Foundation, became popular in the 1960s among groups seeking a progressive alternative to the turbulence of the era and to Old and New Left models of social change. In the 1970s and 1980s "neo-populist" organizers modified and expanded the Alinsky method, hoping to create a grass-roots, majoritarian, Left strategy more effective than the single-interest, single-group efforts characteristic of the 1960s.

Alinsky was a brilliant tactician and demanding organizer whose work, perhaps more than that of any other individual, reflected and advanced the two dominant shifts in organizing since World War II—from the factory to the community as the locus of organizing and from consciously ideological to "nonideological" politics. *See also*: Civil Rights Movement

—Robert Fisher

REFERENCES

Alinsky, Saul. *Reveille for Radicals*. Chicago: University of Chicago Press, 1946.

Bailey, Robert Jr. *Radicals in Urban Politics: The Alinsky Approach*. Chicago: University of Chicago Press, 1974.

Finks, P. David. *The Radical Vision of Saul Alinsky*. Ramsey, N.J.: Paulist Press, 1984.

Fisher, Robert. *Let the People Decide: Neighborhood Organizing in America*. Boston: Twayne, 1984.

ALLERTON AVENUE "COOPS"

Perhaps the most concentrated group of American radicals in a single housing complex, the residents of the Co-ops (pronounced as *coops*, not *co-ops*), on Allerton Avenue of the Bronx, lived in a world where the Left set the cultural tone and the bourgeoisie was conspicuous by its absence.

During the early 1920s, a small number of young activists experimented with a cooperative housing and restaurant arrangement in Harlem. Most came together with wider circles during the summer, in Camp Nitgedaiget, Beacon, New York. They ambitiously planned a housing development for workers in a section of the Bronx still sparsely settled. With the guidance of architect Herman Jessor (he would later design Co-op City), they designed high ceilings, sunshine in at least one room of each apartment, and a common courtyard facing Bronx Park.

The "Workers Cooperative Colony" managed to complete almost 750 apartments with about 2,000 rooms, and to help maintain a group of small cooperative businesses in the surrounding areas—laundry, tailor, grocery, newsstand, cafeteria, and butcher shop among others, and even engaged a physician dedicated to preventive medicine. The Depression eclipsed most of this effort, however, and after a ten-year moratorium of debt payments the directors accepted a private landlord rather than set a bad political example by raising rents.

The political and social atmosphere through the 1940s emphasized versions (mostly the Communist version) of Jewish socialism. Cultural events in the Vanguard Community Center brought radical films, concerts, and a multitude of classes along with socializing. The International Workers' Order commanded great loyalty, as did Yiddish (and English) shuls for children. The library, with some 75,000 books, served the entire northeast Bronx.

Equally important, "Coopniks" acted widely upon the world outside their gates. They were the heart of neighborhood rent strikes (although never against the Co-ops), union drives, May Day Parades, and fundraising for many causes but especially antifascism and the Yiddish Communist daily *Morgen Freiheit*. Political gerrymandering split the coop vote into two districts to prevent a solid bloc of votes for American Labor Party candidates.

The shift to private ownership, McCarthyism, upward mobility and assimilation of young people, and finally the deterioration of the neighborhood ended the experiment. In 1977 a Coop reunion was held. *See also*: Communist Party, Rent Strikes

—Paul Buhle

REFERENCES

The Coops. Great Neck, N.Y.: Semi-Centennial Co-op Reunion, 1977.

ALLIS-CHALMERS STRIKE

This 1945 action, and its aftermath of repression, marked a new phase of conservative counterattack against the CIO, aimed specifically at Communist labor leaders and indirectly aided by CIO chiefs themselves.

Workers at Allis-Chalmers, in West Allis (Milwaukee), Wisconsin, had sought to organize themselves, with limited success, until they received a charter from the UAW-CIO as Local 248. Throughout World War II, the company attempted to provoke a strike, and made quite clear that they would force a strike, to undo the gains, when the war ended. Unwilling to bargain with the union's Left leadership and rejecting arbitration, the company succeeded in promoting a nearly unprecedented campaign of harassment by FBI agents, anticommunist congressional investigators, media witch-hunters, and other conservatives against the strikers. Anticommunist unionists in Wisconsin, including some UAW locals led by Walter Reuther supporters, for a time refused to supply strike support.

After eleven months the strike failed, nearly destroying Local 248 as a result of the firing of almost one hundred of its leaders. Harold Christoffel, the local's first president and most noted public Left figure, was later sent to prison for perjury before the Taft-Hartley Committee. The strike and its defeat—spuriously described by Walter Reuther as a "political" strike in consonance with European Communist-led strikes—delivered a serious blow to the Left in the UAW. Although progressive unions had lent their support to the strike and its leaders (and although Local 248 itself managed to rebuild under Taft-Hartley), the workers had become strategically weaker in the face of the increasingly coordinated repression. *See also*: United Auto Workers

—*Harold Christoffel*

REFERENCES

Levenstein, Harvey A. *Communism, Anticommunism and the CIO*. Westport: Greenwood, 1981.

Amalgamated Clothing Workers of America

Born out of the great risings of needletrades workers that erupted between 1909 and 1913, the Amalgamated was officially founded in 1914 as a new industrial union. Samuel Gompers and the AFL leadership condemned it as an illicit dual unionist breakaway from the Federation's craft affiliate in the men's clothing industry, the United Garment Workers (UGW).

In fact, the Amalgamated originated earlier, during a 1910 mass strike in Chicago against the industry's leading manufacturer, Hart, Schaffner and Marx. The strike was reluctantly endorsed and quickly abandoned by the nativist and corrupt UGW. Like the "Rising of the 20,000" in New York City the year before, the strike had been triggered by accumulated miseries of sweated labor: the petty tyrannies of foremen, the endless hours, the filth and stifling air, the niggardly piece-rates always subject to arbitrary reductions, the precariousness of a livelihood dependent on the wild seasonal and cyclical oscillations of a business subject to the whims of fashion. The strike enlisted the help of middle-class progressives like Jane Addams and the Women's Trade Union League, who were both repelled by the medievalism of the industry and worried that if these abuses were left unchecked the new immigrants of the "rag trade" would become permanently estranged, a chronic source of social instability and even revolution.

Indeed, the rank-and-file garment workers who actually led the strike and the institution to which it gave birth were, without exception, political radicals for whom trade unionism was but part of larger designs for social transformation. Among its founding cadre, nearly every variety of left-wing politics was represented: Lithuanian revolutionary nationalism, Bohemian free-thought, Italian syndicalism, the revolutionary unionism of the Industrial Workers of the World, Jewish and Italian anarchism, the orthodox socialism of the American Socialist Party and Second International, and the tactically bolder socialism of the Jewish Bund. The Wobblies were particularly conspicuous during the Hart, Schaffner and Marx strike and continued to exert influence during the union's formative years. But organized Jewish socialism, in both its Second International and Bundist versions, actually dominated the evolution of the Amalgamated—not surprising for an industry where Jewish workers comprised a plurality of the labor force and included within their ranks a disproportionate number of experienced trade unionists and socialists.

All radicals agreed that the AFL was afflicted by a fundamental elitism, craft parochialism, political conservatism, and anti-immigrant nativism. But the Socialist Party, which included such Jewish notables as Morris Hilquit and Abraham Cahan, was also committed to a strategy of "boring from within," hoping to gradually convert the AFL, if not to socialism, then at least to a position favoring industrial unionism. Cahan and the Jewish socialists who led the trade-union affiliate of the AFL, the United Hebrew Trades, therefore exerted pressure on the fledgling leadership of the Amalgamated to compromise its differences with and rejoin the UGW. But the young men—they were almost all young and male despite the fact that the industry's labor force was nearly half female and, more to the point, that many of the shop-floor leaders at the outset of the Hart, Schaffner and Marx strike were women—were not about to surrender their bitterly contested organizational independence in the higher strategic interests of Abraham Cahan's socialist Tammany Hall on Union Square.

Many, although by no means all, of these founding figures were refugees from the 1905 Russian Revolution, including the new union's president, Sidney Hillman. Like Hillman, they had belonged to the Bund and were familiar both with the tactics of the mass strike and the more centralized discipline of a semi-clandestine political party. Together with a smaller complement of Italian socialists and one-time Wobbly organizers—the Bellanca brothers, Emilio Grandinetti, and others—they fashioned a militant, semi-industrial, and ethnically mixed union that by 1919 managed to consolidate its position in most of the industry's major markets: a remarkable accomplishment when one considers the previous history, stretching well back into the 1890s, of repeated failures to establish a lasting organizational presence among the men's clothing workers.

World War I created an environment conducive to this early success and in several crucial respects was pivotal in the formative life of the union. Because of its wartime concern with labor shortages and unrest, the government sanctioned collective bargaining and actually exerted pressure on uniform manufacturers to negotiate with the Amalgamated. At the same time, echoes of Bolshevism and the radical democratic movements for workers' control, which spread across Western and Central Europe, resonated within the ranks of the ACW. At its founding convention, the union had adopted a militant, class-struggle preamble for its constitution, lifted almost verbatim from the credo of the Socialist Labor Party. (The union's general secretary, Joseph Schlossberg, had in fact until recently been a leading figure in the SLP.) The risings of soviets in Germany and Hungary, the factory occupations in Italy, and the strikes in France all made the most improbable apocalyptic dreams seem suddenly imminent. The Jewish rank and file, in particular, greeted the overthrow of czarism with delirious enthusiasm.

However, the war also generated countercurrents within the union's hierarchy. Hillman depended on the government's support and developed close relations with officials like Felix Frankfurter, Walter Lippmann, and Louis Brandeis, all of whom were sympathetic to trade unionism, even to industrial unionism, but who were averse to radical working-class politics. Frankfurter and others were ideological proponents of "industrial democracy," an antidote to the pervasive crisis of authority in the workplace that recognized the need for autonomous vehicles of working-class representation, but also sought to incorporate such institutions within a broader collaborative program premised on expanded and efficient production and mass consumption. Hillman embraced "industrial democracy" wholeheartedly as the "British road" to industrial equity and peace; that is, as the preferred alternative to the tyranny of the "Prussian method" and the social chaos of Bolshevism. The ACW was quickly lionized by middle-class progressives everywhere as the pioneer of the "new unionism" with a social conscience. It combined innovations in collective bargaining—especially the creation of an elaborate democratic apparatus of grievance mediation and impartial arbitration—

SPRING CREEK CAMPUS
WITHDRAWN

with a broader interest in social welfare. Thus, during the twenties, the Amalgamated was heralded for its introduction of unemployment insurance, cooperative housing, labor banking, and consumer cooperatives.

Even before the Great Depression, then, the contest between reform and revolution was firmly decided in favor of the former. A series of factional battles in the mid-twenties eliminated most anarchist and Communist opposition to the union leadership, an opposition that in any event was itself not always averse to the basic logic of the "new unionism." By 1929 the Amalgamated's "new unionism" foreshadowed the fundamental transformations authored by the New Deal and the CIO, both in the field of industrial labor relations and in the wider arena of social welfare. The Wagner, Social Security, and Fair Labor Standards acts encoded in federal statutes reforms first enacted in microcosm by the ACW. Orchestrating the diverse motivations of numerous ethno-occupational groups into a coherent movement for industrial justice and economic well-being was the Amalgamated's central accomplishment, one that paved the way for all the new industrial unions of the CIO.

For all these reasons, Sidney Hillman played a conspicuous role during the New Deal and World War II and embodied the critical political link between the CIO and the New Deal Democratic Party. He staunchly defended the New Deal against all its enemies on the Right and Left. As the chairman of CIO-PAC he helped institutionalize the relationship between the new labor movement and the Democratic Party. Hillman's career and that of the ACW encapsulated the political trajectory of much of the industrial labor movement in mid-twentieth-century America. Beginning as an avowedly socialist union, excluded from the mainstream of American industrial and political life, it had become, by 1945, integrated into a new industrial order, renouncing its more visionary aspirations for a share in the cornucopia of mass production and consumption. *See also*: American Labor Party, Italians, Socialist Party, Workers Control, Yiddish Left

—*Steven Fraser*

REFERENCES

Fraser, Steven. "Dress Rehearsal for the New Deal: Shop-Floor Insurgents, Political Elites, and Industrial Democracy in the Amalgamated Clothing Workers." In *Working-Class America: Essays on Labor, Community and American Society*, edited by Michael H. Frisch and Daniel J. Walkowitz. Urbana: University of Illinois Press, 1983.

———. "Sidney Hillman: Labor's Machiavelli." In *Labor Leaders in America*, edited by Melvyn Dubofsky and Warren Van Tine. Urbana: University of Illinois Press, 1987.

Josephson, Matthew. *Sidney Hillman: Statesman of American Labor*. Garden City: Doubleday, 1952.

AMERASIA

A monthly magazine (1937–47) devoted to the Far East and the American involvement therein, *Amerasia* had a limited but prestigious readership, most of which consisted of Far Eastern specialists in the official and academic worlds. It was started by Frederick V. Fields, the secretary of the American branch of the Institute of Pacific Relations, an academic organization, and Philip J. Jaffe, a businessman long a student of the Far East. Both had been editors of *China Today*, a left-wing journal covering somewhat the same area, which ceased publication in deference to the new venture.

Under the guidance of an editorial board of Far Eastern specialists, *Amerasia* presented a broad political analysis of the realities of the Far Eastern situation (e.g. the developing Chinese Communist revolution and Japanese imperialist invasion of China) and its implications for American policy. With the coming of World War II, the journal's contents increasingly discussed anticipated postwar problems. At the same time many members of the editorial board resigned to join in the war effort; others withdrew as objections to the founders' left-wing connections were brought into greater prominence.

In June 1945, in one of the government's first noisy salvos into what was later recognized as the Cold War, the FBI arrested the two remaining editors, three officers of the government, and a journalist, accusing them of trying to pass government secrets to a foreign power. Several thousand allegedly confidential papers were seized as evidence. After a few months of sensational headlines, the *Amerasia* Case, as it became known, petered out. The great bulk of papers turned out to be not so secret. On the contrary they proved to be an embarrassment to the government because they revealed the true situation in China, which the government had gone to great lengths to conceal from the American public. Neither side wanted a lengthy, expensive, and highly publicized trial, so a compromise was reached whereby two of the defendants paid a nominal fine and the government dropped the case. *See also*: Asian Studies, McCarthyism

—Frederick Vanderbilt Field

REFERENCES

Field, Frederick V. *From Right to Left*. Westport: Lawrence Hill, 1983.

Jaffe, Philip J. *The Amerasia Case from 1947 to the Present*. (privately published, 1979).

Klehr, Harvey, and Ronald Radosh. "Anatomy of a Fix, the Untold Story of the *Amerasia* Case." *The New Republic*, April 21, 1986.

U.S. Congress, Senate. *Institute of Pacific Relations Hearings before Subcommittee to Investigate the Administration of the Internal Security Act*. 82nd Cong. 1st sess. Washington, D.C.: Gov. Printing Office, 1951.

American Committee for Protection of Foreign Born

For almost fifty years, the ACPFB battled the federal government's attempts to deport and denaturalize foreign-born Americans. Founded in 1933, largely on the initiative of Roger Baldwin of the American Civil Liberties Union, the committee came to specialize in the defense of radical aliens. During periods of political repression, the organization's caseload increased, but even during the relatively liberal New Deal years the federal government was under pressure to crack down on the Left; and the ACPFB soon found itself defending Harry Bridges and some other Communist and left-wing labor leaders against deportation. The anticommunist furor of the McCarthy period in the late 1940s and early 1950s inundated the organization with business, especially since mainstream civil liberties organizations refused to defend Communists.

The organization was closely allied with the Communist Party and its conception of its mission drew heavily on the Party's theory of "labor defense," which required a two-pronged campaign to mobilize public opinion against political deportations as well as challenge them in the courts. The ACPFB's success, however, depended more on the overall political climate than it did on the organization's ability to win mass support or on the legal skills of its attorneys. In the early 1940s, during the high point of U.S.-Soviet friendship and tolerance for the CP, the organization was able to win some important legal victories as well as attract the assistance of such eminently respectable Americans as Wendell Wilkie, the Republican presidential candidate in 1940, who helped the organization litigate a successful Supreme Court case against the denaturalization of the California Communist leader William Schneiderman.

With the onset of the Cold War, the federal government began an intensive drive against foreign-born radicals. By the beginning of 1947, the Immigration and Naturalization Service (INS) had initiated deportation proceedings against more than a hundred people, many of whom it tried to detain without bail. The ACPFB handled most of these cases, litigating several of them all the way to the Supreme Court. The pace of deportation activity increased during the early 1950s with the passage of the McCarran Internal Security Act in 1950 and the McCarran-Walter Immigration Act in 1952. By 1953, Eisenhower's attorney general, Herbert Brownell, was threatening to deport 10,000 "subversive" aliens.

Though a few hundred foreign-born leftists did have to leave the country, most of the people threatened with deportation for political reasons were able to remain. The ACPFB handled many of their cases, though it is unclear how helpful the organization's efforts were. Until the late 1950s, the federal judiciary's reluctance to curb the government's anticommunist campaign meant that ACPFB attorneys were able to win few victories in the courts. Nonetheless, the slowness of the judicial process and the technicalities that the organization was able to exploit kept many otherwise deportable aliens in this country until changes in the political climate ended the danger.

The committee's activities as a mass-action organization were less successful. Its leaders, especially its executive secretary, Abner Green, and the heads of its Detroit and Los Angeles chapters, Saul Grossman and Rose Chernin, labored valiantly, lobbying against repressive legislation and organizing support groups for the people threatened with deportation. But because the organization was considered by the federal government and by those mainstream liberals who knew of its work to be a Communist front, it was never able to broaden the opposition to political deportations from its beleaguered enclave on the far Left.

In addition, the organization was severely handicapped in all its activities by official harassment. Individual leaders were called before congressional committees or were themselves threatened with deportation. Abner Green actually spent three months in Danbury Federal Penitentiary for refusing to give a federal grand jury a list of contributors to a bail fund for CP leaders indicted under the Smith Act; and Rose Chernin had to fight off a Smith Act prosecution as well as an attempt to denaturalize her. The organization was harassed as well. Attorney General Tom Clark put it on his list of subversive organizations. The New York State attorney general revoked its status as a charitable organization, and in April 1953 Attorney General Brownell tried to make it register with the Subversive Activities Control Board as a "Communist-front organization." The ACPFB successfully fought the registration order, but the struggle lasted for thirteen years and severely drained the organization's resources.

Even so, the American Committee did not fold. Though the pace of politically motivated deportations did begin to slacken by the late 1950s, there were still enough new cases as well as old ones to keep the ACPFB busy throughout the sixties. By the 1970s, however, the political deportations that had been the ACPFB's main concern had largely ended and the group shifted its focus to that of organizing opposition to sanctions against employers of illegal aliens. In 1982 it merged with the National Emergency Civil Liberties Committee and went out of business. *See also*: Communist Party, McCarthyism

—*Ellen Schrecker*

REFERENCES

Smith, Louise Pettibone. *Torch of Liberty*. New York: Dwight-King, 1959.

AMERICAN EXCEPTIONALISM

The notion of American exceptionalism is an old one with many meanings. In its strictest form, it refers to the apparent departure of the United States from certain assumed historical norms or laws of development. For one reason or another, so the notion goes, the United States has failed to produce ever-sharper antagonisms between capital and labor (as measured, most commonly, by the rise of a viable socialist movement). Hence, it appears that America is an exceptional historical case, quite different from other capitalist nations. The search for reasons why this is so has taken scholars and pundits in numerous directions, searching for the flaws (or, depending on the writer, the strengths) that are unique to American politics, culture, and social relations. As a result of these searches, observers have often diluted the concept of American exceptionalism to mean something closer to American distinctiveness, concerned with all the ways the United States is different from other countries.

In some respects, claims about American exceptionalism date back to the earliest days of European settlement on these shores—at least as far back as John Winthrop's famous remark to his fellow Puritans in 1630, that they would establish a "city upon a hill," a clear break from the corrupt world they had left behind. Through the age of revolution, travelers, colonists, and home-grown *philosophes* explored what was special about the North American continent and its inhabitants—inquiries that culminated in Crèvecoeur's *Letters from an American Farmer* and Jefferson's *Notes on the State of Virginia*. By the nineteenth century, America had come to loom large in the imaginations of European thinkers as different as Hegel and Tocqueville, as some sort of exceptional image of the future. Americans, for their part, proudly proclaimed theirs a unique political society, freed from the shackles of Old World superstition and tyranny.

The coming of industrialism to the United States, the emergence of labor movements from the 1820s to the 1890s, and the demise of slavery forced observers to rethink some of these assumptions, in light of the passing of long-established regimes. Mainstream writers, while foreseeing the closing of the American frontier and the rapid growth of manufacturing, celebrated America's supposedly exceptional lack of fixed social classes and its opportunities for social mobility. American radicals, however, measured some of the new industrial realities against the legacy of the American Revolution, and found that the nation had departed in decisive ways from its highest ideals of personal independence. European radicals, meanwhile, tended to respond ambiguously to American events: while none could deny the liveliness of American labor movements, they also tended to believe that American workers were far more attached to bourgeois political and social ideals than their European counterparts were—and therefore proved an "exceptional" kind of working class.

In this century, the notion of American exceptionalism has gathered enormous strength from writings all across the political spectrum. Conservative writers, sometimes mingling nostalgia with analysis, have kindled the ideal of America as a providential nation, set apart from the rest of the world as a bastion of freedom. Liberals have preferred to focus on economic growth and cultural pluralism as the keys to understanding American distinctiveness. Mostly, however, the modern discussion of exceptionalism has revolved around issues first raised on the Left.

The German socialist Werner Sombart's *Why Is There No Socialism in the United States?* (1906) became a classic statement of the problem. Sombart's answer to the question he posed—that American class-consciousness had been wrecked on "shoals of roast beef and apple pie"—reflected both the economism of the Second International and the German ascendancy within the international socialist movement. The émigré Selig Perlman, a product of the Russian social revolutionary movement, restated matters somewhat in *A Theory of the Labor Movement* (1928). Perlman stressed both the importance of political citizenship and the power of "pure-and-simple," "bread-and-butter" unionism as major factors undermining American working-class radicalism and assuring American exceptionalism. Somewhat later, the question reappeared in various dissident corners. Of special note were the writings of Leon Sampson, which argued that "Americanism" had become a kind of substitutive socialism for American workers. In a rather different vein, writers grouped around the anti-Stalin Bukharinite opposition of the 1930s—including Bertram Wolfe and Lewis Corey—wrote explicitly of "American exceptionalism" while drawing on Bukharin's general theory of exceptionalism.

Since the 1930s, what had once been a debating point for left-wing intellectuals has entered the mainstream of academic controversy. Young liberal historians and sociologists who had been influenced by the 1930s Left (notably Richard Hofstadter, Louis Hartz, Daniel Boorstin, and Seymour Martin Lipset) refashioned the exceptionalism idea in the 1950s, in their explanations for the apparent overriding consensus in American political life. The more celebratory strain in this scholarship lives on today in the writings of historians like Boorstin, as one of the animating concepts behind academic neoconservativism.

The New Left of the 1960s and early 1970s, while arguing against the so-called consensus school, carried on with its own versions of the exceptionalism argument. While insisting that class divisions are central to American life, New Leftists also contended that one or another social or cultural factor (ethnicity, racism, party politics, mass culture) has effectively muffled working-class consciousness. Explanations for what various scholars called "the historical incorporation of the American working class" remained very much a part of New Left historical and sociological writing, whether couched in the Gramscian vocabulary of "hegemony," in borrowings from the Frankfurt School, or in some other idiom.

More recently, the entire concept has come under further scrutiny—and considerable attack. At the core of the exceptionalism problem, some scholars have argued, is a fallacious, teleological assumption that the past and present ought to judged against some preconceived notion of what *ought* to have happened. Continuing events in Europe and elsewhere have made the United States seem far less "exceptional" than ever before. The criteria for assessing normality—what C. Wright Mills once called a "labor metaphysic," which quickly turned into a socialist metaphysic—no longer appear as self-evident as they once did. Discarding their blinders, several historians have located a powerful, recurrent strain of American working-class consciousness, rooted in the very concepts of democratic equality that older historians misconstrued as "bourgeois." Without denying the obvious differences between the United States and other industrial capitalist countries—the heritage of slavery, the impact of mass immigration, the changing structure of American politics—historians, literary critics, and social scientists have begun looking at class relations and social development without judging them against some predetermined model of supposedly normative results.

Not that the idea of American exceptionalism has entirely disappeared. The picture of America as a shining city on a hill, standing virtually outside of history, retains a powerful cultural appeal. Plainly, the differences between characteristically American ideas and situations and those in other countries are open to comparative study. There are still some scholars and activists who think the exceptionalism question a useful entryway into larger problems of United States and world history. At the moment, however, the whole matter would seem to be more important as a myth that needs analysis than as a fixed historical reality requiring some global explanatory theory. *See also*: History, U.S.

—*Sean Wilentz*

REFERENCES

Foner, Eric. "Why Is There No Socialism in the United States?" *History Workshop Journal*, no. 17 (Spring 1984).

Laslett, John H., and Seymour Martin Lipset, eds. *Failure of a Dream? Essays in the History of American Socialism*. Garden City: Doubleday, 1974.

Perlman, Selig. *A Theory of the Labor Movement*. New York: A. M. Kelley, 1928.

Sombart, Werner. *Why Is There No Socialism in the United States?* 1906. Reprint. White Plains: International Aptitudes & Science Press, 1976.

Wilentz, Sean. "Against Exceptionalism: Class Consciousness and the American Labor Movement, 1790–1920," with critiques by Nick Salvatore and Michael Hanagan and reply by Wilentz. *International Labor and Working Class History*, no. 26–27 (1984–85).

AMERICAN GUARDIAN: see

AMERINGER, OSCAR

AMERICAN INDIAN MOVEMENT

This was the most effective, militant, and popular organization fighting for Indian self-determination in the twentieth century.

Resistance by American Indians had been localized and diffuse until the early 1960s, when struggles over fishing and hunting rights took place in Oklahoma, the Northwest, and other places in Indian country. At that time a new organization called the National Indian Youth Council (NIYC) was formed, primarily by disenchanted children of the tribal chairmen who functioned as colonial puppets of the Bureau of Indian Affairs. NIYC was the first modern pan-Indian organization not controlled by the United States. The only other significant organization at this time was the Native American Church, whose membership was made up of traditional Indians, many of whom were spiritual leaders of their nations.

These groups were limited in their potential, NIYC because of its essentially elitist base, and the Native American Church because of the isolation of its members.

In 1968 Indians who more often than not shared a history of prison and urban poverty formed the American Indian Movement (AIM) to fight for the rights of the Indian community in Minneapolis. The goals of AIM were to combat police brutality and improve opportunities for Indian people. The early leaders were Clyde Bellecourt and Dennis Banks. In 1969 AIM participated in the occupation of Alcatraz Island in San Francisco Bay, and by 1970 AIM had a national reputation among Indians. Most of its membership was composed of younger, alienated, urban Indians unlike the college-educated NIYC members or the traditionals of the Native American Church. AIM's militant style, its willingness to go anywhere to support Indians in struggle, and the desperate conditions on reservations and in urban Indian communities made AIM attractive to a new generation of activists. Russell Means, Carter Camp, and John Trudell became leaders during this time.

With the "Trail of Broken Treaties" in 1972, a national caravan focusing on treaty rights that ended with the occupation of the Bureau of Indian Affairs in Washington, D.C., AIM became a force to be reckoned with. The U.S. government negotiated an agreement to end the occupation. Documents obtained by AIM during the occupation and later released showed widespread corruption and mismanagement within the BIA.

A year later at the village of Wounded Knee AIM seized worldwide attention when it supported traditional Oglala Sioux residents of Pine Ridge in their struggle against the dictatorial rule of the BIA-supported tribal chairman, Dick Wilson. During the seventy-one day seige Phantom jets, armored personnel carriers, federal marshals, and units from the Eighty-second Airborne Division were arrayed against Indians armed with shotguns and .22s, and the entire operation was directed from the basement of the Nixon White House.

AIM sponsored a conference on the Standing Rock Sioux Reservation in the summer of 1974 that drew thousands of Indians and established the International Indian Treaty Council (IITC) to work for international recognition of Indian treaty rights. By the end of that year the IITC had an office across the street from the UN and was pursuing support among Third World and nonaligned countries much as SNCC had done a decade earlier.

In the years following Wounded Knee AIM organized in Indian communities throughout North America, ran survival schools where political economy was one of the subjects, and held conferences that featured speakers from the African National Congress and the Zimbabwe African National Union. Despite these achievements, AIM never coalesced into a strong national organization.

Even at its height of popularity it remained a movement with no formal membership, accountability by its leaders, or clear political agenda. Wounded Knee earned AIM the support of perhaps most Indians in the United States, but the cost was high as dozens of activists faced trial in Rapid City, Sioux Falls, Cedar Rapids, and St. Paul over a two-year period. The trials drained most of the movement's resources and placed AIM in a defensive position.

At the same time repression against AIM increased, with activists facing harassment, surveillance, and frame-ups. An aide to AIM leader Dennis Banks whose title was Director of Security was revealed as an FBI agent, and was indicative of the level of government infiltration AIM experienced.

Political contradictions increased during this time as well, as some leaders adopted a spiritualist approach and denounced alliances with U.S. progressives, and others moderated their views and worked within tribal governments.

By the late 1970s AIM ceased to be a major factor in Indian country, and existed only through the rhetoric of national leaders who pretended AIM was still viable and the existence of a few institutions such as the survival schools and the IITC. *See also*: FBI

—Paul Smith

REFERENCES

Matthieson, Peter. *In the Spirit of Crazy Horse*. New York: Viking, 1983.

Ortiz, Roxanne Dunbar. *The Great Sioux Nation: Sitting in Judgment on America*. San Francisco: American Indian Treaty Council Information Center/Moon Books, 1977.

Talbot, Steve. *Roots of Oppression: The American Indian Question*. New York: International Publishers, 1981.

AMERICAN LABOR PARTY

This important but short-lived party was founded in 1936 by an amalgam of hitherto Socialist Party-related trade unions and fraternal organizations. The primary purpose of the ALP's founders—David Dubinsky and Alex Rose—was to provide an electoral line where the traditionally Socialist-voting constituencies could comfortably vote for Franklin Delano Roosevelt. Running only Roosevelt and Herbert Lehman for the U.S. Senate, it achieved its goal: it provided 274,925 votes for Roosevelt, mostly from New York City's working-class Jewish neighborhoods and at the permanent expense of the SP.

The ALP forwarded a left-leaning nonsocialist program. Its 1937 Declaration of Principles stipulated that there should be a "sufficient planned utilization of the natural economy so that coal, oil, timber, water, and other natural resources [that] belong to the American people . . . shall be protected from predatory interests." But in practice the ALP fought harder and louder for the New Deal program. Led by Vito Marcantonio, a radical New York City politician, the Communist-influenced wing had gained ascendency by 1941, which ultimately caused the Social Democratic wing to exit in 1944 and form the Liberal Party. From 1941 until the ALP's demise, foreign policy issues and black rights became central. What most distinguished the ALP, however, was its open class bias: its name said "Labor" and it used the slogan, "Don't Scab at the Ballot Box."

Although the ALP never fostered the national labor party some envisioned, it almost immediately outgrew the narrow confines of its origins. Its creation coincided with the rise of the Popular Front: New York State's Communist Party at once saw building the ALP as its major electoral priority. The ALP also proved critical to the electoral requirements of Fiorello LaGuardia and Marcantonio, both of whom became registered members. In the New Deal era, their political identification as Republicans—regardless of how maverick they were—had become an insuperable obstacle.

In 1937 the ALP polled 482,790 mayoral votes for LaGuardia, more than 21 percent of his vote. The new party also provided almost 45 percent of Marcantonio's votes for his 1938 reelection to Congress from East Harlem. Although its main political bases continued to be working-class Jewish neighborhoods (where on occasion its vote reached 50 percent), El Barrio, East Harlem's Puerto Rican community, was the only place where it became the majority party. After World War II, the ALP vote in the black communities exceeded city-wide averages. In the nine elections between 1938 and 1949, citywide the ALP averaged 13 percent of the vote, from a low of 9.6 percent during the fractious period of the Soviet-German Nonintervention Pact to 19.2 percent for LaGuardia's third mayoral election. Upstate in the six statewide elections contested between 1938 and 1948 the ALP averaged only 3.1 percent of the vote.

The ALP did not fully operate as an independent party. For the most part, it was a satellite party proffering endorsements to candidates of the Democratic Party, and to Republicans considered sufficiently progressive. When the major parties forwarded unacceptable candidates, the ALP ran its own. The

ALP did win public offices: before the abolition of proportional representation in 1947 it had members on the New York City Council, on occasion it elected state assemblymen and senators, and in a special election in early 1948 it elected Leo Issacson to Congress from the South Bronx. Without the ALP, LaGuardia almost certainly would have been a one-term mayor. At a time when almost every major American city continued to be ruled by a political machine, the ALP allowed a different kind of municipal politics to endure in New York City.

But most critically, it provided margins of victory, and after the passage of the Wilson-Pakula Act in 1947 (which effectively abolished the open primary) an electoral line to Marcantonio. The ALP also provided him with its citywide human and financial resources. Furthermore, it traded endorsements so that at first the Republican and then the Democratic parties ran sham or weak candidates and campaigns. In 1948, for example, the ALP endorsed the Democratic Party candidates for the other three congressional seats in Manhattan and in most other state legislative contests. In return, the Democrats ran a lackluster candidate who ran a feeble campaign. Vito Marcantonio, the closest thing to a national spokesman for the Left during this period, was inconceivable without the ALP.

By presenting black and Hispanic candidates, the ALP forced the issue of minority political representation. The first Puerto Rican officeholder in the continental United States, Oscar Garciá Rivera, was elected to the state assembly in 1937 from El Barrio with a majority of his votes garnered on the ALP line. The ALP also ran the first African American candidates for surrogate judge and borough president in Manhattan, forcing the Democratic Party to follow suit with their own African American candidates who became the first to be elected to those posts. The ALP also played a central role in having Adam Clayton Powell elected to Congress in 1942. Most critically, the ALP gave the Left's trade union and organizational work an electoral focus. In part, this accounts for Henry Wallace in 1948 having received one-half his vote in New York, where he ran on the ALP line.

In the postwar period, the press increasingly identified the ALP as "Communist dominated" or "Communist led." Registered ALP voters received solicitations asking them to disavow their connections with a Communist front. The trade union and fraternal organizations that provided the backing for the party were being dismantled. The ALP's voter registration fell by one-half between 1948 and 1950. Nonetheless, Marcantonio conducted a remarkable campaign in 1949 as its mayoral candidate. The party's percentage of the vote actually increased over 1948, and great gains were registered in black-populated areas. Marcantonio's defeat in 1950 to a coalition candidate of the Democratic, Republican, and Liberal parties, however, took much of what remained out of the ALP. By 1953, the CP concluded that fascism was imminent and the ALP simply served to expose its cadre to further legal jeopardy. Acrimoniously disagreeing, a loyal group around Marcantonio persisted. Unable to convince the CP to remain, he resigned in 1953, a year before his death. The ALP ceased running candidates after 1954, when its candidate for governor polled fewer than the 50,000 votes necessary to maintain ballot status. In 1956, at the dawn of a historic revival of the American Left, the ALP officially dissolved. *See also*: Amalgamated Clothing Workers; Communist Party; Marcantonio, Vito; Socialist Party; Yiddish Left

—Gerald Meyer

REFERENCES

Meyer, Gerald. *Vito Marcantonio, American Radical.* Albany: SUNY, 1989.

Waltzer, Kenneth Alan. "The American Labor Party: Third Party Politics in New Deal-Cold War New York, 1936–1954." Ph.D. diss., Harvard University, 1977.

American League Against War and Fascism

The League was formed at a U.S. Congress Against War held in New York City in the fall of 1933, and attended by over 2,600 delegates from trade unions and women's, farm, religious, and political organizations. They gathered in response to a call signed by three widely read authors of the time—Sherwood Anderson, Theodore Dreiser, and Upton Sinclair—following an international antiwar congress in Amsterdam in August 1932. It became one of forty-three national committees of a World Committee Against War and Fascism centered in Paris and headed by Lord Robert Cecil of Great Britain and Pierre Cot, a prominent French Socialist.

The Japanese invasion of northern China, Hitler's rise to power in Germany at the beginning of 1933, and maneuvers of the Western powers, including the United States, to use international disarmament conferences as screens behind which each participant sought to promote its own military superiority were seen by the Amsterdam and New York meetings as signs of an impending world war that only mass action by all peoples might derail. Since the Nazis had built their movement around the goal of destroying "Bolshevism" within Germany and internationally with at least the tacit approval of the other capitalist powers, the first League program warned that the immediate danger of war proceeded from Western determination to overthrow the sixteen-year-old Soviet government.

In addition, the founding program called on the people "to oppose the policies of American imperialism in the Far East, in Latin America, especially in Cuba" (where thirty U.S. warships were then stationed as threats to the revolutionary movement for democracy). While the initial program reflected the influence of the Communist Party, the need for a coalition that went far beyond traditional peace organizations and left-wing political parties was widely accepted. The rise of an antiwar movement in which Communists were conspicuous participants paralleled what was happening in the anti-Depression activities that led to the passage of unemployment insurance and social security, the rise of the industrial union movement and the founding of the Congress of Industrial Organizations, and the creation of a united student movement, the American Student Union, out of the Socialist-led Student League for Industrial Democracy and the Communist-led National Student League.

Among those who addressed the founding congress of the new League were Devere Allen, editor of the pacifist *World Tomorrow*; the feminist leader Harriot Stanton Blatch; Communist Party general secretary Earl Browder; NAACP field secretary William Pickens; American Federation of Hosiery Workers president Emil Rieve; A. J. Muste, head of the Conference for Progressive Labor Action; and Professor Reinhold Niebuhr of Union Theological Seminary. Support by adherents of the Socialist Party was reflected in sponsorship of the League by the Norman Thomas–led League for Industrial Democracy and the naming of J. B. Matthews, a prominent SP member, as first national chairman. When Dr. Harry F. Ward—professor of Christian ethics at Union Theological Seminary and author of *In Place of Profit*, based on his sabbatical year in the Soviet Union—replaced Matthews after the latter's resignation some months later, the League began attracting extensive support among Protestant and Jewish religious leaders and organizations.

Besides seeking affiliation of existing organizations that approved of its policies and activities, the League built citywide membership groups through which it conducted such activities as promoting a boycott of Japanese consumer goods, halting the sale of war materials to Japan, and providing assistance to the Spanish Republic and opposition to antidemocratic legislative probes and legislation. Its efforts to bring together trade unionists and members of the largely middle-class peace organizations was reflected in those membership groups as well as in the speakers who addressed its national congresses and wrote for its monthly publication, *Fight Against War and Fascism*, or *Fight*, as generally referred to. These included CIO president John L. Lewis, American Newspaper Guild founder and president Heywood Broun, and A. J. Whitney, president of the Brotherhood of Railway Trainmen. Leading artists including William Gropper, John Groth, Harry Sternberg, Art Young, and Moses Soyer were regular contributors to the magazine, as were prominent American and foreign authors.

Pioneers in understanding that special efforts had to be made to bring young people into the peace movement, the League's founders set up a youth section to do so. This section began its existence by organizing a campaign against proposals to turn the Civilian Conservation Corps, set up early in the Roosevelt administration to provide work for unemployed youth, into military training camps. Despite widespread political and press support for this diversion, it failed. The Youth Section worked against military training in the schools and sent delegates to World Youth Congresses in Geneva in 1936 and at Vassar College in 1938 and participated in student antiwar strikes. The broad constituency the League appealed to was reflected in its organizational structure, which included trade union, women's, and religious committees on national and local levels.

The organization's name was changed to American League for Peace and Democracy in 1936 to emphasize its commitment to "protect and extend democratic rights for all sections of the American people," with special emphasis on defending trade unions from corporate and legislative assault and winning passage of an antilynching law. With the outbreak of war in Europe in the fall of 1939, the American League for Peace and Democracy had lost its reason for existence and folded soon after. Before its end, the organization registered support of over four million people at its annual congresses. *See also*: Peace Movements

—*James Lerner*

REFERENCES

Klehr, Harvey. *The Heyday of American Communism*. New York: Basic Books, 1984.

American League for Peace and Democracy: see American League Against War and Fascism

American Negro Labor Congress

Formed in Chicago in October 1925 under the auspices of the American Communist Party and the Trade Union Educational League, also a Party organization, the ANLC in effect replaced earlier attempts by the Party to organize black laborers along what might be termed (for lack of space) "left Pan-Africanist" lines into the African Blood Brotherhood. According to its constitution, the stated goals of the ANLC were

> to unify the efforts . . . of all the organizations of Negro workers and farmers . . . as well as organizations composed of both Negro and white workers and farmers . . . for the abolition of all discrimination, persecution and exploitation of the Negro race and working people generally; . . . to bring the Negro working people into the trade unions and the general labor movement with the white workers; . . . to remove all bars and discrimination against Negroes and other races in the trade unions; . . . and to aid the general liberation of the darker races and the working people throughout all countries.

The first congress convened on October 25 at the Metropolitan Community Center on Chicago's South Side, under the leadership of Lovett Fort-Whiteman, national organizer; H. V. Phillips, national secretary; and organizing committee members Edward Doty and Harry Haywood. Haywood reported that, although he estimated the opening-night crowd to be around 500 people, the majority of these were from the surrounding community; the following morning, only 40 or so delegates participated in the actual work of the congress. Not too surprisingly, there were no farmer-delegates. Robert Minor claimed that black federal union members of the American Federation of Labor had been scared off by the anticommunist baiting of AFL president William Green in the press.

Viewed from a historical perspective, the organizational plan of the ANLC proposed by the October conference is familiar enough: it called for the formation of "united fronts"—dubbed "local councils"—in all centers of black population, with special emphasis on the role played by labor unions. Organizations composed of black and white workers were to be admitted, as were unorganized black workers. "Local councils" were not to compete with existing black or labor organizations, but rather were to help coordinate the work of such bodies. And finally, the councils were to facilitate the admission of black workers into existing trade unions by forming "interracial labor committees," the ultimate purpose of which was to halt practices that divided white and black laborers and to support those that united them: the elimination of trade union discrimination and the undercutting of wages, struggles against lynching and race riots, and the like.

The inauspicious beginnings of the ANLC set the tone for its future work: "Few local units were formed," wrote Haywood, "resolutions and plans were never carried into action. Only its official paper, the *Negro Champion*, subsidized by the Party, continued [sporadically] for several years." The principal and perhaps only center of "effective" organizing appears to have been Chicago, whose "local council" included some fifty members at the end of 1925. Attempts were made to organize workers as far away as Jamaica, B.W.I., but efforts failed there as well. The ANLC lasted until 1930, and was succeeded by the National Negro Labor Congress the following year. *See also*: Communist Party, Garveyism, National Negro Labor Congress

—*Ernest Allen, Jr.*

REFERENCES

Draper, Theodore. *American Communism and Soviet Russia*. New York: Random House, 1986 (1960).

Fort-Whiteman, Lovett. "The Negro and World Changes." *Amsterdam News*, August 19, 1925.

———. "American Negro Labor Congress." *International Press Correspondence*, August 27, 1925.

Haywood, Harry. *Black Bolshevik: Autobiography of an Afro-American Communist*. Chicago: Liberator Press, 1978.

Huiswood, Otto E. "ANLC Organizes Labor Unions in West Indies." *Liberator*, December 7, 1929.

Minor, Robert. "The First Negro Workers' Congress." *The Workers Monthly*, December 1925.

Rabinovitch, M. "The American Negro Congress." *International Press Correspondence*, December 10, 1925.

Spero, Sterling D., and Abram L. Harris. *The Black Worker*. New York: Columbia University Press, 1931.

AMERICAN RAILWAY UNION: see DEBS, EUGENE V.

AMERICAN SLAV CONGRESS

In the wake of the Nazi attack on the Soviet Union in June 1941, labor activists of East European origin laid plans for an organization to mobilize mass support for the war effort as a whole and for the American-Soviet alliance in particular. At core was the realization that Slavic Americans represented the vast majority of workers in key defense industries such as coal, steel, auto, electrical equipment, and rubber. Yet many Slavic groups were torn by internal dissension over the issue of Soviet claims to certain territories in Eastern Europe and separated by interethnic conflicts.

The first congress was held in Detroit on April 25, 1942, attended by 2,458 official delegates and over 500 guests. Prior to this meeting, the Polish Section of the IWO had sponsored a three-month lecture tour by two Polish CIO organizers—Stanley Nowak and Bolesław (Billy) Gebert—to raise interest in the proposed organization. Twelve ethnic groups sent representatives to the first congress: Bulgarians, Carpatho-Ruthenians, Croatians, Czechs, Macedonians, Montenegrins, Poles, Russians, Serbs, Slovaks, Slovenians, and Ukrainians. The delegates elected Leo Krzycki (vice president of the Amalgamated Clothing Workers of America) president of the ASC and Blair Gunther (a Pittsburgh judge active with the Polish National Alliance, the largest Polish American fraternal) chair. Grigori Pirinski, a Macedonian, was chosen secretary-general. The first ASC platform called for member organizations to organize war-bond drives, Russian war relief, anti-Nazi propaganda, and demonstrations supporting the Roosevelt administration's alliance with the Soviet Union. Later statements by ASC leaders addressing the issue of postwar Soviet boundaries were seen by some member organizations as favoring Soviet claims at the expense of other national claims, those of the Poles in particular.

Though the 1942 congress succeeded in attracting the interest of a broad spectrum of Slavic American fraternals as well as Roman Catholic clergy, by the second congress, in September 1944, many of those organizations and individuals (including Blair Gunther) had abandoned the ASC. Controversy surrounding visits by the distinguished economist Oskar Lange and a Roman Catholic priest, Rev. Stanislaus Orlemanski (both prominent supporters of the ASC), with Stalin in the spring of 1944 had contributed to the decline of the ASC's influence. By 1944 ad hoc leftist organizations created by the founders of the ASC predominated, e.g., the Kosciuszko Patriotic League (est. 1943) and the American Polish Labor Council (est. 1944). Leo Krzycki remained president of the ASC until 1950. *See also*: Croatians, Poles, Slovenes

—*Mary Cygan*

REFERENCES

Gebert, Bolesław. *Z Tykocina za Ocean*. Warsaw: Czytelnik, 1982.

Irons, Peter H. "'The Test Is Poland': Polish Americans and the Origins of the Cold War." *Polish American Studies* 30, no. 2 (Autumn 1973).

Lukas, Richard C. *The Strange Allies: The United States and Poland, 1941–45*. Knoxville: University of Tennessee Press, 1978.

Miller, Eugene. "Leo Krzycki—Polish American Labor Leader." *Polish American Studies* 33, no. 2 (Autumn 1976).

Nowak, Stanley. "Wspomnienie" nos. 115–126. *Głos Ludowy* (Detroit), February 1978–January 1979.

Sadler, Charles. "'Pro-Soviet Polish-Americans': Oskar Lange and Russia's Friends in the Polonia, 1941–1945." *Polish Review* 22, no. 4 (1977).

American Soviet Friendship

Following the Russian Revolution of 1917, American peace activists, labor organizers, and intellectuals sympathetic to socialism formed a succession of organizations to promote cultural interchange between the Soviet Union and the United States in order to enhance popular understanding of and sympathy for the U.S.S.R. and to influence official U.S. policy favorably toward the Soviet Union.

The earliest of these was the Friends of Soviet Russia. Formed in 1921 to help the Soviets combat widespread famine resulting from drought and foreign blockade, this organization raised relief, sent tractors, and established children's homes. Between 1924 and 1929 there was a lull in its activities.

Two events catalyzed a new friendship effort. In November 1927 delegates from fifty-one countries including the United States attended a Labor Congress in Moscow organized to form a world labor league of "Friends of Soviet Russia," whose purpose would be to defend the Soviet Union against an anticipated rhetorical and possibly military attack by united capitalist powers. Then, in 1929, a group of Russian airmen billed as the Soviet Round-the-World Fliers visited the United States. Shortly thereafter, Friends of Soviet Russia was reorganized as the Friends of the Soviet Union to follow the aims of the 1927 Labor Congress. The American Friends of the Soviet Union affiliated itself with similar groups in twenty different countries and with the International Friends of the Soviet Union, headquartered first in Berlin and later, after Hitler expelled it, in Amsterdam. Its first campaign organized mass receptions for the visiting Soviet fliers.

The stated goals of the Friends of the Soviet Union (FSU) were (a) to mobilize the masses for militant action against war and in defense of the Soviet state through meetings and organization of FSU Anti-War Committees in all basic industries, (b) to encourage normal trade relations with the USSR, and (c) to popularize the successes of socialism in the USSR through lectures, pamphlets, leaflets, films, and magazines. While the organization saw itself as having a base in the working class, it saw intellectuals and professionals as having an important role in cultural activities.

The Friends sponsored a broad program of activities. Since collectivization of agriculture was just beginning in the USSR, the group raised funds for the purchase of tractors to be sent as a present to the first collective farms. The FSU also sponsored trips by delegations of trade unionists to study the conditions of workers in the USSR and held mass-action rallies. Its principal publication was *Soviet Russia Today*, an illustrated monthly first published in February 1931, which contained articles about the Soviet economy, political administration, life, and culture. (This magazine severed relations with the FSU in December 1937, became *New World Review* in the 1950s, and ceased publication in 1986 as *Update/USSR*.)

In the 1930s the FSU was quite radical, holding mass meetings where speakers denounced religion, advocated defense of the Soviet Union, and urged preparation for class war. Speakers included William Z. Foster and James Ford, former Communist candidates for president and vice president, respectively, and Charles Smith, president of the American Association for the Advancement of Atheism. After 1934, however, meetings became more moderate in tone. To mark the twentieth anniversary of the Russian Revolution, the FSU prepared a *Golden Book of American Friendship with the Soviet Union*, published in November 1937. Thereafter, the organization was largely inactive, becoming defunct in 1939.

In July 1938 Mary Van Kleeck, associate director of the International Industrial Relations Institute, chaired a dinner conference on Soviet progress at which announcement was made of the formation of a new American Council on Soviet Relations, whose purpose would be to direct a program to encourage American-Soviet relations. There was some continuity of participation from the Friends organizations to the new Council, notably including author and lecturer Corliss Lamont, who had been involved in the previous groups and was an organizer—and in 1941 became national chair—of the new group.

The National Council on Soviet Relations brought together largely professional people desiring to increase understanding of the USSR in the United States and believing that, in the struggle against fascism, American interests coincided with those of the Soviet Union. In response to the German invasion of the Soviet Union in 1941, the Council organized a mass meeting in Madison Square Garden in July to promote American-Soviet cooperation against Hitler, and, later that year, another rally to publicize the need for prompt American military aid to the Soviet Union. After the United States entered the war, the Council advocated a second front in Europe and a declaration of war against Finland.

In November 1942 the Council sponsored a Congress of American-Soviet Friendship at Madison Square Garden that was attended by several thousand people. It featured addresses by Vice President Henry Wallace and the presidents of the American Federation of Labor and the United Auto Workers, and messages of greeting and support from President Franklin D. Roosevelt and General Dwight D. Eisenhower. Mayor Fiorello LaGuardia declared November 8, 1942, "Stalingrad Day" in New York. Corresponding meetings were held simultaneously in several other U.S. cities.

The success of the Congress affirmed the notion that American-Soviet cooperation was important to the maintenance of world peace and corresponded to American policy and interest. The official sanction of the cause of American-Soviet friendship inspired the leadership of the Council to establish a permanent organization, and the National Council of American-Soviet Friendship was incorporated a few months later. The five incorporators included the chair of the Congress, Corliss Lamont, Dr. Harry Grundfest, Rev. William Howard Melish, George Marshall, and William Morris, Jr.

Local affiliates sprang up quickly. Some were independently formed language and cultural groups, while others were more political; still others had their origins in local Russian War Relief committees, many of which re-formed as local Councils of American-Soviet Friendship when President Truman cut off aid to the Soviet Union in August 1945. By the mid-forties, there were thirty-two active Council affiliates across the country.

Three deserve particular mention. In Chicago, leaders of three local organizations—the Friends of the Soviet Union, the Chicago Forum on Russian Affairs, and Russian War Relief—established a Chicago Society for American-Soviet Relations early in 1943, which affiliated with the National Council and changed its name to the Chicago Council of American-Soviet Friendship later the same year. A Los Angeles Society for Cultural Relations between the U.S. and the U.S.S.R., founded in 1939, and the American-Russian Institute of San Francisco, founded in 1931, similarly affiliated with the National Council around 1943. These three groups, along with the National Council itself, are apparently the only Soviet friendship organizations to have survived from WW II to the present time.

The program of the National Council of American-Soviet Friendship emphasized cultural interchange as a means of strengthening bonds of understanding between the U.S. and the U.S.S.R. The Council sought to counteract negative propaganda about the Soviet Union by means of a broad spectrum of public-information activities. These included annual mass rallies, usually in Madison Square Garden in November, in celebration of anniversaries of the Russian Revolution; the publication of numerous pamphlets such as *Women in the Soviet Union* and *The Voice of American-Soviet Friendship*; and sponsorship of study tours to the Soviet Union and speakers' tours around the United States. Pictorial exhibits focusing on various aspects of Soviet life and culture were also developed for public view; the most significant of these was the "American-Soviet War Exhibit," shown at the Museum of Science and Industry in New York City in 1943 with the active cooperation of the War Department and the Lend-Lease Administration.

Although the National Council enjoyed widespread support from government officials and business and labor leaders during the early forties under the chairmanship of Corliss Lamont (1943–46), groups such as the America First Committee, Committee to Defend America, Fight for Freedom, Incorporated, and the Friends of Democracy denounced the Council from the outset as the "Voice of Stalin in America." After the war, a radical shift in American foreign policy toward the Soviet Union and the growing hostility of the Cold War brought the organization under increasing attack. The Truman administration moved from its earlier position of support for the National Council to an attitude of outright opposition, and in 1946 the House Committee on Un-American Activities began a formal investigation of its activities. The initial phase of this investigation resulted in a HUAC demand for the surrender of all correspondence and financial records of the organization. The Council refused on constitutional grounds, and both the Council's chair, Corliss Lamont, and its executive director, Richard Morford, were cited for contempt of Congress. The National Council was officially placed on Attorney General Tom Clark's list of Subversive Organizations proscribed for federal employees in 1947, and in 1954 the Subversive Activities Control Board declared the Council to be a Communist front organization.

Much of the energy of the Council and its active members during the ensuing decade and a half was absorbed in suits and appeals associated with these actions. Morford was convicted of contempt of Congress in 1950 and served three months in Manhattan's West Street Jail. In 1951, however, the U.S. Supreme Court ruled that the U.S. attorney general had acted in a capricious, arbitrary, and illegal fashion in designating the National Council a subversive organization, and in 1963 the Second District Court of Appeals overturned the Council's designation as a Communist front.

In the Cold War atmosphere of the fifties and sixties, public interest in and support for the Council declined sharply and the number of local affiliates shrank to three, from a high of thirty-two. Monetary support dwindled similarly. Nonetheless, under the successive chairmanships of Dr. John Kingsbury (1949–56) and artist Rockwell Kent (1957–71), the Council continued to pursue a program of public information activities aimed at fostering greater cultural understanding between the Soviet and American peoples and closer cooperation between their governments. Rallies and festivals of Soviet Friendship were held periodically, and the Council's Committee of Women was one of fourteen cooperating organizations that sponsored an International Women's Exposition for Peace and Friendship in 1952. The Council sponsored regular study tours to the Soviet Union and maintained a lending library of literature as well as more than sixty different photographic exhibits of aspects of Soviet life. Other projects included art exhibits, Soviet film festivals, a speakers' bureau, forums, and rallies. During this time the Council also actively supported the broader-based U.S. movements for disarmament and a nuclear test ban, and worked against the McCarran-Walter and Smith acts.

A new period of growth for the Council began in the early seventies, partly as a consequence of the official abolition of the Subversive Organizations list. Under successive chairmanships of William Howard Melish (1971–78),

Ewart Guinier (1979–84), John Cherveny (1985–87), and actor John Randolph (1988–), twenty-four new local affiliates were formed, making a total of twenty-seven by 1988. The first national convention was held in 1977, and the governing structure was reorganized to provide for more local participation and control. In January 1981 Alan Thomson became the new executive director, replacing Richard Morford, who had served in that capacity continuously for thirty-four years.

The Council's programs include an American-Soviet exchange of teenage youth, in cooperation with the Soviet organization Sputnik; sponsorship of young Americans at Artek, a Soviet youth camp on the Black Sea; a speakers' program, which sponsors lecture tours of Soviet students and professionals at U.S. colleges; and maintenance of a lending library that makes available an extensive collection of publications and films to Russian studies programs in the United States.

Improvement in official U.S. relations with the Soviet Union has also fostered the creation of other American groups interested in American-Soviet friendship. These represent a very diverse range of endeavors; exemplary are Anniversary Tours, founded by Lem Harris in the early seventies, which specializes in package tours to the Soviet Union; Promoting Enduring Peace, established in Connecticut by Jerome Davis in the late seventies, which sponsors a Volga Peace Cruise and a Mississippi Peace Cruise in alternating years for joint groups of Soviet and American citizens; and Soviet American Woolens in Kezar Falls, Maine, founded by Marty Tracy and Peter Hagerty, which sells blended skeins of Soviet and American wool marketed as Peace-Fleece through American church and community groups. *See also*: Peace Movements

—*Joanne Melish*

REFERENCES

Files, National Council of American-Soviet Friendship, through 1975, Tamiment Collection, Bobst Library, New York University. Post-1975 files, National Council of American Soviet Friendship, 85 East Fourth Street, New York, N.Y. 10003.

Also in NCASF files, Tamiment:

Butkovich, Catherine. "An Approach to American-Soviet Understanding Through Cultural Interchange." Seminar paper, Northwestern University, April 24, 1949. Typescript.

National Committee, Friends of the Soviet Union, "Who Are the Friends of the Soviet Union?" n.d. (c. 1931).

National Council of American-Soviet Friendship. "We Proudly Present: The Story of the National Council of American-Soviet Friendship." n.d. (c. 1953).

AMERICAN STUDENT UNION: see STUDENT MOVEMENTS, 1930S

AMERICAN WORKERS PARTY

AWP was a short-lived (December 1933–January 1935) revolutionary organization headed by A. J. Muste. Radical intellectuals James Burnham, Sidney Hook, and V. F. Calverton were AWP leaders, and radical writers Travers Clement, Lillian Symes, and James Rorty were also "Musteites." Prominent labor writers J. B. S. Hardman and Louis Budenz took charge of the group's propaganda and publications. The AWP leadership and rank and file also included a number of young working-class graduates of Brookwood Labor College, which Muste headed from 1921 to 1933. The AWP succeeded the Conference for Progressive Labor Action (CPLA), a Brookwood-initiated insurgent group calling for industrial unionism. Founded in early 1929, the CPLA became actively involved in strikes and organization campaigns, and evolved from reformism to Marxism.

The AWP strove to offer a thoroughly American radicalism, "rooted in American soil," as articulated mainly by Budenz, the editor of the party's weekly newspaper *Labor Action*. It professed to be more militant than the Socialists, and more practical and flexible than the Communists, its two chief rivals on the Left. Notwithstanding this "American orientation," the AWP attracted small groups of older immigrant Finnish-, German-, Yiddish-, and Italian-speaking radicals who also stood apart from the Socialists and Communists. For example, several predominantly German bakery- and food-trades unions in New York, under the influence of longtime radical editor Ludwig Lore, were in the AWP orbit.

The American Workers Party succeeded in competing with the SP and the CP most convincingly in the field of unemployed organizing. The "Musteite" National Unemployed League organized on a township- and countywide basis in areas of Ohio, Pennsylvania, West Virginia, North Carolina, and several other states, and won a number of demands from local and state relief agencies. In the Toledo Auto-Lite strike of spring 1934, Muste, Budenz, and local leaders of the Lucas County Unemployed League organized mass picketing by the unemployed in support of a striking AFL local, gaining national attention when the National Guard was sent in and the union achieved recognition.

From its beginning, the AWP received overtures from the American Trotskyists, and after the latter led another victorious 1934 strike, of the Minneapolis teamsters, merger talks began. In early 1935 the AWP combined with the Trotskyist organization the Communist League of America to form the Workers' Party of the United States. However, the core group of Musteites soon became dissatisfied with the new organization, and left to go in various political directions, Muste himself into radical pacifism, Budenz and others into the Popular Front–era CP, and many AWP rank and file into union work. *See also*: Muste, A. J.; Trotskyism

—*Jon Bloom*

REFERENCES

Myers, Constance. *The Prophet's Army: Trotskyists in America, 1928–1941*. Westport: Greenwood Press, 1977.

Robinson, Jo Ann Ooiman. *Abraham Went Out: A Biography of A. J. Muste*. Philadelphia: Temple University Press, 1981.

AMERICAN WRITERS CONGRESS

In January 1935 a "call for an American Writers Congress" went out from the pages of the *New Masses* in an effort to mobilize writers into a revolutionary cultural movement aimed at accelerating "the destruction of capitalism and the establishment of a workers' government." The "call," signed and answered by some of America's most prominent literary figures, led to the creation of the League of American Writers, an organization affiliated with the International Union of Revolutionary Writers. Through "collective discussion" among congress and league participants, its organizers hoped to reveal the most effective ways in which "writers, as writers," could function in the "rapidly developing crisis." While the call reflected the desire of the Communist Party to expand its influence and appeal beyond an already committed cadre of revolutionary writers, a practice characteristic of emerging Popular Front policies, the tightly planned and executed congress resembled, to some, an auxiliary organization of the Third Period more than an inclusive Popular Front one.

The birth of the American Writers Congress and the League of American Writers also sounded the death knell for the John Reed Clubs, organizations for aspiring young radical intellectuals. At a 1934 conference of John Reed Clubs, Alexander Trachtenberg, head of International Publishers, the CP-oriented publishing house, instructed the national committee to organize a national congress of writers. Trachtenberg's plans became clearer at a Party caucus when he informed those in attendance that with the advent of the Popular Front policy, the John Reed Clubs would be dissolved. Richard Wright, who was among the small group who attended the caucus, was shocked at the decision. He inquired what would become of the young writers whom the CP had implored to join the clubs but who would be excluded from the proposed new organization composed only of established "writers who have achieved some standing in their respective fields." Wright received no reply and no one seconded his protest. Neglected and abandoned by the CP, some of these young writers would soon leave the movement or go over to the Trotskyists.

The decision to disband the John Reed Clubs and to focus on enrolling writers of "some standing" reflected a new tack but not a complete turnabout. The Party was not yet ready to make the first congress as broad or as popular as some of the organizing committee desired it to be. Many of the sixty-two writers who signed the call—Granville Hicks, Joseph Freeman, Mike Gold, Richard Wright, Joshua

Kunitz, Malcolm Cowley, Lincoln Steffens, Theodore Dreiser, John Dos Passos, Erskine Caldwell, James Farrell, and John Howard Lawson—were members or trusted friends of the Party. Two nonwriters joined them—Earl Browder, CP secretary, and Trachtenberg. Trachtenberg restricted invitations to congress membership to "reliable" writers, checked delegates carefully, and screened the outlines of papers to be delivered. Although Waldo Frank, a non-Party writer, was nominated as the league's chairman, most of the 17 on the executive committee were Party members or fellow travelers. Browder's appearance before the 216 congress delegates only served to signify what was clear to all, the centrality of the Party in the league.

In his speech at the opening session on May 1, 1935, Browder sought to reassure non-Communist delegates that the Party did not intend to put them into "uniform," but rather to provide an organizational means for cooperating with "all enemies of reaction in the cultural field." He went further in clarifying the Party's position that there was no fixed "Party line" about good or bad works of art. The Party, he declared, did not "want to take good writers and make bad strike leaders of them." To serve the Party, Browder argued, the aim of writer-members should be to become "constantly better writers." The delegates welcomed these remarks.

As might well be expected of any gathering of intellectuals, disputes arose during the congress. James Farrell was the harshest critic of the Party's cultural stance, denouncing "that species of overpoliticized and ideological schematized criticism that had been too dishearteningly frequent in the literary sections of revolutionary journals." The greatest disagreements, by far, were aroused by Kenneth Burke's paper on "Revolutionary Symbolism in America." Burke exposed himself as a premature adherent of the Popular Front when he suggested that the symbol of "the worker" be replaced with that of "the people." Such an exchange of symbols, Burke argued, might enlist lower-middle- and middle-class allegiance to revolutionary thought. In making such a suggestion, Burke unintendedly affronted the sectarian thinking habits so well established during the Third Period and was reminded of a similar usage of the term "the people" made by Hitler. In this transitory period to the Popular Front, Burke's comments, while thoroughly criticized, were forgiven.

By the time of the Second American Writers Congress in 1937, the openly pro-Communist tone of the 1935 meeting had vanished. The Second Congress was dominated by the theme of fighting fascism and displayed a noticeable absence of revolutionary rhetoric. Also absent from the list of signers were the Party politicians and intellectuals. The declarations by several participants, in a session on criticism, of support for Trotsky, however, demonstrated the degree to which the league had drifted from the Communist orbit. Defections by members over political issues, the Moscow trials, and Trotsky, as well as the refusal of the New York John Reed Club, and its journal, *Partisan Review*, to disband, hurt the League. The final blow came with the signing of the Nazi-Soviet Pact in 1939, but by that time many of the most prominent members had left. *See also*: American Artists' Congress; Farrell, James T.; Gold, Mike; Hicks, Granville; Lawson, John Howard; *The New Masses; Partisan Review*

—Robert Macieski

REFERENCES

Aaron, Daniel. *Writers on the Left*. New York: Avon Books, 1965.

Cowley, Malcolm. *The Dream of the Golden Mountains: Remembering the 1930s*. New York: Viking Press, 1980.

Hart, Henry. *The Writer in a Changing World*. New York: Equinox Cooperative Press, 1937.

Klehr, Harvey. *The Heyday of American Communism: The Depression Decade*. New York: Basic Books, 1984.

AMERICAN YOUTH CONGRESS:

see STUDENT MOVEMENTS, 1930S

AMERINGER, OSCAR (1870–1943)

The "Mark Twain of American Socialism," Socialist literary comedian of an age, raconteur, editor, labor organizer, and occasional Socialist city official, Ameringer was one of the most colorful characters of the American Left.

Born in 1870 in Bavaria, son of a cabinetmaker and a freethinking mother, Ameringer later recalled that he sought out the company of the despised village Jews, studying the forbidden "pulp" literature with them. His parents were told he had a future at the end of a rope—or in America, where they sent him at age fifteen. There he spent his *Wanderjahre* as portrait painter, itinerant musician, hobo, and lover. He settled down as a furniture maker, only to be blacklisted after leading a strike. Living as a musician, he studied English by reading *Mark Twain's Library of Humor*, the finest anthology of its type at that time. He soon submitted his first successful literary humor, a satire on the wedding of a Cincinnati heiress to a British duke, to *Puck* magazine.

Meanwhile, Ameringer returned to Bavaria in 1890, increasingly interested in the socialist movement. A convinced socialist back in the United States in the first years of the new century, he became editor of a Columbus, Ohio, union weekly and moved from there to attempting to organize New Orleans brewery- and dockworkers, advocating interracial cooperation. In 1908 he moved to Oklahoma, where his socialist sentiment intensified rapidly. There his fame rapidly grew, both for his political talent and for his versatile public appearances for socialism as speaker, impresario, and musician. By 1911 Ameringer himself nearly won the mayorality of Oklahoma City, and his paper, the *Oklahoma Leader*, soon had a fervent following across the region, second only, among socialists, to the *Appeal to Reason*. More than any other intellectual, he mastered the art of explaining socialism in common-sense terms for the lower-class, even agrarian, reader, as in his famous tract, *Socialism for the Farmer Who Farms the Farm*.

Ameringer's major literary contribution, *Life & Deeds of Uncle Sam*, first published in 1909, stood in the tradition of satirical histories of America and in the then-current fashion of muckraking. By 1917 it had sold some half-million copies, achieved translation into fifteen languages, and become the favorite book given by the socialist to the nonsocialist prospect for conversion. Its hilarity disguised, to the unwary, the power of its critique ("When somebody talks about carrying the cross, the flag, freedom, or civilization to some heathen nation you bet your bottom boots that that heathen nation has got something the other fellow wants"). A new edition appeared as late as the 1930s.

Fleeing a destructive factional brawl and the anticipation of government repression in the Oklahoma socialist movement, Ameringer moved on to Milwaukee, where he aided the *Milwaukee Leader*, under pressure for its antiwar positions. He returned to Oklahoma City, helping to defeat a Ku Klux Klan candidate for governor in 1920, and traveled on to Springfield, Illinois, where he edited the *Illinois Miner*, a dissident weekly aimed at toppling United Mine Workers president John L. Lewis, until 1931.

Returning a last time to Oklahoma, he established the *American Guardian* that year, directing it for a decade mostly to a constituency of old-time Plains States socialists. For the *American Guardian*, Ameringer wrote some of his most brilliant satirical essays under the nom de plume "Adam Coal Digger," essays unremitting in their attacks upon American capitalism but somewhat mellow toward the Soviet Union. His autobiography, *If You Don't Weaken* (1940), recounting his experiences, reached new audiences, and was widely accepted as the most witty and engaging book of its kind ever written by an American radical. Unwilling to countenance socialist support for war, he lost many readers (and even more when his son, taking over the paper for an ill Oscar, announced a pro-war position). The paper closed in early 1942, and Ameringer lived scarcely more than a year longer. The *National Guardian* (today the *Guardian*) took its name from Ameringer's paper. *See also*: Agrarian Radicalism, Humor, United Mine Workers

—*Paul Buhle*

REFERENCES

Ameringer, Oscar. *If You Don't Weaken*, new edition with introduction by James R. Green. Oklahoma City: University of Oklahoma Press, 1983.

Buhle, Paul. Introduction to *Life & Deeds of Uncle Sam*, by Oscar Ameringer. New ed. Chicago: Charles H. Kerr, 1985.

ANARCHISM

The political state has not always existed. Most leftists have believed that the State came into existence when civilization began to produce surpluses controlled by elites who found it useful to create coercive institutions to protect their privileges from internal and external challenges. Many revolutionaries, from the late eighteenth century onward, argued that with the elimination of such privileges, the State might be "transcended" or "abolished." Friedrich Engels, Marx's collaborator, predicted that the State would "wither away" to be placed into "the museum of antiquities, next to the spinning wheel and the bronze axe."

But one sector of radicals began to suggest, especially from the 1840s, that socialists might replace the old State with something yet more oppressive. Pierre Joseph Proudhon, the first popular French spokesperson for the antistatists, wrote that Marxism in particular was a dogmatic religion that would encourage "the indivisibility of power, all-consuming centralization, systematic destruction of all individual, cooperative, and regional thought, and inquisitorial police." The result would be "the socialism of the barracks." As an alternative, Proudhon urged the creation of local and regional confederations of voluntary associations.

Such views were introduced into the United States as early as the 1850s by Wilhelm Weitling. By the late 1860s and early 1870s, several French immigrant branches of the First International pronounced themselves Proudhonites, and joined with anarchist-minded spiritualists and individualists to establish a short-lived anti-Marx federation. American anarchism gained its foremost advocate in the U.S. translator of Proudhon, polemicist-publisher Benjamin R. Tucker. Tucker drew both upon Proudhon and upon a native tradition of extreme individualism expressed by such varied figures as Stephen Pearl Andrews, Lysander Spooner, and Josiah Warren, as he produced his influential newspaper, *Liberty: Not the Daughter but the Mother of Order* (1881–1908).

For the majority of anarchists, especially immigrant anarchists, a society based upon communes would be reached by violent struggles against capitalism. The ideas of Mikhail Bakunin and his allies reached U.S. shores through the formation of the Black International, with its American devotees Burnette Haskell and Joseph R. Buchanan, and with the arrival of Johann Most and his incendiary newspaper, *Die Freiheit*, in 1882. The well-attended Pittsburgh Congress of 1883, although unsuccessful in bringing about a confederation of American anarchists, promoted in its manifesto such goals as "equal rights for all without distinction of sex or race" and "regulation of all public affairs by free contacts between the autonomous (independent) communes and associations, resting upon a federalistic basis."

This anarchist movement, arguably the most influential in U.S. history (especially among workers), reached its apex in 1886. Chicago "social revolutionaries," as they styled themselves, drew upon various sources including Marxism, Bakuninism, and Natural Rights theory as they promulgated doctrine in five newspapers (German-language, Bohemian, and English), directed the Central Labor Union, and played a key role in the eight hour struggle. Scattered across the East Coast and Midwest, smaller groups varying in background and doctrine from followers of William Morris to Bakuninites established propaganda groups and likewise sought to intervene in labor.

The suppression of the radical movement following the Haymarket incident reduced anarchism from a mass cause to a collection of groups and publications,predominantly immigrant in origins. Among the groups, Germans (still in control of the Chicago weekly *Vorbote*), Jews (with their weekly *Freie Arbeter Shtimme*, after 1890), Italians (with a proliferation of papers, mostly ephemeral), and Spaniards had a following, and a press that translated classics into various tongues. "Propaganda of the deed" held a special allure in the desperate 1890s and at the turn of the century. Alexander Berkman (1870–1936) attempted to assassinate Henry Clay Frick, plant manager of the steel plant at Homestead, Pennsylvania, after Frick's private guards and the state militia fired on striking workers; and

Leon Cołgosz (1873–1901) succeeded in assassinating President McKinley. After the McKinley assassination, most anarchists concluded such activity was ineffective and counterproductive.

Anarchist activity took a number of fresh directions. Emma Goldman established cultural respectability for anarchist ideas in the Little Theater movement and parts of the art world at large. The Yiddish *Freie Arbeter Shtimme* cultivated the experimental poets of the community, *di yunge*, and earned itself a niche as avant-garde. Anarcho-syndicalists had wide influence in the Industrial Workers of the World, especially through the Italian Socialist Federation and its weekly, *Il Proletario*, and through the efforts of individual anarcho-syndicalist leaders such as Carlo Tresca. Anarchism played an independent and important role in linking American and Mexican radicals through the Magon brothers and their newspaper, *Regeneracion*. Anarchists deeply influenced even Labor Zionists, beginning to elucidate their vision of *kibbutzim* in Palestine. And anarchists provided some of the fiercest opposition to the coming of war, with Luigi Galleani's followers joining in desperate appeals for mass disobedience. The major theorist for many in this period was Peter Kropotkin (1842–1921), a scientist who wrote such works as *Factories, Fields and Workshops* (1891) and had challenged Darwinian thought in *Mutual Aid* (1902).

Government repression fell with great severity during WWI. Newspapers closed, foreign-born militants were in many cases deported, and entire groups (Galleani's following in particular) were assaulted. The war also brought internal splintering. Following Kropotkin, a handful of anarchist leaders (most notably, Jewish leaders) endorsed the Allies, provoking wide discouragement and disillusionment. Many anarchists, some initially drawn to the Russian Revolution, found anarchism's status permanently altered by the Bolshevik regime and by Communist parties usurping the space left of the socialist movement. Anarchism's most celebrated event of the 1920s, the trial and execution of Sacco and Vanzetti, was also a terrible defeat. The destruction of Spanish anarchism, in the following period, left anarchists with only propaganda and aid to surviving victims.

Anarchist writers like Goldman continued to uphold "the old-fashioned idea that life without freedom is a monstrous delusion even if 'the trains run on time' and 'our beloved comrade in the Kremlin has made Russia the most comfortable and joyous country on earth.'" American anarchism continued to survive through such institutions as the Modern School in Stelton, New Jersey, from which old-timers continued to publish the *Road to Freedom* newspaper, various other organs such as the *Man*, the Italian-language *Adunata de Reffratari* and *Il Martello*, the Yiddish *Freie Arbeter Shtimme*, and assorted ghetto freethought societies and clubs. The most influential of quasi-anarchist papers, the *Catholic Worker*, and its assorted Hospitality Houses, was ideologically anathema to old-time anarchists: religious (even papal) anarchism.

Anarchism enjoyed a mild revival in the 1940s–1950s through a proliferation of pacifist, literary avant-garde, and antistate sentiments and accompanying publications. Especially notable in the Bay Area following World War II, anarcho-pacifism prompted the birth of Pacifica Radio, and encouraged writers later associated with the Beat generation. In New York, Dwight Macdonald published *Politics*, an approximately anarchist magazine with a small but intensely intellectual (and in the long run, influential) following. In the subsequent era, *Liberation* magazine, roughly anarcho-pacifist, seeded the ground for the New Left, as did one of its leading figures, Paul Goodman, with his influential tract *Growing Up Absurd* (1961).

Anarchist ideas continued their revival with the mounting skepticism about both "democratic people's republics" such as the USSR, and of "free-world governments" such as those of France and the United States, which conducted vicious colonial wars. The largest radical organization of the 1960s, Students for a Democratic Society, advocated an anarchist-influenced "participatory democracy" where people controlled the institutions that concerned their daily lives. Anarchist ideas, as such, found a place in *Anarchos*, published by Murray Bookchin's circle, and anarcho-syndicalist ideas in Black and Red publications, and in the later *Fifth Estate* newspaper from Detroit, both heavily influenced by the work of Yugoslav-born Fredy Perlman. Numerous New Left journals, including *Radical America*, sought to draw upon anarchism's heritage along with other sources.

After the collapse of the New Left proper, anarchism found a new haven in the ecology movement, especially in its militant, direct-action wing among groups such as Friends of the Earth. Murray Bookchin's works did much to inspire this movement, while Edward Abbey's *The Monkey Wrench Gang* (1975) offered helpful tactical suggestions. Here, as nowhere else, "propaganda of the deed," nonviolently directed against machines to save nature, had a lasting and potentially mass appeal. To a considerably lesser extent, anarchist ideas along with religious-mystical notions and many others influenced feminism's attack upon Marxism and its advocates' effort to establish a theoretical and practical approach to liberation. Punk rock, with its inspired nihilism, more directly and consciously carried anarchist ideas forward.

The results of this history cannot yet be fully assessed. Anarchism is no mass movement, has no stable class base, lacks unified theory, posits uncertain tactics, and has no long-term organizations. Its power resides in its basic critique and the conviction that even if it may never be realized in ideal form, its definitions of liberty can only perish when people have been reduced to robots. Specifically, anarchists have asked whether the future should be deeded to the numerous militaries, privileged bureaucrats, and authoritarian religions. Must agribusiness and collective farms be dominant modes of food production? Must democracy remain an indirect exercise in which casting ballots is the major duty of citizenship? Must the environment be plundered for short-term statist or corporate needs? The search for alternatives continues.

See also: Anarcho-Syndicalism; Black International; Goldman, Emma; Haymarket Incident; *Mother Earth*; Pacifism

—*David DeLeon*

REFERENCES

DeLeon, David. *The American as Anarchist: Reflections on Indigenous Radicalism*. Baltimore: Johns Hopkins University Press, 1978.

Guerin, Daniel. *Anarchism: From Theory to Practice*. Translated by Mary Klopper. New York: Monthly Review, 1970.

Marsh, Margaret. *Anarchist Women, 1870–1920*. Philadelphia: Temple University Press, 1981.

Veysey, Laurence R. *The Communal Experience*. New York: Holt & Rinehart, 1973.

Woodcock, George. *Anarchism*. New York: Penguin, 1986.

Anarcho-Syndicalism

The origins of anarcho-syndicalism are found in the discussions and resolutions of the First International's Congress at Basel (1869) and the schism they later initiated. At this meeting collectivist anarchists and revolutionary socialists within the trade union movement challenged the International's foundation principles. In his report to the congress, Eugene Hins called for the abandonment of political action and introduced into discussion for the first time the idea of workers' councils as the weapon of class struggle and the structural basis of the coming libertarian society. These ideas derived from the writing and activities of Mikhail Bukunin and had gained support in the sections of the International in Belgium, Holland, the Swiss Jura, France, and Spain. Following the London Conference of the International, these sections formed the Antiauthoritarian International in response to an attempt by Karl Marx and Friedrich Engels to broaden the powers of the General Council.

In the 1870s there appeared numerous Antiauthoritarian or Federalist sections of the International in New York, Boston, and other American cities. The *Word*, a libertarian monthly magazine founded by Ezra Haywood in Princeton, Massachusetts, began publishing Bakunin's writings. *Woodhull and Claflin's Weekly* and the *Word* became the unofficial organs of the International. These journals defended the principles of decentralist socialism and criticized the authoritarian orientation of the General Council. Among foreign-language groups in the United States were also a number of adherents of the Bakuninist wing of the International. Principally refugees from the Paris Commune, these immigrants established sections in New York and New Jersey and sent delegates to the Antiauthoritarian International that met in St. Imier, Switzerland, in 1872.

In the 1880s and 1890s revolutionary syndicalism became a worldwide movement. Carried by immigrant-worker intellectuals, anarcho-syndicalism spread through intricate patterns of "cross-fertilization." Revolutionary syndicalism did not represent a closed system of ideas, a definite philosophy or theory, but rather paralleled a movement within the working class itself that developed and changed over time. Increasingly international in influence, this movement opposed Marxian socialism and sought a more revolutionary orientation for the trade union movement. In France this trend coincided with widespread disillusionment with terrorist tactics. In the 1890s many anarchists entered the trade union movement while others immigrated to escape police repression and continue their activity. Anarchists like Fernand Pelloutier and Emile Pouget had a great impact on the trade union movement. Through their efforts, the idea that a general confederation of labor unions could manage the economy in a stateless society gave birth to the Confederation Generale du Travail in 1895.

In the United States, similar ideas were beginning to take root among native and immigrant labor activists. Among immigrant revolutionaries the German anarchist Johann Most played a decisive role. Immigrating to the United States in 1882 he became involved with the social revolutionary movement and more than any individual was responsible for its growth. Drafting the "Pittsburgh Manifesto," which sought unsuccessfully to confederate U.S. anarchist groups unto the London-based Black International. Most galvanized the social revolutionary movement. Most and his followers objected to any form of compromise with existing institutions and declared their opposition to trade unions and the struggle for immediate economic gain. Albert Parsons and August Spies, however, opposed Most's position on the trade union question. Midwestern social revolutionaries advanced the idea that labor unions represented the instrument of social revolution and would eventually replace capitalism with a cooperative commonwealth in which workers would administer the economy for their own needs. Endorsed by a majority of delegates attending the Pittsburgh congress, the "Chicago idea" represented an amalgam of socialist, anarchist, and other radical ideas derived from both American and European sources of labor lore.

The "Chicago idea" called for a free society in which the labor union represented the formative cell. The new movement was intended to be a loose federation of autonomous groups having as its connecting link an information bureau located in Chicago. The "Pittsburgh Manifesto" rejected all political parties, including the necessity of a revolutionary party of the proletariat, and called for direct action in the industrial field. The official organs of the "syndico-anarchists" were the *Alarm*, an English-language weekly, the *Arbeiter-Zeitung*, a German paper published on weekdays, the *Vorbote*, published on Saturday, and the *Fackel*, published on Sunday. The Metal Workers Federation of America, organized in 1885, came closest to realizing the "Chicago idea."

Italian immigrants, working in mining or on track gangs, or settling in large towns to become factory workers, were also significant carriers of syndicalist politics and culture. Italian and Spanish anarchists in Paterson, New Jersey, agitated for a workers' union organizational model based on anarcho-syndicalism toward the close of the nineteenth century. In Paterson the group formed the Universita Populare, which organized public lectures, discussions, social gatherings, and study groups. *La Questione Social* (*LQS*), organ of the "Right to Existence" group published many articles reporting on the European revolutionary syndicalist movement as well as appeals to striking silk workers to adopt syndicalist tactics in their struggles against manufacturing magnates.

Under the direction of the Spanish anarchist Pedro Esteve, the Paterson group became involved with the struggles of both soft- and hard-rock miners in Colorado, sending monetary support and publicizing their struggles in the pages of *LQS*. Esteve and other Paterson anarchists spent months in the western part of the United States supporting the Western Federation of Miners in their union-forming activities.

The spread of syndicalism was not limited to immigrant anarchist groups, which underscores its ubiquitous presence and influences on the American labor and political community in the twentieth century. Among the left wing of the Socialist Party were many revolutionary socialists who leaned toward a anarcho-syndicalism version of industrial unionism, while within the Socialist Labor Party a Marxist version of syndicalism emerged. The former tendency is best represented in the writings and activities of William E. Trautmann, the latter by Daniel DeLeon. Both played instrumental roles in founding the Industrial Workers of the World.

Among the anarchists active in the industrial union movement, Thomas J. Hagerty, who authored the IWW "Preamble," played a principal role. Hagerty's revolutionary attitude toward socialism had been formed through his contact with the Chicago anarchists, participation in the "eight hour" movement, and through his reading of Benjamin Tucker's semimonthly publication, *Liberty*. Forming alliances with revolutionary socialists and trade unionists, Hagerty became one of the earliest advocates of industrial unionism. Writing for the *American Labor Union Journal* and later serving as editor of the *Voice of Labor*, Hagerty advocated a form of industrial unionism that not only drew from the ideas advanced by the Chicago anarchists but incorporated the experience of French and Spanish anarcho-syndicalists.

Although American and European anarcho-syndicalism deeply influenced the Wobblies, the IWW's conception of industrial unionism did not reflect commitment to a single ideological position or source. While on a formal, or policy, level the IWW did not declare itself anarcho-syndicalist, among the Wobblies were many advocates of anarcho-syndicalism. The IWW press frequently ran news articles on the revolutionary syndicalism movement in Europe and published excerpts from the writings of Emile Pouget, S. Nacht (Arnold Roller), C. Cornelissen and others making propaganda for the revolutionary syndicalist movement. One may also find in the IWW's strike tactics and activity the influences of anarcho-syndicalism.

Following the Russian Revolution, America's entry in the world war, and the passage of criminal syndicalist legislation, anarcho-syndicalism as a tendency within the labor movement entered a decline in the United States but reemerged in Europe in the form of the International Workingmen's Association and the Spanish Confederación Nacional del Trabajo (CNT). Although anarcho-syndicalism currently lacks a visible presence in the United States, the ideas of international solidarity, pluralistic authority, and the industrial form of labor organization continue to exert influence on social movements and the labor community. *See also*: Anarchism; Black International; Father Hagerty's Wheel; Giovannitti, Arturo; Haymarket Affair; Industrial Workers of the World; Paterson Anarchists; Tresca, Carlo

—*Sal Salerno*

REFERENCES

Avrich, Paul. *The Haymarket Tragedy*. Princeton: Princeton University Press, 1984.

Brissenden, Paul. *The IWW: A Study in American Syndicalism*. New York: Columbia University Press, 1919.

Reichert, William O. *Partisans of Freedom: A Study in American Anarchism*. Bowling Green, Ohio: Bowling Green University, 1976.

Roediger, Dave, and Franklin Rosemont, eds. *Haymarket Scrapbook*. Chicago: Charles H. Kerr, 1986.

Salerno, Sal. *Red November, Black November: Culture and Community in the IWW*. Albany: State University of New York Press, 1989.

Animal Rights

Although an extensive literature questioning anthropocentrism and urging greater harmony in the relations between humankind and other animals has existed in the Western world for centuries, the modern movement for animal rights emerged only in the late nineteenth century. At first the notion that animals too had rights was little more than a side issue in platforms of other reform movements regarded as major, notably abolitionism and woman suffrage. One of the first Americans to declare that animals, even insects, "have the same right to life that I have" was Unitarian antislavery spokesman William Ellery Channing, but he gave little emphasis to this aspect of his thought in his published writings. Similarly, Susan B. Anthony, Elizabeth Cady Stanton, Frances Willard, and many other feminists took up the cause of vegetarianism (a current closely allied to animal rights) but it never became a focus of their agitation.

The American Society for the Prevention of Cruelty to Animals, the first organization in the Western Hemisphere devoted to better treatment of other species, was founded in New York in 1866, and like-minded groups soon formed all over the country. Such groups were not concerned with defending animals' rights in the broader sense, but rather in securing legislation against what they regarded as excessive cruelty. A major function of the Humane Society, founded in Chicago in 1877, was to provide public water-troughs for horses in crowded downtown areas.

With the 1892 publication in London of the book *Animals' Rights* by British socialist Henry S. Salt (a New York edition appeared two years later), animal rights came to be recognized as a distinct movement, and it began to attract the active support of other reformers. Popular feminist author Elizabeth Stuart Phelps Ward wrote tales and tracts depicting the horrors of vivisection. All through the nineties, feminists, dress-reformers, and pioneer conservationists joined animal rights advocates in an eventually successful campaign against the use of stuffed birds and exotic plumage in women's hats.

Significant as it is that the international animal rights movement was founded by a socialist, it is no less significant that Salt's socialism was rooted in the pre-Marxian radicalism of two poets: the militant vegetarian Shelley and that ardent champion of wilderness, Thoreau. The notion of a reconciliation of humans and other animals figured prominently in much utopian literature, notably in Charles Fourier's dream of "universal harmony" (which had reverberated throughout the pre-Civil War United States) and in the works of Edward Bellamy, especially with the publication of his *Equality* (1897), in which America's greatest utopian made it clear that recognition of animals' rights was a key feature of the new society. As Marxism became the dominant mode of socialism, the question tended to be shoved aside. Neither Marx nor Engels ever troubled to write on the subject in detail, but their scattered references to vegetarians and antivivisectionists are not sympathetic. This seeming indifference on the part of Marxism's founding fathers made it easier for later guardians of Marxian orthodoxy to dismiss any interest in the rights of other species as merely another form of "petit-bourgeois deviation." Of the major figures in the Marxian tradition, only Polish-born Rosa Luxemburg, in some of her letters, approached a conception of animal rights. In this area as in others, utopian dreams survived far from the Marxist mainstream, in various heretical currents and such as the Frankfurt School, Wilhelm Reich's "Sex-Pol," and above all in the anarchist movement.

In pre-World War I American socialism, at least in part because of Bellamy's enduring legacy and because of the tolerance of diversity in such mass movements as Eugene Debs's Socialist Party and the Industrial Workers of the World, animal rights was, albeit marginal, not so taboo a topic as it was in the narrower, more ideology-conscious European movement. In 1906 America's premier socialist publishing house, Charles H. Kerr's cooperative, brought out *The Universal Kinship* by Chicago high school zoology teacher J. Howard Moore—a work highly praised by Henry Salt himself as a major contribution to the animal rights cause. Moore's book was promoted in the influential *International Socialist Review* as well as in the IWW press, and Kerr, who was himself a vegetarian, published several other books by the same author. More dramatically, the last major work by America's best-known socialist writer, *Michael, Brother of Jerry* (1917) by Jack London, was a militant animal rights novel, portraying the evils of circus animal-training. In his preface London urged one and all to join the struggle for animal welfare.

But the voices for animal rights never were more than a faint undertone in the SP's heyday. Many socialists doubtless agreed with Upton Sinclair that "some day" society would be able to get along "without the maintenance of the slaughterhouse," but persuaded themselves, as the author of *The Jungle* persuaded himself, that the question could safely be postponed till "after the Revolution." For the Communists who seized the mantle of Marxism in the early 1920s and held it for decades, the question did not even exist.

Interestingly, however, as the socialists' involvement in the animal rights movement all but ceased, the movement itself virtually collapsed. Older groups grew increasingly conservative and made their peace with a social order that required the brutal exploitation of animals. Gassing to death stray dogs and cats became the chief work of many "anticruelty" societies, and in some states such groups made a business of supplying strays to laboratories for "experimentation." From the Great Depression through the Vietnam War the cause of animal rights in the United States was in eclipse.

Not until the 1970s, after a decade of civil rights, New Left, and antiwar agitation, did a new and even more radical animal rights movement arise. An important link between the older struggle for socialism and the new animal rights activism were Helen and Scott Nearing, whose radicalism extended back decades—in Scott's case to Debsian days—and whose later vision of decentralism and "the good life" involved them in a two-person crusade against the "slaughterhouse diet." As they wrote in 1979, "We cannot conceive of kindly, considerate, aware people consuming carcasses of perceptive, defenseless animals who were raised in captivity for slaughter."

Vastly larger than the movement of Salt's day (the Coalition for Nonviolent Food comprises more than 400 organizations with a membership in the millions), the new animal rights movement has acknowledged a far-reaching range of inspirations, including Salt himself (his *Animals' Rights* was reprinted in 1980), Thoreau and Gandhi and the whole current of nonviolence, Eastern religions (especially Taoism and Buddhism), and above all radical environmental movements such as Greenpeace and Earth First! These last have provided more recent activists not only with impressive examples of the effectiveness of direct action, but also with a broad, nonanthropocentric, radical ecological perspective. The new movement has tended to be a youthful one, and has readily employed methods of struggle learned from civil rights and student struggles of the 1960s: sit-ins, boycotts, blockades, sabotage, etc.

Cutting across social classes and conventional political affiliations, the movement continues to be as diverse organizationally as it is ideologically. One of its most prominent spokespersons, longtime radical labor activist Henry Spira, coordinator of many notable struggles (including the successful campaign against experimentation on cats at New York's Museum of Natural History in the 1970s), has expressed an orientation that seems to be shared by a great majority of activists: that the end for which the movement was formed—reduction of the slaughter and suffering of our fellow creatures—should never be obscured by the particular ambitions or needs of any of its constituent groups. Diversity as well as decentralization thus remain essential features of this movement, whose adherents range from traditional anti-vivisectionists with a focus on education to the clandestine "guerrillas" of the Animal Liberation Front, who conduct "raids" on animal-testing laboratories, filming their cruel procedures, seizing incriminating files, and liberating captive animals (finding homes for them later via "underground railway").

In lively book, pamphlet, and periodical literature modern animal rights activists set forth polemics against the movement's opponents—the hunting and gun lobby; the fur, meat, and cosmetics industries; the Christian churches; and the scientific establishment—and elaborate their critique of the effects and implications of the mass slaughter of animals in advanced industrial society. The monthly *Animal Agenda* appeared on popular newsstands. Without abandoning their traditional moral/ethical emphasis, they have carefully detailed the environmental devastation and health hazards wrought by animal abuse. Earlier advocates were often content simply to point out the moral wrong of meat eating and the nutritional superiority of a vegetarian diet. Newer activists tend to be more aggressive, and their view of the larger picture more concrete. In discussing the link between a meat diet and cancer, for example, recent animal rights literature points to the fact that over half the public land in the United States is heavily subsidized by the federal government to promote the billion-dollar cattle industry, thus relating the questions of meat diet and cancer to a wider context of industrial/corporate abuse of the entire planet.

The movement's leading manifesto, *Animal Liberation*, by the Australian Peter Singer, appeared as a mass-market paperback in 1975. The book popularized the term *speciesism* (by analogy with racism and sexism) to signify human arrogance toward other species. Its first chapter, titled "All Animals Are Equal," argues that "supporters of liberation for Blacks and women should support Animal Liberation too." Other animal rights activists have adopted the IWW slogan: "An injury to one is an injury to all." *See also*: Radical Environmentalism

—*Franklin Rosemont*

REFERENCES

Boyd, B. R. *Animal Rights and Human Liberation*. San Francisco: Taterhill Press, 1986.

"Singer Talks with Spira." *Animal Liberation* (Australia) January–March 1989.

ANTHROPOLOGY

Since the 1960s leftist scholarship has had a positive impact on anthropological discourse by raising questions about how the societies anthropologists study are connected to larger domains of power shaped by colonialism, the articulation of modes of production, and gender. Additionally, it has motivated a self-critical and reflexive line of inquiry into how mainstream anthropology is itself colonialist, classist, and sexist. Hence, in the last two decades, anthropology has recovered at least a part of the critical function it enjoyed at the end of the nineteenth century and the start of the twentieth, when L. H. Morgan was a major shaping influence on socialist thought and when the work of Franz Boas provided a scientific challenge to and refutation of the prevailing racism of the epoch.

After World War II anthropology became above all an academic discipline, and it was only between the demise of McCarthyism and the rise of Reaganism that Marxist anthropologists in U.S. universities could openly unveil a Left perspective. During the 1950s students of Julian Steward, notably Sidney Mintz and Eric Wolf, laid the foundation for an alteration of traditional approaches to community studies by situating the people studied in the broader context of U.S. hegemony and international capitalism. The customary objects of anthropological investigation were recast as colonized and proletarianized subjects rather than as exotic tribes or backward peasants. By the 1970s this perspective was clearly articulated by anthropologists who argued that the societies under study were not being transformed through the value-neutral processes of assimilation and acculturation, but through oppressive and exploitative colonialist and imperialist projects.

Innovative work by dependency and world-systems theorists and French structural Marxists (nonanthropologists and economic anthropologists alike) encouraged a return to the writings of Marx and Engels, above all Engels's *Origin of the Family . . .* , the four volumes of *Capital*, and Marx's *Grundrisse* (translated into English only in 1973). The Marxist concepts of mode of production and social formation assumed a saliency for understanding the societies anthropologists looked at. Marxist anthropologists were able to examine the dependent status of Third World societies in which class differentiation has assumed a variety of trajectories and where people confront different forms of capitalism. In this vein, theoretical and substantive advances have been made toward a historical anthropology, toward understanding the effects of merchant capital in "the periphery," and regarding other topics that much pre-1970s anthropology ignored or refused to problematize.

Feminist anthropologists have examined how colonialism, imperialism, and different modes of production shaped what was for long a classic topic of anthropological research, relations between men and women. Writers and activists such as Eleanor Leacock have argued that relationships between men and women are historically variable and that gender relations in some noncapitalist societies are more egalitarian than in capitalist societies. At the same time, recognizing that patriarchy antedates capitalism, leftist feminist anthropologists have demonstrated how the interaction of patriarchy with capitalism is particularly oppressive for women. An important line of research has undermined the modernization theorist's assumption that women's status improves with the development of capitalism. Scholars have noted how the entrance of women into the labor market does not lead to an improvement in their status position, since they get the lowest-paying jobs and bear the double burden of having to perform domestic work as well as wage labor.

Feminists have not only developed alternative analytical approaches to mainstream anthropology, but have questioned fundamental aspects of the discipline. Some have challenged anthropology on the grounds of its manifest male bias. This was particularly evident in androcentric kinship studies and analyses of marital alliances, in which women figured as mere tokens of exchanges controlled by men, or in studies of economic contributions to the reproduction of society, where women's roles had been glossed-over, underanalyzed, or ignored.

Other Left anthropologists have criticized the way colleagues have wittingly or unwittingly been implicated in colonialist, imperialist, and hegemonic projects. The participation of anthropologists in U.S. Department of Defense and CIA efforts to undermine popular protest in Chile and Thailand during the 1960s were revealed, and ethical guidelines for the profession were redrawn to condemn anthropological research conducted for the purpose of oppressing and exploiting the people being studied. This has had important consequences for the shape of the discipline and contributed to the creation of an intellectual space within anthropology in which leftist analysis has been able to develop. It is less clear, however, whether Marxist and Left criticism has reshaped mainstream anthropology to the extent some scholars have claimed. While issues of domination and power have secured recognition in anthropological debates, few anthropologists have explicitly politicized their own work. However, those who have no longer simply write about the people they study; they also seek to empower them. *See also*: Leacock, Eleanor; Morgan, Lewis Henry

—*Ana Maria Alonso, Teresa Murphy, Daniel Nugent*

REFERENCES

Asad, Talal, ed. *Anthropology and the Colonial Encounter*. London: Ithaca Press, 1973.

Engels, Frederick. *The Origin of the Family, Private Property, and the State*. 1884. Reprint. New York: International Publishers, 1942.

Leacock, Eleanor. "Marxism and Anthropology." In *The Left Academy: Marxist Scholarship on American Campuses*, edited by Bertell Ollman and Edward Vernoffs. New York: McGraw Hill, 1982.

Social Responsibilities Symposium. *Current Anthropology* 9, No. 5 (1968).

Wolf, Eric. *Europe and the People Without History*. Berkeley, University of California Press, 1982.

ANTICOMMUNISM

Marx and Engels announced in the *Communist Manifesto* that communism was a "specter" haunting Europe. If so, anticommunism has been the turning of that specter into a master ideology of the present epoch.

Anticommunism needs to be distinguished from radical criticism of existing "communist" societies, and from the posing of utopian alternatives to the present order everywhere. The distinction is crucial because anticommunism has frequently disguised itself in such modes. Properly speaking, anticommunism knows "communism" only to destroy it. Everything takes a bipolar coding: down with communism = up with capitalism (or rather, "Freedom" and "Democracy," purportedly realized only under capitalism). No essential complexity, no important evolution of "communist" societies themselves can be accommodated in this system, and above all,

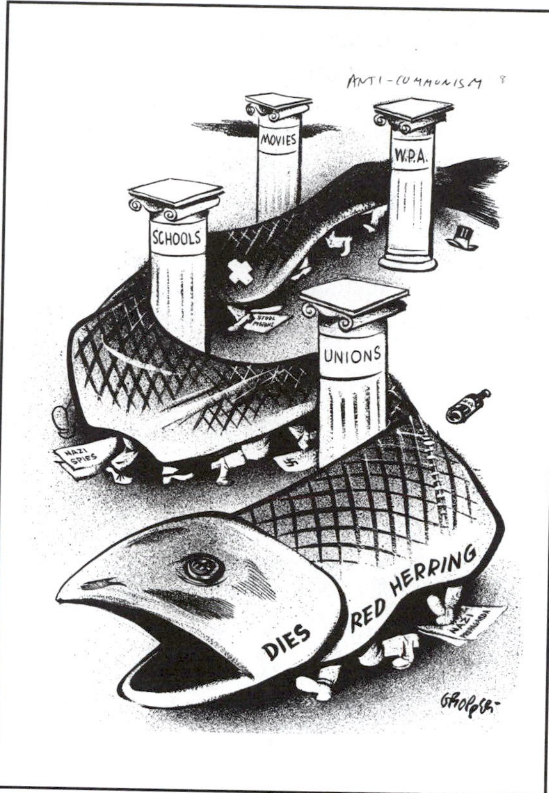

no consideration of capitalism as a doomed social order. The traits adduced to demonstrate the evil of communism make up something frozen out of time. Rather than being seen concretely in its real relations, it is seen as a manifestation of deep and fixed essence.

Anticommunism concerns, then, not communism at all but rather its own internal needs. Anticommunism is not a matter of fact, but of how facts are constructed, and the framework in which they are placed. Full-blown anticommunist discourse is notable for the presence of what can be called the "black hole" effect—the sense that communism represents some absolute, infinitely dense standard of evil into the evaluation of which all critical distinctions disappear.

This may also be called the ABC effect: Anything But Communism. Or, in its most pathological form, Better Dead Than Red. Its threat outweighs all other considerations, and justifies all acts to combat it, from support of tyrants and the launching of support of actions that cause massive civilian casualties and the devastation of human environments to preemptive nuclear war.

One aspect of anticommunism, its dominant part, is made up of the instrumental activities of ruling elites. Another part, quite separate in origin and functions, is made up of subjective popular dispositions to embrace what may be called anticommunist theology.

Instrumental anticommunism obeys the logic of political calculation. By projecting all sin to the other side, agents of ruling elites can create a climate in which political opposition is effectively silenced and the severe contradictions between democratic ideology and actual behavior apparently nullified. The use of atomic weapons against Japan, nominally to end World War II but actually to announce postwar U.S. hegemony over Asia, offers a striking case in point. Only by portrayal of Stalin's crimes as somehow worse could the contradiction between American ideals and American practices be reconciled.

An understanding of subjective anticommunism, on the other hand, requires a cultural and psychological critique. Cultural, first of all, because anticommunism is contiguous with certain "paranoid" features of American society going back to the colonial era, or earlier, to the roots of Western civilization. The continual repression of religious heretics, the frenzy of the Crusades, the repeated witch trials, among other events, have been persecutory premonitions of anticommunism. In American history, the process has often overlapped with waves of nativism, fears of loss of community and family, reactions against bureaucratization, and unfulfilled religious impulses. Despite the calculations of a less fanatical anticommunism, the demonology frequently breaks loose, blinding policy elites and undercutting their objectives.

The precursors of what crystallized into anticommunism with the emergence of the Bolshevik state can be seen in many forms earlier in American history: in the defense of slavery against allegedly "fanatical" abolitionists; in anti-Catholic agitation; in the racist and xenophobic outbreaks following the Civil War and episodically thereafter (leading to the formation of the Ku Klux Klan and similar movements); and, throughout, in the defense of capital against a rising and militant working class. The police raids on radical organizations following the Haymarket rebellion of 1886, and the resulting execution of innocent anarchists, established the basic plan to be followed.

At least three major Red Scares have exhibited the major symptoms. In 1919–20, with the Bolshevik Revolution providing the symbolism, the U.S. government, the press, and big business joined forces against a labor movement that had grown strong enough to launch a general strike in the city of Seattle. The resulting hysteria and gross violation of civil liberties set a specifically anticommunist pattern. In the wake of the Second World War, a second Red Scare crushed the progressive wing of the New Deal, integrated the labor movement once and for all into corporate strategy, and legitimized the policy of Soviet containment by any means necessary. This spate combined the zeal of influential Cold War liberals and testimonializing former Communists with the other elements, culminating in massive FBI searches, employment blacklisting, union expulsions, the persecution of figures such as Alger Hiss, and the execution of the Rosenbergs.

A third wave of anticommunism, in part a reaction to the rise of new social movements in the sixties, has had a basically different focus from the first two—owing in some degree to the successes of earlier phases in vitiating the Left. The anticommunism of the Reagan era (although it began in the last years of the Carter administration) set its sights more exclusively on the external enemy than the internal Red threat. The basic instrumental purpose has been twofold: to overcome the "Vietnam syndrome" of reluctance to engage in anticommunist and imperial wars; and to legitimize the monstrous military expenditures as a kind of Keynesian approach to a stagnant economy. As in previous crusades, a number of former liberals and former radicals have played a role. However, in this phase the cultural front has been largely occupied by the religious Right and its attack upon the modernizing sexual forces that erupted in the sixties.

The latest Red Scare seems nearly to have run its course. Yet anticommunism has at many times virtually carried the day in the United States. It has played a great role in destroying the Left outright or, more subtly, setting the terms of debate upon and within the Left. To the degree that ideology becomes internalized, it defines parameters of thought across most of the political spectrum, while escaping scrutiny itself. The result has been a tremendous loss of political intelligence—a failure of critical power, and a failure of vision and hope. *See also*: FBI, McCarthyism

—*Joel Kovel*

REFERENCES

Caute, David. *The Great Fear*. New York: Simon & Schuster, 1978.

Navasky, Victor. *Naming Names*. New York: Viking, 1980.

Schrecker, Ellen W. *No Ivory Tower: McCarthyism and the Universities*. New York: Oxford University Press, 1986.

ANTIFASCISM

One of the most important and certainly the most popular policies of the post-1920 Left, antifascism made possible in the late 1930s and World War II years an unprecedented coalition of Left sympathizers, from middle-class intellectuals to blue-collar immigrants. For a short time, it brought Communists a respectability they had not previously sought, and which would remain out of their grasp afterward.

Antifascism actually began more than a decade before the announcement of the Popular Front, in the Italian-American response to Mussolini's 1922 seizure of power. Communists, socialists, anarchists, and Wobblies sought to combine in local coalitions to propagandize against fascism, and to mobilize against local pro-Mussolini demonstrations. These coalitions proved difficult to maintain (as did their sister movement, the Sacco-Vanzetti mobilizations of Italian-Americans), due to internecine differences. Yet a range of participants, including Carlo Tresca and local Italian-American Communists, managed a rough working relationship through much of the 1920s–1930s. More directly, Italian-American antifascists, as individuals or in groups, confronted local fascist paraders with fists and clubs, driving them in many cases into private meetings.

American Socialists urged antifascist mobilizations, especially from the inception of Hitler's regime, but Communists in their ultra-Left phase (1928–33) generally resisted cooperation and even engaged in sectarian sniping at Socialist events. With the Seventh Congress of the Comintern in 1935, and the articulation of a world antifascist policy, significant changes began. For a few years, Communist sectarianism continued to hold back appeals to fellow immigrants, to liberals, and (more pointedly) to their socialist rivals for antifascist solidarity. By 1936–37, antifascism had become a defining purpose and a distinctive rhetoric.

When fully adopted, the appeal worked brilliantly. In virtually every Eastern European community, it gathered fresh support behind the Communists. Across the intellectual and arts worlds, it gave Communists and their supporters a battle cry. The Spanish Civil War provided, for the moment, the epiphany. But the broad spirit of antifascism also acutely identified antiracism, anti-Semitism, and various xenophobic internal enemies of democracy in the United States as the local variants of fascism.

Antifascism had three great failings for the Left. First of all, it placed antiwar sentiment into abeyance, and discredited the widespread mobilization in the early to mid-1930s against war-profiteer capitalists and against the system that made them possible. This popular view, once eroded, would be most difficult to resurrect. Second, antifascism as practiced seemed aimed at preservation of the Western democracies in a world of non-whites still largely oppressed by colonialism and neo-colonialism. Communists seemed to place aside the anti-imperialist clarion call so obvious in earlier years. Black nationalism within the United States, once seen sympathetically, was viewed as an obstacle to needed unity. Third, as a consequence of these and other shifts, the necessity for a socialist transformation tended to disappear from Communist plans and rhetoric. Once discussed unrealistically as a short-run possibility, socialism now all but vanished as an American prospect in the foreseeable future.

The Hitler-Stalin Pact reversed virtually all these policies, but only briefly and incompletely. Antifascist mobilization fell to others, such as the Socialist Workers Party, able to call successfully for demonstrations against mass meetings of the German-American Bund in New York and elsewhere. But as intellectuals and others deserted Communist ranks, they found no other site for a concentrated Left antifascism.

Antifascism reached its apparent apex in the Second World War. Communist Party cooperation with the war effort, if not crucial to government success, was nonetheless very important in major industries and many ethnic communities. In the glare of antifascist solidarity, Communists helped to erect new sweeping alliances (such as the American Slav Congress) and revive old contacts. Beneath the surface of events, anticommunist (or Cold War) liberalism began to take shape with an anti-Russian antifascism, however. The return of Republicans to congressional control in 1942 marked the emergence of a conservative-liberal consensus that equated antifascism with free-enterprise "Americanism," linked Stalinism with Hitlerism, and considered American Communists along with Fascists as potential traitors.

The decisive weakening of antifascist sentiment just following WW II foreshadowed the isolation and destruction of the Left. Communist efforts to point to the integration of erstwhile Nazi officials and collaborators into the NATO governments and CIA European agencies made little popular impression outside Jewish circles, and even here the empowered Cold War liberalism stoutly ignored the implications. Newer European immigrants to the United States, including many Nazi collaborators or sympathizers, helped reverse the tide of ethnic support built in antifascist days. U.S. investigative agencies now included antifascist organizations, present and past, under the rubric of Communist fronts. Spanish Civil War veterans, already known as "premature antifascists," were considered as nothing more than Communists or Communist dupes for opposing a dictator who became a staunch Cold War ally of the United States.

Later attempts to revive versions of antifascist style, against U.S. racism, South African apartheid, or even the fascist-sounding rhetoric of America's chosen Third World leaders, proved unsuccessful. Antiracism would prove an intermittantly powerful sentiment, but the "lessons" of fascism were mired in a national memory confused with contradictory judgments and slipping quickly away. *See also*: American League Against War and Fascism; American Slav Congress; American Writers Congress; Hitler-Stalin Pact; North American Committee to Aid Spanish Democracy; Popular Front; Student Movements—1930s

—*Paul Buhle*

"ANTIREVISIONISM" (MAOISM)

In 1956, at the twentieth Congress of the Communist Party of the Soviet Union, Khrushchev delivered his famous speech denouncing Stalin. It signaled a general policy of seeking accommodation with the West in order to provide space for Soviet economic growth. Khrushchev's policy found its greatest support in the Communist parties of the advanced capitalist countries, which welcomed a program of constitutionalist reform and transition to socialism without civil war. At the same time it provoked opposition, especially in Asia, where armed struggle based in the countryside had shown or was showing itself successful. The leaders of the Chinese CP from the first identified with the opposition, which labeled Khrushchev a "revisionist," after the turn-of-the-century German Social Democrat Bernstein. Because Khrushchev had flung down the gauntlet over Stalin, the "antirevisionists" took up the task of defending the reputation of the man who had led the world communist movement for thirty years.

"Antirevisionism" found expression in the United States in several small splitoffs from the CP: Turning Point in 1956, the Provisional Organizing Committee in 1958, Hammer and Steel in 1960, and Progressive Labor in 1962; each of these groups involved individuals who would later play a prominent role in building new communist organizations.

At the same time the "revisionism" controversy was raging within the communist movement, other forces were developing that would contribute to the emergence of a new communist movement in the United States: the shift of the Afro-American freedom movement into a more radical phase with the birth of the Student Nonviolent Coordinating Committee in 1960; and the break with social democracy by Students for a Democratic Society in 1962. These two moments marked the birth of a "new left" in the United States.

"Antirevisionism" reached the Afro-American movement in the early 1960s through the Revolutionary Action Movement (RAM), and the white student milieu a few years later through the Progessive Labor Party. By identifying with China and orienting toward workers' struggles, as well as by its leadership of important student struggles, most notably for black studies at San Francisco State (which it later repudiated), the PLP was able to establish itself as an important pole within SDS. Although it was never truly Maoist, the PLP became the most important bridge between the "antirevisionism" of the 1950s and the Maoism of the 1970s.

Maoism at first was not distinguished within the general "antirevisionist" tendency that has become known as Stalinism. It was only after the impact of the Cultural Revolution began to be felt outside China that Maoism emerged as a distinct and recognizable current, leaving its initial sponsors behind and attracting new supporters in the period of militant Afro-American rebellions and widespread campus unrest. Since Maoism was the principal expression of Stalinism within the New Left, it is necessary to look at the elements that made it attractive.

First was populism. Deeply rooted in American tradition, populism offers in place of Marxian notions of class conflict a struggle of "the people" against "the interests." In that it is open to a variety of interpretations. However, since the traditional language of class often serves, especially in Europe, to limit the movement to the corporate contention between employers and workers, its absence in the United States may, paradoxically, remove a barrier to the emergence of a revolutionary vision that transcends present class divisions. Maoism, with its deliberate blurring of class lines (appropriate to a philosophy of *national* rebirth influenced by a variety of Western thinkers from Marx to Emerson), was readily adopted by American middle-class radicals raised outside the tradition of fixed and hereditary stations.

The second element was thirdworldism, which viewed the revolution as a struggle between rich and poor nations. This current, which arose after the Bandung Conference and the Algerian and Cuban revolutions, reached its greatest popularity in the United States when thousands of middle-class radicals began to identify with Vietnamese peasants. Maoism reinforced their view of the world by declaring that Europe and North America were the cities of the world while Asia, Africa, and Latin America were the countryside surrounding them.

The third element was voluntarism and its concomitant moralism. In China the revolution had been made by intellectuals going to the people, overcoming by the force of will the limitations of backwardness, remaking themselves through criticism and self-criticism. They were now engaged in the Cultural Revolution, a project aimed at no less than the remolding of the entire Chinese people. What could be more appealing to the land of Puritans and pietists, a land of Great Awakenings and Great Revivals, whose people once dared to attempt prohibition by legislation? To radical intellectuals Maoism offered a faith that the suburbs they grew up in could no longer provide.

Maoism is Stalinism shaped by backward, even primitive, material conditions—Marxism-Luddism. It upholds the characteristic Stalinist view of the vanguard party at the head of the "masses." But it gives this dogma a distinctive reading. For one thing, Maoism is more confrontational and militant, less interested in maneuvers, than traditional Stalinism. For another, it places unusual stress on the repetition of slogans and standard phrases in mobilizing people. Finally, it preserves the rituals of "criticism and self-criticism" and "summing up experiences" that have fallen into disuse elsewhere.

The first formal Maoist organization in the United States—as distinct from earlier "revisionist" and later pro-China groups—was the Bay Area Revolutionary Union, founded in San Francisco in 1968 by several New Leftists with the behind-the-scenes guidance of former CPUSA members recently returned from China.

BARU distinguished itself among New Left groups of the day by what it called its "style of work"—base building, which it first attempted among oil workers in Richmond, California. It advocated "summing up of experiences" as a means of developing politics, which seemed to place it above the polemical sordidness that characterized most other left groups. Its working relations with the Black Panther Party helped BARU gain national recognition. Its foremost public spokesman, Bob Avakian, was elected to the eleven-person National Interim Committee at the final SDS convention in 1969. His election, like that of others elected at that time, signaled the turn of student activists' attention toward industrial settings and working-class neighborhoods. Over the next several years BARU—now RU—spread to most major cities through locally based Revolutionary Worker newspapers and base building. It passed through several regroupments and splits, with some of the veterans of the Black Workers Congress (some of whom had earlier been influenced by RAM) and with the Puerto Rican Revolutionary Workers Organization and the August 29th Movement in the Southwest, eventually emerging in 1975 as the Revolutionary Communist Party, which at its peak attained a membership of 500–700. (It was during this period that the group came out publicly against school busing in Boston and Louisville, which earned it the enmity of most Left activists.) Following the overthrow of the "gang of four" in China the RCP split in two, leaving the pro-Mao faction headed by Avakian in control of the organization. Shortly thereafter the group shifted its concentration from large plants in heavy industry toward youth and less protected workers. It embarked on a campaign of intensified militancy, exemplified by calls for May Day actions and a brief occupation of the Alamo as a demonstration against U.S. expansionism. The RCP was by the late 1980s the only avowedly Maoist organization in the United States; notwithstanding the paradox of Stalinism without a country, it claims ties with similar groupings elsewhere, most notably the Shining Path guerrillas in Peru.

Maoism was not the only current within what was known as the "antirevisionist Left" or the "new communist movement." The CP(M-L), more properly designated as "pro-China" than "Maoist," grew out of the October League in Los Angeles and the Georgia Communist League in Atlanta, both of which had come into existence following the demise of SDS. Its earliest leaders were people who had been prominent in SDS, such as Mike Klonsky, Lyn Wells, and Carl Davidson, but it soon drew in well-known individuals from other traditions, for example, Nanny Washburn, Harry Haywood, Sherman Miller, and Bob Zellner. The CP(M-L) sought to mobilize people behind specific demands through which they would come to appreciate the need for socialism and the leading role of the Party. This policy achieved its greatest confirmation at the Fightback Conference, held in Chicago in 1976, which brought together 1,500 people from all around the country in support of a comprehensive program in opposition to the capitalist offensive. The figure of 1,500 gives some idea of CP(M-L) numerical strength, since not all those at the conference were Party members, nor were all Party members in attendance. (As with the RCP, membership figures are estimates, since neither group revealed numbers, even to their members; moreover, their centralized structures made it difficult for members in one area to gain any real idea of the state of the organization in another area, and sometimes even in another part of the same city.)

From their inception the RCP and CP(M-L) had competed for the franchise from China as the "official" U.S. Marxist-Leninists. The victory of the latter was signaled by Klonsky's visit to China, where he had his picture taken with Hua Kuo-feng, Mao's heir-apparent. Decline followed swiftly. Hua was removed, as China embarked on a policy of encouraging private enterprise and developing military and diplomatic collaboration with the United States. The CP(M-L) exploded in the ensuing ideological crisis, dragging down with it the U.S.-China People's Friendship Association, delayed only slightly by a partial rapprochement with the pro-China wing of the RCP. The remnants of "pro-China" politics are to be found in the Progressive Student Network and in some secondary leadership of the trade union movement.

As China's foreign policy evolved, a group came together that called itself the "antirevisionist, antidogmatist" current. It was critical of both China and the Soviet Union, while declaring adherence to the traditional principles of Marxism-Leninism as enunciated by the CPSU up to 1956. The Philadelphia Workers Organizing Committee was the flagship of this tendency, which took the form of local collectives grouped together in the Organizing Committee for an Ideological Center. Although it enjoyed the support of the *Guardian* newspaper, the OCIC and most of the local groups dissolved in a welter of factionalism, "rectification," and bitterness. Line of March was able to gather in the fragments; it is active in various local struggles and anti-imperialist solidarity organizations. From its birth, Line of March kept close links with sections of the Filipino Left, and this has been important to its survival and growth.

Another of the "antirevisionist" groups was the Communist Workers Party, which formed around the same time and attained national prominence through the fatal shooting of five of its members and supporters by Nazis and Klansmen at Greensboro, North Carolina, in 1979. Following the Greensboro massacre, the CWP reversed its political line and later dissolved entirely.

The longest-existing "antirevisionist" group is the Communist Labor Party, whose roots go back to the 1950s. Like Line of March, the CLP adheres to a pre-Khrushchev Marxism-Leninism and an orientation toward the milieu of the CP. It includes a number of experienced and capable individuals, including some who were prominent in black workers' struggles in Detroit. It is active in local labor struggles, and in the Jobs With Peace campaign.

During the late sixties and early seventies a number of Chinese-American radicals were influenced by Maoism. They formed I Wor Kuen, which later merged with the Congress of African People, led by Amiri Baraka, to form the League of Revolutionary Struggle. The LRS was able to distance itself from CCP policy, and maintains a presence in the student movement and in struggles in Chinese communities around the country.

The Marxist-Leninist Party began in the early seventies as the Central Organization of U.S. Marxist-Leninists. Formerly linked to the Canadian Marxist-Leninists headed by Hardial Bains, the group for a short time published a daily newspaper based in Cleveland. It has declared Albania the only true workers' state and fortress of internationalism. *See also*: Communist Party, New Left

—*Noel Ignatiev*

REFERENCES

Costello, Paul. "A Critical History of the New Communist Movement, 1969–1979." *Theoretical Review* 13 (November-December, 1979).

Proletarian Unity League. *Two, Three Many Parties of a New Type? Against the Ultra-Left Line*. New York: P.U.L., 1977.

ANVIL AND NEW ANVIL

These two magazines were the most successful and vigorous among a group devoted to proletarian writing in the 1930s. Other such periodicals included *Left Front* (Chicago), *Left Review* (Philadelphia), *Leftward* (Boston), *New Force* (Detroit), *Blast* (New York), and *Rebel Poet* (Northern Minnesota). One of the features of the *Anvil*s was that they only published creative work—fiction and poetry—and no criticism. Editor Jack Conroy has written that his magazines were "rough-hewn and awkward, but bitter and alive from the furnace of experience—and from participants, not observers, in most instances."

The first issue of *Anvil* (1932–35) consisted of 1,000 copies. While widely read by Left writers, the magazine increased circulation only modestly until an ill-fated merger with *Partisan Review*. That fusion proved so unsatisfactory to many *Anvil* contributors that they regrouped to issue 2,500 copies of *New Anvil* (1939–40), the first of what would be six issues. Poet-publisher Ben Haggland, who had produced *Rebel Poet* prior to the founding of *Anvil*, handprinted both magazines as well as playing an editorial role.

The *Anvil*s published many of the Left writers of the 1930s. *New Anvil* published Richard Wright for the first time and published stories of Erskine Caldwell considered "too hot" for the big-circulation magazines Caldwell had access to. J. D. Salinger had the dubious honor of having a story rejected but commented on the helpful rejection letter sent by Conroy. Among poets published by the magazines were John Malcolm Brinnin, Langston Hughes, Tom McGrath, Kenneth Patchen, and Karl Shapiro. Short story contributors included Nelson Algren, Caldwell, Conroy, August Derleth, Stuart Engstrand, James T. Farrell, Michael Gold, Meridel LeSueur, William Carlos Williams, and Frank Yerby. *See also*: Algren, Nelson; Conroy, Jack; *New Masses*

—*Dan Georgakas*

REFERENCES

Conroy, Jack, and Curt Johnson, eds. *Writers in Revolt, The Anvil Anthology*. Westport: Lawrence Hill, 1973.

Conroy, Jack. *The Jack Conroy Reader*. New York: B. Franklin, 1979.

APPEAL TO REASON

No newspaper was as much identified with the early-twentieth-century socialist movement in America as the *Appeal to Reason*. Published from 1895 to 1922, the *Appeal* preceded the formation of the Socialist Party in 1901 and, more than any socialist institution, the weekly *Appeal* gave ongoing life, power, and sense of community to insurgent native-born radicals. Headquartered after 1897 in Girard, Kansas, the *Appeal* reached a paid circulation of over 760,000 in 1913, a figure that remains greater than any Left publication has reached since in America. During political campaigns and crises, copies of single issues reached 4,100,000—a world record, the paper's staff liked to comment, that broke totals the *Appeal* itself had earlier set. The *Appeal* succeeded at a time when millions of people spoke of the "cooperative commonwealth" with hope, expectation, and meaning.

The *Appeal's* primary purpose was to convert readers to socialism. If "common sense" and "an appeal to reason" had propelled an earlier American revolution, their reapplication, it was thought, would hasten the transition from capitalism to socialism. The *Appeal*'s founder and publisher was J. A. Wayland. Born into poverty in Indiana, successively a printer, publisher, land speculator and capitalist, communitarian militant Socialist, and propagandist, Wayland was harassed into suicide in 1912. Wayland had been converted to socialism by reading, and he and the *Appeal* staff explained socialism in a plain, passionate idiom that swelled the socialist ranks. The *Appeal* publicized all manner of social and economic injustice: if working conditions or a strike needed to be publicized in West Virginia or Colorado, the *Appeal* was there; if Milwaukee, Schenectady, and Butte were voting Socialist, *Appeal* correspondents reported the victories and the strategies that could be used elsewhere; and if states were without socialist papers, the *Appeal* made up and printed individual state editions. A vital political advocate and radical institution rather than simply a newspaper, the *Appeal* community included an "Appeal Army" of men and women, 80,000 at its highest point, who sold subscriptions and dropped extra copies at hotels and union halls—wherever the paper could be read. The *Appeal* published Marx, Engels, and Kautsky; Dickens, Ruskin, and William Morris; Upton Sinclair, Jack London, W. D. Howells, Kate Richards O'Hare, and Eugene Debs; as well as scores of American political and literary writers now little known or unknown to history.

Although never an official vehicle for the SP, the *Appeal* was nevertheless dependent on its fate. After Wayland's death and editor Fred Warren's departure, the paper was edited by Louis Kopelin and sold to Emmanuel Haldeman-Julius, neither of whom had the editorial capacity, writing skills, or commitment to socialism of Wayland and Warren. When Socialists opposed World War I, American capitalism and its political institutions crushed domestic radicalism. The *Appeal* initially opposed WW I and America's participation in it, temporarily supported it in the form of the *New Appeal*, and then, with hostilities concluded, reverted back to its condemnation of WW I as a grim battle for economic supremacy between competing capitalist nations. The *Appeal* never regained its prewar vitality and closed in November 1922. *See also*: Agrarian Radicalism, Ruskin Colony, Socialist Party

—*John Graham*

REFERENCES

Graham, John, ed. *Yours for the Revolution: The Appeal to Reason, 1895–1922*. Lincoln: University of Nebraska Press, 1989.

Shore, Elliot. *Talkin' Socialism*. Lawrence: University Press of Kansas, 1988.

Aptheker, Herbert (b. 1915)

One of the most prolific American historians of the twentieth century and longtime prominent member of the Central Committee of the Communist Party, Herbert Aptheker was born in Brooklyn, New York, and educated at Columbia University, where he received a B.A. in 1936 and a Ph.D. in 1943. He served in U.S. Army Intelligence in Europe during World War II and was honorably discharged with the rank of major.

From the beginning of his career, Aptheker has been devoted to Afro-American history. His *Negro Slave Revolts* (1943) has attained the status of a classic, and his three-volume *Documentary History of the Negro People in the United States* (1951–74) is regarded as a landmark collection.

Into the 1950s Aptheker helped to edit the journal *Masses and Mainstream*, which was closely associated with the CPUSA. During this period he also attacked intellectual repression in volumes such as *Laureates of Imperialism* (1954) and *Era of McCarthyism* (1955). Some of his essays and books of this time were sharply polemical, such as *The Truth About Hungary* (1957). His *World of C. Wright Mills* (1960) was a friendly critique of the sociologist's ideas.

By the end of the 1950s, Aptheker began to publish a projected twelve-volume Marxist history of the United States. The series includes *The Colonial Era* (1959), *The American Revolution* (1960), and *Early Years of the Republic* (1976). He also completed books on the abolitionist movement and the Civil War.

During the 1960s, Aptheker was often invited to college campuses to represent the views of the CPUSA. At this time he also visited the Democratic Republic of Vietnam and described it in *Mission to Hanoi* (1966). He founded the American Institute of Marxist Studies in New York and edited its newsletter and series of publications for many years.

The crowning achievement of Herbert Aptheker's career has undoubtedly been his editions of the works of his friend W. E. B. DuBois, for whom he has also served as literary executor. In addition to a bibliography of DuBois's published work, published in 1973, he edited DuBois's correspondence in three volumes (1973–78) and his complete works in forty volumes, a project completed in 1988. Aptheker has continued to defend DuBois's importance in the Harlem Renaissance, the black scholar movement, and the Pan-African movement, hailing him as "the father of the black intelligentsia." *See also*: Communist Party; History, U.S.; *Science and Society*

—*Fred Whitehead*

REFERENCES

Aptheker, Bettina. "Bibliographical Comment." In *The Unfolding Drama*, edited by Herbert Aptheker. New York: International Publishers, 1978.

Aptheker, Herbert. Interview. *People's Daily World*, February 25, 1988.

ARAB AMERICANS

An estimated 100,000 Arabs immigrated to the United States between 1880 and 1910. By the 1980s Arab Americans numbered two to three million. Known as "Syrians," the early immigrants were mostly unskilled, semiliterate males, drawn mainly from the ranks of the landed peasantry in Ottoman-ruled Syria, Lebanon, and Palestine. Information on their involvement in worker movements is scant and subject to filtering by contemporary accounts. The early period is often romanticized by post–World War II accounts that project images of Arab immigrants as dry-goods peddlers or grocery store owners. The reality was that most worked in New England textile factories, Pittsburgh iron works, and Detroit and Cleveland auto plants. The silk factories of Paterson and West Hoboken, New Jersey, are estimated to have employed 80 percent of the Arabs living in those cities. Arabs also found employment in farming as seasonal workers, truck farmers, and homesteaders in various parts of the country. Philip Hitti, the eminent Princeton historian, determined in 1924 that fully one-fourth of the seasonal agricultural workers in the vicinity of Oneida, New York, were Arabs.

These early immigrants could not have escaped the radical and socialist political currents of the times. This is partially borne out by reports of individual Arabs in various locales. In 1912, for example, an Arab striker was killed in the famous IWW-led Lawrence Strike. In the 1930s Arab-American George Addes played a major role in the Left coalition within the leadership of the UAW.

Significant waves of Arab organization occurred during the 1970s in Michigan and California, primarily among Yemeni workers, the least literate and skilled group of recent Arab immigrants. In August 1973 Nagi Daifallah, a Yemeni farm worker active in the United Farm Workers Union, was brutally gunned down with another union organizer by a county sheriff. California had become, by then, a center for several thousand Yemeni farm workers.

Detroit and its nearby industrial suburbs remained the site of the largest community of Arabs in North America, including a sizable Arab working class. The 200,000-strong Detroit community was composed of Lebanese, Palestinian, Yemeni, Iraqi, and Egyptian immigrants and their descendants. During the October 1973 Arab-Israeli War, 2,000 Arab workers protested the purchase of Israeli government bonds by the UAW. On November 28, 1973, a group calling itself the Arab Workers Caucus asked fellow autoworkers to boycott the production lines and attend a mass rally to protest the UAW's Israel-bond purchase. Production at one auto plant was severely hampered and 2,000 workers gathered outside a dinner honoring then–UAW president Leonard Woodcock. Embarrassed company and union officials retaliated by disciplining and laying off hundreds of workers. These and other retaliations contributed to a lessening of Arab worker militancy in the 1980s.

Arab Americans in the late 1960s and 1970s formed several ethnic political organizations in response to issues and negative stereotypes emanating from the Arab-Israeli conflict. Headed mostly by professionals and academics, these organizations have become recognized as part of the American progressive community. Prominent among them are the American-Arab Anti-Discrimination Committee, founded by former Senator James Abourezk and the Association of Arab-American University Graduates. The most notable examples of the continuing tradition of individual activism are Palestinian-American scholar Edward W. Said, who is a member of the Palestine National Council and ADC activist Alex Odeh, killed in an anti-Arab bomb blast in Santa Ana, California, on October 11, 1985. *See also*: United Auto Workers

—*Nabeel Abraham*

REFERENCES

Abraham, Nabeel. "Detroit's Yemeni Workers." *MERIP Reports*, no. 57 (May 1977).

Abraham, Sameer Y., and Nabeel Abraham, eds. *Arabs in the New World*. Detroit: Center for Urban Studies, Wayne State University, 1983.

"Arab Workers." (Special Issue), *MERIP Reports*, No. 34 (January 1975).

Friedlander, Jonathan, ed. *Sojourners and Settlers: The Yemeni Immigrant Experience*. Salt Lake City: University of Utah Press, 1988.

Hitti, Philip K. *The Syrians in America*. New York: Doran, 1924.

Sawaie, Mohammed, ed. *Arabic-Speaking Immigrants in the U.S. and Canada: A Bibliographical Guide with Annotation*. Lexington, Ky: Mazda Publishers, 1985.

Hooglund, Eric J., ed. *Crossing the Waters: Arabic-Speaking Immigrants to the U.S. before 1940*. Washington: Smithsonian Institution Press, 1987.

Arbeiter Kranken- und Sterbekasse der Vereinigten Staaten von Amerika (Workmen's Sick and Death-Benefit Fund of the United States of America)

This organization was founded in New York in 1884 by a small group of Germans who had been forced into exile under the Anti-Socialist Laws passed in Germany in 1878. Modeled after a similar fund in Hamburg-Altona, the organization grew from 116 members to approximately 50,000 in 1937, and it had paid out over $20 million in benefits by that time. In that year, the fund held $4 million in reserve. Its primary purpose was to provide mutual aid for workers and protection from financial disaster in times of sickness and death. After enrolling, members were covered for all illnesses and accidents, pregnancy, and periods of up to 100 weeks of sickness. Life insurance for adults and children was available, office visits to a physician were fully covered upon payment of a small additional charge, and a special fund protected members who became unable to pay their monthly fee. The fund was administered by officials who were elected every two years by the membership. Men and women of all professions, races, and nationalities were eligible for membership.

The fund was not limited to insurance purposes, for its members also conceived of it as part of the progressive workers' movement of the time. It maintained rest homes (*Erholungsheime*) and homes for the elderly in several locations, and summer camps for children such as Camp Solidarity in Columbus, Ohio, and the Recreation Farm in Fosterdale, New York. These establishments functioned as gathering places for people of different ages who shared a common political point of view and commitment. Many branches of the *Krankenkasse* maintained free German schools or participated in popular amateur theaters. The *Krankenkasse* also gave significant support to the German-American working-class and socialist press through direct financial support and through advertising. It published its own official organ, *Solidarität*, as a monthly from 1906 to 1954. This journal printed informational and feature articles and advocated the creation of an adequate social-security system and general measures to improve the situation of lower-income citizens. *See also*: German-Americans, *New York Volkszeitung*, Socialist Labor Party

—*Carol Poore*

REFERENCES

Keil, Hartmut. "German Working-Class Immigration and the Social Democratic Tradition of Germany." In *German Workers' Culture in the United States, 1850–1920*, edited by Hartmut Keil. Washington: Smithsonian Institution, 1988.

ARBEITERBILDUNGSVEREINE, SOZIALISTISCHE SCHULVEREINE, ARBEITERHALLEN (WORKERS EDUCATION ASSOCIATIONS, SOCIALIST SCHOOLS, WORKERS' HALLS)

Characteristically, the German-American socialists created many different types of organizations as alternatives to similar activities among nonsocialist groups. From the earliest days of the socialist movement, there were workers' gymnastic societies (*Turner*), singing societies, amateur theaters, and special organizations for socialist women. Fitting into these attempts at creating an alternative culture were the various efforts to provide educational opportunities compatible with socialist principles, including *Arbeiterbildungsvereine*, socialist schools for children and adults, and large labor lyceums or workers' halls. As in Germany, such institutions represented attempts at self-help and self-education by peers, as well as havens of escape from the religiously and patriotically slanted education offered in the public schools, and opportunities to acquaint participants with the fundamentals of socialism. Networks of socialist schools for children were established by the socialists in most large industrial cities, often in cooperation with groups of *Freidenker* (free thinkers). For example, in New York there were approximately twelve such "*freie deutsche Schulen*" in 1890, established by members of the *Sozialistische Arbeiter-Partei* (Socialist Labor Party) and staffed mainly by women teachers. These schools had a twofold purpose: to familiarize the children of immigrants with German language and literature, thus preserving this part of their cultural heritage; and to acquaint them with basic socialist principles of economic and historical development. To this end, children from the socialist schools frequently participated in socialist festivals, presenting plays, songs, declamations, or gymnastic exercises.

In addition to these educational and recreational activities for children, *Arbeiterbildungsvereine* and *Arbeiterlesezimmer* (workers' reading rooms) were founded in most large cities by socialists or trade unionists to provide adults (primarily men) with a chance for further political education and self-improvement. In some cities (New York, Philadelphia) where the German working-class community was large enough to support such an effort, labor lyceums or workers' halls were established as centers for all the progressive workers' groups and unions of the city. Perhaps the largest and most important of these was the Brooklyn Labor Lyceum, which reported in 1889 that it served as a meeting place for twenty-eight various groups with a total of 4,000 members. Such lyceums housed socialist schools for children and adults, along with party and trade union sections, and musical, theatrical, gymnastic, and other social groups. Also, they presented their own program of lectures and entertainment and provided space for large meetings and opportunities for socializing and communication. *See also*: German-Americans, Socialist Labor Party

—*Carol Poore*

REFERENCES

Douai, Adolf. "Kindergarten und Volksschule als sozialdemokratische *Anstalten*." Leipzig: Verlag der Genossenschaftsbuchdrückerei, 1876.

Nelson, Bruce. *Beyond the Martyrs: A Social History of Chicago's Anarchists, 1870–1900*. New Brunswick: Rutgers University Press, 1988.

ARBEITER-SÄNGERBUND DER VEREINIGTEN STAATEN (WORKERS' SINGING SOCIETIES OF THE UNITED STATES)

Although workers' singing societies were associated with the German-American socialist movement from its beginnings in the 1860s and 1870s, it was in 1892 that the *Arbeiter-Sängerbund der Nordöstlichen Staaten* was formed as a central federation of these societies, and it was followed in 1897 by the *Arbeiter-Sängerbund des Nordwestens*, centered in Chicago. Midnorthern (Detroit) and

Pacific regional organizations also existed. In the late 1920s these groups came together to form regional branches of the *Arbeiter-Sängerbund der Vereinigten Staaten*. In terms of numbers, these singing societies were the most important cultural organization of the German-American socialists. Approximately every three years, until the Second World War, each region held a singers' festival that could attract three to four thousand participants and a much larger audience. The repertoire for these concerts, which before World War I consisted almost solely of the songs of German Social Democracy and songs by German-American socialist writers, with time drew more and more from the standard *Liedertafel* (song society) repertoire (*Heimatlieder*—homeland songs; *Jägerlieder*—hunting songs; *Trinklieder*—drinking songs). However, although this trend came to dominate the larger national group, there were smaller local societies affiliated with the German-American section of the Communist Party in the 1920s and 1930s, whose members continued to emphasize the performance of political, revolutionary workers' songs.

Socialists involved in these singing societies viewed both their repertoire and the close connections to the socialist political movement as necessary alternatives to what they saw as bourgeois or petit-bourgeois culture. As was also the case with their theatrical groups, festivals, educational clubs, and schools, socialists found it imperative to break away from nonsocialist German-American groups and establish a certain autonomy. With respect to singing societies, which were extremely popular among all classes of German-Americans, socialists formed their own rather than join the large, more conservative *Nordamerikanischer Sängerbund*. In their press, socialists criticized the latter organization for its "philistinism," its indifference to progressive ideas and important social questions, and the presence of religious and nondemocratic songs in its repertoire. As an alternative to this type of cultural organization, the workers' singing societies emphasized the singing of *Freiheitslieder* (freedom songs) within the context of the socialist movement, with the goals of providing alternative leisure opportunities to workers who might otherwise be attracted to the more conservative groups, and thus of winning more participants to the socialist movement. There is scattered evidence that a few singing societies required their members to join one of the parties they were connected to, but this generally does not seem to have been required. However, with their active and passive members in every city with a significant German-American population, the singing societies encompassed a wide variety of people beyond the narrow circles of party membership and drew them into socialist political events. This is shown most clearly by the participation of workers' singing societies in festivals or meetings designed to raise money for the socialist press or other activities, and in turn, it was these joint performances that led to the formation of the citywide and regional federations.

Through the performance of *Arbeiterlieder* (workers' songs), these socialists had two complementary purposes in view, political influence and "aesthetic education." On the one hand, their goal was to expose social contradictions, to invest the working-class singers and audience with a sense of their rights, and to create feelings of solidarity, enthusiasm, and courage. On the other hand, through the artistic experience of performing choral works, socialists hoped to create an aesthetic sensibility, a sense for the "beautiful" and for "higher ideals." They viewed this goal as a viable function of performing music, in particular, which they hoped would then lead to moral and social improvements over the former vices of those people held at the lowest levels of the social pyramid. That is, they viewed the singing societies and their repertoire as a means to an end, as a means of creating a desired political response, but they also saw them as a way of furthering a contemplative attitude of appreciation for art in the participants. After World War I, the latter goal predominated as these singing societies became more and more similar to nonsocialist groups, and the sense of class identification dissipated as the ethnic group became more assimilated into the mainstream of American society. *See also*: German-Americans, Socialist Labor Party

—*Carol Poore*

REFERENCES
Poore, Carol. *German-American Socialist Literature, 1865–1900.* Bern: Peter Lang, 1982.

Armed Struggle—1960s and 1970s

The organized American Left has always been wary of schemes involving or advocating armed struggle. This view stems from the conviction that political persuasion must be the central focus of radical education, organization, and agitation. Armed struggle, if necessary at all, would be the last stage of conflict, coming when the Left had an overwhelming popular mandate and was being kept from assuming political authority by a self-evident governmental abuse of military power. Short of this unlikely scenario, violence has been judged as likely to have a negative public-relations effect that only serves as a pretext for oppression of the Left as subversive and lawless. The frequent use of agents provocateurs by employers and the state has reinforced this perspective.

Radicals of the 1960s and 1970s largely held to the traditional Left view, but the mass media gave inordinate amounts of publicity to miniscule groups that advocated violent methods of one kind or another, and the media usually obscured the difference between self-defense and aggression. Almost all the violent incidents involving civil rights organizations were linked to self-defense. In the student, antiwar, counterculture, and New Left groups, violent tactics were a distinctly minority activity and mainly emerged as the movement began to wane.

From its onset the civil rights movement spotlighted courtroom battles and nonviolent resistance. Its goals were to fulfill constitutional rights, not to reject legitimate authority. The bulk of the Reverend Martin Luther King, Jr.'s followers may not have shared his philosophical belief in the redemptive power of nonviolence, but they did agree that nonviolent resistance was the most effective political tactic. Even in the face of incredible police and vigilante violence, extending from beatings to bombings and assassinations, the movement retained its nonviolent orientation until the late 1960s.

Students for a Democratic Society 1608 West Madison Chicago, Illinois

SDS NEW LEFT NOTES

Vol. 4, Number 6 LET THE PEOPLE DECIDE February 1969

NIC notes

(See Page 9)

Huey rallies to stress self-defense

SDS and the Black Panther Party will celebrate Huey P. Newton's birthday (Feb. 17) at rallies across the country. The theme will be the Panther concept of self-defense based on the active participation of the community in its own protection. The rallies can also be used as part of a program to attack institutional racism, and can serve as an occasion to help build a working relationship with the Panthers on local levels. The NIC last weekend voted to encourage SDS chapters to participate in rallies, or sponsor them alone if there is no local active black group. (For related stories, see pages 6 and 7.)

Although King's views and tactics dominated the movement, they had always been contested. One of the earliest challenges came from Robert Williams, who had served as a marine in Korea and in 1959 was head of the NAACP chapter in Monroe, North Carolina. Williams stressed the constitutional right of self-defense and organized armed units to protect civil rights workers. An incident in 1961 moved the debate with King to newspaper headlines. The federal government charged that Williams had kidnapped a white couple during a racial incident. Williams maintained that he saved the couple from an angry black mob. As the dispute unfolded and a long prison term for Williams seemed likely, he fled the United States, finding sanctuary first in Cuba and then in China. From these locations he published a newsletter titled the *Crusader*, which urged and described various forms of armed struggle that went beyond self-defense to guerrilla war.

Williams's ideas inspired the creation of the semiclandestine Revolutionary Action Movement (RAM), which advocated an amalgam of black nationalist and Marxist views. RAM had some momentary influence in the Atlanta office of SNCC, among founders of the League of Revolutionary Black Workers, and in various groups in the Philadelphia area. RAM never attracted a large membership and retained a low profile, but it was consistently cited in FBI reports as the kind of militant organization that must be kept under the strictest surveillance and destabilized as soon as possible.

The progression made by Williams from self-defense to guerrilla war was not inevitable. The Deacons for Defense, which organized in Louisiana in 1964, remained a group that simply protected the black community and its militant leadership from outside assault. The Deacons encouraged the formation of similar independent groups and in many areas this occurred even if the self-defense units had no name or formal structure. Activists in SNCC and CORE became disillusioned with nonviolent resistance as a philosophical concept relatively early in the struggle, and some began to carry weapons even though continuing to practice nonviolent tactics. Famous media personalities taking part in demonstrations in the South or appearing at rallies often carried weapons, sometimes with legal permits, sometimes not.

The black nationalist wing of the liberation movement never accepted nonviolence as a strategy, holding that self-defense was a moral and a constitutional right. The Nation of Islam under the practical leadership of Malcolm X became renowned for its defense units even though it rarely became involved in violent clashes. Other nationalist groups, such as the New Republic of Africa, which originated in Detroit, clashed with police repeatedly in incidents that sometimes resulted in death. Such groups insisted that the incidents were provoked by the police in an attempt to wipe out organizational nuclei. The view that united the various nationalist groups was that the white power structure of America was not morally redeemable and that white people would only "behave" or "get right" when faced with physical force comparable to their own.

Any assertion of the right of self-defense got considerable media coverage. A photo flashed around the nation in April 1969 showed Cornell University students armed with shotguns and strapped with bandoleers demonstrating for their constitutional rights. This brandishing of weapons in public got its greatest exposure on the West Coast with the formation of the Black Panther Party (BPP). Based in young gangs and having an agenda of organizing the subproletariat or "street people," the BPP was adamant on self-defense and hinted that a little violence might be appropriate to speed the course of freedom.

The BPP outfitted its youth in quasi-military black berets and leather jackets, and it raised one of the most unfortunate slogans of the era: "Off the pig." Street language of the time rendered *off* as a substitute for *kill* and *pig* meant *cops*. BPP leaders defended the slogan as symbolic language that meant the black community demanded an end to police abuse. Most police and the media took the slogan literally. Violent incidents with law enforcement groups, other black liberation groups, and with the immediate community plagued the BPP throughout its heyday. When the organization shattered in the early 1970s, BPP leaders were recorded making death threats to one another over the phone. Deaths, in fact, had resulted in a clash within the US organization of Los Angeles, and on December 4, 1969, Chicago BPP leader Fred Hampton was killed in a highly controversial raid by the Chicago police. A year earlier, following a BPP trial in Oakland, the courthouse had been bombed in an act attributed to a Persian exile supposedly in league with the BPP. In the wake of these and other incidents the BPP was often perceived by friend and foe as a nascent guerrilla organization.

A widely used phrase by many black activists was the ambiguous "by any means necessary." This formulation was often depicted as code for the willingness to use violence. Despite its somewhat ominous overtones, such an assertion was almost obligatory. A mass movement was battling for its constitutional rights through constitutional means. If the system ultimately betrayed its own principles and proved unreformable, the option had to be left open to proceed to other forms of rebellion. Malcolm X put the issue most dramatically with his battle cry, "The ballot or the bullet."

The black masses ran out of patience with the system long before the official movement did and the reaction was stronger in the North than in the South. Riots in Harlem (1964) followed by the Watts Rebellion (1965) going through to the Newark and Detroit insurrections (1967) and dozens of outbreaks following the murder of King (1968) were the costliest in U.S. history. A new aspect of these disturbances was that unlike previous riots that had mainly pitted one race against another, the 1960s' violence was usually directed against property. In Detroit, site of the most extensive rioting, blacks and whites in many areas looted stores side by side. Arrest records show that more whites than blacks were apprehended for shooting at police. These violent outbursts, if anything, attested to the moderate nature of the means advocated by the major civil rights organizations.

One of the most violence-prone sectors of the movement was that involving black convicts. The BPP and sections of the Left tried to politicize black inmates by distributing free literature, taking up individual cases, and occasionally becoming involved in educational programs conducted behind bars. Reviving language from the early 1900s, some political groups began to refer to inmates as "class-war prisoners." Sometimes this was reserved for class-conscious prisoners whatever the reason for their incarceration but generally it was used to describe all nonwhite convicts.

Prison writers like George Jackson in California argued that the economic system had led them to their antisocial behavior and that jails systematically encouraged racism and brutalized nonwhites. Jackson set up a prison unit of the BPP. His posthumously published *Blood in My Eye* is dedicated thusly: "To the black Communist youth—To their fathers—We will now criticize the unjust with the weapon." Jackson was the object of a failed armed-rescue attempt by his brother and was subsequently killed on August 21, 1971, by San Quentin guards in an incident still shrouded in controversy. Communist Angela Davis would be catapulted to international fame through her involvement with Jackson and his defense committee.

The Attica Prison uprising of 1971 further reflected the militancy of urban blacks and activist prisoners. The Left charged that it was no accident that the violent repression of the riot at the order of Governor Nelson Rockefeller resulted in the death of almost all the politically active prisoner leaders. Shortly thereafter the Left led the resistance to the attempt by New York State to open a facility dedicated to behavior modification programs that would include electric shock treatments and possibly lobotomies. The leader of the prisoner resistance was Martin Sostre, a black Puerto Rican who had run a radical bookstore in Buffalo but was in jail on drug charges he called a frame-up. Also active in the anti-behavior modification campaign were committees supporting Puerto Rican militants and a defense group formally headed by Angela Davis and under the day-to-day leadership of Communist Charlene Mitchell. The state's plan was defeated; and Sostre was eventually released from prison after efforts on his behalf by Phillip Berrigan and Amnesty International.

The interaction of political militants and individuals with a criminal history led to a blurring of whether some acts were politically or criminally motivated. A number of armed-car and bank robberies on the East Coast were said to be the work of black or Puerto Rican revolutionaries seeking funds for the movement. The most famous of these involved the "Black Liberation Army" led by Joanne Chesimard. Rarely was it possible to definitely judge if the political purpose claimed was an attempt by superficially politicized robbers to gain public sympathy, a device of the authorities to discredit the civil rights movement, or a genuine guerrilla action.

The most problematic example of this phenomenon was the emergence on the West Coast of the Symbionese Liberation Army. Like most of the so-called armies, the SLA seems to have had no more than a dozen members and perhaps as few as eight. Some had radical histories but there was no organizational link to any preexisting Left group. The SLA gained fame out of all proportion to its acts when it kidnapped media heiress Patty Hearst in 1974 and momentarily converted her to its views. Most of the SLA personnel were killed in police assaults in which little effort was made to take live prisoners. Hearst pleaded that her brief career as a revolutionary bank robber had been the result of "brainwashing" and she soon returned to the kind of life she had led before the kidnapping. Many Left and counterculture newspapers of the time believed that the SLA was the creation of the government. Only seventeen months elapsed between its first appearance and its demise.

Documents obtained through the Freedom of Information Act and evidence surfacing at various trials have shown that many violent plots were, in fact, the work of police "Red squads" or federal security agencies. A case in point was the attempt to blow up the Statue of Liberty in the early 1960s. The instigator of the plot who recruited coconspirators in New York's Lower East Side radical hangouts was in the pay of the police from the start. Others involved in the plot would reappear in other cases of like nature. The New York Police Department has also acknowledged that it controlled the central staff of the local BPP from the first day it opened an office in Harlem. Any violent plots attributed to that milieu would, at the very least, have been known about from their earliest genesis.

Two New York Panthers convicted of violent crimes presented new evidence in the late 1980s that they had been framed. Herman Ferguson had been convicted in 1968 for being part of a conspiracy to murder moderate civil rights leaders Roy Wilkens (NAACP) and Whitney Young (Urban League). He had jumped bail and fled to Guyana, where he became a citizen under a new name. Ferguson voluntarily returned to the United States in 1989 to establish his innocence. Central to his defense was evidence in newly released documents from the counterintelligence program set up by J. Edgar Hoover to destabilize militant organizations. Imprisoned Richard (Dhoruba) Moore sought a reversal of a twenty-five-year-to-life conviction for machine-gunning two policemen in 1973. He cited the same federal documents as Ferguson, but even more important to his case were passages from a book written by former Deputy Police Commissioner Robert Daley stating that prosecutors had concealed evidence that could have exonerated him. The two cases were among many cited by civil libertarians to indicate that federal and local authorities had used charges of violence to systematically fabricate conspiracies and frame black militants in an effort to dismantle the civil rights movement.

The course toward violent acts within the New Left followed a different pattern. While most organization against poverty, racism, and the war in Vietnam employed conventional methods, there was always a revolutionary undertow expressed in admiration for developments in Cuba and China. Rhetoric, however, ran far ahead of action. Although a scattering of very small groups called for "Victory for the Vietcong," the dominant slogan in the antiwar movement of the early 1960s was the decidedly mild "Negotiations Now," which then shifted in the late 1960s to a more demanding but quite reasonable "End the War" and "Bring the Boys Home."

As sentiment against the war deepened and significant counterculture communities emerged in urban and university centers, the government became ever more adamant in insisting that it would not be swayed by mass demonstrations or resistance to the draft. The more militant ranks of the antiwar movement responded with the call "Bring the War Home." For some that simply meant nonviolent means must be escalated until politics- and business-as-usual became untenable. For others the slogan suggested that the American power elite would only listen when it began to suffer physical losses on the home front.

By late 1966 in places such as New York City and the San Francisco Bay Area, segments of demonstrations began to break away from the main body to rampage through the streets. At the first mammoth peace parade led by Martin Luther King, Jr., thousands of demonstrators followed the lead of marchers from Harlem and a contingent dedicated to liberation movements around the world to bolt the Central Park staging area and romp along avenues the police had prohibited to the official parade. No violence ensued from this "taking of the streets," but the precedent was set for smaller groups to do as they wished during mass rallies. Thereafter any large demonstration was likely to have breakaway groups that tried to demolish army recruiting booths or shatter the windows of banks and major corporations. This was called "trashing." Parade organizers did all they could to discourage the phenomenon but "trashing" became increasingly popular and acceptable.

Concurrent with the trashing tendency was a rash of bombing incidents. These were directed at military installations, pylons holding power lines, courthouses, university war research centers, and corporate offices. The bombings were usually carried out in a way that only affected property, but in some instances caretakers and passersby were hurt or killed. The bombings were the work of a variety of independent and extremely small groups, most numbering half a dozen persons or less.

The bombings had a mixed reception from activists. There was some satisfaction that the antiwar effort was finally "getting serious," particularly among those unhappy with the "flower power" and pacifist components of the movement. At the same time there was considerable apprehension that violent acts would alienate a general public that had been growing more receptive. Over the years as various bomb cells were caught or surrendered, the individuals involved usually stated that they had not been particularly concerned about building a mass movement. They frequently compared themselves with those Germans who had worked against the Nazis in the 1930s and 1940s.

By far the most important and largest group of this kind was the Weatherman faction that formed within SDS. In contrast to rival factions calling for stronger ties with workers and the poor, Weatherman considered the American public to be substantially corrupted by the economic prosperity generated by the military-industrial complex and hopelessly confused by anticommunist sentiment. The only honorable recourse was thought to be a guerrilla war that supported the revolutionaries in Vietnam and elsewhere, whatever the immediate political cost in the United States. This strategy was also considered to be a means of connecting with the most militant sectors of the black movement, which Weatherman thought would also gravitate to armed struggle. Mark Rudd and Bernardine Dohrn became the best known Weather spokespersons.

Weatherman set out to create incidents that would result in police repression. They believed a persecuted movement would then split and the most militant fighters would become part of the Weather underground. The first major manifestation of this approach was the Chicago Days of Rage in 1969, which were billed as a movement accounting for the police riot of the previous year during the Democratic convention. Weather activists and supporters mounted demonstrations and parades focused around large city parks and engaged the police in violent confrontations. In the following weeks Weather units appeared in various cities to create incidents designed to put the local SDS chapters under tremendous public and government pressure. This course of action proved disastrous, alienating most individuals not only from SDS and Weatherman but from political activism of any kind.

The decline of Weathermen thinking was sealed by the Town House Explosion of March 1970, in which Weather cadre who were working on making bombs accidentally set off an explosion that killed or maimed most of those present. A sinister aspect of the incident was the revelation that the group had been producing antipersonnel bombs as part of its arsenal. The surviving Weatherpeople carried on a score of bombings and other unlawful acts, but their support and activity fell off rapidly. The greatest revolutionary skill demonstrated was the ability to avoid arrest. Most remained underground for a decade only to resurface voluntarily in the 1980s with the admission that their strategies had been erroneous.

A number of affinity groups that did not gain the notoriety of Weatherman were also prone to guerrilla tactics. Among the most visible was Up Against the Wall, Motherfuckers, organized on the Lower East Side of New York by anarchist Ben Morea. The group's objective was to achieve de facto control of its region of the city. Based on a core of about a dozen persons but able to attract considerable community support for any given action, the group was a kind of leftist street gang that operated in the area of St. Mark's

Place and Second Avenue for approximately a year. The group became involved with drugs, frequently clashed with police, alienated potential allies with strongarm methods, and collapsed with the demise of the larger student New Left movement. Similar groups appeared briefly in other localities at various times between 1968 and 1971.

Closer to the Weatherman model were affinity groups like the seven or so individuals led by Raymond Luc Levasseur in Ohio. Beginning in 1968 they were thought to have bombed a score of corporate, government, and military structures. Police also accused them of robbing banks to finance their efforts and bankroll aboveground groups they supported. At various trials Levassuer, without admitting or denying any specific acts, linked his group's activities to the "international war against imperialism." Similar groups existed on the fringes of the Puerto Rican independence movement and various radical centers. Their ideological orientation tended to be toward the considerable literature on armed struggle and urban guerrilla warfare then appearing in Latin America.

Operating under a cruder strategy was the FALN—Fuerzas Armadas de Liberaction Nacional (Armed Forces of National Liberation), a small group dedicated to Puerto Rican independence. The FALN, operating in an area from Chicago to New York and Boston, was believed to have been involved in a hundred bomb incidents throughout the 1970s. Unlike other groups using bombs, the FALN seemed unconcerned about harming innocents. In 1974 the FALN placed a bomb that killed four and wounded fifty-four persons dining at Fraunces Tavern, a Wall Street restaurant-bar. A bitter irony was that the four dead were Puerto Rican secretaries on a lunch break. The group became inactive in the 1980s after the government captured or identified most of its cadre.

Established Marxist organizations shunned armed struggle. Communists and members of the Socialist Workers Party were often derided by militant antiwar demonstrators for being allied with the pacifists and "doing the man's work" when they struggled to maintain order at mass demonstrations. Smaller Marxist groups like Youth Against War and Fascism and the Progressive Labor Party tried to create a more dynamic image for themselves, but they, too, assailed provocations and violence as "adventurism." With the exception of the 1979 Communist Workers Party shootout with the KKK in Greensboro, North Carolina, Marxist organizations managed to avoid armed confrontations and loose talk of armed insurrection.

Given the frequency with which the word *revolution* was evoked and the considerable anger, frustration, fear, and rebellion within the various mass movements, the amount of New Left violence was remarkably small. As was the case in the movement for black liberation, many of those who advocated confrontational policies and denounced other strategies as "selling out" proved to be police agents. The antiwar movement had activated hundreds of thousands of Americans and at one time SDS claimed 150,000 members. In contrast, the total number of those who participated in armed struggle remained in the low hundreds. The next phase of radical activism would not involve guerrilla war but an attempt to form a new Communist Party based on the strictest adherence to Marxist-Leninist principles. One of the tenents of the new movement that would involve thousands of activists was an echo of that of the established Marxist groups: that advocates of immediate armed struggle in the United States must be regarded as either infantile leftists or agents provocateurs. *See also*: Antirevisionism; Attica; Black Panther Party; Civil Rights Movement; Davis, Angela; Direct Action; Federal Bureau of Investigation; Greensboro Massacre; League of Revolutionary Black Workers; New Left; SDS

—Dan Georgakas

REFERENCES

Anthony, Earl. *Picking up the Gun*. New York: Dial Press, 1970.

Becker, Howard. *Campus Power Struggle*. New Brunswick, N.J.: Transaction Books, 1973.

Copeland, Vincent. *The Crime of Martin Sostre*. New York: McGraw-Hill, 1970.

Graham, Hugh Davis, and Ted Robert Gurr (compilers). *Violence in America: A Report to the National Commission on the Causes and Prevention of Violence*. New York: Signet, 1969.

Grathworth, Larry. *Bringing Down America: An FBI Informer with the Weathermen.* New Rochelle, N.Y.: Arlington House, 1976.

Jackson, George. *Blood in My Eye.* New York: Random House, 1972.

Miller, James. *"Democracy Is in the Streets"—From Port Huron to the Siege of Chicago.* New York: Simon & Schuster, 1987.

Newton, Huey P. *Revolutionary Suicide.* New York: Harcourt Brace & Jovanovich, 1973.

Sale, Kirkpatrick. *SDS.* New York: Random House, 1973.

Sostre, Martin. *The New Prisoner.* New York: Martin Sostre Defense Committee, 1972.

Williams, Robert. *Negroes with Guns.* New York: Marzani & Munsell, 1962.

X, Malcolm. *The Autobiography of Malcolm X.* New York: Random House, 1964.

ARMENIAN AMERICANS

Large numbers of Armenians immigrated to the United States in the late nineteenth and early twentieth centuries. Most of them came from the Ottoman Empire, fleeing the persecutions and massacres of 1895–96 and 1908, and finally, the 1915 Armenian Genocide. Many of these immigrants, especially those who were educated and lived in cities, were influenced by the cultural and political awakening of the Armenian people, which had taken place in the nineteenth century in Western (Turkish) and Eastern (Russian) Armenia dominated during this period by the Ottoman and Russian Empires, respectively.

In the 1880s and 1890s politicized Armenians in the Turkish- and Russian-dominated homeland, disillusioned by the broken promises of the major Western powers (England, France, and Germany) to guarantee them cultural and political autonomy—the question of complete independence and sovereignty was not raised at this time—began the formation of political parties for the achievement of their goals. The two major groups established in the late nineteenth century were the Social Democrat Hunchak Party (Hunchaks) and the Armenian Revolutionary Federation (Dashnaks).

Founded in Geneva in 1887, the Hunchaks were influenced by Marxist thought, the party being the first Armenian socialist organization. Their energies were directed at Turkish Armenia as the most oppressed sector of the historic homeland. They believed that only through revolution and an international socialist perspective could the historic homeland be liberated. On the other hand, the Dashnaks, founded in Tiflis (modern Tbilisi, Soviet Georgia) in 1890, had a much more nationalistic perspective. Their goal for the liberation of the historic homeland was envisaged in the context of a sovereign nation-state rather than a world federation of socialist states (which the Hunchaks advocated). However, the two organizations were able to cooperate in certain political activities, since both advocated the accomplishment of their goals through revolutionary means (political agitation, violence when and if necessary, illegal action, etc.).

Both the Hunchaks and Dashnaks established branches of their respective political organizations in the United States in the 1890s. Since Worcester, Massachusetts, was the first Armenian center on the East Coast, it was in that city that the first Hunchak (1890) and Dashnak (1895–96) branches were established. As the Hunchak Party was a member of the Second International, many of its members cooperated with the American Socialist Party. In 1906 the Socialist Armenian Organization of the United States was founded, which was affiliated with the left wing of the SP. Eventually this group was absorbed into the Communist Party.

World War I brought new hope to both the Armenian nationalists and socialists. The nationalists, led by the Dashnaks, pinned their hopes and aspirations on the Allied powers. Their party was able to establish a short-lived independent Armenian state in Tanscaucasia between 1918 and 1920, oriented to the Allies. The socialists, led by the Hunchaks, Armenian Bolsheviks, and others, looked to the newly formed Soviet state for help in attaining their goal of a liberated socialist Armenia. Invaded by Kemalist Turkey and pressured by the Soviets, the Dashnak-led Republic of Armenia collapsed and was replaced by a soviet socialist republic in November 1920, with the full support of the Hunchaks and Armenian Bolsheviks.

After WW I and the collapse of the Second International the socialist movement split, with the formation of Socialist and Communist parties throughout the world. In 1921, with the fusion of two groups, America's Communist Party was formed and, as noted above, the Socialist Armenian Organization of the United States united with it. In the same year the CP established an Armenian bureau that carried on agitation work among more than 50,000 Armenian-American workers. Due to the activities of Armenian Communists, an "Armenian Labor Union" was formed in 1921 and tried to persuade Hunchaks and Armenian workers to join. This in turn led to the formation of the Armenian Labor Party in 1922. In 1923 this party joined with the Hunchaks in founding the Armenian Federation of the American Workers Party, which fell apart soon after its inception.

The internal conflicts of the CP in the 1920s and the subservience of the Party to the Soviet Union and Stalin in the 1930s had a profound effect on its national sections, including the Armenian, so much so that by the beginning of WW II these sections were no longer operative. With the disintegration of the Armenian section of the CP, a group of former members, uniting with Armenians sympathetic to the Soviet Union and to communist ideology, formed the Armenian Progressive League (Progressives) in 1938. This organization supported the efforts of the Soviet Union in its fight against fascism in WW II, as well as being an ardent defender of the Armenian Soviet Socialist Republic.

Since the 1950s there has been a general dearth of Left politics and activities among Armenian-Americans. This is due in part to the general conservative nature of the 1970s and 1980s and in part to the profound changes that have taken place in the Armenian socialist and communist organizations. The Hunchaks, due to ethnocentric and ideological pressures, have tended to de-emphasize socialism and instead have promoted Armenianism, conforming to the nationalistic ideology of the two other major Armenian political parties, the Dashnaks and the Ramkavars (Ramkavar Freedom Party), a bourgeois-liberal organization. These organizations publish a number of papers, both Armenian and English, in this country. The Hunchaks publish a weekly called *Massis* (Ararat) on the West Coast and a monthly, *Eritassard Hayastan* (Young Armenia), on the East Coast (both in Armenian). The Dashnaks publish a daily called *Asbarez* (Combat) on the West Coast and a daily, *Hairenik* (Fatherland), on the East Coast (both in Armenian, with *Asbarez* having an English section), as well as an English weekly called the *Armenian Weekly*. The Ramkavars publish a daily called *Baikar* (Struggle) in Armenian, as well as an English weekly called the *Armenian Mirror Spectator*. The Progressives publish a weekly called *Lraper* (Reporter) in Armenian and English, and both they and the Hunchaks have been uniquely (among long-established radical groups of immigrants in the United States) revived to a degree from a new influx of recent Left-minded refugees, immersed in Armenian language and culture. *See also*: Communist Party, Socialist Party

—*Ara Dostourian*

REFERENCES

Atamian, S. *The Armenian Community*. New York: The Philosophical Library, 1955.

Mirak, R. *Torn Between Two Lands: Armenians in America, 1890 to World War I*. Cambridge: Harvard University Press, 1983.

Nalbandian, L. *The Armenian Revolutionary Movement*. Berkeley and Los Angeles: UCLA Near Eastern Center, 1963.

Walker, C. J. *Armenia: Survival of a Nation*. New York: St. Martin's Press, 1981.

"The Armenians in the USA," in *The Armenian Soviet Encyclopedia*. Vol. 1 (in Armenian). Yerevan: 1974.

"The Communist Party of the USA," in *The Armenian Soviet Encyclopedia*. Vol. 1 (in Armenian). Yerevan: 1974.

ARONSON, JAMES: see NATIONAL GUARDIAN

ART MOVEMENTS

Certain conditions had to exist before art movements connected to or expressive of the American Left could come into being. First, artists had to experience and be conscious of the external economic, political, and social conditions that the Left political movement was either exposing or attempting to reform and overthrow; and second, there had to be a large art-conscious audience and patronage in order to encourage the efforts of the artists and, when necessary, offer political and ideological leadership.

In the last quarter of the nineteenth century American artists such as John Ferguson Weir and Thomas Anshutz painted industrial workers, but no one attempted an ambitious critique of the capitalist system until Robert Koehler painted *The Strike* in 1886. By upbringing and inclination he was a product of the socialist movement. His parents were sympathetic to radical ideas when they emigrated from Germany to Milwaukee during Koehler's childhood; later, returning to Germany to complete his art training, he was drawn to socialist ideas. In 1885 he showed *The Socialist* at the National Academy of Design—a picture depicting a fiery orator vehemently gesticulating to make a political point. The following year he exhibited *The Strike* at the National Academy. This painting was the first to depict not just the dignity of labor (a concept that emerged during the rise of the bourgeoisie) but *class struggle*, as a group of workers gather to confront the factory owner. Koehler realistically shows many degrees of commitment, from militant anger to puzzled questioning among workers and their wives, with the more firmly committed strikers arguing with others in order to achieve solidarity. *Harper's Weekly* reproduced *The Strike* as a centerfold in its issue of May 1, 1886, the day designated by labor leaders across the country for a general strike for the eight-hour day.

During the Progressive era (1890–1920), liberal-minded patrons increasingly paid attention to images of immigrants, child laborers, and industrial workers, particularly those seen in the photographs of the reforming social photographers Jacob Riis and Lewis Hine. Whereas Riis's photographs often reinforced the widely held belief that the slums could breed criminality, Hine focused on the dignity of poverty and documented working conditions that needed correction. Conservative patrons particularly appreciated more upbeat pictures, ones of workers shown in harmonious relationship with management and the machinery of industry. Edwin Austin Abbey designed a large mural, *The Spirit of Vulcan, the Genius of the Workers in Iron and Steel*, executed between 1904 and 1908, for the State Capitol rotunda in Harrisburg, Pennsylvania. In 1911 Everett Shinn painted a mural for the City Hall Council Chambers of Trenton, New Jersey, representing steel production and pottery making, both important industries of the state.

The images that came closest to a content of class struggle appeared in the popular press. Shinn was one of the Philadelphia newspaper artists who along with George Luks, William Glackens, and John Sloan had followed their mentor, realist painter Robert Henri, to New York City at the turn of the century. Like Henri, they undertook to show in their paintings (as they had in their newspaper illustrations) the "spirit of the people" rather than labor per se. Dubbed the "black revolutionary gang" when they showed together as "The Eight" in 1908 at the Macbeth Gallery in New York, they diverted American painting away from academic impressionism to "ashcan realism," even though few of their paintings sold. There was not yet an audience for fine arts paintings that celebrated "the other half."

Political ideologies then in currency affected the new subject matter. Henri was a philosophical anarchist; Sloan, the most talented, joined the Socialist Party in 1908. Sloan consciously declined to put "propaganda" into his art; he was not about to carry on the tradition of Koehler. Yet he did not hesitate to draw vivid graphic cartoons of the class struggle for the *New York Call* and the *Masses*, the radical monthly edited by Max Eastman. Sloan was, in fact, the unpaid art editor of the *Masses* from about 1913 through 1915, after which his involvement waned along with his withdrawal from SP activities.

While the audience of the *Masses* was limited to middle-class radicals and bohemians, other New York intellectual impresarios attempted to reach out to a broad audience through exhibitions. John Weichsel, a Polish émigré who wrote on aesthetics and taught engineering at the Hebrew Technical Institute, founded the People's Art Guild in early 1915. The purpose of the guild was to overcome the elitism of artists and to educate the masses who might be moved toward their own creative self-expression by good artistic examples. To this end, the Guild mounted over fifty exhibitions in its first two seasons in settlement houses, public libraries, newspaper offices, YMHAs, and coffeehouses in the Bronx and on the Lower East Side. The climax came with the exhibition of eighty-nine artists and over 300 works held in the offices of the *New York Jewish Daily Forward* in May 1917. The Guild folded in 1918, but during its heyday its membership included Henri and Sloan (who was given one of his first solo exhibitions under Guild sponsorship) along with early American modernists John Marin, Max Weber, Marsden Hartley, Charles Demuth, and Stuart Davis, all committed at that time to the proposition of bringing art to the people.

The first self-conscious "movement" of Left artists can be dated to October 1929—not because of the stock market crash (which occurred that month), but because a group of Communist Party artists, writers, and their sympathetic friends, meeting informally in the offices of the *New Masses* for discussions about the function of art in the revolutionary class struggle, decided to rent their own space and to form their own club. Called the John Reed Club, its aims were: ". . . The development of a cultural movement dedicated to advancing the interests of the working class . . . [and] the defense of the achievements of the Union of Soviet Socialist Republics [and] the development of new working-class writers and artists, as well as alignment of all artists, writers, and intellectuals to the side of the revolutionary working class, stimulating their participation in revolutionary activity."

Members of the John Reed Club, including the artist-cartoonist William Gropper, traveled to the Second World Plenum of the International Bureau of Revolutionary Literature held in Kharkov, USSR, in November 1930. They returned with suggestions for a cultural program along the lines of the experimental, Proletcult movement—a program of Marxist theory and practice—to bring art *to* the people and encourage art *of* the people. Soon John Reed Clubs sprang up across the country, and a convention was held in 1932, representing eleven such clubs. The John Reed Club artists put on exhibitions of socially concerned art, some of which traveled to workers' clubs and to the Soviet Union. The New York club even started its own art school, which included as instructors Nicolai Cikovsky, Anton Refregier, Louis Lozowick, and Raphael Soyer. Although the CP influenced their political activities, many John Reed Club artists maintained to this writer that a Party "line" was rarely imposed on their art, since the spirit of individualism exerted a strong force. As might be expected, the most consistently "revolutionary" content is found in the graphics of the period.

The clubs were disbanded in the winter of 1935, in line with the CP's new Popular Front policy, formulated in August 1935 at the Seventh World Congress of the Communist International, which called for broad alliances with other socialist and democratic groups to fight against fascism. The new line was incompatible with the John Reed Clubs, which had been associated with a more narrowly political outlook.

When the John Reed Clubs folded, artists turned their attention to the American Artists Congress, an organization formed in the fall of 1935 to include acknowledged professional artists of all political persuasions. At that time the goal was to organize for a large conference later held in February 1936 in New York City. The theme of the conference was the struggle against war, fascism, and, as artist Stuart Davis stated, "every manifestation of war-mongering reaction." The published papers, *First American Artists' Congress*, 1936, constitute an important document of the times. The congress, which put on exhibitions and was a significant forum for ideas, continued until early 1940 when a faction of the membership forced a split over the issue of the Russian invasion of Finland.

Crucial to the Left art movement's success throughout the 1930s was an audience and a patronage favorable to these artists of social issues. The audience consisted of great numbers of the urban intelligentsia: critics, dealers, curators, and labor unionists as well, all of whom encouraged the expression of revolutionary ideas in art. New public patronage also benefited such artists. By the mid-1930s the government had thousands of needy artists on its payrolls through such programs as the Federal Art Project of the Works Progress Administration (or, for photographers, the Farm Security Administration). In return, artists such as Allan Rohan Crite, Philip Evergood, Jacob Lawrence, Jack Levine, and Alice Neel periodically submitted artwork or taught in community art schools. Through these programs hundreds of thousands of artworks (murals, easel paintings, sculpture, posters, prints) found their way to hospitals, post offices, municipal and federal buildings, schools, and airports, where they could be viewed by the broadest spectrum of people. This experience of having a common employer—the government—contributed to the artists' camaraderie and identification with workers. (However, by the end of the 1930s these programs were under attack by Red-baiting congressmen such as Martin Dies of Texas.)

Fostering such camaraderie was the Artists Union, formed in September 1933 as the Emergency Work Bureau Artists Group to act as bargaining agent for artists on the government projects. The union, along with the Artists Committee of Action, organized the publication of *Art Front*, the first issue of which appeared in November 1934 and which continued as a monthly until December 1937, when it ceased publication. During its existence *Art Front* was the premier magazine for Left artists, containing news items, reviews of exhibitions and books, announcements of meetings and rallies, and polemical essays on the political and aesthetic issues facing artists. Many of the major artists and critics of the 1930s wrote for the magazine, including Harold Rosenberg, Meyer Schapiro, William Phillips, Kenneth Rexroth, Irwin Edman, and Elizabeth McCausland (under the pseudonym "Elizabeth Noble"), and artists Louis Lozowick, Philip Evergood, Moses Soyer, Max Weber, Fritz Eichenberg, and many others.

The Public Use of Art Committee of the Artists Union cooperated with trade unions to bring workers art that would have popular appeal. An article in the December 1936 issue of *Art Front* reported that the Union of Dining Car Employees had suggested "works showing the effect of speed-up on dining car employees; the battle for union recognition on the Santa Fe; antiwar subjects; exploitation of women employed in hotel dining rooms and kitchens; antilynching subjects; scenes in the culinary industry; Negro discrimination." The Brotherhood of Sleeping Car Porters explicitly implored: "Kindly have running through the entire series of paintings relative to the Pullman porters and the Brotherhood a pattern of struggle, sacrifice, and fighting." The trade unions were mandating social realism with a content of class struggle, and many artists took their requests seriously.

However, the Popular Front policy eventually acted to modify critiques of capitalism since its aim was to unite the workers' movement with "progressive" capitalists and liberals in the fight against fascism. Also, social realist artworks depicting strikes and lynchings or lampooning well-known capitalists and politicians were unacceptable as WPA submissions. Thus, both the CP and the government encouraged artists to back away from proletarian politics and to support Roosevelt's efforts to reform capitalism. As the CP lost its vanguard edge, it was only a matter of time before it lost its cultural influence with artists as well. Later, when the United States entered the arena of World War II, it seemed unpatriotic to paint pictures of class struggle. Many artists further repressed their radical views when they joined the war effort: designing posters, going to the front as artist-journalists, or simply serving in the armed forces.

The rise of abstract expressionism in the post–WW II years was one manifestation of the eclipse of the Left; a new era had arrived, concerned less with social issues and more with aesthetic form, concerned less with collective goals and more with individualized insight. Many reasons have been advanced for this change and its relationship to Cold War ideology; among them are: the conditions of a new private patronage that supplanted government patronage; the promotion of new, individualist philosophies such as existentialism and a redefinition of the meaning of "avant-garde"; the corresponding political swing to the Right, the failure of a Left party to rally against political reaction, and anticommunist pressures on critics and writers; and the new obsession with consumerism, affluence, and control of world markets.

Artists on the Left since the 1930s have generally shunned the leadership of a party devoted to working-class struggles. Moreover, while they may have embraced some Marxist theories, they often have not had direct experiences in working-class issues such as unemployment, cutbacks, and deteriorating health care. Finally, such artists are unsure of their audiences. While many radical artists work in communities making art (street art, performance art, murals) for an alternative or potentially oppositional culture, a large number of "political artists" still look to the commercial art galleries, the museum world, and an international, elite group of patrons for validation.

—*Patricia Hills*

REFERENCES

Baigell, Matthew, and Julia Williams, eds. *Artists Against War and Fascism: Papers of the First American Artists' Congress*. New Brunswick: Rutgers University Press, 1986.

Foner, Philip S., and Reinhard Schultz. *The Other America: Art and the Labour Movement in the United States*. London: Journeyman Press, 1985.

Harrison, Helen A. "John Reed Club Artists and the New Deal: Radical Responses to Roosevelt's 'Peaceful Revolution.'" *Prospects* 5 (1980).

Hills, Patricia. *Social Concern and Urban Realism: American Painting of the 1930s*. Boston: Boston University Art Gallery, 1983.

———. "The Fine Arts in America: Images of Labor from 1800 to 1950." In *Essays from the Lowell Conference on Industrial History*, Part I, *The Arts and Industrialism*, edited by Robert Weible. North Andover, Mass.: Museum of American Textile History, 1985.

Weichsel, John. Files. Archives of American Art, Smithsonian Institution.

ARTEF

The ARTEF, a Yiddish workers' theater company existing from 1925 to 1940, combined left-wing politics, Soviet-inspired aesthetics, and Jewish folk culture into innovative productions that drew large Jewish immigrant audiences while influencing the New York theatrical scene of that period.

Begun during a period when the Jewish Left was in its heyday, the founders of the ARTEF, the *Arbeiter Theater Verband* (Workers Theater Group), sought to create a theater in Yiddish, reflecting the lives and struggles of the Jewish working class. They also set high dramatic standards, hoping to provide an alternative to the popular commercial Yiddish theater of "Second Avenue," which they derided for its vaudevillesque, off-color, melodramatic style.

Following up efforts of the Yiddish communist daily, the *Freiheit*, to establish a dramatic studio, a group of young workers, led first by Jacob Mestel and then joined by Benno Schneider of the Soviet Jewish folk troupe Habima, spent three years (1925–28) undergoing intense dramatic training. Known as the "ARTEF Studio," they began with twenty-six students who worked days and studied nights and weekends, supporting the studio's costs largely from their day jobs as shop workers.

From this, an Actors Collective was formed, producing its first play, *By the Gate*, in 1928. Praised by New York theater critics, it was criticised by Communist Party cultural officials for emphasizing Jewish folk themes over the "ideals of class struggle." Nevertheless, the ARTEF was closely associated with the CP's Jewish Bureau, receiving the bulk of its audience and publicity through affiliate organizations. This support was crucial, as the more moderate, social democratic, Jewish organizations, such as the *Jewish Daily Forward*, banned ARTEF reviews and advertising, while the Hebrew Actors Union denied affiliation to ARTEF members.

The ARTEF was strongly influenced by Soviet theater, incorporating styles of Stanislavsky, Vakhtangov, and Meyerhold, and combining elements of realism, naturalism, impressionism, and agitprop. Dramatic emphasis was on the actors' ensemble as opposed to "stars," integrating dance, music, and song, set off by modernist, multilayered scenic design by M. Solatoreff. Along with regular performances in several New York theaters, the ARTEF toured major cities, including Philadelphia, Boston, Montreal, and Toronto.

While the ARTEF saw its mission as educating the Jewish working class to left-wing ideology, its overriding commitment to high dramatic standards and experimental forms resulted in its recognition as a popular Yiddish "art theater," which also attracted leading figures of the American theater.

Most of its plays dealt with the conditions of Jewish life in eastern Europe, adapted from stories by popular Yiddish writers such as Sholem Aleichem. Its other plays were taken from the Soviet stage. Of the eighteen plays presented to 1937, only two dealt with conditions of the Jewish-American worker, and these were considered dramatic failures.

By 1940 the ARTEF folded. Improved conditions of the late 1930s removed the pressing social issues of the Depression and receptivity to radical ideas. A number of ARTEF actors left the company, joining the WPA's Federal Theater Project. The ARTEF's move to a larger theater in the mid-1930s raised operating costs, which they couldn't cover. The biggest factor was the Hitler-Stalin Pact of 1939, which alienated a large portion of their Jewish audience because of their association with the CP. *See also*: Yiddish Left

—*Joel Saxe*

REFERENCES

ARTEF. *Ten Years ARTEF: Published for the Tenth Anniversary of the ARTEF*. New York: Posy-Shoulson Press, 1937.

Kline, Herbert, ed. *New Theatre and Film, 1934–1937, An Anthology*. New York: Harcourt Brace Jovanovich, 1985.

Rifson, David, S. *The Yiddish Theatre in America*. New York: Thomas Yoseloff Ltd., 1965.

Sandrow, Nahma. *Vagabond Stars: A World History of Yiddish Theatre*. New York: Harper & Row, 1977.

Asian Studies

Response to events in Asia, particularly the war in Vietnam and the Cultural Revolution in China, played a central role in the development of the New Left in the United States. One of the main catalysts of that response was the Committee of Concerned Asian Scholars.

CCAS's founding in March 1967 by some thirty American graduate students studying in Taiwan came at a time when Asian studies had been stripped by the ravages of McCarranism of any voices even vaguely critical of American policy. For a number of years, CCAS succeeded in developing both a community and a journal in which people interested in Asia—not as something exotic, nor as a route to a career in the military or in the State Department—could develop their critical analyses of U.S. policy into a coherent antiimperialist view and explore the potential of the Cultural Revolution for social change in a professional way within their field.

CCAS first came to the public eye on campuses. At the spring 1968 Association of Asian Studies convention in Philadelphia, its members began to confront AAS on its role in the destruction of the critical, but not leftist, Institute of Pacific Relations. Many CCAS members helped to organize the teach-ins on Vietnam that swept the country in 1968 and 1969. At the 1969 Boston convention of AAS, CCAS's panel on the effects of McCarranism on Asian studies and "moral detention"—the fear of criticizing American policy—drew nearly 2,000 people.

Following the Boston convention, CCAS began to be viewed as a threat, even a violent threat, to U.S. policy. One of its leaders was falsely accused of murder and CCAS was accused of plotting to bomb the bookstalls at the 1970 AAS convention in San Francisco.

CCAS's vocal opposition to the Vietnam War, its advocacy of recognition of the People's Republic of China (PRC), and its critique of the detachment, irresponsibility, and sycophantism of establishment scholarship continued unabated through both its journal and such publications as *The Indochina Story* and *America's Asia* in the late sixties and early seventies. CCAS attracted the attention of the wider public in 1971 when a small delegation was invited to visit the PRC, the first Americans to visit China—aside from the Ping-Pong team startlingly invited several months before—in nearly twenty years. This trip resulted in the publication of *China: Inside the People's Republic* and an invitation for a second delegation. But future relations with China deteriorated as CCAS moved from the relatively naive and uncritical positions in *Inside the People's Republic* to positions questioning China's policies on issues ranging from the handling of homosexuality to her support for Pakistan against Bangladesh.

Following its short period in the limelight, CCAS and other groups of progressive Asian-studies students continued their organizing, working with a wide range of groups, from the U.S.-China Peoples Friendship Association to various organizations teaching about China to some of the pre-party formations of the seventies and even to attempting to establish a boycott of nonunion grapes in Hong Kong in support of the United Farm Workers. Although CCAS was never pulled apart by the factionalism that split many of the other groups of the Left, it too reflected the changing times. Many supporters of Mao and the Cultural Revolution became strong critics. By the late seventies, with the reduction in funding for Asian studies in the United States following the end of the war in Vietnam, the reversal of Maoist policies, the rise of Reaganism, and the accompanying change in the focus of many students of China from social change and revolution to business administration, CCAS disappeared as a membership organization. The *Bulletin of Concerned Asian Scholars*, however, has continued to flourish, with a circulation of some 2,000. It continues to develop many of the themes that dominated the earlier works of CCAS—including the analysis of the role of imperialism in the development of Asia and the critique of the focus on leaders as the key point in history in favor of analyses of the linkages between people, classes, governments, and parties.

As with many other Left groups, CCAS combined a sense of vibrancy, optimism, and excitement with a sense of seriousness and dedication. Professors and politicians were directly and personally confronted with the responsibility for their work, thus breaking with many of the niceties of academic life. A not insignificant number of progressive Asian-studies students sacrificed jobs in elite universities to teach in more working-class settings. Others gave up promising academic careers for more political jobs. And some were effectively forced out of the field and/or blacklisted for their political views and activities. Others, from the least well known to Noam Chomsky, have continued through the years, both from inside and outside of academia, to present a critical view both of social, economic, and political changes and the U.S. role in those changes not only in China and Vietnam, but also in the rest of Southeast Asia, Japan, Korea, and India.

Although the legacy of CCAS and the Left in Asian studies is hard to pinpoint, it did help give legitimacy to a unity of personal, political, and professional goals in favor of meaningful social change. It helped make large amounts of critical information about Asia's past and present accessible both to the Left and to large segments of the American public. It provided the support for those who produced and continue to produce critical studies of China, Southeast Asia, Japan, Korea, and India. Perhaps most important, it helped this critical view of Asia to become rooted in both academia and the wider public, so that many people who may not even know what the New Left is can read materials that are products of that experience and be taught by people who formed and were formed by that experience. *See also*: *Amerasia*; "Antirevisionism" (Maoism); New Left; Snow, Edgar; Strong, Anna Louise

—*Rich Levy*

Atheism

The denial of a god has varied meanings for the U.S. Left—theoretical, political, and cultural. Atheism formed the primary philosophical premise accepted by the Marxist and Bakuninist tendencies in the U.S. section of the First International. Marx has always been infamous in the United States for disparaging religious beliefs as incompatible with any genuine amelioration of proletarian misery. Bakunin argued that God was incompatible with human freedom and must be rejected by all true revolutionaries. Their U.S. comrades and successors tended to espouse a similar atheism, not only to draw the workers away from the soporific influence of the churches, but also to encourage them to claim their legitimate inheritance from the scientific enlightenment. A revolution in its own right, atheism was also an educational gain for working-class people, who for the first time had access to a curriculum aimed at liberating them rather than controlling them.

A second facet of importance is summed up in the practical materialism of the U.S. labor movement and political Left. Disregarding alleged spiritual or mystical goods and rewards, the Left expresses a practical atheism by demanding concrete economic and social benefits for the workers who actually produce real goods. In the programs of unions and political parties from the very beginning of the Left movement, the demand was for the product of labor rather than of prayer. Likewise, the demands for justice, equality, freedom, and peace are made exclusively in concrete terms even though spiritual versions of such goods are offered by the churches as preferable. Much working-class culture of the early twentieth century, especially humor, made constant reference to the contrast between the two modes of satisfaction—the "pie in the sky" motif.

Another major facet of atheism is its use, *against* the Left, as an accusation or indictment to attack individuals, organizations, or whole classwide movements. Communists, anarchists, and socialists are portrayed as godless and morally depraved by nearly all "Red-baiters" and all reactionary propaganda. The most visible early examples of this tactic were provided by the churches themselves, as in the U.S. Catholic hierarchy's attack on the Paris Commune and the Knights of Labor. The systematic promotion of religion in periods of economic crisis and its growing use as an ideological fulcrum by the Right have greatly aided this tactic. But by the New Deal era labor had already toned down explicit criticism of the churches. Left political movements did likewise and in recent decades, the 1970s and 1980s, even the Left intelligentsia has begun to accommodate to religion as social theory in general inclined to anthropologist Emile Durkheim's view of religion as a sociological absolute independent of the validity of theism or any creed whatsoever.

Another major factor was the gradual liberalization of religious attitudes toward social change. Key denominations progressed from support for social reforms to acceptance of unionism and finally, in the 1970s and 1980s, segments of the Christian community offered controversial support for liberation movements in the Third World, notably Southern Africa and Latin America. White mainstream Christians were moved to this policy in some measure by the example of black churches and ministers in the civil rights movement. This was reinforced by the activities of small groups of antiwar Christians in the United States and even more so by the emergence in Latin America of "liberation theology," which espouses a radical social gospel.

But despite this tendency, the dominant experience in the late twentieth century has been that movements and governments based on religion tended to be overwhelmingly reactionary and extremely hostile to secular radicals and their goals. Examples can be drawn from nations as diverse as Iran, Poland, India, Lebanon, and Israel. In contrast to the Latin American support work of a few U.S. churches, the dominant U.S. religious trend has been rightist.

Throughout the post-World War II era, atheism was not moribund on the Left. But it existed in a latent, diffused form within the most radical branches of nonconformist youth culture. The great wave of cultural and moral experiment that accompanied the political New Left in effect attempted to live out the Old Left atheist proposition that human beings can be free and masterless and yet still be happy, productive, and just. Among the themes that have dominated the Left since the 1960s has been the belief that the revolutionary process should lead to the full imaginative as well as material enfranchisement of all. Surrealists have enriched the debate on the subjective factor in revolution by emphasizing such often-repressed psycho-social phenomena as poetry, dream, spontaneous revolt, love, madness, eroticism, and irreverence. These features restore a more anarchist color—the libertarian bloom—to a drab socialist rose and are perennially attractive to rebel youth repulsed by the restrictions of religious creeds. *See also*: Anarchism, Free Thought

—*Joseph Jablonski*

REFERENCES

Garon, Paul. *Blues and the Poetic Spirit*. London: Eddison Press, 1975.

Harrington, Michael. *The Politics at God's Funeral*. New York: Holt, Rinehart & Winston, 1985.

Jablonski, Joseph. "The Haymarket Atheists." In *The Haymarket Scrapbook*, edited by David Roediger and Franklin Rosemont. Chicago: Charles H. Kerr, 1986.

Most, Johann. *The God Pestilence*. Reprint. Tucson: The Match, 1983.

ATTICA

This upstate New York town has been the site of a maximum-security state prison since 1931. On September 13, 1971, it was the scene of a slaughter of 29 prisoners and 10 prison guards during a six-minute-long assault by state troopers and correctional officers. The attack ended a four-day takeover of the institution by 1,281 prisoners, who took 43 guards hostage after a series of minor incidents had escalated into a full-scale prison riot on September 9.

The driving forces behind the takeover were the conditions and treatment of prisoners inside the institution, and the perceived inequities in the criminal justice process that had delivered them to Attica.

> We are MEN! We are not beasts and do not intend to be beaten or driven as such. The entire prison population has set forth to change forever the ruthless brutalization and disregard for the lives of the prisoners here and throughout the United States. What has happened here is but the sound before the fury of those who are oppressed. [From *Five Demands*, issued to "the people of America" by rioting prisoners at Attica on September 9, 1971.]

Between the time of the uprising and the assault by state troopers, prisoners and prison officials attempted to negotiate a peaceful resolution to the situation through a committee of outside observers brought to Attica at the inmates' request. Most of the prisoners' demands related to changes in prison policies or practices (nutritional food, religious freedom, etc.), but negotiations deadlocked on the demand for amnesty from prosecution for events connected with the uprising. Because a guard had died of injuries sustained in the events leading up to the takeover, prisoners risked potential murder charges. However, despite desperate pleas from both the observers' committee and from his own corrections officials that he come to Attica to show his concern, Governor Nelson Rockefeller gave up on negotiations and ordered the state police to "reopen the institution."

The issues behind the uprising itself, the barrage of state firepower leveled against a virtually unarmed population of prisoners and hostages in an enclosed area, the brutal and massive retaliation inflicted on prisoners afterward, and the convictions relating to these events obtained later against prisoners—but not against any state officials—brought the inequities of the criminal justice system furiously to the front burner for the American Left. Analyses pinpointing the roots of crime in social, racial, political, and economic inequality brought some organizations to adopt the position that all prisoners in America were political prisoners. Particularly, the connection between racism and the role of prisons in the United States, which black activists had been articulating for years, was grasped in a new way by white leftists and mainstream liberal groups after Attica.

The issue of amnesty symbolized the political forces that were in contention at Attica. The logic of the demand for amnesty centered on the position that prisoners were already paying for their crimes by serving sentences, but crimes had been and were being committed against *them* routinely by agents of the state. In taking over the institution, inmates were seeking a forum not available to them through legitimate means, through which they might speak out on their own victimization. Amnesty seemed required by simple fairness. For the state of New York, however, amnesty meant the surrender of legal control over its citizens. Not even to save the lives of its own employees, the hostages, could the state consider amnesty for the prisoners without opening to question the legitimacy of state authority per se. *See also*: Armed Struggle, Civil Rights

—Jill Raymond

REFERENCES

Wicker, Tom. *A Time to Die*. New York: Quadrangle/The New York Times Book Co., 1975.

Attica/The Official Report of the New York State Special Commission on Attica. New York: Bantam Books, 1972.

B

BAKER, ELLA (1903–86)

The "godmother" of the Student Nonviolent Coordinating Committee (SNCC), Ella Baker was a major influence on political activists from the 1930s to the 1980s. She encouraged hundreds of students and community people to organize and take what was legally theirs, particularly in the area of civil rights. In addition to her work with SNCC, Ella Baker was national director of the Young Negroes' Cooperative League, director of branches of the National Association for the Advancement of Colored People (NAACP), executive director of the Southern Christian Leadership Conference (SCLC), a coordinator of the Mississippi Freedom Democratic Party (MFDP), and a staff member of the Southern Conference Educational Fund (SCEF).

Granddaughter of slaves who had acquired the land in North Carolina on which they had slaved, Ella Baker grew up with a strong sense of a black community who shared what they had. After graduating from Shaw University in Raleigh, North Carolina, she moved to New York City, where she worked for the *American West Indian News* and the *Negro National News*. Because few jobs were open to black women, she did factory work and waitressing to survive. In 1932 she helped organize the Young Negroes' Cooperative League, a consumer cooperative, and did consumer education for the Works Progress Administration.

From 1940 to 1946 Ella Baker traveled in the South for the NAACP as field secretary and then director of branches to recruit members and stimulate local campaigns. She was involved in the antilynching campaign and the equal pay-for-black-teachers movement. Her strength was to evoke in people a feeling of common need and the belief that people together can change the conditions under which they live. During these years, she formed a network of politically active people throughout the South who proved invaluable during the civil rights struggles of the 1950s and 1960s. In 1946 Baker resigned from her leadership role in the national NAACP because she felt it was too bureaucratic. She also took on the responsibility of raising her niece. She did, however, work with the NAACP in New York City on school desegregation and served as president of the city's branch.

In 1958 Ella Baker became executive director of SCLC, founded by Martin Luther King and other ministers in 1957 immediately after the Montgomery bus boycott. Although SCLC believed voter registration to be primary, this priority did not become a reality until SNCC was formed in 1960. Baker was instrumental in inviting to a conference the hundreds of black students and some white students who had participated in the sit-ins at lunch counters throughout the South, and out of which came SNCC and its philosophy of nonviolent direct action. Although Baker did not personally believe in nonviolence, she saw it as a tactic that could accomplish voter registration and one in which many of the students believed. During this first SNCC conference, Baker broke with SCLC and Martin Luther King, who wished her to influence the SNCC students to become a youth wing of SCLC. In the following years, Baker was the older person behind SNCC who listened, counseled, advised, and nurtured the civil rights workers who organized the freedom rides, worked in voter registration, and broke segregation in the South. Baker saw securing the vote as a necessary step for black people to take, but did not idealistically believe it would cure their problems.

The MFDP was organized by SNCC as an alternative to the regular Democratic Party in Mississippi. Ella Baker set up the Washington office of the MFDP and keynoted its Jackson, Mississippi, convention. Although the MFDP delegates were not seated at the National Democratic Convention, the influence of the MFDP was felt in the election of many local black leaders to office in Mississippi. But the Democrats' rejection of the MFDP also disillusioned many young activists about the possibilities of working within the system.

Ella Baker continued her political work with SCEF, an organization dedicated to helping black and white people work together. She also was a supporter of freedom struggles in Africa, a national board member of the Puerto Rican Solidarity Committee, and vice-chairperson of the Mass Party Organizing Committee. In her last years she continued to nurture, inspire, scold, and advise the numerous young people who worked with her during her long career of political activism. *See also*: Civil Rights

—*Susan Gushee O'Malley*

REFERENCES

Cantarow, Ellen, and Susan Gushee O'Malley. "Ella Baker Organizing for Civil Rights." In *Moving the Mountain*. New York: The Feminist Press, 1980.

Fundi: The Story of Ella Baker. Directed and produced by Joanne Grant. 1980. Sixty minutes. Distributed by Icarus/First Run Features.

Baran, Paul (1910–64)

A leading Marxist economist, Baran was born in Nikolaev, Russia, to Jewish-Polish parents. He attended universities in Moscow, Berlin, and Frankfurt, where he was much influenced by the "Frankfurt School." As a youth he joined the German Communist Party (KPD), but later, protesting its position on fascism, switched to the Social Democrats (SPD). In 1939 he emigrated to the United States and, after studying at Harvard University, he assumed positions in war-related projects, including the Office of Strategic Services (OSS) and the U.S. Strategic Bombing Surveys. In 1948 he joined the Economics Department at Stanford University; until his death, Baran was probably the only public Marxist economist teaching in an American university—and he keenly felt his isolation. Moreover, during much of the 1950s the government denied him a passport. In 1960, however, he traveled to Cuba and wrote warmly of the new revolution.

Although his writings were not voluminous—two books and a posthumous collection of essays—Baran's influence has been far-reaching. *The Political Economy of Growth* (1957) and *Monopoly Capital* (1966, with Paul M. Sweezy) are classics, widely read and translated; for countless students they have served as a nondogmatic education in Marxism, virtually inaugurating American Marxist discussions of Third World underdevelopment and advanced, or monopoly, capitalism. In both books Baran introduced the category of economic "surplus." For Baran "surplus value" insufficiently comprehended Third World dependency as well as the prodigious waste that besets monopoly capital. A rising "surplus" registered the wasted work and productivity, measured not by rates of exploitation but by human and social needs. For more orthodox Marxists, however, "surplus" sounded too philosophical and moral—the last chapter of *Monopoly Capital* is called "The Irrational System." Despite this criticism Baran was an original Marxist economist, perhaps without peer in the United States, whose writings ranged over underdevelopment, militarism, racism, advertising, and monopoly; he was a classical Marxist who rethought the theory for the contemporary world. *See also*: *Monthly Review*, Radical Economics

—*Russell Jacoby*

REFERENCES

Paul A. Baran: A Collective Portrait. Edited by Paul M. Sweezy and Leo Huberman. New York: Monthly Review Press, 1965. (*Monthly Review* 16, [March 1965]).

Clecak, Peter. *Radical Paradoxes*. New York: Harper and Row, 1973.

Foster, John Bellamy. *The Theory of Monopoly Capital*. New York: Monthly Review Press, 1986.

THE BEATS AND THE NEW LEFT

The first major post–World War II literary rebellion, the Beat Generation of the 1950s, was a cultural rather than a political movement. Based on a highly individualistic anarchism, the Beat movement denounced capitalist Moloch without the slightest hope for a Marxism whose authoritarianism was frequently assailed. Beat opposition to militarism, racism, and economic injustice was consistent and fervent, but it was generally secondary to celebration of hallucinatory drugs, homosexual sex, mystical religion, and exotic experiences of all kinds. The term *Beat* refers to the state of beatitude originally set as a prime goal of the movement's originators. The issues and style of the Beats are relevant to discourse about the Left primarily because the Beats set the tone for the counterculture of the 1960s with which the New Left was intimately bound.

The Beats came from various parts of the country, but they had clustered in San Francisco by the mid-1950s. Unable to find acceptance in either the commercial or literary press, the Beats took up two artistic activities that would have a profound influence on the burgeoning counterculture—public performance and self-publishing. Public performances originated in coffeehouses but moved to all manner of public forums. Poetry was projected by the Beats as a spoken or sung art best experienced in a public place and not as an individual and silent act of reading. When the original Beats generated a following throughout the nation, poetry readings became a fixture in the alternative culture. With the development of various political movements in the 1960s, the reading of poetry at rallies, teach-ins, demonstrations, and other political events became commonplace. The style of reading and the sense of poetry as a social force were directly related to the Beats.

Self-publishing had been critical to American literary innovation since at least the time Walt Whitman self-published *Leaves of Grass*. Drawing on that tradition, Beat poet Lawrence Ferlinghetti opened the City Lights bookstore in 1953 and inaugurated a Pocket Poets Series with his *Pictures of a Gone World* (1955). The small books that fit easily into pants pockets totally bypassed the established publishing and review complex. What soon differentiated the venture from similar efforts was that Allen Ginsberg's *Howl* (1956) sold first in the thousands and ultimately nearly a million copies. Ferlinghetti had defied the cultural hegemony of the dominant culture yet had reached a mass audience. Coming at a moment when new printing technology was greatly reducing the labor and cost involved in self-publishing, Ferlinghetti's success spawned the creation of new presses whose numbers reached into the high hundreds by the late 1960s. This movement, in turn, meshed with the creation of the alternative weekly newspapers that were such a vital force in the late 1960s and early 1970s.

Ferlinghetti retained his commitment to an alternative press. Long after he and other writers he first published were famous enough for the commercial press to take on, he continued with independent publishing. A full quarter of a century after *Howl*, he was publisher of *Free Spirits: Annals of the Insurgent Imagination*, an anthology featuring anarchist, Beat, surrealist, eccentric, and independent Marxist artists of various nations and disciplines.

The Beats first achieved national attention when Ginsberg was charged with obscenity for reading *Howl* in a San Francisco coffeehouse. The long poem was featured in the special issue of *Evergreen Review* (vol. 1, no. 2, early 1957), which was totally dedicated to the Beat movement and included Ferlinghetti, Jack Kerouac, Michael McClure, Robert Duncan, Brother Antoninus, Gary Snyder, Philip Whalen, and other new writers. Editors Barney Rosset and Donald Allen posited a tradition for the Beats by publishing selections from Henry Miller and Kenneth Rexroth as well. Miller was included because of the language precedent he had set in *Tropic of Cancer* and Rexroth linked the Beats to political dissent. In a San Francisco "literary letter," Rexroth berated American Marxist writers as authoritarian and obsequious to political power; and in a poem Rexroth paid homage to the Kronstadt insurrection, Peter Kropotkin, Makhno's peasant anarchists, Carlo Tresca, and Alexander Berkman.

None of the Beats possessed the ideological sophistication of Rexroth, but they shared his disdain for the established Left. Ginsberg wrote negatively of the regimes in Czechoslovakia and Cuba, and he lamented Che Guevara as a tragic hero on a futile mission. Such immediate political concerns continued to crop up in his life and work. In the 1967 siege of the Pentagon by the antiwar movement, Ginsberg led a group that sought to levitate the Pentagon by humming *OM*, a beatific Buddhist-derived incantation. Whether that act was scene-stealing performance or religious conviction, Ginsberg was present not only to end a specific war but militarism itself. His advocacy of poet as spiritual guru, as acknowledged legislator of morality, was easily translated into more political terms by radical writers.

Other themes of Beat culture prefigured and entwined with political issues of the 1960s and 1970s. Gary Snyder wrote often about the need to defend the environment and respect the rights of other animals. William Everson, a lay monk who also published as Brother Antoninus, sought to reconcile traditional religions such as Roman Catholicism with the new mysticism, sexual liberation, and social activism.

William Burroughs and Jack Kerouac, the two major prose writers of the Beats, were more problematic for the Left. Kerouac's *On the Road* (1957) lauded individual freedom and mobility, but the more Kerouac wrote, the more his various right-wing sentiments became evident. His personal influence faded quickly and he became a heavy drinker who had little contact with other Beats. In novels like *The Naked Lunch* (1959) Burroughs used obscene and surreal images to assault the generic police state, but his vision remained essentially nihilistic. While Ginsberg enjoyed being a celebrity, Burroughs avoided the limelight and admitted much of his life was a personal disaster. He had accidentally killed his wife while playing with a pistol and spent many years severely addicted to drugs. More so than any other Beat ikon, however, Burroughs insisted on the necessity of maintaining a permanent alternative culture. He has said his work is "directed against those who are bent, through stupidity or design, on blowing up the planet or rendering it uninhabitable."

On some issues, the New Left took strong exception to Beat thinking. The attempt to achieve change through mystical means was an obvious sore point. A deeper concern was the debate on how society should deal with drugs. Drug use was a taboo in the traditional Left, but recreational drugs became an accepted element in the New Left environment. How far such usage should go, especially in the face of the destructive role of drugs in much of society, pit the freedom of individual choice against the self-protective needs of society. Ginsberg and Burroughs wrote extensively of their pursuit of exotic drugs, often in travels to developing nations. Their indifference to the political oppression in those nations seemed like that of other Westerners who exploited the Third World for personal, economic, or recreational purposes. Feminist critics found Beat culture not only to be mostly male but also male chauvinist.

On the other hand, the New Left responded positively to the dynamic language and theatrics of the Beats. This was most evident in the ploys of Abbie Hoffman and Jerry Rubin, but generally speaking the freewheeling nature of the New Left style owed far more to the Beats than any leftist influence. Beat celebration of homosexuality broke ideology and artistic barriers of the Left as well as the Right and fed currents that would culminate in the gay liberation movement. The antiorganizational bias of the Beats was reflected, for better and for worse, in radical groups like Students for a Democratic Society, which rejected the discipline of Marxist-Leninism. Many New Left activists expressed mixed feelings when referring to the Beats, saying that they reacted as much against the Beats as with them, but acknowledging it had been the Beats who shattered the conformity of the Eisenhower era and dramatically rekindled vital themes in the broad tradition of American dissent. *See also*: New Left

—*Dan Georgakas*

REFERENCES

Burroughs, William. *Junky*. New York: Penguin Books, 1977.

Evergreen Review: San Francisco Scene, V. 1 #2, 1957.

Free Spirits: Annals of the Insurgent Imagination. Edited by Paul Buhle, Jayne Cortez, Philip Lamantia, Franklin Rosemont, Penelope Rosemont, and Nancy Joyce Peters. San Francisco: City Lights Books, 1982.

Gitlin, Todd, ed., *Campfires of the Resistance: Poetry from the Movement*. Indianapolis: Bobbs-Merrill, 1972.

Herman, Jan, ed. *Something Else Yearbook—1974*. West Glover, Vt.: Something Else Press, 1974.

Lewis, Roger. *Outlaws of America: The Underground Press and Its Context—Notes on a Cultural Revolution*. New York: Penguin Books, 1972.

BEDACHT, MAX: see INTERNATIONAL WORKERS ORDER

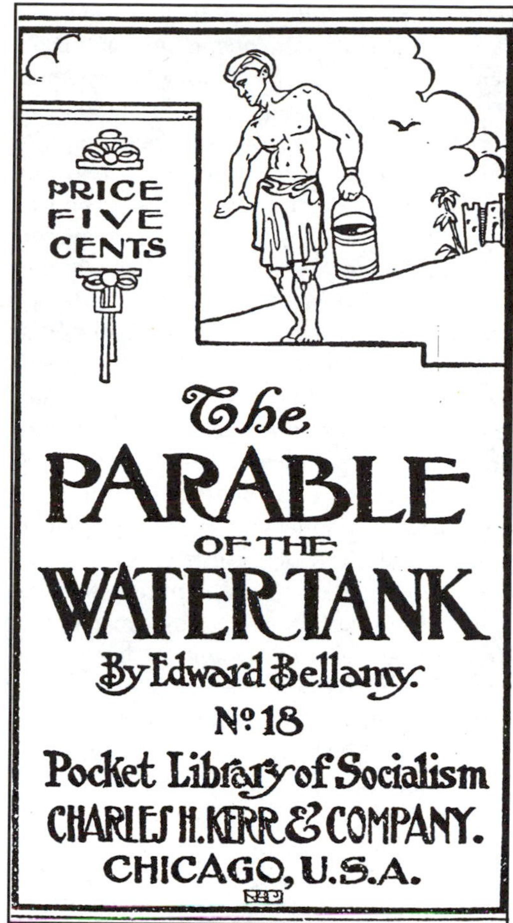

Cover drawn by Ralph Chaplin

BELLAMY, EDWARD (1850–98)

America's best known and most influential utopian socialist, author of *Looking Backward* and *Equality*, Bellamy was born in the rapidly industrializing village of Chicopee Falls, Massachusetts, where, except for brief visits to Germany, Central America, Hawaii, and New York, he lived nearly all his life. He attended Union College in 1867 and was admitted to the bar in 1871, but abandoned law as a career after his first case. He made his living thereafter as a journalist and writer of fiction, first on the editorial staff of the New York *Evening Post*, and in 1872 as editor of the Springfield (Massachusetts) *Daily Union*, where he remained for five years. The first of his twenty-two published short stories, "The Cold Snap," appeared in *Scribner's* in 1875; the first of his six novels, *Six to One: A Nantucket Idyl*, was published three years later. In 1883 he married Emma Sanderson, with whom he had a son, Paul, and a daughter, Marion.

His preeminence as a utopian social critic has tended to obscure the fact that Bellamy was first and foremost a writer of imaginative fiction—second only to Hawthorne, in the opinion of so demanding a critic as William Dean Howells. Hints of his later radicalism are discernible in some of his lyceum lectures and editorials from the early 1870s, and especially in his novel *The Duke of Stockbridge* (1879), a markedly sympathetic portrayal of Shays' Rebellion, the 1786 Massachusetts uprising of debtor-farmers and poor mechanics. But the truly distinctive and even unique qualities of Bellamy's utopia were prefigured, rather, in his science-fiction and fantasy tales. These weird stories, most of them involving disturbing reversals of everyday assumptions, often with an unmistakably satirical intent, reveal his abiding interest in the phenomena and problems of abnormal psychology (somnambulism, hypnotism, hysteria, hallucinations, altered states of consciousness, ventriloquism, etc.) as well as a philosophical passion for surmounting the contradictions of what he later called the "Jekyll-Hyde existence" of modern capitalist society. In these tales, which were essentially philosophical puzzles—"attempts to trace the logical consequences of certain assumed conditions"—he elaborated elements of a revolutionary critical theory and even a kind of experimental morality. The radical social views advanced in *Looking Backward* and *Equality* can be seen, in turn, as the logical consequences of the moral/psychological radicalism of these tales. Central and recurring themes of his nonutopian fiction—supersession of memory by imagination, transcendence of the tyranny of linear time, reintegration of the personality, and the need for wilderness ("I wouldn't give much for a country in which there are no wildernesses left") became key notions of his utopia. This double critique of the mind's war with itself and of society's war with itself—a critique resembling, in many respects, that of the much later surrealists and Freud-influenced Marxists such as Herbert Marcuse—constituted Bellamy's real originality and the essence of his thought.

By far his most famous book, *Looking Backward* (1888) is the story of a lone survivor of 1880s capitalist Boston who awakens in the year 2000, after more than a century of sleep, to find that a nonviolent revolution has completely changed the conditions of society and therefore the relationships between people. Having abolished private ownership of the means of production, the new society has done away with social classes, exploitation, poverty, starvation, sex slavery, war, slums, crime, jails, buying, selling, money, banks, censorship, charity, corruption, taxes, custom duties, advertising, housework, air pollution, politicians, merchants, servants, lawyers, the militia, the army, the navy, and the State Department. Government itself, reduced to the coordination of industrial production and distribution, hardly exists. The new society is wholly free of coercion, everything having become "entirely voluntary, the logical outcome of the operation of human nature under rational conditions." Starting at twenty-one, everyone works; at forty-five everyone retires. Work has become greatly simplified and even pleasurable. Workplace health and safety are assured for all. Working hours are short; vacations are long.

The social transformation described in *Looking Backward* has in turn transformed, or rather liberated, the human personality. In Bellamy's vision of the year 2000, selfishness, greed, malice, insanity, hypocrisy, lying, apathy, the lust for power, the "struggle for existence," and anxiety as to basic human needs are all things of the past. The new education aspires to "the highest possible physical, as well as mental, development for everyone" and "free play to every instinct." In contrast to the sickly and downcast wage-slaves of the nineteenth century, the inhabitants of the new society are infinitely freer, happier, healthier, brighter, and friendlier people, enjoying active, playful, adventurous, and creative lives.

Denounced as dangerously revolutionary in daily papers and from pulpits across the land, this "fairy tale of social felicity," as Bellamy himself called it, became a best-seller and inspired a movement. "Although in form a fanciful romance," Bellamy explained in a postscript to the second edition, *Looking Backward* was "intended, in all seriousness, as a forecast, in accordance with the principles of evolution, of the next stage in the industrial and social development of humanity. . . ." In the immediate aftermath of the Haymarket tragedy and America's first Red Scare, Bellamy proposed what he called "Nationalism" as a peaceful alternative to the ruinous and undemocratic system of private capital or wage-slavery. Without economic (or industrial) democracy, he argued, political democracy is a sham. The aim of Nationalism was to organize the people so that, united and therefore invincible, they could make industrial democracy a reality. Founded on his fundamental principle of "production for use, not for profit," Bellamy's Nationalism was a radically egalitarian system of public ownership and operation of industry, a distinctly American variant of the municipalization and nationalization programs advocated by other socialists of the period. As set forth in the form of a dramatic love-story and dream-tale, embellished with colorful touches of science fiction, Nationalism took the public by storm and rapidly became the leading current of social radicalism in the United States.

The Nationalist movement passed through two distinct phases before dissolving into the current of Debsian socialism at the turn of the century. In the comparatively brief initial phase (1889–90), exemplified by the Boston Bellamy Club, which held its first meeting in January 1889, the movement was almost exclusively middle-class in composition (the Boston Club's founders included such well-known genteel reformers as Edward Everett Hale, Thomas Wentworth Higginson, and retired General Arthur Devereaux, "hero of Gettysburg"), dominated by Theosophists (Madame Blavatsky had praised Bellamy's novel and urged her followers to lead the movement), and pursued a purely literary activity consisting of lectures and publication of a ponderously preachy journal, the *Nationalist,* in which Nationalism tended to be presented as a patriotic, nonrevolutionary, explicitly antisocialist solution to the "Social Problem." Bellamy himself was far from happy with the Boston Club and had little to do with it.

The second phase of organized Bellamyism, in which Bellamy played a far more active role, but which has received much less attention from historians, was brought about by the growing participation of working people in the movement. "Debated by all down to the bootblack on the corner," as Henry Demarest Lloyd remarked, *Looking Backward* naturally proved attractive to many working-class readers, and quickly won the endorsement of many American Federation of Labor and Knights of Labor officials, some of whom helped found Nationalist clubs. Doubtless workers' interest was heightened by the fact that, during labor's mounting crusade for the eight-hour day, the novel took for granted a vastly greater reduction in the hours of labor.

As more and more workers identified themselves with the Bellamyist cause, the movement underwent significant change. Dissatisfied with the pompous dullness of the monthly *Nationalist,* which specialized in tedious texts of patronizing edification, Bellamy started his own lively activist-oriented weekly, the *New Nation* (its first issue is dated January 31, 1891), which regularly and prominently featured labor and strike news under such headings as NOTES FROM THE FRONT and GUERRILLA WARFARE BETWEEN CAPITAL AND LABOR. A few weeks later, the *Nationalist* folded; most of the Theosophists and elite reformers had dropped out. "Nationalism can no longer be twitted as a 'kid-glove' movement," Bellamy declared, "the workingmen are swelling its ranks very rapidly."

The mass influx of workers changed not only the Bellamy movement but Bellamy himself, who moved steadily Left all through the nineties. He who, in *Looking Backward,* had written disparagingly of labor parties and "the followers of the red flag," and who, in pre-*New Nation* days, had declined to call himself a socialist, now declared Nationalism to be "the only really practical labor party in the world" and "the most radical form of socialism." The *New Nation* saluted "Labor's May Day" as "the most significant and important anniversary of the year," and welcomed the activity of "nationalist coal-miners in Cherokee County, Kansas." All through the 1890s, as reported in the *New Nation* and other movement papers, unions were taking action along the lines Bellamy proposed, especially demanding collective ownership of railways, the telegraph, and utilities.

The impressive rise and ignominious collapse of the 1890s Populist movement, in which Bellamy and his comrades had formed an important part of the extreme Left, confirmed and deepened his growing revolutionary inclinations. His writings of the mid- and late 1890s affirmed the primacy of the working class as the agent of revolutionary social transformation, and the need for a specifically revolutionary party. Increasingly antireformist in his last years, he remained till the end a merciless critic of both the Democratic and Republican parties, which he saw as two pillars of capitalism, and strongly opposed those would-be radicals whose efforts served only "to help capitalism obtain a longer lease on life by making it a little less abhorrent."

Bellamy's revised and expanded radicalism was set forth in imposing detail in his last and longest book, *Equality*, a sequel to *Looking Backward* published in 1897. The definitive expression of his utopian vision, *Equality* shows that this author, who, in the last decade of his life, was unceasingly reviled in the mainstream press, responded positively only to criticism from the Left—from workers, anarchists, Marxists, and feminists. A number of incongruously authoritarian elements that had disfigured *Looking Backward*—the "industrial army," for example, which was perhaps borrowed from the Marx/Engels *Communist Manifesto* or from Fourier, and the weird system of "alumni" voting—virtually disappear in the sequel.

In *Equality*, moreover, new emphasis is given to the central role of women in radical social change. Feminists had hailed *Looking Backward* as a book of their own, and were instrumental in organizing the Bellamy movement, but the feminism of *Equality* was immeasurably deeper. Affirming women's "absolute sexual autonomy" in everything, the book includes a strong discussion of reproductive rights: "Prior to the establishment of economic equality by the great Revolution, the non-childbearing sex was the sex which determined the question of childbearing." In the new society, however, women are "absolutely free agents in the disposition of themselves."

Finally, *Equality* surpassed all the social radicalism of its time in its bold affirmation of animal rights and wilderness conservation. In portraying the new society "blending with the face of Nature in perfect harmony" in a deurbanized, decentralized America, utilizing a technology at last brought under human control, and no longer at war with the natural environment, Bellamy was among the first to pose fundamental questions that rank high on radical political agendas of our own time. His pages on "The Reforesting," urging that wilderness should not only be preserved but vastly enlarged, introduced a theme not found again in socialist discourse until the 1980s.

Equality is, in fact, one of the most forward-looking works of nineteenth-century radicalism. It is not hard to understand why the anarchist Peter Kropotkin found it "decidedly admirable" and even "much superior" to *Looking Backward*, stressing indeed that he knew "no other Socialist work . . . that equals Bellamy's *Equality*" as a critique and analysis "of all the vices of the capitalistic system."

Equality was written after the movement had spread across the continent and stirred the American imagination as it had not been stirred since the days of the abolitionists. Altogether some 165 Bellamy Clubs were formed, in Washington, D.C., New York, Chicago (where young Clarence Darrow was an active member), and elsewhere throughout the country; in just a few months, seventeen groups were formed in California alone. Scores, maybe hundreds, of newspapers took up the cause. Most of these were short-lived; Bellamy had to give up the *New Nation* in 1894 because of illness. One cannot, however, gauge Bellamy's impact solely on the basis of groups and publications that took his name, for in the later period of the movement, Bellamyists tended more and more to call themselves simply socialists. Unlike most utopians, Bellamy did not regard his own work as an infallible revelation but rather as a contribution to a discussion, definitely subject to change. Notably, in this regard, he recognized many "sequels" to *Looking Backward* by other authors, some of them featuring views sharply differing from his own on important points, and promoted them in the *New Nation* as worthy contributions to the movement; two of these, Ludwig Geissler's *Looking Beyond* (1891) and Archibald McCowan's *Philip Meyer's Scheme: A Story of Trade-Unionism* (1892), are especially significant for their emphasis on the working class as the vital force of the Revolution.

Every current of American radicalism was strongly marked by Bellamy's utopian dream. His influence was unmistakable, in many cases paramount, in the People's Party, Farmers' Alliance, trade unions, women's clubs, several utopian communities, other socialist groups, and in such papers as the *Coming Nation* and its successor, the *Appeal to Reason*. Few social movements have been so heterogeneous. Trade unionists, Unitarians, feminists, populists, Knights of Labor, Christian Socialists, spiritualists, Theosophists, temperance advocates, dress-reformers, vegetarians, antivivisectionists, a handful of communitarians, and many who thought of themselves as Marxists were all able to fight the good fight together under the Bellamy banner. Egalitarian, feminist, nonviolent; an open system, always more counterinstitutional than narrowly political; imaginative and undogmatic, one of the all-too-rare combinations of the visionary and the practical; expressing itself largely through poetry, parables, and fiction—Bellamyism was the characteristic American socialism of the 1890s, and exerted an influence on radical thought, on radical lives, and on the broader culture, that in many respects has never been surpassed.

Well into the new century, up to the eve of the First World War, the great majority of those who brought something new and original to the cause of working-class emancipation in the United States—Daniel DeLeon, Eugene Debs, Frances Willard, Charles H. Kerr, Julius Wayland, Gaylord Wilshire, Charlotte Perkins Gilman, George Washington Woodbey, William C. Owen, Upton Sinclair, Austin Lewis, Scott Nearing, Oscar Ameringer, and Elizabeth Gurley Flynn are only a few—were those whose first steps as radicals had been guided by what Elizabeth Cady Stanton called "Edward Bellamy's beautiful vision of the equal conditions of the human family in the year 2000."

Bellamy's influence, moreover, has not been confined to the United States. Despite the unfortunate "Nationalist" label that he gave to his movement, which has doubtless injured his reputation among later generations of radicals here and abroad, his perspectives and legacy were truly *inter*national. Bellamyism was a major radical current throughout the English-speaking world, especially in Canada, England, and Australia, and played a significant role in the radical and intellectual history of many other countries, including Hungary, Holland, Japan, Indonesia, and Russia, where *Looking Backward* was a favorite of workers in the Petrograd Soviet during the Revolution of 1905. Bellamy's impact on the U.S. immigrant community has not been well studied, but the fact that his works were translated into at least twenty-six languages (as well as Esperanto) and praised by such world-renowned foreign radicals as Tolstoy, Maxim Gorky, and Jean Jaurès, suggest that this impact may have been considerable.

Bellamy died on May 22, 1898, after a long illness. The movement he inspired largely passed into the Socialist Party (Eugene Debs was one of Bellamy's most ardent admirers) and the Industrial Workers of the World. For many years his writings held their high place on radical best-seller lists; Charles H. Kerr's socialist publishing house in Chicago was still reprinting a pamphlet of *The Parable of the Water-Tank* (a chapter from *Equality*) in editions of many tens of thousands well into the 1910s. After the Bolshevik Revolution of 1917 the new style of Marxism made all forms of utopian socialism unfashionable, though the Great Depression witnessed a modest Bellamy revival, in which Heywood Broun of the Newspaper Guild took an active part. In the non-Leninist Left, most notably the IWW, Bellamy continued to be appreciatively studied and cited all through the 1930s and 1940s; longtime labor activist Stan Weir recalls that it was an old Wobbly seaman who sparked his own radicalism by urging him to read *Looking Backward*. Walter Nef, who directed the IWW's single largest organizing drive—agricultural workers, 1915—later devoted himself to a purely Bellamyist agitation, and was still issuing his *Equalitarian Bulletin* in the 1950s.

Bellamy's influence on more recent radicalism is not easily measured, although it is interesting to note that at least one founder of the Students for a Democratic Society (SDS), Al Haber, has acknowledged *Looking Backward* as the book that made him a radical. First published over a century ago, *Looking Backward* has never been out of print since—seven editions are currently available, four of them inexpensive paperbacks—and never has it ceased to make readers question the dominant values and institutions of modern capitalist society. Earlier American socialists reached thousands. Bellamy reached millions. *See also*: Spiritualism, Utopianism

—*Franklin Rosemont*

REFERENCES

Bowman, Sylvia et al. *Edward Bellamy Abroad: An American Prophet's Influence.* New York: Twayne, 1962.

Morgan, Arthur E. *Edward Bellamy.* New York: Columbia University Press, 1944.

Patai, Daphne, ed. *Looking Backward 1988-1888: Essays on Edward Bellamy.* Amherst: University of Massachusetts Press, 1988.

Rosemont, Franklin, ed. *Apparitions of Things to Come: Edward Bellamy's Tales of Mystery and Imagination.* Chicago: Charles H. Kerr, 1989.

Benjamin, Herbert: see

Unemployed Movements, 1930s

Berger, Victor L. (1860–1929)

One of the pivotal leaders of the Socialist Party of America, along with Eugene V. Debs and Morris Hillquit, in its most expansive era, Berger was a founder of the national party and the key figure in shaping the Milwaukee branch, which held power in that city for over three decades. His career—as editor, party leader, and public officeholder—paralleled the rise and fall of the socialist movement.

Born in the Nieder-Rehbach region of the Austro-Hungarian Empire, Berger was the son of conservative innkeepers whose fortunes declined during his childhood. He briefly studied at universities in Vienna and Budapest, and in 1878 he emigrated to the United States with his family, settling in Milwaukee, where the German ambience and radical-oriented labor movement soon enveloped him. He became a language teacher and was active in the local *Turnverein*, and in 1889 joined the Socialist Labor Party. Soon driven from it by the tight centralization and ideological rigidity he perceived, but committed to socialism, he became an editor and publisher of various German- and English-language socialist newspapers. He edited the *Wisconsin Vorwärts* (1893–98), the *Social Democratic Herald* (1900–1913), and the *Milwaukee Leader* (1911–29), as well as the more ephemeral sheets. In the meantime, he dabbled in Populism, then joined the Social Democracy and was a founder of the Social Democratic Party in 1898 and of the Socialist Party of America in 1901.

Berger was a political reformist and a revisionist who supported the theoretical views of Eduard Bernstein of the Second Reich's SDP but departed from them as he deemed necessary. Berger advocated educating the enfranchised proletariat while pursuing electoral politics. As a pragmatist, he believed that Marxist principles must be modified to meet the opportunities presented by changing political and economic conditions, an approach that led orthodox Marxists to call him an opportunist. He viewed the triumph of socialism as inevitable and yet he argued that the transformation of the system should be directly encouraged at the ballot box. He maintained that the eventual socialist system would permit a degree of individual ownership within a democratic structure, and throughout his career opposed communism for he thought that nationalization of all property would be retrogressive.

Berger supported the American Federation of Labor and for twenty years was a delegate to its conventions, where he pursued a policy of "boring from within" while simultaneously opposing the industrial unionism of the IWW. On the issue of race, Berger was a virulent bigot, believing that groups were innately unequal. He argued that "white civilization" in the United States was threatened by the influx of "new immigrants" and he was convinced of the absolute inferiority of American blacks. On female emancipation, he accepted the party position in support of universal suffrage but privately he was concerned that enfranchised women would be a conservative force in politics. In Milwaukee Berger shaped a uniquely integrated movement in which the local Socialist Party and the trade unions cooperated fully on policy, finances, and electoral politics. Berger's success there rested firmly on the German roots of each organization. The Milwaukee Social Democratic Party first elected a member to the city council in 1904, and later won many offices, including the mayor's office, 1910–1912 and 1916–40. Berger always sought to protect his Milwaukee base by stressing the principle of local autonomy within the national party. While he himself served briefly on the city council, he was essentially active behind the scenes, thereby inviting charges of bossism.

In the national party Berger was a fixture on the National Executive Committee and the National Committee, was usually a convention delegate, and served on ad hoc committees. He was known as an intense but honest infighter, a good negotiator, skilled debater, and an intellectual. Not personally charismatic, he was nonetheless influential and was never hesitant to assume individualistic positions, however unpopular. As examples, he supported the idea of national self-defense, arguing that workers identified with their nations, and he favored citizen-armies and public service conscription. He also flaunted party policy against class collaboration with reformers and peace groups.

Berger was elected to the U.S. House of Representatives in 1910, the first of only two Socialists, and was elected five additional times. In Congress he introduced measures addressed to the condition of workers, sponsoring bills promoting public-work jobs, old-age pensions, and shorter workdays, and he successfully pushed through hearings on issues related to the McNamara–*Los Angeles Times* bombing case and the Lawrence strike of 1912. His efforts were criticized as counterproductive by the socialist Left but he did serve to introduce a class perspective into congressional debates.

During World War I Berger opposed preparedness, endorsed his party's major antiwar statement, and was a founding member of the socialist People's Council that sought to coordinate the peace movement. He conducted a strong campaign for the U.S. Senate as a peace candidate in 1918, and was elected to the House that same year. But the war cost his newspapers their second-class mailing privileges and he, with other party officials, was convicted of conspiracy under the Espionage Act, a verdict later overthrown by the Supreme Court. Because of his conviction, however, the House of Representatives twice excluded him from his seat, and he was unable to represent his constituents during the war era.

After the SP schism and Red Scare, Berger remained with the rump party. He warned his comrades against the folly of imitating Soviet models, condemning the concept of the dictatorship of the proletariat, and he opposed membership in the new Communist International. In the 1920s he served three terms in Congress and was a founder of the Conference for Progressive Political Action, a farmer-labor coalition. He died on August 7, 1929, the victim of a traffic accident. *See also*: Municipal Socialism, Socialist Party

—*Sally M. Miller*

REFERENCES

Miller, Sally M. "Casting a Wide Net: The Milwaukee Movement to 1920." In *Socialism in the Heartland: The Midwestern Experience, 1900–1925,* edited by Donald T. Critchlow. South Bend: University of Notre Dame Press, 1986.

Miller, Sally M. *Victor L. Berger and the Promise of Constructive Socialism, 1910–1920.* Westport: Greenwood, 1973.

BERKMAN, ALEXANDER: see

ANARCHISM; GOLDMAN, EMMA

BERRY, ABNER WINSTON (BABA SUFU) (1902–87)

An Afro-American revolutionary born in Texas, Berry grew up in New Orleans, St. Louis, and Chicago, where he followed his father into work at the Armour packing plant. After the sixth grade, Berry educated himself primarily with the Haldeman-Julius "Little Blue Books" available on the streets of Chicago.

In 1929, while a reporter for a black weekly in Houston, Berry joined the Communist Party, impressed by what he read in exchange copies of the *Daily Worker*. In 1931 Berry moved to Kansas City. There he adeptly united blacks and whites into a militant Unemployed Council. He was elected to the CP Central Committee in 1934.

In late 1934 Berry moved to New York City, where he became CP section organizer for Upper Harlem until 1940. An effective "behind the scenes" facilitator and coalition builder, he forged the alliance between Harlem's Italian community and black nationalist Garveyites to protest Mussolini's invasion of Ethiopia.

Berry was drafted into the U.S. Army in 1942 while a reporter for the *Daily Worker*.

After he returned from the war in Europe, he resumed work at the *Daily Worker*, reporting on the black freedom movement and the South, including the 1955 Montgomery bus boycott. Called the "layman's theoretician" by his colleagues, Berry authored a regular column in the *Daily Worker* and was editor of the weekly *Harlem Worker*.

Berry resigned from the CP in 1957. From 1960 to 1968 he worked as the United Nations correspondent for *Antara*, the Indonesian news service. From 1969 to 1973, he ran Afro World Associates news service at the UN, supplying many articles to *Muhammed Speaks* concerning the Third World.

Influenced by Malcolm X and the black liberation movement of the 1960s, Berry taught Marxism to young activists in the black Left. He joined the African Peoples Party and took the name Baba Sufu. He was an organizer and speaker at the 1974 African Liberation Day in Washington, D.C.

Though wheelchair-bound due to a 1977 stroke, Berry moved to Rocky Mount, North Carolina, in 1981 to work in the "black belt" South. There he helped found the Black Workers for Justice. He was a plaintiff in the 1983 voting rights suit in Rocky Mount that overturned the at-large method of city council elections. Berry guided the BWFJ in establishing the Workers School in 1985, the monthly newspaper *Justice Speaks*, and the cultural ensemble Fruit of Labor. The BWFJ opened the Abner Berry Freedom Library and Workers Center in Rocky Mount in 1986. *See also*: Communist Party, *Daily Worker*

—*James Wrenn*

REFERENCES

Naison, Mark. *Communists in Harlem During the Depression*. Urbana: University of Illinois Press, 1983.

Charney, George. *A Long Journey*. Chicago: Quadrangle, 1968.

Bimba, Anthony (1894–1982)

Leading Lithuanian-American radical activist, journalist, and Communist labor historian, Bimba was among the handful of immigrant Left leaders known widely outside their communities.

Born in Rokìškis, the son of a skilled wood-carver of sacred images, Bimba arrived in the United States in 1913, working in a New Jersey steel mill and a Maine paper mill before becoming a truck driver for a cooperative bakery. In 1915 he enrolled at Valparaiso University (Indiana), then a popular spot for Lithuanian immigrants bent on self-improvement. He studied history and sociology, and joined the socialist movement. He began writing for Lithuanian Left publications, was arrested for a speech to Gary steelworkers in 1918 and expelled from Valparaiso the following year. He moved to New York to become editor of *Darbas*, the Lithuanian-language organ of Amalgamated Clothing Workers Local 54.

Soon a committed Communist, Bimba became national secretary of the Lithuanian federation and edited *Kova*, its organ. He led the federation's merger with the communist movement and in 1922 became editor of the Lithuanian Communist daily *Laisve*, a post he retained until his death in 1982. Only Paul Novick, editor of the Yiddish *Morgen Freiheit*, had a longer tenure in the U.S. Left press. Bimba also edited the quarterly cultural journal *Sviesa* from 1936 onward. He wrote more than twenty books in Lithuanian, his earliest, published in 1923, a description of working women's condition.

As a public Communist spokesman, Bimba was notable first for his 1926 arrest—the earliest in the United States—under 1919 laws forbidding seditious utterance. The case was dropped. In 1927 Bimba's *History of the American Working Class Movement* marked the American Communists' entry into the writing of working-class history. Rigidly doctrinaire, Bimba's history was nevertheless more single-mindedly class oriented than later Communist versions, and remained the standard, through a second edition, for almost a decade. His *Molly Maguires* (1931), a slight text, commemorated the miners' uprising. In short, Bimba the Lithuanian-American journalist had also been the first substantial American Communist historian. *See also*: Communist Party, Lithuanian Americans

—*Rudolf Baranik*

REFERENCES
"Bimba Library Acquired." *Spectrum* (publication of the Immigration History Research Center) 5 (Winter 1988).

Bimba Library Collection. Immigration History Research Center, University of Minnesota, St. Paul.

Mizara, Eva. Interview by Paul Buhle. Oral History of the American Left, Tamiment Library, New York University.

Raguotis, Bronius, *Antanas Bimba: Gyvenimo, Veiklos, Kurybos Bruozai*. Vilnis, Lithuania: Mintis, 1974.

Birmingham, Alabama

Center of the 1930s–1940s southern Left, and often referred to as the "Pittsburgh of the South," the Birmingham-Bessemer industrial complex has had a history of working-class militancy dating back to the late nineteenth century. The Knights of Labor and the United Mine Workers of America initiated a tradition of interracial unionism, but southern racial mores and vicious antilabor repression made it difficult to sustain. Despite the sentiment against interracial unionism, or anything else perceived to represent working-class radicalism, there was an active Socialist Party in Alabama. In 1908 the Socialists claimed 400 members organized in twenty locals, and two years later William Raoul began editing the Alabama Socialist weekly the *People's Voice*. Unlike Louisiana and parts of Texas where southern Socialists organized blacks, albeit in separate locals, in Alabama the SP was exclusively white.

Outside of disparate meetings of Socialists during the 1920s, there was no left-wing movement in the Birmingham area before Communist organizers arrived very late in 1929. The Central Committee of the CPUSA chose to concentrate much of its southern organizing efforts in Birmingham because of the city's level of industrial development as well as its proximity to the rural "black belt" counties. It was in these cotton-producing counties that the Party, in its official documents and formal pronouncements after the Sixth World Congress of the Comintern in 1928, demanded the right of self-determination for the black majority. As early as 1930, Birmingham was designated the headquarters for District 17, encompassing Alabama, Georgia, Louisiana, Florida, Tennessee, and Mississippi.

Other than the handful of white Communists from the North and a few native white southerners, the overwhelming majority of pioneering Communists in Birmingham were black Alabamians. Most of its rank-and-file membership typified black working-class life and culture in the South. The majority were semiliterate churchgoing Christians who combined the Party's politics and ideology with black folk culture.

Between 1930 and 1933, the Party concentrated most of its efforts on organizing the unemployed. Attracting predominantly black groups of unemployed workers, as well as a significant cadre of whites in the industrial suburb of Tarrant City, Communists led numerous demonstrations during this period, the largest drawing an estimated crowd of 5,000 on November 7, 1932. However, most of these events led to arrests and severe beatings inflicted on local Party activists. By 1933, with the passage of New Deal legislation sanctioning the right of workers to organize, Birmingham Communists shifted their focus from the unemployed to the industrial working class.

Although Communists formed "rank-and-file committees" within various industrial unions, particularly in the United Mine Workers of America in Birmingham's coal mines, they were most influential in the international Union of Mine, Mill, and Smelter Workers, in part because black workers in Jefferson County constituted the vast majority in both the industry and the union. Several Communists, both black and white, held low- and middle-level positions in the union as open Communists. And with the assistance of the Unemployed Councils, the Party was active in a series of strikes that had erupted in the ore mines in 1934. During the Popular Front and afterward, especially with the election of left-wing labor leader Reid Robinson to the position of international president, Communists constituted the main body of local leadership in the Birmingham area.

Despite an intensification of jailings, beatings, and intimidation during the strike wave of 1934, the Communist Party and the International Labor Defense in Birmingham increased its membership to approximately 1,000 and 3,000, respectively, by May 1934. The changing character of the ILD partly explains its growing popularity in the early 1930s. After brief experiments with chapters of the American Negro Labor Congress and the League of Struggle for Negro Rights, the ILD became Birmingham's "Negro rights" organization. While it was active in local cases prior to the spring of 1931, the celebrated Scottsboro case marked a turning point in the nature of ILD activity, transforming Birmingham's tiny legal-defense auxiliary into a very localized, mass organization. The Birmingham ILD defended members of the Share Croppers Union involved in violent confrontations with authorities and investigated numerous other local police brutality cases, lynchings, alleged rape cases, and extralegal mob violence directed at the black community.

While the Popular Front was a reflection of international antifascist sentiment, for local Birmingham Party leaders it was an opportunity to demobilize massive anticommunist repression in the South by gaining the support of southern liberals and labor leaders. Communists and left-leaning activists not only faced police repression, they also confronted violent reprisals from the Ku Klux Klan and the White Legion. In 1935 a tentative alliance was formed in opposition to a statewide antisedition bill as well as a number of local seditious-literature ordinances. Toward the end of 1934 and in the early part of 1935, Birmingham Communists drew up a "united front agreement" with a handful of southern Socialists, most of whom were affiliated with the Highlander Folk School and were openly supportive of the left-wing Revolutionary Policy Committee within the Socialist Party. Although most state Socialist leaders denounced the agreement, a good portion of rank-and-file Socialists joined the Communist Party soon afterward.

The local "Third Period" leadership, steeped in the militant left-wing and radical Afro-American traditions, was replaced by a more sober, liberal-intellectual leadership during the Popular Front. Robert Fowler Hall (who initially arrived under the name "Bill Moseley"), a graduate of Columbia University and a native southerner, replaced Nat Ross as district organizer. In order to attract liberal and mainstream political attention, Alabama's new leadership hoped to turn the Communist Party into an open, legal organization. Entire families of Party activists were encouraged to participate in open Communist meetings that included singing and political lectures.

In September 1937 the Party held its first *open* All-Southern Communist Party Conference. The participation of Earl Browder and James Ford signaled the growing importance of the South to the Communists during the Popular Front. Despite attempts to court white liberals, which included dropping its staunchly militant stance against racism, the Communist Party as an organization failed to establish a serious working relationship with the southern liberal intelligentsia. Instead, individual Communists often kept their affiliation to themselves and worked with liberal southerners behind the scenes.

Undoubtedly, the most influential Alabama Communist among liberal and New Deal circles was Joseph Gelders, a former physics professor from the University of Alabama. As the southern secretary of the National Committee for People's Rights (an organization that superseded the southern chapter of the National Committee for the Defense of Political Prisoners and the International Labor Defense in Birmingham), Gelders fought on behalf of police-brutality victims and individuals incarcerated for violating seditious-literature ordinances. Because of his activities in support of jailed Communist Barton Logan (alias Jack Barton), Gelders was kidnapped and severely beaten by vigilantes in 1936. The beating outraged the southern liberal community and, in part, contributed to renewed attempts for a united front between liberals and left-wingers. Gelders went on to help found the Southern Conference for Human Welfare in 1938.

In addition to becoming a support organization for southern liberal activities, Birmingham Communists continued to organize WPA workers through the Workers Alliance and played pioneering roles in the development of the Congress of Industrial Organizations, particularly in the steel and red ore mining industries. However, since Communist leadership in Birmingham no longer emphasized Party autonomy, several local Party activists—especially black Communists—chose to devote nearly all of their time to the labor movement or other allied organizations. After 1937, the Party lost a large proportion of its black Birmingham membership.

When the Nazi-Soviet Pact was signed in 1939, its impact was felt only among the tiny circle of liberals the Party was trying to influence. Compounded by an intensification of anticommunist activity spurred on by the Dies Committee, the Communists in Birmingham were becoming more isolated than ever. The Party proper diminished rapidly, its Birmingham membership declining from approximately 400 or 500 paid-up members in 1938 to approximately 60 or 70 active members by 1940. The absorption of black Communists into the CIO at the expense of Party activity, growing anticommunist sentiment, and the district leadership's initial willingness to subordinate its militancy, particularly on racial issues, were the central reasons for the Party's rapid decline during the late 1930s. Nevertheless, movements that were led by Communists, or in which Communists played an important part, were becoming much more prominent in the overall fight for civil liberties and in the struggle to organize the industrial working class in the South. In addition to the CIO, the Communist-led Southern Negro Youth Congress, the League of Young Southerners, the Jefferson County Committee Against Police Brutality, and the Right to Vote Club were attempts at mass-based political organizing in the Birmingham community.

In June 1941, just when the Party was in the midst of rebuilding itself by taking up the issues of suffrage and the extension of citizenship to blacks, the Soviet Union was drawn into the international conflict. Birmingham Communists, therefore, turned most of their energies toward supporting the "people's war against Hitlerism." Although the suffrage campaign dwindled during the war, the Alabama cadre continued concentrating on the needs of the black working class and made civil rights a central issue. Nonetheless, the Communist Party was only a shadow of its former self. In line with Browder's position, in 1944 Rob Hall liquidated the Party and formed the Alabama People's Educational Association. The APEA did not attract any considerable number of people, and most active Communists during the war kept a low profile and became untiring organizers for the SCHW. Black Communists who did not enlist remained active in the CIO and the Southern Negro Youth Congress. Indeed, it was the talents of women such as Esther Cooper Jackson, Dorothy Burnham, and Augusta Strong that sustained and strengthened the SNYC during the war.

The period from 1945 to 1950 marked the last vestiges of Communist activity in Birmingham. In the South, where vehement anticommunism and segregationist thought were inseparable, open Communists faced fierce, violent opposition from authorities, vigilantes, and even conservative white labor leaders. Communists were expelled from nearly all CIO unions, and the predominantly black, left-led International Mine, Mill, and Smelter Workers actually faced direct violence from white organizers in the United Steel Workers of America in Birmingham. Under the leadership of Sam Hall, the Party in Birmingham tried to breathe life into Henry Wallace's faltering 1948 presidential campaign, and it faced violent reprisals when it attempted to organize several peace demonstrations in the city streets.

Although several individual Communists and left-leaning activists chose to leave Birmingham, many of those who remained continued their activity as silent civil rights activists during the late 1950s and early 1960s. But as the McCarthy era began to take on a clearer form and definition throughout the nation, Birmingham became one of the most untenable places for Communists. When the Alabama Communist Control Act became law in 1951, it was only the beginning of a flurry of antiradical legislation, marking the end of an era. *See also*: Communist Party; Hudson, Hosea; International Labor Defense; Southern Conference for Human Welfare; Southern Negro Youth Congress; Western Federation of Miners/Mine, Mill and Smelter Workers

—*Robin D. G. Kelley*

REFERENCES

Carter, Dan T. *Scottsboro: A Tragedy of the American South*. 2d ed. Baton Rouge: University of Louisiana Press, 1984.

Kelley, Robin D. G. *Hammer and Hoe: Alabama Communists During the Depression*. Chapel Hill: University of North Carolina Press, 1990.

———. "'Comrades, Praise Gawd for Lenin and Them!': Ideology and Culture Among Black Communists in Alabama, 1930–1935." *Science and Society* 52 (Spring 1988).

Painter, Nell Irvin. *The Narrative of Hosea Hudson, His Life as a Negro Communist in the South*. Cambridge: Harvard University Press, 1979.

Williams, John [Hosea Hudson?]. "Struggles of the Thirties in the South." In *The Negro in Depression and War: Prelude to Revolution, 1930–1945*, edited by Bernard Sternsher. Chicago: Quadrangle, 1969.

BIRTH CONTROL

Birth control is an ancient practice, but political movements for birth control are modern, originating in the early nineteenth century. There were at least six separate movements with different political content, and only some of them were left-wing. Indeed, the organized Left has been deeply ambivalent about birth control, at best confused about its political significance, and at worst opposed to its association with autonomous women's organization and feminist goals.

The phrase "birth control" has been attributed to Margaret Sanger, but it has since become a generic term for reproduction control. In some ways this usage is unfortunate, since the phrase encourages grouping together distinct political phenomena. The first "birth control" campaigns were extremely varied, including the secular and the religious, the reformist and the visionary. British Neo-Malthusians in the early nineteenth century, among whom Francis Place was the leading figure, sought to increase the standard of living among the poor, and to strengthen the working class socially and politically, by reducing births. This "bottom-up" Neo-Malthusianism was soon joined by middle- and upper-class reformers with different motives: hoping to pacify and control the working class by reducing its numbers, and to increase its standard of living without redistribution. By the late nineteenth century, British imperialists were already advocating population control as a means of pacifying subject peoples.

At the same time "utopian" socialists, both secular and religious, began advocating birth control for various reasons: to control their populations, to prevent the spread of hereditary disease, to liberate women from reproductive drudgery, and sometimes to permit greater sexual freedom. In the United States in the 1820s, Neo-Malthusian ideas were integrated into the experimental, non-class-conscious socialism associated with Robert Dale Owen (whose father, Robert Owen, had been directly influenced by Place) and Frances Wright, a socialist feminist.

These secular socialists were soon joined by religious radicals who also promoted birth control, but in different forms. The Second Great Awakening had given rise to a "perfectionist" mode of thought, heretical in relation to orthodox forms of Protestantism because it emphasized possibilities of perfecting earthly life. Also committed to improving women's condition and public health generally, these religious socialists sought other means of birth control than contraception, which they considered artificial. The birth control methods they favored involved changing the nature of sexual activity itself. For example, the Oneida Community in the 1840s, ruled by John Humphrey Noyes, practiced male continence, a regimen in which men refrained from ejaculation altogether. Noyes and his supporters believed that the practice not only built self-discipline but actually heightened sexual pleasure. In the second half of the century, "free lovers" further developed these noncontraceptive forms of birth control, recommending withdrawal or sexual activity other than intercourse. Feminist socialist physician Alice Stockham designed a sexual system called "Karezza" that required both men and women to avoid orgasm and resulted, she believed, in the intensification and prolongation of pleasure.

Even more conservative feminists shared with these early socialists the view that the discipline and self-control required by such noncontraceptive birth control was liberating in itself. By the 1870s, a flourishing feminist movement transformed this tradition of thought into a new and more political demand, with the slogan "voluntary motherhood." These feminists, like their socialist predecessors, opposed contraception because they feared it would merely license more predatory male sexual aggression. Also, like most radicals until the twentieth century, they opposed abortion, which, they believed, would further disadvantage women by removing a lever for enforcing male responsibility in sex. Instead they proposed abstinence for birth control. Their proposals and rhetoric have been maligned as prudish, and there is truth in this characterization, since they were expressing many women's negative experiences of sex as oppressive, pleasureless; yet viewed in their historic context, they can also be characterized as spokeswomen for women's sexual liberation. They understood that women could not find and defend their own sexual desires until they gained the power to reject men's. At the sex-radical fringes of the feminist movement, some openly advocated greater sexual experience and pleasure for women. Elmina Slenker, "free love" and voluntary-motherhood advocate, wanted "the sexes to love more than they do; we want them to love openly, frankly, earnestly; to enjoy the caress, the embrace, the glance, the voice. . . . We oppose no form or act of love between any man & woman." Their arguments for abstinence as a form of birth control thus had two meanings: one was voluntary motherhood, opposition to coercive childbearing; another was voluntary sex, opposition to men's traditional prerogatives of demanding sexual submission from wives. Moreover, some voluntary-motherhood advocates developed a deep critique of male sexuality, prefiguring much that late-twentieth century feminists argued regarding the obsessiveness and dominance embedded in much of what men experience as sexual desire. Unlike their Neo-Malthusian predecessors, voluntary-motherhood advocates were not concerned with population size nor with working-class power; they were resolutely pro-motherhood and, far from challenging the Victorian romanticization of motherhood, they manipulated it to increase women's power.

Throughout the nineteenth century the growing class-conscious socialist movement was in the main hostile to Neo-Mathusianist, perfectionist, and feminist birth control programs. Most unionists and party socialists saw birth control as a conspiracy to weaken the working class, and autonomous women's movements as attempts to undermine class consciousness. Indeed, many of them supported the "race suicide" panic of the first decade of the twentieth century. Sparked by no less a figure than Theodore Roosevelt, moralists propagandized against the "selfishness" of women who refused their maternal duties with birth control, deploying racist fears (in a period of heavy immigration) that WASP dominance would be undermined by the high birthrates of those of "inferior stock."

Nevertheless it was from within the Socialist Party and socialist unions that a mass movement for birth control arose between 1914 and 1916. As the nineteenth-century woman's rights organizations had devolved into a relatively conservative suffrage movement by the 1890s, many more Left feminists had been attracted to socialist women's groups and causes. Here they grew restive and rebellious under the male leaderships' attempts to subdue and channel their political energies. While urban radicals grew more daring sexually, they also discovered the widespread promotion of contraceptives sponsored in Europe by unions and SD parties. Emma Goldman of the IWW and Margaret Sanger of the SP visited clinics in Holland where women were fitted with diaphragms. When they decided upon civil disobedience as a means of dramatizing the issue in the United States, distributing prohibited leaflets about contraception and opening illegal birth control clinics, the Left leadership remained uninterested—but rank-and-file women responded with passion. Within a few years there were birth control leagues in every major city and most large towns of the United States. When these activists offered contraceptive information and services, they were deluged with clients; when arrested, their political defenses publicized contraception and created an even more avid demand for it.

The leaders of the hundreds of birth control leagues in 1916–17 were radicals—feminists and usually socialists. The mass response, the thousands who eagerly sought out contraceptives, were women wanting a very personal sort of help. Thus the pressure for the movement to become a social service was great. Most groups began to plan ways of opening clinics or otherwise providing actual birth control information. Responding thus to a concrete, immediate, and fillable need, the radical birth controllers did not effectively resist incorporation of their demands into professional, physician-dominated lobbying organizations during the 1920s and 1930s. Their destiny might have been different if—if the Socialists had supported the demand for legal contraception, if the Communist Party (which did on the whole discuss birth control in a favorable light) had made it a high-priority part of its program, if there had not been such a vicious and effective attack on radicalism, including feminism, after World War I.

Instead, birth control during the next two decades was adopted by liberal groups and assimilated to mainstream, even anti-Left causes. The leadership of the main national birth control organization, led by Sanger, deserted the earlier demand for women's right to reproductive choice and endorsed a compromise: physician's discretion, making birth control appear—as it still does to many today—a medical issue. Moreover, birth control leaders kept the eugenic arguments that had dominated social thought for several decades (arguments used to support many progressive reforms, since they did not originally rest on exclusively hereditarian principles) and used them in racist ways, building on fears of high birthrates among immigrants and blacks to support the case of legalization of contraception. The adoption of statutes providing for forcible sterilization of the feebleminded, degenerates, and some other groups by many states, with special alacrity in the southern states, was also part of this redefinition of the function of birth control. These choices further estranged leftists from the birth control cause, especially black radicals, who viewed birth control propaganda as potentially genocidal.

The WW II period gave birth to two new birth control movements: Planned Parenthood and population control. These were distinct but related, two faces of a similar analysis. The former was a renewed campaign for the legalization and promotion of contraception, arguing not from a feminist analysis but as a campaign for family stability. Unlike the conservative profamily backlash of the early twentieth century, these "family planning" advocates recognized that marital "adjustment" must rest on a permissive attitude toward sex without fear of conception. Planned Parenthood, unlike the voluntary motherhood movement, endorsed lots of sex as a sign of health and did not raise issues of women's sexual exploitation. In its domestic campaigns, Planned Parenthood promoted small families and planning. In its international aspects, it argued a renewed Neo-Malthusianism: it blamed Third World poverty on overpopulation, and advocated population control as a cure for poverty. Like nineteenth-century Neo-Malthusianism, it simply passed over individual bases of pro–birth control attitudes, such as women's desire for control, which might have challenged fundamental gender power-structures, just as it attempted to increase standards of living without challenging class power-structures. By 1960 population control had become such an unchallenged ideology in the United States that many used this phrase interchangeably with the earlier "birth control."

By 1960 birth control appeared, at best, just another commodity. Then a renewed women's liberation movement once again changed the terms of understanding of the reproduction-control project. The women's movement viewed birth control as part of an overall campaign for women's self-determination. The feminist birth control program was not at its outset theoretically or historically knowledgeable about the many meanings of reproduction control. Nevertheless, it immediately began to undo the ideological knot that united and subordinated these many meanings under the rubric of population control. The feminist campaign coalesced around the issue of abortion. Previously only a few marginal radicals endorsed legal abortion (for example, Antoinette Konikow), and the Left participated in the general hypocritical denial of what was in fact a widespread practice. Moreover, the campaign for legal abortion in the 1960s did not begin with feminists but, rather, with civil-libertarian physicians. But women's liberation soon achieved hegemony in defining the meanings of legal abortion (just as the greatest victory of the Right to Life movement since then has been in redefining their position as defining the rights of fetuses). Although abortion remained the focal, defining issue, the women's movement began to describe a position of general support for reproductive self-determination, criticizing forced sterilization, unsafe contraception, unnecessary hysterectomies, and cesarean sections. By the mid-1970s, most Left organizations in the United States supported these demands. Thus despite the powerful antifeminist backlash against reproductive freedom, by the 1980s the Left as a whole had developed a reasonably clear understanding of the political importance of these issues to a democratic movement. *See also*: Free Love; Goldman, Emma; Sanger, Margaret; Women's Liberation

—*Linda Gordon*

REFERENCES

Gordon, Linda. *Woman's Body, Woman's Right: A Social History of Birth Control in America*. Rev. ed. New York: Viking/Penguin, 1976.

———. "Malthusianism, Socialism and Feminism in the United States." In *History of European Ideas*, vol. 4, no. 2. Oxford: Oxford University Press, 1983.

———. "Why Nineteenth-Century Feminists Didn't Support 'Birth Control' and Twentieth-Century Feminists Do." In *Rethinking the Family*, edited by Thorne, Barrie. White Plains, N.Y.: Longman, 1981.

Petchesky, Rosalind Pollack. *Abortion and Woman's Choice: The State, Sexuality, and Reproductive Freedom*. White Plains, N.Y.: Longman, 1984; Boston: Northeastern University Press, 1986.

Sears, Hal. *The Sex Radicals. Free Love in High Victorian America*. Lawrence: Regents Press of Kansas, 1977.

Black International

Formed in London in 1881 to promote a revived and radicalized version of previous leftist internationalism, the International Working People's Association found its largest potential following and its gravest political disappointments in the United States. In the end, the American anarchist experience had produced most of all a martyrology that anarchists around the world could share. Along the way, immigrant and American-born anarchists around the Black International had translated and published an extensive literature of Bakunin, Kropotkin, and other leading anarchist intellectuals.

The largest segment of U.S. adherents existed in Chicago, and gathered there to endorse the new international movement formally. Its inspiration had coincided with the disillusion of Chicago "social revolutionaries" with political socialism in general and with the Socialist Labor Party in particular. Inheriting and transforming various local socialistic institutions—craft union locals, social *Vereins*, and free-thought schools among others—the Chicago anarchists gathered elements of a mass movement that anarchism scarcely possessed anywhere in Western industrial societies.

Fidelity to Black International principles remained very much in the eye of the beholder. To more extreme anarchists, especially among the readers and the editors of the English-language *Alarm*, the actual anarchism of the dominant "social revolutionary" movement remained ambiguous, not wholly differentiated from the socialistic assumptions of a few years earlier. (And, indeed, discussion of the Black International in most of the Chicago revolutionary-socialist movement was not extensive.) To the tabloid press and moderate labor leaders, who associated "anarchists" with bomb throwing, these differences seemed irrelevant or mere disguise.

A second segment of adherents took their cues from popular lecturer-thespian Johann Most and his *Freiheit* newspaper. Unwilling to work within unions, given to considerable rhetoric about violence, Most's fellow anarchists established themselves as propaganda groups, mostly across the East Coast but also in other scattered cities. Wide varieties of anarchists, including near-individualist Americans, English former comrades of William Morris, Proudhonists, and others, mixed into these groups. To such propaganda clubs, the translation and publication of anarchist writings had the overwhelming value of making the great ideas accessible to their communities—with Bakunin's *God and the State* the most popular of all.

The third segment, not actually an affiliate, claimed to be a surviving section of the First ("Red") International. These western IWA "divisions" owed their development to two extraordinary individuals, Joseph R. Buchanan and Burnette Haskell, and their vigorous activities in the middle 1880s. Buchanan, a former printer who turned to the rhetoric of violence after himself being exposed to armed attack by western strikebreakers, published the important regional labor paper from Denver, the *Labor Enquirer*, and led its supporting group, the Rocky Mountain Social League. Haskell, son of a prominent lawyer (and lawyer himself), provided initiative and skills for the formation of a West Coast sailors' union, and published the *Truth*, a most philosophical agitational paper, from his political base in San Francisco.

Buchanan and Haskell proclaimed revolutionary-messianic doctrines inspired by Bakunin. Both papers urged the dissemination of anarchist ideas (offering extensive lists of English-language publications imported from England) and the formation of secret societies set upon direct—including violent—action when the final crisis of capitalism approached. In 1881 Haskell had unsuccessfully proposed the federation of U.S. anarchists and revolutionaries into one autonomous body with its own information bureau. Failing this, the two leaders jumped at the chance to affiliate with the Black International. Their own followings formed the first two official American divisions (Pacific Coast and Rocky Mountain). For a few years, their groups contained a few hundred, perhaps a few thousand members, with a mixture of natural-rights propaganda, labor-education advocacy, and direct-action doctrine that resembled later IWW expressions. So influential did they become that Buchanan in particular posed a threat to the moderate Powderley leadership of the Knights of Labor.

Efforts to coordinate these various tendencies into a single U.S. anarchist movement prompted the Pittsburgh conference of social revolutionaries in 1883. Unable to resolve key differences between the three disparate tendencies, the Conference issued an important manifesto stating that only through force could workers obtain their just deserts, and the meeting closed sine die.

In the aftermath of the Haymarket events and accompanying mass repression, anarchist tendencies retreated to propaganda and occasional "propaganda of the deed." Buchanan and Haskell had already gone over to popular anti-Chinese sentiment, Haskell indeed playing a central propaganda role on the West Coast. Thereafter, Haskell and his following relocated into a utopian colony and disappeared politically. (His paper briefly appeared as a tiny proto-feminist sheet, *Truth in Small Doses*.) Buchanan, bringing his *Labor Enquirer* to Chicago, broke with the Chicago anarchists and drifted toward the Democratic Party.

Seen in retrospect, the formation of the Black International had actually tended to isolate anarchists from the radicalized workers in the new socialist movements. By 1889 and the formation of the Second International, the IWPA had given up the ghost. But during its brief history in the United States, the Black International had served as a symbolic meeting point of potential allies at anarchism's highest level of mobilization. *See also*: Haymarket Affair; Most, Johann; Parsons, Albert; Socialist Labor Party

—*Paul Buhle*

REFERENCES

Avrich, Paul. *Anarchist Portraits*. Princeton: Princeton University Press, 1988.

Quint, Howard. *The Forging of American Socialism*. New ed. Indianapolis: Bobbs-Merrill, 1963.

Saxton, Alexander. *Indispensable Enemy*. Berkeley: University of California Press, 1971.

"Shall the Black and White Unite? An American Revolutionary Document of 1883." In *American Radicalism, 1865–1901*, edited by Chester M. Destler. New ed. Chicago: Quadrangle Books, 1966.

BLACK NATION

Perhaps no concept in the history of American radicalism has been more maligned or misunderstood than the concept of the "black nation." The quest of the Afro-American people for some form of territorial integrity and national self-determination has had a long and winding history. Long before the American Communist Party seized the concept as an organizational tool to mobilize the Afro-American masses, they had given the concept its own historical validity. From Paul Cuffe's emigrationist efforts in the late eighteenth century, through the nationalist and emigrationist sentiments that threatened to splinter the abolitionist movement, to the postbellum era with its "exodus" movement, Chief Sam's "Back to Africa" endeavor, or E. Sutton Griggs's "Imperium in Imperio," the Afro-American people have given the concept of the "black nation" their own definition, utility, and both an organized and unorganized expression of its political intent.

It was not until the end of World War I, however, that the white Left comprehended the potential appeal of the concept to the Afro-American masses. This era was marked by a series of internal and external circumstances that would give the "black nation" concept an opportunity to be fulfilled. First, the crisis of plantation agriculture in the southern states stimulated widespread migration to the industrial cities of the Northeast and Midwest, while those who remained behind slumped further in their semifeudal status. Second, the Bolshevik Revolution and the ensuing crisis of the European nation-state unleashed the powerful force of self-determination for the oppressed nationalities of eastern Europe, the decaying Ottoman Empire, and the Far East. It was the Afro-West Indian radical Cyril Briggs who, in a 1917 editorial in the *Amsterdam News*, proclaimed, "SECURITY OF LIFE" FOR POLES AND SERBS—WHY NOT FOR COLORED AMERICANS. It was Briggs's radical organ, the *Crusader*, that initially articulated a separate state for Afro-Americans, from its founding in 1918 until 1920, when he denounced the idea as "unsatisfactory." It was revived by his fellow traveler Hubert Harrison in 1924 as the foundation of the International Colored Unity League, whose main objective was the establishment of a separate state in the continental United States for Afro-Americans.

Meanwhile, the newly founded Communist Party of the USA had taken up the question at the Comintern's Second Congress, where Lenin presented his "Thesis on the National and Colonial Question." Point 14 was devoted to a synopsis of the position of "The Negro in America." By 1928 a subcommittee on the "Negro question" was formed to prepare a resolution for the Comintern's Sixth World Congress. Harry Haywood, a member of the subcommittee, submitted an article in which he argued for the "national minority status" of the Afro-American people. He advocated a "national revolutionary" movement for self-determination and an autonomous republic to be established in the "black belt" of the American South. By 1930 self-determination in the black belt became the official position of the CP in its attempt to organize the Afro-American masses. The concept of national self-determination in the black belt was pronounced dead by Earl Browder in 1943. Haywood continued to support the position until his ouster from the Party in 1959. He would argue that self-determination and territorial autonomy were the only mechanisms that would guarantee the security of the Afro-American people.

By no means did the concept die when the Party abandoned it. Elijah Muhammad's Nation of Islam had a separate state as the foundation of its redemptive program. Malcolm X supported a version of territorial autonomy, while a generation of revolutionary nationalists continued to support the goal of a separate state in the South throughout the 1960s and early 1970s—from Max Stanford's RAM (Revolutionary Action Movement) to the Republic of New Africa, the All-African People's Party, and the Black Liberation Army. The idea of a "black nation" has not disappeared but has taken on an even newer expression. *See also*: Communist Party; Crusader; Garveyism; Harrison, Hubert; Haywood, Harry; Moore, "Queen Mother" Audley

—*William Eric Perkins*

REFERENCES

Bracey, John, August Meier, and Elliott Rudwick, eds. *Black Nationalism in America*. Indianapolis: Bobbs-Merrill, 1970.

Foner, Philip, and James Allen, eds. *American Communism and Black Americans: A Documentary History, 1919–1929*. Philadelphia: Temple University Press, 1987.

Haywood, Harry. *Negro Liberation*. New York: International, 1948.

Vincent, Theodore, ed. *Voices of A Black Nation*. San Francisco: Ramparts Press, 1973.

Black Panther Party

Founded in October 1966 by Huey Newton (1942–1989) and Bobby Seale (b. 1936), the Black Panther Party for Self-Defense became the most widely known black militant political organization of the late 1960s. The Black Panthers attracted widespread support among young urban blacks, who wore the group's distinctive black leather jackets and black berets and often openly displayed weapons. Also attracting the attention of local police and the FBI, the group declined as a result of deadly shootouts and destructive counterintelligence activities that exacerbated disputes between Panthers and other black militant groups.

Newton was already a black militant activist in 1961 when he met Seale, a fellow student at Oakland's Merritt College. Both joined the Afro-American Association, a black cultural organization led by Donald Warden, but they became dissatisfied with Warden's procapitalist form of black nationalism. Their sentiments were more in accord with those of Malcolm X, especially after his 1964 break with Elijah Muhammad's Nation of Islam, and of Robert F. Williams, the then Cuban-based guerrilla warfare advocate. After affiliations with the Merritt's Soul Student Advisory Council and with the Williams-inspired Revolutionary Action Movement, Newton and Seale created the BPP in order to expand their political activity, which mainly involved "patrolling the pigs"—that is, monitoring police activities in black communities to ensure that civil rights were respected.

The BPP dropped "for Self-Defense" from its name in 1967, but the group remained a paramilitary organization held together by Newton's eclectic ideas, which were drawn from Marxist-Leninist and black nationalist writings and from the examples of revolutionary movements in Asia and Africa. Although Newton and Seale once gained funds and notoriety by selling books containing the quotations of Mao Tse-tung, the revolutionary tract that most influenced Panther leaders during the mid-1960s was Frantz Fanon's *Wretched of the Earth* (1965). The party's appeal among young blacks was based not on its unrefined ideology but on its willingness to challenge police power by asserting the right of armed self-defense for blacks. The explicit political goals of the Panthers were summarized in the last item of their ten-point Platform and Program: "We want land, bread, housing, education, clothing, justice, and peace. And as our major political objective, a United Nations–supervised plebiscite to be held throughout the black colony in which only black colonial subjects will be allowed to participate, for the purpose of determining the will of black people as to their national destiny."

Button, late 1960s

On October 28, 1967, the development of the BPP was profoundly affected by Huey Newton's arrest on murder charges after an altercation with Oakland police that resulted in the death of one policeman and the wounding of another. With the party's principal leader in jail, the role of spokesmen increasingly fell to Seale and Eldridge Cleaver

(b. 1935), a former prison activist and Malcolm X follower who became the Panthers' minister of information. Cleaver, a writer for the New Left journal *Ramparts* and a powerful public speaker, increasingly shaped public perceptions of the Panthers with his calls for black retribution and scathing verbal attacks against black counterrevolutionaries.

During February 1968, former SNCC leader Stokely Carmichael (b. 1941), who had been asked by Cleaver and Seale to appear at "Free Huey" rallies, challenged Cleaver's role as the dominant spokesman for the party. Carmichael's Pan-African perspective, emphasizing racial unity, contrasted sharply with the desire of other Panther leaders to emphasize class struggle and to attract white leftist support in the campaign to free Newton. Although Carmichael downplayed his policy criticisms of the party until he resigned as the Panther's prime minister in the summer of 1969, the ideological and personal tensions between Carmichael and other Panthers signaled the beginning of a period of often vicious infighting within the black militant community. A SNCC-Panther alliance announced at the February rallies broke apart by the following summer. After the Panthers branded Ron Karenga, the head of a Los Angeles-based group called US, a "pork-chop nationalist," escalating disputes between these two organizations culminated in January 1969 with a gun battle on the UCLA campus that left two Panthers dead.

Police raids and the covert efforts of the FBI's counterintelligence program contributed to the tendency of Panther leaders to suspect the motives of black militants who did not fully agree with the party's strategy or tactics. In August 1967 the FBI targeted the Panthers when it launched its COINTELPRO operations designed to prevent "a coalition of militant black nationalist groups" and the emergence of a "black messiah" "who might unify and electrify these violence-prone elements." FBI-inspired misinformation, infiltration by informers, and numerous police assaults contributed to the Panther's siege mentality. On April 6, 1968, police attacked a house containing several Panthers, killing the seventeen-year-old treasurer of the party and wounding Cleaver, who was returned to prison as a parole violator. In September 1968 Newton was convicted of voluntary manslaughter and sentenced to from two to fifteen years in prison. The following December, two Chicago leaders of the party, Fred Hampton and Mark Clark, were killed in a police raid. By the end of the decade, according to the party's attorney, twenty-eight Panthers had been killed. At that time, Newton was still in jail (his conviction was reversed on appeal in 1970); Cleaver had left for exile in Algeria rather than return to prison; and many other Panthers elsewhere were facing long prison terms as a result of intense repression. In 1970 Connecticut authorities began an unsuccessful effort to convict Seale of the murder of a Panther in that state.

During the early 1970s, the BPP, weakened by external attacks, legal problems, and internal schisms, rapidly declined as a political force. After Newton was released from prison in 1970, he sought to revive the party by rejecting Cleaver's inflammatory rhetoric emphasizing immediate armed struggle. In place of police confrontations, Newton stressed community service, such as free-breakfast programs for children and, during the mid-1970s, participation in electoral politics. These efforts to regain popular support were negated, however, by published charges that Newton and other Panthers engaged in extortion and assaults directed against other blacks. By the mid-1970s, most Panther veterans, including Seale and Cleaver, had deserted or were expelled from the group, and Newton, faced with various criminal charges, fled to Cuba. Upon his return to the U.S., Newton remained a controversial figure. Although he completed a doctorate and remained politically active, he was also involved in the drug trade. He was shot to death in Oakland in the summer of 1989 in a drug-related incident. *See also*: Armed Struggle, Civil Rights, New Left, Student Nonviolent Coordinating Committee

—Clayborne Carson,
David Malcolm Carson

REFERENCES

Anthony, Earl. *Picking Up the Gun*. New York: Dial, 1970.

Coleman, Kate, with Paul Avery. "The Party's Over." *New Times*, July 10, 1978.

Foner, Philip S. *The Black Panthers Speak*. Philadelphia: Lippincott, 1970.

Newton, Huey P. *Revolutionary Suicide*. New York: Harcourt Brace Jovanovich, 1973.

Scheer, Robert, ed. *Eldridge Cleaver: Post-Prison Writings and Speeches*. New York: Random House, 1969.

Seale, Bobby. *Seize the Time: The Story of the Black Panther Party and Huey P. Newton*. New York: Random House, 1970.

BLACK WORKERS CONGRESS: see LEAGUE OF REVOLUTIONARY BLACK WORKERS

BLATCH, HARRIOT STANTON (1856–1939)

Daughter of the nineteenth-century feminist Elizabeth Cady Stanton, Blatch was herself a major leader of the twentieth-century suffrage movement. She was one of the pioneers in bringing working-class women into the movement and in adapting the modern, militant style of the British suffragettes to the American scene. Born in 1856 to Elizabeth Cady and Henry Brewster Stanton, she graduated from Vassar in 1878 and shared with other early college women a deep faith in science, including social science. She went to Europe to continue her studies and in 1882 married a wealthy Englishman, William Henry Blatch. For twenty years she lived outside of London and was active in the British suffrage movement and the Fabian Society. She also had two children, one of whom, Nora Stanton Barney, went on to become a feminist activist like her mother and grandmother. The other, Helen, died at age three.

When her mother died in 1902, Harriot moved back to the United States. She was swept up in New York City reform activism, especially anticorruption politics and the Women's Trade Union League, but within the suffrage movement she found existing organizations too tradition-bound. In 1907 she organized the Equality League of Self Supporting Women, dedicated to recruiting wage-earning women and building links between them and professional women. The Equality League introduced to America the innovations of British suffrage militants. It also played a major role in reinvigorating the movement in New York but in the process was itself transformed. By 1910 Blatch was relying increasingly on upper-class women, who had enough money to organize a winning campaign; she also believed that the work of recruitment and "propaganda" must now give way to more explicitly political efforts.

In 1910 Blatch changed the name of her organization to the Women's Political Union and began to concentrate on getting a woman suffrage referendum before the state's voters, a lobbying effort that took three years. In 1913 the Women's Political Union began to canvass the entire state for a 1915 referendum on woman suffrage. The measure lost by a significant margin, and Blatch's democratic faith was temporarily weakened. While Blatch shifted her own efforts to votes for women at the national level, other New York suffragists resumed the state battle, and in 1917 a second referendum passed.

Meanwhile, Blatch and her followers joined forces with Alice Paul, Lucy Burns, and the Congressional Union, who were determined to force President Wilson to support a woman suffrage amendment to the federal Constitution. While Paul preferred civil disobedience, Blatch advocated the strategic deployment of women already enfranchised to put pressure on the national Democratic Party. Embracing Blatch's ideas, the Congressional Union renamed itself the National Woman's Party. Blatch and Paul also differed over U.S. entry into the First World War, which Blatch supported, believing that unified civic purpose and a powerful state would rebound to women's benefit. By the end of the war, she was profoundly disillusioned, and this, along with attacks on radicals and the impending enfranchisement of women, led her to join the Socialist Party, as a way of declaring both her belief in the political process and in the need for a fundamental redefinition of its purposes. In 1924 she played an important role in the independent, prolabor presidential candidacy of Robert LaFollette.

Meanwhile, Blatch was also involved in the post-enfranchisement women's movement's redefinition of its agenda. Although an early critic of sex-based protective labor legislation (she wanted such laws to be extended to all workers), she did not support the Equal Rights Amendment advocated by Paul, because she did not think "equality" could be understood abstractly or legislated categorically. Her own agenda stressed economic independence for women, with special emphasis on the dilemmas of the working wife and mother, but these issues got little attention until the Great Depression. By then, Blatch was close to eighty, and her waning energy went to her own autobiography, *Challenging Years*, and to documentation of her mother's historical contributions. She died in 1939 of complications resulting from a fall. *See also*: Socialist Feminism

—*Ellen Carol DuBois*

REFERENCES

Blatch, Harriot Stanton, and Alma Lutz. *Challenging Years: The Memoirs of Harriot Stanton Blatch*. New York: Putnam, 1940.

DuBois, Ellen Carol. "Working Women, Class Relations and Suffrage Militance: Harriot Stanton Blatch and the New York Woman Suffrage Movement, 1894–1907." *Journal of American History* 74 (June 1987).

Blitzstein, Marc (1905–64)

The first theater composer to set to music the authentic American language as spoken by all social classes from immigrant laborers to society matrons, Blitzstein devoted the bulk of his career to topics of social commentary and political satire. Born in Philadelphia into a banking family with socialist leanings, he was a child prodigy at the piano. He attended the University of Pennsylvania and the Curtis Institute of Music, studied with Nadia Boulanger in Paris and Arnold Schoenberg in Berlin. Early works include settings of poetry by Cummings and Whitman, instrumental pieces and short operas. One opera, *The Condemned* (1932), obliquely refers to the Sacco and Vanzetti case.

With *The Cradle Will Rock* (1936), a musical about a CIO-type union struggle in Steeltown, USA, that draws strong portraits of the

sold-out middle class, Blitzstein joined the Left wholeheartedly. (His wife, Eva Goldbeck [1901–36], was one of the first Americans to understand Bertolt Brecht's esthetic approach; she wrote about Brecht and translated him into English.) In *I've Got the Tune* (1937), a radio song-play, he showed the odyssey of a composer finding his true home in the protest movement. He wrote scores for the labor films *Valley Town* and *Native Land*, and incidental music for numerous plays. In *No for an Answer* (1941) he again approached working-class organizing issues, but in a more folk-operatic style. He was a Communist Party member from 1936 or 1938 until 1949.

During World War II, Blitzstein served in London in the U.S. Army Air Force; he wrote incidental music for troop shows, researched French Resistance music, composed an orchestral piece, *Freedom Morning*, and a cantata for male chorus and orchestra, the *Airborne Symphony*. After the war he helped organize the American-Soviet Music Society. *Red Channels* gave him a four-page listing; he gave private testimony, without naming others, to HUAC in 1958.

His major later works include *Regina* (1949), an opera based on Lillian Hellman's *The Little Foxes*; *Reuben Reuben* (1955), a Faustian musical about the life urge overcoming the death wish; *Juno* (1959), a musical version of Sean O'Casey's *Juno and the Paycock*; *Idiots First* (1963), a one-act opera based on Bernard Malamud's story; and the uncompleted *Sacco and Vanzetti* (1960–64), commissioned for the Metropolitan Opera.

In 1952 Blitzstein premiered his English adaptation of Bertolt Brecht and Kurt Weill's *Threepenny Opera*, which went on to a nearly seven-year run off-Broadway. Blitzstein left a solid repertory of humanistic work for the American stage, opening up new possibilities in subject and style, that no one has equaled since. *See also*: Seeger, Charles

—*Eric A. Gordon*

REFERENCES

Dietz, Robert J. "The Operatic Style of Marc Blitzstein in the American 'Agit-Prop' Era." Ph.D. diss., University of Iowa, 1970.

Gordon, Eric A. *Mark the Music: The Life and Work of Marc Blitzstein*. New York: St. Martin's Press, 1989.

Talley, Paul M. "Social Criticism in the Original Theatre Librettos of Marc Blitzstein." Ph.D. diss., University of Wisconsin, 1965.

BLOOR, ELLA REEVE (1862–1951)

Labor organizer, journalist, and advocate of women's rights, "Mother" Bloor achieved heroic status within the Communist Party of the USA and served as its model of Communist womanhood. Born on Staten Island, New York, to middle-class parents, she worked her way through the suffrage and temperance movements into the Social Democratic Party of America in 1897 and the Socialist Labor Party in 1898. Throughout her life she maintained her first political concern, the condition of women and their children. As late as 1934 she organized the U.S. delegation to the International Women's Conference Against War and Fascism, held in Paris. In her seventies she conducted a major lecture tour for International Women's Day.

In 1902 Bloor joined the Socialist Party and became a devoted follower of Debs. She ran for state office on the SP ticket, served as a union organizer in the machine, mining, and garment trades, and campaigned militantly for woman suffrage. After the publication of Upton Sinclair's *The Jungle* in 1906, Bloor assisted the author in verifying his descriptions of conditions in Chicago's stockyards for a government investigating commission. Openly opposed to World War I, she helped to form the Workers Defense Union.

In 1919 Bloor became a founding member of the CPUSA and served on its Central Committee from 1932 to 1948. In 1921 she made her first trip to the USSR as an American delegate to the First Congress of the Third International of Labor Unions. Throughout the 1920s she worked for industrial unions in textiles and mining. At age sixty-three she hitchhiked across the country to distribute the *Daily Worker*. By the 1930s this venerable radical became known as "Mother" Bloor. She continued to maintain an active schedule, taking part in hunger marches, demonstrating on behalf of unemployed workers, and helping to build the Farmers National Committee for Action. At age seventy-two she was arrested for assault and inciting a riot and imprisoned for a month.

In 1937 Bloor returned to the USSR, this time to be an honored celebrant of the twentieth anniversary of the Bolshevik Revolution. Upon her return she wrote *Women in the Soviet Union* (1938), a short pamphlet extolling its model programs of child-care and protection of motherhood.

Married three times, the mother of eight children, Bloor managed a busy schedule throughout her life. Elizabeth Gurley Flynn met her in 1910 and recalled that Bloor, then in her late forties, "moved as if she were flying rather than walking." In addition to her lecture and organizing tours, Bloor wrote for Left newspapers as well as such mainstream publications as *Pearson's Magazine*. During WW II she conducted her final lecture tour to build support for the war against fascism. As a testament to her lifelong work, she left an autobiography, *We Are Many* (1940), and wrote: "It has been a privilege and joy to carry the torch of socialism. . . ." *See also*: Agrarian Radicalism, Communist Party

—*Mari Jo Buhle*

REFERENCES

Ella Reeve Bloor Papers, Hollins College, Roanoke, Va.

Barton, Anna. *Mother Bloor: The Spirit of '76*. New York: Workers Library, 1937.

Flynn, Elizabeth Gurley. *Daughters of America: Ella Reeve Bloor and Anita Whitney*. New York: Workers Library, 1942.

Bohemian Americans (*Czechs*)

Despite their relatively small numbers in the United States (310,000), Bohemian Americans were quite prominent in the Left of several American cities—particularly in Cleveland and Chicago—in the late nineteenth and early twentieth centuries. The Czech-American Left first made its influence felt in the wave of strikes that accompanied the Great Railroad Strike of 1877. In Chicago, Czechs dominated both the leadership and the rank and file of a major strike in the lumberyards. In Cleveland, Czechs were similarly noticeable in the coopers' strike at Standard Oil. In both cities, strike activity carried over into politics and the Workingmen's ticket fared well in predominantly Czech neighborhoods.

Less conspicuous, but no less important, was the role of Czech skilled workers who labored in smaller manufacturing establishments. It was these individuals who furnished a large and influential part of the core membership of Czech socialist clubs and fraternal societies. Also important in the 1870s were a small number of worker-intellectuals such as Lev Palda and Frank Škarda who attempted to organize and politicize Czech immigrant workers. The Czech Left also found allies in the liberal editors of the influential Czech anticlerical newspapers. These included Charles Jonáš of *Slavie* (Racine, Wisconsin), Václav Šnajdr of *Dennice Novověku* (Cleveland), Frantisek Zdřubek of *Svornost* (Chicago), and John V. Čapek of *New York Listy*.

After suffering a decline in the early 1880s, the Czech Left reemerged in the mid-1880s with renewed vigor as a result of the rise of the Knights of Labor as well as the immigration of several Czech socialist anarchists to the United States. The Czech anarchists are most famous for their role in the Haymarket affair in Chicago in 1886. Some of the most notable Czech immigrant anarchists included Robert Zoula, Joseph Pečka, Jakub Mikolanda, and Leo Kochman. In large part due to the Haymarket fiasco and the setbacks faced by the Knights of Labor, however, the more revolutionary wing of the Czech-American Left found itself replaced in influence by more moderate socialists in the late 1880s and 1890s.

Events in the Czech homeland also help explain the ascendance of the moderate socialists within the Czech-American Left. The legalization of the Social Democratic Party in Austria in 1889 allowed for the construction of socialism as a mass movement in the Czech homeland. The revolutionary tactics of the 1880s now appeared anachronistic as party members reveled in the newfound vitality of the Czech socialist movement.

The moderation of the socialist movement in the homeland in the 1890s was mirrored in the United States. Large numbers of socialist Czechs made their way to the United States from 1890 to 1914. By the early part of the twentieth century, Czech socialist immigrants had created a durable subculture within urban Czech communities. They sponsored a number of organizations and institutions including several newspapers such as *Spravedlnost* (published daily in Chicago beginning in 1905), *Americké Dělnické Listy* (Cleveland), and *Obrana* (New York). They also established a wide array of gymnastic, theater, music, and social clubs. By the 1910s, Czech socialists numbered perhaps 10,000 of the approximately 150,000 Czechs living in American urban centers.

Despite suffering a decline in the late 1880s and 1890s, the more revolutionary Czech socialist faction reemerged with renewed vigor in the first two decades of the twentieth century. Its renewed strength was fueled largely by the push toward industrial unionism that was occurring in the years from 1900 to 1920 in both the United States and Europe.

Revolutionary and moderate socialists appear to have been relatively equal in influence within the Czech-American Left on the eve of World War I. Differences in political hue were apparent, however, between Czech socialists from one American city to the next. New York Czech socialists had the most radical reputation in the years before WW I, Czech socialists in Cleveland were the most moderate, and Chicago Czech socialists were made up of significant numbers of revolutionaries and moderates. After WW I, New York, Chicago, and Detroit Czech socialists joined the Communist Party, while those in Cleveland remained with the Socialist Party.

The Czech-American Left maintained its influence within urban Czech communities in the United States until well into the 1950s. By that time, the deaths of most first-generation Czech socialists combined with the left-wing purges of the McCarthy period spelled the end for the Czech-American Left. *See also*: Anarchism, Socialist Labor Party

—*Gregory M. Stone*

REFERENCES

Capek, Thomas. *Čzechs in America*. Boston and New York: Houghton Mifflin, 1920.

Chada, Joseph. *The Czechs in the United States*. Chicago: Czechoslovak Society of Arts and Sciences, 1981.

Schnierov, Richard. "Free Thought and Socialism in the Czech Community in Chicago, 1875–1887." In *"Struggle a Hard Battle": Essays on Working Class Immigrants*, edited by Dirk Hoerder. DeKalb: Northern Illinois University Press, 1986.

BOOKCHIN, MURRAY (b. 1921)

The foremost contemporary anarchist theorist, Bookchin was born in New York of Russian Jewish immigrant parents. During the 1930s he was a militant in the Young Pioneers and the Young Communist League. He later entered the Trotskyist movement, worked in an iron foundry and auto plant, and organized for several unions, including United Auto Workers locals. By the 1950s he was writing extensively for the libertarian Marxist journal *Contemporary Issues*.

In the 1960s Bookchin emerged as a central figure in contemporary anarchism. He was a force in various anarchist organizations, including the Radical Decentralist Project, the third largest faction of Students for a Democratic Society. As both a theorist and an indefatigable speaker, he exerted a major influence on the revival of anarchism as both a cultural tendency and a political movement.

By the 1970s Bookchin's theoretical work became his prime focus. While his pioneering work in ecology began in the early 1950s, it came to maturity with his founding of the Institute for Social Ecology in 1974 and in a series of major works on ecological social theory, including *Post-Scarcity Anarchist* (1971), *Toward an Ecological Society* (1980), and his magnum opus, *The Ecology of Freedom* (1982). In other writings he established his place in radical urbanism and the critique of technology.

Bookchin's work continued to evolve in the 1980s. He developed a theory of libertarian municipalism, a full-scale critique of nature philosophy, and the defense of radical ecology ("fundamentalism") within the Green movement. He is director emeritus of the Institute for Social Ecology in Vermont. *See also*: Anarchism, Radical Environmentalism

—*John P. Clark*

REFERENCES

Clark, John P. *The Anarchist Moment*. Montreal: Black Rose Books, 1984.

BOROCHOV, BER: see SOCIALIST ZIONISM

BOUDIN, LOUIS B. (NÉE L. BUDINOFF) (1874–1952)

For a time the foremost Marxist economic theoretician in the United States, Boudin played an ambiguous role in the Left-Socialist and Communist movements, reemerging later as a rare scholar of U.S. legal history. All the while a prominent lawyer, he may also be considered the earliest important constitutional theorist within the U.S. Left.

Born into a middle-class family in Russia, Boudin immigrated to the United States in 1891. He quickly began legal studies, entering New York University, gaining a master's degree from that institution and admittance to the New York bar in 1898. In this period, he was already a major theoretician in Yiddish, writing under his own name in such publications as *Di Zukunft* and *Di Naye Geist* on aesthetics and historical materialism. He played a minor role in the Socialist Labor Party.

Boudin found himself a Left dissenter within the Socialist Party, and a contentious theoretician in the Yiddish and English-language press. From his perspective, the naive SP lacked theoretical rigor, and made too many compromises with perceived American reality. His essays on economics in the *International Socialist Review* (where he was recognized as one of the very few sophisticated theoreticians that the SP could boast of) grew into his classic, *The Theoretical System of Karl Marx*. Essentially an "answer" to Ernst Böhm-Bawerk's contemporary challenge to Marxism's predictions, *The Theoretical System* placed itself ambivalently upon the key question of the "falling rate of profit." He offered the suggestion, often repeated later (by Paul Sweezy and Harry Magdoff among others) that capital used its surplus in war making, and rebuilt its profitability during the period following.

Notwithstanding the international repute of *The Theoretical System* (especially its German edition), Boudin gained little popular recognition among American socialists. He wrote widely for the New York daily *Call*, the *New Review*, and *Di Zukunft*, however. In 1917 he joined with Louis Fraina and Ludwig Lore to launch the *Class Struggle*, a proto-Bolshevik monthly. Yet fixed upon a vision of Marxian precision, he disputed the SP antiwar stance with his own (he also defended radicals arrested on wartime charges); and he viewed the Russian Revolution as an impossible attempt to create socialism under primitive capitalist productive conditions. He therefore stalked out of the 1919 Communist Labor Party convention, separating himself from any section of the fractured Left.

In later years, Boudin shied away from formal political involvement, although he taught at the Communist-led Workers School in the later 1920s and occasionally wrote for the *New Masses* in the middle and late 1930s. By 1940 he had repudiated Communism, while adamantly defending individual Communists' constitutional rights. For the most part, Boudin shifted to legal activities and to his own scholarship. As a lawyer, he won several important cases for the rights of specific sectors of workers to organize. As an author, he supplied two large volumes of *Government by Judiciary* (1932), the only thoroughgoing Marxist historical account of American jurisprudence ever attempted.

Government by Judiciary was in fact a rather Beardian effort to reveal usurpation of democratic prerogatives by a vested, aggressive elite. In his view, the Federalist attempt to graft English Common Law upon the American system ended in a collision with "the people," i.e., Jefferson and his mass support, with an accompanying loss of prestige to the Supreme Court. Chief Justice Marshall succeeded where his predecessors had failed, however, in turning people's rights to property rights. Despite a fresh challenge to the courts by popular Jacksonianism, a rising sense of Court prerogative, capped by Chief Justice Taney's Dred Scott decision, prepared the Court's later role in overturning democratic decision-making. Never widely read in Left circles, *Government by Judiciary* remained in use among law students for decades. Boudin himself, largely active in refugee efforts after World War II, was by his death a figure forgotten in the Left but for his family, one of the most prominent in Left law to date. *See also*: Communist Party, Socialist Party

—*Paul Buhle*

REFERENCES

Boudin Papers, Columbia University.

Buhle, Paul. *Marxism in the US*. London: Verso, 1987.

Braden, Anne (b. 1924) and Braden, Carl (1914–75)

These two prominent journalists joined forces in Louisville, Kentucky, where they met as education and labor editors, respectively, for the *Louisville Times*. Anne Gamrell McCarty, the college-educated daughter of a relatively privileged family, was raised in Mississippi and in Alabama. As the result of her upbringing and the Episcopal church, her education at Stratford and Randolph-Macon (Virginia) colleges, contact with a young black woman in New York, and her experiences as a reporter in Anniston and Birmingham, Alabama, she came to abhor the ugly effects of the South's segregation system on whites and its humiliating impact on blacks. She returned to Louisville, her birthplace, in 1947 at age twenty-three. There she met thirty-three-year-old Carl Braden, who had already been married and divorced, had organized unions, and had worked his way up through a variety of newspapers in Harlan County, Knoxville, and Cincinnati. Carl came from Portland, a poor white section of Louisville. His father, a railroad shop worker and factory hand, imbued him with the socialist teachings of Eugene Debs, while his Catholic mother taught him the social gospel. Carl attended Catholic schools and proseminary, but abandoned plans to join the priesthood and instead went to work in 1931 as a newspaper reporter. He and Anne married in 1948, and the couple became public relations directors for Left-led CIO unions and worked in the Progressive Party campaign. During the rest of their adult lives, the Bradens remained at the center of battles to transform the South, and were repeatedly attacked as subversives for their work supporting black freedom.

Mississippi authorities jailed Anne in 1951 for leading a delegation of southern white women to the governor's office to protest the scheduled execution of Willie McGee, a black man charged with raping a white woman. Following the Supreme Court's *Brown* desegregation decision in 1954, Kentucky state prosecutors arrested the Bradens and charged them with plotting to incite insurrection when they bought a home in a white neighborhood and sold it to a black family. Local newspapers blacklisted them from employment, prosecutors confiscated their books as "evidence," and racists bombed the home they had purchased for Andrew Wade. Held on $40,000 bail, Carl served eight months of a fifteen-year prison sentence for state sedition before a higher court overturned his conviction. Anne popularized the case in a book about segregation titled *The Wall Between* (1958).

Unable to secure employment as journalists, the Bradens became field organizers and writers for the integrationist Southern Conference Educational Fund (SCEF), which James Eastland's Senate Internal Security Subcommittee (SISS) and the House Un-American Activities Committee had called a Communist front. In 1958 HUAC called the Bradens to Atlanta to testify about the integration movement in the South. In the hearings, Carl stated, "My beliefs and my associations are none of the business of this committee," and refused to testify based on his right to freedom of speech and association contained in the First Amendment. He and anti-HUAC organizer Frank Wilkinson nearly succeeded in winning their First Amendment test case against HUAC but lost it in a celebrated 5–4 decision before the Supreme Court in 1961. As in the Louisville case, authorities put off questioning or prosecuting Anne. She meanwhile wrote and circulated 200,000 copies of a pamphlet *HUAC: Bulwark of Segregation*, and traveled across the country in a clemency campaign. Rev. Martin Luther King, Jr., and other black leaders held a dinner honoring Braden and Wilkinson before they entered prison to begin serving eight months of a year's prison sentence for contempt of Congress.

From that time forward, the Bradens continually upheld the position that protection of the First Amendment guarantee for freedom of belief and association, like the struggle for black rights, was integral to all other struggles. They helped launch the National Committee to Abolish HUAC, and throughout the 1960s organized support for most of the major civil rights campaigns. State and federal authorities continually attacked the Bradens and attempted to isolate them from the civil rights movement (Alabama even enjoined Carl from working in the state) and from southern whites. However, the Bradens used every attack against them and against the movement as a platform to raise issues. More than others on the Left, they perfected the use of media and the written word to fight back against repression. In 1967, during a period of increased radicalization in the southern movement, the Bradens became executive directors of SCEF. In the same year, Kentucky authorities again arrested them on sedition, this time for setting up a community organizing project among poor whites in Appalachia. The courts ultimately overturned the law as unconstitutional.

In 1972 the Bradens retired as SCEF directors, Carl setting up a training institute for activists and Anne returning to full-time editing of SCEF's paper, the *Southern Patriot*. By this time factional and ideological splits of the New Left had torn SCEF apart. Carl resigned to protest what he considered Red-baiting within the organization, and Anne left shortly thereafter when the SCEF board voted down a proposal to renew the organization's formal commitment to interracialism. Carl directed the Training Institute for Propaganda and Organizing, initiated the fight to free North Carolina's Wilmington Ten, and became one of the leaders of the National Alliance Against Racist and Political Repression. He died suddenly of a heart attack in 1975 at age sixty, embittered with much of the New Left but never backing down from his participation in the movement. Anne, along with others who had been in SCEF, formed a new group, the Southern Organizing Committee for Economic and Social Justice (SOC). She continued to build interracial coalitions, to work against racist violence, and to support Rev. Jesse Jackson and other black leaders.

For many on the Left, the Bradens became the symbol of radical challenge to the segregation system from within the white South. Although the FBI and other authorities warned black civil rights leaders not to work with them, the Bradens developed close working relations with black activists throughout the region, and supported the Student Nonviolent Coordinating Committee and the Black Power movement when many liberals turned away. They were widely respected for their unwavering commitment to the struggle against racism, and despite the inquisitions and arrests directed against them, the Bradens never rejected Marxist politics. As principal victims of anticommunism in the South, the Bradens never affirmed or denied whether they ever held membership in any Left party. At the same time, they steadfastly worked with and supported Communists and others on the Left, and stated their own socialist beliefs when they thought them relevant to the struggle at hand.

However, their main focus remained on the struggle for racial justice as the key to changing the South and the nation. As Anne Braden explained her antiracist commitment in the *Louisville Defender* in 1978, "Our future and that of our children rides with the fate of the Black struggle for progress, and [we must] join in that struggle as if our very lives depend on it. For, in truth, they do." *See also*: Civil Rights, House Un-American Activities Committee, Southern Conference Educational Fund

—*Michael Honey*

REFERENCES

Anne and Carl Braden Papers, Wisconsin Historical Society.

Braden, Anne. *The Wall Between*. New York: Monthly Review Press, 1958.

BRAVERMAN, HARRY: see

RADICAL ECONOMICS

BREITMAN, GEORGE (1916–86)

A socialist writer, editor, and organizer, Breitman may be best known for his work in helping to disseminate and popularize the works and ideas of the revolutionary black nationalist Malcolm X, making them available to perhaps millions of people through his edition of *Malcolm X Speaks* as well as his influential study *The Last Year of Malcolm X: The Evolution of a Revolutionary*. In addition, he was chief editor of the fourteen-volume *Writings of Leon Trotsky (1929–40)*.

Breitman joined the Workers Party of the United States in 1935 and was also a leading activist in the New Jersey section of the Workers Alliance. A founding member of the Socialist Workers Party, he was an organizer of the Newark and Detroit branches of the SWP, also serving on the National Committee and Political Committee of that organization. He functioned at various times as editor of the weekly *Militant*. In the late 1960s Breitman became centrally involved in the SWP's Merit Publishers (soon renamed Pathfinder Press), helping to expand greatly its titles—not only works by such people as Trotsky, James P. Cannon, Che Guevara, and Ernest Mandel, but also a variety of pamphlets on black liberation, feminism, the youth radicalization, and socialism (plus a few innovative cultural works on Afro-American poetry and jazz, Lenny Bruce, and surrealism).

In 1984 Breitman was expelled from the SWP (along with many others) as a result of opposition to policies of the party's new leadership. He became a leader of the Fourth Internationalist Tendency, a small group that sought to reunify revolutionary socialists in the United States around the program of the Fourth International. *See also*: Socialist Workers Party

—*Paul Le Blanc*

REFERENCES

Allen, Naomi, and Sarah Lovell, eds. *A Tribute to George Breitman, Writer, Organizer, Revolutionary*. New York: Fourth Internationalist Tendency, 1987.

Le Blanc, Paul, ed. *The Revolutionary Traditions of American Trotskyism*. New York: Fourth Internationalist Tendency, 1988.

BRIDGES, HARRY (b. 1901)

Because he and the International Longshoremen's and Warehousemen's Union (ILWU) have usually stood on the left of the American labor movement, Harry Bridges spent nearly twenty years under threat of deportation and the ILWU was expelled from the CIO. After 1960, however, Bridges received broad-based acclaim as a labor leader.

Born in Australia, Bridges rejected the white-collar career planned by his middle-class parents. He went to sea in 1917, shipping from American ports after 1920. Exposure to Australian socialism and his seafaring experiences produced a brief affiliation with the Industrial Workers of the World in the early 1920s. In 1922 he began to work as a longshoreman in San Francisco.

In 1933 San Francisco longshoremen formed a local of the International Longshoremen's Association (ILA). Bridges worked closely with Communist Party members to develop a militant longshore union with strong rank-and-file control. During the maritime and general strikes of 1934, he rose rapidly to leadership in the San Francisco local and the West Coast ILA. In 1937 Bridges led the West Coast ILA into the CIO as the ILWU; he became ILWU president and CIO regional director. Activism exacted a toll; Bridges developed severe ulcers and his marriage disintegrated.

From 1934 onward, business leaders, the press, and elected officials labeled Bridges a Red and urged deportation. He denied Party membership, but openly supported many Party positions. In 1939 a hearing produced no grounds for deportation, leading Congress to adopt new criteria. A second hearing went against Bridges. The Supreme Court reversed that decision and Bridges became a citizen in 1945.

During World War II, Bridges opposed strikes but refused to compromise on conditions. After the war, he came under renewed attack for his political views. In 1949 Bridges was charged with lying on his naturalization papers regarding Communist affiliations. The Supreme Court ruled in his favor in 1955; federal attorneys filed new charges but they were quickly dismissed.

In the 1950s Bridges concluded that mechanization of longshore work was inevitable; he led negotiations that produced the Mechanization and Modernization Agreement (M&M) in 1960. The ILWU accepted increased use of machinery on the docks; employers agreed to generous pensions, no layoffs, and guaranteed pay. *Fortune* called Bridges "the union leader who did best" for his members in 1960. A few ILWU members, especially Communists, criticized the M&M for reducing the size and hence the political clout of the ILWU, producing a brief rift between Bridges and the Party.

His continued admiration for the Soviet Union notwithstanding, Bridges came increasingly to be hailed as a "labor statesman" and was appointed to a city Charter Revision Commission in 1968 and to the San Francisco Port Commission in 1970. He retired as ILWU president in 1977. In 1988 Bridges gave his blessing to ILWU affiliation with the AFL-CIO.

As ILWU president, Bridges never accepted a salary higher than the best-paid longshoremen and eschewed perquisites routine among some union leaders. In retirement, Bridges stands somewhere between living legend and mythological hero, but accolades bring his standard response: all honors properly belong to the rank and file. *See also*: California Left, Hawaii, International Longshoremen's and Warehousemen's Union (ILWU), Smith Act Defendants

—*Robert W. Cherny*

REFERENCES

Kutler, Stanley I. "'If at first . . .': The Trials of Harry Bridges." In *The American Inquisition: Justice and Injustce in the Cold War*. New York: Hill and Wang, 1982.

Larrowe, Charles P. *Harry Bridges: The Rise and Fall of Radical Labor in the United States*. New York: Lawrence Hill, 1972.

Schwartz, Harvey. "Harry Bridges and the Scholars: Looking at History's Verdict." *California History* 59 (Spring 1980).

Ward, Estolv E. *Harry Bridges on Trial*. New York: Modern Age Books, 1940.

"Bring the Boys Home" Movement

The largest-scale rebellion in U.S. military history, the victorious post–World War II "Bring the Boys Home" movement began in the fall of 1945, after the unconditional surrender of Japan. Timing of demobilization of the remaining twelve million men and women in the U.S. armed forces depended on a point system based on length of service, number of dependents, combat duty, and decorations. Most combat veterans believed that newly inducted replacements would occupy the former enemy territories and that they would be sent home rapidly. Instead, they were told that points had stopped accumulating on V-J Day. Many found themselves on cross-country trains to the West Coast, where they were loaded on ships headed for the Pacific theater for occupation duty in friendly liberated nations like the Philippines.

At railroad stations men propped up homemade signs in the train windows: SHANGHAIED FOR THE PACIFIC, while cheering crowds on the platforms held up their own signs: THE WAR IS OVER. BRING 'EM HOME! Reporters attempting to interview the soldiers were arrested and detained by the Army Security Guard. In October, General Douglas MacArthur announced that 200,000 men would be required in the Far East. President Harry S. Truman publicly contradicted him by stating that two and a half million men were needed. Congressmen were deluged with protest letters and hundreds of "Bring Back Daddy" clubs sprang up all over the country.

The Bring the Boys Home movement gained momentum and was best organized in Manila, in the Philippines, where a friendly population had fought an underground war against the Japanese invaders. On Christmas Day 4,000 men marched to protest the cancellation of a troopship sailing. Their commander ordered them back to their barracks and dismissed the demonstration as "a college rally."

But when, on January 4, 1946, the War Department announced that 300,000 men per month would be going home from the Pacific instead of the previously projected 800,000, spontaneous demonstrations cropped up all over Manila. On January 7, more than 2,500 men distributed leaflets calling for a mass meeting that night. "The State Department wants the army to back up its imperialism," the leaflet stated, contradicting reports that the swelling tide of protest reflected nothing but homesickness. Twenty thousand men came to the rally. Although the basic demand of the speakers was lower critical point scores, there were many angry denunciations of the U.S. policy and military involvement in North China, where U.S. troops were aiding Chiang Kai-shek against the Communist supporters of Mao Tse-tung, and in Indonesia, where they were helping in the Dutch attempt to defeat the nationalist forces of Sukarno. The men cheered when speakers informed them that the only purpose for the continued American occupation of the Philippines was to put wealthy landowners who had collaborated with the enemy back in power. Money was collected for a full page ad in the *New York Times* and thousands of trade union members stationed in Manila contacted union leaders. The National Maritime Union responded with a nationwide one-day strike and AFL president William Green issued a public statement of support for early demobilization. On January 10, 158 delegates elected by 139,000 men formulated a program to present to the members of the Senate Subcommittee on Surplus Materials. A nine-soldier delegation told the visiting senators that members of one "railroad battalion are being held in Luzon as potential strikebreakers on a native railroad" and added that many of the soldiers interpreted the special combat training of the Eighty-sixth Infantry Division, which had already fought in Europe, as preparation for the repression of possible uprisings by disgruntled farm tenant groups.

By January 8, the Bring the Boys Home movement had spread throughout the Pacific—to Luzon, Hawaii, and Guam. In Japan, Secretary of War Paterson was greeted by a demonstration when he visited Yokohama and the provost marshal of the U.S. Army Service Command told the press that the demonstrations were "a near mutiny stirred up by a lot of Communists and hotheads." That night, President Truman told the American people that demobilization was taking place "as fast as possible" and that there was "a critical need for troops overseas," while soldiers protested at nearby Andrews Field. By morning the movement had spread to Europe.

Military leaders and government officials could arrive at no consensus on methods of dealing with the Bring the Boys Home movement. They wavered between the carrot of concessions and the stick of punishment, censoring Army newspapers, telling the men their protests were futile, and calling them everything from "Reds" to "sissies." Technically, participants could have been prosecuted under Article 66, the mutiny provision of the Articles of War, but these men were war heroes in the eyes of the public.

At the end of the second week in January, without reference to the burgeoning movement, the War Department instituted a new point system that would release the men more quickly, and efforts to recruit new forces were stepped up. Previously empty ships soon filled up with troops for the voyage home. On January 17 Eisenhower banned GI demonstrations. In Manila, court-martials were ordered for any soldiers who continued agitation for demobilization. But by then, the aim of the Bring the Boys Home movement had clearly been achieved and could not be reversed without great political cost. Nine months after V-E Day and five months after V-J Day, the U.S. WW II veterans had won a stunning victory and were finally going home. *See also*: Peace Movements

—*Hedda Garza*

REFERENCES

Garza, Hedda. "The 'Bring the Boys Home' Movement." *American History Illustrated*, June 1985; *The New York Times*, December 1945 through January 1946; *St. Louis Post-Dispatch*, January 8, 1946.

BRITISH AMERICANS

British socialism and British immigrants affected the U.S. Left for the most part in the early period, with a special influence on the artisanal-oriented, gradualistic vision of socialism.

Before the establishment of a regular English-language socialist book-publisher, British volumes and pamphlets served an American audience of the 1880s–1890s. William Morris's *News from Nowhere* and Robert Blatchford's *Merrie England* enjoyed wide circulation, as did a number of newspapers from the earliest British Marxist organizations, such as William Morris's *Commonwealth*. A few survivors of Chartism or later British laborism took important roles in the small English-language wing of the Socialist Labor Party. The most prominent, Thomas J. Morgan of Chicago, conducted the "regular" wing of the local socialist movement against the social-revolutionaries and sought to direct socialist trade union work into the mainstream union groups rather than competing socialist trades-bodies. Elsewhere, British (along with "Lancashire Irish," i.e., Irish who had come to America by way of Lancashire) labor activists sought the establishment of strong craft unions and (if socialists) an educational effort aimed at the community.

British influences also had a special importance, in some areas, for the growth of libertarian or anarchist ideas. In Chicago, several of the leading Social Revolutionaries (including Samuel Fielding, son of a Chartist and himself a former Lancashire prelate) had known political activity earlier in England. British-born anarchists, many of them veterans of William Morris's movement, were active in propaganda groups of the 1880s–1890s. They had the most concerted influence in Boston, where they outnumbered other contributors to Benjamin Tucker's *Liberty* magazine and where, through influence on the local printers' and tailors' unions, they exerted significant influence upon the Central Labor Union.

By the 1890s, the rise of Fabianism and the inability of American ethnic socialists to reach the native-born with an acceptable doctrine brought many American intellectuals in contact with the English socialists. The most prominent American by far, Woman's Christian Temperance Union leader Frances Willard, converted to Fabian Socialism while on an extended visit. Fabian ideas meanwhile penetrated the Nationalist Clubs evoked by Edward Bellamy's *Looking Backward*, prompting the formation of the *American Fabian* in 1896. A humorous contemporary account probably captures (and caricatures) the intellectual atmosphere:

> The former president, Mr. Crosby, sued to say emphatically, thinking probably of the "class struggle," the "social revolution," and the tactics and tone of the SLP: "No, I am not a socialist"; and then, fixing his eyes on the ceiling, he would reflect upon "the Brotherhood of Man," and "Equality Before God" . . . and would murmur dreamily: "Why, yes, I am a socialist; really, of course, we all are."

While the *American Fabian* did not survive the reorganization of the socialist movement in the last years of the century, Fabian and Guild ideas flowed into the new Socialist Party. Gaylord Wilshire, John Spargo, William English Walling, A. M. Simons, Harry Laidler, and other important intellectuals were devout Anglophiles; the journals they edited (or to which they contributed) also featured articles by George Bernard Shaw, H. M. Hyndman, Keir Hardie, Ramsay MacDonald, E. Belfort Bax, Tom Mann, and even Oscar Wilde, and were frequently illustrated by Walter Crane's Morrisian drawings. The *Comrade*, edited by Spargo, was the most beautiful U.S. Left magazine until the *Masses*, and was also the most British-influenced.

After 1900, British-American anarchist intellectuals concentrated their efforts upon establishing "Modern Schools" and anarchist colonies in Stelton, New Jersey, and Moghegan, New York, among other places. (One of the prominent figures, William Bridge, was the grandfather of Joan Baez.) Especially in the aftermath of World War I and the Russian Revolution, these institutions became the major points of survival for English-language anarchism, and the publications from them (such as the *Road to Freedom*, published partly from Stelton in the 1920s–1930s) the chief evidence of intellectual vitality.

The American movement in part outgrew its early dependence upon British writers, and also drew increasingly apart on tactical lines. With WW I, most of the Anglophile writers, whatever their factional orientation, defected to pro-War positions. The major exception and new source of British influence was the pacifist current and the collegiate socialism around the *Intercollegiate Socialist* and its 1920s successor, *Labor Age*. Harry Laidler, editor of the *Intercollegiate Socialist*, would for decades pursue the themes of nationalization as a road to American socialism, and the Independent Labour Party's strategy (through the mainstream labor movement's own political institutions rather than outside) as suitable. Labor education, such as fostered at the Brookwood Labor College in partial imitation of British workers' education, was the other strand of this program. As late as the 1950s, the League for Industrial Democracy (of which Laidler remained secretary) urged nationalization of the steel industry as the key transition to a more cooperative order.

It could be said that another British phase (or miniphase) ensued with the later 1960s–1970s, when U.S. radical scholars in a number of fields looked to English theoretical expeditions. English historian and peace leader E. P. Thompson, very likely the most influential Anglo-American historian after Charles Beard, erected new scholarly paradigms with his *Making of the English Working Class* (1963), a book of particular importance to a New Left generation deeply drawn to social history. The *New Left Review*, sometimes correctly viewed as Thompson's nemesis, became for a time a principal fount for Althusserian, structuralist theorizing on both sides of the Atlantic. Other areas of postmodern radical scholarship, literature to psychology, also looked to specific British intellectuals. On the political front as such, several brands of American Trotskyists found their ideological motherland in England, where Trotskyism achieved an intellectual influence rare elsewhere. *See also*: Anarchism, Socialist Labor Party, Socialist Party

—*Paul Buhle*

REFERENCES

Anderson, Perry. *Western Marxism*. London: Verso, 1981.

Avrich, Paul. *Anarchist Portraits*. Princeton: Princeton University Press, 1988.

Brodsky, Joseph (1889–1947)

A founding member of the Communist movement, the International Labor Defense (ILD), and the International Workers' Order (IWO), attorney Joseph Brodsky was involved in hundreds of political cases from the time of the Palmer Raids through to the early years of the Cold War. But he gained his greatest fame for his work on behalf of the Scottsboro Boys. Born in Kiev, Russia, he immigrated to New York City with his parents at age two. Benjamin Brodsky, his father, was a shirtmaker and a militant Socialist who was a founder of Branch 1 of the Workmen's Circle. Joseph Brodsky was a socialist soapboxer by age thirteen and a formal member of the Socialist Party when he began to practice law in 1912. Along with brother Carl Brodsky, Joseph was soon a delegate to the City Central Committee, where they both came into conflict with the SP's moderate wing. The brothers joined John Reed, Jim Larkin, and other Left socialists who left the SP in 1919 to form the Communist Party.

The immediate impulse to the creation of the ILD in 1925 was the government persecution of Communists who had attended the "secret" 1922 Unity convention in Bridgman, Michigan. Drawing on the tradition that had created defense networks for persecuted labor activists such as the McNamaras, Mooney, and the Centralia IWWs, the ILD brought seventy-eight delegates from trade unions and fraternal organizations together with twenty-three delegates from the Labor Defense Councils set up by the CP to defend its leaders. One of the first cases taken on was support of Sacco and Vanzetti. The strategy involved massive public demonstrations to buttress the actual legal maneuvers. That defense approach remained a hallmark of a Brodsky defense.

Through the years, Brodsky would be the general counsel of the IWO, adviser to many trade unions, and attorney for Communists such as C. E. Ruthenberg, William Z. Foster, Robert Minor, and Rose Pastor Stokes. His cases usually entailed conspiracy charges that resulted from strikes or demonstrations. His legal thrust was always aimed at exploiting what he considered a fundamental contradiction between the constitutional guarantee of political equality and an economic system that guaranteed social inequality. He also thought it was possible, at times, to appeal to the better instincts of judges who were upset by gross inequities and wished to preserve social stability. One of his assets in arguing a case was a charming personality and an infectious sense of humor. Joseph Brodsky remained a Communist militant his entire life. At the time he suffered his fatal heart attack, he was working on the defense of Eugene Dennis and he had just raised $24,000 for the United Jewish Appeal in a speech at the Mohegan Colony in rural New York. *See also*: International Labor Defense

—*Dan Georgakas from materials provided by Ann Fagan Ginger*

REFERENCES

Daily Worker, July 31, 1947, and August 1, 1947.

Brookwood College: see Workers Education

Brotherhood of Timber Workers

The BTW was a radical, interracial industrial union that organized thousands of lumberjacks and sawmill workers in the Louisiana/Texas piney woods region. Founded in December 1910 in Carson, Louisiana, by the socialist sawmill workers Arthur Lee Emerson and Jay Smith, the BTW was, according to an opponent, "covering the country like a blanket" by 1911. At first a semisecret society replete with Knights of Labor–derived rituals, it was forced entirely underground in early 1912. However, during the spring of that year an open, official BTW convention was held in Alexandria, Louisiana. Persuaded by speeches from William "Big Bill" Haywood and the southern poet, organizer, and editor Covington Hall (1871–1952), the delegates voted to affiliate with the Industrial Workers of the World. The convention further adopted the IWW practice of integrated organization and voted to accord membership rights to working-class women, including the wives of timber workers. Black workers joined the union in force, along with "redneck" whites and some Mexicans and American Indians. During a series of bitter strikes and lockouts in 1912 and early 1913, the union's fortunes fluctuated greatly. It grew to include as many as 20,000 members. Nearby tenant farmers supported BTW actions and even joined the union themselves. Local residents, including many farmers who became timber workers, often resented the lumber corporations as "intruders" who brought in strikebreakers, interfered with traditions regarding common use of the woods, and destroyed the environment. However, the union suffered from fierce repression by public agencies and private police, especially in Louisiana at Grabow, the scene of a large gun battle, and Merryville, the scene of a violent strike. Legal defense came to take much of the time and money of the union, while race-baiting, blacklists, and the massive importation of strikebreakers exacted a heavy toll. By March 1913 the BTW had lost its struggle for egalitarian industrial unionism in the piney woods. *See also*: Industrial Workers of the World

—*David Roediger*

REFERENCES

Green, James R. "The Brotherhood of Timber Workers, 1910–1913." *Past and Present* 60 (August 1973).

Roediger, David R., ed. *Dreams and Dynamite: Selected Poems of Covington Hall*. Chicago: Charles H. Kerr, 1985.

Browder, Earl (1891–1973)

One of eight children, Browder was from a British family that immigrated to America before the Revolution, a fact that Communist propaganda of the Popular Front rarely failed to mention. Son of a teacher who became invalid and grandson of a Methodist circuit-riding minister, Browder was born in 1891 into a poor farming family in Wichita, Kansas, his ancestors having moved from Virginia to the Midwest. Forced to leave school before the age of ten, he worked first as an errand boy and then bookkeeper while he completed a law correspondence course.

As in much of Kansas before World War I, populist and socialist tendencies were present in his family. Before finding his way into the Communist movement—as did several of his siblings—Browder passed through the Socialist Party (he left after William D. Haywood's recall) and then a local Kansas group, the Workers' Educational League, which followed the line of William Z. Foster's Syndicalist League of North America of working within the AFL. In 1914 Browder became president of his local of the AFL Union of Bookkeepers and Stenographers and in 1916 worked for a farmers' cooperative store in Kansas City. Arrested in 1917 for his opposition to the war, he served two jail sentences of more than a year each, which limited his political involvement. Influenced by the Russian Revolution, he rejoined the Socialist Party and, with James Cannon, took over the Kansas City local for the left wing. In 1919 he put out the *Workers' World*, one of the first procommunist newspapers outside New York. In jail, as the first Communist groups had been formed, he entered the United Communist Party in January 1921 and accepted the offer to organize an American trade union delegation—of which Foster would become part—to the first Congress of the Red International of Labor Unions (Profintern) to be held in Moscow in July 1921.

Elected an alternate member from Kansas of the first Central Executive Committee of the Workers Party (WP) at its December 1921 founding convention, Browder appeared to be a quiet and unassuming second-level functionary. He helped edit the *Labor Herald*, the monthly of the CP-founded Trade Union Educational League, and was considered Foster's chief lieutenant and part of the latter's trade union group against the more "political" WP leadership of C. E. Ruthenberg and Jay Lovestone.

American representative to the Profintern in 1926, he worked for its Pan-Pacific Secretariat in the late twenties and served as part of a mission to China in that crucial period. Absent at the height of the factional struggles in the American Party, Browder came directly into the leadership supported by the Comintern, which appreciated his organizational abilities. Already prominent at the June 1930 Seventh Convention, he was elected general secretary at the following convention four years later.

In the early New Deal, he moved the Party out of its isolation and fought against sectarian tendencies still strongly present: he indicated that the New Deal, though moving in the direction of fascism, had not yet arrived there; he pushed forward United Front activities in 1933–34 around farm and unemployment questions; and he opposed underestimating work in the AFL. The Labor Party policy in early 1935—adopted naturally after consultation with Moscow but perhaps initiated by Browder himself—attempted to transfer the United Front approach to the electoral arena.

The CP in the second half of the thirties emerged under Browder, through its presence in the trade union and cultural worlds and its increasing connection to the New Deal, as a genuinely American political force on the national level and in various local situations. After the official launching of the Popular Front policy, he increasingly noted the positive tendencies in the administration—especially as a seemingly antifascist foreign policy emerged. The Communist secretary showed great capacity for interacting with various New Deal and left-of-center political exponents, religious leaders, and intellectuals as well as for finding wealthy financial backers for Party enterprises. Putting forward with vigor the Party's Popular Front image and its claim to be the continuer of the eighteenth-century revolutionary tradition, he stated in 1935 that "we are the Americans and Communism is the Americanism of the twentieth century" (later he was compelled to recognize the "limitations" of this formulation). As to the final direction of the Communist movement, he maintained somewhat lamely that whatever strengthened the working class also went in the direction of socialism.

After the 1939 German–Soviet Pact, as part of a general crackdown on Communists, Browder was arrested for a minor passport violation committed in the twenties. Sentenced in 1940 to four years in jail and a fine, he received 14% of the vote in a special congressional election on New York's Lower East Side in the same year. Partially reflecting neutralist sentiment, this electoral energy also indicated that Communist strength in this working-class-immigrant area had remained constant despite the German-Soviet Pact and opposition to Roosevelt.

In May 1942, Franklin Roosevelt commuted Browder's sentence. In these years the Communist secretary willingly put himself forward as a sort of unofficial spokesman not only for Stalin but also Mao Tse-tung and Tito among others. On this basis he corresponded and met with Undersecretary of State Sumner Wells about various international questions.

During the war, Browder's ideas moved ever further away from classical Marxism and Leninism: as part of an all-out win-the-war effort he put forward an incentive-pay proposal to increase productivity and also supported Roosevelt's war-service one; he supported a national unity that included not only monopoly capitalists but also reactionaries in the Democratic Party; and he denied the relevance of the right to national self-determination for the black population. Americans were now, he believed, subjectively unprepared for the discussion of socialism.

After the "Teheran meeting" in late 1943, Browder affirmed not only that the Big Three would remain allies after the war and that Europe would be reconstructed on a nonfascist, capitalist basis but that an identity of interests existed between American capitalism with its increased productive capacity and the progress of the war-torn and undeveloped world in need of capital and goods. Within the United States, labor-management cooperation was to continue while the Party would dissolve organizationally with members operating in existing organisms as a left-wing pressure group.

The opposition of Foster in early 1944 to this latter proposal found support neither in Moscow nor in the CP leadership: Browder's positions seem to have corresponded to a widespread desire of members for full political integration and acceptability and to have been in step with the Party's general direction. In the late spring of 1945, however, Browder fell from power as an article by French communist leader Jacques Duclos, undoubtedly inspired by Moscow, criticized his interpretation of the Teheran conference as something more than a diplomatic agreement between governments. Despite the existence of a genuine cult of personality, Browder's total rejection of this criticism made removal obligatory. In July 1945 a special convention reconstituted the Party. Knowledge that Foster's criticism had been suppressed and that Moscow did not support the ex-secretary added to the developing Cold War and the strike wave of 1945–46, which negated Browder's predictions of international and domestic tranquility, all contributed to the membership's acceptance of this turnabout.

Browderism received little support from abroad. With its virtual elimination of anti-imperialism, it could never be very popular in Latin America, while in Europe Communist forces, although following a policy of unity, showed no intention of prematurely disbanding as an independent political force. Nor was previous friendship with the Chinese Communists sufficient to bring them in on his side.

Expelled from the Party in February 1946, Browder held a position for a few years as U.S. representative for Soviet publishing concerns, but this in no way led to his political rehabilitation. In the years of his withdrawal from all public life, he published *Marx and America* and worked on several versions of an uncompleted autobiography. Although his name had been bandied about during the 1956 upheaval in the Party, his death in 1973 went largely unnoticed.

During the favorable conjuncture of the thirties and the war his line stimulated Party growth in numbers and influence and its entry into mainstream politics. Never considered the direct representative of a politically conscious working-class minority nor an apostle of a new socialist society, Earl Browder was primarily an able tactician capable of developing theoretical justifications. *See also*: Communist Party; Foster, William Z.; Popular Front

—Malcolm Sylvers

REFERENCES

Isserman, Maurice. *Which Side Were You On? The American Communist Party During the Second World War*. Middletown: Wesleyan University Press, 1982.

Klehr, Harvey. *The Heydey of American Communism: The Depression Decade*. New York: Basic Books, 1984.

Brown, Bishop William Montgomery (1854–1937)

An important radical-religious pamphleteer, Bishop Brown popularized the Russian Revolution and personally dramatized the continuing appeal of "free thought" to millions of readers.

Brown had grown up poor in Ohio, then met a wealthy Cleveland patroness who made possible his education and whose niece became Brown's supportive wife. Educated at Kenyon College and ordained an Episcopal priest in 1884, Brown quickly gained a reputation for attracting converts. Appointed Bishop of Arkansas, Brown began to oppose racism openly, with *The Crucial Race Question* (1907). Resigning under fire in 1912, Brown returned to his Galion, Ohio, home to study and to write prolifically. He wrote in favor of birth control, against abuse of Native Americans by whites, and—greatly influenced by World War I—for socialism.

Brown's *Communism and Christianism* (1920), calling on humanity to "Banish the Gods from Skies and Capitalists from the Earth," was instantaneously popular. Over the next twenty years, it would be translated into more than a dozen languages and go through numerous editions totaling more than a million copies. *Communism and Christianism* made Brown an important public figure. A decade earlier, he might have joined the then-considerable Christian Socialist milieu. An enthusiast of Russia, he ill-fit a young Communist movement with little room for popular eclectics.

Brown achieved his greatest celebrity as martyr to free thought. Brought up on heresy charges by the U.S. House of Bishops in 1925, he was defended by Joseph Sharts, noted attorney for Eugene Debs. After seven months' deliberation and much public controversy, he was removed (he was installed as bishop in the small Old Catholic movement).

Thereafter, Brown spoke widely for Communist causes, from the *Daily Worker* to International Labor Defense, as public lecturer an extraordinary figure in his ecclesiastical garb. He also continued with his personal sense of mission, supporting Irish and black revolutionaries and (with the onset of the Depression) the poor in his own Galion. Loyal to the Communist Party, he bequeathed it virtually his entire estate. The "Brownella Cottage," where he lived and to which many famous visitors came, remained for decades abandoned. Local friends managed, in recent years, to add the cottage to the National Public Registry and to convince the local Galion Historical Society to reopen it as a museum, with the Bishop's personal library and papers intact. *See also*: Christian Socialism, Communist Party

—*Paul Buhle*

REFERENCES

Haferd, Laura. "The Heresy Trial of Bishop Brown." The *Beacon* (Columbus, Ohio), September 12, 1982.

Roy, Ralph Lord. *Communism and the Churches*. New York: Harcourt, Brace, 1960.

Bryant, Louise (1885–1936)

Born Anna Louise Mohan in San Francisco, the daughter of a newspaperman, she took the name Bryant from a stepfather when her mother remarried. She graduated from the University of Oregon in 1909, married a Portland dentist and with him raised Persian cats. When John Reed came to visit his mother in Portland, they met, and within weeks she went to New York City at his urging. As soon as her divorce became final, she married Reed.

Her life with the tumultuous Reed caused her to be slighted, both by her Greenwich Village contemporaries and by subsequent historical (including media) treatments. She was, however, a talented journalist in her own right—she went with him during the Russian Revolution of 1917 and had a series of newspaper stories already in print when he arrived home. The book she wrote, *Six Months in Russia*, won praise for clear information, and she addressed large, enthusiastic American audiences on a whirlwind tour.

Bryant viewed Reed's death of typhus in Russia in 1920, but stayed on to write for King Features, a Hearst syndicate, and International News Series. Among the first Western reporters to travel to the vast stretches of eastern Russia, she remained an outstanding observer. Later, increasingly wearied and reportedly depressed, she traveled frequently, spending much time in Paris. After her death, she became almost immediately an obscure figure, her acclaim of the 1920s forgotten next to John Reed's deathless (and much deserved) reputation. *See also*: Greenwich Village; *The Liberator*; Reed, John

—*Virginia Gardner*

REFERENCES

Gardner, Virginia. *Friend and Lover, the Life of Louise Bryant*. New York: Horizon Press, 1983.

Bulgarian Americans

The major period of Bulgarian immigration was between 1900 and 1920. Most of these immigrants settled in industrial centers to become factory workers while a smaller number worked in railroad construction. Having participated in progressive movements in their native land, Bulgarians early joined the ranks of American labor and by 1910 had established Marxist groups in many of their communities.

The most famous personality in the early period was George Andreytchine, who was drawn to the Industrial Workers of the World and became a key leader in the IWW-led strike of 16,000 Mesabi Range miners in 1916. A year later he was among the 101 IWWs convicted in the infamous Chicago mass trial, where he received a sentence of twenty years in prison and a $20,000 fine. While fighting the conviction in higher courts, he worked with

John Reed during the founding of the American communist movement in 1919. When his appeal process ran out two years later, he was among 8 IWWs to choose exile in the Soviet Union with William D. "Big Bill" Haywood rather than returning to Leavenworth Prison.

In the succeeding decade politically progressive Bulgarians gravitated to the Worker Education Clubs founded in Detroit, Michigan, in 1925 and the Macedonian-American League founded in Gary, Indiana, in 1931. They also gave considerable public support to compatriot George Dimitrov during the time of the Reichstag Fire case. Detroit's *Suzanni* (*Consciousness*), a weekly newspaper, was particularly aggressive in supporting Dimitrov.

During the early 1930s Bulgarians were active in hunger marches. Later in the decade they participated in sit-down strikes in auto and steel, where they were staunchly CIO. Although the smallest of the Slavic groups (100,000), Bulgarians played an important interethnic role by helping to unite the organizations of ten million Slavic Americans on behalf of the war effort. This achievement was greatly appreciated by the Roosevelt Administration as Slavic Americans then made up 51 percent of the work force in heavy industry.

At war's end the influence of progressive thought among Bulgarians, as among other Slavic groups, was substantial. Some sixteen thousand persons, for example, attended a September 1946 rally in Madison Square Garden sponsored by the Slav Congress. At the rally Paul Robeson sang on behalf of world peace and various speakers urged continued cooperation among the wartime allies and the emerging socialist regimes in Eastern Europe. This political current ebbed considerably with the coming of McCarthyism and the Cold War. A number of Bulgarians were deported and radical organizations went into a decline from which they have never recovered. *See also*: American Slav Congress, Communist Party

—*George Pirinsky*

Bulosan, Carlos (1911–56)

When Bulosan landed in America in 1930, nearly 100,000 young men like him had been recruited from Filipino peasant villages to run Alaska's canneries and work the plantations of Hawaii and the West Coast. But in search of two brothers who had migrated earlier, Bulosan had also come to complete his education and become a writer.

It was not a time to become a writer for oneself. Caught in the maelstrom of the Depression, Filipinos (then called "Pinoys") faced irregular underemployment, exploitation by labor contractors and large-scale growers, unmitigated racism, and vigilante violence. The Tydings-McDuffie Act limited Filipino immigration yearly to fifty in 1934, and the Repatriation Act of 1935 threatened Pinoys with deportation. Bulosan eventually gave up his plan to finish school and helped organize Filipino resistance against these oppressive practices and moves.

Bulosan scholar Susan Evangelista has traced Bulosan's radicalization to this period, when he had lived with his brothers Dionisio and Aurelio in California and seen firsthand the vicissitudes of Filipino migrant life. Indeed, by this time, Bulosan had served as a publicist for the organization of what was later to become the United Cannery, Agricultural, Packing and Allied Workers of America (UCAPAWA). He had also put out a short-lived bimonthly called the *New Tide* and written scathing pieces for local newspapers about the problems of Pinoys. Turning to self-education, he had begun reading intensively at the Los Angeles Public Library, this time to become a writer for his countrymen.

From 1934 to 1937, strikes by Filipino workers broke out in California, persisting far into the beginnings of World War II. According to Evangelista, it was within this period that Bulosan forged his lasting friendship with Chris Mensalvas, an active Filipino unionist based in Seattle. By publishing the *New Tide* he came to know literary figures and the struggling socialist writer Sanora Babb. While confined for tuberculosis at the Los Angeles County Hospital from 1936 to 1938, Bulosan read and wrote intensively, guided by Dorothy, Babb's sister, and urged by Harriet Monroe, editor of *Poetry*.

It was from this period until 1946 that Bulosan published widely. His career peaked with the best-selling *The Laughter of My Father*

(1944) and his revered ethnobiography of Pinoys, *America Is in the Heart* (1946). Bulosan wrote about Filipinos in America and peasants in the Philippines and used himself, his family, and friends as paradigms for the characters who peopled his writing. His autobiographical mode of writing wedded fact and fiction tightly, and sought to symbolically transcend the boundaries that separated him from his peasant heritage and ethnic group.

Perpetually sickly, Bulosan was not exactly the itinerant worker-narrator of *America Is in the Heart* in real life. Also, his early grasp of writing even as a young emigrant had set him on a different track from that of his countrymen. But once awakened by the plight of Pinoys in America, Bulosan never wavered in his identification with them. In 1943 the Philippine government-in-exile offered him a comfortable sinecure in Washington D.C. While Bulosan visited the then-ailing president-in-exile, he spurned the offer.

Unable to accept the compound of history and biography in Bulosan's work, critics on both sides of the Pacific accused him of dishonesty and commercialism. After a dubious plagiarism charge in the late forties ruined his career, Bulosan fell into alcoholism, illness, obscurity, neurosis, and despair, according to Bulosan's friend Dolores Stephens Feria. Evangelista points out that it was Chris Mensalvas who asked Bulosan to move to Seattle in 1950 to edit the yearbook of the International Longshoremen and Warehousemens Union (ILWU), Local 37. Bulosan then resumed his writing and his participation in the collective struggles, which continued as Filipino unionists and their American sympathizers braced for the McCarthy era.

Bulosan died from pneumonia in 1956, leaving behind fragmentary and finished manuscripts, including a novelette on the 1950s communist rebellion in the Philippines. Both Feria and Evangelista say that surviving associates remain silent on Bulosan's rumored ties with the American Communist Party yet do not deny that he was drawn to proletarianism. Evidence also suggests some contact between him and Amado V. Hernandez, a labor leader, journalist, and poet in the Philippines who was imprisoned in the fifties, courtesy of the Filipino version of the McCarthy witch-hunts.

Bulosan's writing was rediscovered by Asian-American and Filipino scholars in the sixties. At least six collections of his short fiction, poetry, letters, and essays have been published, mostly under the editorship of Bulosan scholar Epifanio San Juan, Jr. *America Is in the Heart*, which Carey McWilliams has dubbed a "social classic," has been reissued several times in the United States and the Philippines.

—*Oscar V. Campomanes*

REFERENCES

Bulosan, Carlos. *The Power of the People*. Ontario: Tabloid Books, 1977.

———. *Sound of Falling Light: Letters in Exile*. Edited by Dolores Feria. Quezon City: University of the Philippines Press, 1960.

Evangelista, Susan. *Carlos Bulosan and His Poetry: A Biography and Anthology*. Seattle: University of Washington Press, 1985.

San Juan, Epifanio, Jr. *Carlos Bulosan and the Imagination of the Class Struggle*. Quezon City: University of the Philippines Press, 1972.

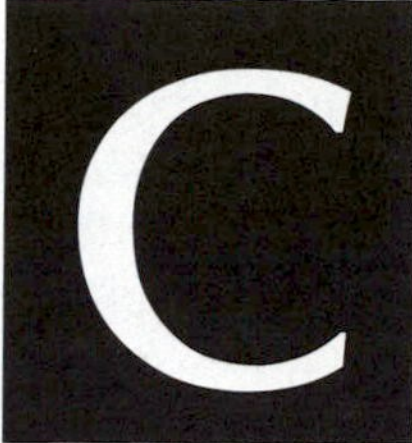

Cacchione, Peter V. (1897–1947)

One of the most charismatic of local Communist politicians, and one of their few Italian leaders, Cacchione became the first Communist elected in a major American city (New York City councilman 1941–47). He embodied the folksy popularity of the Left in the ethnic groups of the neighborhoods and especially among their labor movement activists.

An Italian immigrant raised in a Pennsylvania railroad town, son of the owners of a small grocery store and bakery, Cacchione worked in the railroad and had no special political involvements until his move to New York in 1932. The Depression brought him into contact with the Unemployed Councils, and there he emerged as a minor leader in the Bonus March on Washington. He joined the Communist Party and moved from the Bronx to Brooklyn, where he quickly became the leader of the borough Communist organization. Attaching himself to Mayor Fiorello LaGuardia, Cacchione learned much from the mayor's showmanship and his shrewd use of Italian symbolism.

Although unsuccessful in 1937 and 1939 campaigns for the New York City Council on the American Labor Party ticket, Cacchione attracted increasing attention and support with his attention to the detailed concerns of his neighborhood constituents, his public leadership of struggles over such matters as subway fares and his clever campaign tactics. Under the Proportional Representation system, he received more than 24,000 write-in votes in 1939, despite the difficulty of his name's spelling. His vote pattern, highest in Jewish neighborhoods, was nevertheless higher in Italian districts than any other Left politician but Vito Marcantonio could muster.

In 1941, under the slogan of "Unity Against Hitler," Cacchione was elected to the city council. There he threw himself into such practical concerns as the integration of the Brooklyn Dodgers, the breakdown of racial discrimination in city-assisted housing, and the maintenance of living standards in wartime inflation. (Nor did he lose the common touch: his favorite radio show was the *Lone Ranger*.) Joined by Benjamin Davis, he formed a small but true Communist bloc. He fought, after the war, especially against the rise in prices, and against the concerted anti-Left move to eliminate proportional representation. At his death, the New York City Council, breaking precedent and rule, refused to seat a Communist Party replacement for the remainder of Cacchione's term. *See also*: American Labor Party, Communist Party, Benjamin Davis, Popular Front

—*Paul Buhle*

REFERENCES

Gerson, Simon W. *Pete: The Story of Peter V. Cacchione, New York's First Communist Councilman.* New York: International Publishers, 1976.

CAHAN, ABRAHAM (1860–1951)

Best known to the American public as the author of the highly praised immigrant novel *The Rise of David Levinsky* (1917), Cahan was also the longtime editor of the influential social democratic Yiddish language newspaper the *Jewish Daily Forward*, in its day the most widely read Yiddish publication in the world. Cahan helped found the paper in 1897 with a group of Jewish trade unionists and Socialist Labor Party members who had become estranged from Daniel DeLeon and the SLP as too rigid and sectarian. Thereafter, for about five years, Cahan pursued a literary and journalistic career in English, returning to reign as editor of the *Forward* from 1903 until his death.

Born near Vilna in Lithuania, Cahan joined a revolutionary reading group while a student at the Teachers Training Institute, and feared arrest after the assassination of the czar in 1881. He fled to the United States in 1882, became one of the very earliest American socialist agitators in the Yiddish language, and was active in the New York of the 1880s–1890s in Jewish labor and socialist politics. Sent as a delegate to the second and third congresses of the Socialist International in 1891 and 1893, he worked as editor and writer for five Yiddish radical periodicals, including the earliest journal, *Di Zukunft*, and the earliest notable newspaper, *Di Arbeter Zeitung*.

Cahan's politics evolved from the pre-Marxist amalgam of idealized socialism and anarchism he brought from Russia to an increasingly right-wing social democratic position. He welcomed the Russian Revolution in 1917, but from the middle 1920s onward was bitterly and actively anticommunist, a position the *Forward* urged upon the Jewish public. Nominally a socialist all his life, Cahan helped found the American Labor Party in 1936 along with Sidney Hillman and David Dubinsky, primarily to support Roosevelt and the New Deal.

At least as important as his formal politics was Cahan's view of Yiddish and *Yiddishkayt* (culture using Yiddish language in daily life and arts). He advocated that the Jewish immigrant masses Americanize themselves as rapidly and effectively as possible, even though his own literary work frequently showed the social and psychological price such a course exacted. Cahan's position put him severely at odds with Yiddishists, many religious groupings, Zionists, and other advocates of Jewish cultural autonomy (including some Marxists). Paradoxically, by its use of Yiddish—however Americanized or vulgarized—and by its attention to Jewish workers' lives, the *Forward* heightened and has maintained to date a considerable degree of Jewish consciousness. *See also*: Yiddish Left

—*Jules Chametzky*

REFERENCES

Cahan, Abraham. *Bleter fun Mayn Lebn* (Pages from my life, an autobiography), 5 vols. New York: Forwards Publishing Association, 1926–31.

Chametzky, Jules. *From the Ghetto: The Fiction of Abraham Cahan*. Amherst: University of Massachusetts Press, 1977.

Howe, Irving. *World of Our Fathers: The Journey of the East European Jews to America and the Life They Found and Made*. New York: Harcourt Brace Jovanovich, 1976.

Sanders, Ronald. *The Downtown Jews: Portraits of an Immigrant Generation*. New York: Harper & Row, 1969.

CALENDARS

Long a primary form of literary expression and outreach for ethnic-radical movements, calendars reappeared during the 1960s among environmental, feminist, labor-political, and other progressive movements. In each case marking special memorial days and showcasing particular illustrations, calendars made a political point with ease and subtlety.

The German-American socialists, borrowing upon their home traditions, produced the first important radical calendars, and some of the most lasting series. From 1882 to 1933, the *Pionier-Kalendar* appeared, published by the *New Yorker Volkszeitung* (People's newspaper). Over a hundred pages in length, this creation featured topflight illustrations and writings by many of the outstanding intellectuals of the movement. Generally, a title-page portrait of a major figure such as Marx or Ferdinand Lassalle would be followed by the actual calendar section with dates of important socialist events included, reading material (generally preceded by a poem of the year), then some pages of advertising and greetings from socialist, labor, and fraternal groups. Outright political expressions were integrated into a popular reading-matter context of stories, jokes, and poems—ranging from class-conscious to love and nature themes—and historical, economic, and popular-scientific essays.

The *Pionier*, more thoroughly than any of its successors, urged self-improvement upon its working-class audience. Essays on art and literature encouraged readers to develop their own aesthetic understanding. In later years, the works of artists like Käthe Kollwitz were frequently reproduced in the *Pionier*. Women's rights, applied specifically to the housewife who likely referred most often to the calendar, grew in importance over the decades, conveying a desired empowerment in daily life. By its final decade, ending with the outbreak of World War II, authors and audience had become *alte Genossen*, old-timers in a fast-disappearing milieu. Yet it continued until the end to express a motto it claimed for itself: For the Worker the Best Is Just Good Enough!

Other socialist ethnic groups, imitating the *Pionier* or in some cases continuing their own homeland-ethnic traditions, published calendars in proliferating numbers by the 1910s. These had relatively less importance for groups that were large in numbers and semi-assimilated, than for smaller and more insular groups who had few linguistic alternatives. Among Slavs, for instance, even the Socialist Labor Party's sectarian "South Slavonian Federation," from their headquarters in Cleveland, continued into the 1930s to publish and sell door-to-door in Slovenian neighborhoods their calendar with American holidays, socialist and labor memorial days, and Slovenian saints' days intermingled, facing a popular homeland illustration.

Although rarely successful among English-language radical groups, calendars began to reemerge as fundraising efforts for 1960s–1970s movements. Sometimes, as with the City Lights Bookstore calendars, more emphasis would be placed upon the literary avant-garde, but with a socialistic (or anarchistic) political undertone. Sometimes, as with the *Mill Hunk* calendars from Pittsburgh's blue-collar organizing project, much emphasis was placed upon labor history. Frequently, as with a variety of feminist calendars, "recovered" lives of radical women and women's history events saw the light of day. Environmental groups placed special emphasis upon nature pictures, with a preservationist undertone. Only a relatively few calendars emphasized immediate political concerns; audiences were not only too small for such a strategy, but as with the ethnic calendars, the politics of daily life continued to predominate in a successful calendar. *See also*: German Americans, *New Yorker Volkszeitung*

—*Carol Poore and Paul Buhle*

REFERENCES

Poore, Carol. "The *Pionier Volks Kalendar*." In *The German-American Radical Press*, edited by Ken Fones-Wolf, James Dankey, and Elliot Shore. Urbana: University of Illinois, 1990.

CALIFORNIA

Despite a geographic isolation that separated the state from the mainstream of the American Left until well into the twentieth century, California contributed its share of political leaders, writers, and organizers to the growth of American radicalism. With the national headquarters of most major Left organizations located either in the Midwest or East, Californians found it difficult to exert the degree of influence on party policies that New York or Chicago radicals wielded. They did, however, set forth a political style of openness and experimentation that offset the more insular and doctrinaire methods of their eastern comrades.

The California Left dates from the flight of European refugees following the revolutionary upheavals of 1848. In 1869 German followers of Ferdinand Lassalle established a section of the International Workingmen's Association in San Francisco, the second section formed in the United States. French- and English-language sections soon followed, but by the mid-1870s the English section dominated and foreign-language units of succeeding Left organizations had a less significant role in California than they would have in eastern states.

The English section became the California branch of the Workingmen's Party of the United States, actively organizing labor unions in San Francisco, most notably the Sailors Union of the Pacific. Socialist influence ebbed during the 1877 rail strike when San Francisco's working class was co-opted by Denis Kearney's nonsocialist, anti-Chinese Workingmen's Party of California.

Burnette Haskell revitalized socialism in the 1880s. Under his direction, radicals were active in the Knights of Labor and Edward Bellamy's Nationalism, briefly led the anti-Chinese movement, organized the Kaweah colony, and created the short-lived but influential International Workmen's Association.

As with Haskell and his following, many Californians bridged the gap between utopianism, woman's rights, and socialism. Women in the Kaweah Colony themselves published a short-lived gender-conscious version of Haskell's paper, *Truth*, as *Truth in Small Doses*. Older California women, sometimes removed East Coast Yankee veterans of abolitionism, suffrage, and spiritualism, played a major role in the Bellamy movement and in Point Loma, a Theosophist-Socialist colony headed by Katherine Tingley. Bellamy Nationalism was especially strong in California, with Socialists in many leading positions in the local leadership. With many of the same followers, and under the slogan "Let the nation own the trusts," Gaylord Wilshire conducted the first vigorous and well-funded American Socialist congressional campaign in 1890.

Influenced by California's largely agrarian economy, the Left from 1880 to 1900 was involved with farm protest movements, closely paralleling the path of socialism in other farm states. At the 1896 Populist National Convention, California Socialists sought to convert the party into a socialist organization and opposed the endorsement of Democratic presidential candidate William Jennings Bryan. With the collapse of Populism, California radicals turned to the Socialist Labor Party, running their first gubernatorial candidate, Job Harriman, in 1898. Harriman opposed Daniel DeLeon's policy of dual unionism and worked actively in the secessionist movement that split the national SLP (1899). When SLP defectors united with Eugene Debs's Social Democracy in a joint presidential ticket, Harriman received the vice-presidential nomination (1900).

The California SLP entered the newly formed Socialist Party of America virtually en masse. At the 1901 founding convention a black California delegate, William Costley, successfully urged adoption of the only party resolution dealing specifically with black rights passed by the SP during the first decade of its existence. During that early period, the California Left had an especially close relationship with the trade union movement. In a rare move, the AFL and Samuel Gompers endorsed Job Harriman's 1911 Los Angeles mayoralty campaign. Running at the head of a ticket that included both socialists and unionists, Harriman and his slate led all candidates in the primary, benefiting from widespread labor unrest in the city. The platform pledged support to James and John McNamara, union leaders then on trial for the dynamiting of the *Los Angeles Times*. When the McNamaras unexpectedly entered a confession shortly before the final election, the entire ticket went down to defeat.

Despite the shattering loss, the SP not only survived but elected city council members and three state assemblymen in subsequent elections. Other notable victories included Berkeley, where they elected Christian Socialist J. Stitt Wilson mayor (1911) and won control of the school board (1913). California Socialists who won elections generally came from the reformist element, relatively close to the trade union movement, that dominated the party before World War I. The party press and conventions were caught up in a constant debate between the reforming "opportunists" and the "impossibilists," who shunned reform platforms and worked for "scientific socialism." Throughout this prewar era the California SP grew rapidly in membership and voting strength. In 1902 California ranked first among the states, with 1,600 members. It was again first in 1910 with 6,000 members, one-tenth of the national total. Membership peaked in 1914 with 8,200 members and 300 locals.

While the mainstream of the California Left was close to the AFL, another segment supported the Industrial Workers of the World, which had significant strength in the lumber camps and among farm workers. The free-speech struggles at Fresno (1910) and San Diego (1912) drew attention to the activities of the IWW, but the "Wheatland Riot" (1913) found the union involved in a bitter struggle to improve conditions among migrant hop workers in the Sacramento Valley. This militancy was rewarded by a growing attitude on the part of left-wing socialists to support industrial unionism. By 1915 membership in the California IWW had grown to 4,500. This growth of the Left, accomplished despite a strong reform movement among California progressives, was stifled by the coming of WW I. California Socialists were as badly divided over the war as the Socialist movement elsewhere. War supporters included Jack London and several party officials. Other California radicals actively opposed the war, among them Baptist minister Robert Whitaker, who was jailed for war resistance.

During the war the reformist leadership was replaced by a more radical group (including James Dolsen, Max Bedacht, and John Taylor) closely identified with the Bolshevik Revolution in Russia. At the 1919 Socialist convention in Chicago they took the California SP into the newly formed Communist Labor Party. Meanwhile, growing animosity toward the California Left, beginning with the war, resulted in a series of repressive actions. Socialist Tom Mooney was convicted of bombing a preparedness-day parade in San Francisco (1916). Forty-three Wobblies were tried and convicted in a mass trial at Sacramento (1918–19) on federal charges involving the Espionage and Selective Service acts. In Oakland on Armistice Day (1919) a mob wrecked CLP headquarters.

The state government moved against the Left, passing a Criminal Syndicalism Act (1919) that made membership in a group that sought change in industrial ownership by force or violence a crime. Moving at first against members of the SP and then against the newly formed CLP, the state secured enough convictions to virtually drive the CLP out of existence. The U.S. Supreme Court (1927), in the case of CLP member Anita Whitney, found the act constitutional. Four decades later the court would void the act.

The Depression years saw a resurgence of activity, particularly among Communists, who were singled out for repression under the criminal syndicalism law for their agitation on behalf of farm workers. Formation of the CIO and increasing unionization of industry during the New Deal years also increased the Left's influence, particularly that of Communists, in the labor movement.

Some Leftists supported Upton Sinclair's unsuccessful 1934 California campaign for the governorship on the Democratic ticket. The former Socialist captured the nomination on a platform that emphasized the state's duty to provide work for the unemployed, but his "End Poverty in California" movement was considered too reform-minded to be considered a part of the Left, a judgment that many California radicals, including Communists, later regretted. Never again would a Left figure so nearly approach state leadership.

Communist reorientation to the Popular Front plunged the Left into the liberal wing of the Democratic Party, where it played an influential role for several decades. Social agencies of the New Deal provided opportunities for some of the Left. Others gained positions in the administration of Culbert Olson, whose election in 1938 returned a Democrat to the governorship for the first time in three decades. But the political success of Democratic reformers weakened any general appeal that the Left might itself have made to the electorate. Instead, Communists concentrated their strength, by the 1940s, in the California Democratic Council (CDC), an influence group.

Dissatisfaction with the postwar Truman administration led much of the California Left to support Henry Wallace's 1948 presidential bid. Called the Independent Progressive Party in California, it gave the Left a place on the ballot for the next two decades. During the forties and fifties the IPP was closer to the Communists than to the Socialists, who did not identify with it.

California Communists, in contrast to their eastern comrades, peaked in numbers and influence during the 1940s, and retained their strength well into the 1950s. With the *Daily People's World*, widespread influence in the International Longshoremen's and Warehousemen's Union among other labor organizations, and the capable state leadership of Dorothy Healey, they epitomized the more flexible side of American Communism.

The Red Scare of the 1940s and 1950s was symbolized by the anticommunist loyalty-oath fight that rocked the University of California. Despite a general complacency on campuses in the 50s, toward the end of the decade there was a revival of student awareness, particularly over campus racial discrimination and regulations that seriously limited free speech.

By the 1960s the IPP had lost its ballot status due to declining voter strength, and the Left was further splintered by the emergence of numerous factions within both the Socialist and Communist camps. To unify the movement, the Peace and Freedom Party was organized in response to the civil rights struggle and the Vietnam War. While it continued to function into the 1980s, it remained largely a paper organization utilized only at election time. Members of the Left continued to work within the old Socialist and Communist organizations or in new ones, such as Democratic Socialists of America, into which longtime California Communist Dorothy Healey moved in the 1980s.

The turmoil of the 1960s and 1970s brought forth other organizations that drew a disproportionate amount of publicity by virtue of their activities. The Black Panthers and the Symbionese Liberation Army were on the fringe of the California Left. Still other organizations directed at economic, social, or antiwar goals had a strong Left leadership but remained apart from traditional sectarian politics. *See also*: Communist Party; *People's World*; Sinclair, Upton

—*Ralph E. Shaffer*

REFERENCES

Cross, Ira. *A History of the Labor Movement in California*. Berkeley: University of California Press, 1935.

Richmond, Al. *Native Daughter*. San Francisco: Anita Whitney 75th Anniversary Committee, 1942.

Shaffer, Ralph E. "Communism in California, 1919–1924." *Science and Society* 34 (Winter 1970).

Weintraub, Hyman. "The I.W.W. in California, 1905–1931." M.A. thesis, UCLA, 1947.

California Labor School

This progressive labor school, which opened in 1946, grew out of the increasing strength of the San Francisco labor movement and the "united front" against fascism before and during World War II. It had been founded in 1942 as the Tom Mooney Labor School, in a loft, with a student body of one hundred and a curriculum that included women's history, black history, labor organization, journalism, public speaking, economics, and training in industrial arts (plastics, ceramics, construction, photography, and graphic arts). By the time of its renaming, the school had expanded tenfold and moved to larger quarters on Market Street, with an auditorium, art gallery, and substantial library.

Uniquely among progressive labor schools of the time, the CLS gained approval for study under the GI Bill, offering opportunities for veterans otherwise unable to gain a higher education.

Most of the faculty was made up of union officials from the then-separate AFL and CIO. They were joined soon by teachers from nearby universities such as Stanford and the University of California. The student population of some 2,600 per semester included not only workers but also housewives, young professionals, and students attending other schools. The curriculum had four major divisions: labor organization, social sciences, creative writing, and industrial arts. So well did it place emphasis upon black history and black participation that the President's Commission for Fair Employment Practices presented the CLS an award for its efforts to make "America a place where groups can live together in harmony." The school's first play, *Stevedore*, was about interracial struggles on the New Orleans waterfront. The CLS theater and the Labor School Chorus, both composed of union members, entertained widely at mass meetings, in union halls, and on picket lines.

By 1948 the school had added extension

courses in many neighborhoods and attracted celebrities for lectures, including Frank Lloyd Wright, Muriel Rukeyser, Eric Sevareid, and Orson Welles. Financial support came from many sources, including Frank Sinatra's RKO film *The House I Live In*. But in 1948 the U.S. attorney general, without notice or public hearing, placed the school on its "subversive" list. The Treasury Department, revoking the school's tax-exempt status retroactively, demanded $7,000 in back taxes. Attacks continued and in 1954 the CLS was ordered to register as a "Communist front" organization. The school fought back gamely, maintaining itself on a smaller scale (and engaging in cultural activities such as publication of Malvina Reynolds's first songs, in 1954). In May 1957—after the school had been declared by the Subversive Activities Control Board to be "Communist-dominated" and could not raise sufficient funds to fight the ruling—it closed its doors for a final time. *See also*: California

—*Pele deLappe*

REFERENCES

Cerney, Isobel. "California Labor School." In *The Cold War Against Labor*, edited by Ann Fagan Ginger, 2 vols. Berkeley: Meiklejohn Civil Liberties Institute, 1987.

CALVERTON, V. F.: see MODERN QUARTERLY

CAMPBELL, HELEN STUART (1839–1918)

Social reformer and noted home economist, Campbell became a prominent member of the Edward Bellamy Nationalist movement. Born in Lockport, New York, and raised in New York City, Campbell turned to issues of poverty and unemployment while working in a waterfront mission and recorded her observations in *Darkness and Daylight; or, Lights and Shadows of New York Life* (1891). She published several landmark studies of wage-earning women, her major subject of investigative journalism. A series of descriptive articles published originally in the *New York Tribune* were collected as *Prisoners of Poverty* (1887). A sequel, *Prisoners of Poverty Abroad*, followed in 1889. Campbell's *Women Wage-Earners* (1891) won a prize from the American Economics Association and played an instrumental role in the formation of the first consumers' leagues in the 1890s.

Campbell began her career by writing children's stories and returned intermittently to fictional forms. *Mrs. Herndon's Income* (1886) joined her concern for women to a nascent faith in socialism. This allegorical novel relates interlocking stories about two unhappily married women of different class positions. By showing how a common condition of economic dependence on men shapes their lives, Campbell concludes with a critique of capitalism and remakes each into a socialist appropriate to her station. The middle-class heroine finds companionship with a Christian socialist, her working-class alter ego with a German-born revolutionary.

Campbell wrote for such journals as the *Nationalist*, *American Fabian*, and the *Arena*. *See also*: Christian Socialism, Radical Novel 1870–1920

—*Mari Jo Buhle*

REFERENCES

Buhle, Mari Jo. *Women and American Socialism, 1870–1920*. Urbana: University of Illinois Press, 1981.

CANNON, JAMES PATRICK (1890–1974)

The foremost leader of U.S. Trotskyism, Cannon was born in Rosedale, Kansas, and grew up in a working-class family in which his mother's Catholic religious convictions coexisted with his father's deep-rooted labor radicalism (from the Knights of Labor to the Socialist Party of Eugene V. Debs). Cannon became an organizer for the Industrial Workers of the World, trained by IWW leaders William D. "Big Bill" Haywood and Vincent St. John in militant strikes, revolutionary agitation, free-speech fights, and patient working-class organizing. A midwestern leader of the SP's left wing after Russia's 1917 revolution, he helped establish the early communist movement, serving as the first national chairman of the Workers Party in 1921. Cannon was an American delegate to the Com-

Pamphlet cover by Laura Gray

munist International on five occasions, once spending eight months in Moscow on the Comintern's executive committee. In the United States he headed the International Labor Defense from 1925 to 1928, organizing campaigns to defend such "class-war prisoners" as Sacco and Vanzetti, Tom Mooney, and others. With William Z. Foster he led a faction in the American Communist Party that saw itself as more grounded in U.S. labor-radical experience.

While attending the 1928 Sixth World Congress of the Comintern, Cannon obtained a copy of Leon Trotsky's critique of Stalin's bureaucratic policies in the USSR and the Communist movement. Agreeing with the exiled Trotsky's defense of "Bolshevik-Leninist" principles, he quietly circulated the document among comrades back in the United States. This resulted in a rash of expulsions and the organization of the Communist League of America. Through a complex process of splits and fusions, in which Cannon played a leading role, the Trotskyists significantly increased their numbers and influence by the time they established the Socialist Workers Party in 1938. Cannon was its national secretary until his semi-retirement in 1953. Even afterward he played a substantial role in helping the SWP survive the intense pressures of the Cold War period. He was also active in the leadership of the Fourth International, a worldwide organization established by Trotskyists in 1938. In the early 1940s Cannon was one of the first victims of the Smith Act.

As an orator and writer, Cannon distinguished himself as an accomplished popularizer of revolutionary Marxist ideas that were strongly flavored by a blending of the Bolshevik and U.S. labor-radical traditions; for example, in *The Struggle for a Proletarian Party* (1943), *America's Road to Socialism* (1953), and *Speeches for Socialism* (1971). *See also*: Smith Act, Socialist Workers Party, Trotskyism

—*Paul Le Blanc*

REFERENCES

Breitman, George, ed. *Don't Strangle the Party: Three Letters and a Talk by James P. Cannon*. New York: Fourth Internationalist Tendency, 1986.

Cannon, James P. *The First Ten Years of American Communism*. New York: Lyle Stuart, 1962.

Evans, Les, ed. *James P. Cannon as We Knew Him, by Thirty-Three Comrades, Friends, and Relatives*. New York: Pathfinder Press, 1976.

Le Blanc, Paul, ed. *The Revolutionary Traditions of American Trotskyism*. New York: Fourth Internationalist Tendency, 1988.

Wald, Alan. *The New York Intellectuals, The Rise and Decline of the Anti-Stalinist Left, from the 1930s to the 1980s*. Chapel Hill: University of North Carolina Press, 1987.

Cape Verdean Americans

Hailing from the Cape Verde Islands situated off the west coast of Africa, Cape Verdean Americans represent the only major community of Afro-Americans to have voluntarily made the transatlantic voyage to this country. Pioneering this migration in the first half of the nineteenth century were young men from Brava Island, who were recruited by U.S. whaling vessels during stopovers in the Cape Verde Islands. Some of these recruits eventually became permanent settlers, particularly in and around the ports of New Bedford, Massachusetts, and Providence, Rhode Island. In the late nineteenth and early twentieth centuries, increasing numbers of Cape Verdean immigrants arrived as cheap sources of labor for the expanding textile mills, the cranberry industry, and the maritime-related occupations of southeastern New England. Thus began the establishment of a Cape Verdean-American community that grew by the 1980s to nearly 300,000, a figure roughly matching the total population of the Cape Verde Islands.

The earliest account of labor unrest among Cape Verdean settlers dates to 1900, when a riot at a cranberry bog was reported. Not until the Depression years did more organized action take place, led in part by the local Left. In 1933, 1,500 workers from forty bogs struck, demanding a wage increase, guaranteed employment until the end of the season, and recognition of their right to union representation. The labor dispute escalated, with charges of "outside agitators," until violence erupted. The cranberry bog struggle, primarily involving Cape Verdean immigrants, was also the first strike by agricultural workers in the history of Massachusetts. Subsequently a number of Cape Verdeans in New Bedford and elsewhere joined or supported the Communist Party. A larger number reportedly joined the Left-led International Workers Order.

Left activity among Cape Verdeans resurfaced in the late 1960s and early 1970s in two areas of political life, the New Bedford chapter of the Black Panther Party and the American Support Committee of the PAIGC, the African Party for the Independence of Guinea Bissau and Cape Verde. In the revolutionary struggle for black liberation, primarily young Cape Verdean community leaders joined members of the Afro-American population in New Bedford to form the Black Panthers. Urban riots broke out, resulting in the wounding of several Panthers and the death of a Cape Verdean youth. Two other Cape Verdeans, brothers Parky and Ross Grace, were charged with murder and imprisoned. During the early 1980s a movement to free Parky Grace—who maintained his militancy and Left politics during his years of incarceration—was initiated on grounds that he had been framed. In 1984 the group succeeded in obtaining Grace's release.

In the 1950s, under the leadership of the revolutionary Amilcar Cabral, the Cape Verde Islands and Guinea Bissau together created a national independence movement, including a protracted armed struggle to overthrow Portuguese rule. While Cape Verdean-American support for the PAIGC was never widespread, a small group of political sympathizers formed in New England to disseminate information and raise funds for the independence movement. The identification with Cabral's revolutionary ideology and with African liberation movements represented a departure from the primarily Portuguese identification that had historically characterized much of the Cape Verdean immigrant population. Since the successful revolution and the establishment of a socialist government, Cape Verdean Independence Day, July 5, 1975, has been celebrated in this country with well-attended picnics, speeches, and cultural events in New England and California. *See also*: Portuguese Americans

—*Marilyn Halter*

REFERENCES

Cabral, Amilcar. *Unity and Struggle*. New York: Monthly Review Press, 1979.

Halter, Marilyn. "Working the Cranberry Bogs: Cape Verdeans in Southeastern Massachusetts." In *Spinner: People and Culture in Southeastern Massachusetts*, vol. 3. New Bedford: Spinner Publications, 1984.

Lobban, Richard, and Marilyn Halter. *The Historical Dictionary of the Republic of Cape Verde*, African Historical Dictionaries 42. Metuchen, N.J.: Scarecrow Press, 1988.

Catholic Worker Movement

Founded on New York's Lower East Side during the depths of the Depression in 1933, the anarchistic Catholic Worker movement was the brainchild of two colorful personalities: Peter Maurin (1877–1949), an eccentric French émigré philosopher, and Dorothy Day (1897–1980), a Brooklyn-born former Wobbly and Socialist with Communist sympathies who had become a Catholic convert in 1927. It embraces four basic tenets: voluntary poverty (to build solidarity with the oppressed), and the achievement of social justice through nonviolent activism, pacifism, and personalism (a stress on the individual's responsibility to remake society through direct, personal intervention). Primary sources for the Catholic Worker movement's ideas are the life of Jesus, as recorded in the four Gospels of the New Testament, as well as papal encyclicals such as *Rerum novarum* (1891) and *Quadragesimo anno* (1931). In addition, the lives of such saints as Teresa of Avila and Thérèse of Lisieux and the writings of Fyodor Dostoyevsky, Jacques Maritain, Emmanuel Mounier, and others have been important influences. Catholic Worker Houses of Hospitality, which feed and shelter the poor, first appeared in 1933 in New York City and then throughout the United States (especially in the Northeast and Midwest) as well as, to a lesser degree, abroad. Today the Houses of Hospitality in the United States number about one hundred. Less long-lived have been the dozen or so Catholic Worker farming communes that have appeared in the United States since 1933.

Inspiring Day with his ideas, Maurin left the practical execution of them largely to her. In the Catholic church of the 1930s, such a role at the helm of a radical lay organization was rare for a woman—especially one who, like Day, was a Catholic convert, single parent, and veteran of the Old Left. For Day, the Catholic Worker movement united the secular radical activism of her youth with the traditional Catholic piety of her later adulthood. Indeed, as a Catholic Worker she continued her civil-disobedience activities, including several arrests and jailings in the period 1955–60 resulting from her protests against civilian defense air-raid drills in New York City.

A former writer for the Socialist *Call*, the *Masses*, and the *Liberator*, Day instinctively recognized the centrality of reform journalism to the Catholic Worker cause. On May Day, 1933, the first issue of the movement's tabloid-size paper, the *Catholic Worker*, was distributed in Union Square. Day remained publisher, editor, and chief writer until her death, living in voluntary poverty at St. Joseph's, the Catholic Worker House of Hospitality in New York City. She attracted artists such as Fritz Eichenberg, Adé Bethune, and Rita Corbin, and writers such as Jacques Maritain, J. F. Powers, Lewis Mumford, Claude McKay, Catherine de Hueck Doherty, Danilo Dolci, Daniel and Philip Berrigan, Thomas Merton, and Michael Harrington. Through the Spanish Civil War, World War II (when internal discord over the pacifism issue threatened to split the movement and subscriptions plummeted to 50,500), the Korean War, and the Vietnam War, Day hewed the editorial line to social justice and pacifism. Circulation peaked at about 100,000, where it remains today, and the *Catholic Worker* may be considered one of the most significant (and editorially consistent) advocacy publications in U.S. history.

Over the years, the radical stance of the Catholic Worker movement and its paper has attracted the close scrutiny of both the Catholic church hierarchy and J. Edgar Hoover's FBI. However, the *Catholic Worker* has survived to challenge several generations of Americans to strengthen their commitment to social justice and peace. It has invigorated Catholic, non-Catholic, and secular justice and peace activism. *See also*: Day, Dorothy; Irish Americans

—*Nancy L. Roberts*

REFERENCES

Coy, Patrick G., ed. *A Revolution of the Heart: Essays on the Catholic Worker.* Philadelphia: Temple University Press, 1988.

Klejment, Anne, and Alice Klejment. *Dorothy Day and "The Catholic Worker": A Bibliography and Index.* New York: Garland, 1986.

Miller, William D. *A Harsh and Dreadful Love: Dorothy Day and the Catholic Worker Movement.* New York: Liveright, 1973.

———. *Dorothy Day: A Biography.* San Francisco: Harper and Row, 1982.

Piehl, Mel. *Breaking Bread: The Catholic Worker and the Origin of Catholic Radicalism in America.* Philadelphia: Temple University Press, 1982.

Roberts, Nancy L. *Dorothy Day and the "Catholic Worker."* Albany: State University of New York Press, 1984.

Stoughton, Judith L. *Proud Donkey of Schaerbeeck: Ade Bethune, Catholic Worker Artist.* St. Cloud, MN: North Star Press, 1988.

Chaplin, Ralph H. (1887–1961)

Radical labor artist, journalist, songwriter, and poet, Ralph Hosea Chaplin was born in Cloud County, Kansas, in 1887 but grew up primarily in Chicago. A working artist interested in socialism and poetry, Chaplin and his wife, Edith, formed a close friendship with William D. "Big Bill" Haywood in 1907 that lasted until the latter's death in 1928. Chaplin formally joined the Industrial Workers of the World in Chicago in 1913; by then, he had visited revolutionary Mexico and reported U.S. labor strikes for radical journals. In 1915 he wrote the famous labor anthem "Solidarity Forever" and early in 1917 became editor of the Wobbly paper *Solidarity*. He was among the more than 150 IWW leaders who were charged and convicted under the Espionage Act during the repression accompanying U.S. involvement in World War I. Sentenced to twenty years, Chaplin was imprisoned at the federal penitentiary in Leavenworth, Kansas. Out on bond in 1919 pending appeal, he traveled nationally supporting IWW defense efforts and reported the Red Scare trial and trumped-up murder convictions of the Wobblies at Centralia, Washington. Holding the general IWW position of wariness toward Communism, he declined to join Haywood and several others who forfeited bond and fled to the USSR in 1921. Returning to prison, he was pardoned in 1923 along with the other Wobbly victims of the federal government.

Chaplin actively backed various radical defense endeavors and, maintaining his IWW position, became increasingly critical of the Communists. From 1932 to 1936, he edited the Wobbly *Industrial Worker* but left the IWW in 1936, feeling it could never revive. In 1937 he edited the *Voice of the Federation* (Maritime Federation of the Pacific Coast), but conflicts with Communists resulted in his ouster. In 1941 Chaplin began editing the AFL *Tacoma Labor Advocate*, continuing this for half a decade. He then published his extensive autobiography, *Wobbly*, in 1948; converted to Roman Catholicism; continued to back grass-roots unionism and libertarian radicalism and to publish poetry; and lent his efforts to American Indian rights. Chaplin died in Tacoma in 1961. *See also*: Industrial Workers of the World

Cover of pamphlet written by Ralph Chaplin; cover drawing by Ralph Chaplin

—*John R. Salter, Jr.*

REFERENCES

Chaplin, Ralph. *Wobbly: The Rough and Tumble Story of an American Radical*. Chicago: University of Chicago Press, 1948.

———. "Why I Wrote 'Solidarity Forever'." *American West* (January 1968).

Salter, Jr. John R., "Reflections on Ralph Chaplin, the Wobblies, and Organizing in the Save the World Business—Then and Now." *Pacific Historian* (Summer 1986).

Chicago Star

This Left weekly tabloid (1946–1948) was supported primarily by the progressive unions of the Chicago area such as Farm Equipment,

United Auto Workers, United Packinghouse, Fur and Leather, Food and Tobacco, Longshoremen and Mill, Mine. Left fraternal bodies, including then-important affiliates of the International Workers Order, as well as the Communist Party of Illinois, also vigorously supported the paper. Grant Oakes, international president of FE, was elected president of the People's Publishing Association. At its peak, the paper attained a 25,000 circulation, with special enlarged editions for independent election campaigns.

Issues, news, and editorial coverage of the *Star* reflected the domestic and international concerns of the postwar recovery period. The paper highlighted the postwar strikes, and the problems of inflation, unemployment, housing, and rent control that these strikes reflected. It documented racial discrimination in Chicago and elsewhere, and championed equality. It called for intensified unionization, defense of civil liberties, and greater independent political activity. The *Star* warned in an editorial that postwar U.S. foreign policy was leading to the "preservation of the prewar status quo or its replacement by a new American big money imperialism."

After nearly two years of publication, the *Star* agreed to sell the paper to a newly formed group within the emerging Progressive Party. Renamed the *Illinois Standard*, it was short-lived, and merged into the national progressive publication the *National Guardian*. In that sense, the *Chicago Star* offered a preview and an important boost to the *National Guardian* as well as to the PP throughout the Midwest. *See also*: *National Guardian*, Progressive Party

—*William Sennett*

REFERENCES

Belfage, Cedric, and James Aronson. *Something to Guard—The Stormy Life of the "National Guardian," 1948–1967*. New York: Columbia University Press, 1978.

Children's Literature (English Language)

Both the Socialists and Communists produced children's literature to transmit radical ideas to children. During the first half of the twentieth century more than forty children's books were published whose characters, plots, and settings were intended to help children identify with the radical movement, and to absorb its ideology and culture.

The first socialist children's book, Nicholas Klein's *Socialist Primer* (1908), was published by the *Appeal to Reason* newspaper and was modeled on the simple school reader. Following Klein, John Spargo's *Socialist Readings for Children* (1909) included short biographies of Robert Owen and Karl Marx, descriptions of socialist meetings, and a "little talk on evolution."

Caroline Nelson's *Nature Talks on Economics* (1912) and Mary Marcy's *Stories of the Cave People* (1912) and *Rhymes of Early Jungle Folk* (1922) all used science to explain the logic of socialism to children. In Nelson's book the lessons of biological evolution and cooperation are used to show children why socialism is the next, necessary step in social evolution. Mary Marcy, an editor of the *International Socialist Review*, used a kind of socialist anthropology, borrowed from Engels and Lewis Henry Morgan, to show how human society originated and evolved, and to make the point that further social evolution was necessary.

The first Communist children's book, *Fairy Tales for Worker's Children* (1925), by Herminia zur Muhlen, was originally published in German. It was followed by *Battle in the Barnyard* (1932), by Helen Kay, which contained stories of working-class children engaged in political struggle, as well as fables and fairy tales with socialist morals.

The Communists published the works of Geoffrey Trease, a British author who later went on to become quite well-known for his mainstream historical fiction for young adults, the first among radical children's books to move beyond the simplistic Sunday-school lesson or fairy tale. *Bows Against the Barons* (1934), for example, was a radical retelling of the story of Robin Hood, while in *Call to Arms* (1935) three young people in a Central American country are drawn into a revolution.

U.S. Communist writers during the 1930s

and 1940s also created stories for young adolescents. Eric Lucas's *Voyage Thirteen* (1946) described the adventures of two boys serving on a merchant marine ship in the closing days of World War II. Its form is similar to many boys' stories of ship life, except that the seamen include a Spanish republican, a militant Afro-American, and a Communist, who teach the boys about life from a class-conscious, antifascist perspective. Jean Karsavina's *Tree by the Waters* (1948) is about the ethnic and class conflict between Polish-American workers and Yankees in a New England mill village.

The attention given to biological evolution in the books by Caroline Nelson and Mary Marcy was an expression of the socialist belief that evidence for evolutionary change in the natural world supported the possibility, and necessity, of social evolution. In only one Communist children's book, *Science and History for Boys and Girls* (1932), by the former Episcopal archbishop-turned-Communist William Montgomery Brown, did Darwinism play as important a role.

The Communist children's books were more focused on teaching children about class divisions in capitalist society and the importance of activism in the radical movement. Furthermore the Communist children's books contained more on current social problems, and included ethnically and racially diverse characters.

The children's literature published by the Socialist and Communist movements was an example of how radicals in the United States attempted to provide an alternative culture for their children to grow up into. The authors of these books believed that the ideas of socialism were accessible to children, and that exposing children to radical ideas when they were young would predispose them to political radicalism as they grew older. *See also*: Yiddish Left, Yiddish Language Schools

—*Paul C. Mishler*

REFERENCES

Mishler, Paul C. "*The Littlest Proletariat: American Communists and Their Children, 1922–1950.*" Ph.D. diss., Boston University, 1988.

Miegs, Cornelia et al. *A Critical History of Children's Literature*. New York: Macmillan, 1969.

Chinese Americans

Chinese immigrants came to the United States in large numbers during the California gold rush in the late 1840s, and were employed as cheap labor by the railway companies in the 1860s and 1870s. The Chinese Exclusion Act of 1882 restricted the immigration of Chinese laborers to the United States for more than half a century. Until World War II, most Chinese Americans lived in ghettos—the so-called Chinatowns—in the big cities and were engaged in low-paying jobs such as restaurant and laundry work.

The experience of being excluded, exploited, and discriminated against in America strengthened Chinese Americans' tendency to look to China for their future. Thus, the first Chinese-American socialist/Left organizations were inspired by the revolutionary movements in China, and they accepted Marxism as a solution not only to the problems that existed in the Chinese-American community but also to those that their motherland confronted. This China-orientation made the Chinese-American Left vulnerable to the vagaries of Chinese politics, and political splits in China always caused Chinese Americans to divide into factions whose history was complicated and often confusing.

The radical organizations that emerged in the Chinese-American community in the 1920s to support the Chinese Revolution included San Francisco's Sanminzhuyi Yanjiushe (Association for the Study of the Three Principles of the People, 1926; later reorganized and renamed the Kung Yu Club, 1927, and Chinese Workers Club, 1928), San Francisco Chinese Students Club (1927), and the Grand Revolutionary Alliance of Chinese Workers and Peasants (1927, reorganized as the Chinese Anti-Imperialist Alliance of America [CAIA] in 1930). The CAIA's organ, the *Chinese Vanguard* (Philadelphia, 1929–30; New York, 1930–38), was the first Marxist Left weekly newspaper published by Chinese Americans, and it received some help from the CPUSA. Some Chinese leftists joined the CPUSA and established a branch of the Party in San Francisco's Chinatown in the late 1920s.

In the 1930s the Chinese-American Left successfully combined its efforts to organize Chinese workers to survive the hard times of the Depression with its Popular Front movement to save China from Japan's invasion. The Left also inspired and promoted the establishment of many labor organizations. Among them the Chinese Workers Mutual Aid Association in San Francisco, and the Chinese Hand Laundry Alliance (CHLA) in New York City were the most influential. The CHLA provided essential support to establish the first Chinese radical daily newspaper—the *China Daily News* (1940–present). The Chinese Youth Clubs in both S.F. and N.Y.C. were also active in supporting China's war efforts against Japan and participated in the American youth movement. In addition they initiated many cultural programs and activities.

Even in the peak years of their influence in the Chinese community, leftist activities weakened but could never shatter the established power structure in U.S. Chinatowns. Nor was the Left ever able to seize the leadership of the Chinese community or successfully mobilize the masses as they hoped to do. There were many reasons for this: limited membership, factionalism, dogmatism, a militant tone that was alien to most ordinary Chinatown residents.

After the outbreak of the Korean War, Chinese leftists were harassed by U.S. government agencies because of their sympathetic attitude to the New China. Many of them were China-born and subject to immigration officials' endless investigations and harassments. Some were deported or jailed, many were forced to remain silent. Their organizational membership declined and most of their newspapers closed. By the mid-1950s, many Chinese left-wing organizations were dissolved.

The 1960s and early 1970s saw the emergence of New Left activists in Chinese-American communities. They were inspired by the civil rights movement and consisted of native-born students and professionals. Unlike the Old Left, these New Left activists concentrated more on community issues and sought more direct participation in American politics. *See also*: Asian Studies

—*Renqiu Yu*

REFERENCES

Kwong, Peter. *Chinatown, New York, Labor and Politics, 1930–50*. New York: Monthly Review Press, 1979.

Lai, Him Mark. "A Historical Survey of the Chinese Left in America." In *Counterpoint*, edited by Emma Gee. Los Angeles: UCLA Asian American Studies Center, 1976.

Chomsky, Noam (b. 1929)

In the 1960s–1980s arguably the foremost public, radical critic of U.S. foreign policy and the ideological system that supports it, Chomsky has also become one of the most- (or best-) hated radical writers of the era. He was a veritable symbol for the "Vietnam Syndrome" of popular revulsion at U.S. intervention into and subversion of the Third World.

A Depression child of liberal, Zionist parents, Chomsky attended the University of Pennsylvania, from which he gained a Ph.D. in 1955, and studied linguistics with Zellig Harris. Vaguely anarchistic (or anti-Leninist) in orientation, he lived in an Israeli kibbutz in 1953 and planned a long-term settlement but abandoned the idea. He emerged during the later 1950s and 1960s as perhaps the most internationally famous linguistic theorist, literally changing the nature of linguistic study from classification of speech elements to a major challenge of behavior science models. His "generative grammar," explained in *Syntactic Structures* (1957) and other works, has been widely called the "Chomskyan Revolution" in thought.

Chomsky was first drawn into public political debate by the Vietnam War. His writings on Indochina, especially *American Power and the New Mandarins* (1969), were among the most rigorous and well documented of any written for a general audience. He became an important political speaker, particularly but not only in the Boston area. He also became a much-admired figure by the New Left because of his uncompromising moralism and his anarchist-influenced sense of social alternatives. His sympathetic treatment of the Asian revolutionaries inspired a special admiration among blossoming New Left Asian scholars. It also inspired hatred in the White House (he was placed on Nixon's "Enemies

List"), and the beginnings of attacks upon him from Cold War liberals who viewed his sympathy for American foes as proof of Chomsky's "totalitarianism."

As the Vietnam War wound down, Chomsky turned his attention to the roots of foreign policy, the dynamics of the Cold War, and the role of the intelligentsia. While he followed other Left scholars in an examination of unequal exchange and U.S. support to Third World dictatorships, Chomsky offered original insights into the logic and role of the State in decisively reducing human rights. Next, Chomsky examined the sources of the Cold War, arguing that it was in fact functional for the superpowers both as a means of popular mobilization and (particularly in the United States) a technique of economic management. He also sought to define precisely the content and limits of the doctrinal system to which all "responsible" criticism of U.S. foreign policy must conform, i.e., the assumption of American good intentions and the ascription of accompanying atrocities to error rather than modus operandi.

With *Towards a New Cold War* (1982), Chomsky had become a pariah of neo-liberalism, especially Jewish neo-liberalism. Chomsky's entanglement in a freedom-of-expression case involving a French scholar whose work denied the Holocaust offered the *New Republic* among other journals the opportunity to attack Chomsky as an enemy of Western values and of Jewish life. He ceased to be invited as contributor to major liberal outlets, and reviews of his books from those outlets virtually disappeared.

Chomsky's recent attention to the Middle East and Central America has deepened both admiration for him on the Left and hatred of him in neo-liberal circles. As an imminent critic of existing Zionism who views liberal intellectuals' uncritical support of Israel as similar to uncritical support of Stalinist Russia in the 1930s–1940s, he has been fearless. As a supporter of Third World causes in the face of post-1960s apathy and repugnance, he has been unbendingly strident. As a radical scholar with roots in the anarchist, moralist critique of the Security State, he has remained unique.

See also: Anarchism, New Left, Peace Movements

—*Paul Buhle*

REFERENCES

Chomsky, Noam. *The Chomsky Reader*. New York: Pantheon, 1987.

Chomsky, Noam. *Language and Politics*. Edited by C. P. Otero. Montreal: Black Rose Books, 1989.

CHRISTIAN SOCIALISM

Nearly forgotten until quite recently, Christian Socialism has played a vital role in life and on the American Left. Several of the most popular and widely read U.S. theologians of the first half of this century were outspoken Christian Socialists, Walter Rauschenbusch (1861–1918) and Reinhold Niebuhr (1892–1971) above all. While rarely holding high party (or union) offices, Christian Socialists have served to connect radical ideas with sections of the working class—especially the

Cover of "Bad Bishop" Brown's most popular book

poor and racial minorities—and with a wide stratum of intellectuals.

William James, Sr., was the first prominent American to argue (in 1848, that fateful year) that the goals of Christianity and socialism are identical. Christians heavily populated the utopian socialist settlements across the continent. But with a few exceptions, abolitionism absorbed and drained the reform energies of mainstream northern churches at midcentury. In 1872 a group of Bostonians led by the Congregationalist Rev. Jesse H. Jones founded the Christian Labor Union and published the first two Christian Socialist periodicals, *Equity* and the *Labor Balance*. These institutions had faded by 1879.

During the 1880s, a large number of crusading ministers joined reform and radical movements. The vast majority of the Social Gospel advocates opposed radical ideologies. But a minority of New England Social Gospelers, including Jones, spread the evangel of Christian Socialism. W. D. P. Bliss, a Massachusetts Episcopal pastor, became a prominent figure in the New England Knights of Labor, and later editor of the *Dawn: A Magazine of Christian Socialism and Record of Social Progress*. The reform writings of Richard T. Ely, and the utopian burst of activity following the publication of Edward Bellamy's *Looking Backward*, helped ministers such as Bliss develop both public interest and Christian approbation for a cooperative, spiritually inspired solution to the "Social Question."

Christian Socialism (intermixed with Bellamy nationalism, British-inspired Fabian socialism, and radical offshoots of Christian Science) had a special appeal to women reformers repelled by the class-struggle doctrines of the generally patriarchal immigrant socialist milieu. Several of the most prominent women leaders of the day, including Woman's Christian Temperance Union leader Frances Willard and Civil War–era Sanitary Commission leader Mary Livermore, publicly announced themselves for a cooperative solution. Vida Scudder, English professor at Wellesley College with extended experience in the settlement house movement, would continue these themes of class reconciliation in religious understanding for decades into the twentieth century.

In 1901 Congregationalist minister George D. Herron (1862–1925) played a leading role in the convention that united various rival factions of the Socialist Party. As the *Worker*, a contemporary socialist weekly, noted, his selection as temporary chair of the party "was unanimous and satisfactory to all parties. . . . He steered the convention through some threatening breakers during the opening and most trying hours. . . ." One of the most effective agitators of the day, he did much to bridge the gap between presumably "atheistic" immigrant socialists and frequently evangelical American radical reformers.

Although Herron lost his public position and his ministry due to a divorce scandal, the ranks of American-born socialists, especially in the Plains States and the Southwest, filled with churched and unchurched Christians. While much socialist rhetoric (including that of Eugene V. Debs) turned upon Christian metaphors, organized Christian Socialism had a special role to play. The *Christian Socialist*, published by the Reverend Edward Ellis Carr in Danville, then Chicago, Illinois, achieved a circulation of 20,000, including 2,000 ministers, and led to the formation of the Christian Socialist Fellowship (1906–17) with twenty-seven chapters and 1,500 members. The *Christian Socialist*, devoting special numbers to various denominations, shrewdly played to its appreciative audience. But it also took moral positions advanced even for the socialist movement.

Of these, its antiracism was easily the most important. Nearly all the early black socialists of note were Christian ministers, such as George Washington Woodbey (1854–?), a San Diego Baptist, contributor to the *Christian Socialist*, and former slave. One of Woodbey's converts, George Slater, achieved special prominence. Pastor of the Zion Tabernacle in Chicago and active in that city's Socialist branches, he was elected to the executive committee of the Christian Socialist Fellowship and made CSF Secretary for the Colored Race. Slater published several popular socialist pamphlets, notably *Blackmen, Strike for Liberty*, and also a prosocialist monthly, the *Western Evangel*.

Rev. Carr, accusing a Socialist Party national figure of moral turpitude, ran afoul of the organization. Expelled and then restored by the national party, he was expelled again by the immigrant-dominated Chicago party branches. In any case, much of the Christian Socialist milieu left the SP in order to support the First World War, while a small section of young Christian intellectuals became socialists as a result of their wartime pacifist commitments. The ranks of religious-influenced rural and semirural Socialists, their newspapers repressed through government action and their faith shattered by the precipitous decline of the SP, turned quiescent or joined the farmer-labor movements active during the 1920s.

But in a diminished SP—its militantly atheistic wing now a part of the Communist movement—the prestige of Christian Socialism grew relatively. Former Presbyterian minister Norman Thomas, the party's perennial presidential candidate from 1928 onward, imparted a spiritualistic or moral tone to even the most economic-political message. Around Thomas ranged such institutions as the *World Tomorrow*, a highly influential monthly drawing the energies of Christian pacifists and veteran travelers through the impoverished colonial world. At the local level, many Socialist branches gained the active participation of clergy, especially during the Depression and the years shortly before the U.S. entry into World War II. Especially in the South, where a handful of Christian Socialists and Communists such as Claude and Joyce Williams, James Dombrowski, and Howard Kester headed important political institutions, the message carried a strongly interracial gospel.

For the broader Christian public, the works of Rauschenbusch and Niebuhr exerted significant influence. Never joining the SP, Rauschenbusch argued vigorously for the idea of socialism and sometimes for public support of the party. Niebuhr, an editor of the *World Tomorrow*, founded in 1931 the Fellowship of Christian Socialists and served as editor of its publication, *Radical Religion*. A prolific writer, teacher, preacher, and activist, he resigned from the SP in 1940 in order to support armed resistance to fascism but remained a socialist until 1948. Considered thereafter to be a theological mentor of the Cold War neoconservatism, he returned to dissent with belated opposition to the U.S. war in Vietnam. His successors at the Union Theological Seminary published *Christianity and Crisis*, an influential monthly that bridged the religious gap between Old and New Left. Meanwhile, one section of Christian Socialists, led in part by former New Haven SP luminary (and CIO chaplain) Willard Uphaus, militantly opposed the Cold War and sought to guide Christian Socialism toward Soviet-American reconciliation. Others, dedicated pacifists, participated in antiwar and anti-Bomb activities and organizations such as the Fellowship for Reconciliation.

Christian Socialists, as individuals, played a notable role in the civil rights and 1960s antiwar movements, but remained ideologically in the background. With the collapse of the 1960s movements, they assumed greater importance in the 1970s, around such campaigns as the United Farmworkers' grape boycott and the empowerment of women clergy. By the later 1970s, they had become key backers of Third World support movements such as the North American Committee on Latin America. Their prestige and ideological clarity arose with the forceful appearance of liberation theology movements in Latin America, Africa, Asia, and the Philippines. Christians for Socialism (1974–83), a network of activists, never achieved wide support. But Christian Socialist ideas found their way into major denominational publications, and fairly dominated such Left-leaning journals as *Sojourners*, the *Witness*, and *Christianity and Crisis*. The Democratic Socialists of America has maintained a Religion and Socialism Commission, and published the newsletter *Religious Socialism*. *See also*: Liberation Theology; Pacifism; Peace Movements; Soviet-American Friendship; Spiritualism; Thomas, Norman; World Tomorrow

—*Paul Buhle, John Cort*

REFERENCES

Cort, John. *Christian Socialism*. Maryknoll, N.Y.: Orbis Press, 1988.

Quint, Howard H. *The Forging of American Socialism*. Chapel Hill: University of North Carolina Press, 1953.

Civil Rights Congress

It was called the most successful "Communist front" of all time. Dashiell Hammett, author of *The Thin Man* and longtime companion of Lillian Hellman, went to jail because of his association with it. Paul Robeson was stoned at Peekskill as he raised money for it. What stirred such passion was the Civil Rights Congress (CRC), which during its existence from 1946 to 1956 fought for and established a number of civil rights and liberties rulings that expanded the rights of all in the United States.

CRC was formed in the early postwar period when the impending Cold War and McCarthyism could be sensed but had not yet been established. It was formed as a result of a merger among the International Labor Defense (which was catapulted to prominence as a result of its vigorous defense of the Scottsboro Nine and Angelo Herdon, among others), the National Negro Congress (an early effort to form a "Black United Front" among Afro-Americans), and the National Federation for Constitutional Liberties. Early on they developed a specialty in fighting "black" and "red" cases.

One of CRC's earliest black cases was that of Willie McGee, Mississippi truckdriver whose white lover accused him of rape after her husband discovered their affair. In their attempt to save McGee's life, CRC launched a national and international campaign that made his name a household word. They helped to publicize the fact that rape of white women had been used historically as a reason to lynch or execute black men. A significant percentage of their cases had this theme, including the Martinsville Seven—another one of their more significant cases. Even in their declining days, they were still able to mobilize masses around the case of black teenager Emmett Till, the Chicago resident who was lynched on an ill-fated trip to Mississippi in 1955 after allegedly "getting fresh" with a white woman. The flip side of this emphasis was their defense of Rosa Lee Ingram, the black female sharecropper from Georgia who was assaulted by her white landlord, whom she then fatally dispatched. This emphasis touched a raw nerve in the national consciousness among blacks and whites, as CRC linked sensitive questions of race, sex and exploitation.

Long before Montgomery, CRC was "softening up" the racists in the Deep South for the subsequent onslaught led by Rev. Martin Luther King, Jr. In the early 1950s they led "Freedom Rides" to Virginia to save the Martinsville Seven. But their success in bringing domestic racism to the international arena may have been their most significant contribution. In the postwar period Jim Crow was becoming an aching Achilles heel in the execution of U.S. foreign policy. How could hearts and minds be won in an increasingly "colored" world when people of color were being subjected to such pernicious discrimination here? CRC seized upon this contradiction when it published the landmark study *We Charge Genocide*, which detailed the heinous crimes committed against Afro-Americans and was filed at the United Nations. Reprinted in many languages and many thousands of copies, this work was an international embarrassment for the U.S. government and was a factor in bringing down the walls of Jim Crow.

Still, as dramatic and riveting as their "black" cases were, perhaps more controversial were their "red" cases. CRC was the major organization fighting the Smith Act frameups, the McCarran Act, the Communist Control Act, the House Un-American Activities Committee, and the panoply of laws and institutions formed to enforce a Cold War consensus. Their opinion was that defense of the Communist Party was the first line in the defense of civil liberties generally. Hence, they were avid in their defense of the CP leadership, which ultimately involved imprisonment for scores of activists on the grounds of "teaching and advocating" Marxism-Leninism—not seeking to overthrow the government, as is commonly misunderstood. Despite this gargantuan labor, a number of Communists in CRC felt that not enough attention was paid to these cases or to repression of the labor movement, as evidenced by the passage of the Taft-Hartley Act. Others felt that the battle for Afro-American equality was the cutting edge in the battle for democracy generally, thus justifying this emphasis. The fact that the beginning of the end for HUAC came when they brought their traveling road-show to Atlanta and encountered a united civil rights leadership does lend some credence to the last notion.

The practical and theoretical battles were conducted within an organization that at its zenith may have had 10,000 members, during a time when progressive organizations were not proliferating. The CRC's strongest chapters were in such critically important cities as New York, Detroit, Seattle, the San Francisco Bay Area, and Los Angeles. Though it was derided as a "Communist front," a number of the Party's internal weaknesses did not unduly influence CRC negatively. For example, during a time when the CP was conducting a vigorous campaign to uproot white chauvinism that was later deemed by the leadership to have been conducted improperly, the brunt of the deleterious impact managed to escape CRC despite—or perhaps because of—their own vigorous campaigns on behalf of McGee, Ingram et al.

CRC had titanic clashes with both the ACLU and the NAACP. "Free speech" for racists and the Ku Klux Klan was a bone of contention with the ACLU, though that organization's ingrained anticommunism certainly played a role in their conflicts. CRC's conflicts with the NAACP were more complex. That group was avowedly "anti-imperialist" and experienced tremendous growth during those days of lessened anticommunism, 1941–45. This was the time when black Communist Ben Davis was elected to the New York City Council from Harlem with the support of NAACP executive secretary Roy Wilkins; but the alliance was not able to withstand the blows of the Cold War. Nevertheless, just as Booker T. Washington publicly disdained battles against aspects of Jim Crow while secretly funding them, the NAACP maintained forms of cooperation with CRC while hewing to the official line publicly. This was aided by the contradictions of Jim Crow itself; Wilkins lived across the hall from CRC leader William Patterson in a segregated Harlem apartment building, 409 Edgecombe Avenue.

The U.S. government, a major target of CRC broadsides, was a major factor in bringing on their dissolution. The Subversive Activities Control Board, in particular, forced the liquidation not only of CRC but also the Council on African Affairs (the premier organization pushing decolonization and antiapartheid) and other Left-led organizations. Yet, there was significant continuity between CRC and the post-Montgomery movement, as many who had honed their skills fighting for McGee went on to press for the Civil Rights Act of 1964, the Voting Rights Act of 1965, and counsel the Black Panther Party. This was CRC's ultimate legacy. *See also*: Civil Rights; Communist Party; Patterson, William L.

—Gerald Horne

REFERENCES

Horne, Gerald. *Communist Front? The Civil Rights Congress, 1946–56*. Rutherford: Fairleigh Dickinson University Press, 1987.

CIVIL RIGHTS MOVEMENT

The movement to uproot segregation laws in the South and obtain full civil liberties for African Americans in all states was sparked by a 1954 Supreme Court decision that declared segregated schools unconstitutional. Despite the seemingly modest aim of simply obtaining rights already guaranteed by existing federal law, the movement's goals could not be realized without a fundamental change in American society. Massive popular resistance to that change was immediate and was vigorously supported by local and state governments, which often tolerated antimovement vigilante violence. The federal government, while ostensibly supportive of the movement, usually intervened belatedly and halfheartedly.

From the onset the civil rights movement was "charged" with being Communist-inspired and subversive. The struggle would indeed attract many radical activists, and rebels of varied ideological orientation and in specific locales would reactivate radical-liberal alliances destabilized by McCarthyism. Three major currents came to dominate a multifaceted and national movement. The largest group accepted the leadership of the Rev. Martin Luther King, Jr., and his Southern Christian Leadership Conference (SCLC), which was founded in 1957 following the successful Montgomery bus

boycott of 1955–56. From this general orbit came the younger and more dynamic Student Nonviolent Coordinating Committee (SNCC), founded in 1960. Separate from the two southern-based organizations but converging with them over a period of time were black separatist currents, mainly headquartered in northern cities and informally recognizing the Harlem-based Malcolm X as their major spokesperson.

Martin Luther King first came to prominence when the leadership of the Montgomery bus boycott was all but forced on him. Many of his closest advisers were also Baptist ministers, but two, Bayard Rustin and Stanley D. Levison, were representatives of what came to be called the Old Left. Rustin, who had been a Communist for a brief period in the 1930s, was closely allied with the most militant pacifist organizations, while Levison had been a fundraiser for Communist Party causes for many years and still retained informal ties to the party.

The tradition represented by Rustin was not new to King. He had studied the ideas of Walter Rauschenbusch, Reinhold Niebuhr, Mahatma Gandhi, and A. J. Muste while in college and had concluded that the Hegelian dialectic could be interpreted in a Christian context. King believed nonviolent resistance to evil could activate the moral center of humanity, effecting a profound and lasting change in human relationships. This view would be the hallmark of his political commitment. Rustin provided King with a direct link to the established pacifist Left and served as a logistics officer for specific campaigns such as the historic 1963 march on Washington.

Levison embodied the Popular Front approach in which the interests of labor, the nation, and racial minorities were seen as convergent. With ties to various elements of the New Deal coalition, he was a highly sophisticated and successful fundraiser. A nearly irreplaceable figure in the early years, he was sought for advice on all major problems, and like Rustin, he edited some of King's writing. When the issue of his CP links was raised by the FBI, the Kennedy brothers forced King to promise that he would cease consulting with Levison, but King continued to do so in a semisecretive fashion. Levison ended his informal CP ties in 1963.

Another SCLC staffer with Communist links was Jack O'Dell, a black organizer recruited by Levison. O'Dell had been active in Communist causes throughout the 1950s, and FBI reports stated he was a concealed CP member with a seat on the National Committee. For a short time, Levison and O'Dell constituted the New York SCLC, and various appointments and contacts flowed through their office. O'Dell eventually resigned his post under the pressure of the Communist issue because SCLC was determined to avoid being labeled "subversive."

King never made a public statement that he was a socialist, but he had questioned capitalist ethics as early as college and often told his aides that he was indeed a socialist. Under Levison's advice he adopted the term "socialized democrat" for public utterances. King was greatly impressed by the social democracy he witnessed in Scandinavia when he accepted the Nobel Peace Prize (1964) and in the United States he had contacts with socialists such as Michael Harrington. Late in 1967 various radicals approached him about heading a third-party effort, a course he ultimately rejected.

The war in Vietnam was another radicalizing force on King. Conservative civil rights leaders urged him to remain silent on the issue because opposition to the war would further strain the already fragile federal support for the movement and would surely alienate some segments of the general public. Although he held the view that the war was a moral blight for many years, he did not make a public statement until 1966. After that his leadership of parades and other antiwar efforts brought him more deeply into the orbit of traditional radical-liberal coalitions.

Leftist influences, however, had been present in King's movement from its very genesis. Rosa Parks, the woman whose refusal to move to the back of the bus set off the Montgomery boycott, had previously attended training classes at the radical Highlander Folk School, and a major boycott organizer, E. D. Nixon, had been a lifelong associate of A. Philip Randolph. SCLC would have continuing contacts with Highlander and with Left support groups such as the Southern Conference Educational Fund (SCEF). Although the NAACP and other established civil rights organizations had expelled Communists from their ranks to accommodate McCarthyism, any local campaign was likely to include radical veterans of battles in which the CP had played a major role.

The perspective of SNCC was different. Rather than concentrating on building campaigns around a single issue and a celebrated leader, SNCC organized communities for long-term structural change. SNCC organizers lived in the communities being mobilized and tried to develop indigenous leaders. Nonviolence was less a philosophical imperative than a chosen tactical option given that the immediate opposition was often led by sheriffs, police chiefs, or officers of the National Guard. Rather than taking counsel from the Old Left, SNCC proved to be a model for some of the founders of the New Left. Tom Hayden, for one, has stated that SDS's concepts of participatory democracy and organizing oneself out of the organizer's job were directly inspired by SNCC. A number of early SDS activists—Casey Hayden, Betty Garman, Jim Onsonis, Bob Zellner, and Maria Varela—had first been active in SNCC.

Unlike SCLC, which was terrified of being tarred as Communist-dominated, SNCC adopted a policy of barring no one on ideological grounds. Against the advice of and occasional threats by established leaders, SNCC accepted the assistance of radical groups such as the National Lawyers Guild. FBI reports stated that children of prominent Communists could be found working on SNCC projects and that SNCC facilities carried literature from many radical groups, including the CP. The FBI also noted that SNCC knowingly cooperated with the CP-sponsored W. E. B. Dubois Clubs during demonstrations at Texas Southern University, allowed the Socialist Workers Party and its youth group, the Young Socialist Alliance, to raise funds on its behalf, and sent representatives to SDS conventions.

The origins of SNCC, however, had not been ideological. SNCC had come into existence as a response to segregation laws in the South and what was perceived as inadequate militancy on the part of SCLC. Disappointed that the United States failed to live up to its ideals when called to account, and themselves victims of state-sponsored and state-tolerated violence, SNCC activitists sought philosophical and ideological grounding. Frantz Fanon and Che Guevara were more widely read than Marx, and current events in China, Africa, and Cuba seemed far more relevant than the October Revolution. SNCC representatives accepted invitations to visit North Vietnam, Cuba, the Dominican Republic, Japan, Israel, and the USSR. SNCC became involved with the War Crimes Tribunal headed by Bertrand Russell and administered at the time by Trotskyist Ralph Schoenman. The most frequent of the SNCC travelers was Stokely Carmichael, who began to shape a Pan-Africanist Marxist perspective. His most dramatic foreign appearance was at a congress of intellectuals held in Havana in 1967.

No single ideology ever captured the SNCC core. In some areas of Mississippi, activists were inclined to the perspectives of the Industrial Workers of the World, while in Atlanta, one of the major SNCC centers, influential individuals had ties with the Revolutionary Action Movement. At the same time black Trotskyists were active in SNCC's National Black Antiwar Antidraft Union, other SNCC members attended youth conferences in Moscow. This internal search for a unifying political perspective ultimately was resolved not by the adoption of a revolutionary theory but by the sense that the time had come for an all-black organization whose message to would-be white allies was to organize their own communities. This concept emerged into public view as the "Black Power" slogan of 1966 and soon swept the entire civil rights movement.

The appeal of Black Power was directly related to the murders, bombings, beatings, and other brutal reactions to the voter registration drives, the failure of the federal government to protect the constitutional rights of activists, and the rejection of the Mississippi Freedom Democratic Party at the 1964 National Democratic Convention. Disillusionment with what could be expected from white power-structures also amounted to a de facto repudiation of nonviolence. In 1967 SNCC came out in support of the Puerto Rican independence movement and signed "treaties" of cooperation with Hopi leader Tomas Banyaca and Mexican-American rebel Reyes Tijerina. But Black Power cost SNCC dearly. Trusted white organizers had to leave and former sources of financial support dried up. Most damaging of all was the disaffection of large segments of a black southern constituency whose desire remained integration, not voluntary separatism.

If SNCC were to survive, it would have to find a new base of African-American support. Stokely Carmichael believed the future lay in an alliance with the Black Panther Party founded in Oakland, California, in 1966. The BPP founders had said SNCC was their direct inspiration and that their logo had been taken from SNCC graphics found in Lowndes County, Alabama. The appeal of the BPP was that it was in a period of rapid growth and its strength in the black community was augmented by good relations with white radicals organized in groups such as California Newsreel and the Peace and Freedom Party.

California was also home to black groups hostile to the BPP. Among these was the Los Angeles–based US, an organization espousing a blend of black nationalism and socialism created by its flamboyant leader, Ron Karenga. US and the BPP had had physical as well as verbal confrontations. Carmichael believed a revitalized SNCC could halt such infighting and meld militant local groups scattered throughout the country into a powerful national presence. He agreed to a fusion of SNCC and the BPP as a starting point, and he presided over a large rally in Los Angeles in which US and other smaller organizations peacefully participated alongside the BPP.

The fusion with the BPP was mainly a one-man show, for most of the SNCC core no longer recognized Carmichael's leadership, much less supported his nearly unilateral dissolution of their group into another. The official SNCC leader was H. Rap Brown but he soon went into hiding when car bombs killed his closest associates, one of whom was long-time SNCC activist Ralph Featherstone. James Foreman tried to guide SNCC toward organizing black workers and eventually led a number of associates into the Detroit-based League of Revolutionary Black Workers as a prelude to building a socialist Black Workers Congress. Frances Beal used SNCC elements to build the Third World Woman's Alliance, an organization that would have considerable impact. Other SNCC workers persevered in local projects that often included municipal or state electoral campaigns. The various SNCC pieces went in so many different directions that a 1971 FBI report declared that the organization had ceased to exist.

The Congress of Racial Equality experienced a process similar to that of SNCC. When James Farmer became head of CORE in 1961, he and Bayard Rustin organized conferences in various cities with the cooperation of direct-action pacifist groups. The result was the Freedom Rides campaign, which was modeled on an earlier effort organized by the

Fellowship of Reconcilation, the group from which CORE originated. The heroic Freedom Rides established CORE as a major civil rights group. The most racially integrated of the action organizations, CORE played a role in community organizing, voter registration, and support of the MFDP. But as beatings and murders mounted without adequate federal response, many CORE cadre became disenchanted with nonviolence as a way of life and began to carry arms. In 1964 whites were asked to play a less prominent public role at the urging of James Farmer, who wished the organization to remain racially integrated, but in 1967, under the leadership of Floyd McKissick, CORE became all-black. Its influence faded quickly. Roy Innis became leader in 1968 and transformed CORE into a black nationalist organization without any ties to its pacifist origins. The organization survived as a personal forum for Innis but without any mass base.

The separatist tide that prevailed with the "Black Power" slogan was linked to a black nationalism that went back to 1920s activists such as Marcus Garvey and black scholars such as J. A. Rogers, who had traced the contributions of Africans throughout world history. During the years when SCLC, SNCC, and CORE were most active, their strategy was to confine actions to the South and use the North to raise funds and recruit volunteers. Their target constituencies for organization were churchgoers and the college educated. One result of this perspective was that direct action in the North was mainly left to local groups, and the needs of the most blighted sectors of the black community, particularly the population that came to be called the underclass, were rarely addressed.

The organization that emerged to fill some of the political vacuum in the North was the Nation of Islam, much of whose appeal was a black separatism based on personal regeneration and discipline. Popularly called the Black Muslims, the Nation of Islam was highly unorthodox in its teaching that white people were representatives of the devil. Although the formal leader was Elijah Muhammad, an aged figure who spent most of his time in Chicago, the charismatic leader of the Black Muslims was Malcolm X. Like many Black Muslims, Malcolm X had been a criminal. Under his direction the Nation of Islam intensified an already vigorous recruitment in urban ghettos and prisons. While espousing a communal self-sufficiency that was sometimes dubbed "black capitalism," the Muslims offered a merciless attack on America's racial hypocrisy at home and abroad, and the Muslims were adamant about their right to self-defense. Many African Americans who could not accept the Muslims on religious grounds admired their pride, militancy, and self-sufficiency.

Malcolm X developed a speaking style that provided a systematic critique of U.S. foreign and domestic policies in terms easily comprehended by urban audiences of limited formal education. His speeches also began to attract the admiration of radicals. The SWP, in particular, believed he would eventually drop his separatist views and become a major leader of black America and perhaps the socialist movement itself. Acting on this premise, the SWP sponsored forums at which he spoke and diligently collected his writings and made recordings of his key speeches. While Malcolm X was not about to join the SWP and it is not clear exactly what he thought about Trotskyism, he was certainly aware that socialists were responding to his message.

Following a 1964 trip to Mecca and extensive travel in North Africa, Malcolm X set out in a new political direction. He broke with Elijah Muhammad on grounds of religion and personal corruption. Although he remained an orthodox Muslim himself, Malcolm X's new political base, the Organization of Afro-American Unity, had no religious or ideological criteria. He was now ready to mobilize a vast range of admirers, including leftists such as actor Ossie Davis, militant writers such as James Baldwin, influential journalists such as the *Amsterdam News*'s James Hicks, and prominent nationalists such as Harlem bookstore owner Louis Micheaux. Although Malcolm X expressed a growing interest in what was happening in China, no less a figure than Martin Luther King announced his pleasure that Malcolm X had joined the mainstream civil rights movement.

Malcolm X undertook a speaking tour of college campuses, where enthusiastic audiences were often predominantly white. He was also the object of constant death threats. As he dictated his autobiography to Arthur Haley, he said he did not expect to live long enough to read his own book. He was assassinated in 1965 just as the book was becoming available. Black Muslims were eventually convicted for the murder, but there is considerable scholarship that points in other directions. Before his death, Malcolm X had said he had created the military apparatus of the Nation of Islam and knew what it could and could not do. In his opinion, the attacks and pressures he had experienced were beyond their power and could only be possible through governmental assistance.

The anger that Malcolm X had sought to channel into political action exploded in the Watts riots of the summer of 1965. A string of uprisings followed, culminating in the massive Newark and Detroit rebellions of 1967, the costliest in American history. These insurrectional outbursts made it evident to all that urban blacks had not been appeased by the passage of the Voting Rights Act (1964), school desegregation efforts, and other gains secured by the King-led movement. King himself thought the concessions he won were often only sops to stave off more violence. While King accepted any gains that were available, the advances were not the result of the moral regeneration he had sought to foster through nonviolent resistance. He also understood that the personal respect shown to him was often a means of keeping the spotlight from more volatile leaders. While personally willing to suffer whatever misfortune might flow from continued nonviolent resistance, he questioned how long he could continue to ask others to follow a course that was inevitably met by violent counterattacks. Whatever viability remained in the nonviolent tradition was largely dispelled when King was assassinated in 1968.

No successor to King was able to emerge from the SCLC milieu, and, like SNCC and CORE, SCLC was doomed to political oblivion. New organizations such as the Black Panther Party and the League of Revolutionary Black Workers were unable to regroup the collapsing movement. Malcolm X would prove as irreplaceable as King despite the attempts of Eldridge Cleaver, George Jackson, and Stokley Carmichael to carry his banner. The Nation of Islam also split, with the largest formation becoming totally orthodox in its teachings but also largely apolitical.

Rather than expanding to ever larger arenas in the 1970s, the civil rights movement contracted to local venues. Many individual activists and grass-roots organizations took part in efforts to win city, county, and state offices. In the North as well as the South, there was a rising tide of black mayors and state legislators along with a minor uptick in black congressmen. During the Carter administration, there were some opportunities at the federal level as well, the post of UN ambassador going to Andrew Young, one of King's closest advisers. The ultimate heir of the electoral tradition, however, was to be Jesse Jackson, formerly one of SCLC's younger staffers and not especially close to King.

After creating a self-help group in Chicago, Jackson emerged in the 1980s as leader of the Rainbow Coalition, a vaguely defined movement that sought to unite various dissident sectors of American society with a sharp focus on race, class, and sexual exploitation. Some members of the coalition hoped it would become a third party while others saw it as a pressure group within the Democratic Party. Whatever the ultimate fate of the Rainbow Coalition, the black voting blocks made possible through the civil rights agitation centered around SCLC and SNCC had become the most dependable Democratic constituency and the most liberal voters in the United States.

The phase of the historic drive for racial equality that began in the 1950s and persisted to the early 1970s had always been a house of its own, a reaction to American injustice under the direct inspiration of American ideals as stated in the Declaration of Independence and codified in the Civil War amendments to the Constitution. Many radical individuals and organizations were attracted to its massive and heroic efforts to redress historic wrongs. These radical forces never dominated, much less led, the movement, but they were part of the broad process of change, their ideas influenced by, as well as influencing, the dramatic course of events. *See also*: Armed Struggle; Baker, Ella; Black Panther Party; Braden, Anne and Carl; Highlander Folk School; League of Revolutionary Black Workers; National Lawyers Guild; Pacifism; Randolph, A. Philip; Rustin, Bayard; Southern Conference Educational Fund; Student Nonviolent Coordinating Committee

—*Dan Georgakas*

REFERENCES

Breitman, George. *The Last Year of Malcolm X: The Evolution of a Revolutionary*. New York: Pathfinder Press, 1967.

Breitman, George, Herman Porter, and Baxter Smith. *The Assassination of Malcolm X*. New York: Pathfinder, 1976.

Carson, Clayborne. *In Struggle—SNCC and the Black Awakening of the 1960s*. Cambridge: Harvard University Press, 1980.

Garrow, David J. *Bearing the Cross—Martin Luther King and the Southern Christian Leadership Conference*. New York: William Morrow, 1986.

———. *The FBI and Martin Luther King*. NY: Norton, 1981.

X, Malcolm (with the assistance of Alex Haley). *The Autobiography of Malcolm X*. New York: Random House, 1965.

Classics

Critics on the Left have never been entirely comfortable with the idealized image of ancient Greek and Roman civilization captured in the famous verse, "the glory that was Greece and the grandeur that was Rome." According to this story, Greece is the fountainhead of democratic values and institutions, as well as of literature, philosophy, art, and history, while Rome is the model of a stable and powerful empire, bestowing the benefits of peace and Hellenic culture upon the known world. As the twin sources of "Western Civilization," the virtues of Greece and Rome have been appealed to as evidence of the superiority of European over other cultures.

There is, however, an alternative picture: Greek and Roman civilization was built upon a brutal system of slavery; women were excluded from civic roles; both Athens and Rome developed empires that were perceived as tyrannical by their subject populations; the Roman aristocracy was as greedy, arrogant, and powerful a ruling clique as any; so great a thinker as Aristotle believed that "barbarians" were biologically inferior and thus naturally fit to be slaves of the Greeks. Oddly enough, much of what was truly democratic about classical culture, like its theater and sculpture, has been perceived in modern times as elite art, known through difficult languages or stored up in museums.

Recent decades have seen the emergence of a critical perspective on classical civilization that has focused attention on oppressed and marginalized populations in the ancient world. Scholars on the Left, especially feminist critics, have to a large extent inspired this new approach, and it has begun to affect the teaching of the classics in colleges and schools.

In the 1960s, the Women's Classical Caucus was formed within the professional society of classicists (the American Philological Association) in order to address the status of women in antiquity in a critical way. These women and men did not take it for granted that, in classical Athens, a respectable woman did not appear alone in public, and rarely appeared in public at all; that she was deprived of juridical as well as civic rights (in the law courts, it was considered indecent even to mention the name of a citizen woman); that in all legal transactions she was represented by a guardian (called the *kyrios*), who, in marriage, transferred her to the authority of a husband, who in turn became her *kyrios* (women in Rome suffered comparable disabilities, although they were not so rigorously segregated from male social life as they were in Athens). Feminist scholars were not content to describe such oppression; they were also concerned to understand how it was legitimized. As a result, a new word has entered the vocabulary of classicists: *ideology*. The great texts of antiquity, from Aeschylus to Virgil, are now seen, by some, as complicit in sustaining or reproducing systems of domination, and not just as timeless repositories of high values; the sexist aspects of ancient medicine, or of Aristotelian biology, are increasingly being subjected to critical scrutiny. To address the problem of ideology, classicists borrowed from other disciplines, such as anthropology and semiotics (the analysis of language and meaning); new journals came into being to accommodate the new methods (in this country, especially *Arethusa*), and the whole field became the scene of political, as well as antiquarian, controversy. In this way, classics responded to the new currents of women's liberation, and a self-consciously Left-oriented women's tendency within the discipline remains the most important stimulus to reevaluating the classical heritage.

The role of ideology was not restricted to the domination of women; ethnic exclusivism has also become the focus of critical attention, and ancient prejudice toward "barbarians" is no longer simply reproduced in modern scholarship. The societies conquered by Alexander the Great and later by the Romans were often at as high a material and cultural level as their conquerors, and historians have begun to investigate how the Greeks and Romans rationalized slavery and imperialism, as well as the social bases of internal and external exploitation.

Leftist scholars have brought a new sophistication to the analysis of the ancient economy, and have elucidated the class structure of classical societies. In the process, another term has entered the lexicon of classical scholarship: *class struggle*. Wealth in ancient Greece and Rome primarily took the form of land, although there was some manufacture and export of commodities like pottery. Poor citizens, struggling to maintain a small plot, constantly ran the risk of falling into debt and thus being expropriated by the rich, who exploited dependent labor on their estates. Materialist historians have shown how ancient democracy was the result of a collective effort by the lower and middle strata to protect their interests, and how the failure of democracy coincided with the victory of the large landowners. Under the Roman Empire, there was a progressive lowering of the status of the average citizen, under competition from mass slavery and intensive exploitation, until the condition of tenant farmers and serfs was socially and legally little better than that of slaves. It remains controversial among leftist scholars to what extent slavery may be understood as a specific "mode of production" in antiquity.

Slavery was, as one ancient testimony by a slave informs us, the worst catastrophe that could befall a human being. Slaves have had little chance to have their own voice recorded in the annals of history, but scholars are collecting what evidence they can, often in the form of inscriptions, to understand how slaves responded to a condition in which marriages were regarded as mere cohabitation, and slave children were said to be fatherless. In Rome, manumitted slaves received citizen rights, and could aspire to decent livelihoods, but the condition of the free poor was by and large miserable, especially in overcrowded cities like Rome, where work was scarce.

Thus, scholars responding to feminism, the civil rights movement, and new developments in Marxist theory have begun to correct the glorified or sanitized notion of classical antiquity. The plight of slaves, the poor, women, foreigners, and other oppressed groups is at last receiving some of the attention it deserves, and has in turn called into question the notion of a privileged and superior "Western" tradition. *See also*: Anthropology

—*David Konstan*

REFERENCES

Arthur, M., and D. Konstan. "Marxism and Classical Antiquity." In *The Left Academy: Marxist Scholarship on American Campuses*, edited by B. Ollman and E. Vernoff. Vol. 2. New York: Praeger, 1984.

de Ste Croix, G. E. M. *The Class Struggle in the Ancient Greek World*. Ithaca: Cornell University Press, 1983.

Finley, M. I. *The Ancient Economy*. 2d ed. Berkeley: University of California Press, 1985.

Peradotto, J., and J. P. Sullivan, eds. *Women in the Ancient World: The Arethusa Papers*. Albany: SUNY Press, 1984.

Cleveland Citizen

"America's Oldest Labor Newspaper," as its subtitle still proclaims, the *Cleveland Citizen* played an especially important role in socialist and trade union movements of 1891–

1920 through the political influence and personal forcefulness of its leading editor, Max Hayes (1866–1945).

Founded as an organ of the new Central Labor Union, which had broken from the Knights of Labor in 1887 and adhered to the AFL, the *Citizen* was simultaneously prosocialist and pro-AFL. Despite Hayes's national reputation of leading socialist opposition to Samuel Gompers for three decades, Hayes consistently argued against any break with the AFL. He adamantly opposed the Socialist Trades and Labor Alliance in the 1890s, the Industrial Workers of the World in the 1900s and 1910s, and the CIO in the 1930s.

During the 1890s the strongest and most durable of many local socialistic labor papers, the *Citizen* functioned as an organizing tool for the CLU and for national AFL unions in the Cleveland area, and as a free, open forum for discussion of all the hotly debated issues in the working class and the Left. In addition to a wide range of national and international labor news, the weekly characteristically covered the economic, political, social, and cultural activities of Cleveland's multi-ethnic labor and community groups—with special emphasis upon those involved in the skilled trades. Reputedly, Gompers began publishing the *American Federationist* in 1894 to counter the *Citizen*. On the other side of the political lines, in 1895–96, Hayes was among the first important union leaders to break with Daniel DeLeon's Socialist Labor Party, and to call for an alternative socialist movement more accepting of labor's institutional autonomy. The *Citizen* fended off several further threats from Right and Left in subsequent decades, losing the subsidy of the Central Federation of Labor but not its endorsement.

In 1920 the *Citizen* again took the national spotlight when it became the official organ of the Cleveland and Ohio Labor Party with Hayes the candidate for the national Farmer-Labor Party ticket. Hayes did not run for office again, and the communist movement eclipsed the *Leader* and its milieu in the surrounding ethnic community. Hayes remained at the helm of the paper, advocate of the AFL and of independent political action, until incapacitated by a stroke in 1940. The paper subsequently lost its socialistic character, and was purchased in 1977 by the Cleveland Building Trades Council. *See also*: Socialist Labor Party, Socialist Party

—*Jean Tussey*

REFERENCES

Dick, William M. *Labor and Socialism in America: The Gompers Era*. Port Jefferson, N.Y.: Kennikat, 1972.

Sidlo, T. L. "Socialism and Trade Unionism: A Study of Their Relation in Cleveland." *Western Reserve University Bulletin* 12 (November 1908).

Tussey, Jean. "Max S. Hayes." *Encyclopedia of Cleveland History*. Bloomington: Indiana University Press, 1987.

Cloth Hat and Capmakers

In its formation and early years an almost classic Jewish socialist union, the Capmakers suffered from inordinate Left infighting and drifted under moderating leadership toward the center of the political spectrum.

Heir to a succession of unsuccessful or short-lived union efforts and an increasingly successful (but hardly socialist) Hatters Union among blocked hat makers, the Capmakers grew up economically out of a vast expansion of the headwear industry in the New York area. Cloth Hat and Cap Operators Local #1 organized in 1887 and, although it turned to the Socialist Labor Party for aid, it resisted by a majority an affiliation with the Socialist Trades and Labor Alliance as destructive of union autonomy. Led entirely by socialists, however—some of the most important being former DeLeonites—the union also resisted affiliation with the AFL until 1905. By then, the union had been rechartered (in 1901, as United Cloth Hat and Cap Makers of America) and had thrown its energies against the efforts of the Industrial Workers of the World (perceived as a newfangled DeLeonism) to create a presence in New York through a Wobbly capmakers' affiliate. Intent upon a more "constructive" socialist labor policy, the Capmakers enthusiastically endorsed Socialist Party candidates and participated widely in New York socialist activities into the 1930s.

The union came of age under the unchallenged leadership of Max Zaritsky. Erstwhile underground revolutionary and son of a prosperous Minsk merchant, Zaritsky had entered the trade from the business side and rapidly rose to leadership. Enjoying a small-scale version of Amalgamated Clothing Workers president Sidney Hillman's success, Zaritsky in 1917 became the union's first president and directed it through its World War I–era growth and consolidation.

By the 1920s, when Zaritsky had considerably moderated his socialist practice, he faced opposition from undiminished old-time Socialists and from younger Communists, both emboldened by deteriorating conditions. Winning abandonment of the piece rate, he soon insisted on its return for the sake of labor productivity and manufacturing profits. He resigned in 1925, taking a position with the *Jewish Daily Forward*, but returned in 1927 and remained for the duration of his career. The Trade Union Education League had organized against him from the early 1920s, at one point nearly taking a majority of cap-makers' locals. Led by organizer Gladys Schechter, the Communists again challenged in 1926–27, but were beaten back through the gerrymandering of locals.

The Communist shift to the dual unionism of the Trade Union Unity League, and Zaritsky's subsequent expulsion of dissidents, virtually destroyed Left influence in the trade. Zaritsky's own loyalties had by this time become markedly Zionist, and he later abandoned socialist ideas altogether for something approaching a corporate view of labor and management.

Unlike the case in a number of other needle trades, the Left posed no further threats to Zaritsky's leadership of the proliferating unionization under the New Deal. Politically a wholehearted supporter of the American Labor Party, he led his troops in alliance with the David Dubinsky wing of the ALP. After Sidney Hillman's death, Alex Rose (a leader of the millinery workers, a Labor Zionist, and a bitter anticommunist crusader since the early 1920s) maneuvered the formation of the Liberal Party, dedicated to a Cold War liberalism and to patronage. Into the 1940s–1950s, a persistent strain of Jewish (especially Yiddish) radicalism, in all varieties from anarchist to communist, nevertheless remained among the old-timers. Although the union cooperated widely with employers in the postwar years, the shrinking of the hat trade dramatically reduced the size of the UCHCM. Merger with the Amalgamated Clothing Workers Union (later Amalgamated Clothing and Textile Workers Union) brought them back eventually toward a progressive milieu. By that time, Jewish membership—concentrated in the leadership—had diminished within the union, which was itself to become steadily weaker because of the incoming rush of imported goods. *See also*: Amalgamated Clothing Workers of America, Yiddish Left

—*Paul Buhle*

REFERENCES

Robinson, Donald H. *Spotlight On a Union*. New York: Dial Press, 1948.

COLD WAR REVISIONISM

In the early 1950s, Cold War assumptions dominated American public life. Almost unnoticed, three books were published, one by a young, unknown academic, one by a jailed Communist, and one by a maverick reporter. These books began the effort to break through the closed-mindedness of American public opinion about the "struggle for freedom" with the Soviet Union. They marked the first appearance of Cold War Revisionism—an argument against the virtually unanimous view that Soviet expansionism and worldwide subversion had necessitated a defensive military buildup by the United States and its allies and even defensive wars in Greece, Korea, and French Indochina.

Professor William A. Williams authored *American-Russian Relations, 1787–1947* (1951). He placed the beginning of the Cold War in the broad historical context of U.S. imperial concerns. The U.S. government had tried to reverse the revolution in Russia after 1917 and was aggressively opposing Soviet interests in Eastern Europe. The book was a strong scholarly rejoinder to the George Kennan school of containment. In the era of the Truman Doctrine and Korean War even such a measured critique was too much for the establishment. The publisher submitted the chapter on Kennan to *Foreign Affairs,* the magazine of the foreign policy elite, but they returned it to Williams stating it was interesting and provocative but too personal in its rebuttal of Kennan (whatever that meant!). The book made no apparent impact in academia, but was approvingly reviewed in the small left-wing press.

Carl Marzani, serving a prison sentence for contempt of Congress, wrote *We Can Be Friends* (1952) from published sources available in the prison libraries. This book showed that a careful reading of U.S. government documents, speeches of politicians, memoirs like those of Winston Churchill, and the *New York Times* could cast doubt on the consensus about Soviet blame for the Cold War. Meanwhile, journalist I. F. Stone, no supporter of Stalin, had discovered that the Korean War may very well have been caused by intra-Korean issues and not by the Soviet Union. Furthermore, he argued that the intervention of the Chinese was a result of legitimate Chinese security concerns. With no one willing to publish his book, Paul Sweezy and Leo Huberman of the *Monthly Review* took his manuscript as the first Monthly Review Press book. Stone's *Hidden History of the Korean War* (1953) provided a useful summary of evidence suggesting that the Korean War was not necessarily a case of unprovoked aggression.

In historiography, revisionism means just what it sounds like. It represents the revising of previously accepted interpretations—a challenge to "received doctrine"—on the basis of new evidence, previously ignored evidence, new interpretations of agreed-upon evidence, or some combination. New material becomes available. The bias of earlier historians may have blinded them to some evidence. The passage of time permits perceptions of events to become more detached, and the issues of succeeding eras to shed new light on those of the past. Thus, our understanding of historical events change quite drastically as time passes. In the case of judgments about the origins and course of the Cold War, this is a particularly important phenomenon because one's beliefs about the history of the Cold War can lead to two possible conclusions. Either history provides evidence to support policies necessary for the continuation of that confrontation, or provides a way of exposing policies adopted in furtherance of U.S. imperial ambitions having nothing whatsoever to do with the needs of the American people.

I. F. Stone went on to found *I. F. Stone's Weekly,* which regularly pricked holes in the various balloons of disinformation loosed onto an unsuspecting public. William A. Williams expanded his investigations to include U.S. foreign policy in general. After publishing a number of articles he put out a book-length interpretation, *The Tragedy of American Diplomacy,* in 1959. In 1960 Professor D. F. Fleming published a two-volume work, *The Origins and History of the Cold War.* These two books mark the upsurge of post-McCarthy Cold War Revisionism, with different emphases. Whereas Williams put the Cold War in the context of long-term U.S. economic and political expansionism—in a word, imperialism—Fleming felt that the Cold War was a serious departure from the more cooperative policy with the Soviets that had been followed by Franklin Roosevelt during the wartime alliance. In the early 1960s, opposition to U.S. moves against the fledgling Cuban Revolution (as opposed to the virtual silence in this country as the United States toppled governments in Iran and Guatemala in the early 1950s) provided a context in which such revisionism could resonate. Williams brought out a second, expanded edition of *Tragedy* in 1962 and published *The United States, Cuba, and Castro* with Monthly Review Press in the same year. In 1964 Gar Alperovitz wrote *Atomic Diplomacy,* which interpreted the decision to use the atom bomb at the end of World War II as the opening salvo in the postwar struggle against the Soviet Union.

The intellectual anti-interventionism of the early 1960s grew with opposition to the Vietnam War into a fuller critique. Writing in the revisionist tradition expanded. Williams's colleagues and students even constituted a "school" within Cold War Revisionism, emphasizing the concept of an "open door" empire that had been implanted into the ideology of American leaders at least as early as the late nineteenth century. By 1968, Cold War Revisionism was so successful in challenging "received doctrine" that Arthur Schlesinger, Jr., published an article saying "it's time to call a halt" to this subversive, revisionist doctrine. Meanwhile, the Fleming and Williams strands of Cold War Revisionism were joined by a third in 1969 when Gabriel Kolko published *The Politics of War*, which opposed Fleming's interpretation by tracing U.S. hostility to the Soviets and radical nationalist movements back into the years of the wartime alliance. Kolko eschewed the Williams "open door" imperialism interpretation. He gave no credence to the rhetoric of idealism sounded by individuals like Woodrow Wilson. To Kolko such verbalizations merely represented the most cynical of manipulations and not a genuine contradiction of ideals and practices as in Williams. This approach is also taken by that meticulous foreign policy critic Noam Chomsky. (See, for example, *American Power and the New Mandarins* [1968] and *Turning the Tide* [1987].)

In 1973 Princeton University Press published an attack on Williams, Kolko, Fleming, and others for committing fraud by deliberate misquotations, etc. (James Maddox *The New Left and the Origins of the Cold War* [1973]). The book received a favorable front-page review in the *New York Times Book Review*. Despite such attacks, revisionism has continued to develop. Graduate students and even undergraduates are at least aware that there is an alternative interpretation of the role of the United States as an alleged "defender of the Free World." Writers who don't accept revisionism have to respond to it with their own writings. Scholarship in the revisionist tradition has informed the movement against intervention in Central America in the 1980s.

Williams had argued that when the expansionist impulse contradicted our national commitment to self-determination, we sacrificed that alleged commitment. As congressional hearings during the 1980s indicated, pursuit of certain imperial aims in Central America caused collaboration with drug runners. Meanwhile, the Chomsky/Kolko school have seen this as evidence for their view that our nation's idealistic commitments are the rhetoric of imperial self-justification and nothing more. Cold War Revisionism remains alive and well. *See also*: *In These Times*; *Monthly Review*; Stone, I. F.

—*Michael Meeropol*

REFERENCES

Noble, David W. "William Appleman Williams and the Crisis of Public History"; Bradford Perkins, "'The Tragedy of American Diplomacy': Twenty-Five Years After"; and William G. Robbins, "William A. Williams, 'Doing History Is Best of All. No Regrets.'" In *Redefining the Past: Essays in Diplomatic History in Honor of William Appleman Williams*, edited by Lloyd C. Gardner. Corvallis: Oregon State University Press, 1986.

COMING NATION: see APPEAL TO REASON, RUSKIN COLONY

COMMITTEE OF CONCERNED ASIAN SCHOLARS: see ASIAN STUDIES

COMMUNIST/POLITICAL AFFAIRS: see COMMUNIST PARTY

COMMUNIST LABOR PARTY (OF 1919 ORIGINS): see COMMUNIST PARTY

COMMUNIST LABOR PARTY (OF POST–WW II ORIGINS): see LEAGUE OF REVOLUTIONARY BLACK WORKERS, ANTIREVISIONISM

COMMUNIST LEAGUE OF AMERICA: see TROTSKYISM

COMMUNIST PARTY, USA

The CPUSA was the most important American radical organization from its factionalized 1919 origins well into the 1950s. Since that time, the Party has played a far more modest but not unimportant role within various social movements. During its most dynamic periods, the CP guided a multitude of non-Party organizations and alliances with a far greater following and more impact than

Cover drawing by Robert Minor

the Party proper. At less auspicious times, the CP has isolated itself or, worse, expended most of its energies simply to survive government persecution. Through good and bad times, the Party has had to combat the charge that its politics simply reflect directives passed down from Moscow.

The origins of the Communist movement can be found in the left wing of the Socialist Party and in the alternative political and industrial movements that sometimes cooperated with and sometimes combated the Socialists. This radical spectrum of groups and individuals did not ultimately set Communist policies, especially after the first turbulent years, but they did provide the first wave of American Communists. Their struggles and disputes also underscore the complex native-born and immigrant roots of the new movement.

Left disaffection with the SP had two large components. By emphasizing an electoral politics, Socialists alienated members of the Industrial Workers of the World and many other militants who believed the road to revolution lay through direct or "mass" action. The same critics generally upheld industrial unions as the primary means of organizing and preparing the masses for revolutionary activity.

In contrast to the IWW's sanguine expectations, Socialists generally held a more realistic view of the problems to be confronted in creating mass industrial unions, and the long-run uncertainty of those unions' political commitment. But in minimizing the importance of the foreign-born, and maintaining a bureaucratic leadership drawn for the most part from the early years of the movement, the SP alienated the post-1912 influx of new members, who felt themselves less than fully welcome. The SP position regarding world war, crucial elsewhere in fostering Left and Communist dissent, was not a major factor in the United States, despite rhetorical attempts to make it so. The precipitating factor, the October Revolution and the resulting Comintern, did not so much create as bring together earlier dissent and give it the slogans for a formal split.

The Socialist Propaganda League, located in Boston with the support of the strongly pro-Lenin Latvian-American socialists, was the first to send out a call for American Socialist adherence to the principles of the Bolshevik Revolution. The Friends of the Russian Revolution, or Friends of New Russia, formed at the end of 1917, and the American Bolshevik Bureau of Information formed in 1918. Both provided positive information about the Russian Revolution to the general American public. Like the first book popularizing the event, Louis Fraina's anthology *The Proletarian Revolution in Russia* (1917), these phenomena were American in origin rather than responses to Russian initiatives.

Although the Bolsheviks anticipated splits within the socialist movements as precursive to new communist parties, they had less direct influence in the United States than elsewhere. The course of the conflicts among the language-federation groups and those groups' largely Pyrrhic triumphs within the SP proved decisive. Furious factionalism and preparations for a split incited moderate, essentially parliamentarist-inclined Socialists to stage their own walkout and to maneuver against a Left seizure of organizational power. Over a six-month period in 1919, a rump National Executive Committee was able to expel or suspend approximately two-thirds of the SP membership.

The left wing now quarreled over the best course to pursue. A majority favored a continuing struggle within the SP, at least until the time of the next national convention. A substantial minority, led by the large and prestigious Russian Federation, called for the immediate abandonment of the SP. Naming itself the Communist Party, this group immediately turned its most bitter attacks upon rival left-wingers. The other, largely English-language group remained in the SP until duly expelled at the 1919 SP convention after a notable floor-fight; it then formed the Communist Labor Party. These battling twins faced, in turn, the Palmer Raids, which (along with the mass strikes of the day, and the brief anticipation of the Russian Revolution sweeping Europe) temporarily reinforced a near-insurrectionary sentiment.

For the next three years, mostly "underground" but under the close watch of federal spies, the Communists accelerated the internecine propaganda war, largely against each other or against other Left groupings. Each of the parties sought membership in the Comintern, and each was told that Moscow would not favor one over the other and that they would have to unify. Each of the original Communist organizations suffered various schisms with departing groups often appropriating the organizational name. Efforts also continued to unite the multiplying factions into a single organization. In 1922 those who had remained in the original Communist Party of America joined with the United Communist Party (a merger of the Communist Labor Party and a faction of the Communist Party of America) to establish the Workers Party of America as a unified aboveground entity. The Workers Party of America was able to gain the adhesion of most other Communist formations within a matter of years, most notably the United Toilers of America, which had also presented itself in 1922 as an aboveground Communist party seeking unification. The new merger was named the Workers (Communist) Party, a name which prevailed until 1929 when it was changed to Communist Party, USA.

During the underground period, the Communists had lost some five-eighths of their initial Left adherents within the SP, including the vast majority of American-born and older-generation supporters. Two of the most significant segments, the Jewish and German federations, sat out most of the warfare, negotiating their entry at a late point in the process. Much of the working-class membership had in practice done the same, ignoring the internecine political excitement for the more customary Left social and cultural activities.

The emerging Workers (Communist) Party bore the stamp of a new Communist international strategy, the United Front. Conceived by the Comintern to meet the perceived delay in the world-revolutionary process, this policy entailed a strategic reorientation of major proportions. Unlike the old left-wing Socialists and the IWW, the Communists would work within non-Left, mass institutions, including the AFL and labor or labor-farmer parties. Many moderate socialists had long urged these policies, but with their revolutionary aims, Communists were forced to carry out their work in semiconcealed fashion. The tarring of Bolsheviks as bearded bomb-throwers had by this time been so successful, and the general defeat of the revolutionary Left so complete, that concealment of one's affiliation and ideology seemed necessary. No satisfactory theoretical articulation followed from the Communist leadership to address the complex and difficult implications of this maneuver. At a minimum, it tended to make the Communists' electoral efforts in their own name essentially propagandistic and pro forma. Communists did not seriously expect to be elected, and for that matter no longer held the socialist faith in transforming society primarily through patient, open educational efforts.

Through much of the 1920s, the Communists' own internecine warfare continued unabated, although with shifting lines of controversy. Midwestern enthusiasts of industrial unionism put most of their energies into the International Labor Defense, while mostly Eastern and predominantly Jewish veterans of the needle-trades struggles called for a more directly political-educational approach. The second group, more content in a sense with the enclave status of the Party's stubborn ethnic support, proclaimed an "American Exceptionalism" based on the unique status of being the home base of the foremost capitalist power and prescribed a patient, strategic advance upon state power. This view was tolerable to the Comintern during the brief ascendence of Bukharin, but it could not ideologically survive Stalin's wide Left turn in 1928, and seemed disproved in actuality by the stock-market crash of 1929. The Communist theoretical monthly, the *Communist*, a generally difficult publication reached its apex of readability during this period but swiftly declined thereafter to wild attacks upon perceived heretics (such as literary editor V. F. Calverton) and reaffirmations of current doctrine.

The Communist factions thus engaged in organizational jousting and traded fierce polemics over the appropriate application of the Russian example to the American scene. With the dubious counsel of Comintern representatives (themselves actors in a far larger, international factionalism), American Communists struggled first of all to create a Left presence within the AFL. The Trade Union Educational League, the most successful of their efforts, indeed rallied many traditional unionists for a fighting program. The rightward retreat of the AFL, along with a number of Communist tactical blunders, ended the adventure and returned many activitists back to the budding fraternal, ethnic institution-building over which the Party had little direct control. The second major effort at mass influence, the formation of a Left-oriented farmer-labor movement, failed for the same internal and external reasons, resulting in the Communists' isolation from the Progressive Party campaign of 1924 headed by "Fighting Bob" LaFollette. The third and last major effort, the Trade Union Unity League, set out to form new unions of unorganized and unskilled workers. The TUUL filled some of the vacuum left by the IWW collapse and by AFL indifference toward the unskilled. It would be remembered, in later years, for the "shop papers" published by activists with particular grievances aired—a clear anticipation of and preparation for the CIO. On the debit side, the TUUL's presence tended to pull Left activists away from some important points of influence (such as the needle trades) without being able to build up self-sustaining organizations.

Along the way, the Party had critically reduced its ethnic base in a variety of ways. "Bolshevization"—an attempt to eradicate the Balkanization of the Party and produce a single, unified leadership—proved widely unpopular and among some groups catastrophic. The attempted breakup of language sections in favor of geographic organizations successfully discouraged for a time the insular cultural activity derided as "Banquet Socialism," and demonstrably weakened language-federation authority. But in the hostile political climate of the 1920s, public activity proved difficult and even economically hazardous to immigrant workers and their middle-class supporters. In any case, the struggle to build up ethnic radical institutions had its own dynamic within working-class life, a factor often regarded too casually by Communist leaders in these early years. In deprecating the priority of choral and theatrical groups, literary circles, clubhouses, language schools for children, and the like, Party political decisions weakened the capacity of the working-class Left to speak for, and build a lasting base within, the immediate community. Ethnic workers, for their part, often came to regard the Russian authority as unerrant, but the American Communist movement as confused and misled.

Among the casualties of this cultural conflict could be counted the Italian group, mostly older men who had never entirely given up the anarcho-syndicalist faith of their younger days; and the Finns, who bolted in large numbers at the insistence upon Party control of their cooperatives' financial resources. The simultaneous emigration of Finns by the thousands to work in Soviet Keralia permanently weakened the Finnish-American Left. The Party also lost widely on several other fronts, for a variety of international reasons. Polish nationalism, detached from socialism, buried Left influence for some years to come. South Slavs, who had supported World War I for nationalist reasons, remained largely in the SP or became politically inactive. Jews, bitterly alienated in large numbers by the Party's characterization of the 1929 Palestinian riots as a liberation struggle rather than a pogrom or manipulated conflict between two oppressed peoples, fled the Party and (perhaps more important) its mass organizations in significant numbers. Even Armenians, roused to a high level of mobilization by the Turkish slaughter of homeland nationals and by the Red Army defense of Armenians, lowered levels of activity by the end of the 1920s as the Armenian crisis eased.

Relative to these major losses, the expulsions of "Left" and then "Right" deviationists was less destructive in terms of numbers or influence immediately lost. Only in the needle trades did the expelled carry many members out of the Party with them, and those were mainly a thin stratum of leaders. The long-term impact of the expulsions, however, was considerable. The actions were judged to be the result of direct Soviet interference in leadership of the American Party and reflected struggles about the direction of the USSR rather than that of the United States. Those driven from the Party charged that its basic policies were now being set by the Comintern and that the Comintern reserved the right of final approval of Party leadership. These accusations reinforced popular perceptions of Communism as an inauthentic national movement.

The rightest group led by Jay Lovestone soon formed a relationship with anticommunist labor leaders and would play a major role in the continuing effort to deny Communists any role in the trade union movement. Lovestoneites became particularly influential in the post-1950s reunited AFL-CIO. The Left faction headed by James Cannon founded American Trotskyism, which presented itself as a genuine Leninist movement and a democratic alternative to the Stalinist policies of the CP. The Trotskyists provided a continuing critique of the USSR that gradually won a wide intellectual following. Many of the charges brought against Stalin by the Trotskyists would be validated by future Soviet leaders, tentatively by Khrushchev in the late 1950s and more emphatically by Gorbachev in the late 1980s.

In short, Communists entered the era of the Great Depression—at approximately 18,000 members and a following perhaps five times that size—considerably weaker than might have been expected from earlier levels of activity. They had made, however, several important gains. Despite much confusion and sectarian posturing, they had placed black liberation on the Left political agenda as it had not been placed before, and had taken preliminary steps to appeal to poor blacks north and south. Second, they had in their labor work increasingly encouraged the cadre whose groundwork most definitely prefigured the CIO. Third, they had regularized many internal institutions (such as the *Daily Worker*) and functions (such as the ethnic-based International Workers Order established in 1932) that could serve better as the Party emerged from sectarianism.

That emergence took some years and exacted considerable costs. William Z. Foster's 1932 book, *Towards a Soviet America*, demonstrated little appreciation for the unique qualities of the American mentality even in a potentially prerevolutionary situation. His presidential campaign of that year, despite the backing of noted intellectuals, had little impact relative to Norman Thomas's Socialist effort, which recorded almost a million votes. Moreover, wild sectarian attacks upon Socialists and reformers delayed or prevented potential alliances against the worst effects of the Depression. Marches upon city halls frequently evoked more violence than a wide potential following felt itself prepared to accept. Some of the best work, rent strikes and related neighborhood relief efforts, grew up among the unprestigious women supporters of largely Jewish neighborhoods, and the lessons sunk in slowly. Veteran youth leaders, such as Gil Green, seemed to grasp most readily the need for a broad new orientation. Hundreds of young Communists entering factories strove to put their ideas into practice, but without a general Party line that would facilitate this work. Perhaps only southern Communists, offering a virtual black insurrectionary line, found a constituency whose dire condition might instill faith in Communism—and here, with repression so intense, little opportunity for open organizing existed.

The San Francisco General Strike of 1934 signalled the changing attitudes. Labor activists fought their way to rejoin a sluggish but awakening left-of-center. Permitted to move into wider spheres, with fewer ideological restrictions, activists in many arenas began to find a wide acceptance. Communist participation in the movement for social security indicated another measure of political realism. Harlem activists dared to work with controversial evangelist Father Divine on the one hand, and invite the participation of noted jazz musicians to protest events on the other. Ethnic fraternalists, now striving to reinterpret their cultural traditions in a radical way and to argue openly for the survival of these traditions, began to find new links with economic discontent and labor yearnings around them. Students of socialist, communist, and liberal leanings started to share podiums and finally united a few years later into one organization.

The Communist approach to the 1936 election set the tone for the virtual abandonment of its traditional strategies and slogans. Roosevelt's promulgation of a "Second New Deal," replete with real and promised social benefits, had won over millions of immigrant voters (or previous nonvoters), including the mass base of industrial unions. As veteran SP notables abandoned their party to support Roosevelt, Communists pronounced a de facto support of Roosevelt against Alf Landon—the first time an official U.S. Marxist organization had taken such a position. In a broader sense, the Communists had gone over to a Center-Left alliance with measured emphasis upon the Left.

Shifts in the Communist press reflected this broad reorientation. The *New Masses* became a popular magazine among the left-liberal middle classes, especially in the East, and the *Daily Worker* toned down its earlier sensationalism for a more workmanlike approach to creating a solid Left journalism. The *Communist*, however, revealed the most dramatic shift. Long an arid mechanism of doctrinal self-justification, in the hands of political-intellectual chief Alexander Bittelman the monthly became notably more strategic and tactical-minded. His own editorial essay, considered at the time the definitive up-to-the-moment political statement from the Party, shrewdly argued for something like an advanced social democracy.

At the climax of this reorientation, in the later 1930s, the Party reached 65,000 members and attained a very wide following in many sections of American life. Providing national, regional and local leadership of many important industrial unions as well as liberal, student, and cultural organizations, Communists and "fellow travelers" served as a dynamic wedge of radicalism within the dominant New Deal liberalism. Left activists had, in an important sense, followed the inclinations of their own constituencies toward Roosevelt. For the moment, this strategic adaptation largely coincided with imperatives set out by the Comintern.

Influence in labor, especially, grew rapidly after John L. Lewis agreed to use Communist organizers in the nascent CIO. Communist leaders, rising out of the ranks, won wide approval through their fearlessness and their dedication. Communists in New York State's American Labor Party (which repeatedly sent the radical Vito Marcantonio to Congress), in Minnesota's Farmer-Labor Party, and in the progressive wing of the Democratic Party, came to be looked upon as agents not of Moscow but of the democratic agenda. Influential Communists could be found in cinema, the theater, music, and the graphic arts. The vital social theater and mural art of the Works Progress Administration, especially, were at their highest creative levels, often quite pro-Communist in sympathies. Communist identification of racism as the running sore of democracy and the mark of incipient fascism, combined with Communists' ardent efforts to uplift the cause of minorities both politically and culturally, prompted liberal respect almost bordering upon awe.

Communist efforts in international affairs had more mixed results. The Spanish Civil War became a liberal cause célèbre, and its fallen heroes the martyrs of a generation—even if millions of unquestioning American Catholics did not think so. For many East European immigrants, anti-Nazi Russia with all its flaws seemed vastly preferable to its alternative—such as the collaborationist regimes in Hungary, Yugoslavia, Lithuania, and other nations. Liberals, dismayed by the lack of resistance against fascism from democracies like France and Great Britain, were likewise willing to forgive Soviet shortcomings. Jewish support for the Communist movement rose precipitously.

On the other hand, the public portrayals of Russia as a virtual paradise for workers and peasants required great credulity, even in the best of times, and the later 1930s were far from the best of times. Stalin's purges of the "Old Bolsheviks" through the Moscow Trials required ideological overkill from American Communists, which baffled and pained their liberal allies. The unquestioning acceptance of such positions by ordinary Communists raised serious questions for nonmembers. The undemocratic character of American Communism's inner organizational life did not greatly exceed that of the Republican or Democratic parties, but the perceived gap between deed and word expanded just as Communists staked their claim upon being the tribunes of democracy.

The Hitler-Stalin Pact and the turn of Communists to extreme antiwar positions permitted conservatives their long-awaited opportunity at legal repression. The pact might have been defended as a forced necessity, but Communists mercilessly attacked those who held to the anti-Hitler front, alienating themselves from the very groups with whom they had been most intimate. Loss of Party membership was slight, but sympathizers were stunned at the sudden shift in directions, broadly rekindling old fears of American Communism as a Soviet pawn. Opponents of the Party within the CIO and liberal circles took advantage of the opportunity to puncture Communist moral authority. Congressional committees played upon public fears to savage the most left-leaning New Deal programs. Party leader Earl Browder went to jail on a passport violation, reminding Communist regulators that their gains in American life had never been secure. Roosevelt's new "Doctor Win-the-War" strategy signaled the virtual collapse of the liberal agenda, but Communists had long since come to the point of no return. To remove themselves from the Democratic Party coalition meant isolation.

Following the German invasion of the USSR, the Communists again switched their line to unrelenting opposition to the Nazis. Under the Democratic Front policy the Party worked with all other democratic forces to rally new levels of popular support for Soviet-American cooperation. Party membership would hit its all-time peak of 85,000 in 1942. If there was a moment when the Communists might have totally surfaced all their members in the trade union movement and other organizations, this was it. Earl Browder, in fact, attempted to tailor his organization to American conditions by formally abandoning the designation of "party" for the Communist Political Association, which indicated the organization would now function as a political pressure group.

The Communist influence in certain regions became considerable in the 1940s. In New York City neighborhoods where housing struggles continued to be popular and where Communists offered the only thoroughgoing perspective for the creation of a multiracial and multicultural democracy, Communist candidates were elected to municipal offices. Moreover, major social-political figures considered close to the Party, notably Harlem's Rev. Adam Clayton Powell, exerted even wider influence. Simultaneously, and for the first time, Communist spokespersons, such as Elizabeth Gurley Flynn in her *Daily Worker* column, began to argue for a forceful advancement of women's rights, not merely protective legislation or special consideration as women workers. In such matters, especially in relation to liberal organizations of many types, subtle shifts from proletarian to lower-middle-class orientations served the Party well.

Despite the obvious strengths of the Communist movement, there were numerous handicaps. The frequent zigzagging in political line, with equal ferocity brought to instantly changing positions, had sapped its intellectual credibility. The near-fanatical attachment to wartime national unity seemed all too characteristic of past adaptations. Across a wide spectrum of efforts, the Party paid a heavy price, as Popular Front organizations (e.g., the Congress of Spanish Speaking Peoples) that had been created under difficult conditions were now suddenly abandoned or dissolved. In like manner, Communist insistence upon the no-strike pledge in war industries and other curbs on militancy, while not universally applied, nevertheless created hostility among some of the most militant industrial workers. Support of the Smith Act usage against Trotskyists and support of the confinement of Japanese Americans raised serious doubts about Communist commitments to civil liberties.

The Party also had an unrepresentative geographic spread, being concentrated mainly in a few urban areas, particularly New York. Communist membership on the New York City Council and a factory base not unlike modest-size European Communist parties were totally unrepresentative of national Communist strength. A majority of the Party was female and worked from neighborhood rather than factory bases. Many male Communists who joined the armed forces would return from war greatly changed and in many instances would be propelled from the working class by benefits offered in the GI Bill.

By the time the war drew to a close, the Communist accommodation to the liberal and labor establishment swelled to a crescendo without, however, winning over or neutralizing stubborn opponents who awaited an opportunity to isolate the Party. The emerging Cold War soon placed Communists at an enormous disadvantage. The problem was compounded when Browder was removed as leader of the Party after Russian disfavor was signaled via a critical letter issued by the head of the French CP. Considerable internal confusion ensued and Americans already skeptical of CP independence saw Browder's fall as another sign of the Party's domination by a foreign power.

The Party, now gravely weakened, reestablished its form in 1945, but its leadership was in disarray. Organizational feuding resulted in numerous individual expulsions and in collective cynicism among many longtime supporters. Left ethnics faced a considerable influx of new, largely middle-class, and in some cases, formerly collaborationist refugees bitterly hostile to Communism. They, as Communists in general, also faced the hard reality of oppressive Russian rule in Eastern Europe and growing perceptions about the long-term prospects for Stalinist restrictions on rights and liberties. Rapid reorientation of the Left under these conditions became almost impossible.

The first hints of a cohesive anticommunist campaign—from Cold War liberals and social democrats to far Right organizations to government agencies—offered disturbing glimpses of the future in store. The Union for Democratic Action, predecessor of the Americans for Democratic Action, announced Communist exclusion as one of its main tenets. The more conservative CIO and AFL leaders began to pinpoint Communist centers of influence to be eliminated, and to buttress significant labor support (the Association of Catholic Trade Unionists offered a semimass base, while liberals such as the Reuther brothers supplied organizational muscle) behind a drive to marginalize the Party faithful.

In response, the Party led a spirited anti-Cold War effort across many sectors. Among liberals who hoped for postwar détente between America and Russia, the Progressive Citizens of America used celebrities such as Frank Sinatra and a compulsive mobilization of well-placed activists to fight the lure of President Truman's mix of domestic reforms and international aggressiveness. The American Veterans Committee, farm groups, race leaders, and others rallied opponents of American leaders' de facto plan to dominate the postwar world through economic power and atomic weapons.

The Party threw itself desperately into the Henry Wallace campaign of 1948, and suffered dire consequences both before and after Wallace's ignominious defeat. By pressuring friendly union leaders to support Wallace, at a time when the CIO had shifted rightward on foreign policy and was simultaneously cracking down bureaucratically on its own rebellious ranks, the Party propelled some of its former stalwarts and their unions out of the Left orbit. Individuals who accepted CP positions faced expulsion from the CIO in 1949, either from their office or with their entire unions. With ever fewer institutional defenses to support liberal and labor activists, the Red Scare tactics of government and business found ready prey. Thousands of activists, members and former members of the CP or Left-linked movements, were grilled by FBI agents, their family and fellow workers intimidated, mail and phone service intercepted, and (especially for those in conservative districts) a public outcry incited against them by the active Right.

Desertions accelerated on all sides. For instance, while the Party shifted away from support of third parties after the Wallace defeat, many "progressives" such as those grouped around the *National Guardian* asserted their independence, taking up causes such as Vito Marcantonio's last Congressional campaign, which was viewed askance by the Party. For such people, the Communists had ceased to be the center-point of progressive politics, not only because of the Party insistence upon unquestioning loyalty to Soviet pronouncements, but also because Communists could no longer deliver organizational muscle.

The anticommunist movement that had been building since the 1940s with a full panoply of public and private acts thus fell upon the Party at its weakest moment. With most leaders and celebrities already gone, investigators could pick off remaining supporters through a combination of jail threats and deprivation of public access. Communist opposition to the Korean War impelled wide fears about a coming world conflict, with American Communists as a "Fifth Column" subverting defense efforts. Newspaper tabloids whipped up a frenzy, with headlines like FBI TO STRIKE AT 20,000 REDS, identifying Communists with potential military subversion. The Hiss case, the Rosenberg case, and a host of others were orchestrated—with careful preparation by the FBI, often in the form of prompting witnesses with pat answers—to demonstrate that America had "lost" China and the A-bomb secrets due to Communist infiltration of government. Meanwhile, fishing-expedition hearings essentially demanded of witnesses that they repudiate their past Left activities, and furthermore give testimony against their trusted friends and co-workers of many years.

Two sectors suffered especially from these varied forms of repression. The fraternal International Workers Order, a financial backbone of the Party and a symbol of Communist respectability among aging European immigrants and many of their descendants, was quashed. Communists lost contact with several generations of working-class activists who, without joining, had taken Party teachings and local representatives seriously. Fraternal and folk-dance groups, summer-camps, shuls, choruses, and other activities remained, but far smaller and more insular. Second, the youth sector, reorganized in 1949 as the Labor Youth League, practically had to operate underground. The Party lost, in effect, virtually an entire generation that might have bridged the gap to the New Left.

Political opportunities to advance the Left-liberal program therefore fell by the way. Urgently needed contemporary reform projects—such as the National Negro Labor Congress, established with wide black support to further racial equality within the labor movement—attracted only hostility from liberal-minded non-Communists. Remaining local activists worked on their own at any rate, as the foremost Party leaders had gone underground, and (preparing for the worst by reducing themselves to hardened cadres) the organization dropped many faithful members who had merely neglected their membership renewals.

Two international events of 1956 brought new chaos to the Party: the Soviet suppression of the Hungarian Revolution and revelations of Stalin's misdeeds at the Twentieth Soviet Congress. Individuals long faithful to the Party now felt betrayed and wondered privately and openly if their political lives had been built upon self-delusion.

Self-appointed reformers centered around the *Daily Worker* briefly sought an internal transformation into an open, democratic movement. An unprecedented wave of collective self-criticism appeared in the pages of the Party's national organ. The departure of many like-minded members, filled with despair or disgust, contributed to their defeat by doctrinaire loyalists. With the victors stood a considerable section of the ethnic faithful, many of whom had personally experienced the Palmer era repressions and now refused to be cowed by or to accept the various revelations as sufficient cause to leave the movement. Their now increasingly prominent presence, in a smaller organization, revealed a new demographic reality: the Party had been aging. This process was not as abrupt as it seemed. Recruitment of young people had peaked in the 1930s. That tendency would now become a dominant trend.

Greatly weakened as the Party ranks were, they still included many extraordinary individuals, and within the Party's surviving peripheries were many more. Ironically, the Party's weakness made for better work in alliances. Party activists rarely felt the necessity, much less the opportunity, to impose their positions on non-Communists. Some of their opponents in mass movements had also grown weary of ideological and organizational struggle, frequently having moved upward to bureaucratic office or occasionally recognizing the harm done to labor and reform movements by the old internecine squabbling. Anti-Stalinism lacked left-wing credentials in a society whose obsessive anticommunism had become a primary public rationale for the arms industry, unrecalcitrant racial segregation, and the unhampered political activity of FBI and CIA operatives. All this did not mean that future fellow activists with Communists accepted the persistently claimed virtues of the Communist-led nations, only that the issue had been put aside as less pressing than matters at hand.

As the Cold War eased, and Third World liberation struggles replaced great power face-offs as the immediate focus of foreign policy, Communists began to reemerge. Communists played a key role in the new Africa-support movement, in many cases educating church people to the real effects of neo-colonialism and helping to establish liaisons between liberals and the newly independent states. CP supporters, meanwhile, continued their longtime pioneering work in the South, quietly establishing themselves within the new civil rights movement, although never becoming the dominant or manipulative force that conservatives imagined. *Freedomways* magazine, established with Party assistance, had an authoritative quality among many, especially older, black activists. Comparable political work was accomplished in northern industrial areas with minority populations and militant trade unions. The Party retained pockets of labor strength, especially among officials and older rank-and-filers among the West Coast longshoremen, but also in other scattered industries and locations. The ethnic networks, however reduced, continued to maintain a sufficient following for a dozen daily presses and a variety of other activities.

When a renewed radical movement took shape in the 1960s, the CP—for the first time in its existence—was not the dominant force on the Left. In major cities, the CP network of trade union contacts—seasoned veterans of Left-liberal coalitions and ethnic activists—could be counted upon to form broad alliances against war and racism, but there were other radical formations of equal or greater strength. Frequently, Party commitment to work within the Democratic Party and the broad liberal spectrum put local Communists at a disadvantage within the embryonic New Left. In 1964 nearly all activists could agree upon the defeat of Barry Goldwater as a pressing priority. Thereafter, the role of the Democratic Party mainstream gave the arguments for liberal coalitions more obvious contradictions. Communist political sniping at New Leftists, while never reaching the orchestrated heights of 1930s–1940s anti-Trotskyism, precipitated an uncomfortable generation gap between many veteran militants and their own children or grandchildren, a conflict that New Leftists' own youthful arrogance personalized and exacerbated.

As a result, while Communists took a leading role in some specific fronts of the anti–Vietnam War movement, pacifists and Trotskyists ultimately staffed most of the movement's infrastructure. The new W. E. B. DuBois Clubs (organized in 1965) renewed campus activism but with far fewer members than Students for a Democratic Society and fewer chapters than the Young Socialist Alliance. Successful CP mechanisms among youth, such as the Che-Lumumba Club of Los

Angeles, tended to be local in nature and dependent upon particularly accommodating CP leaders. One strong point, the Party's fraternal links with revolutionary movements in Vietnam, Mozambique, South Africa, Cuba and elsewhere in the Third World, gave the Party its highest contemporary prestige and influence, without however prompting any wide-scale recruitment even among Third World support activists.

The Communists had few contacts with the emerging sexual liberation movements, notwithstanding the past Party membership of the Mattachine Society founders and past Popular Front links with some senior women's liberation figures such as Bella Abzug. While some parts of the now "Old Left" would rally to the gay movement as it emerged, the CP remained aloof. Likewise, while the CP had long supported women's rights as part of the progressive agenda, it was not prepared for an autonomous feminist movement that appeared to replace class with sex as the primary contradiction. Like the painfully antifeminist perspectives of some black liberation leaders, Communist fears of black women not supporting black men's activities betrayed a lack of fundamental commitment to gender issues. Communists could not place themselves on record for so mild a measure as the Equal Rights Amendment, and therefore benefited little from the women's liberation movement with all its ramifications.

Little improvement could be seen with the collapse of the New Left. Trotskyists and, especially, Maoists rather than Communists recruited most of the New Left activists turning toward Leninism in the late 1960s and early 1970s. Intense factionalism and disillusionment with the Chinese regimes soon destroyed hopes for a "new communist party" with the strength of the old CP, but relatively few younger activists on campus (many now notably influenced by religious ideas) or in communities turned to the Party for leadership. Continuing uncritical support for the USSR, especially in the face of Eastern European dissent and occasional uprising, sustained the anxieties of the middle 1950s and provoked further internal discontent. The resignation of West Coast leader Dorothy Healey in 1973 was taken as a signal to many outsiders that the established Party leadership had determined to remain impervious to the democratic challenges heard in Eurocommunism.

Nevertheless, American Communism had over the decades acquired an invaluable asset upon which it would now draw freely. The most historical-minded generation in the American Left, graduating from campus and community activism, collaborated with Party stalwarts and sympathizers as well as non-Communist radicals in celebrating American traditions of militancy. A wave of documentary films, written histories, memoirs, and public events, some widely acclaimed and even government-funded, commenced in the middle 1970s. At the local level, high officials turned out for prestige banquets to sanctify and vindicate the lives of elderly Communists. Over the objections of many critics, and despite the virtual end of controversial public funding in the Reagan era, American Communism became a recognized and even respected part of American reform history.

Communists also gained from long-standing political contacts in the black community. Victories of black mayoral and congressional candidates with decades-old ties to the CP—a short list would include Coleman Young and George Crocket in Detroit, Gus Newport in Berkeley, and somewhat more ambiguously, Harold Washington in Chicago—helped to rehabilitate the Party image. Like the continuing struggle against racism within unions, this public vindication brought a trickle of new black and Latin members, although never enough to compensate for the attrition in the aging fraternal networks.

The CP managed to emerge from the 1970s in far better organizational shape than might have been expected and much stronger than any of its immediate political rivals. The perenially fractured SWP had shrunk to its pre-1960s size and influence, and was in the odd ideological position of emphasizing the theories of Fidel Castro over those of Leon Trotsky. None of its numerous breakaway groups, all of which were closer to original Trotskyist doctrine, had attracted a significant following. The Maoists, whose various organizations had had a combined membership in the thousands, had all but disappeared as had would-be successors to SDS. The only other large Left group was the Democratic Socialists of America (DSA), which remained smaller than the CP (which still claimed it had over 10,000 members), and had a less activist rank and file. Both DSA and the CP could boast of more than a few trade union members, officials, and sympathizers. But only the CP was strong enough to maintain a daily newspaper, the *Daily World*.

The emergence of Mikhail Gorbachev as leader of the USSR in 1985 gave American Communists an unexpected, if also sometimes unnerving burst of new interest and new issues. With the Cold War fast fading and the USSR increasingly seen as the superpower most committed to ending the nuclear arms race, the CP could claim vindication for its long-term foreign-policy orientation. As many Americans voiced enthusiasm for Gorbachev's reforms, the CP stood to gain more public visibility. Although Communists were no longer central to movements such as those opposing apartheid in South Africa or supporting the Sandinista revolution in Nicaragua, they had placed themselves respectably within those broad currents. CP influence also extended into the newer political refugee communities (notably the Chilean, but also the Salvadorean, among others). Like smaller ideological groups but with generally more public impact, the CP campaigned vigorously against political repression of native-born and immigrant racial minorities.

The new Soviet candor also freed the Communists, at least in theory, from the need to support every regime in Eastern Europe and from the need to maintain that the Bolsheviks executed by Stalin had been truly the "agents of capital." By the end of the 1980s, the Party had not yet embarked upon its own programs of *glasnost* or *perestroika*, and the Gus Hall leadership evinced little eagerness to do so. Yet an avenue for internal reform had been opened. The irreversible decline of the Communist Party into insignificance—long predicted with great confidence by its critics—seemed at the very least decidedly premature.

See also: Abraham Lincoln Brigade; African Blood Brotherhood; Allerton Avenue Co-ops; American Committee for Protection of the Foreign Born; American League Against War and Fascism; American Negro Labor Congress; American Slav Congress; American Soviet Friendship; American Student Union; American Writers Congress; Anticommunism; Antirevisionism; Aptheker, Herbert; Armenian Americans; Berry, Abner; Birmingham, Alabama; Bloor, Ella Reeve; Bridges, Harry; Brodsky, Joseph; Browder, Earl; Bulgarian Americans; Cannon, James P.; Chinese Americans; Civil Rights Congress; Congress of American Artists; *Daily Worker*; Davis, Angela; Davis, Benjamin; Federal Bureau of Investigation; Flynn, Elizabeth Gurley; Foner, Philip; Foster, William Z.; Fraina, Louis C.; *Freiheit*; Gastonia Strike; Gellert, Hugo; Gold, Michael; Green, Gil; Grey, Eula; Hall, Gus; Haywood, Harry; Healey, Dorothy; Hitler-Stalin Pact; Hollywood Blacklist; Hollywood Left; Hudson, Hosea; Hungarian Americans; ILGWU; ILWU; Inman, Mary; International Publishers; International Workers Order; Jefferson School; Jones, Claudia; Krushchev Revelations; Latvian Americans; Lawson, John Howard; Lithuanian Americans; Lore, Ludwig; Lovestonites; McCarthyism; *Mainstream*; Minor, Robert; Moscow Trials; National Maritime Union; National Woman's Commission; *New Masses*; Olgin, Moissye; Paterson, William; Patterson, Louis Thompson; Peekskill; *People's World*; Popular Front; Progressive Party; Public Sector Unions; Puerto Ricans; Rapp-Coudert; Radical Filmmaking; Red Daiper Baby; Red Scare; Reed, John; Rent Strikes; Robeson, Paul; Rosenberg Case; Ruthenberg, Charles; San Francisco General Strike; Scales, Julius Irving; Share Croppers Union; Southern Negro Youth Congress; Southern Worker; Rose Pastor Stokes Summer Camps; Taft-Hartley Loyalty Oath; Teachers Union; *Toveritar*; Trade Union Educational League; Ukrainian Americans; Unemployed Movements of the 1930s; United Farm Equipment and Metal Workers Union; UCAPAWA; UPOWA; Vanguard Party; Williams, Claude; Winston, Henry; Workers Schools; *Working Woman/Woman Today*; Young Communist League

—*Paul Buhle,*
Dan Georgakas

REFERENCES

Bart, Philip, Theodore Bassett, William W. Weinstone, and Arthur Zipser, eds. *Highlights of a Fighting History: Sixty Years of the Communist Party, USA*. New York: International Publishers, 1979.

Buhle, Paul. *Marxism in the USA: Remapping the American Left*. London: Verso, 1987.

Draper, Theodore. *American Communism and Soviet Russia*. New York: Viking Press, 1960.

———. *Roots of American Communism*. New York: Viking Press, 1957.

Green, Gil. *Cold War Fugitive: A Personal Story of the McCarthy Years*. New York: International Publishers, 1984.

Isserman, Maurice. *If I Had a Hammer: The Death of the Old Left and the Birth of the New Left*. Middletown, Conn.: Wesleyan University Press, 1982.

———. *Which Side Are You On? The American Communist Party and the Second World War*. New York: Basic Books, 1987.

Klehr, Harvey. *The Heyday of American Communism: The Depression Decade*. New York: Basic Books, 1984.

Starobin, Joseph. *American Communism in Crisis: 1943–1957*. Cambridge: Harvard University Press, 1972.

COMMUNIST WORKERS PARTY:

see GREENSBORO MASSACRE

COMPOSERS COLLECTIVE

Between 1933 and 1936, the collective brought together in New York a dozen or more conservatory-trained composers to create a body of music for use as a weapon in the class struggle. Originally an offshoot of the Pierre Degeyter Club, named for the composer of the "Internationale" (1871), the collective was affiliated to the Workers Music League, which published music and coordinated the activities of proletarian choruses, mandolin orchestras, and other groups.

The tradition of revolutionary music in America consisted largely of lyricists, like Joe Hill, writing new words to old hymns and popular melodies. With his hour-long cantatas *October* and *Storm*, Jacob Schaefer was one of the few who wrote original music for left-wing audiences. But in the 1930s, when mass organizations of the Left arose in response to Depression conditions, sympathetic musicians wanted to contribute their skills to the cause. Some of the Composers Collective members, comfortable with brasher twentieth-century harmonies and even atonalism, followed European models such as Hanns Eisler, Stefan Wolpe, and Dmitri Shostakovich in trying to amalgamate modern musical idioms with proletarian texts. In form, their work consisted of rounds, mass songs, four-part choruses, and solo songs; some of these composers found a large new public at demonstrations, picket lines, and benefit concerts. The Composers Collective sent out "shock troops" with programs of varying length and content to support the Left movement.

Aside from Schaefer, other members of the Composers Collective included Lan Adomian, Charles Seeger, Elie Siegmeister, Norman Cazden, Alex North, Herbert Haufrecht, Henry Leland Clarke, and Earl Robinson. Marc Blitzstein served as secretary. Hanns Eisler and Aaron Copland attended occasional meetings. For subject matter, they turned to themes such as the Scottsboro Boys, Lenin, strikes, proletarian internationalism, unemployment, and satires of the bourgeoisie. For texts they took poems by such writers as Langston Hughes, Alfred Hayes, and the Communist Party's chief cultural authority, V. J. Jerome. In 1934 and 1935 the collective issued two volumes of the *Workers Songbook*. Collective members also wrote instrumental music with social content, such as Siegmeister's symphonic movement *May Day*.

In 1935–36 the CP shifted its strategy to the Popular Front. In this more populist phase, almost all of the collective members retracted from their international beaux-arts style and began turning toward native American folk music for their inspiration. Shortly thereafter, they went their separate ways and the collective fizzled out. None of the sophisticated, crafted music of the Composers Collective period, with its supermilitant texts, ever truly took root in the working class. But the collective was an important proving ground for its members, leading to such major statements in music as Blitzstein's *The Cradle Will Rock* and Robinson's *Ballad for Americans*, and to the ideas in Siegmeister's essay *Music and Society* (1938). *See also*: Blitzstein, Marc; Copland, Aaron; Jewish Folks Chorus; Robinson, Earl; Siegmeister, Elie; Seeger, Charles

—*Eric A. Gordon*

REFERENCES

Achter, Barbara. "Americanism and American Art Music, 1929–1945." Ph.D. diss., University of Michigan, 1978.

Blitzstein, Marc. "The Composers Collective of New York." *Unison* 1 (1936).

"Composers Collective of New York." In *The New Grove Dictionary of American Music*, edited by Stanley Sadie and H. Wiley Hitchcock. Washington D.C.: Grove's Dictionaries of Music, 1986.

Dunaway, David K. "Unsung Songs of Protest: The Composers Collective of New York." *New York Folklore* 1 (1977).

CONFERENCE FOR PROGRESSIVE LABOR ACTION: see MUSTE, A. J.

EL CONGRESO DEL PUEBLO DE HABLA ESPAÑOLA (THE SPANISH-SPEAKING CONGRESS)

The exact details on the origins of El Congreso are obscure, but the initial and main organizer was Luisa Moreno. Born in Guatemala, Moreno emigrated first to Mexico and then to the United States in 1928. Moreno was educated in the United States and graduated from the College of the Holy Names in Oakland, California. In a 1976 interview with Albert Camarillo, Moreno noted that she had worked as a seamstress in a New York City garment factory near Spanish Harlem. Sweatshop conditions plus association with leftist Latino workers led to her radicalization. Moreno first worked as an organizer for the Needles Trades Workers Industrial Union in the early 1930s and then with the AFL organizing Florida cigar workers. Moreno joined the CIO in 1937. She helped organize striking Mexican pecan shellers in San Antonio as an organizer for the militant United Cannery, Agricultural, Packing, and Allied Workers of America (UCAPAWA). Living and working with Spanish-speaking people, Moreno recognized the need for a mass organization of the Spanish-speaking in the United States.

In 1938 Moreno traveled throughout the Southwest as well as to other parts of the country organizing Committees for a National Congress of Spanish-Speaking Peoples (Comités en Pro del Congreso). She received support from a variety of sources: Mexican-American community groups, CIO unions, and progressive whites. The founding national convention of El Congreso took place in Los Angeles on April 28–30, 1939, with an estimated 1,500 people in attendance. While the exact role of the Communist Party in the establishment of El Congreso is not clear, the congress largely reflected a Popular Front strategy linking radical and liberal elements in the Mexican communities on a range of issues affecting Mexicans in the United States. It stressed the unity between Mexican-American workers and Mexican immigrant workers. Besides their common working-class roots, Mexicans were further united by history, culture, and oppressed conditions. Instead of regarding Mexicans in the Southwest as constituting a nation, El Congreso viewed Mexicans as a national minority that possessed inextricable ties with the rest of the American working class.

Between 1939 and the commencement of World War II, El Congreso engaged in a number of activities, principally in the greater Los Angeles area, aimed at protecting the rights of the Spanish-speaking as well as providing effective organization. These included relief assistance; protesting antialien legislation, police abuse, and the lack of low-cost housing; education; youth activities; the right to unionization; the rights of women; the neutrality movement; and wartime employment for Mexicans.

During its existence, El Congreso was led by its executive secretary, Josefina Fierro de Bright. At age eighteen Fierro became the main organizer and fundraiser for El Congreso. Born in 1920, in Mexicali, Fierro had fled the Mexican Revolution of 1910 with her parents. Her mother had been a follower of Ricardo Flores Magón, who represented the anarchosyndicalist faction of the revolution. Politicized by her mother, Fierro later married the Hollywood screenwriter John Bright, who, according to Nancy Lynn Schwartz in *The Hollywood Writers' Wars*, was an early member of the CP's Hollywood branch.

Although portrayed as a national organization, El Congreso consisted primarily of the California organization headquartered in Los Angeles. At least twelve branches of El Congreso functioned. These included branches in Central Los Angeles, East Los Angeles, Watts, Lincoln Heights, San Pedro, San Fernando, Wilmington, and Anaheim. Additional branches operated in Sacramento, Shafter, San Francisco, and San Diego. It is difficult to determine the exact number of members affiliated with each branch; however one branch reported a membership of two hundred in 1940.

El Congreso's shift from workers' struggles to wartime unity led to its demise. Militant reformism during the war, it was believed by Popular Front groups, would only play into the fascist's hands. By the middle of 1942, El Congreso effectively ceased to function. Still, activists such as Fierro did not remain dormant when particular cases of social discrimination surfaced. Fierro helped organize the Sleepy Lagoon Defense Committee in 1942 to defend several young Mexican Americans who were unjustly accused of murder. During the "zoot-suit riots" in Los Angeles the following year, Fierro personally flew to Washington to appeal to Vice President Henry Wallace to help put a stop to the attacks started by servicemen against young Mexican Americans.

Following WW II and the commencement of McCarthyism, El Congreso leaders such as Moreno and Fierro suffered political harassment and persecution. Luisa Moreno exiled herself to Mexico. Josefina Fierro de Bright, who had never become a U.S. citizen, left the United States for Mexico because she did not want to remain, face arrest, and possibly incriminate friends if subpoenaed.

—*Mario T. Garciá*

REFERENCES

Camarillo, Albert. *Chicanos in California: A History of Mexican Americans in California*. San Francisco: Boyd and Fraser, 1984.

Garciá, Mario T. *Mexican Americans: Leadership, Ideology, and Identity, 1930–1960*. New Haven: Yale University Press, 1989.

Ruiz, Vicki L. *Cannery Women/Cannery Lines: Mexican Women, Unionization, and the California Food Processing Industry, 1930–1960*. Albuquerque: University of New Mexico Press, 1987.

Oral history interviews with Luisa Moreno and Josefina Fierro de Bright are in the private possession of Albert Camarillo, Mario T. Garcia, and Vicki L. Ruiz.

Congress of American Artists

A smaller and less-remembered version of the Congress of American Writers, this congress rallied a wide variety of greater and lesser notables for an antifascist program.

The John Reed Clubs, primarily literary in purpose, had launched numbers of exhibitions in 1933–34 showcasing political, class-oriented work. With the turn toward the Popular Front and the convocation of the first National Writers Congress in 1935, leading figures of the Reed Clubs sought a more inclusive artistic expression. Stuart Davis, one of the prominent *Masses* artists twenty years earlier, served as executive secretary for a proposed artists' congress. Committees including Hugo Gellert, George Ault, Louis Lozowick, Ben Shahn, and others put together a planning committee (which also included former *Masses* artist Henry Glintenkamp). Many notables, such as Moses Soyer, Raphael Soyer, and Max Weber participated in the "call" for a congress.

The first meetings of the congress, held at New York's Town Hall and the New School for Social Research in February 1936, emphasized solidarity against fascism and war, so much so that the usual Left artists' criticisms of conservative regionalism or American Scene art virtually ceased. With the disappearance of that familiar critical edge, the avid Left promotion of social realist art practically faded from the CAA also. The lionization of the Soviet approach to social art, by Margaret Bourke-White and Louis Lozowick, only hinted at the utility of social realism for U.S. artists. Censorship (such as the effacement of Diego Rivera's Rockefeller Center murals) was viewed as a facet of the imminent danger fascism posed to world culture. Max Weber delivered the rhetorical high note of the congress, connecting art with the revolutionary transformation of society and embracing modern art's innovations as essential. Artist groups' representatives spoke at length about the economic and social conditions of their members, and efforts at collective improvement. Leading figures of the congress described it as the greatest event in American art since the Armory Show of 1913.

After the congress, working CAA branches sprang up in New York, Cleveland, St. Louis, New Orleans, Los Angeles, and Chicago, symposia were widely held, and various shows (including a noted print show, "America—1936") and annual exhibitions were opened. Meanwhile, the congress lobbied for a permanent federal arts program, helped establish an American Artists and Writers Ambulance Corps for Spain, and defended controversial art from suppression.

From 1937 to 1939, the same type of activity continued, with lower-key national meetings and much local politically oriented activity. Meanwhile, critics increasingly charged Communist domination (a prospect that Stuart Davis, promised autonomy, had resisted in practice). Ultimately, the compulsion to defend the Moscow Trials and the Hitler-Stalin Pact proved too much. Davis himself grew weary of Communists' bloc-voting, and sought to reduce the CAA's purview to solely artistic affairs. A 1940 vote to approve a report favoring Russia's invasion of Finland precipitated Stuart Davis's resignation and a minority report charging Communist Party domination of the CAA. The organization limped on, with Henry Glintenkamp as chairman, and a variety of loyalists (including William Gropper, Raphael Soyer, Philip Evergood, and Art Young) in tow. It officially dissolved in 1942. *See also*: Congress of American Writers; Gellert, Hugo; Gropper, William; Rivera, Diego (Murals); Young, Art

—*Paul Buhle*

REFERENCES

"The American Artists' Congress: Its Context and History." Introduction to *Artists Against War and Fascism: Papers of the First American Artists' Congress*, edited by Matthew Baigell and Julia Williams. New Brunswick: Rutgers University Press, 1986.

Congress of American Women

This short-lived organization (1946–1950) was founded as the U.S. branch of the Women's International Democratic Federation, a post-war, anti-fascist alliance of eighty-one million women in forty-one countries dedicated to women's equality, security and opportunity for children, and peace for all. The founders and leaders of CAW were a group of prominent American women, black and white, of left-liberal to Communist political orientations. Among them were Cornelia Bryce Pinchot, a suffrage leader and wife of a former governor of Pennsylvania; the aviator Jacqueline Cochran, a director of Eastern Airlines; Communist Party leaders Elizabeth Gurley Flynn and Claudia Jones; the actress Faye Emerson Roosevelt; anthropologist Gene Weltfish, author with Ruth Benedict of *The Races of Man*; black leaders Dr. Charlotte Hawkins Brown, Thelma Dale, and Vivian Carter Mason; and Muriel Draper, chairperson of the women's division of the Soviet-American Friendship Council.

In 1949 CAW claimed 250,000 members, and branches in the major industrial cities. On the grass-roots level, in neighborhood clubs, CAW organized black and white women around civil rights issues, against lynching, for lowering the cost of living, and against the Taft-Hartley Act. More than any feminist organizations before or since, CAW incorporated black women in its leadership and made racial equality an important plank in its program. The foreign-policy platform of CAW, like other American Popular Front organizations of its time, was dedicated to the fight against fascism, friendship with the Soviet Union, and international peace. What was distinct about CAW, however, what that in its program, rhetoric, and tactics, it combined a simultaneous demand for women's rights, world peace, and economic and social justice at home.

CAW supported the principle of equal pay for equal work, called for free public child-care centers, low-cost carry-home dinners and low-cost in-plant feeding for industrial workers, and large-scale kitchens and dining halls in every public housing project. The CAW Commission on the Status of Women supported an Equal Rights Amendment, but not in the form proposed by the National Women's Party, charging that the NWP amendment would wipe out protective legislation "built up over the past fifty years." With a sense of women's history rare for its time, the preamble to the CAW constitution invoked the memory of such historic women as Anne Hutchinson, Harriet Tubman, Sojourner Truth, Lucretia Mott, Harriet Beecher Stowe, Susan B. Anthony, Elizabeth Cady Stanton, and the Lowell mill girls. A CAW pamphlet proclaimed, "In the past the fight for women's rights was part of the fight against slavery and economic exploitation; today it is also part of the fight for peace and security everywhere."

As the Cold War escalated, the issue of world peace became the central focus of CAW. Its active opposition to the Truman Doctrine and the Marshall Plan and the frequent visits by its leading members to WIDF conferences in Communist countries provoked an investigation by the House Committee on Un-American Activities. Ironically HUAC singled out for attack Susan B. Anthony II and Nora Stanton Barney, granddaughter of Elizabeth Cady Stanton, who were both active members, and charged CAW with exploiting the legitimate women's rights movement for Communist gain. "There is even an Elizabeth Cady Stanton branch of CAW in the Bronx," HUAC complained in its report. CAW withstood the HUAC attack, but it could not survive the 1950 order by the Justice Department to register its officers and its board as foreign agents. At that point CAW voted, reluctantly, to sever its ties to WIDF. But there was no way of continuing the organization without a legal battle, which the officers and the CP decided would be too expensive, too draining, and probably futile in the political climate of the day. In late 1950 CAW voted to disband, and with it went the connection between the suffrage generation, the Old Left, and women's peace activism. *See also*: Peace Movements

—*Amy Swerdlow*

REFERENCES

Foster, Catherine. *Women for All Seasons: The Story of the Women's International League for Peace and Freedom.* Athens: University of Georgia Press, 1989.

Congress of Industrial Organizations: see Communist Party, Popular Front, FBI, Individual Unions

Connolly, James (1868–1916)

Irish Left-socialist with an international impact, Connolly ended a life of industrial and political struggle in an act of violent revolution. A leader of Ireland's Easter Rebellion, he was captured by British troops, later taken from a hospital bed, propped up in a chair, and shot.

Already a figure in the Irish nationalist and socialist movements, Connolly emigrated to the U.S. in 1902 and immediately began touring for the Socialist Labor Party. An outsider to the conservative Catholic leadership of most Irish-American communities, he proclaimed a message of industrial unionism, women's rights, and Irish consciousness. Most Irish-American workers, steeped in parochialism and racial values, could not accept his vision of socialism. Yet he was a widely admired figure for his personal courage and moral vision.

He found too little common ground with most of the U.S. Left. The SLP—and its leader, Daniel DeLeon, in particular—could barely tolerate his nonreductive view of nationality, his spiritual predilections, and above all his opposition to divorce. Not inside or outside the SLP did Connolly find sufficient support for his small, short-lived newspaper, the *Harp*, the sole Irish-American socialist publication of the time. After 1906 he turned his attention to the Industrial Workers of the World, in 1910 becoming editor of the *New Castle Free Press*, a Wobbly-oriented newspaper published in the heart of the area dominated by the Steel Trust.

Thereafter, he considered his American sojourn "a mistake" and said he "never ceased to regret it." Perhaps most difficult to him, beyond penury and political problems on the Left, was the general indifference of Irish-American nationalists to class exploitation and to the suffering of the poor. He returned home to become a beloved (and hated) figure in Ireland and England, with increasingly mythic proportions after his martyr's death. *See also*: Irish Americans

—Al McAloon

REFERENCES

Morgan, Austen. *James Connolly: A Political Biography.* New York: Manchester University Press/ St. Martin's Press, 1988.

Reeve, Carl, ed. *James Connolly and the U.S.* Atlantic Highlands, N.J.: Humanities Press, 1978.

Connolly Clubs: see Irish-Americans

Conroy, Jack (*b. 1899*)

A premier midwestern novelist, editor, and folklorist, Conroy was connected with the region from the time of his birth in the Monkey Nest coal camp on the outskirts of Moberly, Missouri. His Irish immigrant father, who had studied for the priesthood, died in a mining accident when Conroy was quite young, as did a brother and two half-brothers. In his teens, Conroy started work as an apprentice carman in the Wabash Railroad shops in Moberly and served as recording secretary for his union local. After joining the great strike of 1922, Conroy found himself blacklisted from any further railroad employment. He spent much of the 1920s as a migratory worker, sometimes riding the rails with Wobblies. His main source of education was the famous "Little Blue Books" of E. Haldeman-Julius.

After writing some poetry and deciding it was not his genre, Conroy joined with Ralph Cheney in establishing the *Rebel Poet* group and magazine in 1928. This magazine proclaimed "The Internationale of Song," and it established Conroy as the center of an energetic, talented, and discontented group of writers and artists, including H. H. Lewis, "Plowboy Poet of the Gumbo" (Conroy himself later became known, in Populist fashion, as the "Sage of Moberly"). During this period, Conroy coedited militant anthologies entitled *Unrest*, 1929–31. After differing with Cheney, Conroy began a new magazine called the *Anvil* (1933–35), a parallel experiment to the John Reed Clubs. The *Anvil*'s motto was We Prefer Crude Vigor to Polished Banality, and it attracted both readers and contributors from a widespread working-class audience. Its authors included Richard Wright, Kenneth Patchen, and Meridel LeSueur. Communist Party support made possible a circulation of some 5,000.

Meanwhile, Conroy's stories and sketches of working-class life had caught the eye of H. L. Mencken, who published several of them in his *American Mercury*. With Mencken's encouragement, Conroy drew these together for his best-known work, *The Disinherited* (1933), a novel. Widely praised as a broad-ranging chronicle of a young worker's exposure to life in rural and mining villages in the context of deepening economic and social crises, *The Disinherited* was one of the most authentic and important "proletarian" novels of the age.

Conroy successively worked on the staff of the Federal Writers Project, where he became the center of a rowdy, dissident group of midwestern bohemians called the "Parallel Centrists," gave an address at the American Writers Congress in 1935, and left Missouri for Chicago. In the meantime, he had been pressured by Communist cultural functionaries to relinquish control of the *Anvil* to a group of New York editors and writers around Philip Rahv and William Phillips, who excluded Conroy and soon transformed the project into a modernist-Trotskyist magazine, the *Partisan Review*. In Chicago, Conroy joined Nelson Algren in publishing the *New Anvil* (1939–40), which continued the earlier project of publishing working-class writers, this time including Frank Yerby, Margaret Walker, Tom McGrath, and Karl Shapiro. He also collected stories of industrial folklore (some of which appeared in B. A. Botkin's *Treasury of American Folklore*) and befriended Arna Bontemps, with whom he wrote an account of the rural-to-urban migration of black Americans, *They Seek a City* (1945).

In order to support his family, Conroy became the literary editor of an encyclopedia in Chicago for two decades, returning home to Moberly in 1966. He continued to play an important role encouraging younger writers, during a career in which by his own account he "must have written a million letters." In 1984 Moberly honored her "Sage" with a day of celebrations and discussions. *See also*: *Anvil and New Anvil*, John Reed Clubs, *Partisan Review*

—*Fred Whitehead*

REFERENCES

Conroy, Jack, and Curt Johnson, eds. *Writers in Revolt: The Anvil Anthology*. New York: Lawrence Hill, 1973.

New Letters magazine (special issue), 39 (Fall, 1972).

Wixson, Douglas. Introduction to *The Weed King and Other Stories*. Westport: Greenwood, 1985.

Copland, Aaron (b. 1900)

Composer and self-styled "good citizen of the Republic of Music," Copland devoted his talent as both composer and musical commentator to the cause of political music in the mid-1930s. He spent a comfortable childhood in Brooklyn that included piano study at an early age. By 1917 he had begun to define his personal sensibility as a modernist in response to the more traditional aesthetic of his teacher, Rubin Goldmark. Between 1920 and 1924, Copland studied with Nadia Boulanger at the American Academy at Fontainebleau. The years after his return from Paris saw the flowering of Copland's talent as an advocate for modern American music. He was a member of the League of Composers and a major contributor to *Modern Music*. A founder (with composer Roger Sessions) of the Copland-Sessions Concerts, he helped to bring new music to New York, and he lectured on music at the New School for Social Research from 1927 to 1937. In the late 1920s, Copland was among a group of American modernist composers who incorporated the sounds and technical features of jazz into his works for the concert hall. In the mid-1930s, he was associated with left-wing musical activists as a participant in the Composers' Collective and a writer for *New Masses*. He asserted the importance of mass singing as a vehicle for communicating the "day-to-day struggle of the proletariat" as part of the development of a working-class movement in the United States and asserted that American workers needed a music appropriate to their own struggles. In 1934, Copland's setting of "Into the Streets, May First!" (text by Alfred Hayes) won a song competition sponsored by *New Masses* and was subsequently published in the collective's second *Workers Songbook* (1935). A year later, Copland composed an opera for children, *The Second Hurricane*, that includes a chorus of parents. This work, along with the "Outdoor Overture," written in 1938 for New York City's High School of Music and Art, serve as examples of Copland's commitment to making concert music accessible to wide audiences and groups of performers. During the following decade, Copland's explicitly political activity was transformed into an effort to incorporate American folk and popular music along with regional settings into many of his concert and stage works. His ballet scores for *Billy the Kid* (1938), *Rodeo* (1942) and *Appalachian Spring* (1943–44) all reflect the composer's interest in portraying regional history in music and in treating songs that might be familiar to American audiences as materials for motivic development. The *Lincoln Portrait* for speaker and orchestra (1942) utilizes popular tunes of the famous president's time as well as his speeches and writings. While Copland's concern with class struggle as reflected in art did not continue beyond the period of the mid- to late-1930s, he made a significant contribution to music on the Left and helped to bring the popular music of the American people into the concert hall. *See also*: Composers' Collective Popular Front

—*Barbara L. Tischler*

REFERENCES

Copland, Aaron, and Vivian Perlis. *Copland, 1900 Through 1942*. New York: St. Martin's/Marek, 1984.

Reuss, Richard A. "American Folklore and Left-Wing Politics." Ph.D. diss., Indiana University, 1971.

Tischler, Barbara L. *An American Music, The Search for an American Musical Identity.* New York: Oxford University Press, 1986.

Zuck, Barbara Ann. *A History of Musical Americanism.* Ann Arbor: UMI Research Press, 1980.

CORE: see CIVIL RIGHTS

COUNCIL COMMUNISM

Council communism emerged in Germany and Holland in the 1920s, spreading to the United States by the time of the Great Depression. Though council communists never built organizations of any size or led struggles of particular note, they kept alive a vision of self-emancipatory communism that, at key points in American history, connected with oppositional movements. Independent of both the reformist and the Leninist Left, council communists have long offered a vision of a "third path," both Marxist and libertarian.

Council communism as a body of ideas was constructed on two pillars: (1) that the spontaneous explosions of working-class activity that characterized the Russian Revolution of 1905, the Industrial Workers of the World mass strikes of 1909–13, the Russian Revolution of 1917, and the German revolution of 1918–19 showed the way forward; in particular, that workers could organize themselves directly at the point of production and then connect organizations to challenge for social power; and (2) that vanguard parties constructed on the Leninist model would stifle and subvert such activity, block self-organization, and blunt any thrust toward self-emancipation.

The council communists locked horns with the Bolsheviks when the Third International insisted that all communist parties enter the trade union movement and participate in parliamentary politics in their own countries. The councilists argued that Western capitalism had entered a stage of crisis in which no reforms were possible, and that it was therefore counterproductive to rebuild reformist institutions like trade unions and parliamentary parties, particularly when workers themselves had shown an ability to transcend those institutions in the heat of struggle.

In 1921 Lenin read the council communists out of the Third International when he published *Left-Wing Communism: An Infantile Disorder*. Herman Gorter, the famous Dutch poet, answered that a model based on a largely peasant country ought not be imposed on an industrialized one (*Response to Lenin*, 1921). By the 1930s, the councilist critique of Leninism had deepened into a reinterpretation of the Russian Revolution. In his "Theses on Bolshevism" (*International Council Correspondence*, October 1934), Anton Pannekoek argued that the Bolsheviks had actually carried through the tasks of the bourgeois revolution—"the destruction of absolutism, the abolition of the feudal nobility as the first estate, and the creation of a political constitution and an administrative apparatus that would secure politically the fulfillment of the economic tasks of the revolution." Otto Rühle argued in "The Struggle Against Fascism Begins with the Struggle Against Bolshevism" (*Living Marxism*, September 1939) that the Communist parties in the West had become a major obstacle to the development of the self-emancipatory tendencies expressed in the revived labor movement.

It was in the 1930s that council communism reached America, as part of the diaspora of the European Left. There were some contacts made with the IWW and the Proletarian Party. But the councilists' main activity remained the circulation of ideas within fairly small circles, primarily through their own journals (*International Council Correspondence, New Essays*, and *Living Marxism*), occasionally in journals with a broader audience (V. F. Calverton's *Modern Monthly* or Dwight Macdonald's *Politics*), and through books (Karl Korsch's *Karl Marx* [1936] and Anton Pannekoek's *Worker's Councils* [1946]). Council communism's emphasis on spontaneity and self-organization, as well as its critique of bureaucracy and institutionalized leadership, touched responsive chords in the sit-down strikes of 1936–37 and the wildcat strikes of WW II.

Council communism again touched oppositional movements in America during the 1960s and 1970s. Its emphasis on self-emancipation and direct democracy, as well as its critique of bureaucracy and reformism, resonated with the outlook expressed by the campus-based New Left. A new journal and pamphlet series was begun (*Root and Branch*), which reissued Pannekoek's *Workers' Councils*, and explored the American student movement and Afro-American history. Jeremy Brecher's *Strike* (1972) presented a councilist interpretation of American labor history. It was originally subtitled *The True History of Mass Insurgence in America from 1877 to the Present* and was published by Straight Arrow, then connected with *Rolling Stone* magazine. Over the next two decades, *Strike* sold more than 35,000 copies and helped to shape a new activist generation's understanding not only of labor history but of the role of the working class in future social change.

The best known of all the council communists in America was Paul Mattick. Born in Germany in 1904, he worked as a skilled tool-and-die maker and participated in Rosa Luxemburg's youth group before WWI. He played an active role in the revolutionary events of 1918–21 and helped build Left (KAPD) and mass syndicalist (AAUD and AAUD-E) organizations in the 1920s. Mattick emigrated to America in 1926, where he collaborated with cultural radicals like Max Eastman and labor radicals like the IWW in Chicago before assuming responsibility for editing councilist journals. He became best known in the 1960s and 1970s as a Marxist economic theorist.

Mattick applied and elaborated Henryk Grossmann's interpretation of Marxist crisis theory—that the falling rate of profit resulted from the "overaccumulation" of capital and would lead to a "breakdown" in the capitalist economy. It was during such a crisis, Mattick posited, that spontaneous working-class revolutionary activity could be expected to revive (*Critique of Marcuse*, 1971). Mattick made an original contribution in his analysis of Keynesian economics. At a time when many on the Left as well as in the mainstream argued that state intervention and economic "fine-tuning" had banished all threats of depression to the historical past, Mattick applied a rigorous Marxist framework of value analysis and concluded that state intervention would soon reach its own "limits" in which the expenses of state expenditures would come to be viewed as a drag on corporate profits, as a syphon on investment capital (*Marx and Keynes: The Limits of the Mixed Economy*). Mattick's framework continues to prove useful in the analysis of the "stagflation" of the 1970s and the Reaganite "supply-side economics" and "deregulation" in the 1980s. *See also*: Industrial Workers of the World, Proletarian Party, Vanguard Party

—*Peter Rachleff*

REFERENCES
Rachleff, Peter. *Marxism and Council Communism*. Brooklyn: Revisionist Press, 1976.

Coxey's Army: see Industrial Armies

Criminology

During the post–World War II period, up to the mid-1960s, criminology was an extension of the theoretical perspectives that were formulated in the 1930s. This was a liberal criminology that sometimes stressed the social sources of crime, but focused primarily on the individual pathologies of the offender and promoted rehabilitation of criminals. Although radical ideas about crime existed among nineteenth-century utopian socialists, anarchists, and Marxists, these ideas had little effect on mainstream criminology in the United States during this period.

Early Marxist thinkers had not given much attention to crime. A few late nineteenth-century and early twentieth-century scholars who wrote about crime had been influenced in a rudimentary way by Marxist ideas. The Italian socialist Enrico Ferri rejected the biological determinism of Lombroso and sought the causes of crime in the social and economic conditions of the criminal. Willem Bonger argued that competitive capitalism gave rise to selfish individualism and the egoistic act of crime. There were studies by others of the relationship between crime rates and various economic conditions, including unemployment and food prices. In the United States at the turn of the century, reformist penologists and lawyers, especially Clarence Darrow, related crime to the economic conditions of the country. Later, in the 1930s, the critical thinkers Georg Rusche and Otto Kirchheimer, drawing from the Frankfurt Institute, documented the relationship between penal sanctions and the labor market.

Eventually, at the end of the 1950s, academic criminological research began to take a radical turn as it gave attention to the legal system, uncovering its social and economic sources and its selective definition of crime. However, it was with developments in the larger society of the 1960s that a truly radical criminology emerged, responding to the civil rights movement, the antiwar movement, the student movement, black power, and the feminist movement. Many criminologists—still largely educated in sociology departments—began to reject the belief in a benevolent state and a capitalist economy that had informed a liberal, positivistic criminology.

The "new" criminologists—variously called conflict, radical, critical, or Marxist criminologists—had a marked influence on the criminology of the 1970s. Mainstream criminology was severely challenged as the ideas of the New Left provided criminologists with new and controversial ways of understanding crime. At the beginning of the 1970s, criminologists began to read Marx for the first time and to apply Marxism to law and crime. Crime was understood in relation to the underlying mode of production and to class struggle. The solution to crime was seen in the transformation of society, and in the creation of socialist political and economic institutions. The new criminology brought into mainstream academic criminology the realization that as capitalist society is further threatened by its own contradictions, "criminal justice" is increasingly used to protect and legitimize the capitalist system.

Marxist criminology, among many of its practitioners, continued to emphasize the material foundations of crime and criminal justice. At the end of the 1980s, however, there emerged a new appreciation of the cultural and spiritual aspects of human existence and the appropriateness of such an appreciation in a developing Marxist criminology. This happened at the same time that mainstream criminology was being released from a decade of conservative thinking, a repressive perspective fostering deterrence and punishment, and systematically excluding the economic, political, and cultural sources of crime. The latest direction of Left criminology is toward peacemaking, a criminology that employs such ideas and practices as mediation, reconciliation, abolition of punishment and the death penalty, and humanist actions of various kinds. It is a criminology that is based necessarily on human transformation in the achievement of peace and justice.

The ideas of radical criminologists have reached several generations of college and university students in the United States and Canada, Europe, and Latin America, presenting a new message regarding the nature not only of crime but of capitalist society. Criminology has thus become part of the larger humanist and socialist movement. The struggles for liberation around the world—in response to repressive regimes and capitalist domination—are integral to the most recent developments in a criminology of the Left. *See also*: Sociology

—*Richard Quinney*

REFERENCES

Chambliss, William J., and Robert B. Seidman. *Law, Order, and Power*. 2d ed. Reading, Mass.: Addison-Wesley, 1982.

Currie, Elliott. *Confronting Crime: An American Challenge*. New York: Pantheon, 1985.

Greenberg, David F., ed. *Crime and Capitalism: Readings in Marxist Criminology*. Palo Alto, Calif.: 1981.

Quinney, Richard. *Criminology*. 2d ed. Boston: Little, Brown, 1979.

CRITICAL LEGAL STUDIES

This political-intellectual movement in legal thought took root in U.S. law schools in the late 1970s. Its original proponents had been influenced by the experience of the antiwar and particularly the civil rights movements, where appeals to legality played an important part in assisting organizing efforts and were sometimes successful in the courts.

Most of its proponents found the formulations of classical Marxism attractive but ultimately unsatisfyingly rigid, and an important theme in some works is the importance of abandoning grand social theories in favor of close attention to the details of particular historical moments.

Critical legal studies focuses on several propositions, though they are not all linked together in a tight logical unit: (1) Law is rife with contradictions. In particular, law attempts to express both our fear of and our dependence upon other people. At any single time, individual legal rules may subordinate one pole of the contradiction to the other. But other legal rules will reverse the hierarchy, and over time even the rules dealing with a single topic may flip from preferring one pole to preferring the other. (2) As a result, law is indeterminate, at least in any socially significant case. No single legal outcome or rule is required to the exclusion of other, often radically different, outcomes or rules. (3) When people assert that the law requires some result, several things might be going on: (a) If the people are members of the dominant class, they are attempting to construct a coherent ideological universe in which their positions of power are seen to be both justified and inevitable. (b) If they are members of subordinate classes, they may be deceiving themselves, making their lives more bearable by persuading themselves that there is nothing that can be done about their circumstances. (c) Or, more important, they may be appealing to the currently subordinated pole of the contradictions inherent in law. When they do so, appeals to legality take on a valuable utopian cast by demonstrating that within the present forms of law there are opportunities for radical change.

By the end of the 1980s, critical legal studies became a persistent irritant to mainstream legal thought, which responded by attempting to domesticate weaker versions of the ideal of indeterminacy while rejecting the other themes in critical legal studies, and by using traditional forms of Red-baiting and job-related penalties. *See also*: Boudin, Louis B.; National Lawyers Guild

—*Mark Tushnet*

REFERENCES

Kelman, Mark. *A Guide to Critical Legal Studies*. Cambridge: Harvard University Press, 1987.

Tushnet, Mark. *Red, White, and Blue: A Critical Analysis of Constitutional Law*. Cambridge: Harvard University Press, 1988.

Unger, Roberto. *The Critical Legal Studies Movement*. Cambridge: Harvard University Press, 1986.

CROATIAN AMERICANS

The Croatian-American community included a significant Left presence that grew out of both Old Country politics and the American experience. Socialists pioneered labor mobilization and secular education. Especially during the 1930s–1940s, the Left provided much of the community's leadership. Throughout, radicals played important cultural roles. After the Second World War, American cultural and political influences, along with the burgeoning of a powerful Croatian-American Right, cut many of the old ties. Unlike that of most other European communities, however, Croatian-American cultural life retained roughly social-democratic influences of enduring significance.

The Croatian Left was deeply rooted in the historical conflicts of the Old World. An internally diverse group, Croatians had struggled for a thousand years to rule themselves. The Austro-Hungarian Empire had abridged their freedom in the nineteenth century, and the Serbs took control after World War I. A radical peasant movement developed in response, pursuing economic justice and political democracy as much as national autonomy. Participants in this movement emigrated to America, and organizers frequently visited the "colonies" to proselytize and raise funds. They helped form radical culture clubs—especially around the famed *Tamburitza* (mandolin) orchestras—which grew up in Croatian-American neighborhoods and which, like the German-American *Turnvereins* before them, effectively bridged the gap between recreational activities and socialist politics. In 1907 a Croatian socialist movement, the Croatian Workers Organization and Political Association, officially formed, with *Radnicka Straze* (Workers' Outlook) its organ. Croatian immigrants, numbering perhaps a quarter-million in the U.S., were handicapped by their widespread lack of education; unlike their sister nationality, they had little exposure to European urban life and education. Jurisic Glumac, a noted Croatian intellectual who came to the U.S. to edit their paper, helped Croatian-American socialism make its first significant progress.

Drawn primarily to three industries—coal, steel, and meat-packing—and to such associated districts as Pittsburgh, Cleveland, and Chicago, Croatians became active in the radical industrial unionism of the 1910s and in the all-Yugoslav (but in practice, mostly Croatian and Slovene) South Slav Socialist Foundation. Their industrial lives, dominated by large corporations, high injury rates, and low wages, instilled the need for strong mutual-benefit associations and job protection. It also inspired, to a considerably greater degree than the more politically minded Slovenes, a spirit of syndicalism or revolutionary unionism. This experience, and the events in Europe, evoked a deep sympathy with the new Soviet Union. Of the South Slav groups, only Croatians joined the Communist movement in considerable numbers, publishing *Radnik* (Worker), *Glas Radnika* (Voice of the Worker), and *Radnicki Glas* (Workers' Voice) over the decades as Left influence rose and fell.

Unique in another sense, Croatian radicals remained active within the generalized, secular, and ostensibly nonpolitical Croatian Fraternal Union, whose leadership shifted from one broad orientation to another without demanding adherence at the local level. The CFU, ardently supporting industrial unionism, helped unite Croatian Left and mainstream industrial workers in common tasks of labor and politics. The New Deal seemingly answered all needs. Later, the CFU's ardent support of Tito and its participation in the American Slav Congress caused it to be placed upon the attorney general's List of Subversive Organizations as a Communist-linked group. Obtaining legal extrication from the list, the CFU went on to prosper in future generations of Croatian Americans, noted for its large membership (more than 100,000 in the middle 1980s), its *Tamburitza* bands, and its mildly left-of-center national leadership. Its national weekly, *Zajednicar* (Unity), has continued (in Croatian and English) to urge upon its readers a generally progressive perspective. In the face of conservative, post–WW II immigration from Yugoslavia, the growing strength of the Croatian Catholic Union, and occasional right-wing bombing incidents, the survival and positioning of the CFU is (along with that of its sister SNPJ) unique within the European-American ethnic world. *See also*: American Slav Congress, Slovenes

—*Peter Rachleff*

REFERENCES

Barrett, James, Rob Ruck, and Steve Nelson. *Steve Nelson: American Radical*. Pittsburgh: University of Pittsburgh, 1982.

Rachleff, Peter. "The Croatian Fraternal Union in the Great Depression." In *The Ethnic Enigma*, edited by Peter Kivisto. Philadelphia: Balch Institute, 1989.

THE CRUSADER

This monthly magazine was one of a group of black radical Harlem periodicals that gave voice to the militant New Negro movement while also propagating Socialist causes. Founded by Cyril Briggs (1887–1966), who edited it throughout its three-and-a-half-year run (1918–22), it was first the organ of the nationalistic Hamitic League of the World, then of the African Blood Brotherhood, a black affiliate of the Communist Party. The magazine reflects the important influence of West Indian immigrants on black radicalism in America, the intersection of a class analysis with Negro nationalism, and the organization of a black radical opposition to the policies of Marcus Garvey.

Briggs emigrated from the West Indies in 1905, and was a reporter and editor for the New York *Amsterdam News* before beginning the *Crusader*. He made the *Crusader* both a political organ and a journal of black culture, featuring African history essays intermixed with radical editorials and coverage of Harlem dramatic, musical, literary, artistic, sports, and business affairs. The magazine also carried original and reprinted fiction and poetry, as well as a short-lived women's department edited by Bertha De Basco. Featured writers included T. Thomas Fortune, Andrae Razafkeriefo, Paul Laurence Dunbar, Claude McKay, John E. Bruce, Eugene Debs, Agnes Smedley, Richard Harding Davis, Maxim Gorky, W. A. Domingo, and Charlotte Perkins Stetson. Gertrude Hall and Ben and Theo. Burrell were among the regular members of the editorial staff.

The proclaimed goals of the magazine, as stated in the November 1918 issue, were the "renaissance of Negro power and culture throughout the world," and propagation of "the doctrine of self-government for the Negro and Africa for the Africans." Briggs offered his readers both Pan-African and Socialist means to achieve these goals. From December 1918 to December 1920 the *Crusader* was identified as the official organ of the Hamitic League of the World, an Ethiopianist organization founded by George Wells Parker. It carried regular articles by Parker and advertisements for his *Children of the Sun*, which chronicled Africa as the ancient source of civilization. While celebrating African heritage, Briggs also urged class consciousness and support for Socialist candidates, including the 1918 New York races of A. Philip Randolph, Chandler Owen, and George Frazier Miller, and the 1920 presidential bid of Eugene Debs. Briggs told his readers that the Socialist Party platform represented equal opportunities for laborers of both races as well as an end to the special forms of oppression—lynching, segregation, disfranchisement—faced by blacks. Importantly, it also advocated self-government among blacks in Africa and areas of the Caribbean.

Briggs's central themes of class alliance and nationalistic self-determination were underscored by news coverage of the Sinn Fein and other nationalist liberation movements, as well as of the foreign policy of the Soviet Union. By 1921 Briggs was advocating a dual strategy of embracing Communism at home, while also backing the establishment of an independent black state (to be located in Africa, Latin America, or, as he had suggested earlier in his career, within the territory of the United States). His 1921 editorials further praised Bolshevism for its anti-imperialist stance, and urged alliance between the Soviet Union and African nations seeking liberation from colonial rule.

The increasingly militant tenor of the magazine coincided with the announcement in June 1921 that the *Crusader* had become the organ of the African Blood Brotherhood, soon followed by Briggs's open rejection of the American Socialist Party, his call for support of the Third International, and his participation in the founding of the Workers Party. Briggs had begun advertising the ABB in the magazine in October 1919, urging a policy of active self-defense in reaction to racial violence. The ABB was primarily a propaganda organization, but it also functioned as a radical underground society open to the participation of both men and women of the Negro race, organized internationally in local posts with a New York-based administration. Estimates of the size of the secret fraternity at its peak range widely, from 1,000 to 50,000 members.

While the platforms of the Hamitic League and the ABB characterize the first two phases of the publication of the *Crusader*, the final phase was devoted to attacks upon Marcus Garvey. *Crusader* coverage of the Garvey movement had originally been positive. In December 1919 Briggs described Garvey's Universal Negro Improvement Association (UNIA) and the ABB as two "parts of one movement." By 1921, however, this support had shifted to open animosity. Briggs attacked Garvey's reliance on capitalistic enterprise as a means of African liberation, and the UNIA leader's autocratic refusal to participate in black coalition politics—a line of criticism exacerbated by Garvey's expulsion of ABB and Workers Party members from the 1921 UNIA convention. The last four issues of the *Crusader* were devoted to exposés of the fraudulent administration of the UNIA, including articles by prominent ex-Garveyites who had moved to the ranks of the ABB. The propaganda war was carried on between the *Crusader* and the *Negro World* until February 1922, when Garvey was indicted on the fraud charges that would eventually lead to his deportation, and the *Crusader* ceased publication.

In the early twenties Briggs continued to operate the radical Crusader News Service.

The ABB slowly dissolved as a separate organization, its members merging with the WP and later the American Negro Labor Congress (ANLC). Briggs edited the organ of the ANLC and in 1936 became a contributor to the *Negro Worker*, the organ of the International Trade Union Committee of Negro Workers. He was expelled from the CPUSA in 1939 for his continued support of black nationalist policies. He rejoined the Party in the late 1940s, and worked as a functionary in the Los Angeles area during the McCarthy era. *See also*: Black Nation; Domingo, W. A.; Garveyism

—*Barbara Bair*

REFERENCES

Foner, Philip, and James Allen, eds. *American Communism and Black Americans*. Philadelphia: Temple University Press, 1987.

Hill, Robert, comp. *The Crusader*. Facsimile reprint. New York: Garland, 1987.

Hill, Robert, and Barbara Bair, eds. *Marcus Garvey: Life and Lessons*. Berkeley: University of California Press, 1987.

Cuban Americans

The presence of this group in the U.S. Left dates to the 1820s, with the publication of the radical exile paper *El Habanero* in Philadelphia, no doubt intended to be smuggled into Havana to promote independence. The modern movement began under the inspiration of the Cuban workers' movement and the Paris Commune. The failed Cuban insurrection (1868–78) greatly expanded the Cuban-American community by way of emigration to Key West, Tampa, and New York, where cigar manufacturers had located in search of docile labor forces. The failed French insurrection popularized anarchism (and nonparliamentary versions of socialism) as an ideology of the undefeated romantic Left.

All sections of the heterogeneous emigrant generation sought to dislodge the colonial tyranny from Cuba, but they did so from a variety of political standpoints. Spanish and Cuban tobacco workers, centered in Florida, created a culture of labor organizations and of learning imparted through readers to the tobacco operatives. Separately, a rather more petit-bourgeois emigrant Cuban-American community, based in the greater New York area, promoted philanthropy and Cuban independence. The link between them, the Cuban Revolutionary Party (PRC), was founded in 1892 and directed by the anarcho-mystic intellectual and journalist José Martí. Simultaneously, *La Liga* (The league) was founded by Rafael Serra, with the help of Martí, for the education and achievement of black Cubans, of whom there were many among the *independentista* generation. *La Liga* rapidly became a center for PRC enthusiasm and multi-racial Cuban identity.

While Martí himself was a nationalist-romantic-utopian at best, his Florida comrades took a more socialistic turn. Carlos Baliño (1848–1926), their outstanding personality, represented cigar workers at the memorable 1886 Knights of Labor convention in Richmond, Virginia. A founding member of the PRC, he often accompanied Martí on tours through Florida, Baliño the practical agitator and Martí the visionary. Eager to establish a Cuban presence apart from the sweatshops of Tampa, Baliño organized a community of PRC-oriented families in Thomasville, Georgia, and another, Martí City (where he became the first mayor), in a township of Ocala, Florida. His newspaper, *La tribuna del Pueblo*, published intermittently in Tampa during the 1880s–1890s, made him the godfather of Cuban socialism. Meanwhile, a multitude of socialist and anarchist institutions included a Ferrer school and a cultural center, *Antorcha*, whose main patrons were Spaniards and Cubans, and whose leader was the famed Spanish anarchist exile Pedro Esteve.

New factors emerged in the radical equation. Thousands of Spaniards, many with experience in anarchist movements, emigrated to Cuba and thence to the United States. Black Cubans, excluded from political participation after a failed uprising in 1912, also fled in numbers to the United States. Meanwhile, the intended Cuban revolution of the day, and its would-be facilitator, the PRC, had decisively lost out to the expansive American empire. The intensification of political-cultural activity presaged a chilling repression. No sector of U.S. radicalism suffered more from the effects of government and private vigilantism of the war years and afterward.

Over the following decade of enforced silence, the older, more anarchist-oriented generation of Cuban-American radicals gradually faded away. The Russian Revolution stirred a smaller, mostly younger group to new anticipations. According to oral testimony, an autonomous Communist Party was formed by Spanish-Cubans in the Tampa area wholly out of touch with the splits and factionalism of the mainstream U.S. communist movements. Not until the end of the 1920s did CP regulars seek to absorb this local movement of several hundred individuals, and at that, their rigorous ideological demands lost the majority of previous enthusiasts.

Communism continued to appeal to Cuban Americans, but rather in the fashion of Popular Front and labor-oriented radical cadre. Antifascist sentiment directed at Franco and the Spanish Civil War sparked widespread support, despite differences among Communists and surviving anarchist factions. Most attention went into civil liberties efforts against omnipresent repression, into union activity (first inside the "red" Tobacco Workers International union, and after its collapse, in the mainstream labor organizations), the distribution of the *Daily Worker*, and financial support to Communists active in Cuba. Spanish Cubans maintained a small IWO sector, mostly in New York and Florida. Unlike other, more substantial groups, they published no distinct Spanish-language Communist organ, although they took part in the short-lived Congress of Spanish-Speaking Peoples.

By the 1930s, meanwhile, a new, more middle-class exile culture solidified in Miami and New York. The later opponents of Batista, as of Machado, included Communists, but less prominently in the U.S. than in Cuba. Ybor City, a section of Tampa dominated by radical Cuban workers and Cuban-American workers' culture, became far less central.

By the 1950s, Fidel Castro, like so many other revolutionaries of the preceding half-century, made public appearances, raising money for his newer revolutionary-nationalist movement. A movement greatly reduced by McCarthy-era repression, by removal of the tobacco industry from Tampa, and by the aging process greeted the Cuban Revolution with excitement. Soon, however, new waves of repression, and the intimidating presence of right-wing, often violent anti-Castro Cuban exiles, effectively eclipsed the Cuban-American Left. While a small anarchist (anti-Fidel) tendency could be found in Miami of the 1980s, ultraconservative politics with a few endangered strands of liberalism dominated the life of Cuban Americans, by this time easily the wealthiest and most Republican of Spanish-speaking exile groups. *See also*: Anarchism; Martí, José; Ybor City

—Thomas Fiehrer

REFERENCES

Foner, Philip. Introduction to *Our America: Writings on Latin America and the Struggle for Cuban Independence*, by José Marti. New York: Monthly Review Press, 1977.

Mormino, Gary, and George Pozzetta. *The Immigrant World of Ybor City: Italians and Their Latin Neighbors in Tampa, 1885–1985.* Champaign: University of Illinois Press, 1987.

CUBAN REVOLUTION

The triumph of the Cuban Revolution in January 1959 coincided with a thaw in the Cold War, the beginnings of a political stirring in the student population, and a general feeling that it was time to get out of the malaise that had hung over the body politic during the nasty years of the Korean War and the rampages of Joseph McCarthy.

Fidel Castro became an instant hero in the United States as the romantic guerrilla chief who had led the fight against Fulgencio Batista, a universally hated dictator (except by the CIA and the U.S. State Department). The Old and the nascent New Left in the United States found the Cuban leader appealing. Castro seemed to epitomize popular democracy and economic and social justice without the ideological baggage of Marxism-Leninism. He also believed that Cuba could not be independent unless it controlled its own economy, whereas U.S. leaders had never believed that a small country inside its sphere should achieve real independence. Fidel Castro's ideology, before and after he became a communist, was designed to bring the Cuban people into the course of history from which they had been

"I envy you. You North Americans are very lucky. You are fighting the most important fight of all - you live in the heart of the beast." Che, *1964*

From *The Old Mole* (Boston, late 1960s)

excluded first by Spanish and then by U.S. domination.

Most of what was first known about the Cuban Revolution came from the *New York Times*. Herbert Matthews, a senior reporter, had snuck into the Sierra Maestra Mountains and interviewed Castro in early 1957, just months after Fidel had brought his guerrilla troops to Cuba from Mexico on a yacht called *Granma*. Matthews created, and other reporters then strengthened, a popular image of Fidel, one that lasted a short time with the mass media but endured for some of the young people who went to visit Cuba during the first two years of the revolution.

The excitement of a people that had taken the first step toward nationhood and the energy that emerged from revolution was a "turn-on." Thousands of students who returned from Cuba joined the Fair Play for Cuba Committee, or the Student Fair Play Committee. During 1960 this organization was in the forefront of the "Hands Off Cuba" campaign. Writers such as James Baldwin, C. Wright Mills, and Jean Paul Sartre, all of whom had visited Cuba, gave prestige to the organization.

By mid-1960 most of the mass media journalists, except for a few like Matthews, followed the U.S. government line. American officials had been upset by Castro's first moves—slashing rents, taking over the public utilities, and beginning an anti-Yankee campaign. Their feeling was translated into a campaign of public opposition when in March the Cuban revolutionary tribunals ordered the execution of 500 Batista officials, an event that turned public opinion.

The Cuban Revolution also coincided with the birth of the New Left in the United States and energized many of those who came to play leadership roles. For the first year and a half the Cuban Revolution was the delight of anarchists and Trotskyists. As soon as the Soviet Union made clear its intention to provide Cuba with basic economic and military aid, the Communists also joined the pro-Castro front.

By summer 1960, Paul Sweezy and Leo Huberman, the editors of *Monthly Review,* had correctly diagnosed the Cuban Revolution's character: socialist. By the fall of 1960, Ballantine Books had published both C. Wright Mills's *Listen, Yankee,* which characterized Fidel and the revolution as democratic, populist, and quintessentially just, and Jean Paul Sartre's *Sartre on Cuba.* The French philosopher proposed that the Cuban Revolution was existentialist in nature, a social movement whose leaders reacted to human need.

SARTRE: And if the people asked you for the moon?

FIDEL: It would be because they needed it.

On the other side, more than half a million Cuban exiles poured into the United States to join an already well established anticommunist movement. The Fair Play Committee was faction-ridden and subjected to enormous pressure from federal police and anti-Castro groups. Under such pressure, both oddballs and agents joined or formed Fair Play chapters. Such characters included Lee Harvey Oswald, unknown by any of the national officers, who opened a Fair Play office in New Orleans.

By April 1961, when the CIA launched the Bay of Pigs invasion, New Left enthusiasm for the Cuban Revolution had waned. The Soviet Union was clearly involved, and the New Left eschewed association with the repressive nature of the Soviet regime. The revolution itself had also begun to harden: It no longer fit the suit tailored by Mills and Sartre. It had taken on a socialist character in the Soviet sense of the word.

Later, some New Leftists regained their earlier enthusiasm for Cuba as they became disillusioned by the nature of the U.S. system, and as they began to learn about the difficulties involved in confrontations of Third World revolutions with the U.S. empire. By 1968 the Cuban Revolution had become not only permanent but a downright nuisance for the U.S. government's international policies. Havana offered inspiration for anti–Vietnam War activists to be ever stronger in their own struggles. *See also*: Cuban Americans, *Monthly Review*, Regroupment, Trotskyism

—*Saul Landau*

REFERENCES

Brenner, Philip. *From Confrontation to Negotiations: U.S.-Cuban Relations.* Boulder, Colo: Westview Press, 1988.

Brenner, Philip et. al. *Cuba Reader.* New York: Grove, 1989.

Lockwood, Lee. *Castro's Cuba; Cuba's Fidel.* New York: Vintage, 1969.

Morley, Morris. *Imperial State and Revolution.* New York: Cambridge, 1987.

O'Connor, James. *The Origins of Socialism in Cuba.* Ithaca: Cornell University Press, 1970.

Smith, Wayne. *The Closest of Enemies.* New York: Norton, 1987.

Curran, Joseph: see National Maritime Union

Czołgosz, Leon (1873–1901)

Commonly depicted as the "crazed anarchist assassin" of President William McKinley, American-born Leon Czołgosz, the son of immigrant working-class parents, explained his rationale for the deed: "I killed the president because he was the enemy of the good people—the good working people." Exposed to politics by his father, who belonged to a Polish branch of the Socialist Labor Party in Cleveland, he became an avid reader of radical literature in English and Polish. Not long after hearing a speech by Emma Goldman, he traveled to Buffalo, where he shot McKinley at the Pan American Exposition on September 6, 1901. His "*attentät*" resulted in an upsurge of antiimmigrant hysteria and a nationwide roundup of anarchists suspected of conspiracy in the assassination. His trial lasted less than eight hours and he was electrocuted on October 29, 1901. He was roundly denounced by spokespersons of the Left, with the lone sympathetic exception of Emma Goldman, who nonetheless advised against individual acts of political violence. *See also*: Anarchism

—*Bill Falkowski*

REFERENCES

Clarke, James W. *American Assassins*. Princeton: Princeton University Press, 1982.

Falkowski, Bill. "The Dubious Legacy of Leon Czołgosz: The Hegemony of Capital and Class Formation Within Buffalo Polonia." Paper presented at the annual meeting of the Polish-American Historical Association, New York, 1985.

Fine, Sidney. "Anarchism and the Assassination of McKinley." *American Historical Review* 60 (July 1955).

Goldman, Emma. *Living My Life*. Garden City, New York: Doubleday, 1931.

———. "The Tragedy at Buffalo." *Mother Earth* 1 (October 1906).

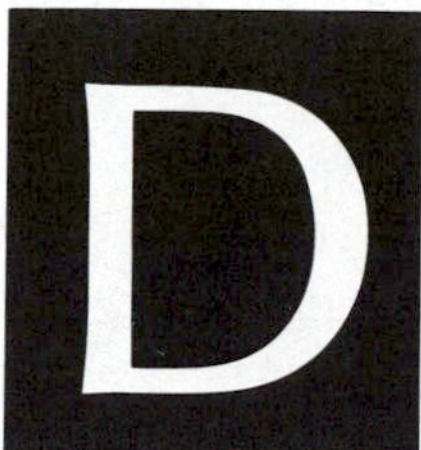

Dada

Started in Zurich in 1916 by the Romanian Tristan Tzara, the Alsatian Hans Arp, the German Hugo Ball, and other expatriate antiwar artists, poets, and performers from many countries, the dada movement quickly spread across Europe and even to Japan and the United States before it disintegrated in the mid-1920s. Defiant yet playful, its best manifestations were characterized by a wild humor all its own. "No one can escape from Dada," wrote Tzara, the movement's most persistent promoter. "The real Dadas are against Dada. . . . Dada is opposed to the future. Dada is dead. Dada is crazy. Long live Dada."

Antiacademic, anti-institutional, antiesthetic, in most countries dada tended to be antipolitical as well. In Berlin, however, a Central Dada Council for World Revolution issued incendiary tracts in 1918, and in Cologne leading dadas helped found the Communist Party of the Rhineland. The dadaists' pranks and practical jokes revealed their hostility to the bourgeois order and clearly appealed to revolutionary-minded youth; it is not surprising that Hitler denounced the movement in *Mein Kampf*. Even where dada did not engage political questions as such, it still functioned as a subversive force. In 1921, for example, the Paris dadas—André Breton, Benjamin Péret, and others who would soon proclaim themselves surrealists—staged an elaborate, prolonged mock trial of best-selling nationalist author Maurice Barrès that provoked a huge scandal.

Dada manifestations in the United States, centered in New York, were fewer and less impressive than those in Europe. Most of what passed for American dada activity was little more than a casual by-product of often brief sojourns of such globe-trotting exemplars of the movement as Marcel Duchamp and Francis Picabia, of France; the eccentric German baroness Elsa von Freytag-Loringhoven; Swiss-born poet/pugilist Arthur Cravan and his English companion, poet/painter Mina Loy. America's ephemeral dada periodicals—the *Blind Man* (two issues, 1917), *Rongwrong* (one issue, 1917), and *New York Dada* (one issue, 1921)—lacked the punch of their European counterparts, and their influence was negligible. More significant was the aggressive vehicle of Cravan's views, the *Soil*, edited by Robert Coady, which, with its passion for jazz, George Herriman's *Krazy Kat*, silent film comedies, boxing champion Jack Johnson, and other liberatory aspects of popular culture, actually was closer to the consciously revolutionary orientation of the later surrealists than to the dadaists' naive nihilism.

Unlike such earlier currents as symbolism, futurism, and cubism, in which the role of women was greatly restricted, dada from the start enjoyed the active participation of many women, and the New York dada milieu was no exception. It is a notable if rarely acknowledged fact that dada entered the English language most vigorously through poetry written by Loy and Freytag-Loringhoven in New York in the late 1910s. Interestingly, some of the latter's poems were published in the socialist magazine the *Masses*.

In a list of active dadas published in the Berlin *Almanach Dada* in 1920, Tzara included such Americans as the wealthy art collector W. C. Arensberg, socialite Mabel Dodge, novelist Hutchins Hapgood, abstract painter John Marin, and photographer Alfred Stieglitz—not one of whom can be said to have reflected more than the faintest traces of a dadaist outlook. In Chicago, Ben Hecht, who had taken part in the First International Dada Fair in Berlin, 1920, started his *Literary Times* a few months later, with Max Bodenheim; more provocative than the New York productions, it was no less eclectic.

America's most notable dadaist was Man Ray. Painter, collagist, photographer, filmmaker, and writer, he was born in Philadelphia in 1890 and grew up in New York. Already painting as a child, by 1909 he was attending night classes taught by Robert Henri and George Bellows at the art school of the anarchist Francisco Ferrer Social Center, where he held his first exhibition in 1912. The following year he met the poet Adon Lacroix, who introduced him to the work of Lautréamont and other forerunners of the European *avant-garde*, and became his "wife." A link between New York's anarchist and dadaist circles, Man Ray drew covers for Emma Goldman's *Mother Earth*, issued the protodadaist *Ridgefield Gazook* in 1915, and four years later, with the anarchist poet/sculptor Adolph Wolff, produced a one-shot anarchist/dadaist review titled *TNT*.

In 1921 he moved to Paris and joined the dadaists there. Three years later he helped found the surrealist movement, of which he became a prominent figure. More works by Man Ray were reproduced in *La Révolution Surréaliste* than by any other artist, and it was a one-man show of his that inaugurated the Galerie Surréaliste in 1925. Although he never shared the Marxist orientation of his surrealist comrades, he regularly collaborated on surrealist books and journals, and participated in the movement's collective exhibitions until his death in 1976. *See also*: Anarchism, Surrealism

—*Franklin Rosemont*

REFERENCES

Hecht, Ben. *A Child of the Century*. New York: Simon & Schuster, 1954.

Motherwell, Robert. *The Dada Painters and Poets*. New York: Wittenborn, 1951.

Ray, Man. *Self-Portrait*. Boston: Little, Brown, 1963.

Schwarz, Arturo. *New York Dada*. Munich: Prestel-Verlag, 1973.

DAILY WORKER (AND SUCCESSORS)

The most important literary-political expression of the Communist movement, this New York–based daily newspaper has generally echoed the orthodoxy at the center of the Party political apparatus. But it has also sought, in different ways at different times, to become a popular newspaper of the Left and (mostly in hope rather than expectation) of a broader "progressive" audience. These two aims, often if not always in conflict, have supplied the dynamic tension in the newspaper's life.

The *Daily Worker* reflected a historical weakness of the Left English-language press. Only during the heroic era of the Socialist Party (and again, in the political sector of the 1960s "underground" press) could an English-language paper gain a sufficient popular following and advertising base to pay for its production. Heavy subsidies, from readers and Communist sympathizers, made up the difference, but even so the specter of financial crisis never disappeared. The staff received meager wages, just sufficient (with the occasional contribution of a week's pay) to qualify for Newspaper Guild membership. Although rarely trained within the commercial presses, the staff remained largely stable over a considerable period and gradually acquired increased skills. Political demands, however, repeatedly frustrated the tailoring of styles to a sustained perspective.

The *Daily Worker* was launched in 1924 with $100,000 raised from the Communist-led language-federation groups, which were already supporting their own dailies. During these early years, the publication seemed most intent upon its official status as Party organ, publishing documents and official

Cartoon by Jacob Burck from the *Daily Worker*

theoretical interpretations. Among the competing factions of the 1920s it was a fiercely desired object (at one point, William Z. Foster's supporters occupied the newspaper's office at gunpoint) whose proprietership depended upon the factional control of Party leaders, which in turn depended ultimately upon Comintern favor. These tensions stifled the paper's effort to reach out to a wide audience.

A shift of the paper from Chicago, where it was founded, to New York in 1927 brought early hints of a different journalism. Harvey O'Connor, professional newspaperman and Federated Press wordsmith, joined the staff for a time, as did wry humor columnist Sendar Garlin and a number of talented young writers. With Communist leadership that looked more to the long haul than immediate revolutionary prospects, the *Daily Worker* sought to become more of a radical labor paper, with a somewhat popular appeal. Continued factional fighting and the opening of the Third Period in 1928 returned the paper to a wild stridency. Yet it had improved, or at any rate had become popularized, as its internal, theoretical character passed to more specialized publications (especially the monthly *Communist*) and open factionalism ended with the departure of the Trotskyists. Subjects such as developing battles in the Third World against imperialism gained coverage unimaginable in the commercial U.S. daily press.

Like the CP generally, although in more elusive ways, the paper started to shift toward yet a different kind of newspaper style closer to that of the commercial daily press in the early 1930s. Earl Browder, a competent functionary who established his claims over rival candidates for Party leadership, brought with him Clarence Hathaway (1884–1963), a former leader of the Minnesota Farmer-Labor movement, as editor of the *Daily Worker*. A skilled editor, he provided a continuity and modest support for "Americanization" that took root and developed within the Party. Indeed, the early 1930s *Daily Worker* had a tabloidlike flavor no more hysterical in tone, certainly, than the New York *Daily News* or *Mirror* in their antiunion anticommunism.

By 1935–36, the *Daily Worker* had palpably improved. Writing and design had become more professional, and the tone had begun to lighten somewhat with the addition of a sports column and comic strips. If these two features can be considered emblematic, sportswriter Lester Rodney may himself have been the clearest sign of a changing attitude toward Left journalism. Avid sports fan (especially of the Brooklyn Dodgers) and mostly self-taught journalist, Rodney carried on a protracted internal struggle with newspaper staffers and die-hard old-fashioned readers who disdained sports as pure escapism, or as activity best confined to the intramural events of the ethnic Left's soccer leagues. By 1937–38, Rodney's column was widely noted, among sports fans considerably outside Communist circles, for his feeling for the players, his sensitivity to race and ethnic issues, and his close observation of details. His ten-year struggle for the integration of major league baseball has been widely noted by sports historians, and considered by many to have been crucial. In the same years, *Little Lefty*, drawn by Louie Furstadt (by the 1940s assisted by, among others, Harvey Kurtzman, later *Mad Comics* editor) emerged as the most interesting—if somewhat predictable—Left comic creation since the IWW's *Mr. Block*. By contrast, *Daily Worker* film reviewing tended almost unfailingly toward the heavy-handed didactic. Daily circulation, generally in the 20,000 range, reached above 30,000, with a weekend-edition circulation about twice that figure—the maximum ever attained.

The *Daily Worker*'s labor coverage had always been intense, especially in regard to strikes and the activities of Communist-led unions. In the 1920s and early 1930s, it was nevertheless often marred by extreme exaggeration and by a lack of on-the-spot, investigative reportage. A larger staff, both paid (if scarcely) and volunteer, provided more detailed and more accurate coverage—no less accurate in its own way, even at its worst, than the commercial dailies. Sometimes, as Communists covered and simultaneously promoted the new industrial unions and their struggles, the paper became an important tool in providing information and adding a sense of experience to local militants. Communists or near-Communists rising within the CIO in turn became the paper's venue to the heart of industrial unionism.

By contrast, although this became rather more clear in retrospect, the paper (in articles by Anna Louise Strong and others) maintained a ferociously optimistic perspective of Soviet public cheer and economic growth. The Moscow Trials, demanding vast credulity, brought out the worst in Russian-based American workers and exposed the *Daily Worker* to charges of smearing honored revolutionaries while glorifying Joseph Stalin to superhuman heights. The cooperation of Left-leaning public intellectuals so marked in the earlier 1930s dissipated.

Such features existed side by side, with little sense of apparent contradiction. At the apex of the Popular Front, Woody Guthrie's regular appearance signified a kind of translation of Communist doctrine into something approaching a radical democracy. Mike Gold's "Change the World" column, in earlier years dour and full of charges against liberals, grew positively rosy in its hopes for American democracy leavened (if not revolutionized in any foreseeable short run) by the active presence of Communism. Even coverage of the Democratic Party's liberal wing developed a sophistication, as Communist journalists pinpointed the contradictions within the electoral system, and made themselves the forceful supporters of Vito Marcantonio's righteous voice in Congress and of many other noncommunist but progressive public officials (especially in New York State) and candidates.

Most of all, however, the *Daily Worker* made itself authentically "American," in the sense of native radical traditions, in support of black causes, especially close at hand in Harlem. During earlier years, the absence of any but the rarest black journalists (and not many black readers) had handicapped the paper; political insistence upon "self-determination" of "black belt" southern counties had an air of unreality about it. The Popular Front's insistent promotion of blacks into the center of American life had a magnetic appeal to the black middle class, and to many white liberals and radicals. The Scottsboro, Angelo Herndon, and other legal cases, the exposure of human tragedies caused by discrimination and segregation, and the promotion of black candidates for office, all gave the paper an impact far beyond its circulation. No other paper cared so much; none, not even the commercial New York papers with their extensive music coverage, had such feelings for the importance of blues and jazz in American culture. No paper in the country could boast a reporter with the brilliance of Richard Wright (*Daily Worker* Harlem editor) on the Louis-Schmeling fight.

These tendencies generally magnified during the Second World War, after the brief, confusing, and politically costly Hitler-Stalin Pact ended with Germany's invasion of Russia. The paper was stymied, however, when Hathaway was replaced as editor by the journalistically incompetent Louis Budenz, who sought for a time to ride herd politically upon a staff grown more self-consciously professional. Pressed to glorify the Red Army and, soon, U.S. military triumphs, the *Daily Worker* retreated to a kind of shrillness even when—relative to other American papers—its interpretation of unfolding world events gave a more correct balance of Russia's importance in defeating Naziism.

At the same time, coverage of women's issues grew dramatically—most notably in the advocacy of women's improved status by Elizabeth Gurley Flynn and others—as women became a major component of the wartime Party and of its middle-level leaders. And in spite of a fanatically single-minded devotion to military victory over Germany (miners' leader John L. Lewis was roundly condemned for leading a major strike, the imprisonment of Minneapolis Trotskyists lauded, and the internment of Japanese Americans not opposed), the paper found space to maintain a vital sports section. It did not, although urged by distributors, seize the United Front moment to install a racetrack tip sheet, which would surely have proved yet more popular among the working-class readership.

Once again after the war, for the second time since the later 1930s, the *Daily Worker* gathered the momentum to nearly become a solid, professional daily. When Budenz suddenly returned to Catholicism in 1945, the editorship passed to Morris Childs, later famous as a reported FBI informant, then in 1947 to a young John Gates, shaped politically in the Browder era. In terms of sheer journalistic competence, the *Daily Worker* grew by leaps and bounds. But it found itself pressed hard on two sides. The Party entered the Cold War era disoriented and internally divided, increasingly unable after 1948 to meet the pressures of public anticommunism and the increasingly undeniable revelations about Russian misdeeds. Alarmed at the rightward shift of America, convinced fascism might be only months away, Party leadership isolated the organization and the paper unnecessarily. On the other side, the *Daily Worker* endured heavy competition, during the 1940s, from *PM*, a liberal New York daily, and its short-lived successor, the *Daily Compass*. By 1950, many middle-class "progressive" readers in particular, were frightened of receiving a Communist paper and switched to the weekly *National Guardian*, because of McCarthyism. Party membership fell drastically, and circulation of the *Worker* dipped below 10,000.

The Twentieth Soviet Congress brought Gates and his political following into direct conflict with the more hard-line supporters of the Russian successors to Stalin. For a moment between 1956 and 1958, the *Daily Worker* became a semi-independent player in the Left, condemning the Russian invasion of Hungary and defending dissent within the Party press, even encouraging readers to write in with their opinions about American Communism's true status and its past mistakes. Gates's staff, notably the veteran journalist Max Gordon, used the opportunity to explore the contradictions of Communists less democratic in their internal life than the capitalism they deplored.

As the Party lost members and supporters, the *Daily Worker* lost readers, and despite a reduced page-size and staff, soon could no longer maintain production without rocketing subsidies. For political and editorial reasons, the daily closed in 1957, and with it, the independent status of the Communist press.

No Communist daily appeared in a decade marked by fresh and unpredicted developments. In 1967 the *Daily World* took the field, enabled by a union agreement that permitted maximum automation of the office (in advance, one might say, of other dailies). While no other Left daily existed, the *World* lacked the influence of its predecessors upon the political scene. Young people, who in any case had little attraction to Communist politics, soon formed their own local press, with a vastly greater influence. The *Daily World,* mostly sold or given away by staunch Communist veterans of many years' standing, seemed pallid by comparison. In the wake of the New Left collapse, it gained new talent (such as Terry Cannon, formerly a New Left journalist of note) and a somewhat greater weight in the Left circles that remained active. It experienced rare moments of triumph, albeit vicarious, in the election of local black officials—themselves or their long-standing allies close to the CP of an earlier age, and loyal to the sense of multiracial devotion in Communist circles. On international affairs, after the Vietnam War, it found no issue of equal appeal, despite heavy promotion of the African National Congress. Frequent attacks on Israeli policies, and praise for Israel's avowed enemies as well as internal critics, continued to cost the Communist press dearly among once-faithful Jewish readers. Perhaps its most touching pages were devoted to late-life public celebrations of sturdy militants, often by local public or union officials. Then again, by way of comparison, Maoist groups, even before the Chinese turn away from world revolutionism, had no luck at founding a U.S. daily; as a communist organ, the *Daily World* remained singular if hard to find among the nation's shrinking supply of independent-minded news vendors.

In 1986, against the wishes of many West Coast Communists and their longtime liberal allies, the *People's World* merged with the *Daily World* to become the *People's Daily World,* with color outside pages and center spread. Although some cultural writers came over from the *People's World,* the New York–based paper was actually a somewhat expanded version of the *Daily World,* with a daily readership of perhaps 15,000, including many gift subscriptions, and a weekly paid readership of perhaps twice that. In an exceptionally difficult era for the Left, the *PDW* lionized Jesse Jackson and the Rainbow Coalition (while maintaining fervent loyalty to Communist political candidates), and castigated anticommunism as a fatal concession to Reaganism. *Perestroika* and *glasnost,* Gorbachev's appeals to the West, and Western popular fascination with unfolding Russian events seemed to catch the *PDW* somewhat ill-prepared, if game, to explain the latest developments. *See also*: Communist Party; PM

—*Paul Buhle*

REFERENCES

Levenstein, Harvey A. "The *Worker/Daily Worker.*" *The American Radical Press, 1880–1960, I,* edited by Joseph Conlin. Westport: Greenwood Press, 1974.

Rodney, Lester. Interview by Paul Buhle and Michael Furmanowsky. Los Angeles: UCLA Oral History Project, 1981.

Garlin, Sendar. Interview. Oral History of the American Left archives, Tamiment Library. New York University.

Davis, Stuart: see Masses

Davis, Angela (b. 1944)

One of the few Communists to become a national political figure in the period of the New Left, Davis was the defendant in two major legal cases involving civil and political rights. She was born in Alabama to a black middle-class family whose social circle included Communist activists. A scholarship from the American Friends allowed her to attend high school in New York, where she lived with the family of Reverend William Melish, an individual known for his radicalism. Davis was exposed to socialist thought while in high school and attended meetings for a Communist Party youth group. At Brandeis University, she became a student of Marxist Herbert Marcuse, who influenced her decision to do her graduate studies at Frankfurt University (1965–67). During her time in Europe, Davis attended the World Youth Festival in Helsinki and took part in anti–Vietnam War demonstrations. Upon her return to the United States, she again studied under Marcuse.

With the civil rights movement at full steam, Davis joined several organizations, the most important being the Student Nonviolent Coordinating Committee, the CP, and the Black Panther Party. She made a visit to Cuba in 1969 and that autumn caught the political spotlight for the first time. She had been hired to teach philosophy at the University of California-Los Angeles while she completed her doctoral dissertation. Ronald Reagan, then governor of California, protested the appointment, citing a state law that banned CP members from teaching at state universities. Davis publicly acknowledged her CP affiliation and was immediately dismissed. In the ensuing litigation, which engaged civil libertarians of various tendencies, the law was declared unconstitutional.

Davis intensified her work with the Black Panthers, becoming ever more involved with the plight of black inmates who had begun to call themselves class-war prisoners. She was most passionate about the situation of a group called the Soledad Brothers, inmates charged with killing a prison guard, and she became personally involved with their leader, George Jackson. In August 1970, Jonathan Jackson sought to force the release of his brother by seizing hostages at the Marin County courthouse. During the subsequent gunplay Jonathan and a judge were killed. Angela Davis was immediately accused of involvement in the affair and formally charged with conspiracy, kidnapping, and murder. Within a short time the entire civil rights and New Left movements were mobilized in her defense by the National United Committee to Free Angela Davis. Massive national and international protests soon made Angela Davis a name recognized in millions of American households.

When the case went to trial in 1972, Davis was acquitted of all charges. She subsequently toured the U.S. to thank her supporters and then traveled around the world, including stops in the Eastern bloc. Her defense committee was renamed the National Alliance Against Racist and Political Repression. With Davis as co-chair, the alliance, like the International Labor Defense of old, took on a variety of political cases that did not necessarily have any direct links to the CP. The majority of those actively defended were blacks and Hispanics. Although it has had some successes, the alliance has never gained the wide support enjoyed by its predecessor. Davis has remained active in the CP, running as its vice-presidential candidate in 1980 and 1984, but she has gradually lost her public prominence.

See also: Civil Rights, Communist Party

—*Dan Georgakas*

REFERENCES

Davis, Angela, Y. *Angela Davis: An Autobiography* New York: International Publishers, 1964.

———. *Women, Culture, and Politics.* New York: Random House, 1989.

Davis, Benjamin Jr. (1903–64)

A two-term Communist representative on the New York City Council (1943–47), Davis grew up in a privileged black family in Atlanta. His father, a Republican national committeeman, was able to send him to Amherst College and Harvard Law School. Davis's radicalization began when he assumed the defense of Angelo Herndon, a black Communist charged with "attempting to incite insurrection" as a result of his Depression-era organizing among Atlanta's unemployed. Conducting his defense before a white-supremacist judge and jury, Davis found inspiration in the Communist Party's advocacy of interracial solidarity and its outspoken criticism of racial segregation. He joined the Party during the trial, but was forced to leave Atlanta shortly after Herndon's conviction because of threats to his life.

Moving to New York, Davis became editor of the *Harlem Liberator* and an editor of the *Daily Worker*. Active in the National Negro Congress and numerous Harlem campaigns against racial discrimination, Davis became a popular figure in the community, with ties to ministers and politicians as well as Party activists. When Adam Clayton Powell, Jr., launched his campaign for Congress in 1942, he designated Davis as his chosen successor on the New York City Council. Winning Communist and American Labor party endorsements, Davis won the election and was reelected by a larger margin in 1945. Popular with his constituents, Davis only lost his seat in the midst of Cold War tensions that led most of his former allies to break with him. In 1948 Davis was indicted under the Smith Act along with other members of the CP's National Committee. He was convicted and spent several years in the federal penitentiary in Terre Haute, Indiana. When he was released, he returned to Harlem, but with the CP a shell of its former self, he never recovered his popularity or influence. *See also*: Herndon Case, Communist Party

—*Mark D. Naison*

REFERENCES
Davis, Benjamin J. *Communist Councilman for Harlem*. New York: International Publishers, 1969.

Drawing of Eugene V. Debs by Art Young

DEBS, EUGENE V. (1855–1926)

Eugene Victor Debs, the closest thing to a folk hero ever produced by the American Left, was born to French parents in Terre Haute, Indiana, where his father ran a small grocery store. Named for the Frence novelists Eugene Sue and Victor Hugo, young Debs was a bright and inquisitive student who enrolled in high school briefly in 1870 before deciding to enter the world of work as a locomotive paint-scraper while continuing his studies as a nighttime business student. He joined the Brotherhood of Locomotive Firemen, not as the youthful firebrand of later legend, but more for the social and civic exposure and benefits that might accrue from membership in a mutual-benefit type of association.

Debs nurtured an idealistic worldview of harmony between employer and employee, with both groups obligated by mutual responsibilities to one another and the community around them. Debs toiled long and hard to fulfill his part of this social contract. He was elected city clerk and state representative in 1879 and 1884, respectively, with majority support in working-class and upper-class wards. The local newspaper christened him "the blue-eyed boy of destiny," as his oratory and political acumen hinted at fame and fortune to come.

His trade union career similarly proved a double helix of success. Debs was appointed editor of the Brotherhood's national journal in 1880 and became secretary-treasurer in 1885. He meted out his conservative philosophy to readers and members with a hiring-hall mentality, so that railroad managers could secure the best and brightest for the aristocracy of the rails. Debs pontificated against strikes in general and labeled the portentious 1877 general railroad walkout as signifying "anarchy and revolution" despite the cumulative wage reductions imposed on railroad workers. The Haymarket martyrs also received his scorn a decade later as upsetters of the social order. Debs's embrace of individual social mobility and liberty within a context of class cooperation became anachronistic in the confines of the Gilded Age's industrial vagaries. He never quite abandoned these youthful philosophies although he reluctantly began to criticize the growth of monopoly and the demise of individual freedom.

As corporate power increasingly threatened traditional American values by employing federal troops, court injunctions, and blacklists against workers, Debs slowly agonized over the changing situation. He reluctantly envisioned a federation of railroad workers to balance the growing power of industry rather than individual, centripetal craft unions. This was no sudden change on his part, but a poignant, time-consuming transformation in outlook much different from the "born radical" image of his contemporary biographers and followers. Nor was this Debs the Christ-like figure of legend. He often attacked his foes unscrupulously, supported Jim Crow, and embraced nascent American imperialism.

By 1892 the contradictions between Debs's idealistic, old-fashioned belief system clashed irrevocably with the dictates of a changing world. He sadly resigned from the Brotherhood and developed a new type of organization, an undertaking that would propel him onto the national political scene for the next three decades.

As Debs reevaluated his earlier stands against strikes and union militance, he searched for the ingredient that would provide labor with the unity and power enjoyed by the industrial trusts without unleashing the mob atavism that haunted his visions of an enlightened socialist commonwealth. Abandoning his old emphasis on a skilled and elite work-force, and blaming the new industrial order for undermining the skills of that workforce, Debs created the American Railway Union in 1893, an industrial-style federation open to all train workers who received a paycheck from a railroad corporation. The fledgling organization, as its first order of business, engaged the Great Northern Railroad, the bastion of the powerful James Hill, who had cut wages and fired union supporters in a familiar Gilded Age scenario. Debs wisely bridled the de facto and undisciplined militance of the rank and file into a peaceful and solid phalanx of support among competing crafts, Knights of Labor assemblies, and unskilled laborers. More important, he tactfully turned merchants, most notably Charles Pillsbury—the grain merchant dependent on timely transportation for his perishable product—against Hill and his policies, thus breaking capitalist unity in the strike.

The conflict was eventually settled in arbitration, but an arbitration imposed by the unity of the union. When the arbitrator ruled in its favor and restored wage levels, new members stampeded into the ARU not unlike the deluge the Knights of Labor had experienced in the first blush of their success in the mid 1880s. The boom raised the union's membership to a remarkable 150,000, outstripping the combined forces of all the other brotherhoods, which stood at just below 100,000. Debs still continued to blame individual robber barons like Hill for the ills of industrial society, rather than the system itself. On the heels of this major victory he boldly and prematurely proclaimed a new dawn of cooperation between management and labor through the collective-bargaining and arbitration process. Strikes, he stated, would soon be a thing of the past, a flash of wishful thinking reminiscent of the idealism of Terrence Powderly of the Knights of Labor.

The victory over James Hill, rather than serving as a harbinger of a new day in industrial relations, indirectly led to one of the greatest labor confrontations in U.S. history. The liberal membership policy of the ARU led to affiliation by factory workers at the Pullman car company in Chicago, who went on strike in 1894. The diet of wage cuts in an oppressive company town—"Pullmedown," as the residents sarcastically called it—provided an emotional backdrop to the ARU convention in June of that year. The delegates voted to initiate a national boycott against all trains with Pullman sleepers, which were still rented individually by the various railroads.

The General Managers Association, the governing body of railroad capital in the United States, saw an opportunity to destroy the upstart labor Lilliputian. As the boycott spread, the railroad chieftains had the government cynically invoke the Sherman Anti-Trust Act against the union, the first time that particular legislation was employed. Thousands of federal troops were sent into Chicago despite the lack of violence there. The presence of soldiers ironically engendered rioting, and Debs, like the Haymarket martyrs before him, was indicted for influencing the course of events.

Debs was sentenced to six months in jail in 1895 despite the courtroom heroics of defense lawyer Clarence Darrow. He spent his fortieth birthday there and read *The Communist Manifesto*. He left as a hero, with 100,000 citizens hailing his release in an impressive rally in Chicago on November 22, 1895. Debs became such a popular symbol that he was offered the Populist Party nomination for president the following year, but turned it down. The McKinley victory finally turned him leftward.

In the waning years of the nineteenth century, Eugene Debs was a soul in search of an institutional anchor and a meaningful ideology after the defeat of the American Railway Union, which never resurrected itself from the debilitating Pullman showdown. He briefly instituted a quasi-political party, the Social Democracy of America, and flirted with a colonization scheme in the western United States. However, he soon gravitated to Victor Berger's new Social Democratic Party, the precursor to the Socialist Party. Debs had finally found the political antidote to the dislocations of the new industrial order.

Debs's own philosophical confusion in these years reflected the uncertainty in his audiences and seemed to create a sympathetic bonding with working-class America, which collectively shared his own anomie. In 1900 Debs was the standard-bearer for the SDP, the first of five runs for the nation's top office. He barely polled 100,000 votes but managed to double that four years later. By 1912, Debs had garnered almost a million votes, 6 percent of the votes cast that year and the electoral highwater for the American Left. His lingering belief in the American Dream, an unsettled ingredient in his own socialist psyche, found sympathetic listeners outside the narrow circle of the already convinced.

Although he remained uneasy with union heirarchies, Debs tried to find a home with the infant Industrial Workers of the World, attending the founding convention in 1905. He remained close to the rank and file of that organization but was unable to handle the fractious personalities that made up the IWW leadership. By the eve of World War I, the SP had a flourishing media, a coterie of successful local candidates, and over 100,000 duespaying members. Debs, while the titular head of the party, suffered greatly from insecurity and uncertainty. His marriage to Kate Metzel in 1885 had quickly turned to one of convenience. Debs often retreated from depression by visiting bordellos or bars. He also detested the internecine battles that rumbled through the SP and the American Left like thunderstorms on the western prairie. He often sacrificed himself as a peacemaker who never really brought peace but only an expedient, temporary truce.

As the capitalist parties appropriated the demands of the socialists, populists, and trade unions into their own platforms, considerable venom was taken from the socialist sting. When the Progressive era stumbled into World War I, Debs and the American SP held firm against imperialist war. Debs was determined to take a stand, even as the hard-won socialist gains unraveled in the growing wartime hysteria. Debs, who had always possessed a martyr complex, foresaw his own crucifixion—indeed toiled for it—as the once-powerful European socialist parties succumbed to individual nationalisms. In one of his most quoted passages he wrote: "I am not a capitalist soldier; I am a proletarian revolutionist. I am opposed to every war but one; I am for that war with heart and soul, and that is the world wide war of the social revolution. In that way, I am prepared to fight in any way the ruling class may make necessary, even to the barricades." That rhetoric was designed to rally the socialists and taunt the authorities, who responded soon after American troops had been dispatched to Europe. Debs was arrested for sedition after a militant antiwar speech in Canton, Ohio, in June 1918.

At the age of sixty-three, with his beloved party hounded and repressed, Debs was sentenced to ten years in federal prison. He believed his incarceration might at least rally his followers and provide the cure to the political impotence he felt. He had proved his citizenship once again and earned the approbation of Lenin in revolutionary Russia. He began his sentence on the eve of the Red Scare, in April 1919, when it seemed that rebellion might shake America too. But he rode to prison in a union train with not so much a whisper of protest from his former coworkers.

Once ensconced at Atlanta Penitentiary, Debs became a protest candidate for the U.S. presidency for the fifth and last time in 1920. He railed at the system from within and taunted the prosecutors: "There are no bars and no walls for the man who in his heart is free, and there is no freedom for the man who in his heart is a slave." His followers wore buttons, much prized by collectors today, that proclaimed VOTE FOR PRISONER 9653. Debs polled more than 900,000 votes, about the same as his 1912 total. He was pardoned on Christmas Day, 1921, in an unusual gesture by President-elect Harding. The convict sent his five dollars release money to the Sacco Vanzetti Defense Committee. The Debs that left Atlanta Penitentiary in 1921 was a different person from the one who had left the Chicago jail in 1895, and it was a different country as well. A large throng greeted him upon his return to Terre Haute, as others had earlier in Chicago, but Debs was in his twilight years now and the promise of social victory so alive a generation earlier had given way to despondency and defeat. He and his party had lost despite the intense loyalty of remaining members. The Russian Revolution had become the standard-bearer of the world Left and eclipsed the native socialism of Debs. He died on October 20, 1926. *See also*: Socialist Party

—*Scott Molloy*

REFERENCES

Debs Papers, Cunningham Library, Indiana State University, Terre Haute, Indiana.

Ginger, Ray. *The Bending Cross: A Biography of Eugene Victor Debs*. New Brunswick: Rutgers University Press, 1949.

Salvatore, Nick. *Eugene V. Debs: Citizen and Socialist*. Urbana: University of Illinois, 1982.

DE CLEYRE, VOLTAIRINE (1866–1912)

One of the most prolific anarchist writers of her time, de Cleyre was educated in a Catholic convent. When her father converted from Free Thought to Catholicism while she was still in her early teens, he sent her to a Catholic convent in Sarnia, Ontario, Canada. Despite her protests and those of her mother, Voltairine's father insisted his daughter must become a nun. She remained in the convent for more than three years, sometimes running away, always disobedient, and forever despairing that she had no means of permanent escape. When she emerged at age nineteen, she was a crusading atheist who believed religion was a repulsive and oppressive institution. Upon hearing a speech by Clarence Darrow, she decided that capitalism should be added to the litany of world evils. She was soon reading Benjamin Tucker's *Liberty*. Her commitment to anarchism was sealed by the Haymarket affair.

Through the years she moved from individualistic anarchism tinged with pacifism to the direct-action approach of the IWW. In addition to European influences, she posited American roots for her ideas in the work of Thoreau, Jefferson, Paine, and Emerson. Whatever the momentary emphasis, she always directed her efforts to working-class audiences. She was enthusiastic about the educational ideas proposed by Francisco Ferrer and was among the first writers to argue that detective stories, sports writing, pornography, and even advertising could be regarded as literature in that they reflected the lives of common people. She frequently criticized anarchists such as Emma Goldman for being too elitist and directing their work to intellectuals and the middle class.

De Cleyre's personal life was tragic. Most men were put off by her learning and her lack of physical beauty; and the one man she felt she loved died when she was only twenty-seven. She later had an affair that resulted in the birth of a son. When she refused to live with the child's father, the baby was taken from her and she did not see her son again for seventeen years. This harsh collision with sexist laws and culture reinforced a feminism that found expression in poetry, oratory, fiction, and essays. A second tragedy took place in 1902 when she was shot by an opposing anarchist. Although she recovered, her always fragile health was shattered. Characteristically, she refused to press charges, stating her assailant should be sent to a mental facility, not a prison.

Her base of operations from 1889 to 1910 was Philadelphia, where she lived among poor Jewish immigrants. She taught English and music, and she learned Yiddish well enough to add the *Freie Arbeiter Shtimme* to the many journals to which she contributed. As she grew closer to anarcho-syndicalism, she began to study Spanish in order to participate directly in the Mexican Revolution. Before she could relocate to Mexico she became ill from "brain fever" and died in Chicago on June 12, 1912.

De Cleyre's work soon went out of print and she was rarely cited. More than fifty years passed before her writing enjoyed a revival in conjunction with the reemerging women's movement. In many ways her chief work seemed to be the uncompromising manner in which she had led her life. A statement she had made shortly before her death spoke directly to the new feminists: "I die, as I have lived, a free spirit, an Anarchist, owing no allegiance to rulers, heavenly or earthly." *See also*: Anarchism

—*Dan Georgakas*

REFERENCES

Avrich, Paul. *An American Anarchist: The Life of Voltairine de Cleyre*. Princeton: Princeton University Press, 1978.

Shulman, Alix. "Viewing Voltairine de Cleyre." *Women: A Journal of Liberation* 2 (Fall 1970): 5–7.

DeLeon, Daniel (1852–1914)

The first English-speaking intellectual to influence long-run trends in the American Left, DeLeon could not build a successful socialist movement but he did elucidate powerful notions about the evolution of industrial society. He also created, within severe limits, a model "vanguard" party and a resolutely uncompromising daily press generations before the Communist Party undertook these tasks.

Apparently born to Sephardic Dutch-Jewish parents on the Caribbean island of Curaçao, DeLeon went abroad with his mother, attending European schools (albeit not the prestigious Leyden Academy, from which he later claimed to have graduated). Arriving in the United States between 1872 and 1874, DeLeon taught secondary school in Westchester County, New York, attended Columbia Law School and graduated with honors, opened law offices first in Texas then New York, and finally gained a prize lectureship in International Law at Columbia. There, he lectured notably on the oppression of Latin America. He also was elected president of the new Academy of Political Science, and was one of the earliest contributors to the *Political Science Quarterly*.

Growing interested in the Henry George mayorality campaign of 1886, DeLeon abandoned his faith in patrician reform and commenced public activity for the Left. Denied the usual offer of a professorship following two terms as lecturer, DeLeon resigned from Columbia in 1889. By this time, he had already been converted to socialist ideas through reading Edward Bellamy's *Looking Backward*, and he plunged himself into the New York Nationalist Clubs. Disappointed with the unclarity of the milieu, DeLeon pressed on to the Socialist Labor Party, joining in 1891.

DeLeon would gain much by a close reading of Marx and other socialist writers. But he carried within him the outlines of a general theory formulated in terms of contemporary natural science and social science. Like Charlotte Perkins Gilman and her evocative *Woman and Economics* or August Bebel and his *Frau und Der Sozialismus* (of which DeLeon himself would make the first American translation), DeLeon looked to Darwinian "natural laws" of evolution and to the anthropology of Lewis Henry Morgan, which hinted at a return of humanity to a collective stage abandoned eons ago at a lower level of social development. DeLeon expounded this theory of socialism's approach with a brilliance of logic no previous English-language speaker could summon.

Almost immediately, he added life to the SLP's municipal campaigns through multilingual oratory. Within months, he had become a touring lecturer, and soon after, the official editor of the new weekly, the *People*. This paper he transformed into a stern analytic sheet, improving labor reportage but writing editorial matter largely himself. With relatively few socialist papers in English, and most of those filled either with hayseed sentimentalism (as the *Coming Nation*) or local labor news (such as the *Cleveland Citizen*), the *People* appeared more socialist, more Marxist.

Convinced that the severe economic depression of the 1890s meant the end of capitalism, DeLeon pursued a political agenda not unfamiliar to veteran socialists. Above all, he intended to throw off the caution accrued in decades of slight success, and the timid unwillingness to criticize the craft unions for their refusal to endorse the socialist movement (as was standard for most European labor). Like earlier dissenters from the SLP's main policies, he therefore called for aggressive political campaigns and a break with AFL conservatism. The exclusion of an SLP delegate from the 1890 AFL convention in Detroit seemed to demonstrate the hopelessness of the familiar tactical approach. DeLeon's work from within the Knights of Labor, likewise drawing upon traditions of hostility toward purely economic unionism, eclipsed in 1895 when the Knights' leadership reneged on a promise to make a socialist the editor of their official journal. Breaking off with the AFL the same year, DeLeon personally led the creation of the Socialist Trades and Labor Alliance as the alternative to both existing organizations.

DeLeon's insistence upon the absolute political fealty of ST&LA leaders doomed the new movement after a few years. Meanwhile, opponents of DeLeon had more and more abandoned the SLP, a development he greeted with jeering attacks upon the personalities of his critics. The SLP might have failed entirely but for a modestly rising vote and DeLeon's own powerful rhetoric. During the 1890s and first years of the new century, he delivered a series of addresses that—reprinted in the *People* and virtually innumerable SLP pamphlets—demonstrated his oratorical abilities and clarified his revolutionary perspectives.

DeLeon's celebrity can be traced in no small part to the form of his lectures. He notoriously shunned the familiar crowd-pleasing devices, discouraging applause and seeking earnestly to provoke his audience into hard thought. In one of his most celebrated ruminations, *Two Pages from Roman History: Plebs Leaders and Labor Leaders* (1902), DeLeon used the historical example of the Gracchi brothers in Rome to argue his main strategic point. The proletariat, the first social class to emerge heir apparent yet collectively pauperized, had to compensate for its tactical weakness with an absolute clarity of aims. "The proletarian revolution . . . must avoid, as it would a pestilence, all alliance with any other class," any sign of weakness or dependence upon others. Only a political party with unity and clarity, DeLeon's followers believed, could prove equal to the task of leading this vulnerable but potentially all-conquering class. Little real evidence of Marxist orthodoxy for these innovations could be demonstrated from doctrine, but DeLeon had, like Lenin after him, genuinely captured a sentiment in Marx's interpretation of the Paris Commune as the wholesale replacement of the bourgeois order.

By the turn of the century, the SLP had been reduced to only a few thousand members, soon to be far outdistanced by the growing Socialist Party. Some of DeLeon's trusted functionaries deserted him shortly. Efforts by immigrants of various kinds to attach their groups to the SLP rather than the SP generally ended in disappointment, with DeLeon's stern unwillingness to yield any meaningful autonomy. But he and his faithful survived in a kind of splendid isolation. Reduced to personal penury, DeLeon managed to bring out a *Daily People*, ultrarevolutionary if most unentertaining for a daily paper. He translated some thirteen volumes of Eugène Sue's "Proletariat Across the Ages" series, and Ferdinand Lassalle's play of bourgeois revolution, *Franz von Sickingen*. He made appearances at the Socialist International's European meetings, forcefully backing the sentiments of Lenin and Luxemburg. To the DeLeonite, typically a self-educated member of the working class, DeLeon seemed to incarnate the true revolutionary dedication to knowledge and proletarian strategy.

DeLeon's last major political opportunity loomed with the 1905 founding of the Industrial Workers of the World. DeLeon delivered perhaps his most heralded address, "The Preamble to the IWW," at the time of the convention, adding to Wobbly determination a social science-like perspective. The evolution of society, DeLeon insisted, had outmoded the political state, and prepared the working class to abolish it in favor of a noncoercive, merely economic mechanism. This view had special attraction for socialists who observed the apparent electoral indifference or cynicism of the American working class at large, and who believed the SP was foolish to seek the impossible. Within industrial life itself—as many socialists and more conservative trade unionists had long since concluded—must therefore lie the answer to class injustice. DeLeon supplied the theoretical formula with engaging logic of industrial inevitability, much as Gilman had depicted the emancipation of women through economic self-support.

At first, a certain reconciliation with Left-socialists such as Eugene Debs and the Western rank and file (largely spared the earlier rounds of faction fights) appeared in the offing. DeLeon seemingly urged the unification of the Socialist and Socialist Labor parties, but obviously allowed for unity upon SLP principles.

Meanwhile, the fledgling IWW, beset by defections and splits (some of them encouraged by DeLeon), absorbed this logic even while throwing off the SLP and its leader. The organization had formed just a few years too early for the strike wave of the unskilled and mostly foreign-born workers, 1909–12, which gave flesh to the Wobblies' institutional and ideological bones. By that time, DeLeon had been purged, and his small following had formed the "Detroit IWW" upon SLP principles—but not with any significant encouragement from DeLeon himself.

Ironically, as DeLeon faced maximum isolation, erstwhile disciples and others deeply influenced by him went on to become outstanding articulators of the industrial socialism idea. Justus Ebert and Ben H. Williams, acting within the IWW as pamphleteers and newspaper editors, interpreted the coming of the proletariat into its own. Frank Bohn and Austin Lewis, within the SP, urged a pro-IWW course, and Lewis in particular went further to reconcile IWW ideas with the main course of Marxist logic. Louis C. Fraina, who had joined the SLP at a tender age and served as the *Daily People*'s correspondent during the Lawrence, Massachusetts, textile strike, made himself the proto-communist intellectual par excellence, interpreting the Russian soviets as workers' councils, as the IWW had hoped to see them. Even at the fringes of mainstream labor, longtime SLP loyalist Joseph Schlossberg served as radical second to Sidney Hillman in the Amalgamated Clothing Workers, urging forms of workers' control as a transition to true socialism.

The *Daily People* suspended in 1914, and DeLeon died not long after. Some 30,000 people appeared at his funeral, a remarkable tribute to the respect he had gained from people not remotely willing to join or at least to remain in the SLP. The party remained, after his death, utterly dedicated to his principles and memory, reprinting his essays in every *Weekly People* for generations and circulating his pamphlets widely. *See also*: "Detroit IWW," Industrial Workers of the World, Socialist Labor Party, Socialist Trades and Labor Alliance

—*Paul Buhle*

REFERENCES

Buhle, Paul. "Marxism in the United States, 1900–1940." Ph.D. diss., University of Wisconsin, 1975.

Daniel DeLeon: The Man and His Work, a Symposium. New York: New York Labor News, 1918.

Seretan, L. Glen. *Daniel DeLeon: The Odyssey of an American Marxist*. Cambridge: Harvard University, 1979.

Socialist Labor Party Papers. State Historical Society of Wisconsin.

Dell, Floyd: see Greenwich Village, Masses

Dellinger, David (b. 1915)

Editor, activist, and one of the Chicago Seven, Dellinger has provided continuity in publishing and activism between the pacifist Left of the 1940s and the radical movements spawned in the 1960s. Born to a family with roots in colonial New England, Dellinger graduated from Yale (1936), studied at New College, Oxford (1936–37), Yale Divinity School (1938), and Union Theological Seminary (1939–40). This background led him to be active in draft resistance during World War II.

In 1945 Dellinger was the moving force in the founding of *Direct Action*, a journal of radical pacifism. Three years later, as leader of a faction of the Committee for Nonviolent Revolution, he fostered a merger with Peacemakers, a group enjoying the support of A. J. Muste, Dwight Macdonald, and Milton Mayer. The resulting pacifist current, much influenced by Gandhi, viewed pacifism as an active movement for change, not simply a reactive defense against injustice. Pacifists would not only refuse any cooperation with the armed forces, but they would also attempt to close down missle bases nonviolently, refuse to pay the portion of any tax that went to the military, and hold vigils at factories producing chemical weapons such as poison gas. Concepts such as participatory democracy and civil disobedience were to be at the heart of all activity. To promote such views, Dellinger helped found and became the first editor of *Liberation*, a journal that influenced many individuals who were to be prominent in the early phases of the New Left. A regular *Liberation* contributor was anarchist Paul Goodman.

With the advent of the Vietnam War, Dellinger became a well-known public figure. He was a featured speaker at the first teach-in at Berkeley (1965) and was co-chair of the Spring Mobilization to End the War in Vietnam (1966). He also visited Hanoi in 1966 and set up a relationship that would bring numerous antiwar Americans to Vietnam and would lead to the release of some American prisoners of war. Dellinger became especially noted as a reliable debunker of State Department disinformation regarding the war. Following the street riots connected with the Democratic National Convention in 1968, Dellinger and six others were arrested for conspiracy to ferment riot in what became the landmark legal battle of the era. The successful defense of the Chicago Seven, or Conspiracy Seven, took on international dimensions and became the subject of at least two films.

In the decade of the 1970s Dellinger was involved in the ill-fated attempt to establish *Seven Days* as a radical slick weekly on the model of *Time* and *Newsweek*. Since that time he has concentrated his efforts on various aspects of the nuclear energy problem, from preventing nuclear war to closing down nuclear power plants. *See also*: Pacifism, Peace Movement

—*Dan Georgakas*

REFERENCES

Dellinger, David. *Revolutionary Nonviolence*. Indianapolis: Bobbs-Merrill, 1970.

———. *More Power than We Know*. Garden City, N.Y.: Anchor Press, 1975.

Democratic Socialists of America: see Socialist Party

Dennis, Eugene: see Communist Party

Detective Fiction

This literary genre owes its existence to the urban, industrialized society of the late nineteenth century. Earlier, Edgar Allan Poe had used several stories to show the wear and tear modernization exacted upon American culture, and such neo-Gothic radicals as George Lippard framed their novels around the investigation of crime. The last decades of the century saw the appearance of Cap Collier and other urban heroes wrestling with corruption and communism. Despite the formidable (and politically ambiguous) place of Sherlock Holmes in Anglo-American detective fiction, the predominant mode remained a conservative defense of existing standards.

Public disillusionment following the First World War changed the detective story forever. A group of writers around the new pulp publication *Black Mask* (1921–54) "put murder back where it belonged," out of the suites of the cerebral master sleuth and into the streets with the cynical, hard-working private eye. In this version, the evil of society itself confronts the detective, whose story becomes the vehicle for a penetrating social commentary. Dashiell Hammett's earliest novel, *The Red Harvest*, thus focuses upon the corruption unloosed in Butte, Montana, by the destruction of unionized mining. Hammett's other novels, such as *The Maltese Falcon*, elaborate the ultimate fetishization of capital (the falcon, after all, proves worthless), the multiple betrayal of friendships and love for material gain, and the compulsive morality of the protagonist who will not permit himself the luxury of bourgeois romanticism. Hammett himself, romantic about the Left, served on countless committees, taught at the radical Jefferson School, and eventually served six months in prison for refusing to turn over the names of contributors to a bail fund for Smith Act defendants.

Meanwhile, the hard-boiled detective, almost a living metaphor of antifascist determination in the film personage of Humphrey Bogart, dominated the genre from political Right to Left. At least one detective (as novelized by a onetime editor of the *Socialist Call*) strongly resembled Norman Thomas. Two others—Coffin Ed Johnson and Grave Digger Jones—represent the black nationalist impulse of disillusioned radical author Chester Himes. Even moderate liberal and conservative writers such as Raymond Chandler and Ross Macdonald nevertheless offered an occasionally striking picture of society turned inside out by the revelations of carefully hidden secrets.

No American literary innovation, it is safe to say, has had quite as much international influence on popular culture. (Albert Camus once ascribed the origins of existentialism to the hard-boiled novel.) To the present day, the detective story remains the primary genre where political themes survive as the subtext of modern alienation, and in which the mores and conspiracies of capitalism, ever-more troubling to the average citizen, can be worked out in fiction. *See also*: Jefferson School of Social Science; Popular Culture

—*Robert Greene*

REFERENCES

Shaw, Joseph, ed. *Hardboiled Omnibus*. New York: Simon & Schuster, 1946.

The Detroit IWW, or, the Workers International Industrial Union

At the 1905 founding convention of the Industrial Workers of the World, the Socialist Labor Party's Daniel DeLeon wrote the "political clause" of the constitution's preamble, which advocated organizing politically as well as economically. In 1908 anarcho-syndicalists claimed that this clause would allow the SLP to control the IWW. Supporters of Vincent St. John and William Trautmann barred DeLeon from being seated as a delegate and eliminated the clause.

Outraged advocates of political action reconvened in Paterson, New Jersey, and denounced the "Chicago IWW" for "seating fictitious delegates while refusing seats to duly elected ones." The new organization's original New York headquarters were changed to Detroit within a few months. Starting with twenty-two locals, the Detroit IWW was strongest on the East Coast and began publishing the *Industrial Union News* in 1912. Peaking at 11,000 members in 1912, it attained a size roughly one-third that of the Chicago faction's.

Wage increases won at the Michigan Malleable Iron Co. and strikes by New York structural-iron painters and Ohio machinsts contradict the misconception that the Detroit IWW existed only on paper. Its most extensive activity was in organizing strikes by Paterson silk workers in 1911–12, though the bulk of those strikers sided with the Chicago IWW. The last publicized flurry of Detroit IWW activity came with 1913 strikes by Connecticut textile workers, Philadelphia mechanics, Baltimore cigar-makers, and San Francisco tailors.

In 1915 the union condemned the Chicago group for "disgracing" the IWW name, and changed its own name to the WIIU. The Detroiters rejected sabotage as incompatible with preparing the working class to run industry. Their hallmark was insistence on the independent socialist vote.

Though the Detroit IWW is identified with the name of Daniel DeLeon, he actually did not favor its creation. Eugene Debs thought the 1908 split was a "terrible blunder" and preferred a united movement including both IWWs, the Western Federation of Miners, and the United Mine Workers.

Before the WIIU disbanded in 1924, it had organized affiliates in Canada and South Africa. The Detroit-affiliated Industrial Workers of Great Britain was involved in major strikes in Glasgow and Edinburgh. The "political" IWWs were stronger than their anarcho-syndicalist rivals in Australia and Great Britain. *See also*: Industrial Workers of the World, Socialist Labor Party, Socialist Trades and Labor Alliance

—*Don Fitz*

REFERENCES

Brissenden, Paul. *The IWW: A Study of American Syndicalism*. New York: New York Labor News Co., 1919.

Johnson, Olive M. "The SLP: 1890–1930, Part II." In *Four Decades of the Socialist Labor Party*. New York: New York Labor News Co., 1930.

Renshaw, Patrick. *The Wobblies: The Story of Syndicalism in the United States*. Garden City, N.Y.: Doubleday, 1967.

DEWEY COMMISSION: see DEWEY, JOHN; TROTSKYISM

DEWEY, JOHN (1859–1952)

One of the most influential philosophers, educators, and social reformers in the United States, Dewey was a member or founder of innumerable political organizations and a lifelong defender of unpopular causes. He intervened on every major social issue—from the Great Depression and the world wars to the Spanish Civil War and the Moscow Trials—with a progressive viewpoint that consistently rooted social conflicts in the workings of the capitalist economy.

Initially, Dewey flirted with socialist ideas such as guild socialism and nationalization of key industries. But with the rise of "totalitarianism" in Germany and Russia, Dewey, like so many other intellectuals, softened his earlier radicalism and concluded that the most urgent task was to defend existing democratic rights, however imperfect. Yet he never went so far, unlike his student Sidney Hook, as to enlist in the Right. As a testament to his enduring progressivism, at the age of seventy-eight Dewey traveled to Mexico in 1937 to head the commission investigating the charges against Leon Trotsky in the Moscow Trials, publishing *Not Guilty* the same year.

A central figure of the philosophical school known as pragmatism, Dewey argued that philosophy should abandon its sterile metaphysical pursuits and apply itself in a practical manner toward the amelioration of social life. While Dewey made major contributions in virtually every area of philosophy, he is best known for his philosophy of education, which stated that the evils of capitalism could be remedied through the proper imbuing of creativity, democratic values, and scientific intelligence.

There are strong similarities between Dewey's philosophy and that of Karl Marx (whom Dewey misinterpreted as a mechanistic materialist). These include a common heritage in Hegel, a strong historical sense, a repudiation of individualism as anathema to democracy, a rejection of all dualistic categories, and a belief in evolution and naturalism (self-realization through interaction with nature). Such parallels have led many writers to seek a rapproachement between the two thinkers. Philosopher Sidney Hook has gone so far as to argue that Deweyism is the genuine fulfillment of Marxism. But the similarities end abruptly on a key point: Marx insisting on the revolutionary overthrow of capitalism, and Dewey embracing pragmatic reform and rejecting Marxism as "unscientific utopianism."

Trotsky, who engaged in a famous debate with Dewey on the question of means and ends in the revolutionary process (Dewey insisting that a democratic result required a democratic process), saw an extreme danger in Dewey's philosophy insofar as it seduced radicals into accepting a reformist program. At Trotsky's urging, George Novack wrote a powerful Marxist critique of Dewey's philosophy. Novack, later to be a leading intellectual in the Socialist Workers Party, emphasized the virtues of Dewey the man and the considerable value of his philosophy over previous bourgeois philosophies, but sharply condemned pragmatism as an insidious apology for capitalism and class collaboration. It remains a contradiction of pragmatism that the experimentalism it championed was not rigorously applied to the socialist experiment itself. *See also*: Sidney Hook, Moscow Trials

—*Steven Best*

REFERENCES

Bernstein, Richard. *John Dewey*. New York: Washington Square, 1966.

Bullert, Gary. *The Politics of John Dewey*. New York: Prometheus Books, 1983.

Hook, Sidney. *John Dewey: An Intellectual Portrait*. New York: John Day Company, 1939.

Novack, George. *Pragmatism Versus Marxism*. New York: Pathfinder Press, 1975.

Thomas, M. H. *John Dewey: A Centennial Bibliography*. Chicago: University of Chicago Press, 1962.

Direct Action

This concept was widely circulated within the American working class by the Industrial Workers of the World during its 1905–24 heyday as a mass organization. The essence of the doctrine was that workers should strive for immediate redress of grievances at the point of production rather than pinning their hopes on third parties such as courts, government, mass media, or even union officials. Slowdowns and strikes of every kind were the most common form of direct action. Whether violent acts were permissible remained unclear, and some IWW speakers complicated the issue by using *direct action* and *sabotage* as interchangeable terms. The most typical IWW direct actions were massive nonviolent parades and civil disobedience; IWW literature stressed that workers had to learn how to use "mental" dynamite such as striking with their fists in their pockets. Nonetheless, some IWW songs and literature implied that there were circumstances where violence could not be ruled out. The reality was that the IWW was purposely ambiguous about its definition of *direct action* and *sabotage* in much the way civil rights leaders of the 1960s were ambiguous about the meaning of the phrase "by any means necessary." IWW activists got additional psychological mileage out of this verbal ambiguity by using a menacing black cat and the slogan "We never forget" on agitational literature. Direct action again became a frequently urged tactic during the formative years of the CIO—this time without the complementary evocation of the word *sabotage*. Since that period, direct action is most likely to be advocated by militant caucuses and other groups seeking to revive the trade union movement. In those situations, rank-and-file members may be urged to take direct action against their own leadership as well as management and the state. *See also*: Anarcho-Syndicalism, Industrial Workers of the World

—*Dan Georgakas*

Silent Agitator stickers drawn by Ralph Chaplin

REFERENCES

Bird, Stewart, Dan Georgakas, and Deborah Shaffer. *Solidarity Forever: An Oral History of the IWW*. Chicago: Lake View Press, 1985.

Kornbluh, Joyce. *Rebel Voices—An IWW Anthology*. Rev. ed. Chicago: Charles H. Kerr Co., 1988.

Salerno, Sal. *Red November, Black November: Culture and Community in the Industrial Workers of the World*. Albany: State University of New York Press, 1989.

DISSENT

In early 1954 the first volume of this new independent socialist journal, edited by Irving Howe and Lewis Coser, appeared on a few select newsstands. It was not the most auspicious season for launching a new radical quarterly, and the editors were suitably modest in their initial statement of purpose. *Dissent*'s editors were only too aware that "in America today there is no significant socialist movement and that, in all likelihood, no such movement will appear in the immediate future." *Dissent* began with a dual purpose in mind: to reexamine the socialist tradition and to challenge the prevailing conservative tide in American political and intellectual life. Most of the journal's founders had come out of the Trotskyist movement (with representatives of both American and European Trotskyism among them); while they remained anti-Stalinist and (for the most part) socialist in conviction, they believed that all the leading variants of Marxist orthodoxy had proven inadequate guides to understanding the tragedies confronted by the Left in the twentieth century.

For all its gloomy prognoses about the future of socialism, from its earliest issues *Dissent* offered a combative and forward-looking political vision. In Harold Rosenberg's 1955 article "Couch Liberalism and the Guilty Past," *Dissent* took aim at the liberal capitulation to McCarthyism; in Norman Mailer's "The White Negro," published in 1957, *Dissent* anticipated the appearance of a new radical movement that would challenge the cultural as well as political status quo. The journal enthusiastically welcomed the appearance of the civil rights movement and the revival of campus activism in the early 1960s. As the journal's circulation and influence rose, *Dissent*'s editors began to speak optimistically about the prospects for the "democratic Left": "Perhaps," Irving Howe wrote in 1963, "we should venture a little into hypothetical 'program-making'—what we would say if there were a significant socialist movement in the U.S." But Howe and *Dissent* grew critical of the New Left, as young radicals increasingly looked to Cuba, Vietnam, and China for models of revolutionary heroism and development. The journal's commitment to anti-Stalinism remained fierce and inflexible. Although the journal opposed the Vietnam War, it was reluctant to see the Left sever useful connections with liberals in the Johnson administration. As a result, it was largely ignored when not denounced by the New Left, and it increasingly commented on contemporary events in a distant and embittered tone. Howe later decided that he had "overreacted" in some of his disputes with the New Left: "I told myself that I was one of the few people who took the New Left seriously enough to keep arguing with it. Cold comfort."

Unlike most New Left publications, *Dissent* survived the 1960s and continued to serve as the most important American journal espousing democratic socialism. Closely associated with Democratic Socialists of America in the 1980s, it attracted new contributors and editors, as it attacked Reaganism with the same fervor that it had earlier devoted to its challenge of McCarthyism. *See also*: Howe, Irving; Socialist Party

—*Maurice Isserman*

REFERENCES

Bloom, Alexander. *Prodigal Sons, The New York Intellectuals and Their World*. New York: Oxford University Press, 1986.

Howe, Irving. *A Margin of Hope, An Intellectual Biography*. New York: Harcourt Brace Jovanovich, 1982.

Isserman, Maurice. *If I Had a Hammer, The Death of the Old Left and the Birth of the New Left*. New York: Basic Books, 1987.

Pells, Richard. *The Liberal Mind in a Conservative Age, American Intellectuals in the 1940s and 1950s*. New York: Harper, 1985.

Wald, Alan. *The New York Intellectuals, The Rise and Decline of the Anti-Stalinist Left from the 1930s to the 1980s*. Chapel Hill: University of North Carolina Press, 1987.

DISTRICT 65, UAW

This union traces its origins to the Wholesale Drygoods Workers Union (WDGU), organized in September 1933 at H. Eckstein, a dry goods warehouse on New York's Lower East Side. The union was founded by male Jewish workers led by Arthur Osman, a salesperson at the firm. At the same time, textile warehouse workers were organizing in New York's garment center. Led by a young radical, David Livingston, their militant activities won them a CIO charter from Sidney Hillman as Local 65 of the Textile Workers Organizing Committee. In August WDGU merged with the smaller CIO Textile House Workers to become the Wholesale and Warehouse Employees Union, Local 65, CIO, and membership began to increase dramatically. In September 1937 Local 65 came under the jurisdiction of the newly chartered CIO national union, United Retail and Wholesale Employees of America (URWEA).

The beginning of World War II ended the first phase in the union's growth. Along with other CIO unions, 65 adopted the "no strike" pledge and vigorously supported the war effort. The war period was characterized by a dramatic shift in union tactics. Instead of confrontation the union turned to the War Labor Board to resolve conflicts. Over 10,000 members served in the armed forces or joined war-related industries, depleting the ranks of the union pioneers. Women became a majority (which they remain today) and took increased leadership roles.

From the outset the new union had combined an ideological emphasis on democratic, mass participation and left-wing politics. Local 65 maintained very close ties to the Communist Party USA. The union generally followed Party policies until 1950. What distinguished Local 65 from many other left-wing unions was the consistent effort to generate support from the rank and file for these policies.

Between 1937 and 1948, Local 65, the largest local in URWEA, was at the center of a group of left-wing locals in New York City that were locked in a bitter conflict with their International. Local 65's influence far exceeded its size and its importance in the city economy. Particularly close cooperation developed between Local 65 and the Department Store Workers Union.

Differences between the left-wing New York locals and the national leadership, including a dispute over compliance with the Taft-Hartley Act, led to a split in the Retail, Wholesale, & Department Store Employees of America in September 1948. Eight of the largest New York locals, representing 30,000 workers (including the department stores), seceded to form the Distributive Trade Council with Arthur Osman as president.

In February 1950 the Distributive Workers Union (DWU), a new international union outside the CIO, was formed by the dissident locals. Osman headed the international and David Livingston became president of Local 65. In 1950 DWU leadership signed the non-Communist affidavits required by the Taft-Hartley law to minimize the danger of raiding by CIO locals protected by the NLRB.

In 1950 the DWU merged with the remnants of the United Office and Professional Workers of America (UOPWA) and Food, Tobacco, and Agricultural Workers Union (FTA), both expelled from the CIO for Communist domination, to form the Distributive Processing and Office Workers of America (DPOWA). This grouping may have been an effort to build a left-wing alternative to the CIO. Local 65, now District 65, DPOWA, became the dominant force within the DPO. Conflict quickly developed between the merged unions. The UOPWA and FTA membership had been decimated and they provided little in actual resources or members. Additionally there was a clash of organizational cultures between the rank-and-file character of Local 65 and the "top down" structure of the UOPWA.

In early 1952 District 65 openly broke with the CP over the issue of reunification with the CIO. A short internal struggle for control of the union ended with the defeat of Communist candidates in the unionwide election in June 1952. The contest was never in doubt. Most union staff and active members, many of whom were Communists, chose to remain with the union rather than continue to ally themselves with the increasingly faction-ridden and vulnerable CP.

At the same time, the union was being investigated for its left-wing activities by a federal grand jury (April 1952) and congressional committees (July 1953). With the approval of the membership, the national leaders refused to answer questions regarding their political beliefs or associations.

With the effective demise of the Left, District 65 sought affiliation with the CIO. The DPOWA rejoined the Retail, Wholesale and Department Store Union in 1954, becoming District 65, RWDSU, CIO, with David Livingston as president.

Following the merger District 65 turned inward. The union's priorities became the efficient servicing of the membership, consolidation of new industries (direct mail), and new organization. With a strong and viable base in New York, the union expanded to New Jersey and then nationally. The union integrated its leadership ranks, advancing black leaders to important organizational positions to represent the shift in the racial composition of the membership.

District 65 remained active in progressive politics, particularly civil rights. The union provided money and early support for Rev. Martin Luther King, Jr. Cleveland Robinson, secretary-treasurer of District 65, was a national coordinator for the March on Washington in 1963. Opposition to the war in Vietnam led 65 to become one of the founding unions in Labor for Peace. In that capacity David Livingston traveled to Hanoi in 1969. The union's consistent opposition to AFL-CIO conservative policies heralded the entry of "sixties issues" into the labor movement even while supporting the Democratic Party.

In 1969 District 65 again disaffiliated from the RWDSU over differences on civil rights, foreign policy, and commitment to new organizing. It formed the Distributive Workers of America (DWA) with ten other seceding locals in seven states. Notably the Department Store Workers, with 10,000 members, refused to leave the International and ended their formal ties with District 65. The new DWA joined with the UAW and the Teamsters to form the short-lived Alliance for Labor Action (ALA). The DWA remained unaffiliated until 1981, when the DWA formally affiliated with the United Auto Workers to form the current District 65, UAW. *See also*: Communist Party; Food, Tobacco, and Agricultural Workers Union; Peace Movements; Taft-Hartley Loyalty Oath; United Office and Professional Workers of America

—*David Paskin*

REFERENCES

Cook, Alice. *Union Democracy: Practice and Ideal, An Analysis of Four Large Local Unions*. Ithaca: Cornell University Press, 1963.

Paskin, David. "District 65: A Serialized History." *Distributive Worker* (Official Publication of District 65/UAW) (November 1983–April 1986).

Rogow, Robert. "Relationships Among the Environment, Policies, and Government of a Labor Union: A Study of District 65, Retail, Wholesale and Department Store Union, AFL-CIO." Ph.D. diss., New York University, 1965.

Tabb, Jay. "A Study of White Collar Unionism: Tactics and Policies Pursued in Building the Wholesale and Warehouse Workers Union of New York." Ph.D. diss., University of Chicago, 1952.

Dobbs, Farrell (1907–83)

Best known as a talented trade union organizer—particularly in the International Brotherhood of Teamsters—and as a leader of the Socialist Workers Party (SWP), which sought to apply the ideas of Lenin and Trotsky to U.S. conditions, Dobbs was born in Queen City, Missouri. The son of a lower-level manager in the coal industry, he began his political career as a registered Republican and supporter of Herbert Hoover. His thinking changed during the Depression, however, and his first contact with left-wing ideas occurred in 1933 when he became involved in Teamsters Local 574 while working as a coal heaver at the Pittsburgh Coal Company in Minneapolis, Minnesota. Key activists in the local were the well-known Dunne brothers (Vincent R., Miles, and Grant) and Carl Skoglund, all of whom were seasoned veterans of the IWW, socialist and communist movements, and were Trotskyists. Admiring the leadership these activities displayed in a successful coal strike in early 1934, Dobbs decided to join the Minneapolis branch of the Communist League of America, which was the forerunner of the SWP.

The Dunne brothers and Skoglund went on to initiate the Minneapolis Teamsters strike of 1934; the struggle turned into a militant general strike that ultimately made Minneapolis a union town. Dobbs was centrally involved in this struggle as chief picket dispatcher, helping to pioneer techniques such as the "flying wedge" that were instrumental in the workers' victory. In 1935 Dobbs and his comrades fought off attempts by International Brotherhood of Teamsters (IBT) president Dan Tobin to drive the Trotskyists out of Local 574. Reconstituted as Local 544, the Teamsters local elected Dobbs as its recording secretary.

Dobbs played an important role in Teamster organizing drives of 1936 and 1937, which drew into the IBT 125,000 new members covered by a pioneering master contract over an eleven-state area. The impact and success of the Trotskyist organizers moved Tobin to hire Dobbs as an IBT staffer in 1939, though he resigned the following year to devote his energies to working as the SWP's trade union director. During this period he journeyed to Mexico to discuss issues facing the labor and socialist movements with Leon Trotsky. Convicted under the first Smith Act trial, in 1941, he served thirteen months in Sandstone Prison in 1944–45 for defending revolutionary socialist ideas.

Dobbs was an increasingly prominent leader of the SWP. An editor of the weekly *Militant* during the 1943–48 period, he became the party's first candidate for the U.S. presidency in 1948 (and again in 1952, 1956, and 1960). He and Tom Kerry—a veteran from the SWP's martime faction—became the organization's central figures during the 1950s, after party leader James P. Cannon went into semiretirement. Dobbs served as the SWP's national chairman from 1949 to 1953 and as its national secretary until 1972. Between 1972 and 1977 the organization published his valuable four-volume history of the Teamster struggles, although after the mid-1970s he became relatively inactive in party work. Dobbs spent his last ten years in California and died October 31, 1983. *See also*: International Brotherhood of Teamsters, Socialist Workers Party, Trotskyism

—*Paul LeBlanc*

REFERENCES

Dobbs, Farrell. *Teamster Rebellion*. New York: Monad, 1972.

——. *Teamster Power*. New York: Monad, 1973.

Le Blanc, Paul. *Trotskyism in America, The First Fifty Years*. New York: F.I.T., 1987.

Dombrowski, James Anderson (1897–1983)

For thirty-seven years, between 1929 and 1966, Dombrowski sought to build United Front coalitions in the South, first among the region's few progressive religious leaders, then during industrial union drives, and finally, during the civil rights movement. A Christian Socialist, he was reviled by the South's elected politicians as "Public Enemy Number One." He was equally anathema to much of the political Left, scorned by Communist Party members as a liberal while feared by many liberals as a Communist.

Dombrowski was born in Tampa, Florida, the only son of first-generation English and Polish immigrants. His mother died when he was five, and his father, who owned a jewelry store, died ten years later. The Methodist Church dominated young Dombrowski's early years, first in Tampa, and later, after World War I, when he enrolled at Emory University. Through Dr. Harry F. Ward at Union Theological Seminary in New York, and the social turbulence of the 1920s, Dombrowski became an organizer. He was arrested in Elizabethton, Tennessee, in 1929 during strikes at three rayon mills. He joined the Highlander Folk School in 1933, teaching miners and mill and farm workers leadership and organizing skills until 1942, when he became director of the Southern Conference for Human Welfare.

Determined that SCHW would challenge the exploitation of labor, blacks, and women, either through organizing, political education, or electoral politics, Dombrowski was soon under fire. In 1948 he was hauled before a Nashville, Tennessee, grand jury investigating subversion. The same year he was arrested for violating the Birmingham, Alabama, Jim Crow law while speaking at the all-black Southern Negro Youth Congress. A year later, he was ousted from the SCHW in a bitter membership fight, mostly over his United Front views.

Without pause, he founded the interracial Southern Conference Education Fund to confront racism. As with SCHW, SCEF's influence extended beyond its membership or resources. In 1954 Dombrowski refused to give the U.S. Senate Internal Security Subcommittee SCEF's membership list. In 1963, having arranged a conference on civil rights attended by black and white lawyers in New Orleans, he was arrested for subversion by Louisiana officials, who seized all SCEF's records, handing them over to U.S. Senator James Eastland.

On grounds that his first amendment guarantees had been violated, Dombrowski took his argument to the U.S. Supreme Court, which found in his favor in 1965 in *Dombrowski* v. *Pfister*, which concluded that the arrest had "a chilling effect" on freedom of speech.

A year later, Dombrowski, hobbled by arthritis, left SCEF, devoting his remaining years to less direct civil rights activities, mostly in New Orleans, and to oils and watercolors that evidenced his strongly held social views. *See also*: Birmingham, Communist Party, SCEF, Southern Negro Youth Congress

—*Frank Adams*

REFERENCES

Adams, Frank. "Dombrowski: Portrait of an American Heretic." *Southern Exposure* 10 (July–August 1982).

Domingo, Wilfred A. (1889–1968)

A Jamaican nationalist and journalist, Domingo was associated with a series of West Indian-led movements as well as with the Socialist Party in Harlem, and participated in the publication of the *Negro World, Emancipator, Messenger*, and *Crusader*. He was instrumental in shaping the young Marcus Garvey's ideas on race consciousness and later fostered Garvey's political career in New York by introducing him to leading activists. He became the first editor of the *Negro World*, but his class-conscious editorials soon drew Garvey's ire. Abandoning Garvey's Universal Negro Improvement Association in 1919, Domingo continued as a member of the SP's speakers' bureau, and taught at the SP's Rand School in New York. He castigated the party's failure to make organization among blacks a priority, and cautioned in a 1919 essay seized in a Lusk Committee (an anti-red investigative body) raid that this avoidance would result in blacks continuing to serve as strikebreakers without class identification with white workers, and, potentially, as a capitalist-led mercenary army in the event of social revolution. He was active in Cyril Brigg's African Blood Brotherhood in the early 1920s. In the thirties he returned to his earlier focus on Jamaican nationalism, and in 1936 formed the Jamaica Progressive League (JPL) with other New York–based West Indian immigrants. The self-described "militant liberal" JPL platform supported self-government, universal suffrage, unionization, and the organization of consumer cooperatives, arguing that in Jamaica the primary conflict was not between capitalists and an industrialized, urban proletariat, but between imperialist powers and a large peasantry combined with an undeveloped petite bourgeoise. A JPL branch was founded in Jamaica in December 1938 and soon merged with Norman Manley's People's National Party. Domingo participated in these changes in Jamaica as vice-chair of the Trades Union Advisory Council and as contributor to the *Labour Weekly*. He returned to New York in 1947 and in the 1950s opposed the PNP leadership. *See also*: Garveyism

—*Barbara Bair*

REFERENCES

Foner, Philip S. *American Socialism and Black Americans*. Westport: Greenwood Press, 1977.

Foner, Philip S. and James Allen, eds. *American Communism and Black Americans*. Philadelphia: Temple University Press, 1987.

Hill, Robert, and Carol Rudisell, eds. *The Marcus Garvey and UNIA Papers*. Vol. 1. Berkeley: University of California Press, 1983.

Post, Ken. *Arise Ye Starvelings: The Jamaican Labour Rebellion of 1938 and Its Aftermath*. The Hague: Nighoff, 1978.

Dos Passos, John (1896–1970)

A leading writer of the Great Depression, Dos Passos forged a career that spanned from the post–World War I years to the Vietnam War era. Admired for his experimental techniques, he published more than a dozen novels dramatizing major episodes in twentieth-century America. He also traversed the political spectrum from far Left to far Right.

Born the illegitimate son of the mistress of a married Portuguese immigrant who had become a successful corporation lawyer, Dos Passos spent his early years traveling semiclandestinely about the United States and abroad with his mother. It was to these unusual circumstances of his birth and childhood that he would later attribute his lifelong sense of rootlessness.

After graduating from Harvard in 1916, he served as a volunteer in ambulance units in war-torn Europe and then was inducted into the U.S. Army. His first novels, *One Man's Initiation—1917* (1920) and the far superior *Three Soldiers* (1921), established the predominant antiwar and semianarchist themes of his radical period. *Manhattan Transfer* (1925) dramatized the isolation and rapid movement of city life.

His masterwork was *U.S.A.*, a 1,450-page trilogy consisting of *The 42nd Parallel* (1930), *1919* (1932), and *The Big Money* (1936). Conceived as a new kind of book that interweaved the historical and personal, *U.S.A.* introduced new formalistic devices such as a "Newsreel" and "Camera Eye," which were mixed with poem-biographies and traditional realistic narrative.

In the 1930s the politics of *U.S.A.* seemed to confirm Dos Passo's growing connections with the far Left. In 1926 he had assisted in founding the *New Masses*, soon a Communist Party–affiliated magazine. In 1927 he was arrested while picketing on behalf of the incarcerated anarchists Sacco and Vanzetti, and his *New Masses* articles on the subject were published as *Facing the Chair*. In 1928 he took an extended trip to the Soviet Union, and his reports were sufficiently favorable to be published in the Party press.

In 1931 he traveled to Harlan County, Kentucky, with a Communist-initiated delegation to investigate the condition of striking miners, where he was indicted for "criminal syndicalism." In 1932 he publicly endorsed the CP's presidential candidate. As late as 1937, *The Big Money* was voted the best novel of the year by the Communist-led American Writers Congress.

Nevertheless, the trilogy embodied ambiguities that are clearer in retrospect. While the first volumes affirm a Marxist class analysis—emphasized by the sympathetic biographical portraits of John Reed and Randolph Bourne—the final volumes shifted toward a view of corruption, power, and greed as the eternal enemies of freedom. He was influenced as much by Thorstein Veblen as Karl Marx.

In the year of *The Big Money*'s publication, Dos Passos enthusiastically voted for Franklin Delano Roosevelt. In 1939 he published *Adventures of a Young Man*, depicting the de facto execution of an American volunteer in the Spanish Civil War by Communists who suspect him of political deviation. After the 1930s, Dos Passos moved steadily to the Right, becoming an associate of *National Review* and the Young Americans for Freedom, as well as an admirer of Barry Goldwater, Richard Nixon, and Ronald Reagan.

Adventures of a Young Man was the first volume of a trilogy that included *Number One* (1943) and the *Grand Design* (1949). Despite steady productivity, Dos Passo's literary reputation passed into a decline in the 1940s. Interest in his work was briefly rekindled in 1961 by *Midcentury*, an antilabor novel recalling some of his earlier techniques and vitality.

See also: Partisan Review, Proletarian and Radical Writers

—*Alan Wald*

REFERENCES

Luddington, Townsend. *John Dos Passos: A Twentieth Century Odyssey*. New York: Dutton, 1980.

Rosen, Robert C. *John Dos Passos: Politics and the Writer*. Lincoln: University of Nebraska Press, 1981.

Drug, Hospital, and Health Care Employees Union, Local 1199 of the Retail, Wholesale, Department Store Union: see Local 1199

Dual Unionism

Participation in the labor movement presented revolutionaries with a paradox. Unions were the characteristic form of organization for wage earners under capitalism, bringing workers together on the basis of shared interests and grievances and in the process contributing to a sense of working-class solidarity. To separate oneself from the unions was to cut oneself off from the heart of the working class and to abandon perhaps the most important potential base for the creation of a revolutionary movement. On the other hand, labor unions were by their nature reformist organizations. Designed specifically to win limited concessions from employers, they undercut the revolutionary potential of the working class. When such organizations were dominated by conservative business unionists, as was often the case in the American Federation of Labor, it was extremely difficult for revolutionaries to function within them. This contradiction—the vital role of the unions in working-class life and the difficulty that revolutionaries had working within them—provides the key to understanding the history of dual unionism in the United States.

During the 1880s anarchists established separate union federations in Chicago, New York, and other cities. The social basis for such federations can be explained partly in ethnic terms—they tended to be based largely on Germans, Bohemians, and other nationalities with strong radical subcultures. But there was also a revolutionary principle involved—the anarchists hoped to harness the power of the unions to a movement that would destroy the capitalist state and the basis for private property.

While the impulse to establish separate revolutionary union federations is easily understood, there is little question but that the decision frequently led to splits within the revolutionary movement as well as further alienation from the mainstream unions. In the case of the Socialist Labor Party's establishment of the Socialist Trades and Labor Alliance in 1895, for example, the move failed to win not only most trade unionists but even some of the party's own members, who preferred to fight it out with Samuel Gompers and his allies within the AFL. The issue of dual unionism precipitated a debate within the SLP that helps to explain the foundation of the Socialist Party in 1901.

By far the most famous of the dual union efforts was the Industrial Workers of the World, an anarcho-syndicalist organization that won considerable strength among diverse groups of unorganized workers between its birth in 1905 and its virtual destruction during the 1920s. IWW activists provided brilliant leadership in a series of mass strikes by immigrant workers in textile, steel, and other industries between 1909 and 1913, but their local organizations were either destroyed in ferocious employer counterattacks or simply proved incapable of maintaining their membership.

As an alternative to dual unionism, William Z. Foster and a group of syndicalist militants developed a strategy that came to be known as "boring from within." Foster argued that the mainstream unions could indeed be radicalized but only through long-term agitation by a "militant minority" within the regular trade union organizations. Foster and his group developed their critique of dual unionism first within the IWW and then through a series of organizations they formed between 1911 and 1920. The boring-from-within strategy, endorsed by Lenin, had a major impact on early Communist trade union policy.

From its inception in 1919 until the end of 1928, the Communist Party firmly rejected the concept of dual unionism, though its members were constantly at odds with the conservative leadership of the AFL. At the end of 1928, however, in response to a change in the Comintern line and mass expulsions of left-wing activists from several unions, the Party established the Trade Union Unity League (TUUL), a separate federation of revolutionary industrial unions. The league was liquidated in 1935 and many of its activists went on to play important roles in the development of the Congress of Industrial Organizations (CIO), which set out to organize mass-production workers throughout American basic industry and competed with AFL organizers in several sectors of the economy.

These radical dual unions were never successful in the ultimate sense that they won the mass of workers over to a revolutionary trade union program. Their failures, however, should not obscure the important role they played in organizing groups of workers otherwise ignored by the mainstream movement: in developing new strategies and forms of organization that helped to reshape the labor movement in the long term, and in persistently arguing for a radical vision of the labor movement as an agent of social and political transformation. *See also*: Industrial Workers of the World, Socialist Trades and Labor Alliance, Trade Union Unity League

—*James R. Barrett*

REFERENCES

Foster, William Z. *American Trade Unionism*. New York: International, 1947.

Saposs, David. *Left Wing Unionism*. New York: Russell & Russell, 1926.

Du Bois, W. E. B. (1868–1963)

Undoubtedly the most influential black intellectual of the twentieth century and one of America's finest historians, William Edward Burghardt Du Bois maintained an ambiguous relationship with Marxism and the Left throughout much of his career. An advocate of elite dominion in black politics (the so-called Talented Tenth theory), he initially mistrusted mass movements and Left appeals. Yet he eventually emerged a peerless voice in Western Marxism, the "father" of Pan-Africanism, an adversary of Cold War cultural assumptions, and a vocal advocate for peace. He died a dedicated Communist.

Born in Great Barrington, Massachusetts, the descendant of a well-established Berkshire black family and a Bahamian plantation owner, he grew up with an impoverished and crippled mother utterly dedicated to her only offspring. He had few bouts with racism as a child and graduated from high school a promising scholar. After two years at Fisk University (Du Bois's first introduction to the world of southern black culture and religion), he went on to graduate cum laude from Harvard, where he worked closely with William James, and advanced his study of German philosophy at Fredrich Wilhelm University in Berlin in 1892. Although he studied more of Hegel than Marx and Engels, Du Bois occasionally attended rallies of the German Social Democratic Party, displaying an early interest in socialism. He then returned to receive his Ph.D. from Harvard. His prodigious dissertation, "The Suppression of the African Slave Trade to the United States of America, 1638–1870," whose detached empiricism barely veils its ringing moral condemnation of slavery, was published as the first in the Harvard Historical Series volumes. In 1896, after a teaching stint at Wilberforce University, he was commissioned by the University of Pennsylvania to undertake a study of black Philadelphia, resulting in the classic sociological treatise *The Philadelphia Negro: A Social Study* (1899).

This book, in which he suggested that the black elite had an obligation to uplift the race, marked an important stage in his political evolution, essentially planting the seeds for his Talented Tenth thesis. Though still wedded to the idea that education and scientific inquiry were liberating, during his tenure at Atlanta University, beginning in 1897, Du Bois began to reassess the complexity of black consciousness in light of widespread racial violence and segregation. Although indifferent to religion, he grasped the significance of black faith as a response to American racism. And in an 1897 essay entitled "Strivings of the Negro People," he articulated the concept of double consciousness, the need to reconcile the African-American's quest for assimilation with his/her African identity. First published in *Atlantic Monthly*, it became the basis for a series of essays published as *The Souls of Black Folk* (1903), which not only developed Du Bois's early ideas on cultural pluralism but presented unique perspectives on black religion, culture, politics, and history, positing the color line as the great question of the dawning century.

Du Bois's prominence as much as his political orientation automatically made him a rival of reigning black elites, such as those represented by Booker T. Washington and T. Thomas Fortune, who had placed their stake in accommodation. Searching for like-minded allies in his fight against lynching, segregation, and the "Tuskegee Machine," Du Bois teamed up with Boston *Guardian* editor William Monroe Trotter, whose militancy contributed to Du Bois's prolonged shift away from enlightened leadership to self-activity and open rebellion. Together they established the short-lived Niagara movement in 1905, comprised of black educated men opposed to Booker T. Washington. Hardly a movement of radicals, it did attract a few black socialists, such as the Reverend Reverdy C. Ransom. More important, Du Bois was moving toward socialism independently. He began reading the works of Henry George, Jack London, and John Spargo, and by 1907 had described socialism as the "one great hope of the Negro in America."

The collapse of the Niagara movement coincided with growing white liberal and radical concern over American racism (sparked by racial violence in Springfield, Illinois, in 1908), thus opening doors for Du Bois to build new alliances with white progressives. He joined Socialists William English Walling, Mary White Ovington, and several other progressives to form the National Association for the Advancement of Colored People in 1910. Appointed director of publicity and research, Du Bois agreed to edit its journal, the *Crisis* (whose name Walling had suggested). Although in no sense avowedly radical, the *Crisis* was regarded as inflammatory by white southerners and by the Bureau of Investigation, predecessor to the FBI. Under Du Bois's strong editorial guidance it spoke primarily to the Talented Tenth, but attracted many white socialists and liberals. Meanwhile, Du Bois began to contribute to an array of radical periodicals, joined the editorial board of the *New Review*, and devoted an entire issue of the *Crisis* to woman suffrage.

When Du Bois joined the Socialist Party in 1911, his ideas did not change significantly. He viewed the party as another vehicle for racial and economic emancipation and remained close to his moderate Socialist coworkers in the NAACP, namely Walling, Ovington, and Charles Edward Russell. He left the party after a year, however, prompted partly by racism within the organization and primarily by his decision to endorse Woodrow Wilson's 1912 presidential bid, though he continued his contributions to the socialist press and remained an independent socialist.

The First World War fixed Du Bois's pacifism, deepened his anti-imperialism, and intensified his Pan-African sentiments. His 1915 essay "The African Roots of War" recognized the critical role European imperial designs played in the conflict. Although he initially opposed the war and viewed it as an opportunity for increased agitation for civil and political rights, in 1918 he joined his familiar (and now ex-socialist) allies around the *New Republic* in championing America's entry. He was so sure that black participation would make a claim for democracy that he actually requested federal support for the coming 1919 Pan-African Congress. But his call to "close ranks," for which he was sharply criticized by contending black radicals, did not lead to the intended results. As he learned, even the most modest Pan-African proposals for a moderated colonialism aroused racist suspicions, and postwar "race riots" revealed the true fruit of international conflict. At the war's end, Du Bois urged blacks to defend themselves against racial attacks and became a more assiduous proponent of Pan-Africanism—the Second Pan-African Congress in 1921 displaying a greater militance than the previous meeting.

By the early 1920s, Du Bois's public prominence was clearly on the decline. He sustained attacks from several circles, ranging from rising black-nationalist leader Marcus Garvey to Harlem Renaissance writer Claude McKay. Militant black Socialists A. Philip Randolph and Chandler Owen dismissed Du Bois as virtually another Booker T. Washington, and the revolutionary African Blood Brotherhood assailed him for ignoring black workers in favor of the Talented Tenth. An advocate of pragmatic, Fabian socialism, Du Bois was initially skeptical of the Russian Revolution, which made him a target of criticism from the emerging Communist movement. Although a visit to the USSR in 1927 inspired Du Bois to proclaim it "the most hopeful vehicle for the world," he still regarded Communism as inappropriate for African Americans. He won even fewer allies by preaching social tolerance in the intolerant twenties, and his assault on racism in the AFL prompted counterattacks from white labor leaders.

The Great Depression threw the *Crisis* into economic peril, and Du Bois's preliminary proposals for black survival irked most NAACP leaders, both of which contributed to his resignation as the journal's editor in 1934. In a series of articles in 1934–35, he had advocated a form of urban black self-determination, based on the creation of economic cooperatives, in which communities could wrest control of and collectivize local economies. It was a kind of Talented Tenth–tainted socialism, revealing Du Bois's belief that black petit-bourgeois leadership could implement socialist strategies in urban America. While considered too radical for NAACP tastes, Du Bois's vitriolic attacks upon the International Labor Defense's role in the Scottsboro case made him an adversary of the Communists. Seemingly isolated from the world of politics, he returned to Atlanta University's Sociology Department.

Du Bois quickly immersed himself in the works of Marx and Engels (and even taught a course in 1933 on "Karl Marx and the Negro"), thus laying the foundation for what could be described as the most important Marxist work on U.S. history, *Black Reconstruction* (1935). Adopting a truly independent approach to Marxism, *Black Reconstruction* antedates the works of Eric Williams, Oliver Cox, and Immanuel Wallerstein by placing American slavery and emancipation at the center of the emergence of world capitalism and imperialism. If the Southern revolution had been successful, it would have shaken the power of Northern capital, democratized America, and obliterated prevailing racist notions—notions that justified colonial expansion. It was no coincidence, therefore, that direct colonialism replaced American slavery as the principal generator of primitive accumulation. The failure of American labor to support black reconstruction, Du Bois argued, had been a calamity for all of humankind, for it could have altered the balance of social and economic democracy across the planet if it had succeeded.

Aside from its general thesis, *Black Reconstruction* contributed startling insights into the nature of revolutionary consciousness. First, Du Bois recognized that the black elite not only betrayed the movement but advocated only political solutions for fundamentally economic problems. It was ex-slaves, in fact, who forced the land issue to the fore. As C. L. R. James would repeat three years later, Du Bois demonstrated that slaves and agrarian workers displayed even greater revolutionary force than urban industrial workers or their elite leaders. Second, Du Bois's narrative suggested that the development of revolutionary consciousness did not precede the revolution but was the *result* of it. Moreover, this consciousness was not, in Marx's sense, a "mirror of production," but rather a partial reflection of religious and cultural traditions derived from an African past—hence, it was a consciousness outside the logic of bourgeois thought.

Black Reconstruction was not well received in Communist circles but it did cause a stir, prompting Party activist James S. Allen (Sol Aurebach) to produce the hastily written *Reconstruction: The Battle for Democracy*. Nevertheless, by the late 1930s Du Bois found himself more and more in agreement with Communist positions. He defended the Nazi-Soviet Pact, called for American intervention when Germany invaded Russia in 1941, and read more deeply about communism as a world movement. After retiring from Atlanta University in 1944, and returning to the NAACP, he focused his attention on colonialism and imperialism as the basic causes of war. He also participated in the historic Fifth Pan-African Congress in Manchester, England (1945), which had attracted Africa's most prominent nationalist leaders. Stung by the Western powers' unwillingness to relinquish their colonial (and neocolonial) claims, Du Bois turned sharply left for the last time. Dismissed from the NAACP in 1948 for his views, he became honorary vice-chair, under Paul Robeson, of the avowedly anti-imperialist Council on African Affairs and actively raised funds for the council's African Aid Committees. As an early advocate of the Progressive Party, a delegate to the Paris World Congress for Peace (1949), and chairman of the antinuclear, anti–Cold War Peace Information Center (1950), he became a prime victim of McCarthyism and endured attacks from a panoply of black leaders who had been drawn into the Cold War campaign. He refused to cower to political repression and emerged a staunch opponent of McCarthyism, contributing numerous critical essays to such Left publications as *Jewish Life*, *Freedom*, and the *National Guardian*. His stand exacted a heavy price: among other things, he and his second wife, Shirley Graham, had their passports revoked by the State Department in 1953 for refusing to submit anticommunist affidavits.

In 1950 the eighty-two-year-old scholar-activist made his first bid for public office. A candidate for Senate on the American Labor Party ticket, he received more than 200,000 votes from New Yorkers, concentrated mainly in Harlem. Although he grew steadily closer to the Communist Party and less tolerant of black anti-Marxist intellectuals, Du Bois remained independent very late in his life. In 1958, for example, he joined a number of Trotskyists, ex-Communists, and independent radicals to propose a united left-wing coalition for the New York State elections. Nonetheless, he became increasingly dedicated to the promises of socialism as a worldwide system, and to existing communism as a stage toward its evolution.

In 1961, three years after his passport had been reinstated, Du Bois accepted Kwame Nkrumah's offer of citizenship in Ghana, to produce a project conceived decades earlier but long abandoned, the *Encyclopedia Africana*. He died in 1963, the encyclopedia unfinished, but *Freedomways* magazine (with his wife, Shirley Graham Du Bois, at the helm) was founded to carry on his work. He had joined the CPUSA just prior to his departure for Africa, and that act became his final political testament. *See also*: American Labor Party; Communist Party; *Freedomways*; History, U.S.; Progressive Party

—Robin D. G. Kelley
Paul Buhle

REFERENCES

Du Bois, W. E. B. *The Autobiography of W. E. B. Du Bois: A Soliloquy on Viewing My Life from the Last Decade of Its First Century*. Edited by Herbert Aptheker. New York: International Publishers, 1968.

Horne, Gerald. *Black and Red: W. E. B. Du Bois and the Afro-American Response to the Cold War, 1944–1963*. Albany: State University of New York Press, 1986.

Marable, Manning. *Black Radical Democrat*. Boston: Twayne Publishers, 1986.

Robinson, Cedric. *Black Marxism: The Making of the Black Radical Tradition*. London: Zed Press, 1983.

DUNAYEVSKAYA, RAYA (1910–87)

Noted philosopher and political activist, Dunayevskaya (née Rae Spiegel) is best remembered as one of the major figures in the 1940s–1980s effort to revive the Hegelian legacy and to create a "Marxist humanism." For her, more than for any other activist-thinker, dialectics *is* revolutionary thought.

Born in Russia, Dunayevskaya emigrated to the United States in 1922 and rapidly became involved in radical activities, including Communist efforts to reach black workers. Expelled from the Communist Party's youth section in 1928, she turned to Trotskyism, for a time in the 1930s serving as Trotsky's secretary in Mexico. Dunayevskaya broke with Trotsky over the nature of the Soviet Union and returned to the United States, where she developed her theory of the USSR as a state capitalist social formation. Active in Trotskyist circles, she helped found the "Johnson-Forest Tendency" (taking a party name of "Freddy Forest") with C. L. R. James. Their group passed through the Socialist Workers and Workers parties, 1940–51, producing bulletins to develop their own perspective. As an independent entity, they published the newspaper *Correspondence* from Detroit to express workers' own views. Following James's deportation, Dunayevskaya and others formed their own entity, the News and Letters Committees. For thirty-two years, she led the committees in their publication of many pamphlets and several books, and the monthly paper *News and Letters*.

As a political philosopher, Dunayevskaya proposed returning to the early Marx and his Hegelian roots, centering on the Marxist critique of alienation and its overcoming. Her best-known work, *Marxism and Freedom* (1958), was for her admirers (who included many New Leftists in the United States and abroad just learning about Marxism) an incisive introduction to Marx's thought and to the continuity of the Hegelian-revolutionary tradition. Among her other works, *Philosophy and Revolution* (1973) theorized the era of Third World revolution, beginning in Cuba and extending to Vietnam and elsewhere. She again sought to show the linkage between actual revolutionary struggles and revolutionary philosophy as guidance for contemporary theory and praxis. Her final major work, *Rosa Luxemburg, Women's Liberation and Marx's Philosophy of Revolution*, emphasizes the new social forces of revolt, and the relevance of Marx and Luxemburg for the women's liberation movement.

While small in numbers and modest in general impact, her News and Letters group had (and following her death, still has) a worldwide influence on individuals drawn to Dunayevskaya's ideas. She pioneered women's leadership of radical activity prior to the New Left, and attempted to realize the unity of theory and practice, which she took to be the core of the revolutionary Marxism. *See also*: James, C. L. R.; Trotskyism

—*Douglas Kellner*

REFERENCES

Raya Dunayevskaya Collection, Wayne State University.

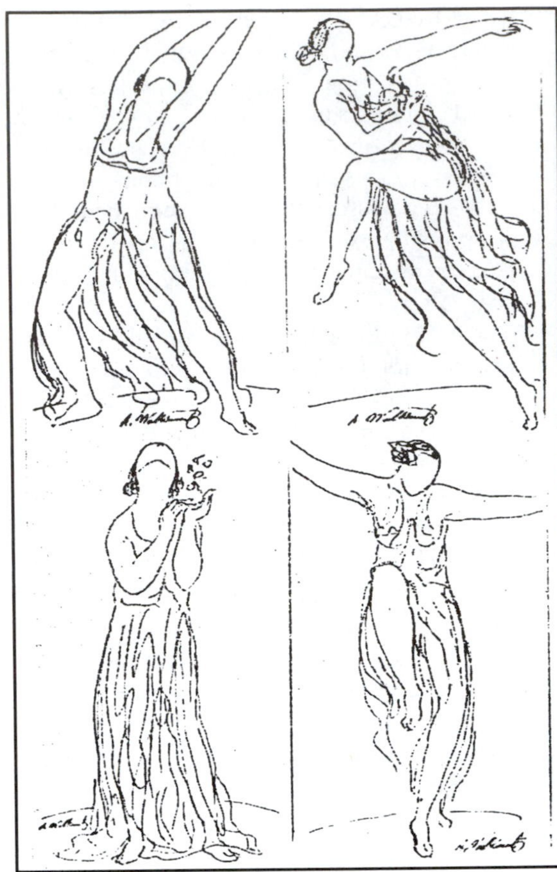

Sketches by Abraham Walkowitz

DUNCAN, ISADORA (1877–1927)

A dancer and writer, Duncan was born and raised in the San Francisco Bay Area. Unhappy at school, she was educated largely by her freethinking mother, whose instruction focused on classical music and the great poets; notably, all four Duncan children pursued careers in theater. By her early teens, Duncan had discovered the fundamentals of what would later be called modern dance, based not on the restrictive traditions of ballet but on free, natural, expressive movements.

Universally regarded as revolutionary, Duncan's new dance was derided by conservative critics but hailed as a liberating force by the rising generation of avant-garde poets and painters as well as by political radicals. As has so often been the case of American innovators in the arts, she was famous throughout Europe before attaining even modest recognition in her native land.

Her American admirers and supporters covered the entire spectrum of the Left, and included Max Eastman, Floyd Dell, and John Sloan of the *Masses* group, the poets of the Yiddish *di Yunge*, anarchist Alexander Berkman, single-taxer Bolton Hall, socialist-feminist Antoinette Konikow, and John Collier, lifelong agitator on behalf of American Indians.

Although in later years she liked to boast that she had been a revolutionist since the age of five, her social radicalism deepened appreciably in the course of a performance tour of Russia in the wake of the 1905 Revolution. From the 1910s on she was world-renowned not only as a dancer but as a living symbol of revolt, revolution, and women's emancipation. Duncan-style dance was taught at the

Socialist Party's Rand School in New York and at the anarchists' Modern School at Stelton, New Jersey.

An outspoken defender of the Bolshevik Revolution of 1917, in spring 1921 she accepted the invitation of Soviet diplomat Leonid Krasin to establish her school of dance in Moscow. Warmly welcomed by Commissar of Fine Arts Anatoly Lunacharsky, Duncan always insisted that her several years' Soviet sojourn, marred though it was by frustrations and disappointments, was the most exciting and rewarding period of her life. In the USSR she choreographed dances for the workers' hymn "The Internationale", as well as for peoples' songs such as Ireland's "Wearin' o' the Green" and France's "Carmagnole", and two funeral marches for Lenin.

Duncan lived most of her later life in Europe and the USSR, but returned to the United States many times for extended tours, often giving benefits for Russian famine-relief and other Left causes. Her last tour, in fall/winter 1922–23, with her companion, Soviet poet Serge Esenin, was a disaster. A grueling interrogation at Ellis Island because of her pro-Bolshevik views set the stage for a campaign of vilification against her, not only by the American Legion, the Ku Klux Klan, and evangelist Billy Sunday, but also by editors of America's largest dailies, who denounced her on their front pages as a dangerous "agent of Moscow." In many cities her performances were canceled. Finally, deprived of her U.S. citizenship, Duncan fled what she called the "narrow-minded, hypocritical, loathsome United States," vowing never to return.

Persecution by reactionaries did not diminish her revolutionary ardor, however; she remained steadfastly on the far Left. In the last years of her life, her Paris apartment served as unofficial headquarters of the Sacco-Vanzetti Defense Committee.

Isadora Duncan's epoch-making achievements as a dancer have unfortunately tended to obscure her considerable qualities as a thinker and writer. Her posthumously published *My Life*, probably the most widely read autobiography in English after Benjamin Franklin's, reflects the originality and boldness characteristic of all her essays and speeches. One of the most inspired writers on dance, she was also a penetrating critic of modern education, the situation of women in patriarchal society, and other aspects of repressive culture. *See also*: Modern Dance

—*Franklin Rosemont*

REFERENCES

Duncan, Isadora. *My Life*. New York: Liveright, 1927.

Rosemont, Franklin, ed. *Isadora Speaks*. San Francisco: City Lights Books, 1981.

Seroff, Victor. *The Real Isadora*. New York: Dial, 1971.

E

EASTMAN, MAX: see GREENWICH VILLAGE, PSYCHOANALYSIS, MASSES

EDUCATION

Two fundamental and in many respects contradictory perspectives underlie virtually all of Left educational theory since the 1930s: liberatory pedagogy, which emphasizes the possibility of social change through critical teaching and learning; and social reproduction, which analyzes the ways in which schools as institutions reproduce existing class, gender, and race structures. Underlying both of these perspectives is the question of the extent to which schools and universities as institutions within sexist and racist capitalist society are controlled by the demands of capital and the dominant ideology and the extent to which they provide the spaces for critical and political work.

In the early twentieth century the Progressive education movement and in particular the educational thought of John Dewey influenced liberal experiments in curriculum and pedagogy; more clearly Left experiments such as the anarchist Modern Schools and worker education programs in urban unions developed more politicized alternative pedagogies. But the first clearly articulated analysis and program for schools from the Left is found in the 1930s, in the work of George Counts and the social reconstructionist movement and in their journal, *Social Frontier*. Counts called capitalism "cruel and inhumane" and called for teachers in the public schools to "build a new social order." But while the social reconstructionists called for the political transformation of the schools, they did not provide a theoretical analysis of the role of the schools in the existing social order.

After the Second World War and in the emerging Cold War, the creation of a permanent war economy increasingly tied the universities to the demands of the defense industries and military research, while reformers like James Conant called for the reform of the public schools to better meet the needs of an industrialized, capitalist state. At the same time, schools and universities became the focus of right-wing attacks. Conservative groups began to monitor textbooks, liberal and Left professors and teachers were condemned as Communists and in some cases lost their jobs. Throughout this period, Left intellectuals used their energies to defend themselves from attack and to fight for rights of free expression. The major exception to this defensive stance were desegregation struggles, which, in challenging racism, *were* calling for a new social order, but in racial rather than class terms. Except for the powerful educational writings of W. E. B. Du Bois (collected as *The Education of Black People: Ten Critiques 1906–1960*), there was no direct Left analysis of race, class, and schooling in this period.

The call for a politicized pedagogy and the development of a Left critique of the existing educational system emerged from the

New Left social protest movements of the 1960s—the civil rights movement, the antiwar movement, and the women's movement. Freedom schools in the South, teach-ins around the Vietnam War, and women's consciousness-raising groups provided examples of teaching and learning outside formal educational institutions and led to calls for more relevant and politicized teaching within the colleges and universities and to anarchist calls for the abolishment of formal state schools. The activists of the late 1960s and early 1970s who founded libertarian free schools, radical alternative programs in colleges, and journals such as *Radical Teacher* argued that a critical and liberatory schooling could be created to replace the old. Theoretically, the basis for a Left pedagogy was found in the work of Paulo Freire, whose *Pedagogy of the Oppressed* was translated into English in 1968. In his emphasis on the power of a politicized literacy to contribute to revolutionary movements, Freire provided a theoretical and practical model for Left teachers and intellectuals in the United States. His work has influenced Left Catholic movements and a number of teachers in literacy programs and community colleges.

New Left critics also turned to an analysis of the role of schools in reproducing class and, to a lesser extent, race oppression. As the fundamental nature of U.S. society as a capitalist and imperialist power was explored, the ties of the universities to the state and the role of the public schools began to be examined and critiqued. A number of first-person accounts exposed the racism of public schools. Left historians of education challenged the dominant consensus in educational history that the schools were central institutions in providing social mobility and preserving democracy; instead, they asserted that schools as institutions must be viewed in relation to developments within capitalism and to the growth of the state. Michael Katz is perhaps the best known of a number of Left historians who examined such topics as the development of urban school systems as a struggle among competing groups, the growth of scientific management and control, and the ties between the schools and capitalist elites. A number of Left theorists addressed the ways in which curriculum and social relationships inside schools reproduce class structure. One of the most influential analyses of schools in relation to political economy was Samuel Bowles and Herbert Gintis's *Schooling in Capitalist America*, published in 1975. Bowles and Gintis argued that there is a functional correspondence between what is learned in working-class schools (work discipline, acceptance of monotonous work outside of individual control, bureaucratic authority) and what is experienced in the workplace. Thus the schools as state institutions reproduce the class structure of capitalism. While Bowles and Gintis's study has had a powerful influence on subsequent Left analyses, it has also been criticized for an implicit functionalism and failure to address the struggles over schools documented by Left educational historians or to recognize the various forms of radical pedagogy developed by the Left.

In the 1980s, critiques by the black, gay, and women's movements as well as other disempowered groups challenged traditional Left analyses of schooling. While these critiques have not always been tied to a class analysis, the criticisms of white feminists and both men and women of color have called into question the adequacy of a Left analysis of education in solely class terms and have pointed to the need for a Left analysis to address all forms of oppression. Despite the contributions of both the civil rights movement and the women's movement in creating liberatory and democratic forms of pedagogy, often these contributions have been ignored in white male calls for a socialist pedagogy or in analyses of education that discuss class exclusively without considering the fact that most teachers are women, or that the structure of schooling in the United States has been consistently racist. Henry Giroux and Michael Apple have been the best known of a number of Left theoreticians attempting a synthesis that would take into account the social-reproduction theories of writers like Bowles and Gintis, the liberatory pedagogy of Freire, and gender and racial struggles around teaching and schools that take place in terms of actual practice. *See also*: Teachers' Unions

—*Kathleen Weiler*

REFERENCES

Apple, Michael. *Teachers and Texts*. London and Boston: Routledge and Kegan Paul, 1986.

Aronowitz, Stanley, and Henry Giroux. *Education Under Siege*. South Hadley, Mass.: Bergin and Garvey, 1985.

Bunch, Charlotte, and Sandra Pollack, eds. *Learning Our Way*. Trumansburg, N.Y.: The Crossing Press, 1983.

Weiler, Kathleen. *Women Teaching for Change*. South Hadley, Mass.: Bergin and Garvey, 1987.

EINSTEIN, ALBERT: see SCIENCE

EMBREE, A. S. (1877–1957)

A foremost radical western organizer, Embree spanned the generations and movements from the Industrial Workers of the World to the Congress of Industrial Organizations. He also led the last of the major IWW strikes, far past the zenith of that organization's influence.

Born in Newfoundland, Embree graduated from college in 1897 and joined the Western Federation of Miners in British Columbia in 1899. He came into the emergent IWW in 1905. A key leader in the 1917 copper strike, he was among 1,200 unionists deported from Bisbee, Arizona, and later played an important role as IWW defense coordinator for the Espionage Act defendants. Convicted in Idaho on state criminal-syndicalism charges in 1921, Embree spent four years in prison. On his release, he began organizing southern Colorado miners, who for three days responded to the IWW appeal for strikes to support Sacco and Vanzetti. This militancy and cohesion prompted Embree and others to urge a statewide coal strike, which was successful in shutting down all three Colorado fields simultaneously.

Bitterly attacked by mine and public officials, miners responded with mass parades, auto caravans of singing miners, the formation of "Junior Wobblies" branches, and other creative actions. Repression escalated into the "Columbine Massacre," with state police machine-gunning strikers, killing six and wounding dozens, yet miners stood firm and won major concessions. Few Wobblies had been recruited during the strike, and some IWW national leaders privately charged Embree with a plan to "take over" the locals for Communist labor organizations. In fact, Embree remained with the IWW until 1937, when he joined the Western Federation of Miners' successor, the Mine, Mill, and Smelter Workers (IUMMSW). He continued as a Mine, Mill organizer into the 1940s, and his daughter, Una, married one of the union's most prominent (and Left-identified) figures, Maurice Travis. *See also*: Western Federation of Miners/ Mine, Mill and Smelter Workers

—*John R. Salter, Jr.*

REFERENCES

Gambs, John. *The Decline of the IWW*. New York: Columbia University Press, 1932.

McMahon, Ronald. "Rang-U-Tang: The IWW and the 1927 Colorado Coal Strike." In *At the Point of Production—the Local History of the IWW*, edited by Joseph Conlin. Westport: Greenwood, 1982.

Solski, Mike, and John Smaller. *Mine Mill: The History of the International Union of Mine, Mill and Smelter Workers in Canada—Since 1895*. Ottawa: Steel Rail Publishing, 1985.

EMMA LAZARUS FEDERATION OF JEWISH WOMEN'S CLUBS

Named for the Jewish poet whose lines are inscribed on the pedestal of the Statue of Liberty, the Emma Lazarus Federation (ELF) was founded in 1951, rising from the ashes of the Women's Division of the Jewish People's Fraternal Order of the International Workers Order when McCarthyism liquidated that organization. Under the dynamic leadership of June Gordon (1901–67) and, since 1967, of

Rose Raynes, the federation developed a program of cultural and sociopolitical activism.

ELF commissioned and sponsored the publication of Eve Merriam's biography (1956) of Emma Lazarus (1849–87) and Yuri Suhl's biography (1959) of Ernestine L. Rose (1810–92), and kept in print into its fifth edition (1982) Morris U. Schappes's *Selections from the Prose and Poetry of Emma Lazarus* (1944). In 1955 the ELF also published Aaron Kramer's translation of Yiddish poems by Morris Rosenfeld (1862–1923).

In 1957 ELF established the Emma Lazarus Day Nursery for working mothers in Jaffa (now Tel Aviv) and became a founder of the Museum of Immigration in the Statue of Liberty. ELF's several thousand members nationwide in the 1950s and 1960s campaigned on behalf of the foreign born, civil rights, women's rights, child welfare, and consumer protection. ELF stressed opposition to the nuclear arms race and favored a political solution to the Palestine-Israel conflict that would guarantee Israel's security and Palestinian national rights. By 1989, ELF, having failed to attract younger women to its ranks, had closed its national office, with clubs continuing in New York, Los Angeles, Miami, and Chicago. *See also*: *Jewish Life/Jewish Currents*, Yiddish Left

—*Morris U. Schappes*

REFERENCES

Hutchins, Grace. *Women Who Work*. New York: International Publishers, 1952.

Equi, Marie D. (1872–1952)

A physician for working-class women and children, a lesbian, and a dynamic and flamboyant political activist, Equi was known as a "firebrand in the causes of suffrage, labor, and peace in Portland in the 'teens, '20s, and '30s." Daughter of working-class immigrants in New Bedford, Massachusetts (her father was an Italian stonemason active in the Knights of Labor, her mother an ardent Irish nationalist), Equi worked in the textile mills during her youth. In 1890 she moved to Oregon and in 1903 graduated from the University of Oregon's medical school. By 1905 Equi was active in both the woman's suffrage movement and the Progressive Party. In 1911 she helped found Oregon's Eight-Hour Day League. During this period she began her lifelong work of distributing contraceptive information and performing illegal abortions. She also lived openly as a lesbian.

Equi's radicalism was sparked in 1913 by a militant strike of immigrant women cannery workers, led by the Industrial Workers of the World. Thereafter she worked mainly with the IWW regarding lumber workers, the unemployed, and the homeless. She also provided care to victims of the 1916 Everett Massacre and, as Oregon's representative, scattered Joe Hill's ashes to the wind in an international ceremony to commemorate the first anniversary of his execution. Shifting her focus from suffrage work, Equi championed direct action to hasten women's full emancipation. In 1916 she revised Margaret Sanger's pamphlet on birth control, *Family Limitation*, to make it more accurate medically, and the two were arrested at a Portland birth control demonstration that summer.

With the onset of WW I Equi joined the American Union Against Militarism to fight against preparedness, conscription, and imperialism and played an important role in local antiwar rallies. In 1918 she was arrested for making an antiwar speech. Convicted under the Espionage Act, she served time in San Quentin from 1920 to 1921. After her release, Equi grew less active politically. From 1926 to 1936 Elizabeth Gurley Flynn lived with her. In 1934 Equi performed her last documented public political act, giving a large donation to men wounded in a West Coast longshoremen's strike. She also demanded that she be listed at the top of Portland police's "Red List," under the rubric of "Queen of the Bolsheviks." She died a virtually forgotten woman. *See also*: Birth Control

—*Nancy Krieger*

REFERENCES

Gordon, Linda. *Woman's Body, Woman's Right: A Social History of Birth Control in America*. New York: Grossman Publishers, 1976.

Everett Massacre

The Industrial Workers of the World spent considerable energy on free-speech fights in the early 1910s. After 1915, official

organizational policy shifted from "the soapbox to the job," but one of the most important free-speech struggles did not erupt until the spring of 1916. The site was Everett, Washington, a city of some 35,000 inhabitants on Puget Sound. Its port was a strategic center for shipping out lumber, and its hiring halls recruited workers for operations in the interior. On May 1 some 400 shingle cutters went on strike. When Sheriff McRae began to arrest pickets, the local sent out a national call for assistance. Although the local belonged to the AFL, which did not respond to its appeal, the IWW in Seattle sent James Rowan to organize a solidarity campaign. As soon as Rowan stood up to speak in public, he was arrested and a free-speech fight was on.

Local support was considerable, but several efforts to speak in public met with failure. In an effort to build up the free-speech forces, a contingent of 41 IWWs arrived by ferryboat on October 30. They had not even left the dock area when they were surrounded by a sheriff's posse. Shortly thereafter, they were taken to a park on the edge of town and severely beaten. A week later another 250 Wobblies arrived by ferry to challenge the sheriff's lawlessness with a public meeting. As the boat attempted to dock, a drunken sheriff and deputies began to shoot at the passengers. Some of the IWWs shot back, and before the ferry could pull away, there were at least 5 dead, 6 missing, and 27 wounded passengers. On shore, a deputy lay mortally wounded, a lumber company official was already dead and 24 other individuals were wounded. The Everett free-speech fight had become the Everett Massacre.

The immediate aftermath was that seventy-four IWWs rather than the individuals who had shot at them were put on trial for murder. This was the typical IWW experience in which the victim of violence was treated as the instigator. The attempt at repression soon backfired when the IWWs achieved acquittals or dismissal of charges in well-publicized legal proceedings. The IWW victory fueled the determination of timber workers to seek long-sought basic reforms under IWW leadership. In the succeeding years, numerous gains were won through strikes and other direct action. As one IWW put it, the "timberbeast" became "a lumber worker." *See also*: Industrial Workers of the World

—*Dan Georgakas*

REFERENCES

Bird, Stewart, Dan Georgakas, and Deborah Shaffer. *Solidarity Forever—An Oral History of the IWW.* Chicago: Lake View Press, 1985.

Foner, Philip S., ed. *Fellow Workers and Friends—IWW Free-Speech Fights as Told by Participants.* Westport: Greenwood Press, 1981.

Kornbluh, Joyce R. *Rebel Voices—An IWW Anthology.* Rev. ed. Chicago: Charles H. Kerr, 1988.

Evergood, Philip (1901–73)

Beginning in the early thirties and continuing until his death, Evergood painted socially and politically engaging images. His most partisan paintings date from the thirties. During that decade he joined numerous artistic organizations affiliated with the Communist Party, and in many cases he became an active leader in them. In the early thirties he exhibited works at the John Reed Club in New York and attended the club's forums. He helped organize the Artists Committee of Action and the Artists Union and eventually became the president of the Artists Union. He was a member of the executive board of the American Artists Congress during the Popular Front and joined the Artists League of America during the Second World War. Throughout the thirties and early forties, Evergood wrote and spoke prolifically on artists' economic rights and their social and political responsibilities. He also ardently defended social realist art against those who accused it of being propagandistic. His own paintings from the thirties often take up themes of fascism and labor, and he donated a number of these paintings to exhibits organized to raise money for Spanish refugees and Russian relief. Although after WW II Evergood still addressed social and political issues in his paintings, these works are more symbolic and less topical than his works from the thirties. *See also*: Art Movements; Congress of American Artists

—Cécile Whiting

REFERENCES

Baur, John I. H. *Philip Evergood*. New York: Harry N. Abrams, 1975.

Hills, Patricia. "Philip Evergood's *The American Tragedy*. The Poetics of Ugliness, the Politics of Anger." *Arts* 54 (February 1980).

Taylor, Kendall. *Philip Evergood: Never Separate from the Heart*. Lewisburg, PA: Bucknell University Press, 1987.

Factions

Within a radical organization a faction is a group that seeks leadership of the organization, or, if it is already in control, to maintain that control. These groups are usually united around a leader or a specific policy direction on vital issues. Organized factions are permitted in some organizations, prohibited in others. Factions may struggle with one another for years, with various individuals switching sides. When faction fighting becomes acrimonious, the losing group often resigns or is expelled. The ousted faction may then form a new organization or create a publication to advance its views. Ousted factions frequently splinter into ever-smaller groups that soon disappear from the political scene even though individuals may remain politically active and join other groups. Significant faction fights have occurred at various times within the Communist and the Socialist parties in the United States. The Trotskyist movement is particularly prone to faction fighting, a phenomenon that has led to a proliferation of parties and organizations so small that they are dwarfed by the Socialist Workers Party, whose own membership usually ranges between 500 and 1,000. *See also*: Tendencies

—Dan Georgakas

Farmer-Labor Party

Created at a chaotic convention held in Chicago in July 1920, the FLP represented the amalgamation of the Labor Party of Illinois, sister labor parties in Connecticut, Indiana, New York, Ohio, and Utah, and radical elements in the Committee of Forty-Eight, a progressive organization containing the remnants of the "Bull Moose" Progressive Party of Theodore Roosevelt. Positioned close to the Socialist Party on many issues, the FLP seemed to many socialists or former socialists the way forward in American politics. In 1924 Robert M. LaFollette's Progressive ticket would nearly complete the absorption of the badly fading socialist movement into nonsocialist third-party politics. Meanwhile, the farmer-labor movement proved to be the U.S. Communists' first venture, however unsuccessful, into mass electoral maneuvers.

The powerful Chicago Federation of Labor (CFL), with the nonsocialist but radical John Fitzpatrick (1871–1946) in its lead, and the associated Illinois State Federation of Labor, directed by its president, John H. Walker (1872–1955), supplied the FLP its strongest support. In November 1919 the Illinois laborites hosted a convention in Chicago where 800 delegates representing thirty-four states and the District of Columbia created the National Labor Party. Reflecting Fitzpatrick's influence, the new party selected Chicago as its headquarters and made plans to hold a convention in that city in July 1920 to unite with agrarian and progressive groups, draft a platform, and select a presidential ticket. The convention issued a "Declaration of Principles" that called for disarmament, expanded civil rights and civil liberties, the eight-hour day and the forty-hour week, and the nationalization of "all the basic industries."

Similarly, the Committee of Forty-Eight was organized in St. Louis about a month after the Chicago labor party convention. At that time, the 300 delegates in attendance agreed on a platform advocating public ownership of transportation, public utilities, and natural resources; a tax policy designed to force idle land into use; and full and equal civil, political, and legal rights for all, regardless of sex or color. Moreover, the Forty-Eighters also called for the creation of a new, broadly based national party and made plans to meet in Chicago in July 1920 as well.

Though the expressed goal of the two groups, meeting separately but advocating amalgamation, was cooperation and joint action, the relationship between them was tense from the start, and there was mutual suspicion. Some leaders of the Committee of Forty-Eight feared that the new party would be dominated by labor elements who advocated excessive nationalization of the economy. Ultimately, a number of Forty-Eighters bolted their own convention and affiliated with the National Labor Party. The delegates reconstituted themselves as the Farmer-Labor Party, although only a few agrarian organizations, including the Non-Partisan League, endorsed the new party. Moreover, the party was not affiliated with the recently organized Farmer-Labor Party of Minnesota and other similar groups. Initially, most of the delegates favored LaFollette for president. Ultimately, the Wisconsin senator refused the nomination, on the grounds that the platform was too radical, and on the second ballot delegates turned to Parley P. Christensen (1869–1954), a little-known Utah lawyer who had chaired the Forty-Eight convention, to serve as the presidential candidate. Though unknown nationally, Christensen had a long career in Utah politics. Beginning as a Republican, he gradually broke with the party leadership over the issue of political reform, and affiliated with the Progressive Party in 1912. After service in the Utah state legislature, where he championed a number of progressive measures, Christensen helped form the Utah Labor Party in 1919. He had been active as an attorney defending members of the Industrial Workers of the World detained at Camp Douglas, Utah, during the war, and as the legal counsel for the streetcar workers' local in Salt Lake City. Christensen's ties to the labor movement brought him to the attention of the Justice Department, which had him under surveillance prior to his nomination and throughout the campaign.

Though hampered by a lack of funds, few organizers, and the competition of Eugene V. Debs's presidential campaign from prison, Christensen ran a strong campaign calling for large-scale nationalization of the U.S. economy, amnesty for political prisoners, especially Eugene Debs, expanded civil rights for blacks, extension of civil liberties, and recognition of the Soviet Union. His running mate, Max S. Hayes (1866–1945), further emphasized the socialist presence in the campaign: longtime leader of Cleveland and AFL socialists, Hayes had broken with the party over the war issue but remained close to most of its positions. Gathering more than a quarter million votes in eighteen states, the FLP appeared on its way to becoming a major force on the American Left. Moreover, the spread of the Non-Partisan League movement in the Dakotas reinforced the argument for a farmer-labor coalition.

After the 1920 campaign, the FLP captured the attention of American Communists and presented them with an interesting challenge. American Communists lived in a "sort of clandestine contemplation," largely foreign-born in composition and isolated from the labor movement. In the mid 1920s, following the Leninist line to affiliate with broader labor-based groupings, Communist Party leaders saw the FLP as representing such an opportunity. By 1923, FLP strength rested primarily among radical elements in the Northwest, not in Chicago, and while Fitzpatrick was the party spokesman, he failed to realize how radicalized the party membership among agrarian and labor elements in the West and Northwest had become, and that he had little influence in highly autonomous FLP groups across the country. These Farmer-Laborites were sympathetic to Communist viewpoints, and especially favored developments in the Soviet Union.

Communists, increasingly eager for influence in farm regions, had two major centers of activity. In the state of Washington, the farmer-labor movement drew upon long-standing Left traditions, in the Dakotas upon highly placed figures in the Non-Partisan League, in Minnesota upon the Finnish-American "stump farmers" blacklisted out of the mines, and in sections of Montana upon a genuinely charismatic Communist leader of farmers, three-hundred-pound Charles "Red Flag" Taylor (1884–1967). A veteran of Montana's Non-Partisan League, Taylor built his weekly *Producers News* from Sheridan County into one of the best Left papers in the United States, captured the local Republican Party through the NPL, and with his fellow leaders joined the CP but hid his membership for several years, serving as a Republican state senator in 1922. Taylor wielded great influence as an editor, agitator, and organizer.

In March 1923 John Fitzpatrick issued a call for a convention to meet in Chicago in July to build "a broad alliance of workers and farmers." Fitzpatrick himself, a longtime friend of William Z. Foster in the CFL, did not necessarily object to the Communist presence in the coalition, and that presence offered American Communists their most respectable opening hitherto. The Socialist Party's own reservations that the assembled forces were too weak to launch a new, major party caused them to hold back and ultimately persuaded Fitzpatrick that a precipitous move wold be unwise. By this time, however, most delegates—including, but not restricted to, Communists—had decided on a new electoral policy. "Mother" Jones, among other notables, addressed the gathering. Fitzpatrick's group split—the Federated Farmer-Labor Party was formed—and not long after the meeting, many organizations pulled back. The Communist-oriented Federated Farmer-Labor Party virtually dissolved in the face of the LaFollette candidacy.

The Farmer-Labor Party, still in Fitzpatrick's control, supported LaFollette's PP candidacy, as did the SP. And in some states, including Utah, the FLP and the SP worked together, running joint tickets for state and local office. After the disappointing outcome of the LaFollette candidacy and LaFollette's death in 1925, the FLP shifted its headquarters to Ogden, Utah, and gradually died out in the late 1920s. Charlie Taylor, along with a handful of others, continued to run, sometimes successfully, on its party line until the end of the decade. *See also*: Agrarian Radicalism

—*John Sillito*

REFERENCES

John Fitzpatrick Papers. Chicago Historical Society.

Dyson, Lowell K. *Red Harvest: The Communist Party and American Farmers*. Lincoln: University of Nebraska Press, 1982.

Shapiro, Stanley P. "Hand and Brain: The Farmer-Labor Party of 1920." Ph.D. diss., University of California-Berkeley, 1967.

Sillito, John R. "Parley P. Christensen: A Political Biography, 1869–1954." Master's thesis, University of Utah, 1977.

Weinstein, James. *The Decline of Socialism in America, 1919–1925*. New York: Monthly Review Press, 1967.

FARRELL, JAMES T. (1904–79)

A world-famous novelist and literary critic, Farrell was born in Chicago of second generation Irish-American working-class parents but was raised by middle-class relatives. He embraced socialist ideas while episodically attending the University of Chicago between 1925 and 1929. After a year of expatriatism in Paris, he moved to New York City in April 1932, where he became a sympathizer of the Communist Party.

Farrell contributed to the Party's *New Masses* as early as 1930, although his writing only appeared there with frequency in 1934. He also published in the *Daily Worker*, addressed the 1935 American Writers Congress, and regularly contributed a "Theatre Chronicle" to *Partisan Review*, literary organ of the New York City chapter of the John Reed Clubs. In these same years he produced his best-known work, the "Studs Lonigan Trilogy," consisting of *Young Lonigan: A Boyhood in the Chicago Streets* (1932), *The Young Manhood of Studs Lonigan* (1934), and *Judgment Day* (1935).

Farrell considered himself part of the movement of revolutionary writers allied with the Party, but was also fiercely independent about his writing style and judgments about literary practice. Throughout his career, in which he published more than fifty books, he held the conviction that his novels and short stories could improve social conditions by examining the growth and stultification of the human personality.

In the 1930s and 1940s, Farrell steeped himself in the texts of classical Marxism and Leninism, studying the policy and practice of the international Communist movement with care. By 1936 he reached political views considerably influenced by the exiled Bolshevik leader Leon Trotsky, as well as the American Trotskyists, who had recently become a faction in the Socialist Party. That year Farrell issued *A Note on Literary Criticism*, a major text in the development of Marxist aesthetics in the United States. Here he systematically repudiated CP cultural policies, elaborating a perspective compatible with Leon Trotsky's *Literature and Revolution* (1922).

After the autumn of 1936, Farrell more openly became a supporter of the Trotskyists who founded the Socialist Workers Party in late 1937. Until mid-1944, he worked with the SWP on several projects. These included the American Committee for the Defense of Leon Trotsky, organized to allow Trotsky (who had accepted political asylum in Mexico) a hearing during the Moscow Trials, and the Civil Rights Defense Committee, which defended Trotskyist and Teamster victims of the Smith Act.

Following a political dispute in which he accused the SWP of sectarianism, he collaborated with Max Shachtman's Workers Party, which had originally split from the SWP in 1940. Selected essays in Marxist cultural criticism were anthologized in *The League of Frightened Philistines* (1945) and *Literature and Morality* (1947), many of the latter first appearing in the pages of the WP's *New International*.

In the spring of 1948, Farrell changed his views drastically, becoming an anticommunist social democrat. In the 1950s he served as chairman of the American Committee for Cultural Freedom, and in the 1960s he supported Hubert Humphrey. During the final year of his life he belonged to Social Democrats U.S.A., an organization on the far right wing of the spectrum of social democracy. *See also*: *Partisan Review*, Trotskyism

—*Alan Wald*

REFERENCES

Branch, Edgar M. *James T. Farrell*. New York: Twayne, 1971.

Wald, Alan M. *James T. Farrell: The Revolutionary Socialist Years*. New York: New York University Press, 1978.

Fasanella, Ralph (b. 1914)

A 1972 feature article in *New York* magazine first brought Fasanella, a painter, to the attention of the American art public. A seven-page spread heralded him as a remarkable urban primitive painter, a kind of left-wing Grandma Moses. Fasanella's instant success was deceptive, for he had been painting every day for nearly thirty years. His public had been friends and associates who knew him as a member of the Abraham Lincoln Brigade, an organizer for the United Electrical, Radio and Machine Workers of America (UE), and a campaigner for the American Labor Party (ALP).

Fasanella's parents had immigrated to the United States from Bari, Italy. His mother was a left-wing activist and his father an ice man with leftist sympathies. Fasanella's parents eventually separated, partly because the father was resentful of his wife's greater intellectual and political involvements. Fasanella spent some time in a boy's home run by Catholic priests but returned to his mother's household where he continued to be greatly influenced by her views.

While always attracted to Left causes, Fasanella never took extreme positions. Appropriate to that temperament, his political hero was radical New Yorker Vito Marcantonio. Fasanella campaigned for Marcantonio, himself ran for office on the ALP ticket, named his son Marcantonio Fasanella, and put Marcantonio's image into more than one canvas. In the ALP and in his organizing for the UE, Fasanella made extensive use of his Italian working-class ties. During the mid-1940s he decided to dedicate himself to painting. He supported himself with industrial jobs until blacklisted in the McCarthy era and then worked at menial occupations. At the time of his "discovery," he was working for his brother at a Bronx gas station.

The huge and colorful canvases he worked on were crammed with vivid images, details, vignettes, and even printed messages. Many of his themes were decidedly left wing—homages to the Rosenbergs, evocations of May Day, renderings of UE halls, attacks on McCarthyism. He also did cityscapes and sports scenes in which working-class and ethnic motifs dominated. There were depictions of social tragedies like the Triangle Fire and a whole series celebrating the historic Lawrence strike of 1912. His workers were brave but far from invincible. Often he showed them as crucified by ignorance and exploitation. This reflected his Catholic background to some degree, but he first thought of using the Christ image in an artistic manner when he read Pietro Donato's *Christ in Concrete*. Like the characters in that novel, for a time the young Fasanella had become an ice man, replacing his father in the prescribed social order.

More so than that of any other post-World War II painter, Fasanella's work has been almost exclusively dedicated to social and political concerns. It has been widely reproduced and featured at fundraising events for progressive causes. His interests bridge most of the generational and sectarian divisions in the Left, and reproductions of his best known works frequently adorn the office walls of labor educators and trade union officials. *See also*: Abraham Lincoln Brigade; American Labor Party; Art Movements; Marcantonio, Vito; UE

—*Dan Georgakas*

REFERENCE

Watson, Patrick. *Fasanella's City*. New York: Knopf, 1973.

Fast, Howard (b. 1914)

A prolific author of historical novels, biographies, popular histories, children's stories, film scripts, plays, detective fiction, science fiction, and "Zen Stories," Fast also wrote "entertainments" under the pseudonym E. V. Cunningham. In the 1940s, and again in the 1970s and 1980s, he achieved best-seller status with novels explicitly promoting left-wing ideas.

Born the son of a factory worker in New York City, Fast dropped out of high school and published his first novel before he was twenty. Within a few years, he had issued more than half a dozen historical novels about the American Revolutionary War period, including *Conceived in Liberty* (1939), *The Unvanquished* (1942), and *Citizen Tom Paine* (1943). *The Last Frontier* (1941) was an impressive effort to view the effects of the colonization of the continent from the viewpoint of native peoples.

Fast was sympathetic to the antifascist movement and the Popular Front from the onset of his career. In 1943 he joined the Communist Party. In the years of his membership, his most successful books were *Freedom Road* (1944), a novel of the Reconstruction era; *The American* (1946), a fictionalized biography of Illinois governor John Peter Altgeld, who pardoned three of the Haymarket anarchists; and *Spartacus* (1951), a drama of the 71 B.C. slave revolt.

In addition, Fast wrote less successful and more explicitly radical novels such as *Clarktown* (1947), concerning a Massachusetts strike; *Silas Timberman* (1954), depicting an academic victim of McCarthyism; and *The Story of Lola Gregg* (1956), describing the FBI pursuit and capture of a Communist labor activist. Among his Communist nonfiction writings, *Literature and Reality* (1950) is a vulgar treatise on Marxist criticism; *Peekskill, U.S.A.: A Personal Experience* (1951) describes the 1949 attack of anticommunist rioters on a Paul Robeson concert; and *The Passion of Sacco and Vanzetti* (1953) eulogizes the martyred Italian anarchists.

In 1950 the House Committee on Un-American Activities ordered Fast to provide the names of all those who had contributed to the support of a hospital for Spanish Republicans in Toulouse, France, with which he had been associated during the Spanish Civil War. When he refused, he was thrown in jail for three months. Blacklisted upon his release, he initiated his own publishing company, the Blue Heron Press. In 1952 he ran for Congress on the American Labor Party ticket, and in 1954 he was awarded the Stalin Peace Prize.

Immediately following his sensational break with and public excoriation of the CP in *The Naked God: The Writer and the Commu-*

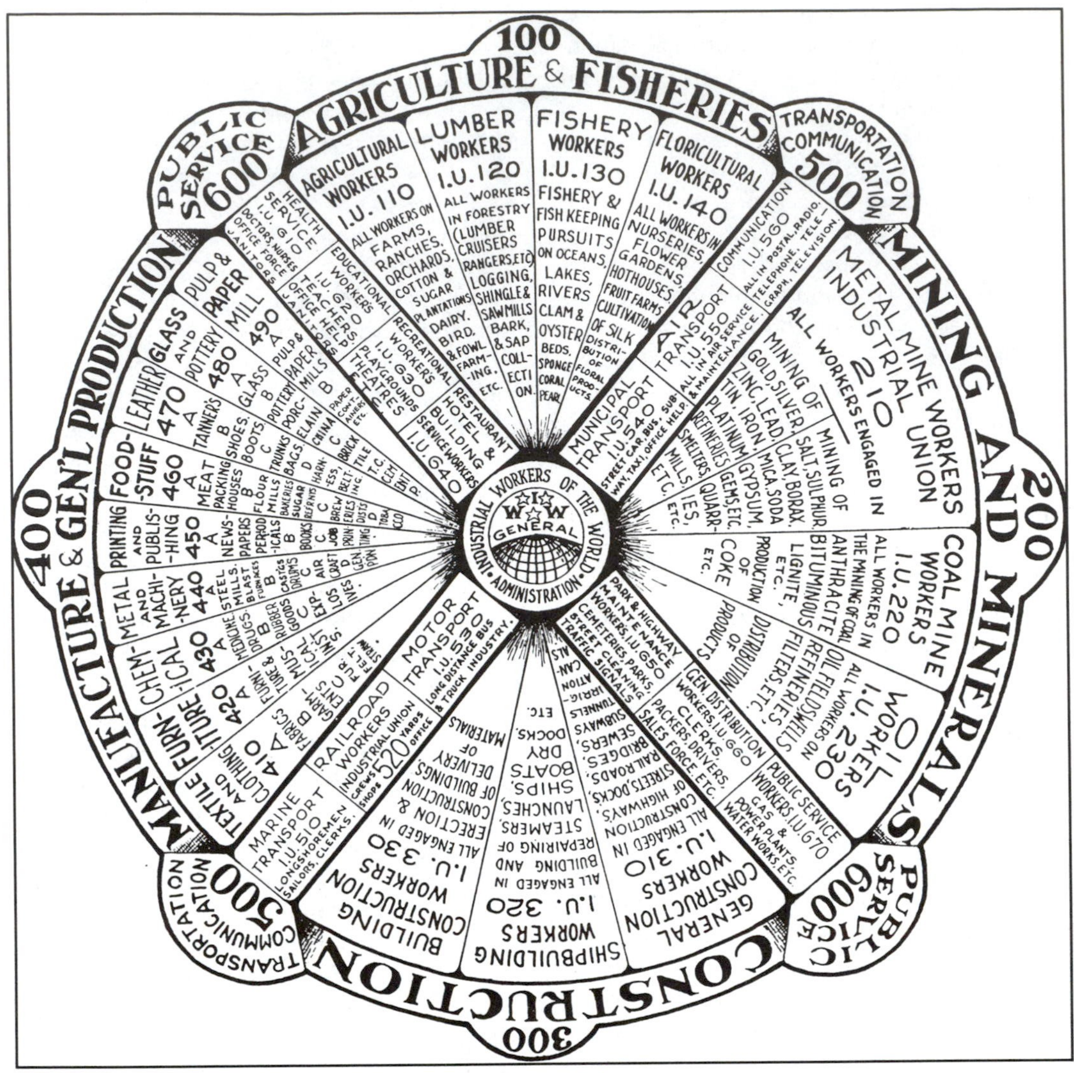

Diagram of the IWW "One Big Union" based on "Father Hagerty's Wheel of Fortune"

nist Party (1957), he moved to Hollywood to begin a new career as a scenarist. Nevertheless, by 1977 his popularity as a novelist was greater than ever when he wrote *The Immigrants*. The book was turned into a two-part television film and became the first of a pentalogy that was animated by left-liberal themes and traced an American family from the turn of the century through the Vietnam War era. *See also*: Proletarians and Radical Writers

—*Alan Wald*

REFERENCES

Murolo, Priscella. "History in the Fast Lane." *Radical History Review* 31 (1984).

Wald, Alan M. "Pictures of the Homeland: The Legacy of Howard Fast." *Radical America* 17, no. 1 (January–February 1983).

Father Hagerty's Wheel

Thomas J. Hagerty had a brief but spectacular impact on the movement for industrial unions that took shape at the turn of the century. At the time of his ordination as a Catholic priest in 1892, Hagerty was already a proponent of Marxist ideas. His consistent agitation among Colorado miners during the succeeding decade led to his formal suspension from the clergy in 1903. Hagerty continued his political activism and is usually credited with being the major author of the "Preamble" to the constitution of Industrial Workers of the World. His greatest fame, however, came from a chart he created to illustrate the nature of the new industrial society he envisioned. His wheel chart first appeared in *Voice of Labor* (May 1905) a month before the founding of the Industrial Workers of the World. Although Hagerty soon disappeared from the labor scene, his wheel was continuously reproduced for many years. It was extremely popular among all those inclined to syndicalism, but it was also used extensively by the Socialist Labor Party. His wheel placed every wage-earning occupation then in existence under one of eight departments that formed the wheel's rim: Manufacture, Public Service, Distribution, Food Stuffs, Agriculture, Mining, Transportation, and Building. The hub of the wheel was labeled "General Administration," and specific job categories were located between the hub and the rim under the appropriate department. In an age when illiteracy was common among working people, the chart proved an invaluable aid to organizers and propagandists. *See also*: Anarcho-syndicalism, General Strike, Industrial Workers of the World

—*Dan Georgakas*

REFERENCES

Doherty, Robert E. "Thomas J. Hagerty, the Church, and Socialism." *Labor History* 3 (Winter 1962).

Kornbluh, Joyce L. *Rebel Voices—An IWW Anthology*. Rev. and expanded ed. Chicago: Kerr, 1988.

FEDERAL BUREAU OF INVESTIGATION

It is difficult to comprehend the history of the twentieth-century American Left without considering that of the FBI. The FBI has not only tried to establish the boundaries of permissible dissent, but has also intervened to change the course of American history. At times it has acted independently of congressional and Department of Justice oversight; at others it has functioned as an arm of the executive branch and within an implicit public mandate.

Founded in 1908, the Bureau of Investigation, as the FBI was called until 1935, first directly affected the American Left during the Palmer Raids. In nationally coordinated raids in November 1919 and January 1920, the Bureau seized at least 4,000 supposed subversives, of whom about 1,000 were eventually deported. From 1920 to 1924 the Bureau continued its "antisubversive" activities: it expanded its files on dissidents, helped break the 1922 railroad strike, cooperated with private detective agencies, and led the federal government's drive to destroy Marcus Garvey and the United Negro Improvement Association.

The Bureau of Investigation's systematic violation of the Bill of Rights, combined with internal corruption at the top and in the ranks, produced significant reforms in 1924. Attorney General Harlan Stone established strict limitations on the Bureau's activities and promoted Assistant Director J. Edgar Hoover to the directorship—the post he held until his death in 1972.

Hoover, born in Washington, D.C., in 1885, was the FBI. Operating from convictions and values established during his childhood and alien-registration work in the Department of Justice during WW I, Hoover almost literally turned Bureau employees into himself. Hoover's supervision of the Palmer Raids, moreover, solidified a mind-set concerning dissent that prevailed until his death.

Two key points stand out about the FBI during the period from 1924 to 1936. First, the Bureau secretly continued its spying, while reducing its scope. (Other agencies, including urban police "red squads," military intelligence, private spy agencies, and right-wing organizations, compensated for the cutbacks.) Second, a variety of circumstances—increased national attention to crime, an adroit public-relations campaign, and a qualitatively improved professionalism—combined to create a superb public image for Hoover and his G-men. Hoover's FBI would live off this ideological and cultural capital for the next forty years.

A new stage in the FBI's antisubversive activities began in August 1936, when President Franklin D. Roosevelt requested a "survey" of Communist and fascist organizations. Hoover soon expanded this mandate and, by the fall of 1938, had reestablished the General

Intelligence Section (dormant since the 1924 reforms) to begin reviewing Left periodicals and creating a filing index for information on individuals and organizations. The Bureau's number of special agents had grown from 391 in 1933 to 898 in 1940; by 1944, it would have 4,886 such agents.

From 1940 to 1946, the Bureau opened thousands of files on individuals and organizations into which it poured information gathered from a variety of sources. From February 1941 thorugh the following year, the FBI opened 60,000 individual files in the "subversive" classification and in the following year, nearly 120,000 files. Among the Bureau's sources were general-circulation newspapers, Left publications, and internal organizational material. "Confidential informants" from the ranks of management, the labor movement, and Left organizations provided still more intelligence. Finally, the FBI gathered much information through barely legal and outright illegal methods. These included tapping telephones and rooms, breaking into domiciles and offices, and examining mail and trash.

In late February 1946, the FBI launched a full-scale offensive against American Communism. Ostensibly developed to prepare the American public for the "flood of propaganda from Leftist and so-called Liberal sources" in the "event of extensive arrests" of Communists during a "serious emergency," the Bureau began preparing "educational materials" to "undermine Communist influence" in unions and "religious circles." The goals were threefold: to separate Communists from those who would work with them; to politically isolate left liberalism; to make Communism the nation's only significant political issue.

The FBI promoted its version of "American" industrial unionism in three specific ways. First, ex-FBI agents became prominent in corporate security and personnel departments; they brought information and informers with them and hired former colleagues to do the same. Still others, such as the New York City ex-agents who founded *Counterattack* and eventually published *Red Channels,* were instrumental in anticommunist organizations.

Second, the FBI leaked information to individuals. As early as 1940, the Bureau could "place" articles and editorials in newspapers across the country; this activity expanded later in the decade. These journalistic arrangements not only helped establish the ideological boundaries of acceptable union activity, but also disseminated information that anticommunists could put to good use. Leaks to the *Milwaukee Journal* in 1946, for example, helped Allis-Chalmers management defeat militant unionism at its West Allis plant.

CIO leaders, both nationally and locally, received FBI help. In 1943 James Carey requested information on CIO personnel; by early 1950, as Carey and other anticommunists stepped up their attacks on the United Electrical Workers (UE), Bureau data was flowing to Carey and his allies. And at the local level, for example, disgruntled members of a Westinghouse local in Erie, Pennsylvania, used such information in a series of unsuccessful efforts to otherthrow the UE leadership.

The FBI also leaked information to Catholic laypersons and priests who were active within the heavily Catholic CIO. Father John Cronin, S.S., who acted as intermediary for the FBI and Richard Nixon during the Alger Hiss case and who later was a speechwriter for Nixon, began receiving and providing information in 1941. Cronin moved into the Social Action Department of the National Catholic Welfare Conference in 1946; there he wrote a series of enormously influential Chamber of Commerce pamphlets, including *Communists Within the Labor Movement* (1947). Some Association of Catholic Trade Unionists members, including Monsignor Charles Owen Rice, provided information to the FBI (and in turn received it).

In Congress, FBI leaks were used in hearings by the House Education and Labor Committee, the Senate Internal Security Subcommittee, and the House Committee on Un-American Activities (HUAC). These committee hearings were central to the attack on the CIO Left; they were often held during or immediately before strikes and/or representation elections, i.e., the 1948 Univis Lens strike in Dayton and the 1952 International Harvester strike. While CIO leaders often condemned these witch-hunt committees, they took advantage of the political fallout during raids on Left-led unions and locals. In 1952 HUAC, with substantial FBI help, focused its Detroit hearings on the huge United Automobile Workers local at Ford's River Rouge plant. Walter Reuther, the UAW president under steady criticism from the River Rouge local, used the HUAC hearings as the occasion to place an administratorship over the local.

Third, some evidence exists to show more direct FBI intervention in trade union politics. In 1952 Hawaii special agents tried to split the Longshoremen's Union by offering to have a Smith Act indictment dropped in exchange for a union official's leading a secession movement. Although the agents thought they had solidified their union support, the plan backfired when union officials legally taped the oral offer of a bribe.

The FBI did not destroy the CIO Left on its own. Many other developments and factors—Soviet foreign policy, an ever-higher standard of living based on the "Pax Americana," internal divisions within unions and the American working class, and antimodernist reactions to changes in gender relations and social mores—contributed to that defeat. The Bureau's tactic of getting out the "facts" was, however, extraordinarily effective, in part because of the Marxist-Leninist strategy of the Communist Party—the leading force on the American Left. Unionists who were members of the CP in general hid that fact. This tactic allowed Party members to gain an enormous amount of influence that would not have been theirs if the issue of communism had been out in the open. On the other hand, when the "facts" came out—and the FBI often did have sound information—the rank and file and secondary leaders often felt a deep sense of betrayal. In contrast, where Party members functioned more or less openly—for example, in the Farm Equipment Workers—unionists often remained steadfastly loyal despite unrelenting attacks.

The FBI intensified its harassment of the American Left in 1956 when it established CONINTELPRO: Counterintelligence Program. First put into effect against the CP and the Socialist Workers Party, then "White Hate Groups," "Black Nationalist Hate Groups," and the "New Left," CONINTELPRO aimed to destroy, by any means necessary, the groups targeted. It was out of this mind-set and organizational effort that Hoover, who as a youth witnessed the formal segregation of Washington, D.C., directed the efforts to get rid of Martin Luther King, Jr., and replace him with more "responsible" black leadership.

Hoover's perspective on the world, frozen at about 1920, grew increasingly out of sync with American society in the late 1950s and 1960s. His FBI was forced to investigate organized crime and the violation of civil rights; that FBI, molded in Hoover's image and ideology, never quite understood that the movements of the 1960s could not easily be fit into a "Communist Infiltration" model. The CONINTELPRO programs often succeeded not because the operating assumptions had some congruence with reality, as had the earlier drive against the CIO Left, but because the FBI had virtually unlimited resources, the ability to function illegally, and sense enough to exploit already existing divisions.

On March 8, 1971, a group calling itself the Citizen's Commission to Investigate the FBI broke into a Bureau office in Media, Pennsylvania. There they pilfered files that revealed the existence of CONINTELPRO-New Left and published them in *WIN* magazine. This incident, according to one of Hoover's aides, was the "turning point in the FBI image." Criticism of the Bureau increased, and in late 1971 a two-day conference at Princeton met to discuss the FBI (Investigating the FBI, 1973). In 1973 and 1974, a lawsuit, filed under the Freedom of Information Act, forced the release of CONINTELPRO documents; in 1975 the Bureau released records documenting its program against the SWP. Finally, the House and Senate Select Committees on Intelligence held fairly thorough hearings on a whole range of FBI activities from the 1930s on.

The Freedom of Information Act has permitted researchers an unparalleled opportunity to investigate the history of the FBI. Although the files released under that law are incomplete and often heavily censored, they show that the histories of the twentieth-century American Left and the FBI are inseparable. They demonstrate, furthermore, that the

FBI, led by a genuinely American totalitarian, has often functioned as a policer of thoughts and a subverter of the Bill of Rights. *See also*: Armed Struggle, Civil Rights, Communist Party, House Un-American Activities Committee, McCarthyism, New Left, Socialist Workers Party

—*Steven Rosswurm*

REFERENCES

Garrow, David J. *The FBI and Martin Luther King, Jr.: From "Solo" to Memphis*. New York: Norton, 1981.

Lowenthal, Max. *The Federal Bureau of Investigation*. New York: Turnstile, 1950.

O'Reilly, Kenneth. *Hoover and the Un-Americans: The FBI, HUAC, and the Red Menace*. Philadelphia: Temple University Press, 1983.

———. "Racial Matters." In *The FBI's Secret File on Black America, 1960–1972*. New York: Free Press, 1989.

Powers, Richard Gid. *Secrecy and Power: The Life of J. Edgar Hoover*. New York: Free Press, 1987.

Theoharis, Athan, and John Stuart Cox. *The Boss: J. Edgar Hoover and the Great American Inquisition*. Philadelphia: Temple University Press, 1988.

FEDERAL THEATER PROJECT

From its inception, the Federal Theater was a "political theater," if we mean by that term a theater that encouraged political awareness and supported political action that could alter the status quo in America. It sought to expose selfishness, special interest, privilege, and injustice. But it also prided itself on exploring and experimenting with the dramatic medium as well as the human material available to it. As Hallie Flanagan, the national director, made clear, the FTP would be a theater that dramatized the search of the average American "for knowledge about his country and his world, to dramatize his struggle to turn the great natural, economic, and social forces of our time toward a better life for more people."

However, fewer than 10 percent of FTP plays dealt with issues such as housing, power, agriculture, public health, or labor. The Theater Project actually produced more plays by Shakespeare than by any other playwright, with the cycles of plays by Eugene O'Neill and Bernard Shaw close behind. So while plays investigating social and economic topics represented only a fraction of the FTP's work, those were the plays used with great success by the Dies and Woodrum committees of Congress to label the entire Theater Project Communist.

In specific areas where the Federal Theater exerted leadership and made substantial artistic strides—the Living Newspaper, the Negro theater, and the Dance Project—the outcries were the loudest. However, among the factual and carefully documented Living Newspaper scripts, only *Injunction Granted* might be considered politically questionable, and Hallie Flanagan closed that play herself. While no Living Newspaper was used as a platform for Socialist or Marxist or Communist party propaganda, this did not mean that individual authors, actors, and others connected with the project did not have Left sympathies. One calls to mind Mary Virginia Farmer, Florence and Burton James, and John Randolph. However, since the FTP was forbidden by law to inquire about an individual's political or religious affiliations, there was really no way of keeping a head count of Democrats, Republicans, Socialists, or Communists.

Among the Negro units of the Federal Theater Project only Theodore Wards's *Big White Fog*, produced in Chicago in April 1937, seriously questioned the viability of capitalism for black people in America. But even that discussion was presented in the context of other political alternatives, Garveyism and African nationalism. Nevertheless, a nervous FTP, even after a successful box-office response, moved *Big White Fog* to a South Side high school, clearly a case of de facto censorship.

How Long Brethren, supported by a Negro choral ensemble and including dances based on Lawrence Gellert's *Songs of Protest*, made a strong racial statement, but the Federal Theater Dance Project in New York included, besides Helen Tamiris, choreographers Gluck Sandor, Felicia Sorel, Don Oscar Becque, and Charles Weidman, and Doris Humphrey as advisers.

Among the new American plays produced by the FTP during its four years, only *Chalk Dust*, about the ills of the public school system, and *Class of '29*, about the anguish of four unemployed college graduates during the Depression, played widely outside New York City. Of the plays produced in New York City, only *America, America* (one performance), *Awake and Sing!* (in Yiddish), *Battle Hymn*, and *Processional* could even be said to express a view from the Left.

Even so, throughout the four years of the project, Hallie Flanagan spent enormous amounts of time and energy writing and speaking against charges that the Federal Theater was a Communist organ. She even had to petition Congress to be allowed to testify on behalf of the project before the Dies Committee. But she lost. After June 30, 1939, no funds were available from Congress for the FTP. Flanagan commented, "Curtains came down on plays. Curtains came down on a coast-to-coast theater plant; on the people; and on the records of the activities of those people."

—*Lorraine Brown*

REFERENCES

Brown, Lorraine, and John O'Connor. *Free, Adult, and Uncensored: The Living History of the Federal Theatre Project*. Washington: New Republic Books, 1978.

Cosgrove, Stuart. "The Living Newspaper: History, Production, and Form." Ph.D. diss., University of Hull, 1982.

Flanagan, Hallie. *Arena*. New York: Duel, Sloane and Pearce, 1940.

Goldstein, Malcolm. *The Political Stage: American Drama and Theater of the Great Depression*. New York: Oxford University Press, 1974.

Himelstein, Morgan Y. *Drama Was a Weapon: The Left-Wing Theatre in New York, 1929–1941*. New Brunswick: Rutgers University Press, 1963.

Mathews, Jane DeHart. *The Federal Theater, 1935–1939: Plays, Relief, and Politics*. Princeton: Princeton University Press, 1967.

Naison, Mark. *Communists in Harlem During the Depression*. New York: Grove Press, 1983.

Williams, Jay. *Stage Left*. New York: Scribner's, 1974.

FEDERATED PRESS

The most enduring and comprehensive Left-oriented press service created in the United States, FP (1919–56), offered detailed alternative news reporting and critical interpretation.

Socialist papers had established cooperative publication arrangements, with outside pages added to local editions, several times from 1890 to the 1910s. None of these proved lasting, and the usual practice of reprinting news from other socialist papers meant delays or dispatches from only a few correspondents. During the 1919 nominating convention of the Farmer-Labor Party in Chicago, newspaper editors from the Committee of Forty-Eight, the Non-Partisan League, Socialist Party, and militant union movements—representing a total of thirty-two newspapers—founded the Federated Press. Robert M. Buck, editor of the *New Majority*, was named editor. FP's activist and educational mission, to raise labor consciousness and assail capitalist propaganda, would not have been possible without editorial insistence that FP's news be as solid, professional, and as cleanly written as that of any wire service in the world.

In 1920 FP began its subscription mail service. It operated three main bureaus, in Chicago, New York, and Washington, D.C. Other bureaus were variously opened in Detroit, Los Angeles, and elsewhere as labor struggles developed. FP supplemented a limited full-time staff with dozens of part-time writers, including Robert Dunn and Len DeCaux. Most of these correspondents worked for little or no compensation. Cartoons and photo mats were also provided to subscribers who could afford them in addition to news stories. Regular columns on foreign affairs, economic trends, labor news summaries, and humor became mainstays of the service. So too did feature stories.

Carl Haessler (1883–1969), former Rhodes scholar and university professor, imprisoned war resister and *Milwaukee Leader* staffer, moved into the central leadership position during the organization's early financial collapse in 1921–22. Haessler shunned formal party allegiance, yet recognized the broad need for working-class unity and cooperation.

Through the 1920s, representatives of AFL union papers joined representatives from independent, socialist, communist, and syndicalist organs on FP's executive board. William Z. Foster sat on the board, as did Vern Smith of the Industrial Workers of the World.

Earl Browder remained on the board until 1929. Fred Hewitt, editor of the International Association of Machinists' *Machinist's Monthly Journal,* served until his retirement in 1941. Labor editors on the board saw the FP as a means of expanding the scope and strength of their own newspapers. They also saw FP as a means of drawing attention and support for struggles their own organizations were undergoing.

Yet the presence of well-known radicals on FP's board drew the attention of more conservative labor leaders and, with the continued rise of red-baiting, open attacks from the right wing of American society. At the behest of Matthew Woll, the AFL conducted an investigation of FP's politics, funding, and labor reporting in 1922–23. Haessler fully cooperated with the investigation, but the AFL created its own *Weekly Service* to compete with FP. FP nevertheless continued to draw support from trade union editors who saw the need for a regular labor news service.

FP thrived as the union movement thrived. From its initial subscription list of 32 labor papers in 1919, it grew to 120 in 1921. The economic crises of that year spelled hard times for organized labor, and the corresponding drop in union membership throughout the 1920s was matched by declining subscriptions. From a low of 59 subscriptions in 1927 FP rebounded to just over 100 in the first year of the New Deal's protection of collective-bargaining rights for workers. Subscriptions continued to grow, and reached an all-time high of 250 in 1946.

FP correspondents served as articulate firsthand reporters, following the rise of union struggles well before they were reported by the mainstream press. Many went on to serve as editors of the CIO union papers. Thus Haessler was also able to encourage continuity and help coordinate the news received and used by the *CIO News, Guild Reporter,* the *United Mine Workers Journal,* and the *United Automobile Worker*. These papers, as much as anything else, were vital keys to information and organizing in the movement.

Two noted writers for FP, Harvey and Jessie O'Connor, illustrate the remarkable quality of the collective effort. Jessie, the granddaughter of reformer-journalist Henry Demarest Lloyd, began working for Haessler in 1928 and continued off and on for more than a decade, covering strikes and labor conditions, most notably the famous Gastonia, North Carolina, conflict. Harvey O'Connor, youthful participant in the Seattle General Strike and for a time a staffer for the *Seattle Union Record,* became FP's Eastern Bureau Chief and remained a correspondent until its demise. In later years especially, the O'Connors helped make the financial continuation of FP possible. In part on his experience gained there, Harvey became one of the outstanding muckrakers of the 1930s–1950s, with a series of popular books about family fortunes.

Yet oligopolization of the commercial press in the 1940s and 1950s concentrated the force of opposition against FP. Section 304 of the Taft-Hartley Act (1947) forbade unions from making direct contributions for political purposes, drawing the wrath of those opposed to FP's explicit political reporting. So too did the stabilization and bureaucratization of the labor movement, whose leaders increasingly sought better ways of controlling their unions and the information about them. Organized labor's in-house papers developed internal resources, and politics, capable of excluding the need for FP's news service. Similarly, the advent of radio and television supplanted community reliance on newspapers for local news; workers, like other Americans, became less dependent on and less willing to read local papers, even though popular press, radio, and television reporting was increasingly hostile to labor.

The Cold War's red scare tactics above all spelled the end of FP. The CIO's expulsion of Communists, and Communist-influenced unions, made FP's role as labor's Left voice insecure. Willingly, CIO leaders sought a secure and respectable place in American society. This contradicted FP's philosophy of labor as a movement. Between 1940 and 1950 the number of independent labor papers decreased by half as labor leaders came to grapple with dissent. Under attack by labor leaders, Congress, and McCarthyism, FP officially disbanded on October 29, 1956. *See also*: *Daily Worker*, Liberation News Service

—*Doug Reynolds*

REFERENCES

Dilling, Elizabeth. *The Red Network*. New York: self-published, 1935.

Haessler, Stephen J. "Carl Haessler and the Federated Press: Essays on the History of American Labor Journalism." Master's thesis, University of Wisconsin, Madison, 1977.

O'Connor, Jesse Lloyd, Harvey O'Connor, and Susan Bowler. *Harvey and Jesse: A Couple of Radicals*. Philadelphia: Temple University Press, 1988.

FELLOW TRAVELERS

Persons who sympathize with a political party (usually a Marxist group) and tend to follow its political line but are not formal members are known as fellow travelers. Although they may contribute to party causes, they pay no dues, have no party card, and are not bound by party discipline. Individuals may remain in this status rather than becoming members for many reasons. Most common are that they simply are unwilling to undertake the rigors of party life or have a disagreement on some aspect of the party's structure or agenda. In some cases the party may prefer persons to remain outside its formal ranks. In the case of famous persons, this is done in order that a celebrity may be seen as uncompromised by organizational affiliation or simply to protect that person from ideological attack. During the 1950s the term *fellow travelers* was used in a pejorative way by anticommunists. Fellow travelers were attacked for lacking the courage of their conviction or alternatively for hiding their true convictions from the public through a technicality.

—*Dan Georgakas*

FELLOWSHIP OF RECONCILIATION: see PACIFISM; PEACE MOVEMENTS; RUSTIN, BAYARD

FEMINISM: see WOMEN'S LIBERATION, SOCIALIST FEMINISM

FIFTH AVENUE PEACE COMMITTEE: see PEACE MOVEMENTS

FILM AND PHOTO LEAGUE: see PHOTOGRAPHY, RADICAL FILMMAKING, 1930s

FINNISH AMERICANS

During the 1890s Finnish immigrants in Massachusetts and New York founded two workingmen's associations, the Saima Aid Society and the Imatra Society, designed to serve workers' educational and fraternal needs. These two organizations became models for later socialist organizations. In 1899 Antero F. Tanner established a socialist club in Rockport, Massachusetts. He and a follower, Martin Hendrickson, published a socialist newspaper for a few editions in 1900. Both "Apostles of Socialism," as Finns later called them, began nationwide organizing tours in 1901. Matti Kurikka, a utopian socialist, also crisscrossed the country after the failure of his utopian community, Sointula, in British Columbia. All three of these Finnish radicals

From 1915 *Lapatossu*

spoke to workingmen's associations, temperance groups, church bodies, and to anyone else who would listen.

Spurred by the agitational efforts of Tanner, Hendrickson, and Kurikka, and aided by leftist exiles from Finland who began to arrive regularly in Finnish communities in the United States in the wake of czarist pressure in Finland, Finnish Socialists formed a national organization in Hibbing, Minnesota, in 1906. Called *Suomalainen Sosialistijärjestö* (Finnish Socialist Federation), the organization grew by 1913 to 260 chapters with 13,000 members throughout the nation. The federation was supported by three newspapers, *Työmies* (Workingman, 1903) *Raivaaja* (Pioneer, 1905) and *Toveri* (Comrade, 1907). In 1907 federation members gained control of *Työväen Opisto* (Work People's College) in Duluth, Minnesota, from a Finnish religious organization and used the school partly to train socialist functionaries.

Finnish socialists were active in the 1907 Mesabi Range iron miners' strike in Minnesota and the 1913–14 copper miners' strike in northern Michigan. On the heels of the copper strike, a split occurred in the federation. The more radical left-wing socialists backed the Industrial Workers of the World. In 1914 4,000 members withdrew from the federation, took control of Work People's College, and began publishing *Industrialisti* (Industrialist, 1915–75), which by 1920 had more than 20,000 readers. Government pressure on the Left during and after World War I caused the arrest of five Finnish IWW members, who were tried and convicted in the infamous mass trial of IWW leaders in Chicago. After WW I industrial unionism began a decline.

The Bolshevik Revolution in Russia gave the left wing of the federation a new cause. Supporters of Lenin gained control and withdrew from the Socialist Party. The federation amalgamated with the American Workers Party. Several years later the federation was reorganized separately as the Finnish Workers Federation. During the 1920s federation members worked assiduously to promote consumers' cooperativism as a weapon in the class struggle and to strengthen Central Cooperative Wholesale, located in Superior, Wisconsin. In 1930, however, because of their close association with the American Communist Party, Finnish federation members were driven from CCW at its annual meeting.

In the early 1930s, in response to Russian requests for aid to develop the timber resources of Soviet Karelia just across the border from Finland, about 6,000 to 10,000 Finnish-American men, women, and children migrated to Karelia from the United States and Canada. Later in the 1930s, during the Spanish Civil War, approximately 400 Finnish-American volunteers fought in the International Brigades on the side of Republican Spain. In 1941 the Finnish Workers Federation merged with the International Workers Order, a move that tended to diminish separate ethnic identity for Finnish-American members. While *Työmies-Eteenpäin* is still published in Superior, Wisconsin, it is read by a diminishing number of supporters.

The left-wing proletarian internationalism of federation members irritated right-wing socialists, who made their objections known through their newspaper, *Raivaaja*. The right wing established a new federation within the SP but withdrew in 1937 and became the Finnish-American League for Democracy, a strictly independent socialist group. *Raivaaja* is still published in Fitchburg, Massachusetts; its readership, too, is declining.

After its internal struggle with the left-wing labor movement, the consumers' cooperative movement grew impressively. By 1940 it had well over 100 member societies in the Midwest and published two Finnish- and English-language newspapers. In 1962 it merged with a large midwestern agricultural cooperative and, for all practical purposes, lost its ethnic identity. *See also*: Communist Party, Industrial Workers of the World, International Workers Order, Socialist Party, *Toveritar*

—*Michael Karni*

REFERENCES

Karni, Michael, and Douglas Ollila, eds. *For the Common Good: Finnish Immigrants and the Radical Response to Industrial America*. Superior, Wis.: Tyomies, 1977.

Karni, Michael, ed. *The Finnish Diaspora*, 2 vols. Toronto: Multi-Cultural History Society of Ontario, 1981.

FIRST INTERNATIONAL: see INTERNATIONAL WORKINGMEN'S ASSOCIATION

FLYNN, ELIZABETH GURLEY (1890–1964)

Christened "the Rebel Girl" by Wobbly bard Joe Hill, Flynn was a "jawsmith" for the Industrial Workers of the World (1906–28) and a great orator, which in the era of street life and mass strikes was like being a media star today. In the major East Coast strikes—Lawrence, Massachusetts, and Paterson and Passaic, New Jersey—she agitated and led the immigrant workers. To her, labor defense was vital to organizing and in this capacity she participated in the free-speech fights in Missoula, Montana (1908), and Spokane, Washington (1909–10), and brought to the English-speaking public the case of Sacco and Vanzetti, with which she was intimately involved for seven years (1919–26). She organized the Workers Defense League to fight for the victims of the Palmer Raids and was one of the founders of the American Civil Liberties Union, which ousted her in 1940 because she was a member of the Communist Party.

Pamphlet addressing persecution of the Communist Party

Flynn's life was illustrious and stormy. Her parents were radical Irish immigrants, and although born in Concord, New Hampshire, she grew up in the poverty of the South Bronx. After a brief marriage she left her husband and returned to her family, and remained with them most of her life. Her mother and her sister Kathie, a schoolteacher, raised her son, Fred (1911–40), who died tragically as the result of an operation. From 1928 to 1938 Flynn rested and recovered from physical and mental exhaustion due to fatiguing labor battles and a tragic love affair with the anarchist organizer and womanizer Carlo Tresca.

After this breakdown she joined the CP (although she occasionally claimed to have joined in 1928) and rose quickly, joining the party's National Board in 1941. In the CPUSA, she was mainly a figurehead and rarely dissented from the major party line, avoiding conflict and feeling outclassed intellectually by the sophisticated, college-educated city folk. Having no base of support, Flynn always felt uncomfortable in the CPUSA, having come in at the top instead of having risen from the ranks. She was one of their most popular speakers and columnists, faithfully writing two to four times a week for twenty-six years for the *Daily Worker*. Her constituency were the rough-and-tumble miners and immigrant workers, and she preferred militant organizing to bureaucratic and reform work.

Flynn was indicted with the top Party leadership under the Smith Act and endured, with great flair and eloquence, a nine-month trial, where she provided her own defense. She was sentenced to a three-year term in the Alderson Federal Penitentiary and served from January 1955 through May 1957. When she returned to active political life, the Party was in disarray. She had missed the vital 1956 period of reassessment and reevaluation, which served her well, since it meant she wasn't connected with either the hard-line,

Moscow-oriented William Z. Foster faction or the more reform John Gates group. She sided with the middle-of-the-road, compromise Eugene Dennis position and in 1961 became the first woman selected as national chairman. She ran for state assembly, headed the Woman's Commission, and traveled abroad.

Flynn grew discouraged with the Party's tired old leadership, policy, and morals, but only criticized Party policy privately. She still saw herself as part of an international movement, but she longed to retire and write the second half of her memoirs. While awaiting jail in 1955 she had written the autobiography of her "first life" (1906–26), *Rebel Girl* (1955), and after, a prison memoir, *Alderson Story* (1963).

She died in the Soviet Union and was given an elaborate state funeral. However, she always felt part of the American people and had requested that her ashes remain near the Haymarket martyrs in Chicago. She was no feminist, but she was an exceptional woman in the male-dominated IWW and CPUSA. In her later life she regretted that she hadn't fought more against male chauvinism. She inspired many women, however, with her colorful speeches and example. *See also*: Communist Party, *Daily Worker*, Industrial Workers of the World, Irish Americans, Lawrence Strike

—Rosalyn Fraad Baxandall

REFERENCES

Baxandall, Rosalyn. *Words on Fire, the Life and Writings of Elizabeth Gurley Flynn*. New Brunswick: Rutgers University Press, 1987.

Elizabeth Gurley Flynn Papers. Tamiment Library, New York University. Microfilm.

Flynn, Elizabeth Gurley. *The Rebel Girl, An Autobiography, My First Life (1906–1926)*. New York: International Publishers, 1955.

———. *The Alderson Story, My Life as a Political Prisoner*. New York: International Publishers, 1963.

The Trial of Elizabeth Gurley Flynn by the American Civil Liberties Union. Edited by Corliss Lamont. New York: Monthly Review, 1968.

Folk Music

Americans have been creating and sharing music since the arrival of the earliest settlers. Encompassing musical styles derived from American Indian, English, European, Asian, and African traditions, topical American folk music often takes its musical form from earlier pieces and its content from the events of the day. In the early 1930s, as the Depression worsened, there was much to chronicle in topical music, and American farmers, workers, and unemployed citizens often put new words to old and familiar hymns, marches, and popular tunes. They were renewing the tradition of black soldiers in the Civil War who created the "Marching Song of the First of Arkansas" from "John Brown's Body"; miners who sang "Miners' Lifeguard" in the 1880s to the tune of "The Vacant Chair," written after the assassination of Abraham Lincoln; and members of the Industrial Workers of the World who sang "I'm Too Old to Be a Scab" to the tune of the Civil War ballad "Just Before the Battle, Mother."

In the early part of the decade, the organized Left had expressed little interest in folk music as a vehicle for advancing class struggle. The Communist ideological line of that time downplayed the importance of regional or national cultural expressions, and some of the highly trained modernist composers of the Composers Collective disdained folk music in favor of the more complex styles they had recently studied in Europe. But this music was less than effective in organizing working-class audiences. In 1933 Mike Gold recognized the problem when he asked in the *Daily Worker*, "Why don't American workers sing? The Wobblies knew how, but we still have to develop a Communist Joe Hill."

The shift to the ideas of the Popular Front in 1935 had a profound impact on left-wing American music. Composers in the Collective began to include folk music in their *Workers Song Books* and to popularize the folk musics of Afro-Americans, farmers, miners, and urban workers in their concert pieces. Left-wing performers such as Paul Robeson, Cisco Houston, Aunt Molly Jackson, and many others gave voice to the protests and celebrations of these constituencies in music that once again relied on older hymns, familiar tunes, and the talkin' blues to communicate the political messages of the latter part of the decade.

Among the important performer-creators of the 1930s were Huddie Ledbetter (Leadbelly) and Woody Guthrie. Each had a broad repertoire of songs and each placed his songs in political and social context with recorded monologues about the conditions that inspired the music. A blues player and singer from Louisiana as well as a performer on the twelve-string guitar, Leadbelly recorded his music for the Library of Congress in 1933 and again in 1935–40 under the direction of John Lomax. Woody Guthrie hailed from Oklahoma, knew the dust bowl region firsthand as a hobo in the 1930s, and wrote more than one thousand songs. Guthrie, who had painted "This Machine Kills Fascists" on the body of his guitar, made recordings with Alan Lomax for the Library of Congress in 1940.

During World War II, Southern topical music, often called hillbilly or country music, began to reach a broader audience as service personnel from the region helped to expand the popularity of such performers as Roy Acuff and Ernest Tubb. Later performers and composers of protest music would return to the tradition of the narrative ballad and other forms common in country music.

Between 1941 and 1942, the Almanac Singers, founded by Pete Seeger, Lee Hays, Millard Lampell, and Woody Guthrie, and deriving their name from the *Farmer's Almanac*, sang for CIO organizing campaigns and other political functions. The group consisted of about twelve singers and players who lived together in a loft commune near New York's Union Square. They performed topical songs about life in the Depression as well as union songs. From time to time the group included Burl Ives, Cisco Houston, Bess Lomax, and composer Earl Robinson. From 1941 to 1946 Elie Siegmeister led the American Ballad Singers in performances of traditional American music throughout the country. This group foreshadowed the trend toward performing folk music in arrangements for more than one voice, often with instrumental accompaniment.

People's Songs emerged after WW II as a loosely knit group of folk musicians whose purpose was to present occasional performances and develop a library of protest songs that could be used by trade unions and other groups. The group elected officers and published a monthly bulletin whose first issue declared that "the people are on the march and must have songs to sing. Now, in 1946, the truth must assert itself in many singing voices. . . ." Members of the Almanac Singers participated in People's Songs, as did younger singers and folk dancers such as Irwin Silber. The lyrics to the popular "If I Had a Hammer" were written by Seeger and Hays at a board of directors' meeting of People's Songs.

Perhaps the most significant contributing group in the "folk revival" of the 1950s and 1960s was the Weavers, founded in 1948 by Seeger, Hays, Ronnie Gilbert, and Fred Hellerman. Strong left-wing political convictions and associations led both to the blacklisting and FBI investigation of this group and to its popularity among progressives during the McCarthy era. The Weavers performed and recorded traditional topical music as well as contemporary songs composed by members. Political pressure forced the Weavers to disband in 1953 because they could not find a hall in which to perform. The Weavers reformed in 1955 and continued performing until 1963, even after Seeger's departure in 1958. A special reunion concert of the Weavers was chronicled in the film *Wasn't That a Time* (1981).

With the popularization of folk music presented in more formal arrangements came a variety of groups such as the Kingston Trio and the New Christy Minstrels, whose music reached broad audiences largely because of accessibility and the absence of a strong political perspective. The new popularity of folk-music styles helped gain acceptance for folk and topical music that dealt with significant social issues. Singers like Josh White, Big Bill Broonzy, and Odetta brought the blues, religious music, and freedom songs of the civil rights movement to a public that was accustomed to the folk sound. In addition, composers of new topical songs such as Malvina Reynolds, Seeger, and Bob Dylan communicated significant messages in their songs as they and others performed them. A humorous critique of social and political conformity, a denunciation of the evils of war, and the perspective of a new generation reached the public in "Little

Boxes," "Where Have All the Flowers Gone?" and "The Times They Are A-Changin'." Traditional folk pieces and new topical songs were published and discussed in *Sing Out!* magazine, from which many amateur and professional folk performers learned of the newest developments in folk and protest music.

In the mid-1960s, lines between the folk-music and popular-music *genera* were bridged for a time as folk performers and their songs achieved significant popularity. The music of Seeger and Dylan, for example, was heard by large audiences through recordings by such diverse artists as Judy Collins, Joan Baez, the Byrds, and Peter, Paul, and Mary. As the civil rights movement had contributed new verses to familiar songs as well as newly composed songs to the folk-music repertoire, the protest against the war in Vietnam inspired music by Seeger and Baez, Phil Ochs, and Tom Paxton. The popularity of antiwar songs such as Arlo Guthrie's "Alice's Restaurant Massacree," first performed at the Newport Folk Festival in 1967, and "Fixin' to Die Rag," sung by Country Joe McDonald and the Fish, particularly in the version sung at Woodstock in 1969, gave these pieces near-folk status with a public that associated antiwar sentiments with music. The 1960s also saw the fusion of folk styles with rock music in the work of the Byrds, Simon and Garfunkle, and Crosby, Stills, Nash, and (sometimes) Young.

If the decades since the 1960s have not inspired a sustained public interest in topical songs with clear political messages performed in a folk style, there is no lack of contemporary folk music. The women's movement has given inspiration to many composers and performers. The antinuclear movement has a topical music of its own, as do various labor, community, and environmental groups. As long as there are social issues to serve as the subject of new music, folksingers will keep alive the traditions of the past as they adapt old styles to meet new political challenges. *See also*: Guthrie, Woody; Seeger, Pete; *Sing Out/Broadside*

—*Barbara L. Tischler*

REFERENCES

Denisoff, R. Serge. *Great Day Coming, Folk Music and the American Left*. Urbana: University of Illinois Press, 1971.

Dunaway, David K. "A Selected Bibliography: Protest Song in the United States." *Folklore Forum* 2 (1977).

Klein, Joe. *Woody Guthrie: A Life*. New York: Knopf, 1980.

Reuss, R. A. "American Folklore and Left-wing Politics." Diss., Indiana University, 1971.

Rodnitzky, Jerome L. *Minstrels of the Dawn: The Folk-Protest Singer as a Cultural Hero*. Chicago: Nelson-Hall, 1976.

Silber, Irwin. "The Weavers: New Find of the Hit Parade?" *Sing Out* 1 (1951).

Foner, Philip Sheldon (b. 1910)

Since the late 1930s Foner has been a prominent Marxist intellectual and one of the most prolific of American historians. In a career connecting scholarship with the activity of movements for social change, he has been writer, teacher, editor, and publisher.

Born in New York City, Foner was educated at the City College of New York and Columbia University, where he received the Ph.D. in 1941. He began his teaching career at CCNY in 1933 but in 1941 became one of the victims of the legislative Rapp-Coudert purge of Communists and other radicals teaching at New York's public colleges. Employed for a period in labor education, he was later a partner in the Citadel Press publishing firm. From 1967 to 1979 he was professor of history at Lincoln University in Pennsylvania and as emeritus professor has continued to lecture and teach at numerous universities, both in the United States and abroad.

From his first book, *Business and Slavery: The New York Merchants and the Irrepressible Conflict* (1941), Foner has repeatedly broken new ground. In 1947 the first volume of his *History of the Labor Movement in the United States* appeared, and this multivolume work stands as a formidable challenge to the orthodox John R. Commons interpretation of labor history. In *The Life and Writings of Frederick Douglass* (1949–52) he provided the basis for major scholarly attention to the life and career of this great leader of nineteenth-century African Americans and champion of the antislavery struggle. Other important works written by Foner include *Women and the American Labor Movement* (1979, 1980), *Organized Labor and the Black Worker, 1619–1973* (1974), *History of Black Americans* (1975, 1983), and *A History of Cuba and Its Relations with the United States* (1962, 1963). He has edited numerous documentary collections. *See also*: Communist Party; History, U.S.; Rapp-Coudert; *Science and Society*

—*Herbert Shapiro*

FOOD PROTESTS

In February 1917 thousands of immigrant Jewish women in New York City erupted in protest against the high cost of living. They successfully enforced a citywide boycott that shut down sales of chicken, fish, and vegetables in Jewish neighborhoods for over two weeks.

The women's protests posed an immediate challenge for New York's vibrant Socialist Party. How would the party respond to the concerns of militant housewives in their own backyard? The uprising offered the Socialists not only a huge pool of female potential members, but also a chance to link bread-and-butter issues to a long-term socialist vision.

The February 1917 women's uprising was not a unique one. New York's Jewish women had imposed a previous boycott on their city's kosher butchers in 1902. Toronto's Jewish women similarly boycotted their city's butchers in 1908 and again in 1914. And in 1917, protests nearly identical to those in New York broke out in Philadelphia, Boston, and Chicago.

Between February 19 and 21, the idea of a boycott in response to rapidly escalating prices spread like wildfire across New York's Lower East Side, Williamsburg, and parts of the Bronx. Structurally, boycott activities included neighborhood-level mass meetings to drum up support, groups of pickets roving the streets to accost boycott violators, and observers posted at key sites to ensure constant vigilance over fellow shoppers. Violence was frequent; arrests of protesters mounted to over a hundred a day. By the end of the boycott's first week, these localized street actions spilled over into an irate and insistent march on city hall.

Participants in these protests were almost entirely married immigrant Jewish women, usually in their thirties or forties, with several children. When queried by reporters, they articulated no elaborate structural theories as to the political economy of food. They merely stressed their own families' need for an adequate living, and asked that prices be lowered.

New York's SP responded swiftly to the challenge presented by these women's protests. They immediately organized a new body, the Mothers' Anti–High Price League, and called for a "mass meeting" in Madison Square on February 24 to protest the high cost of living. The meeting, however, just as quickly revealed the tensions between the boycotters' organizing style and goals, and those of the Socialists. Thousands of tired, upset women, wearied of merely listening to approved Party speakers, spilled over from the official meeting to precipitate a riot at the Waldorf-Astoria Hotel where, they erroneously believed, government officials were housed. The Socialists, meanwhile, sent a polite delegation to confer with officials in the correct hotel.

The subsequent weeks' activities highlighted the divergent perspectives of the two groups. On the one hand, the women continued their localized, at-times violent street vigilance, merely appropriating the legitimacy of the Mothers' Anti–High Price League to strengthen their position. As prices did indeed begin to fall after two weeks (albeit temporarily), their boycott activities rapidly dissipated.

The SP's activities, meanwhile, grew increasingly bureaucratized and distanced from street militance. Carefully appointed committees composed of high-ranking labor leaders, Socialists, and Progressives continued with formalized lobbying and with orderly meetings designed to draw protesters into Party work. Their model, however, gave little role to the housewives whose activism had sparked the cost-of-living movement. The Party carefully selected all speakers in advance. Guards banned potential "disrupters" from "public" meetings. Perhaps most important, doorkeepers barred babies from protest meetings. Yet the women boycotters had conspicuously brought their children along to their own previous actions.

The Socialists' commitment to the cost-of-living issue ultimately proved a quickly moving bandwagon on and off which the local Party's leadership quickly leapt. For male Socialists, protest against imminent U.S entry into WW I took precedence. All preferred, in their discussions of the price issue, to encourage trade unionism or the election of Socialist officials as the proper channels for Socialist agitation. The Party's activist women persisted longer than their menfolk but sought, similarly, to divert cost-of-living protests into their own preferred channel, suffrage work.

Ultimately, the Socialists' basic theoretical structure proved inadequately flexible to accommodate and build a mass movement out of the housewives' concerns. Such women could directly engage in neither electoral work (without the vote) nor trade union activism (as workers in an unwaged workplace)—the two basic strategic arms of the Party. For the boycotters, the high cost of living was an immediate and pressing concern. *See also*: Consumers' Movements, Rent Strikes

—*Dana Frank*

REFERENCES

Frank, Dana. "Housewives, Socialists, and the Politics of Food: The 1917 New York Cost-of-Living Protests." *Feminist Studies* 11 (Summer 1985).

Freiburger, William. "War, Prosperity, and Hunger: The New York Food Riots of 1917." *Labor History* 25 (Spring 1984).

Hyman, Paula. "Immigrant Women and Consumer Protest: The New York City Kosher Meat Boycott of 1902." *American Jewish History* 70 (1980).

Food, Tobacco, Agricultural, and Allied Workers (FTA-CIO)

The origins of the FTA-CIO can be traced to efforts by various radical and trade union groups to organize agricultural workers during the Great Depression. The United Farmers League and the Trade Union Unity League's Cannery and Agricultural Workers Industrial Union represented the Communist Party's early efforts in this area. The Party's adoption of a Popular Front strategy gave rise to the National Committee for Unity of Rural and Agricultural Workers, later the National Committee of Agricultural Workers (NCAW), which provided the structure and leadership for the United Cannery, Agricultural, Packing, and Allied Workers of America (UCAPAWA). Donald Henderson, a former economics instructor who had been fired by Columbia University for activities on behalf of the unemployed and New Jersey migrant workers, headed the NCAW. Henderson attempted to put together a coalition of NCAW-affiliated unions and independent AFL locals and seek a charter from the AFL. When that failed the NCAW called a national convention and voted to affiliate with the CIO.

The formation of the UCAPAWA brought together a diverse group of local unions. Beet workers from the Rocky Mountains joined forces with Filipino fishermen, Mexican and Japanese field workers, and former lettuce pickers from the Industrial Workers of the World on the West Coast. Members of the Southern Tenants Farmers Union came together with mushroom workers from New York. The CIO's John L. Lewis funded a major organizing drive, and thousands of workers joined UCAPAWA. Agricultural workers were excluded from the provisions of the Wagner Act, as well as from most other federal protective legislation. They were among the nation's most exploited citizens, in many cases living and working in a state of virtual peonage. Their work was seasonal and many workers lacked a home base, moving from farm to farm as the season progressed. UCAPAWA's leadership subsequently concluded that organizing field workers required the organization of more stable workers one step removed from the harvest, in the fisheries, canneries, and processing sheds.

World War II greatly aided UCAPAWA's efforts as labor shortages and the activist role of the War Labor Board increased workers' bargaining power. Among the key victories of this period were the organization of workers at R. J. Reynolds Tobacco Company in Winston-Salem, North Carolina, Campbell Soup in

Chicago and Camden, New Jersey, and workers in the cigar factories of the American Tobacco Company. To reflect the changing composition of the membership, the union changed its name to Food, Tobacco, Agricultural, and Allied Workers (FTA) at its convention in 1944.

One reason for FTA's success was the union's policy of nondiscrimination in industries dominated by women and minority workers. Locals were organized on an interracial basis, and regional and national meetings were integrated. The union actively promoted women and minorities to leadership positions at the local and national level. In 1947 the international vice-presidents were a black tobacco worker, a Mexican-American woman organizer, and a Cuban cigar worker.

The postwar reaction hit FTA particularly hard. From its inception, FTA was a union of the Left. Donald Henderson had been an active CP member during the early 1930s, and many of the union's leaders shared Henderson's political sympathies, if not his Party membership. As a result, the union's position on national and international issues generally reflected the thinking of people in the Communist movement. Such ideas were not to be tolerated in the ensuing Cold War years. An equally important reason for the postwar attack on FTA (and other Left-led unions) had to do with its growing success in organizing low-wage, women, and minority workers. Democratic unions threatened management authority on the shop floor, and the increased political activism of FTA members, particularly among blacks in the South, challenged the power of local elites.

FTA refused to support the Marshall Plan and the growing anticommunist stance of Harry Truman and in 1948 supported the Progressive Party candidacy of Henry Wallace. Like other CIO unions, FTA did not sign the non-Communist affidavits required by the Taft-Hartley Act. By 1949 FTA faced raids not only from AFL unions but from unions in the CIO. In 1950 the CIO expelled FTA and the union merged with the Distributive Workers Union and the United Office and Professional Workers Union to form the Distributive, Processing, and Office Workers Union. *See also*: Migratory Farm Workers, Southern Tenant Farmers Union, Taft-Hartley

—*Bob Korstad*

REFERENCES

Honey, Michael. "Labor and Civil Rights in the South: Black Workers and the Industrial Labor Movement in Memphis, Tennessee." Ph.D. diss., Northern Illinois University, 1986.

Korstad, Robert. "Daybreak of Freedom: Tobacco Workers and the CIO, Winston-Salem, North Carolina, 1943–1950." Ph.D. diss., University of North Carolina, Chapel Hill, 1987.

Ruiz, Vicki. *Cannery Women, Cannery Lives: Mexican Women, Unionization, and the California Food Processing Industry, 1930–1950*. Albuquerque: University of New Mexico Press, 1987.

FOSTER, WILLIAM Z. (1881–1961)

The rise and decline of a radical labor movement in the twentieth-century United States was encapsulated in the life of Foster, who stood at the center of each of the key radical movements of this era: socialism, syndicalism, and communism. His early career, through the 1920s, demonstrates the strong roots that such ideas had within some working-class communities and among certain groups of workers, while his later life, especially during the late 1940s and early 1950s, exemplifies the increasing isolation of Marxist radicals through the ascendancy of Stalinism as well as government repression.

Raised in an Irish Catholic home in the slums of Philadelphia, Foster left school after the third grade and drifted around the country, working at jobs ranging from deep-water sailor to locomotive fireman. His intimate knowledge of a wide variety of jobs and his sensitivity to the ways that workers thought about their work and their problems made him a talented organizer.

Foster joined the Socialist Party just after the turn of the century and became a member of the Industrial Workers of the World in 1909, playing a key role in the Spokane free-speech fight of that year. He taught himself to read in German and French, read the classic works of Marxism, and then traveled throughout Europe, studying the ideas and strategies of labor movements there.

In 1911 Foster split from the IWW over the issue of dual unionism, which he vigorously opposed. Deeply influenced by French syndicalists, he developed the concept of "boring from within" the mainstream labor organizations to win them over to a revolutionary program. He established a series of organizations designed to accomplish this goal. Both the Syndicalist League of North America (1912–14) and the International Trade Union Educational League (1915–17) remained small "militant minorities" based largely in midwestern industrial cities, but their strategies and personnel played important roles in later movements and organizations, including the Communist Party. By the First World War, Foster had emerged as a leading theorist of American syndicalism and during the war he earned a national reputation, directing drives to organize unskilled immigrant and black workers in the meat-packing and steel industries. He visited Russia during 1921 in the wake of the Bolshevik Revolution, was won over to the revolutionary cause, and joined the CP later that year. Foster was still highly regarded by many labor activists as a creative and talented organizer with firm roots in the mainstream labor movement long after he had joined the Party.

During the 1920s Foster was instrumental in building the Trade Union Educational League (TUEL), the most important Left opposition group within the American Federation of Labor. Throughout the early twenties Foster worked with John Fitzpatrick and other figures in the Chicago Federation of Labor to create a national Farmer-Labor Party, but when a shift in Communist strategy in 1923 undercut his relationship with Fitzpatrick and other mainstream labor progressives, Foster found himself more and more isolated. The TUEL provided leadership in several of the most important strikes of the decade, however, and kept alive the goal of industrial over craft organization.

Beginning in the late 1920s, as a result of Comintern policy formulations and factional conflicts within the American Party, Foster became the spokesman for a narrow, sectarian line. After bitterly opposing its formation in 1928, he eventually became the leading figure in the Trade Union Unity League (TUUL), a separate federation of dual, revolutionary unions. Foster campaigned as the Party's presidential candidate in 1924, 1928, and 1932 and directed its trade union work throughout the 1920s and the early years of the Great Depression. A severe heart attack during his 1932 presidential campaign slowed him down considerably, though he turned much of his attention to writing and remained a leading figure in the Communist movement. Although he was a prolific author of books and pamphlets throughout his long career, Foster produced his most ambitious works on the history of communism, labor, and Afro-Americans during the forties and fifties.

Foster was the Party's chairperson between 1932 and 1957, from its dramatic growth and increasing influence in the Depression and war years through its isolation and decline during the McCarthyism of the 1950s. He played a central role in the expulsion of Earl Browder, architect of the Party's Popular Front policies, and led the organization's reversion to a more sectarian line in the postwar era. When Khrushchev revealed the extent of Stalin's crimes in a 1956 speech before the Soviet CP's Twentieth Congress, a reform group sought to reconstruct the American Party along more democratic lines and to make it more independent of Soviet influence. Foster successfully resisted these efforts, however, and the failure of the reform movement fueled a precipitous decline in membership. His own physical collapse in the late 1950s paralleled that of the movement he had done so much to build. William Z. Foster died in Moscow on September 1, 1960, and his ashes were placed near the monument to the Haymarket martyrs in Waldheim Cemetery outside Chicago. *See also*: Communist Party, Syndicalist League of North America, Trade Union Educational League

—James R. Barrett

REFERENCES

Draper, Theodore. *American Communism and Soviet Russia*. New York: Viking, 1960.

Foster, William Z. *From Bryan to Stalin*. New York: International Publishers, 1937.

———. *Pages from a Worker's Life*. New York: International Publishers, 1939.

Isserman, Maurice. *Which Side Were You On? The American Communist Party During the Second World War*. Middletown: Wesleyan University Press, 1982.

Zipser, Arthur. *Working-Class Giant: The Life of William Z. Foster*. New York: International Publishers, 1981.

The Fourth International

On September 3, 1938, delegates from eleven nations voted to adopt the founding document of the Fourth International, entitled "The Death Agony of Capitalism and the Tasks of the Fourth International," more popularly known as "The Transitional Program." The chief author of the document was Leon Trotsky. At the Founding Conference, U.S. Marxists played an unprecedentedly important role. The Socialist Workers Party was among the larger groups to participate (because of legal restrictions in the United States, the SWP has never been a formal member of the FI, but has been in fraternal solidarity with it).

The FI was established in the wake of what was perceived as a retreat from international revolutionary struggle on the part of the Soviet Union under Stalin (now defined as a degenerated workers' state), and the parties of the Third International that were in broad agreement with the Soviet line. Its strategy is summed up in the opening sentence of the Transitional Program: "The world political situation as a whole is chiefly characterized by a historical crisis of the leadership of the proletariat."

The parties associated with the FI faced an immediate test in the outbreak of the Second World War and the pact between Stalin and Hitler, which was the basis for a series of splits within the Trotskyist movement, including the SWP. After the war, when Trotsky's expectation of political revolution in the Soviet Union failed to be fulfilled, and in the wake of the Sovietization of states in Eastern Europe, the main body of the FI, with its Secretariat located in Paris, adopted the thesis developed by Michel Pablo that deformed workers' states might last for centuries, with the concomitant strategy of deep entry into the parties of the Third International. In 1951 the Secretariat expelled the majority section of the French party, which opposed Pablo's doctrine, and in 1953 the SWP openly joined the opposition, along with an important group in Great Britain, forming a public faction of the FI known as the International Committee for the Fourth International.

The FI subsequently abandoned the Pabloist position, and relations between the SWP and the Secretariat improved during the 1960s. The British section was now the dominant group within the ICFI, and two tendencies sympathetic to it were expelled from the SWP in 1963. The SWP subsequently reestablished a fraternal association with the FI. In recent years, three other groups in the United States have also been recognized by the FI as sympathizing organizations. *See also*: Socialist Workers Party, Trotskyism

—*David Konstan*

REFERENCES

Documents of the Fourth International. New York: Merit Publishers, 1970.

Fraina–Lewis Corey, Louis C. (1892?–1953)

The first major ideologue of American communism, Fraina combined in himself the various contradictions of 1910s proletarian enthusiasm, cultural avant-gardism, and political overreach. Lewis Corey, more liberal socialist than Marxist, similarly epitomized the course of the intellectual first drawn to and then repelled by the 1920s–1930s Left.

Louis Fraina was born in Galdo (Salerno), Italy, probably in 1892 (he sometimes gave the year as 1894), son of a radical republican who emigrated to New York in 1897. Young Fraina, newspaper seller and factory worker, grew close to the Socialist Labor Party, in which he rapidly rose to become an ace reporter and a protégé of Daniel DeLeon. Breaking with the SLP, he became an editor and in a few years the primary editor of the political and cultural avant-gardist *New Review*. Excited by the widespread mass strikes, and intellectually active in support of the Russian Revolution, he formulated early communist theories in *Revolutionary Socialism* (1918) and in his annotated edition of Russian writings, *The Proletarian Revolution in Russia* (1918). Concurrently, he edited a few issues of *Modern Dance* magazine, and served as one of three editors of the proto-communist *Class Struggle*.

Fraina fell afoul of early Communist factionalism. Disillusioned by a tour of Comintern duty in Mexico, he recrossed the border as Lewis Corey, obtaining work as proofreader at the *New York Times*. He reemerged in the 1920s–1930s as an economist, editorial worker at *The Encyclopedia of Social Sciences*, author of *The House of Morgan* (1930), *The Decline of American Capitalism* (1934), *The Crisis of the Middle Class* (1935). Stung by repeated unsatisfying experiences with the Communist Party, Corey became a spokesman of Left-leaning liberalism in the 1940s–1950s, with *The Unfinished Task: Economic Reconstruction for Democracy* (1942), and with *Meat and Man* (1950), a history of the meat-cutters' union. Corey died of a stroke, at work on a biography of utopian Frances Wright and awaiting deportation for revolutionary political activities he had repudiated decades earlier. *See also*: Communist Party, Modern Dance

—*Paul Buhle*

REFERENCES

Draper, Theodore. *Roots of American Communism*. New York: Viking, 1957.

Corey, Esther. "Lewis Corey (Louis C. Fraina), 1892–1953: A Bibliography with Autobiographical Notes." *Labor History* 4 (Spring 1963).

FRANCO-AMERICANS

Relatively small in number and widely varied in culture and location, Francophones (including those speaking various dialects) have played a minor, but not insignificant, role in the U.S. Left.

French settlers, especially Icarians and the followers of Victor Considerant, took part in early utopian colonization during the 1840s–1850s. Charles Fourier's doctrines reached many more via American intellectuals' popularizations, and the efforts by middle- and working-class Americans to establish phalanxes. But the modern influence of Francophones begins, properly, with the First International. New York, key gathering place for political refugees especially after the repression of the Commune, mixed French anarchists and socialists as wide in their variety as their potential mass following was scarce (relative to other immigrant-radical population bases) in numbers. In New York, housepainter Joseph Dejacque coined the word *Libertaire*, and New York presses printed for the first time a French exile's composition, "L'Internationale."

The French sections of the International briefly played a most notable role at the front of the famous New York parade in memory of the Paris Commune. In New York, but also in Boston, New Orleans, Chicago, and elsewhere, they soon allied with the anarchist or libertarian wing against the undemocratic internal regime of the mostly German Marx loyalists. As much as expelled, most French sections sought, with the forces led by Victoria Woodhull, reentry into the International, or the establishment of a democratic, pluralistic American section independent of the Marxists. The presidential campaign of Woodhull in 1872 proved, however, too much for many of the French immigrants, and organized activity passed to the local level. Several of the former International sections, notably New York Section 2 (mostly Commune refugees), Section 29 of Hoboken, and Section 42 of Paterson, adhered to the anarchist international.

Among those who did not return to France, socialist branches survived for several years, cooperating with local efforts of other ethnic groups, and supporting more anarchistic or libertarian tendencies. A small fraction of the First Internationalists resumed activity with the founding of the U.S. "Black International" and the rise of revolutionary socialism in Chicago and elsewhere. Most French socialists would act as individuals within the socialist movement, unconnected with any radical Francophone institutions. A few, such as Socialist Labor Party theorist Lucien Sanial, became leaders. More—like the freethinking father of Eugene Victor Debs (named for Eugene Sue and Victor Hugo)—passed their legacies privately on to new generations.

In the latter decades of the nineteenth century, Francophone activity established itself on two small fronts. In and around New Orleans, a Creole cultural upsurge prompted free-thought literary and debate societies and a scattering of publications with a radical edge. In the mine fields of Pennsylvania, meanwhile, Edouard David published, from 1885, *La Torpille* (The torpedo), a Blanquist sheet influenced by Johann Most, assailing mine owners and praising the ideals of socialism. From Pennsylvania it reached correspondents, some of them active in small Francophone radical groups, from New Jersey to Illinois and Iowa to Wyoming. Ardently defending the Haymarket martyrs, this paper ceased amid the wave of repression, only to reappear under a new title and a nearby location, as *La Reveil des Mineurs* (Miners' alarm). In 1893 David published one last paper, *La Crise Sociale* (The social crisis), for a short time in New York.

A Belgian anarchist, Louis Goaziou, followed David in establishing *L'Ami des Ouvriers* (The friend of workers) in Hastings, Pennsylvania, in 1894, succeeded by *La Tribune Libre* (Free tribune) in 1896, maintained until 1901 with an eclectic mixture of doctrine. *L'Union des Travailleurs* (The workers' union), established by Goaziou in Charleroi that year, had special appeal to Franco-Belgian glassblowers, who had carried their socialist faith from the motherland to the American labor movement and support of the Socialist Party. Goaziou's final paper, *The Union Worker*, formed in 1915 in place of *L'Union des Travailleurs*, suggested that its constituents had already displaced the French language and integrated themselves in the American labor and socialist movements—as did the French-American members of the Industrial Workers of the World who had briefly published *Germinal* from Paterson, New Jersey. By that time, most of the Francophone anarchist circles consisted of aging comrades eager to see Emma Goldman on tour or to receive news of French anarchism, but strictly marginal in political terms.

Another, quite distinct wing of Francophones, Quebecois immigrants to New England in the latter decades of the nineteenth and early twentieth centuries, were widely noted for their social and political conservatism. However, in certain circumstances they worked closely with noted radical leaders in establishing militant industrial unions, most notably in Woonsocket, Rhode Island, where an Independent Textile Union (growing out of riots against mill owners in 1934) briefly succeeded in organizing much of the town's work force and projecting a vision of a cooperative order with union-sponsored housing and medical care.

In recent years, cultural movements of Creole and Cajun descent in Louisiana have (with the support of the French Socialist government) allied themselves with ecology and other regional reform forces in an effort to preserve their geopolitical linguistic-cultural island of autonomy in an endangered physical and social environment. *See also*: Textile Unions

—Paul Buhle,
Thomas Fiehrer

REFERENCES

Creigh, Ronald. "Socialism in America: The French-Speaking Coal Miners." Unpublished essay.

Gerstle, Gary. "The Mobilization of the Working-Class Community: The Independent Textile Union in Woonsocket, 1931–1946." *Radical History Review* 17 (Spring 1978).

Frank, Waldo (1889–1967)

An influential novelist, essayist, and social-cultural historian, Frank was born to a comfortable Jewish middle-class family in Long Branch, New Jersey, and raised in New York City. He received B.A. and M.A. degrees simultaneously from Yale University in 1911.

In the fall of 1916, Frank became an associate editor of the *Seven Arts*, a short-lived but influential arts/cultural magazine that had taken a pacifist position toward the U.S. entry into World War I. Frank later served as a contributing editor of the *New Masses* and *New Republic*.

In 1917 Frank published *The Unwelcome Man*, the first of a series of innovative fiction titles that culminated with *Chalk Face* (1924). Though marred by a naive romanticism, these works were perhaps the first American use of stream-of-consciousness technique. Frank developed a synthetic style in which poetry mixed with prose and varieties of typographical styles and layouts. The small school of like-minded writers around him included Jean

Toomer, Evelyn Scott, Cyril K. Scott, Sam Ornitz, and Isidor Schneider. Like several of these writers, Frank was deeply concerned with social and political problems, above all the integration of the individual into the modern social order. The major themes of his novel *Holiday* (1923) involved race relations, for whose understanding Frank had disguised himself as a Afro-American during a tour of the South with Jean Toomer.

After 1924, Frank turned increasingly to nonfiction. His first in a series of historical-social studies, *Our America* (1919), reflected his characteristic concern with the destructive individualism of U.S. society and the antidotes he found in elements of apparently archaic societies elsewhere. Several of his later books—*Virgin Spain, America Hispana, South American Journal,* and *Cuba, Prophetic Island*—dealt with Iberian and Latin American cultures. Throughout, he sought to discover and explain alternative modes of civilization; increasingly, he denounced the effects of U.S. imperialism upon these still incompletely modernized, rationalized, and bourgeoisified systems. Within the United States, these works were generally misunderstood as mere travel literature. He intended to show, as he argued forcefully at the 1935 American Writers Congress, that the building of socialism had never been understood as a cultural and human problem and that even American Left intellectuals had allowed themselves to be "taken over [by] the philosophy of the American capitalist culture that we are sworn to overthrow."

Intermittently, Frank threw himself into political activism. As an organizer for the Nonpartisan League in Kansas (1919), as a lecturer for the Friends of the Soviet Union (after a trip to Russia in 1931), as chair of the Independent Miners Relief Committee in Harlan County (for which he was assaulted by vigilantees) in 1932, and as protest leader against mistreatment of such varied victims as Chinese intellectuals and the "Bonus Marchers," he played an important role. Like many other writers, he had a tumultuous relationship with the American Communists. A significant figure in the 1932 League of Professional Groups for Foster and Ford, he toured with Earl Browder in Browder's 1936 campaign, and served as outstanding spokesman at early Congress of American Writers events. Questioning Russian policies as early as 1935, he broke with Communist politics in his report to the International Committee for the Defense of Political Prisoners, protesting Stalin's purges, and abandoned Popular Front organizations in 1939. After World War II, Frank was less politically active. Yet, he was an early, if critical, supporter of Fidel Castro, serving as 1960 temporary chair of the Fair Play for Cuba Committee.

—*Harvey Pekar*

REFERENCES

Bittner, William. *The Novels of Waldo Frank*. Philadelphia: University of Pennsylvania Press, 1955.

Carter, Paul J. *Waldo Frank*. Boston: Twayne, 1967.

Trachtenberg, Alan, ed. *Memoirs of Waldo Frank*. Amherst: University of Massachusetts Press, 1973.

Free Love

A concept originated in the mid-nineteenth century, Free Love meant an absence of legal ties rather than promiscuity, as frequently misunderstood and more frequently charged in the anti-socialist press. A mark of bohemianism until the 1960s, Free Love had become by the 1970s-80s a historical predecessor of the radical critique of sexuality notably carried on by feminist and homosexual liberation movements.

A number of the utopian movements, religious and nonreligious, had endorsed such sexual practices as celibacy, polygamy, and complex marriage which were at odds with Christian norms. Abolitionism reinforced incipient Free Loveism through a critique of southern sexual slavery. Free Love entered the socialist movement via spiritualism, a veritable hotbed of Free Love doctrine, when Victoria Woodhull endorsed Free Love in *Woodhull & Claflin's*. The open statement of such policies justified—in the eyes of Marx's American allies—the expulsion of the Woodhull group and its supporters from the First International. To the respectable public, Woodhull herself became "Mrs. Satan," mirror of socialism's

"Mrs. Satan" cartoon by Thomas Nast, 1872

infidel status, when she not only justified philosophically her own practices but also made known the affair of noted minister Henry Ward Beecher with the wife of prominent reform editor Theodore Tilton, an ally of Beecher. Meanwhile, among German freethinkers and socialists, Free Love continued to be practiced, especially among intellectuals, but only rarely was it articulated in theory.

Until the end of the century, anarchists of varying backgrounds carried on the Free Love agitation without notable socialist support. Moses Harman, Lois Waisbrooker and Ezra Heywood among other late nineteenth century individualist anarchists, conducted a vigorous protest of the 1873 Comstock Act, which prohibited broadly-interpreted "obscenity" from the mails. They meanwhile published periodicals such as *Lucifer, the Light Bearer*, pamphlets addressing questions of birth control, and a lively correspondence with the liberal press (such as the more open-minded of woman suffrage journals). Among the Germans, Robert Reitzel and his weekly *Arme Teufel* perhaps best captured the poetic possibilities of the entire subject, and placed it in the heroic traditions of German literature.

In the early years of the twentieth century, anarchist Emma Goldman became the celebrated spokesperson of the Free Love cause, the most popular speaker and the darling of the surviving anarchist groups. Anti-socialist journals and lecturers meanwhile charged, despite the frequent denials of the Socialist Party, that socialism meant the end of the family. Casually at first, and then with some momentum, a movement of cosmopolitan intellectuals within or around the Socialist Party began to revive the subject in another light, attaining their major influence in Greenwich Village and the *Masses* magazine. With their philosopher the English homosexual writer, Edward Carpenter, their international sexologist Havelock Ellis, and such noted writers as Upton Sinclair providing literary credence, they marshalled a powerful case for Free Love as the soul of modernity.

The splintering of the Socialist movement and the rise of a Communist movement with little concern for personal (especially women's) issues once more thrust Free Love issues back into private life—except for anti-communists, who predictably charged that young revolutionary Russia had "nationalized" its women. During the 1920s, American bohemianism meanwhile gained a mass following of sorts, mostly hedonistic but connected in part with the Harlem Renaissance and the wish to escape the stifling American commercial culture. A small group of Left intellectuals around the *Modern Quarterly*, seeking to integrate sexology into a heavily anthropological "science of society," had little short-run impact upon the Left political movement. They did, however, help to keep alive a sexual element in the radical attack upon American racism. While Leninist workerism forbade the open return of the Free Love subject, a subterranean connection had already been made between interracialism and the principles of Free Love. Further connections, with jazz, poetry and anti-war sentiments, flourished in the bohemian and Beat movements of the late 1940s to early 1960s, with

Free Love (including homosexuality) a measure of cultural bravado and a practical arrangement for transient lifestyles.

During the later 1960s, revolt against the Vietnam War, the overall Youth Culture sensibility and the commercial sexualization of culture together conspired to return Free Love toward the center of the radical picture. "Make Love Not War," a slogan of Antiquity renewed by John Lennon and Yoko Ono among others, seemingly embodied the ultimate rejection of capitalist culture. An evocative photo of a young couple kissing at the barricades of May, 1969, Paris, became overnight an icon of popular New Left sentiment.

The women's liberation movement, following upon the efflorescence and decline of youth culture, made a strident critique of Free Love as practiced by the New Left. These objections, mounted in polemical essays and pamphlets, themselves become important new statements of Free Love principles. A proposed permanent revolution of sex radicalism to overthrow patriarchal practices wherever they occurred, the Feminist view of sexuality led directly to the commentaries by gay and lesbian spokespersons on the authoritarianism of heterosexual domination, and to widespread movements to decriminalize homosexual activity.

By the 1980s, gay liberation had become inseparable from other issues on the Left, substantially because gay activists had become a presence in virtually every field of struggle. At times and places (such as San Francisco), major gay political figures served doubly as socialist influentials. Meanwhile, Free Love (in the sense of an absence of legal bonds) had become paradoxically impeccable in Left (and liberal) attitudes toward private life, and somewhat more scarce in the practice of generations seeking economic and emotional security. *See also*: Birth Control, Emma Goldman, Moses Harmen, Lois Waisbrooker, *Woodhull & Claflin's*, Women's Liberation Movement

—*Mari Jo Buhle*

REFERENCES

Hal D. Sears, *The Sex Radicals: Free Love in High Victorian America* Lawrence: Regents Press of Kansas, 1977.

Free Speech Movement

In the fall of 1964, white student veterans of the civil rights movement led University of California students in the postwar era's first major northern student uprising. When UC Berkeley administrators tried to halt growing civil rights activism among UC students by banning campus fundraising activity for off-campus causes, activists from the Friends of the Student Nonviolent Coordinating Committee (SNCC) and the Congress of Racial Equality (CORE) mobilized a coalition of groups from the Young Republicans to the Independent Socialists and the youth group of the Communist Party to defy the ban. On October 19, campus police arrested Jack Weinberg for staffing a CORE fundraising table; but when they tried to put him in their car and drive him away, hundreds of students spontaneously sat down around the car and prevented it from leaving. In the course of a thirty-six-hour sit-down, the students won Weinberg's release and initiated a dynamic campaign that came to be known as the Free Speech Movement (FSM).

Over the next three months the FSM battled the university with rallies, marches, sit-ins and, ultimately, a massive student strike. UC administrators, led by Chancellor Clark Kerr, alienated many UC students with their refusal to consider any concessions and their clumsy attempts at forceful repression of the FSM. When administrators suspended Mario Savio and other FSM leaders, thousands of students responded with a massive December 5, 1964, rally and occupation of Sproul Hall. By calling in the police and the National Guard to arrest those sitting in, administrators prompted a student strike and faculty walkout that ended only when UC gave in to FSM demands for campus freedom of political activity.

Over the course of the campaign, the FSM developed a pointed critique of the university as a servant of the status quo and a tool of social control. Analyzing the writings of Chancellor Kerr, who minimized undergraduate education and boasted instead of the university's service to corporations and the State, former Shachtmanite Hal Draper and other FSM leaders developed an ideology that

The Mailed Fist of the Law.

linked student dissatisfaction at UC to the larger political and economic forces changing the university and American society. The transformation of students' individual concerns into collective political issues was essential to the FSM's success in building a broad-based campus movement.

The other key factor undergirding the FSM's success was its ability to adapt the tactics, philosophy, and organizational structure of the civil rights movement to a new context and constituency. Many key FSM activists had taken part in local civil rights campaigns, and leaders such as Mario Savio had gone South to work with SNCC in the 1964 Mississippi Freedom Summer. Drawing on this experience, the activists built a highly democratic, almost anarchic organizational structure, prefiguring their goal of a university where students could participate in the decisions that shaped their lives. Like early SNCC activists, they gained a wide audience by using the language of traditional American values such as democracy, community, and freedom, and avoiding the "alien rhetoric" of class conflict.

The size and militancy of the FSM startled observers who still thought that America's white college students were politically conservative and apathetic. Intensive media coverage of the FSM broadcast the unexpected image of bright, white young Americans braving arrest to mount a radical challenge to a highly respected liberal institution. Many veterans of the student movement of the late '60s in America and Western Europe have since recalled that watching news reports on the FSM encouraged them to begin thinking of themselves as radical student activists.

A few months after the triumph of the FSM, the United States escalated the war in Vietnam, and student protests helped initiate the antiwar movement. In the years that followed, student activists across the country drew upon the fresh language, tactics, and organizational style modeled by the FSM in protesting campus militarism, racism, and authoritarianism. The FSM not only revealed the contradictions of the modern "multiversity," but also demonstrated that white, middle-class students could be a significant force for social change in the postwar world. Historically linking the civil rights protests of the early 1960s to the antiwar and student power demonstrations of the later years, the FSM served as a catalyst for the explosive growth of the New Left in America and around the world. *See also*: Civil Rights, New Left

—Bret Eynon

REFERENCES

Draper, Hal. *Berkeley: The New Student Revolt.* New York: Grove Press, 1965.

Heirich, Max. *The Spiral of Conflict: Berkeley, 1964.* New York: Columbia University Press, 1971.

Jacobs, Paul, and Saul Landau, eds. *The New Radicals: A Report with Documents.* New York: Vintage Press, 1966.

Wolin, Sheldon, and John H. Schaar. *The Berkeley Rebellion and Beyond.* New York: New York Review of Books, 1970.

Free Thought

The English-language anticlerical freethought movement revived in post–Civil War America parallel to the labor and socialist movements. Although no merger took place, these movements converged on issues of atheism, secularism, free love, and some aspects of women's rights. In organized free thought, sympathy for labor's cause dates to the debates at the Free Thinkers' Convention at Watkins, New York, in 1878 in the aftermath of the

Great Strike of 1877. Such leanings continued into the Haymarket era with free-thought organs such as the *Truth Seeker* (New York), *Lucifer* (Kansas), and the *Word* (Massachusetts) speaking out for the Chicago anarchists. These publications were associated with the names of their libertarian founders—D. M. Bennett, Moses Harman, and Ezra Heywood—who were forceful critics of both church and capitalist state.

From 1887, Left free thought influenced notable women, such as Lucy Parsons, Voltairine de Cleyre, and Emma Goldman. Emma Lazarus, Elizabeth Cady Stanton, Susan B. Anthony, Josephine Tilton, Matilda Joslyn Gage, Helen Keller, and other Left-oriented women of the Progressive era were also freethinkers.

Free thought flavored the rebirth of the radical labor movement with the forming of the Industrial Workers of the World in 1905. The Wobblies, most notably songwriter Joe Hill, aggressively attacked the theory of religious compensation in many writings and songs.

Free thought deeply influenced attorney Clarence Darrow, ardent defender of the labor Left in the Debs case of 1894 and the Haywood case of 1907. Theodore Schroeder (1864–1953), who aided Emma Goldman in San Diego and Denver trials, helped in free-speech fights in Chicago and Paterson, New Jersey. Schroeder also defended "Bad Bishop" William Montgomery Brown, expelled by his church for attacking religion from the communist viewpoint in *Communism and Christianism* (1920).

Publishers Emanuel Haldeman-Julius (1889–1951) and the Charles H. Kerr Company brought numerous scientific free-thought and socialist texts on the religious question to radical readers. After World War II the United Secularists of America, founded by socialist William McCarthy, brought out the journal *Progressive World* (1947–81). The 1980s elicited strong convergences of socialist democratic and freethinking tendencies in humanism, while the anarchist-atheist affinity kindled the new series of the *Match* (1982–).
See also: Free Love, Free Speech

—*Joseph Jablonski*

REFERENCES

Brown, Marshall G., and Gordon Stein, eds. *Free Thought in the United States: A Descriptive Bibliography*. Westport: Greenwood Press, 1978.

Jablonski, Joseph. "The Haymarket Atheists." In *The Haymarket Scrapbook*, edited by David Roediger and Franklin Rosemont. Chicago: Charles H. Kerr, 1986.

Warren, Sidney. *American Freethought, 1860–1914*. New York: Gordian Press, 1966.

FREEDOMWAYS

For much of its lengthy publication life (1961–85) the most distinguished African-American political-cultural journal, *Freedomways* was also something that the Left had lacked since the 1930s, a forum for some of the most prestigious American intellectuals to meet and mingle with Marxists.

Freedomways' lineal predecessor, *Freedom* (1951–55), had been a Cold War casualty. The notable Committee for Negroes in the Arts had swung behind the new publication and above all its publisher, Paul Robeson. Contributors John Killens, Lorraine Hansberry, Shirley Graham, Julian Mayfield, Ruby Dee, John Henrik Clarke, and W. E. B. DuBois among others would carry on to *Freedomways*. The demise of *Freedom*, however, cruelly deprived Robeson of a final major literary outlet for his talent. Louis Burnham, the paper's main editor, moved on to the *National Guardian*.

Freedomways, opening its doors in the more hopeful period of the early civil rights movement, had vastly more opportunity to succeed both financially and editorially. *Freedomways'* founding editorial proclaimed "we are African-American," and promised to "explore, without prejudice or gag, and from the viewpoint of the special interests of American Negroes . . . the new forms of economic, political, and social systems now existing in the world," and "to offer a medium of expression for serious and talented authors." W. E. B. DuBois contributed the opening essay, "The United States and the Negro." Shirley Graham and Esther Jackson served as founding editors, joined by Schomburg librarian Ernest Kaiser, the Southern Christian Leadership Conference's J. H. O'Dell, and an array of contributing editors that in later years included Ruby Dee, Angela Davis, Alice Walker, and Selwyn R. Cudjoe among others.

Freedomways distinguished itself by linking culture to politics. It published many important special issues on leading figures—including DuBois, Robeson, Hansberry, and artist Charles White—and on such select topics as the Caribbean people (with such contributors as C. L. R. James, Eric Williams, and Derek Walcott) and the crisis in education. It conducted a pioneering effort at the public recognition of African American women, in particular black women writers, from its earliest issues onward. And it effectively promoted African-American art in many forms, at one point establishing its own management bureau to arrange lectures and public performances.

Perhaps most impressive, however, was *Freedomways*' breadth of prominent commentators from African-American life, and the diversity of its political discussion. A short list of noted contributors would include Ossie Davis, Harry Belafonte, Nikki Giovanni, Richard Hatcher, Vincent Harding, Shirley Chisolm, George W. Crockett, Jr., Ron Dellums, Jesse Jackson, James Baldwin, James O. Killens, Sterling Brown, and Wyatt Tee Walker. If, as critics sometimes charged, *Freedomways* had little expressed empathy for separatism or militant black nationalism (until Malcolm X was assassinated in 1965), remaining generally true to a political perspective formed in the orbit of the 1940s Popular Front, the magazine nevertheless radiated an openness sufficient to draw New Leftists and even an occasional black political veteran such as C. L. R. James, earlier linked with Trotskyist dissent from the Old Left mainstream.

Freedomways' circulation, peaking at 6,500 or so, rarely sustained the magazine unaided. A generational gap and a crisis of funds generally overtook staff regulars, at a time when the proliferation of newer black publications such as the *Black World* and the *Black Scholar* offered alternatives for the younger reader in particular. Growing noticeably thinner in its final issues but never losing its sense of the immediate political questions (indeed, Jack O'Dell's reports on the Rainbow Coalition offered an insider's look at the foremost movement of the day), *Freedomways* passed from the scene, leaving a vacuum in its wake. It had been, in some ways, the finest intellectual product of the Popular Front, speaking with a distinctive voice about matters that concerned African Americans.

—*E. Ethelbert Miller,*
Paul Buhle

REFERENCES

Kaiser, Ernest. "25 Years of Freedomways." *Freedomways* 24 (Third Quarter 1985).

Freie Arbeter Shtimme (1890–1976)

The outstanding anarchist publication in the Yiddish language, and the most popular anarchist publication of any kind in America, the *FAS* long served as central mechanism for anarchist ethics and aesthetics within the Jewish immigrant world. It also epitomized the adaptation of many anarchists to the reality of shrinking influence, a strategy that matched accommodation to middle-of-the-road unionism with undaunted philosophical discourse.

The *Freie Arbeter Shtimme* began as an American version of the highly successful London *Arbeter Fraint* (Workers Friend), intended, like the *Fraint*, to bring together anarchists and socialists under one editorial roof. But in America, the socialists had the upper hand in resources and editorial talent. The outstanding early contributor to the *FAS*, poet David Edelstadt, died of tuberculosis at the age of twenty-six after composing verses that became classics in the Yiddish choral repertoire. His comrade Joseph Bovshover, the earliest bohemian Jewish radical and the other outstanding anarchist poet, was soon confined to a mental institution. The *FAS* disappeared for a few years at the end of the century, only to return under the hand of experienced London editor Sh. Yanofsky, who dominated the paper until his departure in 1920.

In the meantime, the *FAS* and its constituency had adjusted themselves to a narrower political gauge. Active within the Jewish socialist fraternal movement and unions, they adamantly opposed the extreme Left embodied in the Socialist Labor Party and the revolutionary garment unions formed by the Industrial Workers of the World. They aligned themselves, informally and almost unconsciously, with the *Poale Tsion* (Labor Zionist) movement, many of whose members shared a vague utopianism and a desire to make practical changes in daily life.

The *FAS*, its pages studded with *di yunge*, young rebellious poets of the ghetto, reached a circulation of 30,000 amid the last major Jewish diaspora. But Yanofsky's support of American entry into World War I (following anarchist Peter Kropotkin's similar endorsement) disheartened many readers. Others felt drawn, although sometimes only temporarily, to the Russian Revolution and the new Yiddish Communist *Freiheit*.

The *FAS* struck early and hard at the new Russian regime, and its followers could be counted upon to support the garment union mainstream against Communist challenges. Its own anarchism became steadily more philosophical and reactive. It retained perhaps 10,000 readers as a "free thought" forum for the older reader and the shrinking but still significant numbers of young Yiddish writers; and for the last outstanding "Yiddish" anarchist luminary, the gentile German intellectual Rudolf Rocker. But it remained a beacon of traditional anarchism as well, albeit mixed increasingly with a liberal anticommunism and a crypto-Zionism. Its activist readers, comfortable with the fraternal Yiddishist atmosphere of the Workmen's Circle, convoked anarchistic study groups within the Circle, raised funds for the Spanish anarchists, and accommodated themselves to an amiable libertarianism.

By the 1940s–1950s, the *FAS* became increasingly a newspaper of anniversaries and reprinted poems or essays. Several of the distinguished old-time Yiddish writers, such as Abraham Raysen, continued to write for the paper until their deaths. A handful of younger writers, such as the melancholy eccentric A. Almi, contributed fresh essays on a variety of subjects, from music to literature. For the most part, the *Freie Arbeter Shtimme* (Free voice of labor) celebrated its own, the great individuals and causes past or passing. As the present dimmed, in a world diminished by the Holocaust and by the passing of Jewish labor into the middle classes, the past grew brighter. In the paper's last years, anarchist historian Paul Avrich became a major interpreter of tradition, his essays translated from the English for the faithful. In 1976 the final editor, Arne Thorne—syndicalist by inclination and typesetter at the *Jewish Daily Forward* by occupation—closed the paper for lack of finances and readership. *See also*: Anarchism, Yiddish Left

—*Paul Buhle*

REFERENCES

Biolostotski, B. I., ed. *Dovid Edelshtot Gedenk Bukh* Los Angeles: Edelstadt Memorial Committee, 1952.

Cohen, Josef. *Di Anarchistishe Bevegung in Amerika*. Philadelphia: Radical Library Branch #243, 1945.

Yanofsky, Sh. *Ershte Yorn fun Yiddishe Freiheitlekhe Sotsialism*. New York: Freie Arbeter Shtimme, 1948.

Freie Gemeinden and Freidenker (Free Congregations and Freethinkers)

The development of *Freie Gemeinden* or "free congregations" in Germany was tied to the growing conservative influence of the established Catholic and Protestant churches during the Restoration after 1815. During the 1840s, *Freie Gemeinden* were formed by members of both church groups as a protest against strict orthodoxy and the conservative political position taken by the church hierarchies. These free congregations attempted to avoid hierarchical structures by having "speakers" who substituted for clergymen, and their members arrived at decisions in a democratic way on matters affecting them. The free congregations were by no means atheistic, but they advocated the practice of religion tempered by reason and science. In Germany, the high point of membership in the *Freie Gemeinden* occurred in the early 1850s, when they claimed approximately 150,000 adherents. After this point, these groups either lost members or evolved into *Freidenker-Vereine* (Freethinker societies), which were decidedly more atheistically oriented. The purpose of these latter groups was to free people from religious misperceptions, proceeding from a rational and scientific perspective, and to champion the absolute freedom of religious belief or nonbelief.

Among German immigrants to the United States, several free-thought papers existed prior to 1850. The most important of these was the journal *Die Fackel* (The torch) published by Samuel Ludvigh from 1843–69. However, it was the immigration of radical "Forty-Eighters" that gave impetus to the founding of *Freie Gemeinden* in many cities around the country. The first *Freie Gemeinde* in the United States was formed on November 6, 1850, in St. Louis, by Franz Schmidt, member of the Frankfurt Parliament in 1848. Several attempts were made to unite local groups into a national organization, but these larger groups generally did not cohere for long. For example, in 1897 the *Bund der Freien Gemeinden und Freidenker-Vereine von Nord-Amerika* (Association of free congregations and freethinking societies of North America) was founded in St. Louis, reporting that it had eight congregations with a total of 814 members but that more congregations existed outside it. Many of the most well known German Americans of the day were connected with the free congregation movement, including Eduard Schroeter, Friedrich Schünemann-Pott, Karl Heinzen, Adolf Douai, and Robert Reitzel. The freethinkers published a large number of papers and journals in cities around the country, most importantly the *Freidenker* (The freethinker, 1872–1942, published in Wisconsin and Minnesota). After the turn of the century, membership in these groups declined, and there are no longer any active congregations.

As in Germany, the *Freie Gemeinden* tended to develop into *Freidenker-Vereine* with a more atheistic viewpoint. The main principles of the *Freidenker* with respect to religion were that they did not think that belief in God, immortality, and the divinity of Jesus was necessary to lead an ethical life. Placing their main emphasis on rationality and a scientific approach to the world, they argued against revealed religion and advocated the total separation of church and state. Politically, the *Freidenker* supported the equality of the races, sexes, and classes. They were in agreement with German-American socialists on the necessity of a shorter working day, free public education, and other issues affecting the working class. Also, they were often allied closely with German-American *Turner* groups until the latter became more conservative after the American Civil War and the unification of Germany. The *Freidenker* often established free schools for children (sometimes in conjunction with the socialists) that offered instruction in German, English, and the natural sciences.

In the United States, free thought was also a significant movement among English-speaking citizens and other ethnic groups (especially the Bohemians) in the late nineteenth century. Thus, the German *Freidenker* were part of a much larger context of groups advocating atheism, rationalism, or secular humanism. *See also*: German Americans, Socialist Labor Party

—*Carol Poore*

REFERENCES

Brown, Marshall G., and Gordon Stein, eds. *Freethought in the United States: A Descriptive Bibliography*. Westport: Greenwood Press, 1978.

Was sind die freien Gemeinden? St. Louis: Bund der Freien Gemeinden und Freidenker-Vereine von Nord-Amerika, 1902.

Freiheit**:** see Olgin, M. J.; Yiddish Left

Fromm, Erich (1900–80)

Born in Frankfurt, Germany, Fromm was one of the first to carry through a synthesis of Marx and Freud, and to develop a Marxian social psychology. Trained in psychoanalysis and affiliated with the Institute for Social Research in Frankfurt from 1930–1938, Fromm combined Freudian psychology with Marxian social theory. In his early essays, he indicates the common dialectical and materialist elements in Marx and Freud, and applies his Marxian social psychology to interpret such phenomena as religion, the sado-masochistic roots of the authoritarian personality, and the dominant bourgeois character types.

Forced to flee from Nazi Germany in 1933, Fromm settled in the United States and lectured at the New School for Social Research, Columbia, Yale, and Bennington. In the late 1930s, he broke with the Institute for Social Research and with *Escape from Freedom* (1941) began publishing a series of books that would win him a large audience. *Escape from Freedom* argued that alienation from soil and community in the transition from feudalism to capitalism increased insecurity and fear. Documenting some of the strains and crises of individualism, Fromm attempted to explain how alienated individuals would seek gratification and security from social orders such as fascism.

His post–World War II books, *Man for Himself* (1947) and *The Sane Society* (1955), applied Fromm's Freudian-Marxian perspectives to sharp critiques of contemporary capitalism. Fromm popularized the Neo-Marxian critiques of the media and consumer society, and promoted democratic socialist perspectives during an era when social repression made it difficult and dangerous to advocate radical positions. Although his social critique was similar in many ways to that of his former colleague Herbert Marcuse, the two thinkers engaged in sharp polemics from the mid-1950s into the 1970s. Marcuse began the polemic by attacking Fromm as a Neo-Freudian revisionist, and Fromm retaliated by calling Marcuse a "nihilist" and "utopian." Marcuse claimed that Fromm's emphasis on the "productive character" simply reproduced the "productivism" intrinsic to capitalism, and that his celebration of the values of love, in books like *The Art of Loving*, and religious values simply reproduced dominant idealist ideologies.

Fromm continued to be a prolific writer until his death in 1980, publishing a series of books promoting and developing Marxian and Freudian ideas. He was also politically active, helping organize SANE and engaging in early "Ban the Bomb" campaigns, as well participating in the antiwar movement of the 1960s. Fromm continued to argue for a humanistic and democratic socialist position, and claimed that such elements were intrinsic in Marxism. His many books and articles had some influence on the New Left and continue to be widely read and discussed today. *See also*: Marcuse, Herbert; Psychoanalysis

—Douglas Kellner

REFERENCES

Funk, Rainer. *Erich Fromm: The Courage to Be.* New York: Continuum, 1982.

Landis, Bernard, and Edward S. Tauber, eds. *In the Name of Life: Essays in Honor of Erich Fromm.* New York: Holt, Rinehart and Winston, 1971.

Schaar, John H. *Escape from Authority: The Perspectives of Erich Fromm.* New York: Basic Books, 1961.

FRONT GROUPS

Radical organizations often seek to influence political events by creating groups that deal with only one aspect of their general program. Such groups are called *fronts*. In this context *front* does not indicate a facade but a broadly-based coalition. *Front* may also indicate a general policy of working with other groups on commonly held positions even if there is no formal organization. Fronts take on issues such as opposition to nuclear war, defense of political prisoners, and promotion of civil rights in a manner that unites persons who would not join a political party or might disagree on other issues. The group(s) that originates the front tries to give it direction, but if the front succeeds in attracting wide participation, the sharing of decision-making becomes essential if the front is to survive. Activists in a front are usually aware of the forces that shaped the front, but the general public is likely to perceive the organization as spontaneously formed. Organizations and individuals within a front usually have a similarity of views on more than the issue at hand, but many fronts contain forces otherwise antagonistic to one another.

—Dan Georgakas

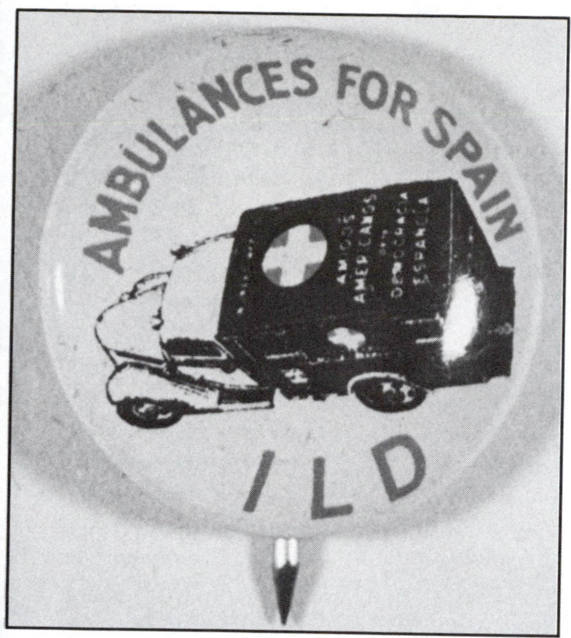

International Labor Defense, a front organization to defend political prisioners, took part in a wider front to defend the Spanish Republic

Frontier Films: see Radical Filmmaking, 1930s

Fur and Leather Workers

The International Fur and Leather Workers Union (IFLWU) is a prime example of a successful Communist-led American trade union. Its success was largely due to the efforts of Ben Gold and close associates such as Irving Potash, Jack Schneider, and Joseph Winogradsky. Gold joined the Communist movement from its inception and remained a member until compelled to resign in 1950.

The fur workers union of the 1910s was controlled by right-wing Socialists and trade union bureaucrats. Gold, who had been born in Bessarabia in 1898, entered the fur industry in 1912 and quickly drifted into the orbit of the left-wing Socialists. In 1917 he served as a leader of militant fur workers in a Montreal strike. Returning to New York, he became head of a progressive faction that sought to take over the leadership of the union. Through considerable courage and the skillful handling of strikes, Red-baiting, and other political challenges, the Gold group won the loyalty of the predominantly Jewish rank and file.

Typical of the leadership's foresight and determination was the organization of some 300 shops employing 1,500–2,000 Greek workers. Strikes had previously been lost or weakened when work at struck shops flowed to the nonunion Greek sector. The former leadership considered the Greeks unorganizable, but Gold, using Greek-speaking organizers from the Communist Party, unionized the Greek shops in a brief whirlwind campaign in 1926.

Shortly after the Greek shops were organized, the union called an industrywide strike. A bitter and difficult conflict was capped by a substantial victory that firmly established the Gold leadership. The forty-hour work week was won, wages raised, legal holidays obtained, working conditions improved, and job security protected. In subsequent years the union would build upon this base to establish wages, hours, and conditions that were among the best in the garment industry.

Employers had often used gunmen and "sluggers" to work their will in the garment districts of New York. During the 1930s the fur bosses hired gangs led by Louis (Lepke) Buchalter and Jacob (Gurrah) Shapiro. The union formed defense units and bested the hoodlums in a bloody series of confrontations that resulted in serious injuries and deaths on both sides. Almost alone among the garment unions, the fur workers could boast that they had defended their interests against gangsters without having to hire gangsters of their own to do the job. The battle with hoodlums is a central theme in Leonard Kriegel's *Quitting Time* (1982), a novel loosely based on the union's leaders and history. Lepke would become notorious in later years as the main figure in Murder, Inc.

By the end of the 1930s the fur workers had organized 100 percent of their industry and had become pioneer members of the CIO. Their success in fur led to a request by leather workers for affiliation. Wages, conditions, and hours for leather workers were despicable, and the existing union was collapsing rather than growing. Under the Gold administration, the new International Fur and Leather Workers Union was able to win benefits for leather workers that were comparable to those of the fur workers. Membership in the IFLWU swelled to 100,000.

While the union focused most of its energies on trade union issues, it was part of the Left culture of its time. The union sent an ambulance to the Spanish Republic, and some of its leaders and members fought in the Abraham Lincoln Brigade. The union later sent funds for a hospital in China set up by Doctor Norman Bethune for use by Mao Tse-tung's guerrilla army. In later years the union would question the Korean War and offer guards for Paul Robeson's threatened concerts in Peekskill, New York. While only a few members were African American, the union was a strong advocate of full civil rights for all races and elected African Americans to union posts. The Greek section of the union was the focus of Left cultural life of New York City's Greek community and the leader in Greek war-relief work directed through the trade union movement. More broadly, the fur workers had close working relations with the ALP and its various initiatives.

In the postwar era, the IFLWU came under heavy pressure due to the Taft-Hartley Act. Gold had always avowed his Communist views and had held visible posts in the CP, but his leadership group was a true alliance of Communists, Socialists, and liberals. The union was a model of internal democracy and was free of economic scandals. Gold voluntarily resigned his CP membership to comply with provisions of Taft-Hartley, but he did so in a letter that praised Communist objectives and practice. His resignation was termed "fraudulent" and "insincere" and led to long court battles in which radical East Harlem politician Vito Marcantonio served as Gold's counsel. Although Gold ultimately won in the courts, the survival of the IFLWU required additional concessions to the reunited AFL-CIO.

Other IFLWU leaders with past or present Communist affiliations had to resign their posts. Some of the Greek Communists would, in fact, be deported under the McCarren-Walter Act. Thus purged of card-carrying Reds, the IFLWU made an accommodation in 1955 by which it became the Fur and Leather Department of the Amalgamated Meat Cutters. Patrick Gorman, the secretary-treasurer of the Amalgamated, was a longtime socialist and a militant trade unionist. He integrated the IFLWU staff into important posts in the Amalgamated, which grew rapidly and took progressive stances on civil rights and was an early opponent of the war in Vietnam. In 1979 the Amalgamated merged with the Retail Clerks to form the United Food and Commercial Workers International Union, the largest in the AFL-CIO. The remaining fur and leather locals, greatly reduced in size due to contraction of their industry, retained some sense of their special history and a commitment to a socially oriented labor movement. *See also*: American Labor Party, Taft-Hartley Loyalty Oath

—Dan Georgakas

REFERENCES

Foner, Philip S. *The Fur and Leather Workers Union*. Newark, NJ: Nordan Press, 1950.

Ginger, Ann Fagan, and David Christiano, eds. *The Cold War Against Labor*. 2 vols. Berkeley: Meiklejohn Civil Liberties Institute, 1987.

Gold, Ben. *Memoirs*. New York: William Howard, 1988.

Galleani, Luigi (1861–1931)

The dominant figure of the Italian antiorganizational anarchist movement in the United States, Luigi Galleani was less a theorist than an agitator and propagandist who believed that ideas without action were sterile. His anarchism was of Bakuninist derivation but strongly influenced by Peter Kropotkin's *The Conquest of Bread*. For Galleani, anarchism was simply the absolute negation of authority and the autonomy of the individual in free association with others. But he rejected individualistic anarchism, emphasizing the solidarity of the proletariat as the basis for anarcho-communism. The anarchist society, in his opinion, could only be realized through social revolution, which required the violent and total destruction of the existing social order. Galleani hailed all spontaneous expressions of the revolutionary spirit, including the individual violent acts of Gaetano Bresci and Leon Czołgosz, as preparation of the masses for the final battle, the general strike that would bring about the collapse of the capitalist system. A charismatic orator, facile writer, and fierce polemicist, Galleani for a half century exerted a powerful influence over a substantial segment of the Italian workers in both Italy and the United States.

Born in Vercelli (Piedmont) on August 12, 1861, in a middle-class and monarchist family, Galleani received a good bourgeois education. But as a student of law at the University of Turin, he was swept up in the socialist ferment of the 1880s. His writings in the labor press, his speeches in the *piazza*, his prominent role in workers' organizations and strikes quickly established Galleani as a fiery leader of the emerging radical movement in northern Italy. These activities also brought him to the attention of the authorities, resulting in arrests, imprisonments, and a period of exile. In the split between anarchists and socialists that culminated at the Congress of Genoa in 1892, Galleani, then an organizational anarchist, was a leading exponent of the intransigent, antiparliamentary position. During the

Crispian reaction of the nineties, he was sentenced to prison and confinement, but escaped after several years from the island of Pantelleria.

Upon his arrival in the United States in October 1901, Galleani immediately resumed his work of agitation and propaganda. He became editor of *La Questione Sociale* of Paterson, New Jersey, but because of his dramatic part in a violent silk-workers' strike fled to Canada in 1902. Reentering the United States under the pseudonym Luigi Pimpino, he began publication of *Cronaca Sovversiva* in Barre, Vermont, on June 6, 1903. For sixteen years, *Cronaca* was Galleani's pulpit, from which he preached the gospel of anarchism and lashed his enemies, particularly the socialists. Although he successfully solicited articles from such notables as Peter Kropotkin, Galleani complained that "the *Cronaca* in spite of the variety of pseudonyms ends up being the work of only one person." The newspaper had a circulation of some 5,000 with wide distribution in Europe as well as both Americas.

Cronaca bore the stamp of Galleani's mind and character: forceful, polemical, passionate. Although his avowed purpose was the intellectual and moral elevation of the workers, one wonders how many of the semiliterate immigrants were able to master his elegant, sometimes ornate, prose. Many of his writings were subsequently republished in book or pamphlet form, as were tracts by other leading anarchists. Copies of these could be found in libraries of the *circoli di studi sociali* and in the homes of ordinary workers. Galleani also vigorously carried on the propaganda of the spoken word, delivering thousands of speeches in meeting halls and miners' shacks in the course of frequent tours. Wherever there were labor struggles, he leaped into the fray, suffering arrests and jailings. While it is difficult to measure the efficacy of this propaganda, the scores of autonomous groups of "Galleanisti" that sprang up around the country were evidence of conversions.

When the Great War broke out, Galleani, vehemently antimilitarist and antinationalist, took an uncompromising position. It was a quarrel among the bourgeoisie for power and profits. Rather than use arms against other workers, the proletariat should use them to reclaim its land, bread, and liberty, he believed. Galleani published antiwar tracts in which he sought to dissuade immigrants from returning to Italy for military service. In a May 26, 1917, issue of *Cronaca*, American military conscription was condemned as a form of slavery and thus contrary to the Constitution! During the war, Galleani and *Cronaca* came under increasing scrutiny by federal intelligence agencies. Galleani himself was arrested, as were hundreds of subscribers, and *Cronaca* was eventually suppressed. Its last regular issue was that of July 18, 1918, but two clandestine issues appeared in March and May 1919. Defiant to the last, Galleani called upon the comrades to avenge themselves upon their tormentors. Whether by coincidence or not, a series of bombings took place in the spring of 1919, culminating with explosions in eight cities on June 2. On June 24 Galleani was deported, but the United States had not heard the last of him. He resumed publication of *Cronaca* in Turin in April 1920 with a special American edition under the masthead *"A Stormo!"* Galleani was finally silenced by the Fascist regime. Sentenced repeatedly to prison and confinement, he lived the last years of his life ill and destitute; he died alone at Caprigliola (Tuscany) on November 4, 1931. Meanwhile, the "Galleanisti" in America had established a new publication, *L'Adunata dei Reffratari* (The gathering of the refractories). Published from 1922 to 1971, *L'Adunata* continued to propagate Galleani's ideas. The "Galleanisti" persisted as a militant and troublesome presence in the Italian-American Left until well after World War II. As their dreams of anarchism receded in the face of twentieth century realities, they became more and more sectarian, devoted to maintaining the purity of the ideals that Galleani had taught them. *See also*: Anarchism, L'Adunata dei Reffratari, Italians, Peace Movements

—Rudolph J. Vecoli

REFERENCES

Avrich, Paul. *Anarchist Portraits*. Princeton: Princeton University Press, 1988.

Fedeli, Ugo. *Luigi Galleani*. Cesena: Edizioni "L'Antistato," 1956.

Masini, Pier Carlo. "La giovinezza di Luigi Galleani." *Movimento Operaio*. New series, VI (May–June, 1954). VI (1974).

Molinari, Augusta. "Luigi Galleani: un anarchico italiano negli Stati Uniti." *Miscellanea Storica Ligure*. Universita di Genova, Istituto di Storia Moderna e Contemporanea, Genova, XI, 1974.

Nejrotti, M. "Galleani L." In *Il movimento operaio italiano. Dizionario biografico 1853–1943*, edited by Franco Andreucci and Tommaso Detti. 5 vols. Rome: Editori Riuniti 1976, 2: 418–24.

GARVEYISM

A grassroots black nationalist political movement and a sociocultural philosophy of racial pride and dignity, Garveyism arose during World War I and burgeoned in the early interwar years. Given structure by the black militancy of the New Negro movement, Garveyism was radical in its early manifestations, but also carried with it reactionary elements of thought and practice. It is the early radical ideals of Garveyism, however, that have primarily been maintained in black folk culture and as an international political legacy. These ideals of black unity and resistance became important factors in the thought and formation of the black power movement in the United States, and in black liberation movements in Africa and the Caribbean.

Garveyism takes the name of its primary figure, Marcus Garvey (1887–1940), who was born to peasant parents in Jamaica, was influenced by Pan-African thought in London in 1912–14, and founded the Universal Negro Improvement Association with Amy Ashwood in Kingston in 1914. The UNIA was initially a benevolent self-help or uplift organization, which provided a forum for black culture, performed charitable activities in the black community, and worked toward a goal of establishing a technical school for blacks in Jamaica based on the Tuskegee model—a plan for which its members sought white patronage. The organization took on more radical overtones when it was reformulated by Garvey in Harlem in 1917–18. Garvey traveled to the United States in 1916 to raise funds for the school. Although the emphasis on black education remained a part of Garveyism, it soon became a secondary aim, as Garvey—influenced by the militant rhetoric of fellow West Indian immigrants like Cyril Briggs, W. A. Domingo, and Hubert Harrison—decided to remain in New York and build the UNIA as a political organization. In the early years of the movement in Harlem, Garvey praised the Bolshevist government and endorsed nationalist and anticolonial liberation movements in India, Japan, Ireland, Morocco, and elsewhere, instilling the motto of Africa for the Africans in his followers. In the heated context of postwar racial violence, the earlier philosophical aims of the organization, which had been directed at the development of racial consciousness and pride in African heritage, took on more radical meanings. Garveyism in these years came to encompass the idea of overcoming racial domination through the formation of a united front of people of African descent, who would build a powerful independent black empire in Africa, resist white-defined cultural norms, and identify with the anti-imperialist struggles of other politically subordinated peoples, particularly people of color. Garvey's Black Star Line—a UNIA shipping company designed to develop commerce between black producers in the Caribbean and consumers in the United States, and, eventually, it was hoped, to serve as a passenger line between the Americas and Africa, assisting the UNIA's Liberian colonization program—captured the popular imagination and served as a propaganda tool to organize local divisions of the movement.

The radicalism of Garveyism was underscored by the surveillance and repression of the movement by British colonial and American governmental officials. The UNIA organ, the *Negro World*, which reprinted news of liberation and labor struggles in all parts of the world, was banned in several African, Central American, and Caribbean countries as seditious; organization of local divisions of the UNIA was also prohibited in some areas. The newspaper was nevertheless passed from hand to hand, and helped foster the outgrowth of Garveyism in many regions under colonial rule, including western and southern Africa and the West Indies. In the United States, the UNIA was soon identified as a radical organization by government officials, its headquarters infiltrated, and Garvey placed under surveillance with the aim of building a case for his deportation. The pursuit of Garvey was directed by the young J. Edgar Hoover, first as special assistant to the attorney general, and later with the Department of Justice General Intelligence Division and finally the Bureau of Investigation, forerunner of the FBI.

As a direct result of this program of political repression, 1921 was a turning point in the development of Garveyism in America. After organizing hundreds of local divisions, beginning negotiations with the Liberian government to institute UNIA colonies there, and holding a successful international UNIA convention in New York in 1920, Garvey left the United States in 1921 on a scheduled one-month tour to organize for the movement in the Caribbean. Hoover used the opportunity of Garvey's voluntary departure to attempt to deny his reentry into the country. Backed by the Bureau of Immigration, Hoover was able to block Garvey's reentry for several months. The effort at exclusion was eventually overruled by the State Department, but had a lasting effect on the politics of the movement.

After his delayed return to the United States, Garvey developed an increasingly conservative tone. His speeches took on a blatantly patriotic rhetoric; he endorsed candidates of mainstream political parties; and he focused more on the anti-intellectual and commerical aspects of Garveyism. He praised men like Rockefeller and Carnegie as role models, and professed a Horatio Alger–like belief in free enterprise, capitalist investment, and individual effort, telling Garveyites that hard work and wealth were the best routes to power and rights. In doing so he voiced a conservative strain that had always been a factor in the movement, and was in part the product of the early influence of Booker T. Washington on Garvey's thought. This pro-enterprise element of Garveyism was accented by the executive power structure of the UNIA. While many Garveyites were industrial, service, or agricultural workers—many of whom seized upon the separatist self-pride aspects and communitarianism of Garveyism with religious fervor—the leadership of the UNIA was drawn primarily from a petit-bourgeois base. Thus Garveyism as manifested in the United States had strongly capitalistic as well as overtly cultural and political orientations, and became closely identified in the popular mind with the operation of the Black Star Line and other UNIA businesses.

In the years after 1921, Garvey's earlier politics of resistance were channeled more and more into bitter infighting with other black leaders, factionalization within the leadership of the UNIA, and renewed stress on policies of racial purity and separate institution building. An emphasis on racial separatism had always been a key part of Garveyism. However, the conflict between separatist and integrationist strategies became a heated subject of debate within the black political community when Garvey made statements that seemed to associate separatism with accommodationism and mass African repatriation. In 1921 Garvey denounced the principle of social equality and such efforts as residential desegregation as equivalents to miscegenation and race suicide. At the same time that he eschewed coalition politics with other black activist organizations, he began seeking informal alliances with leading white racists. In a move that caused a furor among Afro-American activists, he arranged a meeting with the acting imperial wizard of the Ku Klux Klan in June 1922, and defended his negotiations with the virulently antiblack organization by declaring the KKK the invisible government of the United States, and further pointing out similarities between the aims of the UNIA and the KKK as separatist organizations. "The KKK desires to make America absolutely a white man's country," he told a Liberty Hall audience in July 1922, and "the UNIA wants to make Africa absolutely a black man's country." In the mid-twenties he continued this tactic, corresponding with white supremacists such as Senators Theodore Bilbo of Mississippi and John Powell (president of the Anglo-Saxon Clubs of America) and Ernest Sevier Cox (author of *White America*). He also expressed admiration for Thomas Dixon, author of *The Clansman*. Years later the UNIA would work in support of Bilbo's 1938 Greater Liberia repatriation bill, an aspect of UNIA activism that, in combination with the earlier operation of the Black Star Line, would help to simplistically label Garveyism as a "Back to Africa" movement.

If Garvey's gestures of support for the radical Right were meant to conciliate government opposition, they were unsuccessful. Six months before his meeting with Acting Imperial Wizard Edward Young Clarke in 1922, Garvey was arrested on mail-fraud charges stemming from sale of Black Star Line stock. He was tried and convicted in 1923, denied an appeal and imprisoned in 1925, and deported in late 1927, instituting a new phase in the history of the movement. Tensions between the American-based and Jamaica-based wings of the movement resulted in a formal split in the UNIA in 1929, with some American divisions remaining loyal to Garvey and others backing the leaders at the UNIA headquarters in New York. Garvey remained president general of the splintered UNIA, and in the late 1920s pursued a career in electoral politics in Jamaica. His People's Political Party (PPP) sought a coalition of small proprietors, peasants, agricultural labor, and the urban working class, and in 1929 presented a platform in a Legislative Council campaign that included land reform, urban renewal, public health and education measures, a minimum wage, and an eight-hour day. The PPP was short-lived, and in 1935 Garvey relocated to London, where he remained throughout the Jamaica labor rebellions of 1938. UNIA conventions were held under his leadership in Jamaica in 1929 and 1934, and in Toronto in 1937 and 1938. The Canadian conventions were attended primarily by those active in the movement in the United States. After his conviction and deportation Garvey's writings and speeches contained anticommunist and anti-Semitic messages; and in the years prior to his death in 1940, while continuing to denounce colonial domination of Africa, he also wrote of the black need to manifest power and organization like that shown by Hitler and Mussolini.

The major principles of Garveyism—a profound racial consciousness, Pan-African unity, the development of a strong black economic sector and international trade, knowledge and pride of black history, African liberation, resistance to white standards of beauty, and the fostering of positive black concepts in literature, the arts, and religion—remain the primary legacy of Marcus Garvey's varied career. This legacy has had a diverse and widespread political impact, helping to shape Black Muslim and Rastafarian belief, and contributing forcefully to the growth of black nationalism in the 1960s, and to anti-imperial movements in the Third World. The positive import of Garveyism as a philosophy of cultural resistance, revising negative self-concepts and instituting the teaching and writing of black history, is an equally crucial and far-reaching contribution. *See also*: *Crusader*; Domingo, W. A.; Harrison, Hubert; Haywood, Harry; Moore, Audley; "Queen Mother"

—*Barbara Bair*

REFERENCES

Hill, Robert A. "The Foremost Radical Among His Race: Marcus Garvey and the Black Scare, 1918–1921." *Prologue: Journal of the National Archives* 16 (Winter 1984).

Hill, Robert A., and Barbara Bair, eds. *Marcus Garvey: Life and Lessons*. Berkeley and Los Angeles: University of California Press, 1987.

Lewis, Rupert. *Marcus Garvey: Anti-Colonial Champion*. London: Karia, 1987.

Lewis, Rupert, and Maureen Warner-Lewis, eds. *Garvey, Africa, Europe, the Americas*. Kingston, Jamaica: University of the West Indies, 1986.

Martin, Tony. *Race First*. Westport: Greenwood Press, 1976.

Stein, Judith. *The World of Marcus Garvey*. Baton Rouge: University of Louisiana Press, 1986.

Gastonia Strike

The Loray Mill strike in Gastonia, North Carolina, in the spring and summer of 1929 was largely the result of a decision made by the American Communist Party, following a shift in Comintern policy, to reverse its strategy of "boring from within" existing unions in favor of "dual unionism." The first of the separate revolutionary unions was the National Textile Workers Union, created in September 1928. Among its major goals were solidarity with the USSR and the organization of textile laborers in the American South. NTWU agents selected Gastonia's Loray Mill, the largest in the area, with 3,500 workers, as a prime target.

Fred Beal, a New Bedford strike leader

and CP member, was selected to lead the Gastonia effort. Residing in nearby Charlotte for three months prior to the strike, Beal established contact with Loray workers, convincing them of the advantages of a union. On April 1, both shifts walked out, demanding increased wages, a forty-hour week, abolition of the notorious stretch-out system, and union recognition. Rejecting their demands, mill owners organized a "Committee of One Hundred" to fight the union. The local press incited citizens to violence, urging destruction of the strike and the "Red Russianism" inspiring it; the governor called in the National Guard to break up the picket lines.

While the AFL denounced the strike, CP officials in New York sent representatives of the Workers International Relief, the International Labor Defense, the Young Communist League, the Young Pioneers, and the *Daily Worker* to Gastonia. Directions from central headquarters, in accord with goals of the international Communist movement, often proved inappropriate for the Gastonia situation. Despite insufficient funds for the Loray strike, Party leaders called for a general strike throughout the textile South. Although only two blacks worked in Loray Mill, the Party made racial equality a central issue in the rhetoric surrounding the strike, antagonizing white mill-workers as well as the "uptown" community.

Intent on ending the strike, policemen terrorized picket lines composed largely of women and children, an armed mob demolished union headquarters, and mill owners evicted strikers from company houses. In an exchange of gunfire on the night of June 7, the chief of police was slain. Sixteen strikers and leaders, including Beal and three women organizers—Vera Buch, Sophie Melvin, and Amy Schecter—were charged with first-degree murder. In major cities throughout the Western World, groups of the political Left gathered petitions and demonstrated in the streets on behalf of the accused.

At the trial, the defendants confined their testimonies to the facts of the case, but witness Edith Miller shocked the courtroom by denouncing capitalism and religion, and proclaiming the virtues of the Soviet system. Seven of the accused were found guilty of second-degree murder, charges having been dropped against the other nine. Released on bail provided by the ACLU, the defendants fled to the Soviet Union, where four remained permanently. In contrast, when mill worker and ballad singer Ella May Wiggins was slain in a hall of gunfire on September 14, the five Loray employees indicted for her murder were never convicted.

Although Loray Mill workers gained a slightly reduced work week and the eventual abolition of night work for women and children, the strike of 1929 was a failure. Throughout the South, textile labor remained unorganized. Yet the Gastonia strike left its mark on proletarian literature. In the very year of the strike, Michael Gold, editor of the *New Masses*, urged young American writers to "go left" for a firsthand knowledge of working-class life.

To go left was to go South, to Gastonia for rich material that fed the imaginations of novelists eager to employ "art as a class weapon." The political issues and violent drama of the Gastonia strike inspired no fewer than six novels in the 1930s: Mary Heaton Vorse, *Strike!* (1930); Sherwood Anderson, *Beyond Desire* (1932); Fielding Burke (Olive Tilford Dargan), *Call Home the Heart* (1932); Grace Lumpkin, *To Make My Bread* (1932), recipient of the Maxim Gorky Award for the best labor novel of the year; Myra Page, *Gathering Storm: A Story of the Black Belt* (1932); and William Rollins, *The Shadow Before* (1934).

For realistic portrayals of mill workers, the four women novelists surpassed the more experimental novels of Rollins and Anderson. Vorse, Page, Lumpkin, and Burke were especially sensitive to the problems of women as mill workers and activists. Lumpkin and Vorse portray fictional representations of strike martyr Ella May Wiggins; Burke feminizes her rebellious heroine; and Page makes the problems of black women central to her work. In addressing issues of gender as well as class, women novelists added an essential dimension to proletarian fiction. *See also*: Textile Unions, Trade Union Unity League

—*Christina L. Baker*

REFERENCES

Beal, Fred E. *Proletarian Journey, New England, Gastonia, Moscow*. New York: Hillman-Curl, 1937.

Cochran, Bert. *Labor and Communism: The Conflict That Shaped American Unions*. Princeton: Princeton University Press, 1977.

Lacey, Candida Ann. "Engendering Conflict: American Women and the Making of a Proletarian Fiction (With Particular Reference to the Period 1929 to 1935)." Ph.D. diss. University of Sussex, 1985.

Pope, Liston. *Millhands and Preachers: A Study of Gastonia*. New Haven: Yale University Press, 1942.

Weisbord, Vera Buch. *A Radical Life*. Bloomington: Indiana University Press, 1977.

Gay/Lesbian Liberation Movement

On June 27, 1969, the patrons of the Stonewall Inn, a gay bar in New York's Greenwich Village, reacted angrily and violently to a police raid. The unprecedented response to police harassment sparked three days of rioting. That revolt is now recognized as the inception of a process that has transformed gays and lesbians into a minority group with its own issues, culture, and a politics very much on the Left of the U.S. political spectrum. Every year on the last Sunday of June, Stonewall is commemorated by massive Gay Pride marches in New York City and San Francisco as well as smaller manifestations throughout the United States. These events constitute some of the largest political mobilizations since the anti–Vietnam War rallies.

Intellectual and political developments in Europe prior to Stonewall, particularly in the USSR and Germany, had enormous impact on the way gay liberation in the United States evolved. The conceptualization of "homosexual" as an identity as opposed to isolated sexual acts occurred for the first time in the second half of the nineteenth century. In 1869 Karoly Benkert, a Hungarian doctor, coined the word *homosexual*. Recognizing the scapegoating function that the homosexual served for a repressive society, Benkert joined the Scientific Humanitarian Committee, founded in 1897 by a German doctor Magnus Hirschfeld, to further tolerance toward gays and lesbians.

The committee's efforts remained focused on circulating a petition among prominent people calling for the removal of the paragraph from the German criminal code criminalizing homosexual acts. Socialist August Bebel spoke in favor of the petition in the Reichstag on January 13, 1898, and from that time leaders of the Social Democratic Party, including Karl Kautsky and Eduard Bernstein, became its primary supporters. From abroad this campaign was supported by Emile Zola, Leo Tolstoy, and Sigmund Freud, who insisted that "inverts cannot be regarded as degenerate."

The SDP took up the cause and *Die Neue Zeit*, its newspaper, carried news of the gay movement. In its pages, Bernstein defended Oscar Wilde (who had propagandized for socialism and protested against the execution of the Haymarket martyrs). Bernstein argued against the notion that homosexuality was unnatural by noting that "moral attitudes are historical phenomena" and reflect a society's stage of development rather than any genuine state of nature.

Hirschfeld's work led to the founding of the World League for Sexual Reform, which at its peak had affiliated organizations with a total membership of 130,000. The Nazis' rise to power forced Hirschfeld—triply threatened as a Jew, a Leftist, and a homosexual—into exile. On May 6, 1933, at 9:30 A.M., storm troopers raided the Institute of Sexual Science, which housed the World League for Sexual Reform. A few days later, in a torchlight procession, the Nazis impaled on a pike a bust of Hirschfeld and threw it on a pyre with the institute's 10,000 books. In 1935, while trying to reestablish the institute in France, Hirschfeld died.

The Nazis, extending penalties against homosexuals for actions that included thinking homosexual thoughts, murdered tens and perhaps hundreds of thousands of homosexuals. They summarily shot those homosexuals found in the military and delivered those found in the general society to concentration camps. Tagged with the pink triangle, homosexuals inhabited the ninth circle of this hell. Even to this day, organizations speaking for other categories of Holocaust victims have difficulty acknowledging their sharing the pyre with homosexuals.

The Soviet Union had sent official delegations to the world conferences of the World

League for Sexual Reform. The League held Soviet law as the model because legislation by the Bolshevik government in December 1917 treated sodomy exactly the same as vaginal intercourse. The German Communist Party had supported the movement to decriminalize homosexuality and under the leadership of Wilhelm Reich had formed the *Deutscher Reichsverband für Prolitarische Sexualpolitik*, which attracted more than 20,000 members.

Shortly after the Nazi constitutional coup, however, the CP of the Soviet Union altered its official ideology to define homosexuality "the product of decadence in the bourgeois sector of society." Moreover, it increasingly linked homosexuality to counterrevolution. Mass arrests of gays began and in March 1934 the state introduced a law punishing homosexual acts with imprisonment up to eight years.

Individuals elsewhere had taken up this cause. Most notably Edward Carpenter (1844–1929), an English man of letters, envisioned a revolution destroying the existing "commercial regime" and replacing it with a new society embodying "to the fullest extent the two opposite poles of Communism and Individualism in one vital unity." But it was only in Germany where a sustained movement existed. Furthermore, although the gay rights movement had attracted the positive attention of many liberals, it was clearly a manifestation of the Left. The Soviet Union's repudiation of civil equality for gays and lesbians caused the Left to withdraw from this struggle.

Within the United States, expressions of support for homosexuality were limited to passages from Walt Whitman's poems, certain writings and lectures of Emma Goldman, and a short-lived Society for Human Rights established in Chicago in 1923. Therefore the United States was an unlikely place for the reemergence of the gay and lesbian movement. Even more unlikely was the time—1950.

In Los Angeles, a long-term CP member, Harry Hay, invited four friends to discuss the formation of an organization for the purpose of "liberating one of our largest minorities from . . . social persecution." By 1951 under Hay's leadership, several Communists and Leftists founded the Mattachine Society (named after *mattachines*, mysterious medieval figures in masks who Hay surmised were homosexual). Mattachine viewed gays and lesbians as an oppressed cultural minority suffering from a false consciousness caused by the internalization of the dominant culture's defamatory conception of gays and lesbians. Further borrowing from the Marxist-Leninist ideological armature, it saw the task of liberating homosexuals as the responsibility of homosexuals themselves, who alone could substitute for lives based on "self-deceit, hypocrisy, and charlatanism" an "ethical homosexual culture" based on a "new pride . . . in participating in the cultural growth and social achievements of . . . the homosexual minority."

The Mattachine Society's highly centralized structure, reflecting the CP background of its founders, consisted of a pyramid of five "orders" of membership with increased levels of responsibility. The fifth order, comprising the founders, had representatives in the fourth order, representatives from the fourth had representatives in the third, etc. The leadership expected this structure to duplicate itself as the society grew.

At this time all but two states classified sodomy as a felony, with only murder, kidnapping, and rape eliciting heavier sentences. Psychiatry branded the homosexual as pathological, and religion castigated homosexual activity as sinful. The entire culture of the fifties reaffirmed traditional gender roles, casting further outside the pale those who deviated from the sexual norms.

In tandem with the anticommunist hysteria of the time, the government conducted an as yet largely unacknowledged, antihomosexual witch-hunt. In 1950 the chair of the Republican Party asserted that "sexual perverts who have infiltrated our government in recent years . . . [are] perhaps as dangerous as the actual Communists." That same year, the Senate authorized an investigation into the presence of homosexuals "and other moral perverts" in the government. Its report argued that homosexuals lacked the "emotional stability of normal persons" and had a weakened moral fiber and warned that even "one homosexual can pollute a government office." By emphasizing the risk that homosexuals could be lured or blackmailed into betrayal of the United States, the Senate report directly linked the homosexual, the sexual subversive, to the Communist, the political subversive.

Starting in 1950 the number of homosexuals dismissed from the federal government's employ rose from 5 to 60 per month. Under Eisenhower, the loyalty-security program explicitly listed "sexual perversion" as sufficient cause for disbarment from federal jobs. Contrasting with the relatively tolerant attitudes during World War II in the military, the number of "undesirable discharges" (an administrative remedy that precluded all due process guarantees) for homosexuality doubled to 2,000 per year and then rose to 3,000 in 1960. The FBI fed the Civil Service Commission an endless stream of names of alleged homosexuals garnered from its contacts with local police departments. The Postal Department added to this blacklist by putting tracers on the mail of subscribers of suspect magazines. During the fifties, arrests of homosexuals—many through entrapment—exceeded 1,000 per year in Washington, D.C., and 1,200 per year in Philadelphia.

Defying the powerful currents that were causing all manifestations of nonconformity to retreat, the Mattachine Society grew. The Society's semipublic discussion groups had a profound impact on their participants, many of whom for the first time found themselves together with others who affirmed their homosexuality.

When in February 1952 one of Mattachine's founding members became a victim of entrapment by the Los Angeles Police Department, the fifth order decided to fight back by organizing a front group, the Citizens Committee to Outlaw Entrapment. Gays and lesbians responded to Mattachine literature: they joined in increasing numbers and contributed generously to the legal defense fund. The defendant admitted to the court that he was homosexual but denied the charges against him. A deadlocked jury—eleven for acquittal—caused the district attorney's office to drop the charges. This absolutely unprecedented fightback in the history of gay and lesbian people caused Mattachine to grow to more than 2,000 participants organized into nearly 100 discussion groups.

In January 1953 members of the Mattachine founded *One*, the first homosexual magazine, whose circulation soon reached 2,000. In October 1954, the Los Angeles postmaster seized copies of *One* as "obscene, lewd, lascivious, and filthy." The editors contested the supression of their journal and in January 1958 the U.S. Supreme Court unanimously reversed the findings of the lower courts.

Hay and the other original leadership cadre (who had already resigned from the CP) became the target of increasingly pointed Red-baiting by the press and within the Society's ranks. At Mattachine's first convention, held in Los Angeles in April 1953, the delegates supported the leadership's positions opposing McCarthyite attacks on the Society and affirming the conception of gays and lesbians as a minority with its own culture. Nonetheless the leadership's fear that their recent political affiliation with the CP would destroy Mattachine caused them to resign. Into the vacuum stepped the conservative spokespersons whose ideological positions had just been defeated.

Within a short time the new leadership replaced Mattachine's radical imprint with an orientation that viewed gays and lesbians as individuals who, except for their sexual preferences, were just like everyone else. Its political thrust consisted of attempts to enlist leading academics and legal experts in the cause of legal equality for gays and lesbians. Now Mattachine published pamphlets reassuring their readers that "homosexuals are not seeking to overthrow or destroy any of society's existing institutions, laws, or mores, but to be assimilated as constructive, valuable, and responsible citizens." The membership and presence of the Mattachine Society declined precipitously. By 1955, however, membership began to increase again and the publication of the *Mattachine Review* gave renewed impetus to the organization.

Lesbians had participated in the Mattachine Society in small numbers. From the first, it became clear that the Society's agenda did not coincide with the central needs of lesbians. Overriding concern with legal entrapment and persecution resulting from cruising and patronizing gay bars remained irrelevant for lesbians, whose lives tended to be organized around long-term relationships and friendship networks. Lesbians shared the castelike status as legal and moral pariahs, but they also experienced oppression as women. Even within organizations dedicated to gay and lesbian rights, women were often patronized and marginalized.

The Daughters of Bilitis and its publication, the *Ladder,* were founded in 1955 to forward the specific needs of lesbians within the context of the movement for equality for all regardless of sexual orientation. DOB worked closely with *One* and Mattachine. Nonetheless, as late as 1959, Del Martin, one of the founders of DOB, had to remind the delegates to a Mattachine Convention: "Lesbians are not satisfied to be auxiliary members or second-class homosexuals." Mattachine and DOB subsidized their publications, provided support for their membership, and attempted to influence opinion makers. Outside events would soon engulf these enclaves.

The effort to have gays and lesbians recognized as nonconformists rather than deviants began to gain scientific support when Alfred Kinsey (whose studies revealed a much more widespread incidence of homosexual behaviors than previously estimated) and Evelyn Hooker (whose pioneering sociological studies of the gay community suggested no greater incidence of psychological disturbance than in the general population) challenged the psychological and genetic understanding of homosexuality.

The emergence of an openly gay and lesbian community provided a haven where life independent of the straight world could be contemplated. An early expression of this lifestyle was practiced by Beats in the 1950s, who propounded a way of life defying society's conventions—including its rules and regulations about sexual relationships. Many of the most important figures in the beatnik movement were gay, including its poet laureate, Allen Ginsberg.

The Beat Generation's effect was largely limited to relatively small groups in some of the largest cities, and it had nothing to offer to women (that is, "chicks"), no less lesbians. The counterculture of the sixties with its rejection of the conventional view of respectability and promotion of individualistic, sensual, and spontaneous expression provided a larger space within which gays and lesbians could begin to live openly. The counterculture's respect for diversity encouraged many gays and lesbians to see their sexuality as something other than an affliction.

That a great center of the Beat Generation and the nascent counterculture, San Francisco, first experienced a mass gay and lesbian movement is no coincidence. Police raids on gay bars—always a problem for gays—reached extreme proportions in 1960. Misdemeanor charges resulting from raids began to total forty to sixty per week. In August 1961 the police arrested more than one hundred patrons of a gay bar. In October the Alcoholic Beverages Commission revoked the liquor licenses of twelve gay bars. Resistance originated when the ABC started proceedings against the Black Cat as a "resort for sexual perverts." José Sarria, a performer at the Black Cat, achieved great fame within the gay and lesbian community for his consciousness-raising satires. He is especially remembered for ending his performances by having the audience rise, hold hands, and sing "God Save Us Nelly Queens." In 1961 he ran for city supervisor as an open homosexual and a drag queen and garnered 6,000 votes.

Subsequently, the homosexual rights organization Society for Individual Rights and the publication *Vector*—with the support of the tavern owners—emerged out of the bar milieu with participation and circulation greatly exceeding those of the traditional homophile movement. This underscored the centrality of the bars for gays and to a lesser extent for lesbians. It was only in the bars that gays achieved a public space that they controlled. For many it was only place they could feel truly comfortable, at home, and not alone. By the 1980s there were a greater variety of institutions—churches, community centers, restaurants, political clubs—that served these purposes.

The early organization of gays out of the

somewhat unedifying bar milieu explains why gay political power first developed in San Francisco. It also indicated that the gay and lesbian political movement would grow out of an approach that affirmed and helped develop the community while fighting political battles with the straight world.

One of those battles was to elect gay activists to public office. The landmark event in that effort was the election in 1977 of Harvey Milk as city supervisor of San Francisco. Milk's achievement was given a tragic dimension when shortly after taking office he was murdered by a defeated right-wing candidate. The light prison sentence given to his killer led to serious riots in the Bay area. Since Milk's election, a number of politicians at various levels of government had been open about their homosexual orientation. The most prominent of these is Congressman Barney Frank of Massachusetts.

The liberalized milieu of the sixties gave rise to the women's movement—somewhat in advance of the gay liberation movement. From the beginning these movements showed certain tensions, and only gradually their underlying broader unity of purpose. The publication of Betty Friedan's *Feminine Mystique* in 1963 and the founding of the National Organization of Women in 1966 announced the existence of a women's movement. In the June 1967 issue of the *Ladder,* Del Martin registered one of the first responses to the new feminism from within the growing gay and lesbian movement: "The Lesbian, after all, is first of all a *woman*—an individual who must earn her own livelihood . . . much more concerned with problems of inequality in job and educational opportunities." The logic of this position led Martin to argue in favor of lesbians leaving homophile organizations in order to participate in NOW, the League of Women Voters, and women's professional organizations.

NOW's ambivalence towards open lesbianism within its ranks surfaced when conservatives led by Friedan made efforts to purge lesbians from elected office. Friedan's effort was defeated and in 1971; and NOW went on record to acknowledge "the double oppression of women who are lesbians" and that "the oppression of lesbians [is] a legitimate concern of feminism." Nonetheless, most straight women cringed when Ti-Grace Atkinson declared that "feminism is the theory; lesbianism is the practice."

The subordination of lesbian issues to those of heterosexual women within the woman's movement established the need for gay men and women to remain united against homophobia and for antidiscrimination legislation. Within this natural alliance, however, gay men had to struggle to overcome their own male chauvinism and acknowledge independent lesbian concerns. Both gay men and gay women got their most consistent nongay support from feminists. The mutual concern was patriarchy, defined as the supremacy of the masculine gender with rights conceded to inherent violence and superior physical strength. Gays and lesbians benefit enormously from the blurring of gender categories in daily life. The diminution of sexual stereotyping particularly reduces their being targeted as freaks. Only when women are no longer devalued will genuine equality for gays and lesbians be possible.

In the same way that "Black Is Beautiful" encapsulated the Black Power movement, "Gay Is Good" epitomized the outlook of the new gay and lesbian politics. Modeling itself on the concepts of the black militants, this branch of the gay and lesbian movement no longer sought acceptance by the dominant culture. The evolving gay and lesbian minority demanded respect for its own lifestyles however much at variance with those of the wider society. It demanded equality, not acculturation and total integration.

Organized shortly after Stonewall, the Gay Liberation Front forwarded a politics that joined the gay and lesbian movement to other movements committed to the radical reordering of society. The openly gay contingents at peace marches and pro–Black Panther demonstrations often met hostility. Most wrenching of all were the verifications of widespread persecutions of homosexuals in Cuba.

In response, the Gay Activist Alliance (GAA), founded in 1970, focused solely on the needs of the gay and lesbian community. It set out a clear statement of principle: "We as liberated homosexual activists demand the freedom for expression of our dignity and value as human beings through confrontation with and disarmament of all mechanisms which unjustly inhibit us." (The GAA first used the now-universal symbol the Greek letter *lambda*, because in physics it symbolized wave length.) The GAA began circulating petitions to public officials calling upon them to introduce legislation to eliminate discrimination against gays and lesbians.

Directly inspired by the civil rights movement, from which it frequently borrowed its tactics and strategies, the GAA's focus on antidiscrimination legislation has provided the arena for the greatest degree of unity between gay men and lesbians and the various ideological tendencies and lifestyles present in their communities. The passage of antidiscrimination legislation represents the most visible expressions of progress. Half the states have decriminalized homosexual acts, and fifty counties and municipalities (which comprise 10 percent of the country's population) have passed legislation barring discrimination against gays and lesbians.

Of inestimable importance to the progress of the gay and lesbian movement was the declaration in 1973 of the American Psychiatric Association and the American Psychological Association that homosexual orientation was not, in itself, an illness. The removal of the stigma of homosexuality as a mental illness has not been met by a similar move to eliminate homosexuality as a sin by organized religions. The Unitarian Church and the Metropolitan Community churches accept homosexual marriages, and liberal Protestant denominations—especially the Quakers, the Disciples of Christ, and the United Church of Christ—have supported antidiscrimination campaigns, but the largest denominations—especially Orthodox Judaism, Roman Catholicism, and the fundamentalist Protestants—remain a mass ideological base for the perpetuation of the oppression of gays and lesbians.

The strengthening of the gay and lesbian community has increased its power to fight for its rights. The gay and lesbian newspapers, softball teams, choruses, Democratic Party clubs, bars, and AA meetings provide the basis for self-affirmation, self-expression, and the ability to lead lives not twisted out of shape by fear, self-loathing, and hiding. Although gay men and lesbians are found in every class, as an organized political force they inevitably become part of the liberal to radical side of the country's political life. As the stewards of tradition and nostalgia, the Right can never concede "the family"—that is to say, patriarchy. In ways far more radical than even the feminist movement, gays and lesbians represent a subversion of the patriarchal family. Support for even the most minimal degree of gay and lesbian rights is inconceivable from this quarter. Moreover, the Right seems unable to resist active gay-baiting. The religious Right would be at a serious loss to fill its television slots without homophobia, which in its sermons and tracts rivals abortion for condemnation.

Support for the gay and lesbian movement has grown within liberal institutions such as the American Civil Liberties Union, which in 1964 reversed its 1957 policy sustaining the constitutionality of the sodomy statues and the security regulations barring gays from federal employment. In 1980 the Democratic Party included a gay-rights plank in its national platform.

Marxist organizations have had a mixed record regarding gay rights. The Communist Party has not supported the movement in any fashion and barely mentions it in its press. The various Maoist groups have generally followed in the same mold. During the 1970s, when some 3,000 or so activists oriented toward Maoism tried to form a new Marxist movement, many of the participating groups did not allow gays as members and considered homosexual behavior to be antisocial. This antigay position derived from the conviction that political organization must be based on class and that any deviation from that outlook was a bourgeois luxury. Gay rights are seen as civil rights issues at best with a good possibility that gayness may indeed be a psychological illness.

Trotskyism, which in its totality in the 1970s also numbered about 3,000, had a different evolution. The major Trotskyist group, the Socialist Workers Party, was antigay until a major shift in the mid-1970s. At that time some SWP leaders revealed that they were gay, and gay issues have since been energetically advanced as part of the SWP program. Most of the smaller Trotskyist sects also support gay liberation, the Workers World Party being particularly vigorous.

Democratic Socialists of America, the largest socialist organization, has leaders who are gay and supports gay rights without making them prime issues. The Socialist Party has run a gay for president. The two Left newspapers of highest circulation, the *Guardian* and *In These Times* promote gay liberation, as have many of the radical quarterlies. *Radical America*, in the 1980s, has been especially strong in its advocacy. The same is true of Left cultural organs such as *Jump Cut, Heresies*, and *Ikon*. The first radio programs devoted to gay rights were aired in 1962 on WBAI, the New York station of the Pacifica Foundation.

The more gays and lesbians organize on their own behalf, the more they find their affinity with other despised minorities. The system's tolerance of the failure of the public school system in the ghettoes is mirrored in the indifference of the system to the AIDS epidemic. As a result of this reality, African-American leadership has accepted gays and lesbians as full-fledged members of the Rainbow Coalition. For example, black congresspeople almost without exception have co-sponsored legislation to outlaw discrimination against gays. To date, the Rev. Jesse Jackson is the only leader of national prominence who has embraced the movement's full agenda, including spousal rights, the rights of gay and lesbian parents to claim custody of their children, and the decriminalization of sodomy. His 1988 campaign platform stated: "Historically, lesbians and gay men have made great contributions to humankind, yet they have often had to live under conditions of intense oppression. . . . The humanity of lesbians and gay men must be recognized and their rights fully respected." He addressed over half a million demonstrators at the October 11, 1987, National March on Washington for Lesbian and Gay Rights who mobilized around a platform that included a call for an end to sexism, racism, and apartheid. Not surprisingly, gays and lesbians constituted a major portion of Jackson's white supporters.

Organizations in the forefront of the struggle to advance gay liberation include the Lambda Legal Defense and Education Fund, which provides legal support for test cases; the Gay and Lesbian Task Force (the first gay and lesbian group with a paid staff and national mission), which provides lobbying resources for initiatives such as the statistical basis for the inclusion of gays and lesbians in antidiscrimination measures; and the Gay and Lesbian Alliance Against Discrimination, which has convinced a score of major newspapers and television stations to provide balanced reporting on gay and lesbian issues. The many gay and lesbian caucuses in organizations such as the American Library Association and the Democratic Party are also making significant contributions.

The assertion of homosexual identification ("coming out") has been recognized as the prime step in the emancipation from the internalization of society's homophobia. What appears to be a personal act is, in fact, a profoundly political act. The potential risks include loss of employment, ostracism from family and community, excommunication from churches, and being targeted for violence. This set of circumstances usually leads to an identification of gay and lesbian communities as the primary sources of support and compensation. Organizations based on those communities become the political vehicles for establishing basic political and human rights.

The agenda of the gay and lesbian movement is a long one. Like rape, violence against gays is underreported. The National Gay and Lesbian Task Force found that more than one in five gay men and nearly one in ten lesbians had been physically assaulted in some manner. The murder of gay men is not uncommon and their perpetrators are most often lightly punished.

The federal government explicitly discriminates against gays and lesbians in the military, the CIA, the FBI, the National Security Agency, and the State Department. It refuses to give security clearance to gays and lesbians. Discrimination continues by state and local governments, private employers, landlords, immigration and naturalization agencies, insurers of all types, and custody and adoption organizations.

Antisodomy laws applying to same-sex adult couples are on the books in twenty-four states and the District of Columbia. These laws, though often no longer enforced, create a devalued sexual category. The movement to remove these statutes has come to a halt because the 1986 Supreme Court decision on *Bowers* v. *Hardwick* found that the Constitution does not "confer a fundamental right upon homosexuals to engage in sodomy."

The response of the gay and lesbian community to the AIDS epidemic is one of the best examples of communal self-organization in modern United States history. The Gay Men's Health Crisis (founded 1981) has pioneered in every aspect of the AIDS epidemic. ACT-UP (AIDS Coalition to Unleash Power) has taken to the streets to demand that the federal Food and Drug Agency release drugs suspected of combating some aspect of the AIDS syndrome prior to the completion of the total testing process, and that housing be created for people with AIDS.

The most unifying issue arising from the gay and lesbian community is the demand for legal recognition of "domestic partnerships." Berkeley, California, has passed domestic-partner legislation giving gay couples the same rights to city benefits as married couples. San Francisco's Board of Supervisors approved a law allowing unmarried partners, both heterosexual and homosexual, to register their relationships with the city. The AIDS epidemic has been responsible for thrusting this issue to the forefront. Innumerable gays have been denied visitation rights in hospitals where their life-partners lay dying. Lovers and friends have been denied access to funerals of gay men by families who previously had shunned the deceased. There are constantly cases in which bereaved gay or lesbian partners have to leave their homes after the death of their loved ones because there was no legal way of getting their name on the lease. This fight by gays and lesbians for recognition of their relationships has potentially wide import in a nation where only 27 percent of the households contain two parents living with children.

Increasing numbers of lesbians and gays are determined to obtain custody and visitation based solely on their parenting. Gays and lesbians are also demanding the right to adopt and to care for foster children. The growing visibility of stable gay and lesbian families with children threatens a liberalism that can tolerate deviant sexual relationships but may not be prepared to grant equal status to those hitherto marginalized by their sexual orientation. A wider consequence of the insistence of gays and lesbians for recognition of their relationships as familial has been the expansion of the rights of other nontraditional households through court decisions, union contracts, legislation, and executive orders. Gays and lesbians have been in the forefront of those demanding that society define "family" as an affectional and economic unit committed to the mutual benefit of its members and not a patriarchal relationship sanctioned by tradition, church, and state.

By the end of the 1980s, activists had identified the forces opposing gay liberation as the same forces opposing greater rights for other minorities and oppressed groups. As the Right increasingly stressed traditional values and social structures as a means of attracting and holding electoral support, gays and lesbians found their natural allies to be somewhere on the Left. Radical and liberal organizations, in turn, increasingly accepted gay rights as givens of the progressive agenda. *See also*: The Beats and the New Left, New Left, Socialist Feminism, Stonewall Riots, Women's Liberation

—*Gerald Meyer*

REFERENCES

Altman, Dennis. *The Homosexualization of America*. Boston: Beacon Press, 1983.

D'Emilio, John. *Sexual Politics, Sexual Communities: The Making of a Homosexual Minority in the United States, 1940–1970*. Chicago: University of Chicago Press, 1983.

Fernbach, David. *The Spiral Path: A Gay Contribution to Human Survival*. Boston: Alyson Publications, 1981.

Lauritsen, John, and David Thorstad. *The Early Homosexual Rights Movement (1864–1935)*. New York: Times Change Press, 1974.

Marotta, Toby. *The Politics of Homosexuality*. Boston: Houghton Mifflin, 1981.

Mieli, Mario. *Homosexuality and Liberation: Elements of a Gay Critique*. London: Gay Men's Press, 1980.

Mohr, Richard D. *Gays/Justice: A Study of Ethics, Society, and Law*. New York: Columbia University Press, 1988.

Von Praunheim, Rosa. *Army of Lovers*. London: Gay Men's Press, 1980.

Weiss, Andrea, and Greta Schiller. *Before Stonewall: The Making of a Gay and Lesbian Community*. Tallahassee: Naiad Press, 1988.

GELLERT, HUGO (1892–1985)

Famous as one of the least overtly political artists of the *Masses* magazine, Gellert devoted most of his long political life to the Communist movement and in particular to its Hungarian language group, of which he was unquestionably the most famous member.

Born in Budapest, the son of a tailor, Gellert moved with his family to New York at the turn of the century. By his teens, he had developed a double life. He Americanized himself easily, through literature, work as a machinist, and early design work on posters. Simultaneously, he became active with his older brothers in the Hungarian language federation of the Socialist Party, where he gained minor celebrity as an amateur athlete.

Gellert reached his artistic turning point when he attended the National Academy of Design and won a prize trip in 1914 to Paris. He intended to enroll at the Académie Julian, but instead was drawn to the sweeping style of contemporary commercial art, specifically the Michelin tire posters. After a walking tour across Europe, he returned to New York to begin antiwar cartoons for the Hungarian-American daily *Elöre*, while making his living in commercial lithography. In 1916 he gravitated to the *Masses*, and while not joining the staff, he contributed some of the most memorable drawings, famous for their innocence, occasional abstraction, and apparently nonpolitical character.

Capitalism's favorite method of disposing of unneeded labor power: War
From *Karl Marx's Capital in Lithographs*.

With the *Liberator*, Gellert became more directly political, drawing its first cover and serving on its editorial board until the magazine's last days. Its absence "keenly felt," as he recalled, he helped found the *New Masses* and contributed illustrations in a variety of styles to its pages. He made a commercial living contributing generally realistic illustrations to the *New York World* and the *New Yorker*. During the Depression, he exercised wide influence as director of the John Reed School of Art, chair of Artists Committee of Action, and initiator and prominent activist of the American Artists Congress and a founder of the Mural Artists Guild of the United Scenic Painters, AFL-CIO. As an artist, he created the billboard design for the Sacco-Vanzetti defense campaign, painted murals for the workers' cafeteria (at CPUSA headquarters), did lithographs for a 1933 edition of *Capital*, and exhibited his work widely.

Gellert was also extremely active with the Hungarian-American Left, drawing frequently for *Elore* and campaigning on nationally related issues. He played a key role in the 1927 formation of the Anti-Horthy League (against the existing Hungarian government), the second antifascist movement after the Italian-

American anti-Mussolini efforts. During the Second World War, he joined actor Bela Lugosi, composer Béla Bartók, and others in a wide Hungarian-American mobilization.

During the 1950s–1970s, he continued to contribute his art widely, on racism, militarism, and (in a noted poster for Local 1199, Hospital Workers) the cause of unionism. *See also*: Congress of American Artists, *Liberator, Masses, New Masses*

—*Paul Buhle*

REFERENCES

Deak, Zoltan, ed. *This Noble Flame: An Anthology of a Hungarian Newspaper in America, 1902–1982*. New York: Heritage Press, 1982.

Gellert, Hugo. Interview by Paul Buhle. OHAL Archives, New York University.

General Strike

A general strike occurs when all the workers in a given industry, region, or nation strike simultaneously with the same demands. As far as leftists are concerned, the general strike may be regarded as a tactical or a strategic weapon. If tactical, the general strike, like other strikes, has limited objectives. General strikes of this nature have occurred in various American cities, most notably in Seattle (1919) and San Francisco (1934). In movements influenced by anarcho-syndicalist theories, the general strike is viewed as a revolutionary weapon capable of ending capitalism. This view is distinct from the parliamentary strategy associated with the Socialist Party or the vanguard party concept of Marxist-Leninists.

Anarcho-syndicalists reject the parliamentary road on the grounds that worker power is maximal at the point of production, not at the ballot box. Elections are seen as based on relatively meaningless geographic divisions and conducted in a manner that favors middle- and ruling-class interests. At the turn of the century, when anarcho-syndicalism was strongest in the United States, the electoral road appeared particularly unappealing and essentially undemocratic. Women, workers under the age of twenty-one, and most new immigrants could not vote. Millions of migratory workers did not have a stable address to use for registration purposes, and minorities such as blacks were prevented from voting in the very venues where they were a majority or a significant percent of the population.

Leninism was rejected on the grounds that a genuine transvaluation of old values could not be accomplished by a group of highly trained and professional revolutionaries, however well intentioned. Change must flow from the direct action of millions of workers satisfying their needs and honing their skills through democratically operated unions. Each strike would serve as a training ground in self-management in an ever-expanding movement that would culminate in the national general strike. The last strike, the ultimate revolutionary moment, would succeed only if each individual union had already developed a constellation of leaders from its own ranks. Common sense and direct-action experience—not abstract ideology, organizational discipline, or parliamentary guile—would distinguish these leaders.

The strategy of the general strike was most aggressively put forth in the United States by the Industrial Workers of the World during its peak period of 1905–23. The IWW "Preamble" stated that the solution to economic and social injustice lay in the creation of a worker-controlled system called industrial democracy. The primary task of revolutionaries was to create industrial unions that would fight for gains within the system until strong enough to call a general strike able to bring all economic life to a halt. The conditions for returning to work would be the substitution of industrial unions for all business enterprises and governmental activity. The means of production would then be run by unions to satisfy social needs rather than private profit. What had been done in one nation would be duplicated throughout the globe. *See also*: Direct Action, Industrial Workers of the World, Vanguard Party

—*Dan Georgakas*

REFERENCES

Chaplin, Ralph. *The General Strike*. New ed. Chicago: IWW, 1982.

Krimerman, Leonard I., and Lewis Perry, eds. *Patterns of Anarchy*. New York: Anchor-Doubleday, 1966.

German Americans

The first important ethnic socialist group in the United States, German Americans established institutions, styles, and a political-cultural perspective that remained substantially constant for most immigrant groups until 1920 and in subtle ways continuous to the 1940s–1950s.

Arriving in several large waves of immigration from the 1830s to the 1890s, reaching a peak of a quarter-million in 1882 alone, Germans would differ in important respects from most other immigrant-radical groups. First of all, they came from a political culture that, despite its internal divisions, bore little resemblance to an oppressed nationality. German working-class immigrants, however personally impoverished, carried their particular socialist heritage of German culture in a proud, sometimes imperious way. They sought and succeeded to a large extent, until the 1890s, in imposing their standards upon other nationalities, as did German-speakers in the Austrian socialist movement.

Second, Germans brought skills and a tradition of industrial organization that enabled them to take a leading role in the development of craft unions and a variety of labor-related social institutions. Toward the end of the century, German immigration patterns had turned heavily from a mostly rural origin to a mostly industrial-urban one. But even in earlier days, the 1840s–1870s, a sufficient quota of the German immigrants had artisan background of some kind to extend their role in the fledgling American labor movement far in proportion to their actual size. Not only unions proper but newspapers, halls, public labor forums, and a variety of socialist-laborist institutions bore their stamp.

Third, in matter of timing, German-American socialists moved into the forefront as the older "natural rights" radicalism (highlighted in the Civil War crusade to abolish slavery) ran aground on the increasing division of social classes. German-Americans established the first Communist Club, by way of relations with Marx himself, and outnumbered all others in the American wing of the First International. As the small numbers and occasional enthusiasm of native-born socialists waxed and waned erratically, Germans resigned themselves to the task of bellwethers. Like Jews in the 1910–40 period, but with a class-cultural autonomy in mass society later inconceivable, they tended rightly or wrongly to judge all phases of American radicalism by their own standard.

This hegemony proved remarkably enduring also because German Americans proved the most stable socialist grouping, in class and political terms. Working-class households tended to remain so, as years and a generation or so passed. Political loyalties altered very little, relative to the fast-paced American scene. As late as the 1910s, Germans (by this time mostly well into middle age) dominated the membership rolls of the Socialist Party in greater New York. As late as the 1920s–1930s, Milwaukee, the Germanic city of beer making and *Turnvereins* (gymnastic societies), continued with a municipal socialist experiment abandoned or never approached elsewhere.

All this success, it might be argued, came at a considerable price. German-American socialists suffered, through the entire history of their collective organization, from a sense of insularity within the more chaotic, less generally class-conscious American society (and working class) at large. The problem that therefore posed itself from the 1860s onward was how German radicals might reach out to the wide potential constituency of American socialism, and yet maintain a clear class orientation.

During the German-American movement's first major phase, of the early 1870s, their leaders (principally Friedrich Sorge) desperately feared the prospect home-grown radical reformers overwhelming the immigrant socialists, and consequently expelled a majority of the First International's American section. In the second phase, the socialists, responding to the Railroad Strike of 1877, sought to encompass the most radical class forces within their own circles by opening the socialist movement to political action, American style. They watched as their newfound comrades melted away. In the third phase, of the middle 1880s, they earnestly sought to promote local labor tickets, as in the Henry

George mayorality campaign in New York City, and to coordinate craft union activity with that of the Knights of Labor. Whether socialist or "revolutionary socialist" (anarchist), they felt the cold breath of repression and public hostility fall upon them after 1886, and they withdrew to their tents for regrouping.

The German-American socialists succeeded more readily along different lines. Upbuilding their own institutions, especially the daily and weekly press in a half-dozen cities, they created a presence in the labor movement and in the German-American community that could be denounced but not easily vanquished. German culture in America, from the theater to literature to choral groups, all felt their influence. The weekly *Vorbote* (Herald) and daily *Chicagoer Arbeiter-Zeitung* (Chicago workers news), a case in point, grew out of the depression of the 1870s and consolidation of immigrant Left resources around an increasingly solid labor movement. Modeled in format and internal structure after the homeland socialist press, enjoying wide support in their neighborhoods, they survived the extreme repression following the Haymarket tragedy, and remained (*Arbeiter-Zeitung* expired in 1919, *Vorbote* in 1924) until the great majority of their readers had reached ripe old age.

Such institutions made possible the development of some of the finest leaders, both lecturer-agitators and thinkers, of the entire American Left saga. These men, largely trained in Germany, also stood in place of Left theoreticians and even Left artists in later generations, as they variously interpreted socialist doctrine in the light of American conditions, and wrote plays and poetry. One of the most distinguished, Adolph Douai, had been a noted pedagogue of the "Forty-Eighters" generation, editor of an abolitionist paper in Texas, and a writer of American travelogues for the German reader. Editor of several early German-American socialist papers, he remained the tireless editorialist at his post until his death in the late 1880s. August Otto-Walster, one of the pioneer playwrights and fictionalists of the early German Social Democracy, not only edited American socialist papers in New York, Cincinatti, and St. Louis but continued his short-story production, while serializing many of his own classics. Josef Dietzgen, widely known as an independent discoverer of historical materialist principles, in 1886 took over the Chicago *Vorbote* as its editors faced extreme persecution. Paul Grottkau, once a noted labor leader in Berlin, became a prominent anarchist-leaning editor in Chicago and Milwaukee. By the 1890s, with the end of the Bismarkian repression, the stream of such men was largely cut off. Yet figures such as the *New Yorker Volkszeitung*'s (New York people's news) Alexander Jonas remained with the paper through the 1910s, succeeded by younger German immigrant Ludwig Lore, growing old with American socialism's most venerable aging constituency.

In consolidating their own forces during the late 1870s to early 1890s, the German-American socialists also placed themselves ideally to promote smaller and newer immigrant-radical entities. In Chicago, especially, the Czech Left community accepted an avuncular relationship with the German socialists as early as the 1880s. German Jews eased the way for the new Yiddish-language institutions, including newspapers, fraternal benefit societies, and social halls. To a lesser but still important degree, German radicals helped orient incoming Slavs, Hungarians, Finns, and the emerging mass English-language socialist movement.

According to their critics, who included Friedrich Engels, they had retarded the specifically American working-class developments with their insistence upon retaining socialist political leadership for themselves. In the 1870s–1880s, a strong argument could be made for this contention (although not the same argument Engels himself would make): the growingly exclusionary approach of craft unions had made cooperation with the largely Irish-American (but also significantly black, and female) Knights of Labor problematic, limited to moments of high mobilization. For that matter, socialism at large, in order to gain a wide following in the United States, needed to lay claim to republican traditions, as the SP would do forcefully after 1900. Lacking the capacity or will to do so, German-American socialists froze their movement within a segment of the working class.

On the other hand, German-Americans rather eagerly handed over leadership of the socialist movement, i.e., the Socialist Labor Party, to non-Germans during the 1890s, with results disastrous on all sides. Embracing the young intellectual Daniel DeLeon and his short-lived following in the ghetto Jewish environment, the Germans in effect encouraged an extreme sectarianism posing simultaneously as Americanization and political-class clarification. At the end of the experiment, most Jews and others having already withdrawn, the German loyalists split with the SLP. Henceforth they would settle for a narrower gauge, in the socialist movement led by Eugene Debs. They would live out their socialist beliefs as merely one (if the most venerable) of the ethnic socialist groups that, like most others, chose the Communist alternative in the 1920s—and unlike most others, withdrew its main institutions from the Communist apparatus, to continue as an independent socialist entity to the end. *See also*: Anarcho-Syndicalism; Arbeiterbildungsvereine; Arbeiter-Sangerbund der Vereinigen Staaten; Calendars; Freie Gemeinden (Freidenker); Greie-Cramer, Johanna; Haymarket Episode; International Workingmen's Association (First International); Lehr- and Wehrvereine; Lilienthal, Meta Stern; Lore; Ludwig; Milwaukee; Most, Johann; *New Yorker Volkszeitung*; Reitzel, Robert; Socialist Labor Party; Socialist Party; Sozial-revolutionare Clubs; Sozialistischer Turnerbund; Spies, August; United Brewery Workers; Woodworkers Union.

—*Paul Buhle*

REFERENCES

Dankey, James, Ken Fones-Wolf, and Elliot Shore, eds. *The German-American Radical Press*. Urbana: University of Illinois Press, 1990.

Keil, Hartmut, ed. *German Workers' Culture in the United States, 1850 to 1920*. Washington, D.C.: Smithsonian Institution Press, 1988.

Nelson, Bruce C. *Beyond the Martyrs: A Social History of Chicago's Anarchists, 1870–1900*. New Brunswick: Rutgers University Press, 1988.

Ghent, William J.: see

Rand School

GI Coffee House Movement

In 1968 Fred Gardner opened the UFO Coffee house in Columbia, South Carolina. Its staff of anti–Vietnam War activists had the modest goal of making friendly contact with GIs from the local Fort Jackson Army base. They quickly discovered that antiwar and antiauthoritarian sentiments were almost as widespread inside the Army as out—and deeper. They were amazed at the risks GIs were willing to take in order to be part of "The Movement."

An organization called the United States Serviceman's Fund was established to help support GI activists. By 1971 the USSF was providing small grants to thirty-four GI coffee houses near Army, Navy, Air Force, and Marine bases. Some, like the Oleo Strut in Killeen, Texas (Fort Hood), and the Shelter Half in Tacoma, Washington (Fort Lewis), served hundreds of cups of coffee a night, showed movies, and provided live music on the weekends. Many of the other "coffee houses" were actually bookstores, counseling centers, or simply a house near the base with a mimeo machine.

By 1971 the USSF was also providing tiny stipends to forty-three regularly appearing GI newspapers. *FTA*, originally printed in June 1968 at Fort Knox, is sometimes cited as the first GI newspaper of the era. But the movement was so widespread and spontaneous—one incomplete survey counted 300 periodicals—that it would be risky to call any one GI

Advertisement for American Deserters Committee, late 1960s

paper the first. Titles like *Left Face, Fed Up, Fatigue Press, All Hands Abandon Ship,* and *POW* ("Every GI Is a Prisoner of War" said its masthead) indicate their tone.

As a loose fundraising organization, USSF set no program for the coffee house movement. In the "let the people decide" spirit of the time, the coffee house staffs supported a range of GI-initiated activities from mutinies to pray-ins.

As a part of the broader civilian movement, GIs joined farm workers to protest the Army's enormous purchases of grapes and lettuce. They organized mess-hall boycotts and in some cases threw the offending produce around the base. In protest against their own exploitation, a group at Fort Hood boycotted a chain of credit jewelers that preyed on servicemen in isolated base towns. Black GIs refused riot duty after Martin Luther King Jr.'s assassination. The "Fort Hood Forty-Three" were arrested for refusing duty that might put them in conflict with demonstrators at the Democratic National Convention in Chicago.

Stateside GIs invented new forms of protest ingeniously attuned to base life. One company collectively canceled their U.S. Savings Bonds, another group changed their military life-insurance beneficiary to the Black Panther Party. An Air Force nurse leafletted her base from a plane.

In Vietnam itself, antiwar activity was more dangerous and emotionally complex. Though there were coffee houses near U.S. bases in Germany and Japan, the coffee houses were never able to bring the support of lawyers, mimeograph machines, or entertainers directly into the war zone. (They tried.) Still there were several well-publicized mutinies and countless negotiated refusals that took the form "You let us sit here, and we'll let you report a body count." By the end of the war many commanders complained openly that a combination of dope and disaffection made the Army on the ground just about useless.

In movies of the 1970s and 1980s, Vietnam GIs were characterized as either betrayed patriots or confused victims—drafted, drifting, and drugged. There is some truth to each of those stereotypes. But it is also true that tens of thousands of Americans in uniform took organized, brave, and dramatic actions to end the war and to assert their own worth. *See also*: New Left, Peace Movement, Socialist Workers Party, Trotskyism

—*Barbara Garson*

REFERENCES

Cluster, Dick, ed. *They Should Have Served That Cup of Coffee*. Boston: South End Press, 1979.

Cortright, David. *Soldiers in Revolt*. New York: Anchor-Doubleday, 1975.

GILMAN, CHARLOTTE PERKINS (1860–1935)

An exceptionally popular and prolific writer on the "woman question," Gilman influenced many thousands of women through her sociological studies, novels, stories, poems, and lectures. Gilman had little direct influence upon political movements, choosing to remain unaffiliated most of her life. Her best work seemed dated by the late 1910s. But she had already created an analytical bridge between the views of the nineteenth-century woman's movement and the "scientific" socialist conceptions of woman's advance common to the early twentieth century.

Grandniece of Harriet Beecher Stowe, Gilman spent most of her economically impoverished childhood in Providence, Rhode Island. After attending college briefly, she married a local artist, and the next year gave birth to her only child. Shortly thereafter, she fell into extreme despondence, leading to near nervous collapse. Relocating to California, she gained a divorce and returned her daughter to the care of her husband, a fact treated as scandalous by Boston and California papers. Throughout the rest of her life, she suffered from the aftereffects of these experiences.

Shifting her base to the Bay Area and desperate to earn money, she turned to storywriting of an almost science fiction–like character. (Her best known story, "The Yellow Wallpaper," recounts her own mental breakdown.) A volume of poetry earned praise, and for a short time she joined the socialistic Helen Campbell in editing the organ of the Pacific Coast Woman's Press Association. Most important, she had been attracted to Edward Bellamy's ideas, and made herself a lecturer on them to groups of all kinds. As her reputation spread and she became known for her discussion of women's topics as well, she devoted most of her time to the national lecture circuit. Although little inclined to become active in the sectarian Socialist Labor Party, she attended the Second International Congress in 1896 in London as an American delegate, and contributed to the short-lived *American Fabian*.

With *Woman and Economics* (1898), she emerged as a pioneer sociologist of women's topics. Much influenced by Lester Frank Ward's *Dynamic Sociology* and providing a "scientific" socialist text paralleling August Bebel's *Frau und der Sozialismus*, she broke decisively with the earlier communalistic-utopian views of work and the home. Women's emancipation, rather than coming through men and women sharing the "unproductive" labor of homemaking, would come through equal engagement in productive labor, she insisted. In her wider view, the era of extreme individualism had in any case passed with the evolution of modern economics. Woman's status would now change dramatically if social evolution were properly guided. The greatest need, she believed, was to set women on the path to earn their own livelihood. Shortly after the turn of the century, she broadened this argument to advocate communal nurseries and kitchens to replace individualized homes entirely and to eclipse motherhood as a social specialization.

Remarried to her first cousin in 1900, she assumed the name Charlotte Perkins Gilman, by which she would be principally known thereafter. She lived in New York City, later Norwalk, Connecticut, where she and her husband were joined by Helen Campbell, who cooked and cleaned while Gilman wrote essays and prepared *Human Work* (1904), an exaltation out of tune with the coming times.

She also edited, largely wrote and published the *Forerunner* (1909–16), one of the most unusual of independent socialist magazines, equally devoted to improving the status of women and promoting social evolution. She filled the magazine's pages, in part, with manuscripts of her own rejected by other publications or never submitted. She boasted of "no capital except a mental one," and met half the magazine's expenses through her continual lecturing and writing. Much as Walt Whitman's literary executor, Horace Traubel, conducted his personal socialistic journal, the *Conservator*, Gilman filled the pages of the *Forerunner* with her own literary and cultural commentary on the age, addressing herself directly to her few thousand readers. She also frankly addressed questions of private morality, such as prostitution, social diseases, and marriage. For the *Forerunner*, she serialized some seven novels, including her major fantasy contribution, *Herland*, a visit to an island community of women governed by the principle of the New Motherhood, in which cooperative ideals (and parthenogenesis) have replaced the male-dominated competitive social-sexual order.

Joining Jane Addams as a founding leader of the Women's Peace Party in 1915, Gilman fell into obscurity with the sharp decline of socialistic sentiment and the upswing of Freudianism in the 1920s. Placing herself as an old-fashioned scientific evolutionist who held to the decreasing significance of gender differences, she and her emphases had been effectively bypassed. Nevertheless she dedicated herself to her autobiography, *The Living of Charlotte Perkins Gilman*, at last published posthumously. Overwhelmed by spreading disease, she preferred "chloroform to cancer," taking her own life in 1935. *See also*: Campbell, Helen; Utopianism

—*Mari Jo Buhle*

REFERENCES

Degler, Carl. "Charlotte Perkins Gilman." *Notable American Women*. Vol. 2. Cambridge: Harvard University Press, 1971.

Gilman, Charlotte Perkins. *The Living of Charlotte Perkins Gilman: An Autobiography*. New York: Appleton-Century, 1935.

Hill, Mary A. *Charlotte Perkins Gilman: The Making of a Radical Feminist, 1860–1896*. Philadelphia: Temple University Press, 1980.

Lane, Ann J. Introduction to *The Charlotte Perkins Gilman Reader*, edited by Ann J. Lane. New York: Pantheon Books, 1980.

Stern, Madeleine B. "The Forerunner." In *The American Radical Press, 1890–1916, II*, edited by Joseph Conlin. Westport: Greenwood Press, 1974.

GIOVANNITTI, ARTURO (1884–1959)

Poet, playwright, editor, IWW orator-agitator, and union official, Giovannitti gained the admiration of many. His politics were sometimes more passionate than consistent and, as a result, it was not unusual for a wide spectrum of the American Left—socialists, revolutionary syndicalists (Industrial Workers of the World), anarchists, Greenwich Village bohemians, and trade unionists—to consider him one of their own.

Son of a modest doctor/pharmacist, Giovannitti was born in Ripabottoni, a small hill town of southern Italy in the region of Abruzzo-Molisee. Upon completing school he emigrated to Canada.

Little is known about Giovannitti's Canadian years, but, some time after his arrival, he became interested in the Protestant church and studied in several theological seminaries near Montreal. By the time he left Montreal for New York City in 1904, he was fluent in both French and English.

The great metropolis of New York completely captivated Giovannitti and he called it home for the rest of his life. At first he resumed his university studies at Columbia, but he soon became so deeply involved in radical politics within the Italian community that he never completed his degree. After convincing his comrades that he was no longer religious, he joined the *Federazione Socialista Italiana* (Italian Socialist Federation) in 1907. He always retained, however, a certain religious temperament, which manifested itself particularly in his poetry. By 1909 he had changed from a reformist socialist into a firm proponent of revolutionary syndicalism and had been chosen a member of the editorial committee of *Il Proletario*, the Italian-language journal of the IWW. In 1911 Giovannitti became the paper's sole editor and it was in this capacity that he went to Lawrence, Massachusetts, in January 1912 to aid in the great textile strike that had just begun.

The effectiveness of Giovannitti and fellow IWW organizer Joe Ettor during the bitter Lawrence strike of 1912 made them marked men. During a confrontation with the state militia, a young girl among the striking demonstrators was killed. Although Ettor and Giovannitti were not present at the shooting incident and evidence indicated that a police officer's bullet had actually killed the young girl, they were arrested and charged as accessories to murder. This blatant effort to break the strike by framing its leaders on false charges, a not unusual occurrence in that period, catapaulted their case into national attention and turned their names into a rallying cry for the IWW and American labor. After almost a year of imprisonment, Ettor and Giovannitti were found innocent by a jury and set free.

THE GENERAL STRIKE IS THE KEY THAT FITS THE LOCK TO FREEDOM

Cartoon from *Industrial Worker*, August 15, 1912

Upon his release from prison Giovannitti chose not to reassume his position as editor of *Il Proletario*, though he still continued to work closely with the IWW and with his earlier comrade-in-arms, Ettor, and with the IWW's Carlo Tresca, Elizabeth Gurley Flynn, and William Haywood. He now began to frequent the American radical and cultural circles that were then flourishing in Greenwich Village and associated with such American writers and artists as Max Eastman, John Reed, Floyd Dell, Robert Minor, Art Young, Mike Gold, and Boardman Robinson. He was one of the few Italian-born radicals of his generation who moved easily through the wider world of American culture. He started to write regularly for the *Masses* and even the usually conservative *Atlantic Monthly* published his poem "The Cage," which dealt with his imprisonment during the Lawrence strike. In 1914 Giovannitti published his first book of poems (in English) *Arrows in the Gale*, which had an introduction by Helen Keller.

Giovannitti, like most of the American Left, fought fervently against America's entry into World War I and undertook a tremendous schedule of antiwar agitation. He managed at the same time to write prolifically for the socialist and anarchist press, to edit two short-lived Italian-language political-cultural journals, *Il Fuoco* (1915, New York City) and *Vita* (1916, New York City) and to stage the first of many Italian-language dramas, *Tenebre Rosse* (Red shadows).

Upon the entrance of the United States into World War I, the American Left was fiercely, and often illegally, attacked by the federal government for its antiwar position. The Red Scare, the great, irrational fear that shook American society as a result of the Bolshevik revolution, also unleashed a political reaction against the Left. Giovannitti, one of the prominent targets of the authorities, was able, only by chance, to escape the arrest and imprisonment that was the fate of most of the IWW leadership.

At war's end, the political activity of Giovannitti changed direction. With the IWW essentially destroyed as a major force within the ranks of labor by governmental repression, he began to move from his almost total involvement with revolutionary syndicalism into a closer association with the main labor union movement. He played an important role in establishing Local 89, the Italian Dress Makers Union, of the International Ladies Garment Workers Union. As a writer he became a contributing editor to Max Eastman's *Liberator*, a member of the Workers Drama League, and a contributor to the *New Masses*, all groups that in time became more or less connected with the Communist Party. With the sponsorship of the union-backed *Camera Del Lavoro* (The Italian Chamber of Labor, New York City), he undertook his last major editorial effort, the Italian-language cultural journal *Il Veltro*, 1924–25.

During 1925 Ettor and Giovannitti reunited and fought together for a radical cause one last time. They made public appearances on behalf of two other Italian-born radicals, Sacco and Vanzetti, whose murder trial would not have the fortunate outcome of their own. (After 1925, Ettor essentially disappeared from the stage of radical politics, fading into the anonymous life of a farmer and wine maker in California. He lived quietly among Italian comrades, selling them wine, and died unnoticed in 1948.)

After 1930, Giovannitti no longer wrote much for the American press, radical or cultural. His activities became centered almost exclusively around organized labor—ILGWU, ACWA, AFL—and his writings now appeared mainly in union journals and obscure Italian-language publications. As part of the *Alleanza Anti-Fascista di Nord America*, he did play a role in the antifascist activities that were centered in New York City, but by now Giovannitti spent more time associating with figures of the labor establishment—Luigi Antonini, David Dubinsky, Sidney Hillman, August Bellanca, Norman Thomas. He was appointed the secretary of the Italian Labor Education Bureau (New York City), but a certain fire and direction had disappeared from his life. He had become more of a romantic symbol of the past than an energetic actor in the politics of the present.

Max Eastman once commented that the names of Ettor and Giovannitti were as well known to American radicals as Lenin and Trotsky. Their voices, which had been among the most intelligent and the most energetic in the fight for freedom and social justice in the beginning of this century, faded, however, into obscurity, melancholy examples of how difficult it is to sustain a lifelong radical posture in America. *See also*: Anarcho-Syndicalism, Industrial Workers of the World, Italians

—Robert D'Attilio

REFERENCES

"Omaggio a Arturo Giovannitti." *La Parola del Popolo* (February–March 1962).

Tusiani, Joseph. "La poesia ingelse di Arturo Giovannitti." *La Parola del Popolo* (November–December 1978).

Gold, Michael (1893–1967)

Born Itzok Granich to impoverished Jewish immigrants on Manhattan's Lower East Side, Gold derived the major themes of his long career from those roots and reflected them most prominently in his major literary work, the fictionalized autobiography *Jews Without Money* (1930). Like the boy in that novel, Gold dropped out of school in the eighth grade, but in real life, he also had a year of journalism classes at New York University (1912–13) and a traumatic year as a special student at Harvard (1914). His novel concludes with a political rally that leads to a leftist conversion. The origin of that account was a rally in 1914, but Gold was not as politically naive as his fictional counterpart. He had considerable exposure to radical ideas through his younger brother Manny, who was active in the Industrial Workers of the World. Even after Gold became associated with the Communist Party, anarchist and syndicalist ideas would retain some appeal, for he remained an unsystematic and eclectic thinker.

Gold's first radical publication was in the *Masses* (1914–17) and in the Sunday supplement of the *New York Call* (1916). Three of his one-act plays were performed by the Provincetown Players in 1916, 1917, and 1920, respectively. The entire period was filled with political and personal anguish. In 1918 he went to Mexico to avoid the draft, and during the Red Scare of 1919–20 he changed his name to Michael Gold as a protective measure. Nonetheless, in 1920 he became editor of the *Liberator*, successor to the *Masses*, which had been suppressed in 1917. Six years later he became editor of the *New Masses* (1926–47), which succeeded the *Liberator*. His period of greatest literary influence would be from the founding of the *New Masses* until the mid-1930s, a time when he was identified as the leading American advocate of proletarian literature.

The high point of his most fruitful period was publication of *Jews Without Money*. In addition to the work's considerable intrinsic merits, its appearance coincided with the deepening of a depression that made a novel about poverty pertinent to a mass audience. Friends hailed him as the American Gorky, but Gold was never to fulfill his promise as a writer of fiction. Although he published short stories and left versions of partly completed novels at his death, there would be no second novel. His energy seemed to flow more naturally to editing and journalism than to fiction. He became a columnist for the *Daily Worker* in 1933, a role he would retain until the end of his life. As a columnist he could write in the short spurts that came easily to him and he could make immediate comments on ongoing political and literary controversies.

His columns were always provocative. He loved a literary fight. Max Eastman, his old mentor at the *Masses*, Thornton Wilder, and James T. Farrell were early targets. His grounds for attack were usually more ideological than literary and he became increasingly ascerbic as he took up the bitter task of denouncing "renegades" whom the Moscow Trials and Hitler-Stalin Pact had alienated from the CP. His views on the inadequacies of Ernest Hemingway, Archibald MacLeish, Waldo Frank, Robinson Jeffers, Sherwood Anderson, and Granville Hicks are found in *The Hollow Men* (1941), a collection of his *Daily Worker* columns. Another bitter dispute came in 1947 when he lashed out at Albert Maltz, radical novelist and screenwriter, who advanced the view that the politics of a writer did not necessarily determine the quality of that writer's work. Gold's last decade was spent in the San Francisco Bay Area, where he worked on a memoir, which he never completed. He died in quiet obscurity, one of the few literary radicals of the 1920s and 1930s who never left the Communist movement. Ironically, he is now most respected not for his theoretical polemics but for his novel. *Jews Without Money* remains a classic account of the Jewish ghetto during the first years of the twentieth century.

See also: Congress of American Writers, *Daily Worker, New Masses*, Radical and Proletarian Writers

—*Dan Georgakas*

REFERENCES

Folsom, Michael, ed. *Mike Gold: A Literary Anthology*. New York: International Publishers, 1972.

GOLDMAN, EMMA (1869–1940)

More than any woman in Progressive America, the anarchist Emma Goldman captured popular imagination as a symbol of working-class militancy and female revolt. Many Americans, equating anarchism with terrorism, blamed her for inspiring the assassination of President William McKinley despite the absence of evidence connecting her with that act. Others admired her courage in standing up to police harassment, her daring lectures on topics ranging from anarchism and syndicalism to free love, homosexual rights, and the modern European drama. She endured repeated arrest, imprisonment, deportation, and exile without losing her enthusiasm for the anarchist ideal, which she saw briefly realized in Spain, at the start of the Spanish Civil War. A follower of Peter Kropotkin, Goldman called herself a communist anarchist. Yet her thought retained a strong individualist strand, and she took pride in her role as a "free lance." She also brought to the movement a new stress on sexual and psychological liberation. Her sex radicalism, controversial even among anarchists, influenced many young early twentieth-century feminists who admired her challenge to Victorian values and celebrated her as a feminist heroine, despite her outspoken criticism of the suffrage movement.

Goldman was born in Lithuania in 1869, to a Russian-Jewish family of shopkeepers. Educated in East Prussia, she also attended high school in St. Petersburg. Here she first heard of the Russian Narodniks, whose women members became her lifelong heroines. As an immigrant factory worker in Rochester, New York, Goldman was radicalized by the trial and hanging of the Haymarket anarchists in 1886–87. In New York City, she joined the German anarchist movement and, under the tutelage of Johann Most, rapidly became known as a witty, provocative speaker. Her complicity in her lover Alexander Berkman's attempted assassination of steel magnate Henry Clay Frick, during the Homestead Steel strike of 1892, sealed her commitment to the movement. While Berkman spent fourteen years in prison, Goldman rose to national attention

Emma Goldman caricatured in Yiddish press

through her coast-to-coast lecture tours. Routinely arrested and denied access to halls, she waged imaginative free-speech fights, often in alliance with the Industrial Workers of the World. She served one year in prison on charges of "inciting to riot" during an 1893 hunger demonstration, and two weeks in 1916 for her role as an early campaigner for birth control. For opposing the draft during World War I, she served two years in the Missouri State Penitentiary.

Revolutionary anarchism in America was largely an immigrant phenomenon. Goldman hoped to Americanize anarchism by appealing to English-speaking audiences, especially to intellectuals. From 1906 to 1917, she published an influential "little" anarchist monthly magazine, *Mother Earth*, which attempted to link European anarchist thought with American traditions of dissent. She also expanded her lecture into two books, *Anarchism and Other Essays* (1911), and *The Social Significance of the Modern Drama* (1914) offered a useful introduction to European playwrights such as Ibsen, Strindberg, and Hauptmann. She attracted many native-born admirers, especially among the pre-WW I bohemian intellectuals and artists, including Floyd Dell, Eugene O'Neill, the painter Robert Henri, and Margaret Anderson, editor of the avant-garde *Little Review*. But unlike Goldman's protégé Roger Baldwin, founder of the ACLU, many remained personal admirers who disclaimed her radical politics or identified anarchism with personal rebellion. The heart of the anarchist movement in America remained in the Russian, Jewish, Spanish, Italian, and other foreign-language groups with whom Goldman maintained ambivalent relations.

At the height of the Red Scare in December 1919, Goldman was deported to Soviet Russia, along with Alexander Berkman. She had ardently defended the Bolsheviks while in the United States. But she was shocked by the catastrophic conditions in Civil War Russia, and by the harsh politics of "war communism." She was especially outraged at the persecution of Russian anarchists, who had initially supported the October Revolution. She rapidly lost confidence in the Bolsheviks, but continued to work with them, withholding public criticism until the Kronstadt uprising of March 1921, when both Goldman and Berkman became outspoken critics. They left Russia in December 1921 to settle temporarily in Berlin. Here Goldman wrote scathing indictments of the Bolshevik regime, including an emotional book, *My Disillusionment in Russia* (1923), which combined trenchant criticism of early Bolshevik repressiveness with a misleading picture of social, economic, and cultural conditions.

Granted a British visa in 1924, Goldman worked in London to mobilize public protest against Soviet imprisonment of left-wing oppositionists. Her efforts were hindered by her wholesale attacks on Bolshevism, which alienated British Socialists initially sympathetic to her aims. With the failure of her anti-Soviet campaign, Goldman tried lecturing on drama and other subjects in Britain, and later in Canada. Her epic autobiography, *Living My Life* (1931), celebrated her dramatic public career while documenting her conflicted personal affairs, including her tormented passion for Dr. Ben Reitman.

Goldman lived to see a successful anarchist revolution in part of Spain, precipitated by the fascist rebellion of July 1936. She was thrilled by the sight of anarchist collectives, Barcelona in the hands of the working class. She made three visits to Spain in the course of the civil war, returning each time to London to act as publicist and fundraiser for the Spanish anarcho-syndicalist organizations, the Confederación Nacional del Trabajo-Federación Anarquista Ibérica. Despite strong reservations about the decision of the Spanish anarchists to enter the Popular Front government, Goldman defended the CNT-FAI within the bitterly divided international movement as well as in public, while privately urging the Spanish militants against further concessions. With the defeat of the Republic in 1939, Goldman traveled to Canada, where she continued her efforts on behalf of Spanish anarchist refugees. She insisted she would oppose any support for the Allies in the approaching war, as she had in 1917. Yet the violent anti-Semitism of the Nazis made her antiwar position personally problematical. She was torn by conflicting loyalties she could not reconcile.

The consistency of Goldman's commitment to anarchism masked a considerable confusion in her ideas and her life. She never resolved the contradictions of her thought, which swung between extremes of faith in and contempt for the masses, between belief in revolution and despair of its benefits, between voluntarism and resignation to "fate." During her years in exile, a shrill anticommunism dominated her politics, although she remained a sharp critic of capitalism. What stands out in her fifty years of militance is her extraordinary energy and tenacity in the face of persecution, isolation, and loneliness.

Goldman died of a stroke in Toronto in May 1940. Although she had been denied entry into the United States except for one brief visit in 1934, death granted her a permanent visa. She was buried in Waldheim Cemetery in Chicago, in the country she always regarded as her home. *See also*: Anarchism, Free Love

—*Alice Wexler*

REFERENCES

Drinnon, Richard. *Rebel in Paradise*. Chicago: University of Chicago Press, 1961.

Falk, Candace. *Love, Anarchy, and Emma Goldman*. New York: Holt, Rinehart & Winston, 1984.

Porter, David. *Vision on Fire: Emma Goldman on the Spanish Revolution*. New Paltz: Commonground Press, 1983.

Wexler, Alice. *Emma Goldman in America*. Boston: Beacon Press, 1984.

———. *Emma Goldman in Exile*. Boston: Beacon Press, 1988.

Goodman, Paul (1911–72)

Widely acknowledged as "the philosopher of the New Left," Goodman had already run through several careers before his decade of fame as the author of *Growing Up Absurd* (1960). Critics charge that he spread himself too thin. He was trained as a philosopher at City College in New York and the University of Chicago, where his mentors were Morris Cohen and Richard McKeon, and went on to teach mathematics and the Greeks to ninth graders at a progressive school and literature at various colleges. He was fired three times for his open homosexuality. (Goodman was bisexual—a family man, twice married and father of three.)

With his architect brother Percival Goodman he collaborated on *Communitas* (1947), a classic of community planning. With Fritz Perls he wrote *Gestalt Therapy* (1951), the theoretical cornerstone of the movement that went by that name, and he practiced psychotherapy for a decade. *The Structure of Literature* (1954) and *Speaking and Language* (1971) were equivalent tours de force in literary criticism and philosophical linguistics. He also published stories, novels, and poems. His plays were produced by the Living Theater, where he was a kind of guru-in-residence. Adding his social criticism, his output was over thirty volumes.

The foundations of his anarchism had been laid in his youth, but he always spoke of himself as "apolitical," and it was not until World War II threatened to gobble him up in its armies that he set himself to formulate his radicalism. He became a central figure among the New York anarchists and published chapters of his manifesto *The May Pamphlet* (1946) in magazines like *Why?*, *Retort*, and *Politics*. During this period his circle overlapped with the War Resisters League and the Committee for Nonviolent Revolution, where many leaders of the antiwar movement served their apprenticeships.

Goodman joined the editorial board of *Liberation* shortly after its founding in 1956 and was active there until the late 1960s, when he and the New Left parted company over the Leninist tactics and anti-intellectualism that, as he saw it, were betraying the spirit of the Berkeley Free Speech Movement and the Port Huron Statement. Soon after, he suffered his first heart attack, and although he continued to speak out on radical issues, especially in *New Reformation* (1969), he now turned to work that was more congenial. His last books were poetry and apologia. He described himself as "a man of letters in the old sense," explaining that he had only one subject in all his multifarious works, "the human beings I know in their man-made scene." *See also*: Anarchism, Pacifism

—*Taylor Stoehr*

REFERENCES

Dennison, George. "A Memoir." In Goodman, Paul. *Collected Poems*. New York: Random House, 1973.

Wieck, David. "Goodman's Flag." *Telos*, No. 35 (1978).

Gray, Eula (1912–?)

The descendent of poor, black tenant farmers, Gray was born in Tallapoosa County, Alabama. At the age of nineteen Gray became a leader of the Communist-led Share Croppers Union and subsequently joined the Communist Party. The daughter of SCU leader Tommy Gray, she held the union together in rural Alabama after her uncle, Ralph Gray, a Communist and union cofounder, was killed in an armed confrontation with local police in 1931. Besides serving as ad hoc secretary of the SCU until the spring of 1932, she organized and led the Young Communist League in the "black belt." Once she took up residence in New York (ca. 1935), her public esteem diminished, though she continued to raise money for the Alabama SCU. *See also*: Share Croppers Union

—*Robin D. G. Kelley*

REFERENCES

Gray, Tommy. "Brother Ralph Gray's Story." *Labor Defender*, 11/8 (August 1935).

Kelley, Robin D. G. "Hammer and Hoe," *Alabama Communists During the Depression*. Chapel Hill: University of North Carolina Press, 1990.

Rosen, Dale. "The Alabama Share Croppers Union." B.A. Honors Thesis, Radcliffe College, 1969.

Greek Americans

Approximately half a million Greeks emigrated to the United States between 1900 and 1940. Although the post–World War II generation would emerge as one of the most affluent and best-educated ethnic groups, the initial immigrants were mainly unskilled male workers who were regarded as only quasi-European and were harshly discriminated against in local statutes and hiring. The first political clubs, while mainly concerned with republican versus royalist struggles in Greece, also served as centers for domestic politics. Through the 1930s, worker-led struggles against the Ku Klux Klan and state militias for political rights were as ardent as the battles waged on economic issues.

The first American radical organizations to reach Greeks were the Socialist Labor Party and the Industrial Workers of the World. The SLP developed a Greek-language section and a newspaper with some influence in New England. Two IWW pamphlets appeared in Greek, and there was IWW impact on miners in the West, loggers in the Northwest, and food handlers in the East. Militant Greek workers played major roles in the Bingam Canyon, Utah, copper strike of 1912, the Lowell, Massachusetts, textile strike of 1912, and the Ludlow, Colorado, coal strike of 1913. The most vibrant radical presence, however, formed around a New York group that published *Phone tou Ergatou* (Voice of the worker), 1918–23; *Embros* (Forward), 1923–38; *Eleftheria* (Freedom), 1938–41; and *Helleno-Amerikaniko Vima* (Greek-American tribune), 1941–53. These papers, sometimes daily, usually weekly, reflected the views of the Communist Party with name changes indicating policy shifts. Top weekly circulation of approximately 10,000 occurred in the 1940s when liberal and conservative dailies printed approximately 15,000 copies each. During the period when the CP had ethnic units, there were some 500 members in the Greek section. Organizational life revolved around publishing ventures and organizing worker clubs. These clubs, most of which were east of the Mississippi and north of the Mason-Dixon line, became the backbone of the thirty Greek lodges of the International Workers Order.

Greek Communists led Local 70 of the Fur Workers Union, which became a fulcrum for Greek radicalism in the East. Greek-speaking radicals, primarily Communists, were also active in organizing CIO locals in the steel, rubber, mine, textile, food, maritime, and electrical industries. The Trotskyist-oriented Communist League of America had a number of Greeks who led a successful general strike of New York hotel workers in 1934. Some Greeks were founding members of the SWP and the Workers Party, but they had little impact on the Greek community. Other radical activity included a continuing attraction of intellectuals to various forms of anarchism, Greeks for Norman Thomas, Greek candidates for the American Labor Party and the Progressive Party, and a cooperative system of profit-sharing among Greek sponge divers in Tarpon Springs, Florida.

The Greek Left reached its peak of influence in the early 1940s when a liberal/radical coalition led community support of EAM-ELAS (the National Liberation Front of Greece) and the war effort at home. This respectability was shattered at war's end by the impact of the civil war in Greece and McCarthyism in America. A number of Greeks, nearly all involved with the labor movement, were deported and Greek dissent was chilled. No further Left initiatives among Greeks took hold until liberals and radicals created the antijunta movement of 1967–74. Among the lasting consequences were Left organizations in the Astoria community in Queens, New York, and a strong radical presence in both the English-language and Greek-language ethnic press.

See also: Fur and Leather Workers, International Workers Order

—*Dan Georgakas*

REFERENCES

Georgakas, Dan. "The Greeks in America." *Journal of the Hellenic Diaspora*, 14 (1/2) (Spring–Summer 1987).

Moskos, Charles C. *The Greek Americans*. Rev. ed. New Brunswick, NJ: Transaction, 1989.

Psomiades, Harry J., and Alice Scourby, eds. *The Greek American Community in Transition*. New York: Pella, 1982.

Green, Gil (b. 1906)

An early member of the Communist Party, Green has been a lifelong activist and is currently a member of the CP's National Committee. He was one of the architects and executors of the policy evolved at the Seventh World Congress (1935) of the Communist International that reversed the "narrow 'class against class' political line into one that sought unity of Communists, Socialists, and all democratic forces into an all-inclusive people's struggle against fascism and war." He wrote in his book *Cold War Fugitive* that this reversal of policy derived in large measure from experiences of the Communist youth movement in the USA (especially with groups such as the American Youth Congress) and the Popular Front movement in France.

Green was born in Chicago in 1906 to working-class Jewish parents. After his father died when Gil was nine, his mother supported herself and three children by doing housework and receiving home relief (welfare).

In 1924 Green joined the Young Communist League and rapidly rose to become its national leader in 1931. The Comintern elected him as one of three youth leaders to the executive committee in 1935. Shortly after, at the Sixth World Congress of the Young Communist International, he was elected to the executive and secretariat of that body. In 1936 he was part of the U.S. delegation to the World Youth Congress in Geneva. In 1937 Green was one of three YCI delegates to a meeting of representatives from the YCI and the Socialist Youth International that drew up a unity pact to aid the Spanish Republic. In 1938 he was a U.S. delegate to the World Youth Congress, held at Vassar College.

After he graduated from the youth movement, Green became a member of the National Board of the Communist Party (USA) and served as district organizer in New York and in Illinois. He was indicted by the federal government in July 1948 under the Smith Act for being both a leader and a member. The trial started on January 17, 1949, in New York and he was found guilty on October 14. Selected by the CP to remain outside of prison and work as a leader in the underground movement, Green became a fugitive until he surrendered voluntarily on February 27, 1956. He was imprisoned until July 29, 1961. Since then he has been active as a writer about the Party and as a national leader.

A prolific writer, he has written many pamphlets and seven books: *The Enemy Forgotten* (1956), *Revolution Cuban Style* (1970), *The New Radicalism* (1971), *Portugal's Revolution* (1976), *What's Happening To Labor* (1976), *Cuba at 25, the Continuing Revolution* (1984), and *Cold War Fugitive* (1984). *See also*: Communist Party, Young Communist League

—*Ruth F. Prago*

REFERENCES

Green, Gil. *Cold War Fugitive*. New York: International Publishers, 1984.

Greensboro Massacre

An anti-Klan rally organized by the Communist Workers Party in a black housing project in Greensboro, North Carolina, on November 3, 1979, was attacked by an armed nine-car caravan of Ku Klux Klan and Nazi Party members and supporters. The Klan-Nazi caravan was led to the rally site by a Klansman acting as a paid informant of the Greensboro police. After eighty-eight seconds of gunfire, five CWP members and supporters were dead or dying, seven others wounded.

The five murdered CWP members were: Dr. James Waller (president, ACTWU Local 1113-T), William Sampson, Sandra Smith, Cesar Cauce, and Dr. Michael Nathan. All were veterans of the radical student antiwar and black liberation movements of the late 1960s who developed into Marxists in the

1970s. In North Carolina, activists from both white and black Left groups in Durham and Greensboro began organizing in textile mills and hospitals beginning in 1974. By 1977, these forces had been consolidated into the Workers Viewpoint Organization, a national communist grouping that became the Communist Workers Party in October 1979. The WVO initiated the Trade Union Educational League, which in addition to gaining leadership in several local unions in North Carolina, organized support for six labor strikes across the state in 1978 and four in 1979.

The CWP's anti-Klan rally was organized in the context of an upsurge of Klan and racist violence that swept across the Piedmont South during 1978–79. Blacks organized armed self-defense patrols against the Klan in Tupelo, Mississippi, Decatur, Alabama, and China Grove, North Carolina. In China Grove, the CWP (WVO) assisted black residents in a militant confrontation at a Klan rally at the town's community center on July 8, 1979. Retaliation for the humiliation at China Grove may have been one motive in the Klan attack on the Greensboro rally.

In organizing the Greensboro rally and conference that was to have followed, the CWP sought to consolidate anti-Klan activists in the South who upheld the right of armed self-defense, as opposed to the anti-Klan network of the Southern Christian Leadership Conference, which promoted unarmed pacifist opposition and reliance on the police. The CWP (WVO) anti-Klan campaign was led by Nelson Johnson, a longtime black community organizer from Greensboro, and Paul Bermanzohn, a Jewish doctor from Durham who suffered permanent injury from wounds received in the November 3 attack.

Of the five CWP members who died, four were rank-and-file union leaders and organizers. After this, CWP activity in the unions in North Carolina declined.

After two all-white juries acquitted Klan-Nazi defendants of criminal charges in the Greensboro murders, a third jury held two Greensboro police officers, the Klan-police informant, and four Klan-Nazi gunmen liable for wrongful death in a civil suit that ended on June 8, 1985. As a result, the city of Greensboro paid $351,000 to Dr. Martha Nathan, widow of Dr. Michael Nathan, in the final settlement of the case. *See also*: Civil Rights, "Revisionism" (Maoism)

—*James Wrenn*

REFERENCES

Alvarez, Sallyann, and Carolyn Jung. *Red November, Black November.* (film) 1981.

Bermanzohn, Paul C. and Sally A. Bermanzon. *The True Story of the Greensboro Massacre.* New York: Cesar Cauce Publishers, 1980.

Institute for Southern Studies. "Third of November" report. 1981.

Parenti, Michael, and Carolyn Kazdin. "The Untold Story of the Greensboro Massacre." *Monthly Review* 33, (1981–82).

Taylor, G. Flint. "*Waller* v. *Butkovich*: Lessons in Strategy and Tenacity for Civil Rights Litigation." *Police Misconduct and Civil Rights Law Report* 1, no. 13, (January–February 1986).

Wheaton, Elizabeth. *Codename GREENKILL: The 1979 Greensboro Killings.* Athens: University of Georgia Press, 1987.

Greenwich Village

The intellectuals who gathered in Greenwich Village in the 1910s celebrated creative individuality over social adjustment, urban diversity and turmoil over middle-class assimilation and tidiness, radical dissent over bureaucratic regulation, improvisation over expertise, artistic vision over political pragmatism. Their traditions have since inspired the American Left, old and new: movements for women's and sexual emancipation; the artistic avant-garde, to the extent that one has existed in America; and many of the ensuing efforts to redefine American culture as pluralistic, diverse, and cosmopolitan. These struggles have included movements for civil rights, civil liberties, and increased democratic participation by all members of our society—regardless of race, class, gender, or sexuality.

These rebels are often referred to as "the Greenwich Village Left"—although there were other and earlier centers of rebellion, notably Chicago in the first decade of the century. Still, by 1912 or so, most of the cultural radicals of this generation had made their way to New York, and many stayed on for the next five or more years, before disbanding for

Paris, Moscow, Taos, Croton-on-Hudson, Provincetown, or the more disciplined socialist community on New York's Lower East Side. The names of some of the leading participants will suggest the variety of careers and backgrounds that came together in this "rebellion": Max Eastman, Crystal Eastman, John Reed, Emma Goldman, Floyd Dell, Mabel Dodge, Alfred Stieglitz, Margaret Sanger, John Sloan, Hutchins Hapgood, Dorothy Day, Randolph Bourne.

What drew this community of artists, journalists, activists, poets, organizers, and malcontents together and to the Village in the years after 1910? Most came from elsewhere—the majority of the rebels grew up in provincial American towns, children of respectable but often marginal or even downwardly mobile parents. Some historians have suggested that a characteristically shared experience of the rebels, male as well as female, was that they grew up in mother-dominated homes, with absent or failed fathers. Even if such circumstances were not as unusual in late-Victorian America as some historians would make them seem, there is merit to the speculation that such an upbringing produced in the children, especially the sons, a sense of alienation from the more traditional male modes of success in late-nineteenth-century America, as well as an unusual willingness in both genders to accept the possible equality of women.

Although many of the male rebels were products of Ivy League educations (Eastman, Reed, Bourne, Van Wyck Brooks) and several had continued on to advanced graduate work, most shunned the newly emerging routes to professional success—whether through university appointments, government service, the professions, or even conventional journalism. Instead, they sought to combine politics and art, advocacy and poetry, life and work—to reject predictable careers and to improvise. That explains, in large part, the appeal of the Village, where rents were still cheap, studio space and a sense of community still possible, and where the ethnic diversity and marginality of the neighborhood might shelter the "bohemian rebels" from the prying eyes of disapproving bourgeois neighbors. (The Italian immigrants in the Village disapproved, too, but their opinions clearly carried less sanctioning weight.) The women rebels were more likely to be professionals—lawyers, social workers—than were the men, but for a woman to enter these professions in 1910 was hardly to surrender to conventionality. In their private lives, these women defied more conventions than did their male comrades, as they challenged the double standard of Victorian sexual morality; advocated birth control, woman suffrage, and an end to traditional marriage and the conventional sexual division of labor; and probably to a greater degree than the men, experimented with homosexual and homoerotic relations as well as heterosexual liaisons.

These experiments were not without their complications and emotional costs; conventional mores may be flouted while still maintaining a powerful hold on peoples' imaginations, fears, and aspirations.

Perhaps the most characteristic unifying belief of the rebels, an idea that united people as different as Max Eastman and Emma Goldman and movement organs as various as the *Masses* and the *Seven Arts*, was their linking of artistic experiments—modernism—and an eclectic array of radical political positions—generally some variation on anarcho-socialism—in a sweeping belief in the primary necessity of a revolution in consciousness. In so doing, many rejected the means if not always the goal of the Marxist socialists' more disciplined advocacy of organization toward a class revolution fueled by the inescapable contradictions of capitalism. Simultaneously and more consistently, the Greenwich Village intellectuals criticized the Progressives' liberal faith in adjustment, expertise, and reform from within the existing political and economic arrangements. Crucial to this faith in the transformation of consciousness was the rebels' sense that the individual consciousness would be the source of revolutionary (usually nonviolent) action. Modern art, liberated sexual energies, cultural criticism, and intellectual dissent would inspire the rejection of materialism, conventional morality, traditional gender relations, and the political status quo. This transformed consciousness would ignite a revolution that would somehow liberate both the individual genius and the oppressed classes of the world. Writers, artists, poets, intellectuals, and critics, of course, would play a defining role in any such reconstruction of consciousness, since they were already exploring the revolutionary implications of modernist literature and syndicalism, surrealism and feminism, Freud (in an often distortedly optimistic and therapeutic sense), and the connections between free love and the demise of private property. These radical aspirations clearly appealed as much to the various personal discontents of these writers, artists, and intellectuals as they did to the larger problem of a transformed social order. To the rebels, this would not have indicted their intentions but justified them, since personal disaffection and unhappiness were—as social scientists had taught them—a direct product of social alienation, political oppression, and economic dislocation. The famous Paterson Pageant of 1913, a rally for striking silkworkers of the Industrial Workers of the World orchestrated by John Reed and other *Masses* writers, was just one example of the Villagers' effort to join their political and artistic ideals, their personal desires and social commitments.

In the ensuing decades of this century and for several different generations of the American Left, Greenwich Village has had a continuing and storied importance. But for the celebrated generation of radicals who gave the Greenwich Village "rebellion" its name, the First World War brought an end to this phase of the history of the Left in the Village. With the federal government's wartime suppression of dissent, including the Post Office's battle against the *Masses* in 1917–18, with the imprisonment of pacifists and the deportations of alien radicals like Emma Goldman, many of the Village rebels lost heart. Often they found their already fragmented and improvised political positions increasingly under attack or untenable, and turned to private lives and solutions, to art for its own sake, to postwar Paris or revolutionary Moscow, but in most cases away from the faith in the spontaneous liberation of human consciousness that had once united and inspired them. *See also*: Free Love; Goldman, Emma; Giovannitti, Arturo; *The Liberator, The Masses*, Reed, John; *Seven Arts*

—*Tara Fitzpatrick*

REFERENCES

May, Henry F. *The End of American Innocence*. New York: Knopf, 1959.

Fishbein, Leslie. *Rebels in Bohemia*. Chapel Hill: University of North Carolina Press, 1982.

Abrahams, Edward. *The Lyrical Left*. Charlottesville: University Press of Virginia, 1986.

Trimberger, Ellen Kay. "Feminism, Men, and Modern Love in Greenwich Village." In *Powers of Desire*, edited by Ann Snitow et al. New York: Monthly Review Press, 1984.

Greie-Cramer, Johanna (1864–?)

Born of middle-class parents in Dresden, Germany, Greie emigrated with her husband to the United States, where she became a leading socialist writer and lecturer on the "woman question." She played an instrumental role in supporting German-American socialist women in their establishment of separate organizations within the Socialist Labor Party of the 1880s. Although Greie shared the commonplace opinion that women's emancipation depended upon the overthrow of capitalism, she readily challenged many of her contemporaries by extolling men as women's enemy.

In 1888 Greie spearheaded the formation of the *Frauen und Mädchenbund*, the first federation of socialist women's clubs centered in the Northeast and industrial Midwest. For one year she traveled to address these clubs only to witness their demise by the next. Following the Second International's adoption in 1896 of Clara Zetkin's resolution favoring women's organization, German-American women organized the Social Democratic Women's Federation and once again provided Greie-Cramer (by this time widowed and remarried) with a platform. She edited a women's column in the *New Yorker Volkszeitung* and resumed her lecture tours.

Johanna Greie-Cramer played an instrumental role in building a base for women's organization among the German-American and Yiddish-speaking socialists who would form the Socialist Party after the turn of the century. *See also*: *New Yorker Volkszeitung*, Socialist Labor Party

—*Mari Jo Buhle*

REFERENCES

Buhle, Mari Jo. *Women and American Socialism, 1870–1920*. Urbana: University of Illinois Press, 1981.

GROPPER, WILLIAM (1897–1977)

One of the most important illustrators for the American radical press, William Gropper sharpened his pen against potbellied politicians and bloodthirsty fascist leaders, while honoring the heroism of the worker and the rituals of Jewish life. He also drew humorous caricatures of literary figures and flappers in the twenties for literary magazines such as the *Bookman*, *Broom*, and *Dial*. Throughout his lifetime, Gropper experimented with a variety of techniques including pen and ink, lithography, etching, and painting. Despite his numerous works on canvas, however, Gropper was most gifted as a political illustrator. Critics have often compared his drawings with works by Francisco Goya and Honoré Daumier.

Born and raised in a working-class family on the Lower East Side of New York City, Gropper developed an allegiance to the radical Left in 1912, when at age fifteen he began to study art with Robert Henri at the Ferrer School. He did not, however, start drawing leftist illustrations until 1918, when while working as a feature artist for the *New York Tribune* he did a story on the Industrial Workers of the World and discovered that his political sympathies lay with the Wobblies. He began producing illustrations for the IWW's newspaper, *Rebel Worker*, which eventually cost him his job at the *Tribune*. During the 1920s Gropper contributed political drawings to the *Liberator*, *Revolutionary Age* and the *Freiheit*, and in the 1930s he became one of the principal illustrators for the *New Masses*.

The Depression decade marked Gropper's greatest involvement in radical politics. Although he never officially joined the American Communist Party, he was in 1927 an American delegate to the Tenth Anniversary Celebration of the October Revolution, and in 1930 he attended the Kharkov Conference. During the late 1930s and Second World War Gropper devoted his art to the antifascist cause. One of his antifascist cartoons published in 1935 by *Vanity Fair* provoked a minor international controversy. The illustration depicted a series of "five unlikely events" and included a picture of Emperor Hirohito pulling a rickshaw loaded with a scroll labeled "Nobel Peace Prize." The Japanese government, offended by the image of the emperor performing the task of a coolie, protested to the United States. Secretary of State Hull offered an "informal" apology.

Due to his involvement with leftist politics during the 1920s and 1930s, Gropper was called before the House Un-American Activities Committee in 1953, accused of drawing maps for the CP. The document in question was a map of the United States with an American folklore hero drawn over each state. Between 1953 and 1956 Gropper did fifty lithographs entitled the *Caprichos* based on the McCarthy inquisition.

Gropper never gave up his commitment to the Left. After the Second World War he traveled to Poland in 1948 to attend the Congress of Intellectuals for Peace at Cracow, Poland, as well as the unveiling of the Warsaw Ghetto monument. Afterward he decided to pay tribute to the Jews who died in the Holocaust by painting one picture on the theme of Jewish life every year. Overall, Gropper's drawings and paintings became less topical after the war, dealing instead with general themes of suffering and exploitation. *See also*: *Liberator*, *New Masses*

—*Cécile Whiting*

REFERENCES

Freundlich, August L. *William Gropper: Retrospective*. Los Angeles: Ward Ritchie Press, 1968.

Gahn, Anthony J. "William Gropper—Radical Cartoonist." *The New York Historical Society Quarterly* (April 1970).

Lozowick, Louis. *William Gropper*. Philadelphia: The Art Alliance Press, 1983.

GROYSSER KUNDES

The "big wise guy," or "big stick," in Yiddish, the *Groysser Kundes* (1909–27) was the leading satirical weekly in that language, and thereby one of the most widely read leftish satirical publications in the United States.

Founded and published by a melancholy poet, Jakob Marinov, the *Groysser Kundes* (first called the *Groysser Kibitzer*, "big kibitzer") was at once the weekly sitcom and the conscience of the Lower East Side. It pilfered jokes or reprinted cartoons from the British *Punch* and *Simplissimus*, usually on such standard themes as jilted romances. But it also dwelt in loving detail on the contemporary personalities and problems of the ghetto. Its artists caricatured every literary or theatrical notable, often with scathing satire but also as a form of Jewish celebrity-recognition. Its writers similarly analyzed cultural developments through witty poems and feuilletons. In effect, they upheld a standard of moral or aesthetic purity and commitment to Jewish culture against which they judged their own, often quite harshly.

The *Kundes* therefore for a long period found its most serious and continued butt of satire in the *Jewish Daily Forward* and above all the *Forward*'s editor, Abe Cahan. According to the *Kundes* artists in particular, the *Forward* had been founded on socialist principles but conducted itself as a mere capitalist enterprise, with the production of literary *shund* (trash) a primary means of gaining readers and advertisers. The *Kundes* considered the *Forward* to be an organ, in essence, of assimilationism. In later years, the *Kundes* turned its barbs against the opponents, inside and outside the ghetto, of the proposed Jewish state in Palestine.

But the *Kundes* may be best remembered for its two great public campaigns: for Jewish labor, and against war. Its sentimental cartoons about Jewish martyrdom refocused attention upon socialism and the Jewish labor movement as the modern guides out of Pharaoh's Egypt. Its caricatures on World War I borrowed from the Yiddish literary tradition, which had since the 1870s detached Jewish interests from armies and fighting. For writers and cartoonists of the *Kundes*, militarism became the enemy and iconoclastic humor a chief Jewish strategy for survival. In its special "War Edition," August 1914, the *Kundes* cover shows "Brutality" (male) and "Civilization" (female) superimposed upon a map of Europe. As "Civilization" is overrun by shovelsful of soldiers, "Brutality" gloats: "Ah, now I'll get even with my enemy: I'll bury her alive!"

Jewish radicals sympathetic to the Russian Revolution, themselves (like most younger Yiddish intellectuals of note) former contributors to the *Kundes*, tried several times to launch pro-Communist versions of the *Kundes*. All failed, although the editor of *Der Humorist* (1922), Sam Liptzin, became humor columnist for the Communist *Morgen Freiheit* for a half century. With the disappearance of *Kundes*, a popular humor tradition on the Left came to an end.

—*Aaron Lansky, Paul Buhle*

REFERENCES

Howe, Irving. *World of Our Fathers*. New York: Simon & Schuster, 1976.

GUTHRIE, WOODY (1912–67)

Woodrow Wilson Guthrie, known as Woody, was the best known of the folksingers associated with the American Left during the 1940s. He subsequently emerged as a popular-culture hero whose reputation spread far beyond left-wing circles, serving as a model for politically oriented "singer-songwriters" such as Bob Dylan and Phil Ochs.

Born into an Oklahoma family rich in musical talent but dogged by tragedy (his father squandered all his money in losing political campaigns, while his mother's illness put her in an asylum), Woody spent his youth on the fringes of society, consorting with hoboes and itinerant laborers who added to his already growing repertoire of songs and stories. He began playing "hillbilly" music in local bands as a teenager, then drifted to California with other "dust-bowl refugees," where he became a popular country performer at a progressive radio station (KFVD) in the late 1930s.

His sympathy for the displaced farmer led him to write protest songs such as "Talking Dust Bowl" and "Do Re Mi" (which were apparently very well received by his Okie audience), and he soon became involved with union functions, strikes, and Communist Party rallies. Woody's charm and "authenticity" endeared him to left-wing intellectuals; he began writing a regular column, "Woody Sez," for the newspaper *People's World*, and entertaining at Hollywood political fundraisers. After a while, political performances were his primary source of income.

In 1940 Guthrie went to New York City, where he became a dominant member of the developing folk movement; he recorded his *Dust Bowl Ballads* for RCA Victor, performed at union functions with Pete Seeger and the newly formed Almanac Singers, wrote for the *Daily Worker*, and at times even appeared on network radio, something that filled him with apprehension and conflict. As the war effort grew, Woody (who was never quite a pacifist) gave himself wholeheartedly to it, inscribing "This Machine Kills Fascists" on his guitar; he eventually entered the merchant marines, and finally, the Army (this last with great reluctance though, and only when he was drafted and had no choice). He also authored a popular autobiography, *Bound for Glory*, during the war years, but the postwar witch-hunts, combined with chronic, degenerative illness, made his later career progressively more difficult.

Although Guthrie periodically flirted with conventional success, it seemed to make him sufficiently uncomfortable that he preferred to avoid it. He was handicapped throughout his career by an unwillingness to compromise, a singlemindedness that also (fortunately) helped preserve the purity of his music. He alienated socialists by refusing to denounce the Hitler-Stalin Pact, radio sponsors by refusing to soften his protest lyrics, and his wives and friends by refusing to stay put (although many of his later personal difficulties can be attributed to the onset of Huntington's chorea, a condition that finally caused his death). Generally weak on strategy, Guthrie had a credo that simply said, "Let's give up our selfishness and differences, and work together"—he left the details to others. Ideologically, he was as much a populist as a communist; in fact, he perceived the communist ideal to be identical with the Christian, often referring to Jesus as a "socialist outlaw."

Like the hoboes he traveled with, Guthrie was quite willing to blend fact with fancy, and he willfully encouraged sycophants who portrayed him as the archetypal American worker-hero; it was good business to do so. Yet within such hyperbole lay more than a kernel of truth: both his art and his politics *were* deeply rooted in American tradition.

Woody's songs were generally based either on standard Anglo-American ballads or blues structures; he often parodied the popular hillbilly song hits of the time, yet he managed inadvertently to write a couple of those himself: "Philadelphia Lawyer" and "Oklahoma Hills." Although he produced his share of transitory agitprop material, his best lyrics captured the spirit of America in a style so highly poetic and yet so extremely direct that one of them, "This Land Is Your Land," has often been proposed as a replacement for "The Star-Spangled Banner." He had that talent (possessed by great revolutionary poets) for fusing abstract political concerns with the minutiae of daily experience, plus a particularly marvelous sense of humor. Yet even when most of his songs are forgotten, he will be remembered for having created an activist role for folksingers in U.S. politics. *See also*: Folk Music

—Joseph Blum

REFERENCES

Guthrie, Woody. *Bound for Glory*. New York: New American Library, 1943.

Guthrie, Woody. *Dust Bowl Ballads* (LP). Folkways Records (FH 5212).

Guthrie, Woody. *Library of Congress Recordings*. Elektra Records (EKL 271/272).

Klein, Joe. *Woody Guthrie: A Life*. New York: Ballantine Books, 1980.

GUTMAN, HERBERT: see
HISTORY, U.S.

Hall, Gus (b. 1910)

Born Arvo Halberg, Hall has been the official leader of the Communist Party of the USA since 1959. He personally symbolizes both the victory of Leninist orthodoxy over a more flexible and open style of Communist politics advocated during the later 1950s, and the relative insularity of American Communists from the New Left, feminism, gay liberation, and Left ecology movements of the 1960s–1980s.

Raised in a Finnish-American home on the Mesabi Iron Range of Minnesota, Hall grew up in a Communist home, surrounded by one of the most intensive Left subcultures in the United States. By age seventeen he had joined the Young Communist League and soon toured the often-radical mining towns of Michigan, Wisconsin, and Minnesota for the Young Communists. As a YCL leader, he became deeply involved in Minneapolis of the early 1930s, participating in hunger marches, farm protests, and the famous 1934 Teamster strike led by Trotskyists. On strike-related charges, he served a six-month prison sentence.

Reassigned to the Ohio-Pennsylvania district, Hall took a leading role in the organization of the Youngstown Sheet and Tube plant where he had gone to work. He reached his apex of labor influence as a leader of the Warren-Youngstown area 1937 "Little Steel" strike and as a staff member of the Steel Workers of America. Soon after, he resigned to become Communist leader of Youngstown, from which he rose to section organizer and finally leader of the Cleveland branch.

Elected to the Party's National Committee in 1944, while serving in the Pacific, Hall reentered civilian and Party life two years later at a most critical point. The ouster of CP general secretary Earl Browder and the resulting political confusion and disintegration over the next few years discredited or demoralized a number of familiar leaders and the validity of seemingly time-tested approaches. Under these conditions, Hall rapidly gained the reputation of a supreme Party loyalist and a deputy to Browder's successor, Eugene Dennis. Elected to the National Executive Board in 1946, he faced indictment under the Smith Act in 1948. Convicted in 1949 and sentenced to a five-year term, he became acting national secretary in 1950 (replacing the jailed Dennis), while appealing his sentence.

In this period of Hall's leadership, the Party—faced with multiple legal threats—adopted the view widely known as "five minutes to midnight," i.e., the time had arrived to prepare an underground movement. Many leaders became "unavailable." Hall himself, choosing the underground rather than prison, was arrested in Mexico City during a failed effort to reach Moscow, and sentenced to an additional three years in prison.

On his release in 1959, Hall found a Party still further diminished by the upheavals after the Hungarian Revolution and Khrushchev's denunciation of misdeeds by Stalin. Hall himself was indicted once more, in the early 1960s, under the McCarren Act, but escaped prison with the Supreme Court's ruling against most of that act. Winning the office of general secretary, then held by Eugene Dennis, Hall rapidly placed his stamp upon the movement. Like those within the main branch of socialism, he and his fellow Communist leaders on the one hand chose to remain committed fundamentally to reorienting the liberal wing of the Democratic Party. (Hall's own repeated candidacies since 1972 constituted a largely symbolic side-gesture.) On the other hand, Hall stoutly resisted the polycentrist impulse known abroad as Eurocommunism. His style of leadership brought great stability, if few dramatic openings.

While Hall's health sometimes suffered in later years, his speeches and writings remained, in the *Daily People's World, Political Affairs,* and in pamphlet and book form, the authoritative Communist political statement of the moment. *See also*: Communist Party

—*Dan Georgakas*

REFERENCES

Starobin, Joseph. *American Communism in Crisis, 1943–1957.* Cambridge: Harvard University Press, 1972.

Halstead, Fred (1927–88)

A leading member of the Socialist Workers Party, Halstead served on its national committee for many years and was its presidential candidate in 1968. In the 1960s he became the most visible of the hundreds of SWPers who maintained the structural heart of much of the anti-Vietnam War movement. His most important work was the leading role he played with the Fifth Avenue Peace Parade Committee, which organized major demonstrations in Washington, D.C., and New York City. For the first time in the postwar era, Marxists from competing parties worked together and in alliance with liberals, pacifists, and other activists in the same organization. Halstead spoke extensively throughout the United States and traveled to Vietnam. When the war ended he wrote the 759-page *Out Now!—A Participant's Account of the American Movement Against the Vietnam War.*

Halstead came from a radical background. His mother, an immigrant Jewish garment worker, had been a Debs socialist, and his father, a machinist of Irish extraction, had been in the Industrial Workers of the World and in the forerunners of the SWP. Halstead served in the Navy during WW II and was affected by the "Bring the Boys Home" movement. His SWP membership prevented him from getting seaman's papers or a teaching job. He became a garment cutter and was a member of the International Ladies Garment Workers Union for most of his working life. In 1954 he was a volunteer activist in the bitter Square D strike in Detroit when management sought to eradicate a local of the United Electrical Workers. Through the years, Halstead was an on-site reporter for the *Militant* for major civil rights, environmental, and labor issues. He wrote pamphlets on the Harlem Rent Strike movement of the 1960s, the Three Mile Island accident, and the Hormel meatpackers' strike of 1985–86. *See also*: Peace Movements, Socialist Workers Party

—*Dan Georgakas*

REFERENCES

The Militant, June 24, 1988.

Hansberry, Lorraine (1930–65)

Best remembered for her play *A Raisin in the Sun*, Hansberry was also a talented poet, essayist, feminist, and political activist. In much of her writings, art and politics were inseparable themes. If her impressions of the African-American experience provoked controversy, they also revealed universal truths without sacrificing integrity or artistic conviction.

Daughter of a successful Chicago businessman who was unflinching in his quest for civil rights, Hansberry was nurtured in a highly conscious and politically aware household. She was fond of recalling how her determined father, after moving his family into a restricted neighborhood where blacks were unwelcome, proceeded to fight the case all the way to the Supreme Court. Eventually the case resulted in a decision against restrictive covenants and became famous as *Hansberry* v. *Lee.*

Aspects of this incident are vitally interwoven in *A Raisin in the Sun*.

At a very early age Hansberry decided on a career as a writer. "I think since I was a child, I have been possessed of the desire to put down the stuff of my life," she said at the beginning of her book *To Be Young, Gifted, and Black*. Her ability as a writer flowered right along with her political development. The aspiring writer was nineteen when she attended Paul Robeson's riot-marred concert at Peekskill, New York, in 1949. Three years later, at a mass meeting in Manhattan, she publicly assailed the witch-hunts of the House Un-American Activities Committee. By the time she was twenty-four, having studied at the University of Wisconsin and the Jefferson School of Social Science, Hansberry, now married to Robert Nemiroff, was active as director of special events at Camp Unity, conducted and attended by leftists and based in upstate New York. It was through her initiative that W. E. B. DuBois appeared at the camp to speak on political affairs in 1954.

During this period her writing consisted mostly of poetry and occasional journalistic assignments, particularly for Paul Robeson's newspaper, *Freedom*. As an activist-journalist, Hansberry moved swiftly from front to front, covering and participating in numerous social and political events. All the while she was honing her skills as a playwright. In 1959 her first play, *A Raisin in the Sun*, which featured Claudia McNeil and Sidney Poitier, was highly acclaimed, earning her the New York Drama Critics Award, a first for a black playwright. This historic success marked the emergence of a new movement in black theater. "She broke new ground," observed playwright/actor Douglas Turner Ward, who met Hansberry when she first arrived in New York City in 1950. "She crossed new frontiers . . . created new possibilities. Her impact and influence upon her own generation and succeeding ones are historic."

Hansberry, however, was too busy to enjoy her new celebrity. She continued her involvement in the growing civil rights movement, writing articles, marching, speaking at benefits, and when she could, working on her next play. She was, as the late author Julian Mayfield recalled, "living each moment as if it were her last." Because of this uncommon energy and enthusiasm for life, it was doubly shocking for those who knew her to hear she was stricken with cancer and dead at thirty-four. Hansberry's short but remarkable life has left an indelible imprint on the world of letters. *See also*: Civil Rights; Robeson, Paul

—*Herb Boyd*

REFERENCES

Freedomways (Lorraine Hansberry Special Issue) 19 (1979).

Hansberry, Lorraine. *Les Blancs: The Collected Plays of Lorraine Hansberry*. Edited by Robert Nemiroff. New York: Random House, 1972.

HARBURG, EDGAR Y. (1898–1981)

A lyricist who called for theater that presented the "guts of life," "Yip" Harburg began writing song lyrics while a student at the City College of New York. In the early years of the Depression, he collaborated with composer Jay Gorney on several musical revues. One of these, *Americana* (1932), included "Brother Can You Spare a Dime," which has long been associated with the Depression in the United States. A 1932 collaboration with Vernon Duke (Vladimir Dukelsky) produced *Walk a Little Faster*, the show that included "April in Paris." Duke and Harburg also wrote the 1934 Ziegfeld Follies. Harburg's career also included long working relationships with composers Harold Arlen and Burton Lane. He worked with Arlen on the 1934 production of *Life Begins at 8:40* and brought his satirical pen to a discussion of the prewar arms race in *Hooray for What!* in 1937. His films written in collaboration with Arlen included *Gold Diggers of 1937, At the Circus* (1939), *The Wizard of Oz* (1939), *Cabin in the Sky* (1943), *Meet the People* (1944, with Sammy Fain and Burton Lane), and *Gay Purr-ee* (1962).

Harburg continued to write for the stage, and his most famous work, *Finian's Rainbow* (book by Harburg and Fred Saidy, music by Burton Lane), ran on Broadway for 725 performances, starting on January 10, 1947. Using a fantastic setting and fanciful characters,

Finian's Rainbow confronted the issues of segregation and race relations in American society. Commenting on Broadway theater in the 1940s, critic Brooks Atkinson noted that "Harold Arlen's *Bloomer Girl* and Burton Lane's *Finian's Rainbow,* full of political satire and comic caprice [both with lyrics by Harburg], helped to redeem Broadway from drudgery." When *Finian's Rainbow* was revived in 1967, Harburg told the *New York Times* that his goal as a writer was to create "entertainment that brings people laughter and hope, but also spurs them to action." *Finian's Rainbow* received an award in 1967 from *Ebony* magazine for the play's contribution to improving interracial understanding. *Finian's Rainbow* was released as a film in 1968.

Harburg remained dedicated throughout his career to the causes espoused by various groups on the Left, although he did not have a specific party affiliation. As did those in *Finian's Rainbow,* the lyrics in *Bloomer Girl* (with S. Herzin and Fred Saidy, with music by Harold Arlen, 1944) and *Jamaica* (with Fred Saidy, music by Harold Arlen, 1957, starring Lena Horne and Ricardo Montalban) encouraged audiences to think critically about social problems and to consider seriously the writer's not-too thinly veiled critique of capitalism while enjoying the highest quality theatrical productions. He worked tirelessly in the American Society of Composers, Authors, and Publishers (ASCAP) to improve royalty payments to composers and writers, who often lost control over their creative work when it was produced on recordings. In addition to his work for stage and screen, Harburg published two volumes of poetry, much of which focused his wit and satire on current social issues. *Rhymes for the Irreverent* (1965) was dedicated to his wife, and he published *At This Point in Rhyme* in 1976. Harburg was closely associated with many members of the staff of *Monthly Review* and composed a "Birthday Song" for the journal's fifteenth anniversary in 1964. It was reprinted in tribute to Harburg in April 1984, one month after his death. *See also*: Monthly Review

—*Barbara L. Tischler*

REFERENCES

Bordman, Gerald. "E. Y. Harburg." In *The New Grove Dictionary of American Music,* edited by H. Wiley Hitchcock and Stanley Sadie. London: Macmillan, 1986.

Claghorn, Charles Eugene. *Biographical Dictionary of American Music.* West Nyack, N.Y.: Parker Publishers, 1973.

Harrington, Michael (1928–89)

For years America's best-known "bright young socialist," Harrington inherited the mantle of Norman Thomas and Eugene Debs. Although never the leader of a large movement, he was the only socialist after 1960 whom many Americans could identify and trust.

Born in St. Louis in 1928, the only child of a teacher mother and lawyer father, he remembered a boyhood among the "lace-curtain Irish." His Jesuit education at Holy Cross College trained him well for a life of debate and battle in the socialist movement. After a year at Yale Law School, which he entered as a Taft Republican and left as a democratic socialist, he enrolled at the University of Chicago, where he earned a master's degree in English. He moved to New York's Greenwich Village in 1949 and led the life of a bohemian, writing poetry and spending late nights at the White Horse Tavern.

Two years (1951–53) as a volunteer at the anarchist-pacifist Catholic Worker house on the Lower East Side, where he was associate editor of the *Catholic Worker,* marked him profoundly. He drew on those years for *The Other America* (1962), his ground-breaking book on poverty in America, and returned there twenty years later for research on *The New American Poverty.*

In between those two books and subsequent ones came a lifetime of socialist organizing and activism as well as writing and speaking about social issues that took him to thousands of lecture halls and college campuses. When he left the *Catholic Worker* and the Catholic faith, he became organizational director for the Workers Defense League in 1953. From 1954 to 1962 he supported himself as a researcher and writer for the Fund for the Republic. In 1957 he published a long article on poverty in *Commentary,* from which grew the book *The Other America*. This period coincided with changing political alliances and faction fights. As a leader of the Young People's Socialist League (YPSL), the youth section of the Socialist Party, Harrington differed with Norman Thomas over the latter's critical support for the American war in Korea and took the New York YPSL into Max Shachtman's Independent Socialist League in 1954. He was YPSL national chairman until it dissolved in June 1957. Starting in September 1958, Harrington and other ISL-YSL members entered the Socialist Party as a bloc. From 1960 to 1962 he edited *New America,* the SP's official paper.

With the publication in 1962 of *The Other America,* Harrington stepped into the national limelight. The book was read by President John F. Kennedy and is considered the intellectual force behind the antipoverty programs of his administration and of Lyndon Johnson's War on Poverty. As the *Boston Globe* editorialized in 1987, Medicaid and Medicare, food stamps and expanded social-security benefits are "directly traceable" to it. Harrington was also active in the civil rights movement and served on Martin Luther King, Jr.'s Advisory Committee.

During the 1960s Harrington's rigid anticommunism and thus his inability to support an unconditional withdrawal of U.S. troops from Vietnam contributed to divisions on the Left that haunted him for years. As liaison for the League for Industrial Democracy, he came into conflict with the LID's youth section, Students for a Democratic Society. He was upset that SDS allowed the Communist Party an observer at its Port Huron convention in the summer of 1962. Harrington had come to believe in realignment, that the seeds of a labor or socialist party existed within the Democratic Party and could be nurtured by coalition work with Leftists. He therefore believed that sections of the SDS Port Huron Statement would offend the liberals with whom he hoped to work, because they took an insufficiently critical attitude toward the Soviet Union and other authoritarian regimes. Later, Harrington would call his actions "stupid" and publicly berate himself for this blunder, but at the time he was a key force in the split between the Old Left and New Left.

He was elected SP chairman in 1968 as it debated its stance toward the Vietnam War. Harrington's Realignment Caucus opposed the war, but did not support unconditional withdrawal. (Shachtman continued to give critical support to the U.S. efforts, while the Debs Caucus was militantly antiwar.) Although he split with the Realignment Caucus and formed the Coalition Caucus—which backed George McGovern—Harrington did not resign as SP cochairman until October 1972, two months before leading his caucus out of the party convention to become, in February 1973, the Democratic Socialist Organizing Committee, of which he was chairman.

DSOC pursued its Democratic Party strategy through such projects as Democracy '76 and Democratic Agenda, which were program and policy coalitions within the party. In the 1980s, the successor coalition was called New Directions.

A rapprochement between some members of the Old Left and New Left occurred when Harrington supported the merger of DSOC and the New American Movement in 1982. Now he was working with many who had disdained him during the 1960s, but whose politics had come closer to his and his to theirs. The new organization, Democratic Socialists of America, claims to be the largest democratic socialist organization in the United States since the SP of 1936. Harrington cochaired it with socialist feminist Barbara Ehrenreich until his death.

Although widely known for his work on domestic issues, Harrington took great pleasure and pride in DSOC's, and then DSA's, participation in the Socialist International. As secretary of the Resolutions Committee at the SI Congress in 1983, he drafted the Manifesto of Albufeira, a political resolution adopted by the sixty-five parties, and served as coordinator of the Committee on a New Declaration of Principles.

In 1972 he became a professor of political science at Queens College. Harrington's contribution to American society through his writing and speaking helped legitimize left-wing discourse in American politics. Unlike many intellectuals, he was more than willing to participate in the tedious work of building an organization. Colleagues marveled at his patience and conciliatory skills and chafed at his inability to share power. Despite a losing battle with cancer of the esophagus, Harrington maintained a grueling writing and speaking schedule and remained active in DSA. He joked that he hoped to stave off death by writing so much. His sixteenth book, *Socialism: Past and Future*, was published in July 1989. He died on July 31, 1989. *See also*: Realignment, Socialist Party

—*Maxine Phillips*

REFERENCES

Chernow, Ron. "An Irresistible Profile of Michael Harrington (You Must Be Kidding)." *Mother Jones* (July 1977).

Harrington, Michael. *Fragments of the Century*. New York: Saturday Review Press, 1972.

———. *Socialism Past and Future*. New York: Arcade/Little, Brown, 1989.

Miller, Jim. *Democracy Is in the Streets: From Port Huron to the Siege of Chicago*. New York: Simon and Schuster, 1987.

Harrison, Hubert H. (1883–1927)

The Socialist Party functionary whom historian Joel Rogers described as "perhaps the foremost Afro-American intellect of his time" was a self-educated journalist and orator whose activism helped lay the groundwork for the New Negro movement in Harlem. Originally from the Virgin Islands, Harrison joined one of two Harlem branches of the Manhattan local of the SP in 1909, and soon distinguished himself as a speaker. In 1911 he published two editorial letters critical of Booker T. Washington's accommodationist philosophy. Subsequent pressure from members of the Tuskegee political machine resulted in the loss of his job with the U.S. Post Office, and he was hired as an organizer by the New York local of the party, working in the black community to win Socialist votes for the municipal campaign of 1911. His success led to his assignment to establish the Colored Socialist Club in Harlem. He wrote for the *Call*, and became an assistant editor of the *Masses*.

Harrison protested the local's quick abandonment of the recruitment campaign among blacks in 1912, but continued as a lecturer while openly criticizing the racial prejudice manifested by some party leaders. His support for Bill Haywood and the SP's pro-IWW (Industrial Workers of the World) wing, including his participation with Haywood and Elizabeth Gurley Flynn in the silk-workers' strike in Paterson, New Jersey, in 1913, further alienated him from the executive committee. He was suspended in 1914, and withdrew from the party. He returned to street speaking in Harlem, emphasizing black history and racial issues central to the black community. In the wake of the extreme racial violence of 1917 he launched the nationalist Liberty League of Negro-Americans, and edited its organ, the *Voice*, urging a stringent self-defensive response by the New Negro to white-instigated attacks. Marcus Garvey met Harrison in these years, and later recruited him to edit the *Negro World* (1920–22). In the mid-twenties Harrison advocated the creation of a separate black state within the territory of the United States, and in 1925 he founded the International Colored Unity League and a new periodical, the *Voice of the Negro*. His publications include *The Negro and the Nation* (1917) and *When Africa Awakes: The Inside Story of the Stirrings and Strivings of the New Negro in the Western World* (1920). *See also*: Garveyism, Socialist Party

—*Barbara Bair*

REFERENCES

Foner, Philip. *American Socialism and Black Americans*. Westport: Greenwood, 1977.

Hill, Robert A., and Carol A. Rudisell, eds. *The Marcus Garvey and Universal Negro Improvement Association Papers*. Vol. 1. Berkeley: University of California Press, 1983.

Rogers, Joel A. *World's Great Men of Color*. Vol. 2. New York: Macmillan, 1947.

HAWAII

The unique political economy of these islands has meant a quite different political spectrum from the rest of the United States throughout most of Hawaiian history. From 1850 to the end of World War II, Hawaii was ruled by a very small oligarchy that controlled both the political system and the plantation economy. Entirely dependent upon imported Asian labor, the planters established a firm grip on the political system—a grip that was only dislodged by the climactic attack on Pearl Harbor. The stark contrast between the opulence of the small ruling class and the destitution of the Asian workers made for a greater degree of class consciousness in Hawaii. The plantation camps and villages further promoted solidarity among the workers, who slowly learned to eliminate ethnic and racial animosities. Resistance to the political system was perforce confined to individual plantations until 1900.

The U.S annexation of Hawaii in 1900 brought federal law to Hawaii. Workers promptly took advantage of the freedom from indenture contracts and formed strikes organized around issues and goals. Convinced by strikes in 1909 and 1920 that a radicalism similar to that perceived on the mainland was coming to Hawaii, authorities introduced a wave of repressive legislation to eliminate plantation labor unions. The fear of radicalism was spurred by the development of the Japanese-language press. Of the fourteen such newspapers, three were distinctly Marxist in orientation. A handful of AFL craft unions struggled for survival in Honolulu. The Socialist Party that had put in a brief appearance in 1910–12 disappeared from the scene in World War I. The military, always prominent in Hawaii, viewed the large, non-Caucasian population as potentially radical. Military intelligence monitored labor activity closely.

The Great Depression began the effective alteration of the oligarchical structure in Hawaii. The final cutting off of imported labor supplies in 1934, New Deal subsidy legislation, and the growing militancy of the American labor movement were the principal agents in this process. Radical sailors organized a weekly newspaper, the *Voice of Labor*, in 1937, which reflected the militancy of the maritime labor community of the Pacific Coast. The Communist Party in New York sent Bill Bailey to Hawaii in 1937 to organize a chapter. Recruiting members on the waterfront and in Honolulu, Bailey also served as a writer for the labor paper. He and seaman Jack Hall (1916–72) were sent to Maui by the newly opened CIO office to assist the Filipinos in the last ethnic strike in Hawaii. For the first time the planters sat down and negotiated with the workers.

Hall began to organize plantation workers for United Cannery, Agricultural Packing and Allied Workers (UCAPAWA) on Kauai and to bring workers' political pressure to bear on the oligarchs with the Kauai Progressive League. The strong Marxist message appealed to the group-conscious Japanese and Filipino workers. There were enough citizens in the plantation work force to replace Kauai's two aristocratic senators with labor representatives in 1938 and 1940.

The International Longshoremen and Warehousemen's Union responded to local workers and led a sweeping organization of agricultural and maritime workers. Between 1944 and 1946, all but one of the sugar plantations were organized. Frank Thompson, veteran of the Industrial Workers of the World and the California Agricultural Industrial Workers Union, led the field organizing, while Jack Hall handled the very effective political organizing. Union-endorsed candidates were elected in 1945 in sufficient numbers to secure passage of a "little" Wagner Act, which closed the loopholes of the national act and permitted the effective organization of fieldworkers along with the sugar-mill workers.

All of this activity came to a focus in the first industrywide sugar strike of 1946. The ILWU effectively shut down the industry and defied the companies to use the old technique of eviction from plantation housing. The 79-day strike won union recognition and significant changes in the work situation. This victory gave the union the strength and base to conduct a 1949 strike in which longshoremen effectively curtailed shipping for 179 days. Solidarity with West Coast maritime workers made it impossible for the usual employer tactics to succeed.

Reflecting the rising antiradical sentiments in Washington, the territorial governor launched a Red-baiting assault in 1947, targeting two prominent schoolteacher-activists—John and Aiko Reinecke. Their dismissal, despite the complete lack of evidence in the "hearing," launched a vigorous antiunion campaign in the press and the legislature. An effort was made to split the Filipino workers away from the supposedly radical Japanese by forming an anticommunist rival to the ILWU. A parade of congressional committees, both House and Senate, linked the labor movement to Communism with a variety of paid informers.

The indictment of Jack Hall, regional director of the ILWU, and six of the leading members of the Hawaii CP in 1951, came as no surprise. The indictments charged the "Hawaii Seven" with "conspiring to teach and advocate the need to overthrow the government of the United States by force and violence," as well as with a variety of other crimes. Other than their membership in the CP and labor organizing, the evidence against the seven consisted solely of reading from Marxist-Leninist works, day after day, in the lengthy trial.

Although the convictions were overturned, the trial eroded public support for the labor movement. It had little impact on the loyalty of ILWU members. The democratic structure of the union and the continuing impressive contract gains turned aside all efforts to split the workers away from the union. The influence of the CP had been strongest among secondary leaders of the ILWU. As mechanization of the plantations reduced the work force, the sugar and pineapple workers were converted into something approaching mass-production industrial workers. The locus of radical activity shifted to the urban community.

Active Left-oriented groups have continued in Hawaii since the 1960s. A University of Hawaii firing of a young assistant professor over the Vietnam War issue in 1966 mobilized the heretofore tranquil student body to win his reinstatement after a two-year struggle.

The decade of the 1970s was a time of transition from the old Marxist Left to a younger, more environmentally oriented Left with few connections to the labor movement. This shift is reflected in the history of radical newspaper publishing in Hawaii. The *Honolulu Record*, edited by Koji Ariyoski, one of the Hawaii Seven, between 1948 and 1953, was financed by the ILWU. A recent Left-oriented newspaper was *Ka Huli'au* (1982–86), edited by a young radical environmentalist and supported by public contributions; the editor then won election to the state legislature.

Land utilization, environmental issues, and, since the 1970s, the rights of native Hawaiians, have been major issues. Much of the post–Vietnam War progressive spirit was evident in the successful campaign organized by former Communist leader Howard "Stretch" Johnson for a state holiday in honor of Martin Luther King, Jr. *See also*: ILWU

—*Edward Beechert*

REFERENCES

Beechert, Edward. *Working in Hawaii: A Labor History*. Honolulu: University of Hawaii Press, 1985.

Fuchs, Lawrence. *Hawaii Pond: A Social History*. New York: Harcourt, Brace & World, 1971.

Kent, Noel. *Hawaii: Islands Under the Influence*. New York: Monthly Review Press, 1982.

Zalburg, Stanford. *A Spark Is Struck! Jack Hall and the ILWU in Hawaii*. Honolulu: University of Hawaii Press, 1979.

Hawes, Elizabeth (1903–71)

One of the few fashion designers to involve herself with politics, Hawes not only believed the two were necessarily interconnected, but spent most of her working life trying to show how. A progressive political program, she argued, *had* to include the right to things that pleased the eye and heart, and not just the stomach.

Born to a well-respected Ridgewood, New Jersey, family, Hawes graduated from Vassar College in 1925, when she left for Paris to train as a traditional couturiere. It was a demystifying experience, which she detailed in reports to the *New Yorker* magazine in 1927 and 1928 under the pen name "Parisite." Ultimately, disgust with the French fashion scene moved her to return to the United States in 1928.

Hawes opened her own couture business in New York just as the Great Crash was wiping out many of her potential customers. Throughout the 1930s, she supplemented her income by doing design commissions for mass-market manufacturers. In 1935 she was the first foreign dress designer invited to show her work in the Soviet Union, where she traveled with the man who would become her husband in 1937, the stage (and later film) director, Joseph Losey.

In her first book, the 1938 best-seller *Fashion Is Spinach*, Hawes stripped the fashion business naked, revealing both its corrupt practices and its essential indifference to the needs of consumers. Fashion was a commodity, she argued, and like other commodities, it had to change incessantly, to keep people buying.

Men Can Take It—Hawes's argument against the oppression of men—followed in 1939. She suggested men try skirts and bright colors and not worry so much about their masculinity. In January 1940, Hawes closed her business, restructuring it as a collective, and joined the founding board of *PM* newspaper. As editor of the "News for Living" section, Hawes transformed the traditional women's page into a kind of populist guide to better living, focusing on education and consumer rights, as well as affordable entertainment and clothing. In this period Hawes also worked for the Committee for the Care of Young Children in Wartime.

Realizing her need for some firsthand experience of ordinary working life, Hawes took a night-shift job as a grinder at the Wright Aeronautical plant in Paterson, New Jersey, which formed the basis of her 1943 *Why Women Cry, or Wenches with Wrenches*. In one of the rare "war plant diaries" that rose above propaganda, Hawes laid out a "bread and roses" platform of radical proportions.

In 1944 Hawes was hired by the education department of the United Auto Workers in Detroit as a troubleshooter for women workers in UAW locals across the country. At the same time, she wrote a hard-hitting weekly column for the *Detroit Free Press*, where she confronted Detroiters with her ever-progressive ideas. By mid-1945, Hawes was Red-baited out of the UAW and her job at the *Detroit Free Press*. She returned to New York, where she wrote up these experiences in her 1946 *Hurry Up Please It's Time*.

Ever since her *PM* days, however, the FBI had been collecting a file on Hawes's activities, a file that seemed doubly dangerous since they had confused Hawes with another radical woman of the same name. While Hawes herself was not aware of the file, some of her business associates were, and she found difficulties returning to her former fashion work.

As the Cold War climate in America became unbearable, Hawes looked for alternatives. Her choice was St. Croix, the Virgin Islands, where she taught herself to live as a self-styled bohemian. Her 1948 *Anything But Love* was a sarcastic exposé of the new mythology of contented postwar womanhood.

Life in the Caribbean also opened her eyes to the fact of American imperialism, which she discussed in her 1951 *But Say It Politely*. Uncomfortable with the contradictions of her position as a "Continental," Hawes moved to California in the early fifties, where she became the inspiration for younger designers such as Rudi Gernreich. But it was not until her 1967 retrospective at the Fashion Institute of Technology that the depth and consistency of Hawes's design work was finally recognized. Her more central vision—of the necessary unity of art and politics—remains to be appreciated. *See also*: *PM*

—*Bettina Berch*

REFERENCES

Berch, Bettina. *Radical by Design: The Life and Style of Elizabeth Hawes*. New York: E. P. Dutton, 1988.

Hayden, Tom: see Students for a Democratic Society

Hayes, Max: see Cleveland Citizen

Haymarket Incident

On May 4, 1886, a bomb was thrown as local police attacked an anarchist-led labor demonstration in Chicago's Haymarket Square. Eight policemen died as a result of the bombing and of crossfire among police. An undetermined, but probably larger, number of demonstrators lost their lives amidst the tumult and police gunfire. The identity of the bomb-thrower remains a mystery, but the events leading up to Haymarket, and the tremendous repercussions of the bombing, are more clear.

The Haymarket Square demonstration grew out of a massive nationwide movement of working people demanding the eight-hour working day. That demand had begun to attract support during the Civil War as workers identified their long hours as a kind of "slavery" from which they could be "emancipated" by legislation. After the war, Eight-Hour Leagues boomed in membership and successfully lobbied for eight-hour laws in several states. But these laws almost all featured gaping loopholes. In Illinois, Chicago Eight-Hour Leagues were instrumental in securing the passage of a shorter-hours law in 1867, albeit an unenforceable one. On May 1 of that year, tens of thousands of Chicago workers attempted to make the statute apply by striking. Their actions failed, largely as a result of police violence, but the episode in that booming industrial city presented in microcosm trends that would mature in the next twenty years and lead toward Haymarket.

By the early 1880s, radical workers in Chicago and elsewhere had accumulated further grievances against the political system, especially in the bloody suppression of the 1877 railroad strike and in subsequent local elections in which socialist candidates charged that fraud had "counted them out" of victory. Three separate national organizational responses resulted, all of them seeking to reconcile republican citizenship with industrial society and to address the question of how the labor movement should interact with a government hostile to labor action. The oldest of these organizations, the Knights of Labor (founded 1869), preached the virtues of cooperatives, of working-class self-education, of agitation for political reform, of cultivation of good relations with local politicians, of organization of both skilled and unskilled workers, and of caution in undertaking strikes. Irish-American workers strongly supported the Knights of Chicago. The Federation of Organized Trades and Labor Unions (founded 1881, evolved into the American Federation of Labor in 1886) stressed trade union organizing and sought to avoid politically divisive issues and reliance on the state in labor-reform matters. The smallest organization, the International Working People's Association (founded 1881) mixed anarchism, socialism, and syndicalism. The IWPA utterly rejected both politics and reform while embracing revolutionary self-defense and writing romantically about the possibility of dynamite as a tool for labor militants. It attracted substantial support among German, Czech, and Scandinavian immigrants. Its Chicago branch, led by Albert Parsons, Lucy Parsons, and August Spies, emphasized the role of industrial unions and farm organizations in providing the basis for a new and stateless society.

Lines dividing these various approaches to labor organization were extremely fluid, with many activists easily switching organizational affiliations or even belonging to different groups simultaneously. In Chicago, with the approach of the May 1, 1886, date designated by the FOTLU for transition to an eight-hour day, Knights, craft unionists, and the IWPAers who helped lead the large Central Labor Union joined forces to build a huge strike involving perhaps 80,000 workers.

During this strike, it became apparent that Mayor Carter Harrison, who earlier had urged restraint in the policing of labor disputes, had abandoned such a policy in favor of the stance of his appointee, police captain John Bonfield, who held that "the club today saves the bullet tomorrow." On May 3, lumber workers rallying for the eight-hour day joined strikers from the McCormick Harvest Works, involved in a separate labor dispute, to harass strikebreakers at the latter establishment. Police fired into the crowd, killing at least two and wounding many strikers. The anarchist leader August Spies had spoken to the lumber workers and witnessed the bloodshed. The IWPA, which had promised to defend the eight-hour strikes against the kind of police, Pinkerton, and National Guard violence that had caused scores of workers to die in the 1877 strike wave, called the May 4 meeting at Haymarket to protest police violence and to memorialize the victims at McCormick Works. Tensions ran high as employers' associations and the press demanded decisive antistrike measures while one version of the IWPA's leaflets against police violence bore the headline: REVENGE! WORKINGMEN, TO ARMS!!!

The demonstration in Haymarket Square was itself uneventful until the police attacked. Rain was heavy and attendance light. Mayor Harrison, who came as an observer, found the gathering peaceable and orderly. But after the mayor and most of the demonstrators had departed, Captain Bonfield led 180 police in an attempt to break up the rally. Moments later, the bomb exploded, sparking a police riot.

The first fruits of the bombing were accelerated campaigns of repression against the eight-hour strikers, anarchists, and labor leaders in Chicago and, to an extent, nationally. Chicago's press mixed anti-immigrant, anti-labor union and antiradical stereotypes in a hysterical campaign against anarchist "serpents," who were seen as the "offscourings of Europe." Police for weeks kept up a steady pattern of raids on Chicago labor leaders' homes and labor organizations' headquarters, and their spurious reports of finding caches of arms and explosives just as steadily splashed across front pages of the city's daily papers.

Eight IWPA members were prosecuted in this atmosphere for conspiracy to murder policeman Mathias Degan, who died at Haymarket. In their trial, State's Attorney Julius Grinnell affirmed that "anarchy" was the real defendant and, as Paul Avrich has recently put it, Judge Joseph E. Gary "flaunted his bias against the defendants" at every turn. All eight defendants received guilty verdicts in August 1886, though no evidence specifically linked them to the bomb. In November of the following year, four of them—August Spies, Albert Parsons, George Engel, and Adolph Fischer—were executed by hanging. A fifth condemned anarchist, Louis Lingg, killed himself in jail. Oscar Neebe, Samuel Fielden, and Michael Schwab stayed in jail until released in 1893 by Illinois governor John Peter Altgeld, whose stinging pardon message acknowledged the injustice of the trial.

Haymarket's bomb echoed long and deep. The explosion and ensuing repression decimated the anarchist labor movement, though the martyred defendants became heroes to many and inspired countless individual conversions to anarchism and to socialism. Victimized too were the Knights of Labor, who suffered both from the general repression of worker's organizations and from the refusal of their national leadership to endorse the broad-based campaign in defense of those accused as a result of the bombing. The pardons ruined Altgeld's promising political career. The tactic of the mass strike was far less appealing to pragmatic U.S. labor leaders after Haymarket, and the idea of self-defense by labor never again received so broad a hearing on the national scale. On an international scale, the Haymarket events and 1886 eight-hour strikes contributed to the 1889 decision of the Second International to adopt May 1 as World Labor Day. *See also*: Anarchism; Black International; May Day; Parsons, Albert; Parsons, Lucy; Spies, August

—*Dave Roediger*

REFERENCES

Avrich, Paul. *The Haymarket Tragedy*. Princeton: Princeton University Press, 1984.

David, Henry. *The History of the Haymarket Affair*. New York: Russell and Russell, 1958.

Foner, Philip S., ed. *The Autobiographies of the Haymarket Martyrs*. New York: Monad Press, 1969.

Nelson, Bruce C. *Beyond the Martyrs: A Social History of Chicago Anarchism 1870–1900*. New Brunswick: Rutgers University Press, 1988.

Roediger, Dave, and Franklin Rosemont, eds. *Haymarket Scrapbook*. Chicago: Charles H. Kerr Company, 1986.

Haywood, Harry (1898–1985)

Of all the Afro-American figures in the history of American Communism, none was more important in ultimate impact than Harry Haywood. Born to a sharecropping family that fled the South at the turn of the century, Haywood came to Chicago as a young man following World War I. He joined the Communist Party in 1925 and in 1926 sojourned to Moscow, where he was strongly influenced by the first generation of anticolonial revolutionaries (among them M. N. Roy of India, Tan Malaka of Indonesia, and Ho Chi Minh). During his years of study in the Soviet Union his peasant background merged with this anticolonial tradition to crystallize his major theoretical contribution to American radicalism—the theory of self-determination in the "black belt" of the American South for the Afro-American people.

Haywood initiated the debate on self-determination within the Party during the 1930s and vigorously fought for this position until his expulsion in 1959. Accused of "Left sectarianism," Haywood continued to be one of the most astute observers of the civil rights and black power movements from an independent standpoint during the later 1950s and 1960s. His work on the insurrectionary potential of the black masses bore fruit in the "long, hot summers" of 1965–68; on the revolutionary implications of black nationalism with the emergence of Malcolm X, the Revolutionary Action Movement, and the League of Revolutionary Black Workers; and finally, his cautious warning about the co-optation and subversion of an independent black mass movement. During the last years of his life, he was instrumental in nurturing a new generation of Afro-American radicals, exposing them to the intricacies of his own experience in party politics, while exposing them to the dangers of the integrationist dogma of liberal and radical alike. His major works include *Negro Liberation* (1948) and his autobiography, *Black Bolshevik* (1978) in addition to numerous articles, pamphlets, and political tracts. Ernest Allen of the University of Massachusetts is preparing a collection of his lesser-known writings for eventual publication. *See also*: Communist Party, Garveyism

—*William Eric Perkins*

REFERENCES

Baraka, Amiri [LeRoi Jones]. "*Black Bolshevik: Autobiography of an Afro-American Communist*, by Harry Haywood." *Daggers and Javelins: Essays, 1974–1979*. New York: William Morrow & Co., 1984.

Haywood, Harry. *Black Bolshevik: Autobiography of an Afro-American Communist*. Chicago: Liberator Press, 1978; distributed by Lake View Press.

———. *For a Revolutionary Position on the Negro Question*. Chicago: Liberator Press, 1975. This was written and circulated in 1957.

———. *Negro Liberation*. International Publishers, 1948. Reprint. Chicago: Liberator Press, 1976.

HAYWOOD, WILLIAM D. (1869–1928)

A hard-rock miner, "Big Bill" Haywood became the leader and symbol of the Industrial Workers of the World during the IWW's brief heyday as a power in American industrial relations. William Dudley Haywood was born in Salt Lake City, Utah, on February 4, 1869, the son of a South African woman and a Kentucky miner who had also worked as a Pony Express rider. In 1884 the young Haywood went to work as a miner's helper in Nevada, where he learned the rudiments of industrial unionism and the principles of socialism from a member of the Knights of Labor. He soon married Nevada Jane Minor, the daughter of a rancher, and filed for a homestead near the Idaho line. The land was lost when the federal government recalled it for use as an Indian reservation. With his wife ailing with chronic arthritis, Haywood returned to mining, settling in Silver City, Idaho.

He quickly rose to be head of the Western Federation of Miners in Silver City. He was an excellent administrator, maintaining virtually total organizational control of the town, supervising the hospital, and negotiating peacefully with employers. In recognition of his success, Haywood was brought to Denver in 1901 to be secretary-treasurer of the national WFM, which had become the target of an aggressive regional campaign by employers and state governments out to break its power in the mines, mills, and smelters. Over six feet tall, well over two hundred pounds, and with a glowering glass eye (the consequence of a boyhood accident), Haywood soon earned a reputation as a resolute crisis leader. He went about his rounds armed with a revolver and ready to exchange blows and epithets in his capacity as editor of the *Miner's Magazine*. An increasingly militant socialist, he was also a heavy drinker and a womanizer. Nevada Jane

Sabotage Sticker

converted to Christian Science and the Haywoods became estranged.

In 1905 Haywood was the keynote speaker at the founding convention of the IWW, which he called "the Continental Congress of the working class." His immediate role in the union was aborted when in 1906, along with WFM president Charles Moyer, he was charged with the bombing murder of former Idaho governor Frank Steunenberg, arrested, and irregularly extradited to Idaho. Defended by Clarence Darrow, Haywood was acquitted in July 1907, but his career in the WFM had ended due to a falling out with Moyer, the causes of which are obscure.

As a radical cause célèbre, Haywood found himself in a wider world of agitation. Vaudeville operators offered him thousands of dollars a week in fees if he would appear on their circuits. Haywood, who had stood as Socialist candidate for governor of Colorado while in prison, chose to lecture for the Socialist Party. At one meeting in Chicago's Riverside Park he addressed 60,000 paid admissions and in Milwaukee 25,000. Haywood also contributed to the *International Socialist Review*, which supported the "revolutionist" wing of the SP, was elected to the party's national executive committee, and twice represented the SP at meetings of the Second International. In the course of representing the SP abroad, he met many prominent revolutionaries, trade unionists, and intellectuals. Among these were George Bernard Shaw, V. I. Lenin, Rosa Luxemburg, Ramsey MacDonald, Jean Jaures, and Clara Zeitkin. Haywood addressed large gatherings in Scandinavia and Great Britain.

By 1912 Haywood was an organizer-at-large for the IWW. He played the leading role in the successful Lawrence, Massachusetts, textile strike of 1912 and in the unsuccessful but historic IWW strikes in Akron, Ohio, and Paterson, New Jersey, in 1913. Although a favorite of the fashionable Greenwich Village Left of Mabel Dodge and John Reed, Haywood irritated "reformist" Socialist leaders such as Morris Hillquit and Victor Berger. They disapproved of his militant rhetoric on behalf of sabotage, which they interpreted as meaning violence, and by his disdain for their electoral approach to socialism. While never rejecting electoral politics, Haywood emphasized that revolution could be affected only by workers at the point of production working through their industrial unions.

When their expectations for the election of 1912 were unrealized, the reformers blamed the shortfall on the public's association of the SP with the IWW. In early 1913 they arranged to recall Haywood from his party office, the main complaint being that he would not unambivalently disavow the use of violent sabotage. Haywood did not resist and soon succeeded Vincent St. John as secretary-treasurer of the IWW. He soon led the union to significant organizational successes, especially among western loggers, copper miners, and migrant farm workers. The IWW had reached its peak membership of approximately 100,000 when the "preparedness" campaign and American intervention in World War I presented it with a mortal challenge. The IWW opposed the war but, largely at Haywood's behest, did not agitate against it nor forbid members to comply with the draft. Nevertheless, politicians, patriotic organizations, and employers' associations attacked the union as disloyal and dangerous. A series of raids resulted in the indictment of Haywood and most of the union's leadership under the Sedition Act. After a long and celebrated trial in Chicago, infamous for its lack of hard evidence, Haywood was sentenced to a fine of $20,000 and twenty years imprisonment.

Haywood had urged IWWs to submit to arrest and a mass trial, convinced that the government's case would collapse and the subsequent IWW victory would launch it into an era of renewed growth. In March 1921, with his strategy discredited and himself ailing with diabetes, Haywood jumped bail and fled to the Soviet Union while most of his co-defendants languished in prison. IWW morale was shattered. Although individuals remembered him affectionately and excused his action without justifying it, his influence on the American Left had all but vanished.

Haywood's years in the Soviet Union have been a subject of dispute in the Left. Those opposed to the Communist Party have claimed Haywood was extremely unhappy in Moscow and perhaps disillusioned with the Bolsheviks. Others have written that his major problems in the USSR had to do with his health. What is clear is that after failing as a manager of a factory complex, Haywood spent most of his time in Moscow, where he chiefly mixed with journalists such as Walter Duranty of the *New York Times* and radicals like Harry Haywood (no relation), who had come to study in the Soviet Union. He was not entirely idle politically. James Cannon credits him with launching the idea for the International Labor Defense and Harry Haywood has written that Big Bill often met to discuss political issues with Moscow-based Communists. While in Moscow, Haywood wrote an autobiography, *Bill Haywood's Book*, which has become a focus of partisan acrimony. Anticommunists reject it as inauthentic or at best, heavily edited to serve the purposes of the CP. The book comes to a climax with Haywood's arrival in Moscow and a meeting with Lenin, feeding the speculation that someone other than Haywood completed the book or that Haywood rushed the final parts due to illness. He suffered two strokes in the spring of 1928 and died on May 18. He is interred in the Kremlin wall. *See also*: Industrial Workers of the World, Socialist Party

—*Joseph R. Conlin*

REFERENCES

Carlson, Peter. *Roughneck: The Life and Times of Big Bill Haywood*. New York: Norton, 1983.

Conlin, Joseph R. *Big Bill Haywood and the Radical Labor Movement*. Syracuse: Syracuse University Press, 1969.

Dubofsky, Melvyn. *"Big Bill" Haywood*. New York: St. Martin's Press, 1987.

———. *We Shall Be All: A History of the Industrial Workers of the World*. Chicago: Quadrangle Books, 1969.

Haywood, William D. *Bill Haywood's Book*. New York: International Publishers, 1929.

HEALEY DOROTHY (b. 1914)

Postwar leader of the southern California Communist Party, Healey was a full-time Party activist and spokesperson for over forty years. She was born in Denver, Colorado, and raised in Oakland, California. Her mother was a founding member of the CPUSA. Shortly after joining the Young Communist League in 1928 Healey became known as a popular and effective organizer of migrant farm-workers in the agricultural valleys of California, and in 1940 she was appointed a deputy labor commissioner by liberal Democratic governor Culbert Olson. Healey quietly opposed Earl Browder's dissolution of the CPUSA during WW II, and in 1945 she emerged from the intra-Party factional struggle as a compromise candidate to head the Los Angeles branch.

In 1952 Healey was among a large group of Party leaders arrested under the Smith Act. Following her release in 1952, she began to campaign within leading Party circles for a more flexible and independent approach toward the USSR. In the years after Khrushchev's revelatory speech in 1956, she became something of a maverick figure in the CPUSA, concentrating most of her energies on southern California.

In the early- and mid-1960s Healey became widely known for her frequent appearances on college campuses and her strong support for the student-led antiwar movement. These activities, however, increasingly brought her into open conflict with the national Party leadership, and in 1969, having openly opposed the Soviet invasion of Czechoslovakia, she effectively removed herself from the CPUSA. Following her formal resignation in 1973, Healey became active in the New American movement and the Democratic Socialists of America. *See also*: Communist Party, Migratory Agricultural Labor

—*Michael Furmanovsky*

REFERENCES

Healey, Dorothy Ray. *Tradition's Chains Have Bound Us*. University of California at Los Angeles Oral History, 1982.

HEALTH LEFT

The health field, long dominated by the medical profession and its institutional and commercial allies, has a widely recognized and well-deserved reputation for political conservatism and for obstruction to meaningful social change in and outside the health field.

This dominance has obscured the existence during the past 100 or so years of a line of Left physicians, nurses, dentists, and other health professionals who have held contrary views and have played important political roles in and outside the health field. They have joined various people's movements in resisting economic exploitation and other social injustices and in fighting for improved health services and better health for all.

Usually unnoticed in labor and political history are the health-policy proposals and health-service programs that originated in Left unions, women's clubs, political parties, and other peoples' organizations. These groundbreaking efforts, often marginal in their original settings, significantly influenced the thinking and products of mainstream health reformers in contemporary and later periods.

Environmental health concerns were a high priority among the measures formally proposed by the Left political parties of the 1870–1900 period for "improving the conditions of the working classes." Typical is item 2 in the eleven immediate demands specified in the "Declaration of Principles of the Workingmen's Party of the United States," adopted July 22, 1876: "Sanitary inspection of all conditions of labor, means of subsistence ['victuals'], and dwellings included."

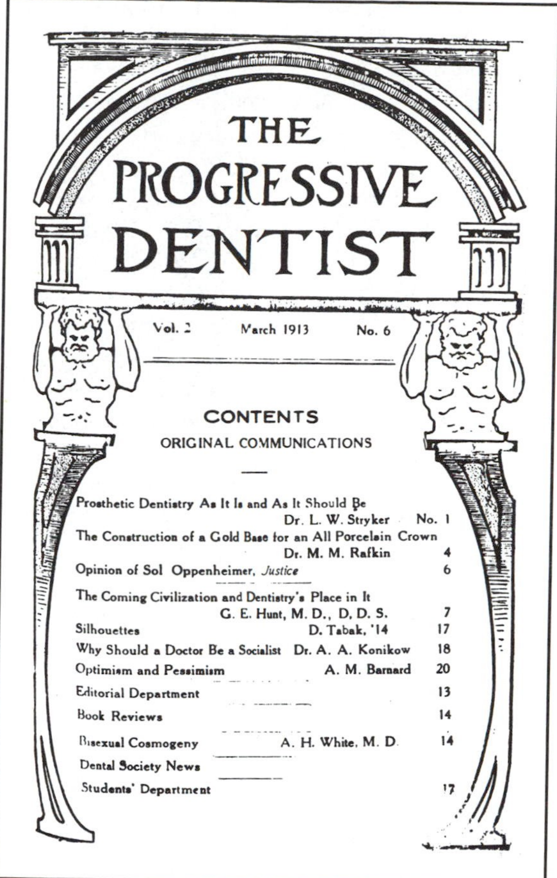

THE PROGRESSIVE DENTIST

Vol. 2 March 1913 No. 6

CONTENTS

ORIGINAL COMMUNICATIONS

Prosthetic Dentistry As It Is and As It Should Be	Dr. L. W. Stryker	No. 1
The Construction of a Gold Base for an All Porcelain Crown	Dr. M. M. Rafkin	4
Opinion of Sol Oppenheimer, *Justice*		6
The Coming Civilization and Dentistry's Place in It	G. E. Hunt, M. D., D. D. S.	7
Silhouettes	D. Tabak, '14	17
Why Should a Doctor Be a Socialist	Dr. A. A. Konikow	18
Optimism and Pessimism	A. M. Barnard	20
Editorial Department		13
Book Reviews		14
Bisexual Cosmogeny	A. H. White, M. D.	14
Dental Society News		
Students' Department		17

Journal for Socialist Dentists, 1913

Radical women activists and union leaders were prominent in the efforts to press this demand, particularly the elimination or control of hazards in sweatshops, factories, and mines. A significant example of such work is the 1891 report *The New Slavery: Investigation into the Sweating System*, by socialist Elizabeth Morgan and comrades, published by the Chicago Trade and Labor Assembly; the associated campaign resulted in the 1893 enactment of the Illinois Factory Inspection Act.

Left workers also helped organize and run unions and mutual-aid societies that, among their functions, provided death (funeral) and disability benefits and paid for general physician care, medicines, and sometimes other medical services on a group-payment (insurance) basis.

In a few such situations hospitals were built and operated, the first being established in 1891 by the Coeur d'Alene Union of the lead and silver miners in northern Idaho. The Left-dominated Cuban and Spanish societies of the cigar makers of Ybor City (Tampa) furnish another early example (1904) of worker-controlled medical-benefit activities expanding into hospital ownership and management.

In the late nineteenth century socialist and other Left health practitioners, dismayed by the underserved needs of the poor, provided care in their private offices or at dispensaries and hospitals to those who could not get it otherwise. Physicians, in particular, also gave money and the prestige of their names to mass events and campaigns organized by the Left. A few assumed leadership positions in local and national political parties.

Physicians were especially numerous among the politically influential veterans of the 1848 revolution in Germany who emigrated to the United States. One such physician was Ernst Schmidt, who in 1879 ran for mayor of Chicago on the Socialist Labor Party ticket and in 1886 chaired the defense committee for the Haymarket martyrs.

When the Socialist Party was founded in 1901, the immediate demands again included environmental health concerns, this time recognizing existing but inadequate government efforts: "more effective inspection of workshops and factories." In addition, the Socialists' increased reliance on government for solution of social problems resulted in two further health demands of substantial magnitude and political significance: (1) "compulsory insurance against . . . illness, accidents, invalidism" [as well as 'unemployment, old age, and death'], and (2) "the creation of a [federal] department of public health."

Essentially similar positions were expressed by progressives generally. Theodore Roosevelt accepted fully the counsel of Socialist social welfare experts (John A. Kingsbury, I. M. Rubinow et al.) as reflected in the platform of the Progressive Party (1912); this includes a commitment to (1) "a system of social insurance [that would protect] home life against the hazards of sickness" [as well as 'irregular employment and old age'] and (2) "the union of all the existing agencies of the federal government dealing with the public health into a single national health service . . . with such additional powers as may be necessary [for] the protection of the public from preventable diseases. . . ."

The heyday of Socialist electoral politics enabled some demonstration of a Socialist health program. For instance, George R. Lunn, the Socialist mayor of Schenectady, addressed that city's Aldermanic Council in 1912 as follows: "We place health in our administration as the one consideration that should outweigh all others. As Socialists, we recognize it as part of the duty of the twentieth century State to assume the responsibility for the health of its citizens. . . . We propose to use the whole force of the Health Department as an educational power. Through lectures, demonstrations, and exhibits, we shall seek to enlighten people as to those social conditions which are the root of so much disease. . . . A maternity and infancy nurse trained also as a social worker, will be appointed. . . . In the public schools rigid inspection by qualified physicians will begin—cases of illness and deficiency will not only be reported but will be followed up by nurses. . . . Hindered though we are by unjust laws, we shall nevertheless use every available power to make it possible for the people to maintain their homes in the face of the deplorable conditions that tyrannize over them. . . . We assert as Socialists that tuberculosis is due to economic and social causes. The community is, therefore, responsible for the disease, and must act upon that responsibility by remedying the vile living and working conditions which produce it. So far as the laws permit we shall work with prevention as our first aim. . . . The disease must be wiped out."

The most creative and challenging contribution of Socialists of this period to the health field was the comprehensive neighborhood health center under the control of those it served. This concept was developed by Socialists Wilbur C. Phillips and his wife Elsie Cole Phillips. After an abortive first try to establish such a center in Milwaukee at the request of that city's Socialist administration, they were able to try again in Cincinnati. In three years there, 1917–20, they did create a functioning, democratically elected Citizen's Council to govern the enterprise. Despite strong neighborhood support, this unique experiment in social organization for health service was killed by postwar Red-baiting conservatism.

Left physicians, men and women, of a variety of political perspectives were frequently zealous participants in union health services, abortion and birth control services, and public education/advocacy campaigns about tuberculosis, mental health, sexual health, healthful living, and national health insurance.

Not surprisingly, in this period emerges the first (and rarely replicated) avowedly Socialist organization of health workers—the Dentists Study Chapter of the Intercollegiate Socialist Society. The chapter, organized in 1910, was located in New York City and its active members were both dental students and dentists. In addition to educational meetings, social events, and distribution of literature (including their own leaflet on "oral hygiene from the Socialist standpoint"), they published the *Progressive Dentist*, the first Left health-workers' periodical. Like most Socialist enterprises with strong antiwar positions, both the chapter and the magazine did not survive long after the war started.

The Russian Revolution was a powerful and complex stimulant to the Health Left and its visions of greatly expanded governmental health responsibilities. In the 1920s and early 1930s a few health professionals, after visiting the Soviet Union, reported enthusiastically on the potential if not the actuality of the first completely nationalized system of medical practice, training of health workers, scientific research, and public health.

Such laudatory education reached maturity in the systematic studies and prolific writings of Henry E. Sigerist, internationally recognized medical historian and sociologist; he was a temporary but influential American, imported from Europe in 1932 by Johns Hopkins University to head its Medical History Institute. Sigerist's *Socialized Medicine in the Soviet Union* was published in 1937 by a major commercial publisher and was immediately accorded authoritative status by the health field and the general public. (He appeared on the cover of *Time* magazine.) This book begins with a forty-page "Background of Soviet Medicine," which sympathetically presents the history of the Revolution and the Marxist political foundations of the Soviet health system.

Sigerist followed this up in the 1940s by helping organize and guide the American-Soviet Medical Society and its journal, the *American Review of Soviet Medicine*. This enterprise provided Western medicine for the first time extensive reports about Soviet medical research, medical practice, and the organization of health services. It prospered for four years and then became a Cold War fatality.

Far more simple politically but much more engaging personally for the Health Left was the Spanish Civil War. Medical/surgical units for the Abraham Lincoln Brigade were organized by the Medical Bureau to Aid Spanish Democracy with major leadership from Communist Party physicians. Those who risked their lives for their political convictions on the battlefronts in Spain numbered about sixty-five nurses, about thirty physicians, and about forty other health professionals, technicians, and ambulance drivers. In addition, the bureau raised money at medical institutions across the country to purchase and send to the Spanish Loyalists seventy ambulances and large quantities of medicines and medical/surgical supplies.

On the home front, the detrimental impact of the workplace on the health of workers continued to receive intensive attention from the Left. A unique expression of this priority was the Workers Health Bureau of America, organized in 1921 by several women with experience in the consumers' and labor movements. It served as the research, education, and advocacy arm of organized labor for workplace health and safety. At its height, it had the support of 190 labor organizations in twenty-four states. It viewed workers' health and safety as class issues to be controlled by unions and workers themselves; this distinguished it from most contemporary and subsequent occupational-health efforts premised as the province of special technicians and professionals. It organized the first national labor health conference in 1927. A year later it disbanded when hostility from conservative AFL leadership resulted in loss of its union support.

Perhaps the most significant attempt at education of the general public about health matters from a Left perspective was the magazine *Health and Hygiene*. It was published monthly for about four years beginning in 1935. It provided up-to-date advice on personal health matters as well as coverage of the political aspects of the health field.

The International Workers Order, the Communist offspring of the Workmen's Circle, and other Left union and mutual-aid societies, with substantial support of Left physicians, revitalized the medical benefit programs traditional among immigrant working people.

In the 1930s and 1940s Left physicians provided leadership to the development of short-lived federal medical-care programs for the poor and long-lived group-practice health-insurance plans for the middle class—the earliest precursors of HMOs. Several of these—in Washington, D.C., the Midwest, and Far West—were organized on the consumer cooperative model. Inspiration and guidance came from James P. Warbasse; out of political conviction and personal wealth, he retired from a successful surgical practice in Brooklyn in 1916 to become the protagonist, major funder, and first president of the Cooperative League of the USA, a position he held for twenty-five years. He authored the first monographs on "Cooperative Medicine"; having rejected strongly both the competitive for-profit and the total government approaches, he believed the only salvation for American medical care was the local consumer-controlled approach.

Among the unions organized in the 1930s with CP leadership was Local 1199, the union of New York City pharmacists and drugstore clerks. Its founding raised the fundamental issue for Left health professionals then and ever since—do health professionals, mostly not working class by background, income, or social status, belong in unions? Decades later this union expanded to include other kinds of health workers and is now the National Union of Hospital and Health Care Employees, still known as 1199.

Left physicians did not join unions but were responsible for a variety of political organizations; notable among these for its program scope and longevity is the Physicians Forum, now almost fifty years old. The forum's central commitment was to national-health-insurance education and advocacy but it did pioneering work on racial discrimination in the health field and premiered the concept of nuclear weapons testing and use as a major public-health issue. This last was picked up brilliantly early in the 1960s by Physicians for Social Responsibility; many of its leaders were veterans of Left medical-student activities in the 1930s and 1940s, one of whom, Bernard Lown, received the Nobel Prize for Peace in 1986.

Beginning in the 1940s, Left public-health workers—academic physicians, health administrators, and others—invested considerable energy in the internal affairs of the American Public Health Association, making it the major left-of-center political force in the health field. Several of its presidents were known leftists and in recent years it has even flaunted a large and energetic Socialist Caucus.

The Medical Committee for Human Rights was started by Left and liberal physicians in 1964 as an adjunct to the civil rights movement. Initially its main contribution was "medical presence": the physical presence of white physicians and other health professionals at major demonstrations in the South added credibility to the events and increased the safety of all the participants; first aid and limited medical and surgical care were also furnished. A community clinic was established in a poverty-stricken rural county of Mississippi.

With the withdrawal of northerners from southern civil rights activities, MCHR experienced intensive and prolonged internal review and upheaval, becoming a multi-issue, radical-style, Left-oriented organization; in the process, it lost most of its liberal support. Chapters in different parts of the country continued to provide "medical presence" at movement demonstrations, but they also developed special proficiency in organizing and furnishing emergency medical care required by police brutality, one particularly notable example being the demonstrations at the 1968 Democratic convention in Chicago. Although racism in the health field was a principal concern, MCHR's agenda included opposition to the Vietnam War and support of government policies and programs to eliminate or ameliorate the plight of the poor. It created an occupational health and safety project that was reborn as independent COSH groups (Committees on Occupational Safety and Health) in a number of large cities and it developed principles for a national health service that were the basis for the NHS Bill introduced by Congressman Ronald Dellums, an avowed socialist.

The New Left—with essential, unpaid enthusiasm and the skills of its medical-student wing—spawned the "Free Clinics" in San Francisco's Haight-Ashbury and in other cities with medical schools. Dependent on the available time and continuing commitment of unsettled health professionals in training, these efforts were tenuous in scope, quality and permanence. An important variant were those clinics established by the Black Panthers in the black ghettos of Chicago, Oakland, Philadelphia, and other big cities. They were the most authentic, albeit brief, demonstration of health care organized and delivered by the population it served.

Left health professionals, most also active in MCHR, organized and staffed the health/medical unit of Ralph Nader's Public Citizen and a health think-tank/professional journal, *Health/PAC* (Policy Advisory Center). These and related efforts nourished the concept of health rights, which soon became formalized, at times legalized, and in the case of hospital patient rights, taken over and grossly distorted by hospital administration.

Two other Health Left journals were founded and are still guided by academic physicians with different Left credentials predating the New Left: *International Journal of Health Services* (Vicente Navarro) and *Journal of Public Health Policy* (Milton Terris). Both of these editors with their own extensive research and publications have shed much rose-colored light on the politics and economics of the health field. They and several other younger and older physicians as teachers in medical and public-health schools have immeasurably influenced the thinking and practice of a host of health professionals.

During this period many Left health professionals were ardent supporters of solidarity with the successful socialist revolutions in China, Cuba, Nicaragua, and Vietnam and the people's liberation struggles in Central America, South America, and southern Africa. Some of the solidarity organizations had a medical/health focus only. The educational work of the solidarity organizations highlighted socialized health systems as well as the people's health needs and were usually based on visits of health professionals in both directions. These organizations also raised substantial amounts of money for medicines, medical/surgical supplies, and professional textbooks and journals; in a few instances they funded the construction of a clinic or hospital.

The emergence of the women's self-help/mutual-aid health groups in 1969 and subsequently the women's health movement constituted a profound ideological challenge to modern health care—who owns medical science as well as who owns the body needing care? Although such radical (but not so new) ideas did not appear in Left party platforms, many in the leadership of the women's health movement, both with and without academic health-care training, were on the Left as traditionally defined. The full impact of this challenge is yet to be experienced. *See also*: Scientists, 1930–50

—*Walter J. Lear*

REFERENCES

Ehrenreich, Barbara, and John Ehrenreich. *The American Health Empire: Power, Profits and Politics* (A Health-PAC Book). New York: Random House, 1970.

Elling, Ray H., ed. *National Health Care: Issues and Problems in Socialized Medicine*. Chicago: Aldine-Atherton, 1971.

Kotelchuck, David, ed. *Prognosis Negative: Crisis in the Health Care System*. New York: Vintage, 1976.

Krieger, Nancy. "Queen of the Bolsheviks: The Hidden History of Dr. Marie Equi." *Radical America* 17 (1983).

Lear, Walter J., guest ed. *Health & Medicine* (History Issue) 4, no. 1 (Spring 1987).

McKinlay, John B., ed. *Issues in the Political Economy of Health Care.* New York/London: Tavistock Publications, 1984.

Mullan, Fitzhugh. *White Coat, Clenched Fist.* New York: Macmillan, 1976.

Roemer, Milton I. *Social Medicine: The Advance of Organized Health Services in America.* New York: Springer, 1980.

Rosner, David, and Gerald Markowitz, eds. *Dying for Work: Workers' Safety and Health in Twentieth Century America.* Bloomington: Indiana University Press, 1987.

Sidel, Victor W., and Ruth Sidel. *Reforming Medicine: Lessons of the Last Quarter Century.* New York: Pantheon Books, 1984.

HELLMAN, LILLIAN (1907–84)

When Hellman met Dashiell Hammett in 1930, she was unknown and he was a famous writer. At the age of twenty-three, she had sold a few short stories to obscure magazines and worked as a press agent and a reader for a publishing house, various theatrical producers, and, concurrently, for MGM Studios. Hammett at thirty-six was already started on his final book but finding it difficult to write or to stop drinking.

By 1934, that last book, *The Thin Man,* was out, but his writing block had grown so severe he never functioned professionally again. Her play *The Children's Hour,* about the evil power of slander against two women accused of lesbianism, was banned in several cities but was a Broadway hit, and she was on her way to becoming the leading writer of her sex in the English-speaking theater.

By her own testimony, he was not only her love and political mentor but a critical and editorial influence on her plays. A Marxist and professed Communist, he guided her from a loose set of liberal leanings to an understanding of historical materialism and an appreciation of the role of the Soviet Union in the struggle for collective security against Hitlerism. In a sense, the intelligence and energy he had put into creative writing and political activism was diverted into her career as a playwright and celebrity spokesperson for the American Left.

After *The Children's Hour,* she wrote *Days to Come,* a drama about a strike. Then traveling to Spain, she co-wrote Joris Iven's movie *The Spanish Earth,* returning to the United States to campaign for Loyalist aid. *The Little Foxes,* a drama about Southern money and power, was an enormous success. Her most political play, *Watch on the Rhine,* which treated a German antifascist refugee and his encounter with a middle-class American family, won the New York Drama Circle Critics Award. Among her other works, *The Searching Wind* treated the appeasement of Hitler before the war. After Hammett's death in 1961, she wrote only one play, *My Mother, My Father and Me.*

Instead, she showed her brilliance as a prose writer in the volumes of reminiscence, *An Unfinished Woman, Pentimento,* and *Scoundrel Time,* all based upon real events but reworked for dramatic effect, which Hellman always preferred to the literal truth. Her "Julia" story was rendered into a film starring Jane Fonda. A number of plays were also adapted for films, most notably *Watch on the Rhine.*

Perhaps her most memorable line was not in any of her plays but in the letter she addressed to the House Committee on Un-American Activities to explain why she would not talk about other people in her testimony. "I cannot and will not cut my conscience to fit this year's fashions." *See also*: Detective Fiction, Hollywood Left, Jefferson School

—*Ring Lardner, Jr.*

REFERENCES
Rollyson, Carl. *Lillian Hellman: Her Legend and Her Legacy.* New York: St. Martin's Press, 1988.

HERBST, JOSEPHINE (1892–1969)

An important Left journalist of the 1930s, Herbst was one of the most accomplished of the "proletarian novelists" around the peripheries of the Communist Party and Popular Front. Born in Sioux City, Iowa, and raised in near-poverty, Herbst attended several colleges between periods of work, and graduated from the University of California at Berkeley in 1919. That year she moved to New York City, and almost immediately became involved in the circles around the *Liberator* and later, the *New Masses.*

Following an unhappy affair and near-breakdown, Herbst moved to Berlin in 1922 to pursue full-time writing. There she met a writer she later married, John Hermann, an alcoholic eight years her junior. By 1928 she settled down in Erwinna, Pennsylvania, which became her lifelong residence and the site of her most productive literary work.

Shifting from the Hemingway orientation of the 1920s that marked her first two novels, Herbst took up proletarian literature for her monumental trilogy, *Pity Is Not Enough* (1933), *The Executioner Awaits* (1934), and *Rope of Gold* (1939). These family sagas from the Civil War to the then-present were widely recognized at the same time as manifesting the maturity, the breadth, and the careful style lacking in nearly all other full-scale proletarian literary efforts.

As her marriage to Hermann broke up in the middle 1930s, Herbst also became a noted journalist on such topics as the farm crisis, the Cuban uprising, German antifascism and the civil war in Spain. Especially as a writer for the *New Masses*, she drew wide praise. Her experience in Spain in 1937 left her in personal despair and distanced her from formal political involvement (although she had never joined the CP, she had been very close for several years).

From 1942, when she lost a government job for political reasons, to 1954, she endured government harassment in a variety of forms. Her further literary work meanwhile received scarce recognition. Although little more was published before her death, she began to enjoy a literary revival, with her own Pennsylvania home an informal center for once-radical writers such as Alfred Kazin and Saul Bellow. *See also*: Proletarian and Radical Writers, 1930s–1940s

—*Mari Jo Buhle*

REFERENCES

Langer, Elinor. *Josephine Herbst*. Boston: Little, Brown, 1982.

HERNDON CASE

In 1932, Angelo Herndon, a 19-year-old black Communist, helped organize an interracial hunger march in Atlanta, Georgia. Less than a week later, Atlanta police arrested him when picking up mail at his post office box, held him without bail, and charged him with "attempting to incite insurrection," a capital crime.

Thus began one of the legal cause célèbres of the 1930s. The International Labor Defense, the Communist Party's legal defense arm, took charge of Herndon's defense, retaining a young black Atlanta attorney, Benjamin Davis, Jr., to try his case. Davis challenged the constitutionality of Atlanta's jury and grand jury systems (which excluded blacks), the constitutionality of the insurrection law, and the employment of racial epithets in court by prosecutor and judge, but his arguments were swept aside by a white-supremacist judge and jury who convicted Herndon and sentenced him to twenty years on a chain gang. The outrageous conduct of the judge, as well as the extraordinary severity of the sentence (for organizing a peaceful demonstration) prompted a nationwide movement in Herndon's behalf, including black organizations, labor unions, and religious groups as well as the CP. Appeals on the Herndon case lasted for four years. Finally, in 1937, the Supreme Court, by a five to four margin, ruled that the Georgia insurrection law was unconstitutional and secured Herndon's release. The trial, the appeals, and the movement in Herndon's defense helped educate the northern public about abuses in the southern legal system and strengthen liberal opposition to racial segregation. *See also*: Communist Party, International Labor Defense

—*Mark D. Naison*

REFERENCES

Herndon, Angelo. *Let Me Live*. New York: Random House, 1937.

HEYWOOD, EZRA (1829–93)

An individualist anarchist, Heywood participated in the abolitionist, labor reform, and free-love movements of the nineteenth century. He lived in Princeton, Massachusetts, with Angela Tilton Heywood, his companion for twenty-eight years. A Garrisonian nonresistant, Heywood broke with the abolitionists over their support for the Civil War. Subsequently he embraced the anarchist philosophy of Josiah Warren. Branding marriage a form of slavery, Heywood was a key figure in the postwar free-love movement, which called for social, political, economic, and sexual equality between men and women.

Heywood organized reform leagues and created the Cooperative Publishing Company. His writings addressed labor reform, free love, temperance, and free speech. From 1872 to 1893, Heywood edited and published a monthly paper, the *Word*. Published in 1876, Heywood's *Cupid's Yokes* denounced marriage, and the Victorian enforcer of virtue, Anthony Comstock, arrested him for selling it. Heywood only became a more aggressive advocate of woman's rights, including her right to birth control. Comstock was responsible for arresting Heywood five times for various obscenity charges. Two of those arrests resulted in prison terms. *See also*: Anarchism, Free Love

—*Martin Blatt*

REFERENCES

Blatt, Martin. *The Collected Works of Ezra Heywood*. Weston, Mass.: M&S Press, 1985.

———. *Free Love and Anarchism: A Biography of Ezra Heywood*. Urbana: University of Illinois Press, 1989.

Sears, Hal. *The Sex Radicals: Free Love in High Victorian America*. Lawrence: Regents Press of Kansas, 1977.

Hicks, Granville (1901–82)

One of the most influential practitioners of the Marxist literary criticism developed in this country during the 1930s, Hicks was ideologically located somewhere between the hardline leftism of Michael Gold and the liberal Marxism of Edmund Wilson and Malcolm Cowley. He tried to practice a criticism that brought social and economic questions to the center of the critical debate.

Hicks studied theology for two years after graduating from Harvard in 1923, but abandoned his plans to become a minister, returned to Harvard for an M.A. in English, and took a job at Rensselaer Polytechnic Institute, where he taught until he was fired for political reasons in 1935. He joined the Communist Party in the early 1930s, became the literary editor of the *New Masses* when it reappeared as a weekly on January 2, 1934, and helped to make it one of the best Left literary journals of the 1930s. During this crucial period, in addition to his numerous articles and reviews, Hicks produced three important books: *The Great Tradition: An Interpretation of American Literature Since the Civil War* (1933/revised 1935), a biography of John Reed (1936), and *Figures of Transition: A Study of British Literature at the End of the Nineteenth Century* (1939). Hicks quit the CP after the Hitler-Stalin Pact in 1939, and repudiated his own Marxism in autobiographical works after that (like *Part of the Truth*, 1965), but he continued as a literary critic until 1977 (most notably as a literary columnist for the *New Leader* during the 1950s and the *Saturday Review* during the 1960s), and his Marxist orientation was one important underpinning of his later critical practice.

Hicks's limitations as a Marxist critic are clear. His Marxism was often puritanical in bias and mechanical in application. Worse, by demanding that literature be used as a class weapon, he limited its range and possibilities. "The critic will demand," he wrote in "The Crisis in American Criticism" (1933), "that the author's point of view be that of the vanguard of the proletariat." On the other hand, his support for proletarian literature helped encourage some of the younger writers who emerged in the 1930s, and his discovery of a social-realist past (in the literature of Whitman, Sinclair, London, et al.) gave them an American literary tradition to join. *See also*: Literary Criticism, *New Masses*

—*David Peck*

REFERENCES

Aaron, Daniel. "The Arrival and Departure of Granville Hicks," Chapter 16 of *Writers on the Left*. New York: Avon, 1961.

Bicker, Robert J. *Granville Hicks: An Annotated Bibliography*. Emporia, Kans.: Emporia State Research Studies, 1968.

Long, Terry L. *Granville Hicks*. New York: Twayne, 1981.

Robbins, Jack Alan, ed. *Granville Hicks in the New Masses*. Port Jefferson: Kennikat, 1974.

Highlander Research and Education Center

Highlander Folk School opened in a two-story frame house in Monteagle, Tennessee, on November 1, 1932, as a residential adult-education center. Since that time, uncounted southern activists from labor, the civil rights movement, and Appalachian mining or land struggles have used the school to learn from each other's experience demanding social change.

Highlander's purposes, the people who have learned and taught there, and the radically different educational philosophy undergirding what is taught and how, as well as its durability despite attack from government and allies, place Highlander uniquely within, yet apart from, the American Left.

Founded by southerners who met at Union Theological Seminary at a time when the nation's economic and political institutions were in disarray, Highlander was one of nearly 250 operating labor colleges. Many had been started by the Socialist Party, unions, immigrants, or the IWW to counteract the failures of public education, or to train new leadership. From the start, Highlander's purposes differed in part. For Myles Horton, Elizabeth Hawes, James A. Dombrowski, Rupert Hampton, and Malcolm Chisholm, the founders, the school's ideology welled up from people rather than party, platform, or proclamation. They believed poor people themselves knew best what they needed to learn, and when, and could determine their own goals. Music, games, washing dishes, making a play, and traditional storytelling were as valued for their educative outcomes as books or lectures. Doing these activities together, the founders reasoned, was the means by which the poor learned the power of unity and organization, as well as the capacity of self. And when enough "students," all deliberately recruited from "the underclass," put these lessons into action, the founders' vision for a socialist revolution would be realized.

Barney Graham, leader of miners striking for union recognition in Wilder, Tennessee, was one of the first persons to shape Highlander's work and history. Besides leading the strike, Graham had been teaching Highlander students. He was shot to death by gun thugs on May 2, 1933. Other Highlander students experienced nonfatal intimidation while participating in historic conflicts: Paul Christopher, Esau Jenkins, Rosa Parks, Buck Maggard, Pedro Arculeta, Fanny Lou Hamer, Florence Reece, Stokely Carmichael.

With these and other equally determined activists coming and going, Highlander inevitably attracted both loyal support and fierce reaction. Perhaps as many as 3,000 persons, and a handful of foundations, have kept the school in operating cash. Others, however, including the State of Tennessee, Ku Klux Klan, the Federal Bureau of Investigation, the Internal Revenue Service, and several congressional investigating committees have tried to shut the school, sometimes with temporary success.

Highlander Folk School was raided and padlocked in 1959 during an interracial voter-education workshop. After a long, losing court fight, Highlander Research and Education Center opened in an abandoned whorehouse in Knoxville, Tennessee, operating there until the city used its power of eminent domain to seize the property. The school moved to New Market, Tennessee, its present location, in 1972. Internal conflicts have gripped Highlander from time to time, and were equally threatening, especially as the region's two principal social movements—the union drives of the thirties and the civil rights movement of the fifties and sixties—ebbed or welled. Communists have spurned the school as reformist. Many unions repudiated Highlander as Communist controlled.

The school's pedagogy, which predates what has come to be called the Freirian model, holds that education is a tool for social change, rather than the means by which labor and power relationships are reproduced in a capitalist wage and industrial system. To some extent, Highlander's original aims have been, and continue to be accomplished. New leaders have forged significant changes through unions, voter drives, music festivals, blockading strip mines, or taking polluters water they poisoned. The second aim, social reconstruction ending exploitation of labor, race, and gender, as yet eludes the still-functioning school.

Highlander outlived its peers, including many of the better known and connected among them, such as Brookwood, the Work Peoples College, and Commonwealth. Its unexpected survival for over a half-century may be its most important achievement. *See also*: Braden, Carl and Anne; Civil Rights; Dombrowski, James; Horton, Myles; SCEF; West, Don

—*Frank Adams*

REFERENCES

Adams, Frank, and Myles Horton. *Unearthing Seeds of Fire: The Idea of Highlander*. New Market, Tenn.: Highlander, 1975.

Glen, John M. *Highlander: No Ordinary School, 1932–1962*. Lexington: University of Kentucky, 1988.

Hill, Joe (1879–1915)

The most popular songwriter and most celebrated martyr of the Industrial Workers of the World, as well as one of the union's early cartoonists, Hill was also very much a hobo and "lone wolf" and, as such, has long been the despair of biographers, for, as is generally true of migratory workers, very little is known of his life.

He was born Joel Emmanuel Hägglund in Gävle, Sweden, of Swedish Lutheran parents. As a child, after his father's death in 1887, he worked in a rope factory and as fireman on a steam-powered crane. In his teens he was stricken with tuberculosis and hospitalized in Stockholm. In 1902 he emigrated to the United States.

For the next eight years almost nothing is known of his doings except that he made his way across the continent working as a porter, harvest-hand, longshoreman, and at various other odd jobs. He lived in New York for a year, working on the Bowery, and in the course of his wanderings spent time in Philadelphia, Pittsburgh, Cleveland, Chicago, the Dakotas, Spokane, and Portland. In 1906 he wrote a firsthand account of the San Francisco earthquake that was published in his hometown paper in Sweden.

Exactly when and where Hill joined the IWW is not known (the union's records were seized by the U.S. government in 1918 and later destroyed) but it seems to have been sometime in 1910, and possibly in San Pedro, California, where he lived for several years and served for a time as secretary of the IWW local. In 1911 he and other Wobblies took part in the Mexican Revolution in Baja, and in the following year we find him in British Columbia writing songs for strikers on the Canadian Northern railroad.

Hill contributed to the IWW cause primarily as wordsmith and artist rather than as organizer or soapboxer. He loved to draw (his home in Sweden, now the Joe Hill Museum, has an oil painting that he did as a young man) and his cartoons show that he carefully studied the work of such pioneering exemplars of the cartoonist's art as F. B. Opper and Rube Goldberg. He played piano, accordion, guitar, and banjo, and clearly enjoyed the popular music of his day. He also had a natural ear for slang that gave his lyrics an added "punch." The few articles that he wrote—such as his celebration of Wobbly sabotage, "How to Make Work for the Unemployed," published in the *International Socialist Review* in December 1914—reveal the same qualities evidenced in his songs and cartoons: a vivid, overriding hobo humor, and an extraordinary ability to express revolutionary ideas with a simplicity as compelling as it is appealing. Hill's first contribution to the IWW press, a letter to the editor, appeared in August 1910. His first song published in the IWW's *Little Red Songbook*, "The Preacher and the Slave," appeared in 1911. Another edition of the songbook, in 1912, carried his first Wobbly cartoon.

By mid-1913 Hill was one of the better known Wobs, admired in IWW halls and hobo jungles and on picket lines throughout the land above all for his rousing "songs to fan the flames of discontent." Hill's songs, raucously comic ballads, mostly sung to popular tunes ("Casey Jones, the Union Scab," "Mr. Block," "Scissor Bill") or revolutionary rewrites of old hymns ("The Preacher and the Slave," "There Is Power in a Union," "Stung Right") quickly became Wobbly favorites; the union's 1913

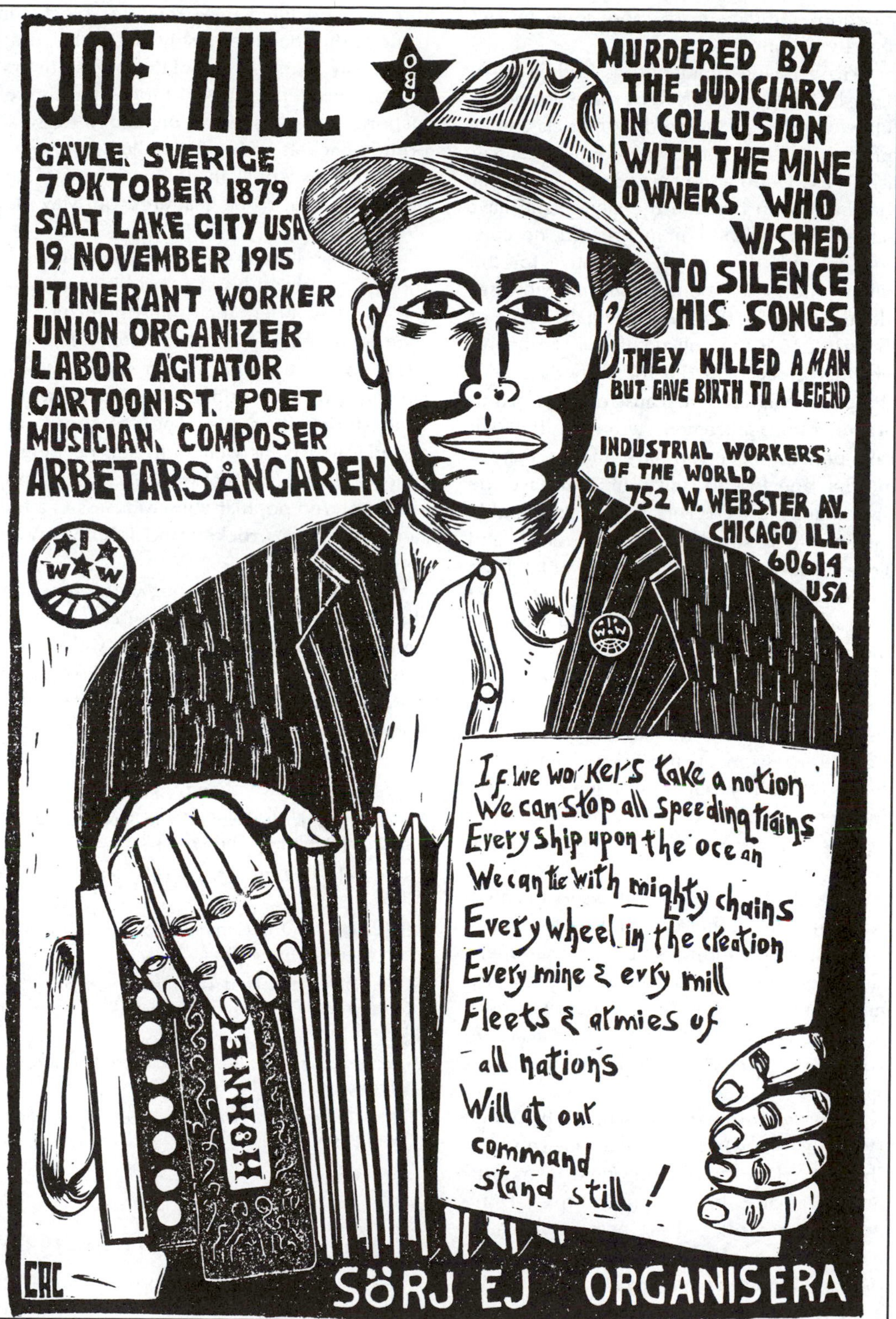

Linocut poster by Carlos Cortez

songbook contains many more songs by Hill than by anyone else.

His growing reputation as leading IWW bard did not go unnoticed by those he and his fellow workers recognized as their class enemies. In January 1914 he was arrested near Salt Lake City, Utah, and charged with a murder that had taken place in the city several days earlier. Hill had no criminal record, no connection with the victim, no motive for the killing; moreover, none of several witnesses identified him as the man leaving the scene of the crime. But the police chief of San Pedro, who had once held Hill for thirty days on a charge of "vagrancy" because of his efforts to organize longshoremen, wrote to the Salt Lake police: "I see you have under arrest for murder one Joseph Hillstrom. You have the right man. . . . He is certainly an undesirable citizen. He is somewhat of a musician and writer of songs for the IWW songbook." Utah "public opinion," dominated by the Copper Trust and the notoriously antiunion Mormon church, followed this cue in a case that nearly all historians have come to recognize as one of the worst travesties of justice in American history. After a trial riddled with biased rulings, suppression of important defense evidence, and other violations of judicial procedure characteristic of cases involving labor radicals, Hill was convicted and sentenced to death.

The IWW's vigorous defense campaign, exposing the "frame-up" and demanding a new trial, won enormous support. The American Federation of Labor, the Swedish government, and even President Woodrow Wilson intervened on Hill's behalf, but to no avail. On November 19, 1915, Hill faced the firing squad.

Shortly before his execution he wired IWW Secretary-Treasurer Bill Haywood, in Chicago: "Don't waste any time in mourning—organize." In shortened form—"Don't mourn, organize!"—these became the most famous "famous last words" in U.S. labor history, and remain a battle cry not only for militant labor but for oppressed people throughout the world.

Many thousands had to be turned away from Hill's funeral service in Chicago, and the throngs who filled the streets for blocks en route to the cemetery, lustily singing his songs all the way, made up one of the largest funeral processions in the city's history. After his cremation, his ashes were divided into small printed packets and sent to fellow workers in every state except Utah, and in dozens of foreign countries, to be scattered on May Day 1916.

Hill was already something of a legend in the last months of his life, and his legend—as the Wobbly poet, the poet-organizer, and "the man who never died," after a line in a 1925 poetic tribute by Alfred Hayes—has steadily grown ever since. Honored in novels, short stories, films, plays, poems, songs, and the plastic arts, as well as in several biographies and collections of his work, he has long since entered popular consciousness as a folk hero like Davy Crockett and Johnny Appleseed.

It was above all as a songwriter, however, that Joe Hill was best known in his lifetime, and his songs—recorded by many well-known singers and still popular on picket lines today—remain his greatest legacy. *See also*: Folk Music, IWW, IWW Cartoonists

—Franklin Rosemont

REFERENCES

Foner, Philip. *The Case of Joe Hill*. New York: International Publishers, 1965.

———, ed. *The Letters of Joe Hill*. New York: Oak, 1965.

Kokk, Enn, ed. *The Complete Joe Hill Song Book*. Stockholm: Prisma, 1969.

Nolan, Dean, and Fred Thompson. *Joe Hill: IWW Songwriter*. Chicago: Industrial Workers of the World, 1979.

Rosemont, Franklin, ed. *The Cartoons of Joe Hill*. Chicago: Charles H. Ken, 1989.

Smith, Gibbs M. *Joe Hill*. Salt Lake City: Peregine Smith, 1984.

Hillquit, Morris (1869–1933)

Popularist, politician, consummate adaptationist of European-style social democracy to Jewish American life, Hillquit played a leading role in the Socialist Party from its formation until his death.

Born Moses Hillkowitz in Riga, Latvia, of assimilated Jewish parents, he attained an exceptional education for a Jew in the Russian school system, and immigrated to the United States in 1885. Working in the garment trades of the Lower East Side, he joined the Socialist Labor Party, and soon helped to organize the United Hebrew Trades. Less a journalist than an organizational talent, he was named manager of the weekly *Arbeter Zeitung*, and meanwhile studied law at New York University. Passing the New York bar exam in 1893, Hillquit became the most prominent of a handful (later, a far larger number) of Jewish former workers turned lawyers but still loyal to the socialist cause. In the following decades, he would handle many hundreds of worker's injury or civil liberty cases with only the smallest of fees.

Meanwhile, he emerged as an orthodox Marxist in his own terms, a "centrist" in the 1890s political lineup of loyal DeLeon followers on the Left and independent socialists (mostly but not entirely native-born) on the Right. This perspective placed him roughly with Karl Kautsky of the German Social Democrats, against Bernstein's "revisionism," which denied the efficacy of socialist orthodoxy, but also more forcefully against the proponents of the general strike or other mass, direct actions. Officially taking the name "Hillquit" in 1897, he led the "Kangeroo" rebellion within the SLP two years later, splitting the organization roughly in half. Hillquit dominated this dissident SLP in strategy and in theoretical perspectives. Along with other leaders of his group, he bargained intensively before agreeing to unity with Eugene Debs's Social Democracy of America in 1901. Through that agreement, he emerged a foremost leader of the New Yorkers in the new SP.

According to his critics, Hillquit's factional maneuvering did not cease, but only changed form. He reluctantly accepted the titular party leadership of Eugene Debs, and sought occasionally to put up other candidates for the presidential race. He was an inveterate foe of the Industrial Workers of the World and of the SP faction that urged labor activity independent of the AFL. He led the bitter internal party struggle to renounce the theory of sabotage, precipitating William D. Haywood's removal from the National Executive Committee and the abandonment of the party by many revolutionary socialists. On the other hand, Hillquit had personally defended Haywood in the 1907 Steuenberg case, and he earnestly opposed, at Socialist International congresses and elsewhere, efforts by Milwaukee leader Victor Berger to urge immigration restriction to curry favor with the AFL and supposedly raise the living standard of American workers. He also generally resisted calls for socialists to merge their efforts into a labor party. In the war years, Hillquit took a courageous antimilitary position, doing much to shape the official party posture and the extraparty antiwar groups such as the People's Council of America.

As a public figure, Hillquit proved an attractive political candidate, if not the equal of Berger or of Meyer London. His runs for Congress in 1906 and 1908, although unsuccessful, garnered wide public interest (including the endorsement of noted liberal and radical intellectuals) and helped lay the basis for London's victory in the Lower East Side a few years later. Hillquit's New York City mayoral candidacy in 1918 was widely viewed as a referendum on the First World War, his more than 20 percent of the total vote a strong signal to Washington and his forceful campaign an inestimable assistance to numerous Socialist candidates elected to New York city and state offices that year.

Hillquit also emerged, in these years, as the earliest official historian of American socialism, and as one of its prime popularizers of socialist theory. *The History of Socialism in the United States*, published in 1903 and revised for a new edition in 1910, had the memoirist's touch, but also the preliminary scholar's dedication. His primary perspective, dividing early "utopian" from later "scientific" socialism, was consistent with Friedrich Engels's brief *Socialism, From Utopia to Science*. Rather unfair to his factional opponents (especially DeLeon), the book was in many other respects a remarkable intellectual achievement for its time. Hillquit's 1912 theoretical study, *Socialism in Theory and Practice*, on the other hand, was not greatly different from or superior to a half-dozen other contemporary American efforts along the same lines. Like the others, it had its following, mainly among Americanizing Jewish immigrants.

Hillquit suffered his major and permanent political defeat with the Russian Revolution's impetus to American Bolshevism, and with the ascendency of a new generation of Jewish radicals no longer sharing his calm confidence in socialism's inevitable, peaceful, parliamentary advance. In another sense, the defection of liberal middle classes from municipal socialism to mainstream politicians and to Woodrow Wilson's war policies had already restricted Hillquit to the Jewish ghetto. Stricken by tuberculosis in the late 1910s, Hillquit hoped in vain for an amicable separation of Communists and Socialists. Following the split, and following many savage verbal attacks upon him by the Communists (including Lenin himself), Hillquit became bitterly anticommunist, penning in 1923 *From Marx to Lenin* as a formal denunciation of Leninism.

Hillquit meanwhile had become the reigning senior figure in the reduced SP. He led the Socialists in supporting Robert LaFollette's 1924 Progressive campaign, and once again in nominating Norman Thomas as a titular leader to fill Debs's shoes. A partial SP revival, ironically, found many critics regarding Hillquit as an obstacle to the successful Americanization of the movement. After a political brawl, he won a Pyrrhic victory in 1932, retaining his post as national chairman but helping to set the stage for the ultimate Socialist faction fight of 1935 in which his fellow "Old Guard" activists withdrew themselves and most New York socialist institutions from the SP. In a last electoral effort for mayor in 1933, campaigning heroically despite his illness, Hillquit won a quarter-million votes. A few months later, his autobiography, *Loose Leaves from a Busy Life*, appeared, an anecdotal treatment not destined to become a classic of American socialist literature. Almost within weeks, he died of tuberculosis. *See also*: Socialist Labor Party, Socialist Party, Yiddish Left

—*Paul Buhle*

REFERENCES

Hillquit, Morris. *Loose Leaves from a Busy Life*. New York: Macmillan, 1933.

Kipnis, Ira. *The American Socialist Movement: 1897–1912*. New York: Columbia University Press, 1952.

Pratt, Norma Fain. *Morris Hillquit: A Political History of an American Jewish Socialist*. Westport: Greenwood, 1979.

Hiss Perjury Trials

The conviction on perjury charges in 1950 of Alger Hiss, a high-ranking State Department official during the New Deal, is pivotal to any understanding of Cold War America. A grand jury indicted Hiss for perjury for his denials of allegations made by Whittaker Chambers in a controversy originating in testimony before the House Un-American Activities Committee (HUAC). There were two counts: his denial that he had ever given State Department documents to Whittaker Chambers for transfer to the USSR and his denial that he had ever seen Chambers after joining the State Department in September 1936.

The first trial began on May 31, 1949, in New York City. Assistant U.S. Attorney Thomas F. Murphy, in charge of the prosecution, told the jurors, "If you don't believe Whittaker Chambers then we have no case under the federal perjury rule." Focusing on this formulation, Lloyd Paul Stryker, counsel for Hiss, elicited from Chambers admissions that on sixteen separate occasions Chambers had given perjurous testimony. The jury was unable to agree on a final verdict.

In the four-month interval before the retrial, two events exacerbated political hysteria: detonation by the USSR of its first atomic bomb and the Communist victory in China by the forces led by Mao Tse-tung. Right-wingers vied with one another in blaming "Communist spies" for these developments. The "treachery" of Alger Hiss, who had been convicted of nothing, was bruited about as the chief cause of what mainstream America perceived as two catastrophes.

The second trial lasted twice as long as the first, produced a several-million-word record and several thousand pages of exhibits, featured more than a hundred witnesses, and resulted in wholly irreconcilable testimony about the events in question. Chambers was the only witness to accuse Hiss of any wrongdoing and the only witness to give evidence on both counts of the indictment. Chambers's statements about his own Communist past and how it supposedly impinged on Hiss was irreconcilable with his former HUAC testimony.

Chambers's "proofs" consisted of sixty-five typed sheets he had produced in November 17, 1948, as a defendant in a libel suit initiated by Hiss but discontinued after Hiss's perjury indictment. Characterized as the "Baltimore Documents," these papers were copies or paraphrases of State Department cable traffic during the first four months of 1938. Chambers testified that they had been typed by Hiss's wife, Priscilla, and given to him by Hiss. They were said to be "like" the material he had been collecting since 1934 as part of a Soviet spy operation.

Ramos C. Feehan, an FBI document examiner, testified that in his opinion Chambers's documents and the papers typed on a Woodstock typewriter that the Hisses owned in the 1930s had been typed on the same machine. The defense conceded this vital point, but argued that the issue was not the machine on which the documents had been typed but the person who had been the typist and where the machine was when the papers were typed.

Also offered as evidence by the prosecution were two strips of film that proved to have no meaningful significance to the case. Some were films of documents to which Hiss had never had access, many of documents given to the press, and all had been distributed to many persons, as many as 150 State Department staff officers. Four slips of paper in Hiss's handwriting were in a shorthand gibberish indecipherable to anyone but Hiss and consistent with notes to himself that Hiss used to brief his State Department superior.

Chambers testified that the films, the handwritten notes, and the sixty-five typed sheets had been stored in a nine by twelve manila envelope that he had given in 1938 to his wife's nephew, Nathan Levine, for safekeeping. Levine testified that he never saw or knew what was inside the envelope, either when he received it or when it was retrieved in 1948.

Collaborating Chambers's story was Julian Wadleigh, a forty-four-year-old Oxford-educated economist. He testified that although he had never been a member of the Communist Party he cooperated with the Party in the mid-1930s by assisting a member of the CP underground whom he knew only as "Carl." After identifying Chambers as "Carl," Wadleigh testified that from 1936 to March 1938, while he was assigned to the Trade Agreement Division of the State Department, he had handed over to "Carl" documents that came across his desk that he thought would be of interest. The defense did not challenge Wadleigh's testimony other than to show it had no connection to Hiss and indicated a person who might have been the source of *all* the material produced by Chambers.

The remainder of the evidence related to count two of the indictment, whether or not Hiss had ever seen Chambers after joining the State Department in 1936. The "proofs" offered were unrelated to espionage or to charges specified in the indictment. They were all circumstantial and related to purchases of a car, a New England vacation, and the sale of a rug. Chambers's wife, Esther, testified to a close relationship with the Hiss couple from 1934 through to the spring of 1938. Having never been a Communist and admitting no knowledge of her husband's self-confessed espionage activities, Esther Chambers's evidence bore only on count two of the indictment.

Some of Esther Chambers's testimony was clearly a by-product of knowledge acquired in the 1940s. When describing a Hiss home she claimed to have visited in late 1937 she said it was white with a stone fence, changes that had been made in 1946, eight years after the last claimed meeting and three years after the Hisses left the premises. In the 1930s the house had been natural red brick.

Hiss's testimony was consistent with that previously given to HUAC. He said he had met Chambers in 1935 in the office of the Nye Committee, the Senate body he served as counsel in its investigation of the munitions industry. Chambers had introduced himself as George Crosley, a free-lance writer planning a series of magazine articles on the investigation. Hiss stated that he had sublet an apartment on Twenty-eighth Street in Washington, D.C., to the "Crosleys" for six weeks in 1935 at a time when the lease had not yet expired and the Hisses had moved to a new address. Hiss stated that he had seen Whittaker and Esther Chambers no more than a half dozen times.

Regarding the Woodstock typewriter, the defense showed that it was no longer in the Hisses' possession at the time Chambers said it had been used to type federal documents. Five witnesses—Alger and Priscilla Hiss; Clidi Catlett, their former houseworker; and Mike and Pat Catlett, sons of Clidi who had been teenagers at the time—gave evidence that the typewriter had been given to the Catlett boys in December 1937 when the Hisses moved.

Another aspect of the defense was the testimony of two psychiatrists of international distinction, Drs. Carl Binger and Henry Murray. They gave evidence that Chambers's was a psychopath whose mental makeup was so skewered that it made him wholly unreliable as a witness. The government made no effort to call psychiatrists of its own and simply stressed that the doctors had no experience in examining Communist espionage agents.

The political hysteria of the times, the skulduggery of the prosecution and FBI (first revealed a quarter of a century later through documents obtained under the Freedom of Information Act), and the acceptance without challenge that Chambers had been a paid CP functionary for some fourteen years, six of which were spent as part of a spy apparatus, proved too much to overcome. Alger Hiss was found guilty on both counts and eventually sentenced to five years in prison. The Supreme Court refused to review the case and Hiss served forty-four months at the federal penitentiary at Lewisburg, Pennsylvania (March 1951–November 1954).

Although the offense for which Hiss was found guilty was perjury, in the public mind he had been convicted as a "Communist spy." Conservatives had a field day connecting him (and, by osmosis, the New Deal, the Democratic Party, liberals, Communists, and a wide variety of radicals) to espionage and treason.

The complete record based on evidence discovered since the conviction has established that the case against Hiss was based on fraud. In 1952 Hiss filed for a new trial based on posttrial discoveries of documents proving that by early 1938 Chambers was totally opposed to communism and out of the CP, that the documents produced by Chambers were forgeries, that the materials could not possibly have been stored for ten years as claimed, that Priscilla Hiss could not have typed any of the Baltimore Documents, and that the typewriter introduced at the trial was a fake machine planted on the defense to incriminate Hiss. This startling array of evidence from an impressive range of experts was denied without even granting the defendant a hearing.

In 1978, based on FBI and Justice Department documents obtained under the Freedom of Information Act, Hiss made another attempt to have his 1950 conviction set aside by filing a *coram nobis* petition in federal court. New evidence showed the prosecution had suppressed exculpatory evidence, made false representations to the court, knew certain evidence to be perjurious, permitted its witnesses to give false testimony, exploited the presence of a typewriter it knew to be a fake machine, placed informers in the defense camp, intimidated document examiners from giving evidence for the defense, and had Hiss and his counsel under physical and electronic surveillance throughout. The massive documentation for this petition consisted of 129 documents from the government's own files. All the exhibits plus the legal arguments have been published in two volumes under the title *In Re Alger Hiss* (Hill and Wang, 1980).

The petition was denied, without hearing, in a twenty-five-page opinion written by federal judge Richard Owen and dated July 15, 1982. The opinion was affirmed without additional opinion of its own by the Court of Appeals and later by the U.S. Supreme Court. It may be appropriate that the last legal word on the case was written by a judge appointed by President Richard Nixon after impeachment proceedings against Nixon had begun. Nixon, a freshman Congressman in 1948, had been the individual who launched the campaign to convince the American people that Alger Hiss was a Communist spy, a campaign begun months before any evidence to support such a charge was "discovered." *See also*: Anticommunism; Federal Bureau of Investigation; House Committee on Un-American Activities; McCarthyism; Nixon, Richard, Whittaker Chambers, and the Hiss Case

—*William A. Reuben*

REFERENCES

Cook, Fred J. *The Unfinished Story of Alger Hiss*. New York: Morrow, 1958.

Hiss, Alger. *In the Court of Public Opinion*. New York: Knopf, 1957.

———. *Recollections of a Life*. New York: Seaver Books/Holt, 1988.

Jowitt, The Earl. *The Strange Case of Alger Hiss*. New York: Doubleday, 1953.

Navasky, Victor. Review/essay on Allen Weinstein's *Perjury*. *Nation*, April 12, 1978.

Reuben, William A. *The Atom Spy Hoax*. New York: Action Books, 1955.

———. *Footnote on an Historic Case*. New York: The Nation Institute, 1983.

———. *The Honorable Mr. Nixon*. Rev. ed. New York: Action Books, 1960.

Smith, John Cabot. *Alger Hiss: The True Story*. New York: Holt, Rinehart Winston, 1976.

Zeligs, Meyer. *Friendship and Fratricide*. NY: Viking, 1967.

HISTORICAL MATERIALISM

Historical materialism designates what Marx himself called the "guiding thread" of Marxist studies. Unlike most previous theories of society, this one considers the means of production to be the fundamental basis of society. It further postulates that the relationships and values generated by production process condition the "social, political, and intellectual life process in general." Within the development of the forces of production—runs the theory—contradictions increasingly divide society at large into classes and prepare the conditions for the next phase. With capitalism, class society reaches its ultimate stage of development; the proletariat, carrying in itself the legacy of all human development, stands next in line to take control and, in so doing, abolish the tyranny of economics over common life.

While accepting the general outlines of this theory, different elements of the U.S. Left have emphasized its importance to a greater or lesser degree and one aspect over another. During the early era, roughly 1870 to 1890, eclecticism ran rampant. For approximately the next thirty years, the "scientific" materialism of the Second International blended comfortably with the crude materialism of grassroots radicals. The "dialectical materialism" of Lenin and especially Stalin, superimposing upon the "copy theory" of reality a view of the "vanguard" at once predestined by cosmic forces and yet also guiding history, prevailed until the 1950s. The popular view of historical materialism, faced with the advance of nuclear weapons and with the twists and turns of unpredicted events, has never subsequently recovered. And yet from the standpoint of methodological sophistication of intellectual practice, historical materialism has retained and even expanded its value.

Much of the interpretation of historical materialism depended upon the central sources for inspiration. Among German-Americans in the early days, Ferdinand Lassalle easily figured with Marx as a champion of labor vision, and the *Vormärz* poets' lyric idealism held no small influence. *The Communist Manifesto*, clarion call to revolution, had far more effect than *Capital* for some time to come. Native-born Americans of the "revolutionary socialist" faction most thoroughly dedicated to class struggle occasionally drew their inspiration directly from idealist sources. For instance, Burnette Haskell, U.S. formulator of anarcho-syndicalism and editor of the San Francisco–based newspaper the *Truth*, looked to the relentless dialectical development of history; his key collaborator, Joseph R. Buchanan, editor of the Denver *Labor Enquirer*, relied more characteristically upon the cruel realities of frontier labor and the degradation of the American republic to spell out an insurrectionary conclusion. Utopians of the Bellamy Nationalist and successive movements freely acknowledged Marx but in proposing a characteristically American-style, voluntary escape from history made a decisive judgment upon the theory's efficacy. William Morris, more than Marx, gave them clues to overcoming the intrusion of capitalism upon humanity.

In the era to follow, popularization of doctrine predominated in virtually every quarter. The rise of American social science coincided with the translation of European socialist classics, above all the new *Socialism, Utopian, and Scientific* from Engels's *Anti-Dühring* (1893). Engels's pamphlets upheld by Daniel DeLeon as the key source of "scientific socialism," provided an open sesame to popular explanation and also reduction. Among English-language socialists in particular, the local study class became a medium for teaching the "science of society," Lewis Henry Morgan to Karl Kautsky. Behind the study club stood the richly didactic, colloquial explanation of social exploitation and inevitable economic decline in the pages of *The Appeal to Reason* and its many less-popular counterparts. Heavily proletarian immigrant movements tended to emphasize the reality of the daily class struggle over the finer points of doctrine. Yet even here the goal of workers' education remained.

More detailed and controversial discussion of materialism failed to elicit wide interest. The *International Socialist Review*, founded in 1900 with social-science enthusiast A. M. Simons at its helm, brought the prestige of German theorists to Americans firsthand. There and in the pages of the Yiddish *Zukunft* the details of historical materialism received a most vigorous debate: Did the theory apply equally to all individuals or nations? Did it reconcile the question of European and American colonialism as the absorption of backward societies into more materially advanced ones? What application could be given to art and science? But such discussions appealed largely to intellectuals.

By the approach of the First World War, the theoretical solidity of Engelsian doctrine had been breached from several angles. Feminists and bohemians raised up idealist theorists and theories more akin to utopianism than to Marxism. Immigrants in particular faced the ambivalent possibilities of nationalism for their flocks, and the limits of generalized Marxism to interpret the danger of world powers dominating lesser peoples. The Russian Revolution at first glance seemed to deny the efficacy of historical materialism by projecting a backward nation into the first self-proclaimed socialist society.

Leninism affixed a patchwork solution to the theoretical dilemmas, never fully restoring the simple class content or teleology of the older model. Amended to encompass the struggle of the superexploited races and peoples, "dialectical materialism" (as it had been redesignated) no longer spoke consistently or convincingly of the "advanced" proletariat's central role in bringing world revolution. The Soviet Union, in theory now exempt from class conflicts if not historical materialism, nevertheless obviously underwent traumatic struggles to raise up its own forces of production by which, logically, its course should not be determined. Leninism's "vanguard party" concept and its affirmation of the Russian Revolution as central event in modern history provided a solution so convincing to a generation of revolutionaries that every political alternative to the Communist Party ended with essentially the same philosophical propositions.

The unmatched example of the Russian Revolution, however constrained or corrupted (according to different theories) continued to rule triumphant in the Left so long as capitalism seemed on a downward economic spiral. The renewal of capitalism after World War II snapped the last barrier against the collapse of historical materialism as an all-sufficient explanation. Attempts to extend historical materialism into a true world-system, with the "proletariat" in effect the Third World population at large, brought Leninist theory to a conclusion but did nothing to restore expectations for the proletariat in the most highly mechanized nations. Substitutions of a revolutionary peasant army or peasantry at large (China and Vietnam, or Ghana) validated one aspect of the theory at the expense of other aspects.

The effect of these revolutionary developments, combined with the Khrushchev revelations of 1956 and the character of newer mass movements (above all civil rights) in the United States, all tended to discredit theoretical assumptions that had remained dominant in the American Left since 1917. Unlike such European heretics as Cornelius Castoriadis or

Jurgen Habermas, Americans did not generally confute historical materialism outright or seek to substitute technology for production. They simply abandoned the particulars of historical materialism.

By the later 1960s, discussions of contradictions centered in capitalism's "superstructure" drew alike upon Gramsci and Althusser for justification in setting aside traditional historical-materialist analyses, affirming a wider and more eclectic view of class, race, and gender exploitation in whatever studies were pursued. Culture and religion began therefore to be viewed as highly significant factors that could essentially be autonomous from economics. Not even the radical economists of New Left vintage looked to a definitive capitalist breakdown (whose last major theorist, as of the Labor Theory of Value, passed with Paul Mattick, Sr.) as the source for socialist transformation.

Not surprisingly, as the older socialist organizations rooted in traditional theory tended to diminish in importance, their own theorists tended to de-emphasize (without drawing broad, heretical conclusions) the old theories of historic materialism save in the most general sense of world-capitalist crisis. More generally, Left groups' concentration upon peasant-based revolutionary movements (or governments) abroad, and imperialism or racism and sexism and environmental degradation at home, precluded the older theoretical framework. While labor-oriented activities therefore continued, especially among sectors accessible to organization and reform, deeper theory became increasingly a minor concern.

Within the academic world, historical materialism remained alive as a conditioning factor for radical history, sociology, literary theory, and even psychology. Indeed, certain trends in the transition to poststructuralism and postmodernism raised up explicitly historical materialist readings of "culture" in the broadest anthropological (as well as the more customary) sense. Here and there, as in the writings of Michael Buroway, Marxist theory even enjoyed a measure of revival in something like its original form. For the most part, historical materialism served as a rallying point and an antidote (not to be taken whole) to the more extreme idealism of theory inspired by the apoliticized, French-oriented, intellectual avant-garde. *See also*: Philosophy

—*Paul Buhle*

REFERENCES

Buhle, Paul. *Marxism in the United States*. London: Verso, 1987.

Buroway, Michael. *The Politics of Production*. London: Verso, 1985.

History, Europe

American left-wing historical scholarship on Europe is mostly a post–World War II phenomenon, with a few roots going back to the Popular Front period of the 1930s. Many of the pioneers found a forum in *Science & Society*, and they later suffered severely during the McCarthyite purges of the early Cold War. The scholarship that followed has generally been the province of academics (and a very few journalists, notably those associated with *Monthly Review*), and it burgeoned on American campuses during the 1960s and 1970s, parallelling the rise of the New Left.

The bulk of this research has concerned France, most probably because of its rich revolutionary and left-wing traditions and because of already well established indigenous left-wing scholarship. From the beginning, American left-wing scholars concerned themselves with the French revolutionary tradition, the origins of working-class movements, and the rise of socialist movements. However, they were relatively less concerned with the Great Revolution (1789–99) than non-leftist American historians, probably because French Marxists themselves so dominated the study of that period. Samuel Bernstein, one of the founding editors of *Science & Society*, led the way in the post–World War II period with a number of studies stretching from the Revolution of 1789 and the revolutionary tradition of the nineteenth century to the development of a socialist movement at the beginning of this century.

No one had a greater impact on the field than Harvey Goldberg (1922–87), whose *atelier de l'histoire sociale* at the University of Wisconsin from 1963 through 1987 trained over fifty doctoral candidates in a variety of topics on the French working class and left-wing history, ranging from socialist, communist, and syndicalist movements, to local, oral, and quantitative histories, to studies of the women's movement and French imperialism. Goldberg himself was a brilliant and extremely popular lecturer who drew hundreds of students and other interested people to his lectures. The author of a definitive study of Jean Jaurès, he eschewed great theories in favor of meticulous archival research. The topics and methods of research he directed varied as foci of interest changed over the years, and both he and his protégés have been well received by the left-wing scholarly community in France. Joan Wallach Scott, who eventually went to the Institute for Advanced Study, was Goldberg's prize student, producing a first-rate study of French glassmakers, *The Glassworkers of Carmaux* (1974).

More prolific than Goldberg, but with less of a following, was Charles Tilly, who at the University of Michigan and later at the New School for Social Research produced a number of socio-historical studies, with a quantitative orientation, of the revolutionary tradition and working-class actions in France, including a celebrated study of the uprising in the Vendée during the French Revolution, *The Vendée* (1964). Louise Tilly collaborated with him on nineteenth-century revolutions, and then separately studied grain riots in France and the working class in Milan before turning to studies of women, work, and the family.

Bernstein, Goldberg, and Charles Tilly generally set the tenor of the other left-wing studies of France that have concerned primarily politico-social history: the revolutionary tradition, the working-class movement, the Socialist and Communist parties, imperialism, and the women's movement. Besides Wisconsin, Columbia University produced a relatively large number of these historians. They differ from their predecessors only in their emphases on local, regional, ethnic, oral, and quantitative studies. Nobody seems much interested in formulating grand syntheses.

American left-wing scholars have paid much less attention to other parts of Europe. England, in particular, is one of the least studied areas, except for a recent interest in women's history, possibly because British Marxists, themselves, have so thoroughly combed that field.

Germany has attracted both a few left-wing historians and literary scholars from the United States. For the historians the chief foci are the twentieth-century crises in German socialism and communism, National Socialism and the Third Reich, and women's history, Jost Hermand, at the University of Wisconsin, the leading left-wing literary scholar, has supervised some forty doctoral candidates and has written about thirty books, focusing principally on a historical analysis of German literature and culture since the 1870s. The *New German Critique*, founded in Wisconsin in 1973, an interdisciplinary journal of German studies, strongly influenced by the Frankfurt School and primarily interested in mass culture, has provided a forum for a number of left-wing scholars and has produced special issues on Germans and Jews, Nazism, and German feminism. In the past twenty years, a number of Americans, some of whom are left-wing, have taken a keen interest in the history and literature of the German Democratic Republic.

American left-wing interest in Russia and the Soviet Union goes back to the Popular Front period of the 1930s, particularly to two very prolific men: Frederick Schuman of Williams College, a political scientist, and Ernest Simmons of Cornell, a literature specialist. Both men also wrote to promote better, and more sympathetic, American understanding of the Soviet Union and its people. Several other scholars have followed in their paths, frequently in the pages of *Science & Society*. They have concerned themselves with a number of topics ranging from Soviet literature to the Soviet ecology movement, from Kerensky to the Sino-Soviet dispute. Of course, there is also increasing interest in Soviet women.

Finally, there are a few outstanding left-wing generalists, most notably Arno Mayer of Princeton, who has written major studies of World War I such as *Wilson Versus Lenin* (1959), the Paris Peace Settlement, and the counterrevolutionary movements following the war. Gabriel Kolko, primarily an Americanist, did major books on the European politics of World War II and the early Cold War. Immanuel Wallerstein, too, has not neglected Europe in his studies of the world capitalist system. *See also*: Radical Professional Journals

—*Edward Rice-Maximin*

REFERENCES

Abelove, Henry, Betsy Blackmar, Peter Dimock, and Jonathon Schneer, eds. *Visions of History: Interviews with E. P. Thompson, et al.* New York: Pantheon Books, 1983.

HISTORY, U.S.

In most eras of the Left, U.S. history has served as the predominant form of political-scholarly popularization. For the New Left phase of the 1960s–1970s it became the most prestigious form of intellectual expression. The radical interpretations of history have, however, varied enormously era by era.

Left history of the United States began with the somewhat educated newspaper editor/lecturer/political leader seeking to explain current events against the background of American history. From American socialism's earliest days, opinion sharply divided on the history of the Republic. Had American history, from at least the Revolution onward, been acted out as a class drama in deceptively "democratic" packaging? Or alternatively, had the great advances of American democracy been made but subsequently squandered by the consolidation of a class system? Neither immigrant or native-born socialists had a monopoly on the alternative interpretations, although immigrants leaned toward the former and native-born toward the latter.

The Socialist Party, shortly after the turn of the century, provided encouragement for book-length efforts. Algie M. Simons, who studied with Frederick Jackson Turner, wrote the most popular scholarly study, *Social Forces in American History* (1911), said to have been used in some 4,000 local socialist study classes. Oscar Ameringer's wry *Life & Deeds of Uncle Sam* (1909), translated into some fifteen languages, reached a readership of a half-million. These two works, along with the first socialist history of American labor, James Oneal's *Workers in American History* (which grew, similarly, from an agitational newspaper series), leaned heavily upon the muckraking Progressive historians of the era, above all Charles Beard. Gustavus Myers's *Great American Fortunes* (1910), which most successfully survived into the next period, summed up the message: "History, in the main, thus far, has been an institution for the propagation of lies. . . . Since the private property system came into existence, an incessant, uncompromising warfare has been going on between oppressors and oppressed."

The relative handful of Communist historians at first continued in this vein. Anthony Bimba, editor of the Communist Party's Lithuanian daily, thus gathered the *History of the American Working Class* (1928) almost directly from the old socialist material, with a sprinkling of "vanguard" concepts. By the mid- and late-1930s, the attraction of a handful of academic writers and the gravitation of the CP toward the Popular Front stress upon "democratic forces" in the nation's past drastically altered the view of American history. The most formidable inspiration, V. L. Parrington, had provided in his *Main Currents of American Thought* (1928) a model of progressive and reactionary intellectual traditions. Earl Browder's 1938 pamphlet *Traitors in American History: Lessons of the Moscow Trials* suggested how far along the method could be taken, by the line of the day, into caricature. By 1940, Communists had embraced Charles Beard (who notably disdained class concepts) as the finest example of an American mainstream scholar.

But the Popular Front also promoted black history as had no previous Left tendency. It received W. E. B. DuBois's monumental *Black Reconstruction* (1935) with mixed emotions, fearing the author's political popularity and his stress upon the absence of progressive white, lower-class forces in the South. James S. Allen's *Reconstruction: The Battle for Democracy* (1937) might be considered almost a "correction" from the class standpoint. A young Herbert Aptheker published his first studies of slave revolts under these auspices, in *Science & Society*. At a broader level, by urging Black History Week, Communists and their allies made a major contribution to the changing perception of race.

During the approaching Cold War epoch and its immediate aftermath, Aptheker and Philip Foner delivered, between them, a veritable library of Marxist historical studies marked by voluminous research and strictest orthodoxy. Only *The Bending Cross* (1948), a popular biography of Eugene Debs by independent radical Ray Ginger, reached a larger audience with militant tales of the past.

The chief labor and social-historian mentors of the New Left, David Montgomery and Herbert Gutman, grew out of and beyond the Popular Front milieu, attempting to bring a more flexible (but no less radical) view of race, class, and ethnicity into consonance with current methodological advances. Montgomery, a former Communist and longtime machinist, brought to labor history a keen sense of factory details, especially in the work process. Gutman, whose Yiddish-Left background had a sustaining influence on his life, became the *magus* of social history, discoverer and promoter of hidden history in the submerged life of the masses. These two men dominated the newer, radical views of social history at large. Eugene Genovese, eventually a master scholar of slavery, graduated from CP circles with a Gramscian turn of mind unique for the middle 1960s, and wrote classic works—most notably *Roll, Jordan, Roll* (1981)—elucidating slave life and the relations between whites and blacks in the antebellum South.

A separate current, no less important but more clearly in the indigenous radical vein, provided the key intellectual inspiration for the antiwar New Left campus movement. William A. Williams's volumes on U.S. foreign policy, and the works of his highly influential graduate students, recuperated a sturdy isolationism with a close (and surprisingly sympathetic) study of early elites so as better to criticize the twentieth century "corporate" order. This style of history, close to Herbert Marcuse's critique of contemporary America, inspired voluminous Left studies of militarism, advertising, education, prison and mental institutions, even of unions as integrating elements in the tightly woven "system." The precocious New Left journal *Studies on the Left* (1959–66) initially spread the evangel of this movement, and its lineal successor, *Socialist Revolution* (later renamed *Socialist Review*), especially in its first years emphasized similar themes.

By 1970, an activist movement of mostly current or former graduate students shaped radical history networks within and outside the universities. Regional groups, most prominently the Mid-Atlantic Radical Historians Organization (MARHO), held conferences and lectures, agitated on questions of common concern, and fostered or encouraged the publication of new journals. *Radical America*, which grew initially out of a national study group within Students for a Democratic Society in 1967 and maintained informal links with that organization until 1970, urged labor, black, and women's history as critical sources of insight for the spread (soon, the renewal) of the radical movement from the campuses and ghettos into a deeply rooted, powerful force. The *Radical History Review*, although aimed from its beginnings in 1970 rather more toward academic networks, also urged organizing strategies integrated with the pursuit of knowledge.

By the later 1970s and 1980s, immediate political expectations had diminished, but activity proliferated in several important ways. At the local level, radical historians became extremely active in public history programs ranging from labor history, race and ethnic history, and women's history to urban history and gay history. They held public discussions, mounted exhibitions, worked with filmmakers on prestige documentaries, and by the end of the 1980s found themselves well situated to speak (albeit sometimes in Aesopian tones) publicly about the past lives of ordinary peoples and the often bitter struggles for economic and political democracy. At a national level, they advanced the scholarly dialogue via important forums, such as the Berkshire Women's History conferences, the American Social History Project (which produced classroom visual aids and a landmark textbook of labor and social history), and even the Smithsonian Museum's exhibits. In a scholarly sense, such additional "new" areas as Asian-American, Native American, gay history, and environmental studies, among others, have likewise found their Left scholars, often central to the respective fields. Along with such subject areas, methods such as oral history became for the first time major interests of radical scholars. If radical history had once been rare in the authoritative *Journal of American History*, it now became commonplace.

On the other hand, not even scholarly optimism about the validity and radical uses of class, race, and gender perspectives could be maintained in light of the conservative drift from the White House to undergraduate students. Fields established at great personal cost, such as women's studies and black studies, often found themselves besieged by student disinterest and the long-run effects of insufficient university commitment. The single most notable scholarly success—forcing the concept of class upon an unwilling historical profession—suffered by the late 1980s fresh attacks from scholarly Right and even sections of the Left restive at white racism and the apparent eclipse, with de-industrialization, of the proletarian project. Despite the scholarly elaboration of women's history in particular, and the appearance of such major class- and race-oriented works as Eric Foner's *Reconstruction* (1988), the momentum of radical history had been decisively slowed.

By the mid-1980s, a growing popular disbelief in historical process, and a growing interest in apparently transhistorical or nonsequential cultural subject-matter, tended to overshadow historical-minded studies. And yet the enduring role of history in popular explanation remained, by now spread to such once-unlikely fields as the histories of rock 'n' roll or television. Meanwhile, a corresponding methodological crisis in history's main polemical opponent, French-oriented structuralism, pointed to the likelihood of some postmodernist terrain on which radical scholars of various disciplines, ranging from communications to literature to history, would find common points of intellectual rendezvous and common political objectives in the next radical upsurge. *See also*: Cold War Revisionism, Historical Materialism

—*Paul Buhle*

REFERENCES

Abelove, Henry, Betsy Blackmark, Peter Dimock, and Jonathon Schneer, eds. *Visions of History: Interviews With E. P. Thompson, et al.* New York: Pantheon Books, 1983.

Buhle, Paul. "American Marxist Historiography, 1900–1940." *Radical America* 4 (November 1970).

HITLER-STALIN PACT

Also known as the Molotov-Ribbentrop Pact, this agreement on August 23, 1939, announced a cessation of war preparations by each side against the other, and meant the division of Eastern Europe into two spheres of control.

The pact came as a shock to almost everyone in the United States Left, but its impact varied greatly from sector to sector. From the mid-1930s onward, the Communist Party of the USA had devoted a substantial amount of time and energy to the struggle against fascism, internationally as well as against such domestic pro-Nazi organizations as the Silver Shirts, the Coughlinite Social Justice movement, and the Ku Klux Klan. Many American liberals had joined or allied themselves with the CPUSA largely because of its leadership in this struggle. The Soviet Union was generally accepted as Nazism's archenemy if not as leader of international opposition to fascism. On the other side, Hitler's emphatic anticommunism was, explicitly or implicitly, accepted as sufficient reason for benevolent neutrality by more respectable rightist groups such as the Liberty League.

Most leftists had been well aware of the frustration the USSR had met with in its repeated attempts to form alliances for collective security against the Nazis, and, likewise, of the Neville Chamberlin–led British government's refusal to give any serious consideration to Soviet proposals for a mutual-aid pact. There seemed, in short, good reason to heed Soviet fears that Britain's rulers would welcome, or even actually support, a Nazi drive to the East.

The startled leadership of the CPUSA therefore accepted the strategic value of the amazing countermove Stalin had apparently engineered, and most U.S. Party members reluctantly endorsed the pact as a defense necessity for the Soviet Union, whose survival was considered the decisive priority. The Party therefore suffered no substantial immediate loss of actual membership. But the sense of disorientation and of total CPUSA adherence to Russian leadership took a heavy toll in the long run.

For three feverish days, the Party leaders remained sharply divided as to their own propaganda line. General Secretary Earl Browder advocated continuation of anti-Nazi campaigns, presenting the pact as a tragic military necessity forced upon the USSR by the Allied nations. A large section of the Party "old guard," never entirely comfortable with the Popular Front, insisted that primary emphasis be placed upon the imperialist nature and essential equivalency of the Wall Street-Downing Street axis and the Rome-Berlin-Tokyo axis, and called for a denunciation of the attempt of the Allies to repeat the fraudulent moral claims of World War I. It rapidly became clear that the Soviet Union had adopted the latter stand and expected its sister movements to follow.

The result would have been catastrophic in any case, but was made even more so by the ways in which Party members active in mass or liberal-Left movements found themselves directed to implement the new line. In many cases, as in the League of American Writers, they were instructed to introduce totally inappropriate motions on the pact or the nature of the impending war. Such motions generally passed by narrow majorities, Pyrrhic victories followed by the near-complete exodus of all those opposed. The work of years was thereby lost almost overnight.

The breakdown of such relations and its devastating results are well exemplified by the fortunes of the strongly antifascist faculty committee built up at the City College of New York. Here, as generally, the actual core of Party membership remained intact. But the shock and disillusionment precluded any united action, even in self-defense. When, in 1940, the Rapp-Coudert Committee initiated a political witch-hunt at City College, no organized faculty opposition emerged and no protest developed against the summary dismissal of many highly respected colleagues.

Despite a real period of effective united-front action and even CP respectability (or popularity) during the war, a strong residue of distrust remained among the non-Communist Left and liberals, a sense of Party direction by outside forces and of Party members following a hidden agenda in mass organizations. The reservoir of suspicion was soon tapped and effectively exploited by Senator Joseph McCarthy and others in the domestic Cold War. *See also*: Communist Party

—*Annette Rubinstein*

REFERENCES

Richmond, Al. *A Long View from the Left*. Boston: Houghton Mifflin, 1973.

Starobin, Joseph. *Crisis in American Communism, 1943–1957*. Cambridge: Harvard University Press, 1972.

Hoan, Dan: see Milwaukee, Municipal Socialism

Hoffman, Abbie (1936–89)

A cultural revolutionary who came to prominence in the 1960s, Hoffman once wrote that "a modern revolutionary heads for the television station, not for the factory." Using ridicule and audacity as potent weapons against the political, military, and judicial systems that were helping to prosecute the Vietnam War, Hoffman worked to transform the antiauthoritarian sentiments of many young people of the '60s counterculture into political consciousness and a mentality of resistance. "Personally," he wrote in his autobiographical *Soon to Be a Major Motion Picture* (1980), "I always held my flower in a clenched fist. A semi-structure freak among the love children, I was determined to bring the hippie movement into a broader protest." This politicizing impact upon the drugs-and-rock 'n' roll counterculture significantly offset the polarizing or alienating aspects of his unruly anarchism, as beamed to mainstream America by the electronic media. His hilariously communicated revulsion at the corporate American culture, moreover, had deep impact upon the entire '60s generation.

Abbott Hoffman was born on November 30, 1936, in Worcester, Massachusetts, the oldest of three children of a Jewish family whose living derived from a family drugstore and then a medical supply company. Expelled from Classical High School after a fight with his English teacher, Hoffman finally graduated from a private academy and then attended Brandeis University, from which he graduated in 1959 with a B.A. in psychology. He became active in the civil rights movement and was arrested in Mississippi during Freedom Summer, 1964; in 1966 he founded Liberty House, a crafts store in New York City that sold the products of poor people's co-ops in Mississippi. It was as an organizer against the Vietnam War, however, that Hoffman won media attention and found a constituency for his brand of protest.

In April 1967, Hoffman and cohorts threw dollar bills from the visitors' gallery to the floor of the New York Stock Exchange, provoking chaos as traders scrambled for the money. His wedding to Anita Kushner (his second marriage) in Central Park that August attracted over 3,000 people, as did the "be-ins" he helped organize in the park. During the antiwar demonstration of over 50,000 in Washington, D.C., in October of that year, Hoffman led an "Exorcism of the Pentagon" (surrounding the Pentagon to levitate it by mental force). On New Year's Day, 1968, Hoffman, Jerry Rubin, and other activists proclaimed themselves "Yippies," and shortly thereafter founding the Youth International Party, a conceptual community that instigated many street demonstrations and media events. These culminated in the "Festival of Life" at the 1968 Democratic National Convention in Chicago, during which the Chicago police under Mayor Richard Daley indulged in what a government report called a "police riot." Hoffman nominated a pig, "Pigasus," for president and was arrested for having "Fuck" scrawled across his forehead.

The violence in Chicago's streets led to the Chicago Eight Conspiracy trial (eventually called the Chicago Seven trial, as Bobby Seale of the Black Panthers was bound, gagged, and railroaded separately to four years in prison for contempt of court). Hoffman's talent for guerrilla theater gave rise to radical mockery of courtroom decorum (he claimed, among other things, to be trial judge Julius Hoffman's illegitimate son). Dozens of well-known political and cultural figures testified on behalf of the defendants as the trial became a showcase for Left politics and the counterculture.

Hoffman spent the next years as a full-time agitator, speaker, and writer, logging dozens of arrests and facing serious harassment from police. In 1973 he was arrested for participating in the sale of cocaine to undercover agents. (He always maintained the anticipated profit from the sale had been earmarked to finance movement activities.) Facing a mandatory life sentence with no possibility of parole before fifteen years, he vanished in February 1974 and spent more than six years underground. These years included plastic surgery, many aliases, a long companionship with a woman, Johanna Lawrenson, two nervous breakdowns, and some serious and very public environmental activism under the name "Barry Freed" in upstate New York near the St. Lawrence River.

Hoffman emerged from hiding on national television on September 3, 1980. He served less than a year in prison after pleading guilty to a lesser charge, became a popular college campus speaker, was arrested (with former president Jimmy Carter's daughter, Amy) protesting CIA recruitment at the University of Massachusetts (Amherst), and remained active, especially on environmental issues. His endurance as an organizer and his continued commitment to political causes well beyond the heyday of the 1960s and 1970s were inspiring to many of his contemporaries and instructive, especially, to college-age people of the 1980s.

His suicide on April 12, 1989, shocked most of his admirers and friends. At the time of his death he had been taking lithium and other prescribed drugs to deal with his manic-depressive cycles and injuries from a serious automobile accident of the previous year. The coroner's report of April 18 found cause of death to have been "massive doses" of phenobarbital and alcohol.

In classic anarchist tradition, Hoffman viewed his radicalism as a way of life and distrusted activists whose lifestyles did not, in his judgment, incarnate their ideologies. His ideas were most effectively presented in direct action, but he wrote a number of books, including *Revolution for the Hell of It* (1967), *Woodstock Nation* (1969), *Steal This Book* (1971), *Vote!* (1972), *To America with Love: Letters from the Underground* (1976), and *Steal This Urine Test* (1988).

—*Lawrence Bush*

REFERENCES

Hoffman, Abbie. *Woodstock Nation*. New York: Viking, 1969.

Jones, Jeff. "Abbie's Legacy." *Guardian*, April 26, 1989.

HOLLYWOOD BLACKLIST

The investigation of Hollywood radicals by the House on Un-American Activities Committee in 1947 and 1951 was a continuation of pressures first exerted in the late 1930s and early 1940s by the Dies Committee and State Senator Jack Tenney's California Joint Fact-finding Committee on Un-American Activities. HUAC charged that Communists had established a significant base in the dominant medium of mass culture. Communists were said to be placing subversive messages into Hollywood films and discriminating against unsympathetic colleagues. A further concern was that Communists were in a position to place negative images of the United States in films that would have wide international distribution.

Totally ignored in the hysteria generated by HUAC were the realities of the Hollywood studio system of the 1930s and 1940s. That system's outstanding characteristic was the hands-on control by studio bosses who ran their business as a strictly entertainment industry and shared Sam Goldwyn's often quoted sentiment that, "If you want to send a message, use Western Union." When films did have a political edge, studio bosses were personally involved in every phase of production, including the vital final cut. This was decidedly the case with the most notoriously pro-Russian film ever made in Hollywood, *Mission to Moscow* (1943). The film, undertaken by Jack Warner at the request of the Roosevelt administration, combined an all-out assault on American isolationists with a complete acceptance of the Stalinist account of the Moscow purges. Warner considered his film to be a patriotic service to the New Deal in the war against fascism.

Evidence of leftist images and dialog in Hollywood films was extremely slim. HUAC had to resort to citing the smiling children in *Song of Russia* (1944) and noting that Russian workers shouted *"tovarich"* (comrade) as American merchant ships that had run the Nazi submarine blockade entered a Soviet port in *Action in the North Atlantic* (1943). Even committee members struggled to keep a straight face when Ginger Rogers's mother complained that her daughter "had been forced" to speak the subversive line "share and share alike, that's democracy" in a 1943 film scripted by Dalton Trumbo.

Contrary to the HUAC contentions, Communist Party policy in Hollywood had been largely defensive. Film workers were instructed that their primary responsibility was to keep anti-Soviet and anti-Left sentiment out of films, a kind of esthetic Hippocratic Oath to First, Do No Harm. On the positive side of the ledger, radicals were urged to advance a democratic and populist ethos that was totally in accord with the New Deal and popular culture. Melvyn Douglas, a leading Hollywood liberal, commented years later that the Communists had been fellow travelers of the liberals and not vice versa. Liberalism, not Communism, may, in fact, have been the true target of the HUAC investigators. The Right wished to discourage any Hollywood impulse to make films advocating social change at home or critical of foreign policy. The task of intimidation was focused on the role Communists played as screenwriters. Nearly 60 percent of all individuals called to testify and an equal percent of all those blacklisted were screenwriters. Only 20 percent of those called and 25 percent of those blacklisted were actors.

When the first subpoenas were issued the Hollywood impulse was to fight back. Defense committees were formed and efforts to purge various guilds defeated. Eric Johnston, president of the Motion Picture Association of

America, pledged that he would "never be party to anything as un-American as a blacklist." The will to resist was put to the test when some of the first writers called refused to cooperate and tried to read statements condemning the committee in sessions that often turned into shouting matches. The result was bad press for Hollywood and a feeling by producers that their radical writers were vying with the committee for sensational headlines at the industry's expense. On November 24, 1947, Congress cited ten screenwriters for contempt. Producers meeting at the Waldorf Astoria hotel two days later signaled their capitulation to the investigators by announcing that "no Communists or other subversives will be knowingly employed by Hollywood." An appeal by the "Hollywood Ten" was turned down and by mid-1950 most of them had begun to serve one-year terms in prison.

HUAC returned for a second Hollywood round in 1951 but the proceedings were not true investigations. The political views of those called were already known and the people they were asked to name as comrades were also known. The hearings amounted to a kind of ideological exorcism. Witnesses were expected to state they had been misled or confused in the past and were now regretful. They could prove their sincerity by naming others who had been with them in Communist organizations or at Communist functions.

Response to the hearings took many forms. Most Party members and sympathizers had never hidden their views but did not accept the right of HUAC to question their right of political association. Civil libertarians could easily back this view on the basis of the First and Fifth amendments. Others like actor Zero Mostel said they would gladly discuss their own conduct but were prohibited by religious convictions from naming others. Individuals who had only been involved with antifascist front groups or had left the Party for ideological reasons did not wish to martyr themselves for a cause they had never embraced or had now renounced, but naming names seemed morally wrong. Other ex-Communists such as Budd Schulberg and Elia Kazan felt there was a Communist conspiracy and that it was proper, if not patriotic, to expose it.

Whatever one's convictions, there was little room for maneuvering once called, yet two out of three who testified were unfriendly or uncooperative. A few, like Lucille Ball, were allowed to pass with garbled and meaningless testimony, but most were pinned down. Fame was no protection. A lifelong non-Communist progressive like Sam Jaffe was blacklisted for refusal to cooperate. Jaffe, who had been nominated for an Oscar for *The Asphalt Jungle* (1950) and was famous for roles in *Lost Horizon* (1937) and *Gunga Din* (1939), was reduced to teaching high school math and living with his sisters. He would eventually make a comeback as Dr. Zorba on the successful *Ben Casey* television series. Lee Grant, nominated for an Oscar for her role in *Detective Story* (1951), was blacklisted for refusing to testify against her first husband, screenwriter Arnold Manoff. Grant would eventually return to Hollywood and win two Oscars, one for acting and another for directing a documentary.

The most defiant Hollywood actor was gravel-voiced Lionel Stander, who had been in comedies directed by Ben Hecht, Frank Capra, and Preston Sturgis. Active in the Salinas Valley lettuce strike, the Tom Mooney case, the Scottsboro defense, guild campaigns, antifascist work, and other left-wing causes, Stander said he had not joined the CP because he was to the left of it. He said he had been blackballed for his politics for over twenty years and that the only "un-Americans" active in Hollywood that he knew of were members of the committee. Blacklisted anew, Stander became a successful Wall Street broker, later starred in European films, and still later returned to American prominence as the chauffeur in *Hart-to-Hart*, one of television's top ten programs during the early 1980s.

Few of those blacklisted would prove as resilient as Stander, Grant, Jaffee, and Mostel. No more than 10 percent would be able to return to careers in Hollywood. Even the biggest names were vulnerable. Larry Parks, fresh from triumphs in two films about Al Jolson, was banned for his brief membership in the CP and did not appear onscreen again until getting a small role in *Freud* (1962). Charles Chaplin, the most famous face in the world, had remained a British citizen and a firm believer in the Popular Front. Although he had never been in the CP, Chaplin was not allowed to reenter the United States following a trip to Europe. He did not return to the United States until 1972, when an apologetic Hollywood honored him with a life achievement award during the Oscar ceremonies. His *A King in New York* (1957) satirizes HUAC. In like manner, Bertolt Brecht, one of many anti-Nazi refugees working in Hollywood, had such a bad taste from his HUAC appearance that he repatriated to East Berlin to become an in-house critic of socialism.

Performers who had already established some kind of name might survive through work on the stage, but those at the beginning of their careers had few options. Technical workers faced an even more difficult time, as there was no alternative industry for them to turn to, and Roy Brewer, head of the Hollywood craft unions, remained fiercely anticommunist. Ronald Reagan, then head of the Screen Actors Guild, kept in touch with the FBI about "disloyal" actors. Dozens of blacklistees lost spouses due to the hearings and even more suffered irreparable financial loss. Mental and physical distress was common. Clifford Odets never again wrote effectively and the deaths of John Garfield, J. Edward Bromberg, Canada Lee, and half a dozen others are linked to their committee appearances.

The group that came to exemplify resistance was the Hollywood Ten and their writing colleagues, many of whom had been in the Party. The Ten consisted of Alvah Bessie, Herbert Biberman, Lester Cole, Edward Dmytryk, Ring Lardner, Jr., John Howard Lawson, Albert Maltz, Sam Ornitz, Robert Adrian Scott, and Dalton Trumbo. They had scripted or directed hundreds of Hollywood films. Trumbo was one of the highest paid Hollywood writers and Lawson had been the first president of the Screen Writers Guild. Most of the Ten's best films had dealt with antifascist themes. These included *Hotel Berlin* (1945), *The Master Race* (1941), *Crossfire* (1947), *Sahara* (1943), *Pride of the Marines* (1945), *Destination Tokyo* (1944), and *Thirty Seconds Over Tokyo* (1944). Lardner had scripted the Academy Award–winning *Woman of the Year* (1942), Maltz the well-received *This Gun for Hire* (1942), and Trumbo the Academy Award nominee *Kitty Foyle* (1940). The Ten also worked on genre film such as Lester Cole's script for *The Invisible Man Returns* (1940).

Scriptwriters had the most options to continue working during the blacklist period. Performers could not change their faces nor could directors wear masks, but writers could use pseudonyms. This proved a profitable strategy for many. Abraham Polonsky, Walter Bernstein, and Arnold Manoff wrote most of the *You Are There* segments, a series of historical events re-created for television with a strong focus on cultural martyrs such as Socrates, Galileo, Joan of Arc, and the Salem witches. Ring Lardner, Jr., and Ian McLellan Hunter wrote *The Adventures of Robin Hood* series. The phenomenon of using phony names and surrogates became the basis of *The Front* (1976), which starred Woody Allen. The film was written by blacklistee Walter Bernstein, produced and directed by blacklistee Martin Ritt, and featured blacklisted actors Zero Mostel, John Randolph, Lloyd Gough, Joshua Shelley, and Herschel Bernardi.

Other blacklisted writers found work in Mexico and Europe. Notable among these are Hugo Butler, who wrote scripts for Luis Buñuel in Mexico City, and Jules Dassin, who scored box-office hits with his French-made *Rififi* (1954) and the Greek-made *Never on Sunday* (1960). A few writers worked behind the scenes in Hollywood in an effort to wear down the blacklist. One of Trumbo's pseudonyms, Robert Rich, won an Academy Award for *The Brave One* (1956), and as the decade drew to an end Hollywood insiders became aware that Nathan E. Douglas, the Academy Award writer of *The Defiant Ones* (1958), was really blacklisted Nedrick Young. In 1960 Otto Preminger officially broke the blacklist by crediting Trumbo for scripting *Exodus*. It was then revealed that Michael Wilson had written the blockbuster *The Bridge on the River Kwai* (1957) and had completed a script that would become *Lawrence of Arabia* (1962).

Another consequence of the investigations was a series of anticommunist films: *The Red Menace* (1949), *I Married a Communist*

(1950), *I Was a Communist for the FBI* (1951), *Walk East on Beacon* (1952), *My Son John* (1952), *Big Jim McClain* (1952), and *Trial* (1955). A labor leader modeled on Harry Bridges was the main villain in *I Married a Communist*, Hawiian Communists were exposed by a two-fisted John Wayne in *Big Jim McClain*, and Communist defense efforts for a Mexican-American were depicted as insincere political and mercenary opportunism in *Trial*. All of the films took it as a given that Communists were de facto agents of the USSR. *On the Waterfront* (1954) had no Communist characters but its emphasis on the need to testify before federal investigating committees was widely interpreted as a reference to HUAC. Scriptwriter Budd Schulberg has repeatedly denied that connection but director Elia Kazan has stated that for him the parallel was explicit. Kazan also directed *Viva Zapata!* (1952), in which the visionary revolutionary anarchist Zapata is favorably contrasted with a Communist-style bureaucratic revolutionary.

The Hollywood Left began to revive in the late-1960s and, unlike the student New Left, the new Hollywood rebels, although not connected with the CP, felt warmly toward their predecessors and occasionally worked with them on joint projects. Films with radical bite began to appear with some regularity in the 1970s and 1980s. Ring Lardner, Jr., scripted *M*A*S*H* (1970), a satire on the Korean War that became the basis for one of the most popular of all television series. Labor themes were addressed in *The Molly Maguires* (1970), *Norma Rae* (1979), *Silkwood* (1983), and *Matewan* (1987). The Rosenberg case was reviewed in *Daniel* (1983) and John Reed celebrated in *Reds* (1982), a film that incorporated interviews with real-life radicals such as Scott Nearing. Nuclear power was attacked in *The China Syndrome* (1979) and the Vietnam War critiqued in *Go Tell the Spartans* (1978), *Coming Home* (1978), *Apocalypse Now* (1979), and *Full Metal Jacket* (1987). Capitalism itself was indicted in *Wall Street* (1987) and Latin American intervention assailed in *Missing* (1982), *Under Fire* (1983), *El Salvador* (1986), and *Latino* (1986). The blacklist itself was the subject of *The Way We Were* (1973), which starred Barbra Streisand as a totally sympathetic Communist married to a liberal screenwriter.

The new Hollywood activists were not immune from career threats. Jane Fonda, famous for her opposition to the Vietnam War, was forced from some shooting locations by irate Vietnam veterans. Ed Asner, president of the Screen Actors Guild and a supporter of medical aid to left-wing rebels in El Salvador, had his *Lou Grant* television show canceled after an active protest campaign by right-wing groups. Vanessa Redgrave, a member of a Trotskyist group in England and a vocal opponent of Israel, had contracts aborted and projects threatened with boycotts by Zionist groups. Liberals Robert Redford, Jack Lemmon, and Gregory Peck were criticized for participation in film festivals held in Cuba. While such pressures were not nearly as destabilizing as the blacklist-period tensions had been, awareness of the dangers associated with political activism had its effect on how filmmakers addressed political issues, the kind of film projects undertaken for production, and the particular personnel chosen for given projects.

What the blacklist entailed and its effect on Hollywood has generated a large body of writing by those directly involved. Lillian Hellman's *Scoundrel Time* (1976) and Dalton Trumbo's *The Time of the Toad* (1949) are classics of this genre. Hellman and writers such as Lester Cole and Walter Bernstein have been unforgiving of those who cooperated. In similar fashion, Elia Kazan insists in his autobiography, *A Life* (1988), that he did no wrong in being a friendly witness even though he writes movingly about the traumatic effect the testimony had on his life and that of others who were called before HUAC. Individuals such as Albert Maltz and Jules Dassin have commented on the terrible cost of broken relationships and upended careers with varying degrees of forgiveness for the "friendlies." Dalton Trumbo has been the most generous in this regard by rendering his final judgment that "we were all victims." *See also*: Lardner, Ring, Jr.; Lawson, John Howard; Radical and Proletarian Writers; Radical Filmmaking, 1930s; Union Sponsored Films

—*Dan Georgakas*

REFERENCES

Ceplair, Larry, and Steven Englund. *The Inquisition in Hollywood: Politics in the Film Community, 1930–1960*. Berkeley: University of California Press, 1983.

Culbert, David, ed. *Mission for Moscow*. Madison: University of Wisconsin Press, Wisconsin/Warner Bros. Screenplay Series, 1980.

Navasky, Victor S. *Naming Names*. New York: Viking Press, 1980.

Sayre, Nora. *Running Time: Films of the Cold War*. New York: Dial Press, 1980.

Trumbo, Dalton. *Additional Dialogue, Letters of 1942–1962*. New York: M. Evans, 1970.

HOLLYWOOD LEFT

The organized Left in the Hollywood motion picture industry enjoyed a brief existence (from 1936 to 1949) and a limited influence. It centered around the 300 or so studio employees who belonged to the Communist Party.

Although many Communists were active in organizing guilds and unions, they were not the sole source of trade union militancy. The two most militant labor organizations, the Screen Writers Guild (SWG), organized in 1933, and the Conference of Studio Unions (CSU), established in 1941, were organized by non-Communists. However, a Communist, Jeff Kibre, did mastermind the ultimately unsuccessful effort to organize a CIO-affiliated studio union movement between 1937 and 1939.

Militancy or activism began in Hollywood in 1933, coincident with the New Deal. The most militant talent guild, the Screen Writers Guild, was organized in February, and later that year Lou Goldblatt began to organize the Motion Picture Workers Industrial Union (Association of Motion Picture Employees), under the auspices of the Communist Trade Union Unity League.

The MPWIU lasted one year, recruiting about one thousand members and issuing a publication, the *Motion Picture Worker*. In its second number, dated August 1, 1934, it called on studio workers to adopt industrial union tactics, form industrial unions, and take "control of their unions out of the hands of the misleading bureaucratic fakers and [place] it where it should be—with the 'rank and file' and rank-and-file committees." However, before the MPWIU had attracted enough members and strength to test the gangster-dominated, AFL-affiliated International Association of Theatrical Stage Employees (IATSE) and the studios, the TUUL was dissolved, in March 1935.

From strike literature issued by the Screen Cartoonist's Guild during the strike against the Disney Studio, c. 1940

Meanwhile, Socialist Upton Sinclair's 1934 campaign for the governorship of California, the studios' refusal to recognize the SWG, the continued influx of writers from New York with backgrounds in guilds and left-wing theaters, and the arrival of refugees from Europe noticeably increased the radical temperament in Hollywood. The CP's interest in writers, especially successful writers, had also heightened. In May 1935 a call for a national writers' congress was issued. Although only two screenwriters signed the call, early the following year the CP's "cultural commissar," V. J. Jerome, and an experienced organizer, Stanley Lawrence, journeyed to Hollywood. They laid the foundations for the Hollywood pattern of organizing by talent branches (writers, directors, actors).

The CP's support for black rights, unskilled and semiskilled workers, and women, its antifascism, its connection with what seemed to be the one progressive country in a world saddled with a massive economic depression and collapsing democracies, and its disciplined organization convinced many screenwriters that Communism represented the best vehicle for defending democratic values in the United States. Party hierarchs believed that Hollywood offered skilled writers and speakers and money for party-backed causes.

Between 1936 and 1946, approximately 300 movie studio employees joined the CP (about 1 percent of the work force). They joined for various reasons and stayed for varying lengths of time. Screenwriters predominated (145); there were about 60 actors, 20 directors and producers, and somewhere between 50 and 100 backlot, sound stage, or front-office workers.

Although they had little impact on the political content of movies, Communists contributed to the slight studio trend toward more realistic treatment of some topics. The main political influence of Hollywood Communists occurred in union and guild organizing, support for antifascism, and the election of progressive candidates to public office.

Communists were active in the fight to gain recognition for the SWG, they helped organize other guilds, they were the core elements in the struggle to supplant the gangsters who dominated the IATSE and restructure the federation on a democratic basis, they aided the effort to organize agricultural workers, and they helped the CSU in its major postwar strikes.

The single Communist-initiated trade union effort began in the spring of 1937. Jeff Kibre, a miniature-props worker, member of IATSE Local 37, and a Communist, with a small group of dissidents, launched a campaign to transform the IATSE. Kibre received advice and a meager amount of money from the leaders of the CIO organizing effort in California (Harry Bridges, Goldblatt, and Philip Connelly), and the CP made him a "protected member," freeing him from usual Party duties and attendance, but provided very little else.

Although Kibre would prove endlessly imaginative and undauntingly optimistic in his two-year effort, he failed to find a means to break through the craft consciousness of studio workers or counter the power and ruthlessness of the IATSE-studio combination. When his main weapon, an unfair labor practice complaint filed with the National Labor Relations Board, bogged down in NLRB efforts to achieve a settlement, and the IATSE had brought the studio labor situation to the verge of chaos, Kibre filed for a representation election. The IATSE, with open studio backing and promises of a wage raise if it won, ran a vicious red-baiting campaign, winning 4,460 to 1,967.

Kibre did not enjoy the support of Communists in other parts of the country or in Hollywood. The other movie-industry Communists were, for the most part, caught up in their own guild recognition battles, fighting, in the case of the screenwriters, a studio-created rival union and an industry blacklist. In addition, the CP did not make an effort to unite its union-building forces in Hollywood or to mobilize its supporters in the projectionist branches of the IATSE. Communist leaders seemed content with the galaxy of names that could be mobilized behind Party-supported campaigns and the amount of dollars flowing from the movie industry to those campaigns. During the height of the Popular Front era, 1936–39, the members of the Hollywood branches contributed more to (people's front) causes than any other geographical group.

A host of Popular Front organizations sprung up in Hollywood. The largest and most effective were the Hollywood Anti-Nazi League, the Motion Picture Artists Committee, and the Motion Picture Democratic Committee. Communists provided much of their organizational backbone. They did not dominate them, but they had a strong influence over them when, and only when, Communist and non-Communist policies coincided. When they did not, as happened in the wake of the Nonaggression Treaty signed by Germany and the Soviet Union in August 1939, the organizations splintered.

Although there was not a mass exodus from the CP in September 1939, when the party line changed from antifascism to anti-imperialism and antiwar, Communists were isolated and their Popular Front groups became powerless rumps. The German invasion of the Soviet Union in June 1941 and the Japanese attack on Pearl Harbor in December 1941 altered the situation and a wartime popular front of left-wing forces was constructed. The Hollywood Left dove into the cause of victory, but not to the exclusion of its prewar beliefs. Communists were very active in the efforts to stanch the racism generated by the Sleepy Lagoon case and the Zoot Suit riots, both of which involved Mexican Americans. A small number wrote scripts for radio plays, critically examining the nature of the peace that was coming; a larger number became active in the various electoral organizations formed by "progressives" to continue the New Deal and block the conservative political trend building since the election of 1938; and almost all supported, in guild meetings and on the picket lines, the Conference of Studio Union strikes that erupted between 1945 and 1946.

The defeat of the CSU coincided with the onset of the domestic Cold War, which would strike Hollywood first and hardest. A coalition of the militant Right (the Motion Picture Alliance for the Preservation of American Ideals), the House Committee on Un-American Activities, the IATSE, and, after a short resistance, the producers' associations combined to destroy the organized Left in Hollywood. The Taft-Hartley Act and the blacklist effectively removed radicals from guild and union offices and isolated unions with militant leaders, thus eliminating the Left's main organizational base in Hollywood. *See also*: Hollywood Blacklist, Popular Culture

—*Larry Ceplair*

REFERENCES

Ceplair, Larry, and Steven Englund. *The Inquisition in Hollywood: Politics in the Film Community, 1930–1960*. Garden City, N.Y.: Anchor/Doubleday, 1980.

Talbot, David, and Barbara Zheutlin. *Creative Differences: Profiles of Hollywood Dissidents*. Boston: South End, 1978.

HOME COLONY: see UTOPIANISM

HOOK, SIDNEY (1902–89)

Born and raised in New York, Hook was exposed to radical ideologies and activism early in his life. He received his M.A. (1926) and Ph.D. (1927) in philosophy at Columbia University, completing his dissertation (*The Metaphysics of Pragmatism*) under the direction of John Dewey. After receiving his doctorate, Hook went to Europe to study at the universities of Berlin and Munich and at the Marx-Engels Institute in Moscow. He returned to America in 1933 and taught philosophy at New York University, one of the first Marxist professors in the United States. He subsequently became a preeminent member of the "New York Intellectuals" and one of the most notorious renegades from the radical cause.

Deeply influenced by Karl Marx and John Dewey, Hook believed that philosophy is not a pursuit of abstractions disconnected from social life, but rather the development of a critical and scientific intelligence applied toward the clarification of human values and concrete social problems. He believed the philosopher's task is to criticize all ideologies and conventions that militate against the development of the human individual. Throughout the sharp ideological changes in Hook's life, this general belief remained constant.

Hook began his academic career as a Marxist in the late 1920s with a translation of Lenin's *Materialism and Empirio-Criticism* and critical defenses (particularly against Max Eastman) of dialectics. He soon proved himself a superb interpreter of Marx. Early works such as *Towards an Understanding of Karl Marx* (1933) and *From Hegel to Marx* (1936) were the best U.S. scholarship on Marx at the time. They were heavily influenced by Georg Lukacs and Karl Korsch (with whom he studied at the University of Berlin in 1928). Following the lead of these first "Western Marxists," Hook rejected the prevailing reformist and deterministic interpretations of the Second and Third International, and emphasized the revolutionary, humanist, philosophical, and nondeterminist aspects of Marxism.

During the early 1930s, Hook was a member of the Communist Party. But because of his philosophical heresies and his defense of Trotsky's right to asylum in 1932, he was expelled. He then helped organize the American Workers Party and wrote its political program. For the moment, Hook upheld revolutionary strategy and supported the idea of a Fourth International.

Hook's revolutionary outlook began to wane in the late 1930s. By 1940, in *Reason, Social Myths and Democracy,* he announced his break with radicalism by fully embracing a Deweyian pragmatism, claiming that everything good in Marx had been independently and more rigorously developed by Dewey. With his best years behind him, Hook produced no major writings, limiting himself to essays and polemical disputes, many of which tried to define the role of the liberal intellectual in postwar America and to explain the need to defend capitalism against the evils of "totalitarianism."

In the 1950s, Hook became a fanatical anticommunist and completely reversed his earlier views. Where in 1934 he wrote that "only Communism can save the world from its social evils," in 1953 he concluded that "Communism is the greatest menace to human freedom in the world today." While intoning platitudes about freedom and democracy, Hook began a crusade to banish leftist professors and students from the university. In 1972, Hook supported Nixon's presidential campaign and in 1980 and 1984 he supported Reagan. *See also*: Dewey, John; *Partisan Review*; Philosophy

—*Steven Best*

REFERENCES

Bloom, Alexander. *Prodigal Sons: The New York Intellectuals and Their World.* New York: Oxford University Press, 1986.

Buhle, Paul. *Marxism in the United States.* London: Verso, 1987.

Pells, Richard H. *Radical Visions and American Dreams.* Middleton: Wesleyan University Press, 1973.

Wald, Alan. *The New York Intellectuals.* Chapel Hill: University of North Carolina Press, 1987.

Horton, Myles (b. 1905)

Little in Horton's heritage suggested his subsequent lifetime of activism, either as an organizer or founder of Highlander Research and Education Center.

He was born July 5, 1905, in Savannah, Tennessee, the first of four children. At times, his father taught school, sold insurance, or was a county clerk. His mother taught school, too, before rearing children. The family was Cumberland Presbyterian, a restrained, virtuous faith with small-town, superficial concern for surrounding poverty but which ignored equally evident segregation or exploited labor. In 1928, as the South's economy was collapsing, Horton graduated from Cumberland Presbyterian College. He got work with the YMCA but soon enrolled at Union Theological Seminary in New York City.

As a seminarian, Horton encountered the ideas of Christian socialism and Marx, other equally serious southerners, the Danish Folk High School movement, and Dr. Harry F. Ward's unremitting calls for ethical service and labor. Horton returned to Tennessee dedicated to teach a social gospel blending these influences. With other southerners, including Don West, James A. Dombrowski, and John Thompson, he founded Highlander Folk School in 1932 at Monteagle. His propelling impulse was a mixture of Christ's teachings with socialist theories.

Horton quickly became a controversial figure, first during a bloody miner's strike only weeks after Highlander opened, but subsequently as well, during the CIO's drive to organize the South, in the Southern Conference for Human Welfare, the McCarthyism of the 1950s, and the Eastland hearings into subversion and the civil rights movement. Often at odds with allies on the left, Horton, a radical individualist in spirit and deed, remained unswerving in his faith that collective action could, and did, issue from hard-pressed people learning from their daily struggles. This stubborn belief reinforced his reputation as a loner undisciplined by ideology.

By 1982, when Highlander celebrated its fiftieth anniversary, Horton had been arrested, beaten, smeared as a Red, rebuked by union leaders and socialists, hated by segregationists, observed by government agents, and feared. He had seen the vision of interracial coalitions battered, if not set aside, and any hope of a thoroughgoing social reorganization postponed, if not daunted. Highlander had been firebombed, seized by the State of Tennessee, which sold the school and its possessions at public auction, and ousted by the City of Knoxville through a fraudulent urban renewal scheme. The school is now located in New Market, Tennessee, where Horton lives.

Frustrated by biracial quiescence in the South, and labor's diminished role within Appalachia, Horton has sought peripatetically to link Highlander with revolutionary struggles in Cuba, China, Central and Latin America. In recent years, during these travels, he has won deserved recognition, chiefly within the field of adult education. *See also*: Highlander Research and Education Center

—*Frank Adams*

REFERENCES

Glen, John M. *Highlander: No Ordinary School, 1932–1962*. Lexington: University of Kentucky, 1988.

Poster protesting the jailing of CP leader Eugene Dennis

House Committee on Un-American Activities, aka House Un-American Activities Committee (HUAC)

This was the prototype of the inquisitorial committees that infested the legislative branches of national and state governments during the McCarthy era. It was the forerunner of the McCarthyite inquisitorial techniques immortalized by the query, "Are you now, or have you ever been a Communist?", and the mentor of the art of Red-baiting, guilt by association, and the political smear.

After uncertain beginnings as the Fish Committee (1930–32) and the McCormack-Dickstein Committee (1934–35), the renewed Committee on Un-American Activities hit its full stride under the flamboyant Texan Martin Dies in 1938. When the United States became a participant in World War II, as an ally of the Soviet Union against the Fascist Axis of Germany, Italy, and Japan, Dies' strident anticommunism and divisive attacks on the Roosevelt administration were out of step with the times.

The Cold War emerged before the end of World War II, reversing America's political direction. Erstwhile enemies became allies, and former allies, the Soviet Union and the emerging countries of the Third World, became the enemy. The chief threat facing the United States was the "worldwide international Communist conspiracy," the Internal Security Act of 1950 proclaimed as the finding of Congress. This and the Communist Control Act, an amendment to the ISA enacted in 1954, are the only significant pieces of legislation generated by HUAC in its thirty-year history.

With the changing political climate, HUAC became a permanent standing committee in 1946, mandated to investigate "subversive and un-American propaganda activities." Unlike other committees of the House, HUAC was not primarily concerned with the legislative purpose mandated by the Constitution but with the ideological mission of chilling dissent and inculcating anticommunism.

Orchestrated by HUAC and its counterpart committees in the Senate and state legislatures (with the covert assistance of the FBI), the surge of anticommunism engulfed the nation. Since guilt was ideological, it mattered little to the inquisitorial committees whether a person was an actual member of the Communist (or other Left) Party, or a "fellow traveler" who participated in a CIO union or other progressive cause. Countless Americans found themselves enmeshed in the dragnets of the subversive-hunters.

HUAC was armed with the power to compel testimony anywhere in the United States under subpoena, and to enforce its rules with citations for contempt of Congress. In the classic confrontational hearings, witnesses summoned before it were of two classes, "friendly" and "unfriendly."

The "friendlies" were the informers who named names in well-rehearsed testimony. Most often these were paid FBI infiltrators; others were persons supportive of HUAC's aims and purposes who volunteered their cooperation, as did former Screen Actors Guild president Ronald Reagan (FBI code number T-10). Some were frightened individuals who gave reluctant testimony to escape being fired, blacklisted, or, in some cases, deported with their families. The "unfriendly" witnesses were pilloried in proceedings lacking every element of due process and fairness. To avoid being compelled to be a witness against themselves and others, they most often "took the Fifth Amendment," which provided the only sure means of avoiding a year in prison for contempt to those who refused to answer the committee's questions.

Until the mid-sixties, the news media usually played a supportive role, headlining HUAC charges and giving full and uncritical coverage to informer witnesses, while downplaying or ignoring the testimony of "unfriendly" witnesses.

The Los Angeles-Hollywood area was the movie capital of the world. During the Depression and war years, many progressive writers, actors, directors, and technicians won fame and fortune. In 1947 HUAC undertook to cleanse the industry of such "subversive" influences, to redirect the movie industry as a propaganda instrument for the Cold War.

A group of writers and directors known as the "Hollywood Ten," resisted, with the support of many celebrities, citing their First Amendment rights as grounds to refuse to answer the committee's questions. When the U.S. Supreme Court rejected their claim, and they were sentenced to prison, the "Hollywood blacklist" emerged to punish all who failed to answer the committee's questions. Resistance crumbled. HUAC went on to scour the nation, exposing "subversive" activities in unions, cultural groups, schools, orchestras, plays, organizations of the foreign born, and civil rights groups in hearings held throughout the nation.

In the late 1950s, the Los Angeles area again became the center of organized resistance to the committee, giving birth to the National Committee to abolish HUAC. Community opposition was organized wherever HUAC hearings were held, and political pressures were transmitted to the House of Representatives. By 1969, HUAC was forced into a tactical retreat, adopted the sanitized name of "House Committee on Internal Security," and stopped issuing subpoenas to hostile witnesses. In 1975, as part of a structural reorganization of the House of Representatives, the committee was eliminated, and its files, including index cards on 750,000 "subversive" Americans, were consigned, under seal, to the National Archives.

When the Freedom of Information Act was amended in 1976 to permit a limited public access to FBI records, it revealed the full scope of the illicit partnership between HUAC and the FBI, which began in 1947 in conjunction with HUAC's purge of the movie industry. Without this vast storehouse of political intelligence dating back to the early 1930s, HUAC would have been largely impotent. Thereafter, HUAC became an adjunct to the operations of FBI director J. Edgar Hoover.

Hoover needed HUAC as an instrument in his illegal "neutralization" programs, which were intended to destroy individuals and organizations targeted by Hoover, against whom evidence was lacking for lawful prosecution. The notorious Counterintelligence Program brought to public attention in the 1970s by hearings of the Senate Select Committee on Intelligence headed by Senator Frank Church was only one of many neutralization programs. By placing FBI informer testimony in the public record, HUAC acted as the laundry transforming confidential data into "public source information," which the FBI could more safely leak to its favored news media contacts. By giving HUAC its lists of individuals to subpoena as its "unfriendly witnesses," the FBI could effectively damage those it sought to neutralize. Information covertly passed along to the HUAC staff director included informer-derived and wiretap information on the contemplated moves of congressional opponents of HUAC. *See also*: Hollywood Blacklist; Lawson, John Howard; McCarthyism; National Lawyers Guild; Odets, Clifford

—*Richard Criley*

REFERENCES

Final Report of the Select Committee to Study Governmental Operations with Respect to Intelligence Activities, United States Senate, Supplementary Detailed Staff Reports of Intelligence Activities and Rights of Americans. Book III. Washington, D.C.: Government Printing Office, 1976.

O'Reilly, Kenneth. *Hoover and the Un-Americans*. Philadelphia: Temple University Press, 1983.

HOWE, IRVING (b. 1920)

The most prestigious American socialist literary critic of the 1950s–1970s, Irving Howe long remained one of the most controversial figures on the Left. According to his supporters a defender of socialism's roots in liberal values, he was to others a foremost defender of a socially constructed "West" (principally the United States, Europe, and Israel) in the era of imperial decline and cultural de-centering.

The child of an East Bronx Jewish proletarian family, Howe precociously joined the Young People's Socialist League and attended City College, where he became a Trotskyist student leader. Like most of the other Trotskyist "youth," he left the Socialist Workers Party in 1940 for the newly founded "Third Camp" Workers Party led by Max Shachtman. The next year Howe became editor of the weekly *Labor Action*, remaining until his departure for military service in 1941, and then again returning briefly in 1946. Soon Howe felt restless in the movement and began to ease out, turning his attention to mostly literary essays for liberal, anticommunist journals, and for *Time* magazine, where he wrote reviews from 1948 to 1952.

With McCarthyism and the disintegration of the American Left, most of Howe's intellectual milieu lost interest in socialism. Many, including some of Howe's protégés and closest allies, went on to careers as prestige ideologues of neoconservatism. He separated himself from them politically, but continued to share much of their culture bent. Therefore, he straddled literary-critical pursuits—taking up a wide range of subjects but concerned above all with the "modern," where aesthetics increasingly escaped political judgment—and political polemics, directed mostly against the surviving Communist Left, but also against the general backsliding of his own milieu. By 1953, Howe had come to support the United States in the Korean War, albeit critically, and had resigned from the fading Independent Socialist League. He attacked McCarthyism and attacked cultural "conformity," however, and sought to advance an independent position on domestic and international matters. Accepting a position with Brandeis University that year, he launched *Dissent* magazine as a voice of anticommunist, democratic socialism.

He continued with a variety of literary criticism, his political essays seeking to define democratic socialism (increasingly in later years, liberalism), and with several anthologies of basic socialist writings. In all this, his most distinctive work, in collaboration with editor-poet Eliezer Greenberg, was to help return Yiddish literature (even when regarded, as by Howe himself, as hopelessly vanishing in any live language sense) to dignity among educated Jews. As anthologist and critic-historian, he thereby offered a popular paean to a socialistic past quickly vanishing.

Howe returned to New York in 1963 to teach at Hunter College. To his considerable surprise, much of his particular anti-communist style had become an intellectual vogue among an important stratum of liberals. He found himself reciprocally sympathetic, while correspondingly hostile toward the New Left as it increased in size and importance. Howe's support, until 1970, of the U.S. presence in Vietnam, his *New York Times Magazine* savaging of the antiwar movement, and his literary attacks on angry black and feminist writers, marked an almost complete break between himself and the New Left.

In subsequent years, through the Democratic Socialist Organizing Committee and its successor, Democratic Socialists of America, Howe and a section of New Left survivors effected an uneasy peace. Howe's versions of democratic socialism, often shifting subtly during his career, remained unsettled. By virtue of intellectual alliances and personal ties, he appeared prominently identified with extreme rightward edge of liberalism in the pro-contra, Cold War hard-line position of the *New Republic*, owned and directed by Howe's former student Martin Peretz. On the other hand, he stood firm with his status in the relatively pluralistic liberal-socialist milieux of *Dissent* and DSA.

Howe's literary-critical status bore other contradictions. His methods were considered outdated by newer generations of Marxist, feminist, and Third World critics. His favorite authors—V. I. Naipaul and Saul Bellow prominent among them—were taken to be symbols of Western contempt for the submerged cultures. Yet he retained into advanced middle age extraordinary prestige in leading liberal publications, and a wide (especially Jewish) audience outside the academy. Still bearing the scars of earlier eras, reputedly shifting leftward again, Howe remained at the end of the 1980s the avatar of Jewish radical-liberalism in transit from ghetto socialist culture to some uncertain destination. *See also*: *Dissent*, New International, Trotskyism, Workers Party

—*Mari Jo Buhle*

REFERENCES

Howe, Irving. *A Margin of Hope*. New York: Harcourt, Brace Jovanovich, 1982.

Wald, Alan. *The New York Intellectuals: The Rise and Decline of the Anti-Stalinist Left from the 1930s to the 1980s*. Chapel Hill: University of North Carolina Press, 1987.

HOWELLS, WILLIAM DEAN (1837–1920)

Born on the frontier in Ohio, Howells was the son of a crusading abolitionist printer and newspaper editor. Young Howells picked up rough-and-ready radical politics even before his teens. By 1861 he had written a campaign biography of Lincoln and was rewarded with an appointment as U.S. Consul in Venice. When he returned to the United States in 1865, still a radical Republican, he quickly landed on his feet as assistant editor of the prestigious *Atlantic Monthly*, where he remained until 1881, publishing well-received novels and critical essays, basking in the company of Boston Brahmins, and learning how to be genteel and politically orthodox. Even during his Boston years, Howells still used his position in the world of letters to champion unorthodox writers. His defense of the new realists, people like Rebecca Harding Davis, Hamlin Garland, and Ed Howe, reflected ambiguities within Howells. While he was proclaiming that "the smiling aspects of life are the more American," the writers he praised and published were dealing with the dark side of emerging industrial capitalism, with poverty, ignorance, and oppression in mills, in city slums, and on the farms. By 1885 Howells experienced savage attacks from critics in England and America for the realism he defended as well as the realism in his own novels. "Practical atheism" and "mental and moral pathology," one critic, Hamilton Wright Mabie, snarled about *The Rise of Silas Lapham*. One event in 1887 precipitated Howells again into the public world of radical politics. When seven Chicago anarchists were sentenced to death for the "Haymarket Affair" of May 4, 1886, Howells, alone among the established literary lights, defied his publishers, his fellow writers, the press, and his readers by speaking out in defense of the condemned men. On November 6, 1887, Howells wrote in the New York *Tribune* that the trial had not established the guilt of the defendants, and he urged the commutation of the sentences. On November 12 four of the condemned were hanged. Howells continued to agonize about the injustice: "It blackens my life," he wrote. "This free Republic has killed 5 men for their opinions." For his courageous action Howells had to endure a storm of criticism, but he stood his ground. From 1887 on, his writing assumed a darker tone, a recognition that something had gone deeply wrong with the system. His novels, *Annie Kilburn* (1888), *A Hazard of New Fortunes* (1890), *A Traveler from Alturia* (1894), and *Through the Eye of the Needle* (1907) dealt with strikes, with class injustice, with socialism. Deeply influenced by Tolstoy and William Morris, Howells now began to commit himself more earnestly and publicly to radical writing and radical politics. He championed black writers, Paul Laurence Dunbar and Charles W. Chesnutt, recommended realistic novels about slum life, Stephen Crane's *Maggie* and Abraham Cahan's *Yekl*, spoke out for equality for blacks and suffrage for women. In 1898 he publicly opposed the Spanish-American War and became president of the Anti-Imperialist League. He called himself a socialist although he never joined any socialist groups.

In old age Howells became an odd mixture of radical and conservative. President Taft spoke at his seventy-fifth birthday fete about his lucid style and kindly humor, but W. E. B. DuBois also praised the seventy-five-year-old writer for his humanity and justice: "When a band of earnest men" spoke for Negro emancipation, "William Dean Howells was among the first to sign the call. From this call came the National Association for the Advancement of Colored People." And at seventy-five Howells marched in a parade for woman suffrage. While remaining unrepentant for his stance on America's imperialist war in 1898, he became an enthusiastic supporter of the Allied cause in World War I. *See also*: Peace Movements

—*Fay M. Blake*

REFERENCES

Cady, Edwin H., and Norma W. Cady. *Critical Essays on W. D. Howells, 1866–1920*. Boston: G. K. Hall, 1983.

Cady, Edwin H. *Young Howells and John Brown: Episodes in a Radical Education*. Columbus: Ohio State University Press, 1985.

Hough, Robert L. *The Quiet Rebel: William Dean Howells as Social Commentator*. Lincoln: University of Nebraska Press, 1959.

Howells, Mildred. *Life in Letters of William Dean Howells*. 2 vols. New York: Doubleday, Doran, 1928.

Hudson, Hosea (b. 1898)

Retired iron molder, Communist, and former official of the United Steel Workers of America (USW) in Birmingham, Alabama, Hudson represents the hundreds of working-class, urban black southerners who joined the Communist Party of the United States between the two wars. A labor leader in the late 1930s and early 1940s and also a prominent local Communist, he belongs to the generation forced early in the Cold War to choose between the CPUSA and the labor movement. Hudson chose the CPUSA, although he continues to be active in organized labor through the Coalition of Black Trades Unionists.

Like many southerners in his generation, Hudson was born in a rural area (Wilkes County, Georgia) and left sharecropping in 1923 for wage work after the boll weevil and a family crisis aggravated the oppressive social and economic system that he had long resented. In Atlanta he worked as a laborer at a railroad roundhouse, in the hazardous working conditions common at the time. He and his family moved to Birmingham in 1924, attracted by the prospect of high wages.

In Birmingham, Hudson became a skilled iron molder and continued with his passion for singing in quartets, distinguishing himself in both roles and hoping that his vocal talent would lead to a singing career on the radio. In early 1931, however, the Scottsboro case attracted his attention. Hudson saw this as another barely legal lynching that blacks were afraid to protest. The CPUSA's civil rights division, the International Labor Defense (ILD), defended the "Scottsboro Boys," kept them from being executed, made the case internationally known, and brought many American blacks like Hudson into the Party. After Al Murphy, a fellow black ironworker, invited him to a Party meeting in 1931, Hudson joined immediately. Until he encountered the CPUSA, Hudson had angrily questioned the southern status quo—economic and racial—without discovering any remedies available to working-class blacks who felt uncomfortable in the Interracial Commission or the National Association for the Advancement of Colored People.

One of Hudson's activities as a Communist entailed organizing the Right to Vote Club in 1938 that attempted to teach literate blacks how to qualify to register to vote. Hudson himself had only recently learned to read at a CPUSA National Training School near

Ossining, New York. Between 1938 and 1940 Hudson worked on the Works Progress Administration, serving as vice president of the Birmingham and Jefferson County locals of the Workers Alliance, the WPA workers' union that was heavily CP-influenced.

When the need for war material brought him back into iron molding, Hudson became active in the USW, serving first as recording secretary of Local 1489 then as founder and president of Local 2815. He was also chairman of 2815's grievance committee and delegate to the Birmingham Industrial Union Council. During 1944–45, while the CPUSA was reorganized nationally as the Communist Political Association, Hudson was vice president of the Alabama section, known as the Alabama People's Educational Association.

The Cold War years inflicted a series of injuries on Hudson from which he never completely recovered. Weakened by his immersion in the Party and many absences from home, his thirty-year-old marriage broke up in 1946. In 1947 he was expelled from the Birmingham Industrial Union Council, fired from his job, stripped of his offices in Local 2815, and blacklisted for being a Communist. In 1950 he went underground and worked for CPUSA as a southern liaison until he moved to New York City in 1954. He remained in the North, working on two autobiographies, and moved to Gainesville, Florida, in 1985.

He sees recognition by the city of Birmingham as vindication; Mayor Richard Arrington proclaimed February 26, 1980, as Hosea Hudson Day, honoring Hudson as a civil rights pioneer and founder of the Right to Vote Club. *See also*: Birmingham, Civil Rights, Communist Party, Western Federation of Miners/Mine, Mill

—*Nell Irvin Painter*

REFERENCES

Hudson, Hosea. *Black Worker in the Deep South*. New York: International, 1972.

Painter, Nell Irvin. *The Narrative of Hosea Hudson: His Life as a Communist in the South*. Cambridge: Harvard University Press, 1979.

———. "Hosea Hudson and the Progressive Party in Birmingham." In *Perspectives on the American South*, edited by Merle Black and John Shelton Reed. Vol. 1, London: Gordon & Breach, 1981.

HUGHAN, JESSIE WALLACE (1875–1955)

A founder and first secretary of the War Resisters League (WRL) in 1923, Hughan saw her pacificism and socialism as integrally related. The profit motive, she believed, was the cause of both war and economic injustice.

Hughan was born in Brooklyn, New York, to parents who became active in Henry George's "single tax" plan and came to share their perspective on social inequality. When Hughan studied economics at Columbia University, she wrote her master's thesis on Henry George's place in the field of economics. She turned to the subject of socialism for her doctoral dissertation, and in doing her fieldwork attended meetings of New York Socialist Party locals. She became a member of the SP in 1907 and ran several times for office on the party ticket. She wrote several books on socialism in the United States, including *American Socialism of the Present Day* (1913), a revision of her doctoral dissertation, and *The Facts of Socialism* (1913).

Following the outbreak of World War I, Hughan joined the antipreparedness movement and helped to organize the No-Conscription League in 1915. She also became a founding member of the Fellowship of Reconciliation, which in 1922 brought representatives from several peace societies together as the WRL. The WRL staged antiwar parades and conducted a mass pledge drive, asking individuals to sign a statement reading: "War is a crime against humanity. We therefore are determined not to support any kind of war and to strive for the removal of all causes of war." The WRL collected more than 12,000 signatures on its pledge by 1937. In 1942 she published *Three Decades of War Resistance*.

During WW II, Hughan supported pacifists and called for an early armistice to forestall on the further destruction of Europe's Jewish population. In 1945 she resigned as secretary of the WRL, although she remained member of its executive committee until her death. *See also*: Peace Movements, Socialist Party

—*Mari Jo Buhle*

REFERENCES

Chatfield, Charles. *For Peace and Justice: Pacificism in America, 1914–1941*. Knoxville: University of Kentucky Press, 1971.

Wittner, Lawrence S. *Rebels Against War: The American Peace Movement, 1941–1960*. Philadelphia: Temple University Press, 1985.

Hughes, Langston (1902–67)

Afro-American poet, playwright, novelist, and journalist, Hughes was born in Joplin, Missouri, but grew up in Lawrence, Kansas, and Cleveland, Ohio, before settling later in Harlem. His dedication to the ideal of social justice was first developed by his maternal grandmother, Mary Langston, whose first husband had died at Harpers Ferry in John Brown's band, and whose second husband (Hughes's grandfather) had also been an ardent abolitionist. In Cleveland, Hughes was introduced to socialism by certain high school classmates, many of whom were the children of immigrants from Eastern Europe and Russia. As an emerging poet, he was shaped decisively by the democratic modernist Carl Sandburg but also found Claude McKay, then an associate of Max Eastman and other New York Leftists, an ideal role model of the black writer committed at once to socialism, black progress, and literary excellence.

After a year at Columbia University (1921–22), Hughes undertook a series of menial jobs that increased his ties to the black working class. A trip in 1923 down the west coast of Africa intensified his dislike of European colonialism, and on his return he began to publish in radical journals such as the *Messenger*, in addition to his usual showing in the NAACP and Urban League magazines. Two books of verse, *The Weary Blues* (1926) and *Fine Clothes to the Jew* (1927), as well as the novel *Not Without Laughter* (1930), established him as the major young writer of the Harlem Renaissance. But the onset of the Depression, the decline of the Renaissance, and a traumatic experience with a wealthy white patron drove him about 1930 to reassess his art and life.

Turning sharply leftward, in 1931 he visited Haiti and Cuba and denounced American imperialism there in the *New Masses*. Also visiting the "Scottsboro Boys" in prison in Alabama, he openly sided with their Communist lawyers in their controversy with the NAACP over the case. He spent a year (1932–33) in the Soviet Union, to which he had gone to help make a film (soon abandoned) about American race relations. Warmly received, he wrote several radical poems, including "Good Morning Revolution" and "Goodbye Christ," as well as a short book, *A Negro Looks at Soviet Central Asia* (1934), in praise of the Soviet treatment of its darker peoples. In 1934 he wrote "One More 'S' in the U.S.A." (to make it Soviet) for a national Communist Party convention. The same year, he was elected president of the Communist-backed League of Struggle for Negro Rights. In 1938, after three months in Madrid as a war correspondent, he founded the Harlem Suitcase Theater, which staged his *Don't You Want to Be Free?* This play loosely combined some of his strongest poems about race with the music of the blues and exhortations about class consciousness and unity. The same year, he published a collection of radical verse, *A New Song* (1938), with an introduction by literary radical Mike Gold.

Such involvements made many people think of Hughes as a Communist, but he always denied Party membership. Although he lent his name to many organizations, his personal involvement, as in the case of the League, was usually token. With the Nazi-Soviet Pact taxing his socialist sympathies, World War II found Hughes in retreat from radicalism. An autobiography, *The Big Sea* (1940), contained virtually no reference to the Left. That year, after an attack by a right-wing group, he repudiated "Goodbye Christ" and declared his radicalism an error of his youth. Thereafter he published mainly in centrist journals, where he stressed the evils of Jim Crow. Late in the decade he published his first purely "lyrical" or nonpolitical volume of verse, *Fields of Wonder* (1947), and sounded few pro-Marxist notes in his later volumes *One-Way Ticket* (1949), *Montage of a Dream Deferred* (1951), *Ask Your Mama* (1961), and *The Panther and the Lash* (1967). However, in certain poems during the war, such as "Good Morning Stalingrad," about Soviet heroism, he showed deep admiration of the Soviet people, and now and then he defended the American Left in his weekly column in the Chicago *Defender*. In 1948 he publicly endorsed Progressive Party candidate Henry Wallace for president, and in 1949 Hughes so vividly condemned the prosecution in New York of twelve Communist leaders that the regional CP asked (and received) his permission to reprint the essay.

Toward the end of the 1940s, as his prestige gained with the success of efforts such as the musical play *Street Scene* (1947) with Kurt Weill and Elmer Rice, right-wing harassment at his many public readings increased. He came under closer scrutiny by the FBI. In March 1953 a subpoena brought him before Senator Joseph McCarthy's investigating committee. Hughes named no names, but generally cooperated with McCarthy. Later in the fifties he further offended the Left by omitting leaders such as W. E. B. DuBois and Paul Robeson, long known and admired by Hughes, from certain of his books for young persons in which they clearly belonged. At a public celebration of Robeson's sixtieth birthday, DuBois rebuked Hughes for his treatment of Robeson.

To some extent, Hughes regretted his public break with the Left. But his main commitment from the start had been to black Americans as an embattled group, and his unprecedented career as a black writer living only by his pen depended on his close relationship to local black communities. Psychologically, too, he seemed incapable of enduring the ostracism and isolation visited on leaders like DuBois and Robeson. Instead, he chose to safeguard his position as the most representative and most beloved of black writers. *See also*: Humor, *New Masses*

—*Arnold Rampersad*

REFERENCES

Berry, Faith, ed. *Good Morning Revolution: Uncollected Social Protest Writings by Langston Hughes*. Westport: Greenwood, 1973.

Rampersad, Arnold. *The Life of Langston Hughes, Vol. I: 1902–1941*. New York: Oxford University Press, 1986.

———. *The Life of Langston Hughes, Vol. II: 1941–1967*. New York: Oxford University Press, 1988.

Humor

In written and graphic forms, humor has played a great role in the U.S. Left, although one scarcely recognized in strategic, tactical, or theoretical discourse. Humorists have for the most part warmed up audiences, or filled the back pages of Left publications—the one exception to this rule being the cartoonist's front-page status in some Left papers. These humor workers have, nevertheless, been among the most beloved figures in the Left movements, warmly embraced by the rank-and-file radical.

Left literary humor dates to well before 1870. James Russell Lowell's *Biglow Papers* savagely criticized the Mexican War. David Ross Locke, whose "Petroleum V. Nasby" protagonist epitomized the reactionary stupidity of Confederate sympathizers in the Union states, was considered required reading at Lincoln's White House. Russell B. Nye, writer of comic histories of the United States (and a good personal friend of Eugene Debs) could be racist, but was also militantly antiwar and enormously skeptical about patriotic claims in general. In the final decades of the nineteenth century, Marietta Holley added many volumes of proto-feminist satire, skewering male and female resistance to woman's rights. Mark Twain, the greatest of American humorists (and in old age an avowed socialist) labeled the "Gilded Age" and captured the banality of a reckless materialism.

Building upon these traditions, hayseed socialist commentators beginning in the 1890s press wrote affable jests at American resistance to socialist ideas. The best of the writers, editor J. A. Wayland, had special fun assaulting the aristocratic pretensions of the American new rich, and the vacuousness of continued public democratic rhetoric. Oscar Ameringer swiftly emerged as the stage comic and literary comedian par excellence. In a long career spanning the early years of the century to the verge of U.S. entry into World War II, "the Mark Twain of American Socialism" wrote monologues for many publications (mostly those edited by himself), important humor agitation pamphlets, and one vastly popular comic history, *The Life and Deeds of Uncle Sam*.

Ameringer had many imitators during the "Golden Age" of native-born socialism, 1900–15, perhaps the best known being Henry M. Tichenor, columnist for the *National Rip-Saw* and editor of his own satirical free-thought journal from St. Louis, the *Melting Pot*. The lyrical counterpart to this literary comedy from the Industrial Workers of the World, satirical Wobbly songs in *The Little Red Songbook* reached as many listeners as any document in American radical history. Humorous Wobbly soapboxers also abounded, and a few (notably, T-Bone Slim) became famous for their newspaper or magazine columns.

Cartoonists drew more broadly, it is fair to say, upon international traditions, but by no means entirely so. Although little cartoon work of note appeared in the nineteenth-century socialist papers, the traditions of Breughel, Hogarth, Daumier, Goya, and the contemporary artists of the popular German *Simplicissimus* and its socialistic sister publication, *Die Wahre Jacob*, had an impact in creating an artistic climate of wide commercial work for cartoonists.

Art Young, the most renowned of the old-style newspaper illustrators, had made a name for himself in the commercial press before shifting his activities full-time to socialism around 1910. He went on, after the decline of the socialist movement, to found a short-lived comic weekly, *Good Morning* (1921–22), and to draw occasionally for the *New Masses* while preparing his own book-length Dante-esque version of hellish modern civilization. His mostly younger colleagues at the *Masses* magazine, including Kenneth Chamberlain, Stuart Davis, Henry Glintenkamp, Boardman Robinson, and Robert Minor, fairly invented the "artistic" cartoon later adopted by the *New Yorker* among other publications, of crayon-style sketch and spare (often wry and unconsciously self-satirical) dialogue. Most devoted themselves to artistic work after 1920 (later becoming leading figures in the Congress of American Artists), while the volatile Robert Minor evolved from militant anarchism to Communism and to functionary status within the Communist Party of the United States.

Within the Socialist Party and IWW press, styles evolved closer to the commercial daily comics, albeit oriented toward class consciousness and working-class enlightenment generally. Ryan Walker, publisher for a short time of the Michigan monthly the *Billygoat* (retitled *Prophet and the Ass*), became a staff cartoonist on the daily *New York Call*, and a frequent contributor to the *National Rip-Saw* among other publications. His notable inventions, *The Rip-Saw Mother Goose* (bound separately, and widely distributed) and the un-class-conscious worker "Henry Dubb" (many strips would end with the painful admission, "I'm the Henry Dubb!"), had a considerable following. The IWW cartoonists, drawing for a semiliterate audience often on the move, dedicated themselves to ridiculing capitalism as an economic and moral system, including within its appendages the "American Separation of Labor." Unlike the socialists, whose cartoon talent largely dissipated after 1920, the IWW had a wealth of mostly self-taught artists whose work continued for decades after.

Immigrant humor followed an almost entirely different path, with only an exceptional crossover (such as German-American Oscar Ameringer). From the 1870s, popular German-American theater included socialistic farces, almost invariably set in the old country but sometimes dealing with issues of immigrant life. A number of outstanding poets and journalists of the movement wrote and occasionally played in these dramas, which were enthusiastically received by local working-class audiences. Johann Most, who had abandoned an early thespian career after contracting a disfiguring jaw disease, was undoubtedly the most noted stage raconteur of radical "dirty jokes." (One survives: the difference between a toilet and a stock market crash is that in the stock market, the paper falls before the crash.) After the turn of the century a variety of new immigrant groups, reputedly among the most enthusiastic the small Bulgarian following, ventured into satirical theater aimed at neighborhood audiences. Finnish theater, the most avowedly "workerist," carried comical antibourgeois dramas into the many fraternal halls of the copper-mining districts. New York–based Yiddish theater, vastly popular and tinged with Left views, emphasized mainly social melodrama with only a light sprinkling of radical farce.

A portion of this comedy reached the immigrant socialist press, along with translations from Mark Twain and other capitalism-jibing authors. Morris Winchevsky, the founder of the Yiddish socialist press, contributed the most popular single column, "Di Meshugina Filosofer" (The crazy philosopher), writing on the foolishness of capitalism and its willing wage slaves. Immigrant radicals attained their earliest satirical publication in *Der Tramp* (1879), satirizing the newly rich German immigrant. The next and most important of all distinctly radical immigrant humor magazines, the *Groysser Kundes* (1909–27), held the Lower East Side in rapt attention, while providing literary work for many young radicals. When after World War I the *Kundes* turned against the Russian Revolution, one of the more promising young writers, Sam Liptzin, founded and edited the short-lived *Der Humorist* (1921–22) en route to becoming the staff humorist of the Yiddish *Freiheit* and author of nearly thirty Yiddish volumes of folksy humoristic commentary. The most long-lived immigrant humor publications, the Finnish weeklies *Punikki*, later *Lopotosu*, made the transition from socialist to communist and lasted into the later 1930s. Italian antifascists aimed several ephemeral 1920s publications at ridiculing Mussolini and his American supporters.

Other radical humor made a troubled but at first generally successful transition to the newly ascendent Communist movement of the 1920s. Communist literary comics and cartoonists, such as Fred Ellis, tended to be less humorous and rather more heavy-handed than socialists or Wobblies in their class-struggle treatments. But in the Yiddish press especially, the burst of creative enthusiasm inspired by the appearance of the *Freiheit* helped put a younger generation's talents to work. Moshe Nadir, after Sholom Aleichem the greatest comic writer in Yiddish, gave his full talents to the *Freiheit* during the 1920s–1930s, with feuilletons, literary sketches, and poems. Nadir and a younger contemporary, Chaver Paver, also created popular children's books in Yiddish with humor and political pathos mixed. Cartoonist William Gropper, who also drew frequently for the *Daily Worker*, gained wide reputation (or notoriety) for his puncturing of Jewish socialist moderates' labor misleadership in the needle trades.

The appearance of the Popular Front created a rallying point for talented artists and literary comics, most especially but not only in the *New Masses*. Robert Forsythe's weekly columns (collected in the 1935 volume *Redder than the Rose*) imitated the *New Yorker* style (or that of Canadian left-leaning Stephen Leacock, popular in the Soviet Union), sophisticated and light-handed. At the *New Yorker*, on the distant liberal end of the Popular Front, Robert Benchley lent his talents to the Spanish Civil War, and the darkly ironic Dorothy Parker became a longtime supporter of Left causes (well into the McCarthy era), especially in defense of legal victims. When Forsythe took a leave from his *New Masses* columns, William Saroyan or S. J. Perelman—best known for his screenwriting of several Marx Brothers films—occasionally spelled the regular columnist. In Hollywood, comedy screenwriter Donald Ogden Stewart became one of the film industry's most important intellectual-activists.

The *New Masses*, like the *Masses*, possessed a special attraction for artists only peripherally involved with politics as such. A wide proliferation of styles and themes, abstract or didactic, worldly, near-cynical, and evangelistic by turns, became a principal feature of the weekly. Few noted artists remained after the Hitler-Stalin Pact and the subsequent decline of the magazine. In these days, however, even the *Daily Worker* acquired staff comic artists, the most talented of whom, Louie Furstadt, produced *Little Lefty*, a popularly followed children's strip.

For the smaller Left movements with their weekly papers, an individual cartoonist often gained almost an especially exalted stature. These artists took special pleasure in skewering the Communist movement and the Soviet Union (Stalin in particular) for betraying the cause of the Left. Thus Jesse Cohen, pennamed "Carlo" in the Trotskyist movement's *Labor Action*, not only concentrated the political message of the paper into one terse line-drawing, but reputedly also served as a teller of difficult truths in party ranks through his verbal repartee. Laura Gray, drawing for the orthodox Trotskyist *Militant*, reached the rare status of a leading woman humor artist. Only perhaps the eldest groups, the Socialist Labor Party with Walter Steinhilber and the IWW with a number of artists, continued to cling to the historical themes such as capital stealing from the workers' pockets.

Meanwhile, an entirely fresh genre took the place, so to speak, of the vanishing theatrical farce. Left folksinging had, from its beginnings, a frequent undertone of comic verve. Woody Guthrie, the most creative and popular of the artists, wrote a folksy humor column in the *Daily Worker* and loaded up his often woeful lyrics with wry asides about bourgeois politics and technological fantasy. Burl Ives, Pete Seeger, the Weavers, and others reproducing rural songs and adding to them a revived genre of labor tunes, wove humor into generally serious themes, while widely entertaining the children of the Left.

The Cold War and McCarthyism made radical humor difficult to perform safely. Talented humorists lost their radical connections, or were badly isolated. Ventriloquist Paul Winchell (whose dummy, Jerry Mahoney, was named after a Tammany politician) went from public appearances for Vito Marcantonio to other things. Zero Mostel suffered a prolonged blacklisting for his refusal to appear as a "friendly witness," and sitcom actor Phillip Loeb, at the peak of his fame as a co-starring member of *The Goldbergs*, was driven from television and committed suicide several years later. "Professor" Irwin Corey, later a regular performer at *Jewish Currents*, held fast to Jewish progressivism. Numerous other radical-minded humor writers and actors in Hollywood and elsewhere, simply languished in their careers or steered clear of all political commitments.

With the rest of the Left, radical humor went into hiding. *Mad Comics*, which developed the technique of satirizing commercial mass culture through a close examination of its details, was developed by Harvey Kurtzman, child of the Yiddish Left and teenage assistant to the *Daily Worker*'s Louic Furstadt. After an unsuccessful effort to create a cartoonists' union, several artists came together in *Mad* magazine, which shunned most political issues as such, but flayed Joseph McCarthy. Paul Krassner, close friend of the *Mad* staff, began a nightclub stand-up act and launched the *Realist* in 1957. His determinedly tasteless and vulgar approach to contemporary political-cultural hypocrisy would be followed, some years later, by the Lower East Side musical group the Fugs, whose lyricist, Tuli Kupferberg, had wide political connections. Tom Lehrer, a Yale mathematics instructor whose concerts and records mocked 1950s bomb-culture, racism, and consumerism, had a largely campus following. But perhaps Jules Feiffer, more civil libertarian than radical, made the most popular dissenting statements, generally about the status of artist or intellectual under capitalism run rampant.

Some of the same took place among the small number of African-American Left humorists. Langston Hughes, whose "Semple" series of barroom dialogues on social topics circulated widely in the black press, received little recognition in the mainstream for his biting humor, and himself eased away from open Left involvements. Ollie Harrington, whose radical-humorous *Bootsie* ran for many years in the *Pittsburgh Courier*, moved to East Germany and began decades of drawing mostly bitter issues-oriented cartoons for the American Communist press.

Kurtzman's *Help!* magazine of the early 1960s (staffed for a time by a young Gloria Steinem) introduced to a wider public two of the most famed dissident cartoonists of the New Left days, Gilbert Shelton and R. Crumb. Shelton, a former history graduate student at the University of Texas, had first gained wide recognition drawing for the *Rag*, one of the earliest and most political-minded underground newspapers. Shelton moved between political-cultural satire and a celebration of the hippie lifestyle. Crumb, obsessed with many subjects (especially sexuality), made extended commentaries on social pathology, and nurtured a mostly hidden socialistic sympathy. Along with many of the other underground cartoonists, the two provided the alternative press a staple attraction, and created a new genre of mostly satirical, sometimes broadly political, often ecological, occasionally feminist-inclined comic books. The earliest outright political venture, *Radical America Komiks* (1969), edited by Gilbert Shelton, appeared as an issue of the informal journal of the Students for a Democratic Society. Of more straightforward cartoon work in the underground press, Ron Cobb's mordant commentaries on self-destructive techno-war culture became a signature of the times.

Leftish comedy found its way to performance more difficult, but not impossible. Barbara Garson's *MacBird!* traveled to dozens of campuses and community performances, with most impact before the close of Lyndon Johnson's presidential administration. The San Francisco Mime Troupe put on a larger and more sustained road show, during the time of Vietnam especially antiwar in emphasis. In later years, a series of avowedly radical-political performers who toured many localities with Leftish raps included Flo Kennedy and lesbian Robin Tyler (herself briefly a major television performer). A "First Radical Humor Festival" at New York University, in 1982, sought—sometimes successfully—to combine performers, artists, and audience in a mix of generations and styles.

Somewhat closer to the mainstream, the albums of the Firesign Theatre reflected antiwar, antiestablishment values. Among the mainstream radical-minded comic performers from the later 1960s to the early 1970s, one could include the Smothers Brothers (one of them of a particularly socialistic sympathy) and Dick Gregory. In television, the tastes of the '60s-style baby boomers had become the mainstream, so that an anti-war or anti-racist message could be delivered within existing comedy-drama formats. Hollywood Blacklist victim Ring Lardner, Jr., thus proved instrumental in a critical turn of the media via Larry Gelbart's adaptation of Lardner's *M*A*S*H* film to antiwar progressive Alan Alda's talents. Later, Robin Williams and Richard Dreyfuss made comedy statements in a variety of films considerably to the left.

By the 1980s, Left humor had already taken on an emphatically postmodern edge. *Processed World*, a Bay Area quarterly, characteristically drew upon Situationist styles (which had barely made an appearance in the 1960s) to describe and satirize the world of new-age office work under high-tech conditions. Avant-garde and sometimes Leftish "punkzines" with circulations from a few hundred to a few thousand assumed the post-industrial, catastrophic reality as fixed and sought to locate a space for humor within it. The newest breed of dissenting comic artists to have their work printed into the radical and liberal as well as mainstream press—Nicole Hollander, Matt Groening, Berke Breathed, and Bill Griffith among them—focused on the layered world of images and the surreality of the little, good or bad, that had not become swallowed up by an image-world now patently out of control. *See also*: Ameringer, Oscar; *Groysser Kundes*; Hollywood Blacklist; Hughes, Langston; IWW Cartoonists; Lardner, Ring, Jr.; Popular Culture; Underground Comix; Yiddish Left

—*Paul Buhle*

REFERENCES

Buhle, Paul, ed., *Labor's Joke Book*. St. Louis: Workers Democracy Press, 1986.

Hungarian Americans

The origins of Hungarian radicalism can be traced back to the failed revolution of 1848 and the flight of Lojos Kossuth and others who found asylum in the United States.

But for the most part this immigration followed the general pattern of other eastern and southern Europeans. About 1.7 million Hungarians emigrated from the Austro-Hungarian Empire before World War I and between one-third and one-half of these were Hungarian-speaking Magyars. Most were peasants, but a third were industrial and/or itinerant workers, whose acquaintance with socialism and unions in Budapest and other Hungarian cities laid the basis for the development of the Hungarian-American Left.

The Hungarians concentrated in New York, Newark, Philadelphia, Pittsburgh, Cleveland, Hartford, Chicago, and other large eastern and midwestern cities, working primarily in mining and heavy industry, especially coal, stockyards, iron, steel, and in the 1930s rubber and automobiles. Within these industries Hungarians were frequently given

BÈRMUNKÁS

HUNGARIAN OFFICIAL ORGAN OF THE INDUSTRIAL WORKERS OF THE WORLD  Entered as second-class matter at the Post Office, at Cleveland, Ohio under the Act of March 3, 1879

VOL. XXX. ÉVFOLYAM — CLEVELAND, 1942 OCT 31 — NUMBER 1239 SZAM

A profitharácsolás expertjei vájkálnak az állampénztárban

Mult heti lapszámunkban az elnök beszédével kapcsolatban | ta a más kiadáson kivül. Warren ajánlotta, hogy két millió

T-BONE SLIM

TRAGIKUS HALÁLT HALT AZ IWW IRODALOM LEGKIVÁLÓBB HUMORISTÁJA. MARÓ SZATIRÁVAL OSTOROZTA AZ URALKODÓ OSZTÁLYT

Hungarian IWW Weekly

the most dangerous jobs, with resultant high accident rates. In New York, Chicago, Cleveland, and the smaller cities of New Jersey, skilled workers congregated and worked in trades such as printing, cabinetmaking, and painting.

Although there were at least four Hungarian AFL locals among the printers, carpenters, furniture workers (Wurlitzer piano makers), and miners, the AFL had little impact among Hungarians because the vast majority of Hungarians were unskilled. Many of the unskilled were used as strikebreakers, but some were active in the Industrial Workers of the World and published a Hungarian-language paper in Chicago, *Bermunkas* (Wage worker). In the 1920s Hungarians played a prominent role in the Passaic, New Jersey, textile strike, providing organizers such as James Lustig with more than $15,000 in cash. Since most Hungarian workers were concentrated in the mass-production industries, they also played a role in organizing the most important CIO unions: the United Automobile Workers, United Steel Workers, Fur and Leather Workers Industrial Union, and the United Electrical Workers Union (especially Julius Emspack) as well as continuing involvement in the United Mine Workers, the Painters Union (especially Louis Weinstock), and the Carpenters Union.

Because most Hungarian-American radicals integrated themselves into the union movement, the Socialist Party, the Socialist Labor Party, and the Communist Party, it is difficult to trace their particular ethnic contribution. But involvement in the Left grew out of, and drew strength from, Hungarian sick and benevolent societies (e.g., *Altalanos Magyar Munkas Betegseglyz*, Hungarian Workers Benefit Association), and especially from the Hungarian Left press that developed at the turn of the century.

In 1905 the SP founded its own paper, *Elöre* (Forward), which has continued under various names and radical sponsorships until the present day. From period to period, as the economic or political situation permitted, it came out as a weekly, a biweekly, and a daily. During WW I it became very attentive to American and international issues, with less emphasis on Hungarian nationalist concerns. It also took a strong antiwar and anti-imperialist position and as a result the Wilson government took away its mailing rights and investigated and arrested a number of its editors and supporters. Hungarian-American radicals fought against the restrictions against *Elöre* by delivering the paper by hand and by mailing it to subscribers in other packages.

The postwar repression and Red Scare was more than offset by the excitement generated by the Hungarian Revolution in 1918–19. Readership increased greatly as radicalism and nationalism were joined. The Hungarian Left in America was further strengthened when, after the failure of the revolution, a coterie of intellectuals, artists, writers, and left-wing leaders migrated to the United States. At the same time the Socialists split, the Communist Party was founded. Many of the leaders of the Hungarian-American Left followed the leadership of the CP, including the editors of *Elöre*, which was renamed *Uj Elöre* (New forward) on November 5, 1921. The paper was published in Chicago, New York, Cleveland, and finally back in New York again in 1937.

During the 1920s and 1930s the press and sick and benevolent associations such as *Rakoczi* (named for the leader of the 1903–11 revolution) and certain branches of *Verhobay* helped sustain a sense of community with educational meetings, picnics, and banquets. But the most important unifying force was opposition to the fascist regime of Miklos Horthy that ruled Hungary from 1919 through WW II. The post–WW I period saw a flowering of cultural and political activity. There were about forty weekly papers supported by Hungarian Workers Clubs in dozens of cities from Akron to Hartford to Newark to Elizabeth. In 1927 the Anti-Fascist League in the United States was formed by groups associated with the CP, and in 1937 it met in Buffalo and reorganized as a Popular Front organization, the Hungarian Democratic Federation, which attracted prominent Hungarian-American liberals such as the actor Bela Lugosi, who served as its president, as well as Communists such as the artist Hugo Gellert.

With the war over and the establishment of the Hungarian Peoples Republic, there was a major split in the Hungarian community. One group supported Hungary's ties with the Eastern bloc and the others were very opposed. In the early 1950s, *Uj Elöre*, which had been renamed in 1938 to support the Popular Front, became the weekly *Magyar Szo* (Magyar voice), which openly supported the Communist regime.

The Hungarian American community suffered a major jolt with the brutal Soviet repression of a popular uprising in 1956. The *Magyar Szo* remained supportive of the Communist government and because of its point of view lost a good deal of its readership. But in addition to this political difficulty, there was a natural attrition of the older Hungarian readership, who died or moved to California or Florida. The *Magyar Szo* continued into the late 1980s as a weekly, although in reduced form. *See also*: Gellert, Hugo; "UE" (United Electrical Workers)

—*Gerald Markowitz,*
Alex Rosner

REFERENCES

Deak, Zoltan, *The Gentle Flame: An Anthology of a Hungarian Newspaper in America, 1902–1982.* New York: Heritage Press, 1982.

Hutchins, Grace (1885–1969)

Graduate of Bryn Mawr College and labor economist, Hutchins was the principal writer on wage-earning women for the Communist Party of the United States. She was born in Boston to well-to-do yet reform-minded parents. During her youth, Hutchins aspired to be a Christian missionary, and served for several years as a teacher in China. She returned in 1916, and when the United States entered World War I she voiced her protest by becoming a member of the Socialist Party. During the 1920s, with the guidance of Marxist historian and economist Anna Rochester (1880–1966), Hutchins became active in the Christian pacifist movement and traveled abroad. Taken with the USSR, Hutchins and Rochester both joined the CPUSA in 1927 and formed, with Robert W. Dunn, the Labor Research Association. Hutchins edited numerous pamphlets and papers for trade unions and published an extensive study of industrial conditions, *Labor and Silk* (1929).

Throughout her life, Hutchins researched and wrote on labor, women, and children's issues. In 1934 she published an expanded version of a pamphlet, *Women Who Work* (1932), that stands as a representative work of the CPUSA's Third Period. Hutchins criticized "bourgeois" feminism for its emphasis on property rights and professional opportunities and countered with an analysis of the situation of black and white working-class women. She presented a brief history of their place in the work force and detailed their "double burden" as household- and wage-workers in contemporary society. Against this drama of capitalist injustice, Hutchins continued to insist, following the original formulation of Marx and Engels, that women could achieve emancipation only through social production. To suggest a model, she crafted a lengthy chapter, "How It Is in the USSR," and documented a range of social services that allegedly endowed Soviet women with full equality. In 1952 Hutchins updated her argument in a new, shorter edition that reflected the Party's strong commitment to civil rights and increased tolerance for reformist women's organizations.

Hutchins was also active in the CPUSA, presenting herself several times as a candidate on the New York State Party ticket. She was co-owner of the *Daily Worker* from 1940 to 1956 and raised large funds in the early 1950s to support the Smith Act defendants, including Elizabeth Gurley Flynn. She was a member of the staff of the Labor Research Association until 1967. Hutchins died three years after Anna Rochester, her lifelong companion. *See also*: Communist Party, *Daily Worker*

—*Mari Jo Buhle*

REFERENCES

Grace Hutchins Papers, University of Oregon Library.

Shaffer, Robert. "Women and the Communist Party, USA, 1930–1940." *Socialist Review* 9 (May–June 1979).

The IJA Bulletin

Widely considered the law journal of the Left, the *IJA* was published by the International Juridical Association—American section. The parent IJA was founded in 1931 by German and French lawyers prepared to fight Hitler and defend civil liberties and labor rights. The American section stemmed from a meeting in Berlin between Carol King, a well-known ACLU attorney in New York City, and Dr. Alfred Apfel, head of the IJA.

The American *IJA* attracted a wide range of activist attorneys, legal scholars, and prominent intellectuals whose political ideologies ranged from liberal to radical. These included Carol King (secretary), Nathan Greene (editor), and Sol Cohn (treasurer), Osmond K. Fraenkel (representing the ACLU), Joseph Brodsky (representing the International Labor Defense), Roy Wilkins (representing the NAACP), Professors Paul F. Brissenden, Jerome Frank, and Karl Llewelyn, and writers Sherwood Anderson and Floyd Dell.

While existing law journals focused on defending property rights, the *IJA* specialized in describing cases involving defense of human rights. It also offered an analysis of current economic and social trends and their effect on cases, a practice other legal publications avoided. Peak circulation of 1,450 was achieved in 1938, and copies were to be found in the offices of Supreme Court justices, Department of Justice officials, and many bar association and law school libraries. The dean of the Wisconsin Law School regarded the *IJA* as "the best publication" in its area of specialization. The other major work of the IJA was done in groups researching projects suggested by movements and lawyers too busy in practice to set aside time for the creative thinking and research needed to fashion new ideas to attack old and new problems. This work often found its way into court briefs, legislative committee testimony and reports, and campaign speeches.

The *IJA* devoted considerable space to major civil rights and labor cases, including the "Scottsboro Boys," Angelo Herndon, and Harry Bridges. It also analyzed New Deal legislation such as the Wagner Act, the Fair Labor Standards Act, and the Tennessee Valley Authority. Writers for *IJA* included Abe Fortas (future U.S. Supreme Court justice), Alger Hiss (future presidential assistant), Lee Pressman (CIO general counsel), Thomas Emerson (future Yale Law professor), and Shad Polier (American Jewish Congress). Many law students contributed while working under Professors Walter Gelhorn and Herbert Wechsler to meet the Columbia Law School's student research requirement.

With the advent of World War II, the *IJA* was concerned that legal gains established in the 1930s were not only preserved but extended. The IJA also supported excess-profits taxes, as well as wage increases in munitions industries. Although finances and circulation remained strong, many staff members were drawn into war service in Washington agencies or into military service. As a result, the editorial board decided to cease publication in 1942 in order to merge forces with the National Lawyers Guild. The *IJA* editors felt the Guild association would allow their work to go on "to greater glory." For the next two decades *IJA*-style articles, often written by Carol King, appeared regularly in the *Lawyers Guild Review*. The *IJA*, now available in facsimile edition, remains an outstanding source for research into the legal disputes of 1932–42 that were of most interest to the Left. *See also*: National Lawyers Guild

—*Ann Fagan Ginger*

REFERENCES

Ginger, Ann Fagan. Introduction to and index of *The International Juridical Association Bulletin* (1932–42). 3 vols. New York: Da Capo Press Reprint Series, 1982.

Carol King Collection, Meiklejohn Civil Liberties Institute, Berkeley, California.

Illinois Woman's Alliance

Culminating in the landmark Illinois Factory Inspection Act of 1893, the work of the IWA (1888–94) stands as an early and successful example of a united front. Although delegates from each of thirty organizations in Chicago participated in its governance, socialist and labor activists led its most vital campaigns.

In 1888 the *Chicago Times* published a series of articles, "City Slave Girls," that described the miserable conditions in factories and sweatshops employing women and children. In response, Elizabeth Chambers Morgan, a local socialist and founder of the Ladies' Federal Labor Union 2703, a mixed union of women workers affiliated with the AFL, formed a committee to verify the *Times*'s report. Convinced of its accuracy, the committee called upon a number of women's organizations to form a coalition "to prevent the moral, mental, and physical degradation of women and children as wage-workers."

The IWA, formed in November 1888, waged a major campaign for investigation of factory conditions and for compulsory-education legislation. In Chicago the IWA worked to improve working-class neighborhoods by demanding more and better schools and by calling for the construction of public bathhouses. In cooperation with the Chicago Trades and Labor Assembly and Jane Addams's Hull House, the IWA sponsored a successful legislative bill prohibiting the employment of children younger than fourteen and for the appointment of women factory inspectors. The IWA also campaigned against police harassment of prostitutes.

For its brief life, the IWA stood as a model cross-class coalition. Joining prominent members from the Chicago Women's Club as well as medical, temperance, and charitable societies, the IWA sponsored some of the era's most important political campaigns on behalf of the state's working women and children and the Chicago working-class community. The depression of 1893 and the Pullman strike of the following year exacerbated class tensions and pulled apart members of the coalition, and the IWA collapsed under the pressure. *See also*: Morgan, Elizabeth, and Thomas Morgan

—*Mari Jo Buhle*

REFERENCES

Scharnau, Ralph. "Elizabeth Morgan, Crusader for Labor Reform." *Labor History* 14 (Summer 1973).

Tax, Meredith. *The Rising of the Women: Feminist Solidarity and Class Conflict, 1880–1917*. New York: Monthly Review Press, 1980.

In These Times

For the later 1970s and 1980s, with the Left in a badly reduced state, the weekly tabloid *In These Times* became the most read and discussed socialist paper. Its circulation, only a few thousand at its 1976 inception, reached almost 40,000 by the close of the 1980s. Its independence, eclecticism, and general perspective in fact coincided with much if by no means all of the surviving (and slowly regenerating) radical opinion.

In a political sense, *In These Times* could trace its lineage, through its editor, James Weinstein, to *Studies on the Left*, the journal *Socialist Revolution* (after Weinstein's tenure, *Socialist Review*), and the early years of the New American Movement. Weinstein had moved from institution to institution with the fixed purpose of promoting radical ideas and practice more in line with the pre-1920 Socialist Party than any other precedent. Now hinged upon the revival of anticorporate, anti-Cold War educated opinion. These views, flexible on details, readily encompassed peace movements, environmentalism, labor dissent, feminism, cultural radicalism, and a special concern for radical history. Editorials elaborating these positions, formulated in the paper's early years by fellow *Studies on the Left* veteran Martin Sklar and in later years by Weinstein himself, focused politically on efforts within the Democratic Party.

In practice, the paper's contents and political shading depended very largely on leading editors and individual correspondents. Political columnists, for instance, lined up both for and—in the neo-liberal perspective of staffer John Judis—vitriolically against Jesse Jackson. A strong cultural section, on the other hand, carried much information on radical art and critical opinion on books, films, theater, and (more rarely) television, from a relatively nonpartisan perspective. Reportage on Central America, Western Europe and the Soviet Union, Asia, or Africa sometimes scooped the commercial press with fearless investigative journalism. Mainstream journalists, generally on U.S. issues, themselves contributed occasional essays unpublishable in their normal medium.

True to the majority Left sentiment of the age, *ITT* endorsed no existing radical movement, although it occasionally showed fraternal feelings for (as well as arch criticism of) the Democratic Socialists of America. *In These Times* implicitly and sometimes explicitly looked ahead to future times when the revival of a mass socialist movement would bring its politics into the mainstream. *See also*: *Studies on the Left*

—*Paul Buhle*

REFERENCES

Weinstein, James. Interview by Paul Buhle. Oral History of the American Left archives, Tamiment Library, New York University.

INDUSTRIAL ARMIES

During March and April 1894 America's unemployed organized several "industrial armies" in response to the Great Depression, which had begun the previous June. By massing on Capitol Hill they hoped to pressure Congress into enacting public-works measures designed to provide temporary jobs.

Jacob Coxey (1854–1951), a wealthy quarry owner from Massillon, Ohio, led the most publicized contingent and thereby gave his name to a movement that at its peak numbered a dozen major "armies" and twice as many smaller ones. Although only 300 marchers actually massed on Capitol Hill on May Day, the movement may have enrolled as many as 6,000 members and many times that number of sympathizers.

An estimated 30,000 people gathered to watch Coxey's band march down Pennsylvania Avenue. Several sympathizers clashed with police when they prevented Coxey from speaking on the Capitol steps. Police later arrested Coxey, his associate Carl Browne, and Christopher Columbus Jones, leader of the Philadelphia contingent, and charged them with carrying banners on the Capitol grounds in violation of an act of Congress. They each spent twenty days in jail. The "petition in boots" failed to move Congress, but because of extensive press coverage the industrial army movement dramatized the plight of America's jobless as nothing before had done.

In 1891 Coxey had conceived a program of hiring the unemployed to improve the nation's roads. The AFL endorsed the plan at its 1893 convention. The idea of marching the jobless to Capitol Hill to dramatize Coxey's program originated with Carl Browne, a Californian who met Coxey at a reform congress in Chicago during the summer of 1893. Coxey and Browne spent the following winter in Massillon planning the march. During that time Coxey proposed that Congress issue noninterest-bearing bonds to finance his public-works program.

The novelty of the crusade attracted a phenomenal amount of press coverage. More reporters traveled to Massillon for the start of Coxey's march than covered major party political conventions. Before the protesters reached Washington some major dailies devoted six of their seven front-page columns to the march. Some reporters called it the biggest story since the Civil War. Without question the press manipulated news of the march to create a maximum amount of entertainment and suspense. This was not yet yellow journalism, but in its tendency to sensationalize the march, press coverage revealed a distinct yellowish tinge.

News of Coxey's crusade gave rise to numerous imitators among the jobless of the Midwest and Far West, where the largest contingents formed. Armies numbering 500 to 1,000 men arose spontaneously in Los Angeles, San Francisco, Portland, Tacoma, Seattle, Spokane, Salt Lake City, and Denver. Smaller contingents from places like Reno, Butte, and Omaha joined forces with West Coast armies as they made their way east.

Marchers from the Far West expected to obtain cheap or free rail transportation to Capitol Hill. Failing that, they simply took and operated the trains themselves. Some 50 major and minor incidents of train stealing took place. Sensational chases occurred in Montana, Oregon, Idaho, and California when federal marshals and the U.S. Army sought to recapture trains stolen by industrial armies. U.S. attorney general Richard Olney worked closely with railroad and state officials to crush the movement throughout the West. In Idaho, for example, federal officials constructed a special prison camp to deter armies traveling east from Oregon and Washington. Such deterrents, together with declining press coverage after May Day and growing interest in the Pullman strike, ended the industrial army movement.

The press labeled the protesters "industrials," "Coxeyites," and "Commonwealers," the latter name deriving from Carl Browne's official title for the movement: "The Commonweal of Christ." Reporters also portrayed the protest in military terms. They invariably described marchers as belonging to armies and regiments and bestowed on Coxey the rank of general, although he originally avoided martial terminology.

Almost all marchers were men, but in several places women formed auxiliary units and at least two women served as "generals." These were Carlotta Cantwell, who led the combined Tacoma-Spokane army after her husband abandoned the men in Montana, and Anna Smith, who headed an army of California marchers.

One of those who joined the movement was Jack London, who accompanied a California contingent from Reno to the Mississippi River and recorded his experiences in a diary. Mother Jones encouraged marchers in the Kansas City area.

Upon his release from prison, Coxey returned to Ohio. He campaigned for public office often—distinguishing himself primarily as an indefatigable monetary reformer—and lost, with the exception of being elected mayor of Massillon in 1931. He repeated his march on Washington in 1914, and this time spoke legally from the Capitol steps. On May 1, 1944, on the occasion of the fiftieth anniversary of the great march, he again mounted the steps of the Capitol and with the permission of Speaker Sam Rayburn and Vice-President Henry Wallace completed the protest speech he had attempted to give there in 1894. It was a measure of how times had changed that after the New Deal, his speech hardly seemed radical. *See also*: Socialist Labor Party, Unemployed Movements

—*Carlos A. Schwantes*

REFERENCES

Etulain, Richard W., ed. *Jack London on the Road: The Tramp Diary and Other Hobo Writings*. Logan: Utah State University Press, 1979.

McMurry, Donald L. *Coxey's Army: A Study of the Industrial Army Movement of 1894*. 1929. Reprint. Seattle: University of Washington Press, 1968.

Schwantes, Carlos. *Coxey's Army: An American Odyssey*. Lincoln: University of Nebraska Press, 1986.

Vincent, Henry. *The Story of the Commonweal*. 1894. Reprint. New York: Arno, 1969.

Industrial Unionism

The struggle for industrial unionism has been a central theme in American labor history since the late nineteenth century. Efforts to organize unskilled workers and to confront major corporations have often faced fierce opposition from employers and the State. Not surprisingly, these efforts have often brought the Left into a prominent role within the labor

movement, while they have more often than not been opposed by the official leadership of the organized labor movement. Into the 1980s, the struggle for industrial unionism has continued to be a magnet for militancy and radicalism within the labor movement.

Coal miners and rail workers, employed by America's largest industrial corporations in the late nineteenth century, were the first to try to develop industrial unions. In the early twentieth century, labor activists and radicals attempted to spread industrial unionism throughout America. They argued that organizational and technological changes were destroying the bases for craft unionism. They pointed to the Homestead, Pennsylvania, strike of 1892. There, a strong craft union and a unified community were defeated by their employer's ability to transfer production to other plants and to replace skilled workers with the new technology of the Bessemer furnace. Activists likewise pointed to the hundreds of thousands of new immigrants arriving each year, taking unskilled jobs in the new, expanding industries owned by gigantic, impersonal corporations. A new approach was needed to reach these new workers, the militants argued, as well as to deal with the new corporations and their new technologies.

Experienced unionists, Socialist Labor Party veterans, socialists, anarchists, and labor radicals joined to establish the Industrial Workers of the World in 1905. Their approach—revolutionary industrial unionism, prepared to cripple the American economy through a general strike—was opposed to the conservative craft unionism of the "American Separation of Labor." AFL leaders, in turn, condemned the new organization. Their opposition helped corporations and the State destroy the IWW during World War I and thereby derail the struggle for industrial unionism.

Labor radicals in organizations of all sorts kept alive the idea of industrial unionism during the 1920s and early 1930s. Welfare capitalism, company unionism, and the open shop combined with new technologies and new investment patterns to decimate the organized labor movement. Yet small, committed organizations like the Trade Union Unity League (TUUL), the Communist Party, Trotskyists, and even remnants of the IWW and the old Socialist Party continued to put forward the struggle for industrial unionism, particularly among unskilled workers. Here and there, skilled workers experimented with "amalgamation movements," linking up different groups of skilled workers employed by the same corporation and moving toward collective action and broader-based organization.

During the 1930s, conditions—wage cuts, speedups, deteriorating working conditions, management capriciousness in layoffs and recalls—combined with the more long-term industrial trends we have already noted—technology, managerial reorganization, the emergence of multiplant corporations—made industrial unionism the necessary first step for a labor revival. At the base, the new unions were built by experienced unionists and committed radicals, many of whom had participated in the efforts to keep industrial unionism alive in the 1920s and early 1930s. John L. Lewis of the United Mine Workers was the symbolic figurehead and the ultimate leader of the CIO. Together with union leaders from clothing, steel, rubber, printing, auto, electrical products, and meat-packing, Lewis spurred the greatest union organizing drive in American history. In campaign after campaign, the Left provided organizers, leaflet writers, newspaper editors, resources, and communications networks.

In the aftermath of WW II, the Left was largely exorcised from the CIO, and the CIO unions were gradually incorporated into, first, the systems of collective bargaining and business unionism, and then back into the arms of the AFL. The two labor federations merged in the mid-1950s. As part of the "social contract" in Keynesian and Cold War America, industrial unionism lost much of its historic thrust.

In the 1980s, changing conditions restored the struggle for industrial unionism at the heart of the labor movement. Corporations have diversified and gone multinational, thereby sapping America's industrial base, undermining industrial unions, and confronting industrial workers with unprecedented demands for concessions. Faced with declining manufacturing membership, the AFL-CIO unions have resorted to mergers and amalgamations, and have taken in workers from industries not in the least related to their traditional bases. Industrial workers have found themselves a minority in their own unions, unable to control the decisions that will affect their lives. The Hormel struggle of 1985–86 made this clear. Not surprisingly, this protracted conflict saw expressions of solidarity, militancy, and union democracy rarely seen in fifty years. It also saw a similar return of official union leadership opposition to the struggle for industrial unionism, as well as an opening for the Left. *See also*: Amalgamated Clothing Workers; Brewery Workers; Industrial Workers of the World; Fur Workers; International Brotherhood of Teamsters; International Ladies Garment Workers Union; International Longshoremen's and Warehousemen's Union; National Miners Union; Textile Workers; Trade Union Educational League; Trade Union Unity League; "UE," Western Federation of Miners/Mine, Mill and Smelter Workers Union

—*Peter Rachleff*

REFERENCES

Lewis, Austin. *The Militant Proletariat*. Chicago: Charles H. Kerr, 1911.

Lynd, Alice, and Staughton Lynd, eds. *Rank and File*. Princeton: Princeton University Press, 1982.

Industrial Workers of the World

Meeting in Chicago in 1905, more than 200 socialists and trade unionists launched the IWW, a union based on the principles of Marxist class conflict and the indigenous American philosophy of industrial unionism. Soon nicknamed the Wobblies, the IWW sought to recruit unskilled and exploited immigrants, nonwhites, women, and migrant workers who were excluded from craft unions of skilled workers organized by the AFL.

IWW Silent Agitator sticker

The IWW sought to create "one big union" through which workers would own the means of production and distribution. This transformation of society would stem from a process of nonpolitical revolution and on-the-job actions that would wage effective war on the great combinations of capital. The IWW opposed the conservative defense of exclusive craft interests and the AFL craft structure, which Wobblies claimed were frequently at the expense of unskilled or semiskilled workers.

Delegates to the founding convention included Bill Haywood, then secretary of the Western Federation of Miners (WFM); Eugene V. Debs, the leader of the American Socialist Party (SP); Mother Jones, the legendary fighter for miners' and childrens' rights; Daniel DeLeon, the leader of the Socialist Labor Party (SLP); A. M. Simons, editor of *International Socialist Review*; Charles O. Sherman, secretary of the United Metal Workers; William E. Trautmann, editor of the United Brewery Workers' German-language newspaper; Father Thomas J. Hagerty, editor of the American Labor Union's *Voice of Labor*; and Lucy Parsons, widow of one of the Haymarket martyrs. The struggle over issues of political action and administrative structure that began at the convention were not resolved until 1908. By that time, secretarian socialist feuds and organizational tensions had led to the defection of many groups and individuals. Among these were the SLP, which set up what it called the real IWW in Detroit (1905), and the WFM, which joined the AFL in 1911. Those who remained in the IWW now focused on "building a new society in the shell of the old" through industrial unions that would become the basis of the new "workers' commonwealth." The preamble to the IWW constitution, as amended in 1908, encapsulated the spirit and structure of the IWW in concise but dramatic language. The IWW perspective would not change in any significant fashion thereafter. As amended, it stated:

> The working class and the employing class have nothing in common. There can be no peace so long as hunger and want are found among millions of working people, and the few, who make up the employing class, have all the good things of life.
>
> Between these two classes a struggle must go on until the workers of the world organize as a class, take possession of the earth and the machinery of production, and abolish the wage system.
>
> We find that the centering of the management of industries into fewer and fewer hands makes the trade unions unable to cope with the ever growing power of the employing class. The trade unions foster a state of affairs which allows one set of workers to be pitted against another set of workers in the same industry, thereby helping defeat one another in wage wars. Moreover, the trade unions aid the employing class to mislead the workers into the belief that the working class have interests in common with their employers.
>
> These conditions can be changed and the interest of the working class upheld only by an organization formed in such a way that all its members in any one industry, or in all industries if necessary, cease to work whenever a strike or lockout is on in any department thereof, thus making an injury to one an injury to all.

> Instead of the conservative motto, "A fair day's wage for a fair day's work," we must inscribe on our banner the revolutionary watchword, "Abolition of the wage system."
>
> It is the historic mission of the working class to do away with capitalism. The army of production must be organized, not only for the everyday struggle with capitalists, but also to carry on production when capitalism shall have been overthrown. By organizing industrially we are forming the structure of the new society within the shell of the old.

The IWW soon became known for its revolutionary tactics of direct action, its dynamic leaders, and its inspiring songs and graphics. IWW membership rolls included workers of all occupations, skill levels, races, and national backgrounds. Immigrants with paid-up union cards in their native countries were eligible for immediate membership. Initiation fees and dues were extremely low so as not to be a barrier to poorly paid workers. As labor-management contracts were viewed as an interference with labor's unconditional right to strike, the IWW would not sign contracts, a controversial position it did not abandon until the 1930s. Strikes rather than contracts were the fuel for IWW militancy, for strikes built the experience and perspective needed for the general strike that Wobblies thought would overthrow the capitalist system. Militarism was condemned, and membership could be denied to anyone who joined a state militia or the police. Labor Day was celebrated on May 1 rather than during the first week in September, the choice of more conservative unions.

From 1905 to 1914, economic conditions in the United States aggravated labor discontent with rising prices, stationary or declining wages, a series of depressions, and widespread unemployment. The IWW became a militant expression of class war in the United States, directing or taking part in at least 150 strikes in the pre–World War I period. Among the most significant of these were the Goldfield, Nevada, miners' strike (1906–07), the Lawrence, Massachusetts, textile workers' strike (1912), the lumber workers' strikes in Louisiana and Arkansas (1912–13), the Paterson, New Jersey, silk workers' strike (1913), and the Mesabi Range ironworkers' strike (1916). Important IWW units existed in lumbering, construction, agriculture, dock work and marine transport. The organization was also briefly successful in numerous eastern textile towns, in Colorado's coal mines, in the copper mines of Arizona and Montana, and the oil fields of Oklahoma. Although the organization was criticized for not building stable unions and at its peak had only 100,000 dues-paying members, the IWW shook the nation with an impact disproportionate to its size.

Not least among its accomplishments was the erosion of sexual, racial, and ethnic divisions within the working class. The IWW local that controlled the Philadelphia docks, the IWW cigar-makers' locals in Pittsburgh, and the IWW lumber-workers' union in the South were racially integrated. Ben Fletcher, the African American who was the major leader in Philadelphia, was considered a national IWW leader as well. Women such as Elizabeth Gurley Flynn and Matilda Rabinowitz led not only women workers, but male workers as well. Flynn traveled throughout the nation and was known as "the rebel girl." Rabinowitz organized textile workers in New England, cigar makers in Pittsburgh, and auto workers in Detroit. Thousands of Spanish-speaking workers on the East Coast who had been denied AFL membership on the basis of their ethnic background became the backbone of the IWW mariners' unions. The IWW also had numerous Spanish-speaking members throughout the Southwest.

Widespread labor education was carried on through propaganda leagues, industrial educational clubs, events at ethnic halls, hundreds of thousands of leaflets, national circulation of newspapers (printed in fifteen languages), libraries in union halls, the Work Peoples College in Duluth, Minnesota, clubs and camps for "junior Wobblies," and "entertainments" that included debates, singing, lectures, and skits. Some of the most effective educational material was published in the IWW's *Little Red Songbook*, a major contribution to workers' culture in America. In addition to the prolific and legendary Joe Hill, IWW songwriters and poets included Richard

Brazier, Ralph Chaplin, Covington Hall, Laura Payne Emerson, and T-Bone Slim. IWW songs were sung on picket lines, in hobo jungles, and at mass meetings. Chaplin's "Solidarity Forever" eventually became American labor's national anthem. IWW graphics and IWW cartoons set new standards of excellence and are admired by professional artists and art historians as well as the politically engaged.

When the IWW tried to recruit members in the "slave market" sections of cities where the unemployed gathered between jobs, it found itself drawn into fights to protect the rights of free speech and assembly. From 1907 to 1917, Wobblies conducted some thirty such struggles to protect their right to speak on street corners to fellow workers. During these dramatic confrontations, thousands of IWW members and sympathizers filled city jails. Many were seriously injured and a few killed before the organization generally reestablished the First Amendment rights to assemble peacefully, distribute publications, and address gatherings in public. Americans not otherwise attracted to the IWW philosophy took part in these struggles and respected the IWW's dedication to civil rights. Roger Baldwin, founder of the American Civil Liberties Union, considered the IWW contribution to civil liberties of paramount value.

Preceding and during World War I, the IWW retained its antimilitary stand and opposed U.S. involvement in the war. In contrast to the no-strike policy adopted by the AFL after the United States entered the conflict actively, the IWW continued to lead strikes. These wartime strikes gave employers and the government the opportunity to accuse the IWW of treason. In September 1917 U.S. Justice Department agents raided IWW offices throughout the nation with warrants branding the entire leadership—over 200 men and women—as subversives. In the major trial in Chicago, nearly 100 Wobblies, virtually the entire first and second tier of past and present leaders, were sentenced to federal prison terms of from ten to twenty years, with accompanying fines of $10,000–$20,000.

Little judicial effort went into protecting IWW members from community hysteria. Employer-funded vigilante groups and patriotic leagues were as likely as police units to raid IWW halls, homes, gatherings, and meetings with impunity. The persecution was soon intensified by criminal syndicalism laws passed in many states with the specific objective of destroying the IWW. Every form of intimidation was employed. An infamous incident that took place on Armistice Day, 1919, is indicative of the temper of the anti-IWW campaign. A group of American Legion members in Centralia, Washington, led an attack on the local IWW hall with the goal of destroying furniture and beating up members as had been done in past incidents. IWW Wesley Everest, a war veteran still wearing his uniform, was castrated and lynched for resisting the assault. Seven other resisting IWWs were sentenced to jail terms of from twenty-five to forty years and most remained in prison until 1933.

Legal defense and amnesty campaigns began to sap the strength of the IWW, and controversy over what terms the jailed members should accept for amnesty racked the membership. Further internal discord arose concerning relations with the nascent American Communist movement. At first the IWW was sympathetic to the Bolshevik Revolution, and in 1920 the Bolsheviks asked the IWW to join the Communist International. Prominent Wobblies such as Bill Haywood, George Hardy, Elizabeth Gurley Flynn, and Charles Ashleigh were among those attracted to Soviet communism. The IWW per se, however, became increasingly critical of the Soviet system. Events such as the repression of the Kronstadt revolt of 1921 and the role of Communists in the Italian factory crisis of 1920 fed an organizational alienation that became outright emnity by the end of the 1920s.

The IWW held to its belief in the gradual acquisition of control of industry by economic action on the job. This was in contrast to the Communist position that accepted industrial unionism but insisted that a "vanguard party" built on democratic centralism was necessary for the overthrow of capitalism. More than ever the IWW demanded democratic bottom-up control of organizations and it grew ever more skeptical of political solutions and the influence of outstanding individual leaders.

In the 1920s the IWW became a victim of

changing industrial technology and changes in the labor force that sapped its areas of greatest strength. Other membership losses were suffered through ruthless employer suppression during the "open shop" campaigns of the period and by the appeal to some workers of the CP. Despite these problems, the IWW continued to propagate widely the philosophy of industrial unions, the necessity of absolute solidarity, and the tactics of direct action. It retained an organizational presence at sea and among farm workers, and in 1928 it led an important strike in the Colorado mine fields.

During the Great Depression, the IWW joined with others to set up "unemployed unions" to provide housing and food for the jobless. In 1932–33 the IWW unit in Detroit was active in the growing protests staged by autoworkers. IWW members contributed their militancy and experience in the sit-down strikes and other activities that eventually led to formation of the UAW. IWWs played similar roles in other industrial centers, but rarely ended as the union chosen by the workers. An exception took place in Cleveland, where the IWW gained representation of workers in a dozen or so plants, a representation it would retain until 1950.

Perhaps the IWW's greatest contribution was in laying the foundation for the tactics and philosophy that led to mass organization of the unskilled, foreign-born, nonwhite, and female workers in the CIO and AFL unions of the 1930s and 1940s. IWW strike techniques—the sitdowns pioneered in Schenectady (1906), the chain picketing in Lawrence, Massachusetts (1912), the car caravans in Colorado (1928), and other innovations—once considered revolutionary, became the practice of the labor movement in general.

The IWW also left a mark in the civil rights field, where it aroused liberals to form permanent defense organizations to protect the rights of dissenters. IWW agitation against "employment sharks" led to regulation of commercial employment agencies, and IWW agitation against notorious prison abuses helped bring about more humane prison conditions. The IWW also pioneered in the organization of migratory workers, particularly farm workers. The style and heroism of the IWWs was such that Wobblies have been honored in American literature in a manner unique for labor radicals. Among the many American writers who have written positively about the IWW are Upton Sinclair, John Dos Passos, Eugene O'Neill, B. Traven, and James Jones. Joe Hill has become a martyr for all of labor, and a song in his honor gained great popularity in the antiwar movement of the 1960s.

IWW headquarters has remained in Chicago. Membership has declined to under a thousand and only a few locals have on-the-job representation, but the IWW has retained a vigorous press. Since the 1960s there has been a resurgence of interest in IWW history and philosophy, resulting in a remarkable wave of books, plays, memoirs, oral histories, and films that deal in part or in whole with the IWW and its legacy. Fred Thompson (1900–87), who joined the IWW in the early 1920s, served a sentence at San Quentin, and was first elected to the general executive board in 1928, was an advisor on many of these projects. Thompson, the official IWW historian, was called upon by virtually every researcher on the IWW and dedicated himself to preservation of an authentic IWW history. The single most important element in that effort occurred when the organization donated its archives to Wayne State University in Detroit, where they are available to the general public as well as scholars. *See also*: Anarchism; Anarcho-Syndicalism; Brotherhood of Timber Workers; Chaplin, Ralph; Debs, Eugene; "Detroit IWW"; Direct Action; Dos Passos, John; Everett Massacre; Finnish Americans; Flynn, Elizabeth Gurley; Foster, William Z.; Giovanitti, Arturo; Hill, Joe; Humor; Hungarian Americans; IWW Cartoonists; International Ladies Garment Workers Union; *International Socialist Review*; International Wood Workers; Kerr, Charles H. Co.; Lawrence Strike; Little, Frank; Magon, Ricardo Flores; Mexican Americans; Neff, Walter V.; Parsons, Lucy; Paterson Strike; *Il Proletario*; St. John, Vincent; Seattle General Strike; Sit-down Strike; Taft-Hartley Loyalty Oath; Textile Workers; Tresca, Carlo; Western Federation of Miners/Mine, Mill, and Smelter Workers

—*Joyce L. Kornbluh*

REFERENCES

Dubofsky, Melvyn. *We Shall Be All*. New York: Quadrangle, 1969.

Foner, Philip S. *The Industrial Workers of the World—1905–1917*. New York: International Publishers, 1965.

Kornbluh, Joyce L., ed. *Rebel Voices—An IWW Anthology*. Rev. ed. Chicago: Charles H. Kerr, 1988.

Miles, Dione, comp. *Something in Common—An IWW Bibliography*. Detroit: Wayne State University Press, 1986.

Salerno, Salvatore. *Red November, Black November: Culture and Community in the Industrial Workers of the World*. Albany: State University of New York, 1989.

Thompson, Fred, and Patrick Murfin. *The IWW—Its First Seventy Years—1905–1975*. Chicago: IWW, 1976.

Cartoon by C. E. Setzer (X13) for *The Industrial Worker*

INDUSTRIAL WORKERS OF THE WORLD CARTOONS

The IWW is the only North American labor union that produced a distinctive and enduring tradition of cartooning. In the IWW's heyday, from the early 1910s through the mid-1920s, its cartoons were almost as effective in "fanning the flames of discontent" as the famous Wobbly songs.

The Socialist Party's cartoonists—those of the *Masses*, for example: Art Young, John Sloan, Robert Minor et al.—tended to be professional artists who worked for large commercial dailies and fashionable magazines; their work was slick, stylish, intellectual, subtle, sometimes slipping into preciosity. Wobbly artists, however, tended to be self-taught amateurs, and their art, reflecting the predominance of hoboes in the union's membership during its most active years, was huskier and brasher, or, as some might say, cruder and more vulgar.

At least one of the IWW's founding fathers, Thomas J. Hagerty, had tried his hand at cartooning, and the most famous Wobbly of them all, the martyred Joe Hill, was a cartoonist as well as a writer of songs. Another well-known Wobbly bard, Ralph Chaplin, author of "Solidarity Forever," contributed scores of cartoons to the IWW press over the years.

The following brief accounts of some representative IWW cartoonists should convey something of the range and quality of Wobbly art.

Ernest Riebe

Notwithstanding the fact that he was the creator of the best-known and longest-running IWW comic strip, *Mr. Block*—the slapstick misadventures of a blockheaded worker who believes the boss is always right—little is known of Ernest Riebe other than that he was born in Germany and lived in or near Minneapolis during his IWW years. *Mr. Block* debuted in the Spokane *Industrial Worker*, the IWW's "Official Western Organ," on November 7, 1912, and continued to appear in that paper, and later in other IWW publications, through the early 1920s.

Before Riebe, IWW cartoons were mostly of the serious editorial type. With *Mr. Block* Riebe helped create the distinctively aggressive variety of hobo humor for which the IWW became so renowned. His scratchy energetic drawings were well-suited to his raucous gags.

Inspired by Riebe's work, Joe Hill's "Mr. Block" song recounted several of the strip's early episodes; first published in January 1913, it soon became one of the most popular lyrics in the IWW's *Little Red Songbook*.

A collection of twenty-four *Mr. Block* strips was published as a comic book later in 1913 (evidently the first use of the comic-book format for specifically revolutionary propaganda); a few strips also appeared as postcards. A smaller comic booklet, *Mr. Block and the Profiteers,* was issued in 1919. Riebe also contributed a poem and a play involving Mr. Block to the IWW press. Several other early Wobbly cartoonists, including "Dust" Wallin and Ern Hanson, introduced the Mr. Block character into their own cartoons, and from time to time the strip has been revived in IWW publications, even in recent years.

In addition to *Mr. Block,* Riebe did numerous single-panel cartoons, among them a remarkable antipatriotic series, "Under the Stars and Stripes," featured on page 1 of the *Industrial Worker* from May through July 1913. Later he drew cover cartoons for the *One Big Union Monthly.* His ironically titled *Crimes of the Bolsheviki,* a pocket-size comic booklet published in 1919, was, like all IWW literature at that time, emphatically pro-Bolshevik in content.

Ern Hanson

Of Norwegian descent, IWW cartoonist Ernest Henry Hanson was born June 2, 1889, in Forest City, Iowa. At twelve he moved west with his parents, first to California and then to Portland, where he worked at the printing trade. Introduced to labor radicalism in Arizona in 1914, he soon afterward joined the IWW on his way to the North Dakota harvest. In 1917, while "beating the draft by keeping on the move from job to job," he became an IWW traveling delegate. He took part in the union's famous May Day, 1919, eight-hour strike, in which the "bindle-stiffs" burned their "lousy blankets" in the public squares of large and small towns and logging camps throughout the Northwest.

Hanson was secretary of the Missoula, Montana, IWW local in 1924 but, like thousands of other Wobblies, left the organization in the wake of the so-called decentralist split. After hoboing much of the first three decades of his life, in his Wobbly days he worked mostly as a logger, and off and on as a trapper and trail cook. In the late 1920s he settled in Idaho as an employee of the U.S. Forest Service, from which position he was fired in 1953, evidently at the demand of the FBI, as "a danger to the national interest." Returning to work as a logger at age sixty-four, he retired on a small pension two years later. He died in 1981 or 1982.

Ern Hanson contributed some of the weirdest and most ornate cartoons ever to appear in the IWW press. Most of these were published in the *Industrial Worker,* the union's western organ, which had a large hobo readership. His grotesque portrayal of "Scissor Bill"—the Wobblies' name for any hopelessly nonclass-conscious, boss-loving worker, mercilessly drubbed in one of Joe Hill's songs—was Hanson's greatest creation, and figured in many of his cartoons.

C. E. Setzer

One of the greatest Wobbly cartoonists, North Carolina–born C. E. Setzer (1905?–70?) joined the IWW's Lumber Workers Industrial Union 120 in 1922, and from time to time also worked as a harvest hand, construction worker, and machinist. Over the years he served the IWW as branch secretary, general executive board member, and organizer on the Boulder Dam project in the early 1930s, but his abundant and highly original cartoons were his most enduring contribution. Although he did some notable pen-and-ink drawings, his best work was done in linoleum-block, a medium he originally chose simply to save the *Industrial Worker* the cost of photoengraving. Signed "X13" (from his IWW "red card" number) or with his initials, Setzer's distinctively thick-lined, grotesque cartoons, bristling with an oftentimes savage humor, are unique in the annals of modern cartooning. Reduced versions of several of his linocuts have appeared as IWW "silent agitator" stickers.

William Henkelman

A machine-gun instructor in the U.S. Army during World War I, William Henkelman was among the American Expeditionary Forces who mutinied when sent to Russia at the close of the war in an effort to crush the Revolution. Honorably discharged, he resumed the trade of sign-painter and lined up in the IWW in the early 1920s. Over the years he lettered many signs for IWW halls and meetings, and later for the Veterans Home in Yountsville, California, where he spent the last decades of his life. More important, he became one of the IWW's most prolific and imaginative cartoonists.

The range and power of Henkelman's cartoons reveal his constant search for new and unusual ways of expressing the IWW message of working-class self-emancipation. Among his cleverest cartoons are his Wobbly adaptations of well-known advertisements, in which commercial slogans are humorously made to subserve IWW aims. In 1945 he prepared an IWW calendar to commemorate the union's fortieth anniversary, and he did the cover for that year's edition of *The Little Red Songbook*. For many years he drew, with a stylus, directly on stencils, numerous cover illustrations for the IWW's mimeographed convention proceedings and internal *General Organization Bulletin*.

Carlos Cortez

Foremost of the more recent Wob cartoonists is Carlos Cortez (b. 1923), probably the only IWW artist whose work has been exhibited at New York's Museum of Modern Art. Inspired above all by the work of the famous printmaker of the Mexican Revolution, José Guadalupe Posada, and the German expressionist Käthe Kollwitz—international influences that reflect his own heritage as the son of a Mexican Wobbly father and a German socialist-pacifist mother—Cortez is best known for his large linocut poster-portraits of Joe Hill, Ricardo Flóres Magón, Lucy Parsons and Ben Fletcher. In earlier years he contributed many linocuts to the *Industrial Worker*, but when the paper switched to offset in the 1960s, he began drawing pen-and-ink cartoons. Poet and songwriter as well as artist, Cortez has also served as editor of the *Industrial Worker* and on the union's General Executive Board, and is one of the IWW's most popular public speakers. In 1985, to commemorate the union's eightieth anniversary, he organized an important exhibition, "Wobbly: 80 Years of Rebel Art," featuring original works by many IWW cartoonists of the past and present. *See also*: Chaplin, Ralph; Hill, Joe; Humor; Industrial Workers of the World

—Franklin Rosemont

REFERENCES

Buhle, Paul. *Labor's Joke Book*. St. Louis: Workers Democracy Press, 1985.

Cortez, Carlos. *Wobbly: 80 Years of Rebel Art*. Chicago: Gato Negro Press, 1985.

Riebe, Ernest. *Mr. Block*. Facsimile edition. Chicago: Charles H. Kerr, 1984.

Rosemont, Franklin. "A Short Treatise on Wobbly Cartoons." In *Rebel Voices: An IWW Anthology* edited by Joyce L. Kornbluh. Rev. ed. Chicago: Charles H. Kerr, 1988.

INMAN, MARY (1894–1985)

A Marxist-feminist theoretician, despite her rejection of the "feminist" label Mary Inman covered a broad agenda in her writings on women's oppression. These ranged from decrying the demeaning portrayal of women in the *Maggie and Jiggs* comic strip and protesting "cheesecake" photos in the major Communist Party newspapers to a long-standing and bitter debate with the CP over the correct position on the "woman question." Underpinning all her writings was Inman's argument that the production of life was as important as the production of life's material requirements.

Raised in Oklahoma, Inman personally learned about women's role in social production when she became the "mother of the house" at age thirteen. Three years later, after a short-lived flirtation with fundamentalism, she became a socialist. In 1917 Inman married Frank Ryan, an organizer for the Industrial Workers of the World in Tulsa. Along with other Wobblies, they were both run out of town by vigilantes in November of that year. To escape detection, the couple began to live under her surname and eventually legalized Inman as their family name. In later years, Inman jokingly referred to herself as a "Lucy-Stoner," a woman who kept her own family name after marriage, following in the footsteps of Lucy Stone.

Inman began writing on women in the mid-1930s, after reading Clara Zetkin's conversations with Lenin. When her 600-page manuscript was rejected by the Party, Inman turned to Harrison George, a Wobbly comrade who had become the editor of the *People's World* in San Francisco. He published condensed portions of the manuscript in weekly installments, after which time, in 1940, it went into three printings under the title *In Woman's Defense*. Although it was initially well received by women like Elizabeth Gurley Flynn and Mother Bloor, the Party launched an official attack in 1941 in a series of articles by Ruth McKenney in the *New Masses*. These were eventually followed by the publication of A. Landy's pamphlet *Marxism and the Woman Question*.

The balance of Inman's original manuscript was published in revised form in 1942, under the title *Woman-Power*. Inman's works were banned by the Party and she was forbidden to write on the woman question for one year. Though she was expelled from the Party in 1942, Inman nevertheless honored the discipline, breaking her silence with the pledge that "never again will the woman's movement be without a militant weapon of publicity of its own." Inaugurating her four-page newsletter, *Facts for Women*, in 1943, Inman used its pages for the next three years to both continue her theoretical discussions and to develop programmatic ideas for the organizing of women, including a plan for the formation of a Union of Labor-Power Production Workers (housewives).

Inman's final book, *The Two Forms of Production Under Capitalism*, was published in 1964, but she continued to write about women, carrying her long-standing argument with the CP to Chair Gus Hall in a sixty-six-page letter in 1972 and to the readers of *Political Affairs* in a lengthy 1973 commentary. Although Inman's writing efforts during the last dozen years of her life were primarily autobiographical, she continued to speak out on women's issues almost until her death in 1985. *See also*: Communist Party, *People's World*

—*Sherna Berger Gluck*

REFERENCES

Gluck, Sherna. "Socialist Feminism Between the Two World Wars: Insights from Oral History." In *Decades of Discontent: The Women's Movement 1920–1940*, edited by Lois Scharf and Joan Jensen. Westport: Greenwood Press, 1983.

Inman, Mary. "Thirteen Years of CPUSA Misleadership on the Woman Question." Schlesinger Library and California State University, Long Beach Archives, 1949. Mimeo.

INTERCOLLEGIATE SOCIALIST SOCIETY AND SUCCESSORS

The earliest collegiate radical movement in the United States, the ISS had several important influences. It made socialist ideas intellectually respectable. It brought together a remarkable coalition of socialist revolutionaries and reformers on equal ground. And it established the institutional basis for a particular kind of socialist intellectualism that gained importance to the labor movement during the 1920s and retained a certain political value into the 1960s. By then the ISS had become the lineal ancestor of the most important radical student group of the century, the Students for a Democratic Society.

The original ISS "call" was signed by prominent intellectuals from abolitionist veteran Thomas Wentworth Higginson and feminist-socialist Charlotte Perkins Gilman to reform editor B. O. Flower, lawyer Clarence Darrow, and pulp writers Jack London and Upton Sinclair. Its student representative on the executive committee, Harry W. Laidler, began a lifelong dedication to campus socialist thought and socialist intellectualism.

Jack London's 1906 campus tour initiated the new method of agitation, followed with great success by many other ISS speakers, of rousing students to the realities of poverty and suffering. Soon, chapters were founded at Weslyan and Columbia, followed by Princeton, Harvard, and more than fifty others, mostly concentrated in the Northeast elite schools but important in many state and private colleges. A small bulletin grew into the *Inter-Collegiate Socialist*, a wide-ranging quarterly with contributions from most major U.S. socialist intellectuals and a handful of British leaders.

ISS leaders and members stressed not commitment to socialism, as in the Socialist Party proper, but willingness to discuss the subject. With that perspective, they urged (sometimes successfully, as at Harvard) the introduction of courses on socialism into the regular curriculum. They held forums and, where possible, channeled regular political work such as electioneering into the local

Young People's Socialist League. In a few cases, they launched their own publications, the most famous of which was the New York Dental College's curious monthly, the *Progressive Dentist*. All in all, the ISS had little direct political influence and an inevitably shifting, unstable membership of a few thousand; but its influence upon the emerging generation of intellectuals was often considerable.

World War I, and especially U.S. entry into the war, produced a conservative tide on campus, and a simultaneous defection of leading intellectuals (some of them formerly active in the ISS) to the Wilsonian program. The ISS executive board, divided internally and fearing repression, took no official position on the war. Meanwhile campuses became virtual ROTC camps, and the ISS strove to remain quietly alive.

In the aftermath of the war, the ISS published *Socialist Review* to survey the prospects of the world socialist movement from a reform (rather than a revolutionary, or Communist) perspective. As the ISS became the League for Industrial Democracy in 1921, devoted to the scientific study of social change, so the *Socialist Review* became *Labor Age*, published with the aim of "keeping [American] labor informed of worldwide labor developments." Early writers included carryovers from the *Socialist Review* and a new entity of socialistic (but not necessarily SP) labor researchers, including David Saposs and Theresa Wolfson and an "angel" of the magazine, Prince Hopkins.

Labor Age, professionally one of the most attractive radical monthlies of the 1920s, informed a mostly educated readership about the latest developments in labor. Somewhere to the left of the AFL, it refrained from open criticisms and eulogized AFL president Samuel Gompers upon his death in 1924. Soon after, the magazine began to dissent from the "new era" policies of the new AFL president, William Green, and vice-president, Matthew Woll. *Labor Age*, unlike the AFL, supported industrial unionism, urged U.S. recognition of the Soviet Union, and opposed the American invasion of Nicaragua.

Toward the end of the 1920s, *Labor Age* completed the trajectory from the *Inter-Collegiate Socialist*'s rallying of students to the promotion of labor studies. Brookwood Labor College and its leader, A. J. Muste, became the foremost influence in *Labor Age*. From 1929 to 1933 the official organ of the Conference for Progressive Labor Action (AFL dissidents rallied by Muste), *Labor Age* reported primarily on CPLA organizing efforts. When the CPLA dissolved to become the American Workers Party, *Labor Age* ceased publication. The League for Industrial Democracy, twin descendent of the Intercollegiate Socialist Society, had survived its counterpart by remaining on campus (through the Student League for Industrial Democracy), although in research more than action. *See also*: Laidler, Harry W.; Socialist Party; Student Movements of the 1930s; Young People's Socialist League

—*Jon Bloom, Paul Buhle*

REFERENCES

Weisenberg, Mina. *The L.I.D., Fifty Years of Democratic Education, 1905–1955*. New York: League for Industrial Democracy, 1955.

International Association of Machinists

Launched by southern railroad machinists in 1889, the IAM was by 1900 a national union of skilled machine-shop workers and one of the AFL's largest and most influential organizations. The union's changing politics reflect both the general fortunes of American socialism and the specific history of the machine trades.

The IAM was not, at first, a socialist stronghold. Indeed, the union gained its AFL charter in 1895 at the expense of the International Machinists Union, an industrial organization led by Socialist Labor Party members Thomas Morgan and August Waldinger. By 1903, however, the IAM had become one of the leading socialist opponents of Samuel Gompers within the AFL; supporters of the Socialist Party dominated the union's executive council, and the IAM constitution committed the union to "class struggle upon both economic and political lines" and to using "the means of production and distribution for the benefit of all the people." Between 1904 and 1911, moreover, IAM members were prominent among socialist candidates for municipal office, and in the latter year the union elected as president William Johnston, a socialist and former SP candidate for the governorship of Rhode Island.

This transformation of union politics reflected in part the influence of Eugene Debs's American Railway Union on IAM members employed in railroad shops—members who resented their leaders' failure to support the Pullman strike. More important, populist demands for economic and political democracy had special appeal (and strong roots) among railroad machinists fighting large railway companies. With the demise of the People's Party, the union joined the move of labor's Left to the SP, whose gradualist program particularly suited the IAM's largely Anglo-Saxon leadership. The spread of socialism in the IAM reflected, finally, the obvious failure of pure and simple unionism after 1901, when metal trades employers—with the support of courts and militia—turned to belligerent open-shop policies.

Despite its socialist politics, the IAM remained a highly exclusive union. During the early twentieth century, rapid concentration of capital, technological innovations, and scientific management undermined the privileges and bargaining power of skilled men. These changes reinforced the search for political solutions to workplace exploitation. But the same trends also pitted the sectional orientation of craft leaders against a large minority of IAM members who increasingly turned to industrial unionism and syndicalism as appropriate strategies for preserving control at work. Northern locals proved receptive to influence from the Industrial Workers of the World after 1905, and beginning in 1910 railroad machinists joined all-grades "system federations" and cooperated with activists from the Syndicalist League of North America. Such rank-and-file initiatives were strenuously opposed by conservative and socialist IAM officials alike.

Even before the end of Johnston's presidency (1926), the IAM followed the labor movement's left wing in moving away from socialist politics. As with other AFL unions, Woodrow Wilson's administration (1912–20) drew IAM support away from the SP. Wartime economic conditions and labor policies further moderated union politics. With the IAM gaining new members in war industries and representation on the National War Labor Board, collaboration proved more attractive than the SP's pacifism. Political moderation, in turn, reinforced the union's industrial conservatism. IAM leaders continued to endorse amalgamation among metal trades unions, but they also opposed rank-and-file militancy whenever it threatened war production or, as in 1919–20, it involved cooperation with such radical organizations as the Workers International Industrial Union or the "One Big Union," as IWW offshoots were variously known.

While the IAM strongly supported railroad nationalization in 1920 and the LaFollette candidacy in 1924, by the mid-1920s it had become an exemplar of AFL liberalism—in principle nonpartisan, in practice pro-Democratic, and reserving its strongest political passions for fighting the Communist Party. (The IAM was one of the first unions, in 1925, to make CP membership grounds for expulsion.) IAM executives also played leading roles in the AFL's battle against the early CIO, and they sought employer support as a "responsible" alternative to more radical labor organizations. These policies heightened conflict within the union as conservative leaders suppressed militant action by industrial unionist members and disciplined rebellious locals on the West Coast.

For most of the postwar era, too, IAM politics have remained within the AFL-CIO's liberal wing, with the union a major actor in the Committee on Political Education. But in the late 1970s, amid renewed challenges from antiunion employers and from new technologies (supported once more by government policies), the IAM leadership again moved to the left of the AFL-CIO mainstream. After assuming the IAM presidency in 1977, William Winpisinger became a major figure in the Democratic Socialist Organizing Committee and its successor, the Democratic Socialists of America. While sympathetic to the ideal of an independent labor party, Winpisinger considered it more realistic to push the Democratic Party to the left on issues of social welfare, military spending, and union rights. To this end he strongly advocated building alliances with constituencies outside the union movement (e.g., environmental and peace groups).

These socialist political leanings—unlike those of the pre-World War I IAM—complemented progressive industrial goals, summarized in the union's 1981 "Technology Bill of Rights." This proposed amendment to national labor law called for greater union control over the design and use of new technology, with the participation of citizen action groups outside the labor movement. The best known (if partial) application of these ideals was the Workplace Democracy project launched at Eastern Airlines (1983), in which wage concessions were paired with union representation on the company board and union participation in the implementation of new technology. The union's capacity to sustain such measures in an era of union decline is questionable (the Eastern agreement collapsed in 1986). So, too, is the IAM leadership's willingness to integrate progressive political and industrial goals with rank-and-file militancy—a dilemma familiar from the Johnson era and still commonly resolved in favor of bureaucratic control. It is clear, however, that during the 1980s the IAM reclaimed the vanguard role in the American labor movement that it occupied before World War I. *See also*: Socialist Party, Workers' Control

—*Jeffrey Haydu*

REFERENCES

Haydu, Jeffrey. *Between Craft and Class: Skilled Workers and Factory Politics in the United States and Britain, 1890–1922*. Berkeley: University of California Press, 1988.

Laslett, John. *Labor and the Left: A Study of Socialist and Radical Influences in the American Labor Movement, 1881–1924*. New York: Basic Books, 1970.

Montgomery, David. *The Fall of the House of Labor: The Workplace, the State, and American Labor Activism, 1865–1925*. New York: Cambridge University Press, 1987.

Perlman, Mark. *The Machinists: A New Study in American Trade Unionism*. Cambridge: Harvard University Press, 1961.

Rodden, Robert. *The Fighting Machinists: A Century of Struggle*. Washington, D.C.: Kelly Press, 1984.

International Brotherhood of Teamsters

The Left has long been active in the IBT, which was organized originally as a union of truck drivers and warehouse workers but broadened to include cannery workers, factory operatives, clerical workers, teachers, police, flight attendants, and other occupations.

During the 1930s Trotskyists were especially influential in the IBT. The 1934 Teamster rebellion in Minneapolis, led by Trotskyists, resuscitated the union from its weak state during the early years of the Great Depression. Minneapolis Trotskyists used direct action and secondary boycotts to organize trucking and warehouse workers from Colorado to the Appalachians. During World War II, employers, state governments, the Communist Party, and top union leaders drove many Trotskyists from the union.

During the 1950s and early 1960s the Left was extremely weak in the IBT. In particular locals, such as Los Angeles Local 208, radicals attempted to transform undemocratic, ineffective locals into militant, democratic ones that enforced their demands through strikes and other forms of direct action. Black and Latino radicals were important in these efforts. In many cases, radicals who came to union office through these struggles eventually lost their militancy.

The late 1960s was a period of growing militancy throughout the IBT. This rank-and-file unrest culminated in 1970 in a national wildcat strike that secured improved contracts and revealed the complacency of the union leadership. In its wake employers attempted to intimidate a major center of rank-and-file rebellion in Los Angeles through a two-month lockout, 500 firings, and the later imposition of a trusteeship on a key local by IBT president Frank Fitzsimmons. Teamster rank-and-file militants responded by organizing a national rank-and-file organization, Teamster United Rank and File.

In 1975 Teamster members of the International Socialists set out to establish a national rank-and-file group in the IBT. When they began, there were less than fifty Teamster members of IS, mostly ex-student radicals who were working in the industry primarily to carry on their political work. Their strategy aimed to organize a "Teamsters for a Decent Contract" campaign among freight workers, car haulers, and United Parcel Service employees. Thousands of workers demonstrated and circulated a petition listing contract demands; this campaign dovetailed with a major car-hauler wildcat. Success led to the founding of Teamsters for a Democratic Union.

TDU, a rank-and-file group, boasted several thousand members by the late 1980s. It established itself as a credible and serious opposition to the IBT bureaucracy. TDU served as a source of on-the-job leadership in struggles with employers. It conducted major lawsuits in defense of workers' interests, opposing undemocratic procedures in contract ratification and urine tests to detect drug use. *See also*: Dobbs, Farrell; Minneapolis General Strike; Trotskyism

—Samuel R. Friedman

REFERENCES

Dobbs, Farrell. *Teamster Rebellion*. New York: Monad Press, 1972.

———. *Teamster Power*. New York: Monad Press, 1973.

———. *Teamster Politics*. New York: Monad Press, 1975.

———. *Teamster Bureaucracy*. New York: Monad Press, 1977.

Friedman, Samuel R. *Teamster Rank and File*. New York: Columbia University Press, 1982.

James, Ralph C., and Estelle Dinerstein James. *Hoffa and the Teamsters*. Princeton: Van Nostrand Company, 1965.

International Labor Defense

Founded in 1925, the ILD was a radical legal-action group that specialized in representing jailed union members, immigrants, political activists, and members of minority groups. In the early 1930s it attracted special notoriety through its militant defense campaigns in behalf of black prisoners, which exposed widespread racism in the American South. Less active during World War II, the organization unsuccessfully attempted a comeback at the war's end. In 1946 it merged into the Civil Rights Congress, which continued many of the ILD's original policies.

Cover of pamphlet issued by the ILD, 1920s

The individual most responsible for the establishment of the ILD was James P. Cannon, an influential leader in the Communist Party of the United States. During a visit to the Soviet Union in 1925, Cannon discussed the need for a comprehensive legal-defense organization with William D. "Big Bill" Haywood, the exiled American labor leader. Upon his return, he helped initiate the drive that led to the formation of the ILD at a Chicago convention in June of that year. Elected as national secretary, Cannon remained the dominant influence in the group until 1928, when he was replaced by J. Louis Engdahl after being expelled from the CPUSA. The stated purpose of the new organization was "to defend all persecuted for their activity in the labor movement," including minorities, and to provide aid for their families. The ILD's guiding philosophy was its concept of "mass defense" or "mass protest." This concept taught that since working-class defendants inevitably faced a hostile court system, legal maneuvers alone could not win an acquittal. Instead, legal strategy had to be complemented by a mass protest movement that would mobilize the general public in behalf of the accused. Only through this dual struggle could justice ultimately prevail.

Although there were always several non-Communists on the national executive board, the CP openly dominated the ILD until 1937. Yet the organization's membership not only included Communists but also numerous liberals and radicals of various ideologies. With the exception of Trotskyists, its legal assistance was consistently made available to prisoners on a nonpartisan basis. Soon after its inception, the ILD became quite active in the unsuccessful campaign to save the lives of Nicola Sacco and Bartolomeo Vanzetti. During the late 1920s and 1930s, the ILD mounted major campaigns over such famous political prisoners as Tom Mooney and Warren Billings, James B. McNamara, and the Centralia, Washington, defendants. In 1930, strongly influenced by the CPUSA's new emphasis on Afro-American affairs, the ILD aggressively began to seek out black cases. The promotion of attorney William L. Patterson, an outspoken black Communist, to the national secretary's post in 1932 further underscored this new commitment.

Among the most important black cases handled by the ILD were those of Angelo Herndon in Georgia, Euel Lee in Maryland, Willie Peterson in Alabama, and Jess Hollins in Oklahoma. But by far the most significant such affair was the famous Scottsboro case, in which nine young black men were accused of raping two white women on a freight train in north Alabama in 1931. The ILD vigorously defended the nine in court while its aggressive protest campaign, aided by the CPUSA and many others, developed the case into an internationally known cause célèbre symbolizing southern racism. Through its aggressive tactics and militant ideology, the ILD added a radical dimension to civil rights struggles and exposed many blacks for the first time to Marxist teachings and CP activities.

In 1937 the ILD was reorganized in response to the rise of the Popular Front. Vito Marcantonio, the East Harlem politician, became president and a major force in the group, while Anna Damon, a CPUSA member, was named national secretary. Under their leadership the ILD became even more heavily involved in defending trade union members and officials, especially during CIO organizing drives. In addition, the group expanded its legal assistance to immigrants and resident aliens and conducted an important national campaign against the ubiquitous practice of debt peonage on southern plantations.

With the outbreak of World War II, the ILD went into a slow decline, increasingly relying on volunteer workers rather than paid employees. The group strongly protested wartime violence against blacks and racial discrimination in the war effort. Yet it never formally endorsed the "Double V" campaign of the Afro-American press and was criticized by some blacks for failing to repeat its dramatic campaigns of the 1930s. At the war's end, ILD supporters tried to revitalize the organization, but with limited success. After extended discussions in 1946, the group's leaders, probably with the encouragement of top CP officials, decided to disband. Officially the ILD was merged into the Civil Rights Congress, a new organization that continued the ILD's traditions of "mass defense" and prisoner relief into another era. *See also*: Angelo Herndon Case; Cannon, James P.; Civil Rights Congress; Mooney-Billings Case; National Lawyers Guild; Patterson, William L.; Sacco-Vanzetti Case; Scottsboro Case

—*Charles H. Martin*

REFERENCES

Carter, Dan T. *Scottsboro: A Tragedy of the American South*. Baton Rouge: Louisiana State University Press, 1969.

Martin, Charles H. "The International Labor Defense and Black America." *Labor History* 26 (1985).

Papers of the International Labor Defense. Frederick, Md.: University Publications of America, 1988. Microfilm

INTERNATIONAL LABOR UNION:

see INTERNATIONAL WORKINGMEN'S ASSOCIATION

ILGWU—INTERNATIONAL LADIES GARMENT WORKERS UNION

A major center of Jewish immigrant radicalism and socialistic sentiments, the ILGWU has also been marked historically by bitter divisions among the Left and by particular labor problems of the trade. It has, alongside its dynamism, also manifested a deeply antiradical sentiment and an abiding rule of male officials over a predominantly female work force. As a labor organization, it has nevertheless had many inspiring moments, and made great contributions to its members' welfare. As a factional battleground, it offered sobering lessons in the losses, moral and strategic, self-inflicted by American radicalism.

Mourning the victims of the Triangle Fire. From *Groysser Kundes,* 1919

The early socialism of ILGWU leaders was shaped by their experiences in the Jewish Bund, along with a scattering of other Eastern European revolutionary organizations. The sweatshop, together with popular traditions of Jewish messianism, created the context for garment workers' response to socialistic ideals. Irish, American-born, and (with important exceptions) Italian workers in the industry remained immune to such appeals, even while often willing to follow radical leaders in practical activities.

Early struggles roiled the Jewish Lower East Side ghetto. During the early 1890s, Jewish anarchists and socialists struggled among themselves while they attempted to create garment locals and to promote the much-anticipated revolutionary transformation. In 1896 the Progressive Cloak Makers joined the Socialist Trades and Labor Alliance, only to be denounced by the rival United Brotherhood of Cloak Makers, led by anarchists and parliamentary-minded socialists. The founding of the ILGWU in 1901 left behind the Socialist Labor Party and placed the union in ambiguous relation with the emerging Socialist Party. New York garment local leaders, many of them socialists, intermittently sought a modus vivendi with nonsocialist national leaders of the ILGWU, compromising for practical reasons the vision of a socialist union. Related to political issues stood the problem of organizational structure, acute for an ILGWU divided in locals along craft, sex, or ethnic lines.

The syndicalism of many Italian garment workers, and the radicalism of Jewish veterans of the 1905 Revolution, posed both a serious possibility of defections to the more extreme Industrial Workers of the World, and contradictorily provided shock troops for militant ILGWU advance. With AFL help, and given the IWW's own weakness, the threat of dual unionism receded (ILGWU leaders continued, into the early 1910s, to join in the appeals of employers and religious leaders to IWW strikers to return to work in garment-related trades). Meanwhile, the growing popularity of Socialist electoral campaigns, and the ardent support of ILGWU unionization by the *Jewish Daily Forward,* cemented Jewish loyalties to a political socialism.

The 1909–10 "rising of the twenty thousand" women shirtwaist makers forced the reorganization of the crucial (and radical) Local 25, itself rising to a membership of ten thousand. Socialist agitation for the strike also marked a high point of women socialists' propaganda efforts on behalf of female workers. This strike paved the way for the cloak makers' strike of 1910, involving 50,000 workers, which resulted in the "Protocol of Peace," with improved wages, sweatshop supervision, and a fifty-hour week. The protocol, soon viewed by much of the membership (and leaders of dissident locals) as suspending class conflict by removing the strike weapon from workers' hands, was sustained under the new socialist president, Benjamin Schlesinger, despite management provocations. The ILGWU, by now the third-largest member of the AFL, was also increasingly outright in endorsing socialist policies.

Indeed, in this "Golden Era" of the SP, the ILGWU facilitated through its membership an array of support for radical institutions and movements. Not only socialist candidates and the *Jewish Daily Forward*, but radical cultural societies, woman suffrage campaigns, Yiddish schools, and an array of publications from Italian anarcho-syndicalist to Jewish anarchist to Labor Zionist, all found a day-to-day convergence of supporters at ILGWU-organized jobs and union meetings. Meyer London's 1914 election to Congress owed much to ILGWU members, as did near-misses and strong campaigns by various socialist candidates. Juliet Stuart Poyntz's emergence from prominent research positions to become educational director of the ILGWU, 1915–19, facilitated the formation of Unity House, a summer retreat whose comradely atmosphere (especially for young women of varying ethnic backgrounds) typified the "leisure" side of union work at its contemporary best.

On the other hand, the ILGWU drew increasingly close to AFL leaders on more than a practical basis. While proposing socialist resolutions at AFL conventions, the union leadership ardently defended the AFL against radicals' criticism. This approach alienated many labor activists, not only in the fading IWW but also in independent unions (such as the Amalgamated Clothing Workers) formed where AFL bodies had failed. During the First World War, the robust ILGWU courageously defended official socialist policies and even initially endorsed the Bolshevik Revolution. Yet the challenges rising up from the ferment—the call for more labor militancy, centered in the Current Affairs Club of mostly young women enamored with Russian events—brought ridicule (leaders openly suggested the women were sexually frustrated) and attempted repression. In the recession of the early 1920s, with working conditions deteriorating and wages swiftly declining, political and generational conflicts brought internecine warfare.

The Trade Union Educational League, founded by Communists and led by William Z. Foster, had one of its strongest bases inside the ILGWU, and also some of its most sophisticated opponents. A shop-delegate movement sought to democratize union leadership drastically, returning it to the shop floor (and the hands of many Communist activists), marking a high point of "workers' control" movements in contemporary labor. Charles Zimmerman, a young darling of the trade, was a most energetic Communist union figure, almost Wobbly-like—as he later recalled—in his enthusiasm for rank-and-file democracy. In response, ILGWU leaders divided Local 25 to weaken radicals, demanded all shop leagues cease activities, and amended the constitution to forbid membership to anyone holding a separate labor affiliation. In 1925 Communist garment leader Louis Hyman drew close to Morris Sigman in the balloting for union president. In 1926 Communists led a six-month, unsuccessful general strike of the garment trade in New York, at the end of which many left-wing locals were suspended. ILGWU leaders and institutions had, meanwhile, continued to support socialist candidates, and gave special urgency to the 1924 LaFollette-Progressive campaign. Increasingly, however, they turned toward major-party politics, first of New York governor Alfred Smith, and then Franklin Roosevelt. The vision of socialism remained, but was increasingly a sentimental one.

The ILGWU meanwhile played a major role in 1930s Left politics, both public and internecine. The division of the CP between supporters of Moscow, and supporters of "Right" Communism (in the United States, of Jay Lovestone) in 1928 affected the ILGWU more than any other union, for here Lovestone's intimates, including Zimmerman, had their base in Local 22. When Communists abandoned the ILGWU for the TUUL Needle Trades Workers Industrial Union, Zimmerman and his supporters remained with the union. The return of relative peace to a much-weakened ILGWU facing the Depression made Zimmerman, and Lovestone, valuable commodities to the new leadership of David Dubinsky, himself a former Bundist gone mainstream. Will Herberg, chief Lovestoneite theoretician (and later conservative theologian) became educational director of Local 22. The Lovestoneite weekly, *Workers Age*, operated almost as a house organ within the union's upper ranks. For their part, the Yiddish-speaking anarchists, who also found in Local 22 their main base of union members, had bitterly opposed Communists from the early 1920s and likewise provided Left logic as well as personal enthusiasm to the union, for a time publishing their own anticommunist ILGWU-oriented organ, *Der Yunyon Arbeter*. As it did with the Lovestoneites, the ILGWU leadership reciprocated anarchist affections. Subsidizing the anarchist papers through "greetings" advertisements in the *Freie Arbeter Shtimme*, Dubinsky personally hailed the paper and its champion, Rudolf Rocker, many times in print, at ILGWU expense. This indirect form of subsidy remained, in ever-diminishing form, until the paper's folding in 1976.

Their own union effort a failure, Communists rejoined the ILGWU in 1934, when the beginnings of a massive National Recovery Act-inspired industrywide success made Local 22 for a time the largest union local in the United States. Through the 1930s, Communists campaigned on various issues, for and against administrations, but they no longer seriously threatened Dubinsky's or Zimmerman's authority. As individuals, indeed, many supported the massive expansion of leisure and cultural activities (especially in Local 22) and Zimmerman's generally keen attention to working conditions. As a group, Communists coalesced with Dubinsky's important support for the American Labor Party (ALP), bringing them together with Jewish socialist old-timers in a common cause, and with the general support for the New Deal that this orientation contained. Symbolically, the stage production of *Pins and Needles*—labor's greatest theatrical extravaganza—with a union cast disproportionately taken from Local 22—offered a moment of class unity in a world of political conflicts.

Personal as much as political conflicts within the upper reaches of the CIO seriously affected the Left. In 1937 Dubinsky began to separate himself from John L. Lewis and Sidney Hillman (whom he had earlier seen as his mentor), and became far more willing than his fellow leaders to conciliate differences with the rock-ribbed conservative AFL. In 1938, amid a developing quarrel within the ALP (Dubinsky bitterly opposed the proposal to nominate Sidney Hillman as senatorial candidate, and the old-line socialists, supported by the *Jewish Daily Forward*, lined up with Dubinsky as Communists lined up with Hillman), Dubinsky sponsored Jay Lovestone's guidance of the conservative Homer Martin's short-lived United Auto Workers regime and Martin's own return to the AFL. Dubinsky himself withdrew the ILGWU from the CIO and returned to the AFL, denouncing the CIO as Communist-led.

As tensions grew within the ALP in the early 1940s, Dubinsky scorned all Hillman's offers for conciliation of the AFL and CIO, i.e., "Right" and "Left" wings. When the Hillman wing won a decisive primary victory in 1944, Dubinsky and his allies seceded, forming the New York Liberal Party under ILGWU auspices. The death of Sidney Hillman and the spread of Cold War sentiment doomed the ALP, while the Liberal Party became a patronage machine, depriving both socialists and communists of an electoral arm even semi-independent of the two-party system.

The ILGWU thereafter experienced a major demographic change: the "Jewish trades" ceased to be Jewish in any respect but leadership, as sons and daughters of garment makers were succeeded by Afro-Americans, Puerto Ricans, and others. With the passing of the old generation, socialism dwindled into a sentimental recollection of the union's difficult early days. A final, ironic blow to the union's progressive image came with the vote by its field staff in 1960 for their own unionization. Dubinsky's refusal to negotiate with the staff union, made up largely of young socialists and liberals who had attended the ILGWU Training School during the 1950s, symbolized the chasm between the ILGWU's hierarchical "social unionism" and the nascent New Left. Harsh and telling critiques by Herbert Hill and Paul Jacobs, in the journal *New Politics* and elsewhere, soon followed.

Meanwhile, the ILGWU moved toward protectionism as ever-greater quantities of goods from abroad (produced by both American and foreign manufacturers) increasingly dominated American markets. Between the early 1960s and late 1980s, union membership dropped from an all-time high of 450,000 to 170,000, and as the end of the century approached, industrial homework had reappeared as a major menace to union standards. Occasionally, the ILGWU still provided inspiration and defenses to the impoverished and vulnerable new members of the garment-industry work force, especially in defending their rights against immigration authorities. At the same time, the ILGWU remained scarcely less rigid in its ideological antiradicalism, which had extended from Communist to the New Left and beyond, to internal dissidents of all types. *See also*: Communist Party, Socialist Party, Yiddish Left

—*Paul Buhle*

REFERENCES

Dubinsky, David, and A. H. Raskin. *David Dubinsky: A Life with Labor*. New York: Simon and Schuster, 1977.

Josephson, Matthew. *Sidney Hillman: Statesman of American Labor*. Garden City: Doubleday, 1952.

Stolberg, Benjamin. *Tailor's Progress*. Garden City: Doubleday and Doran, 1944.

International Longshoremen's and Warehousemen's Union

Heir to a long tradition of waterfront unionism and Left politics, the ILWU currently represents some 55,000 workers in the western United States and Canada, predominantly longshoremen, warehouse workers, inland boatmen, and workers in agriculture and the tourist industry in Hawaii.

San Francisco longshoremen first unionized in 1853. The International Longshoremen's Association appeared in most Pacific Coast ports by the early twentieth century, when influences of the Industrial Workers of the World were strong among some longshoremen. An unsuccessful strike in 1919 destroyed most western ILA locals.

In the early 1930s, western longshoremen revived ILA locals and demanded a coastwide contract. When waterfront employers refused, the ILA struck all Pacific Coast ports in May 1934. Other maritime unions also struck with their own demands. During the strike, six workers were killed and hundreds injured. The Communist Party gave strong support to the strikers and advocated a general strike. Following a four-day general strike in San Francisco employers agreed to arbitration.

After the 1934 strike, the ILA sought to unite West Coast maritime unions into a Maritime Federation of the Pacific (MFP), whose newspaper, the *Voice of the Federation*, provided strong advocacy for Left causes. A MFP strike in 1936–37, however, revealed serious conflict between the ILA and the Sailors' Union of the Pacific (SUP). Concurrently, the ILA began a "march inland" from the docks to warehouses. Despite successes in northern California, warehouse organizing elsewhere was blocked by Teamster opposition.

Conflict with the SUP, the Teamsters, and ILA national officers coincided with an ideological attraction among West Coast ILA activists to the recently formed CIO. In 1937 the Pacific Coast District of the ILA voted to enter the CIO and was chartered as the ILWU. Harry Bridges became ILWU president. The ILWU constitution prohibited discrimination based on political beliefs, and CP members came to hold key positions in the ILWU. Leftists promoted a strong role for the union rank-and-file and opposed racial discrimination. Organizing drives east of the Rockies produced a few warehouse locals. During World War II, the ILWU joined other Left unions in encouraging maximum productivity, and Bridges promoted a no-strike pledge. Louis Goldblatt (ILWU secretary-treasurer, 1943–77) protested the wartime relocation of people of Japanese descent.

Late in the war, ILWU leaders decided to organize in Hawaii from the docks up the chain of production to sugar and pineapple field-workers; the ILWU became the first union to achieve lasting success in organizing agricultural field-workers. As Hawaii's economy moved to tourism, the ILWU organized hotel employees and tourism workers. Since the 1960s, Hawaii has claimed nearly half of all ILWU members.

In 1950 the CIO expelled the ILWU as Communist-dominated. Bridges was tried repeatedly and also jailed briefly for urging an end to the Korean War; Jack Hall, ILWU leader in Hawaii, was tried under the Smith Act. Among the unions purged by the CIO, only the ILWU maintained most of its original membership, jurisdiction, and contracts. The Fishermen and Allied Workers Union had joined the ILWU in 1949, and the ILWU became a refuge for other victims of anticommunism. In 1959–61, San Francisco longshoremen elected Archie Brown, an announced CP member, to local office, violating a Taft-Hartley prohibition; in *U.S.* v. *Brown* (1964), the Supreme Court ruled the prohibition unconstitutional.

Ironically, Cold War attacks on the ILWU came as longshore labor relations were improving. In 1948 negotiators refused to bargain with the ILWU so long as Bridges was president. After a three-month strike, the waterfront employers fired their negotiators and created a new employers' organization, the Pacific Maritime Association; since then, longshore labor relations have been generally smooth, characterized even by cordial cooperation.

The "new look" after 1948 laid the basis for successful adaptation to mechanization. After extensive rank-and-file discussion, the ILWU negotiated the Mechanization and Modernization Agreement (M&M) in 1960. Also in 1960, the ILWU and Teamsters began joint negotiations for northern California warehouse workers, ending their jurisdictional disputes.

Since the 1950s, the role of CP members has diminished in the ILWU, coinciding with the Party's general decline, but ILWU politics have remained well to the left. ILWU officers strongly supported civil rights activities in the 1950s, and the union first called for U.S. withdrawal from Vietnam in 1967. However, the same years saw CP attacks on the M&M, and a lawsuit that alleged racial discrimination against eighty "B-men," provisional longshoremen. Bridges had long worked to integrate the ILWU and denied the charge; the lawsuit was decided in favor of the union.

Strained relations between Bridges and Goldblatt contributed in 1975 to a requirement that ILWU officers retire at age sixty-five; both men retired in 1977. James Herman's election to the ILWU presidency brought little change to the ILWU's politics. In 1988 ILWU members voted to join the AFL-CIO by a three-to-one margin. *See also*: Communist Party, Hawaii, Marine Cooks and Stewards Union, San Francisco General Strike

—Robert W. Cherny

REFERENCES

Fairley, Lincoln. *Facing Mechanization: The West Coast Longshore Plan*. Los Angeles: Institute of Industrial Relations, UCLA, 1979.

Kimmeldorf, Howard. *Reds or Rackets? The Making of Radical and Conservative Unions on the Waterfront*. Berkeley and Los Angeles: University of California Press, 1989.

Larrowe, Charles P. *Harry Bridges: The Rise and Fall of Radical Labor in the United States*. New York: Lawrence Hill, 1972.

Nelson, Bruce. *Workers on the Waterfront: Seamen, Longshoremen, and Unionism in the 1930s*. Urbana: University of Illinois Press, 1988.

Oral histories of Germaine Bulcke, Louis Goldblatt, Norman Leonard, and Henry Schmidt. Bancroft Library, University of California, Berkeley.

Schwartz, Harvey. *The March Inland: Origins of the ILWU Warehouse Division, 1934–1938*. Los Angeles: Institute of Industrial Relations, UCLA, 1978.

International Publishers

This Communist-oriented New York publishing house was founded in 1924 by Alexander Trachtenberg—a veteran socialist who joined the Communist Party in 1921—with financial assistance from A. A. Heller, socialist and entrepreneur. IP became the first U.S. publisher to extensively publish the works of V. I. Lenin, Leon Trotsky, Nikolai Bukharin, and other Soviet Communist thinkers in English. Additionally, IP began extensive publication of the works of Marx and Engels, often commissioning new translations and thus becoming the predominant publisher of Marxist classics in the United States, cooperating with Lawrence & Wishart Publishers, Great Britain, and the Foreign Languages Publishing House, Moscow.

During the heyday of the Communist movement in the United States, which occurred in the 1930s and 1940s, IP published Marxist-Leninist classics in large editions in many formats, including the inexpensive Little Lenin Library series, whose titles were sold for only a few cents each. IP also published original works in a variety of subject areas, including the Labor Fact Book series, which was copublished with the Labor Research Association. Leaders of the CP, including Earl Browder and William Z. Foster, were also among its authors.

During this period IP also published works such as Philip S. Foner's *History of the Labor Movement in the United States*, and Herbert Apetheker's *Negro Slave Revolts*, which influenced many outside the Communist movement. IP also published works by black authors such as W. E. B. DuBois, making them available to a larger audience. Distribution was handled, in great part, through a network of left-wing and CP-related bookstores and through the movement apparatus itself. Displays of IP books and related literature were always present at meetings, rallies, and demonstrations, often reaching tens of thousands in this manner.

IP's fortunes waned during the McCarthy period, as Trachtenberg was jailed with other leaders of the CP under the Smith Act for conspiring to teach the advocacy of the overthrow of the government by force and violence. With the decline of the CP and its formidable literature-distribution apparatus, IP's fortunes suffered. Some of IP's original works during this period included William Z. Foster's *History of the Communist Party of the United States*, *History of the Negro People*, and other historical works.

After Trachtenberg's retirement in 1962, he was succeeded by James S. Allen, author of *Reconstruction: the Battle for Democracy.* Allen began to revamp IP's marketing efforts, printing attractive trade paperback editions of Marxist classics, and hiring a marketing staff that concentrated on regular bookstore channels. Subsequently, during the rise of the student movement of the 1960s, IP's fortunes also rose, making possible a wide range of new titles. Among these were a number of works by Antonio Gramsci, Kwame Nkrumah, Franz Marek, and Ernst Fischer. IP also became a copublisher of Marx-Engels' Collected Works in fifty volumes with Lawrence & Wishart and Progress Publishers, Moscow. The use of original Marxist works in college courses not only boosted IP's sales, but prompted publication of a number of titles, such as *Dynamics of Social Change*, as supplementary reading for courses.

In 1973 Allen was replaced by Lou Diskin, who stepped up IP's marketing efforts through the book trade. As the student upsurge of the 1960s waned, sales of Marxist classics flattened. IP continued to publish works of U.S. Communist leaders such as Gus Hall and Henry Winston. Allen began and Diskin continued the publication of biographies and autobiographies of party leaders, including John Williamson, Ben Davis, Hosea Hudson, and William L. Patterson. By the early 1980s Diskin was replaced by Betty Smith, who continued to reprint Marxist classics and publish new works by black authors and younger Marxist scholars. Standard works, such as Foner's *History of the Labor Movement*, grew into eight volumes.

By the end of the 1980s, IP's catalog included works by Angela Davis, reprints of early works on jazz and music criticism, and Albert Soboul's essays on the French Revolution of 1789. Books published by IP could be found in major bookstores in all the leading cities and were utilized as textbooks in classrooms throughout the country. Nonetheless, the impact of Reagan conservatism brought hard times to all left-wing publishers in the United States, and IP was no exception.

Nor was IP alone in making Marxist authors available to the general public, having been joined by several new publishing houses during the 1960s and 1970s, such as Monthly Review, Verso, South End, and others. Additionally, commercial presses and university presses discovered that Marxist works could yield a profit (e.g., Random House published a very respectable edition of Marx's *Grundrisse*). Among the new presses was Marxist Educational Press of Minneapolis, which reflected a close ideological kinship with IP but specialized in more scholarly works. New

Outlook Press in New York, which printed many pamphlets by CP authors in the 1960s and 1970s, took on a new life as publisher of autobiographies of CP leaders, including Jack Kling, Jim Dolson, and Claude Lightfoot. *See also*: Communist Party

—*Jim Williams*

REFERENCES

Allen, James S. Unpublished autobiographical essay.

International Socialist Review

Published by Charles H. Kerr & Company of Chicago, the *International Socialist Review* (*ISR*) still stands as a major chronicle of the American socialist movement in the first two decades of the twentieth century. The monthly's contributors—a virtual "who's who" of international socialism—reported and made comment on every major social, political, and economic development that had some bearing on the movement's direction.

Edited from 1900 to 1908 by socialist intellectual Algie M. Simons, the *ISR* initially served as a sounding board for the numerous theoretical debates facing the international movement. Its primary goal, enunciated at its inception, was to help familiarize American activists with socialist thought. Differing opinion on the strategy and tactics of the American movement and lengthy exchanges on "correct" Marxian or "scientific" positions filled its pages. Additional discussions on the socialist's relation to the American farmer and the "land question," the "Negro problem," women and socialism, and perspectives on organized religion also found a place during those years. In 1902 the International Socialist Bureau at Brussels designated the *ISR* "the official American organ" for its communiqués.

Kerr fired Simons in 1908 and worked to transform the monthly into "the fighting magazine of socialism," a popular monthly "of, by, and for the working class." Liberally illustrated with "action fotos" and original graphics, the revamped *ISR* carried firsthand reports of major strikes, lockouts, organizing drives, and employers' offensives as well as theoretical and political discussions. Kerr's work with

Cover Cartoon by Robert Minor

longtime associates Mary and Leslie Marcy and an editorial board including left-wingers William D. "Big Bill" Haywood, Frank Bohn, and poet/illustrator Ralph Chaplin raised the *Review*'s circulation from nearly 6,000 in 1908 to over 40,000 by 1911.

A national voice for the movement's direct-action, industrial unionist wing, the monthly survived the in-house battle between left and right within the Socialist Party of America in 1912–13, only to fall victim, in 1918, to government suppression for its opposition to U.S. entry into World War I. *See also*: Industrial Workers of the World; Parsons, Lucy; Workers' Control

—*Allen Ruff*

REFERENCES

Gutman, Herbert G. "The International Socialist Review." In *The American Radical Press 1880–1960*, edited by Joseph R. Conlin, vol. 1. Westport: Greenwood, 1974.

Ruff, Allen M. "Socialist Publishing in Illinois: Charles H. Kerr & Company of Chicago, 1886–1928." *Illinois Historical Journal* 79 (Spring 1986).

———. "'We Called Each Other Comrade!'—

Charles Kerr and the Charles H. Kerr & Company, Publishers, 1886–1928." Ph. D. diss., University of Wisconsin-Madison, 1987.

INTERNATIONAL TRADE UNION EDUCATIONAL LEAGUE: see TUEL

INTERNATIONAL TYPOGRAPHICAL UNION

The oldest and historically one of the most democratic unions in the United States, the Typographical Union had many antecendents. Following a journeymen printers' strike in Philadelphia in 1786—recognized as the first recorded strike in U.S. history—many more or less short-lived local printers' unions or benefit societies were organized.

The delegates from fourteen local unions who formed the National Typographical Union in 1852 (it changed its name to International in 1869 after several Canadian locals had affiliated) assembled in response to a militant "Address to the Journeymen Printers of the United States" drawn up in 1850. Written largely by Martin F. Conway, of Baltimore—later renowned as an abolitionist, lawyer, and judge, a close friend of John Brown's and a major figure in Kansas politics—the "Address" noted the "perpetual antagonism between labor and capital" and called for the "ultimate redemption of labor" by workers' self-organization. His class-struggle perspective was quietly ignored by the new organization, but the ITU from the start had many unique features that distinguish it from all other American labor organizations.

ITU law, for example, drawing in part on the oldest traditions of the printers' craft—the "art preservative of all arts," the herald of freedom, and "the tyrant's foe"—going back to its origins in the late Renaissance and early Reformation, has always had a markedly ultra-democratic tendency. Regular "chapel" (*i.e.*, job site) union meetings on company time, as well as direct referendum vote in all elections and on constitutional changes, gave rank-and-file printers a say in everyday decision-making scarcely dreamt of by most American trade-unionists.

Union printers, moreover, exercised a control of the workplace rarely approached and never surpassed by any other sector of the organized labor movement. On daily newspapers, always the ITU's stronghold, ITU law provided for automatic work-stoppage if an employer so much as set foot in the composing room. The closed shop and traveling-card system enabled "tramp printers"—a great majority of ITUers "tramped" for a time after completing their apprenticeships, and not a few for the whole of their working lives—to secure work at newspaper and printing offices throughout the country simply by depositing their card with the chapel chairman, bypassing the personnel office altogether. Well into the 1960s there were many thousands of union printers who had never suffered the humiliation of "applying" for a job.

The ITU's strong internal democracy and high degree of workplace control help explain why so many radicals have found it a congenial organization. The same factors also help explain why, notwithstanding its leadership's often noncommittal and sometimes downright conservative attitude toward controversial national and international political issues, the ITU long remained the most consistently progressive and least corrupt of all craft unions.

A dictionary of American radicals would contain far more members of the ITU than of any other union. From the last quarter of the nineteenth century through the first quarter of the twentieth, when the ITU was one of the largest and most powerful unions in North America, printers were prominent all across the spectrum of the Left, distinguishing themselves especially as editors of influential radical and labor papers. Among the many ITUers who enjoyed national and in some cases even international reputations as radicals in the 1880s–1890s were Joseph R. Buchanan of the International Workingmen's Association (the "Red International"); "single-taxer" Henry George, author of *Progress and Poverty* and many other works; Haymarket martyr Albert R. Parsons; individualist-anarchist Jo Labadie, one of the best-loved personalities of the Detroit Federation of Labor and principal contributor to the Detroit *Labor Leaf*; and Alzina P. Stevens, organizer and Master Workman of the Joan of Arc Woman's Assembly of the Knights of Labor, editor of the Chicago *Vanguard*, and a mainstay of Jane Addams's Hull House.

After the turn of the century, printers provided much of the leadership of the new Socialist Party. A founding member of the SP, and its frequent candidate for office, George Koop was for decades one of the most notable "characters" in the Chicago Federation of Labor. William J. Ghent authored a number of works of socialist theory and criticism, including *Our Benevolent Feudalism*, which influenced Jack London's *Iron Heel*. Ben Hanford was a popular SP pamphleteer and Eugene Debs's vice-presidential running mate in the 1908 election. *Cleveland Citizen* editor Max Hayes, an ITU international officer and Sam Gompers's most serious contender for leadership of the AFL, ran for the U.S. vice-presidency on the Labor Party ticket in 1920.

Emma F. Langdon, socialist author of an admirable firsthand account, *The Cripple Creek Strike*, was Denver ITU Local 49's delegate to the founding convention of the Industrial Workers of the World (IWW). Louis C. Fraina, a principal founder of the Communist Labor Party in 1919, had a card from New York Typographical Union No. 6. The anarchist presence maintained in the union by Labadie was reinforced by Steven T. Byington, an officer of the Cambridge, Massachusetts, local who is best known for his translation of Max Stirner's *The Ego and Its Own*.

Although the influence of radicals within the ITU has varied greatly over the years, union printers have consistently stood in the forefront of the great struggles of the broader labor movement. Their role in the prolonged crusade for the eight-hour day was second to none, and they continued to uphold the demand for still shorter hours after the eight-hour day was won. In 1945, when most unions no longer gave even lip-service to a further reduction of working time, ITUers initiated an eventually successful drive for a seven-hour day.

The ITU was the only craft union that supported the Committee for (later Congress of) Industrial Organizations (CIO); ITU President Charles P. Howard served as the first secretary of that body. Although the printers' union did not actually join the CIO, in 1938 its members refused, by overwhelming referendum vote, to pay the AFL's anti-CIO "war tax," whereupon the AFL expelled the ITU, one of its founding affiliates. According to the study *Union Democracy*, CIO organizers found that "when they entered cities and towns in anti-union areas such as the South, the one place they could obtain any help was the ITU local in town. Many ITU leaders in the South became temporary and in some cases permanent organizers for CIO unions."

No union was hit harder by the 1947 Taft-Hartley "Slave Labor" Act, and no union worked harder to overturn it. One of three unions that refused to sign the Taft-Hartley affidavits—the others were the United Mine Workers and the IWW—the ITU led organized labor's first major anti–Taft-Hartley strike in a twenty-two-month battle with the Chicago newspapers that began in November 1947.

On broader social issues the ITU has generally pursued a policy far in advance of other unions, though not always as far in advance as its more radical members would have preferred. African Americans were welcomed into the union at an early date, but remained a very small minority of the membership. Among black ITUers was West Indian–born Otto Huiswood, pioneer American Communist, member of the African Blood Brotherhood, and the first American black to meet Lenin.

The ITU was the first national union to admit women (1869); the first to elect a woman, Augusta Lewis, to national office (1870); and the first to demand equal pay for men and women doing equal work (1873). More recently, Jean Tussey of Cleveland Typographical Union No. 53 and Mollie West of Chicago Local 16, both longtime radicals, helped found the Coalition of Labor Union Women in 1974.

The ITU's once-numerous foreign-language locals—German, Swedish, Italian, Polish, Czech, and Yiddish—were an important part of the union for many years; only the New York Italian local survives. The German and Yiddish locals tended to be among the most radical printing trade unions. For several years before it received a charter from the ITU in 1894, Chicago Deutsche-Amerikaner Typographia No. 9, of which Haymarket martyr Adolph Fischer was a member, carried on as an independent anarchist union.

The contributions of union printers to workers' culture, and indeed, to American culture as a whole, are enormous. Such popular authors as Mark Twain, Artemus Ward, and Fredric Brown were all card-carrying, dues-paying Typographical Unionists. The clubs that once flourished in every ITU local—chess clubs, singing clubs, athletic clubs, mutual aid societies, the Old-Time Printers Association, etc.—reflected a kind of trade union utopianism in which the union truly was the vital center of working-class life. ITU brass bands were for years an indispensable part of every Labor Day parade. Formed in 1908, the Union Printers International Baseball League is still around today, the oldest amateur baseball league in the country. Finally, it was printers, more than anyone else, who made America's working public conscious of the significance of the union label as an emblem of solidarity and craft pride.

Severely weakened by the ongoing Cold War against labor that started with Taft-Hartley, and ravaged by rapid technological changes in the printing industry throughout the same period, the ITU survived as a dignified but increasingly powerless relic of a once-great union. Several of its strikes in the 1960s and 1970s were notable for their militancy and creativity, and many ITU locals have continued to exemplify the finest traditions of progressive unionism. But steadily declining membership as the industry bows to electronics and computerization has placed ever narrower limits on the printers' field of action. After unsuccessful attempts at merger with the Newspaper Guild, the Graphic Communications International Union, and even the Teamsters, in 1986 the ITU became the Printing, Publishing and Media Workers Sector of the Communication Workers of America. All but a few of its locals, however, have retained the time-honored name of Typographical Union. *See also*: Socialist Party

—*Franklin Rosemont*

REFERENCES

Guerin, Daniel. *100 Years of Labor in the USA*. London: InkLinks, 1979.

Kelber, Harry and Carl Schlesinger. *Union Printers and Controlled Automation*. New York: Macmillan, 1967.

Lipset, Seymour Martin, Martin Trow, and James Coleman. *Union Democracy: The Internal Politics of the International Typographical Union*. New York: Doubleday, 1956.

Rosemont, Henry. *Benjamin Franklin and the Philadelphia Typographical Strikers of 1786*. Chicago: Union Printers' Historical Society, 1980.

Tracy, George A. *History of the Typographical Union*. Indianapolis: ITU, 1913.

International Woman's Day

It is a historical accident that the first International Woman's Day was held on February 23, 1909, by socialists in the United States rather than in Germany, under the leadership of Clara Zetkin. Zetkin had been present on Bastille Day, 1889, in Paris when socialists organized the Second International Working Men's Association, an assembly of socialist parties, trade unions, and political clubs. The group planned May Day, first held in Europe in 1890. Among the goals of the Socialist International and the demands of the first May Day was control of female and child labor and the ten-hour day for all workers. Zetkin was powerless to insure that the women's component remained a focus of May Day, but she never gave up her own consciousness of the connection between working women's rights and the goals of working-class emancipation.

Socialist women caucused on August 17, 1907, in Stuttgart, Germany, before the annual meeting of the Second International. Under the leadership of Zetkin and Louise Zietz, socialist women pledged to fight for equality in every aspect of life. They suggested an annual demonstration similar to May Day to emphasize the needs of working women and to place the support of socialists behind winning rights for women. But the women's demands got lost in the political debates at the 1907 meetings.

Socialists in Europe held their first International Woman's Day in 1911, taking March 18, the fortieth anniversary of the Paris Commune, as the date to commemorate. The U.S. socialists, recognizing a good idea, had already held their first demonstration on February 23, 1909, when they fixed the last Sunday in February as the holiday's annual date. Following the American model, Russian socialists, led by feminist Alexandra Kollontai, began their International Woman's Day celebrations on the last Sunday in February, 1913.

The importance of International Woman's Day became evident when socialist internationalism otherwise collapsed at the outset of World War I. Zetkin's comrades among socialist deputies in Germany and Austria voted war credits for their governments. Socialist women, led by Zetkin, however, attempted to assert their own internationalism on Woman's Day 1915. Meeting in Berne, Switzerland, socialists like Louise Saumoneau of France wrote a manifesto calling on women as wives and mothers to end the war. For her bravery, she suffered two months in French jails.

The most dramatic celebration of International Woman's Day was in 1917 Russia. Deteriorating living conditions and massacres of Russian men at the front led Russian women in Petrograd (formerly St. Petersburg) to take the occasion of International Woman's Day (March 8 in the West, but February 23 on the Gregorian calendar) to demand bread and peace. Against the wishes of the Socialist Party and trade union leaders, the women led marches from the breadlines to the factories. Half a million Russian workers, mostly in Petrograd, were already out on strike, providing the powder keg the women ignited. They launched the February Revolution in Russia. By March 12 (Gregorian February 27), Czar Nicholas II had been forced to abdicate. The provisional government formed to rule until the election of a constituent assembly granted women the right to vote.

Under Zetkin's instigation, in 1922 Lenin established International Woman's Day as a holiday in Communist countries. In 1967, women students in Chicago revived the celebration. Since then, it has become the occasion for a new sense of feminist internationalism. *See also*: National Women's Committee, Second International

—*Temma Kaplan*

REFERENCES

Buhle, Mari Jo. *Women and American Socialism, 1870–1920*. Urbana: University of Illinois Press, 1981.

Kandel, Liliane, and Francoise Picq. "Le Mythe des origines à propos de la journée internationale des femmes." *La Revue d'En Face* (Fall 1982).

Kaplan, Temma. "Civic Rituals and Patterns of Resistance in Barcelona, 1890–1930." In *The Power of the Past: Essays for Eric Hobsbawm*, edited by Geoffrey Crossic, Pat Thane, and Roderick Floud. Cambridge: Cambridge University Press, 1984.

———. "Commentary on the Socialist Origins of International Women's Day." *Feminist Studies* 11 (Spring 1985).

———. "Women and Communal Strikes in the Crisis of 1917–1922." In *Becoming Visible: Women in European History*, 2d ed., edited by Renate Bridenthal, Claudia Koonz, and Susan Stuard. Boston: Houghton Mifflin, 1987.

INTERNATIONAL WOODWORKERS OF AMERICA

The IWA was founded July 20, 1937. An affiliate of the CIO, the IWA had emerged from a secession movement within the AFL's United Brotherhood of Carpenters and Joiners. Many workers active in that movement had been members of the Industrial Workers of the World and the Communist Party's Trade Union Unity League affiliate, the National Lumber Workers Union.

The first president of the IWA was Harold Pritchett, the only Canadian ever to head a CIO-affiliated union. Like most of the union's executive board members, Pritchett was a member of the CP. Between 1937 and 1941 the IWA's Communist leaders were annually reelected to office by rank-and-file referendum elections. During those years the IWA was prominent in coalition organizations such as the Oregon and Washington Commonwealth Federations.

The support for the Communists came primarily from unskilled, immigrant workers in the mill towns and logging camps in which the Communist worked and resided. Opposition to the Communists arose from the ranks of the more skilled and native-born workers and was supported by the CIO national office. Early in 1940, CIO president John L. Lewis put Adolph Germer in charge of the IWA's organizing activities. Germer, an experienced unionist and decidedly anticommunist Socialist Party factionalist, was able to shift the balance of power within the IWA through his staff choices and by identifying pockets of conservative workers to be brought in the union as new members.

Following several years of lobbying by business interests and investigation by the Dies Committee, Harold Pritchett was refused entry from Canada on August 22, 1940. Other Canadian Communists were denied entry during the 1940s. Combined with the effects of the Taft-Hartley Act, these events precipitated an attempt by the Canadians to disaffiliate and form the Woodworkers Industrial Union of Canada in 1948.

A raiding campaign by the International defeated the WIUC and the Canadians remained part of the IWA until 1987, when they attained independent status. *See also*: Communist Party, Industrial Workers of the World, Trade Union Unity League

—Jerry Lembcke

REFERENCES

Abella, Irving. *Nationalism, Communism, and Canadian Labour*. Toronto: University of Toronto, 1973.

Cary, Lorin. "Adolph Germer: From Labor Agitator to Labor Professional." Ph.D. diss., University of Wisconsin, 1968.

Lembcke, Jerry, and William Tattam. *One Union in Wood*. New York: International Publishers, 1984.

International Workers Order

Working-class fraternal societies are nearly as old as the working class itself. Dating back at least as far as the English Friendly Societies of the eighteenth century, fraternal societies helped workers cope with some of the economic insecurities of life and death under capitalism by providing a form of life insurance that assured a proper burial and money for survivors. Occupation, geography, nationality, race, religion, and sometimes politics served as the base for fraternal orders. In the United States, fraternal societies organized along the lines of race and national origin often performed another function besides the economic, which was to provide immigrants and Afro-Americans with a familiar cultural oasis within the larger society. Of the myriad of fraternal orders that have existed, the most important in terms of radical politics and class struggle was the International Workers Order.

The IWO was formed in 1930 by Communist and other left-wing members of the Workmen's Circle, a fraternal society organized in New York by Jewish socialists in 1892. Rubin Saltzman and other founders of the IWO decided to make it unique among fraternal organizations—a multinational and multiracial order that would offer all workers regardless of occupation the most economical insurance possible, and an order that was committed to the class struggle. By 1947 the IWO had 187,226 members. Though the Jewish section remained the largest (50,000) and best organized, the order also contained sections of Italians, Slovaks, Hungarians, Ukrainians, Poles, Greeks, Romanians, Croatians, Russians, Spanish, Carpatho-Russians, Finnish, and Afro-Americans and other English-speaking members.

For as little as $13.68 a year, a twenty-five-year-old could buy $2,000 of term insurance. For slightly more, a worker could buy sickness insurance and tuberculosis insurance. In major cities the IWO provided a panel of doctors for members, and in New York the IWO had medical and dental clinics.

The individual sections of the IWO supported their own foreign-language newspapers and halls. They also sponsored sports teams, choruses, orchestras, cultural schools, dance and theater groups, and children's camps. Such cultural figures as Paul Robeson, Langston Hughes, Rockwell Kent, Jimmy Durante, Irwin Corey, and Zero Mostel were associated with the IWO.

The IWO remained closely aligned with the Communist Party throughout its history. Many of its leaders, such as Max Bedacht, general secretary of the IWO from 1932 to 1946, were also CP leaders.

Though not a political or labor organization itself, the IWO actively supported progressive political causes and labor struggles. In the 1930s the IWO played an active role in the early CIO, particularly in the organization of the steelworkers, and the order campaigned for unemployment insurance and aid to Spain.

In December 1947, the placement of the IWO on the Attorney General's List initiated a series of events that led to the liquidation of the order by the Insurance Department of New York. In 1954, after a number of court cases, the Insurance Department abolished the IWO and turned over its assets to Continental Assurance Company of Chicago. *See also*: Communist Party, Jewish People's Fraternal Order

—*Roger Keeran*

REFERENCES

Goldsmith, William. "The Theory and Practice of the Communist Front." Ph.D. diss., Columbia University, 1971.

Kahn, Albert E. "Canceling Workers' Insurance Policies." In *The Cold War Against Labor*, edited by Ann Fagan Ginger and David Christiano, vol. 2. Berkeley: Meiklejohn Civil Liberties Institute, 1987.

Keeran, Roger. "The International Workers Order and the Origins of the CIO." *Labor History* (Fall 1989).

Walker, Thomas J. E. "The International Workers Order: A Unique Fraternal Body." Ph.D. diss., University of Chicago, 1982.

International Workingmen's Association ("First International")

Established in 1864 as part of the revival of the European labor movement after its defeats of 1848–49 and in tune with the solidarity London and Parisian workers felt for their martyred Polish counterparts in the uprising of 1863, the IWA quickly became dominated by the intellectual-political activity of Karl Marx. He steered the International toward a compromise between socialist ideas and protection against cross-Channel strikebreaking, the primary reason for the presence of British unions in the organization. Marx's subsequent conflicts with various competing personalities and their ideas shaped the course of the International in the United States.

The International in the later 1860s set up lines of communication with leading figures of American labor and labor reform, most prominently National Labor Union leader William Sylvis, who also wanted mainly to prevent immigrant strikebreaking. Only finances prevented an NLU delegate from attending the IWA's 1868 Congress. Meanwhile, a little group of mostly German-American trade unionists, the Communist Club of New York, applied for membership; a successor group became Section 1. Several other sections joined by 1870, spurred by the popular opposition of labor reformers and others to the Franco-Prussian War, and by the increasing attractiveness of the International to eclectic American radicals.

The Central Committee of German, French, and Czech sections faced problems that became in a short time extremely worrisome for IWA leaders. Music teacher Frederich Sorge, destined to become Marx and Engels' most fervent U.S. follower, at first found himself hard-pressed to explain to London officials of the International that U.S. sections were naturally "foreign," i.e., immigrant, because so much of the emerging industrial working class had arrived from Europe. On the other hand, the disintegrating NLU pulled away from the International. In the first year, buoyed by the "eight-hour" movement and by a brief flurry of Irish nationalist activity sympathetic to the International, several thousand members in more than twenty sections joined. Much favorable press coverage appeared. The U.S. branches remained, however, isolated from English-speaking Americans, and, with the prospects for a labor party very much in doubt, uncertain of political direction.

Internationally, the Paris Commune gave the IWA a reputation as a feared (or admired) revolutionary organization, and in doing so badly alienated more moderate—especially British trade unionist—members. While taking no hand in the Commune themselves, IWA activists conducted large-scale relief campaigns, and Marx penned invaluable documents on the significance of these events. In the United States, the Commune became a cause célèbre due to a mammoth New York City sympathy parade, which police authorities first opposed, but which new elements in the U.S. International personally led. These new elements—including a mixed group of

American reformers, woman's rights advocates, and spiritualists—already possessed the most influential organ of any U.S. section, *Woodhull & Claflin's*. The editors, Victoria Woodhull and Tennie C. Claflin, best known for Woodhull's testimony to Congress on behalf of woman suffrage, joined their friends in promoting the Paris Commune commemoration. They quickly established themselves in Section 12, and, with the help of allies, in effect challenged the German-Americans to redefine the International's American mission.

A multitude of differences between the two sides were summed up in the German-Americans' insistence upon a two-thirds majority of wage-earners in each new section, and the reformers' counter-proposal that the word *workingmen* be struck from the statutes. A split appeared inevitable, and Sorge requested permission—which Marx readily gave—to purge the U.S. sections of their middle-class components. In 1872, therefore, the Central Committee divested itself of a majority of American Internationalists, dooming the organization to sectarian isolation.

Marx's decision reflected the internal situation of the International as much as his own disdain for reformers and woman's rights advocates. Mikhail Bakunin and his anarchist allies had challenged Marx's leadership, and Marx very much feared the organization would fall into unfriendly hands. The Bakuninist (really, Proudhonist) element in the U.S. had virtually no significance, however, and the arguments of the reformers (that women, lacking employment opportunities, could not be required the same proletarian status) stood on solid logical ground. Ultimately, Marx's American loyalists had cleared the decks so that trustworthy New Yorkers could accept the near-defunct International's home office, removed from London to prevent a hostile takeover.

In the meantime, two rival organizations took shape in the United States, both weakened by the split. The "Spring Street" faction of reformers had decidedly the most diverse group of varied immigrants, spiritualists, and authentic labor activists. But it was almost immediately diminished by Woodhull's promotion of an Equal Rights Party in the 1872 election, with herself as presidential candidate. The "Tenth Ward Hotel" faction, smaller but homogenously German American, could carry on more steadily. After unity negotiations repeatedly failed, and the Americans' appeals to London fell upon deaf ears, the reformers' movement faded away. The general council, shifted from London to New York in 1872, preoccupied the German Americans with fresh differences and international correspondence. After five trying years, the general council folded the IWA sine die.

The "official" historian of the American Internationalists, Herman Schlüter, decades later looked back correctly at the amount of real knowledge and wisdom that German-American members had added to the U.S. labor movement. On the other hand, the division had paralyzed American socialists at a moment when the United States was entering a deep economic depression, with labor response climaxing in the 1877 railroad strike. The expelled reformers, including not a few labor activists themselves, symbolized the side of Marxist internationalism lost by the unnecessarily sectarian Marxists.

Several contradictory tendencies emerged directly or indirectly from the First International's role in the United States. Despite a healthy local growth of socialist tendencies, especially in Chicago, the U.S. socialists were doubtless weakened in their tasks and opportunities. Not long after, a number of former IWA labor activists joined New England labor reformers in launching the International Labor Union, which during the last years of the 1870s sought to create an industrial union movement principally among textile workers. While unsuccessful after a few major strikes, it seeded the ground for the Knights of Labor in the same vicinities. Some of the same labor activists also became, in due time, a most wage-conscious, antisocialist and exclusionary force within the American Federation of Labor. In a more distant sense, the First International had created the precedent for a weak U.S. Left that appealed to European leaders for a mandate to rule, and utilized the mandate for sectarian infighting. That melancholy development would haunt the U.S. Left of the

1920s–1950s. So would its sister phenomenon, ex-radicals (some still self-described socialists) who had turned themselves into important defenders of American capitalism. *See also*: German Americans, Socialist Labor Party, *Woodhull & Claflin's Weekly*, Workingmen's Party

—*Paul Buhle*

REFERENCES

Bernstein, Samuel. *The First International in America*. New York: Augustus Kelley, 1962.

Schlüter, Hermann. *Die Erste Internationale in Amerika: Ein Beitrag zur Geschichte der Arbeiter-Bewegung in den Vereinigten Staaten*. Chicago: Deutsche Sprachgruppe der Sozialist. Partei der Ver. Staaten, 1918.

International Workingmen's Association Papers, State Historical Society of Wisconsin.

IRISH AMERICANS

The American Irish, third largest ethnic group in the United States, arrived to occupy the lowest occupational categories open to whites. Canal diggers, domestic servants, and common laborers, they can be considered the first large-scale American proletarian group. Their relationship with the Left has been ambivalent. Although active in militant and sometimes revolutionary unionism, Irish-Americans have, to many observers, epitomized the conservative side of the American worker (and, especially, the labor leader). Proportionally to the size of the group, very few have enrolled in Left movements. Yet Irish-Americans have taken their place in the vicinity of the Left, at important times sharing anticapitalist sympathies even while restrained by religious and other reasons from adopting Marxism.

Irish-American labor activity grew with the new industrial society of the early nineteenth century and expanded among the refugees of Ireland's 1840s "Great Famine." Conflicts with Protestant workers (most notable in Philadelphia of the 1840s) and antipathy toward blacks (most notable in New York City of the 1840s–1860s) mixed with class-conscious rhetoric and action. The creation of the "Stage Irish," proletarian archetype or caricature beloved by the rising urban audiences, also provided symbols both sympathetic and ridiculing about the American worker.

In the later 1860s and early 1870s, Fenian conspiracies and proletarian discontent overlapped with early Marxist agitation. The First International made contact with groups of nationalists, and socialist *wunderkind* P. J. McGuire led a mostly-Irish, slum proletariat of New York in dramatic public demonstrations demanding relief. Violent repression followed, and McGuire (who, along with International Labor Union and later Patersen, New Jersey, labor leader J. P. McDonnell, was one of the rare prominent Irishmen in the American socialist movement until the 1880s) recruited few Irish here or elsewhere in his lecture tours to socialist ranks.

Meanwhile, however, the *Irish World and American Industrial Liberator* (1870–1984) championed labor and Irish national causes, its earliest editor, Patrick Ford, sometimes espousing socialistic ideas without describing them as such. The burgeoning of the Irish Land League in the later 1870s and early 1880s laid a political basis for important labor causes shortly to follow.

The Knights of Labor, one of the most universalistic and potentially revolutionary of American social movements, was disproportionately Irish, from leader Terrence Powderly to the local craftsmen and factory operatives who joined with workers of all kinds (including many Irish-American working women) in short-lived but impressive solidarity. In many places, the middle class-oriented Land Leagues flowed into Knights' branches, and in some served as one origin of avowedly revolutionary intent. In Denver, Colorado, the anarchistic Rocky Mountain Social League and its important weekly, *The Labor Enquirer* found strong support in the Irish community. From Saginaw, Michigan, Land League veteran Tom Barry rose to the National Executive Board of the Knights and simultaneously embarced social revolutionism.

Irish Americans took a heavy role in the formation of local labor parties in the mid-1880s. Many won local office temporarily, and forced an accomodation of the Democratic Party to working class demands. The most spectacular, the Single-Tax mayorality campaign of New Yorker Henry George, seemed to merge Irish nationalism and socialist idealism under one banner.

During the confusion after the Haymarket incident, Powderly and most Knights leaders disavowed all radical connections, alienating socialists without slowing the Knights' disintegration. Local labor parties also faded away. However, in a number of industrial localities, individual Irish-American labor activists made common cause with German American socialists, forming "American" branches of the Socialist Labor Party. This was especially so in New England, where shoemakers and assorted tradesmen sent socialists to the Massachusetts legislature during the 1890s and elected several local officials. The socialist-led National Union of Textile Workers, founded in Providence, Rhode Island, in 1896, was a largely Irish effort to revive the spirit of the Knights of Labor.

Socialist success, however limited, alarmed Catholic prelates, affecting no community more than the Irish Americans. Rigorously espousing the social doctrines of Pope Leo XII's *Rerum Novarum,* leading Bishops endorsed the principal of unionism (in the moderate, AFL version) while turning full fury against the Socialist movement and the IWW. Along with the appeal of Democratic Party labor politics, rapidly spreading in the Progressive Era, this pressure limited radical appeal to Irish Americans. Just to the Right of the Socialist Party, however, the more aggressive non-socialist unions (such as those in the Chicago Federation of Labor) and the then-muckraking, anti-war appeals of newspaper magnate William Randolph Hearst, stirred Irish radicalism of another kind. Between the two types stood a barrier as large as that between May Day and Labor Day, or between the neighborhood ethnic Marxist and the occasional "labor priest." Recruitment among Irish was proportionally very small, if not insignificant, into the Socialist Party. James Connolly, in the United States for only a few years, launched his unsuccessful *Harp,* founded the Irish Socialist Federation in 1908, and debated fellow socialists over the morality of divorce. He found fame (and martyrdom) in return to Ireland.

More characteristically, an Irish-American syndicalist spirit operated on the sidelines of political socialism. Connolly himself contributed to that, with his journalism on industrial unionism. Leonora O'Reilly, although a socialist, made her foremost contribution as a luminary of the Women's Trade Union League and speaker-strategist of the 1909 Shirtwaist Strike. William Z. Foster and Jay Fox, true European-style syndicalists urging work within the AFL, pointed toward Communist strategies of the 1920s. Father Thomas Hagerty contributed the famous IWW preamble. Elizabeth Gurley Flynn, the Wobbly "Rebel Girl," was already in her teens a member of Connolly's Federation, before rising to the apex of her fame as agitator and strike leader in Lawrence, Massachusetts and elsewhere. Even Margaret Sanger, pioneer leader of birth control agitation, had her political origins in syndicalist sympathies which strongly colored her short-lived tabloid, *The Woman Rebel.*

Communists like their precedessors recruited relatively few Irish Americans. But William F. Dunne (farmer-labor political leader, and for many years an editor of the *Daily Worker*) and his brothers Grant, Miles and Ray (organizers of the Minneapolis Teamsters Strike of 1934, and among the founders of American Trotskyism) symptomized the trade union orientation of Irish cadre. Michael Quill, who emerged as foremost leader of the Transit Workers Union (TWA) and a most popular spokesman of the American Labor Party, was at all odds the most successful. Irish-American Communists in the National Maritime Union, somewhat greater in number, until the middle 1940s led one of the most powerful CIO organizations.

Neighborhood and community work had less success, despite moments of promise. At the height of the Depression, socialist James Grailton (deported from Ireland) organized Irish Workers Clubs, with branches in Philadelphia, Boston, Chicago, New York and Providence (known there as the Right to Live Club). Grailton himself taught the writings of James Connolly to Mike Quill and a handful of Clan-na-Gael IRA veterans who went on to found the TWA. The Communist Party had meanwhile published *The Irish Worker* sporadically in the 1920s–30s, and promoted Connolly Clubs in the 1930s–40s.

By the later 1940s and early 1950s, antiradicalism held sway. Irish Americans contributed some of the most conservative individuals and institutions, including Joe McCarthy and the Church leadership. In part at least, however, the bitterly anti-Communist but (especially in its leadership) anarcho-radical Association of Catholic Trades Unionists (ACTU), disproportionately Irish and linked to the *Catholic Worker* Movement, embodied much the same ambivalent conservative radicalism as the earlier Hearst following. Some ACTU local members, active past their days of anti-Communist concentration, worked with 1950s–60s Civil Rights movements and, later, the 1970s Grape Boycott campaigns, embracing their once-bitterest foes.

In the late 1960s, Irish-American radicalism revived in homeland-oriented activity, and emphasized a political dimension in the flourishing Irish-American cultural associations. The North Irish Civil Rights Association spawned support groups and Republic Clubs throughout the United States. Irish American support for a united Ireland, long notoriously conservative in political orientation, grew more progressive or socialistic along with developments in the Sinn Fein and the Irish Republican Army. Irish Northern Aid, often embracing New Left veterans and reaching out to the new wave of Irish immigrants, retained an ambivalently radical spirit during the 1970s–80s. *See also*: Connolly, James; Quill, Mike; Transport Workers Union

—*Joe Doyle*

REFERENCES

Sean Cronin. *Irish Nationalism: Its Roots and Ideology*. New York: Continuum Press, 1981.

Joe Doyle. "The American Women Pickets for the Enforcement of America's War Aims." *Irish World and American Industrial Liberator*, five installments. (May-June 1983).

Eric Foner. "Class, Ethnicity & Radicalism in the Gilded Age: The Land League and Irish-America." *Marxist Perspectives* I (Summer 1978).

Joshua Freeman. *Irish American Radicalism and the Transport Workers of America*. New York: Oxford University Press, 1989.

Kirby Miller. *Emigrants and Exiles*. New York: Oxford University Press, 1986.

Sean Wilentz, *Chants Democratic: New York City and the Rise of the American Working Class, 1788–1850*. New York: Oxford University Press, 1984.

Italian Americans

The Italian-American Left institutionalized itself only briefly, and to a small degree, within the Italian-American community. But for that vital period, from the early years of the twentieth century to the early 1920s, radicals exerted influence vastly beyond their numbers, creating popular heroes and creating movements that nearly transformed Italian-American life. In success and failure, they supplied the shock troops and also most of the outstanding intellectuals of class-conscious U.S. anarchism.

The earliest radical activity—part of the demographic cutting edge of an immigrant wave that would surpass any previous ethnic group, reaching nearly two million—developed around trades familiar to radical activity in the homeland. Skilled textile workers flocked to Paterson ("City of Anarchy"), New Jersey; marble and granite workers turned up at quarry sites in New England. Soon, more scattered organization in a variety of trades, against the background of the socialist movement's development in native Italy, tended in the direction of coordination. By 1896, the "Partito Socialista della Pennsylvania" launched the weekly *Il Proletario*, destined to become the leading Italian-American Left publication. Like the homeland movement, growing between bursts of activity and severe government repression, its U.S. counterpart adopted a variety of strategies to meet the special needs of constituents.

Largely illiterate (especially the female population), predominately from the rural and conservative Italian south, these immigrants lacked for the most part the rudiments of Left self-organization, either industrial skills or strong national self-identity. They faced unremitting exploitation at the lowest levels of American industry, their work often symbolized by the shovel of the menial laborer. Indeed, despite their penetration of major industrial labor such as textiles, they would continue to be viewed as a group apart, virtually nonwhite. Anarchism and syndicalism, with an emphasis on explosive rhetoric and direct action, understandably took early precedence over a patient, electoral socialism dependent upon a stable, educated population.

In 1902 the *Federazione Socialista Italiana del Nord America* (FSI) consolidated the leading body of militants. Unique to any major immigrant grouping, they chose a year later to withhold their affiliation from the Socialist Party, seeing the latter as politically timid and near-xenophobic. The Industrial Workers of the World, with its class-conscious strategy, its fierce egalitarianism, and its American version of the extreme anticlericalism native to Italian radicals, became instead the natural ally of the FSI (and again uniquely, its economic expression: all FSI members were mandated to join the IWW).

While the failure of the organization to develop left local Italian-American radicals with no resources and little strategy but agitation against clericalism and for industrial unionism, the eventual upswing of IWW momentum placed them in the forefront of early 1910s labor struggles. The Lawrence, Massachusetts, textile strike of 1912—with Carlo Tresca, Arturo Giovannitti, and Joe Ettor sharing the spotlight and the threat to their personal safety—marked FSI's highest point. With no more than 3,000 members, it managed to direct support and related activities up and down the Atlantic Coast. The defeat of the Paterson strike the following year, and the retreat of the IWW, marked the eclipse of FSI influence and syndicalism at large.

Soon, Italian-American radicalism tended toward two extremes: on the one hand, the more practical and mundane organization of industrial unions within the labor mainstream; on the other, the perpetuation of outright anarchist agitation against the calamities brought by the war years. Through the International Ladies Garment Workers Union and Amalgamated Clothing Workers (ACW), erstwhile anarcho-syndicalists such as Giovannitti attained respectability and considerable influence. New figures of importance, such as Joseph Bellanca of the ACW, emerged at the leftward edge of the SP mainstream. In coal-mining districts, and in the shoe and needle trades, immigrant socialists marched toward their goal of mobilization in unions, organization in Italian Chambers of Labor (a district-wide employment service inspired by homeland activities), and education in socialist principles. By 1919, they had achieved their immediate goals, at least in the New York area, to a surprising degree.

They had succeeded, however, in the wrong industries and the wrong era. Textiles, coal mining, and shoes would soon be "sick" trades, garments in a slump. More important, they had consolidated their energies just as the fierce antilabor "open shop" wave swept across America. In a few years, nearly all their practical accomplishments had been eradicated, their movements virtually destroyed. Fierce struggles in the early 1920s, against the return of wages and working conditions to pre–World War I status, along with the reorganization of leading radicals in the Italian Federation of the Communist movement, marked the final heroic phase. Antifascist agitation, working against the unquestionably widespread appeal of Mussolini to nationalistic sentiments, tended to center in the diminishing organized Italian-speaking Left, with an occasional foray into direct action against fascist parades.

The Sacco-Vanzetti agitation, underscoring the victimization of Italian Americans in general and anarchists in particular, proved the last hurrah. A short-lived Italian-language Communist daily, *Lavoratore Italiano*, closed its doors within a few years, and Italian support of Communism diminished to such inconsequential numbers that not even the later popularity of radical New York City congressman Vito Marcantonio could create a substantial Left cadre.

Surviving Italian-American radicalism tended increasingly toward anarchism of the extreme, almost individualist, varieties. Following the severe antiwar agitation of *Cronoca Sovversiva* editor Luigi Galleani, government repression reached deep into the Italian community, plucking out hundreds for deportation. Eclectic anarchist Carlo Tresca, publisher of *Il Martello,* remained a popular figure for decades, until his mysterious murder (apparently at the hands of the Cosa Nostra) in 1940, but among a severely depleted constituency. Apart from the scattered and aging followings of the Socialist and Communist parties, Italian-American radicalism drifted in its final decades toward a social life in local clubhouses established long before for a more aggressive purpose. *See also*: L'Adunate dei Refrattori; Anarchism; Anarcho-Syndicalism; Galleani, Luigi; Giovannitti, Arturo; Industrial Workers of the World; Lawrence Strike; Marcantonio, Vito; Paterson Anarchists; Paterson Strike of 1913; *Il Proletario*; Sacco-Vanzetti Case; Tresca, Carlo

—*Bruno Ramirez*

REFERENCES

Fenton, Edwin. *Immigrants and Unions, A Case Study: Italians and American Labor, 1870–1920.* New York: University Press of America, 1975.

Ramirez, Bruno. *When Workers Fight: The Politics of Industrial Relations in the Progressive Era.* Westport: Greenwood, 1980.

Vecoli, Rudolph. "Italian American Workers, 1880–1920: Padrone Slaves or Primitive Rebels?" In *Perspectives on Italian Immigration and Ethnicity,* edited by Silvano Tomasi. New York: Center for Migration Studies, 1977.

James, C. L. R. (1901–89)

Best known in U.S. radical history as the author of *The Black Jacobins: Toussaint L'Ouverture and the San Domingo Revolution* (1938), and his prescient essays on black nationalism and black culture, Cyril Lionel Robert James has also made significant international contributions to the fields of sport criticism, Pan African politics, and Marxist theory.

Born in colonial Trinidad, James grew into a cricketer, small-magazine essayist, and teacher. Sailing to England in 1932 in order to pursue a career as a writer, he quickly became immersed in two transformative social movements: Pan Africanism and Trotskyism. For the former, he publicized the cause of West Indian self-government, recovered the history of eighteenth-century Haitian slave revolution, and played a centrol role in the creation of a pioneer organization for African liberation, the African Service Bureau. As a Trotskyist, he lectured widely and penned *World Revolution, 1917–1936* (1937), a sustained account of revolutionary hopes and the Stalinist Thermidor.

James traveled to the United States in 1938 to attract black Americans to revolutionary socialism. In conversations with Trotsky, he outlined policies of independent black radicalism aided but not dominated by the Marxist Left. During 1941, he spent several months in southern Missouri, as lecturer and pamphleteer for striking sharecroppers. His essay "The Revolutionary Answer to the Negro Question in the USA" presciently suggests a major theme of 1960s–1980s Marxism, that black activities will precipitate prospects for an effective radicalism in the United States. During his U.S. stay, he also collaborated with Raya Dunayevskaya and Grace Lee, among others, in the formation of a small political group and intellectual tendency known as the Johnson-Forest Tendency. "Johnson" was the "party name" of James and "Forest" that of Dunayevskaya. The group translated sections of Marx's *1844 Economic-Philosophical Manuscripts*, urged rejuvenation of Hegelian philosophical discussion among Marxists, and publicized the extrapolitical and extraunion activity of militant workers. It developed a "state capitalist" analysis of the Soviet Union and the United States, predicting a mad bureaucratic "rationalism" on both sides of the globe as the final major obstacle to working-class revolution.

Expelled from the United States on passport violations in 1953, James moved back to England (where he prepared his major study of cricket, *Beyond a Boundary*), and on to Trinidad in 1958, where he became a leading intellectual figure in the national independence movement. Breaking with neocolonialist politics, he delivered a savage critique of its limitations in *Party Politics in the West Indies* (1962). A parallel study, *Nkrumah and the Ghana Revolution*, analyzed the triumph and failure of Africa's once-promising independence movement.

During the 1970s–1980s, James taught for a time in U.S. colleges, lectured tirelessly to young radicals (from Africa and England to North America and the West Indies), and wrote many essays on a variety of cultural and political subjects. The London *Times* described James as a "Black Plato." His range, universality, and sculpted prose have made him a most unique éminence grise of the international Left. *See also*: Dunayevskaya, Raya; Philosophy; Trotskyism

—*Kent Worcester*

REFERENCES

Buhle, Paul. *C. L. R. James: The Artist as Revolutionary*. London: Verso, 1989.

Buhle, Paul, ed. *C. L. R. James: His Life and Work*. London: Allison & Busby, 1986.

James, C. L. R. *Beyond a Boundary*. New York: Pantheon, 1963. Reprint 1964.

Worcester, Kent. *C. L. R. James: A Political Biography*. Forthcoming.

JAPANESE AMERICANS

Within the pre–World War II Japanese immigrant communities, the Japanese-American Left consisted of a small but vocal minority whose birth and fortunes reflected developments in both the labor and radical movements in Japan as well as the United States. In stark contrast to the European immigrant Left, however, Japanese-American immigrant leftists were at a special disadvantage because they stood outside the American body politic. As aliens ineligible for citizenship, they could not enter the political arena to participate in the American political process. Furthermore, Japanese-American Leftists, unlike their European counterparts, also stood outside the structure of organized American labor because Asians were excluded by organized labor on racial grounds until the advent of the CIO in the 1930s.

Japanese-American socialist study groups first appeared in San Francisco, Oakland, and other cities shortly after the turn of the century under the influence of the early socialist and labor movements in Japan. In 1906 a handful of Japanese immigrants formed the Social Revolutionary Party in Berkeley. An anarchist organization, it was launched at the behest of Kōtoku Shūsui, the noted Japanese anarchist. In 1908 remnants of the SRP organized the Fresno Labor League, an incipient agricultural labor union of migratory Japanese laborers, under the partial influence of the Industrial Workers of the World. In 1910 Kōtoku and his alleged co-conspirators were arrested on trumped-up charges of plotting to assassinate the Japanese emperor, and in the following year he, along with others, was executed in what came to be known as the High Treason Affair. This marked the temporary demise of the Japanese socialist and labor movements both in Japan and the United States.

The Japanese-American Left resurfaced after World War I under the influence of Sen Katayama, who was one of the founders of the socialist and labor movements in Japan. In 1914 he came to the United States because his life as a socialist in Japan had become intolerable. While residing on the East Coast, he came under the influence of Russian revolutionaries living in exile and became one of the founding members of the American Communist Party in 1919. In New York City, Katayama published a monthly called the *Heimin* [The Commoner] between 1916 and 1919. Under his influence, Japanese immigrant communists, including Okinawans and women, appeared in the 1920s, and by the middle of the decade they organized Japanese Workers Association branches in New York City, Seattle, San Francisco, and Los Angeles.

During the course of the thirties, Japanese immigrant communists were active in the American labor movement and the international struggle against fascism. Some were active in CIO organizing drives, especially among Alaskan cannery workers. In San Francisco, they published a monthly called the *Kaikyūsen* [class struggle] from 1926, renamed the *Zaibei Rōdō Shimbun* [Labor news] in 1928. From 1930 this publication was issued as a semimonthly under the title *Rōdō Shimbun* [The Japanese worker] as the official organ of the Japanese section of the American CP. In 1937 the *Rōdō Shimbun* was redesignated *Dōhō*, meaning brotherhood, in line with the Popular Front policy of the Comintern, and published continuously out of Los Angeles until April 1942. Almost immediately after the attack on Pearl Harbor, the American CP suspended all Japanese-American Party members and their spouses and supported the mass internment of all Japanese-Americans. This racist policy (later acknowledged as an error by the Party), along with the actual mass internment of Japanese Americans during the Second World War, all but spelled the demise of the Japanese-American Left in the continental United States. *See also*: Migratory Agricultural Workers

—*Yuji Ichioka*

REFERENCES

Ichioka, Yuji. "Early Issei Socialists and the Japanese Community." In *Counterpoint: Perspectives on Asian America*, edited by Emma Gee. Los Angeles: Asian American Studies Center, UCLA, 1976.

Isserman, Maurice. *Which Side Were You On?* Middletown: Wesleyan University Press, 1982.

Oda, James. *Heroic Struggles of Japanese Americans: Partisan Fighters from America's Concentration Camps*. Los Angeles: Privately printed, 1981.

Omatsu, Glenn. "Always a Rebel: An Interview With Kazu Iijima." *Amerasia Journal* 13:2 (1986–87).

Yoneda, Karl. *Ganbatte: Sixty-Year Struggle of a Kibei Worker*. Los Angeles: Asian American Studies Center, UCLA, 1983.

Jefferson School of Social Science

This alternative school (1943–56) was established unofficially by the U.S. Communist Party as an expression of its view that Marxism was a legitimate doctrine neglected by conventional schools. It was intended primarily for outreach rather than (as in the case of its predecessor, the Workers School) to train Party cadres or to recruit members. At its Lower Manhattan site, the "Jeff School" offered hundreds of courses each term, boasted of a 30,000-volume library, and put on concerts and theatrical presentations that attracted large audiences. The student body numbered 2,500 at first and went up to 5,000 a term by the peak years, 1947–48. Howard Selsam, the school's director, was a former Brooklyn College philosophy professor. The rest of the administrative and teaching staff (who were offered salaries) and an unpaid board of trustees included several heavily credentialed leftist academics and a number of teachers dismissed from New York's municipal colleges in the Rapp-Coudert purges of 1940–41.

The learning process at the Jefferson School was not entirely political in nature. The introductory twelve-week course on Marxism, "The Science of Society" (fee: $7), covered the basic principles of Marxism, historical materialism, the theory of the state, surplus value, class struggle, and strategy and tactics in the transition to socialism. Advanced courses—hundreds each term—explored such issues as racism, imperialism, the U.S. political system, and trade union tactics. But artists and craftspersons also offered studio art and dance programs for children and adults. Some of the courses seem to have had little direct relation to the kind of political action normally fostered by a CP-run school. For example, in the winter term, 1948, Dashiell Hammett taught "Mystery Story Writing." Students could also take such courses as "How to Decorate Your Home . . . [a] practical course in making a home within a limited budget." There was even a "Beauty and Fashion Clinic: Making the Most of Your Appearance" intended to show "the busy working woman how she can make herself more attractive with the least expenditure of time and money" and thus be more effective in trade union organizing. These courses, along with popular forums, special workshops, and single-admission ($.50) lectures attracted students from the large pool of politically aware office and industrial workers in the city (men and women, black and white), conventionally educated middle-class people, and the inevitable sprinkling of planted FBI agents.

The problems of effective teaching in the Jefferson School's lively, heterogeneous classes of mostly adult students, many with little previous academic experience, soon prompted the faculty to institute teacher-training courses and to prepare learning aids for students. The staff produced a simple yet sophisticated nickel pamphlet, *How to Study*, that sought to demonstrate that Marxism can "be mastered by the average person." The emphasis was on building confidence and putting ability to learn in a political context, countering alleged capitalist propaganda about workers' supposed "limited intellectual abilities."

During the McCarthy era the Subversive Activities Control Board (SACB), the federal apparatus of the FBI, directed the Jefferson School to register as a "Communist-controlled organization." At first the Jefferson School refused to do so and attempted a defense against the SACB (Jefferson School v. SACB, 331 F.2d 76 [1954]). In the end, the Jefferson School succumbed to massive government pressure and permanently closed its doors in 1956. *See also*: Communist Party, Jewish Workers University, Workers Schools

—*Marv Gettleman*

REFERENCES

Jefferson School of Social Science Papers, State Historical Society of Wisconsin, Madison, Wisconsin.

Jefferson School Holdings, Tamiment Institute Library, New York University.

JEWISH AMERICANS: see ARTEF; CAHAN, ABRAHAM; EMMA LAZARUS FEDERATION OF JEWISH WOMEN'S CLUBS; THE FREIE ARBETER SHTIMME; GOLD, MICHAEL; JEWISH LIFE/JEWISH CURRENTS; JEWISH PEOPLE'S FRATERNAL ORDER; JEWISH WORKERS CHORUSES; LONDON, MEYER; MALKIEL, THERESA SERBER; OLGIN, MOISSAYE J.; RIVKIN, B.; ROCKER, RUDOLF; SCHAPIRO, MEYER; SOCIALIST ZIONISM; WINCHEVSKY, MORRIS; WORKMEN'S CIRCLE; YIDDISH LEFT; YIDDISH SCHOOLS; DI ZUKUNFT

JEWISH DAILY FORWARD: see CAHAN, ABRAHAM; YIDDISH LEFT

JEWISH LIFE/JEWISH CURRENTS

The oldest left-wing American Jewish periodical in English, it began in 1946 as *Jewish Life*, the English-language organ of the *Morgen Freiheit*, and it functioned in the orbit of the Communist Party. However, in 1956 the magazine embarked on an independent course, was renamed *Jewish Currents* in 1958, and evolved in the 1970s into a democratic socialist secular Jewish publication with a heavy emphasis on Jewish culture, Jewish history, and support for close black-Jewish relations. Today *Jewish Currents* is acknowledged as being inside the mainstream Jewish community, as its left-wing component.

JL, for the first nine and a half years of its existence, adhered to current CPUSA positions on Jewish and other issues. From 1948 to the middle 1950s, it followed the Soviet view concerning assimilation when, under Stalin, after 1948 all Jewish social and cultural institutions suddenly shut down. *JL*'s explanation for these events was that they merely reflected a natural process of assimilation of Jews into the general Soviet population and thereby should be seen as being a progressive development and a direct result of the building of a new socialist society in the USSR. When the anti-Semitic campaign in the USSR and Eastern Europe reached its zenith during the years 1948–53, *JL* referred to it as being a myth fed by Cold War lies. The publication defended the Prague trials of 1952 and wrote an effusive eulogy on the death of Stalin called "Stalin and the Jewish People." These positions served to isolate *JL* from organized Jewry.

Therefore, in 1956 *JL* faced a severe crisis threatening its survival in light of the revelation of Khrushchev's secret speech denouncing Stalin's crimes and the appearance of an article from a Polish Yiddish newspaper, revealing—from an official Communist source—the destruction of Jewish writers and institutions in the USSR from 1948 to 1953. The magazine and its editors appeared to have become discredited with many readers. While the editors of *JL* officially apologized "for having failed" their readers in not perceiving the crimes against the Jews in the Soviet bloc, it was too late. The magazine lost three-fourths of its readers. It looked like the periodical would have to fold.

But it survived, as Morris U. Schappes became its full-time editor in 1958. It was renamed *Jewish Currents*, with the new editor resolved to "pursue a course of independence of any outside control. . . ." It would be explicitly committed to Jewish survival and opposed to anti-Semitism wherever it occurred, including the Soviet Union and its allies.

JC maintained its editorial independence during the next ten years, while still retaining a correct relationship with the CP and generally supporting Soviet foreign policy. However, the Six Day War of 1967 saw *JC* stand with the rest of American and world Jewry behind Israel, in direct opposition to the positions of the USSR and the CPUSA. This issue, plus *JC*'s condemnation of the rise of official anti-Semitism in the USSR and Poland, and the 1968 Soviet intervention in Czechoslovakia, prompted the magazine and the CPUSA to go their separate ways.

JC has in recent years defined itself as a democratic, socialist, pro-Israel, but non-Zionist, secular Jewish periodical. Schappes has remained editor, and the magazine readership and financial base continues with those subscribers who came out of the progressive Jewish movement. *JC* has supported close black-Jewish relations, and supports the Peace Now movement in Israel and Palestinian self-determination, including independent statehood on the West Bank and in Gaza, next to Israel. It has backed U.S.-Soviet détente, while it has been critical of the Jewish situation in the USSR, supporting the right to emigrate but also emphasizing the right of the majority of Soviet Jews who choose to remain in the USSR to full Soviet citizenship, including the restoration of cultural institutions where Yiddish, Hebrew, Jewish history, and literature will be taught. *See also*: Yiddish Left

—*David A. Hacker*

REFERENCES

Jewish Currents Reader. New York: Jewish Currents, 1966.

"Jewish Life" Anthology, 1946–56. New York: Jewish Life, 1966.

The Third Jewish Currents Reader. New York: Jewish Currents, 1986.

Jewish People's Fraternal Order

Largest affiliate of the International Workers Order by far, the JPFO was the most robust, and at times among the most independent-minded, of the Left fraternal movements after 1920.

The JPFO grew out of a political and generational division within the Workmen's Circle of the 1920s. As leaders of the Workmen's Circle grew more suspicious of the Russian regime they had initially supported, and as Communist unionists in the garment industry and elsewhere squared off against old-line socialist leaders, a split became inevitable. The Left (popularly known as the "linkies") garnered the loyalty of most of the *Shule* teachers and those young people generally most involved with the Yiddish cultural and recreational institutions; the Right, based for the most part in the older immigrant class, conveyed a somewhat more assimilationist impression even while they supported the *Jewish Daily Forward* and the Yiddish day-schools.

A year after their 1929 withdrawal from the Workmen's Circle, the International Workers Order (for the moment Jewish only) applied for an insurance charter, claiming 5,000 members. By the mid-1940s, as its peak, the JPFO (renamed from the Jewish Section of the IWO, during the 1940s, to avoid the stigma of outright Left affiliation) could tally some 50,000 members, far more than any of its sister groups, and more than a quarter of the combined IWO's 200,000 members. Along with insurance policies, the IWO founded—among other institutions—an adult organ, *Undzer Vort*, and a children's paper, *Yung Varg*, also summer camps, sports leagues, amateur and professional theater, and some fifteen choruses. Its schools, central focus of cultural attention, enrolled some 6,000 students. Its health clinics and cultural apparatus, especially apparent in such Jewish blue-collar neighborhoods as the South Bronx and Brighton Beach, were widely regarded as community centers. In 1944 the JPFO even gained official admittance to the American Jewish Congress.

By the early 1940s, as the scale of European Jewry's tragedy began to become known, the JPFO accelerated a turn away from "abstract internationalism" (or "national nihilism") to a progressive recognition of Jewish identity as holding foremost importance.

Itche Goldberg (b. 1906), the JPFO's outstanding pedagogue, declared in 1943 that the melting pot had a "scorched bottom," and that real democracy demanded a multilingual society of the future. No socialist or communist pronouncements on the "national question" had previously gone so far as to reject the finality of ultimate assimilation. In the wake of the Holocaust, the JPFO furiously launched new schools and literary projects to preserve *Yiddishkayt*, the culture associated with the Yiddish language.

With the acceleration of the Cold War, the U.S. Treasury Department and the New York Insurance Department deprived the IWO of its tax-exempt status and its insurance charter. Accepting defeat, the JPFO (now also deprived of its financial advantages) reorganized, much reduced, as the Jewish Clubs and Societies. Although holding only a few thousand members, the Clubs and Societies have remained an important source of support for the *Morgen Freiheit* newspaper, *Jewish Currents* and *Yiddishe Kultur* magazines, Camp Kinderland, and the publication of Yiddish books. *See also*: International Workers Order, Jewish Chorus, Yiddish Left, Yiddish Schools

—*Maurice Isserman, Paul Buhle*

REFERENCES

Buhle, Paul. "Jews and American Communism: The Cultural Question." *Radical History Review* 23 (Spring 1980).

Goldberg, Itche. "Di Yiddishe kultur un di Yiddishe Shule in Amerika." In *In Dienst fun Folk: Almanakh fun Yiddish Folks Orden*. New York: Jewish People's Fraternal Order 1947.

Isserman, Maurice. "Jewish People's Fraternal Order." In *Jewish American Voluntary Organizations*, edited by Michael N. Dobkowski. Westport: Greenwood, 1986.

IWO Collection, Cornell University.

Trauber, Jerry. Interview by Paul Buhle. Oral History of the American Left, Tamiment Library, New York University.

JEWISH WORKERS CHORUSES

From the 1920s through the 1950s, a Jewish workers' choral movement flourished, with thousands singing Yiddish folk and labor songs of Europe and the United States. Developing national networks of affiliated choruses across the United States and Canada, this movement played an important role in sustaining Yiddish secular culture, left-wing activism, and Jewish national identity.

Distinctly different from religious choirs, the Jewish secular choral movement began in Poland in the 1880s, enlivened with the modernist spirit of the Jewish Haskalah (Enlightment). With increasing Jewish emigration to the United States, young immigrants formed Yiddish singing societies to continue a strong, musical tradition that played a central role in Eastern European Jewish life.

As many of these immigrants suffered harsh living and working conditions, the demands and visions of a young, literary, and street-wise Jewish socialist movement were woven into the lyrical themes and social purpose of these new choral groups.

In the early 1910s the New York Workmen's Circle, the first large-scale Jewish workers' fraternal order, established what would become one of the major, long-term choral groupings. By 1914, a Jewish Socialist Workers Chorus had been established in Chicago. In 1918 the Paterson Singing Society was formed in Paterson, a New Jersey mill town that in 1913 saw one of the largest mass strikes in U.S. labor history. Another early chorus, the Poale Zion Singing Society, represented the young Labor-Zionist movement coming out of Russia.

Splitting from the Workmen's Circle in 1923, the left-wing *Freiheit Gezangs Ferain* (Freedom singing club) was established in New York. These choruses stood for a militant, trade unionist, Soviet-affiliated perspective while holding to a "high" theatrical Yiddish standard. The Workmen's Circle opted for a more moderate, reformist approach. Smaller in numbers, the Jewish Farband (Association) and Labor-Zionist choruses held to a vision of Jewish emancipation in a worker-run society in Palestine.

The original choral music that developed out of this movement drew from eclectic sources: Hebrew religious chants, Slavic and Yiddish folk melodies, and Yiddish theater tunes, with lyrics often drawn from Yiddish poets and writers. This completely new and unique Jewish-American musical form melded religious, folk, and revolutionary styles into classically oriented choral arrangements.

The influence of choral leader and composer Jacob Shaefer exemplifies this elevation of Yiddish folk music into a classical proletarian movement. Born in 1888, the son of a poor Jewish carpenter in a small Russian town near Galicia, he split his youth between working in his father's shop and perfecting his recognized musical talents in local synagogues. In his teens he became the cantor of a large synagogue in Galicia. The influence of early religious training would be heard throughout his choral compositions in religious chanting accents and tonalities.

Coming to the United States in 1910, Shaefer studied music at the Chicago Conservatory, continuing work as a carpenter and achieving prominence as the leader of the Jewish Socialist Workers Chorus. In 1925 he went to New York to lead the *Freiheit Gezangs Ferain*. Under his direction, a National Jewish Musical Union was formed and the left-wing choral movement flourished. By the mid-1930s, forty branches of the FGF existed across the United States. Shaefer also encouraged the development of mandolin orchestras, which grew up alongside many of the choruses.

Through the 1940s, the choruses experienced their greatest strength. World War II, the Holocaust, and the founding of Israel brought a new set of choral themes, emphasizing Jewish cultural identity. This return to Jewish roots was reinforced by the revelations of Stalinist terror and repression of Yiddish culture in the Soviet Union. The McCarthyite Red Scare led to the suppression of left-wing idealism. These factors, combined with demographic forces within the American Jewish community—upward mobility, suburbanization, the decline of Yiddish—contributed to the decline of this diverse choral movement in the 1950s.

Yet through the 1980s, several choruses affiliated with the Workmen's Circle and the FGF continued to perform, giving joy and meaning to members and audiences striving to stay connected with Yiddish culture, Jewish identity, and ethics of brotherhood and justice. *See also*: International Workers Order, Jewish People's Fraternal Order, Yiddish Left

—*Joel Saxe*

REFERENCES

Epstein, Melech. *The Jew and Communism, 1919–1941*. New York: Trade Union Sponsoring Committee, 1959.

Liebman, Arthur. *Jews and the Left*. New York: John Wiley, 1979.

Slobin, Mark. *Tenement Songs*. Chicago: University of Illinois Press, 1982.

Yardeni, Mordecai, S., ed. *Fifty Years of Yiddish Song in America*. New York: Jewish Music Alliance, 1964.

Jewish Workers University

The first and only Marxist school in Yiddish, the university prepared hundreds of activists to occupy positions in organizations such as the Yiddish schools of the International Workers Order, unions, Left choruses, and the Left Yiddish theater.

Founded in 1926 in New York City, the university began with about 200 students, immigrants for the most part formally uneducated, save in rudimentary Hebrew (and only for the boys). It taught Yiddish reading and writing, English history of Jews and the working class, anthropology, political economy, and other subjects. It also promulgated its own chorus.

The school's primary director, Israel Ber Bailin (1883–1961), had been an ardent Bundist and political prisoner in Czarist Russia, a translator-secretary for the pre-1919 Socialist Party, and a founder of the Chicago *Gezangs Farein* along with Jacob Shaefer. Educational director of the Workmen's Circle during the 1920s, he helped establish hundreds of Jewish Children's Schools throughout the nation and edited the fraternal monthly *Der Freind*. Driven out for his support of the Soviet Union, he became editor of *Der Hammer* from 1933 to 1939 and, on its closing, a staff member of the *Morgen Freiheit*.

Under Bailin's leadership, the Jewish Workers University continued until 1941, when it was replaced by the School for Jewish Studies, located in the same building (and

with an overlapping staff) with the Communist Party's Jefferson School. The School for Jewish Studies, headed by Chaim Suller, closed with the Jefferson School in 1956 because of McCarthyite pressures. *See also*: Yiddish Left
—*Jeanette Bailin Cohen*

JOHNSON, OLIVE M. (1871?–1952)

One of the most prominent women in American Socialism, Olive Malmberg Johnson was editor of the *Weekly People*, organ of the (American) Socialist Labor Party, from 1918 to 1938. Born in Sweden, she emigrated in the 1890s to the United States, where she joined the SLP. Like many Scandinavian immigrants, she lived in the Midwest. After moving to California, she was elected to the national executive committee. Her marriage to another member broke up and she never remarried.

She was a close friend to Daniel DeLeon and much of their voluminous correspondence still survives. In 1907 she made an unauthorized trip to the NEC meeting in New York to support DeLeon in his conflict with James Connolly over editorial and party policies. Her vote was also crucial in opposing National Secretary Frank Bohn's moves toward unity with the Socialist Party. In 1910 she attended the socialist international congress in Copenhagen with DeLeon. In 1918 she was chosen by the NEC to replace Edmund Seidel, who as national editor espoused pro-unity views.

Her editorial positions were especially hostile to the Communist and Socialist parties and the antipolitical Industrial Workers of the World, but she also condemned the CIO as well as nonrevolutionary movements such as the cooperative movement and the New Deal. She was very active during this period, not only as editor, but also as pamphlet writer, speaker, and candidate for public office. She was a spokesperson for a socialist women's group in greater New York and in 1907 wrote *Woman and the Socialist Movement*. Other works include *The Cooperative Movement* (1924), *Industrial Unionism* (1935), and a history, *Socialist Labor Party 1890–1930* (with Henry Kuhn, 1931).

In the 1930s, she suffered from tuberculosis and carried out her editorial duties more and more at home. This, along with personality differences with National Secretary Arnold Petersen, resulted in her removal as national editor in 1938. Her health continued to deteriorate and she died in Malibu, California. *See also*: Socialist Labor Party
—*Ben Perry*

REFERENCES

"In Memoriam Olive M. Johnson." *Weekly People*, p. 5, July 10, 1954.

Socialist Labor Party Collection, Wisconsin State Historical Society.

"JOHNSON-FOREST TENDENCY":

see JAMES, C. L. R.

JONES, CLAUDIA (1915?–1952)

Born in Port of Spain, British West Indies (Trinidad), Jones was a child when her family migrated to Harlem in the 1920s. Like many working-class black Harlemites, she was attracted to the Communist Party through the International Labor Defense's campaign to free the "Scottsboro Nine." Soon after joining the Young Communist League in the early 1930s, Jones became editor of the YCL *Weekly Review* and the *Spotlight*.

As one of the preeminent young black Communists in Harlem during the Popular Front era, Jones actively supported the National Negro Congress from its inception, serving as a leader of the NNC youth council in Harlem. Although she had been associated with issues pertaining to Afro-American rights and was among the first to criticize Earl Browder's decision to abandon self-determination in the "black belt," during World War II Jones developed a reputation as a relentless critic of male chauvinism and a leading Party spokesperson for women's rights. After the war she was appointed to the Women's Commission, briefly serving as its secretary.

In 1951 Jones was convicted of violating the Smith Act and imprisoned in Alderson Federal Reformatory for Women. Because the prison conditions aggravated her tuberculosis (which she had contracted as a factory worker in Harlem), Jones served only one year and was deported to England soon after her release. Although residence in London did not vitiate her political activities (she edited the left-wing *West Indian Gazette*), her health continued to deteriorate and she died shortly afterward. *See also*: Communist Party, National Negro Congress

—*Robin D. G. Kelley*

REFERENCES

Davis, Angela. *Women, Race, and Class*. New York: Random House, 1981.

Haywood, Harry. *Black Bolshevik: Autobiography of An Afro-American Communist*. Chicago: Liberator Press, 1978.

Johnson, Ron. "A Fighting Caribbean-American Leader." *People's Daily World*, February 10, 1989.

Naison, Mark. *Communists in Harlem During the Depression*. Urbana: University of Illinois Press, 1983.

North, Joe. "Communist Women." *Political Affairs* 51/3 (March 1971).

Jones, "Mother" Mary Harris (1836–1930)

A union organizer and sometime socialist associated primarily with the United Mine Workers of America, Jones was an impassioned and highly effective organizer. A white-haired, grandmotherly figure, she gained prominence during the anthracite strike of 1900, attracting national attention during several other strikes, including the Paint and Cabin Creek strike (West Virginia, 1913) and the Colorado Fuel and Iron strike (1913–14). Her physical courage and flamboyant style became legendary as she waded creeks, defied mine guards, and went to prison in the miners' cause.

The facts of her early life remain for the most part obscure. She was born in Ireland, most likely in 1836, and at age seven came to the United States with her father. As a young woman she taught school and worked as a seamstress, eventually marrying George Jones, a member of the iron moulders' union. He and their four children died in the Memphis yellow fever epidemic of 1867. In 1871 her dressmaking shop burned down in the Chicago fire. Thereafter she became involved with the Knights of Labor, and later with the anti-Chinese agitation that thoroughly infected the labor movement of the 1880s. In the early 1890s she began organizing coal miners.

Although chiefly associated with coal miners, Mother Jones worked with other groups as well. In 1903 she organized a widely publicized march of textile mill children to demonstrate the evils of child labor. She supported various socialist causes, including her one-woman campaign in 1910 for the release of Mexican revolutionaries jailed in American prisons.

Politically, Mother Jones moved in the mid-1890s from populism to socialism, and in 1916 from socialism to support of the Democrat Woodrow Wilson. She held strongly anti-capitalist views along with fervently traditional views on the roles of women, notwithstanding her own nontraditional lifestyle. Mary Harris Jones died on November 30, 1930, and was buried in the miners' cemetery in Mount Olive, Illinois. *See also*: Socialist Party, United Mine Workers

—*Priscilla Long*

REFERENCES

Autobiography of Mother Jones, edited by Mary Field Parton. Reprint. Chicago: Charles H. Kerr, 1972.

Featherling, Dale. *Mother Jones: The Miners' Angel*. Carbondale: Southern Illinois University Press, 1974.

Foner, Philip S., ed. *Mother Jones Speaks*. New York: Monad, 1983.

Long, Priscilla. *Mother Jones: Woman Organizer, and Her Relations with Miners' Wives, Working Women, and the Suffrage Movement*. Boston: Red Sun Press, 1976.

Steel, Edward M., ed. *The Correspondence of Mother Jones*. Pittsburgh: University of Pittsburgh Press, 1985.

———, ed. *The Speeches and Writings of Mother Jones*. Pittsburgh: University of Pittsburgh, 1988.

Keller, Helen (1880–1967)

Almost everyone knows that Helen Keller, born in Tuscombia, Alabama, was stricken at the age of nineteen months by a disease that left her deaf, blind, and mute; that she was brought out of her prison of despair and frustration by Anne Sullivan; and that she triumphed over her disabilities, graduating cum laude from Radcliffe College after mastering Greek, Latin, German, and French. In the years that followed, Keller campaigned for the deaf and blind around the world. She also appeared in vaudeville and motion pictures and wrote books of literary distinction. Her accomplishments led Mark Twain to characterize her as "the greatest woman since Joan of Arc," and to assert that "the two most interesting characters of the nineteenth century are Napolean and Helen Keller." *Good Housekeeping* included her in its selection of "America's Twelve Greatest Women," describing Helen Keller as "A Living Proof of the Divine Spark in the Human Brain."

For all her fame, not many people know that this woman was one of the best known figures in the American socialist movement, a champion of the working class and its struggles against industrial barbarism, a consistent foe of militarism, war, and imperialism, and a militant crusader for a new society. Turning the yellowed pages of radical newspapers and magazines between 1910 and the early 1920s, one frequently finds the name Helen Keller beneath speeches, articles, and letters dealing with major social questions of the era. The radical vision that runs through these writings is the vision of socialism. In the New York *Call,* daily organ of the Socialist Party, Hattie Schlossberg wrote on May 4, 1913: "Helen Keller is our comrade, and her socialism is a living vital thing for her. All her speeches are permeated with the spirit of socialism. . . ."

There is glory for America in Helen Keller's socialism. But there is shame in the fact that until her death in 1967 at the age of eighty-seven, the director of the FBI, J. Edgar Hoover, maintained a detailed investigative file on this remarkable and distinguished American whose triumph over her disabilities was an inspiration to millions the world over. To Hoover, Helen Keller was a "writer on radical subjects," and as such had to have her activities carefully monitored and recorded in an FBI file that is stamped "Security Information Confidential."

When Helen Keller decided after 1921 that her chief life work was to be devoted to raising funds for the American Foundation for the Blind, her activities for the socialist movement diminished but did not cease. No matter what social cause she espoused, Keller was always on the radical side of the movement. A left-wing socialist, she despised "parlor socialists" who quickly abandoned the struggle when the going became difficult and often ended up "hopelessly reactionary." She supported every workers' struggle, but she was "heartily disgusted" with the conservative policies of the leadership of the AFL. "If only

Jehovah in his infinite mercy would take [Samuel] Gompers to Heaven, there might be some hope of an American labor party worthy of the name," she wrote in the early 1920s. Because of the AFL's emphasis on organizing mainly the skilled, white, male workers in craft unions, she lined up with the Industrial Workers of the World. She admired the Wobblies' militant, innovative tactics, their advocacy of industrial unions under which all workers would be organized regardless of skill, sex, and race, and their belief in the ultimate goal of a new society. She was also on the side of the militants in the struggle for woman suffrage, advocating the adoption of the militant tactics of the British suffragettes, including hunger strikes. "I believe the women of England are doing right," she told a reporter for the *New York Times*. "Mrs. Pankhurst [founder of the British movement] is a great leader. The women of America should follow her example. They would get the ballot much faster if they did. They cannot hope to get anything unless they are willing to fight and suffer for it. The pangs of hunger during the hunger strike are a sample of the suffering they must expect."

She did not value militancy for its own sake nor even for the sake only of individual causes. "I am a militant suffragist," she explained, "because I believe suffrage will lead to Socialism and to me Socialism is the ideal cause." *See also*: Industrial Workers of the World

—Philip S. Foner

REFERENCES

Keller, Helen. *Helen Keller, Her Socialist Years: Writings and Speeches*. Edited by Philip S. Foner. New York: International Publishers, 1967.

KELLEY, FLORENCE (1859–1932)

Foremost socialist figure within the world of mainstream American reform, Florence Kelley reshaped the settlement house movement, conducted early factory inspections, and promoted the passage of groundbreaking state, federal, and local labor and social legislation.

Born into an elite Philadelphia family with a strong tradition of Quaker activism—the daughter of William "Pig Iron" Kelley, a radical Republican with fifteen consecutive terms in the U.S. House of Representatives—Kelley graduated from Cornell in 1882. Contact with socialist refugees and students at the University of Zurich in 1884 precipitated her lifelong commitment to socialism.

That year, she married a Polish-Jewish socialist medical student, Lazare Wischnewetzky. She gave birth to three children in three years, and also undertook major translations of the writings of Marx and Engels. Her translation of Engels's *Condition of the Working Class in England in 1844*, first published in New York in 1887, remains the most widely read version of that classic work.

Upon moving to New York in 1887, she and her husband joined the Socialist Labor Party, from which they were soon expelled. The SLP was unaccustomed to women in leadership positions, especially those who challenged their interpretations of Marx and Engels with more authoritative versions. Thereafter, Kelley turned to other avenues of social change, training herself in 1889 as an expert on child labor reform.

Prompted by her husband's physical abuse, late in 1891 Kelley moved to Chicago. There she entered into a lifelong affiliation with the settlement house movement, taking up residence at Hull House with Jane Addams and others. Herself a key factor in their shift from philanthropy to reform, Kelley gained in turn emotional and financial support from her co-workers. Using data she collected as an investigator for the Illinois Bureau of Labor Statistics and as the U.S. Commissioner of Labor, she constructed in the maps of *Hull House Maps and Papers* (1985) the most sophisticated social survey in the United States. Appointed the first chief factory inspector for Illinois in 1893, she and her staff of twelve vigorously enforced a pioneering eight-hour law for working women and children.

Kelley returned to New York in 1898 as general secretary of the National Consumers League, residing until 1926 at Lillian Wald's Henry Street Settlement. Coordinating the efforts of scores of local leagues, she shaped much of the nation's early labor and social legislation. Between 1910 and 1930 she was the most important single lobbyist for the passage of state minimum-wage legislation for women, likewise instrumental in the creation of the U.S. Children's Bureau in 1912, and the Sheppard-Towner Maternity and Infancy Protection Act in 1921 (the only federal precedent for the child welfare portions of the Social Security Act of 1936). As a Socialist Party member, she played an especially important role in the Intercollegiate Socialist Society, frequently speaking at campuses under its auspices. After 1921, much of her energies were absorbed by her opposition to the Equal Rights amendments, which she viewed as a threat to her life's work of advocating protective legislation. *See also*: Intercollegiate Socialist Society, Socialist Party

—*Kathryn Kish Sklar*

REFERENCES

Blumberg, Dorothy Rose. *Florence Kelley: The Making of a Social Pioneer*. New York: Augustus M. Kelley, 1966.

Goldmark, Josephine. *Impatient Crusader, Florence Kelley's Life Story*. Urbana: University of Illinois Press, 1953.

Sklar, Kathryn Kish, ed. *The Autobiography of Florence Kelley: Notes of Sixty Years*. Chicago: Charles H. Kerr, 1986.

KERACHER, JOHN (1880–1958)

Pioneer American Communist, founder/leader of the Proletarian Party, and Marxist pamphleteer, Keracher was born and raised in Scotland. He came to the United States in 1909 and settled in Detroit, where he operated a shoe store for many years. In April 1910 he joined the Socialist Party.

Discouraged by what he regarded as the SP's low theoretical level, Keracher initiated an ambitious statewide party education program, based on the study of the Marxist classics. Out of this program grew Detroit's Proletarian University, a notable experiment in independent labor education, in which Keracher was among the most popular instructors.

With Keracher at its head, the Michigan SP grew to be among the largest and the most radical of the party's state organizations, and was often at odds with the more conservative national leadership, who in fact expelled the entire Michigan membership in May 1919. The ostensible reason for the expulsion was the Michigan section's vehement antireligious stance, in violation of party statutes. Keracher and his comrades maintained, however, that the expulsion was motivated by their militant defense of Bolshevism.

A few weeks later, together with other expelled SPers and a few independents, Keracher helped found the Communist Party in Chicago in September 1919. Unlike most of his newfound comrades, however, Keracher did not believe that communist revolution was imminent in the United States, and he strongly opposed the new party's antielectoral, "underground" and dual-unionist orientation. Because of these and other disagreements, he and the entire "Michigan group," as its opponents called it, though it included supporters outside that state, were expelled from the CP in January 1920. In June of that year Keracher and the others founded the Proletarian Party, of which he remained the principal leader for the rest of his life.

As a major PP publicist, Keracher wrote countless party leaflets as well as articles and editorials for the *Proletarian News* and internal polemics for party convention bulletins. His pamphlets, however—*How the Gods Were Made* (1929), *Producers and Parasites* (1935), *The Head-Fixing Industry*, a critique of capitalist media (1935; revised 1955, with a section on television), *Crime: Its Causes and Consequences* (1937), and *Frederick Engels* (1946)—are surprisingly free of sectarian rhetoric. Enlivened by flashes of soapbox humor—Keracher was a gifted street-speaker and indefatigable cross-country lecturer—these popularizations of Marxism, several of them still in print, were stocked by other socialist groups as well as by IWW locals and free-thought societies.

Keracher's work at the Proletarian University in Detroit had brought him into close contact with Charles H. Kerr's socialist publishing house in Chicago, and it was to Keracher that an aging Charles Kerr, eager to retire after directing the operation for forty-two years, sold the bulk of his controlling shares in the cooperative firm in 1928. Remarkably, during the next forty-two years, when the Kerr Company was run by Keracher and his fellow Proletarians, it was never made into a narrowly "party press." According to Samuel J. Meyers, himself a PPer in the late 1920s, and more recently international vice-president of the largest AFL-CIO union, the Retail Clerks, "the most important contribution of John Keracher to the labor movement" was to keep the old Kerr Company going during those long, hard times.

Keracher left Detroit for Chicago in the 1920s, remaining there through the early 1950s, after which he retired to Los Angeles. Shortly before his death he completed a history of the Proletarian Party, as yet unpublished. *See also*: Proletarian Party

—*Franklin Rosemont*

REFERENCES

Wysocki, Al. "John Keracher: His Life and Work." *Proletarian News* (Chicago), March 1958.

Charles H. Kerr Publishing Company

Founded in Chicago in 1886, the Kerr Company is the oldest socialist publishing house in the United States. Reaching its height in the 1900s and the 1910s, the company specialized in presenting socialism to a popular audience. Faced with government repression after World War I, it struggled for over a half century before rebounding in the 1970s and 1980s.

Charles Hope Kerr was born in 1860, the son of Congregationalist liberals active in the abolitionist movement. After graduating from the University of Wisconsin in 1881, he moved to Chicago, where he established Charles H. Kerr and Company as a publisher of radical Unitarian literature. In the 1890s Kerr's focus shifted from religion to radical politics. In 1891 the Kerr Company published *The Coming Climax*, by labor journalist Lester C. Hubbard, an important book in the movement to pardon the surviving Haymarket anarchists. In 1894 Kerr published *The Pullman Strike*, an exposé of conditions in Pullman by the Rev. William H. Carwardine. In the 1890s Kerr also began offering company stock to the general public at ten dollars per share. Purchasers of the stock received discounts on publications as well as a chance to share in the "cooperative commonwealth." Throughout the rest of the 1890s the Kerr Company offered titles by a wide range of radicals, including populists, anarchists, utopian socialists, and feminists.

c. 1914–15

In 1899 the Kerr Company began publishing "The Pocket Library of Socialism," also known as "little red books" because of their red cellophane wrappers. This series of thirty-two page, five-cent pamphlets on socialist economics and politics included works by Jack London, Clarence Darrow, and Upton Sinclair. In 1900 Kerr began publishing the *International Socialist Review* (ISR), which survived until 1918.

In the early 1900s the Kerr Company continued publishing a variety of radical works, including the original edition of Gustavus Myers' muckraking *History of the Great American Fortunes*, Lewis Henry Morgan's anthropological study *Ancient Society*, Austin Lewis' *The Militant Proletariat*, Edward Carpenter's sex-reform classic *Love's Coming of Age*, Daniel DeLeon's translation of Marx's *The*

Eighteenth Brumaire of Louis Bonaparte, Irish revolutionary James Connolly's *Socialism Made Easy,* and Mary Marcy's pamphlet *Shop Talks on Economics.* The Kerr Company also specialized in printing English translations of major European socialist works, including those of Marx and Engels—Kerr was the first publisher of the complete text of the three volumes of the English-language text *Capital* (1906–09)—Paul Lafargue, Karl Kautsky, Wilhelm Liebknecht, Joseph Dietzgen, and Antonio Labriola. In 1905 Kerr began publishing the multivolume "Library of Science for the Workers" with Wilhelm Boelsche's *The Evolution of Man.* In 1908 the Kerr Company brought out a deck of socialist playing cards illustrated by IWW poet/artist Ralph Chaplin, and a few years later produced a board game called Class Struggle and played like dominoes.

The financial strain of the government's repression of the *ISR* during World War I caused the Kerr Company to cease printing pamphlets in 1917. The company rebounded somewhat after the war, bringing out several new titles in the early 1920s, including Marcy's *The Right to Strike,* former assistant secretary of labor Louis F. Post's *The Deportations Delirium of Nineteen-Twenty,* and *The Autobiography of Mother Jones.* But the company never approached its prewar popularity, and in 1928 Kerr retired and passed control of the company to John Keracher and members of the Proletarian Party. The PPers ran the Kerr Company until 1971, primarily keeping Marxist classics in print and occasionally bringing out new titles. In the 1930s the Kerr Company published Keracher's pamphlet *The Head-Fixing Industry,* a critique of American mass media, and distributed defrocked Episcopalian Bishop William Montgomery Brown's *Communism and Christianism.* In 1935 Kerr brought out the first English translation of Engel's *Anti-Dühring.* By the late 1960s, the company operated only as a small mail-order concern. But in 1971 a group including longtime IWW member Fred Thompson and International Labor Defense leader Joseph Giganti took control of the Kerr Company and brought out a series of new titles and reprints of radical classics. *See also*: Keracher, John; Proletarian Party

—*David Cochran*

REFERENCES

Rosemont, Franklin. "The Charles H. Kerr Company and the Haymarket Heritage." In *Haymarket Scrapbook,* edited by Dave Roediger and Franklin Rosemont. Chicago: Kerr, 1986.

Ruff, Allen M. "Socialist Publishing in Illinois: Charles H. Kerr and Company of Chicago, 1886–1928." *Illinois Historical Journal* 79 (Spring 1986).

KESTER, HOWARD (1904–77)

Presbyterian and Congregational minister, early organizer of the Southern Tenant Farmers Union, and secretary of the Committee on Economic and Racial Justice, Kester was also secretary of the Fellowship of Southern Churchmen and a participant in several important NAACP investigations.

Born into a segregated community to a father who, although opposed to slavery, was also a member of the Ku Klux Klan, Howard Kester, commonly known as "Buck," sought throughout his life to promote interracial unity and to place the problems of the South within a Christian context.

Kester's own conscience was awakened during a 1923 trip to Europe with the YMCA's American Pilgrimage of Friendship. Kester immediately likened the postwar conditions of the Jewish ghettos of Poland to the plight of Afro-Americans in the United States. Returning to Lynchburg College, which he attended on a Presbyterian ministerial scholarship, Kester became active in the YMCA's European Student Relief Project and formed one of the South's first interracial intercollegiate organizations. Through his friendship with George Washington Carver, Kester became the first white "fraternal" delegate to a black YMCA and advocated the desegregation of the YMCA and YWCA as a whole.

After a brief stint in 1925, Kester left Princeton Theological Seminary because of the school's conservatism and enrolled at Vanderbilt's School of Religion. There, along with Ward Rodgers, Claude Williams, and Don West, he came under the tutelage of Professor Alva Taylor. Taylor's teachings, which had a formative influence on Kester's own philosophy, stressed that with modern science and Christianity, mankind could "make the world over into the kingdom of God."

Dismissed from his position within the YMCA, Kester left Vanderbilt (he did return and completed his degree in 1929) for New York, becoming youth secretary of the pacifist organization the Fellowship of Reconciliation. Traveling by rail to colleges throughout the South, Kester used the opportunity to defy Jim Crow laws. He also continued to organize interracial conferences and meetings now in the name of the FOR.

In 1931 Kester, as an anonymous agent of the NAACP, investigated the trials of the "Scottsboro Boys" and the lynching of George Smith in Tennessee. That year Kester also met and came under the influence of Socialist Norman Thomas, who he felt understood the needs of the South. Along with five others, Kester founded the Nashville local of the Socialist Party and unsuccessfully ran for Congress under the party's banner in 1932.

His involvement with the SP increased his radicalism and brought him to the Communist-dominated Congress Against War in October 1933. It also led to his dismissal from the FOR, which did not conceive of itself as the revolutionary body that Kester envisioned. Declaring that revolution was imminent and militancy was required, Kester became part of the Revolutionary Policy Committee representing the SP's left-wing.

Around this time, the NAACP widely distributed Kester's report on the brutal lynching of Claude Neal in Marianna, Florida. Kester also testified at congressional hearings on the Costigan-Wagner antilynching bill, part of an ongoing campaign by Kester against lynching.

At the urging of H. L. Mitchell, Kester became involved in the Southern Tenant Farmers' Union soon after its founding in July 1934. Despite his apparent revolutionary zeal, Kester brought moderation to the STFU in his advocacy of nonviolence. Mitchell described him as an "outside contact man and a spokesman for the STFU." In 1936 Kester wrote the standard work *Revolt Among the Sharecroppers*, which accurately detailed the plight of the sharecroppers. He also served as a STFU representative in its courtship of big-time labor. In October 1935, Kester met with AFL president William Green at the AFL's annual convention. Although giving a symbolic endorsement of the STFU, the AFL withheld financial backing.

In February 1936, Kester, with the assistance of Gardner Jackson, spoke to a group of senators and congressmen. Although Senator Robert LaFollette was later to create a subcommittee to investigate violations of free speech and assembly, the committee did not concern itself with agriculture.

Kester also became embroiled in the disputes within the STFU after its merger with the CIO-affiliated United Cannery, Agricultural, Packing, and Allied Workers of America (UCAPAW) in September 1937. Having witnessed the Trotskyists infiltration and debilitation of Norman Thomas's Socialist Party, Kester, as well as Mitchell, sought to preserve STFU autonomy. This potentially explosive situation led to the expulsion of Claude Williams and E. B. McKinney from the STFU and to a break between the STFU and UCAPAWA in March 1939. Spurned by established labor, without great financial or numerical support, the STFU lost much of its vigor.

Kester for his part devoted himself to his position as secretary of the Fellowship of Southern Churchmen, which he found more grounded in Christianity. The organization coordinated southern relief, attempted to create a volunteer interracial army unit, and sought to dispel commonly held myths concerning lynching.

In 1942 Kester began his career as an educator, serving as principal at Penn School in Beaufort, South Carolina, the first Christian school founded during Reconstruction for blacks in the South. In 1948 he moved to the John C. Campbell Folk School and later he became a professor and dean at Montreat Anderson College in Black Mountain, North Carolina. His time as an educator was interrupted by a return, from 1952 to 1963, to the Fellowship of Southern Churchmen. On June 12, 1977, Howard Kester, the "'Gene Debs of Dixie," died.

See also: Christian Socialism; Mitchell, H. L.; Socialist Party; Southern Tenant Farmers Union

—*Orville Vernon Burton*

REFERENCES

Dunbar, Anthony P. *Against the Grain: Southern Radicals and Prophets 1929–1959*. Charlottesville: University Press of Virginia, 1981.

Mitchell, H. L. *Mean Things Happening in This Land*. Montclair: Allanheld Osmun, 1979.

KHRUSHCHEV REVELATIONS

From the mid-1930s to the mid-1950s American radicalism was dominated, in declining measure, by the Communist Party. At top strength, before the Nazi-Soviet Pact in mid-1939, the Party and its youth division numbered nearly 100,000. It had, as well, several hundred thousand sympathizers, and millions belonged to organizations with Communists among the leaders. All other radical groups combined then numbered a few thousand.

When the Cold War and the accompanying anticommunist hysteria hit high gear in 1948, Communist membership was still 60,000. But by early 1956, when Khrushchev delivered his secret report on Stalin's crimes to the Soviet's twentieth Communist Party Congress, membership had fallen to 20,000, a two-thirds drop. This, however, was still several times greater than any other socialist group. Khrushchev's revelations had their principal impact on this residual Party membership. It was a devastating one.

Two fundamental developments caused the decline in membership and influence: the anticommunist hysteria accompanying the Cold War, and the sectarian policies following replacement of Earl Browder with William Z. Foster as Party leader in 1945. The Party's postwar policies reinforced the isolation imposed upon it by the witch-hunts.

Persecution of Communists expanded rapidly with the arrest of Party leaders under the Smith Act in 1948, and membership began to drop steadily. Around 1953 Party activists began to reexamine the assumptions and policies that had mired it in isolation. The return, early in 1956, to active political life of the leaders jailed under the Smith Act in 1951 gave impetus to this reexamination process. And in April 1956 the first national committee meeting in five years discussed major new directions.

Khrushchev's secret report, delivered in February, was yet unknown to the Americans in April. A summary received from abroad was read to the national committee and the result was shock. These devoted Communists who had dedicated their lives for decades in pursuit of a better society, and had rejected as impossible the widespread reports of Stalin's dreadful brutalities, were now confronted with the truth from a source they could not question. At issue was not only Stalin's paranoia, but the nature of the system that had permitted it.

The immediate consequence was to intensify the internal struggle concerning the extent and direction of Party change. The revelations, by shifting the emphasis of debate to Stalin and the USSR, tended to undercut the independent overall self-examination that, it was hoped, would help to restore the Party's viability. While most leaders remained in the effort to seek change, a membership exodus did set in and those who left were among the supporters of change. Thus, while the Party convention in February 1957 approved sweeping changes, their advocates proved too powerless to make them stick, as members continued to depart in the face of the revelations and the Soviet invasion of Hungary in November 1956. By 1958, the Party was back in the grip of the sectarians. All others had left; the changes were reversed.

The New Left of the 1960s rose largely out of the void created by the essential disintegration of the CP. Many thousands of ex-Communists continued to function actively, however, in the peace, civil rights, labor, political, and other popular movements. Some joined democratic socialist organizations built in the 1970s, following the disintegration of the New Left. *See also*: Communist Party, *Daily Worker*

—*Max Gordon*

REFERENCES

Charney, George. *A Long Journey*. Chicago: Quadrangle, 1968.

Gordon, Max. "The Communists of the 1930s and the New Left." *Socialist Revolution* 6 (January–March 1976).

Nelson, Steve et al. *Steve Nelson, American Radical*. Pittsburgh: University of Pittsburgh Press, 1981.

Richmond, Al. *A Long View from the Left*. Boston: Beacon Press, 1973.

Starobin, Joseph. *American Communism in Crisis, 1943–1957*. Cambridge: Harvard University Press, 1972.

KING, CAROL WEISS (1895–1952)

Born into an affluent Jewish family headed by a man who organized one of the first corporation law firms in New York, King represented radicals throughout her career, keeping them out of jail and from being deported. One of her brothers founded Paul, Weiss, Rifkind, Wharton, which remains a leading, traditional New York firm. A tireless writer who conducted an extensive correspondence, gave innumerable speeches, and was frequently interviewed, King remained an elusive figure for political pigeon-holers. Her frequent defense of Communists led critics to label her a fellow traveler or, as the *Saturday Evening Post* of February 17, 1951, put it, "the Communist's dearest friend." King refused to respond to such Red-baiting. She would not put a corset on her ample figure or her broad mind. Among friends, she was known as an independent radical who saw her role as defending people of various political views, guided by her own convictions, and using her innumerable contacts across political lines to defend constitutional rights.

While attending Barnard College, she became interested in labor union problems through the influence of her history teacher, Juliet Stuart Poyntz. In 1916 she worked as a research fellow for the American Association for Labor Legislation. Feeling she could accomplish even more as an attorney, she entered New York University Law School and became one of the few female graduates in the class of 1920. Her first legal work was defending foreign-born workers who had been victims of the Palmer Raids.

In 1925 King set up a law firm in partnership with Communist Joseph Brodsky and anarchist Isaac Shorr, and from 1924 through 1931 she edited the ACLU *Law and Freedom Bulletin*. After author Gordon King, whom she had wed in 1917, died of pneumonia in 1930, she continued her numerous activities, propelled to an even quicker pace by the Depression and New Deal. One of her achievements was to persuade old family friends like Wall Street attorney Walter H. Pollak to work gratis on constitutional law cases. In 1932 she made a trip to Europe, visiting the USSR, which inspired her, and Germany, which horrified her. On her return to the United States, she started the *IJA* [International Judicial Association] *Bulletin* and was its moving force until 1942, when it merged with the *National Lawyers Guild Review*, published by another organization she helped to found.

Her association with Brodsky brought her into the International Labor Defense and work on the Scottsboro case. King also worked on hundreds of less well known cases. Her most famous client of the decade was Harry Bridges, who was threatened with deportation in 1938 for membership in the Communist Party. He won in his first hearing, based greatly on King's innovative use of expert testimony by university professors on Marxist theory, but he was rearrested and lost his second hearing. King orchestrated a reversal of the deportation order in the U.S. Supreme Court during World War II.

In 1942 King became general counsel for the American Committee for Protection of Foreign Born, a post she held until her death. That same year, her persuasive skills became evident to all when she was representing William Schneiderman, a CP leader whose citizenship the government sought to revoke. As part of the defense effort, King was able to convince Wendell Willkie, 1940 Republican presidential candidate, to represent Schneiderman in the Supreme Court. The case was won in 1943. Her greatest legal triumph came in 1950 when the Supreme Court accepted her theoretical positions and held that the Immigration and Naturalization Service had to obey the same rules as all other administrative agencies, halting all deportations until the service undertook reforms. Congress soon passed an exception for the service, and King returned to the courtrooms to slow down the deportations of thousands of political radicals born abroad. She seldom won, but few clients were actually deported.

King formed a new law partnership in 1948 with Blanche Freedman, a New York lawyer long active in the Women's Trade Union League. The following year King ran unsuccessfully for a municipal judgeship on the ticket of the American Labor Party. The New

York Bar Association rated her as qualified but could not resist questioning her "judicial temperament." In 1951 she made her first argument to the Supreme Court, and in January 1952 she died of cancer in New York City. *See also*: American Committee for the Protection of the Foreign Born, Communist Party, *IJA Bulletin*, International Labor Defense

—*Ann Fagan Ginger*

REFERENCES

Carol King Collection. Meiklejohn Civil Liberties Institute, Berkeley, California. (Including 1,450 pages of FBI files on King.

Ginger, Ann Fagan. Introduction index to *The International Juridical Association Bulletin* (1932–42), 3 vols. New York: De Capo Reprint Series, 1982.

King, Carol, and Walter Nelles. "Contempt by Publication." *Columbia Law Review*, 1928.

Bridges v. Wixon, 326 U.S. 135 (1945).

Schneiderman v. United States, 320 U.S. 118 (1943).

Wong Yang Sung v. McGrath, 339 U.S. 33 (1950).

KNIGHTS OF LABOR: see SOCIALIST LABOR PARTY

KONIKOW, ANTOINETTE BUCHOLZ (1869–1946)

Socialist orator and educator (in several languages), Konikow was a physician who fought for the right of women to have access to birth control. Born in Russia, she came to Boston to 1893 and immediately threw herself into unemployed organizing, learning Yiddish in order to work among immigrants.

Although a mother of two children, Konikow graduated with honors from Tufts University in 1902. She organized sex hygiene lectures for women and was arrested for exhibiting contraceptives.

In 1923 Konikow published a handbook for women, *Voluntary Motherhood*. Particularly concerned about educating physicians about their responsibility to women, she published her *Physicians' Manual of Birth Control* in 1931. Konikow also polemicized against population-control arguments, asserting that the right of women to control their bodies must be the basis for building a movement.

A delegate to the Socialist Labor Party's 1896 convention, she was expelled in 1897. Konikow helped found the Socialist Party, serving on its Woman's National Committee. Identifying with the Bolshevik Revolution, she participated in the 1919 underground convention that formed the Communist Party of the United States.

In 1928 Konikow opposed Trotsky's expulsion from the Communist International and once again found herself expelled. From that point until her death she was associated with Trotskyism. *See also*: Birth Control

—*Diane Feeley*

REFERENCES

Feeley, Diane. "Antoinette Konikow: Marxist and Feminist." *International Socialist Review* 33 (January 1972).

Gordon, Linda. *Woman's Body, Woman's Rights: A Social History of Birth Control in America*. New York: Grossman Publishers, 1976.

KRZYCKI, LEO: see AMERICAN SLAV CONGRESS

Labor Party

A vision or chimera of a "broad front" led by the Left, the hope for a "Labor Party" remained recurrently an issue and source of deep controversy from the early 1870s to the late 1980s.

During the First International phase of Marxist activity, the "Lassallean" wing, especially notable in Chicago, seized up the labor-party concept as means of reaching the masses. The "Workingmen's Party of Illinois," scarcely successful in electoral terms, became a medium for Chicago German-Americans to launch a local socialist press and begin the formation of socialist-led unions. In New York, political survivors of the anti-Marx faction threw themselves into the Industrial Workingman's Party mayoral campaign of 1874, and other local groups with socialist influence organized in Newark, Cincinnati, and Philadelphia. After the formal dissolution of the International, a brief flurry of electoral success in socialism's own name, and a general collapse of this effort, socialists supported the Greenback Labor Party of 1880, resulting in no success and bringing only political fragmentation upon themselves.

Nevertheless, socialists eagerly joined with local labor-party efforts in 1886–88, in many places posting real (if temporary) electoral advances and a working relationship with nonsocialist labor activists. Of these, the United Labor Party campaign by Henry George in New York was the most spectacular and one of the most successful. By the end of the decade, the movement had disintegrated and labor political activity mostly moved back into the two-party system. Bitterly disillusioned with this experience, socialists for the most part (with temporary exceptions, as in Illinois of the early 1890s) opted out of nonsocialist third-party experiments. Populism attracted, however, many who would become socialists by way of reform movements.

The formation of the Socialist Party in 1901 sealed this rejection of nonsocialist parties for a considerable period. Individual local or regional figures defected to labor party movements. But only once—in 1910–12, when the AFL seemed to approach an outright endorsement of a labor party—did prominent socialists (including A. M. Simons and Robert Hunter) suggest the option of sinking socialist support into a broader movement. Party loyalists, Eugene Debs included, opposed this policy as political betrayal. The subsequent rightward shift of the AFL ended the controversy. Only with the virtual collapse of the SP following the 1919 split did many socialists (acting as individuals) support a Farmer-Labor ticket, with erstwhile Cleveland socialist editor Max Hayes, as vice-presidential candidate.

During the 1920s, Communists reluctant to abandon their insurrection expectations were brought into line by Lenin and by Comintern representatives such as John Pepper (J. Pogeny), whose *For a Labor Party* (1922 and 1923) articulated a new official position. Yet this support for a prospective labor party remained abstract, as coalitions of labor reformers and radical intellectuals proved unable to create a new political movement. Only during 1934–36 did the labor party prospect once again look hopeful, as unionists disillusioned with Roosevelt passed many local resolutions calling for an independent labor ticket. In this interim, Communists and many independent radicals expressed great hopes for the labor party prospects ahead.

Roosevelt's deft engagement of reform issues in the 1936 campaign, and the enthusiasm of ethnic constituencies for him, doomed the labor party effort. Communist complicity—through support for the American Labor Party, an indirect support for Roosevelt and a mere half-step from the two-party system—seemed to end all serious prospects. Some observers, including Trotskyists, hoped that John L. Lewis, turning against Franklin Roosevelt's 1940 reelection bid, might lead a new labor party. Lewis supported Wendell Willkie instead. Thereafter, as Communists lobbied within the Democratic Party or attempted to create a transclass alternative (Henry Wallace's Progressive Party), discussion of a labor party became fanciful and remained, in sloganeering terms, largely to the Trotskyists.

By the 1970s–1980s, the discussion of a labor party had become an occasional warning by individual labor leaders to a Democratic Party jettisoning its New Deal commitments, with only a few seriously arguing the point. Tony Mazzochi, sometime high official and perennial influence within the Oil, Chemical, and Atomic Workers, has expressed this view the most forcefully. *See also*: American Labor Party, Communist Party, Farmer-Labor Parties, International Workingmen's Association, Socialist Labor Party

—*Paul Buhle*

REFERENCES

Bernstein, Samuel. *The First International in America*. New York: Augustus M. Kelley, 1962.

Kipnis, Ira. *The American Socialist Movement: 1897–1912*. New York: Columbia University Press, 1952.

Pepper, John. *For a Labor Party: Recent Revolutionary Changes in American Politics*. Chicago: Workers Party of America, 1923.

Labor Youth League: see

Young Communist League

Laidler, Harry W. (1884–1970)

Prolific author, founder and a leader of the League for Industrial Democracy for decades, Laidler epitomized the gradual and scientific strategy of socialization through economic planning.

Laidler, born into a comfortable Brooklyn family with liberal and socialist connections, graduated from Wesleyan University and took advanced degrees at Brooklyn Law School and Columbia University. He joined the Socialist Party in 1903, while attending the American Socialist College in Kansas, and took part in the founding of the Intercollegiate Socialist Society two years later. Named to the ISS executive to represent undergraduates, he became organizational secretary in 1910, and editor of its new *Intercollegiate Socialist* magazine in 1913 (and edited its successor, *Socialist Review*, from 1919 to 1921). With Laidler's leadership, the ISS engaged in a wide range of activities and converted many intellectuals—including Paul Douglas, later a U.S. senator; poet Babette Deutsch; and W. E. B. DuBois—to socialist ideals. The ISS lost many members to pro-war sympathies, and others to Bolshevik sympathies, in 1917–21. With its change of name to the League of Industrial Democracy, in 1921, Laidler became executive secretary, a position he would hold until 1957.

During the 1920s and, especially, the 1930s, Laidler successfully promoted the LID as American socialism's premier educational apparatus. A speakers' bureau, a considerable list of pamphlets, and Laidler's own works purveyed a rational socialist alternative to planless capitalism. In line with this effort, Laidler was president of the National Bureau of Economic Research, 1930–32 and 1948–49, and chair of its board of directors, 1932–34. Politically, Laidler was meanwhile quite active in socialist support for Robert LaFollette in 1924, and helped manage Norman Thomas's 1928 and 1932 presidential campaigns. His own electoral efforts—he was the SP's New York gubernatorial candidate in 1936 and senatorial candidate in 1938—climaxed in his election as American Labor Party nominee from Brooklyn to the New York City Council, where he served in 1940–41. He had become inactive in a splintered SP in 1938, although he retained his basic convictions.

Laidler would be remembered best, however, as durable functionary, as pamphleteer and scholarly author. His works included *Boycotts and the Labor Struggle* (1913), *The History of Socialist Thought* (1927), *Social-Economic Movements* (1944), and a nearly 1,000-page survey, *The History of Socialism* (1968). *See also*: American Labor Party, Intercollegiate Socialist Society, League for Industrial Democracy, Socialist Party

—*Harry Fleischman*

REFERENCES

Karnoustos, Carmela Ascolese. "Harry W. Laidler and the Intercollegiate Socialist Society." Ph.D. diss., New York University, 1974.

LARDNER, RING, JR. (b. 1915)

A leading Left talent in Hollywood's Screen Writers Guild, 1930s–1940s, Lardner might be considered the member of the "Hollywood Ten" whose revenge against political repression was most complete. In *M*A*S*H*, whose film script he wrote, and on which the television series was based, Lardner helped to launch one of the most popular of antiwar epics in American popular culture and to bridge the gap between the ideals of the Old Left and the sentiments of the New.

Son of the famous humorist and short story writer, Lardner went to work for David Selznick in 1935 at the age of twenty, and joined John Howard Lawson and others in the Left-led effort to organize a writers' union. He accumulated several important credits over the next few years, but broke through as coauthor of *Woman of the Year*, starring Katharine Hepburn. This arguably feminist drama, which allowed Hepburn to make speeches on woman's rights while costar Spencer Tracy cooked meals at home, also had a dark side that reminded some later critics of *M*A*S*H*. Lardner shared an Oscar in 1942 for his accomplishment.

Subpoenaed by the House Committee on Un-American Activities in 1947, he became one of the "Hollywood Ten," who, after declining to answer the committee's questions, were prosecuted for contempt of Congress and formally blacklisted by a resolution of the Motion Picture Producers' Association. When the Supreme Court decided in 1950 not to review their case and they went to various federal prisons, Lardner served more than nine months (one of his fellow inmates, convicted former congressman J. Parnell Thomas, had been one of his questioners). A decade later, in "My Life on the Blacklist," written for the *Saturday Evening Post*, he defended the right of free speech and association in the entertainment industry. He had, in fact, left the Communist Party in the early 1950s, but remained active in movements against political repression and continued writing for such Left publications as *Mainstream*. His first novel, *The Ecstasy of Owen Muir* (1954), and his memoir, *The Lardners: My Family Remembered* (1976), were critically well received.

*M*A*S*H* returned Lardner to the entertainment limelight and won him another screenwriting Oscar. A dark comedy about a U.S. medical team in the Korean War, it mixed humor with semidocumentary style and delivered a devastating blow to right-wing patriotism. Pauline Kael called it the "best American war comedy since sound" had been added to film. *M*A*S*H* owed its greatest popularity, however, to its political timeliness. Korea stood in for Vietnam, with the madness of the American presence in Southeast Asia presented clearly and forcefully. As television vehicle for Alan Alda, *M*A*S*H* became the most successful (i.e., sold in the most residual markets) series in the history of American television. *See also*: Hollywood Left, Popular Culture

—*Paul Buhle*

REFERENCES

Ceplair, Larry and Steven Englund. *The Inquisition in Hollywood*. Rev. ed. Berkeley: University of California Press, 1983.

Lardner, Ring, Jr. *The Lardners, My Family Remembered*. New York: Harper & Row, 1976.

LATIN AMERICAN STUDIES

Few scholarly fields have been as sensitive to political events as that of Latin American studies, and few have engendered so many activist scholars. Before the 1960s the study of Latin America in the United States was largely descriptive, and critical study was confined to journalistic approaches, particularly the work of John Reed, Carlton Beals, and Carey McWilliams. The revisionist approach to American foreign policy of William Appleman Williams was of major importance in providing a framework for the analyses of the region that were to be developed in the following decades.

Political interest in the region engendered by the Cuban Revolution gave rise to an increased demand for Latin American policy experts. This in turn stimulated interest in the field in the academic world and generated millions of dollars in foundation and government funding, which led to more dynamic scholars being attracted to it. C. Wright Mills, the leading radical academician of the period, wrote *Listen, Yankee*, a favorable account of the changes taking place in Cuba and a devastating attack on U.S. foreign policy in the hemisphere. The Cuban Revolution also inspired many young scholars to study revolutionary change in Latin America and to seek out their counterparts in Latin America in a period when the civil rights movement was bringing the rise of a radical movement within the United States.

A center for the study of the region had been developed in the 1950s at Stanford University, under the leadership of Spanish language professor Ronald Hilton. Students in the program were responsible for the publication of the monthly *Hispanic American Report*, which featured articles on current events in all the Latin American republics. Although the curriculum did not include theoretical components, much less leftist theoretical perspectives, the attention to the objective reality and the lack of bourgeois methodology imposed by social science disciplines, as well as the influence of Stanford's Marxist economist Paul Baran, attracted a number of students who came with or developed a Left perspective and who made substantial contributions to the ensuing development of radical scholarship on Latin America in the United States. These included Donald Bray, Ronald Chilcote, James Cockcroft, Timothy Harding, Dale Johnson, and Saul Landau, who worked in concert with James Petras and Susanne Jonas, both trained at the University of California at Berkeley.

The theoretical paradigm adopted during this period was dependency theory. This outlook was influenced by the work being done in Latin America by the United Nations Economic Commission for Latin America (ECLA or CEPAL), by the writings of several Brazilian scholars including Fernando Henrique Cardoso, by the thought of traditional Communists, and by the German scholar Andre Gunder Frank. A key work of this period was *Latin America: The Struggle with Dependency and Beyond* (1974), edited by Chilcote and Joel Edelstein, with an introduction by the editors and country studies written by Latin American and North American authors using a dependency framework with emphasis on political economy.

In 1966 the Latin American Studies Association was founded, reflecting the level of importance the field had achieved for academic professionals. At early meetings of the association the radical wing of its membership began successfully to introduce political resolutions critical of U.S. policy in the region. Politicization of all of the social sciences increased as a result of the protests and teach-ins generated by opposition to the Vietnam War. Ultimately, resolutions came to be approved routinely at LASA business meetings with the old guard failing to mount even token objections. The panels at meetings and LASA committees began to include Marxists, radical political economists, dependency theorists, and feminists. Within LASA a coalition of leftist Latin Americanist scholars, the Union of Radical Latin Americanists (URLA), was formed during the period of professional resistance to leftist activity. This group faded as participants' views became less opposed by the mainstream, and PLAN (Progressive Latin Americanist Network), a less explicitly radical coalition, was formed to support scholarship critical of U.S. foreign policy.

Meanwhile, the radicalism of the sixties was replaced by a more rigorous theoretical scholarship, both in Latin America and in the United States. This was stimulated in the United States by the development of the journal *Latin American Perspectives*, which began publishing in 1974. Edited by a collective of editors residing in southern California, with Chilcote as the managing editor and with U.S. and foreign editors who actively participated in the reviewing and editing of articles, this journal sought to be an anti-imperialist, nonsectarian forum for authors of many political persuasions. In its pages a critical assessment of dependency theory was undertaken and articles appeared interpreting Latin American reality from various leftist perspectives by authors from the United States, Latin America, and Europe.

Also during this period, many Latin Americanists, some influenced by Latin American intellectuals, became dissatisfied with the role of scholarly observers of social inequities and theorists of change, with praxis being limited to participation in demonstrations and teach-ins. They helped develop support groups for radical Latin American movements and made propagandistic films. Some began to participate in or organize political groups founded on Marxist-Leninist principles.

In the eighties the concern of North American researchers focused on the crisis in Central America and U.S. intervention there. In addition to participating in support groups, scholars formed the Guatemalan Scholars Network, the Faculty Committee on Human Rights in El Salvador (FACHRES, later FACHRES-CA), and the Central American Resource Center in Austin, Texas, to provide accurate information for public discussion. A LASA task force that observed the 1984 Nicaraguan elections attested to their fairness. A group of progressive scholars (PACCA: Policy Alternatives for the Caribbean and Central America) developed policy proposals as alternatives to the hegemony over policy-making assumed by the governmental establishment.

Thus, in the 1980s, radical Latin Americanist scholarship in the United States, although it was built on the foundation of critical anti-imperialist class analysis constructed in earlier decades, was characterized by a more pragmatic and policy-oriented approach than in the past. Theoretical approaches (for example, work on modes of production and theories of internationalization of capital), while more sophisticated than in the 1960s, were less deterministic. The international conjuncture in which capitalist production was becoming increasingly internationalized, Latin American economies were overwhelmed by impossible burdens of debt repayment, and traditional socialist economies were adopting mixed-economy strategies posed a challenge to North American leftist scholars to adapt to new realities in the radical study of Latin America. *See also*: North American Congress on Latin America

—*Marjorie Woodford Bray*

Latvian Americans

A small Baltic nationality group, Latvians briefly played an important role in the U.S. Left as ardent allies of Bolshevism and financial supporters of the earliest U.S. Leninists.

Latvia, like Lithuania and Estonia, was a buffer zone between major nations. Industrialization and modernization took place in the late nineteenth and early twentieth century only in selected urban districts. Emigration to the United States centered in a very few locations, especially Greater Boston, with immigrants working mostly in light manufacturing.

Like several other immigrant socialist groups, Latvians were organized at first in the United States as a branch of the homeland party. Affiliating with the Socialist Party in 1908, they maintained close European ties. In the Latvian party, the Right had been historically weak, due largely to the difficulty of reforms and of gradual labor improvements. The dominant Left, linked more closely to Lenin than any other national party faction, early on looked to the Bolsheviks for leadership in search of socialism and national independence.

Centered in Boston, the Latvian (or "Lettish," after the German geographical designation of "Lettland") federation claimed 1,600 members by 1915. Its leader, Fricis Rozins, had been a pioneer of Lettish socialism, escapee from Siberia and close ally of Lenin. Rozins edited the federation organ *Stradneeks* (Worker) and finessed a brief takeover of the Massachusetts SP (weak since the early years of the twentieth century) by the Left in 1913–14.

As a result of defeat at the 1915 state convention, the Latvians established an English-language outlet, the Socialist Propaganda League (SPL), whose manifesto boasted the names of long-standing Left-socialists and aimed at capture of the party for the Left.

In the furious factionalism of the next few years, the Latvians and the SPL frequently took the lead in espousing an ultraorthodox Leninism, as understood at the time. Letts sponsored the rise of Louis C. Fraina as a proto-Bolshevik intellectual, and the SPL put forward a campaign to recruit Americans for the armed forces in Russia (although unable to do so over U.S. State Department opposition). The *Revolutionary Age* (1918–19), for a short period the premier English-language Bolshevik organ in America, was published in Boston with Lettish financial backing. In the breakup of the SP, the Latvian along with the Russian Federation and others supported withdrawal from the SP, into a formal Communist Party (rather than awaiting expulsion, for tactical reasons).

Factionalism and repression did not greatly diminish the Lettish following, but in the open Communist movement that emerged in the 1920s, they ceased to play a central role. *Stradneeks,* edited by John Knudsin and Boston-area supporters, nevertheless remained an important source of support for the Massachusetts Left for decades. The successor organ, *American-Latvian,* edited by Edward Maurin, closed its doors only in the 1980s, after Maurin's death. *See also*: Communist Party; Fraina, Louis C./ Lewis Corey

—*Paul Buhle*

REFERENCES

Draper, Theodore. *Roots of American Communism.* New York: Viking, 1957.

Additional information supplied by Anne Burlak Timpson.

Lawrence Strike

Few people anticipated that the operatives in the numerous textile mills that filled Lawrence, Massachusetts, would strike when mill owners instituted a wage cut in January 1912. The working class in the city was composed of at least twenty-five (and estimates go as high as forty) different nationalities; these workers were mostly unskilled and had been beaten down by years of poverty and poor living conditions. But when 3,500 Italian and Jewish operatives, mostly women, marched out of Everett Mill to protest the wage cut, workers in the other mills quickly followed. By January 13 there were 25,000 mill workers out on strike, among them Italians, Jews, Germans, French Canadians, Poles, Lithuanians, Franco-Belgians, Syrians, Greeks, Letts (Latvians) and Turks.

Thus began the strike for "Bread and Roses." The strikers' demands quickly extended beyond restoration of their original wages. At a meeting on January 14, they established demands for a 15 percent wage increase; a fifty-four-hour work week; abolition of the premium and bonus systems; double pay for overtime; and no discrimination against those who struck.

Several factors worked to keep this diverse group of strikers together. As historian Ardis Cameron has pointed out, working-class women in Lawrence had established solid family and community networks that provided an enormously important foundation for the strikers. Women who had befriended each other across ethnic lines before the strike joined together on the picket lines and at the "local centers of female activity" such as kitchens, stoops, and grocery stores to fight for their rights. The strikers were also drawn together by shared symbols such as the ever-present American flag and a wide range of songs they sang regularly. They sang standard songs of solidarity such as "The Marseillaise" and composed their own songs—"In the Good Old Picket Line," for example, mentioned several different ethnic groups, either praising them for their steadfastness or goading them for their lack of class loyalty. The strikers also participated in numerous parades, which allowed them to witness their own strength in a festive setting.

The solidarity of the strikers would not have been what it was, however, were it not for the presence of the Industrial Workers of the World. The strike at Lawrence, to which the IWW sent representatives almost immediately, constituted the radical union's greatest success on the East Coast. In conducting the strike IWW organizers were wonderfully innovative. Joseph Ettor and Arturo Giovannitti established a strike committee composed of two delegates each from twenty-seven different ethnic groups. This ensured the democratic nature of the strike. The frequent parades were organized under IWW auspices. IWW organizers also instituted the moving picket line (to circumvent a court injunction) and the "children's exodus," which sent many of the strikers' children to sympathizers in New York, Philadelphia, and other East Coast cities. Both tactics were unprecedented in American working-class history. These impressive organizing efforts clearly worried unsympathetic city officials. Ettor and Giovannitti were arrested on a trumped-up murder charge. Their places were taken, however, by IWW leaders Big Bill Haywood and Elizabeth Gurley Flynn, who carried on the struggle ably.

The IWW and the strikers faced many opponents: a brutal police force that attacked men, women, and children picketers alike; judges who handed out injunctions and stiff sentences liberally; church leaders, the majority of whom spoke out against the strike and the strikers; the militia, whose presence turned Lawrence into an armed camp. The AFL also voiced its bitter opposition to the strike. John Golden, president of the AFL-affiliated United Textile Workers, declared angrily, "This is a revolution, not a strike."

The strikers held strong in the face of this opposition, however, and the mill owners were forced to settle late in February. The strikers won wage hikes of 5 to 22 percent (those paid the least receiving the greatest increase); time and a quarter for overtime; premium payments every two weeks rather than once a month; and an agreement that the owners would not discriminate against them. The victory was an enormous achievement—Eugene Debs called it "the most decisive and far-reaching ever won by organized workers." Moreover, concerned textile mill owners all over the East Coast reacted fearfully to the events in Lawrence. By April 1, an estimated 275,000 textile workers in New England had received pay increases. The IWW and Lawrence workers continued to press for the release of the still-imprisoned Ettor and Giovannitti. On September 27, 10,000 workers again filled the streets to protest the unjust treatment of the strike leaders. On November 25 both were acquitted.

Although the organization established in Lawrence could not sustain itself—union membership fell sharply shortly after the strike—there is no question that the tactics of the IWW and the tremendous unity of the diverse, largely unskilled working population constituted a landmark in American working-class history. *See also*: Flynn, Elizabeth Gurley; Giovannitti, Arturo; Haywood, William D.; Industrial Workers of the World; Tresca, Carlo

—*Michael Topp*

REFERENCES

Cameron, Ardis. "Bread and Roses Revisited: Women's Culture and Working-Class Activism in the Lawrence Strike of 1912." In *Women's Work and Protest: A Century of U.S. Women's Labor History*, edited by Ruth Milkman. New York: Routledge and Kegan Paul, 1985.

Flynn, Elizabeth Gurley. *The Rebel Girl, An Autobiography: My First Life* (1906–26). New York: International Publishers, 1955.

Foner, Philip S. *The Industrial Workers of the World, 1905–1917*. New York: International Publishers, 1965.

Lawson, John Howard (1894–1977)

Playwright, screenwriter, and theorist, Lawson was one of the dominant figures in the radical art scene associated with the Communist movement. A third-generation American of Jewish background, Lawson was born in New York City into an affluent, progressive household. As a young boy, Lawson went on tours to Europe and Canada and across the

United States. He had resolved to become a playwright by age twelve and entered Williams College at fifteen, the youngest member of his class. By the end of his sophomore year, he had published more than twenty articles in the college literary magazine. He sold his first play, *Standards,* to producers Sam Harris and George M. Cohan in 1915. The next year, he wrote four plays, one of which, *Servant-Master-Lover,* he sold to Oliver Morosco. Lawson seemed poised to become the first serious American-born playwright.

The First World War interrupted his writing. En route to serve with the American Red Cross, he met John Dos Passos, also a volunteer. The friendship proved to be central to Lawson. Staying on in Paris after the war with other artists of his generation, Lawson wrote *Roger Bloomer,* the first expressionist play of the American theater. Also the first of his works to be produced, it ran for two years. In 1925 his play *Processional* ran for ninety-six performances.

Lawson had meanwhile become a Communist and was elected to the national executive committee of the Proletarian Artists and Writers League. He joined with Dos Passos, Mike Gold and others to form the New Playwrights Theater. Its purpose, Lawson explained, was to present "mass plays done for workers at prices that workers can afford." Likewise dedicated to theatrical experimentation, the New Playwrights Theater produced Lawson's *Loudspeaker* (1927) and *The International* (1928) before dissolving later that year.

By 1930–31, Lawson had begun writing for the movies, completing five scripts for RKO, one of which, *Bachelor Apartment,* was produced. His play *Success Story* (later adapted for the screen as *Success at Any Price*) was produced in 1932 in New York. Two more plays, *Gentlewoman* and *The Pure at Heart,* opened in 1934. During the same period, Lawson helped organize the Screen Actors Guild, and in 1933 was elected its first president. Active in the Scottsboro case, he was twice arrested in Alabama, and served as a member of the National Committee for the Defense of Political Prisoners. In 1936 Lawson published his first book, *Theory and Technique of Playwrighting,* which elaborated his desire to explore and expand the formal possibilities of the genre.

His political work began to take a severe toll on his artistic acceptance. In 1937, *Processional* was revived by the Federal Theater Project, and the Group Theater produced *Marching Song,* but these were the last of his plays to be produced in his lifetime. Writing for a time quite successfully for the movies, Lawson saw six of his scripts produced between 1938 and 1943: *Blockade* (1938), *Algiers* (1938), *They Shall Have Music* (1939), *Four Sons* (1940), *Sahara* (1943), and *Action in the North Atlantic* (1943). Despite his apparent respectability, as early as 1944 the Tenney Committee of California targeted Lawson and his activities—in particular his active role in the Writers Congress held in 1943 at UCLA—for investigation.

Lawson suddenly faced criticism on all sides. Against Albert Maltz, who in 1946 argued in the *New Masses* that art had to be evaluated independently of political line, Lawson insisted on the Marxist concept of art as a form of social criticism that did not transcend the environment that creates the artist. Those Hollywood activists and others hoping for a more liberal interpretation of strategic theory in the Communist milieu looked upon Lawson as an aesthetic hard-liner. Only a year after *Cosmopolitan* gave Lawson an award for his cinematic contributions to the war effort, he faced indictment as a member of the "Hollywood Ten." His final film, *Smashup* (1947), produced before the blacklisting went into effect, barely preceded a 1948 conviction on contempt of Congress charges and a one-year jail term (he shared a cell with Dalton Trumbo) beginning in 1950. That year, he finished a book, *The Hidden Heritage,* wrote a never-to-be-produced play, *In Praise of Learning,* edited the prison newspaper, and under a pseudonym penned a movie script for Alan Paton's antiapartheid classic, *Cry, the Beloved Country.*

Released from prison but unable to write for films under his own name, Lawson entered into a secret agreement with Edward Lewis for work to appear under Lewis's name. Under such pen names as James Howard and James Christopher, Lawson completed scripts for a number of films, including *The Careless Years* (1957) and *Terror in a Texas Town* (1957). Lawson also continued to write critical works—*Film in the Battle of Ideas* (1953) and *Film: The Creative Process* (1964)—while lecturing on play- and screenwriting, until his death. He continued to insist that form as well as content be the concern of the committed playwright. *See also*: Hollywood Blacklist; Lardner, Ring, Jr.

—*Norma Jenckes*

REFERENCES

Brown, Richard Peyron. "John Howard Lawson as an Activist Playwright, 1923–1937." Ph.D. diss., Tulane University, 1964.

Ceplair, Larry, and Steven England. *The Inquisition in Hollywood, Politics in the Film Community, 1930–1960*. Rev. ed. Berkeley: University of California Press, 1983.

John Howard Lawson Archive, Morris Library, Southern Illinois University.

Lawson, John Howard. "Organizing the Screen Writers Guild." In *The Cineaste Interviews*, edited by Dan Georgakas and Leonard Rubenstein. Chicago: Lake View Press, 1983.

Leacock, Eleanor Burke (1922–87)

Anthropologist and social activist, Leacock documented the political and economic sources of class, gender, and racial oppression. Leacock authored more than eighty articles and ten books and was internationally respected for her scholarship on Marxist social theory. Her writings on race and class, gender, colonialism, and capitalist development informed a tireless political engagement.

Leacock's 1952 doctoral thesis challenged the prevailing contention that private property was universal. *The Montagnais-Naskapi "Hunting Territory" and the Fur Trade* (1954) analyzed the impact of commodity production on property and labor relations in a foraging society. After eleven years of part-time teaching, and work on the Bank Street School Project, Leacock finally obtained a full-time teaching position at Brooklyn Polytechnic Institute. While there she wrote a critical appreciation of Lewis Henry Morgan concerning egalitarian societies and cultural evolution (1963); numerous articles on race and class stratification in education, as well as *Teaching and Learning in City Schools* (1969); and *Culture of Poverty: A Critique* (1971). In 1972 she was asked to revamp and chair the department of anthropology at City College/CUNY, where she remained until her death while conducting field research in Samoa on capitalist development and teenage suicide.

Leacock was pivotal in the reemergence of the women's movement, and in the development of Marxist feminism and feminist anthropology, beginning with her edition of Engels's *The Origin of the Family, Private Property and the State* (1972). A selection of her essays on ideologies of gender and theories of women's subordination appeared as *Myths of Male Dominance* (1981).

In the 1980s Leacock coedited a series of anthologies: on colonialism and women's status (*Women and Colonization*, 1980), on foraging peoples' resistance to stratification (*Politics and History in Band Societies*, 1982), and on capitalist development and gender (*Women's Work*, 1986). Her purpose in research and writing was human emancipation, and she brought to that endeavor formidable scholarship, insight, and courage. *See also*: Anthropology; Morgan, Lewis Henry

—*Christine Ward Gailey*

REFERENCES

Gailey, Christine Ward. "Eleanor Burke Leacock." In *Women Anthropologists*, edited by Ute Gacs, Jerrie McIntyre et al. Westport: Greenwood Press, 1988.

League of Revolutionary Black Workers

The LRBW was the only Black Power organization of the 1960s to place its major focus on organizing industrial workers while positing a socialist solution to the problems of black America. Although never gaining the kind of mass media exposure given to the Black Panther Party, the League had an enormous impact on black revolutionaries and on Marxist tendencies within the New Left. The League also made contact with extraparliamentary groups in Europe, particularly in Italy. The LRBW strove to take the movements previously identified with the leadership of the Rev. Martin Luther King, Jr., and Malcolm X to a new stage of organization and consciousness. Its history also provides an example of how the black revolutionaries of the 1960s often had links to preceding radical movements.

The LRBW originated in a wildcat strike of black workers in May 1968 at the Detroit Dodge main plant of the Chrysler Corporation. The strike was the first in fourteen years and black radicals were its organizational core. Coming a year after the most extensive and costly radical insurrection in American history, the wildcat was a front-page story in the *Wall Street Journal* and was given extensive coverage in the Detroit press. The wildcatters formed an organization called DRUM (Dodge Revolutionary Union Movement), which expressed as much hostility toward the United Auto Workers (UAW) as to the company. By their actions the DRUM workers indicated they were unwilling to wait for white workers to ally with them and they would not dilute their demands for racial justice for the sake of hypothetical white support.

The anger that erupted at Dodge Main was symptomatic of the frustration felt by Detroit's entire black working class. A series of RUMs were formed in various workplaces. Most were at auto plants (ELRUM: Chrysler's Eldon Avenue Gear and Axle; FRUM: Ford's River Rouge complex; CADRUM: GM's Cadillac plant) but there were nonauto RUMs as well, such as those organized by United Parcel workers and health workers. RUM-like groups also began to appear in other cities, at steel mills in Birmingham, Alabama, and at auto plants in Baltimore, Maryland; Fremont, California; and Mahwah, New Jersey. The Detroit RUMs consolidated into the LRBW with the goal of first organizing the black workers of Detroit and then the black workers of the entire United States.

Although the League appeared to be a by-product of the "Great Rebellion" of 1967 to outsiders, it reflected more than a decade of agitation and education. The black radicals who came of political age in the 1950s had much more of a Marxist orientation than activists in the South and most other northern cities. This was due in part to a vibrant Detroit radicalism that had centered around the Communist Party, black cultural groups, and Trotskyist publishing groups with roots in the Workers Party of the 1940s. Rather than accepting the nonviolent-resistance strategy of King, the Detroit radicals tended to be supportive of the methods of the Chinese and Cuban revolutions. When Robert Williams, head of the NAACP chapter in Monroe, North Carolina, clashed with King over the need for armed self-defense, a Detroit group in support of Williams was formed. The supersecret Revolutionary Action Movement also had Detroit adherents.

Black radicals had been influenced by the Socialist Workers Party's Friday Night Forums; by study groups run by Marty Glaberman of Facing Reality, a local C. L. R. James support group; and by close contact with James Boggs, whose *The American Revolution: Pages from a Negro Worker's Notebook* (Monthly Review Press, 1963) attracted national attention. A group that joined the Student Nonviolent Coordinating Committee was expelled for wishing to do more than fundraising in the North. Radicals were also involved in the Northern High School student strike, Uhuruh (a Detroit action group), and the Freedom Now Party, an all-black political party that achieved ballot status in Michigan. Future League leaders participated in a 1964 trip to Cuba designed to challenge the State Department ban on travel to the island and met with Che Guevara when he appeared at the United Nations. There were also contacts with supporters of Malcolm X and various radical writers and graphic artists from an older generation of militants. Many of the activists took college classes at Wayne State University, but they worked in basic industry to support themselves.

Acting on Lenin's injunction to create a political press, the Detroiters launched the *Inner City Voice* in 1967 with John Watson as editor. The *ICV* was well received but became irregular due to the refusal of various printers to handle such radical material. The paper had to be produced in a Muslim shop in Chicago and trucked back to Detroit. To overcome this problem, a group of Wayne-based radicals organized to have Watson elected the first black editor of the *South End*, the university's daily paper. Arguing that the paper was a community resource, Watson often put its pages at the disposal of various RUMs throughout the 1968–69 academic year. Other radical groups were also welcomed to use the *South End*. Under Watson's editorship, there was considerable agitation against the war in Vietnam, a series of articles supportive of the Palestine Liberation Organization, and a special issue criticizing the military junta in Greece from a Left perspective.

Among the radicals in the plants, the most important was General Baker. ("General" is a given name, not a rank.) Baker had been known for his revolutionary views for years, but following the Great Rebellion of 1967, he began to attract a mass following. Also playing a crucial role in creating the first RUMs in Detroit factories was Mike Hamlin. Yet another major League personality was attorney Ken Cockrel. With his white law partner, Justin Ravitz, Cockrel won a number of celebrated cases with sensationalistic racial and class aspects. He was well known throughout the city for his efforts to curb police abuses, and he often served as the public spokesperson for the League. Unlike other black organizations, the League never had to go outside its own leadership for legal defense.

One problem the organization never resolved was an exact self-definition. The founders knew what the LRBW was not. It was not a political party. It was not a caucus within the UAW. It was not an independent union. In many ways the League was like a latter-day Industrial Workers of the World, an organization willing to address immediate issues in a militant and winning fashion but with its true passion a total transformation of capitalist society.

Tactical problems stemmed directly from the vague self-definition. Should a RUM attempt to capture the UAW local or should it operate as a dual union? Should nonindustrial issues become part of the immediate agenda? RUMs were limited to nonwhites, but how should cooperating whites be handled? This last issue was complicated by the fact that many black workers attracted to the League had intense nationalist feelings. Various solutions were posed at various times at different RUMs, but the League did not survive long enough to have a consistent policy. Thousands of workers would respond to League calls, but contradictory policies and impractical methods ultimately undermined the organization's momentum. Formal membership never ran to more than a few hundred.

The fate of the League was determined in 1969 when James Foreman, a major leader of SNCC, became associated with it. Foreman wanted the League to be transformed into a national organization with various components dealing with the full range of black community needs. In this sense Foreman set out to remold the League as the successor of SNCC just as Stokley Carmichael sought to remold the Black Panther Party to the same end.

Foreman's immediate project was the Black Economic Development Conference, which demanded $500,000,000 in reparations from religious institutions to fund long-term black economic self-sufficiency. BEDC was not to be an independent organization but a conduit to action groups in the field. Foreman was partially successful and approximately $1 million passed through BEDC. Most of this sum was channeled to groups around the country with Foreman connections. A significant amount went to the components and allies of the League.

BEDC money made it possible for the League to have a modestly paid staff and to finance its own printing shop, film company, and bookstore. The goal of the printing component, Black Star Publishing, was to establish a newspaper and to create educational materials without being held hostage to the whims of outside printers. Black Star published a number of leaflets and posters and one book, *The Political Thought of James Foreman* (1970).

The example of the League led other Detroit radicals to form the Motor City Labor League (MCLL), a mostly white organization with independent socialist goals but one supportive of and cooperative with the LRBW. Its most successful undertaking was a radical book club that involved hundreds of Detroiters who met to discuss a series of highly political books. LRBW members worked with the book club. Two radical bookstores and a second radical book club were among the MCLL's longer-term legacies.

Detroit Newsreel was established by whites who came from New York City to make a film about the League. After a volatile relationship, the League took over the film collective as its own and retained three of the white filmmakers as creative and teaching staff. The final product of this effort was *Finally Got the News* (1970), a feature-length documentary designed to spread League views nationwide. Its political impact was lessened by the circumstance that it was released just as the League was going into schism. The film did get shown extensively over the years and was also screened in Europe. It remains a remarkable expression of the times and the one black radical film under editorial control of the organization it endeavored to celebrate. Black Star Productions tried to work with Jane Fonda and other Hollywood personalities on successor films, but the efforts never bore cinematic fruit.

Two factions had developed in the League by early 1970. One, composed mainly of the plant organizers, wanted to concentrate on industrial organization and to solidify the local base. The other, largely involved in outreach and mass education, felt the League could only advance by expanding. The dispute was fed by personal jealousies, the impact of black nationalism at the factory level, and outside radical forces who came to a Detroit they now spoke of as the American Petrograd. Watson, Cockrel, and Hamlin led the League faction that allied with Foreman for a national strategy. Their vehicle was to be the Black Workers Congress (BWC), originally conceived with the League as its central hub. For most of the 1970s the BWC would seek to re-create League-type structures in various localities. It would work closely with Asian and Latino groups with a similar orientation and with Maoists who wished to build a new Marxist-Leninist party. The BWC was never able to become a viable entity and it expired with the collapse of Maoism and the new party movement.

The group that retained the League name was led by General Baker, Chuck Wooten, John Williams, and Luke Tripp. They never affiliated with the BWC and in spite of continued plant actions, the League more or less disintegrated. Contributing to the decline was the defection of some RUM leaders back to the UAW and the activities of the Communist Labor Party, which had originated as a split from the CP and prided itself on its adherence to a pre-Khrushchev style of Communism. The CLP recruited a block of League cadre. The most prominent of these was General Baker, who would later run unsuccessfully for state office under the CLP banner. A split within the MCLL brought additional members into the CLP camp. These included individuals active in the local National Lawyers Guild. The CLP kept most of its membership secret so any influence it might have in the plants was not easily determined. The organization also worked to establish radical bookstores in major cities, but the CLP link was not acknowledged.

The BWC forces soon suffered a split within the split. Cockrel, allied with elements of the MCLL that had not gravitated to the CLP, decided it was wisest to work in the arena of electoral politics. Justin Ravitz ran successfully for a ten-year judgeship in the criminal court (1972) as part of an effort to reform the judiciary and control the police. Two years later Coleman Young was elected Detroit's first black mayor. Like Judge George Crockett (soon to be elected to Congress), Young was from an older generation that had been victimized by McCarthyism. Although his administration was highly supportive of business, Young hired a number of radicals to work in his administration, including some League personnel. He soon established himself as an unbeatable incumbent. Cockrel, who had mayoral ambitions of his own, had to settle for a seat on Detroit's Common Council some years later and eventually chose to go back into private practice. When Cockrel died of a heart attack in 1989 at age fifty-one, the press and elected officials spoke of him as one of the city's most gifted citizens and the man who had been most likely to succeed Coleman Young.

By the late 1980s the League was another chapter in local radical and black history, but more so than in any other major city, many of its activists and allies had achieved a measure of political power without renouncing their radical views. They could be found in the mass media, in the UAW hierarchy, in university administrations, and in public office. The general assumption was that should another wave of rebellion arise, they would be able and willing to help. *See also*: Armed Struggle; Antirevisionism; Civil Rights Movement; James, C. L. R.; Student Nonviolent Coordinating Committee; Workers Party

—*Dan Georgakas*

REFERENCES

Allen, Ernie. "Dying from the Inside: The Decline of the League of Revolutionary Black Workers." In *They Should Have Served That Cup of Coffee*, edited by Dick Cluster. Boston: South End Press, 1979.

Archives of the League of Revolutionary Black Workers. In materials deposited by Dan Georgakas at Reuther Library, Wayne State University, Detroit, Michigan.

Detroit Under Stress. A pamphlet of the From the Ground Up organization, Detroit, 1973.

Georgakas, Dan, and Marvin Surkin. *Detroit: I Do Mind Dying*. New York: St. Martin's Press, 1975.

League of Struggle for Negro Rights: see National Negro Congress

Lehr- und Wehrvereine (Educational and Defense Societies)

The armed workers' societies of the 1870s–1880s typified the boldness of contemporary radical immigrant efforts, and stirred pride among militant workers while provoking fear and hatred among conservatives and business leaders.

As early as 1875, a *Lehr- und Wehrverein* had been formed in Chicago, in response to the excessive violence of the state militia during the wave of strikes in 1873. Continuing brutal treatment of workers by police and militia during the national railroad strike of 1877 spurred the growth of these societies of armed workers in several cities, especially Chicago. Their stated goals were to preserve the constitutional rights of freedom of the press, speech, assembly, and the right to bear arms. In this sense, such groups "educated" their members about the right to class self-defense. Historic links can be traced to the *Turner* tradition, to the Swiss defense league *Hilf Dir*—a militarized association established during the 1860s to found a German republic—and to the ethnic militia units that had fought in the Civil War. The movement spread primarily among German Americans: beyond Chicago, after 1884, there were armed groups in Detroit, Cincinnati, St. Louis (two), Omaha, Newark, New York (two), San Francisco, Denver, and other cities. These groups numbered from less than 20 members to more than 400 in Chicago.

When these armed societies first sprang up, most German-American members of the Socialist Labor Party appeared to believe them necessary to defend workers' constitutional rights and to counterbalance the so-called citizens' militias, which enlisted few workers. Soon, however, the SLP national executive committee began to distance itself from what it considered the confrontational, extremist tactics of the armed organizations. In late 1878 it ordered party members to withdraw from them. The effect of this decree, along with a general disillusionment with electoral politics, caused many individual members and some entire sections of the SLP, especially notable in Chicago, to withdraw from the organization. Until the Haymarket Affair, members of the German and Bohemian *Lehr- und Wehrverein* marched regularly in Chicago socialist demonstrations. Adverse court action, antianarchist hysteria, and a state militia bill put an effective end to this form of organization. *See also*: Anarchism, Black International, German Americans, Socialist Labor Party

—*Christine Hess, Carol Poore*

REFERENCES

Hess, Christine. "German Radicals in Industrial America: The Lehr- und Wehrverein in Gilded Age Chicago." In *German Workers in Industrial Chicago: A Comparative Perspective*, edited by Hartmut Keil and John B. Jentz. DeKalb: Northern Illinois University Press, 1983.

Lens, Sidney (1912–86)

For five and a half decades, Lens was active as a labor organizer, writer, and peace agitator. Born Sidney Okun in Newark, New Jersey, Lens changed his surname in the mid-1930s when he was blacklisted for union activity. The only child of Russian-Jewish immigrants, Lens was three when his pharmacist father died and his mother entered New York City's garment-district sweatshops to support herself and her son.

After graduation from high school at age seventeen, Lens worked as a waiter at an Adirondack resort. In the summer of 1930 he led a strike of fellow waiters and, as a result, was dragged from his bed one night, beaten, and abandoned in the woods by the local sheriff and his deputies. This launched Lens upon his career as a labor organizer. During the Depression he helped organize advertising writers at New York's Hecht Bros., sit-down strikers for the United Auto Workers in Detroit, and cab drivers in Washington, D.C.

In 1934 he joined James P. Cannon's Communist League of America, a precursor of the Socialist Workers Party. Soon thereafter, the League merged with pacifist and labor agitator A. J. Muste's American Workers Party to form the Workers Party of the United States. Deeply influenced by the pacifism of Muste, Lens nevertheless remained active in Trotskyist groups such as the Revolutionary Workers League, which he joined in 1936. After the 1930s, however, he became a largely unaffiliated radical who felt a new socialist party had to be created with labor as its core. To this end he encouraged various third-party efforts for the rest of his life, including Dr. Benjamin Spock's People's Party in the early 1970s and Barry Commoner's Citizens Party in the early 1980s. He was a member of both.

In 1941 Lens successfully organized waiters and retail clerks into Local 329 of the United Services Employees Union (CIO) in Chicago, ridding the union of old Capone mob influence in the process. He became the local's director in 1942 and, until his retirement in 1966, Local 329 remained his base of operations. In 1946 he took Local 329 into the AFL's Building Services Employees International Union to counter isolation from the mainstream of the labor movement.

In 1949 Lens published *Left, Right, and Center: Conflicting Forces in American Labor*, which examined the failures of "business unionism" and which was the first of his twenty books. Other major books included *The Counterfeit Revolution* in 1952, which analyzed the strengths and weaknesses of Stalinism; *Radicalism in America* in 1966, a history of radicalism from before the Revolution to the '60s; *The Military-Industrial Complex* in 1970; *Poverty, Yesterday and Today* and *The Promise and Pitfalls of Revolution* in 1974; and *Unrepentant Radical*, a 1980 autobiography.

In the 1950s Lens helped found the journals *Dissent* with Irving Howe and *Liberation* with A. J. Muste. At the same time he began contributing regularly to the *Progressive* and became a contributing editor of the magazine in the late 1960s. In 1978 Lens was named senior editor of the journal, a position he held until his death.

Lens opposed America's entry into World War II, viewing it as an imperialist conflict, and for the rest of his life he attempted to combine labor organizing with agitation for peace. In 1960 he was a cofounder of the Fair Play for Cuba Committee and soon thereafter became a leader in the anti–Vietnam War movement. In 1962 he was an unsuccessful peace candidate for Congress and in 1980 he ran unsuccessfully for the U.S. Senate. During the 1960s he was cochair of the New Mobilization Committee to End the War in Vietnam, and in 1976 he became a founder of Mobilization for Survival, an antinuclear peace organization. Lens remained active as a respected leader of Left and peace groups until his death, helping to organize New York's first Conference on Socialism and Activism, in 1985. *See also*: Peace Movements, Trotskyism.

—*Eric Leif Davin*

REFERENCES

Lens, Sidney. *Unrepentant Radical*. Boston: Beacon Press, 1980.

Le Sueur, Meridel (b. 1900)

A champion of women and the working class, Le Sueur is a prominent Midwest poet, journalist, short story writer, novelist, historian, and poet laureate of St. Paul, Minnesota. She was born in Murray, Iowa. Her parents were suffragist Marian Wharton, creator of the "Little Blue Books," and Arthur Le Sueur, former Socialist mayor of Minot, North Dakota.

After dropping out of high school, Le Sueur acted on the New York stage and lived there in an anarchist commune with Emma Goldman and Alexander Berkman. She left for Hollywood, where she worked briefly as a stunt woman in silent films. During World War I and the Palmer Raids, Le Sueur witnessed attacks on her parents and on other radicals. She was jailed in 1927 for protesting the executions of Sacco and Vanzetti.

After an early period of writing in the 1920s characterized by themes of sexual awakening and influenced by D. H. Lawrence, Le Sueur emerged as a major proletarian writer in the 1930s. She embraced a creative and political role as "voice, messenger, and awakener" of the oppressed, particularly women. She wrote for the *New Masses* and the *Daily Worker*, reporting on unemployment, breadlines, strikes, and the plight of farmers. Le Sueur became a Communist Party organizer, taught in the Writers Project of the Works Progress Administration, and helped to establish flourishing literary networks through the John Reed clubs and the American Writers Congress. In 1940 she published her best-known anthology of stories, *Salute to Spring*. At this time she also wrote *The Girl* (1978), a novel based on her life among destitute women during the Great Depression, and *North Star Country* (1945), a unique fusion of folklore and history about the Midwest.

With the advent of the Cold War and the McCarthy witch-hunts, Le Sueur, though a prominent literary figure, was excommunicated from the publishing world, hounded and driven out of jobs by the FBI. She remained creatively active "underground," sustained during this dark time by her identification with the collective suffering of women.

Recognition returned for Le Sueur with the resurgence of political activism and the rebirth of the feminist movement in the late 1960s. Many of her writings, long out of print, were reissued and hailed by younger generations who recognized an early champion of the poor and of the "anonymous" woman. Her work derives optimism from her faith in the nurturing potential embodied in women and a belief in the inevitability of working-class victory over capitalism, a system she perceives as antagonistic to the biological and ecological continuum of the individual, nature, earth, and society. *See also*: Communist Party, *Mainstream, New Masses,* Proletarian and Radical Writers

—Prairie Miller

REFERENCES

Hampl, Patricia. "Meridel Le Sueur—Voice of the Prairie." *MS.* 4 (August 1975).

Hedges, Elaine. Introduction to *Ripening: Selected Work, 1927–1980*, by Meridel Le Sueur and edited by Elaine Hedges. Old Westbury, N.Y.: Feminist Press, 1982.

Yount, Neala Janice Schleuning. "'America —Song We Sang Without Knowing': Meridel LeSueur's America." Ph.D. diss., University of Minnesota, 1978.

Lewis, Lena Morrow (1868–1950)

The first woman elected to the national executive committee of the Socialist Party, Lewis was one of the movement's most successful and long-term organizers. Born in Gerlaw, a small town near Monmouth, Illinois, Lena Morrow served for six years as a district superintendent of the Woman's Christian Temperance Union before turning to the campaign for woman suffrage. She soon realized that "women are victims of class distinctions more than of sex distinctions." In 1902 she took her commitment to women's advancement, finely honed organizing skills, and "revolutionary spirit" into the SP. Traveling among distant party locals on the West Coast, Morrow paused briefly in 1903 to marry the well-known socialist lecturer Arthur Lewis. The couple traveled together for a while, but within a few years Lena Morrow Lewis returned to the life of solitary itinerant lecturer for Socialism.

Although Lewis continued to support the woman's movement, particularly the suffrage campaign, she did so with the expectation that educated, enfranchised women would aid the struggle for Socialism. In her mind, the class struggle encompassed women's emancipation. For this reason she did not support autonomous women's organizations within the Socialist movement and directed women as individuals to stand up to male chauvinists within their locals. "The woman who will be a real and permanent service to the party," she argued, "is the one who maintains her place in the movement and her right to work solely and only on the grounds of her merit and fitness to do things." To demand separate clubs seemed to Lewis either a demeaning request or an appeal for special privilege.

In 1910–11, Lewis became a principal in a sex scandal involving national secretary J. Mahlon Barnes. Although renominated to the national executive committee, Lewis returned 1913 to her former position as national organizer and accepted an appointment in Alaska. Among miners and their wives, she found a congenial outpost and stayed there until 1917. She edited the *Alaska Labor News* and ran for Congress in 1916 on the Alaskan SP ticket.

Lewis remained in the SP after the historic split in 1919 and returned to her original setting, the West Coast. In 1925 she became managing editor of the *Oakland Labor World*, an important daily newspaper. When the paper folded during the Depression, Lewis moved to the New York area, where a small group of Socialists could provide financial support. In 1936 she quit the SP and became a founding member of the Social Democratic Federation, the conservative wing of the SP centered in New York's garment trades. She passed her remaining years working at the Tamiment Institute, organizing the papers of defunct Rand School. *See also*: Socialist Party.

—Mari Jo Buhle

REFERENCES

Buhle, Mari Jo. "Lena Morrow Lewis: Her Rise and Fall." In *Flawed Liberation: Socialism and Feminism*, edited by Sally M. Miller. Westport: Greenwood Press, 1981.

Lena Morrow Lewis Papers, Tamiment Institute Library, New York University.

LIBERATION MAGAZINE: see NEW LEFT, PEACE MOVEMENTS

LIBERATION NEWS SERVICE

Founded in the summer of 1967, LNS provided news of the counterculture and the New Left to hundreds of periodicals with a total readership in the millions, thereby serving as an alternative to the Associated Press or United Press International.

LNS was most influential in the late 1960s and early 1970s, but it continued to send material to subscribing periodicals until 1981, when it finally went out of business. Over the years, perhaps 200 people were involved in LNS, usually with 8–20 full-time participants or staff at any one time. Funding came from subscribing periodicals and from a variety of private donors; the organization could not have functioned without significant amounts of volunteer labor.

LNS was founded by Marshall Bloom and Raymond Mungo, staff members of the U.S. Student Press Association (USSPA). Bloom and Mungo, former New England college editors known for their outspoken opposition to the U.S. role in Vietnam, decided to start an alter-

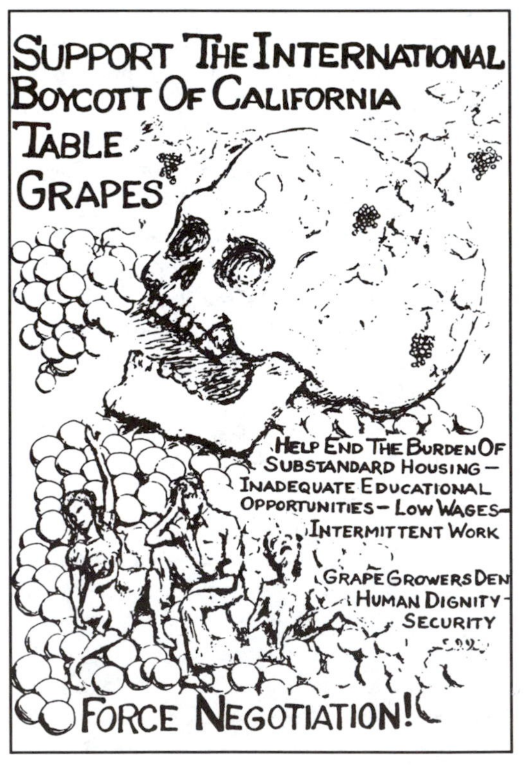

Leaflet by Homer Hurst circulated by Liberation News Service

native press service when Bloom was fired by USSPA for his denunciation of the National Student Association for having accepted funds from the Central Intelligence Agency.

LNS became firmly established after the October 1967 anti–Vietnam War demonstration at the Pentagon, when LNS material documented aspects of the antiwar movement ignored or misunderstood by the "straight media." Starting that fall, printed "packets" were sent out two or three times a week to a mailing list that grew from a few dozen to several hundred subscribers. The packets included hard news of liberation struggles and resistance to oppression in the United States and around the world, plus features, opinion pieces, poetry, photographs, cartoons, and artwork. LNS offered useful copy on national and international affairs to the "underground press," which utilized the technology of inexpensive offset web-press printing to become a fixture in hundreds of cities and small towns.

Several hundred counterculture and movement papers regularly reprinted LNS articles and graphics. The organization operated during its first year in Washington, D.C., where USSPA was located, receiving considerable assistance from the Institute for Policy Studies. LNS relocated in mid-1968 to New York City's Upper West Side, near Columbia University. The move resulted in part from attention LNS received for its insider coverage of the April 1968 student strike at Columbia. Around the same time, LNS merged with a similar press service, Student Communications Network (SCN), launched by the University Christian Movement, and benefited from the new connection by attracting funds from the left-wing sectors of mainstream Protestant churches.

LNS's contribution to American journalism included an advocacy position on formerly taboo topics, such as psychedelic drugs and homosexuality, as well as promoting activism on behalf of movements for social change, especially various Third World liberation movements and feminism. LNS staff members often liked to think of themselves as propagandists in the "good sense of the term," i.e., propagating ideas that would make the world a better place. LNS added a touch of professionalism to the underground press and also sponsored several national get-togethers for writers and activists interested in alternative media. The people of the underground press helped forge a national youth culture and in both subtle and direct ways influenced their colleagues in the "establishment media." The LNS print shop offered its facilities at low cost or no cost to other movement groups, in particular the Black Panther Party, whose position on black issues was supported, almost blindly, by the LNS staff. The lifestyle of LNS staff members mirrored that of many movement activists, including group meals, communal living, subsistence salaries, and considerable interest in mind-expanding drugs, rock and roll, sex, and intimate relationships.

LNS's material represented a broad spectrum of socialist, anarchist, pacifist, civil rights, and "hippie" concerns, but gradually the organization became more decidedly Marxist and more critical of such tendencies as pacifism and the counterculture. Many staff members felt loyalty to Students for a Democratic Society (SDS).

In retrospect, this dichotomy between "politics" and "culture" seems exaggerated, but this was a factor in a serious and unresolved split in the summer of 1968. The increasingly uncomfortable schism motivated a faction, supporters of founder Bloom, to use proceeds from a fundraiser (a showing of the Beatles' *Magical Mystery Tour*) to buy an old farm in Montague, Massachusetts. The split crystallized after a majority of the staff voted for a more structured collective control, undermining the freewheeling style of Bloom and Mungo. For a brief time, news packets were produced in New York City and in Montague, but within a year, the Montague faction ceased publication. Bloom committed suicide on November 1, 1969. In the mid-1970s, residents of the Montague farm became prime movers of the movement against nuclear power when a local utility proposed construction of a nuclear power plant nearby.

Dogmatism on various levels, from obsessive concern about having a correct political line on many national and international issues, to internal organizational matters, such as the distinction between manual laborers (printing press operators) and intellectual laborers (editors and writers), led to internal strife at various times in LNS history. Even after the 1968 split, lengthy, tedious meetings and the often emotional departure of staff members resulted from these internal problems.

In its latter years, with the underground press virtually defunct, LNS served a variety of community newspapers and periodicals serving specialized audiences.

The story of the organization's early years is interestingly and humorously told by Mungo in his book *Famous Long Ago* (though this account is often self-serving and one-sided).

Many copies of periodicals that subscribed to LNS, plus internal papers of the organization, were acquired by the special collections library of Amherst College, where they form a collection named in memory of Marshall Bloom. *See also*: New Left, Underground Press

—*Allen Young*

REFERENCES

Leamer, Larry. *The Paper Revolutionaries: The Rise of the Underground Press*. New York: Simon & Schuster, 1972.

Mungo, Raymond. *Famous Long Ago: My Life and Hard Times with Liberation News Service*. Boston: Beacon Press, 1970.

Peck, Abe. *Uncovering the Sixties: The Life and Times of the Underground Press*. New York: Pantheon, 1985.

Liberation Theology

Vatican Council II (1962–65) not only brought enormous changes to the Roman Catholic church (worship in vernacular languages, respect for religious freedom, openness to human experience) but it also prompted Catholics to ask basic questions. In Latin America church people began to raise questions such as: How should the church relate to the extremes of wealth and poverty? What is the meaning of Christian faith in Latin America today? Out of this questioning came new pastoral strategies, especially in the form of small, lay-led base communities in villages and barrios. Liberation theology was an articulation of the new approach.

In contrast to the time-honored methods of proceeding from doctrine to application, liberation theology insists on the primacy of praxis: it is critical reflection on practice already underway. Out of the suffering and struggle of the poor comes new insight into traditional Christian themes (God, creation, Israel, Jesus Christ, the Church). There is especially a critique of injustice ("structural sin"). In seeking to understand society, church people and theologians make use of Marxism, as do virtually all Latin Americans who are serious about social change. It is significant that this theology emerged just when novelists and social scientists were expressing a new sense of Latin American identity.

Liberation theology is not unique. It has something in common with the "Christian socialism" of the nineteenth century and the "social gospel" prevalent earlier in this century and perhaps with the earlier Reinhold Niebuhr. Similarly, black theologians in the United States (taking their inspiration not only from the Rev. Martin Luther King, Jr., but also from the Black Power movement), Africa, and the Caribbean have produced their own liberation theologies. Insofar as it articulates the experience of an oppressed group, feminist theology is similar and is perhaps the most widespread and most radical liberation theology in the North American context.

The major writings of Latin American liberation theologians are available in English translation, mainly through Orbis Books. More important, several movements and currents in U.S. churches show the influence of liberation theology. Witness for Peace grew out of a 1983 vigil in northern Nicaragua where the contras were expected to attack. Thousands of people have gone to Nicaragua through its programs, which generally include some contact with church groups inspired by liberation theology. Similarly, the Sanctuary movement arose out of efforts to protect fleeing Central Americans from deportation. Indeed, many individuals have become involved in Central America solidarity activities through church contact. Similarly, there is a kinship between liberation theology and the spirit animating church people in the peace movement as a whole. It is not farfetched to see the influence of liberation theology in recent letters of the U.S. Catholic bishops, *The Challenge of Peace* (1983) and *Economic Justice for All* (1986). While the predominant voice in each is liberal, radical questions are raised (e.g., the bishops advocate an "option for the poor" and question the present distribution of wealth in the United States). *See also*: Christian Socialism

—*Phillip Berryman*

REFERENCES

Berryman, Phillip. *Liberation Theology*. New York: Pantheon, 1987.

Boff, Leonardo, and Clodovis Boff. *Introducing Liberation Theology*. Maryknoll, N.Y.: Orbis Books, 1987.

Gutierrez, Gustavo. *A Theology of Liberation: History, Politics, and Salvation*. 1973. Rev. ed. Maryknoll, N.Y.: Orbis Books, 1988.

THE LIBERATOR

Max Eastman and his sister Crystal founded the *Liberator* in March 1918 to print John Reed's reports of the Bolshevik Revolution (which would eventually become *Ten Days That Shook the World*). Reed had originally gone to Russia as a correspondent for the *Masses*, but in August 1917 the postmaster of New York suppressed that magazine under the Espionage Act. The *Liberator* became the *Masses* under a new masthead, and was on the streets before the first trial of the *Masses* editors had even begun.

The *Liberator* was smaller, more focused, and more political than its flamboyant predecessor, but it attracted work from most of the *Masses'* artists and writers, as well as contributions from William Gropper, Reginald Marsh, and Boardman Robinson in graphics, and Edmund Wilson, John Dos Passos, Jean Toomer, and Mary Heaton Vorse in prose and poetry, among many others. The *Liberator*'s primary impact came from its labor reporting, its cultural criticism, and the dissemination of information from the Soviet Union. As staff member Joseph Freeman was to write in his 1936 autobiography of this postwar period, the *Liberator* might have mistakenly ignored Eliot's *The Wasteland* when it appeared in 1922, but "we alone consistently devoted the pages of our publication to the Sacco-Vanzetti case, the partition of China by the imperialist powers, the oppression of Haiti by American bankers, the Garvey movement among the Negroes, the Mexican Revolution, [and] the wage-cut campaign in this country." Mike Gold covered the coal-miners' strike in Pennsylvania and contributed (under his real name, Irwin Granich) the prophetic essay "Towards Proletarian Art" (February 1921), while Floyd Dell produced articles like "Art Under the Bolsheviks" (June 1919) and a series on "Literature and the Machine Age," which ran in 1923–24. Circulation once reached 80,000 (compared with 25,000 for the *Masses*) under the editorship of Eastman and Dell, but the magazine was never finally able to solve the problem that had haunted its predecessor, namely, the split between its art and its politics; the magazine "had one foot in bohemia," Freeman complained, "the other in the revolutionary movement." While the Bolshevik Revolution provided a model for a society in which the two had been fused, as Freeman said, in this country by 1922 "the era of the Tired Radical had begun."

After Eastman himself left to witness the revolution in Russia in 1922, he turned the magazine over to Hugo Gellert, Claude McKay, Gold, and Freeman, who formed two boards, one political and one artistic, under the control of the Communist Party. Such an unnatural arrangement could not long survive, and in the fall of 1924 the *Liberator* was fused with other Communist periodicals, moved its offices to Chicago, and became the *Workers' Monthly*, which continued under the editorship of Robert Minor, Earl Browder, and Max Bedacht. The spirit of the *Masses* and the *Liberator* would be picked up again in 1926 when the *New Masses* began publication with many of the editors, writers, and artists of the *Masses-Liberator* tradition as contributors. *See also*: Communist Party; Dos Passos, John; Gellert, Hugo; Gold, Mike; Gropper, William; *The Masses*; *The New Masses*; Reed, John; Sacco-Vanzetti

—*David Peck*

REFERENCES

Freeman, Joseph. *An American Testament: A Narrative of Rebels and Romantics*. London: Gollancz, 1938.

Klein, Marcus. *Foreigners: The Making of American Literature, 1900–1940*. Chicago: University of Chicago Press, 1981.

LIBERTY BOOK CLUB/MARZANI AND MUNSELL: see UNION-SPONSORED FILMS

LILIENTHAL, META STERN (?–1948)

Writing under the pen name "Hebe" or the surname of her first husband, Stern, Lilienthal produced scores of leaflets, short essays, and pamphlets on women and their concerns for the Socialist Party. She edited a women's page in the *New Yorker Volkszeitung* and a "Votes for Women" column in the *New York Call*, and provided an important link between the German- and English-language sectors of the socialist movement. In 1908 she served briefly on the Woman's National Committee, resigning because she believed its leadership did not sufficiently acknowledge the need for women to organize separately from men.

Born in New York City, Lilienthal grew up in a Socialist environment. Her mother, Augusta Lilienthal, had emigrated from Germany in 1861, joined the Socialist Labor Party, and wrote on woman's rights for *Die Neue Zeit*. Her freethinking parents provided their only daughter with a classical education, including a few years at Barnard College. Lilienthal also devoted one year to studying the major socialist texts before joining the SP. Well versed in history as well as economics, she specialized in writing short pieces of propaganda. Two lengthy pamphlets illustrate her grounding in historical materialism: *From Fireside to Factory* (1916) and *Women of the Future* (1916). In her mind, socialism nevertheless represented "something more than an economic science, or a political theory; it has become a religion, a philosophy of life."

Lilienthal continued her mother's advocacy of woman suffrage and was instrumental in directing SP energies into the major New York suffrage campaigns of 1915 and 1917. She believed that suffrage was a sex, not a class, issue and encouraged SP cooperation with mainstream groups, including the National American Woman Suffrage Association. After the ratification of the suffrage amendment to the U.S. Constitution, Lilienthal edited a short-lived "New Citizens" column in the *New York Call*.

After 1919 Lilienthal turned to the peace movement. She published an autobiography, *Dear Remembered World* (1947), focused on her New York childhood. Writing her memoirs shortly before her death, she raised for posterity her parents' ideals, which she listed as "economic security, physical well-being, and personal happiness for the great mass of mankind." *See also*: *New Yorker Volkszeitung*, Socialist Labor Party, Socialist Party

—*Mari Jo Buhle*

REFERENCES

Buhle, Mari Jo. *Women and American Socialism, 1870–1920*. Urbana: University of Illinois Press, 1981.

LITERARY CRITICISM

Socialist literary criticism in the United States dates from the origins of socialist movements; the stream of book reviews and literary manifestos begins with Orestes Brownson's "American Literature" (1839) and George Lippard's reviews in the *Quaker City Weekly* in the 1840s, and continues through the nineteenth century. However, a distinctive body of socialist criticism does not emerge until the turn of the century along with the Debsian Socialist Party. In his *Forces in American Criticism* (1939), the first major Marxist history of American literary criticism, Bernard Smith points to the founding of the *Comrade* in 1901 and to Emma Goldman's *The Social Significance of the Modern Drama* (1914). Nevertheless, the founding moment for contemporary socialist literary criticism, the source of its paradigms and dilemmas, lies in the controversies of the 1930s, in large part because those debates shaped the birth of modern professional university literary criticism.

There were three main tendencies in socialist and Marxist literary writing in the Depression years. First, there were polemics and exchanges among writers and reviewers, announcing and denouncing strategies of literary production. The controversy over Mike Gold's attack on Thornton Wilder, the debates over the creation of a "proletarian literature," and the exchanges between a host of small magazines issued by the John Reed Clubs had the vitality and vitriol characteristic of literary avant-gardes. Second, there were several major attempts to write a literary history of the United States, all deeply influenced by progressive historiography, and particularly by V. L. Parrington's monumental *Main Currents in American Thought*. The essays of William Charvat and Granville Hicks's *The Great Tradition* remain perhaps the most interesting of these works. Third, there were a few scattered attempts to develop a Marxist poetics, a theory of literary form and a method of reading and interpretation, notably in the essays of Kenneth Burke.

The years of the Cold War saw the institutionalization of professional literary criticism, and the general eclipse of socialist critics. Several of the literary critics associated with the journal *Science & Society* were victims of the anticommunist purge of the academy. The debates among writers and reviewers about socialist writing ceased; the proletarian literature "episode" was caricatured and laid to rest. The Marxist literary histories, and indeed literary history itself, fell from favor, in the turn to the formalism of the "new criticism." There were a few attempts by socialist critics to combine this technical criticism with a historical vision, notably in the American studies tradition inaugurated by F. O. Matthiessen's *American Renaissance* (1940), and in the work of remaining socialists among the "New York Intellectuals," particularly Irving Howe. But for the most part, the literary criticism of the 1950s and 1960s was built around the explicit and repeated exorcism of the themes and methods of socialist and Marxist criticism.

The celebrated "takeover" of the Modern Language Association in 1968 might be taken as the inauguration of a new Left literary criticism, which increasingly found its home in the universities. In part this reflected the professionalization and academization of literary criticism and literary writing generally; in part, it was a result of the social struggles in the greatly expanded postwar university system; and in part it marked the general displacement of *literary* criticism among nonacademic Left cultural critics by a new critical writing about film, television, and rock music. Left literary criticism took two main directions in the 1970s and 1980s: one tendency, represented by the journal *Radical Teacher* and by Richard Ohmann's influential *English in America* (1976), contested the teaching of English in schools and colleges, criticizing the technocratic ideologies of composition instruction, the exclusions of the accepted literary canon, and the politics of established ways of reading. Allied with the emerging programs in Afro-American studies, women's studies, and ethnic studies, the work of these critics in recovering, republishing, and teaching working-class, minority, and women writers began to transform literary education in the United States and provoked one of the central cultural debates of the Reagan era, the controversy over the "canon."

The other tendency, represented by the Marxist Literary Group and by Fredric Jameson's groundbreaking *Marxism and Form* (1971) and *The Political Unconscious* (1981), introduced the literary and cultural theories of European Marxism to an American audience, developed a distinctive way of reading and interpreting literary texts, and sparked theoretical debates over culture and ideology in journals like *Social Text, October, Cultural Critique*, and *ReThinking Marxism*. This work, part of an unprecedented flowering of English-language Marxism in the two decades after 1968, reconstructed Marxist analysis of literary and film form by replacing the class analytic and realist aesthetic of earlier U.S. Marxist critics with a combination of the Frankfurt modernism of Benjamin and Adorno, Lukacs' theory of reification, and Althusser's account of ideology. If the Marxist criticism of the 1930s devoted its energies to literary history, that of the 1980s concentrated on literary theory and interpretation.

Though contemporary socialist literary criticism is dominated by the work of university critics, the tradition of criticism written by poets, novelists, and playwrights is powerfully incarnated in the essays of Tillie Olsen, Amiri Baraka, E. L. Doctorow, and June Jordan, among others. Unlike the university critics whose work addresses the politics of teaching literature and the place of literary scholarship in historical materialism, these essays address the relation of writers to political action, outline the genealogies of a usable past, and suggest the lineaments of a socialist aesthetic. *See also*: Hicks, Granville; Howe, Irving; Matthiesson, F. O.; *Modern Quarterly*; Proletarians and Radical Writers

—*Michael Denning*

REFERENCES

Bullock, Chris, and David Peck. *Guide to Marxist Literary Criticism*. Bloomington: Indiana University Press, 1980.

Denning, Michael. "'The Special American Conditions': Marxism and American Studies." *American Quarterly* 38, No. 3 (1986).

Kavanagh, James H., and Fredric Jameson. "The Weakest Link: Marxism in Literary Studies." In *The Left Academy*, edited by Bertell Ollman and Edward Vernoff, vol. 2. New York: Praeger, 1984.

Lauter, Paul, ed. *Reconstructing American Literature*. Old Westbury: Feminist Press, 1983.

Nelson, Cary, and Lawrence Grossberg, eds. *Marxism and the Interpretation of Culture*. Urbana: University of Illinois Press, 1988.

Newton, Judith, and Deborah Rosenfelt. *Feminist Criticism and Social Change*. New York: Methuen, 1986.

Lithuanian Americans

The first wave of migration from Lithuania to the New World followed the wide famines of 1867 and 1868, although individuals had immigrated to the United States as early as the seventeenth century and in greater numbers following the anticzarist uprisings in Poland and Lithuania in 1795, 1831, and 1863. The majority of later immigrants were young peasants who fled to escape both famine and conscription into the Russian army. They crossed the border into East Prussia mostly on foot, traveled across Germany working often as farmhands, and managed, when they reached Hamburg, to book steerage travel to America.

Most Lithuanians settled first in the mining areas of Pennsylvania. Their communities soon divided into believers and secularists, known as *laisvamaniai* (freethinkers). At the turn of the century, Lithuanian students and other revolutionaries fleeing czarist oppression found a fertile field for organizing among these coal miners, who had already learned some lessons about the class struggle from their Irish and Italian co-workers.

In 1878 *Gazieta Lietuviška* (Lithuanian newspaper) appeared in New York. Its ideology was a joint Lithuanian-Polish nationalism. It closed a year later. In 1884 *Unija* (Union) marked the beginning of the leftist movement among Lithuanian Americans. Between 1894 and 1898 dozens of socialist groups sprang up among Lithuanian workers in Pennsylvania, New York, and other areas of the Northeast. The groups were known as *koupos* (detachments); some were independent, others were loosely linked to the Socialist Labor Party. At the same time, individual Lithuanian Marxists, mostly recently arrived from Lithuania or from exile in Siberia, started to propagate socialism.

In 1904 the Lithuanian Atheist Association of America called a joint socialist conference in New York, where the delegates elected Dr. Šliupas to represent American Lithuanian workers at the Second International congress in Amsterdam, Holland. But Šliupas was not seated because the Social-Democratic Party of Lithuania objected to the representation of a "nongeographic entity." Theoretically, then, Lithuanian socialism was represented in Amsterdam by Rosa Luxemburg, who was seated as the representative of the Socialist Party of the Kingdom of Poland and Lithuania, although her knowledge of Lithuania was minimal.

After the 1905 revolution in Russia, large numbers of educated Lithuanian socialists arrived in the United States and a gradual crystallization of forces took place: the secular camp gradually split into a clearly socialist movement on the one hand and a liberal-bourgeois movement on the other, both confronting the clergy-led Catholic organizations. A clearly socialist publication, *Kova*, appeared at that time in the New York area and another, *Naujoji Gadynė* (New era), began in Pennsylvania. *Kova* published until the start of World War I, when it was forced to close.

The participation of Lithuanian workers in

the American trade union movement was always significant. Among the twenty-one miners who were killed by sheriff's deputies during the Pennsylvania strikes in 1897 were five Lithuanians. Not only in the coal mines but also in steel (Cleveland and Pittsburgh), meat packing (Chicago), needle trades (New York), and textiles (New England), Lithuanians played a role in organizing. In the 1930s Lithuanians were prominently represented in the formation of the CIO, especially in the automobile industry.

Politically the Lithuanian socialist movement had gradually split into right and left wings during the early 1920s with the left taking the majority. Two daily newspapers, *Laisve* (Liberty) in New York and *Vilnis* (Surge) in Chicago, represented the movement. Many organizations came into being, the most prominent being the Lithuanian Workers Literary Society, the fraternal Lithuanian Workers Association, and the Lithuanian Art Union. The right wing of the socialist movement became increasingly conservative.

When Lithuania became incorporated into the Soviet Union in 1940, the Lithuanian-American community split sharply. While the Left greeted the development, the Right saw it as a catastrophe and welcomed the Nazi conquest of Lithuania in 1941. After the defeat of Hitler's Germany, tens of thousands of Lithuanians, among them a number of Nazi collaborators, fled the returning Soviets, and many of these refugees reached the United States. The balance of political forces in the community changed dramatically: the new arrivals, sophisticated and educated, many formerly connected to the government apparatus in Lithuania, inaugurated an atmosphere of fear and quasi-terror, especially in Chicago, where the Left found itself under constant attack. By the 1960s, both sides aging, many retiring to Florida, internecine struggles had ebbed. *Laisve* and *Vilnis*, the former Left dailies, became semiweeklies. In 1988 *Laisve* closed its doors. *See also*: Bimba, Anthony; Communist Party; Socialist Party

—*Rudolf Baranik*

REFERENCES

Buhle, Paul. *Marxism in the U.S.A.* London: Verso, 1987.

Little, Frank (1879–1917)

Hobo agitator and one-eyed rebel, Little was the son of a Cherokee Indian mother and Quaker father. In 1900 he became a metal miner and joined the Western Federation of Miners. A militant direct actionist, Little left the WFM for the Industrial Workers of the World in 1906. A fearless and uncompromising agitator, he was repeatedly beaten and jailed for his union-forming activities. Helping to lead numerous free-speech fights, Little later organized Japanese and Mexican agricultural and construction workers in Fresno into IWW Local 66. Little worked as a "foot loose" organizer bringing harvesters, lumberjacks, and the metal miners into the IWW. In 1914 he was elected to the IWW's general executive board and played a critical role in the formation of the Agricultural Workers Organization and the IWW's job delegate system. In 1916 he resumed his organizing activities among miners, participating in strikes on the Mesabi Range in Minnesota and in Arizona. With a recently broken leg, he traveled to Butte, Montana, to help striking miners shortly after the Speculator Mine fire. The night after his speech, labeled a "treasonable tirade" by the press, Little was brutally murdered by six men. His killers were never identified. Paradoxically, his murder fueled passage of state antisedition laws that were later used to persecute and imprison Wobblies. *See also*: Industrial Workers of the World, Western Federation of Miners/Mine, Mill, and Smelter Workers

—*Sal Salerno*

REFERENCES

Chaplin, Ralph. *Wobbly: The Rough and Tumble Story of an American Radical.* Chicago: University of Chicago Press, 1948.

Little Blue Books

Emanuel Haldeman-Julius (1889–1951) began publication of the Little Blue Books in Girard, Kansas, soon after purchasing the *Appeal to Reason* in 1919. Responding to a request for inexpensive textbooks from Marian Wharton, head of the English Department of the Socialist People's College in nearby Fort Scott, Haldeman-Julius prepared a set of fifty paperbound booklets, three and a half by five inches in size, consisting of the Appeal Pocket Series and the People's Pocket Series. This collection of literary classics and socialist tracts was advertised in the *Appeal* at five dollars per set.

Response from subscribers was immediate and significant. Mass-production techniques had to be utilized to meet mail-order demands. As more sold, prices were lowered and series titles changed to reflect the newer prices (the Ten Cent Pocket Series, etc.). In 1923 the series became the Little Blue Books and expanded into a "University in Print," with original writings substituted for most of the reprint titles. (Shakespeare and Ingersoll were among those authors kept in print even if they did not meet the annual quota of 10,000 sales per title.) Although translations of the Greek and Roman plays (as well as other cultural titles) gave way to better-selling joke books and how-to-manuals, the political integrity of the series was maintained by original contributions from W. E. B. DuBois, Bertrand Russell, Kate Richards O'Hare, Upton Sinclair, Anna Louise Strong, Clarence Darrow, and others. Many young Left writers, such as James T. Farrell, saw their first publications under the H-J imprint. Haldeman-Julius published 2,203 titles in the various series. Nothing was too controversial for him to make available: from Margaret Sanger on birth control (1919) through numerous debunkers of religion and politics (strongest in the 1930s) to critics of the FBI (1948). *See also*: Appeal to Reason

—*Gene DeGruson*

REFERENCES

Cothran, Andrew. "The Little Blue Book Man and the Big American Parade." Ph.D. diss., University of Maryland, 1966.

Haldeman-Julius, Emanuel. *The First Hundred Million*. New York: Simon & Schuster, 1929.

Johnson, Richard Colles, and G. Thomas Tanselle. "The Haldeman-Julius 'Little Blue Books' as a Bibliographical Problem." *Papers of the Bibliographical Society of America* 64 (1970).

LOCAL 1199–RWDSU

Drug, Hospital, and Health Care Employees Union, Local 1199 of the Retail, Wholesale, Department Store Union has experienced a complicated political and organizational history. Founded in 1932 as the Retail Drug Employees Union, Local 1199 emerged out of the efforts of Jewish Communists linked to the Communist Party's Trade Union Unity League to organize New York City drugstores on an "industrial union" model. Combining pharmacists, clerks, soda men, and porters in one organization, the drugstore union also prioritized the goal of equal opportunity for blacks within the pharmaceutical industry, waging significant campaigns on behalf of the employment of black pharmacists in Harlem in the late thirties and early forties. From its earliest days, a key figure in the union's development was its general organizer and president since 1934, Leon Julius Davis, the son of religious Jews from Pinsk, Russia, who had emigrated to the United States in 1921 at the age of fifteen.

While Local 1199 had achieved considerable organizing successes by the early 1950s (signing up over half the independent drugstores in the city and winning a banner forty-hour-week contract from Whelan's, the industry's biggest firm in 1953), the local, which had participated in the formation of the CIO's RWDSU coalition in 1938, was temporarily besieged by pressures from the postwar Red Scare. Forced out of the CIO in 1949, a year later Local 1199 sought protection in the alliance of left-wing locals grouped under Arthur Osman's Distributive, Processing, and Office Workers of America, before eventually returning to the RWDSU (along with Osman's District 65, Wholesale and Warehouse Workers) in 1954. With a stable but restricted jurisdiction in the area's drugstores, Local 1199 membership by the mid-fifties had peaked at 6,000 members.

Its next big move began in 1957–58 when drugstore union leaders in concert with Elliott Godoff, a left-wing castoff from the Teamsters Union, initiated a campaign in the city's voluntary, nonprofit hospitals. After an initial victory at Montefiore Hospital in the Bronx in 1958, Local 1199, Drug and Hospital Employees Union quickly found itself leading a full-fledged crusade among the "forgotten"—and overwhelmingly black and Hispanic and female—hospital service workers. A forty-six-day strike in 1959 at seven metropolitan hospitals highlighted the plight of a work force unprotected by national labor and welfare legislation and earning less than poverty-level wages. Although stopping short of outright recognition, the 1959 settlement provided a crucial foot in the door for a rank-and-file union presence, and through persistent pressure, the union was able to secure legal rights to collective bargaining from Governor Nelson Rockefeller and the state legislature in 1963. A $100-per-week minimum contract in 1968 highlighted the consolidation of the union's strength in the metropolitan area. A year later, a summons from beleaguered nurses' aides in Charleston, South Carolina, would launch the hospital workers' into an expanded organizing drive, formalized in the creation of the National Union of Hospital and Health Care Employees in 1973.

Throughout its history, Local 1199 and the national union it spawned have set an example of political commitment rare on the American labor scene. While 1199 leaders by the early 1950s had largely abandoned ties to the CP, the Left culture in which many of them had matured continued to make an impact. From the beginning, for example, hospital organization was closely and self-consciously tied to the pace of the civil rights movement. Bayard Rustin, A. Philip Randolph, and especially the Rev. Martin Luther King, Jr., and the Southern Christian Leadership Conference acted as close allies in 1199 organizing drives. Likewise, 1199 was the first union to protest U.S. involvement in Vietnam. Later the union actively inserted itself in actions against South African apartheid and American involvement in Central America. As late as 1988, the National Union had become the first in the country formally to endorse the presidential campaign of the Reverend Jesse Jackson.

With the retirement of President Leon Davis in 1982, however, the union encountered a major internal crisis of succession. A failed merger attempt with the Service Employees International Union and hostility between New York district president Doris Turner and National Union leaders touched off several years of bitter racial tension and factional infighting. So inflamed were relations that in 1984 the 1199 National Union formally separated from both the RWDSU and New York Local 1199 (which remained within the international union), although even this settlement did not end conflicting claims to authority within the New York organization.

—Leon Fink

REFERENCES

Fink, Leon, and Leon Greenberg. *Union Power, Soul Power: The Unquiet History of the Hospital Workers*. Urbana: University of Illinois Press, 1989.

Local P-9

Packinghouse Workers Local 9, representing workers at the George A. Hormel plant in Austin, Minnesota, occupies an important place in twentieth-century labor history. In the 1930s Austin unionists played a major role in the organization of midwestern packinghouses. First in the Independent Union of All Workers (IUAW), and later as part of the CIO's Packinghouse Workers Organizing Committee (PWOC), Austin activists helped packinghouse workers form viable unions across the upper Midwest. More recently, Local 9 (now affiliated with the United Food and Commercial Workers) emerged at the forefront of the nationwide fight against concessions. Spurred by wage cuts and new managerial policies, Hormel workers engaged in a protracted but ultimately unsuccessful strike in 1985–86. Despite its defeat, the strike was significant, for it was carried on in open

Cartoon by Mike Konopacki

defiance of the International union and the AFL-CIO.

The Independent Union of All Workers emerged suddenly in the summer of 1933, following a brief work stoppage in the hog-killing department at the Hormel plant. Organized by Frank Ellis, a former member of the Industrial Workers of the World, the fledgling union gained recognition after a successful sit-down strike in November 1933. Influenced by the IWW's "One Big Union" concept, the IUAW quickly expanded beyond the Hormel packinghouse. In Austin and in the nearby town of Albert Lea, the IUAW organized workers in restaurants, taverns, hotels, garages, retail stores, dairies, lumberyards, and small factories. Much of this expansion was sparked by Eva Sauer, a retail clerk who became a full-time IUAW organizer in 1934. Using demonstrations, strikes, consumer boycotts, and, when necessary, the massive presence of unionists from the Hormel plant, the IUAW built a solid regional organization within a few short years.

Although its organizing activities were broad ranging, the outstanding feature of the IUAW was its effort to assist packinghouse workers in the formation of unions elsewhere in Minnesota, Wisconsin, Iowa, and the Dakotas. Constrained by limited funds and ferocious resistance by the packing companies, these efforts met with only partial success. Nonetheless, the nuclei created by the IUAW in many midwestern plants provided the entrée for the CIO when it moved into the meat-packing industry in 1937. Moreover, the IUAW's activities left an indelible mark on the character of packinghouse unionism. The industrial unions they helped found derived their strength from rank-and-file mobilization and powerful shop floor organization, defining characteristics of the future United Packinghouse Workers of America (UPWA), the dominant union in the meat-packing industry through the 1950s.

In the early 1940s, Local 9 and the Hormel Company agreed on an innovative system of profit sharing. Under its terms, Hormel workers became the highest paid packinghouse workers in the country. For more than three decades, relative industrial peace prevailed in Austin. Beginning in the late 1970s, however, new managerial policies started to erode Hormel workers' job security. In 1985, faced with company demands for further concessions, Hormel workers went out on strike. The ensuing conflict, which lasted ten months, involved such tactics as a corporate campaign against Hormel and the First Bank of Minnesota, civil disobedience, and a national boycott of Hormel products. It also divided the labor movement, pitting rank-and-file activists against union officials in a number of international unions. A widespread support network allowed the local to continue its strike despite the intervention of the National Guard, the company's recruitment of replacement workers, and the opposition of the AFL-CIO bureaucracy. The strike ended in May 1986, when the UFCW placed the Hormel local in trusteeship and signed a back-to-work agreement with the company.

—Rick Halpern

REFERENCES

Blum, Fred. *Towards a Democratic Work Process: The Hormel Packing House Workers' Experiment.* New York: Harper, 1953.

Engelmann, Larry. "'We Were the Poor People'—The Hormel Strike of 1933." *Labor History* 12 (Fall 1971).

Halstead, Fred. *The 1985–86 Hormel Meat-Packers Strike in Austin, Minnesota.* New York: Pathfinder, 1986.

London, Jack (1876–1916)

Born in Oakland, California, the bastard son of William Henry Chaney, an itinerant astrologer, and Flora Wellman, a spiritualist mother, he acquired the name London when his mother married his stepfather, John London. Raised in poverty along the docks of the Bay Area, at age fourteen he acquired a small sailboat. He soon began to raid the lucrative oyster beds that lay just offshore but were owned by the railroad interests. Following several close brushes with the police, he gave up pirating and headed for Alaska to participate in the gold rush. After a year of unsuccessful panning for gold, he returned to Oakland and began to write the stories of the North that would make him famous.

The
INTERNATIONAL
SOCIALIST REVIEW

JANUARY, 1917 PRICE TEN CENTS

THE
DREAM
OF
DEBS
BY
JACK LONDON

During the winter of 1900, Jack London wrote *The Call of the Wild*. Published by Houghton-Mifflin the following year, it was the nation's best-selling work of fiction. From that point until the end of his life, London was one of the most widely read writers in the world. Since his death, his best-known works have remained in print in several languages.

Although London's "dog stories" made him famous, his articles, essays, short stories, and novels about the dreadful social conditions throughout the world made him important and somewhat notorious. An avowed socialist from his early teens, London was an ardent supporter of industrial unions and a fierce foe of corruption in government and the power of monopolies. He lectured across the nation on the evils of an economic system that kept almost half the citizenry impoverished at all times. Novels such as *People of the Abyss* about the underclass in London and *The Iron Heel,* a prophetic account of the rise of a fascist state, directly affected the way people looked at the world. London was also instrumental in getting Upton Sinclair's *The Jungle* published, a book that changed forever the American government's role in protecting its citizens from corporate abuse.

Throughout his life London continued to champion the cause of social justice and corporate accountability. The one major inconsistency in his thought was his prejudice against Orientals. At the time of his premature death, he had drifted away from the Socialist Party but he remained an avid admirer of Big Bill Haywood. London's lean prose was greatly admired by the rank and file of the Industrial Workers of the World, and his scathing comic definition of a scab was featured in many IWW publications and songbooks. Following the October Revolution, London became and has remained the most widely read American author in the USSR. *See also*: Industrial Workers of the World, Socialist Party.

—*Chuck Portz*

REFERENCES

Labor, Earle, et al., ed. *Letters of Jack London*. 3 volumes. Stanford: Stanford University Press, 1988.

London, Jack. *American Rebel: A Collection of his Social Writings*. Edited and introduced by Philip S. Foner. New York: Citadel Press, 1964.

———. *Essays of Revolt*. Edited and introduced by Leonard D. Abbott. New York: Vanguard, 1926.

Sinclair, Andrew. *Jack: A Biography of Jack London*. New York: Harper & Row, 1977.

LONDON, MEYER (1871–1926)

Trade union lawyer and Socialist congressman, London favored peaceful and evolutionary methods to achieve the cooperative commonwealth. "As a Socialist," London declared, "instead of denying the existence of the class struggle, I seek to minimize its bitterness."

London was born in Russia and emigrated to New York's Lower East Side in 1891, where his father had published the first radical Jewish newspaper in America. Preferring action to words, he opted for a legal career. Joining first the Socialist Labor Party, London quickly switched over to the new Socialist Party, attracted by its working-class roots and American leadership.

As a lawyer, London's most significant achievement came as counsel to striking cloak-makers in 1910. For eight weeks, 50,000 workers stayed away from their machines, while London negotiated with the employers and mediator Louis Brandeis. The resulting agreement, known as the Protocol, created a mechanism for resolving labor grievances without resorting to strikes. In 1912 London handled the legal work during the twelve-week strike of 7,000 furriers and again emerged victorious.

With strong trade union support, London defeated the incumbent Democratic congressman from the Lower East Side in 1914, making him only the second SP representative ever to sit in the House and the first from the East Coast. He won reelection in 1916. London championed numerous social welfare measures, but his major activity during his first term was vehement opposition to the Wilson administration's preparedness program. He voted against the declarations of war against Germany and Austria-Hungary.

London's positions after April 1917 antagonized both the extreme Right and the extreme Left. He opposed the conscription law and the Espionage and Sedition acts, stands that "100 percent American" groups considered treasonous. Similarly, left-wing Socialists were infuriated by London's decision not to vote against military appropriations and financing bills, but merely to be recorded as "present." Citing his "duty" to American soldiers to "provide them with everything they need," London appealed to his fellow Socialists for "common sense in their attitude in this great crisis of the world." But many radicals believed London had betrayed the St. Louis Platform Declaration to resist *all* wartime activity; they were further incensed by his efforts to keep Russia in the war and his criticism of the Brest-Litovsk treaty. London's opposition to Allied intervention in Russia did not appease them. The congressman also faced attacks from Zionist organizations upset by his refusal to endorse a Jewish homeland in Palestine. With the Democrats and Republicans united behind a single "patriotic" candidate, the Socialists split, and the Zionists hostile, London lost his seat in November 1918.

Two years later, London recaptured his place in Congress. He fought unsuccessfully against the tariff and tax policies of the Harding administration, but did gain passage of the first law sponsored by a Socialist congressman: a measure giving greater protection to workers of bankrupt firms. Gerrymandering of his district's boundaries made reelection in 1922 an impossibility, and London never again held public office. *See also*: Lower East Side, Socialist Party.

—*Mark I. Gelfand*

REFERENCES

Frieburger, William Joseph. "The Lone Socialist Vote: A Political Study of Meyer London." Ph.D. diss., University of Cincinnati, 1980.

Goldberg, Gordon Jerome. "Meyer London: A Political Biography." Ph.D. diss., Lehigh University, 1971.

Rogoff, Harry. *An East Side Epic*. New York: Vanguard Press 1930.

LORE, LUDWIG (1875–1942)

The last leading editor of the influential *New Yorker Volkszeitung* and a precocious formulator of pluralistic or polycentric Communism, Lore stands out as a most unique figure bridging eras of American left-wing activity.

Born to Jewish parents in Friedberg, Germany, Lore graduated from Berlin University and, a committed socialist, worked in the textile industry until emigrating to the United States in 1903. Originally connected with the Industrial Workers of the World, he established himself within the Socialist Party as a New York journalist and supporter of the party's Left. He felt especially drawn to Leon Trotsky, during the latter's sojourn to the United States, and characteristically retained a sense of personal loyalty to the Russian leader even when it had become politically unpopular.

But Lore could in no manner be described as a Leninist or Trotskyist. An early enthusiast of the Russian Revolution, he served as coeditor (with Louis Fraina and L. B. Boudin) of the *Class Struggle*, a pro-Bolshevik monthly, 1917–19, whose pages remained open to eclectic contributions. Meanwhile, Lore's own base of support, German Americans for the most part at least a generation older than himself, looked to him for intellectual and cultural leadership. He guided the *Volkszeitung* into advanced middle age with political dignity and literary style. Executive secretary of the German Socialist Federation, he sought to steer a course between reform socialism and hyper-Bolshevism. After some hesitation, he personally led his troops into the Communist movement.

Within 1920s Communism, Lore remained a rare independent spirit, alternatively pursued and shunned by various factions. His *Volkszeitung* adopted an independent editorial policy, or rather retained its independence of pre-Communist days along with its high literary quality. Repeatedly attacked for "Trotskyism," Lore found himself expelled, through Party manipulation of the German Federation leadership, in 1925. He and the *Volkszeitung* departed with their support virtually intact—a feat not accomplished again until the departure of the Yiddish *Morgen Freiheit* from the Communist movement nearly a half-century later. Due in no small part to his leadership, the paper survived, as a progressive weekly, to see the defeat of Nazism. By the 1930s, Lore himself left the *Volkszeitung* to write an influential daily column for the *New York Post*. According to FBI-released testimony, possibly falsified, Lore also conducted intelligence activity for the Soviet Union, naming Whittaker Chambers as a fellow operative. *See also*: German Americans, *New Yorker Volkszeitung*.

—*Paul Buhle*

REFERENCES

Buhle, Paul. "Ludwig Lore and the *New Yorker Volkszeitung*." In *The German Radical Press in America*, edited by Ken Fones-Wolf and Elliott Shore. Urbana: University of Illinois, 1990.

Draper, Theodore. *American Communism and Soviet Russia*. New York: Viking 1960.

"LOVESTONEITES"

This term is a designation for the "Right Opposition" led in the United States by Jay Lovestone from the time of their collective expulsion from the Communist Party in 1928 to their formal dissolution in 1941. Not a movement like Trotskyism or Maoism, the Lovestoneites distinguished themselves in two regards. First and foremost, their highly placed union connections gave them disproportionate influence in the needle trades and, indirectly, among automobile workers. Their small but vital intellectual following produced work of high quality, if nominal influence within the Left. As unionists and authors after 1940, they also made a significant impact as Cold War operatives.

Jay Lovestone was born 1898 in Lithuania and emigrated to the United States. in 1907. He emerged from City College of New York as leader of the Socialist Club, both articulate and fanatically devoted to the extreme wing of Russian Revolution supporters who favored an "underground" organization. He edited, from the "underground," the *Communist*, noted for its shrillness and factionalism. By the middle 1920s, Lovestone became the chief lieutenant of Charles E. Ruthenberg, whose factional strength centered in the needle trades, i.e., among New York Jews. Upon Ruthenberg's death, Lovestone reached his highest office, deputy secretary-general of the Workers (Communist) Party, from which post he directed the expulsion of real and suspected Trotskyists.

Moving from extreme left to right within the Communist spectrum, Lovestone became the foremost proponent of "American Exceptionalism." According to this perspective, little could be expected from a largely corrupted American population, in the midst of imperialist-laden prosperity, but Communists could cultivate trade union contacts and non-Communist intellectuals. This perspective had the considerable virtue of encouraging a rethinking of Communist policies in a more open fashion, and permitting a hitherto unacceptable latitude in work with non-Communist intellectuals and activists. Thus Bertram Wolfe, Lovestone's ideological aide, led the Party's Workers School into a period of near amity with a variety of Marxist intellectuals; meanwhile Charles (Sasha) Zimmerman, leading figure of International Ladies Garment Workers Union Local 22, sought to apply a policy of stabilization to the generally hectic Communist union politics.

Lovestone's support for Nikolai Bukharin, proponent of "Right" policies within the Comintern, cost him and his followers leadership of the Party in 1929, following a confrontation in Moscow with Joseph Stalin. Expelled, the dissident Communist Party (Majority), so called, actually took only a few hundred members along, but these included Zimmerman and Wolfe. Throughout the early- to mid-1930s, the Communist Party Opposition urged internal reform of the Soviet Union while defending the Russian regime's socialist bona fides from capitalist and Trotskyist criticism. Meanwhile, ILGWU Local 22 became for a time the largest single union local in America, and Lovestone along with his supporters found themselves in steady alliance with ILGWU leader David Dubinsky and the aging but still-vital Yiddish-speaking anarchist faction. Lovestone himself evolved an institutional-syndicalist formula similar to that of earlier pro-AFL anarchists, "everything in and through the unions." Local 22, indeed, conducted an extraordinarily vigorous educational and leisure apparatus, almost rivaling that of the Socialist or Communist movements. Individual Communists, often vigorously in opposition to Zimmerman's policies, for critical periods of the 1930s–1940s supported the Zimmerman leadership.

Meanwhile, the Lovestoneite organ *Revolutionary Age*, later renamed *Workers Age*, became the most literate of the Marxist weeklies in the United States. Bertram Wolfe and Will Herberg (later to become a conservative theologian), among a small crew of others, wrote intelligently on politics, economics, culture, and science. Taking a middle position between Trotskyists and Communist regulars, the Lovestoneites sought to support positive developments in the Soviet Union while increasingly committing themselves to criticisms of bureaucracy. The New Workers School, directed by Wolfe, sought to continue the more open atmosphere of the 1920s efforts and incorporate more Marxism than the increasingly social democratic Rand School.

The Lovestoneites, however, established no significant recruitment either among workers or intellectuals. Like the Trotskyists, they established contacts (some would say "spies") in Socialist Party youth circles of the middle 1930s, most notably in the Revolutionary Policy Committee. Individual Lovestoneites found themselves at the helm of new union locals, but the Lovestoneites lacked a messianic international figure like Trotsky, and a grand strategy such as the formation of a new International. Under the guidance of Lovestone, moreover, they seemed to prefer maneuver among leaders over public appeals for their own cause and organization. *Revolutionary Age/Workers Age* never found its audience beyond "insiders." Nor did Lovestone, Wolfe, Herberg, and the small handful of others distinguish themselves as public intellectuals until they had broken entirely with the Left.

The Moscow Trials and the Spanish Civil War, but also the changing character of American trade unionism, turned the Lovestoneites in a conservative direction. Growing disbelief in the guilt of the defendents of the Trials crystallized a complete hostility to Stalin's leadership. Support for the Spanish Partido Obrero de Unificación Marxista (Workers party of Marxist unification), previously aligned with the thin international stratum of Bukharin supporters (Germany's Heinrich Brandler the most distinguished, with the Indian leader M. N. Roy a close second), reinforced this drift.

Lovestone's own alliance with the American Federation of Labor against the new CIO had a more immediate practical effect upon Lovestoneite activity. Dubinsky, fanatically anticommunist but also deeply resentful of the wide influence exerted by his former mentor, Sidney Hillman, bitterly opposed CIO influence within the needle trades and in its organs, and he often denounced Communist influence on the CIO. With Dubinsky's cooperation, Lovestone therefore placed his personal operatives with Homer Martin, erratic factional leader of the young United Auto Workers, and guided Martin in his group's withdrawal from the CIO union into an avowedly anticommunist (and essentially racist) AFL affiliate.

By 1941, the Lovestoneites (by this time renamed the International Labor League of America) announced dissolution—a virtually unknown act in the Left. While urging members to join the fast-fading SP, the leadership had set itself upon a more severe path.

Lovestone, along with his lieutenant Irving Brown, moved into the highly placed Free Trade Union Committee, originally established to aid European unionists but reorganized as the AFL's anticommunist organ overseas. Working in close concert with the U.S. State Department and Central Intelligence Agency, the FTUC (and later, in a combined AFL-CIO, the International Department) became the bastion of anticommunism within American labor officialdom. Lovestone, intimately close to George Meany and for decades author of his foreign-policy papers, also edited *Free Trade Union News*. In an important sense the personal architect of interventionist trade union policy, Lovestone facilitated the entanglement of the American "New Right" and the AFL-CIO leadership, whose American Institute for Free Labor Development and other regional equivalents received substantial funds from private conservative sources and the National Endowment for Democracy. In essence, Lovestone had established an intelligence community beachhead within labor for such successors, within the AFL-CIO leadership, as Meany's adviser Max Shachtman (architect of AFL-CIO support for the Vietnam War) and teacher's union president Albert Shanker (foremost international neoconservative union leader of the 1980s). Charles Zimmerman, in his later years, was chair of Social Democrats, USA, a socialist split with highly placed representatives and allies in the Reagan administration's foreign policy apparatus.

Bertram Wolfe, himself in later years established at the Hoover Institute, much-touted "think tank" of the "Reagan Revolution," played a similar if considerably less significant role in Russian studies. His notable *Three Who Made a Revolution*, the most scholarly of the early anticommunist studies, may be said to have disappeared among the flock of post-1960s works of varying ideological character. *See also*: Communist Party, International Ladies Garment Workers Union, Socialist Party

—*Paul Buhle*

REFERENCES

Alexander, Robert. *The Right Opposition*. Westport: Greenwood Press, 1981.

LOWE, CAROLINE A. (1874–1933)

A member of the Socialist Party since 1903, Lowe was a well-respected regional organizer in Kansas and Oklahoma. Born in Ontario, Canada, she moved with her parents to Kansas City, Kansas, where she attended public schools. At age seventeen she became a teacher and helped organize a local teachers' association. In 1908 she quit her profession to become a national lecturer for the SP, and toured the Oklahoma socialist encampments during the summer of 1909. She served from 1910 to 1912 as secretary of the Woman's National Committee and managed its offices in the party's national headquarters in Chicago. In 1914 Lowe ran for the Kansas state legislature on the SP ticket and helped launch the People's College of Fort Scott, Kansas.

In 1914 Lowe enrolled in law school; she was admitted to the Kansas bar in 1918. As early as 1914 she joined the free-speech fights and was arrested in Kansas City. During World War I, she defended members of the Industrial Workers of the World in well-publicized trials in Chicago; Wichita, Kansas; and Everett, Washington. In 1923 she joined a law firm in Pittsburg, Kansas, and served as the official counsel for the United Mine Workers-District 14, assisting miners in workers' compensation cases. She retired from practice about one year before her death. *See also*: Socialist Party, Women's National Committee

—*Mari Jo Buhle*

REFERENCES

Buhle, Mari Jo. *Women and American Socialism, 1870–1920*. Urbana: University of Illinois Press, 1981.

Kansas Collection, Haldeman-Julius Room, Southeastern Kansas State University.

LOWER EAST SIDE, NEW YORK: TURN OF THE CENTURY

This was one of the original geopolitical centers of the American Left. Bordered roughly by the East River and Broadway, Chambers and Fourteenth streets, at the turn of the century it was more densely populated than Bombay. Allegedly ruled by unwashed, ignorant, and immoral foreigners in dire need of Americanization, the Lower East Side was indeed an urban hell where thousands of exploited immigrants starved in foul tenements. But thousands of people also created a vibrant, multiethnic cultural life, in which socialism, communism, anarchism, and every form of immigrant radicalism thrived.

In the 1840s, free blacks had established a community in what was a predominantly Irish neighborhood, and the first small wave of German immigrants already foreshadowed the mass influx that was to start four to five years later. Eastern European Jews would not move in in significant numbers until around 1880, Italians and Chinese a little later. Tenements, the notorious "prisonlike structures" that became almost synonymous with the Lower East Side, hardly existed in the 1840s. By 1865, however, more than 15,000 tenements housed 480,000 people. The area had been developed quickly and real estate speculators like the Astors made a fortune with their cheap five-story monstrosities.

The *Socialistische Turnverein* became the cultural center of the German community on the Lower East Side in the 1850s and early 1860s. In the tradition of the German *Turner* movement of the 1830s, this organization promoted "true liberty, prosperity, and free education for all." Its members were not only trained to master the parallel bars but took up fencing and shooting to be prepared for the, as they thought, imminent revolt in Germany. The *Turners*, from their headquarters on Orchard Street, later from a fancy hall "uptown" on Fourth Street, ran a school, a bar, a restaurant, offered drama and poetry classes, and lectures on whatever was in vogue or promised a good laugh—phrenology, vegetarianism, homeopathic medicine, woman suffrage. The *New Yorker Turnzeitung*, the club's publication, introduced the writings of Marx and Engels. The *Turnverein* itself did not have a political arm, but through its members maintained ties to virtually all political organizations and in the 1850s tried to unify the hopelessly chaotic German-American political scene, populated by wings and factions warring over some substantial and many obscure personal and philosophical differences.

After the Civil War, with the *Turnverein* degenerating into just another German "*Verein*," a new generation of immigrant radicalism appeared on the Lower East Side. Its headquarters was the Tenth Ward Hotel on the corner of Broome and Forsythe streets, and its figurehead Friedrich Adolph Sorge, "adjudant of the great Karl and the quintessence of the Prussian gendarme" according to one critic. Competing socialistic groups formed, argued, and split up in rapid succession. The *Soziale Partei* "tried its hand at electoral politics and failed," the *Allgemeine Deutsche Arbeiterverein* initially united communists and Lassalleans, but eventually purged itself of all social-democratic tendencies (and members) to become Section 1 of the International Workingmen's Association. The *Arbeiterunion* was the central body of the German workers, equivalent to the English-speaking Workingmen's Council. Newspapers, a major agitprop medium and a way of transforming often abstract ideas into something tangible, abounded again. The *Arbeiterunion* paper for example was initially edited by Adolf Douai, veteran "Forty-Eighter," supporter of woman suffrage, educator, and textbook author. The difference between the old "romantic revolutionaries," for whom free education for all was a step on the road to liberation, and the new hard-nosed radicals becomes clear in Sorge's opinion on the school war: "Liberation of the workers . . . is not at all dependent on public education. . . . The consciousness of their place in society is completely sufficient."

Outside the Tenth Ward Hotel and its stern politics, the living and working conditions of the immigrants on the Lower East Side didn't improve. Unemployment or twelve-hour workdays in sweatshops and tenements, the five-dollar weekly salaries, infant mortality, typhoid fever, tuberculosis, and industrial accidents still dominated peoples' lives. Although no permanent mass organization developed among the immigrants, thousands of people joined picnics, parades, and protest marches to voice their grievances and to let the outside world know that they were not dumb masses but workers with a clear understanding of their situation and of possible remedies. In the early 1870s, eight-hour agitation began and the Paris Commune raised hopes among the Lower East Side radicals. However serious the theme of these public spectacles, they were always also entertainment, part of the radical culture. During those years, the Germania Assembly Rooms on the Bowery and Houston Street was one of the centers of social life in the German community. A preview to the annual *Allgemeine Arbeiterfest* held at the Germania featured musical and dramatic presentations of works by the old favorites Johann Strauss and Ferdinand Freiligrath, but the highlight of the evening was the premiere of a piece by two local artists, a one-acter aptly titled *Capital and Labor—A Farce*.

The farcical aspects of the struggle between capital and labor, however, became bloody reality once more when the police broke up a demonstration in Tompkins Square Park on the Lower East Side in January 1873. Some 6,000 people—women and children as well as 1,200 members of the German Tenth Ward Workingmen's Association—had assembled to demand public-works programs to alleviate the unemployment and hunger on the Lower East Side caused by the depression. The police moved in and started to beat up the crowd. "In the northwest corner [of the park], however, the Tenth Ward German workers held fast and battled the police" (although their paper, the *Arbeiterzeitung*, had warned against a demonstration). In the first line stood Justus Schwab "carrying the red flag of the Commune." Body count: forty-six people were arrested, twenty-four of them Germans, and Mayor Havemeyer, himself of German descent, could declare that "public works belong to other countries, not ours." Attempts to oust the police board failed. Justus Schwab, who so courageously defended the red flag in Tompkins Square, was a prominent figure on the Lower East Side. He ran a bar on First Street and First Avenue, a radical hangout, frequented by illustrious Emma Goldman and her anarchist friends. The anarchists appeared on the East Side in the 1880s, all bringing their Russian, Italian, or German political traditions along.

By 1880 the ethnic composition of the Lower East Side had started to change. The Germans tended to move uptown, an exodus prompted by the arrival of eastern European Jews, who were viewed with much stronger anti-Semitism than the "more civilized" German Jews. Yiddish became the language of the Lower East Side and Jewish socialism replaced German radicalism.

In Eisl's Golden Rule Hall on Rivington Street in 1882, Abraham Cahan explained the realities of the Lower East Side to the Propaganda Association for the Dissemination of Socialist Ideas Among Immigrant Jews. The leaders of the association were disappointed that their Russian propaganda did not seem to take hold. Here people speak Yiddish, Cahan pointed out—and he was promptly hired as Yiddish-language lecturer. That is how Yiddish radicalism came to the Lower East Side, at least so the story goes. Cahan went on to become one of the heroes of the Lower East Side, powerful editor of the *Forward*, a newspaper housed in a building on East Broadway whose entrance was decorated with reliefs of Marx, Engels, Liebknecht, and Lassalle.

Again, a vibrant culture developed in dire poverty. Yiddish theaters opened along Second Avenue; later on, every better café claimed "Trotsky drank here," from the Garden Cafeteria near the *Forward* building to the Café Royale, in the late 1980s a laundry on Second Avenue. The new forms of popular culture and mass entertainment that developed around the turn of the century immediately became part of the Lower East Side life.

Jewish workers, however, did more than wait "for the paradise promised by the socialists, and while waiting, [singing] Yiddish songs." They had their first big organizing success with the formation of United Hebrew Trades—although a hostile AFL leader claimed that UHT's "entire knowledge of unionism extends from East Broadway to Houston Street and from the Bowery to Sheriff Street." The International Ladies Garment Workers Union won great strikes and in 1914 the Lower East Siders even sent a Socialist, Meyer London, to Congress. He was reelected twice, and died in the twenties, run over by a car on Second Avenue, in his coat pocket a copy of Chekhov's short stories. *See also*: German Americans, Yiddish Left

—*Annette P. Bus*

REFERENCES

Howe, Irving. *Immigrant Jews of New York, 1881–Present*. London: Routledge, 1976.

Nadel, Stanley. "Kleindeutschland: New York City's Germans, 1845–1880." Ph.D. diss., Columbia University, 1981.

Wechsler, Robert. *New York Labor Heritage: A Selected Bibliography of New York Labor History*. New York: Tamiment Library, 1981.

LUCIFER, THE LIGHT-BEARER

A leading anarchist and free-thought newspaper of the late nineteenth century, *Lucifer* was founded by Moses Harman in 1883. After bitter experiences in Civil War Missouri, where he had suffered death threats as an abolitionist, Harman brought his family to Valley Falls, Kansas, in 1879, where he soon established ties with the liberal movement in the state. The greatest contribution of *Lucifer* was its printing of a wide-open letters column that became a national forum, particularly of anguished reports from women of sexual problems. The explicit nature of these letters brought down several prosecutions and jail sentences on Harman, who was charged with sending obscenity through the mail.

During one period when Harman was incarcerated, *Lucifer* was edited by Lois Nichols Waisbrooker (1826–1909), an advocate of free love, spiritualism, and woman's rights. It was Waisbrooker who initiated the infamous "Horse Penis" affair. She printed a graphic paragraph from a U.S. Department of Agriculture book, *Special Report on Diseases of the Horse*, and when the issue was barred from the mail, she ran a streamer in subsequent issues—"Published under Government Censorship"—pointing out that she was being persecuted for printing a paragraph that the government itself had published, and that they seemed much more solicitous of the health of horses than of human beings.

Harman later moved *Lucifer* to Chicago, where prosecutions continued almost to his death in 1910. His newspaper played a dramatic role in the history of free thought in America, particularly with regard to sexual and women's liberation. *See also*: Free Love; Tucker, Benjamin

—*Fred Whitehead*

REFERENCES

Sears, Hal D. *The Sex Radicals: Free Love in High Victorian America*. Lawrence: Regents Press of Kansas, 1977.

Waisbrooker, Lois. *A Sex Revolution*. 2d ed. Topeka: Independent Publishing, 1894.

LUDLOW MASSACRE

An attack on April 20, 1914, by troops of the Colorado National Guard on a tent village inhabited by striking coal miners and their families, mostly Italian, Greek, and eastern European immigrants, gave this incident its name. Two women and eleven children were among those slain. Called a battle by the Guard, it was an incident of the Colorado Fuel and Iron strike (1913–14), a coal strike centered in southern Colorado near Trinidad. Strikers led by the United Mine Workers of America demanded improved safety and living conditions, higher wages, and union recognition. The largest company involved was the Rockefeller-owned Colorado Fuel and Iron Co.

In October 1913 Governor Elias Ammons ordered the Colorado National Guard into the strike region. The Guard, supposedly a neutral force, quickly allied itself with the coal companies. By early April the strike had bankrupted the state, and the governor ordered most troops out of the region. The remaining companies were increasingly joined by mine guards notoriously hostile to the strikers. On the morning of April 20 these troops began circling the Ludlow tent colony. Around nine o'clock the first shot was fired (each side accused the other of it). Troops began firing into the tents as many inhabitants were getting out of bed or getting dressed. Strikers returned fire from a trench dug to one side but were poorly armed and by 4:00 P.M. had run out of ammunition. At dusk the troops entered the tent village with war whoops and burned it to the ground. The dead women and children were found suffocated by smoke in one of the tent cellars dug for them to run into in case of attack. As the news electrified the nation, the miners began an armed rebellion that continued for ten days until President Woodrow Wilson ordered the U.S. Army into the southern Colorado coal field.

In response to Ludlow, reformers, socialists, and others organized protest demonstrations and rallies across the United States. In New York the socialist novelist Upton Sinclair led a silent picket in front of the offices of John D. Rockefeller. The Socialist Party criticized his action on the grounds that the system was at fault, not individuals like Rockefeller. This objection did not prevent similar pickets from appearing in front of Rockefeller's Standard Oil offices in Chicago and San Francisco.

Others prominent in the protests included the reformer Jane Addams, who presided over a large protest meeting in Chicago, and Max Eastman, the socialist editor of the *Masses*. Eastman took the train to Colorado to report on the debacle. Sinclair also went to Colorado and it was on his suggestion that a progressive Denver judge, Benjamin Barr Lindsey, accompanied a group of strikers' wives across the country for the purpose of publicizing the plight of the strikers. Sinclair's novel *King Coal* grew out of his involvement with these protests.

Back in Tarrytown, New York, members of the Industrial Workers of the World picketed the Rockefeller estate, while in New York City four IWW members died in a Lexington Avenue tenement when a time-bomb exploded prematurely. It was generally believed that the bomb had been intended for the Rockefeller townhouse.

Such widespread negative publicity prompted the Rockefellers to launch a pioneering corporate public relations campaign, as well as to institute an important form of the company union in the Colorado coal mines. Although these were largely token efforts, they represented an important ideological shift toward liberalism on the part of some capitalists. *See also*: Industrial Workers of the World; Sinclair, Upton; Western Federation of Miners/ Mine, Mill, and Smelter Workers Union

—Priscilla Long

REFERENCES

Long, Priscilla. "The Women of the Colorado Fuel and Iron Strike, 1913–1914." In *Women, Work, and Protest: A Century of U.S. Women's Labor History*, edited by Ruth Milkman. Boston: Routledge and Kegan Paul, 1985.

———. *Where the Sun Never Shines: A History of America's Bloody Coal Industry*. New York: Paragon, 1989.

McGovern, George S., and Leonard F. Guttridge. *The Great Coalfield War*. Boston: Houghton Mifflin, 1972.

Macdonald, Dwight (1906–82)

Best known as the editor, publisher, and most prolific contributor to *Politics* magazine (1944–49), Macdonald was also among the most radical of the New York intellectuals during the most creative phase of that group. As a Trotskyist he helped edit *Partisan Review*. But Macdonald broke with the other editors when they offered "critical support" of the Allied cause in World War II, and founded his own journal of anarchism and then pacifism. *Politics* enlisted the energies of such European writers as Simone Weil and Albert Camus, as well as refugees from Nazism and Fascism, and was distinguished by an independent effort to reexamine the categories of Marxism and the automatic allegiance to the working class or to trade unions. The monthly (later quarterly) defined the militarism of the modern state and the depersonalization of an apathetic citizenry as the chief evils to be combated. But Macdonald's own radicalism dissipated during the Cold War, when he saw the Soviet Union as the major peril to peace and to individual liberty. By the early 1950s he not only "chose the West" but largely abandoned interest in politics itself, devoting himself to cultural criticism. Macdonald returned to dissent by the middle of the 1960s, putting his polemical bite and graceful wit in the service of opposition to military intervention in Vietnam and in support of the Students for a Democratic Society.

See also: Anarchism, Trotskyism

—*Stephen J. Whitfield*

REFERENCES

Arendt, Hannah. "He's All Dwight." *New York Review of Books* 11 (August 1, 1968).

Glazer, Penina M. "From the Old Left to the New: Radical Criticism in the 1940s." *American Quarterly* 24 (December 1972).

Whitfield, Stephen J. *A Critical American: The Politics of Dwight Macdonald*. Hamden, Conn: Archon Books, 1984.

Magón, Ricardo Flóres (1874–1922)

The political career and ideological evolution of Magón began in the context of the regime of Porfirio Díaz, dictator of Mexico from 1876 to 1911. Like a number of young Mexican intellectuals, he perceived the problems of Mexico associated with the dictator as deriving from the corruption of classical liberalism by this regime, which favored English and American corporations and which crushed any expressions of dissent. In 1903 Magón was expelled from Mexico and in early 1904 he and his brother Enrique crossed the border into Texas and the country he and his compatriots regarded as the model of liberalism. Organizing for the Mexican Revolution from their exile in San Antonio, the Magón brothers, Juan Sarabia, Antonio Villareal, Librado Rivera, Manuel Sarabia, and Rosalio Bustamante reestablished the newspaper *Regeneración* in 1904 and the following year founded the *Partido Liberal Mexicano* (PLM) in St. Louis. At this time these "Liberales" espoused a vague socialism upholding the sov-

Linocut poster of Ricardo Flóres Magón
by Carlos Cortez

ereignty of the people above all else, though asserting the harmony of classes.

Experiencing the work life of a Mexican immigrant and the repressive nature of the American government and law, the PLM junta and Ricardo Flóres Magón, its leader, moved away from their earlier political views and explicitly embraced anarchism in 1908. In this same year they unsuccessfully attempted to spark a revolution in Mexico with a series of border raids around the El Paso area. For this they were convicted of violating neutrality laws and jailed for eighteen months. They had been helped along in their journey to radicalism and in their court trials by the likes of Emma Goldman and other anarchists, the Industrial Workers of the World, and the Western Federation of Miners, all of which contributed to their legal defense.

In 1910 the organization and newspaper moved to Los Angeles, where it continued to propagandize against "clergy, law, and capital." The clarity of their anarchist principles and their advocacy of direct action to secure the means of production for those who worked and to ignite the Mexican Revolution put the PLM outside the mainstream of anti-Díaz activity, which remained concerned primarily with electoral and land reform. In January 1911 approximately 500 Liberales, including nearly 100 Wobbly-affiliated Anglos, attacked Baja California. Briefly successful, the effort soon fell prey to factionalism and desertion. This Baja episode well exemplified the PLM's pattern of inspiring and engineering an effort and then lacking the discipline and organization to carry it through. Their efforts also sparked the vehement opposition of Southwestern newspapers, Mexicans consuls, and American law. In June 1911 their efforts in Baja earned them twenty-three months in jail. Thousands of pro-Magonistas rioted in Los Angeles upon hearing the verdict.

The PLM leaders' theory was as visionary and compelling as their actions. They claimed that their anarchist utopia—in which no bourgeois law ruled people, nor churches fooled them, nor capital oppressed them—was rooted in the traditional Indian communal organization of land tenure. If only the interloper of capitalism could be swept away, human goodness could flourish and produce "a new society of justice and love." This was not mere romanticism to many Mexicans on both sides of the border who had seen the new industrial system erode their independence as artisans, miners, and farmers. While their railings against religion did not resonate with much of the Mexican populace, the PLM's attack on the monopolization of land, of which the Church was a part, did. Propaganda and direct action, not political maneuvering or strategy, would destroy the rule of capital. Then the people, uncorrupted by clergy, law, or capital, would rule themselves with self-governing and autonomous local institutions where cooperation would reign.

Toward this end of cleansing revolution, PLM activists assisted in the organization of Mexican workers into unions, either all-Mexican or in league with the IWW. The IWW's famous Fresno Local 66 included many Mexican agricultural workers thanks to the organizational efforts of the Liberales in 1909 and 1910.

For much of this time the Magón brothers and the rest of the junta were in and out of jail. Thus *Regeneración*, the primary propaganda instrument, languished. In 1918 Ricardo Flóres Magón called upon the workers of the world to reject nationalism and use the world cataclysm to revolt against the bourgeoisie and establish *"la fraternidad universal."* Ricardo was convicted under the Espionage act for hindering the war effort and received twenty years in the Leavenworth Penitentiary, where he died, or was murdered, in November 1922. All the while honoring his martyred name, the generals who eventually controlled the Mexican Revolution cast out the Liberales from Mexico. Magonistas then made Los Angeles their permanent home, where they continued to denounce "clergy, law, and capital." *See also*: Anarchism, Anarcho-Syndicalism, Industrial Workers of the World, Mexican Americans

—*Douglas Monroy*

REFERENCES

Blaisdell, Lowell. *The Desert Revolution: Baja California, 1911*. Madison: University of Wisconsin Press, 1962.

Gómez-Quiñones, Juan. *Sembradores, Ricardo Flóres Magón y el Partido Liberal Mexicano: A Eulogy and Critique*. Los Angeles: Chicano Studies Center, UCLA, 1973. The appendix contains the most important PLM documents, *Regeneración* articles, and some letters of Ricardo Flóres Magón.

Hart, John M. *Anarchism and the Mexican Working Class, 1860–1931*. Austin: University of Texas Press, 1978.

Monroy, Jesus González. *Ricardo Flóres Magón y su actitud en la Baja California*. Mexico City: Editorial Academia Literaria, 1962.

Poole, David, ed. *Land and Liberty: Anarchist Influences in the Mexican Revolution*. Sanday, England: Cienfugos Press, 1977.

MAINSTREAM

During the tumultuous late 1930s, the Communist Party periodical, the *New Masses*, had shifted from monthly to weekly publication, promising to devote considerable space to literary and other cultural fields. The coverage proved uneven and rarely achieved the level of aesthetic sophistication maintained by the then still vaguely Marxist *Partisan Review*. In 1945–46 a group of young writers, largely members of the cultural section of the CP, projected a magazine to publish fiction, poetry, literary and art criticism, and theoretical explorations of a possible Marxist aesthetic. Notable in this group was Charles Humboldt (1910–64), a World War II veteran then studying mural art in Mexico, via the GI Bill.

The first issues of *Mainstream*, especially noteworthy for such authors as Tom Bell, Alexander Saxton, and Meridel LeSueur, evoked considerable enthusiasm. Although circulation began to climb, Party membership and funds had begun to decline, and cultural needs possessed no political priority. The *New Masses*, which had meanwhile lost many readers, merged into the *Masses and Mainstream*, with all four editors carryovers from the *New Masses*. Charles Humboldt was listed merely as part of a cosmetic board of nineteen contributing editors. *Masses and Mainstream*, as unwieldy as its name, floundered until a major reorientation in 1956. Milton Howard remained titular editor but Humboldt was listed as managing editor and became the de facto editor of the monthly, renamed *Mainstream* in September. In 1957 he became sole editor in fact.

Until Humboldt's resignation in 1960, the magazine achieved an extraordinary level of literary sophistication, imaginative breadth, and cosmopolitan interests. Especially notable was its emphasis on Latin American artistic development, a first in the U.S. Left. Through all the financial and political hazards of the Cold War and all the problems of an ever more rigidly philistine Communist leadership, *Mainstream* managed to grow. Humboldt remained responsible for almost every function, meeting weekly with four contributing editors (novelists Barbara Giles and Philip Bonosky and two critics, Sidney Finkelstein and Annette Rubinstein) to secure advice and help in his successful solicitation of material from such distinguished non-CP radicals as John Berger, Joseph Needham, Jean Paul Sartre, David Alfaro Siqueros, Kenneth Tynan, and others.

As early as 1956, the divergence of the official Party outlook and *Mainstream* culminated in a searching effort by Humboldt to question the accepted view of the artist's responsibility to society. After many compromises, ultimatums, and continued financial crises, Humboldt resigned in 1960, along with a number of contributing editors. (He went on to work at the *National Guardian* until shortly before his death.) The magazine grew steadily more characterless and isolated, and expired in 1963, the final notable American Communist literary publication. *See also*: Communist Party; Literary Criticism; LeSueur, Meridel; McGrath, Tom

—*Annette Rubinstein*

MALCOLM X: *see* CIVIL RIGHTS MOVEMENT

MALKIEL, THERESA SERBER (1874–49)

A Jewish immigrant from Bar, Russia, Malkiel arrived in New York in 1891, went to work in the needle trades, and involved herself in the labor movement, socialism, and feminism. Her political activity in the socialist movement epitomizes the difficulties and contradictions encountered by socialists on gender and class issues. Confronting the dilemma of autonomy and integration, she generally opposed women's separatism and, with other women militants, systematically denounced the sex discrimination prevalent among socialists.

Malkiel helped organize the Infant Cloak Makers Union of New York in 1894, led a well-publicized strike, and helped guide the local into the doomed Socialist Trades and Labor Alliance. Breaking with the Socialist Labor Party in 1899, she became the local leader of Socialist women in Yonkers, New York, in the new Socialist Party of America (created in 1901).

In 1908 Malkiel was elected a member of the SP-sponsored Women's National Committee, designed to facilitate national propaganda and support for women.

In those years Malkiel crusaded primarily for the issues of woman's suffrage and work. In 1907 the Second International had ordered all Socialist parties to support votes for women but banned cooperation with the autonomous "bourgeois suffragists." Malkiel herself saw the vote as a crucial stepping stone toward gender equality but primarily as a weapon for the conquest of socialism.

Malkiel denounced the exploitation of women in the workplace and at home. Oppressed as workers, they also had to confront discrimination by workmates and union leaders. Women's only hope, according to Malkiel, lay in collective action and organization. The 1909 shirtwaist workers' strike gave Malkiel, a former shirtwaist worker and a member of a SP women's support committee, the opportunity to involve herself fully with immigrant female workers.

Home was the other facet of women's lives, and Malkiel identified domestic labor—unpaid and unrecognized—as THE specific female oppression and warned working girls against the lures of marriage, doomed to bring a double working day and a more exhausting existence. More privileged in her personal life, Theresa Serber married Leon Malkiel, a socialist lawyer, in 1900. They had one daughter.

When Theresa Malkiel projected herself into an ideal future, freed from industrial and sexual exploitation, she left the family structure more or less unchanged. The decisive factor was the newly won gender equality that would enable wives to carry out their "mission" as mothers and educators with dignity. In Malkiel's *Diary of a Shirtwaist Striker* (1910), the young Jewish heroine experiences liberation from industrial exploitation as well as from patriarchal family relationships. In a new egalitarian context, the heroine fulfills the traditional female mission and guides her meek, male companion toward the Socialist Promised Land.

On the eve of World War I, the SP decided to retrench on women's issues. Committed to pacifism, Malkiel fought on for suffrage and immigrant women. After the war, she became less politically active. *See also*: Socialist Labor Party, Socialist Party, Socialist Trades and Labor Alliance, Women's National Committee

—*Françoise Basch*

REFERENCES

Basch, Françoise. *Theresa Malkiel Journal d'une gréviste*. Paris: Editions Payot 1981.

———. "The Socialist Party of America, the Woman Question, and Theresa Serber Malkiel." In *Women in Culture and Politics. A Century of Change*, edited by J. Friedlander et al. Bloomington: Indiana University Press, 1986.

Buhle, Mari Jo. *Women and American Socialism 1870–1920*. Urbana: University of Illinois Press, 1981.

Miller, Sally M. "From Sweatshop Worker to Labor Leader: Theresa Malkiel, a Case Study." *American Jewish History* 68 (December 1978).

MAOISM: see ANTIREVISIONISM

MARCANTONIO, VITO (1902–1954)

The most electorally successful radical American politician in the twentieth century, Marcantonio, a handsome five-foot-six-inch spellbinder, served as congressman from East Harlem in Manhattan for fourteen years (1934–36, 1938–50). In 1944 his district was expanded to include Yorkville. Marcantonio joined the American Labor Party (ALP) soon after its founding in 1936, becoming at once the leader of its left wing and by 1942 its de facto and by 1948 its elected leader.

Ideologically and organizationally, Marcantonio was closely allied with the Communist Party. He presented domestic issues from a class perspective and approached foreign policy within a Leninist conception, but in general did not attack the capitalist system as a whole nor advocate socialism. He was the only American political figure to consistently insist on the CP's legitimate place in the country's political reality. In 1943, on the floor of the House, for example, he questioned "the war against the Communists, who, as an integral part of 130 million Americans, are fighting and working like all other Americans for victory against the enemy." In 1952 he described the CP as an "American party operating in what it considered to be the best interests of the American working class and people." Marcantonio politically allied himself with the Party within the ALP and held office in or otherwise promoted scores of organizations, unions, and publications associated with the Party, such as the International Labor Defense, the Furriers Union, and the *New Masses*.

Marcantonio, however, was not a Communist. He had occasional disagreements with the Party, including in 1953 an acrimonious and semipublic clash over its decision to withdraw support from the ALP. While accepting the Party's ideological lead and its place in the politics he supported, Marcantonio represented an independent force based on his charisma and his fiercely loyal constituency. For the Party, Marcantonio became a national spokesman for its general program; for Marcantonio, the Party provided the financial and human resources needed to fuel his organization. And it was Marcantonio's political machine that—through its legendary delivery of services and tireless electioneering—converted East Harlem's adulation for its native son into votes.

Driving Marcantonio's politics were the needs of the people—the Italian Americans, Puerto Ricans, and blacks—of East Harlem. Born in the center of its Italian community on East 112th Street, he resided at the time of his death on East 116th Street. In ways small and big he was organically a part of what in the thirties was the largest Italian community in the United States and what has been described as the most Italian community in the United States. He lived in the same house with his grandmother and mother, marched in church processions, socialized with Mafia chieftains, and wore religious amulets. In the House, he upheld the rights of the foreign born and the contributions of Italians to American society with an unrivaled persistence and ferocity. In 1944, when a congressman from Alabama disparaged Marcantonio's nationality, he reminded the House that "while my people did not come over on the *Mayflower*, [they] have always fought for liberty. . . . We are an integral part of the living flesh and blood of our country." Italian Harlem gave a majority of its votes to Marcantonio in all the elections he contested.

By 1936 he had created a second electoral base, East Harlem's El Barrio, the largest Puerto Rican community in the continental United States and the center of Puerto Rican life in New York City. Reflecting the powerful

Left currents in Puerto Rico, this community had a wide array of Left organizations. It became the only place where the ALP was the first party. Marcantonio adopted the Puerto Rican cause as his own: he became co-counsel for Don Albizu Campos, the leader of the independence movement; submitted five bills for Puerto Rico's independence; and in general acted as de facto congressman for Puerto Rico. In 1949, in the center of Italian Harlem before 15,000 people, he shouted: "Yes, I do defend the Puerto Ricans as our most recently arrived, as against the kind of discrimination that was practiced against the Irish, the Jews, and the Italians in the past."

The blacks, though fewer in numbers, added to Marcantonio's coalition. In the House, he was the major proponent of civil rights legislation, serving as sponsor and floor leader for the anti–poll tax and Fair Employment Practices bills. Countless times he proposed antidiscrimination amendments onto appropriations bills and then forced roll-call votes. Shortly after Marcantonio's death, Paul Robeson described him as the "Thaddeus Stevens of the first half of the twentieth century . . . the foremost spokesman for the rights of man the Congress has produced in the twentieth century."

Marcantonio's radicalism engendered an increasingly virulent and determined opposition. In 1944 his district was enlarged to include Yorkville, an area whose majority German- and Irish-American population, largely successful working- and middle-class, proved inhospitable. Nonetheless, his huge majorities in East Harlem returned him to the first Republican Congress since 1928. In 1947 the state legislature passed the Wilson-Pakula Act (which Marcantonio said had everything but his picture on it) abolishing the open primary system. This prevented a candidate registered in one party from entering the primary of another party without the permission of the county committee of that party. Initially, Marcantonio—who had served as LaGuardia's aide de camp in the district while he represented East Harlem in the House from 1922 to 1931—followed in his mentor's footsteps by running as a Republican. Later, despite his ALP affiliation, he contested both major party primaries, winning one (1938, 1940, 1946) or both (1942 and 1944). In 1948, amid a growing press campaign identifying him with Communism and organized crime, he had to seek reelection under the banner of the ALP, which was generally described in the press as Communist influenced, or controlled, or dominated. In a three-way contest, he narrowly won. In 1949, in part to keep alive his only political vehicle, he ran as the ALP candidate for mayor. In a three-way race, he received a majority in East Harlem and a plurality in the district as a whole, but only 13.8 percent of the citywide vote. Finally in 1950, shortly after casting the sole vote in opposition to the Korean War, Marcantonio faced George Donovan, the coalition candidate of the Democratic, Republican, and Liberal parties. Despite an increase in his vote from 1948 (from 36 to 43 percent) and East Harlem's 60-percent majority, Marcantonio could not overcome what he called the "gang up."

After his defeat, Marcantonio became co-attorney for the CP before the Subversive Activities Control Board and represented individuals (including W. E. B. DuBois) whose political views placed them in legal jeopardy. On August 8, while returning from a printer with nominating petitions for an attempted comeback, Marcantonio fell dead of a heart attack in City Hall Park. The Roman Catholic church refused him a Catholic burial. Amid a massive outpouring of people he was buried near LaGuardia in Woodlawn Cemetery, where his epitaph reads: "Vito Marcantonio: A Fighting Congressman." *See also*: American Labor Party, Italian Americans, Puerto Ricans

—Gerald Meyer

REFERENCES

LaGumina, John Salvatore. *Vito Marcantonio, The People's Politician*. Dubuque: Kendall/Hunt, 1969.

Meyer, Gerald. *Vito Marcantonio: American Radical*. Albany: State University of New York Press, 1989.

Rubinstein, Annette, ed. *I Vote My Conscience: Debates, Speeches, and Writings of Vito Marcantonio*, 1935–1950. New York: The Vito Marcantonio Memorial, 1956.

Schaffer, Alan. *Vito Marcantonio, Radical in Congress*. Syracuse: Syracuse University Press, 1966.

MARCH, HERBERT (b. 1913)

One of the Communist Party's most visible and influential trade union leaders, from the early 1930s through the mid-1950s March played a leading role in packinghouse unionism in Chicago and throughout the nation. A powerful speaker and effective mass leader, he helped overcome a long history of mutual antagonism among packinghouse workers through his efforts to forge an interracial, multiethnic alliance.

The son of a Socialist postal worker, March was born in Brooklyn, New York. He became active in the Young Communist League in the late 1920s, and in 1930 moved to Kansas City, where he served as the league's regional director. Under March's leadership the Kansas City YCL involved itself in the organization of the unemployed, the defense of the "Scottsboro Boys," and in a number of regional antilynching campaigns. In 1933 March moved to Chicago and began working at Armour and Company. He led union organizing efforts in the stockyards and, with his wife, Jane, was instrumental in building the CP's meat-packing section.

March served as a ranking official in the Trade Union Unity League's Packinghouse Workers Industrial Union and in the Stockyards Labor Council. He was one of the founders of the CIO's Packinghouse Workers Organizing Committee in 1937, and served as director of the United Packinghouse Workers of America's Chicago-based District One from 1943 until the Taft-Hartley Act forced his resignation in 1948. In this period, March also served as president of the Chicago Industrial Union Council and sat on the CP's Central Committee. After his resignation, he continued to work for the international union for a number of years before being dismissed as a result of pressure from anticommunist elements within the CIO. Immediately after his discharge, Chicago Armour Local 347 hired March as an organizer. He remained an important force in the Chicago district until 1955, when he left both the union and the Party.

In 1956 March moved to the Los Angeles area, where he became a sheet-metal worker and rank-and-file activist in the Sheet Metal Workers Union. He attended law school at night and was admitted to the California bar in 1969 only after a protracted legal struggle. He practiced labor law until his retirement in 1983, negotiating the American Federation of State, County, and Municipal Employee's first contract with Los Angeles County.

—*Rick Halpern*

REFERENCES

Herbert March Interview. On Deposit at State Historical Society of Wisconsin.

MARCH ON WASHINGTON: see
RANDOLPH, A. PHILIP; RUSTIN, BAYARD

MARCUSE, HERBERT (1898–1979)

If anyone warrants the title of *the* theorist of the 1960s New Left, it is the German-émigré philosopher Herbert Marcuse. Many consider this ironic. By the time Marcuse had emerged as the "guru of the New Left" (*Time*), he was *in* his sixties and the movement was notoriously distrustful of "anyone over thirty." The New Left was also known for both its activism and its impatience with intellectuals, while Marcuse's prose is often experienced as forbiddingly Germanic and abstruse. For this reason, too, the affinities between his ideas and the movement are surprising.

The fact is, however, that Marcuse was a New Leftist *avant la lettre*; his links to the movement were deep. Already in the 1930s, in a context of socialism in one country and fascism in several, and through the 1950s, in a context of American consumer capitalism, Marcuse was exploring in theory the prospects of a radicalism beyond not only Stalinism and Social Democracy, but beyond (if still with) Marxism itself. In his writings, the New Left would find coherent expression of some of its own deepest impulses: among them, critique not only of capitalism, but of technological rationality; focus on the sexual nature of both domination and emancipation; preoccupation with culture and consciousness as vital dimensions of revolution; a fusion of pessimism with a will to radical criticism and revolt; and unabashedly utopian tendencies. Likewise, Marcuse would find in the New Left of the 1960s a social embodiment of many of his ideas.

Eros and Civilization: A Philosophical Inquiry into Freud (1955; reissued with an important "Political Preface" in 1966) and *Soviet Marxism: A Critical Analysis* (1958) were in this connection preparatory works. *One-Dimensional Man: Studies in the Ideology of Advanced Industrial Society* (1964), published amid the civil rights movement and the Berkeley free-speech uprising, established direct ties between Marcuse and the New Left. His main subsequent writings—"Repressive Tolerance" (1965); *Essay on Liberation* (1969); *Counter-Revolution and Revolt* (1972); and *The Aesthetic Dimension* (1978)—and the innumerable essays, talks at meetings and rallies, letters, and travels from the late 1960s until his death, constitute a remarkable burst of politically inspired productivity, and reflect his engagement with and hopes for the movement. It is in this specific sense that he was its theorist.

Like many of the student radicals his writings would influence in the 1960s, Marcuse came from a family of means. Born in Berlin on July 19, 1898, he grew up in the comfortable and cultivated confines of the German-Jewish bourgeoisie. This proved to be a fruitful vantage point for critically observing the onset of the "iron cage" of bureaucracy that, during the years of Marcuse's youth, Max Weber had defined as the inescapable destiny of industrialism.

The Great War drew Marcuse toward the political Left. During the revolutionary ferment at the war's end, he participated in a Berlin Soldier's Council and was briefly a member of the Social Democratic Party of Germany. With the ebbing of the revolutionary wave, many in Marcuse's generation of leftists placed their bets on vanguard parties of the Leninist type or gradualist reforms. He turned to aesthetics and philosophy, and entered the University in Freiburg. Many of his writings from the 1920s are weighty works of scholarship: the (unpublished) 1922 doctoral dissertation on the German "artist novel"; the 1925 bibliographic study of Friedrich Schiller, the Romantic dramatist and aesthetic theorist; and the 1932 *Habilitationschrift* (required for eligibility as a university professor) on Hegel's philosophy of "historicity." Nevertheless, these texts indicate the vigor of Marcuse's romantic anticapitalism and his continued effort to articulate the cultural bases of alternatives to the bourgeois order.

Much influenced by Georg Lukacs' *History and Class Consciousness* (1923), and immersed in Hegelian philosophy, Marcuse, in 1927, began several years of close association with Martin Heidegger. His essays in both scholarly and Social Democratic journals, including a brilliant commentary on Marx's "1844 Manuscripts" on alienation, which had appeared in print for the first time in 1932, show Marcuse trying to restore to Marxism an activist philosophy of subjectivity and a culturally radical vision of emancipation. Some see him as having been the first "Heidegerrian Marxist."

Shortly before the Nazi seizure of power in 1933, Marcuse began his affiliation with the "Frankfurt School" of social theory, soon joining its migration to Geneva, Paris, and finally New York. Some of his major essays from this phase of his career appeared in translation in *Negations: Essays in Critical Theory* (1968). *Reason and Revolution: Hegel and the Rise of Social Theory* (1941) is the great work of this period. Under the impact of fascism on the one hand and the leading thinkers of the Frankfurt circle, Max Horkheimer and T. W. Adorno, on the other, the Heideggerian and utopian dimensions of Marcuse's thinking tended to recede, while a more Hegelian and rationalist Marxism, as well as a more intensive critique of industrial society, came to the fore. With *Eros and Civilization* and *One-Dimensional Man,* Marcuse united these elements of his thinking.

During and shortly after the war, he worked, along with other members of the exiled Frankfurt group, in a branch of the Office of Strategic Services, forerunner of the CIA, doing research on Nazi and Fascist ideology in conjunction with Allied plans for occupation and de-Nazification of Germany. His first wife, Sophie, died in 1951. During the early 1950s Marcuse was affiliated with Columbia and Harvard universities, taking a more permanent post in philosophy at Brandeis University in 1955. When Brandeis did not renew his contract in 1964, he assumed his last academic position at the University of California in San Diego, where he became the bête noire of the southern California right wing. Marcuse's second wife, Inge, the widow of Franz Neumann, died in 1973. Three years later, he and Erica Sherover, his longtime student and research assistant, were married. Marcuse died in Starnberg, West Germany, on July 29, 1979. *See also*: New Left, Psychoanalysis

—*Paul Breines*

REFERENCES

Breines, Paul, ed. *Critical Interruptions: New Left Perspectives on Herbert Marcuse*. New York: Herder & Herder, 1970.

Geoghegan, Vincent. *Reason and Eros: The Social Theory of Herbert Marcuse*. London: Pluto, 1981.

Katz, Barry. *Herbert Marcuse: Art of Liberation*. London: Verso, 1982.

Kellner, Douglas. *Herbert Marcuse and the Crisis of Marxism*. Berkeley: University of California Press, 1984.

Lipshires, Sidney S. *Herbert Marcuse: From Marx to Freud and Beyond*. Cambridge, Mass.: Schenkmann, 1974.

Mattick, Paul. *Critique of Marcuse*. London: Merlin, 1972.

Schoolman, Morton. *Imaginary Witness: The Critical Theory of Herbert Marcuse*. New York: The Free Press, 1980.

Marcy, Mary Edna (1866–1922)

A major publicist, pamphleteer, and editorialist for Debsian Socialism's left wing, working-class militant Mary E. Marcy was a central figure at Charles H. Kerr Publishing Company in the 1910s. A key member of the editorial board of Kerr's *International Socialist Review* (*ISR*) after December 1908, Marcy played a significant role in shaping the Left line against war and militarism prior to U.S. entry into World War I. She joined the Socialist Party in 1903 and the Industrial Workers of the World in 1918.

Marcy's muckraking "Letters of a Pork Packer's Stenographer" ran serially in the *ISR* in 1904 and won her instant notoriety within Left circles. She and her husband, Leslie H. Marcy, soon became regular contributors to the Kerr monthly. A student of John Dewey at

the University of Chicago, she maintained a political and pedagogical conviction that Marxian theory had to be presented in a clear, simple fashion if the movement was to make serious headway with American workers. One of her many writings, her now classic economics primer, *Shop Talks on Economics*, first appeared in the *ISR* in 1911 and subsequently went through numerous editions and translations and reached a circulation of over two million by 1922.

Marcy also wrote children's books, and materialist tracts on housework and on sexual relations. *Women as Sex Vendors; or, Why Women Are Conservative* (1918) examined women's subordinate status in relation to sex and morality. She followed this theme in a short dramatic work, *A Free Union: A One-Act Drama of "Free Love"* (1921).

An irrepressible oppositional voice to WW I, Marcy became a target of governmental surveillance and harassment following U.S. entry. Demoralized and exhausted by personal and political losses effected by the war and the onslaught against the Left, she took her own life in 1922. *See also*: Industrial

Workers of the World, *International Socialist Review*

—*Allen Ruff*

REFERENCES
Carney, Jack. *Mary Marcy*. Chicago: Charles H. Kerr, 1923.

Martí, José (1853–95)

Among the most misunderstood radicals in Latin American history, Martí played an important role in Gilded Age America as émigré journalist and labor intellectual.

Born in Havana of Catalan parents, Martí was caught up in the Cuban Revolution of 1868 and exiled to Spain. He traveled widely and made his way to the United States in 1881. His Brooklyn hotel became the headquarters of the new *Partido Revolucionario Cubano* (PRC), the motor of the Cuban independence movement. A correspondent for the *New York Sun* for more than a decade, Martí founded his own newspaper, *Patria*, in 1892. Supported by tobacco workers' contributions, it served as mouthpiece for the movement. From New York Martí often traveled to Tampa, where he rallied Cuban workers and collaborated closely with Carlos Baliño and Vicente Diego Tejera, founders of Cuban socialism, who were active among U.S. workers at the time. Tampa was indeed his most secure political base. Though the Cuban communities in South Florida and New York were roughly the same size, Tampa generated eighty-three PRC affiliates and New York thirteen. Martí forged a link between an extremely radical contemporary Cuban labor movement and the U.S. labor movement, fusing Cuban nationalism with anarcho-socialist ideas, in the process subordinating his own youthful mysticism (he was trained as an aesthete by romantic Cuban intellectuals) to a rationalistic, revolutionary position.

No doubt Martí was influenced by close political associates such as Baliño, president of the PRC in Key West, who later organized a revolutionary community of fifty Cuban families in Thomasville, Georgia, and later was mayor of radical Martí City, Florida. The Cuban exile paper *El Socialista* commented that Martí was no socialist proper, but an ardent ally. An individualist who imbibed Catalan anarchism and collaborated with utopian socialist thinkers and Marxists, he, with his slight charismatic figure, commanded the loyalty of dogmatic radicals and liberal nationalists alike. A bold multiracialist, Martí built the independence campaign on the base of Afro-Cuban worker-soldiers, who ultimately achieved his goals.

Martí posited no systematic social philosophy, but his work is suffused with the constant theme of national liberation and the reconstruction of Cuba along lines of communality and social justice. *See also*: Cuban Americans, Ybor City

—*Thomas Fiehrer*

REFERENCES
Ripoll, Carlos. *José Martí, the United States, and the Marxist Interpretation of Cuban History*. New Brunswick: Rutgers University Press, 1984.

The Masses

This radical magazine reflected the changing relationship between art and politics in the early twentieth century, as did its successor, the *Liberator* (1918–24). The *Masses* was founded in 1911 by the Dutch-born socialist Piet Vlag (with silent backing from Rufus Weeks, vice president of the New York Life Insurance Company) to promote consumer cooperatives in the United States. Modeled after the earlier cultural publication the *Comrade*, it included literature by Tolstoy and Sudermann (translated by the editor, Thomas Seltzer), didactic artwork, and articles in support of cooperatives, right-wing Socialism, woman suffrage, and child labor laws. Its contributors included Marty Heaton Vorse, Walter Lippmann, Art Young, and Josephine Conger-Kaneko. This earnest but dull publication failed in 1912 after attempting to merge with the Chicago-based *Progressive Woman*. Later that year a group of artists revived the *Masses* as an American equivalent to the lavishly illustrated European satiric journals *Simplicissimus* and *L'Assiette au Beurre*; they invited Max Eastman to serve as editor and to raise funds (largely through contributions from wealthy progressives). The artists sought "a magazine we could run around in and be

July 1913 cover by John Sloan

free"—contributors received no pay but exercised artistic control. In protest against the journalistic marketplace, they structured the *Masses* as a worker-owned cooperative with all editorial decisions to be made by group vote. As editor, Eastman moved the magazine away from Socialist Party "dogma" and toward a more wide-ranging program condemning racism, supporting direct action and the Industrial Workers of the World, and advocating a political theory of "hard-headed idealism"—socialism tempered with the pragmatic philosophy of John Dewey. William English Walling contributed a column on European socialism. The strongest writing was labor reportage from Vorse and John Reed, who joined the staff in 1913. After the Chicago critic Floyd Dell became managing editor that year, the literary content expanded to encompass poems by Carl Sandburg, Amy Lowell, and Louis Untermeyer, and stories by Sherwood Anderson, in addition to early attempts at proletarian fiction. Dell, a noted "Greenwich Villager," also brought an interest in psychology, feminism, and free love. The *Masses* soon encountered legal difficulties stemming from its attacks on the capitalist press and organized religion, and its advocacy of birth control. All of these positions were presented with irreverent humor, echoing the editors' promise to "conciliate nobody, not even our readers." The journal soon attracted a reputation and a following far beyond its circulation of between 15,000 and 25,000.

The *Masses* was noted for its art. As official art editor, the painter and illustrator John Sloan redesigned the layout and worked with printers to reproduce vivid two-color covers and the heavy black crayon drawings favored by followers of the socially conscious cartoonist Honoré Daumier. The magazine attracted a group of urban realists who later became known as the Ashcan School (George Bellows, Stuart Davis, Glenn Coleman, and others); their drawings of New York's immigrant neighborhoods in the *Masses* rival their better-known "fine art" paintings and prints. The *Masses* also printed political cartoons "too naked and true for the money-making press" by Robert Minor, Boardman Robinson, Maurice Becker, Kenneth Russell Chamberlain, and Art Young, social satire, and figure studies and landscapes with no overt political message.

The twin goals of "free expression" and "appealing to the masses with the livelier forms of propaganda" led to conflicts that erupted during World War I when most of the art staff "struck" over the issue of adding propagandistic captions to "straight" illustrations. Eastman's efforts to commit the *Masses* to an antiwar position eventually ran afoul of the postmaster general, who revoked the magazine's mailing license under the Espionage Act of 1917. In an early test of free-speech laws, the *Masses* editors were vindicated during a series of well-publicized court cases in 1917 and 1918 but lost access to the mails through a legal technicality; the loss of distribution outlets forced the magazine out of business in December 1917. *See also*: Gellert, Hugo; Giovannitti, Arturo; Greenwich Village; *The Liberator*; Minor, Robert; *New Masses*; Reed, John; Sandburg, Carl; Vorse, Mary Heaton; Young, Art

—Rebecca Zurier

REFERENCES

Eastman, Max. *Enjoyment of Living*. New York: Harper, 1948.

———. *Love and Revolution: My Journey through an Epoch*. New York: Random House, 1964.

Fishbein, Leslie. *Rebels in Bohemia: The Radicals of The Masses, 1911–1917*. Chapel Hill: University of North Carolina Press, 1982.

Zurier, Rebecca. *Art for the Masses: A Radical Magazine and its Graphics, 1911–1917*. Philadelphia: Temple University Press, 1988.

MATTHIESSEN, FRANCIS OTTO (1902–50)

The most prestigious Left academic of the 1930s–1940s, F. O. Matthiessen was also the foremost scholar of American literature. His suicide on April 1, 1950, was widely regarded as a turning point in the intellectual Cold War, dramatizing the precariousness of socialist convictions in the academy.

Born near Pasadena, California, to a cultured eastern mother and the son of a midwestern millionaire industrialist, Matthiessen spent much of his youth in his grandfather's La Salle, Illinois, company town. Early, he affirmed Christian socialist ideas in reaction as he traveled through prep school, Yale, Oxford (as Rhodes Scholar), and Harvard. As a Harvard professor from 1929 onward, he became the main organizer and three times president of the Harvard Teachers Union, the anchor of the Massachusetts American Civil Liberties Union (and frequently a leading participant in nationwide labor defense cases), and the sponsor of numerous Cambridge liberal, pacifist, progressive, and radical organizations. He did so as a homosexual, whose longstanding relationship with the painter Russell Cheney placed both at risk.

Matthiessen's impressive scholarship was marked by a careful approach to a variety of texts, including those (such as T. S. Eliot's poetry or Henry James's novels) apprehended by the contemporary Left only with utmost hostility. His *American Renaissance* (1941), the most influential book in American studies for more than a quarter-century, analyzed the nation's "ruthless individualism" and opposition of practical to intellectual life as fundamentally self-destructive flaws. Turning from simple class reductivism, Matthiessen sought a cultural critique of American civilization both general and particular via the lives, milieu, and work—broadly interpreted—of the Transcendentalists. His imaginative and flexible handling of text as context foreshadowed Raymond Williams's more explicit Marxist studies.

Matthiessen responded to the Cold War, in part, with *From the Heart of Europe* (1948), a journal of personal and political reflection, and with utmost effort for the Progressive Party (he seconded Henry Wallace's nomination). Savage attacks fell upon him from all sides, perhaps the most vitriolic by two young men he had earlier assisted, Irving Howe and Arthur M. Schlesinger, Jr.

Increasingly isolated politically and physically exhausted, Matthiessen took his life by stepping from the twelfth-floor ledge of Boston's Hotel Manger. Characteristically, he refused in his final note to simplify the complex relation between self and society, even under increasingly stressful conditions. "How much the state of the world has to do with my state of mind," he acknowledged, "I cannot know. But as a Christian and a socialist believing in international peace I find myself terribly oppressed by the present conditions." He left behind a bequest that helped the young *Monthly Review* to survive, as he himself could not, the cruel times. *See also*: Literary Criticism, *Monthly Review*

—*George Abbott White*

REFERENCES

Cain, William E. *F. O. Matthiessen and the Politics of Criticism*. Madison: University of Wisconsin Press, 1988.

Marx, Leo. "The Double Consciousness and the Cultural Politics of F. O. Matthiessen." *Monthly Review* 34 (February 1983).

Stern, Frederick C. *F. O. Matthiessen: Christian Socialist as Critic*. Chapel Hill: University of North Carolina Press, 1981.

Sweezy, Paul M. and Leo Huberman, eds. *F. O. Matthiessen (1902–1950): A Collective Portrait*. New York: Monthly Review, 1951.

White, George Abbott. "Ideology and Literature: American Renaissance and F. O. Matthiessen." In *Literature in Revolution*, edited by White and Charles Newman. New York: Holt, Rinehart and Winston, 1972.

MATTSON, HELMI: see TOVERITAR/NAISTER VIIRI

MAURER, JAMES HUDSON (1864–1944)

A machinist and steamfitter, Maurer was a major figure in the Socialist Party and the AFL from 1901 until the early 1930s.

He joined the Knights of Labor in 1880 and held local and regional offices in the Reading, Pennsylvania, area. During the 1890s he was blacklisted because of activities as an organizer for the People's (Populist) Party, Henry George's single tax clubs, and the Socialist Labor Party. In 1901 Maurer joined the SP, eventually serving as its candidate for vice president of the United States in 1928 and 1932. In 1910 Maurer was the first Socialist elected to the Pennsylvania State General Assembly, where he led the fight for workmen's compensation and child labor laws.

Maurer served as president of the Pennsylvania State Federation of Labor (1912–28) and was a founder and first president of Workers Education Bureau (1921–29). During World War I Maurer was an active opponent of U.S. participation. Other activities included campaigning for birth control, serving on the executive board of the 1924 presidential campaign of Robert LaFollette, and participating in a labor delegation to the Soviet Union in 1927. He was elected to the Reading City Council in 1927 on the SP slate. *See also*: Municipal Socialism, Socialist Party

—Alan Singer

REFERENCES
Maurer, James Hudson. *It Can Be Done*. New York: The Rand School Press, 1938.

MAY DAY

Cartoon by I. Swenson (*Industrial Worker*, 1920)

An ancient holiday marked by celebrations in praise of spring and by symbolic evocations of fertility, this day perhaps inevitably became the revolutionary holiday of the nineteenth-century workers' movement. As in British artist Walter Crane's famous May Day drawings (much reprinted in the U.S. socialist press), the vision of socialism seemed to speak at once to the natural yearnings for emancipation from the winter season and from the wintery epoch of class society.

In May 1886 several hundred thousand American workers marched into international labor history when they demonstrated for the eight-hour day. An unusual and informal alliance between the fledgling AFL, local assemblies of the Knights of Labor, and disparate tendencies within the anarchist movement ignited a pent-up demand for shorter working hours. The social and labor ferment that crested in 1885–86 also marked the maturing of the Knights of Labor into the first meaningful national labor organization in the United States. The leadership of the Knights, however, envisioned the eight-hour day as an educational, political, and evolutionary achievement rather than an agitational and revolutionary one. On the other hand, the infant AFL, soon to molt from the impotent Federation of Organized Trades and Labor Unions, tied its star to the militant eight-hour actions. The third grouping in the labor triad comprised that section of the anarchists, mainly European immigrants, who emphasized trade union work as a vehicle to social revolution.

This uneasy and unsettled coalition targeted May 1, 1886, as the day of industrial reckoning. In Boston, Milwaukee, New York City, Pittsburgh, and especially Chicago, tens of thousands of workers rallied and struck for "eight hours for work, eight hours for rest, eight hours for what we will." The nation's newspapers warned that the spirit of the Paris Commune was loose in the land and pointed to specific personalities among the anarchists to prove the point. But the day passed peacefully except in the migrained minds of some employers who reluctantly capitulated to the eight-hour day.

Whether that May day would have been a one-time workers' holiday or "forever remembered," in the words of Samuel Gompers, "as a second Declaration of Independence," is a moot point. The events of a few days later projected it into an international framework and seared the conscience of labor activists ever since. A rally by striking lumbermen near the scene of a labor conflict at the McCormick-Harvester works in suburban Chicago led to a clash with scabs at the famous farm-implement company. Chicago police, already seasoned in labor brutality, mortally wounded several demonstrators.

The Chicago anarchists, who only a few days earlier had organized the peaceful eight-hour parade locally, called for a protest demonstration against the killings. The following night, on May 4, a thousand rallied at Haymarket Square in the city. The mayor of Chicago listened warily in the crowd until a thunderstorm sent His Honor and most of the throng home for the evening. Inexplicably, a large contingent of police seemingly waited for the mayor's departure to forcibly disperse the remaining 200 demonstrators. As the officers sallied into the depleted group, a bomb was thrown into their ranks. Dozens of policemen were injured and eventually seven died, although some may have perished from their comrades' panicked shooting. That response led to widespread but undocumented wounding of many nameless protesters.

The media's failed predictions of violent upheaval for the May Day rallies three days earlier was now easily transferred to the "Haymarket Affair." The forces of law and order understood that the carnage at Haymarket, regardless of who threw the missile, could discredit the labor movement and eradicate its more radical European appendages through a nascent Red Scare. The ensuing show trial in Chicago blessed the miscegenation of May Day and the Haymarket bombing in the popular mind.

The concept of May Day had meanwhile spread rapidly to the international workers' movement, one of American labor's (and radicals') most important innovations. In 1889 the International Socialist Congress in Paris, with full knowledge of the American precedent, designated May 1 as an eight-hour holiday for workers of the world. Already by 1891 May Day became the occasion for violent clashes between police and radicals, as in Rome. Elaborate ceremonies soon evolved, with songs, banners, uniforms, even dioramas to mark the date, often with drawings of the Haymarket victims uplifted as a martyrology. Anarchists, understandably, expressed this particular aspect with the most fervor.

While some labor historians and commentators have claimed that the reaction to the Haymarket bombing debilitated the Knights of Labor and severely curtailed the growing ascendancy of organized labor, the puzzle contains many more pieces than that. The AFL, for example, continued its agitation over the eight-hour day with annual May Day rallies and ceremonies during the 1890s. The proliferation of May Day was thereafter increasingly intertwined with socialist politics, because spiraling conservatism by Gompers and the AFL elevated Labor Day over May Day as the preferred holiday of the American House of Labor.

Immigrants who had participated abroad in May Day events brought the celebrations back to the United States around the turn of the century. More than twenty nationalities held ceremonies—often both miniature versions of events in homelands and a time of joining symbolically with other American workers—from urban neighborhoods to mining camps and farm districts. Finnish Americans, following in part premodern festivities, erected huge bonfires, around which they sang the "Internationale" in Finnish. Immigrant children's musical and theatrical groups, a major focus of leisure activities for all ages, staged their epiphanic performance of the year. Older participants listened to speeches, drank, and danced from night to early dawn.

English-language socialist May Day ceremonies, and even those conducted by the Industrial Workers of the World, although impressive at times, could hardly rival the intensity of the ethnic celebrations. The May Day demonstrations and marches, especially in New York City, perhaps most effectively combined the various groups and sentiments. The advent of World War I, widespread repression, and the division of the movement into Socialist and Communist camps dampened May Day and fairly ended celebrations among mainstream unions. Communists led a partial revival during the 1930s, when the slogan "All Out for May Day" regained a resonance. The Cold War, the isolation of the Left unions, and the aging of the ethnic constituency fairly ended public ceremonies. Radical student-based movements of the 1960s–1970s occasionally attempted, without much success, a revival of the holiday. Most Americans remain oblivious of the continued May Day celebrations of labor, socialist, and communist movements across Europe.

To many Americans (whose elected leaders had, by the 1950s, attempted to institute a celebration of Law Day on May 1), May Day evoked only images of missles and tanks on display in Red Square. The real spirit could be found elsewhere, as among black South African miners who, at tremendous personal risk, took off that day to demonstrate for better working conditions and to remember the Haymarket martyrs. *See also*: Anarchism, Communist Party, Haymarket Incident, Second International, Socialist Labor Party, Socialist Party, Third International

—*Scott Molloy*

REFERENCES

Hobsbawm, Eric, and Terence Ranger, eds. *The Invention of Tradition*. Cambridge: Cambridge University Press, 1984.

Roediger, David, and Franklin Rosemont, eds. *Haymarket Scrapbook*. Chicago: Charles H. Kerr, 1986.

Vecoli, Rudolph. "'Primo Maggio' in the United States: An Invented Tradition of the Italian Anarchists." In *May Day Celebration, Quaderni della Fondazione G. Brodolini*, edited by Andrea Panaccione. Venice: Marsilio Editori, 1988.

McCARTHYISM

During the late 1940s and 1950s, thousands of men and women who were or had been active in the Left fell victim to a massive wave of political repression. Named McCarthyism in honor of the senator from Wisconsin who dominated the news with his reckless charges of subversion in the federal government, the movement was actually a far broader and more effective campaign that not only helped destroy the American Communist Party as an effective political organization, but also drove the Left out of American politics for more than a decade. Nonetheless, when compared with political repression in other societies, McCarthyism was comparatively mild. Only two people (Julius and Ethel Rosenberg) were

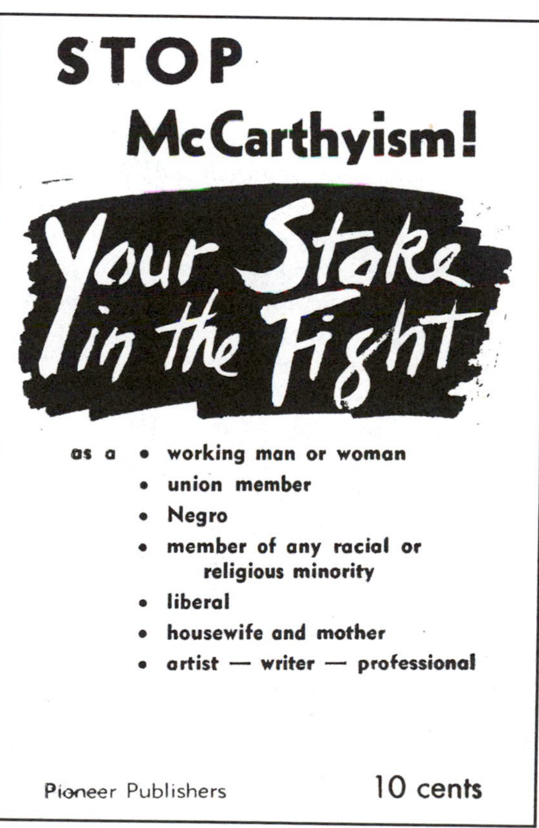

Pamphlet cover, early 1950s

executed and a few hundred others sent to jail; unemployment was the main punishment.

Though anticommunism had long been an important element of American politics, it was not until the United States became involved in the Cold War that it became the dominant element. At that point, the anticommunist program of the political Right was transformed into a national crusade to eliminate Communism and all the groups, individuals, and ideas associated with it from any position of influence within American society. The McCarthyist crusade operated on several levels and contained several different strands. A common thread, however, was the proposition that Communism was such a serious threat to the nation's security that its adherents did not deserve the political and civil rights that other Americans enjoyed. In this period, even the most extreme McCarthyites—like those who felt that the United Nations was as subversive as the CP—often had enough political or economic power to pass legislation or to get people fired.

The McCarthyist crusade began in Washington, D.C., where the Truman administration, under pressure from the traditionally more anticommunist Republican Party, mounted a campaign against domestic Communists as a way of defending itself against charges that it was soft on Communism. The centerpiece of that campaign was a loyalty-security program for government employees. The program, embodied in President Truman's Executive Order 9835 of March 1947, barred Communists, fascists, and other totalitarians as well as anybody guilty of "sympathetic association" with them. Though there was some criticism of E.O. 9835 at the time, most of it was directed against the program's lack of procedural safeguards and reliance on unnamed informers. The core of the program, the institution of a political test for employment, was not seriously questioned and, in fact, quickly spread from the federal government to private employers.

The Truman administration's loyalty-security program made the campaign against domestic Communism a national priority. It also established the two-stage procedure that was to characterize McCarthyism. First the supposed subversives were identified, then they were punished. The first stage, that of identification, was usually handled by some kind of governmental organization, the FBI, for example, or a congressional investigating committee, though conservative journalists and right-wing vigilante groups also fingered people, often with help from the FBI.

The second stage of the McCarthyist process was the application of sanctions. Federal, state, and local governments sometimes administered this stage as well. Most of the time, however, the second stage of McCarthyism was handled by private employers who readily collaborated with the process by firing the individuals who had been identified as politically undesirable during the first stage. Although the first-stage identification procedure is quite well known and is, in fact, what most people usually identify as McCarthyism, it is clear that without the second-stage application of sanctions, the anticommunist offensive would have been much less effective. That second stage not only made it difficult for Communists and other leftists to remain politically active and lead normal lives, but also drew the private sector into the picture.

Most of the people affected were Communists or former Communists who refused to repudiate their past political activities. The Party's leaders probably suffered the most severe penalties. Although the federal government never actually outlawed the Party, it harassed it so severely that it had to devote most of its activities to its own defense. Probably the most significant action in that regard was the indictment and conviction of the Party's top leaders under the 1940 Smith Act for "conspiring to teach and advocate" the forcible overthrow of the government of the United States. Though the Smith Act was a clear violation of the First Amendment's protection of free speech, in 1951 the Supreme Court upheld the Communist leaders' conviction, thus reinforcing the notion that the Party's activities constituted a "clear and present danger" to the nation's security.

Another important element in the McCarthyist campaign were the anticommunist investigations carried out by conservative congressmen. These investigations performed several functions. They not only identified individuals as politically undesirable, but they also provided a forum for the Republican Party's charges that Democratic administrations had tolerated communist subversion. These charges gained substance after the House Un-American Activities Committee's (HUAC) hearings on Communists in government in the fall of 1948 uncovered in the Alger Hiss case what appeared to be an example of high-level espionage. Accused of having been a Communist and then of having passed government documents, Hiss, a former State Department official, denied the charges and was ultimately convicted of perjury, primarily on the testimony of Whittaker Chambers, a self-confessed former spy. The Hiss case not only gave substance to the Republican charges that the New Deal regime had been harboring Communists, but it also enhanced the stature of HUAC and the other anticommunist investigating committees.

Joseph McCarthy was only the most notorious of the congressional anticommunist investigators. He differed from the rest only in that he attacked liberals as well as radicals. But the burden of his charges was the same; he was trying to pin responsibility for such supposed American setbacks as the Communist victory in China on internal subversion. When McCarthy got out of control and continued his attacks even after a Republican administration had taken over, he was finally stopped. But his earlier charges and those of the other congressional investigators did enormous damage, both to the careers and personal lives of the individuals they targeted as well as to the rest of society.

Because employers collaborated with the anticommunist investigating committees by firing the people who refused to cooperate with them, the committees' witnesses had few options. Cooperation, as the committees defined it, meant giving the names of former political comrades, a degrading procedure designed to force people to repudiate their left-wing pasts. Witnesses who named names usually kept their jobs; witnesses who did not usually lost theirs. In addition, they risked going to jail for contempt of Congress. The Supreme Court, whose majority apparently condoned the anticommunist crusade, did not protect people from having to answer the committees' questions about their political beliefs and associations. The only protection the Court upheld was that embodied in the Fifth Amendment's privilege against having to testify against oneself. The committees, which knew that many of their witnesses had invoked the Fifth Amendment only to avoid becoming informers, exploited these people's predicament by branding them as "Fifth Amendment Communists."

Though the men and women who faced congressional investigators received the most publicity during the McCarthy period, thousands of other people also lost their jobs or were harassed in other ways. Loyalty oaths proliferated, especially for government employees at the state and local level. Security clearances for defense-related work affected scientists and engineers. Exact figures are hard to come by, though one source estimates that approximately 10,000 people may have lost their jobs. Unemployment was not the only sanction. The Immigration and Naturalization Service threatened to deport foreign-born radicals and the State Department denied passports to suspected Reds. There were unofficial harassments as well, from the entertainment industry blacklists to anonymous telephone calls. Many people who did not lose their jobs or go to jail, nonetheless suffered considerable personal strain and anxiety.

It is difficult to assess the damage that McCarthyism did to the American Left. Certainly, it contributed to the demise of the American CP as a politically viable movement, though the Party's own internal problems and self-destructive behavior in the face of the campaign against it was also a factor. More important, by increasing the personal risks associated with political radicalism, McCarthyism created a climate that discouraged people from participating in left-wing activities. Those radicals who remained active had to devote most of their attention to self-defense. As a result, it was not until McCarthyism began to subside in the late 1950s that the American Left could again focus on such issues as peace, racial equality, and economic justice. *See also*: Communist Party, FBI, House Un-American Activities Committee, National Lawyers Guild, Rosenberg Case

—*Ellen W. Schrecker*

REFERENCES

Carleton, Don E. *Red Scare! Right-Wing Hysteria, Fifties Fanaticism and Their Legacy in Texas*. Austin: Texas Monthly Press, 1985.

Caute, David. *The Great Fear*. New York: Simon and Schuster, 1978.

Navasky, Victor. *Naming Names*. New York: Viking, 1980.

O'Reilly, Kenneth. *Hoover and the Un-Americans*. Philadelphia: Temple University Press, 1983.

Schrecker, Ellen W. *No Ivory Tower: McCarthyism and the Universities*. New York: Oxford University Press, 1986.

McGrath, Tom (*b.* 1916)

One of America's most prolific and intrepid radical poets, McGrath was born in North Dakota at the outset of the great Non-Partisan League period of the state's history. McGrath's father, a farmer, was sympathetic to the Industrial Workers of the World as well. This rural experience was critical to the formation of McGrath's consciousness and to his sensibility from his literary beginnings to his latest works.

After studying at the University of North Dakota and receiving a B.A., McGrath was awarded a Rhodes Scholarship. Because of World War II, he attended graduate school at Louisiana State University instead. For a time in 1942, McGrath worked as a welder in the shipyards of New Jersey, and became active with the Communist Party. The brutal conditions of work, and penetration of unions by organized crime, helped form the basis of an important collection of poems, *Longshot O'Leary's Garland of Practical Poesie* (1949) and a novel, *This Coffin Has No Handles* (1984).

After the war and Army service in Alaska, McGrath took the Rhodes Scholarship at New College, Oxford, and in 1951 accepted a teaching position at Los Angeles State College. In 1953 he refused in defiant terms to cooperate with the House Un-American Activities Committee, and he was dismissed from his academic position. Regarded on the Left as an especially promising political writer, he continued his work as editorial assistant on the short-lived *Mainstream* (1946–47) and on a science-fiction novel, *The Gates of Ivory, The Gates of Horn* (1957). He also commenced a multilayered narrative "pseudo-autobiography" (McGrath's own description), including narratives from the frontier heritage of North Dakota, the crushing of the IWW, life on the New York waterfront, and the defeat of the Left. This *Letter to an Imaginary Friend* has appeared in 4 sections. Parts I and II were published by Swallow Press in 1969 and Parts III and IV by Cooper Canyon Press in 1985. McGrath has had 3 volumes of his selected poetry published since the early 1960s: *New and Selected Poems* (1964), *The Movie at the End of the World* (1972), and *Selected Poems* (1988). A documentary on his life and work also bears the title *The Movie at the End of the World*. A Soviet edition of his selected work was published in Russian by Raduga in Moscow (1984), and his novel *This Coffin Has No Handles* was published in their journal *Foreign Literature* (1987). *See also*: *Mainstream*, Proletarian and Radical Writers

—*Fred Whitehead*

REFERENCES

"The Dream Champ." Special issue of *North Dakota Quarterly* (Fall 1982).

"Thomas McGrath: Life and the Poem." Special issue of *TriQuarterly* (Fall 1987).

Stern, Fred (ed.). *The Revolutionary Poet in the United States*. Columbia: University of Missouri Press, 1988.

McKay, Claude (1890–1948)

A decisive personal link between the Harlem Renaissance, the West Indies, and the Left, McKay had published two volumes of poetry in Jamaica before arriving in the United States in 1912. Like his literary aspirations, McKay's political tendencies had already developed early in Jamaica, where he came into contact with Fabian socialists through his brother's interest in the ideas of Sir Sidney Oliver and through his own love of the works of George Bernard Shaw.

McKay's first year in America occurred at a moment when socialist thought and action were widely felt. The zeal and unwavering idealism of the Industrial Workers of the World appealed most to him, and by 1919 he had joined their ranks. During this phase, he met and became close friends with Hubert H. Harrison, dynamic Harlem street-corner orator, black socialist, and prolific essayist. When McKay's books later failed to get proper recognition in the black press, Harrison took up the cudgels, extolling McKay as "the greatest living poet of Negro blood in America today."

The *Masses* also deeply influenced McKay with its stirring (if sometimes inconsistent) antiracism. He joined his friend Max Eastman on the board of the *Liberator*, created in 1917 to succeed the repressed *Masses*, and remained an editor into the early 1920s. The *Liberator* in 1919 published his famous poem "If We Must Die," a stirring call to arms against aggressive capitalism. Not yet thirty, McKay was fully committed to the struggle—and to a literary career.

McKay soon joined such Harlem radical figures as Harrison, Cyril Briggs, Richard B. Moore, and Harry Haywood in the African Blood Brotherhood, a small but vital political group that merged with the Communist Party. But he continued to function as a maverick, refusing to submit to Party discipline, determined not to allow his ambitions and ideas to be controlled or subordinated. Meanwhile, he remained a tireless poet, journalist, and black radical. From 1919 to 1923 he traveled to Russia, Germany, and other parts of Europe, making a dramatic appearance at the Comintern and acquiring an international reputation among radical intellectuals. He remained unimpressed by political accolades and attention (possibly, as he suggested in his autobiography, because he could not take the American Communist movement as seriously as it took itself). He achieved the wide literary recognition he had sought with the publication of his poetry volume *Literary Shadows* (1923).

Ironically, the three novels destined to bring McKay lasting fame and notoriety—*Home to Harlem*, *Banjo*, and *Banana Bottom*—were all written and published during a twelve-year hiatus in Europe. He had portrayed black life, in the United States and elsewhere, in many aspects; he had written deeply about the dilemmas of blacks in Western civilization, and about the pleasures of ordinary mass life. But he felt an alienation or melancholy, mirrored in his inability to gain the proper remuneration or royalties from these works. McKay returned to the United States in 1934 a lonely and destitute literary figure, disenchanted with communism.

The remainder of his life would be anticlimactic. Although he continued to write, his creative impulse withered along with his failing health. In 1938 he formed a friendship with Ellen Tarry, a black Catholic writer of children's books. Through her influence, he converted to Roman Catholicism less than four years before his death.

—*Herb Boyd*

REFERENCES

Baker, Houston. *Modernism and the Harlem Renaissance*. Chicago: University of Chicago Press, 1987.

Bontemps, Arna. *The Harlem Renaissance Remembered*. New York: Dodd, Mead, 1972.

Cooper, Wayne. *Claude McKay: Rebel Sojourner in the Harlem Renaissance*. Baton Rouge: Louisiana State University Press, 1987.

McKenney, Ruth (1911–72)

Best remembered for her first and best-selling book, *My Sister Eileen* (1938), which inspired two Broadway plays and a Hollywood film, McKenney joined the Communist Party of the United States in the late 1930s and edited the "Strictly Personal" weekly column in the *New Masses*. Born in Mishawaka, Indiana, and educated at Ohio State University, McKenney worked for a time as a newspaper reporter and contributed short fiction to such mainstream magazines as *Harper's* and the *New Yorker*. In 1937 she married fellow *New Masses* writer Richard Branstein, who wrote under the name Bruce Minton, and later published a fictionalized version of their courtship and marriage, *Love Story* (1950).

When McKenney met Branstein, both were working on books on the American labor movement. McKenney's *Industrial Val-*

ley (1939) recounts the conditions surrounding the Akron, Ohio, rubber workers' strike of 1936. McKenney used articles in local newspapers to piece together a daily journal of the strike. *Industrial Valley* presents a vivid portrait of class relations in Depression America and follows political events into the homes of individual workers. A sociological study and political commentary, *Industrial Valley* was judged at the time of its publication "the most original and readable piece of American labor history every written." The American Writers Congress awarded McKenney its prize for nonfiction in 1938 and again in 1939.

McKenney next tried her hand at a proletarian novel, *Jake Home* (1943), a story about a fictional union organizer and Communist that met, despite favorable reviews, with little popular acclaim. McKenney's unsuccessful novel nevertheless provided a vivid portrait of problematical sex and class relations within the labor movement, a subject that eventually earned McKenney sharp criticism from the *Daily Worker*. While McKenney herself believed her protagonist was too pious, she concluded that her Communist critics required a yet more idealistic and one-dimensional treatment that placed labor organizers "in a sort of left-wing *Little Women* fireside atmosphere."

McKenney wrote several articles in the *New Masses* on the relationship between wage-earning and women's domestic responsibilities. Unlike Mary Inman, she did not value domestic labor and argued to the contrary, that women's emancipation depended upon their equal access to the realm of social production.

In 1946 McKenney and Branstein were expelled from the CPUSA for failing to condemn the discredited leadership of Earl Browder. They drifted in the political wilderness while collaborating on historical fiction and travel literature. *See also*: Communist Party, *New Masses*, Proletarian and Radical Writers

—*Mari Jo Buhle*

McKinney, Edward Britt (early 1900s?–1940s?)

Afro-American preacher and Southern Tenant Farmers' Union organizer, McKinney—called E. B. or Britt by his friends—was a bald, garrulous preacher and a near-legendary organizer for the biracial New Deal–era STFU. McKinney joined the Socialist Party in 1933 and was greatly influenced by Marcus Garvey's black nationalism. He was the first black vice president, and therefore the highest elected Afro-American official of the STFU from its founding in 1934 to 1938. He organized an STFU local in Marked Tree, Arkansas, on the principle of biracial cooperation, inviting whites to Afro-American meetings. Through his leadership, Afro-American and white STFU locals in Marked Tree grew together instead of apart. In 1934 delegates to the STFU Convention elected McKinney as vice president. From 1934 to 1938 he worked feverishly, utilizing his church contacts to enlist members into STFU locals. In 1935 he was among an STFU delegation that traveled to Washington to challenge the Agricultural Adjustment Agency concerning the plight of sharecroppers.

McKinney's longtime Garveyism grew stronger after 1935, however, as he saw African Americans beaten year after year to placate poor whites who were also given slightly better government service. His devotion to black separatism inadvertently led him into the middle of a controversy between STFU leader H. L. Mitchell and Donald Henderson, head of the United Cannery Agricultural Packing and Allied Workers of America (UCAPAWA), both of whom were white. In 1937 STFU leaders had voted reluctantly to enter the CIO-affiliated organization, but Mitchell staunchly resisted UCAPAWA efforts to gain centralized control over STFU operations. In 1938 McKinney attempted to create a separate Afro-American organization within the STFU by gaining separate recognition of thirteen black locals in Arkansas by the UCAPAWA. As a result, Mitchell charged that McKinney was working with Henderson to split the STFU along racial lines. At a special executive council meeting in September 1938, McKinney was expelled from his post as vice president and from the union itself for these activities. McKinney then joined two other ousted white leaders, Claude Williams of Commonwealth College in Arkansas and

W. L. Blackstone of the President's Council on Farm Tenancy, to oppose Mitchell's leadership of the STFU. However, Mitchell courted McKinney at the fifth annual STFU convention at Cotton Plant, Arkansas, in late 1938, and McKinney decided to repudiate Williams and Blackstone.

McKinney's rejection of black separatism won him readmission to the union, although he did not regain the vice presidency. In 1939 McKinney joined other Afro-American STFU leaders in staying with the CIO in the ongoing conflict between Mitchell and the UCAPAWA. This decision virtually ended farm labor organizing efforts in the 1930s. Apparently, no one knows what happened to the dynamic black leader McKinney, known as a "pillar of Granite in a weary land." *See also*: Mitchell, H. L.; Southern Tenant Farmers Union

—*Orville Vernon Burton*

REFERENCES

Canton, Louis. *A Prologue to the Protest Movement: The Missouri Sharecroppers Roadside Demonstration of 1939*. Durham: Duke University Press, 1969.

Grubbs, Donald H. *Cry From The Cotton: The Southern Tenant Farmers' Union and the New Deal*. Chapel Hill: University of North Carolina Press, 1971.

Southern Tenant Farmers' Union Papers, Southern Historical Collection, University of North Carolina-Chapel Hill.

McLEVY, JASPER: see MUNICIPAL SOCIALISM

McNAMARA CASE

On October 1, 1910, two explosions tore into the downtown printing plant of the *Los Angeles Times*. The blasts and a fire they touched off killed twenty-one men. The following April, after an investigation led by private detective William J. Burns, two brothers active in the International Association of Bridge and Structural Iron Workers (BSIW)—Secretary-Treasurer John J. McNamara and his younger brother James B. McNamara—were arrested in the Midwest, brought to Los Angeles, and indicted for murder. Thus began one of the most important legal cases in U.S. labor history.

Unionists of all political persuasions portrayed the McNamaras as victims of a frame-up by their corporate enemies. There was a good deal of circumstantial evidence to support this view. Since 1906, the very existence of the BSIW had been under attack from the National Erectors Association, a management group in which United States Steel, the nation's most powerful open-shop corporation, was a major influence. At the same time, AFL organizers had been engaged, since 1910, in a full-scale and partially successful effort to recruit Los Angeles workers into unions. Harrison Gray Otis, publisher of the *Times*, was a determined foe of organized labor. Convicting the McNamaras for bombing his plant would ruin the local union drive and humble the AFL nationally.

In its breadth and commitment, labor's campaign for the brothers was unprecedented. Samuel Gompers, whom Burns hinted had aided the bombers, declared the McNamaras "innocent victims of capitalist greed," vowed to raise $350,000 for the defense team, and hired celebrated attorney Clarence Darrow to lead it. William D. Haywood of the Industrial Workers of the World called for a nationwide general strike on the first day of the trial; unionists throughout California contributed a full day's wages to the cause; and on Labor Day, 1911 (which the AFL renamed "McNamara Day"), huge crowds in every major American city outside the South gathered to proclaim the brothers' innocence. Across the United States, Socialists and business unionists worked together on the defense. In Los Angeles, they also campaigned to elect as mayor Job Harriman, leader of the local Socialist Party. Harriman won a plurality of the vote in a November primary and was favored to win the runoff election a month later.

However, the entire effort rested on quicksand: the McNamaras were guilty. The testimony of a state's witness named Ortie McManigal and Burns's skillful sleuthing revealed that the *Times* explosion was the crowning blow to a series of eighty-seven bombings that top officers of the BSIW, including John J. McNamara, had carried out since 1906 to force the Natonal Erectors Association to recognize the union. James B. McNamara had placed the dynamite outside the printing plant, intending only to damage the building. But the explosives unexpectedly ignited several drums of highly flammable ink.

On December 1, 1911 (four days before the mayoral runoff), the two brothers came to court and pled guilty—James to the bombing itself and John as an accessory to the dynamiting of a local factory. James received a sentence of life imprisonment, John a sentence of fifteen years. Job Harriman's bid for mayor was decisively defeated. And Los Angeles remained an open-shop stronghold.

But the class hostilities the case revealed did lead, in 1912, to the formation of the prolabor Federal Commission on Industrial Relations and a tacit alliance between the AFL and President Woodrow Wilson. Ironically, the bomb set by James McNamara allowed Samuel Gompers to join hands with those who ruled the progressive state. *See also*: Socialist Party

—*Michael Kazin*

REFERENCES

Foner, Philip S. *History of the Labor Movement in the United States*. Vol. 5, *The AFL in the Progressive Era, 1910–1915*. New York: International Publishers, 1980.

Kazin, Michael. *Barons of Labor: The San Francisco Building Trades and Union Power in the Progressive Era*. Urbana: University of Illinois Press, 1987.

Stimson, Grace H. *Rise of the Labor Movement in Los Angeles*. Berkeley: University of California Press, 1955.

MEMORIAL DAY MASSACRE

Perhaps the most flagrant example of contrived "law and order" against both law and orderly collective bargaining, the Memorial Day Massacre of 1937 in South Chicago also stands out as a major tragedy and defeat to the industrial union movement and progressive forces in that generation.

In the Spring of 1937, the CIO Steel Workers Organizing Committee (SWOC) was completing a nationwide campaign spearheaded by volunteer and paid organizers, including many Communists and radicals. The top officials of SWOC and its parent CIO, however, sought purely economic unionism as chartered in the new National Labor Relations Act. Directly opposing that law, the independent "Little Steel" companies made each plant an arsenal of assorted weapons, grenades, bombs, and tear gas. During the first week of the strike, preliminary skirmishes at several Republic Steel plants pitted armed strikebreakers and police against union pickets. The Republic local of SWOC planned an outing adjoining a neighborhood tavern that served as strike headquarters. The crowd of 2,000 strikers and their families listened to speeches and sang "Solidarity Forever," forming an impromptu parade toward the factory at the close of the event.

Four platoons of Chicago police met them, clubs and guns drawn. A union member asked for the police to stand aside; they answered with gunfire. Amid screaming and outcries, the terrorized paraders fled for their lives, tear gas bombs landing among them. Police followed, bludgeoning the fallen, dragging men and women off to vans. Others, wounded, made the tavern, which became an emergency field hospital. Ten union men had been shot to death.

A later U.S. Senate inquiry traced procative incitements to a police informer of the Industrial Detail (informally, the "Red Squad") of the Chicago police. Chicago police commissioner James P. Allman averred that his men had halted a "communistic parade," operating under "instructions from Moscow."

The "Little Steel" strike was lost, and steel companies held out until forced by wartime pressures to sign a union contract. Tom Girdler, antilabor spokesman of Republic Steel, and the steel companies had in the meantime shocked the nation, disrupted the CIO's momentum, and shattered the nerve of Republic strikers. *See also*: Industrial Unionism

—*S. Carl Hirsch*

REFERENCES

Newell, Barbara Warne. *Chicago and the Labor Movement: Metropolitan Unionism in the 1930s*. Urbana: University of Illinois Press, 1961.

THE MESSENGER: see RANDOLPH, A. PHILIP

MEXICAN AMERICANS

The radicalism of this group has taken four primary forms. Irredentist movements sought to restore the lands taken after the Treaty of Guadalupe Hidalgo; Mexicans organized their own nationals and Mexican Americans for revolution in Mexico; unions have organized both Mexican and mixed locals that were often radical and had ties with American-led organizations such as the Communist Party; and nationalist movements have sought to assert Mexican needs and culture outside of the political and social institutions of the United States.

The Mexican War waged for the lands that are now the American Southwest did not end with its conclusion in 1848. Excluded from, or literally thrown out of, the economic opportunities of the new territories of the United States, several Mexicans became outlaws and popular heroes. Most notably, Joaquin Murieta, Juan Flóres, and Tiburcio Vásquez took to the hills of California in symbolic protest in the two decades after the war in the pattern of the social bandit described in the work of Eric Hobsbawm. In Texas in 1859 Juan N. Cortina raised an army of 1,200 men that captured the town of Brownsville to secure for Mexicans the rights promised them in the 1848 treaty. Himself a member of the wealthy elite, Cortina railed at the lawlessness that characterized the actions of many Anglo-Texans against lower-class Mexicans. Forced across the border in 1860, he fought against the French during their occupation of Mexico. In a more formal fashion, *Las Gorras Blancas* (the White Caps) organized in New Mexico in association with the Knights of Labor in the late 1880s to protest the alienation of their lands. Land grabbers had dispossessed many Hispanic New Mexicans from their ancestral common lands, pressing them into dependence on wage labor, particularly for the railroads. There many, such as *Los Gorras Blancas'* founder Juan José Herrera, became involved in the Knights and were exposed to its philosophy of cooperativism. Their activities, though, centered around cutting the fences that had come to exclude them from their old lands, especially in and around the town of Las Vegas in San Miguel County. In 1890 many of them joined the Peoples Party, which won the county elections, though with little programmatic effect. Factionalized over the use of violence and involvement in elections, *Los Gorras Blancas* faded from the New Mexican landscape by the mid-1890s, though symbolic wire-cutting continued.

In the Rio Grande Valley of South Texas, Mexicans organized a military movement to regain sovereignty over their lands. In 1914 and 1915 *El Plan de San Diego* proclaimed "the independence and segregation of the states bordering on the Mexican nation of which states the Republic of Mexico was robbed in a most perfidious manner by North American Imperialism." Such native *Tejanos* as Aniceto Pizaña and Luis de la Rosa directed armed bands of from twenty-five to one hundred in the valley. By July 1915, raids had become nearly a daily occurrence. By this time over half of the Rio Grande Valley's population left and the area's economy was in ruins. This state of war existed until October, when the border patrols on both sides increased and the raids declined. Again, the land question motivated most of the fighters, though the Texas Rangers—essentially the land-grabbing ranchers' thugs—and the commercialization of life brought by the railroads sparked their actions.

In the late 1950s Reies López Tijerina (b. 1923) initiated new efforts to restore the ancestral lands of New Mexico that had been granted by the Spanish Crown before 1846. Trying to enlist the support of the Mexican government, the United Nations, and the American courts, Tijerina attempted to enforce the Treaty of Guadalupe Hidalgo and the legality of the land grants. Legal channels produced only frustration. In 1963 he organized the *Alianza Federal de Mercedes*, which attracted hundreds of barrio dwellers in Albuquerque who had been pressured off the land and into welfare or wage dependency, and thousands of Hispano farmers from northern New Mexico and southern Colorado who barely subsisted on the remains of their ancestral lands. Through marches on the New Mexico capital, this organization brought mass pressure, albeit futile, on the state government to recognize their cause. Then, in October 1966, Tijerina and 350 *Aliancistas* occupied a portion of Kit Carson National Forest that they understood to be part of the San Joaquin del Rio Chama grant. Arresting two rangers for trespassing, they elected a traditional *alcalde* and *ayuntamiento*. After they were turned out, Tijerina was arrested and released on bail. The state's establishment—Anglo and Mexican—called him a Communist and a "creature of darkness." On June 5, 1967, Tijerina and twenty armed *Aliancistas* captured the Tierra Amarilla Courthouse in an effort to place District Attorney Sanchez under citizens' arrest. The ensuing shootout seriously wounded two officers. The rebels fled to the hills, as a 2,000-man army terrorized the countryside searching for them. After their surrender, a jury remarkably aquitted Tijerina, though he was jailed for the previous incident, effectively causing the demise of the *Alianza*.

Before World War II, the "GI Generation," and the Zoot-Suit Riots of 1943, Mexicans in the United States usually focused their political interests on the events south of the border. The Mexican Revolution (1911–20) particularly fired the passions of Mexicans in the United States, where supporters of all factions could be found. As early as 1891 Catarino Garza, a journalist from South Texas, and 1,000 followers attacked across the border to liberate northern Mexico from the dictator Porfirio Díaz. Most significantly, the anarchist *Partido Liberal Mexicano* organized for the revolution in the American Southwest after its leader, Ricardo Flóres Magón, fled there in 1905.

In the Southwest before the 1930s most Mexicans worked seasonally on the railroads and in agriculture. Thus their union struggles tended to be spontaneous and ad hoc until the Communists' Cannery and Agricultural Workers Industrial Union provided stable leadership in the late 1920s and early 1930s. Several exiled anarchists led such Mexican unions as the *Confederación de Uniones Campesinos y Obreros Mexicanos*, which organized the fields of southern California in the 1930s. American and Mexican Communists, Mexican anarchists, and the Mexican consulate all competed for leadership of this and other agricultural unions.

In urban centers, Mexican workers participated in the unionization drives of the 1930s including "red" Trade Union Unity League unions and Communist-tinged CIO ones. The imminence of the Mexican Revolution drew some Mexicans to revolutionary ideology and rhetoric, or at least they did not fear it as much as their Anglo shop-mates. Two of the most remarkable women in Southwestern U.S. history, Guatemalan-born Luisa Moreno and Emma Tenayuca of San Antonio, state secretary of the Communist Party in Texas, organized in such unions. In fact, the militance and solidarity of Mexican workers proved essential to the organization of several of the CIO's more radical unions in the Southwest, particularly the United Cannery, Agricultural, Packing, and Allied Workers of America; United Furniture Workers; and the International Union of Mine, Mill, and Smelter Workers. The CP recruited some Mexican union leaders to its ranks and pushed for equality within the unions. Such Party organizations as the Workers Alliance and the International Labor Defense participated in Mexican causes where no one else treaded.

This era also saw the emergence of the Spanish Speaking Peoples Congress, which Luisa Moreno organized in 1938. An explicitly radical organization, it took stands on community, labor, legislative, and immigration issues in the Southwest. Red-baiting and factionalism ended its career in 1940, though it had 6,000 members at its peak. Truman-McCarthyism effectively precluded a revival of such Mexican radical activity after World War II, though such groups as the Community Services Organization (CSO), the Mexican American Political Association (MAPA), and the reformist American GI Forum and League of United Latin American Citizens (LULAC) maintained a Mexican political presence in California.

In the 1960s farm workers and youth led the resurgence of a Mexican challenge to Anglo economic, cultural, and political supremacy. Trained at the CSO in San Jose,

César Chávez organized the United Farm Workers in 1962, which eventually brought a modicum of justice to the fields of California through strikes and the famous secondary boycotts of grapes and lettuce. The first Mexican American of true national stature, Chávez inspired a new era of oppositional politics on the part of Mexican Americans.

The Crusade for Justice in Colorado, *El Partido de la Raza Unida* in Texas, the high school student strikes ("blowouts") in East Los Angeles and later in south Texas and Denver, and *el Movimiento Estudiantil Chicano de Aztlán* (MEChA) on college campuses, represented a new nationalism that challenged both Anglo cultural and political dominance as well as the accommodationist views of the 1950s generation of Mexican Americans. The youth took the word *Chicano* to distinguish themselves from assimilationists. (The word derives from the Nahuatl pronunciation of *Mexicano* and usually denoted someone of rough, lower-class origins.) They also took the phrase in use in Mexican communities since the nineteenth century to denote the Mexican people—"La Raza."

Rodolfo "Corky" González, boxer and author of the inspirational epic poem "I Am Joaquín," founded the Crusade for Justice in Denver in 1966. Vigilant in its attempts to "nationalize every school in our community" and in its defense of the Chicano community against the police, the crusade founded its own school, newspaper, and social center.

In 1967 college students in San Antonio founded the Mexican-American Youth Organization, which gained financial assistance from the Ford Foundation. Challenging the Democratic Party in that city, it lost its funding, and one of MAYO's organizers and main spokespersons, José Angel Gutiérrez, then went to Crystal City in South Texas to put MAYO's principles into action in his hometown. In mid-1969 his organization and strategy began unfolding as the majority Chicano population began taking over the school board, city council, and even a few businesses through boycotts, and, with the founding of *La Raza Unida* Party in the spring of 1970, elections. By 1974, Crystal City and *Raza Unida* had become the pride of the Chicano movement in Texas. In 1972, though, other nationalists such as Corky González grabbed hold of the idea and, against Gutiérrez's wishes, thrust the party into national politics. Its zealous supporters' demands for a Chicano third party factionalized Chicano political leaders and essentially doomed *La Raza Unida*. Gutiérrez's efforts did change forever the attitude of Mexican-American politics in Texas. There would no longer be the old deference: "Psychologically," he stated, "if you give in to one of those bastards [the Rangers], you've had it. That's been the life of our parents. That's why they go around with their hats in their hands. This has to be stopped. We've got to be just as arrogant."

In March 1968, 15,000 students walked out of five East Los Angeles high schools protesting the lack of Chicano teachers, the irrelevance of their Anglo-oriented classes, and general disrespect for their culture. The police and arrests and trials of the leaders eventually restored order, but not before students perfected the tactic, using it for two more years to insure the responsiveness of school authorities.

The period from fall 1966 to spring 1967 saw the emergence of the first Chicano student groups on California college campuses. Concerned primarily with issues of cultural identity and a sense of obligation to the barrios from which they came, these students later formed the United Mexican American Students (UMAS) in summer and fall of 1967 at UCLA, from which it quickly spread to other southwestern campuses. Moving away from a service orientation toward political agitation, UMAS, and later MEChA—into which some UMAS chapters had transformed—redefined the goals of education for Chicanos away from preparation for assimilation to "service to the Chicano community . . . and for the purpose of realizing political, social, and economic change." The First Annual Chicano Conference in Denver, which Corky González called forth in 1969 with an attendance of over 2,000, proved the high point of this movement. By the mid-1970s, MEChA chapters had begun to divide between nationalists, often affiliated with *Raza Unida*; Marxists, who also joined Marxist-Leninist groups; and those who wanted a cultural emphasis.

Toward the mid-1970s many Chicano activists shifted their focus to cross national issues. Indeed, they came to reject notions of Chicanismo because it divided those who lived north of the border from those who lived in Mexico. Bert Corona (b. 1918), a veteran of the CIO and organizer of MAPA, organized *Centro de Acción Autonoma-Hermandad General de Trabajadores* (CASA) in Los Angeles to unite all "Mexicanos" against abuses of undocumented workers. *See also*: Communist Party; Magón, Ricardo Flóres; Migratory Agricultural Workers; Spanish-Speaking Peoples Congress; Union Sponsored Films

—*Douglas Monroy*

REFERENCES

Acuña, Rodolfo. *Occupied America: A History of Chicanos*. 3d ed. New York: Harper and Row, 1988.

Castillo, Pedro, and Albert Camarillo, eds. *Furia y Muerte: Los Bandidos Chicanos*. Los Angeles: Aztlan Publications, 1973.

Castro, Tony. *Chicano Power: The Emergence of Mexican America*. New York: Dutton, 1974.

Gómez-Quiñones, Juan. "Research Notes on the Twentieth Century." *Aztlán* 1, no. 1 Spring 1970.

Jarrico, Paul (producer), Herbert Biberman (director), Michael Wilson (writer). *Salt of the Earth*. Film.

Monroy, Douglas. "*Anarquismo y Comunismo*: Mexican Radicalism and the Communist Party in Los Angeles During the 1930s." *Labor History* 24 (Winter 1983).

Rosenbaum, Robert J. *Mexicano Resistance in the Southwest*. Austin: University of Texas Press, 1981.

MIGRATORY AGRICULTURAL LABOR

These workers have faced debilitating problems of chronic migration, job insecurity, low wages, disfranchisement, and racism. Drawn from a labor pool of unemployed and underemployed people, the workers are primarily nonwhite immigrant and native workers who are racially stigmatized, politically disfranchised, and excluded from meaningful federal and state labor legislation. These problems have mitigated against long-term organizations and successful strikes; yet conditions have led to sharp conflicts and radical response.

—Courtesy Workingman's Paper.

The migratory agricultural labor system developed to meet the seasonal demands of large-scale industrialized capitalist agriculture that emerged following the Civil War. The rapidly disintegrating old agriculture provided the migrants: black and white ex-tenants and sharecroppers from the South moved up and down the Atlantic Coast harvesting fruits and vegetables; white farm-workers from the Middle South and Midwest formed another migrant stream into the North Central States; and from Texas and across the border came Mexican workers to work the fields in Texas, California, and the Southwest. California was the most industrialized of the agricultural states, tended by a succession of migrant workers since the 1880s: Indians, Chinese, Hindustanis, Japanese, Filipinos, Mexicans, and Anglos.

The conditions of industrialized agriculture gave rise to organizing, primarily in California. Spontaneous strikes among Mexicans, Filipinos, Japanese, and other groups occurred with the harvest and acted as a de facto form of collective bargaining. Japanese workers used their work gangs as incipient labor organizations. In the 1910s the Industrial Workers of the World worked with migratory agricultural workers in California. The IWW found a base with Mexican workers influenced by the anarcho-syndicalist *Partido Liberal Mexicano* (Mexican Liberal Party) allied with the IWW. Japanese, Chinese, and Filipinos also joined. The brief Wobbly involvement was on a hit-or-miss basis, in part because they avoided tight organization. Their influence came to an end with the 1917 trials of the Wobblies.

By the 1920s, the agricultural industry in Arizona and California had developed industrywide organizations that centralized labor recruitment, set wage rates, and dealt with labor uprisings on an industrywide basis. These effectively squashed spontaneous strikes and necessitated more sophisticated labor organizing. Two forms of organization emerged: ethnic-based organizations and left-wing unions. The two at times worked together, at times conflicted.

Ethnic-based groups established the first permanent agricultural labor organizations. Filipinos organized ethnic organizations. By the late 1920s, Mexican mutual-aid societies, long active in Mexico as de facto labor organizations, began to engage in collective bargaining. In 1927 the *Confederación de Uniónes Obreros Mexicanos* (CUOM), later renamed the *Confederación de Uniónes Campesinos y Obreros Mexicanos* (CUCOM) was formed, uniting Mexican unions and federations in an effort to encourage Mexican labor organization. CUCOM exhibited a mixture of radical rhetoric and adherence to legal and nonviolent tactics similar to its parent organization, the Mexican union, *Confederación Regional Obrera Mexicana* (CROM). CUCOM was active in strikes from 1928 to 1937. In 1936 CUCOM was taken over by anarcho-syndicalist leadership, which worked closely with progressive Anglos, Filipinos, and Japanese.

Ethnic organizations were as ideologically diverse as their communities. While some were conservative, Mexican veterans of the Mexican Revolution, socialists, members of the IWW and the *Partido Liberal Mexicano* (long based in Los Angeles), and Communists provided leadership in the 1920s and 1930s. In the 1920s Mexicans formed all-Mexican cells of the Young Communist League and the Communist Party of the United States. While their relationship with the Party was at times strained, left-wing Mexicans, Japanese, and Filipinos called on progressive Anglos to help in organizing in the 1930s.

In 1928 the CP, following a shift in Party tactics, formed the Trade Union Unity League (TUUL) and, in 1931, the Cannery and Agricultural Workers Industrial Union to organize agricultural workers in California. The militant CAWIU was small, financially limited, and had only a handful of organizers, yet led a series of agricultural strikes. During the Depression, growers slashed wages. Encouraged by the erroneous belief that they were included in Section 7a of the National Recovery Act, workers went on strike in crop after crop in California, resulting in an almost general strike. More than 140 strikes occurred in California between 1930 and 1939. While Mexicans composed the largest group, there were also Filipino, Japanese, and Anglo participants. The strike wave crested in the October 1933 cotton strike by more than 18,000 workers and continued into 1934. In 1934 CAWIU leaders were indicted for violation of the Criminal Syndicalism Act. In 1935 the CP dissolved the TUUL and CAWIU in its move to a "popular front."

With the dissolution of the CAWIU, Filipino and Mexican ethnic organizations and the left wing of the AFL led agricultural organizing from 1935 to 1937. In 1937 veterans of the CAWIU and Filipino and Mexican unions became part of the United Cannery, Agricultural, Packing and Allied Workers of America-CIO (UCAPAWA). UCAPAWA was active in California, Texas, and other states. Although the strongest union to date, the union increasingly focused on cannery and packinghouse workers, and made few substantial gains for field-workers. In 1942 the federal government introduced a contract labor, or "bracero," program that depressed wages and prevented organizing until its demise in 1964. The following year the United Farm Workers (UFW) union was organized.

The UFW picked up from the movements of the 1930s. Composed of Mexicans and Filipinos, the UFW became a social movement in the 1960s. Through public support, the secondary boycott, and gradual political and AFL support, the union obtained contracts and successfully pressured for more favorable pesticide legislation and an Agricultural Labor Relations Board in California. By the 1980s the UFW was no longer a social movement but was declining in strength, in large part due to the problems endemic to agriculture, to increased mechanization, and to the movement of large companies to other countries where labor was cheaper. The migrant streams along the East Coast and from Texas up through the Midwest have not had the same degree of organization found in California. By the 1970s, however, small unions were gaining ground in Florida, Texas, Ohio, and Arizona and were branching out in small, localized strikes in other states.

The increase in undocumented workers in agriculture since the 1950s led to unions such as the Arizona Farm Workers union (AFW), the Texas Farm Workers union (TFW), and the Ohio-based Farmworkers Labor Organizing Committee (FLOC), which have organized undocumented workers and have stressed the need for organizing across international borders. In 1980 these organizations helped sponsor the First International Conference in Defense of the Full Rights of Undocumented Workers, attended by more than sixty organizations in the United States and Mexico, to push for the organization of workers across borders. *See also*: Communist Party; Industrial Workers of the World; Mexican Americans; Mitchell, H. L.

—*Devra Weber*

REFERENCES

Jamieson, Stuart. *Labor Unionism in American Agriculture*. Bureau of Labor Bulletin No. 836, Dept. of Labor. Washington D.C.: U.S. Government Printing Office, 1945.

Kushner, Sam. *Long Road to Delano*. New York: International Publishers, 1975.

McWilliams, Carey. *Factories in the Field: The Story of Migratory Farm Labor in California*. Hamden, Conn.: Archon Books, 1969.

Sanchez, Guadalupe, and Jesus Romo. "Organizing Mexican Undocumented Farm Workers on Both Sides of the Border." *Working Papers in U.S.-Mexican Studies*, No. 27, Program in United States-Mexican Studies, University of California, San Diego, 1981.

Weber, Devra. "The Organizing of Mexicano Agricultural Workers: Imperial Valley and Los Angeles, 1928–1934: An Oral History Approach." *Aztlan* 3 (1973).

MILITANT: see SOCIALIST WORKERS PARTY, TROTSKYISM

MILLS, CHARLES WRIGHT (1916–62)

A leading figure in the revival of radical social thought during the 1950s, Mills published two major books—*White Collar* (1951) and *The Power Elite* (1956)—that analyzed in a fresh and incisive way the class structure of American society. In the first of them he examined the profound changes that had taken place in the nature of the American middle class since the early nineteenth century, from the condition of independent self-employed producers to that of "hired employees." The traditional and prevailing ideology, with its emphasis on independence, individualism, and mobility, more appropriate to the earlier world of small property owners, had become simply a mystification in the mid-twentieth century, and the "new" middle class were "morally defenseless as individuals and politically impotent as a group."

Mills' book on the power elite analyzed another aspect of the class structure, namely the existence in the supposedly "classless" United States of a largely self-perpetuating group that dominates the rest of society. But Mills did not describe this as a "ruling class"; on the contrary, he rejected the Marxist conception of class in favor of a theory of elites, arguing that "'ruling class' is a badly loaded phrase. 'Class' is an economic term; 'rule' a political one. The phrase 'ruling class' thus contains the theory that an economic class rules politically. That short-cut theory may or may not at times be true, but we do not want to carry that one rather simple theory about in the terms that we use to define our problems." His underlying view of American society—and by implication of other modern capitalist societies—was expressed in terms of a division between the power elite and the masses, and of the emergence in the twentieth century of "mass societies" characterized by the powerlessness of isolated, easily manipulated individuals. But critics of Mills's analysis pointed out that he did not provide an adequate account of the bonds that created a single "power elite" out of the three major elites—political leaders, big-business executives, and the military chiefs—that he distinguished; and further, that in European societies and in other regions of the world outside the United States, classes and class conflict still had a predominant role in politics.

In sum, Mills's conception of the "power elite" seemed to many radical critics more simplistic and less profound than Marx's theory of class, and it is the notable revival of Marxist social thought—in sociology, anthropology, and political economy—that has inspired the major radical movements of the past three decades, however much it has been critically revised under the influence of new social movements (especially feminism and the ecology movement). On the other hand, Mills undoubtedly contributed something of great and permanent value to the radical movements of the 1950s and 1960s by his emphasis on the need to create or reanimate voluntary and local organizations through which individuals might acquire a genuine control over decisions of public policy. Implicitly Mills was arguing for the "participatory democracy" that became the ideal of the radical movements in the 1960s and has remained the animating idea of radicalism and socialism in the late twentieth century, in opposition to the existing highly centralized societies, whether they are those of advanced capitalism, dominated by giant corporations, or those of bureaucratic socialism.

Had Mills lived, he would undoubtedly have given a clearer sense of direction to the radical movements of the late 1960s in the United States and would have had a continuing influence on the European New Left, with which he was closely linked. As it is he became in his short lifetime the most powerful and influential critic of American society, and of the "higher learning" in America, since Veblen. *See also*: New Left, Sociology

—*Tom Bottomore*

REFERENCES

Bottomore, Tom. *Critics of Society: Radical Thought in North America*. London: Allen & Unwin, 1967.

Eldridge, John. *C. Wright Mills*. Chichester and London: Ellis Horwood/Tavistock, 1983.

Horowitz, Irving Louis, ed. *The New Sociology*. New York: Oxford University Press, 1964.

MILWAUKEE

Site of electoral socialism's premier achievement in the United States, this heavily German-American city offered a model exception to a generally sorry record.

Socialists held the mayorality of Milwaukee from 1910 through most of the 1930s, and again from 1948 to 1960. Through the 1910s, they regularly elected a substantial minority and sometimes a majority of the city council. In the heyday of the 1910s–1920s, they regularly had a delegation in the state legislature, and they sent Victor Berger to the House of Representatives for six terms. Equally important from a national standpoint, they sometimes delivered up to a third of the local vote for the Socialists' national ticket.

Fundamentally, local Socialists had worked hard to create a unified labor movement in the last decades of the nineteenth century, and had built a powerful educational apparatus with broad appeal to the mostly craft-labor, German-American population. Socialist challenged a notably corrupt Republican Party for local power, thrusting aside a weak Democratic Party machine. Quickly demonstrating their ability to elect candidates and to govern without corruption—a curious procedure in those days—they won over large sections of the middle class and forward-looking business classes. Those who, in other cities, would have bitterly opposed the socialist political movement, learned to accept a social program of advanced progressivism, even when hitched to a rhetoric of eventual socialist transformation.

Several other factors, external and internal, helped to explain the Milwaukeeans' success. A Polish population of Germanic connections, bitterly abused in the strikes of 1886–88, contained an unusually large proportion of Socialist sympathizers, so that the Church had little luck in pitting Catholics against Socialists. A number of other ethnic Milwaukee populations—Croatian, Slovene, and Jewish especially—had strong Socialist followings. The Milwaukee Socialists, for their part, maintained an internal discipline and collective sense of purpose rare in the U.S. Left. "Bundle brigades" regularly leafleted every neighborhood in the city in several languages, proclaiming socialist integrity and idealism. They carefully minimized friction with the Church and professional classes, and aimed their shafts at consensual public enemies, such as the streetcar franchise. They developed a powerful and popular daily, the *Milwaukee Leader*, mostly funded by the labor movement. And when faced with the war crisis, they carefully wove a pattern of legal antiwar protest that further endeared them to the German-American community, even while prominent (American-born) Milwaukee intellectuals went over from socialism to nationalism.

The flagship of a Socialist Party barely surviving in the 1920s, the Milwaukee movement managed a holding action. Popular Mayor Dan Hoan cooperated with progressive council members in such programs as the first low-cost cooperative housing project, and long-range financial planning that allowed Milwaukee to lead American cities in nearly attaining solvency. Almost uniquely among major cities on Lake Michigan, Milwaukee also forbade obstruction of the shoreline from public enjoyment. In a national sense, for the remnants of the Socialist movement, Milwaukee Socialism loomed large by contrast to their own standing. Although with reservations, Milwaukeeans helped facilitate the transfer of party leadership to Norman Thomas, as they sought to restrain disputes arising between the aging "Old Guard" and impatient younger forces.

The Depression brought Dan Hoan near the center of the Socialist maelstrom where SP factions battled each other for control. Moved by their own example and the brief bloom of Socialist fortunes in smaller Wisconsin working-class towns, Hoan and his followers hoped for a Socialist political renewal at the local level. Thomas's strong 1932 campaign and the triumphant municipal showing of Milwaukee Socialist candidates in 1931 made this seem possible. But nationally and locally the new, powerful opposition to the Milwaukee Socialists from the Left (the Communist Party) and from the Right (the New Deal) undercut the effort. Besides, Milwaukee Socialists disagreed bitterly among themselves what strategic course to follow. The labor movement by this time ceased to support the *Leader* (reduced to a weekly in 1929), and abandoned the Socialists without any possibility of strong backing. Important local activists moved on to leadership positions in their growing national unions. Increasingly reduced by this time from a vital mass movement to a club of old-timers and cadre of idealists—albeit still mostly self-taught workers or lower professionals—Milwaukee Socialists entered into the state Farmer-Labor Progressive coalition. Through this shift, Socialists all but lost their remaining identity. Continuing internal disputes, and Mayor Hoan's defeat in 1940, virtually extinguished the movement.

And yet the idea of Milwaukee Socialism did not entirely disappear. Frank Zeidler owed his lengthy administration, 1948–60, both to personal popularity and to an established tradition. His liberal administration, bitterly criticized for its attempts to ease racial relations in changing neighborhoods, continued the main themes of honesty, efficiency, and a vaguely (or at least, abstractly) cooperative spirit. After his years as mayor, Zeidler remained the major personality of a tiny SP and a spokesman for local causes. Running for the U.S. presidency in 1972, he gained the largest number of votes for any Socialist candidate since Norman Thomas—a disproportionate number from Milwaukee, where "socialism" had never become a frightening word.

—*Paul Buhle*

REFERENCES

Beck, Elmer Axel. *The Sewer Socialists: A History of the Socialist Party of Wisconsin*. 2 vols. Fennimore, Wis.: Westburg Associates Publishers, n.d.

Miller, Sally. "Milwaukee: Of Ethnicity and Labor." In *Socialism and the Cities*, edited by Bruce M.

Stave. Port Washington, N.Y.: Kennikat Press, 1975.

Wachman, Marvin. *History of the Social-Democratic Party of Milwaukee 1897–1910*. Urbana: University of Illinois Press, 1945.

Minneapolis Teamster Strikes

Three successive strikes by Minneapolis truck drivers in 1934 resulted in the defeat of the Citizen's Alliance—the dominant employer organization that had broken nearly every major strike in that city since 1916. The strikes also established the industrial form of union organization through the medium of an AFL craft union and set the stage for the organization of over-the-road drivers throughout an eleven-state area, transforming the Teamsters into a million-plus member union. The strikes were notable for their almost unequaled advance preparation, military tactics, and the degree to which they drew the active participation of union, nonunion, and unemployed workers in Minneapolis alike into their struggle. The strikes were led by veteran union militants expelled from the American Communist Party in 1928 as Trotskyists.

Carl Skoglund and V. R. (Ray) Dunne, the central leaders, had been expelled from the AFL Central Labor Union in Minneapolis in 1925 for their political views. In 1931 Skoglund obtained membership in Teamsters Local 574, a small general drivers' local. The president, William Brown, was supportive of their perspective for organizing drivers, helpers, and inside workers into an industrial union formation that could break the hold of the Citizen's Alliance.

By late 1933, working in Minneapolis coal yards, they had consolidated a volunteer organizing committee, including Grant and Miles Dunne (V. R.'s brothers), Harry DeBoer, and Farrell Dobbs. Dobbs, DeBoer, and Shaun (Jack) Maloney became key leaders of the over-the-road-drivers' organizing campaign from 1935 to 1940.

On February 7, 1934, a strike was called in the coal yards, shutting down sixty-five of sixty-seven yards in three hours. Under the leadership of DeBoer, an innovative strike tactic was introduced for the first time—cruising

UNITED LABOR ACTION

THE ORGANIZER 574

SMASH THE CITIZENS ALLIANCE

VOLUME 1 — TWO TWENTY-FIVE SOUTH THIRD STREET

MINNEAPOLIS, MINNESOTA, WEDNESDAY, AUG. 22, 1934 — NUMBER 37

VICTORY!

Settlement Goes Through!

The strike settlement adopted by the Union last night at a membership meeting is a victory for Local 574 and for the cause of trade unionism which was at stake in this strike.

The bosses, led by the Citizens Alliance, forced this strike on us. The Alliance bandits admit that they want to make this an open shop town. The beginning, they thought, would be to smash Local 574. Then they would go on to the rest of the Unions.

They have been defeated in their foul plot!

Battle-scarred and bleeding from many wounds, Local 574 rises from the struggle stronger in the confidence of the workers and more certain of its future than before.

Local 574 has not yet gotten everything for its members that it means to get. The bosses know this and we shall not let them forget it.

But what Local 574 has won is the gain of the whole union movement. All Minneapolis workers rejoice to know that the attempt to break 574 has completely fizzled and that our great union remains in the field to fight the battles of its own members and to point the road of struggle to all workers seeking the benefit of organization and a better life for themselves and their families.

* * *

The walls of Eagles hall shook last night as the members wound up their meeting with the fighting song of 574, "Solidarity Forever!"

When 574 says "Solidarity," it means unison, it means stick together, fight it out, don't give in. And this in turn means 574.

This number is the veritable symbol of unionism and the unconquerable spirit of labor in Minneapolis today.

And not only in Minneapolis.

Local 574's heroic struggle has become a national affair. Minneapolis has shown the country something new, and newspaper front pages everywhere carry our name.

What was new? Not the fact that a few thousand workers, miserably oppressed and exploited, rose to rebel. That happens daily. Everywhere American workers, sick of working like slaves and living like bums, are striking.

The pity is that, as a rule, they are cheated, betrayed or sold out by those they trust and rely on. The bosses crush them, or the leaders betray them, or they get caught in the "National Run Around" of Federal meditation, and before the inexperienced workers know what has happened their strikes are broken and they go back defeated, without conditions, without a union, without anything, as a rule, but an NRA promise worth just about as much as Confederate money.

They tried all that in Minneapolis, but it was no go. That's what was new about our strike. That made the whole country sit up and take notice.

Every means of oppression was brought to bear. They shot our pickets down in cold blood. Two of them lie dead today, victims of the murdering, union-hating conspirators, martyrs to the sacred cause of labor. They flung our pickets and our leader into a military stockade. They raided our headquarters.

But they couldn't break us.

Every dirty trick and maneuver was tried. A Farmer-Labor governor, whom so many workers trusted, turned up as a copper, throwing pickets into the stockade. They put over a "Red Scare" to see if they could catch some suckers and get the union to select a leadership to suit the bosses. Even the Federal Mediators, Father Haas and Mr. Dunnigan, to their shame, tried to go over the heads of our leaders and disrupt our ranks. Such "labor leaders" as Tobin and Smith played the role of Judas.

But they couldn't fool us.

Local 574 stood up and fought back. Rank and file and leaders stood united and nobody could split us. We stuck it out and got a settlement which the whole labor movement will approve.

* * *

Thus the strike ends. But the struggle does not end.

Elections are coming. Local 574 wants to win in every house. Every worker should join the Union. Every union man should speak to his brothers on the job and see to it that 574 gets a unanimous vote. After that we shall remain vigilant and see that all conditions of the settlement are enforced in practice. Local 574 is not going to sleep at the switch.

Let's get out the vote and let's see to it that every ballot cast is marked for 574, a real union.

* * *

And a final word: Mayor Bainbridge has started to yap about driving "Communists" out of the city. We know what he means. He means framing up every worker who fights for his rights. The Citizens Alliance, sore because they had to swallow the settlement, are planning to sic their bloodhound Johannes onto some innocent individual workers and take it out of their hides.

We warn all enemies of labor Local 574 is going to take a hand in the fight against any kind of a frame-up. Those who start this sort of business will be responsible for all the consequences.

* * *

This outlines the immediate program of Local 574.

We are going to see to it that the settlement is carried out.

We are going to see to it that any attempts at discrimination get a crack on the head.

We are going to win the election and build a bigger union than we ever had before.

And we are going to protect every last man of our heroic strikers against any sort of persecution.

The Organizer ceases today to be a Daily Strike Bulletin. It remains the official daily of Local 574. Until the elections have been concluded, we intend to keep in our hands the precious weapon, a daily paper.

Numberless remarks, scores of letters give us confidence that this will be welcome news to the workers of Minneapolis.

Vote for 574 in the Elections
Make Minneapolis a Union Town

Daily paper of the striking Minneapolis Teamster, August 22, 1934

picket squads patrolling the streets by automobile. Cold winter demand for coal brought a quick end to the strike two days later, resulting in a limited victory for the union. Local 574's membership rose to 3,000 by April, as the organization drive continued.

In preparation for a general drivers' strike, 574 got agreement for active support from Minneapolis unemployed organizations and the Farm Holiday Association, allied with the Minnesota Farmer-Labor Party. On May 15, Local 574, now 6,000 members strong, voted to strike all trucking employers, demanding union recognition, the right to represent inside workers, and wage increases.

The union deployed cruising picket squads from strike headquarters, a big garage where they also installed a hospital and commissary. A strike committee of one hundred was elected, with broad representation from struck firms. A women's auxiliary was established at the suggestion of Carl Skoglund.

On Monday, May 21, a major battle between strikers and police and special deputies took place in the central market area. At a crucial point, 600 pickets, concealed the previous evening in nearby AFL headquarters, emerged and routed the police and deputies in hand-to-hand combat. Over thirty cops went to the hospital. No pickets were arrested.

On Tuesday, May 22, the battle began again. About 20,000 strikers, sympathizers, and spectators assembled in the central market area, and a local radio station broadcast live from the site.

Again, no trucks were moved. Two special deputies were killed, including C. Arthur Lyman, a leader of the Citizen's Alliance. No pickets were arrested. On May 25 a settlement was reached that met the union's major objectives, including representation of inside workers.

In the following weeks, it became clear the employers were not carrying out the agreement. Over 700 cases of discrimination were recorded between May and July. Another strike was called on July 16. The union's newspaper, the *Organizer*, became the first daily ever published by a striking union.

Trucking was again effectively closed down until Friday, July 20, when police opened fire on unarmed pickets, wounding sixty-seven, two of whom, John Belor and Henry Ness died. The Minneapolis *Labor Review* reported attendance of 100,000 at Ness's funeral on July 24.

A public commission, set up later by the governor, reported: "Police took direct aim at the pickets and fired to kill. Physical safety of the police was at no time endangered. No weapons were in possession of the pickets."

On July 26, Farmer-Labor governor Olson declared martial law and mobilized 4,000 National Guardsmen, who began issuing operating permits to truck drivers. On August 1, National Guard troops seized strike headquarters and placed arrested union leaders in a stockage at the State Fair Grounds in St. Paul.

The next day, the headquarters were restored to the union and the leaders released from the stockade, as the National Guard carried out a token raid on the Citizen's Alliance headquarters. The union appealed to the Central Labor Union for a general strike and the governor issued an ultimatum that he would stop all trucks by midnight, August 5, if there was no settlement. Nevertheless, by August 14 there were thousands of trucks operating under military permits. Although the strike was gravely weakened by martial law and economic pressure, union leaders made it clear that it would continue.

On August 21 a federal mediator got acceptance of a settlement proposal from A. W. Strong, head of the Citizen's Alliance, incorporating the union's major demands. The settlement was ratified and the back of employer resistance to unionization in Minneapolis was broken. In March 1935 International president Daniel Tobin expelled Local 574 from the IBT. However, in August 1936 Tobin was forced to recant and recharter the local as 544. The leaders of 544 went on to develop the area and conference bargaining that exists today in the IBT.

Local 544 remained under Trotskyist leadership until 1941, when eighteen leaders of the union and the Socialist Workers Party were sentenced to federal prison, the first victims of the antiradical Smith Act. *See also*: Dobbs, Farrell; International Brotherhood of Teamsters; Socialist Workers Party; Trotskyism

—*David Riehle*

REFERENCES

Citizen's Alliance Papers, Minneapolis Central Labor Union Papers, Minnesota Historical Society, Archives and Manuscripts Division, St. Paul, Minnesota.

De Graaf, John. (producer/director) *Labor's Turning Point*. Minneapolis: Labor Education Service, University of Minnesota, 19. Film.

Dobbs, Farrell. *Teamster Rebellion*. 4 vols. New York: Pathfinder Press, 1972.

Taped interviews with Oscar Coover, Jr., Farrell Dobbs, V. R. Dunne, Carl Skoglund. Oral History Collection, Minnesota Historical Society, St. Paul, Minnesota.

Walker, Charles Rumford. *American City*. New York: Farrar and Rinehart, 1937.

MINOR, ROBERT (1884–1952)

A foremost radical cartoonist before 1920, Minor abandoned his extraordinary talent to become a Communist political figure who focused intensely on the "Negro question."

Raised in San Antonio, Texas, a poor lawyer's son, Minor left school at fourteen to take a series of menial jobs. A self-taught artist, he joined the *San Antonio Gazette* in 1904 and the next year moved to the *St. Louis Post Dispatch*. In an age of rapidly changing cartoon work, from the elaborately detailed drawings of the nineteenth century to the simpler, more direct styles of the twentieth, Minor made himself a giant through his intentionally rough lines, his unaffected presentation of human expression, and his keen sense of humor. Perhaps as much as any artist on the Left, he epitomized the adoption of Daumier's passion along with his lithographic crayon work. (A notable technical innovator, Minor himself adapted the metal plates used in cartoon reproduction to simulate the crayon line.)

Converted to socialism in 1907, Minor swiftly moved into the Left. He studied art in Paris in 1911, and there became enamored with anarcho-syndicalism. Returning to the United States the following year, he took a prestigious position at the *New York Evening World*, allowing him to draw antiwar cartoons until an editorial change of heart forced him to the Socialist *Call* (and on the side, the anarchist *Mother Earth*). His fame as a radical artist reached a peak at the *Masses*, whose editorial board he joined in 1916, at a turning point in that magazine. Under the shadow of war, it had lost a lighter tone and some of its more prominent artists; Minor contributed brilliant, bitter satire, especially but not only on the war issue.

At the same time, Minor began to become more active politically. At first, he drew close to anarchist causes, organizing a political defense committee for labor martyr Tom Mooney. Then, visiting Russia as a war correspondent shortly after the revolution, he met Lenin, and began a conversion completed in 1920 with the repudiation of his anarcho-syndicalist beliefs for Bolshevism. He continued to draw cartoons for a time in the *Daily Worker*, but as a busy functionary gave up drawing entirely in 1926. Two years later Minor became editor of the *Daily Worker*, and emerged as a key aid and spokesman for Communist Party leader Earl Browder.

Repeatedly arrested for public agitation in the 1920s–1930s, Minor became known as "Fighting Bob." He ran unsuccessfully several times for office—mayor of New York City, governor of New York, and U.S. senator—and served as correspondent in the Spanish Civil War. When Browder himself was imprisoned in 1941, Minor briefly served as acting general secretary. His close association with Browder, however, removed him from leadership after Browder's 1945 downfall. Made Washington correspondent for the *Daily Worker*, he fell ill and withdrew from political work before his death. *See also*: Communist Party, Humor

—*M. Bird*

REFERENCES

Zurier, Rebecca. *Art of the Masses*. Philadelphia: Temple University Press, 1988.

MITCHELL, H. L. (1906–1989)

Founder of the Southern Tenant Farmers Union, Mitchell has been one of the foremost twentieth-century American socialists engaged in farm activism and multiracial organizing.

Born in Halls, Tennessee, Mitchell worked at farm chores from the age of eight, and after high school graduation tried his hand at a number of jobs, from bootlegging in prohibition days to sharecropping. As an eleven-year-old newspaperboy, he had ridden a special train to Dyersburg, Tennessee, and watched whites lynch a young black man. Searching for some way to understand the world around him, Mitchell became what southerners called a "reading fool." Converted to socialism, he in turn converted his friend, Clay East, and the two created a "Red Square" for Norman Thomas's 1932 presidential campaign in Tyronza, Arkansas, around Mitchell's dry-cleaning shop and East's filling station.

In 1934 the two spearheaded the interracial Southern Tenant Farmers Union. With

Mitchell's organizing skills and and East packing a pistol as the duly elected township constable, the union thrived. By protesting sharecropper evictions, organizing strikes, and lobbying for federal legislation to improve agricultural conditions in the South—with the support and cooperation of black and white farm families—southern radicals forcefully fought the system. Along with strikes to raise wages, their most successful effort culminated in the formation of the Delta Cooperative Farm at Rochdale, Mississippi, by tenants evicted from Arkansas plantations for joining the STFU. This project became the model for the Farm Security Administration, created as a result of growing national concern for the plight of the southern tenant farmer.

At its peak, the STFU could claim 30,000 members, a newspaper, the *Sharecroppers' Voice*, from Memphis, and a series of public-relations successes in the national press and politics (including "Sharecroppers Week" declared by New York mayor Fiorello LaGuardia). Along with the Communists of the Alabama-based Sharecroppers Union, Mitchell and the STFU had effected the most important links of rural, radical southern blacks and whites since Populism, and foreshadowed the future civil rights movement.

Mitchell's hopes for a sustained, mass movement of sharecroppers ran into several formidable obstacles. Franklin Roosevelt's political détente with southern planters forebade any major federal commitment to southern social change, even while Eleanor Roosevelt often expressed her own sympathy for Mitchell's cause. The CIO, absorbing the STFU in 1938, demanded from tenant farmers an impossible style of organization and commitment of scarce resources. Mitchell's relations with Communist labor leaders in the CIO rapidly became unsustainable. Most of all, the low prices for commodities and the impending mechanization of southern agriculture fatally undercut sharecroppers' bargaining power.

Withdrawing from the CIO with his following much weakened, Mitchell opened "Washington's smallest lobby," a little corner of agitation for the tenant farmer and agricultural worker. After the war, he moved the STFU remnant into the AFL, and eventually into the meat-cutters' union. Along the way, Mitchell pioneered the support movement around California farm-workers' unionization, and organized southern fishermen and sugar cane workers.

By the 1970s–1980s, Mitchell set a new and unique task for himself: the public exploration of the STFU's history. As no other American Left figure, he single-mindedly set about speaking on campuses and at scholars' meetings, offering microfilm editions of the STFU papers for sale to libraries, writing his own history, and encouraging media treatment of it. By these efforts and sheer force of personality, Mitchell made an inestimable contribution not only to radical history but also to the sense of continuity among newer generations.

See also: Southern Tenant Farmers Union

—*Orville Vernon Burton*

REFERENCES

Dunbar, Anthony P. *Against the Grain: Southern Radicals and Prophets, 1929–1959*. Charlottesville: University Press of Virginia, 1981.

Grubbs, Donald H. *Cry from the Cotton: The Southern Tenant Farmers' Union and the New Deal*. Chapel Hill: University of North Carolina, 1971.

Mitchell, H. L. *Mean Things Happening in This Land*. Montclair: Osmund, Allenheld, 1981.

———. *Roll the Union On: A Pictorial History of the Southern Tenant Farmers Union*. Chicago: Charles H. Kerr Co., 1987.

Modern Dance

Emerging as a new art in New York in the late 1920s, modern dance was born of the quest to discover the real capacities of the human body as a means of expression, which in turn implied a revolt against the stifling conventions of ballet. The principal initiators of the new movement were Doris Humphrey, Martha Graham, and Helen Tamiris. Although there have been many male dancers of significance, the central and innovative figures of modern dance have been women, exemplifying an important aspect of feminist culture that not only persisted but flourished after the eclipse of organized feminism following the passage of the Nineteenth Amendment in 1920.

Emphasizing that modern dance began as a movement of, by, and for women is the fact that its chief forerunners were two maverick matriarchs. At the turn of the century Isadora Duncan had boldly proclaimed a strong feminist dimension of her own dance, inspiring at least two generations of women—and not only women—to take risks for the sake of freedom and self-fulfillment. An enthusiastic supporter of the Russian Revolution, Duncan left a legacy of wholehearted rebellion.

The less radical Ruth St. Denis also played a liberating role, spearheading exploration of the possibilities of non-Western dance. As it happened, the vaudevillian St. Denis influenced the course of modern dance more directly than the "Divine Isadora," largely because Duncan lived in Europe while modern dance was slowly taking shape in her native land. Duncan's dance, moreover, was the spontaneous and unique result of her own intuition and, as such, unteachable by anyone but her. Of course there were, and still are, some worthy proponents of one variety or another of "Duncan dance": the line of descent from Isadora through Julia Levien to Annabelle Gamson, the outstanding interpreter of Duncan's dances in the 1980s, is straight and unmistakable. Dance à la Isadora was featured at the anarchist Modern School in Stelton, New Jersey, and the "Natural Rhythmic Expression" taught by the little-known Bird Larson at New York's socialist Rand School also owed much to Duncan's example. But the fact that there are so many different versions of Duncan dancing raises doubts about how much of Duncan survives in any of them. Few of the founders of modern dance ever saw Duncan herself dance, and they tended to be unimpressed by what they did see of Duncan-style dancing, which, in any case, has been peripheral to the development of the modern movement.

St. Denis, by contrast, was engaged in the day-to-day business of giving practical, technical dance instruction to pupils who intended to earn their living by dancing. For more than fifteen years, first in Los Angeles and later in New York, she directed (with Ted Shawn) the Denishawn School of Dancing and Related Arts.

St. Denis's own variety of theosophy was an important part of the Denishawn curriculum. Instilled with her belief that Dance (with the capital *D*) was a mystical mission, the best students were expected to remain with the company, not only as teachers, but as propagators of the Denishawn faith on extensive tours. Such a self-effacing regimen was not for everyone, and it is hardly surprising that the most gifted dancers eventually broke away.

Among the graduates of Denishawn were two dancers who, by 1929, were recognized leaders of a "revolution" in dance. A direct descendant of Miles Standish, Martha Graham (b. 1893) was born and raised in a Pittsburgh suburb and moved to California with her parents in 1908. After seven years with Denishawn she set out on her own. By decade's end the very titles of her performances—"Revolt," "Immigrant," "Poems of 1917," "Heretic"—seemed to confirm *New York Times* critic John Martin's remark that her effect "has not been one of warmth and elevation, but rather of tension and disturbed thinking."

Doris Humphrey (1895–1958), who was born in Oak Park, Illinois, and grew up in Chicago, went west in 1917 to enroll in Denishawn, in whose company she remained for eleven years. In 1925–26 she took part in the Denishawn tour of Asia. An outstanding theorist as well as practitioner of dance (her classic treatise, *The Art of Making Dances*, was published posthumously in 1959), Humphrey played a role in the formation and elaboration of the modern movement equal to that of the more-publicized Graham, and not a few dancers and critics have regarded her as the greater choreographer.

Helen Tamiris (1905–1966), a third major figure in the formative years of modern dance, started out as a student of classical ballet in New York City, where she was born. Remarkably versatile, she later choreographed Broadway musical extravaganzas and Hollywood films such as *Show Boat* and *Annie Get Your Gun*. In the late 1920s she was one of the first modern dancers to identify herself with the revolutionary workers' movement. "The validity of the modern dance," she argued, "is rooted in its ability to express modern problems and, further, to make modern audiences want to do something about them."

Although critics applied the term "revolutionary" to any and all modern dancers, Tamiris's avowedly activist orientation was not shared by Graham or Humphrey, who remained aloof to the political turmoil of the Depression years. Graham's biographer, Don McDonagh, notes that "her vision was directed to unlocking the fetters that bound the spirit, not those twisting the social fabric." In a period of mass labor organizing, Humphrey refused to join a union, fearing that such membership might somehow limit her freedom.

The apoliticism of some of its leading personalities notwithstanding, modern dance began as an integral part of the American Left milieu, and was universally regarded as such. "I never heard of a modern pro-fascist dance," wrote Margaret Lloyd, dance critic for the *Christian Science Monitor*. The new movement was repeatedly denounced in the conservative press and, for a time, was treated unkindly in mainstream liberal papers as well. The modern dance audience, moreover, consisted almost entirely of young people who thought of themselves as radicals and revolutionists.

Tamiris welcomed the objective link between social radicalism and the new dance, while Graham and Humphrey can be said to have resigned themselves to it. All three, however, agreed that dance could not and should not be reduced to any sort of propaganda or even to a narrowly "social" esthetic. For her part, Tamiris clearly felt that a certain amount of red-flag-waving was permissible, as in her "Revolutionary March" of 1929, and even Graham and Humphrey sometimes touched on "social" themes. But the heart of their work lay elsewhere. Most of their dances—such as Humphrey's "The Shakers" and "Square Dances," Graham's "Frontier" and "Letter to the World" (inspired by Emily Dickinson), Tamiris's "Circus Sketches," "Prize Fight Studies," "Negro Spirituals," and "Walt Whitman Suite"—were rooted in myths, poetry, folklore, and other magic-laden byways of the American past and present. Left critics tended to be sympathetic to this effort. Recognizing in such dances something of the Left's own striving toward a radical reinterpretation of the American experience, they embraced the new movement as an important component of an emerging revolutionary culture.

For an increasing number of student dancers, however, this vague association of modern dance and social radicalism was not enough. These youngsters, many of whom were members of the Communist or Socialist parties, sought to place the whole modern dance movement at the service of the revolution. Eager to make dance itself play a role in the overthrow of capitalism, they choreographed dances to serve the workers' everyday struggle against the bosses. The CP's ideological tightening-up at the turn of the decade hastened this process. With slogans of "Bolshevization" and the "Third Period" quickening their pulses, young dancers took their cue from manifestoes for "proletarian culture" and proclaimed that "dance is a weapon."

Tamiris, the most politically radical of the elders, was a natural leader of these boisterous troops. Ironically, however, Graham's and Humphrey's students made up much of the active core of such militant groups as the Red Dancers, organized in 1929, the Rebel Dance Group, New Dance Group, Theatre Union Dance Group, Office Workers Dance Group, and nearly a score of others that formed over the next few years. Several of Graham's students, celebrated dancers in their own right in later years, were especially prominent. Jane Dudley danced "In the Life of a Worker" (1934) and "Song for Soviet Youth Day" (1935); Anna Sokolow danced an "Anti-War Cycle" (1937) and Sophie Maslow offered her comrades "Two Songs About Lenin" (1934) as well as a "May Day March" (1936). Eleanor King, a Humphrey student who later established her own school in Seattle, choreographed "A Song About America" (1939), featuring homages to the abolitionists and the Haymarket martyrs; sponsored by the CP, the performance took place on the fifteenth anniversary of the death of Lenin. There were dances to poems by Communist Mike Gold and Socialist Arturo Giovannitti, and others inspired by the Scottsboro and Tom Mooney cases. Is it necessary to add that most of these dances were ultraserious, even somber? Here and there, however, humor was allowed to hold the stage, as in the Red Dancers' "Sell-Out" (1934), choreographed to a parody of "The Man on the Flying Trapeze" and first performed at a textile workers' union meeting in Paterson, New Jersey.

Of the quality of the dancing itself little is known, for these dances long ago disappeared from the repertories, and few if any were filmed. Critic John Martin was probably not far from the mark when he wrote, in *America Dancing* (1936): "In the early stages of the movement, dancing . . . consisted of choosing some literary slogan in conformity with orthodox radical political thinking, and of showing with what energy the dancer or dancers involved agreed with the sentiments thus conveyed. The power of expressional movement, the real stuff of the dance, was not seen to exist."

Undaunted, however, by criticism from anyone other than workers or comrades, the movement spread like wildfire and the modern dance audience, once a mere coterie, grew enormously. The young radicals performed at the New School for Social Research and other educational institutions as well as at trade union picnics, strike meetings, and political rallies. It was said that Graham and Humphrey had a hard time scheduling performances for the first of May because so many of their dancers were away giving performances of their own at May Day gatherings.

The proliferation of radical dance groups around the country inevitably suggested a federation. The SP's Rebel Arts included several dance groups, but the Workers' Dance League, politically allied with the CP, was much larger and more influential. Organized in 1932, the league had more than a dozen affiliated groups in New York City, plus others in Brooklyn, Yonkers, Newark, Passaic, Boston, Washington, D.C., Philadelphia, Pittsburgh, Detroit, Chicago, and Los Angeles. Individual dues were twenty-five cents a year. Its "Aims and Functions" included: "Building a dance art vital and clear, a dance art that is inspired by and useful to workers. Organizing dance groups in working class neighborhoods. . . . Broadening the dance audience by performing wherever workers gather. . . . Educating dancers and audiences to the problems of the working class. . . . Cooperating with artists in other fields of revolutionary cultural activity."

Working conditions in the dance world were generally poor—long hours and low wages prevailed—and the *Workers' Dance League Bulletin* (later *New Dance*) regularly covered dancers' struggles to improve their lot. In November 1934 league members, with Tamiris in the forefront, helped form the New York Dancers' Union, open to all dance-workers. A year later *New Dance* reported that the burlesque dancers were organized but that the effort to line up the taxi-dancers had thus far met with limited success. An ad hoc Dancers' Emergency Association was set up to organize the unorganized dancers but, like many other organizations of "cultural workers" spearheaded by Communists in those years, the "dancers' union" proved ineffectual and ephemeral.

Unemployment during the Great Depression was a serious problem for dancers, and many, including those in the Workers' Dance League, looked to President Roosevelt's New Deal relief programs to solve it. Meanwhile, significant changes were taking place in the Left dance scene. With the advent of the CP's Popular Front line in 1935, the Workers Dance League quietly became the New Dance League, and the shrill rhetoric of its early days was toned down in the process. The accent was no longer on class war and impending revolution but rather on the need to support the CIO and to combat race discrimination and fascism.

This policy doubtless facilitated the administrative involvement of a number of CP members and sympathizers in Works Progress Administration projects. Tamiris helped organize the Federal Theater Project and, by means of a visit to Roosevelt's adviser Harry Hopkins, saw to it that dance was an integral part of the program. Late in 1935 the Dance Project was started in New York, with a hundred dancers; a unit began in Chicago the following year. WPA productions, some of which had impressively long runs, provided work for many unemployed dancers and incidentally introduced modern dance to a substantially larger audience. This experiment in government-subsidized dance proved short-lived, however, for Congress put a stop to it in July 1939. In New York, according to ballet-critic Anatole Chujoy's *Encyclopedia of Dance* (revised edition, 1967), the Dance Project "petered out" even earlier "due chiefly to improved theater business." Other commentators, including many dancers active in the project, maintained that Congress acted in response to prodding by the recently formed House Un-American Activities Committee (HUAC).

If Popular Front strategy eased the entrance of Communist-oriented dancers into the larger society, it also diminished the necessity for an organization made up exclusively of Communist-oriented dancers. In addition to the Workers' Dance League and Rebel Arts there were numerous dance groups linked to unions; the International Ladies Garment Workers Union in New York had an extensive dance program involving more than 200 participants. The National Dance Congress in May 1936 brought together the whole range of American professional dancers and prepared the way for the amalgamation of the league and other groups to form the American Dance Association a year later. The Congress was organized by Tamiris, who became the first president of the new association. Communists, liberals, apolitical dancers, and perhaps even a few conservatives, were now united under one umbrella.

There were many reasons why the explicitly revolutionary political phase of modern dance was of such short duration. The free-spirited young women who made up the great majority of modern dancers could hardly have felt at home for long in any male-dominated political apparatus. A tension that must sometimes have been overwhelming existed between these dancers' well-meaning social aspirations and their fundamentally avant-garde sensibilities. A few may have abandoned dance to work full-time for the Party, but most of them preferred to abandon the Party. By mid-decade, when it became more widely known how severely modern dance was frowned on by the official ballet-loving "socialist realist" aestheticians of the USSR, the romance between dancers and Communists was already declining. Most dancers, in any case, were interested in politics as it affected dance more than in politics as such. "These young rebels," wrote Eleanor King many years later, "were as much against abstraction and mysticism in dance as they were against fascism, exploitation of the workers, and poverty."

It is notable that the decade of "red" dance produced no enduring body of Left dance criticism—a failure all the more striking in view of the pioneering role of socialists in this field. Back in the 1910s, two of the most prominent personalities of the *Masses*—novelist/essayist Floyd Dell and painter John Sloan—had commented insightfully on the dance of Isadora Duncan. In the same years Louis C. Fraina, Marxian economist and a founder of the CP, edited and wrote much of *Modern Dance* magazine; although this publication focused on social dancing, Fraina also wrote of Duncan and other forerunners of the new dance of the late twenties. Another periodical, the *Dance-Lover*, which started in 1923 and evolved into today's *Dance Magazine*, was edited for its first four years by an outspoken leftist, Vera Caspary, best known as the author of the film scenario *Laura*, based on her own detective novel. These promising beginnings, however, were not fulfilled. The Communists' *Daily Worker*, *New Theater* magazine, and especially the *New Masses* (the Socialists' equivalent was *Arise*) included much material on dance, but most of it was mere reportage and the rest tended to be trite superficialities or propagandistic bombast.

As dancers' faith in the Soviet Union diminished, so did their sympathy for the cause of socialism. "There are no reds in modern dance today," Margaret Lloyd wrote in 1948, but in fact the radical dance movement was already over by the start of World War II. The antiwar dancers of the 1930s did not perform their antiwar dances once war had begun. By the end of the decade the character of the entire modern movement had changed beyond recognition. Activist dance largely disappeared: the postwar strike wave and the struggle against Taft-Hartley had to get along without dancers' support. Showing just how far the pendulum had swung, in 1954–56 the once-Red-baited Martha Graham, whose company had included so many emphatically pro-Communist dancers, made several overtly anticommunist overseas tours organized by the U.S. State Department, who touted her as America's "Ambassador of Dance." The sole survivor of the Workers' Dance League, the New Dance Group School in New York, took up nonobjectivism and existentialism. Developed especially by Merce Cunningham, this tendency paved the way for the minimalist and conceptualist dance of the next generation. As dance shrank from real human problems, its audience shrank with it. Modern dance was "no longer a revolutionary emancipating principle," wrote John Martin, but rather "an academic tyranny as binding as that of the traditional ballet against which it originally rebelled."

Exceptions to the rightward trend took unexpected forms that didn't fit any of the existing styles of American radicalism. Perhaps the most innovative and imaginative dancer of the post-1940 years, Chicago-based Sybil Shearer, defied all existing values with the insouciant extremism of a William Blake or a John Muir; baffled critics could not decide whether she represented a return to the simplicity and naturalness of Isadora Duncan or a plunge into the troubled waters of surrealism.

Another nonconformist was California Bella Lewitzky, who had been born in Job Harriman's utopian socialist Llano del Rio colony in the Mojave Desert, and was a member of the Los Angeles New Dance League in the 1930s. Her refusal to testify before HUAC in 1951 ("I'm a dancer, not a singer," she quipped) provoked a barrage of obscene and threatening phone-calls, but she remained a familiar sight at protest meetings and on picket lines. In dance as in life, revolt and freedom have always been her favorite themes, as in "*Tierra y Libertad*" (1941, choreographed by Lester Horton), "Warsaw Ghetto" (1949) and "*Leyendas de Mexico*" (1953, based on the Indians' struggle against the *conquistadores*), danced in an extravagantly antirealistic idiom that had nothing in common with the agitprop of earlier years.

Esther Junger, a student of Bird Larson's who in 1935 had scandalized Boston as the star dancer and choreographer of the Theater Guild's Communist comedy *Parade*, was yet another dancer who bravely resisted the downhill slide of modern dance from poetry to prose. One of the most singular personages of the modern movement, she was for a time choreographer for the Ringling Brothers/Barnum & Bailey Circus. Her dances inspired by jazz, wild animals, Gauguin's paintings, and the lore of indigenous cultures added something new and unsettling to a dance scene increasingly dominated by the predictable.

Black modern dance also challenged the prevalent academicism and Cold War disengagement. Independent of the main currents of the modern movement, Chicago-born Katherine Dunham and Pearl Primus of Trinidad, both with doctorates in anthropology, developed a powerful dance idiom rooted in Afro-Caribbean folklore. Dunham, director of the Chicago WPA Dance Project's Negro Unit and later of the New York Labor Stage, also was choreographer for several Hollywood films devoted to black Americana, including *Stormy Weather* and *Cabin in the Sky*. Primus, widely regarded as the world's foremost authority on African dance, choreographed several Negro spirituals. In recent years the Association for the Advancement of Creative Musicians has featured several innovative dancers in its celebrations of "Great Black Music."

A modest resurgence of radical dance accompanied the social ferment of the 1960s. The Living Theater of Julian Beck and Judith Malina drew more or less equally on Antonin Artaud's dance-based "Theater of Cruelty" and anarchist-pacifist-IWW traditions to produce the Left's most influential dance-theater of those years. Expressive movement has also been central to Peter Schumann's Bread and Puppet Theater. Agitprop resurfaced primarily in mime, most effectively in the popular San Francisco Mime Troupe. A student of Lewitzky's, surrealist Alice Farley, one of the few contemporary dancers to champion the cause of social revolution, has performed extraordinary stilt-dances in New York antiwar parades. In the 1980s dance radicalism survives in widely scattered individuals and companies such as these, isolated in the outermost margins of the dance/theater world. But its heritage is a vital one, and always capable of renewal. *See also*: Duncan, Isadora; Fraina, Louis C.; Political Theater

—*Franklin Rosemont*

REFERENCES

Farley, Alice. *Surrealist Dance*. Chicago: World Surrealist Exhibition/Black Swan Press, 1976.

King, Eleanor. *Transformation: The Humphrey-Weidman Era*. Brooklyn: Dance Horizons, 1978.

Lloyd, Margaret. *The Borzoi Book of Modern Dance*. New York: Knopf, 1949.

Martin, John. *American Dancing*. New York: Dodger, 1936.

Taub, Debra. "Dance and the Transformation of the World." In *Surrealism and its Popular Accomplices*, edited by Franklin Rosemont. San Francisco: City Lights Books, 1980.

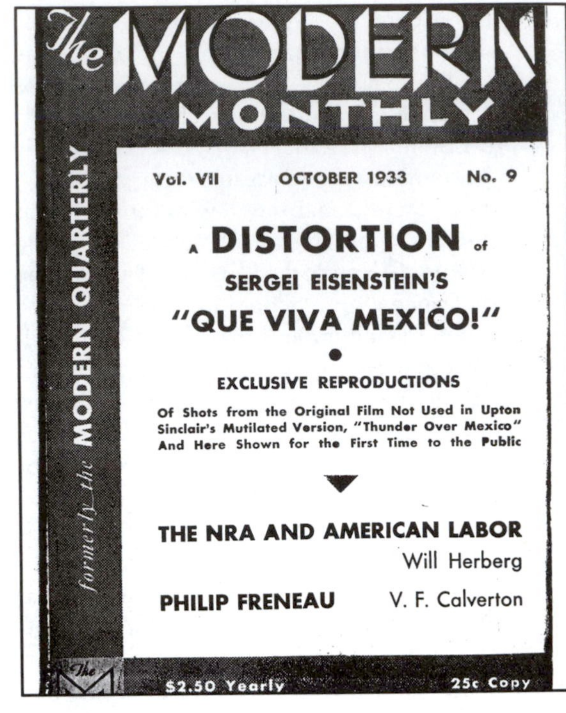
The MODERN MONTHLY

formerly the MODERN QUARTERLY

Vol. VII OCTOBER 1933 No. 9

A DISTORTION of SERGEI EISENSTEIN'S "QUE VIVA MEXICO!"

EXCLUSIVE REPRODUCTIONS

Of Shots from the Original Film Not Used in Upton Sinclair's Mutilated Version, "Thunder Over Mexico" And Here Shown for the First Time to the Public

THE NRA AND AMERICAN LABOR — Will Herberg

PHILIP FRENEAU — V. F. Calverton

$2.50 Yearly 25c Copy

Modern Quarterly/ Modern Monthly

Published from 1923 until its editor's death in 1940, the *Modern Quarterly* was the unique expression of contemporary Left intellectual culture in search of "revolutionary culturism." Its editor, V. F. Calverton (1901–1940), embodied the spirit of the magazine: eclectic, generous-spirited, self-divided between Left politics and Left methodology.

Born George Goetz in Baltimore, Calverton had been successively a semiprofessional baseball player, Johns Hopkins student, and high school teacher. A little too young for the old Socialist Party's glory days and too personally distant for the political split and the formation of American Communism, he came to the Left not with proselytization or "mass action" but rather with intellectual reconsiderations in mind. Earlier, much more widely read publications had appealed mainly to intellectuals, but not by intent. Calverton set out to reach his own class with a message.

The message centered around a radical synthesis of the existing social sciences. History, anthropology, sociology, psychology, and above all, literary criticism had a potentially radical, if by no means necessarily socialist, content. Combined, they could make up a "science of society" to whose scrutiny capitalism would seem a barbaric, outmoded social order. Calverton himself, and to a lesser degree his longtime collaborator Samuel Schmalhausen, gave this argument its most forceful renditions. But a number of outstanding social scientists, such as Harry Elmer Barnes and Arthur Calhoun, drew close.

Two facets particularly highlighted the project. Calverton and Schmalhausen, known informally among their extended circle as the "sex boys," continued the 1910s feminist dialogue (virtually abandoned by the rest of the Left afterward) with historical materialism. No better example of "the modern" could be found than woman's march toward emancipation through participation in the work force and her increasing demands for sexual equality. Each step forward (the two thinkers anticipated no backward steps) further emancipated the race. Second, an understanding of literary modernism would show the casting off of American intellectuals' "Puritan" hangover in favor of realism and radical commitment. With that commitment, Calverton argued in his major work, *The Liberation of American Literature* (1932), would come a recognition of proletarian themes and subjects i.e., the long-awaited socialist cultural imperative. In addition to these themes, the *Modern Quarterly* was especially notable for its embrace of black cultural questions and independent black intellectuals.

Calverton's (and the journal's) ill fortune was to be caught up in the Left's political crosscurrents of the time. He could not accept the discipline of the Communist Party—which would have meant the loss of his editorial freedom, if not the journal itself—and he could find no other movement more appropriate for his project. Early on, Calverton divided his own writing fairly between Socialist and Communist press, wooed by both. In its ultrasectarian phase, roughly 1929–33, the CP (under pressure, evidently, from Comintern officials who sought to eradicate all potential competition) published severe attacks on Calverton's efforts and character. His effort to mediate the differences came to no end, partly because he insisted on his right to publish ex-Communist dissenters (such as Max Eastman and Bertram Wolfe) by this time viewed as dangerous heretics.

Calverton's 1933 decision to publish his magazine monthly (*Modern Monthly*) coincided with an upswing of Left political energies and notable intellectual dissent from the Communist movement. Relentless lecturer, party-giver, intellectual promoter (he took a New York City apartment early on, and made his living partly as a literary agent), he became still more famous as popularizer. F. Scott Fitzgerald called him a "modern Lecky." Meanwhile other Left formations, principally socialist and Trotskyist, either flagged in intellectual energies or devoted them entirely to building the "vanguard party." In any case, the consolidation of the New Deal both recuperated a sector of intellectuals formerly sympathetic to Calverton, and made possible the CP's Popular Front surge.

By the Depression, Calverton's envisioned "revolutionary culturalism" had already lost ground to neo-traditional Marxist economism. By 1936 or so, his effort to create an intellectuals' alternative milieu to that of the CP had been outdated by that Party's own antifascist intellectual appeal. Ironically, Calverton had himself begun a movement toward a more liberalistic socialism, with the Hegelian philosophical backdrop of Marxism sheared away. After 1937, the journal reduced again to a quarterly schedule (and sometimes not even that), and Calverton's compatriot Schmalhausen gone, the project seemingly reduced itself to Calverton's own voice. Rather than the social-scientific confidence of the magazine's early days, Calverton increasingly evidenced an interest in the idealistic, utopian origins of the modern socialist movement. His *Where Angels Fear to Tread* (1940) was to have been the first of a multivolume treatment of that subject.

Like another independent journal of importance, Oscar Ameringer's *American Guardian*, the *Modern Quarterly* nearly expired from readers' (and writers') rejection of the editorial refusal to support the coming world war. Calverton was, in that sense, an old-fashioned socialist to the last. He died from a complication of exhaustion in 1940, leaving a legacy of independent radicalism. Not until Dwight Macdonald's *Politics* magazine would such a journal hold fast to its anticapitalism, refusing to become apologist for Cold War policies and for liberal capitalism. *See also*: Communist Party, Literary Criticism, *New Masses*

—*Paul Buhle*

REFERENCES

Aaron, Daniel. *Writers on the Left*. New York: Harcourt, Brace, and World, 1961.

Gnizi, Halma. "V. F. Calverton, Independent Radical." Ph.D. diss., City University of New York, 1968.

V. F. Calverton Collection, New York Public Library.

Molotov-Ribbentrop Pact:

see Hitler-Stalin Pact

Monthly Review

Subtitled "An Independent Socialist Magazine," *Monthly Review* is known worldwide within the Left as a key source of intellectual support for Third World liberation movements; as a point of origin of much of modern Marxian political economy; and as representing the most irrepressible and independent-minded version of Marxism to be found anywhere in the United States during the post–World War II era.

MR emerged at the dawn of the anticommunist hysteria of the McCarthy era and soon became a major bulwark for a Left threatened by political repression. The magazine first appeared in May 1949 under the joint editorship of historian Leo Huberman and economist Paul Sweezy. Financial backing was provided by literary critic F. O. Matthiessen, who offered $5,000 a year for three years. Albert Einstein wrote an article for the opening issue.

MR's editors each brought a wealth of experience to the magazine. Leo Huberman (1903–68) was chairman of the Department of Social Science, New College, Columbia University from 1938 to 1939. In 1940 he became labor editor of *PM*, and in 1941 a columnist for *U.S. Week*. From 1942 to 1945 he was director of public relations and education for the National Maritime Union; in 1946–47 editor of the pamphlet division of Reynal and Hitchcock. His two most prominent books were *We, the People* (1932) and *Man's Worldly Goods* (1936). Paul Sweezy (b. 1910) taught economics at Harvard and worked for various New Deal agencies from 1934 to 1942. During WW II he served with the Office of Strategic Services in England, France, and Germany. Among his early works was *The Theory of Capitalist Development* (1942). Harry Magdoff (b. 1913), who, following Huberman's death, joined Sweezy as coeditor of *MR*, was hired in 1936 by the Works Progress Administration's National Research Project. He later worked for the Current Business Analysis Division of the Department of Commerce, where he oversaw the publication of the *Survey of Current Business*, and in 1946 was appointed special assistant to Secretary of Commerce Henry Wallace. During the 1950s Magdoff worked as a stockbroker and financial analyst. In 1959 he joined the publishing firm Russell & Russell.

From the first, *MR* was characterized by a nondoctrinaire approach to socialism that did not stop short of criticizing the USSR and other postrevolutionary states, and by a willingness to let the analysis of concrete historical trends dominate over more abstract theory. Eager to reach a wide body of educated readers that included the previously unconvinced, the editors stressed readability, minimizing political and academic jargon. Nevertheless, *MR*—with a circulation that peaked at 12,000 in the late 1970s and fell to 8,000 in the 1980s—was never intended to reach a mass audience. Addressed mainly to intellectuals and activists, the magazine found the most succinct characterization of its practice in the phrase "Better Smaller but Better." Adapted from the title of Lenin's final essay, this slogan was utilized by Paul Baran, professor of economics at Stanford and a close associate of *MR*, to sum up a strategy of putting ideological clarity first and foremost, at a time when the Left was so weak that a search for intellectual common ground with liberals would have meant the silencing of an independent socialist voice in the United States.

Although maintaining a critical distance from "actually existing socialism" as practiced in the Soviet Union, *MR* was sympathetic with the Socialist countries' efforts to curtail the logic of capitalism and implement national planning. It therefore constituted an intellectual political milieu for people moving away from the CP and toward a more independent Marxist position. With the eruption of the Korean War, the coming of the Cuban Revolution, and the beginnings of U.S. intervention in Vietnam (the first article criticizing U.S. involvement in Indochina appeared in 1954), *MR*'s main focus shifted from the internal dilemmas of American socialism to the role of U.S. imperialism. It thus gained the status of *the* Third World journal, and partly as a result exerted considerable influence over the direction of the New Left in the 1960s. Huberman and Sweezy were among the first analysts to recognize that the Cuban Revolution would take a socialist direction. For a time, *MR* identified broadly with the Maoist strategy and critique of Soviet practice. But with the failure of the Cultural Revolution it reverted to a more cautious assessment of postrevolutionary societies. Recently, *MR* has become a forum for the dialogue between Marxism and liberation theology.

In 1951 Monthly Review Press, the book-publishing arm of *MR*, was founded when it became clear that even such a celebrated author as I. F. Stone was unable to find a publisher for his book *The Hidden History of the Korean War* (1952). MR Press's publication of Baran's *The Political Economy of Growth* (1957), marked the beginning of Marxian dependency theory, concerned with the imperialist "development of underdevelopment" in Third World countries. *Monopoly Capital* (1966) by Baran and Sweezy, provided a systematic critique of a U.S. capitalist order that managed to stave off stagnation only through economic waste and military spending. Other key works in the "Monthly Review School" include *The Age of Imperialism* (1969) by Magdoff, and *Labor and Monopoly Capital* (1974) by Harry Braverman—who was until his death in 1976 director of MR Press (a position now occupied by Susan Lowes).

MR's influence over the more academically oriented Left of the 1980s has diminished in relation to the intellectual importance that it gained in the heyday of the New Left. Nevertheless, it remains a bastion for nonsectarian Marxist intellectuals with a leaning toward the Third World and a critical economic focus. A foreign-language edition of *MR* is available in Greek and for a time was available in Italian. *See also*: Communist Party; Economics; Matthiessen, F. O.; New Left

—*John Bellamy Foster*

REFERENCES

Baran, Paul A. *The Longer View*. New York: Monthly Review Press, 1969.

Foster, John Bellamy. "Sweezy, Paul Marlor." *The New Palgrave Dictionary of Economics*, vol. 4. New York: Stockton Press, 1987.

———. *The Theory of Monopoly Capitalism*. New York: Monthly Review Press, 1986.

Resnick, Stephen, and Richard Wolff. *Rethinking Marxism: Essays for Harry Magdoff and Paul Sweezy*. Brooklyn: Autonomedia, 1985.

Sweezy, Paul M. "Interview." *Monthly Review* 38, no. 11 (April 1987).

Mooney-Billings Case

Thomas J. Mooney (1892–1942) was the central figure in the most notorious labor frame-up in the early half of the twentieth century. He and Warren K. Billings (1893–1972) served twenty-three years (1916–39) in California prisons for the death of ten persons killed when a bomb exploded during the 1916

Drawing from Theodore Dreiser's pamphlet, *Tom Mooney*

Preparedness Day Parade in San Francisco. Mooney's actual offense was that he had been de facto leader of the Left wing of the California Federation of Labor and his activities had alarmed some of the most powerful forces in the state. One of his closest associates was Warren Billings.

Mooney had been raised in a Socialist family. At age fifteen, he won a contest sponsored by a Socialist magazine and as his prize enjoyed a free trip to a conference of the Second International in Switzerland. He would soon be an active national campaigner for Eugene V. Debs and an ardent left-wing Socialist. He became editor of the journal *Revolt* in 1912 and won fame as a militant writer and speaker. He did not fear association with anarchists and was not adverse to the doctrine of "propaganda of the deed." At one point he was charged with dynamiting the property of the Pacific Gas and Electric Company in San Francisco; but he was acquitted after three trials. By 1916 he was a dynamic force in San Francisco labor circles. His two major interests that year were opposition to U.S. participation in World War I and a drive to organize the car men of the United Railroads of San Francisco. The bitter unionizing drive, although unsuccessful, took up most of his energies that year as well as those of his wife, Rena, and Warren Billings.

When the fatal bomb went off on July 22, the Mooneys were blocks away, but both Tom and Rena, Warren K. Billings, Israel Weinberg, and Edward D. Noland were arrested for the deed. The common link was association with Tom Mooney. Billings, convicted previously for carrying dynamite on a passenger train, had a reputation for enjoying direct action. Weinberg was a jitney driver who occasionally chauffered the Mooneys, and his son was a pupil of Rena Mooney, who earned a living as a music teacher. Nolan was a Mooney backer in the trade unions. Ultimately only Tom Mooney and Warren Billings were convicted, Mooney for first-degree murder and Billings for second-degree murder.

In less than a year, solid evidence began to surface that the testimony against Mooney and Billings had been perjured. Other evidence substantiated their own account of where they had been. One of the investigating bodies was the federal Wickersham Commission, comprised mainly of conservatives. The commission concluded that the case's sole purpose was to put Mooney and Billings behind bars. Even the trial judge and jurors eventually made public statements that they had erred. National protests flooded the statehouse, including a plea for mercy from President Woodrow Wilson. Mooney's death sentence was commutated to life but no other relief was given. In the two decades that followed, Mooney and Billings came to be viewed as labor martyrs. Their plight remained a major concern of labor, civil libertarians, liberals, and radicals. But it was not until 1939 that Governor Culbert Olsen released them. Mooney was officially pardoned at that time, but Billings would not be formally pardoned until 1961.

Mooney tried to resume his activities but his health was gone. Eighteen months after his release, Mooney was bedridden, and on March 6, 1942, he died in San Francisco at age fifty. Billings went to work as a watchmaker after his release. He avoided radical politics but became vice president of the Watchmakers Union.

—*Dan Georgakas*

REFERENCES

Frost, Richard H. *The Mooney Case*. Stanford: Stanford University Press, 1968.

Gentry, Curt. *Frame-up*. New York: Norton, 1967.

Hunt, Henry Thomas. *The Case of Thomas J. Mooney and Warren K. Billings*. New York: Da Capo Press, 1971.

Mooney, Tom. Film (available at Tamiment Library, New York University) consisting of Mooney giving a resume of his case, 1936.

Ward, Esolv Ethan. *The Gentle Dynamiter: A Biography of Tom Mooney*. Palo Alto: Ramparts, 1983.

MOORE, QUEEN MOTHER (b. 1898)

Born on July 27, 1898, in New Iberia, Louisiana, Audley ("Queen Mother") Moore has been involved in both the Communist and black nationalist movements. While Audley only had three years of formal schooling, her education in southern folkways prepared her for a political life. After marrying at an early age into a black middle-class family, she promptly repudiated this background and joined Marcus Garvey's black nationalist movement in 1919. That same year, Queen Mother organized a massive demonstration of armed blacks to support Garvey's right to speak at Longshoreman's Hall in New Orleans. In the early '20s, Moore, as one of Garvey's most ardent supporters, migrated to New York City to work in the Garvey organization. Garvey's incarceration and subsequent deportation left her searching. In 1936 Moore joined the Communist Party. She was an active street agitator and orator, enjoining Harlemites to come to the aid of Ethiopia after its invasion by Italy. In 1938 she was the Party's candidate for state assembly from the Twenty-first District and in 1940 she ran for alderman from the Nineteenth Assembly District. In 1941 she was elected executive secretary of the Twenty-first District, the Harlem section of the CP. By 1942 she had risen to become secretary of the New York State branch of the Party. In the late 1940s she, along with others, began to assert the Afro-American "national question" within the Party, after its suppression during the Earl Browder years. For this she was ignored, and she finally left the Party in 1950.

In the early 1950s, Queen Mother Moore's political activities took on a decidedly nationalistic bent. She and her sister Eloise, Mother Langley, and Dara Collins founded the Universal Association of Ethiopian Women, which protested the reign of lynch-law in the South. She led the support teams for Robert Williams, an advocate of armed self-defense, after his standoff with the authorities in Monroe County, North Carolina, in 1959. She also tutored the young Malcolm X and prodded Elijah Muhammad to call for a separate state for black Americans in the

South. During the centennial of the Emancipation Proclamation in 1963, she established a Reparations Committee to advocate compensatory payment to descendants of slaves for their ancestors' forced labor and for subsequent social and economic injustice. Throughout the 1960s, Queen Mother Moore's presence became a catalyst for the new generation of "Black Power" advocates. In 1968 she was one of the critical forces involved in the declaration of the Republic of New Africa and initiated its statement of independence. Throughout the 1970s, she was actively engaged in support of nationalist political prisoners.

Queen Mother Moore continues to be active in the nationalist cause today, while continuing her call for reparations. *See also*: Communist Party, Garveyism

—*Muhammad Ahmad (Max Stanford)*

REFERENCES

Moore, Audley. Interviews. Oral History of the American Left, Tamiment Library, New York University.

"Queen Mother Moore." *The New Afrikan* (Detroit), December 18, 1983.

"Queen Mother Moore Receives Garvey Award." *Burning Spear* (San Francisco), January–March, 1987.

Morgan, Lewis Henry (1818–81)

Anthropology in the United States did not begin as an academic discipline but as a scholarly pastime of self-taught amateurs seeking a better understanding of the culture of the American Indians. Its founders included George Catlin, Major John Wesley Powell, Frank Hamilton Cushing and, most influential by far, Lewis Henry Morgan.

Born in Aurora, New York, Morgan graduated from Union College in 1840 and shortly afterward was admitted to the bar in Rochester, where he lived most of his life. Legal adviser to a railroad for many years, he was elected to the New York State Assembly in 1861 and to the State Senate in 1868, but the real focus of his life lay elsewhere. In his early manhood he became interested in "primitive" society, and especially that of his Iroquois Indian neighbors. A chance encounter with a young Seneca, Ely S. Parker, in a bookstore in 1844 quickly led to meetings with other Indians, and started Morgan on the research that would remain his consuming passion for the rest of his days. He was not only a student of Indian culture, but an admirer and defender of that culture; it was largely because of his instrumental role in defeating an effort to seize Seneca land for commercial use in 1847 that he was inducted into the tribe's Hawk Clan.

The Seneca and other tribes of the Iroquois Nation were the subject of Morgan's first book, *League of the Ho-de-no-sau-nee, or Iroquois* (1851), which was followed by three more important anthropological studies: *Systems of Consanguinity and Affinity of the Human Family* (1871), published by the Smithsonian Institution, *Ancient Society* (1877), and *Houses and House-Life of the American Aborigines*, published shortly before his death in 1881. His only nonanthropological book, *The American Beaver and His Works* (1868), was long recognized as the classic monograph on the subject and warmly praised by Charles Darwin; of special interest to modern readers are its lengthy discussion of animal intelligence and its affirmation of animal rights.

In his lifetime Morgan was one of the most respected scientific figures in the United States, and was by no means regarded as a radical. The evolutionary theory of property, the family, and government that he developed in his most famous and later most controversial book, *Ancient Society*, did, however, challenge the prevailing views on these matters, and some passages in the book's 500-plus pages have a distinctly radical ring. His rhapsodic descriptions of primitive "communism in living," for example, and his highly critical estimate of property in civilization, which he concluded by arguing that "a mere property career is not the final destiny of mankind," and that "the next higher stage of society" would be "a revival, in a higher form, of the liberty, equality, and fraternity" of the ancient tribal cultures, suffice to confirm Leslie A. White's contention that *Ancient Society* was "revolutionary in import as well as evolutionary." But such passages did not prevent the book from receiving long and flattering reviews in such mainstream publications as the *Atlantic Monthly*, the *Nation* and the *New York Times*. If Morgan acquired a posthumous reputation as a radical, the credit (or blame) belongs to Karl Marx and Friedrich Engels, who discerned the revolutionary implications of his theories and proclaimed them to the world.

In the winter of 1880–81 Marx made an assiduous study of *Ancient Society*, evidently intending to devote a substantial work to it. The long illness that culminated in his death in 1883 made it impossible for him to complete this task, and his extensive notes were not published integrally until 1972. Engels's *The Origin of the Family, Private Property and the State* (1884) drew on Marx's notes, but was essentially a summary and defense of Morgan's views. Recognized ever since as one of the Marxist classics, Engels's little book set the stage for the enduring socialist interest in Morgan, an interest soon multiplied by other popular works such as August Bebel's *Woman and Socialism* and Paul Lafargue's *The Evolution of Property*. In his book as well as in letters, Engels's praise for Morgan was boundless; indeed, he went so far as to credit him with the independent discovery of the materialist conception of history. Thus, with the possible exception of Benjamin Franklin, Morgan became the only American thinker universally recognized as an important influence on, and contributor to, the Marxism of Marx and Engels.

Well before *The Origin of the Family* appeared in English translation, Morgan's work had an impact on the American movement. In an autobiographical sketch pubished shortly before his execution in 1887, Haymarket martyr August Spies cited *Ancient Society* as one of the three books that had influenced him most. In Daniel DeLeon's Socialist Labor Party, Morgan's work was recognized as a canonical authority equal to the works of Marx and Engels themselves. Again and again DeLeon referred to the "Morgan-Marxian materialist conception of history," or similar formulations, and in later years he boasted that the popularity of *Ancient Society* among American workers was the direct result of his party's educational efforts. Morgan was also boosted in the Socialist Party press; the *Comrade*, edited by John Spargo, offered subscribers copies of the Holt edition of *Ancient Society*.

Morgan's views reached a much larger readership when Charles H. Kerr's Chicago-based socialist publishing house brought out Ernest Untermann's translation of *The Origin of the Family* in 1902, and an inexpensive edition of *Ancient Society* five years later. Promoted in the socialist press as "required reading" for all class-conscious workers, these books were reviewed, summarized, and commented on at length by countless aspiring Marxist theorists over the next three decades. They were used as textbooks at Detroit's Proletarian University, the Work People's College of the Industrial Workers of the World in Duluth, and in socialist study-classes throughout North America. The Kerr edition of *Ancient Society* sold some 4,000 copies in four years, was subsequently reprinted several times, and was still in print in the 1960s.

As Morgan's working-class readership grew, his reputation in academic circles declined sharply. For the socialists and Wobblies of the 1910s, as for the various later factions of Communists, academic disdain for Morgan was regarded almost as proof of his revolutionary correctness. In the Left press the dominant trends in American anthropology—especially the school of Franz Boas—were scornfully dismissed as bourgeois and pro-imperialist, and Morgan's views were defended against all comers. In 1925, for example, the IWW's *Industrial Pioneer* ran a lengthy three-part series titled "Was Morgan Wrong?" Responding to all the arguments of the "anti-Morgan" anthropologists, the author, Vern Smith, concluded that Morgan was, on all disputed points, emphatically right. In 1937 anthropologist Robert Lowie summed up the prevailing academic attitude toward Morgan in his *History of Ethnological Theory*, faulting Morgan's works for their alleged "mystical nonsense" and "fatal errors," though begrudgingly conceding him something of a bumbling pioneer's status. Fifteen years later William Z. Foster, in his *History of the Communist Party*, expressed the sentiment of a sizable segment of the American

Left when he blithely hailed *Ancient Society* as "perhaps the most important book ever written in the Western Hemisphere."

Too often, in these polemics, radicals contented themselves with the simple assertion of Morgan's infallibility, quoting Engels as proof. But there was more than a little truth in their charges that academic anthropology was a deeply conservative discipline, and that the rejection of Morgan by Boas, Lowie, and others was motivated by something more than the disinterested pursuit of Science. Within the field of anthropology itself, in the 1930s, a few independent thinkers arose to challenge their colleagues' conventional wisdom on Morgan. Foremost among these was Leslie A. White, who devoted numerous journal articles to Morgan's vindication, and edited several volumes of his unpublished writings, most notably his *Indian Journals, 1859–62* (1959). Although he was Red-baited because of an early visit to Soviet Russia, White was not particularly interested in Marxism; he tended to avoid the political dimension of the debate on Morgan, and defended the latter's work on strictly scientific grounds.

The Charles H. Kerr Company's advertisements for *Ancient Society* emphasized that the book "points the way to a cleaner, freer, happier life for women," and it is remarkable how many of the best-informed and most militant defenders of Morgan have been women radicals. In a letter to Engels dated June 9, 1886, Florence Kelley noted that "a large section of the Suffrage Association in Iowa took for the subject of its discussions through the winter Morgan's works, especially his *Ancient Society*." In her first exposition of basic Marxist principles, the 1887 essay on "The Need of Theoretical Preparation for Philanthropic Work," addressed to young women entering the field of social work, Kelley strongly urged the reading both of *Ancient Society* and Engels's then-untranslated *Origin of the Family*. In Elizabeth Cady Stanton's autobiography, *Eighty Years and More* (1898), the venerable suffragist who became an avowed socialist in her last years signaled Morgan's work as "truth [that] cannot be questioned" on the subject of matriarchy. Lida Parce, author of *Lesson Outlines in the Economic Interpretation of History* (1908), drew heavily on Morgan in her *Economic Determinism*, an introduction to Marxism published by Charles H. Kerr in 1913.

Morgan's work proved to be of interest to soapbox agitators no less than to theorists. Kate Richards O'Hare, one of the SP's most effective speakers and pamphleteers, outlined the theses of *Ancient Society* in detail in "The Tale of a Rib," an essay on the "woman question" published in the *National Rip-Saw* in 1916. Also based on Morgan's magnum opus was the popular series of *Stories of the Cave People*, by the ebullient Mary E. Marcy, in the *International Socialist Review* (1909–16); published as an illustrated book in 1917, these tales were used in socialist children's classes through the late 1930s.

One of the most zealous and persistent proponents of Morgan was Communist Party activist Mary Inman, remembered today especially for her theories regarding housework as a form of slavery (i.e., unpaid labor). Her books, *In Woman's Defense* (1940) and others, as well as her militant monthly, *Facts for Women*, stressed that *Ancient Society* was a work "highly important to the woman's movement." Morgan's work was a central reference-point in Inman's long intraparty struggle for the creation of a Communist-led national women's organization—a struggle that eventually led her to break with the CP.

A few years later, in the early 1950s, Morgan and Engels's commentary figured prominently in a protracted and heated internal debate (on cosmetics, beauty, and the role of women in the revolutionary movement) between Evelyn Reed, Myra Tanner Weiss, and others in the Trotskyist Socialist Workers Party.

The 1960s and 1970s witnessed a notable revival of interest in Morgan on the part of socialist and feminist scholars and activists. Carl Resek's excellent biography, collections of Morgan's unpublished writings, and English translations of influential studies such as Emmanuel Terray's *Marxism and "Primitive" Societies* (1972) and Wilhelm Reich's *The Invasion of Compulsory Sex-Morality* (1971) provided essential material for a new approach to his manysided achievements. To

Eleanor Burke Leacock, a Marxist anthropologist active in the women's movement, we owe what is probably the most thoughtful and influential critical reassessment of Morgan in recent decades. Published originally as an introduction to a new edition of *Ancient Society* in 1964, and reprinted in her *Myths of Male Dominance: Collected Articles on Women Cross-Culturally* (1981), Leacock argued that *Ancient Society*, while not the unassailable gospel that some of its naive Left defenders have tried to pretend, nonetheless is a book with a "tremendous meaning for today." She concludes, "That the causes of our difficulties lie not in the nature of humanity, but in our social commitment to property, is the profoundly important message." *See also*: Anthropology; Leacock, Eleanor Burke

—Franklin Rosemont

REFERENCES

Krader, Lawrence, ed. *The Ethnological Notebooks of Karl Marx*. Assen: Van Gorcum, 1972.

Resek, Carl. *Lewis Henry Morgan: American Scholar*. Chicago: University of Chicago Press, 1960.

Rosemont, Franklin. "Karl Marx and the Iroquois." *Arsenal/Surrealist Subversion* 4. Chicago: Black Swan Press, 1989.

White, Leslie A. "Morgan's Attitude Toward Religion and Science." *American Anthropologist 46:2* (1944).

Moscow Trials

This series of trials in 1936–38, in which virtually the entire surviving Bolshevik leadership of the October Revolution was charged with having made secret agreements with Hitler and the Mikado to destroy and dismember the Soviet Union, aroused a bitter controversy within the American Left.

The trials occurred during the Great Depression, when the rapid industrialization of the Soviet Union contrasted with the millions of unemployed in the United States. The Nazis had marched into the Rhineland, threatening war, and Communist parties everywhere had ceased their previous ultra-Left denunciations of social democrats as "social fascists" in order to call for "popular fronts" between liberal capitalist parties and the parties of the Left. Under these circumstances, the Communist Party of the United States recruited most of a generation of rebellious youth and was a major force among intellectuals.

The Communists argued that the Soviet judiciary was part of a progressive social system that had brought great gains to the people and could not, therefore, be rotten. The Soviet Union was stronger than ever as a result of the trials. To question them was to break up the unity of the antifascist forces.

The Lovestoneites, the CP faction under whose leadership the Trotskyists had been expelled only to be then expelled themselves by the William Z. Foster faction, at first defended the trials. When, however, Nikolai Bukharin, whose supporters the Lovestoneites were, became a defendant in the third trial, they reversed themselves and declared the trials to be frame-ups.

The Trotskyists called for a commission to investigate the justice of the treason charges against Trotsky. They argued that no evidence had been provided outside of the confessions, that it was preposterous to believe that the entire Bolshevik leadership except for one man consisted of traitors to the revolution, and that allegations in the confessions conflicted sharply with verified facts. The purpose of the trials, they said, was to consolidate the rule of an autocratic bureaucracy that had achieved supremacy as the result of the isolation of a backward country devastated by war and famine and subject to the pressures of its barbaric past and of imperialism's barbaric present. This bureaucracy was faithless to the ideals of the revolution, but the Soviet Union remained a "degenerated workers' state"—just as a trade union under the grip of a bureaucracy that permits no internal democracy and uses gangster methods against the rank and file remains an instrument of the workers even though the union needs to be utterly renovated to function truly as such.

Members of the anti-Stalinist Left who worked with George Novack and other Trotskyists on the Committee for the Defense of Leon Trotsky in setting up an International Commission of Inquiry headed by John Dewey included Max Eastman, James T. Farrell, Sidney Hook, Mary McCarthy, Norman

Thomas, and Edmund Wilson. Frieda Kirchway, the editor of the *Nation*, was for a while a member of the committee but resigned from it under pressure from the Communists, who stated that the *Nation* was acting as the "organ of a counterrevolutionary band of conspirators and assassins."

The liberal fellow-travelers of the CP published an "Open Letter to American Liberals" that urged them to have nothing to do with the Trotsky defense committee, accusing it of interfering in Soviet internal affairs and helping fascism. The eighty-eight signatories included Malcolm Cowley, Theodore Dreiser, Lillian Hellman, Rockwell Kent, Corliss Lamont, Max Lerner, Robert S. Lynd, Carey McWilliams, Dorothy Parker, Henry Roth, Paul Sweezy, and Nathanael West.

The *Nation* and the *New Republic* ostensibly suspended judgment on the trials but in reality were scarcely neutral in the controversy. Both gave as their opinion that, although the defendants might not have been guilty of some of the things they were charged with, they must have been guilty of "something." Both failed to give serious consideration to the findings of the Dewey Commission that led it to declare Trotsky "not guilty." The *New Republic* turned against John Dewey, who was one of its founders, so that he felt constrained to resign from its editorial board, of which he had been a member for twenty-five years.

In the years that followed, many of the members of the CP, the Lovestoneites, and the Trotskyists and their respective peripheries gave up their radicalism. A minority turned conservative. Undoubtedly, the Hitler-Stalin Pact, the war, the postwar boom, the Cold War, and the Soviet repressions of the Hungarians and the Czechs had most to do with this, but the Moscow trials also had their delayed effect. Within two years after Khrushchev's report to the Twentieth Congress of the Russian Communist Party, in which he described the methods of Stalin's GPU in the vast purge that followed the trials—casting doubt by implication on the trials themselves—more than 85 percent of the American CP abandoned it, reducing its membership from 20,000-plus members to less than 3,000.

Fifty years after the first Moscow trial, a U.S. Moscow Trials Campaign Committee, headed by Paul Siegel, Ben Stone, and Marilyn Vogt-Downey, was formed to urge the Soviet government to exonerate the defendants of the Moscow trials. After this was done for all except Trotsky and his son Leon Sedov, it urged the exoneration of these two and the publication of the writings of the principal defendants. Part of an international effort that gained the signatures, among others, of 97 representatives of socialist, labor, and radical parties in the parliaments of nineteen countries, it got the endorsement of more than 225 people of the American Left. Three of the signatories—A. B. Magil, Morris U. Schappes, and Paul M. Sweezy—had been active in support of the trials at the time; one—Mary McCarthy—had been active in opposition to the trials. *See also*: Communist Party, New York Intellectuals, *Partisan Review*, Trotskyism

—*Paul N. Siegel*

REFERENCES

Deutscher, Isaac. *The Prophet Outcast: Trotsky 1929–1940*. New York: Oxford University Press, 1963.

Shannon, David A. *The Decline of American Communism*. Chatham, N.J.: The Chatham Bookseller, 1971.

Wald, Alan M. *James T. Farrell: The Revolutionary Socialist Years*. New York: New York University Press, 1978.

———. *The New York Intellectuals*. Chapel Hill: University of North Carolina Press, 1987.

Warren, Frank A., III. *Liberals and Communism*. Bloomington: Indiana University Press, 1966.

Most, Johann (1846–1906)

A brilliant editor and orator, Most was the leading social revolutionary and anarchist in America during the 1880s. Born in Bavaria, he began his public career as a Social Democrat, serving two terms in the German Reichstag, and was imprisoned in and expelled from both Austria and Germany for his socialist agitation. From London, Most launched his famous paper, *Freiheit* (1879), which he edited until his death. Most's growing extremism and uncompromising calls for violence soon led to a break with the Social Democrats, and Most moved steadily toward anarchism. Following a prison term in England, Most moved *Freiheit* to New York in 1882. The principal author of the Pittsburgh Manifesto (1883), he invigorated the American social revolutionary movement until the Haymarket tragedy (1886). Believing violent revolution was necessary for the working class to liberate itself from capitalism, he denounced trade unions and electoral politics as futile delusions. Most's best-known pamphlet remains his terrorist handbook *The Science of Revolutionary Warfare* (1885); his defense of violent tactics helped perpetuate the popular stereotype of anarchists as fanatical bomb-throwers. A powerful writer and speaker, Most was repeatedly pursued by the police and served three prison terms in New York City. *See also:* Anarchism, Black International

—*Blaine McKinley*

REFERENCES

Avrich, Paul. *The Haymarket Tragedy*. Princeton: Princeton University Press, 1984.

Trautmann, Frederic. *The Voice of Terror: A Biography of Johann Most*. Westport: Greenwood, 1980.

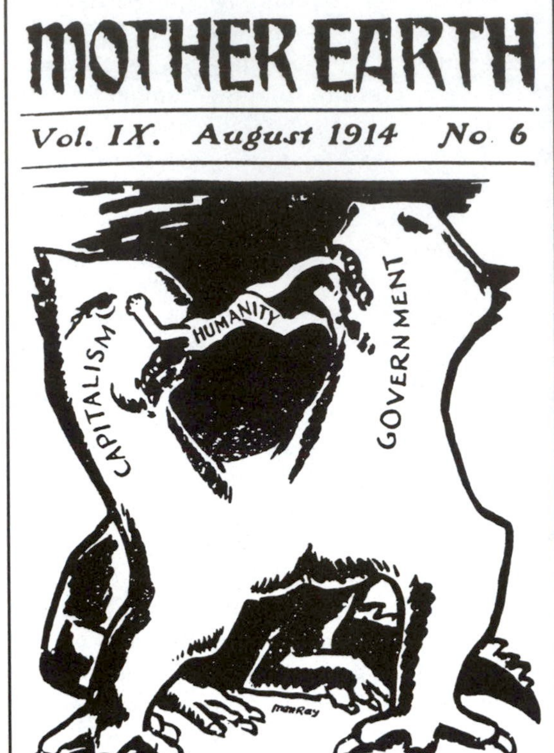

Cover by Man Ray

Mother Earth

Although often edited by others, this anarchist journal reflected the personality and view of Emma Goldman. She was not only the "mother" of the magazine but of the collective that sustained it. This group included Max Baginski, Hippolyte Havel, Harry Kelley, Leonard Abbott, and Alexander Berkman. One of the purposes of their endeavor was to reanimate an anarchist movement that had been on the defensive since the assassination of President McKinley by anarchist Leon Czolgosz. The intent of the collective was to blend social concerns with the arts, but in practice the arts were of secondary interest. Among many well-known contributors were Voltairine de Cleyre, Theodore Dreiser, Frank Harris, Arturo Giovannitti, and the Magón brothers. There were translations of all the leading European anarchist thinkers as well as passages from Nietzsche, Heine, Flaubert, and other European intellectuals. Cover artists included Man Ray and Robert Minor. The magazine's title was generated during a buggy ride in the country by Baginski and Goldman in February 1906. Thrilled to see the soil breaking free of the power of frost and green shoots poking for the sun, Goldman declared "Mother Earth" would be an ideal name for the magazine they were planning. The first issue of sixty-four pages appeared March 10, 1906. Circulating between 3,000 and 5,000 copies, *Mother Earth* continued publishing until 1917, when it was suppressed by the federal government. Goldman and Berkman then published *Mother Earth Bulletin*—to keep in touch "with friends"—until their deportation to Russia in 1919. *See also*: Anarchism; Goldman, Emma

—*Dan Georgakas*

REFERENCES

Wexler, Alice. *Emma Goldman: An Intimate Life*. New York: Pantheon, 1984.

Woodworth, Fred. Cover note to a facsimile edition of *Mother Earth* 2, no. 9 (November 1907), published by the *Match*, May 1, 1986.

Mother Jones: see Ramparts

Municipal Socialism

The greatest gains for American radicals in municipal politics came during the ascendancy of the Socialist Party of America, 1910–15. During these years the party was heavily committed to city elections and was rewarded by an impressive run of electoral successes across the country. Most Socialists understood the limitations of local government, but faced with the task of building a coordinated, nationwide political movement from the ground up, hoped to use municipal politics to build a grass-roots organization. Local campaigns, they felt, could expose exploitation in the neighborhoods, raise working-class political aspirations and confidence, and teach political methods and ideology. Experience at this level would prepare workers for state and national affairs.

In terms of organizational benefits, the party's successes in municipal politics help explain the rapid growth of the movement during the Progressive period. Conversely, the party's inability to consolidate these electoral gains—its failure to build stable grass-roots political organizations—was an important factor in the subsequent decline of the movement. The party entered its most difficult trials during and after World War I with an organization in shambles at the grass-roots level.

Municipal socialism drew upon a long tradition of organized working-class participation in city elections. Local politics, like union organizing, cooperative and utopian programs, and economic boycotts, was part of an evolving search for control at the workplace that spilled over into a drive to control neighborhoods. In the mid-1880s, scores of Knights of Labor assemblies embraced municipal politics through Labor and Workingmen's parties. The most notable results came in 1886. In New York City, "single-taxer" Henry George, running with strong labor backing, nearly defeated Democrat Abram Hewitt, and in Chicago the United Labor Party elected seven assemblymen and five judges. The Knights did not enter local politics with a larger revolutionary goal in mind, yet the similarities between their demands and those of the Socialists three decades later suggest the continuity in working-class republicanism expressed at the local level.

In 1898 Social-Democrat John C. Chase was elected mayor in Haverhill, Massachusetts, along with several Socialist aldermen and councilmen. Socialist Charles R. Coulter became mayor of Brockton a year later. Both candidates received strong union support but were subsequently defeated by fusion tickets composed of Republicans and Democrats. A decade later the SP claimed thirty-five minor municipal offices in eight states.

The party's first major victory came in 1910 in Milwaukee. Building on a history of labor politics, Social-Democrats ran a machinist, Robert Meister, for mayor in 1898 on a platform that included municipal control of public utilities, union labor and the eight-hour day for city work, relief for unemployed workers, heavier taxes for large corporations, and free legal and medical service for needy people. This would become standard Socialist fare across the country. Having secured the union labor vote, the Socialists appealed to liberal middle-class citizens, highlighting a 1903 scandal that involved both Republicans and Democrats. Under the firm hand of Austrian-born Victor Berger, Milwaukee Social-Democrats perfected a remarkable political machine, the most conspicuous feature being a "bundle brigade" that could canvass the entire city with literature in seven languages in a matter of hours.

In 1910 Milwaukee Socialists elected a mayor, Emil Seidel, seven aldermen-at-large, and sixteen councilmen. Two years later a fusion candidate defeated the Seidel administration, but in 1916 the Socialists returned to power and held office until 1940. Their success was partly due to adept handling of the city's diverse ethnic groups. Local Milwaukee's "formula"—a moderate, practical municipal program, close ties with unions, and solid organization—was copied by Socialist locals everywhere, even though many criticized the substance of Berger's reformist municipal program.

Across the nation in 1910–11, Socialists elected more than 400 officials, including 28 mayors and village heads. The prominent victories were in Berkeley, California; Butte, Montana; Flint, Michigan; Granite City, Illinois; Coeur d'Alene, Idaho; Two Harbors, Minnesota; Manitowoc, Wisconsin; Schenectady, New York; Canton, Hamilton, Lima, and Lorain, Ohio; and Reading and New Castle, Pennsylvania. The bulk, however, were in smaller manufacturing, mining, railroad, and lake-shipment communities in the Midwest. Socialists won across a broad range of economic circumstances, but their political strength invariably lay in the factory districts and the "lower ends" of the cities. Their elected officials were likewise generally working people. By 1912 there were more than 2,000 Socialists serving in public office.

In terms of gross numbers of victories, Socialist fortunes in city government, like the party's development as a whole, grew rapidly during the prewar years. But the party's strength in each particular city was far less constant than the national trends. Socialist administrations typically ended with Socialists forced out of office in the first or second election after their victory by a fusion of all nonsocialist parties. This local instability suggests weaknesses in the grass-roots movement.

While the Socialists succeeded in drawing support from working people, they failed to deal effectively with middle-class reformers, who were attracted to the party's immediate demands but repelled by the working-class bias the party showed once in office. Often general reform sentiment fragmented traditional party organizations, and the resulting multiparty elections allowed the Socialists to take office on a plurality based on their strength in working-class wards. The local became entangled in an unstable coalition only partly of its own making, composed of workers and frustrated middle-class voters. Once in power, the Socialists faced a difficult choice between moving to the left to consolidate their working-class support, or broadening their program to include general reform sentiment. Unappeased, middle-class voters gravitated to a fusion ticket endorsed by both major-party organizations and offering a "businessman's" administration with a clear middle-class appeal. Just as damaging were coalitions with middle-class reformers. More than a score of elected Socialist officials, including Schenectady Socialist mayor George R. Lunn, were expelled from the party for adopting middle-class reform issues once in office.

During World War I, Socialists faced state repression, fusion-party opposition, and heightened intolerance. Although victories in smaller communities dropped off accordingly, the Socialist vote in larger cities increased. In New York City, Morris Hillquit came within a few thousand votes of victory in 1917, and six Socialist aldermen were elected. Socialists in Cleveland, Toledo, Dayton, Buffalo, and Chicago received between 20 and 44 percent of the municipal vote, much of it coming from immigrant groups.

Postwar elections brought scattered victories in Wisconsin, Illinois, and Ohio. In Milwaukee, Daniel Hoan, first elected mayor in 1916, held together a coalition of union workers and liberal reformers through the 1930s. Hoan was defeated in 1940, but eight years later Frank Zeidler was elected as America's last old-style big-city Socialist mayor. Zeidler outlasted his SP base and weathered several controversies over his progressive stand on minority rights, slum clearance, and building inspection. He won a third term in 1956 and chose not to run in 1960.

The SP's other notable postwar municipal success came in Reading, Pennsylvania, a working-class city of around 100,000 that elected Socialist J. Henry Stump mayor in 1927. Campaigning against a tax proposal that overburdened working-class homeowners, Socialists promised to equalize property assessments and reduce spending. This limited-government platform, ironically, left the Socialist administration unprepared to deal with destitute workers during the Depression. In 1935 the Reading movement succumbed to a national party split between followers of Norman Thomas and the Old Guard. Although the Old Guard retained control of the local, it was unable to conduct effective campaigns and lost decisively in 1939. Stump was reelected in 1943, but his campaign was largely personal.

Socialists in Bridgeport, Connecticut, led by perennial Socialist mayoral candidate

Jasper McLevy, won office in 1933 after a series of bridge-contracting scandals tarred both major parties. Mayor McLevy, like Hoan and Stump, offered an efficient, responsible government, but nothing distinguished his administration as Socialist. The Connecticut state party censured the conservative administration in the late 1930s, but McLevy, enjoying wide appeal among liberals, continued in office until 1957.

The SP disintegrated as an independent political force between 1948 and 1960. In the late 1970s the political initiative was picked up by a variety of new progressive coalitions in cities like Cambridge, Massachusetts; Ann Arbor, Michigan; and Berkeley, Santa Cruz, and Santa Monica, California. Berkeley progressives won a number of seats on the rent board and city council in the early 1980s, as did Tom Hayden's Campaign for Economic Democracy in Santa Monica. Their concerns ranged from housing reform and rent control to city planning, minority representation, and energy use. The new leadership, drawn from middle-class backgrounds, demonstrated greater flexibility in building coalitions, but lacked the national organizational ties Socialists had formed earlier. Still, they retained the old radicals' faith in social control over economic development and shared a belief that municipal politics could yield tangible organizational benefits and at the same time redistribute, at least in small ways, community wealth through housing reform, improved social services, neighborhood preservation, and other socially responsible actions.

The best known of the new progressive municipal coalitions was ushered in by Bernard Sanders's nine-vote victory over a conservative Democratic incumbent in Burlington, Vermont, in 1981. Sanders, like socialists before him, immediately faced united Republican-Democratic opposition, and like his predecessors responded by taking the council fights into the neighborhoods. Sanders's support came from young professionals, the elderly, students, and working people—a mix that suggests the continuing viability of the old-line Socialist coalitions. Sanders's program, like those of the older Socialist administrations, stressed a concern for more efficient government, equalized tax burdens, improved services for low-income citizens, and popular access to the arts. The administration also focused on regulating speculative development to ensure a social return to the citizens and to protect the viability of older working-class neighborhoods. In May 1985 Burlington's popular mayor was re-elected to a third term. *See also*: British Americans, German Americans, Milwaukee, Socialist Party

—Richard Judd

REFERENCES

Critchlow, Donald T., ed. *Socialism in the Heartland: The Midwestern Experience, 1900–1925.* Notre Dame: University of Notre Dame Press, 1986.

Judd, Richard W. *Socialist Cities: Explorations into the Grass Roots of American Socialism.* Albany: SUNY Press, 1990.

Kaltnick, Arnold. "Socialist Municipal Administration in Four American Cities: Milwaukee, Schenectady, New Castle, and Conneaut, Ohio." Ph.D. diss., New York University, 1982.

Stave, Bruce, ed. *Socialism and the Cities.* Port Washington, N.Y.: Kennikat Press, 1975.

Munro, Evelyn Smith (b. 1914)

Daughter of a New Orleans railroad telegrapher and sometime real estate saleswoman drawn to Huey Long, Munro grew up in Louisiana and Texas and turned radical at an early age. In 1935, recruited through Socialist Party contacts, she became secretary of the Southern Tenant Farmers Union (STFU). For five years she assumed a pivotal role at the center of STFU administration, answering letters, negotiating financial support from liberal allies, writing press releases and even her own sharecropper-related plays. Adept with media and personal relations, she also became head of the Women's Division of the STFU. In these positions, she had a profound influence upon the STFU and radical efforts to create a sharecroppers' social movement.

In 1940 Munro left the STFU, after which she worked for the International Ladies Garment Workers Union (ILGWU) in Knoxville, Tennessee, until becoming disillusioned with union leadership. She worked briefly in New York as assistant executive secretary for the

Workers Defense League, and in Virginia as executive secretary of the Southern Electoral Reform League.

A few years later, moving west with her then-fiancé, radio scriptwriter David Munro, she became educational director of the ILGWU West Coast division. When she and her husband moved on to Washington, D.C., Munro briefly wrote for the STFU's Washington newsletter.

By the 1950s, she had become fully involved in family and career, a Stevenson Democrat who nevertheless continued to view herself as a "Norman Thomas Socialist." During the 1960s–1980s, she raised funds for the United Farm Workers, did volunteer service for the NAACP, served with an agency for the homeless, and joined with such other organizations and movements as Amnesty International, civil rights groups for homosexuals, and a task force on international relations. *See also*: Mitchell, H. L.; Southern Tenant Farmers Union; Workers Defense League

—*Elizabeth Payne*

REFERENCES

Grubbs, Donald. *Cry from Cotton*. Chapel Hill: University of North Carolina Press, 1971.

Mitchell, H. L. *Mean Things Happening in This Land*. Montclair, N. J.: Allanheld, Osmun, 1979.

MURALS

The political and educational dimensions of murals have been utilized by government and ecclesiastic organizations since medieval times. With the Mexican mural renaissance of the 1920s, revolutionary and nationalistic components were added that have made murals an important ingredient in contemporary revolutionary culture. The U.S. mural movement was directly inspired by the three great Mexican muralists—Diego Rivera, David Alfaro Siqueiros, and José Clemente Orozco—particularly during their U.S. period of 1930–34. The Mexican example was especially influential because it promised a means of transforming the best of European modernism (cubism, futurism, and expressionism) into a realistic, popular style that addressed social needs. Both Siqueiros and Rivera were active in the Mexican Communist Party while Orozco was a profoundly humanistic social critic. In creating visual symbolism for revolutionary Mexico each artist attacked capitalism, corruption, imperialism, and the Church. Each had a strong flamboyant personality that sparked controversy and drew attention to his murals and political views.

The American mural movement of the 1930s produced 2,500 works in locations throughout the nation. Most of this work was done between 1933 and 1940 under the aegis of the Works Progress Administration (WPA) as a series of relief programs for artists. The commissions for post offices, schools, and public buildings were awarded through competitions sponsored by the WPA and the Section of Painting and Sculpture of the Treasury Department.

The strongest social and artistic murals were usually the efforts of left-wing artists who had worked directly with Rivera either in Mexico or the United States. These artists included Victor Arnautoff, George Biddle, Lucienne Bloch, Marianne Greenwood, Ben Shahn, Clifford Wight, and Hale Woodruff. One of the most controversial projects was comprised of twenty-six murals directed by Arnautoff for Coit Tower in San Francisco. Murals by Arnautoff, Wight, and Bernard Zackheim were criticized for containing radical images such as that of a worker reading a book by Karl Marx. Only strong protests led by liberals and other artists saved the works from destruction. Another dispute was generated by Rockwell Kent's post office murals in Washington, D.C., which contained an appeal for Puerto Rican independence.

Some of the most artistically successful interpretations of the New Deal's respect for immigrants and workers were rendered by Ben Shahn in murals for the Roosevelt Community Center in New Jersey and the Bronx post office. His design for a mural on the "Passion of Sacco and Vanzetti," exhibited at the Museum of Modern Art in 1932, was finally executed as a mosaic at Syracuse University in 1967. A list of murals with notable social comment would span the nation and would have themes as varied as Lucienne Bloch's *Childhood* at the Women's House of Detention (Rikers Island, N.Y.) and Anton Refreigier's

Mural by Mark Rogovin, Chicago, 1960s

California history series for the Rincon Annex of the San Francisco post office.

With the advent of the Cold War, socially relevant art became suspect in the United States and the dominant style shifted to abstract expressionism. Many WPA murals were either intentionally destroyed or neglected. The Rivera tradition of socially concerned art survived only in the work of black artists such as Hale Woodruff, Charles White, and John Biggers, who painted murals for churches and schools in the South. William Walker, an artist who helped launch the contemporary mural movement, came out of this tradition.

The new mural movement became visible in 1967 when William Walker helped produce the "Wall of Respect," painted on a condemned building in Chicago's black ghetto. This collection of images of black heroes and black struggles was painted by twenty-one black artists shortly after the assassination of the Rev. Martin Luther King, Jr. *Ebony* magazine celebrated the wall with a cover story. Other walls of respect and related murals soon began to appear in ethnic and "hippie" communities throughout the nation.

By 1970 four large murals that epitomized the political activism of diverse neighborhoods had been painted on the sides of Chicago buildings by William Walker, Eugene Eda, Mark Rogovin, and John Weber. Walker's "Peace and Salvation Wall of Understanding" at Cabrini Homes was painted after two white policemen were shot by snipers and an entire housing project was held hostage by police until the suspects surrendered. Eda's "Wall of Meditation" featured Egyptian and Black Panther warriors with portraits of Malcolm X and Martin Luther King in a dramatic style reminiscent of Orozco. Rogovin used a flat Siqueiros-like image of resistance to urban renewal in "Protect the People's Homes," and Weber, working in a neighborhood filled with racial tension, painted a "Wall of Choices." That same year Ray Patlan added a new aspect to the mural movement by evoking Mexican-American history and the struggle of farm workers in murals for the Salón de la Raza at Casa Aztlan in the Pilsen district of Chicago.

Unlike their American predecessors, the murals of the 1960s were undertaken without direct government support. They were community-based and mainly located on the exterior walls of buildings in humble neighborhoods. The creation of murals was often part of a neighborhood struggle, involving active support by community organizations and residents who sometimes participated in the painting. The effect of a mural on local problems like housing, gang warfare, and vandalism become one measure of its success.

Many early muralists were university-trained minority artists who returned to paint for their people as part of the political movement for ethnic pride. These walls often inspired local residents to begin painting and become mural artists. Methods for community projects in which nonartist community residents worked with muralists were developed by groups like Cityarts Workshop in New York. Some projects were painted by youth gang members in Los Angeles to celebrate peace treaties and commemorate dead members. Collective murals were also created by such diverse groups as Artes Guadalupanos de Aztlan (Sante Fe), Mujeres Muralistas (San Francisco), and Peoples Painters (Piscataway, New Jersey). These nonelitist group efforts embodied the philosophy of the counterculture and feminist movements and were an important innovation.

Every style from abstraction to underground-comix images was employed for social murals in the early days of the new movement. In much the same way that the New Left rejected the Old Left, the new muralists, for the most part, rejected the 1930s muralists, especially much of the work done under WPA. But the influence of the Mexican muralists, especially Siqueiros, remained strong. A number of the new muralists went to Mexico to meet the "master" and study his compositions firsthand. Others, especially in the Chicano movement of the Southwest, simply adapted Siqueiros's ideas from films and photographs.

By the mid-1970s government began to see community murals as a means of revitalizing downtown areas, preventing graffiti, and providing constructive experiences for youth. Regular funding became available through the National Endowment for the Arts, local art councils, corporations, foundations, and youth employment programs. Artistic groups, community centers, and galleries that had formed in the early 1970s became established institutions. In Chicago, a center for political murals, there were three major groups: the Chicago Mural Group, led by John Weber, the Public Art Workshop, led by Mark Rogovin, and Movimento Artistico Chicano (MARCH), led by Jose Gonzales and Marcos Raya. New York's Cityarts Workshop became a model for community-participation projects while the Chicano movement in California was mainly organized around community art centers such as Galleria de la Raza (San Francisco), Centro Cultural de la Raza (San Diego), RCAF (Sacramento), and Mechicano Art Center, Goez Gallery, and SPARC (all in Los Angeles).

A national murals network was established at a conference held in New York City in 1976. A second national conference was held two years later in Chicago with representatives from Mexico, England, and France, where similar mural movements had developed. These organizational contacts were buttressed by *Community Murals*, a newsletter begun in the Bay Area in 1978 that soon became a quarterly magazine. The prestige of the muralist movement was further enhanced by two books issued by major publishing houses in the mid-1970s, *Toward a People's Art* and the *Mural Manual*.

When President Carter expanded the federal job-training program to include artists in 1978, mural programs were begun in smaller cities in addition to established programs in Los Angeles, Boston, Philadelphia, Cincinnati, Cleveland, and Baltimore. Although the program was ended by Reagan's election in 1980, it introduced many new artists to mural work. Increasingly, however, government money began to be spent for murals and other public art devoid of social content.

With the ebbing of the protest movements begun in the 1960s there was less demand by community sponsors for issue-oriented murals and more emphasis on permanence, localism, and esthetics. Nonetheless, some sponsorship of political murals continued. Works showing new techniques included a "Song of Unity" mural created in 1978 for Berkeley's La Pena cultural center in memory of the Chilean composer and singer Victor Jara, whose hands had been cut off before he was executed by the Chilean junta that overthrew Allende. This work combined ceramic, paint, and modified papier-mâché techniques to create a three-dimensional surface. A freestanding mural, thirty-three feet by forty-five feet, dealing with the struggle of Central Americans for self-determination was completed by Leo Tanguma of Denver in 1985, and in 1986 a coalition of Bay Area mural artists created a freestanding steel-and-epoxy mural sculpture to commemorate the fiftieth anniversary of the International Longshoremen's and Warehousemen's Union.

California emerged as the undisputed home of the largest and most unusual mural projects. Chicano Park, an ongoing project begun in 1970, has created more than thirty painted freeway pillars on once-disputed land under the Coronado Bay Bridge in San Diego. In Los Angeles by 1980, there were more than 1,000 murals. The Estrada Courts Housing Project of East Los Angeles had become the most densely muralized public housing in the world with more than 90 murals, many with nationalistic and political themes. Los Angeles could also claim the longest mural in the world—a one-half-mile-long "Great Wall" that portrays the history of minorities from the beginning of time through to the 1950s. It was painted over four summers beginning in 1976 by 215 youths supervised by 30 artists under the direction of Judy Baca.

The conservative policies of the Reagan years set off a new wave of art activism in the 1980s. The massive 1982 antinuclear march in New York organized visual and performing artists into support groups for the first time since the Vietnam War era. Similar national activity was stimulated by the 1984 Artists Call Against Intervention in Central America. Nonfunded group projects again became common. In Chicago John Weber organized the World War III project, in which each artist painted one section of a long wall with his or her own antiwar images. In 1984 a coalition of Bay Area muralists put twenty-eight murals on both sides of one of the original Mission District mural sites with images relating to intervention in Central America. Artmakers, a new community mural group in New York City, created the "La Lucha Continua/The Struggle Continues" murals on the Lower East Side in 1985. This thirty-artist project, created under the direction of Eva Cockcroft, placed twenty-six murals dealing with intervention in Central America, apartheid in South Africa, gentrification, and police brutality on four buildings around an empty lot to create a political art park. And in 1988 foreign artists joined U.S. artists in creating a pantheon of international revolutionary heroes on the wall of the New York City building housing Pathfinder Press, the publishing arm of the Socialist Workers Party. *See also*: Gellert, Hugo; Rivera, Diego

—*Eva Cockcroft*

REFERENCES

Barnett, Alan W. *Community Murals: The People's Art*. New York: Cornwall Books, 1984.

Cockcroft, Eva, John Weber, James Cockcroft. *Toward A People's Art: The Contemporary Mural Movement*. New York: Dutton, 1977.

O'Connor, Francis V. *Art for the Millions*. Greenwich: New York Graphic Society, 1973.

Rodriguez, Antonio. *A History of Mexican Mural Painting*. New York: Putnam, 1969.

Rogovin, Mark, Marie Burton, Holly Highfill. *Mural Manual*. Edited by Tim Drescher. Boston: Beacon Press, 1975.

MUSTE, A. J. (1885–1967)

A leader of the labor Left of the late 1920s and early 1930s, Muste also assumed a key role in the pacifist Left of the 1940s–1960s. Unusual for a major figure of the divided and contentious twentieth-century American Left, Muste was highly regarded by many outside his own circle, in part because of his personality and approach. As his co-worker Sidney Lens recounted, Muste "never—absolutely never—deliberately denigrated another person. . . . He argued with political adversaries ranging from traditional conservatives to Stalinists, but no one ever walked away from such an 'argument' feeling hurt or demeaned." Muste was also one of a very few radicals of his era whose long career included neither a pro-Soviet nor a Cold War anticommunist phase.

Born Abraham Johannes Muste in the Netherlands and brought to the United States as a child, Muste grew up in what he later called an "exceedingly orthodox" Calvinist milieu in western Michigan. Though he labored in a furniture factory alongside his father as a child, Muste trained for the Dutch Reformed ministry. A second divinity course at Union Theological Seminary in New York exposed him to the Social Gospel and to a group of classmates and future co-workers including William Fincke, John Nevin Sayre, and Norman Thomas. Though Muste was the only one of the four from a working-class and immigrant background, all were gifted seminarians drawn to urban parish work and soon after to the antiwar Fellowship of Reconciliation (FOR). For Muste and these others, opposition to the First World War ended his short career as a pastor.

Muste's relatively short but noteworthy years in the labor movement began with his leadership of the sixteen-week Lawrence, Massachusetts, textile strike of early 1919, a victory resulting in the attainment of the forty-four-hour week for the Lawrence workers and the formation of the independent Amalgamated Textile Workers of America (ATWA). Throughout the 1920s Muste worked to unify the small and fractious unions in the New England textile industry. Meanwhile, after two years as general secretary of the ATWA, he became the first chairman of the faculty at Brookwood Labor College (Katonah, New York) and a central figure in the flourishing workers' education movement of the period. At Brookwood Muste succeeded in gaining the trust of nonradical officers of the Machinists, United Textile Workers, and other AFL unions, but when he began to write critiques of union-management cooperation schemes and calls for more aggressive organization, Muste and Brookwood were singled out for censure by AFL president William Green.

Disdaining the harsh and polemical Communist denunciations of AFL "misleadership," Muste instead worked to rally critical unionists into the Conference for Progressive Labor Action (CPLA), established shortly before the onset of the Great Depression. Early 1930s conditions drew Muste, like many other radical intellectuals, to Marxist politics and industrial unionism. The most notable contribution of the "Musteite" American Workers Party (successor to the CPLA) was the Toledo Auto-Lite strike, a key pre-CIO victory. However, after a brief sojourn in the Trotskyist movement, Muste abruptly returned to pacifism in 1936.

As executive director of the FOR in the 1940s, Muste defended World War II conscientious objectors and sponsored the founding and early work of the Congress of Racial Equality (CORE). His most remarkable period, however, came after his retirement from the FOR in 1953. In his seventies and early eighties, Muste succeeded in legitimizing antinuclear civil disobedience, conciliating disparate Left elements, and launching a mass movement against the war in Vietnam. He himself took part in widely publicized civil-disobedience actions such as in 1959, when he "hoisted his frail frame over a four-and-one-half-foot-high fence" (in the words of biographer Jo Ann Robinson) at Omaha's ICBM base.

In 1956–57, Muste cofounded the antiwar monthly *Liberation*, which served as an important forum for radical views during the New Left period. With less success, he organized the American Forum for Socialist Education, an attempt to regroup socialists, pacifists, and dissident Communists into a new Left at the beginning of the post-Stalin, post-McCarthy years. A decade later, past eighty, Muste led peace missions to South Vietnam in April 1966 and North Vietnam in January 1967. *See also*: Pacifism, Peace Movements, Trotskyism

—Jon Bloom

REFERENCES

Robinson, Jo Ann O. *Abraham Went Out: A Biography of A. J. Muste*. Philadelphia: Temple University Press, 1981.

Hentoff, Nat, ed. *The Essays of A. J. Muste*. New York: Simon and Schuster, 1967.

Lens, Sidney. *Unrepentent Radical: An American Activist's Account of Five Turbulent Decades*. Boston: Beacon Press, 1980.

Isserman, Maurice. *If I Had a Hammer. . . . The Death of the Old Left and the Birth of the New Left*. New York: Basic Books, 1987.

NAARPR: see DAVIS, ANGELA

NADIR, MOSHE see YIDDISH LEFT

NATIONAL EMERGENCY CIVIL LIBERTIES COMMITTEE

The NECLC was launched in 1951 to fill the void left by existing civil liberties groups that were unwilling or unable to provide vigorous and able defense for targets of the House Un-American Activities Committee, the McCarthy Senate Committee, and the Smith Act. The six founders were all noted civil libertarians: theologian Dr. Paul Lehmann, journalist I. F. Stone, retired banker James Imbrie, sociologist and civil rights activist E. Franklin Frazier, professor Henry Pratt Fairchild, and political scientist H. H. Wilson. The first director was Clark Foreman, a well-known New Dealer and antisegregationist. Under this leadership the NECLC played a major role in the successful drive to eliminate HUAC-type investigations, to overturn the Smith Act convictions, and to end travel restrictions on dissidents.

With the rise of the civil rights movement, the NECLC became involved in various and often unpopular court cases and provided legal assistance to some of the most militant civil rights organizations. During the Vietnam War period, the NECLC joined in early efforts to have the war declared illegal and it supported many forms of opposition to the war, giving special attention to the rights of members of the armed forces and draftees.

The NECLC and the newer NECLC Foundation remained vigorous in the 1970s and 1980s. A major focus of work was to abolish or severely curtail government surveillance of citizens, whether the agency involved was the FBI, CIA, or a local "Red Squad." The NECLC was one of the first organizations to call for and campaign for the impeachment of Richard Nixon. While continuing its efforts in the traditional civil rights areas, the NECLC also put considerable energy into preventing the deportation of political refugees to dictatorships in the Caribbean area and Central America.

A list of prominent individuals and organizations given legal defense by the NECLC would include: Alger Hiss, the National Lawyers Guild, Dr. Benjamin Spock, Dr. Corliss Lamont, the United Farm Workers, Dr. Daniel Ellsberg, and Teamsters for Democracy. Leading NECLC personalities for many years have been Leonard Boudin (general counsel: 1954–1989), Dr. Corliss Lamont (chairperson: 1965–present), and Edith Tiger (assistant director: 1953–69, director: 1970–present).

—*Dan Georgakas*

REFERENCES

National Emergency Civil Liberties Committee, Report, 1971–80.

NATIONAL GUARDIAN AND GUARDIAN

The most longevous and prestigious of the postwar radical newspapers, the *National Guardian* (renamed the *Guardian* in 1967) was founded in 1948 by a triumvirate of James Aronson (executive editor), Cedric Belfrage (editor), and John McManus (managing editor). The immediate objective was to provide a dissenting voice from the Cold War policies then being fixed in place by the government of the United States. A broader goal was to revive the most militant aspects of the New Deal.

The natural political locus for such an undertaking was the orbit of the Progressive Party, and the editors tried to obtain PP funding for their paper. Although this did not come about, most of the original *Guardian* readers were supporters of the PP, and the paper was able to build its circulation by participating in the mass movement associated with the PP. The debut issue of October 18, 1948, headlined an article written exclusively for the paper by Henry Wallace and a contribution from Norman Mailer, already famous as author of *The Naked and the Dead*, and a PP supporter.

At the state level the *Guardian* was aligned with the American Labor Party. Congressman Vito Marcantonio was an enthusiastic *Guardian* supporter and John McManus ran for governor on the ALP ticket in 1950 and 1954. In 1958 the *Guardian* backed the Independent-Socialist ticket, which had McManus as its candidate for governor, Annette Rubinstein for lieutenant-governor, and Corliss Lamont for senator. The McManus vote fell from its 1950 high of 208,000 to 35,000. With the demise of the third parties, Belfrage lamented that the *Guardian* was a journalistic tail without any political dog to wag.

The survival of the newspaper was mainly due to its professional quality. The *Guardian* staff was an amalgam of seasoned journalists and political activists. Aronson, for example, had worked for the New York *Post, Herald-Tribune,* and *Times;* and McManus had worked for *Time, PM,* and the *Times*. McManus had been past president of the Newspaper Guild of New York and Aronson had edited *Frontpage*, the Guild organ. Belfrage had an equally impressive background that included a stint in Hollywood writing for a wire service. Over the years he would also write or edit a dozen books. Other Guardian staff members had worked for *Esquire*, the *Brooklyn Eagle, PM,* the *New York Post*, the *New Republic, Time*, and other well-known publications. The impressive corps of foreign correspondents included Agnes Smedley, Anne Louise Strong, and Wilfred Burchett.

The issues the paper addressed in its first years would continually reappear in new forms. Opposition to the Cold War rendered the *Guardian* virtually the sole public voice opposing the Korean War. A decade later the *Guardian* was among the first publications to go into active opposition to the war in Vietnam, and as American involvement grew, the on-the-scene dispatches of Wilfred Burchett, sometimes written behind communist lines, became must reading for anyone interested in the conflict. The *Guardian* supported national liberation movements whenever they appeared, focusing mostly on Africa in the 1950s, Southeast Asia in the 1960s to mid-1970s, and Latin America thereafter.

Civil rights was another area given considerable space. In the 1950s this involved aggressive reporting on the "Trenton Six," the murder of Emmet Till, and the execution of William Green. Combined with the paper's support of African liberation movements, this work forged a strong working relationship with individuals such as Paul Robeson and W. E. B. DuBois. In the 1960s the paper supported the views of the Student Nonviolent Coordinating Committee, the later positions of Malcolm X, and the Black Panther Party. It also fought against the frame-up of activists such as Angela Davis. During the 1980s the *Guardian* worked to build the multiracial Rainbow Coalition.

A third area of intense concern was defense of political prisoners. The *Guardian* actively defended the Communist Party leadership charged under the Smith Act, Alger Hiss, the "Hollywood Ten," Harry Bridges, Anne and Carl Braden, Corliss Lamont, and Williard Uphaus. In time it would also have to defend close supporters such as Robeson, DuBois,

Marcantonio, and the Rev. Claude Williams, a minister defrocked by the Presbyterian church for his radical views. Each of the *Guardian* editors would also be called before a number of committees. One unhappy result was that rather than languish in prison awaiting a hearing before the Supreme Court, the British-born Belfrage accepted a deportation order in 1955. He was named editor-in-exile and filed stories with datelines from around the world, including nations forbidden to American citizens.

The most historic defense was of Julius and Ethel Rosenberg. At a time when the CP and the *Daily Worker* would not cover the case, the *Guardian* published a William A. Reuben story that sparked what would become an international defense effort. Reuben, who continued to be an important writer on the Hiss case as well, first took the Rosenberg story to I. F. Stone, then an editor of the *Compass*, who turned it down. The *Guardian* role was so vital that after the Rosenbergs were executed, Aronson was named a trustee of the fund established for their children.

The *Guardian* maintained friendly but problematic relations with the CP. A major area of difference was the *Guardian*'s rejection of the CP view that independent political parties were futile and that radicals should work within the Democratic Party. The *Guardian* held exactly the opposite view. In spite of the failures of third parties in the 1950s, the *Guardian* took part in a party-building movement in the 1970s and in the 1980s used its influence within the Rainbow Coalition to keep that movement as independent of the Democratic Party as possible.

In the area of foreign affairs, the *Guardian* refused to be a clone of Soviet policies. It was supportive of Yugoslavia's break from the Soviet orbit and carried on principled coverage of the purges in Eastern Europe and the Hungarian Revolt of 1956. Most important, the editors allowed debate on such subjects to rage in the letters columns. In the winter of 1948–49 when Anna Louise Strong was denounced by the USSR as a spy, the *Guardian* defended her, continued to publish her, and helped initiate the six-year campaign that ultimately led to the accusation being dropped.

Within a few years of its launching, the *Guardian* hit its peak circulation of 75,000. Support of the Rosenbergs, opposition to the Korean conflict, and the repressive atmosphere of the times caused a rapid falloff in readers. In the year the paper took up the Rosenberg defense, circulation fell from 55,000 to just over 20,000. Nonetheless, the paper survived and as radical movements began to stir in the late 1950s better times seemed in the offing.

Despite the death of McManus in 1961, the *Guardian* supported the emerging civil rights, antiwar, and the New Left movements with as much energy as ever. The paper also published Mark Lane's landmark 10,000-word "A Brief for Lee Harvey Oswald," the first in-depth reporting to challenge the "lone gunman" theory of the JFK assassination. Such efforts, however, did not catch the rising tide of radicalism and circulation remained at just under 30,000. Many newcomers to the *Guardian* staff felt the paper was out of touch with the temper and needs of the new era. Individuals later grouped around Irwin Silber, the *Guardian's* cultural editor and a former editor of *Sing Out!*, proposed that the paper provide the New Left movement with direct ideological leadership. Aronson resisted, feeling a newspaper could not substitute for a political party. Internal tensions grew and in April 1967 Aronson and Belfrage decided to resign.

The ensuing reorganization gave the staff working control of the production process and ownership shares. The paper's name was shortened and Jack Smith was elected editor, a post he held until 1981. Under Smith's tenure the paper experienced many swings in format and orientation. As the New Left collapsed, one tendency on the staff wished to transform the paper into a Marxist-Leninist publication while other tendencies wanted to strengthen the reportage tradition or move to the more anarchistic and nonhierarchical forms of the underground press. A schism in 1970 led one group to create the *Liberated Guardian*, a newspaper whose life span was soon cut short by a subsequent schism-within-the-schism. The parent *Guardian* almost folded as well, its circulation dipping to 14,000.

For a large part of the decade that followed, the *Guardian* was a core element in an effort to create a new left-wing party based on Marxist-Leninist principles and the experiences of the Chinese Revolution. The paper began to carry as much editorial and essay material as straight reporting. When the party-building effort failed, partly as a result of changes in China, the *Guardian* struggled to return to its traditional functions. In the 1980s it examined all existing socialist revolutions in a respectful but questioning manner, and it allowed significant editorial space for nonstaff movement activists to express their views, even when those views did not fit the *Guardian* editorial perspective. The Aronson-Belfrage-McManus tradition was underscored in a big thirty-fifth-anniversary supplement. Circulation fluctuated between 20,000 and 30,000, waxing and waning with the mass movements the paper reported on and for. While still highly respected in radical circles, the *Guardian* did not regain the prestige of the *National Guardian* years, which had been greatly diminished in the 1970s.

On the fortieth anniversary of its founding, the *Guardian* could boast of a remarkable consistency. Unlike *In These Times,* the only other independent radical weekly with a national readership, the *Guardian* remained committed to radical alternatives to the two-party electoral system. Strong advocacy of the rights of women and sexual minorities had been melded with its traditional support of civil rights, working-class, antiwar, and national liberation movements. The joy of a fortieth-anniversary banquet planned to underscore the continuity of the paper's politics was sapped when a seventy-three-year-old James Aronson died from a long struggle with cancer just a few days before the celebration.

The memorial services for Aronson illuminated his continuing involvement with quality journalism. After leaving the *Guardian* he had been a teacher of journalism at universities in New York and Peking, had taken part in symposiums on journalism, had written for professional journals, and had been a consultant for journalism departments in Chinese universities. He had also written three important books on American mass media: *The Press and the Cold War, Deadline for the Media,* and *Something to Guard,* a history of the *Guardian* coauthored with Belfrage. His most important legacy, of course, was the *Guardian* itself. *See also*: "Anti-Revisionism" (Maoism), Communist Party, New Left, Progressive Party of 1948, Regroupment

—*Dan Georgakas*

REFERENCES

Aronson, James. *The Press and the Cold War.* Indianapolis: Bobbs-Merrill, 1970.

———. *Deadline for the Media—Today's Challenges to Press, TV, & Radio.* Indianapolis: Bobbs-Merrill, 1972.

Belfrage, Cedric, and James Aronson. *Something to Guard—The Stormy Life of the National Guardian, 1948–1967.* New York: Columbia University Press, 1978.

The Guardian—Thirty-fifth Anniversary Supplement, December 14, 1983.

Bennett, Jonathan A. "James Aronson, *Guardian* Founder, Is Dead at 73," and Cedric Belfrage, "A Personal Farewell to a Rare Friend and Journalist," *Guardian,* November 2, 1988.

NATIONAL LAWYERS GUILD

A professional component of the activist response to the Great Depression in the United States and the rise of fascism in Europe and Japan, the Guild was founded in 1937 to work so that "human rights" would be regarded as "more sacred" than property rights, a principle enshrined in its constitutional preamble. Inspired by the New Deal of FDR, the Popular Front movement launched by the Communist Party, the renewed vigor of the trade union movement, and the increased activity of the NAACP, the Guild also immediately addressed bread-and-butter issues of its specific constituency, including the difficulty many lawyers had making a living and the difficulty black lawyers had in renting appropriate office space in major cities. In a *New York Times* article commemorating the Guild's fiftieth anniversary, David Margolick summarized the Guild's mission of 1937 as an effort to create a progressive and racially integrated alternative to the American Bar Association.

The founding members were an amalgam: a handful of lawyers from affluent families having long involvement with the legal profession and a more numerous group with working-class and immigrant backgrounds, including a handful of outstanding women and members of the Lawyers Security League who got jobs with the Works Progress Administration (WPA) until they could find paying work. Founding members included U.S. senators and congressmen, state court judges, law professors, government officials, and the general counsels of the established AFL and the newly formed CIO. Guild members worked effectively to draft New Deal legislation and then they helped draft and administer regulations to enforce the New Deal statutes.

From the Guild's founding until 1963, it was led primarily by East Coast attorneys involved with the trade union and Left movements. An exception to this geographic rule was Robert Kenny, who served as president of the Guild before being elected attorney general of California. Different Guild leaders were active in the American Labor Party, the left wing of the Democratic Party, the CP, and the Progressive Party of Henry Wallace. During World War II, some Guild lawyers not serving in the armed forces or government jobs began to use traditional law with a working-class twist, choosing to become public defenders for indigent criminal defendants or seeking money damages for people injured in accidents or suffering from defective products. This trend accelerated in the postwar period, as other Guild lawyers moved into international law in the wake of Guild work for the formation of the United Nations.

During the McCarthy era, the Guild and its individual members came under intense pressure because they had repeatedly trounced government agencies such as the FBI and the Immigration and Naturalization Service legally; and they had successfully forged unity between black and white lawyers on civil and economic rights issues. Lawyers for the government and some unions had to resign their membership in order to continue their employment, and students could not join for fear of being rejected for admission to practice law. Private practitioners had to decide whether to represent clients called before the House Un-American Activities Committee (HUAC) and the McCarthy Senate Committee and similar bodies on a state and federal level and thus risk the loss of other paying clients, or to play it safe and get out of the Guild altogether and concentrate on less controversial work. Membership, which had hovered at around 4,000, dwindled to 500.

The Guild proper sued the attorney general when he threatened to place the organization on his list of "subversive organizations," and it carried on a vigorous defense of members called before HUAC and state bar "character" committees or cited for contempt for vigorous representation of left-wing clients. The attorney general dropped his threat in 1957 and the Guild began to regroup.

Organizational leadership shifted in 1964 to a younger group based in Detroit who had survived McCarthyism with fewer casualties than groups in many other cities. More of the new leaders were black and all felt closer to the civil rights struggles within the United States than international movements to which older leaders had long committed themselves. In 1968 a fierce dispute broke out when New Left and anti–Vietnam War activists from California and New York made a bid for control of the Guild. The Old Left versus New Left controversy was officially resolved with a shift from passing resolutions to participating in mass actions and from the filing of friend-of-the-court briefs to direct representation of clients and organizations. Legislative work was virtually ended for a time, as were most scholarly publications.

The Guild has been most successful when participating in and representing mass movements on the rise. Some members have also found it desireable to organize parallel institutions to do still broader or more scholarly work, institutions such as the Center for Constitutional Rights, the Lawyers Committees on Vietnam and Nuclear Policy, the Meiklejohn Civil Liberties Institute, and numerous local special-interest defense groups. Despite changes in the law and in law practice, and changing cycles and styles of American radicalism, which it fully reflected, and in the face of intermittent Red-baiting, the Guild has remained steadfast in its self-appointed role as legal tribune for the nation's movements for social change and to its original preamble. The Guild, virtually the only professional Left organization founded in the 1930s to have survived, moved into the 1990s with 10,000 members organized in 201 lawyer and student chapters in forty-two states and the District of Columbia. *see also*: Communism; International Labor Defense; King, Carol; McCarthyism

—*Ann Fagan Ginger*

REFERENCES

The National Lawyers Guild: From Roosevelt through Reagan, a documentary history edited by Ann Fagan Ginger and Eugene M. Tobin, foreword by Ramsey Clark. Philadelphia: Temple University Press, 1987. Appendix to this volume contains books by Guild committees.

The National Lawyers Guild: An Inventory of Records, 1936–1976, An Index to Periodicals, 1937–1979, compiled by Richard N. Katz. Berkeley: Meiklejohn Civil Liberties Institute, 1980.

National Lawyers Guild Quarterly (1937–40), *Lawyers Guild Review* (1940–60), *Law in Transition* (1961–63), *Lawyers Guild Practitioner* (1965–present). Complete files available at Meiklejohn Institute.

National Lawyers Guild Archives: at Meiklejohn Institute and Martin Luther King, Jr., Center in Atlanta, Georgia.

Ginger, Ann Fagan. *The Relevant Lawyers*. New York: Simon & Schuster, 1972. Sixteen Guild lawyers covered.

Kinoy, Arthur. *Rights on Trial*. Cambridge: Harvard University Press, 1983.

National Maritime Union

From the time of its founding in 1937 until it purged its left wing in the late 1940s the NMU was one of the most radical labor unions in the United States. It was described in its prime (by one of the NMU's founders, Robert McElroy) as a "militant, class-conscious, racially integrated, rank-and-file controlled, revolutionary union of seamen and waterfront workers."

The NMU demonstrably lived up to that combative reputation in its early years. Sitdown strikes were called at sailing time—occasionally involving every ship in port—in order to put pressure on individual shipping lines. A pioneer in integrating the East Coast shipping industry, the NMU fought and won the right of black seamen to work at every job on the ship—previously, blacks had been restricted to working in the stewards department. These gains were contested not only by shipping companies and individual officers aboard the ships, but by some of the union members themselves, as well as the local authorities in many of the southern ports where NMU ships docked.

Rank-and-file democracy was a fiercely cherished ideal of the NMU, which had come into existence in reaction to an undemocratic, racket-ridden predecessor, the International Seamen's Union. NMU members had the right to address union membership meetings, and access to the letters column of an unusually literate union newspaper, the *NMU Pilot*. Efforts were made to involve all members in union affairs. Union meetings were mandatory—one couldn't ship out without proof of attendance, and every ship's crew elected a representative to attend biannual conventions. Contract negotiations were watchdogged by rank-and-file oversight committees—and every union member had the right to demand an impromptu union meeting, right in the shipping hall, when and if violations of the union constitution occurred.

Internationalism was another NMU hallmark. The union was philosophically committed to lending assistance to working-class struggles all over the world, a rare quality among American trade unions. Honoring longshore picket lines in foreign ports was one example of this. A more spectacular example is the heroic role the NMU played during World War II, carrying supplies to Russia, Europe, and the Far East. (Merchant marine casualties were higher, proportionally, than casualties in the U.S. Army, Navy, and Air Force.)

An NMU "leadership school" was established to teach new members a theory of imperialism and colonialism to place in context the exploitation they were seeing in South American and foreign ports. NMU crews even conducted a sit-down strike in Saigon harbor, *in 1945*, to protest U.S. shipment of war supplies to the French during their phase of the Vietnam War.

The Communist Party was the moving force behind the union for most of its early history. A "concentration unit," to organize marine workers, was formed in 1928, evolving into the Marine Workers Industrial Union in 1930, which, in turn, was liquidated in 1935 in order to "bore from within" the AFL International Seamen's Union, the shell from which the NMU emerged. Depression-era shipping was so slow and East Coast seamen so atomized that many founding members say the NMU could not have been organized without Party discipline.

CP strategy for the labor movement as a whole, however, may ultimately have been the union's undoing. The union's proud boast of rank-and-file democracy did not extend to Trotskyists and Wobblies. Excessive rigidity on the part of the overwhelmingly Communist leadership of the union (more than three-fourths of the top union officers by 1947, promoting such unpopular issues as *non-cooperation* with the Marshall Plan) caused a backlash that resulted in a clean sweep out of office of all officials affiliated with the CP.

In 1948–49, NMU president Joseph Curran, having broken with the Left, and backed up by phalanxes of New York City policemen, volunteer muscle from Mike Quill's newly purged Transport Workers Union, and goons recruited from far-flung ports (Phil Murray, president of the CIO, provided funding) proceeded to expell from the union virtually all the founding members who had been in any way radical. The purge was completed in 1950, at the time of the Korean War, when the U.S. Coast Guard declared hundreds of Communists, ex-Communists, and many who were simply principled trade unionists "national security risks" and took away their seamen's papers.

The union drifted in the 1950s into "porkchop" unionism, and degenerated badly in the 1960s—with money scandals, inflated salaries for union officials, and every pretense of rank-and-file democracy stripped away. Down from a wartime peak of over 100,000 members, the NMU in the 1980s had less than 15,000 members and a fraction of that many jobs. The NMU merged with the Marine Engineers Benevolent Association in 1988. *See also*: Communist Party, Irish Americans

—*Joe Doyle*

REFERENCES

Boyer, Richard. *The Dark Ship*. Boston: Little, Brown, 1947.

Kempton, Murray. *Part of Our Time: Some Monuments and Ruins of the Thirties*. New York: Simon & Schuster, 1955.

Nelson, Bruce. *Workers on the Waterfront: Seamen, Longshoremen and Unionism in the 1930s*. Urbana: University of Illinois Press, 1988.

National Miners Union

Founded in Pittsburgh in September 1928, the NMU (1928–33) was an outgrowth of a new direction in trade unionism charted by the Communist Party. In this so-called Third Period, the Party called for the establishment of revolutionary unions that would challenge existing unions affiliated with the AFL. The NMU's first president was John Watt of Illinois, but the real power was wielded by the union's secretary, a Party functionary, and by Party officials in New York. The NMU's program included the following: resistance to wage cuts; a six-hour day; unemployment relief and insurance; use of checkweighmen; rejection of the dues checkoff; abolition of company stores, company towns, and payment in scrip; organization of blacks; industrial unionism; formation of a labor party; and complete emancipation from capitalism.

In its brief existence the NMU waged several strikes, the most notable being in Illinois in 1929, in Pennsylvania, West Virginia, and Ohio in 1931, and in eastern Kentucky in 1931–32. None of these strikes succeeded. The failures owed in part to the sometimes violent opposition of mine owners and government officials, in part to the presence of rival unions such as the United Mine Workers, but also to the limitations of the NMU itself. Strikes were called without adequate preparation. Financial reserves were insufficient to sustain prolonged holdouts. There were too few organizers in the field, especially ones who had a solid base in the communities being organized. While enrolling several thousand miners during the height of strike waves, the NMU proved unable to retain their allegiance. Individual members demonstrated great courage in the face of constant repression, thereby calling attention to the brutality of coal operators and their allies. But such favorable publicity as they received could not offset the forces arrayed against them and their own inherent weaknesses. By 1933 Party leaders had decided to end the effort at dual unionism and return to the goal of unifying all miners in one large organization. *See also*: Communist Party, Trade Union Unity League, United Mine Workers

—*Ralph Stone*

REFERENCES

Draper, Theodore. "The Communists and the Miners, 1928–33." *Dissent* 19 (Spring 1972).

Hevener, John W. *Which Side Are You On? The Harlan County Coal Miners. 1931–1939*. Urbana: University of Illinois Press, 1978.

Wickersham, Edward D. "Opposition to the International Officers of the United Mine Workers of America, 1919–1933." Ph.D. diss., Cornell University, 1951.

National Negro Congress

The key Popular Front entity centered on black rights, and for a few years a powerful force in selected areas, the NNC demonstrated both the strength and the weaknesses of the Communist approach to the "Negro question."

The League of Struggle for Negro Rights, succeeding in 1930 the earlier American Negro Labor Congress, sought with little success to infuse revolutionary and protonationalist themes into contemporary black discontent. With the Popular Front signal to work in broader organizations, the LSNR dissolved in 1935. Communists took a positive but cautious public role in the National Negro Congress, which grew out of the 1935 Howard University Conference on the Status of the Negro in the New Deal, led by Ralph Bunche and John P. Davis. Independent of the Communist Party but not unfriendly to it, the NNC formation in 1936 of a broad reform movement brought together the entire spectrum of Afro-American life except separatist black nationalists and hard-bitten anticommunists. A. Philip Randolph, often hostile to the CP in the past, served as titular leader, defending the right of individual blacks to become Communists if they chose to do so.

In tandem with the Scottsboro and Herndon defense movements, the NNC offered the Party a new, powerful constituency in selected areas. For the first time, the Party entered wide-scale formal or informal relations with black churches, fraternal and cultural organizations. The NNC also successfully lobbied black public opinion for support of the industrial union movement as different from its racist labor predecessors. In Harlem and on Chicago's South Side, Communists black and white shifted the character of their public status from that of virtual outsiders to one of neighborhood club-members throwing their energies into the NNC for such demands as an end to discrimination, more relief for the unemployed, and the abolition of lynching and police brutality. In this atmosphere, Party discipline eased, and Communist affiliation became more casual, for intellectuals and artists perhaps even more than for workers.

Harlemites certainly occupied the most visible section of the NNC. There, the organization embraced some of the most prominent cultural figures in the community, along with many other supporters. But in Chicago the Left depended on black support more than in any other center of mass activity. This strength dated to the early 1930s unemployed movements and rent-strike campaigns that had prompted severe police violence and highlighted the public Communist role. The *Midwest Daily Record*, the least financially successful and most short-lived of the three Communist dailies, found its métier in support of the Chicago NNC's activities and, outside the ethnic pockets of strength, its most loyal readership in the South Side ghetto.

The Nazi-Soviet Pact of 1939 exposed the weakness of Communist influence within the black community and all but destroyed the NNC. Party leaders' dramatically shifting positions and focus upon foreign policy at a time of extreme black hardship alienated many erstwhile followers and allies. Black conservatives and socialists seized the opportunity for an offensive against Communism. Prominent public non-Communist but friendly figures such as Adam Clayton Powell, Jr., denounced the Communists as supine followers of Moscow positions. The alienation of

A. Philip Randolph from the NNC (by now under investigation from the Dies Committee), following a closer open identification of the NNC and Communist positions, spelled virtual doom to old levels of NNC prestige. After the 1940 convention, where his objections to NNC changes were rejected, Randolph denounced the Russian leadership and its American supporters. John P. Davis, succeeding Randolph as president, sought with only limited success to maintain NNC visibility in the black community at large.

Black Communist activity quickly shifted to other fronts. In New York, this shift had considerable success through a variety of cultural and political activities. The NNC remained, although less prominent than hitherto, a locus of struggle against discrimination in the workplace and in public life. In Chicago and many other places, NNC and black public support of Communism did not substantially survive World War II. The Cold War left the NNC a remnant of earlier days, destined to be replaced by the National Negro Labor Council, itself victim not of Communist mishaps but of the climate of McCarthyism and the purge of the Left from the labor movement. *See also*: American Negro Labor Council; Haywood, Harry; National Negro Labor Council; Randolph, A. Philip

—Paul Buhle

REFERENCES

Klehr, Harvey. *The Heyday of American Communism*. New York: Basic Books, 1984.

Naison, Mark. *Communists in Harlem During the Depression*. Urbana: University of Illinois Press, 1983.

National Negro Labor Council

The NNLC was established in Cincinnati, Ohio, on October 27, 1951, at a convention composed primarily of blacks and one-third women from around the country. These delegates included factory workers, teachers, and office workers, among others. As one scholar of black labor put it: "They are continuing a tradition established more than a hundred years before in the National Negro Convention of Pre–Civil War America, and especially in the Colored National Labor Union, founded four years after the war."

A year earlier, 900 delegates had met in Chicago at the National Labor Conference for Negro Rights to discuss a range of problems affecting black workers, such as racial discrimination in hiring and apprenticeship training programs and job upgrading. Most delegates felt that black workers could not depend on traditional black civil rights organizations or predominantly white labor unions, such as the United Auto Workers. Within a year after this conference, a special committee set up twenty-three Negro Labor Councils in major industrial cities and launched a campaign to include a model Fair Employment Practices (FEP) clause into union contracts.

Almost from the beginning traditional white labor leaders attacked these efforts of black workers as "communistically inspired" and "dual unionism." Walter Reuther was a major instigator in this campaign against the NNLC. In spite of these attacks, local Negro Labor Councils played leading roles in supporting the struggles of black workers. For example, the Negro Labor Council in Washington, D.C., contributed to the improved work conditions of black workers in the Bureau of Engraving; the Detroit council started a petition drive for a citywide referendum for a municipal FEP organization opposed by the Reuther leadership. The petition drive failed, but the impetus behind it contributed to the founding of the NNLC in Cincinnati.

Black delegates at the founding convention sent a clear message to white labor leaders: "We wish to say . . . that the day has ended when white trade union leaders or white leaders in any organizations may presume to tell Negroes on what basis they shall come together to fight for their rights."

The "Statement of Principles and Program of Action" adopted by the convention stated that economic and social equality for blacks was attainable only if black workers and their white allies united to protect black Americans from the forces that denied them "full citizenship."

The first elected officers of the NNLC were: William R. Hood, president; Coleman Young, executive secretary; Ernest Thompson, director of organizations; and Octavia Hawkins, treasurer.

The NNLC had two major goals: To "break the patterns of job discrimination against blacks in American industry and to use the trade union base to move the trade unions and our white allies within it into the liberation struggle for black people, with a primary concentration on economic issues as the key."

For the next five years the NNLC struggled against overwhelming odds—including Red-baiting—in championing the cause of black workers. The NNLC helped black workers obtain clerical and administrative jobs in Sears, Roebuck stores, office jobs at the Ford Motor Company, executive positions in banks and hotels, and jobs as streetcar motormen and conductors in cities, baseball players in Detroit, dairy-truck drivers in New York, production-line workers in breweries in Brooklyn, and as airline pilots and stewardesses. The most impressive NNLC accomplishment in their campaign for black jobs occurred in Louisville, Kentucky, in 1954, when the local NNLC orchestrated a broad-based community movement to obtain training for local black workers in preparation for the opening of a new General Electric plant.

NNLC received little support from established labor leaders. NNLC's president, William R. Hood, had a long history of criticizing the UAW leadership for its failure to support the upgrading of black autoworkers and appoint a black vice-president to the international executive board. Walter Reuther's election to the CIO presidency in 1952 destroyed all possibility of cooperation between the two labor organizations.

By 1956, the NNLC's days were numbered. The organization was called before the Subversive Activities Control Board of the House Committee on Un-American Activities to defend itself against charges of being a "Communist-front organization." Burdened with defense costs, the NNLC leadership had no choice but to vote to dissolve the organization. *See also*: Communist Party

—R. W. Thomas

REFERENCES

Thomas, Richard W. "Blacks and the CIO." In *Working for Democracy: American Workers from the Revolution to the Present*, edited by Paul Buhle and Alan Dawley. Urbana: University of Illinois Press, 1985.

NATIONAL RIP-SAW: see AGRARIAN RADICALISM, SOCIALIST PARTY

NATIONAL STUDENT LEAGUE: see STUDENT MOVEMENTS, 1930S

NATIONAL TEXTILE WORKERS UNION: see TEXTILE WORKERS UNIONS

NATIONAL UNION OF MARINE COOKS AND STEWARDS, CIO

Chartered by the CIO in 1937, following the breakup of the AFL's International Seamen's Union (ISU), the National Union of Marine Cooks and Stewards (MCS) was one of the smallest CIO unions (claiming around eight thousand members). It was organized along trade rather than industrial lines and centered on the West Coast. It stood to the left within the CIO, usually following the lead of its larger West Coast ally, the International Longshoremen's and Warehousemen's Union (ILWU).

Communist Party members and sympathizers took prominent roles in the MCS, and played leading roles in breaking down the racial barriers that had characterized West Coast ISU affiliates. By 1950, nearly half of MCS members were black and another fifth or sixth were from other ethnic minority groups. MCS president Hugh Bryson campaigned actively for Henry Wallace in 1948 and helped organize the Independent Progressive Party in California.

The CIO expelled the MCS in 1950 as Communist-dominated. Bryson signed the Taft-Hartley non-Communist affidavit but was charged with perjury and imprisoned. The AFL's Seafarers International Union (SIU) began raids on the MCS membership; the ILWU tried to take the MCS under its wing and to challenge the SIU but lost through a

National Labor Relations Board ruling. Simultaneously, a federal screening program kept Party activists from working aboard ships. Some MCS members found a new home in the ILWU, including future ILWU president James Herman. *See also*: Communist Party, ILWU

—*Robert W. Cherny*

REFERENCES

Nelson, Bruce. *Workers on the Waterfront: Seamen, Longshoremen, and Unionism in the 1930s.* Urbana: University of Illinois Press, 1988.

National Union of Marine Cooks and Stewards Records, Bancroft Library, University of California, Berkeley.

National Union of Textile Workers: see Textile Workers Union

National Women's Commission, CPUSA

Preceded in 1922 by a Women's Department, the Women's Commission was formed in the early 1930s to coordinate agitational and trade union work among women. In 1933 the Communist Party of the United States estimated that women constituted about 16 percent of its membership of 20,000; by decade's end, when the Popular Front was in full swing, the Party claimed that women represented nearly 40 percent of the total. To address and enlarge this constituency, the Women's Commission invited representatives from local CP organizations throughout the country. Its policies and programs appeared in its official organ, *Working Woman*, and in its Popular Front magazine, *Woman Today*.

Directed in the 1930s first by Anna Damon and later by Margaret Cowl, the Women's Commission interpreted its Third Period role as counteracting the appeal of "bourgeois" feminism, especially the Equal Rights Amendment. Much of its work centered in support for working women and recruitment drives around International Women's Day. During the Popular Front, the Women's Commission played greater attention to housewives. By the late 1930s, the *Daily Worker* ran a "Household Corner" column that offered advice to housewives on family finances and health matters. Around the same time and in a few cities, the CPUSA introduced special local organizations to focus agitational work on these issues. These women's organizations involved mainly housewives in community affairs, and they campaigned for improvements in social services and especially for better schools. Antifascism also rallied women, who raised considerable funds to support the Spanish Loyalists.

During the Popular Front the concerns of mothers and children played an important role in the activities of the Women's Commission. Using the Soviet model of maternal protection, American Communists demanded a similar "Mother's Bill of Rights" that would establish in the United States free birth-control clinics, day-care centers, maternal insurance, and an extensive program of social services to assist working mothers.

In 1936 the Women's Commission joined several mainstream women's groups opposed to the Equal Rights Amendment to sponsor an alternative program known as the "Women's Charter." Drafted by Mary Anderson of the Women's Bureau of the U.S. Department of Labor and social worker Mary Van Kleeck, the Women's Charter advocated equal opportunity for women in all areas of economic, political, and social life as well as protective legislation, including special wages-and-hours laws and maternal insurance.

The Women's Commission's participation in the short-lived Women's Charter movement reflected its relatively open Popular Front policy toward middle-class women and mainstream organizations. Director Cowl wrote that "while the Party places central importance on the role played by working-class women, it does not ignore the importance of other sectors of the women's movement. . . ." Such previously maligned groups as the Women's Trade Union League and the Young Women's Christian Association now gained a legitimacy in the Party press for their efforts in behalf of working women. The Hitler-Stalin Pact, however, closed this chapter in its history, and the Party leadership dismantled the Women's Commission in 1940.

The CPUSA reestablished its Women's Commission in 1945, and Elizabeth Gurley Flynn served as its chair until 1953. The role of women in civil rights and in peace movements became its central focus in the postwar period. During the early 1950s the Women's Commission sponsored a woman's page in the *Sunday Worker*, edited by Peggy Dennis and written on alternative weeks by Dennis and the Women's Commission's secretary, Claudia Jones. *See also*: Communist Party; Flynn, Elizabeth Gurley; Jones, Claudia; *Working Woman/Woman Today*

—*Mari Jo Buhle*

REFERENCES

Cowl, Margaret. "Women's Struggle for Equality." *Political Affairs* 53 (May 1974).

Shaffer, Robert. "Women and the Communist Party, USA, 1930–1940." *Socialist Review* 9 (May–June 1979).

Ware, Susan. *Holding Their Own: American Women in the 1930s*. Boston: G. K. Hall, 1982.

NATURE FRIENDS OF AMERICA

In some ways the German-American socialist leisure and cultural equivalent of later, mostly Jewish communist summer camps, Nature Friends was also a historical development in American Left ecological consciousness.

Founded at the turn of the century in Germany by socialists and trade unionists to preserve wildlife and to provide workers with an affordable outdoor recreational organization, the group's popularity spread across Europe to America. By 1910, a U.S. branch was formed by German and Austrian immigrants in the New York area. By 1930 nearly 150 acres, with a clubhouse and hiking trails, were established at "Camp Midvale" and served as a hub for Nature Friends' activities on the East Coast. Nowhere did the Nature Friends receive more attention and support than in the *New Yorker Volkszeitung* and its aging supporters, once the backbone of the New York socialist movement. For many of these comrades and others—mostly skilled workers sympathetic to socialist ideas—hiking in nature offered an escape from the old industrial class conflict to a broader vision of socialist transformation. Nature-lore, rarely seen in Marxist analysis, provided an essentially ecological perspective.

By 1940, Nature Friends' camps sprang up in California, Wisconsin, Pennsylvania, Illinois, and Connecticut, with a wider variety of members. Most held progressive sympathies and only those of "fascist convictions" were excluded by statute. Thus hikers raised funds for such causes as the "Scottsboro Boys," the Abraham Lincoln Brigade, the Committee for the Protection of the Foreign Born, the Committee to Release the Rosenbergs, and the civil rights movement. Placed on the attorney general's list of "subversive organizations" in 1947, Nature Friends saw its members severely harassed and as a result individual camps disaffiliated. Camp Midvale itself was given to the Ethical Culture Society in 1968 in the hopes that it would be preserved as an ecological retreat. The California Nature Friends remain an outdoor organization with no overt political activities or associations. *See also*: German Americans, *New Yorker Volkszeitung*, Radical Environmentalism

—*Andy Lanset*

REFERENCES

Nature Friends Collection, Tamiment Library, New York University.

Lanset, Andy. "Camp Midvale: An Oral History." Created for radio broadcast, 1988. Archived, with interviews of Nature Friends veterans, at the Oral History of the American Left, Tamiment Library, New York University.

NEARING, SCOTT (1883–1983)

The only American radical to be a major figure in the antiwar socialist movement of the 1910s and the alternative-cultural movement of the 1970s and 1980s, Nearing was born into a privileged family in Morris Run, Pennsylvania, where he grew up in an environment of conspicuous class differences. For forty years his grandfather, Winfield Scott Nearing, ruled Morris Run as superintendent of the coal-mining company town. "Czar Nearing," as he was called, broke strikes by evicting workers. Nearing's mother came from a well-to-do banker's family in New Jersey and his father, Louis, operated the Morris Run produce store.

Nearing responded enthusiastically to the social-consciousness doctrines of his mentor Simon Patten, a professor at the Wharton School of Business of the University of Pennsylvania. Patten's guiding principle was that teachers should be "on the firing line of progress." Nearing earned a doctorate in 1909 and taught economics at the Wharton School for nine years. He was fired in 1915 by the university trustees for his outspoken views against child labor; many of the trustees owned manufacturing plants that hired children. His case became nationally celebrated as a major university assault on academic freedom.

In 1917 Nearing was again fired for his political views. This time by the University of Toledo for his outspoken opposition to U.S. preparedness for World War I. Nearing became a prominent figure in the antiwar movement. He characterized war as "organized destruction and mass murder." In 1918, after the American Socialist Society published his forty-four-page pamphlet *The Great Madness*, the U.S. government indicted him for treason. Nearing delivered such an eloquent defense at his trial (February 6–19, 1919) that he was acquitted, the only major pacifist to escape prison.

A member of the Socialist Party from 1917 to 1922, Nearing ran unsuccessfully on the Socialist ticket against Fiorello La Guardia for the Congressional seat in New York's Fourteenth District. In 1927 he joined the Communist Party but left it two years later when officials in Moscow refused approval of the publication of his book *The Twilight of Empire*. He was sufficiently important for the Party to publicly expell him on January 8, 1930, in an announcement published in the *Daily Worker*.

The previous year, Nearing had met Helen Knothe of Ridgewood, New Jersey. He had been separated for five years from his first wife, Nellie Seeds. Helen and Scott bought a farm in Jamaica, Vermont, in 1932 under the assumption that it was better to be poor in the country than in the city. They refurbished the farm and turned it into a showcase organic farmstead and maple sugar orchard. They also wrote exhaustively about their commitment to vegetarianism, organic farming, and a simple life-style. The Nearings moved to Harborside, Maine, in 1951, partly to escape ski development in Vermont. Three years later they published their most widely-read book, *Living the Good Life*. It was reprinted in 1970 and remains a guide for millions of people disenchanted with capitalistic materialism, modern urban life, degradation of natural resources, and the chemicalization of food.

By the 1970s, Scott Nearing had become a living legend among a new generation devoted to personal health and environmental issues, but he had also retained links with his earlier activism. He traveled, lectured, and wrote extensively. In addition to hundreds of newspaper and journal articles, including his "World Events" column in the *Monthly Review* (1953–72), he authored more than fifty books and monographs.

Over the years his respect and hope for civilization dimmed, one reason that led him to a self-sufficient homesteading life in rural New England. Nonetheless, he continued to work as an independent radical for a united world based on a federation of nations. He also became an international spokesperson for the view that vegetarianism and organic farming were essential to solve global food, health, and environmental problems. Two years after he appeared as a "witness" in the film *Reds* about his friend and colleague John Reed, Scott Nearing died at home at the age of one hundred. *See also*: Radical Environmentalism

—*Steve Sherman*

REFERENCES

Nearing, Scott. *The Conscience of a Radical*. Harborside, Maine: Social Science Institute, 1965.

———. *The Making of a Radical, A Political Biography*. New York: Harper and Row, 1972.

Sherman, Steve, ed. *A Scott Nearing Reader: The Good Life in Bad Times*. Metuchen, N.J.: Scarecrow Press, 1989.

Nef, Walter T. (1882–circa 1960)

Widely regarded by his fellow members of the Industrial Workers of the World as one of the greatest of all Wobbly organizers, Nef was the original guiding spirit of the IWW's

large agricultural workers' union. Apart from the fact that he was of German-Swiss background, nothing seems to be known of his pre-IWW life. He took part in the union's Spokane free-speech fight in 1909–10 and later organized for the IWW in the lumber industry as well as in construction, mining, and longshore.

At the IWW Agricultural Workers Organization founding convention in Kansas City, Missouri, in April 1915, Nef was elected general secretary–treasurer and immediately spearheaded an aggressive and innovative organizing campaign. Indeed, much of what became recognized as distinctively Wobbly organizing technique was Nef's creation. Mobile AWO "job delegates" followed the harvest, organizing migratory workers right on the job and taking advantage of the ripening crops to enforce union demands. Starting with 9 members, the AWO had signed up some 18,000 by the end of 1916, making it the largest of the IWW's constituent industrial unions. So great was the IWW's power and prestige among the migratory "wage-slaves" that, according to the testimony of countless old-timers, it was virtually impossible to ride the freight-trains out West unless one had an IWW "red card."

The immense and sudden success of Nef's AWO was, in fact, a major reason for the U.S. government's relentless persecution of the IWW during and after the First World War. It is not surprising, therefore, that in 1918, when he was a leader of the large IWW local in Philadelphia, Nef was one of 101 Wobblies convicted and sentenced to Leavenworth Penitentiary for obstructing the war effort.

Released from prison by the end of 1923, Nef did not resume his activity in the IWW.

Nothing is known of his life during the next couple of decades, though IWW historian Fred Thompson recalled that Nef, regarding the industrial union structure as inherently revolutionary, tried for a time to organize an industrial union movement without the IWW's revolutionary rhetoric. In the 1940s Nef discovered Edward Bellamy's *Looking Backward* and *Equality* and recognized in them the theoretical basis of the ideas that had animated his whole adult life. He at once commenced publication of his own Bellamyist *Equalitarian Bulletin*, which he continued to produce, at first in San Francisco and later in Los Angeles, until his death in the late 1950s or early '60s. The exact date of his death has not been determined, but the reference books which state he died in the 1930s are in error.

—*Franklin Rosemont*

REFERENCES

McGuckin, Henry E. *Memoirs of a Wobbly*. Chicago: Charles H. Kerr, 1987.

Nef, Walter T. "Job Control in the Harvest Fields." *International Socialist Review*, 17 (September 1916).

New Alliance Party: see Psychology

New American Movement

This movement was founded in 1971 to provide an alternative New Left organization in the wake of the collapse of the Students for a Democratic Society in 1969. Its original organizers sought to establish a broad-based "mass organization" that would "overcome the errors of the New Left"—which they identified as including antileadership, glorification of the Third World, and inadequate sensitivity to the interests and needs of American workers. At the founding convention in Davenport, Iowa, in November 1971, many former New Leftists, upset at their perceived defeats in light of the dissolution of SDS and mass defections toward the McGovern campaign for the Democratic nomination for the presidency, argued that NAM was in no position to reach out to American workers, and that it was more important to have an organization that looked inward, spent time defining its politics, and then later moved outward. This position prevailed, and NAM became an organization for former New Leftists, with a national office aimed primarily at serving self-defining local chapters. The local chapters were involved in a variety of locally oriented organizing projects—including building opposition to the continuation of the Vietnam War until 1975, opposing rate hikes for local utilities, opposing nuclear power plants, and opposing nuclear armaments.

NAM cadre were activists in many local struggles, and by the late 1970s NAM saw itself primarily as providing education and political sophistication to these other struggles, rather than as aiming to be the leadership organization itself. From the start, NAM emphasized two ideas that it said had not been adequately integrated into the thinking of the New Left: (1) the importance of socialism as the only possible basis for reconstructing American society; and (2) the centrality of feminism as a core approach that must be integrated into all political work.

NAM emerged in a period of general decline in the Left in the 1970s and did not see itself as capable of attempting to stem that decline. It had no organizational ambitions to become well known outside the Left, and its growth was largely confined to areas with high concentations of former New Leftists. At its height, NAM did not exceed 1,500 members. Yet its spirited internal debates had some influence on the larger protest movements of the late '70s and early '80s.

Meanwhile, Michael Harrington's Democratic Socialist Organizing Committee, occupying very similar ground on most theoretical questions, was gaining many more members—largely because of its strong national organizational focus, its commitment to national leadership, and its orientation toward using the media effectively. In 1982 NAM merged with DSOC to form one organization—the Democratic Socialists of America—though only after an intense internal debate within NAM in which some of the organization's activists quit on the grounds that they feared the new organization would be more "elitist" and less sensitive to feminist issues than NAM had been. Many who supported the merger argued that DSOC's commitment to national leadership and organization were precisely what NAM needed, that NAM had in many ways repeated the fierce antileadership tendencies of the New Left, that NAM had never reached out beyond the immediate constituency of former New Leftists, and that NAM had reacted to the collapse of Left consciousness in the '70s in a passive way rather than providing either strategic or organizational alternatives. *See also*: New Left, Socialist Party

—*Michael Lerner*

The New
INTERNATIONAL
MAY • 1945

NOTES OF THE MONTH
END OF THE EUROPEAN WAR

THE LESSON OF GERMANY
By J. R. Johnson

World Trade Union Conference
By Albert Gates

HISTORICAL IMAGE OF NAPOLEON
By James T. Farrell

BURNHAM'S HEIR TO LENIN
By Ernest Lund

SINGLE COPY 20c — ONE YEAR $1.50

New International/ New Politics

Founded by an early incarnation of the Socialist Workers Party as an "organ of revolutionary Marxism," *New International* (1934–58) was throughout its existence an authoritative expression of U.S. Trotskyist opinion. Leon Trotsky, during his lifetime and after, figured prominently in its pages, as did a host of outstanding U.S. and European intellectuals including George Novack, James T. Farrell, Max Shachtman, Irving Howe, James Burnham, C. L. R. James, Dwight Macdonald, Hal Draper, and Ernest Mandel. Trotsky likened *NI* to "the great masons of the future: Marx, Engels, Lenin." In *Reflections of a Neoconservative*, Irving Kristol recalls that *NI* taught him critical analytic thought.

NI became the authoritative journal of the Workers Party in April 1940, with its editors Shachtman and Burnham in the forefront of the new Trotskyist organization. (Leaders of the orthodox SWP alleged that the WP had misappropriated the publication.) After 1940, *NI* advanced the slogan, "For the Third Camp!" (i.e., the "submerged, smoldering, working masses of the world," as against the first camp, Western capitalism, and against the second, Soviet "bureaucratic collectivism"). As compared with the SWP's new *Fourth International* (1940–56), *NI* was bolder, brasher, and in later years less certain of itself and of Trotskyism.

NI ceased publication when Shachtman's group abandoned vanguard party-building by entering the Socialist Party. The journal's viewpoint on key concerns ("the Russian question," unions, black protest movements, economics, and intellectuals) was continued by a privately published successor, *New Politics* (1961–76 and 1986–present). The primary editor of *NP*, Julius Jacobson, had in fact been the final editor of *NI*. The new journal gathered many familiar figures as writers and editorial associates; its sponsors have included a somewhat broader milieu, including James Baldwin, Jules Feiffer, Erich Fromm, and Norman Mailer. *See also*: Trotskyism

—*Kent Worcester*

REFERENCES

Howe, Irving. *A Margin of Hope: An Intellectual Autobiography*. New York: Harcourt, Brace, 1982.

Wald, Alan. *The New York Intellectuals: The Rise and Decline of the Anti-Stalinist Left from the 1930s to the 1980s*. Chapel Hill: University of North Carolina Press, 1987.

New Left

Based initially on the experience of the civil rights movement, the polyglot radicalism known as the "New Left" centered its influence on the major private or state campus and in communities heavily influenced by campus radicalism and/or youth culture. Its politics, definitely outside the norms of communist, socialist, or other past "Left" movements, stressed human rights and visions of cultural change over the familiar Left struggles of labor and the promise of egalitarian industrial progress. At high tide, in 1969–70, the New Left numbered 150,000 or more steady participants, and a supportive milieu of millions. Unable to expand its popular support beyond young people, it could not, however, attain its goal of revolutionizing campus life by effecting the disengagement of colleges and universities from the military-industrial complex and the commitment of campus resources to social transformation; nor could it reverse a decades-old process of bipartisan coalition around the commitments of the military-industrial complex. Severely pressed by government infiltration and a massive propaganda campaign, the New Left collapsed into fragments of competing sects and a disillusioned, inactive former following.

The final significance of these developments in the history of the Left has yet to be understood. Clearly, however, the New Left managed to dramatize a wide spectrum of issues, from counterinsurgency wars to environmental damage, which have grown from flagrant cases of oppression into evident threats to the survival of the planet. No other constituency of similar size and importance has arisen to replace the New Left, either in the name of resurrected Old Left organizations and ideas or of another, Newer Left.

The New Left began with the avuncular role of important surviving Old Left individuals and institutions. McCarthyism's net, refined by Cold War–oriented college administrators and senior professors, missed relatively little in its search for victims. Not only were jobs lost, but intellectual careers were destroyed and warnings provided against dissent that defied the Cold War consensus. But schools such as the University of Wisconsin, which refused to install loyalty oaths, became meccas for dissenters of all kinds. More important, as McCarthyism eased in the later 1950s, a small-scale renewal of campus activism quickly reappeared, promising greater things. In larger cities or community-campus centers of various Old Lefts, such as Berkeley, California, certain bookstores or cafés provided hangouts where political conversations had never ceased and where bohemian tastes could be indulged. Eating cooperatives and other such institutions carried over from previous generations likewise offered practical networks for political integration.

The "New Left" sobriquet itself came directly out of contemporary British experience, where the emergence of the "Ban the Bomb" Campaign for Nuclear Disarmament, and the breakaway of distinguished Marxist intellectuals from the British Communist Party, marked activist and intellectual components. "New Left Clubs" sprang up on British campuses, and two journals, the *New Reasoner* and *Universities and Left Review* merged in 1960 into the *new left review*, intended to be the intellectual expression of the New Left Clubs. In the United States, the magazine *American Socialist*, formed by a group of activists who had broken from the Socialist Workers Party, took up the cause for an American counterpart.

At this early date, little could be accomplished nationally of an openly New Left character. However, at the local level, sympathy for southern civil rights efforts merged with the political-intellectual evolution of former Labor Youth League members, such as Richard Flacks, who went independent after the Russian invasion of Hungary. These LYL "graduates" had a sophistication in Marxist ideas far beyond those of other radicalized intellectuals, and they had a burning desire to reestablish a radical critique independent of the old Stalin-Trotsky–Social Democracy debates. They also had a strong interest in cultural matters. They played an especially important role in the formation of local "folk music" groups on the campuses in the later 1950s, also in the earliest antimilitarist campus manifestations ("antimilitary balls," posed against the ROTC "military balls" then in vogue), and in the avant-garde cultural/theatrical movements of the time. From their presence can be traced the audacious Fair Play for Cuba Committees and the formation of *Studies on the Left* (1959–66) at the University of Wisconsin, the first sustained intellectual journal calling for a new movement.

If these tendencies touched only a handful of campuses, and a brief Ban the Bomb movement of 1960–61 affected only a few more, they still helped to shape the early 1960s liberal-radical drift. The new Students for a Democratic Society's *Port Huron Statement* (1962), reflecting experience in the civil rights movement and the tones of English New Left manifestoes, was drafted by Catholic moralist Tom Hayden, but bore the stamp of some Marxist sophistication. It appealed for student awareness and for political activity against the dominant ideologies of the Cold War age.

This fresh perspective had a solid basis in the facts of changing campus life. The omnipresent college and university expansion suddenly made the "student," by the early 1960s, a significant demographic segment of the population. The pervasive alienation from bureaucratized U.S. society, well documented in the 1950s, had found its first critics in the faculties, and soon would find its militant opponents among the students. But SDS—lineal successor to the Intercollegiate Socialist Society of the 1910s and the subsequent Student League for Industrial Democracy—lacked the opportunity and perhaps also the inclination to turn the key. For a few years more, campus restiveness remained locked into local, often symbolic issues from dormitory food to censorship.

In a negative sense, the failure of any national Left organization to establish during these years the kind of campus bases suited to seize the Left political hegemony, also proved decisive. The Young Socialist Alliance, which narrowed from an early attempt at coalition to a strict youth component of the Socialist Workers Party, had only very scattered support. The Communist-led W. E. B. DuBois Clubs, only founded in 1965 and even less influential outside the West Coast, reflected in their late appearance and their party-line character the slow and troubled reemergence of the CP from the 1950s repression and internal divisions. The Young People's Socialist League, drifting and faction-ridden, had neither the capacity nor motive for organizing students against Cold War policies. The localism and antiinstitutionalism of the nascent New Left reflected an instinctive rejection of these alternatives, as a rejection of all the efforts of political authorities committed to one kind of bureaucracy or another.

Meanwhile, as SDS turned to community projects in lieu of campus organizing, it sought to carry out a distinctly New Left program. Like other activists operating independently, SDSers aimed at the very poor rather than at the fabled proletariat. Its Education and Research Action Program (ERAP), and especially the Newark Community Union Project (NCUP) and Chicago Jobs or Income Now (JOIN) of 1963–65 highlighted the effort to alert the poor to their own potential power as the southern civil rights movement had done with considerable success. Here, the phrase "participatory democracy," meaning an advance beyond the parliamentary democracy of electing representatives to office, was coined at the University of Michigan. Of major localistic mobilizations, however, perhaps only the welfare rights movement, with its discrete constituency and demands, succeeded in terms of community coalition-building among the poor. The Northern Student Movement, essentially a campus support group for southern struggles, had more success with enrolling dedicated reformers to help the less fortunate elsewhere to free themselves.

A small but sometime influential kernel of self-avowed revolutionaries had meanwhile emerged in Third World–oriented causes of the early 1960s, principally in support of Cuba against the United States and of China against the Soviet Union. In a few years, veterans of these causes, and younger devotees, would enter New Left movements with great impact, positive and negative. The heroic struggles of the Student Nonviolent Coordinating Committee (SNCC) gave radical anti-racism a rallying center, while the self-distancing of liberals from SNCC demonstrated for many the untrustworthiness of Democratic Party politicians. Here and there, a precocious student radicalism emerged. The Rev. Martin Luther King, Jr.'s march in Detroit attracted more than 100,000 and set off high school strikes and Detroit political currents in which white youth joined blacks urging drastic changes in society. Another early indication of national campus interest in more radical views was the rousing campus reception given black nationalist Malcolm X just prior to his 1965 assassination. Yet only rarely could students see social change as coming through their own actions. But they responded with notable warmth to the promise (or threat) of African-American challenges to the American status quo. In this respect, they further distanced themselves from virtually the entire Old Left spectrum, whose leaders had articulated for decades the promise of racial integration and peaceful change through coalitions with liberal and centrist Democrats.

The Berkeley, California, free speech movement of 1964, ostensibly nonpolitical, was the first major campus movement to actually succeed in shutting down a prestige institution. By pitting students of all kinds against the bureaucratic institution of the university, FSM drew the most radical lessons of the civil rights movement and applied them to campus life at large. Shocking many liberal academics with the directness of their demands, which is to say their insistance upon making their own decisions rather than deferring to authority, Berkeley students raised the level of New Left dialogue to a national plane. Hereafter, campus politics took a new direction and a new importance.

The escalating U.S. invasion of Vietnam, from 1965 onward, placed students in direct conflict with the civilian authorities who implemented the guiding military-industrial demands made upon the universities. Confronted with Selective Service and its implications, many young people on campus and off came to see the contemporary uprisings of blacks in Harlem, Watts, and Detroit as movements aimed at the same opponent.

The Selective Service System also played a large role in this alienation. Its class and race bias notoriously favored college students in general. But many who graduated, and more who dropped out, found themselves in uniforms, if rarely on the front lines of jungle warfare. Fear stirred specific resentments, moreover, in a generational sense. Old men (political and military leaders) sent young men to die and condemned young women as well as their mothers to suffer the fears and threats of loss. The older generations, seemingly loyal to the imperatives of imperial war as the price for consumer society, appeared in the eyes of the young as corrupted by age and by power. The forces of age and death seemed, then, counterposed to the forces of life, epitomized in the young. In supporting Lyndon Johnson against Barry Goldwater for the 1964 presidential election, New Leftists (notably, SDS) for the last time assumed a stance on the respectable left edge of liberalism. From 1965 to 1967, with the spreading protest against the Vietnam War, ever larger demonstrations confronted civil authorities and offered right-wing (but also liberal, Cold War) demagoguery a convenient target.

The 1965 Bay Area Vietnam Day Committee (VDC) arranged one of the largest of the early protests aimed at halting the war process or at least constraining active conscription. It was characteristically free of any particular organizational domination, although local SDS, the Young Socialist Alliance, and others participated. That same year, a national demonstration in Washington, D.C., saw radical civil rights, students, and veteran Left leaders denounce the war and trace its origins to the social system. Once again, this demonstration notably lacked any overarching organizational affiliation or ideological inclination.

As SDS began to attract more campus antiwar activists, a national "teach-in" movement on many campuses lifted faculty members to the apex of their influence on the burgeoning protest. By making protest respectable, the teach-ins gave antiwar students and their supporters new national visibility. A handful of varied intellectuals, including Noam Chomsky, Herbert Marcuse, and Staughton Lynd, acquired a national constituency for their speeches, their social theories, and their personalities as campus firebrands. The teaching of Frantz Fanon's *Wretched Of the Earth*, Paul Goodman's *Growing Up Absurd*, and Marcuse's *One Dimensional Man* added intellectual ballast to New Left activism.

In another sense, however, the teach-ins were the last episode in which dialogue served as the major component of New Left activity. Soon, words by themselves would be considered insufficient. SDS, joined by many local groups, coalitions, and spontaneous formations, would become the chief political beneficiary of the new radical enthusiasm.

Unlike the free speech movement, whose tenets became embedded in student movements but whose goals became lost amid other protests, the Vietnam protest spread to most liberal schools and major universities. The media remained, for the most part, locked into the prestige schools such as Columbia. Often scarcely noticed beyond the local scene, the more traditionally conservative campuses such as the average southern black campus (which had hitherto relied on upper-class white tolerance to restrain local whites' violence against black students) and state schools of the South and Southwest, began to take up the issues. By 1969–70, some of the most violent and sustained campus confrontations were taking place in exactly these locations, where authorities responded bluntly with force and students understandably lacked confidence in supposed administrative reforms.

At some point in 1966–69, the popular sentiment on many and perhaps most major campuses turned decisively against the war and against the government determined to prosecute it. Dozens and then hundreds of "underground newspapers"—local tabloids made possible by a technological revolution in the use of newsprint—effectively dramatized the issues and put rebellious intellectual concepts into cultural form. Their combined readership certainly reached the millions. In effect, these sheets (and toned down in rhetoric, often the campus daily, too) created an alternative information system to the hostile reports of the commercial dailies and newsweeklies. They were, like the campus Committees to End the War in Vietnam (frequently a jousting arena for local Trotskyists and Communists) at least as important as SDS chapters in mobilizing discontent.

Material optimism, the sexualization of leisure, and the introduction of "recreational" drugs each also had an important role. The youth of the 1960s had not known economic Depression, and the vast majority had not experienced anything resembling a hard personal upward climb to the middle classes. In their society of peers, leisure had largely taken the place of an earlier generation's long hours of work, and since the early 1960s, had been flooded with the programmed sexualization (at steadily younger ages) of advertising aimed at the "youth market" for consumer goods. Moreover, birth control technologies had drastically improved: if the 1950s coed already wore blue jeans and discreetly engaged in sexual relations prior to marriage, her 1960s equivalent could talk openly about orgasms. The popularization of marijuana and LSD produced less emotional addiction than a loosening of the grip that advanced industrial society, with its project of material "progress," had upon the visions and dreams of the young. Seen through the lenses of LSD experience, the prospect of an executive career appeared less charismatic than it had at any time in modern U.S. society. Drug guru Timothy Leary, Yippie Abbie Hoffman, and even the legacy of the Beat generation writers (continually publicized by traveling poet Allen Ginsberg) found new audiences. Asked in a poll what they most sought in life, a majority of students answered "self-fulfillment," and put material success well down the list. Only a minority believed money meant happiness, and fewer still that opting out meant dire poverty.

Not surprisingly, then, the militant Stop the Draft Week of October 1967 coincided with a year of "be-ins" and a generalized spread of "Youth Culture" from San Francisco's Haight-Ashbury section to little Haight-Ashburys adjoining many campus towns. The two constituencies did not necessarily coincide. Yet politicos in large numbers also smoked marijuana, and "hippies" notoriously appeared in large numbers at political demonstrations. The two types joined in rejecting the view of "democracy" as being limited to the two-party system and of wage or salaried labor as being a worthy personal goal. On the local level, massive political meetings seemed more freewheeling, more leaderless, more spontaneous in generating networks of practical activity, than at any time afterward.

Students who participated in these activities often found themselves simultaneously engaged in militant protests against university functions, and in hard study (and/or classroom participation) that professors would later recall as the most intense in their lengthy careers. Paradoxically, during those semesters frequently interrupted by protest and strike, an eagerness for real learning was widely observed. Classes or professors deemed especially "relevant" (and these might range from U.S. history to black or women's studies to "California culture") drew droves of devoted listeners beyond official enrollment and intense classroom discussions in which students themselves prompted Socratic methods. "Free Universities" with extra classes off campus, in a wide range of subjects, took in the same and other students outside normal class hours. In this sense, the New Left proved, if not as book-oriented as its predecessors on the Left, far more intellectually motivated than generally considered at the time.

Perhaps for that very reason, the split within the campus community now flared as never previously. Those professors openly hostile to student movements—complaining bitterly at what Edward Shils called "temporizing, halfhearted authority" (i.e., an unwillingness to use more severe repressive measures against protesters earlier and more systematically), themselves often taking the disciplinary action of flunking antiwar students—suffered the most from the obloquy. Even more than conservative regulars, self-pronounced liberals who had become attached to the dream of U.S. military victory in Southeast Asia, or who craved revenge against students who now ridiculed their pompousness, seemed most indignant about student uprisings and most public with appeals for repression. Many more faculty members found themselves immensely stimulated if also troubled. Those junior faculty most sympathetic to intellectual integrity and political aims of the students suffered real, if inconsistent, firings, political discrimination, and other penalties over the next few years. Several outstanding careers—such as that of Black History scholar Robert Starobin, a 1971 suicide—ended tragically.

The New Left suffered its own deep internal difficulties at the moment of its triumphs. Students, on strike against some particular outrage (such as police beatings of students who sat-in against recruiters for Dow Chemicals, maker of napalm used in Vietnam), found administrators obdurate on matters of university policy and most professors unchanged if not unshaken by events. Structural reforms envisioned to encompass students in a democratized university could not be implemented. Strikes, even supported by teaching assistants, tended to peter out after a few days or a week. Unlike a labor strike that withholds necessary muscle-power and reduces profits, a student strike depends upon publicity, i.e., embarrassment of the administration. Students returned to classes feeling some sense of triumph (often, amnesty was granted to those committing any but violent acts) but also a continuing frustration. That frustration, especially keen in the minds of political groups on campus, brought ever more frantic visions of America's approaching social transformation.

Years of "hot summers" in the streets of major cities, the 1968 assassination of the Rev. Martin Luther King, Jr., and the hostile response of lawful authorities to even peaceful protest heightened the frustration. Clearly, the empowered section of American society desired no major changes, and was perfectly willing to endorse the use of military firepower, public deceit, conspiracy, invasion of privacy, and even plans for mass detention (drawn up by later Supreme Court Chief Justice William Rehnquist) in order to restore order.

In this circumstance, the practical absence of blacks in large numbers from most campuses mattered less than the symbolic and historical role blacks occupied in U.S. society at large. Black students recruited to campuses in unprecedented numbers as a result of student and urban protests felt deeply ambivalent at their heritage of discrimination and their present opportunity for personal advancement. Many black students tended to resolve this ambivalence with extreme appeals to black nationalism and demands on administrations, occasionally backed up with threats of force. White students felt somewhat in awe of a people seemingly involved in an insurrection; but to a greater degree they felt guilty for America's past sins, and for the present reality of poverty and vast overconcentration on Vietnam's front lines. SDS ideology swerved from Left-liberal to Leninist in order to express opposition to American capitalism and solidarity with the Third World and with black revolutionary movements in the United States.

At times, these feelings inspired race-related student strikes whose main issues and leadership involved internal campus conflicts and personalities only secondarily. In perhaps the outstanding case, the San Francisco State strike of 1968–69, activists' demands also reflected the views of the most militant minority students and faculty. The ferocity of response to such demands (the obdurate president of the college, linguist Sessue Hayakawa, gained fame and senatorial election as the Ronald Reagan of administrators) induced protracted conflict.

Student feelings of rage and helplessness were redoubled by the continuing escalation of the Vietnam War, and by the frustration of political adjustment within the two-party system. President Lyndon Johnson, repeatedly increasing troop strength and promising the "light at the end of the tunnel," dramatically raised the nightly "body count" of killed, as reported on network news. The Vietnamese Tet Offensive, which further bruised the U.S. military's reputation, made continuation of the bloodbath appear hopeless and slightly mad. The unsuccessful peace-candidacy of Senator Eugene McCarthy followed by the assassination of Robert Kennedy ensured the Democratic Party nomination for Senator Hubert Humphrey, a noted liberal Cold Warrior. The "Battle of Chicago," in which Mayor Richard Daley's police violently defended a locked Democratic Party convention from hordes of antiwar demonstrators, worked to the advantage of Richard Nixon and his student-baiting future vice president, Spiro T. Agnew. Against these later-indicted figures, students felt rage and revulsion, but also powerlessness and futility. Indeed, the election of Hubert Humphrey might well have brought a further escalation of the war out of an ideological unwillingness to accept U.S. defeat as Nixon finally did.

The Cambodia bombing of 1970 stirred the last and biggest student uprising of all, highlighted by the authorities' killing of students at Jackson State College and Kent State University. Strikes spread almost universally on campuses. At the same time, student anger seemed impotent and often turned toward "trashing" (throwing rocks at) nearby windows, toward heavier or more continual use of drugs and toward sexual promiscuity in the place of sexual emancipation. SDS, almost fanatically nonideological and decentralist in 1967, had by 1969 divided between opposing Maoist factions by this time claiming rather than representing most campus activists. Rage turned a minority of erstwhile student activists to attempted acts of sabotage, almost uniformly unsuccessful and trivial in effect compared with the U.S. brutality dramatized in the My Lai massacre. These efforts by some student radicals, however, permitted variegated opponents of the New Left, liberal and conservative, to lock arms in denouncing the movement at large, and (where acts had been committed) unleash and legitimize a pattern of police provocations, disruptions, grand jury intimidations, and related actions. As later demonstrated in Freedom of Information Act inquiries, only at the height of the Cold War, or in the 1919–21 wake of the Russian Revolution, had government harassment been so widespread or so flagrantly in violation of constitutional rights.

The collapse of other contemporary movements framed the eclipse of the New Left. SNCC, for example, merged in 1970 with the Black Panther Party, and both disappeared in defeat, disillusionment, and political confusion. The League of Revolutionary Black Workers, which had for a moment offered a serious threat to United Auto Workers leadership, likewise dissipated. Other, more hopeful outcomes of the New Left could still be glimpsed. In Mexican-American and Asian-American communities, young radicals served as community spokespeople. On campuses where activity had begun late, fresh signs of rebellion could be found. In general, however, the "burnout" had become evident and, for a generation of student activists, final.

Only the appearance of the women's liberation movement (and to a lesser extent, the gay movement) brightened a dark picture of campus activism. As a political tendency, this movement was primarily cultural—more concerned with the "sexual politics" of process and everyday life than with presidential elections—but as a cultural movement deeply "political" through its demands upon society. As WLM and GLM banners appeared at the last major demonstrations, and as consciousness-raising groups in a sense took the place of political meetings, as male Left leaders already fumbling now faced critique for their handling of the "woman question," an inner purpose of the 1960s student movement had been nearly realized. But this development had been, tragically, too late to count for much in the great upheavals. *See also*: Armed Struggle; The Beats and the New Left; Black Panther Party; Chomsky, Noam; Civil Rights Movement; Gay Rights Movement; GI Coffeehouse Movement; Hoffman, Abbie; Liberation News Service; New Left Literature; Newsreel and post-New Left Radical Filmmaking; Pacifism; Peace Movements; Political Theater—1960s–1980s; Popular Culture; Students for a Democratic Society; Student Nonviolent Coordinating Committee; Underground Press; Woman's Liberation; Yippies

—*Paul Buhle*

REFERENCES

Fraser, Ronald, et al., eds. *1968: A Student Generation in Revolt*. New York: Pantheon, 1988.

Gitlin, Todd. *The Sixties: Years of Hope, Days of Rage*. New York: Bantam Books, 1987.

Peck, Abe. *Uncovering the Sixties: The Life & Times of the Underground Press*. New York: Pantheon, 1985.

Sale, Kirkpatrick. *SDS*. New York: Random House, 1973.

New Left Literature

The New Left culture of the 1960s did not generate a distinctive literary movement of the kind associated with previous radical movements in the United States. No one work, political organization, geographic location, aesthetic style, or political theme provided a common reference point. Literary people associated with the New Left generally followed individual goals and were more likely to be involved with other writers in feminist, racial, language, or sexual movements than with writers who shared their specific political ideology. In contrast to a parallel phenomenon among radical filmmakers, the diffusion of radical writers tended to subordinate the Left message as such into broader perspectives demanding cultural egalitarianism and equal access of specific constituencies to political and economic power.

While lacking a coherent literary component, the New Left did not lack for creative energy. A common circumstance, in fact, was that many activists wrote poetry or short fiction in addition to doing political and academic work. During the time of the struggle against the war in Vietnam, thousands of poems using radical rhetoric were directed against U.S. policies. This work appeared in the underground press, was read at rallies, and inched its way into literary journals. During Angry Arts Week of 1967 and for some time thereafter, scores of poets in New York City used flatbed trucks to publicly read from at busy intersections throughout the five boroughs. No single voice captured the radical movement as Bob Dylan's songs had at one time, but the totality of the poems had considerable impact. Outstanding antiwar poems from all sectors of the literary world were collected by Walter Lowenfels in *Where Is Vietnam?* (1967). Radical contributors included Lawrence Ferlinghetti, Will Inman, Jack Lindeman, Clarence Major, Tom McGrath, Al Katzman, Dan Georgakas, Denis Knight, Sidney Bernard, Walter Lowenfels, and Leslie Woolf Hedley.

New Left writers were acutely aware of the need for a journal on the model of *Masses*, but their various attempts to create such an organ usually lasted only a few issues and barely got beyond immediate affinity groups. Some of these undertakings were *Crawdaddy*, *TRA* (Toward Revolutionary Art), *100 Flowers*, *Insurgent*, *Treason*, *Weapon*, *Chalk Circle*, *Black Mask*, the *Unrealist*, *Sez*, and *Left Curve*. Few political journals had literary sections although poems occasionally appeared in *The Minority of One* and *Radical America*. The *Guardian*, however, ceased publishing poetry in the 1960s and fiction had to find a place in the few literary journals, like

Minnesota Review, that were open to radical work. More common than creative work in Left cultural publications were critiques of dominant culture, particularly mass media, a tendency that also dominated the journals of the 1970s and 1980s such as *Cultural Correspondence* and *Zeta*. Despite the difficulties of publication, radicals continued to produce an amazing amount of poetry. Todd Gitlin edited an impressive collection in *The Campfires of the Resistance* (1971). Radicals were also included in such textbooks as *The Now Voices* (1971), edited by Angelo Carli and Theodore Kilman, and *The City Today* (1978), edited by George L. Groman.

The single most influential Left literary enterprise was *El Corno Emplumado*, edited by Margaret Randall in Mexico City. Randall had been involved with the abstract expressionists of the 1950s and had close contacts with exiled Spanish loyalists. She began her bilingual journal after moving to Mexico in the 1960s. What distinguished *El Corno* was that it mingled the best of the new Latin American authors, many of whom were active revolutionaries, with American writers of various dissident movements. Randall's criteria were literary but her journal provided a rare cross-cultural writer-to-writer link. The magazine suspended publication in 1969 when Randall received governmental death threats for supporting the rebellion of Mexican students.

Randall tried to return to her native United States but was denied entry because she had given up her citizenship to marry a Mexican writer. Randall was forced to seek asylum in Cuba and in the years that followed she became a New Left Anna Louise Strong, writing of the revolutionary process in Cuba, Vietnam, and Nicaragua with an emphasis on the role of women. She continued to write her own poetry and was a major translator of Spanish-language writers. She was able to return to the United States in the early 1980s but soon became embroiled with the Immigration Service, which wanted to expel her under the provisions of the McCarran-Walter Act. Randall became a major cause célèbre for the radical and feminist movements, and finally had her citizenship reaffirmed in 1989. Her poetry, her nonfiction, and the contents of *El Corno* were cited by the government as proofs of her subversive intentions. Randall, in fact, had become increasingly involved with the woman's movement and her poetry was more personal than political. Her most political writing is found in the collection *Part of the Solution* (1973).

Randall's interfacing with other movements was quite typical of the times and could be applied to radicals as diverse as Susan Sherman, Diane Di Prima, Pedro Pietri, Vincent Ferrini, Etheridge Knight, and Amiri Baraka. Susan Sherman was identified with the women's movement and gay rights, but her *Ikon* magazine took on hard-core political issues such as apartheid in South Africa and she was an editor of the radical poetry anthology *Only Humans with Songs to Sing* (1969). Di Prima had roots in the Beat movement but was best known for her "Revolutionary Poems" cycle, which were a fixture in the 1960s underground press. Pietri was associated with the Puerto Rican movement but wrote in English with such a strong class perspective that Monthly Review Press published his *Puerto Rican Obituary* (1973). Vincent Ferrini pursued ethnic and regional themes related to his home base of Gloucester, Massachusetts, in poetry that he consciously set up as a Left alternative to Gloucester's avant-garde poet laureate, Charles Olson.

Etheridge Knight began publishing poetry while in prison and radicals helped secure his release. Like many prison writers, he linked black crime with capitalism and was representative of the prison writers' movement, which enjoyed Left support. Amiri Baraka had originally won literary fame with plays published under his given name of Le Roi Jones and was loosely associated with the Beats. He later moved into a black nationalist period and was associated with cultural radicals such as Larry Neal. Still later he declared himself a Marxist. Other black writers moved in and around the Left in similar fashion. Among the best known were Sonia Sanchez, Don Lee, Julius Lester, Ishmael Reed, and Clarence Major.

Novels directly about the radical movement were abundant in the 1960s–1970s, but they only occasionally addressed the New Left. A major exception was Max Crawford's *The Bad Communist* (1979), which looked at the cult of "direct action" and at Maoism in a California group focused on black prisoners. Marge Piercy contributed several works related to political movements. *Going Down Fast* (1969), a story of urban renewal reflecting participatory-democracy ideas of the Students for a Democratic Society, was followed with *Dance the Eagle to Sleep* (1970), a novel set in the near future in which an unsuccessful armed rebellion by New Left types is underway, and the science-fiction *Woman On the Edge of Time* (1976). *Vida* (1979) treated the direct action, Weatherman-like minimovement emerging from the disappointments of the New Left. Several other Piercy novels, such as *Small Changes* (1973), *Braided Lives* (1982), and *Gone to Soldier* (1987) touched upon radical movements in passing.

A different body of literature sought to recapture the traditions of the Old Left and relate them in some manner to the New Left. Helen Yglesias's *How She Died* (1972) treated the devastating effect of the Cold War on the cancerstricken daughter of a famous jailed Communist, her New Left–age housekeeper-nurse, and her Old Left savant. K. B. Gilden's *Between the Hills and the Sea* (1971) analyzed the Cold War in a blue-collar Connecticut town, where the approaching victory of the CIO's anticommunist factions leaves little surviving but personal determination. Harvey Swados's *Standing Fast* (1970), focused mainly on a fictionalized version of the Workers Party and the later fate of its activists and sympathizers, down to the tragic murder in Harlem of the most idealistic of their children. Swados's *Celebrations* (1980) had a New Left–style militant redress the accumulated respectability of an aging former radical, and bring the old man (actually his biological father) back toward the fray. Clancy Sigal's *Going Away* (1962), the earliest and perhaps best of the genre, is an on-the-road novel in which the writer crisscrosses America visiting comrades with various reactions to the Khrushchev revelations and the invasion of Hungary. The novel ends with the writer expatriating to England, the path of the author in real life.

A literary device in many radical novels was to have a character who belonged to the Industrial Workers of the World symbolize unblemished American dissent. More rare were accounts of IWW struggles such as Robert Houston's *Bisbee '17* (1979) and Thomas Churchill's *Centralia Death March* (1980). The misfortunes of a Communist-oriented trade union were the subject of Leonard Kriegel's *Quitting Time* (1982). The interaction between immigrant and working-class oppression was a more popular theme. Illegal Mexican immigrants are dealt with in Eugene Nelson's *Bracero* (1973), Chinese railroad workers in Moonfoon Leong's *Number One Son* (1975), and Hispanic migrant workers in Raymond Barrio's *The Plum Plum Pickers* (1972). This was a continuation of a tradition found in earlier works such as Toshio Mori's *Yokohama, California* (1949), a novel about working-class Japanese Americans. Alienation rather than revolution was the theme of most books about the working class. Truman Nelson's *The Torture of Mothers* (1975) dealt with racism in Harlem, Chuck Wachtel's *Joe the Engineer* (1983) with blue-collar workers, John O. Killens's *'Sippi* (1967) with civil rights activists, Toni Cade Bambara's *The Salt Eaters* (1981) with health workers, Denise Giardina's *Storming Heaven* (1987) with coal miners, and Henry Noyes's *Hand Over Fist* (1980) with Sicilians and blacks in Chicago's Forty-second Ward.

Socialists often wrote books in which the Left view was part of the fiction's structure and assumptions rather than a focus of direct discourse. Sol Yurick's *The Bag* (1968) and *The Warriors* (1965) dealt with lumpen street gangs in such a fashion. A film version of *The Warriors* got a controversial homage from the influential film critic Pauline Kael and the publicity led to most of Yurick's fiction being released in paperback for a mass audience. Ernie Brill's *I Looked Over Jordan and Other Stories* (1980) dealt with health-care problems with a similar strategy and one story was excerpted for a television play by Ossie Davis and Ruby Dee. John A. Williams included a devastating critique of the CIA in his *The Man Who Cried I Am* (1967) and celebrated blacks who had fought in the Abraham Lincoln Brigade in his *Captain Blackman* (1972). Meredith

Tax favorably featured radical Jews in her immigrant epics *Rivington Street* (1982) and *Union Square* (1988). Tax wrote a nonfiction account of women garment workers in *The Rising of the Women: Feminist Solidarity and Class Conflict, 1880–1917* (1980). Brill had been on the staff of *TRA* and worked in the Congress of Racial Equality and the Progressive Labor Party. Williams served as a fiction adviser for Monthly Review Press and Yurick spoke often at Marxist forums in New York City.

Science fiction, or what might be called historical fantasy, became, for the first time since the 1910s, a major mode of Left and protest expression in the 1960s–1970s. Along with Marge Piercy's *Woman on the Edge of Time*, this genre saw Ursula K. Le Guin, daughter of noted anthropologist Alfred Kroeber, write several novels analyzing the destructiveness of militarized Western (especially American) culture and seeking out alternatives. *The Word for World Is Forest* (1969) was a thinly disguised allegorical comment on the war in Vietnam, with dreamy creatures brutalized and turned into revolutionary warriors by a galactic invasion from the Earth. *The Dispossessed* (1971) posed the collective effort of planetary anarchism in conditions of scarcity against the rich but corrupt American-like planetary authoritarianism. Philip K. Dick wrote a series of novels about spreading authoritarianism, declining ecological conditions, and the manipulation of the drug culture to make protest and revolt increasingly difficult. *The Three Stigmata of Palmer Eldrich* (1964) and *A Scanner Darkly* (1977) were his most convincing efforts. Ishmael Reed, before abandoning Left ideas entirely for black nationalism, penned the remarkable *Free Lance Pallbearers* (1967), a savage satire of Lyndon Johnson's antipoverty program; *Yellow Back Radio Broke Down* (1969), a caricature of the western novel, with antirealist black and lesbian heroes; and *Mumbo Jumbo* (1972), an imaginative novel about the making of Western civilization and the subversion of it in the 1920s by black culture in the United States. By the later 1970s, this entire phase of Leftish literature had passed.

Another populist blending of art and politics is found in the work of Edward Abbey, a philosophical anarchist and radical environmentalist. His *Monkey Wrench Gang* (1976) combined his major passions by having environmentalists use violent direct action in an all-out effort against developers and other "defilers" of the West. The novel sold half a million copies and made him a cult hero. His *Brave Cowboy* became a 1962 Kirk Douglas western, *Lonely Are the Brave*, and a 1981 TV movie, *Fire on the Mountain*. Abbey's essays were unrelenting in their condemnation of capitalist ethics and economics. Shortly before his death in 1989, Abbey became strongly identified with the Earth First! movement.

Some three decades after SDS's *Port Huron Statement*, the energies that had been generated by the New Left had largely been buffered by dominant culture or absorbed by other movements. Specific writers had gained a measure of influence and even best-seller status but were usually not politically identified as radicals by the general public. The radical movement itself, highly focused on critical analysis of mass media and capitalist cultural hegemony, devoted few of its limited resources to literary endeavors or promotion of radical authors. *See also*: Beats and the New Left; Political Theater of 1960s–1980s; Proletarian and Radical Writers of 1930s–1950s; Swados, Harvey; Underground Press

—*Dan Georgakas*

REFERENCES

Baxandall, Lee, ed. *Radical Perspectives in the Arts*. Baltimore: Pelican Books Original, 1972.

Buhle, Paul, ed. *Popular Culture in America*. Minneapolis: University of Minnesota Press, 1987.

New Left Notes:

see Students for a Democratic Society

New Masses

Following in the direct line of the *Masses* (1911–17) and the *Liberator* (1918–24) the *New Masses* began in May 1926 and ran as a monthly through September 1933, when it was revamped to reappear, on January 2, 1934, as a weekly. While the early editors of this "revolutionary magazine of art and literature" were holdovers from the period of "lyrical radicalism" in the 1910s and early 1920s, increasingly in the late 1920s, as contributing editors like Max Eastman and Floyd Dell drifted away, the *New Masses* was being run by writers like Mike Gold and Joseph Freeman, who argued for stronger revolutionary positions and closer ties to the Soviet Union. In 1930 the International Union of Revolutionary Writers, meeting in Kharkov, urged the magazine to become "in every respect the cultural organ of the class-conscious workers and revolutionary intellectuals of this country," and the editors eagerly accepted this challenge. Gold's campaign for proletarian literature in the late 1920s and early 1930s helped bridge the gap between art and politics that had existed in the earlier *Masses-Liberator* tradition, and when, after 1930, increasing numbers of bourgeois artists and writers moved left under the multiple pressures of the Depression, they discovered a loud and colorful journal with fairly advanced Marxist ideas about both literature and politics.

From 1934 through the decade, during the period of the Popular Front, the weekly *New Masses* enjoyed its peak popularity. (Circulation for the last issue of the monthly in September 1933 was 6,000; the "4th Quarterly Issue" of January 1, 1935, one of a series of literary supplements that appeared after Granville Hicks was named literary editor of the weekly, had a printing of 25,000.) In this period, the *New Masses* was a visually exciting journal (drawing on the graphic skills of William Gropper, Reginald Marsh, and Hugo Gellert, among others) that was at the dynamic center of the literary-political Left in the 1930s. The magazine published many talented writers in this period—not only established authors like Ernest Hemingway ("Who Murdered the Vets?" 1935), Erskine Caldwell, Theodore Dreiser, and Langston Hughes, but newer writers such as Richard Wright, James Agee, Albert Maltz, and Jack Conroy. The *New Masses* sponsored some of the decade's most important literary organizations (the John Reed Clubs in the early '30s, the First American Writers and Artists Congresses in 1935), provoked some of its most controversial literary discussions (on proletarian literature and Marxist literary criticism), and published some of the best radical literature to come out of the '30s (the reportage of Meridel Le Sueur, John L. Spivak, Josephine Herbst, and Agnes Smedley). Stressing sectarian and domestic issues in the first half of the decade, after the opening of the Popular Front the magazine tended to focus more and more on the Spanish Civil War and the growing international fascist threat and became much more conciliatory toward liberals and other journals.

While it continued after the Soviet-Nazi Pact, from 1941 through 1947, as a weekly, the journal's political and literary positions were much narrower and its influence greatly diminished. In March, 1948, the magazine reappeared as the merged *Masses & Mainstream* to run until 1956, under the editorship of Samuel Sillen and Milton Howard. While its influence clearly waned after 1941, in its overall twenty-two-year history, from 1926 to 1948, the *New Masses* must still be considered the dominant radical literary journal in the second quarter of the twentieth century. *See also*: Communist Party; Conroy, Jack; Gellert, Hugo; Gold, Mike; *Mainstream*; McKenney, Ruth; Moscow Trials; Proletarian and Radical Writers; Smedley, Agnes; Wright, Richard

—*David Peck*

REFERENCES

Fitzgerald, Richard. "*New Masses*: New York, 1926–1948." In *The American Radical Press, 1880–1960*, edited by Joseph R. Conlin, vol. 2, Westport: Greenwood Press, 1974.

Klein, Marcus. *Foreigners: The Making of American Literature, 1900–1940*. Chicago: University of Chicago Press, 1981.

North, Joseph, ed. *New Masses: An Anthology of the Rebel Thirties*. New York: International Publishers, 1969.

Peck, David. "'The Tradition of American Revolutionary Literature': The Monthly *New Masses*, 1926–1933." *Science & Society* 42 (Winter 1978–79).

New York Call: see Socialist Party

New Yorker Volkszeitung

The daily *NYVZ* was first published on January 28, 1878, by the Socialist Cooperative Publishing Association of the Socialist Labor Party. It sold 5,500 copies at the beginning and continuously increased its circulation to between 17,000 and 23,000 copies. Economic pressures forced it to close down in 1932; shortly thereafter the weekly *Neue Volkszeitung* appeared as successor. The founding of the *NYVZ* was closely related to the intensification of the class struggle and organizational achievements of the labor movement. A year after the 1875 consolidation of the Eisenacher and Lassallean wings of German social democracy into one party, the united Working Men's Party was established, soon to become the SLP. German workers and emigrant socialists were active in the new party and were soon joined by the exiles from the newly enacted Bismarckian antisocialist laws. The *NYVZ*—jointly with the English-language the *People* (since 1891), later the *Worker*—became the main organ of the SLP. It was supplemented by a Sunday edition (*Sonntagsblatt*) and a weekly edition (*Vorwärts*). Editors were Alexander Jonas, 1878–89, Segius Schewitsch, 1890, Julius Grunzig, 1890–91, Hermann Schlüter, 1891–1919, Ludwig Lore, 1919–31, Siegfried Lipschitz, 1931–32.

Though active in the sometimes acrimonious debates of different SLP wings and outspoken against anarchist tendencies, the daily succeeded in surviving all party splits and sometimes assumed the position of mediator. The paper published German, American, and German-American news as well as international reports. It was the official organ of numerous workers' clubs, mutual aid societies, and unions (ninety-two in 1903). Its cultural pages reprinted classical authors of world literature from Maxim Gorki to Rudyard Kipling to Frank Norris. It published Plechanov, Liebknecht, Kerr, Zetkin, and Trotsky. Women received scant attention until—significantly—a separate women's page was added. The *NYVZ* was banned from Germany under the antisocialist law (though regularly read by Berlin police authorities). U.S. governmental repression during World War I remained limited though the *NYVZ* opposed the war, probably because of its outspoken stand against the German monarch. *See also*: German Americans; Lore, Ludwig; Socialist Labor Party; Sozial-Revolutionäire Clubs

—*Dirk Hoerder*

REFERENCES

Buhle, Paul. "Ludwig Lore and the *New Yorker Volkszeitung*," and Dirk Hoerder, "*The New Yorker Volkszeitung*." In *The German-American Radical Press*, edited by James Dankey, Ken Fones-Wolf, and Elliot Shore. Urbana: University of Illinois Press, 1990.

Newman, Pauline M. (1888?–1986)

The first salaried organizer for the International Ladies Garment Workers Union, Newman campaigned actively for woman suffrage under the auspices of the Socialist Party. She emigrated from Lithuania and within months of her arrival in New York City in 1901 began to work in the garment industry. During the 1909 shirtwaist makers' strike, Newman emerged as a talented speaker and organizer. Although she joined the Women's Trade Union League (WTUL) and remained a member until its demise in 1955, Newman identified foremost with the Jewish labor movement. After the shirtwaist makers' strike of 1909, she left the factory to organize women workers into the ILGWU in New England and the Midwest and played leading roles in strikes in Cleveland, Philadelphia, and Kalamazoo.

In 1908 Newman joined the whistle-stop presidential campaign of Eugene Debs, and later ran for Congress on the New York SP ticket. During the 1915 New York "Votes for Women" campaign, Newman served as a full-time organizer for the SP and toured the state by automobile.

Newman took an active role in the workers' education movement. As early as 1915 she worked with ILGWU Local 25 in establishing a broad educational network of Unity Centers. During the 1920s Newman joined the board of directors of the Bryn Mawr Summer School for Women Workers. She served as an adviser to the U.S. Department of Labor during the 1930s and 1940s.

Newman directed the educational programs of the ILGWU's health center—of which she was a founder—from 1924 until shortly before her death. *See also*: International Ladies Garment Workers Union, Socialist Party

—*Mari Jo Buhle*

REFERENCES

Dye, Nancy Schrom. *As Equals & As Sisters: Feminism, Unionism, and the Women's Trade Union League of New York*. Columbia: University of Missouri Press, 1980.

Wertheimer, Barbara Meyer. *We Were There: The Story of Working Women in America*. New York: Pantheon, 1977.

Newsreel and Post–New Left Radical Filmmaking

The first indication that a radical film revival might be imminent in the United States was Emile De Antonio's *Point of Order* (1964), a documentary using collage techniques to depict the McCarthy-Army hearings. The film not only challenged the Right politically but did so in an innovative film style. *Point of Order* had no spoken narrative, forcing viewers to arrive at their judgments without any directorial coaching on how to interpret the images presented. Variations on this style, particularly the often awkward avoidance of an unseen narrator, would be characteristic of the radical cinema of the 1970s and 1980s. De Antonio, who was personally close to the abstract expressionist painters of the 1950s, would continue to put his political perspectives into controversial forms. His work includes *Year of the Pig* (1968), a minihistory of post–World War II revolution in Vietnam; *Millhouse: A White Comedy* (1971), a critique of Richard Nixon; *Underground* (1976), a clandestine interview with the Weatherpeople; and *In the King of Prussia* (1982), a narrative concerning the Catholic antiwar movement associated with the Berrigan brothers.

The new movement got off to an official start in December 1967 when a group of filmmakers met in New York to launch Newsreel. The new organization sought to record the major events of the time from the point of view of radical dissenters. Films were to be made quickly and put to immediate use by the movement the films also sought to document. Within a year or so of its inception Newsreel had made nearly twenty films of varying lengths and had arranged for films made in Cuba and Vietnam to be distributed under its own auspices or that of allied groups. A dozen Newsreel groups were set up outside of New York, the most important being located in San Francisco, Washington, D.C., Boston, Los Angeles, and Ann Arbor. While aware of their precursors, the Newsreel founders were inclined to anarchistic forms of organization and were generally unsympathetic to the Communist Party, which they judged to be too timid. *Black Panther* (1968) and *Columbia Revolt* (1968) were early Newsreel successes and provided something of a financial base for new projects.

A flickering Newsreel logo whose movements were synchronized to the sound of machine-gun fire began each film. Hand-held cameras, grainy film stock, and bold editing gave the films a battlefield urgency. Indicative of Newsreel's total rejection of dominant culture was its ten-minute *Garbage* (1968). Made during a New York City garbage strike, the film shows radicals dumping their refuse in Lincoln Center, the cultural showcase of the "empire city." Other films addressed every issue of the New Left in the same disrespectful but often jovial manner. The blend of aesthetic and political innovation embodied the defiant and experimental nature of the New Left. Newsreel also attempted fiction films but most were received unenthusiastically by activists and critics.

By the early 1970s Newsreel began to be caught up in the general crisis of the movement. An all-male and all-white leadership that had indulged in marathon decision-making sessions was now challenged by women and nonwhites. These forces demanded a greater voice in Newsreel councils and greater access to equipment. Concurrent with this dissatisfaction was the phenomenon of many Newsreel members drifting away to pursue independent career objectives. The formal Newsreel membership of some threescore evaporated so swiftly that a reorganization conference was held in 1973. The continuing membership was almost entirely of Latin, Asian, or African ancestry. Most were women and none had been Newsreel founders. The new direction being undertaken was codified by a name change to Third World Newsreel.

In addition to making its own films, Third World Newsreel distributed films made by other radicals, kept the Newsreel library in circulation, and imported foreign films. Titles such as *The Steelmakers* (1968) from North Korea and *The Red Detachment of Women* (1968) from Mao's China as well as most of the original Newsreel films have been kept in constant distribution for more than fifteen years. Training sessions aimed at women, the disabled, the aged, and nonwhites were among many efforts to cinematically empower groups usually not associated with filmmaking. Closely allied with this effort were campaigns to create film audiences in nonwhite communities. This often led to the making of films in blunt and confrontational styles that did not always appeal to critics. The skills of Third World Newsreel, however, were being constantly honed and were most obvious in Chris Choy and Renee Tajama's *Who Killed Vincent Chin?* (1988). The film, which deals with race and class violence in Detroit, Michigan, got highly favorable commentary from the entire film community and was nominated for the 1988 Academy Award for Best Picture in the Documentary category.

San Francisco Newsreel proved to be another survivor. Its first film, *Black Panther*, was Newsreel's most widely screened film, but the collective soon moved to taking an economic and sexual issues as its major concern. Eventually the group changed its name to California Newsreel and under that name its best-known work is *Controlling Interest: The World of Multinationals* (1976). Like Third World Newsreel, it continued to distribute radical films made by others and after more than two decades of existence ended the 1980s as an extremely viable and well-respected production company.

The durability of California Newsreel and Third World Newsreel was typical of other filmmaking collectives, many with Newsreel veterans among their members, that sprang up after the demise of the original Newsreel. Concentrated in urban centers throughout the United States, the radical filmmakers took on gender, ethnic, racial, cultural, foreign policy, and sexual topics in what became a multiplicity of submovements, each of which was as prolific as the original Newsreel. The first post-Newsreel phase was marked by the emergence of a feminist film movement. This in turn was followed by movements that focused on Asian Americans, gay liberation, the environment, and Latin America. Characteristic of all the movements was the prominent role played by women. Whatever the specific topic at hand, women as producers, directors, exhibitors, and distributors took on the full range of creative responsibilities that had once been informally restricted to males. In many submovements such as films dealing with the role of the United States in Latin America, radical women dominated the field.

Among the various subgenres developed, one was of particular significance to the Left. This was the attempt to "recover" the history of American radicalism from mass-media distortions or silence. Such films include *Union*

Maids (1976), *With Babies and Banners* (1978), *The Wobblies* (1979), *Free Voice of Labor—The Jewish Anarchists* (1980), *Seeing Red* (1986), *The Good Fight* (1984), and *A Crime to Fit the Punishment* (1984). These feature-length documentaries were augmented by scores of shorter films about individual radicals, specific strikes, or regional organizations. The films tended to be generous in their assessment of the roles radicals had played in past struggles. Their purpose, which was largely realized, was to reestablish radical dissent as an honorable and worthwhile American tradition.

Closely related to the recovery films were films about organized labor and films about foreign affairs. The radicalism in the labor films tended to be implied rather than overt but was unmistakable. *Harlan County—USA* (1976) focused on Appalachian coal miners, *The Life and Times of Rosie the Riveter* (1980) on black and white women in the defense industries of WW II, *Miles of Smiles* (1982) on black Pullman Car porters, and *Northern Lights* (1979) on the Non-Partisan League of North Dakota. The foreign-affairs films were unrelenting in their criticism of U.S. motives and allies but less specific in their evaluation of various reformist and revolutionary movements. The topic of Latin America was of such interest that entire film libraries came into existence around specific nations such as Cuba, Guatemala, Nicaragua, and El Salvador. Deborah Shaffer's *Witness to War—An American Doctor in El Salvador* (1985) won an Academy Award in the documentary category, and films such as *El Norte* (1985) and *When the Mountains Tremble* (1986) were able to gain significant public visibility.

Radicals remained dissatisfied that their films did not get the same distribution as Hollywood-made films but in comparison to the 1930s, they were far more successful in reaching a general audience and in having an impact on the wider film community. In spite of the fact that most radical films were documentaries and that documentaries traditionally do not do well in theatrical distribution, some radical documentaries got theatrical releases and a few, like *Atomic Cafe* (1982), did quite well. More common were screenings on public television, during conferences, in classrooms, and at festivals. Radical films received more than their share of prizes at various competitions at home and abroad, and they were increasingly among the Academy Award nominees and winners. At least one radical film came to be a given at the prestigious New York Film Festival and got national exposure through reviews in mainstream media, including the *New York Times*, *Variety*, and the *Village Voice*.

Concerns about form and other esthetic problems were as intense as political convictions. American filmmakers did not write extensively about their craft but they made frequent appearances at seminars and gave substantive interviews. Radicals were also extremely active in self-distribution, exhibition, and networking. As a result a liberal/radical sensibility became the norm throughout the independent film community and even extended to some degree into the avant garde. A new tendency that began to emerge in the 1980s was the mixing of fiction and nonfiction in the same film, a format boldly probed in *Far from Poland* (1984), a film assessing the Solidarity movement in Poland.

Radical filmmakers were buttressed by a vigorous critical community. The two most important periodicals were *Cineaste* (founded 1967) and *Jump Cut* (founded 1973). *Cineaste* was the self-declared champion of the new movement and by the end of the 1980s enjoyed a worldwide reputation for excellence and was among the highest-circulation film journals in the United States. The more theoretically inclined *Jump Cut* was more directed to filmmakers than film viewers and had a strong commitment to gay films and radical video. Both magazines provided extensive coverage of Third World cinema with an emphasis on Latin America.

Cineaste and *Jump Cut* did not stand alone and their contributors were not isolated from the larger critical community. An associate editor of *Cineaste* became the editor of *American Film*, the organ of the American Film Institute, and later was an editor of *Premiere*, a major commercial publication. Writers who published with *Cineaste*, *Jump Cut*, and a half-dozen smaller journals also published in *Variety, Film Comment,* and the *New York Times.* Film critics for the *Guardian* and *In These Times* had similar access. Film associations and film departments were frequently headed by radicals, and commercial and university presses regularly issued books by radical critics who were often on the cutting edge of film scholarship. Radicals were also extremely active in the editing and publishing of standard reference materials in the field.

The vision of an alternative filmmaking, film distribution, and film exhibition network that was part of the 1960s' Newsreel perspective never fully came to pass, but a strong radical presence in those areas was established in the period from the time of Newsreel's founding to the end of the 1980s. Individual films had moved from one distributor to another and filmmakers had moved into various production organizations, but almost all the radical films made since the 1960s were easily available in the 1980s. In addition to self-distributing collectives such as New Day and the Pacific Street Collective, radical films were available through firms like Cinema Guild, Icarus/First Run, and Kino. Exhibition spaces were still the weakest link. Most were connected to universities or specialty film houses but there were a handful of community groups such as Philadelphia's Neighborhood Film Project. Organizations like Media Network, Women Make Movies, and Global Village provided a wide range of reference and technical services.

The revived film movement of the 1960s proved to be one of the most resilient components of the New Left. By the 1980s many of the movement's filmmakers, critics, and publications had achieved national and even international reputations. Although the cassette revolution had brought new challenges in the educational market and funding had been squeezed during the Reagan era, the radicals had not only survived but had achieved a measure of influence and in some areas leadership in their professions. *See also*: New Left, League of Revolutionary Black Workers, Radical Filmmaking—1930s

—*Dan Georgakas*

REFERENCES

Blackaby, Linda, Dan Georgakas, and Barbara Margolis. *In Focus: A Guide to Using Films.* New York: Zoetrope, 1980.

Cineaste, 5, no. 4 (1973). Special issue: Radical American Film.

Crowdus, Gary. Editorial. *Cineaste* 16, nos. 1, 2 (1987).

Georgakas, Dan. "Malpractice in the Radical American Documentary." *Cineaste* 16, nos. 1, 2 (1987).

Peyton, Patricia, ed. *Reel Change: A Guide to Social Issue Films.* San Francisco: The Film Fund, 1979.

Waugh, Thomas, ed. *"Show Us Life": Towards a History and Aesthetics of the Committed Documentary.* Metuchen, N.J.: Scarecrow Press, 1984.

Zheutlin, Barbara, coordinator. "The Art and Politics of the Documentary: A Symposium of Filmmakers." *Cineaste* 11, no. 3 (1981).

1919 Strike Wave

In 1919 about 20 percent of the nation's workers participated in the largest strike wave in U.S. history. Millions of workers were emboldened by tight wartime labor markets, increased personal savings, and ample union strike funds accumulated during World War I's full-employment economy. Wartime promises by President Woodrow Wilson of a new era of democracy in labor relations as a reward for workers' wartime sacrifices (which included forced purchase of Liberty bonds) also encouraged workers to militant action, as did the sense of change throughout the world created by the Russian Revolution and strikes and revolutionary uprisings in Germany, Hungary, and England. Striking workers in the United States wanted higher wages and shorter hours. They sought to protect unions' wartime gains against a widespread employer union-busting drive and to establish new, independent (not company financed and controlled) trade unions in many industries. Many of the strikes were led by radical activists of one kind or another, especially in newly organized unions, or at the local and regional level.

The year began with a January strike of New York City tugboat workers. In February thousands of textile workers in Lawrence, Massachusetts, and New Jersey's silk factories walked out. Between February 6 and 11, Seattle's transportation, service, and craft workers, including Japanese barbers and restaurant workers, came out in a general strike to support the city's shipyard workers' strike for equitable pay increases, especially for lower-paid workers. During the strike, workers established many cooperative enterprises for distributing consumer goods to the public. Although the strike was beaten by the threat of the deployment of federal troops and the declaration of martial law, Seattle radicals like Anna Louise Strong were heartened because the "vast majority [of Seattle workers] had struck to express solidarity. And they succeeded beyond their expectations."

In May a bitter strike by electrical workers in Toledo, Ohio, led to the deployment of federal troops to prevent what the *New York Times* claimed was an impending union takeover of the city. August saw intense strikes by railroad shopmen in Chicago, subway workers in New York City, and a threat by the national unions representing the operating employees of the railroads to launch a political strike if Congress did not approve the Plumb Plan to nationalize the railroads. California's railroads were paralyzed by a sympathy strike in support of urban streetcar operators' strikes.

September began with the nation's first police strike, as Boston's finest walked out to resist union-busting by the city's police commissioner. On September 22 the great steel strike began. William Z. Foster, a syndicalist who had parted with the Industrial Workers of the World because he favored "boring from within" mainstream labor unions by a class-conscious "militant minority," was the head of the steelworkers' organizing committee, which was created by the AFL. Many striking steelworkers believed victory would inaugurate a new era.

Socialist steelworkers expected more. In October 60,000 metalworkers in the San Francisco Bay Area walked out. The nation's coal miners struck in November. During the coal strike many railroad switchmen staged brief sympathy strikes to prevent the transport of "scab" coal.

Throughout the nation, employers and government officials were alarmed by worker militancy, which gave rise to the view, expressed so succinctly by an Arizona mine manager, that "with Bolshevism increasing every minute all over the world, how can we expect to escape?" Consequently, the U.S. Army was used to break the Toledo electrical workers' strike, the steel strike, and the coal strike (soldiers actually were mining coal in December in some mines). Threats of Navy intervention forestalled strikes by longshoremen and shortened strikes by tugboat operators. The National Guard was deployed to crush the Boston police strike and during the steel strike, various police forces—including the Pennsylvania State Police, the infamous "Cossacks"—brutally assaulted strikers on picket lines, in their homes, and at peaceful assemblies in meeting halls. The counter-offensive against unions and militant union leaders continued in the 1920s, as the Palmer Raids, vigilantee action by businessmen, the revived Ku Klux Klan, the courts, and the military power of the State combined to roll back virtually all the gains unionized American workers had made during the World War I era. But to radicals like William Z. Foster and Anna Louise Strong, the learning experience of the bold efforts of class-conscious workers was more important than the end of the strike wave and the decline of the labor movement. As Strong wrote, "A Great Change is coming over the face of the world . . . which will go deep into the very sources of our lives, to bring joy and freedom in place of heaviness and fear . . . our General Strike was one very definite step towards it." *See also*: General Strike; Strong, Anna Louise

—Robert Asher

REFERENCES

Brecher, Jeremy. *Strike!* San Francisco: Straight Arrow Press, 1972.

David Saposs Papers, State Historical Society of Wisconsin.

Strong, Anna Louise. *The Seattle General Strike.* Seattle: The Seattle Union Record Publishing Co., 1919.

Tom Mooney Scrapbooks, Bancroft Library, University of California, Berkeley.

RICHARD NIXON, WHITTAKER CHAMBERS, AND THE HISS CASE

In his book *Six Crises*, Richard Nixon wrote that had it not been for the Alger Hiss case, he would never have made it to the White House. He rightly observed, "My name, my reputation, and my career were ever to be linked with the decisions I made and the actions I took in that case, as a thirty-five-year-old freshman Congressman in 1948."

The Hiss case erupted on the consciousness of the American people just as the first postwar presidential campaign was getting underway. Beginning in August, the Republican-controlled House Committee on Un-American Activities (HUAC) started a series of hearings that featured ex-Communists Elizabeth Bentley and Whittaker Chambers. Their stories were difficult to disentangle and between them they named scores of former New Deal officials they claimed to have known or known of as Communists. The testimony of the forty-seven-year-old Chambers would have enormous political repercussions. He stated that from 1924 until 1937 he had been a functionary of the Communist Party. He named Alger Hiss, Hiss's younger brother Donald (at that time law partner of future secretary of state Dean Acheson), and six other former New Deal officials as having been part of a secret underground group organized in the 1930s by the CP. Chambers consistently testified that he and the group never engaged in espionage. He said, "I should perhaps make the point that these people were specifically not wanted to act as sources of information."

With the exception of the Hiss brothers, the individuals named by Chambers were publicly known as left-wing activists. Lee Pressman, John Abt, Nathan Witt, Victor Perlo, and Charles Kramer were officials of the newly formed Progressive Party, and Henry Collins was executive secretary of the American-Russian Institute. All six claimed their Fifth Amendment privilege and refused to testify. Donald Hiss appeared before HUAC to deny Chambers's allegations and to state that the only organizations he had ever belonged to were the Boy Scouts of America and the Maryland Yacht Club.

The most prominent of those named was Alger Hiss, then forty-four years old and president of the Carnegie Endowment for International Peace. Previously Hiss had worked as staff counsel for the Agricultural Adjustment Administration and for the Nye senate committee investigating the munitions industry; this had been followed by service with the State Department, beginning in 1936. Hiss had gone to the "Big Three" Yalta conference in 1945 as an adviser to President Franklin D. Roosevelt and had capped his government service by presiding over the founding session of the United Nations as its general secretary. Hiss appeared before HUAC at his own request and denied categorically the Chambers allegations. He denied having known anyone named Whittaker Chambers and he testified that he had never been a member or sympathizer of the CP. Shown a newspaper photo of his accuser, a man he was not alleged to have seen in more than a decade, Hiss requested a face-to-face confrontation. Richard M. Nixon, then a freshman Republican congressman, volunteered to chair a special subcommittee to follow through on the identification. Truman had already held an August 5 press conference in which he berated the HUAC hearings as a Republican Party election-year ploy and a "red herring" to distract the public's attention from the "do-nothing" record of the Republican-controlled eightieth Congress.

Using leaks and statements to the press, Nixon quickly managed to make the dispute between Hiss, president of the nation's leading proponent for world peace, and Chambers, a senior editor of *Time*, the number-one news story of the day. When the confrontation requested by Hiss finally took place on August 17, Hiss identified his accuser as a free-lance writer who had identified himself as George Crosley. Hiss stated that Crosley had said he was planning to write about the munitions-industry hearings and in 1935 had sublet an apartment from Hiss for six weeks.

The Nixon subcommittee's highly partisan activities relating to what it called a "spy" case investigation were published as *Hearings Regarding Communist Espionage in the United States*. The Nixon report stated that the committee had secured from Chambers "testimony regarding Communist espionage activities within the Government" and that its "investigation of espionage" had been "hampered at every turn" by the Truman administration.

The Hiss-Chambers contradictions got into court following statements made by Chambers at the end of August on a *Meet the Press* network radio program. Chambers repeated the charge that he had worked with Hiss in a secret underground CP apparatus that had no espionage function. He said its purpose was to influence policy by getting Communists into key places in government. Unlike his HUAC testimony, these remarks did not enjoy congressional immunity. Hiss filed a $75,000 lawsuit for slander in a federal district court in Baltimore.

The pre-trial sworn depositions of this libel suit (abandoned after Hiss was indicted for perjury) established as a sham every essential element in Chambers's accusations. Chambers was not even able to offer any proof that he had ever been a CP member, much less a full-time employee. For three of the thirteen years he claimed to have been a full-time Communist functionary, Chambers had been employed full-time as a twenty-dollar-a-week clerk in the New York Public Library (1924–27), and for another two years he had been a salesclerk in secondhand bookstores. Another full year had been spent in bed! Chambers testified that the suicide of his younger brother had been so devastating that he had been totally immobilized for a full twelve months. Before being hired by *Time* in 1939, Chambers also had spent considerable time as a translator, beginning with his much-praised translation of Felix Salten's *Bambi* from German to English for Simon & Schuster in 1927. *Books in Print* lists fourteen full-length books translated by Chambers from French or German into English during the next decade—the very period he had testified before HUAC that his only employment was as a CP functionary.

Further complicating his testimony was the fact that Chambers had described himself as an "enemy" of the Party from 1929 to 1932 and an ally of its opponents. His only verifiable links to the Left were four short stories published in *New Masses* in 1931 and a twenty-line poem in the Sunday *Worker* in 1926. Other poems and short stories were published in the *Nation, Poetry, Two Worlds,* and small university magazines. In two days of pretrial dispositions, Chambers said he had been ordered into the CP underground after his short stories were published in *New Masses*. Except for Hiss and Max Bedacht, a longtime CP official whose expulsion from the Party had recently been reported, his only associates in the underground during his claimed five years of such service, 1932–37, were unidentifiable fellow conspirators who had no last names.

At the end of two days of examination by Hiss's lawyer, Chambers was so overcome "with despair" that he contemplated killing himself by taking cyanide, a disclosure made in his 1952 autobiography, *Witness*. Equally depressing for Chambers and for Nixon, HUAC, the Republican Party, *Time*, and others who had championed and exploited his story was the upset victory of Harry Truman in the November elections. Within days there was an indictment on payroll charges of J. Parnell Thomas, chairman of HUAC. Two months later, Thomas was in a federal prison.

On November 17, after a twelve-day recess in the libel suit, Chambers returned for more questioning. He now told a new tale. He produced sixty-five typewritten sheets, dated from January to April 1938, that he identified as copies of State Department documents that "I had forgotten I had." He said they had been given to him by Alger Hiss to be handed over to a Russian agent. At Hiss's insistence all of this material was immediately turned over to the Justice Department. The attorney general asked both sides to say nothing for two weeks until the new development was investigated. One thing was now certain: Chambers had committed perjury. Either his HUAC testimony that he and Hiss had been part of a CP network that did not engage in espionage or his new testimony to the contrary must have been false.

The next public development was an announcement in December that created more headlines than anything HUAC had ever done in its ten-year history. On the evening of December 2 Whittaker Chambers had retrieved from a pumpkin patch on his farm in Westminster, Maryland, five rolls of microfilms (thereafter dubbed the "pumpkin papers"). These were described as "secret" State Department material handed over to Whittaker Chambers by a member of the CP underground. As far as the public could tell, the films verified the spy charges spearheaded by Congressman Nixon and hammered away at by the Republicans in the just-completed presidential campaign. Nixon appeared to be vacationing in the Caribbean. From shipboard he radiogrammed, "Will reopen hearings if necessary to prevent Justice Department coverup." On December 5, the front page of newspapers throughout the country showed a Navy seaplane picking up Nixon in the Caribbean and rushing him back to Washington, where, before examining any new evidence, he told the press that the new materials proved "once and for all that where you have a Communist you have an espionage agent." What only became public after Hiss had gone to prison was that Nixon had visited Chambers in Westminster a number of times while Chambers was preparing his libel-suit defense. Nixon had also gone to see Chambers at the farm the night before Chambers turned over the five rolls of film to HUAC investigators. Nixon had gone back to Washington, written out a subpoena, and then flown to Florida in order to be thousands of miles away on board a vacation ship when the "discovery" of the pumpkin papers was announced.

The Justice Department reconvened a grand jury in New York, but in Washington the Nixon subcommittee held its own hearings. In a two-week attack against the Truman Justice Department, Nixon charged the Democrats were planning to cover up what he called "the most serious series of treasonable activities . . . in the history of America." Front-page photos showed Nixon standing alongside a four-foot-high pile of documents processed from the Chambers films. Nixon would not allow the Justice Department personnel, grand jurors, a federal judge, the press, or anyone to examine this "shocking" evidence for themselves. A quarter of a century later when the films were obtained through the Freedom of Information Act, they were revealed to be information relating to Navy rafts, life preservers, and fire extinguishers. The films were of documents from the Bureau of Standards which had been available to the general public at its library.

On December 15, following a steady barrage of Nixon-generated headlines about treason, the grand jury indicted Alger Hiss for perjury. The first trial lasted seven weeks, from May to July 1949, and ended in a mistrial. Immediately after the decision, Judge Samuel H. Kaufman, a Truman appointee, was subject to a week-long Nixon campaign berating him as "prejudiced for the defense." Nixon called for Kaufman's impeachment. The second trial would be presided over by a seventy-year-old judge who had been appointed by Calvin Coolidge.

Setting the stage for Senator Joseph McCarthy's hallmark cry "twenty years of treason" was the charge leveled by Nixon that the Democrats under the New Deal of Roosevelt and the Fair Deal of Truman were "soft" on Communism. Once the second Hiss trial returned a guilty verdict, there was no restraining the freshman congressman who had made these allegations when no evidentiary justification existed. On January 26, 1950, the day after Hiss was sentenced, Nixon delivered a four-hour House speech that he titled "Lessons of the Hiss Case." The high point of the address was his accusation that in September 1939 Chambers had gone to Washington and presented evidence of espionage and the government had done nothing. Nixon put it thus, ". . . concrete information concerning Communist espionage activities in this country was in the hands of both President Roosevelt and President Truman and still no action was taken." While not true, this was accepted without challenge in many quarters.

In the face of the supposedly proven Communist menace, the existence of treasonous activity, and government laxity in national security matters, Nixon proposed a five-point program. He asked for (1) new legislation to deal with internal security and new types of espionage, (2) unqualified support for the FBI and its chief, J. Edgar Hoover, (3) total support, authority, and funds for congressional investigations of subversives, (4) complete overhaul of the loyalty program so that all doubts could be resolved in favor of the government, and (5) an educational effort to alert the American people to the dangers of the Communist conspiracy.

Nixon himself characterized this speech as the most important of his pre-White House career. The Republican Party published the full text of it in a booklet titled *The Hiss Case*, as the principal campaign document in Nixon's 1952 crusade for the vice presidency. Most significant of all, perhaps, is that the speech provided a point-by-point—and in many passages a word-for-word—agenda for Senator Joseph R. McCarthy, who began his overnight emergence just two weeks later, in a Lincoln Day speech at Wheeling, West Virginia. Forty years later documents presented in connection with Hiss's post-trial appeals have established Nixon's duplicity. *See also*: Anticommunism, Federal Bureau of Investigation, Alger Hiss Perjury Trials, House Committee on Un-American Activities, McCarthyism, Progressives, the Taft-Hartley Loyalty Oath

—*William A. Reuben*

REFERENCES

Andrews, Bert. *A Tragedy of History*. Washington, D.C.: Luce, 1962.

Chambers, Whittaker. *Witness*. New York: Random House, 1952.

Cook, Fred J. *The Unfinished Story of Alger Hiss*. New York: Morrow, 1958.

Hiss, Alger. *In the Court of Public Opinion*. New York: Knopf, 1957.

Reuben, William A. *The Atom Spy Hoax*. New York: Action Books, 1955.

———. *The Honorable Mr. Nixon*. Rev. ed. New York: Action Books, 1960.

Smith, John Cabot. *Alger Hiss: The True Story*. New York: Holt, Rinehart, Winston, 1976.

NORTH AMERICAN COMMITTEE TO AID SPANISH DEMOCRACY

Of those Americans who actively demonstrated concern about the needs of the Spanish people during their civil war, the great majority expressed their sympathy and admiration for the Republic. They participated in and contributed to a number of Left-influenced humanitarian organizations, the largest of which was the North American Committee to Aid Spanish Democracy. It was organized in October 1936, chaired by Bishop Francis J. McConnell. Its secretary was Reverend Herman F. Reissig and it quickly became an umbrella organization with which a number of specialized organizations affiliated.

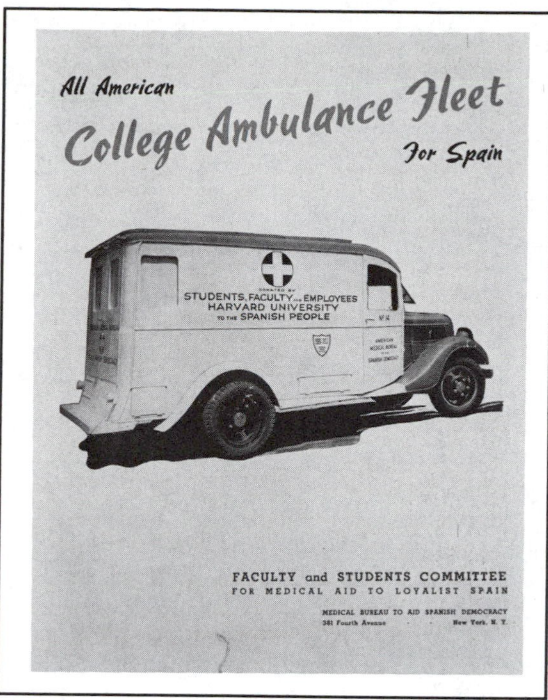

Ambulance donated by students, faculty, and employees of Harvard University

Two of the most important affiliates were the American Friends of Spanish Democracy, headed by Bishop Robert L. Paddock, whose major concern was organizing protests aimed at changing the course of Washington's policy toward Spain; and the other was the popular Medical Bureau to Aid Spanish Democracy, headed by Walter B. Cannon of the Harvard Medical School.

The list of sponsors looks like a Who's Who of the time—with scores of representatives from the arts, sciences, and the professions. The committee was supported by the Socialist and Communist parties as well as by liberals prominent in all walks of life. Never before had so many Americans been so stirred and activized by an event abroad in which the nation was not directly involved.

There were about 150 chapters nationwide raising funds and organizing support for the beleaguered Spanish Republic. In the twenty-one months after its inception, the North American Committee raised more than $1 million (with 1930s purchasing power) in cash and in kind. Hundreds of tons of food, clothing, and medical supplies had been collected; Americans sent to Spain 175 ambulances and motor vehicles; eight hospitals were maintained with personnel of 125 American doctors and nurses; and ten homes housing more than 600 children were established.

All this was accomplished (through special committees such as musicians, trade unions, youth, Hollywood, university faculty, and so on) by means of a variety of functions: fairs, picnics, concerts, lectures, mass meetings—two at Madison Square Garden in New York—dances, concerts, film showings, house parties, street collections, gala benefits with scores of stars of stage and screen (many of whom were subsequently harassed by the infamous House Committee on Un-American Activities) and tours of Spanish delegations. Pamphlets and brochures in the tens of thousands were printed and distributed. Special drives were initiated for funds to aid wounded Americans returning from the battlefields.

Not long after the end of the war (March 31, 1939), most of these humanitarian organizations dissolved, to be replaced by organizations whose aim was to raise funds for the relief of Spanish exiles, especially those in France and in Mexico. *See also*: Abraham Lincoln Brigade

—*Albert Prago*

REFERENCES

David McKelvey White Archives and the Rare Book Division, New York Public Library.

North American Congress on Latin America

NACLA was founded in 1966 by church and academic people as a response to the 1965 U.S. invasion of the Dominican Republic and as an expression of New Left protest. Based in New York City, it has been chiefly known for its magazine, *NACLA Report on the Americas*, although its staff has organized and participated in Latin American solidarity organizations and has undertaken seminars, forums, public speaking tours, and other educational activities.

Since its founding, NACLA has been defined by a concern for the relationship of intellectual work to Left political activism. Using an academic methodology influenced by Marxism but emphasizing empirical data, NACLA has sought to produce information for the progressive community that demythologizes U.S. political and economic institutions that perpetuate exploitation in Latin America and the Caribbean.

NACLA has contributed to a broader comprehension of U.S. imperialism, and of the nature and complexities of Latin American and Caribbean liberation struggles. Important articles and studies it has produced include a number on the Allende period in Chile and its aftermath; the U.S. defense and intelligence establishments; the globalization of U.S. capitalism and the new international division of labor; revolution and U.S. counterinsurgency in Nicaragua, El Salvador, and Guatemala. NACLA's example has also encouraged the development of information centers within the church, labor, peace, and solidarity communities. *See also*: Latin American Studies

—*Robert Armstrong*

Norwegian Americans

Norwegian immigrants who flocked to the United States in the middle and later nineteenth century took a somewhat less prominent role than Danes and Swedes in urban districts such as Chicago, where a Scandinavian Socialist Federation, and later a Scandinavian Communist Federation, were centered and published their various organs. Norwegians were more prominent in the farmer-labor politics of Minnesota and the Dakotas of the 1910s–1920s. The legends of Marcus Thrane, Norwegian founder of Scandinavian socialism (and for a short time a prominent leader of Chicago socialists), and of playwright Henrik Ibsen lived on in the minds of newer generations.

The waves of immigrants after World War I were not as politically oriented as their predecessors, but the Depression of the 1930s impoverished them terribly. By 1930–31, a Scandinavian Workers Club was founded in Brooklyn, New York, and a socialistic newspaper, *Ny Tid*, published in the Swedish, Danish, and Norwegian languages. The leading figures were mostly self-trained intellectuals. Along with the press, Norwegian socialists provided a lively chorus, a classical orchestra, gymnastics facilities, and a clubhouse atmosphere for their unemployed supporters. For several years, a school and recreation club were maintained on Staten Island. Some of the most ardent activists enrolled in the Abraham Lincoln Brigade and were killed in Spain. After a final phase of activity, notably in the peace movement as the Norwegian Labor Club, the group dissolved.

—*Olufson Hauge, translated and transcribed by Einar M. S. Bredland*

Nowak, Stanley (*b. 1903*)

Born into a peasant family in Austrian Poland, Nowak migrated to the Back-of-the-Yards section of Chicago in 1913. Radicalized by the Palmer Raids and by packinghouse strikes, he became a left-wing journalist and speaker in the late 1920s and 1930s and a member of the Proletarian Party. Relocated to Detroit, Nowak turned United Auto Workers organizer, working primarily with Polish and other East European workers. He pioneered the use of ethnic radio programs as an organizing tool.

Elected to the Michigan State Senate (1939–48), Nowak helped found and became an organizer for the American Slav Congress during World War II. From these positions, he exerted great and, among Poles, almost uniquely powerful influence on the Left. Close to the Communist Party, he never officially joined. The government indicted him under the McCarran-Walter Act in preparing his deportation, but the order was overturned in court in 1957. The same year, he became editor of the Left Polish-language paper *Glos Ludowy* (Popular voice), holding that post until 1984. His wife, Margaret Collingwood Nowack, shared these activities and was especially active in the Progressive Party. *See also*: American Slav Congress, Polish Americans

—*Thaddeus Radzilowski*

REFERENCES

Nowack, Margaret C. *Two Who Were There*. Detroit: Wayne State University Press, 1989.

Nykino: see Radical Filmmaking, 1930s

Oakland General Strike of 1946

The last of five citywide general strikes by U.S. workers in 1946, the strike grew out of a walkout by about 1,000 members of the Department Store and Specialty Clerks Union Local 1265 against two downtown department stores. The action eventually paralyzed production for almost four days.

Nonunion truckers from Los Angeles tried to cross union picket lines at Hasting's Department Store in Oakland early on Monday morning December 2, 1946. Strikers tried to block driveways in front of the store, but a squad of Oakland police officers escorted the trucks past the picket lines.

The Alameda County AFL Labor Council officially endorsed a general strike to begin Tuesday morning, December 3, a day after most workers walked off the job on their own. Eventually more than 10,000 joined in the general work stoppage. By Monday evening groups of workers began closing virtually all of the businesses in the city except for pharmacies and grocery stores. Strikers allowed anyone to leave the downtown area, but they allowed only workers with union cards to enter it. A carnival mood prevailed among the strikers as they allowed taverns to remain open, but dragged jukeboxes outside into the streets.

Twenty thousand workers attended a mass meeting on Tuesday night at the Oakland Auditorium, while thousands of others waited outside in the rain, listening to the proceedings on loudspeakers. Representatives from 142 unions voiced support for the retail clerks' strike demands and went on record against police intervention in the strike.

During the next thirty-six hours, workers took diverse actions to enforce their control over the city. They formed patrols to prevent looting, monitored grocery store sales to prevent hoarding, and imposed price controls to prevent price gouging. Five thousand strikers massed in front of the struck department stores and celebrated their control over the downtown area.

Newspaper editorials condemned the strike as "unrestrained" and "juvenile," while Oakland's mayor called the work stoppage an example of mob rule. International Brotherhood of Teamsters national president Dave Beck condemned the strike as "nothing but a revolution," and ordered his members to get back to work. Oakland's Teamsters remained out.

On Thursday morning, December 5, the city manager reached an agreement with Labor Council officials to end the standoff. The city pledged to refrain from using police officers to shepherd strikebreakers across picket lines, while labor leaders pledged to end the general strike. Dissident rank-and-file strikers protested against the agreement because they felt it did nothing to help the striking clerks win their initial demands, but after sporadic picketing and demonstrating on

Thursday and Friday the strike finally came to a close.

Besides paralyzing production in the Oakland area for almost four days, the strike's 100,000 worker participants forced the city police department to assume a more neutral stance in labor-management disputes and they gained a greater sense of the community of interests binding them together. In the aftermath of the strike, four prolabor candidates won election to the Oakland City Council. In addition, the general strike contributed to the nationwide militancy characterizing American workplaces in 1946 and 1947 as the country witnessed the largest wave of strikes in its history. *See also*: General Strike

—*George Lipsitz*

REFERENCES

Lipsitz, George. *"A Rainbow at Midnight": Class and Culture in Cold War America*. Hadley, Mass.: Bergin & Harvey, 1982.

OCTOBER LEAGUE: see "ANTI-REVISIONISM" (MAOISM)

ODETS, CLIFFORD (1906–63)

The most successful Left playwright of the 1930s, Odets was born to Lithuanian Jewish parents and raised in New York City. Abandoning high school in his third year, Clifford dreamed of becoming a poet. He did not turn to the theater until 1928, when he began acting with the Theatre Guild and was inspired by the work of John Howard Lawson. In 1933, Odets began writing plays, his first—*Awake and Sing!*—produced by the Group Theatre in 1935. That same year he wrote in three days his one-act play *Waiting for Lefty*, which won the New York Theatre League contest and brought him to the attention of the theater public. Widely performed as Left theater (sometimes by local union groups) across the United States in the next several years, this labor play (with its actors chanting "STRIKE, STRIKE, STRIKE!" at the conclusion) took its inspiration from a New York taxi strike of 1934.

Odets joined the Communist Party in 1935 and visited Cuba to study the political situation there. He was arrested by the authorities as a Communist. Returning to the United States, he finished three works that would be hits in 1936: *Till the Day I Die*, *Awake and Sing!*, and *Paradise Lost*. Almost singlehandedly, Odets made radical theater a paying concern in New York City, and a prime medium for political expression. He also began work in Hollywood, where he could earn $2,500 a week. His first filmed script, *The General Died at Dawn* (1936), prompted the oft-quoted barb, "Odets, where is thy sting?"

Driven by his need for public acclaim and simultaneously haunted by self-doubts at the cost of his success, Odets returned to Broadway with *Golden Boy* (1937) and *Rocket to the Moon* (1938). Both were critical and popular hits. For the first time, a playwright had brought the Jewish experience to the English-language American stage. Audiences were moved by a rich household vernacular that was permeated with a stark assessment of capitalism's ravages upon the spirit, and no less with a lyrical yearning for a better world. Critics consider these his finest works.

But Odets increasingly felt a sense of futility and self-betrayal in his work, with Hollywood as metaphor of corruption. In 1952 he appeared as a friendly witness for the House Un-American Activities Committee. This destroyed his credibility as a radical, and on his deathbed Odets swore that it had ruined his later life. Evidently, Odets needed Left culture for personal self-worth and as an artistic wellspring. Harold Clurman described Odets's work as a confession of personal anguish "at sharing those values in our civilization that he despised." One of his last serious plays, *The Big Knife* (1949), featured a protagonist who had gone from idealism to cynicism, desperation, and finally suicide. The only play to be produced after his testimony, *The Flowering Peach*, was a folksy retelling of the Noah's Ark legend. *See also*: Hollywood Blacklist; Lardner, Ring, Jr.

—*Norma Jenckes*

REFERENCES

Brenman-Gibson, Margaret. *Clifford Odets: American Playwright*. New York: Atheneum, 1982.

Murray, Edward. *Clifford Odets: The Thirties and After*. New York: Frederick Ungar, 1968.

Williams, Jay. *Stage Left*. New York: Scribner's, 1974.

Oehler, Hugo (1903–83)

An important figure in the Communist Party in the 1920s, Hugo Oehler was especially esteemed by his comrades for his successful efforts as trade union organizer of textile workers in the Deep South and mine workers in Colorado. He was the Party's district organizer in Kansas when he declared himself a Trotskyist in 1930 and joined the U.S. section of the International Left Opposition.

Elected a year later to the National Committee of the U.S. Trotskyists' group, the Communist League of America, Oehler for several years played a key role in the American Trotskyist movement, and was a frequent contributor to its paper, the *Militant*. In 1932 he was sent on a tour of Germany to warn the working class of the impending dangers of Nazism and the ineffectiveness of Communist and social-democratic strategies against it. The following year, back in New York, he helped direct the large hotel-workers' strike, and in 1934 he organized the unemployed as part of the famous strike of the Minneapolis Teamsters.

At an international conference of Trotskyists in October 1934 Oehler spoke against the so-called French Turn—i.e., the entry of Trotskyists into the supposedly leftward-moving social-democratic parties. A year later he and nearly a third of his fellow Trotskyists were expelled from the U.S. Trotskyist group for their opposition to this strategy. Oehler and some 200 other expellees went on to form the Chicago-based Revolutionary Workers League (often called "Oehlerites" by its opponents), whose official publication was the *Fighting Worker*, supplemented by an occasional Spanish-language paper, *Claridad Proletaria*.

Early in 1937 Oehler went to revolutionary Spain as representative of the RWL and wrote extensively of his experiences there. He took part in the workers' revolt against provocations of the "popular front" police in Barcelona in May 1937, and his pamphlet *Barricades in Barcelona* is one of the most valuable firsthand accounts of those events that marked a turning point in the Spanish Revolution. After the Barcelona revolt was crushed, Oehler was arrested, held incommunicado for a month and accused of "spying," but was finally allowed to leave the country.

Oehler continued to head the RWL until he moved to Denver in 1941, when leadership of the group was assumed for several years by Sidney Lens; the RWL disappeared in the 1950s. Increasingly aloof from practical politics, Oehler devoted the last decades of his life to an elaborate project for a scientific philosophy based on his own rather eccentric conception of materialist dialectics. *See also*: Trotskyism

—*Franklin Rosemont*

REFERENCES

Lens, Sidney. *Unrepentant Radical*. Boston: Beacon Press, 1983.

Revolutionary History 34 (Summer 1988).

OFF OUR BACKS

Dubbed by some "the *New York Times* of the women's movement," *off our backs* has been an indispensable guide to anyone interested in understanding the evolution of the women's liberation movement over the past seventeen years. *oob* was founded in early 1970 by veteran New Leftist and *Guardian* correspondent Marilyn Webb, and Marlene Wickes, after Webb, weary of what she de-

1971 cover

scribed as the *Guardian*'s "consistent blackout on feminist news," broached the idea of publishing a women's news journal.

When *oob* began publishing, women's liberationists were typically divided into two camps—Left feminists who believed that women's oppression was largely a function of capitalism and should be fought within the larger radical movement, and radical feminists who believed that it resulted from male supremacy and that its eradication required a separate and autonomous women's movement. Initially, *oob* articulated the former position. Thus, the editorial in its inaugural issue called on women to "oppose and destroy the system that fortifies the supremacy of men while exploiting the mass for the profit of the few." And in an effort to distinguish itself from radical feminism, the staff emphasized that "our position is not antimen but prowomen."

Eager to distinguish itself from liberal feminism as well, the staff made it clear that it took its inspiration from Third World revolutionary women, not Betty Friedan. The paper was filled with glowing reports about women's situations in Vietnam, Cuba, and China, where, if *oob* was to be believed, sexism was rapidly becoming a thing of the past. But the paper was not dogmatically attached to the politico position; within its first year of publication it printed several articles excoriating the male-dominated movement for continued sexism.

As the Left disintegrated and as the women's movement flourished, *oob*ers, like other Left feminists, began to move toward radical feminism. Between 1973 and 1978 *oob* printed some of the most incisive radical feminist writing to be found anywhere. Nor did *oob* repudiate the Left in this period, for, like many radical feminists, its writers believed that radical feminism entailed an expansion rather than a rejection of the Left. Over the years this perspective has receded, as *oob*, reflecting changes within the movement as a whole, has moved closer to cultural feminism—a strand of feminism that among other things believes that feminism and the Left are inevitably antagonistic. *See also*: Socialist Feminism, Women's Liberation

—*Alice Echols*

REFERENCES

Echols, Alice. *Daring to Be Bad: A History of the Radical Feminist Movement in America, 1967–75*. Minneapolis: University of Minnesota Press, 1989.

Willis, Ellen. "Radical Feminism and Feminist Radicalism." In *The '60s Without Apology*, edited by Sohnya Sayres, Anders Stephanson, Stanley Aronowitz, Fredric Jameson. Minneapolis: University of Minnesota, 1984.

O'HARE, KATE RICHARDS (1876–1948)

The Socialist Party's leading female agitator in the Debsian era, O'Hare embodied the best in the American radical tradition while exhibiting many of the contradictions faced by socialists operating in a racist, sexist, and reformist society. A champion of the downcast, O'Hare espoused political activism, mass organization, and education as the means of enacting pragmatic, evolutionary socialism.

Born in Ottawa County, Kansas, Kate Richards taught school briefly before becoming an apprentice in Kansas City, where she joined the International Association of Machinists. She also served actively in the temperance movement, directing her attention to prostitutes and unwed mothers. Disillusion with her church and a talk by Mary "Mother" Jones put her on the road toward socialism.

Training as a SP organizer in 1901, she met fellow radical and Saint Louisan Frank P. O'Hare, who became her husband and partner in political activism until they divorced in 1928. Between 1901 and 1917 the O'Hares raised four children as they spread the socialist gospel, enlisted party locals, wrote voluminously for the radical press, and edited the *National Rip-Saw*. Fiery oratory made Kate O'Hare a star of the Great Plains socialist encampments where poor farmers and migrant workers gathered to hear radical speakers in a carnivallike atmosphere.

While she developed a close attachment to Eugene V. Debs of the party's left wing, her ideology was closer to the more moderate reform-minded Hillquit-Berger faction. O'Hare deplored the direct action of the Industrial Workers of the World, accepted the segregation of the races as a necessity, and backed away from the left wing's demand for the rapid collectivization of agriculture. An outspoken advocate of birth control, she supported suffrage as a way for women to defend their natural sphere, the home, looking to the day when socialism would allow them to concentrate on raising their families.

In April 1917 O'Hare headed the party committee that drew up a statement vigorously condemning participation in World War I. Arrested and convicted under the Espionage Act for speaking out against the war, she began serving a five-year prison term in April 1919, as the Red Scare gained momentum. Released almost fourteen months later, she found what remained of the American Left split into competing factions. The O'Hares launched crusades for prison reform and amnesty for their jailed comrades, and published two books written while she was in prison, *Kate O'Hare's Prison Letters* (1919) and *In Prison* (1920).

Remarried, Kate O'Hare Cunningham worked for Upton Sinclair's End Poverty in California campaign in 1934, served as assistant director of the California Department of Penology under Governor Culbert Olson, and remained active in prison reform until her death. *See also*: Agrarian Radicalism, Socialist Party

—Peter Buckingham

REFERENCES

Basen, Neil K. "Kate Richards O'Hare: The 'First Lady' of American Socialism, 1901–1917." *Labor History* 21 (Spring 1980).

Foner, Philip S., and Sally M. Miller, eds. *Kate Richards O'Hare: Selected Writings and Speeches*. Baton Rouge: University of Louisiana Press, 1982.

OLGIN, MOISSAYE J. (1878–1939)

Yiddish writer and journalist, editor of several Yiddish socialist publications in Russia and the United States, Olgin served as editor of the Yiddish Communist daily newspaper in New York, *Freiheit*, later *Morgen Freiheit*, from its founding in April 1922.

Olgin (family name Moishe Yankl Novomeisky) was born in a small town near Kiev, Ukraine. In 1900 he became a student at Kiev University and was expelled after two years for revolutionary activity. Later, in Vilna (now Vilnius), he became an activist in the Bund, the underground Jewish social-democratic party in Russia. During the 1905 revolution he wrote all the public statements issued by the Bundist leadership and was dubbed the Bund's "golden pen." Following the failure of the revolution he devoted much time to Yiddish education for workers and prepared two Yiddish grammar texts. Beginning in 1910 he studied German literature at Heidelberg University. He arrived in New York in 1915 and became a contributor to the *Jewish Daily Forward* and other Yiddish socialist periodicals. Olgin also studied at Columbia University. His doctoral thesis was issued in book form in 1918 under the title *The Soul of the Russian Revolution*. He spurned offers to accept a teaching appointment at a few American universities, preferring to work with the Yiddish socialist movement.

After the Bolshevik Revolution (November 1917) Olgin became the leader of the pro-Communist faction in the Jewish Federation of the Socialist Party and in 1921 brought it into the Communist Party. Under Olgin's editorship, the *Freiheit* attracted some of the most popular Yiddish writers and poets of the period.

Though Olgin shared the Stalinist viewpoint of the American Communists, he was quick to take advantage of the Party's turn to its Popular Front position in the mid-1930s, when a less rigid sectarian outlook was promoted. In this period Olgin proposed united-front action within the Jewish community against anti-Semitism and fascism and to seek the cooperation of Zionists and even bourgeois spokesmen in this effort. He also expressed appreciation for American democracy in an essay entitled "I Love America," which irritated party hard-liners.

In his last years Olgin became more involved with Yiddish cultural problems. At the World Yiddish Cultural Congress held in Paris in 1937 he delivered the main report, in which he developed a program for the Yiddish secular and progressive cultural movement.

Olgin was also a noted translator in several languages and was among the first translators of Lenin's works into English. He translated a number of important fictional works of European and American writers into Yiddish. During the 1920s and '30s Olgin was an authoritative and much-beloved figure in the Yiddish Left. The procession at his funeral in Manhattan on November 27, 1939, attracted more than 100,000. *See also*: Yiddish Left

—*Sid Resnick*

REFERENCES

Buhle, Paul. "Jews and American Communism: The Cultural Question." *Radical History Review* 23 (Spring 1980).

Olsen, Tillie (b. 1913)

Few American women authors of recent years have underscored the integral connections between feminist politics and working-class realities more forcefully than Tillie Olsen. Now in her mid-seventies, in her career Olsen has largely come to symbolize the deep-rooted societal and cultural obstacles faced by women who create. In nearly everything she has written since the 1930s, Olsen reveals the fundamental conviction that women throughout history have suffered silencing hardships and neglect in their struggles for self-expression. Her career now spans five decades, making Olsen a key figure in the development of a feminist movement concerned with gender, race, and class oppression. Olsen's own life experiences reflect this development.

Olsen was born Tillie Lerner in 1913 in Omaha, Nebraska, the second of seven children. Her parents were Jewish immigrants who fled Russia in 1905 after the failed rebellion. Her father worked at menial jobs while he pursued political activism as state secretary of the Nebraska Socialist Party. The family could not support itself, and Olsen left high school after the eleventh grade to work. When she was seventeen, she joined the Young Communist League, the youth organization of the American Communist Party.

The economic crisis of 1929 and the decision to join the YCL appear crucial in the young author's life. The YCL sent Olsen to Kansas City, where she was arrested for her participation in organizing a packinghouse strike. These experiences led Olsen to begin a novel about a migrant worker family, the unfinished novel *Yonnondio: From the Thirties*.

In 1934 the twenty-one-year-old Olsen published all she would publish during the 1930s. This included two poems, two journalistic accounts (notably "The Strike," a first-hand account of the San Francisco general strike), and a brief excerpt from her novel-in-progress. After that, there were no publications from Olsen for the next twenty-two years.

It was only in 1956, when the short story "I Stand Here Ironing" appeared, that Olsen's writing career resumed. "In the twenty years I bore and reared my children," Olsen writes, "[I] usually had to work on a paid job as well, [and] the simplest circumstances for creation did not exist." Finally, with the assistance of a creative-writing fellowship to Stanford University in 1955, Olsen again turned to fiction writing. In 1961 she published her collection of short stories *Tell Me a Riddle*, and the title story won the O. Henry Award as the best story of 1961.

This success was followed by a Radcliffe Institute Fellowship (1962–64), which allowed Olsen to begin her second book, *Silences*. With this nonfiction work, Olsen explored the special difficulties experienced by women who create. These writings quickly became an inspirational point of departure for many in the emerging women's movement.

In the 1970s Olsen published her unfinished novel, *Yonnondio: From the Thirties* (1974), *Silences* (1978), and a long afterword, "A Biographical Interpretation," to a forgotten nineteenth-century novel, *Life in the Iron Mills*, by Rebecca Harding Davis (1861, reprinted 1972).

In recent years, Olsen has maintained her political identity mainly as an educator and leader within the women's movement, and through numerous benefit readings for a variety of progressive causes. In addition, Olsen has put together *Mother to Daughter, Daughter to Mother: A Day Book and Reader* (1984) as well as an introduction for *Mothers and Daughters* (1987), a photography book on this same theme. This recent work continues Olsen's lifelong commitment to women's studies, and her dedication to "discovering" neglected aspects of women's cultural history.

See also: Proletarian and Radical Writers of the 1930s–1950s, Young Communist League

—*Michael Staub*

REFERENCES

Duncan, Erika. "Coming of Age in the Thirties: A Portrait of Tillie Olsen." *Book Forum* 6, no. 2 (1982).

Orr, Elaine Neil. *Tillie Olsen and the Feminist Spiritual Vision*. Jackson: University of Mississippi Press, 1987.

Rosenfelt, Deborah. "From the Thirties: Tillie Olsen and the Radical Tradition." *Feminist Studies* 7, no. 3 (Fall 1981).

Staub, Michael. "The Struggle for 'Selfness' Through Speech in Olsen's *Yonnondio: From the Thirties*." *Studies in American Fiction* 16, no. 3 (Autumn 1988).

Tillie Olsen Archive: Berg Collection, The New York Public Library.

ORNITZ, SAMUEL (1890–1957)

Novelist, screenwriter, and labor and political activist, Ornitz is most often remembered as one of the "Hollywood Ten." His wider activity made a most extraordinary link between different generations and sections of the political and artistic Left.

Raised in a middle-class family and educated in New York City, Ornitz learned as a social worker about the corruption in the local political and judicial systems. He wrote specifically about this and about labor problems, assaulting the moral descent of bourgeois Jews in particular, in his best-selling *Haunch, Paunch, and Jowl* (1923), which described immigrant life at the turn of the century. This work arguably bridged the gap between that of the older Jewish immigrant writers in Yiddish or English, and the American-Jewish novelists of the 1930s generation, some of whom he knew well in Hollywood.

A children's book, *Around the World with Jocko the Great* (1925), and a portrayal of a Christ-like protagonist martyred by Protestant-Catholic hatred, followed in *A Yankee Passional* (1927). Like *Haunch, Paunch, and Jowl*, *A Yankee Passional* contained strong impressionist and stream-of-consciousness elements, in part influenced by Waldo Frank and James Joyce.

Ornitz shifted his locus to Los Angeles and his work to writing scripts for such generally unpolitical films as *Follow Your Heart*, *The Hit Parade*, *Three Faces West*, and *It Could Happen to You*. He became a pioneer figure, however, in the Hollywood Left. Scholar and voracious writer, a founder of the Screenwriters' Guild and the Anti-Nazi League, he was widely regarded as the Hollywood Communist Party's intellectual guru. With Theodore Dreiser and John Dos Passos, he visited Kentucky to meet with and draw attention to impoverished coal miners, writing about them in his play *In New Kentucky*, printed in the *New Masses* in 1934.

Following World War II, Ornitz faced the House Un-American Activities Committee, whose questions he refused to answer. Convicted of contempt of Congress, Ornitz spent a year in prison. After completing his sentence, he published one more novel, *Bride of the Sabbath* (1951), in many ways a reworking of material from *Haunch, Paunch, and Jowl* and *A Yankee Passional*. *See also*: Hollywood Blacklist

—*Harvey Pekar*

REFERENCES

Miller, Gabriel. Introduction to *Allrightnik's Row* (a reissue of *Haunch, Paunch, and Jowl*). New York: Contemporary Authors, 1986.

Schwartz, Nancy Lynn. *The Hollywood Writers' Wars*. New York: Knopf, 1982.

OVINGTON, MARY WHITE (1885–1951)

Known primarily for her part in forming the National Association for the Advancement of Colored People (NAACP) in 1909, Ovington was a lifelong socialist and strong advocate of women's rights. Born in Brooklyn to well-to-do abolitionist parents, she attended Harvard Annex (later Radcliffe College) for two years. From 1896 to 1903 she expanded her education as head worker at the Greenpoint Settlement in Brooklyn. In 1904 she joined the staff of Greenwich House Settlement and worked mainly with black children. She also began research on the conditions of blacks in Manhattan, a project that resulted in a major publication, *Half a Man: The Status of the Negro in New York* (1911).

Ovington joined the Socialist Party in 1905. She wrote for several Left journals, such as the *New Review*, and frequently for the party press on matters of racial injustice. While an ardent suffragist and pacifist who opposed U.S. entry into World War I, Ovington worked mainly to improve racial relations in the United States. She joined several uplift organizations, including the National League for the Protection of Colored Women. Beginning in 1914 she chaired the NAACP organization for nearly two decades and weathered many political storms, including factional battles of integration, economic radicalism, and Pan-Africanism.

A prolific writer as well as tireless lecturer, Ovington wrote her autobiography, *The Walls Came Tumbling Down* (1947; 1970), which focused on her activities within the NAACP. She also wrote antiracist stories for children and a novel, *The Shadow* (1920). *See also*: Greenwich Village

—*Mari Jo Buhle*

REFERENCES

Mary White Ovington Papers, Wayne State University.

Kellog, Charles Flint. *NAACP: A History of the National Association for the Advancement of Colored People, 1909–1920*. Vol. 1. Baltimore: Johns Hopkins University Press, 1967.

PACIFICA FOUNDATION

Incorporated in 1946, Pacifica put its first radio program on the air on April 15, 1949. The enterprise was primarily the work of Lewis Hill (1919–1957), who envisioned a radio station that was not compromised by advertisers or ratings. His specific political orientation had been taking shape for a decade. In 1937, while studying at Stanford University, he had become attracted to the ideas of the Quakers and had become a pacifist. When drafted into the armed forces in 1941 he registered as a conscientious objector and served in the Civilian Public Service Projects. Following the war he worked as a White House and Senate correspondent for a Washington radio station, but he found attempts to do honest journalism were undercut by commercial concerns. Hill then returned to California with the intent of starting a new kind of radio station.

Drawing upon the radical traditions of the Bay Area, Hill proposed a station that would draw all of its income from listeners and whose programs would thus be dependent upon their pleasure, a form of media direct democracy. The foundation's name reflected rejection of the Cold War and desire for a nonviolent planet. The founding Pacifica station was KPFA of Berkeley, and early supporters and personnel were centered on professors at the nearby University of California campus. Launched in the same period as the *National Guardian* and the *Monthly Review*, KPFA had a strong First Amendment and generally libertarian orientation. Hill had been an officer in the local American Civil Liberties Union and Pacifica supporters were steadfast opponents of McCarthyism in all its forms.

From the start, Pacifica ignored the conventions of the dominant culture. The music of such blacklisted performers as Pete Seeger and Paul Robeson was heard often. Commentary was offered by a wide range of new and old dissident voices, including Alan Watts, Kenneth Rexroth, and the young Pauline Kael. Lawrence Ferlinghetti, destined to play a major role in the Beat Generation and underground press movements, has written that when he first arrived in San Francisco in 1951, the station was the center of intellectual life. Although Hill committed suicide in 1957, the station was able to survive and in 1958 it won a prestigious Peabody Award for public service.

A second station, Los Angeles' KPFK, was added in 1959. That same year a third station came into being under a peculiar circumstance. Louis Schweitzer, an eccentric New York millionaire, was so impressed with Pacifica's programming that he "gave" his WBA station, right in the middle of the New York City FM dial, to the foundation. The station was renamed WBAI and went on the air early in 1960. During the 1970s, KPFT was founded in Houston and WPFW in Washington, D.C. While still excluding all advertising and dependent for survival on listener contributors, the stations had begun to take donations from educational trusts and other charitable institutions.

The New York City station was to be one

of the major cultural institutions of the 1960s, going on the air just as the counterculture and New Left were taking root. The station would provide dramatic coverage of every facet of opposition to the war in Vietnam and the civil rights movement. During the 1970s considerable time would be alloted to feminist and gay liberation programs. During the 1980s the political focus would turn to Latin America and Iran with a number of key programs syndicated to stations outside the Pacifica network. News programs whose time slot was "as long as needed," call-in shows, and multihour segments reflecting a particular and usually highly individualist style were just a few of Pacifica's innovations. The stations also featured a wide range of musical programming that was without precedent and untenable on any other kind of economic base.

Pacifica drew the ire of the Right from its onset and was constantly assailed as "Communist-inspired." License renewals have been held up time and again on a variety of pretexts. An early flashpoint was a two-hour interview first aired on WBAI in 1962 with former FBI agent Jack Levin, who offered an insider's critique of how J. Edgar Hoover ran the Bureau as a despot and intimidated elected officials. The program led to a subpoena for Foundation officials to appear before the Senate Internal Security Committee. The Foundation's license was again threatened in 1970. This time the issue was obscene language. *Variety*, the quintessential nonpolitical show-biz journal, commented at the time that Pacifica's real indiscretion was its vigorous opposition to the war in Vietnam.

The Houston station was bombed twice (1970 and 1971) and threats were made against the Los Angeles station. The Houston bombings kept the station off the air for a time, but Pacifica's integrity had won it considerable mainstream admiration. The Houston *Post* offered a reward of $1,500 for information leading to the arrest of those responsible for the bombing. Of even greater import, the *Post*, CBS, the National Association of Broadcasters, the *Houston Chronicle*, *Broadcasting* magazine, and the *Saturday Review* all extended support when Pacifica stations came under political attack.

Private and governmental attacks have continued, but despite the always tenuous financial realities, the Pacifica stations have survived. Moreover, many aspects of Pacifica programming have been widely emulated. Pacifica-like stations first sprang up in the 1970s in cities such as Seattle, St. Louis, and San Francisco. The development of National Public Radio was influenced by Pacifica concepts, and Pacifica alumni have been prominent not only at NPR but at various commercial stations. Community-access television and noncommercial radio stations of all kinds also reflect the views pioneered by Lewis Hill and the Pacifica founders in the late 1940s.

Celebrating its fortieth year of continuing programming in 1989, Pacifica boasted that it had covered all major events from the Army-McCarthy Hearings through the Iran-Contragate scandal, often offering gavel-to-gavel coverage of hearings and on-the-spot full-time coverage of major demonstrations, parades, and rallies. The Foundation offered 30,000 tapes for use by other stations and the public, and its new programs, augmented by those of independent producers, were being heard on a large number of stations throughout the United States, Canada, and some foreign nations. One of Pacifica's projects for the 1990s was to restore 7,000 tapes from the 1950s and 1960s and make them available to the general public. *See also*: Beat Generation and the New Left, Pacifism, Underground Press

—*Dan Georgakas*

REFERENCES

Armstrong, David. *A Trumpet to Arms—Alternative Media in America*. Los Angeles: J. P. Tarcher, 1981.

Aronson, James. *Deadline for the Media, Today's Challenges to Press, TV & Radio*. Indianapolis: Bobbs-Merrill, 1972.

Monaco, James. *Media Culture*. New York: Delta, 1978.

PACIFISM

A rich worldview that developed from a range of sources, secular and religious, pacifism has the single unifying theme that violence is rejected as a means of resolving social conflict. Uniquely among major radical perspectives, it is "Eastern" as well as "Western," and in that sense among the most thoroughly internationalist. Pacifists differ on whether they might use violence in extreme personal situations such as rape or murder, but agree upon the rejection of violence during civil wars, revolutions, or conflict between nation-states. Whether articulated via Gandhi's Hinduism, Tolstoy's Christianity, or in the secular humanism of the socialist and anarchist movements, pacifism has always emphasized the role of the individual sense of morality against any organized ideology of violence.

Because of their opposition to the State, pacifists have not generally fitted into Marxist-Leninist organizations, but rather allied themselves as loose caucuses within socialist or social-democratic movements. While building some distinct institutions, often at the edges of socialist or liberal religious movements, they have largely acted as individuals upon a wide spectrum of available arenas.

Pacifist influence developed slowly in the modern Left. Although "nonresistant" agitation flourished in reform circles of the 1830s–1850s, pacifists played little apparent role in the immigrant-dominated U.S. socialist movements of the post–Civil War period. Nor did they revive significantly within the new Socialist Party until the nation plunged into war. Widespread antiwar sentiments often took on a semipacifist flavoring within the SP at large, and took organizational form in the Fellowship of Reconciliation and its socialistic magazine, *The World Tomorrow*. Largely Protestant and middle class, a circle of prominent pacifists became increasingly prominent in a reduced SP, especially with the ascendance of Norman Thomas, himself a nearly devout pacifist, to party leadership.

During the Depression, pacifist sentiments fairly swept many college campuses. Asserting a U.S. version of the Oxford Pledge (refusal to "fight for King and County"), undergraduates expressed their fear of the coming war in strikes, marches, and conventions. The threat of world fascism, and the predominance of the antipacifist Communist Party during the later 1930s eclipsed these moods, although Norman Thomas and a badly diminished SP remained pacifistically antiwar until the Japanese invasion of Pearl Harbor. Thereafter, many pacifists did alternative service in mental hospitals (ending the infamous "locked wards") or did time in jail.

Public revulsion at atomic weapons and the devastation of war generally prompted a sharp rise of pacifist sentiments after the war. Pacifists pioneered public radio, an idea germinated during prison terms, by establishing station KPFA-FM in Berkeley, a station that promoted pacifist views and served as a model for other subsequent community-based stations. Likewise, pacifists played an active role in the publication of critical magazines (especially Dwight Macdonald's *Politics* magazine) and many poetry or avant-garde artistic publications, especially in the Bay Area. Out of fundamentally anarcho-pacifist concerns, Lawrence Ferlinghetti's City Lights Bookstore, and its famous poetry series (introducing, among others, anarcho-pacifist Allen Ginsberg) became a major cultural resource of the 1950s–1960s.

The civil rights movement buoyed up the prestige of Gandhi's work and the value of nonviolence, especially in the face of racist attacks. The Rev. Martin Luther King, Jr.'s acceptance and articulation of pacifist philosophy, especially in the face of collapse by existing Left ideologies, provided a new opening for pacifism. The Congress of Racial Equality (CORE), founded by veterans of the Fellowship of Reconciliation (a tax refusal and direct action group), helped launch the civil disobedience tactics challenging segregation in public facilities. The participation of pacifists such as Bayard Rustin in Dr. King's (and other civil rights) campaigns, not greatly noted at the time outside pacifist circles, added to the long-run significance of the civil rights years.

Meanwhile, a socialist-pacifism of sorts had taken various forms. A small group of World War II prison veterans, including Dave Dellinger, Jim Peck, and Ralph DiGia, founded the Committee for Nonviolent Revolution in 1946 with a program that included the nonviolent seizure of the means of production by workers. This small group merged two years later with Peacemakers, a radical pacifist group which A. J. Muste had helped establish and which was moving toward a

"Third Camp" position—rejecting the political leadership of the US and USSR—on the Cold War.

These activists forged a powerful new means of expression in 1956 when, with special support from the War Resisters League (WRL), they set up *Liberation* magazine. At a time of extreme political conformity, *Liberation* found wide acceptance among a proto-New Left, in part by linking the old notions of anti-monopoly and anti-imperialist republicanism with the decentralist and non-hierarchical themes of the new generation. *Liberation* continued to publish until 1977, involving most of the major, national writers around the New Left and establishing a presence far beyond the pacifist community. Among its regular contributors were Paul Goodman, Barbara Deming, Staughton Lynd and David Dellinger. *WIN* magazine, with a smaller but more intensely pacifist following in the 1960s–70s, became in effect a journalistic "Workshop in Non-Violence" (hence its name) for its founding War Resisters League, and a somewhat more general peace publication during later years.

During the 1960s pacifism had an enormous impact upon American political and social movements, ranging from the non-violent campaigns of Martin Luther King to the organization of farm workers by Cesar Chavez. Pacifist organizations such as the War Resisters League experienced their highest membership levels, as WRL itself led the first draft card burnings and attempted direct action "closings" of Army induction centers. Radical pacifists played a central role in the anti-war coalitions, frequently mediating conflicts among other elements and setting the tone of events. Following US withdrawal from Vietnam, pacifist organizations inevitably declined, but continued to exert an influence on the Left. Such varied movements as attempted disruption of missile sites, boycotts against war toys, Greenpeace invasion of nuclear test sites, and non-violent protests by the homeless carried forward crucial elements of pacifism's historical premises. *See also*: Civil Rights; Dellinger, David; Macdonald, Dwight; Peace Movements; Rustin, Bayard; *World Tomorrow*

—*David McReynolds, Paul Buhle*

REFERENCES

Chatfield, Charles. *For Peace and Justice: Pacifism in America, 1914–41*. Knoxville: University of Tennessee Press, 1971.

Wittner, Lawrence. *Rebels Against War: The American Peace Movement, 1933–1983*. Philadelphia: Temple University Press, 1984.

Swarthmore College Peace Collection, Swarthmore, Pennsylvania.

PACKINGHOUSE WORKERS

The United Packinghouse, Food and Allied Workers (UPWA) remained one of the few International unions within the CIO in which an acknowledged left-wing presence played a significant role within the political and ideological life of the organization. What has been called a Center-Left coalition maintained itself as the leading force within the organization from its inception as the Packinghouse Workers Organizing Committee (PWOC) in October 1937 until the merger of UPWA and the Amalgamated Meat Cutters and Butcher Workmen (AMCBW) in 1968. At its peak, the union had approximately 150,000 members in the United States, Canada, and Puerto Rico.

While the Center was clearly the dominant partner throughout the history of the union, the Left contributed much of the energy and ideological support behind the progressive policies and aggressive bargaining posture advocated by International President Ralph Helstein. Helstein led the union from 1946 to 1968. His administration declined to participate in the "red purge" program within the CIO, and took public positions on economic and political issues with which the CIO leadership was not altogether comfortable.

In 1953 the UPWA executive board issued a position paper, "The Road Ahead," which called for an end to the Korean War; for an end to congressional witch-hunts; for recognition of Mainland China; and for a transformation of the American buildup of arms into "a bold program of schools, power projects, housing and hospitals instead of bombers and destroyers." The lengthy manifesto was given display treatment in the union's newspaper and several thousand reprints were distributed widely.

Beginning in 1945, the UPWA executive board set up special procedures for dealing with cases involving racial discrimination, and in 1953 it began to hold an annual Conference on Antidiscrimination and Women's Activities. The intent was to focus on its own nationwide effort behind an aggressive program of "affirmative action" to open up employment and promotion opportunities to minority workers in all of its bargaining units. "Women's Activities" referred to the greater involvement of women members in the life and leadership of the organization at all levels, and to special concern for female-specific plant issues. Through these programs, segregated locker rooms, even drinking fountains then customary in southern plants, were completely abolished. The union also took its program into the communities, both North and South. UPWA was an early supporter of the Southern Christian Leadership Conference. The Rev. Martin Luther King, Jr., addressed the union's 1957 conference, at which he was presented with a check for $11,000 from the UPWA Fund for Democracy.

The union's economic program was characterized by a militant posture and a skillful leadership at the bargaining table, based on an informed membership which was involved as a participant in the decision-making process at all levels. As a matter of policy, the setting of bargaining goals began with a round of membership meetings at the local level at which plant issues were discussed. The next step was a national conference at which local union delegates representing all the employers in the industry agreed on common objectives. All local unions were entitled to participate in their own companywide bargaining sessions. Accordingly, a sophisticated and involved membership brought wages and working conditions in the meat-packing industry from one of the most despised to one of the most desirable.

The ability of the UPWA to operate as a mainstream union with a strong and acknowledged Left element rested on three main factors:

1. Capable Left leaders, who were well identified as such, had made a decisive contribution to the organizing campaigns that had surmounted red-baiting attacks in several key centers; hence significant sections of the union membership had, early on, been inoculated against this form of criticism from the "outside."

2. The meat-packing workers had a strong sense of identity, infused with a strong midwestern and rural populism that found radicalism not too unacceptable. Depression-troubled Iowa farmers had forcibly prevented farm foreclosure sales and dumped milk trucks only a few years before the PWOC was formed.

3. The Left leaders within the UPWA handled themselves tactfully, so that the socialist-oriented Canadians, the "populist" midwesterners, and the Communist-influenced sections in certain metropolitan areas could maintain a mutually respectful working relationship, which allowed President Helstein to chart a course of forward positions on social issues, while building an enviable wage and benefit structure for workers in the industry.

See also: Industrial Unionism

—*Leslie F. Orear*

Paredon Records (1971–88)

For most of two decades Paredon Records was the major American source for politically conscious folk music from around the world. Its founders were Barbara Dane, a progressive folksinger herself, and Irwin Silber, former editor of *Sing Out!* and then an editor of the *Guardian*. The operation, which remained mostly a volunteer effort, was run from Dane's Brooklyn home. Dane was primarily responsible for production and Silber for distribution.

The first Paredon release, *Canción Protesta*, was recorded at a Cuban youth festival and featured the "nueva canción" style. Subsequent albums featured music of liberation movements in nations such as Angola, Vietnam, Ireland, Puerto Rico, Haiti, and Palestine. U.S. artists who were featured included Bev Grant and the Human Condition, Bernice Reagon, and Barbara Dane. The albums contained booklets offering cultural/political background on the music, the original lyrics, and English translations of the lyrics.

In the early 1980s, after having produced forty-six albums, Dane and Silber moved to

California. Silber devoted considerable time to developing the *Line of March* publishing organization and Dane wished to have more time for her own singing. As a consequence the Paredon operation was turned over to Art for Peace and Justice, a Bay Area group. There were new releases offering the music of Nicaragua, Lebanon, and Salvador, but the collective, unable to sustain the enterprise, suspended operations in September 1988. *See also*: Folk Music

—*Dan Georgakas*

REFERENCES

Abelard, Tony. "Song Is Over for Paredon Records." *The Guardian*, October 15, 1988.

Parsons, Albert (1848–87)

Born in Alabama and orphaned as a youth, Parsons went from fighting in the Confederate army to dying on the scaffold as America's leading native-born revolutionary labor leader. He apprenticed as a printer to his brother, who was working in Texas, and followed him into service as a Rebel soldier during the Civil War.

After the war, Parsons was thoroughly radicalized by racial and class conflict, by vigilante violence and state terror. A Radical Republican in Reconstruction Texas, Parsons edited the Waco *Spectator* and fought for black civil rights. He later described the radical movement as a "labor party" for blacks in the state. Parsons, who took a bullet in the leg from white racists for his radical activism, married Lucy Gathings, a woman of black, Indian, and Mexican ancestry, in about 1872. The couple moved to Chicago in late 1873.

In Chicago, Parsons worked as a printer before being blacklisted for his leading role in the 1877 mass strike in the city—a strike whose bloody suppression profoundly influenced him. He was a leading member of the Knights of Labor, Typographical Union No. 16, the Council Trades and Labor Unions, and the Socialist Labor Party in the late 1870s and early 1880s, and he lobbied for the National Eight-Hour Association in Washington, D.C. When Parsons joined the International Working People's Association (IWPA) in 1883, he had already drawn conclusions as to the difficulties associated with electoral politics and the dangers of state-sponsored and employer-initiated violence against the labor movement. In the IWPA he more systematically preached anarchism and self-defense but he never lost his emphasis on trade unionism as the basis for a new society. *See also*: Anarchism, Black International, Haymarket Affair, Socialist Labor Party

—*David Roediger*

REFERENCES

Avrich, Paul. *The Haymarket Tragedy*. Princeton: Princeton University Press, 1984.

Parsons, Lucy E. *The Life of Albert R. Parsons*. Chicago: Lucy E. Parsons, 1889.

Roediger, David, and Franklin Rosemont, eds. *Haymarket Scrapbook*. Chicago: Charles H. Kerr Co., 1986.

Parsons, Lucy (1853–1942)

A woman of color and a working-class revolutionary, Parsons spent her life struggling for the rights of the poor, unemployed, homeless, women, children, and minority groups, and for a future society based on free association of labor organizations.

Born in Texas, possibly a slave, she met Albert Richard Parsons, a militant advocate of the rights of freed people, around 1870, and they moved to Chicago in 1873. In 1877 Albert was blacklisted from the printing trade, and Lucy assumed household financial responsibility by opening a dress shop. She began writing about tramps, disabled veterans of the Civil War, and working women for the *Socialist* in 1878. She soon gave birth to two children.

She joined the anarchistic International Working People's Association in 1883 and the Knights of Labor the following year. In 1884 the IWPA began to publish the weekly *Alarm* in Chicago, with Albert as editor and Lucy a frequent contributor. Her most famous piece was "To Tramps," which advocated propaganda "by the deed" against the rich. On April 28, 1885, she and Lizzie Holmes headed the anarchists' march on the new Board of Trade; on Thanksgiving of that year, Lucy Parsons led the poor people's march down Prairie Avenue, ringing the bells at the homes of the rich.

With other anarchists, she began organizing for the May 1, 1886, general strike for the eight-hour day, concentrating her efforts on sewing women. On May 1, she and Albert led 80,000 workers and supporters up Michigan Avenue. Three days later a labor rally at the Haymarket was the occasion of a fatal bombing incident. Police charged that radical activists were responsible.

As her comrades were rounded up after the May 4 bombing, Lucy began organizing the Haymarket defense. After eight defendants, including Albert, were found guilty of murder, she traveled to many states, pleading her comrades' innocence to the charges, but defending their revolutionary goals. By February 1887, she had given forty-three speeches in seventeen states. When Albert was executed in November of that year, Lucy became a widow with a cause to carry on.

Publisher of the short-lived paper *Freedom* (1892), which attacked the racist lynchings and peonage of blacks, and a member of Eugene Debs's Social Democracy, she was also a founding member of the Industrial Workers of the World and publisher of the *Liberator* (1905–6), to which she contributed a series on famous women. In her role as traveling orator, Parsons reemerged in public notoriety in a 1914 San Francisco demonstration of the homeless and at the head of a 1915 demonstration of the Chicago unemployed and homeless (Jane Addams paid her bail). She took up the cause of Tom Mooney and other imprisoned activists and in 1927 was elected to the national executive committee of the International Labor Defense, a CP front dedicated to defending political prisoners. After years of CP association, she joined in 1939. In 1941, in one of her last public appearances, she addressed strikers at International Harvester, formerly McCormick Reaper, where the events leading up to Haymarket had begun. Lucy Parsons died in a fire in her home on March 7, 1942; her personal papers and books were seized by authorities from her gutted home.

—*Carolyn Ashbaugh*

REFERENCES

Ashbaugh, Carolyn. *Lucy Parsons, American Revolutionary*. Chicago: Charles H. Kerr, 1976.

Participatory Democracy

This phrase first gained currency—as an ideal, and as a rallying slogan of the Left—in the 1960s. Throughout the decade, the term was widely used in the United States by partisans of the New Left, both to suggest the kind of good society they wished ultimately to create, and the political means they deemed appropriate for working toward that end. Although participatory democracy was the property of no single party, it was perhaps most closely identified with the Students for a Democratic Society. It was SDS, in its *Port Huron Statement* of 1962, that first proposed participatory democracy as the focus of a distinctively new, and distinctively American, Left: "We seek the establishment of a democracy of individual participation, governed by two central aims: that the individual share in those social decisions determining the quality and direction of his life; that society be organized to encourage independence in men and provide the media for their common participation."

The chief architect of the *Port Huron Statement*, Tom Hayden, borrowed the phrase itself from his teacher and mentor at the University of Michigan, Arnold Kaufman. In his 1960 essay "Participatory Democracy and Human Nature," Kaufman had argued that active participation in a democracy—in contrast to mere voting—was justified by the way in which it developed the "human powers of thought, feeling, and action." Like such predecessors as John Dewey and Alexis de Tocqueville, Kaufman believed that it was active participation, above all, that enabled citizens to use properly their political rights, including the right to vote.

Although Kaufman was present at the Port Huron conference in 1962—and although Tom Hayden shared Kaufman's faith in the moral and educational benefits of political action—participatory democracy quickly assumed a life of its own as a catchword of the New Left. For some, the phrase was a way of circumventing the tacit American taboo against frankly advocating socialism; assuming that true democracy was incompatible with capitalism, they tended to interpret participatory democracy above all as an implicit call for workers' control of industry.

Soon enough, yet another sense of participatory democracy took hold. By 1964, some within SDS, in an effort to probe the limits in practice of their democratic ideal, began to experiment among themselves with rule-by-consensus, using techniques learned from pacifist activists and religious groups like the Quakers. A growing number of young radicals, stressing face-to-face interaction and sincere mutual counsel, understood participatory democracy to be incompatible not only with capitalism, but also with conventional electioneering: representative democracy was increasingly regarded as a manipulative and hypocritical sham.

For several years, the New Left's experiments in democracy attracted thousands of converts. At the same time, this surge of democratic idealism created an organizational conundrum for SDS that first became acute in 1965, and went unresolved for the rest of the organization's life. By 1965, student sentiment against the war in Vietnam had begun to crystallize; after organizing the first major demonstration against the war in Washington, in April 1965, SDS, virtually overnight, became an influential national group with a mass constituency. Unfortunately, it was unclear how rule-by-consensus—and the dissolution of representative institutions—could be reconciled with leadership of the burgeoning antiwar movement, which seemed to cry out for some kind of disciplined, accountable, traditionally structured mass organization. Debate raged in SDS over whether and how the organization might avoid becoming another illustration of sociologist Robert Michel's famous "iron law of oligarchy." Was participatory democracy compatible with voting and the maintenance of respresentative institutions? Or did it require abolishing such institutions and relying instead on the exemplary élan of collective direct action and the endless meetings that were the embodiment of rule-by-consensus?

These and a host of similar questions were never adequately resolved by SDS or, for that matter, by the New Left as a whole. The resulting confusion was one, though by no means the most important, reason that the movement, large and powerful though it had briefly been, collapsed with such surprising abruptness in the early 1970s.

In the years since, some veterans have come to regard the failed democratic experiments of the 1960s with romantic nostalgia. Others have dug in for the unglamorous work of creating politically effective citizen-action groups at the grass roots, patiently working with poor and middle-class constituents, and addressing a variety of interests, from women's rights to the quality of the environment. Meanwhile, intellectuals, usually writing for readers in the universities, have debated the institutional devices that might make something like participatory democracy into a cogent political goal in a modern industrial state. In the 1980s these debates, and the citizen-action groups that made them seem of practical moment, constituted one of the chief legacies of the New Left—and one of the few systematic alternatives to the oligarchical trends in American political life made apparent in the Watergate and Iran-contra scandals.

See also: New Left, Students for a Democratic Society

—*James Miller*

REFERENCES

Benello, C. George, and Dimitrios Roussopoulos, eds. *The Case for Participatory Democracy*. New York: Grossman, 1972.

Kaufman, Arnold. "Human Nature and Participatory Democracy." In *Nomos III: Responsibility*, edited by Carl J. Friedrich. New York: The Liberal Arts Press, 1960.

Mansbridge, Jane. *Beyond Adversary Democracy*. Chicago: University of Chicago Press, 1980.

Miller, James. *"Democracy in the Streets": From Port Huron to the Siege of Chicago*. New York: Simon and Schuster, 1987.

PARTISAN REVIEW

Born in the world of thirties radicalism, *PR* began in 1934 under the sponsorship of the New York John Reed Club, one of the Left literary groups organized to foster the work of proletarian writers—those aiming to combine literary imagination and class-consciousness. Founded by two young radical critics—Philip Rahv and William Phillips—*PR* announced that it would "concentrate on creative and critical literature, but . . . shall maintain a definite viewpoint—that of the revolutionary working class. . . . The defense of the Soviet Union is one of our principal tasks." While *PR* continued to trumpet the potential and the successes of proletarian art, the editors began to harbor doubts about the quality of much proletarian literature and, especially, the role of intellectuals and critics within the radical-art movement. In 1936 they suspended publication of the magazine.

The "new" *Partisan Review* reappeared in 1937, with four additional editors—F. W. Dupee, Dwight Macdonald, George L. K. Morris, and Mary McCarthy—and a new independent editorial position. The period between its rebirth and Pearl Harbor remains the magazine's most fruitful as a Left journal. Splits in the Left created an intellectual vacuum that *PR* occupied. A great number of important nonaligned leftist writers came to the magazine, including Edmund Wilson, Wallace Stevens, Lionel Trilling, Sidney Hook, and James T. Farrell. In addition, promising writers debuted there: Delmore Schwartz, Saul Bellow, John Berryman, and Elizabeth Bishop among them.

PR also sought to revive the literary reputations of modernist writers, bringing them into a new conception of radical art, a "revolutionary modernism." A radical "sensibility" was just as important as explicit political consciousness. Rahv found that while "reactionary in its abstract content," Dostoyevsky's work was nonetheless "radical in sensibility and subversive in performance." For art critic Clement Greenberg, the avant-garde became a driving radical force in the contemporary world. Middlebrow culture, including proletarian literature, helped perpetuate capitalism. The avant-garde could move the world toward socialism.

This new cultural position corrected the perceived faulty relationship between writer and critic within proletarian art. The critic was now the essential analyst for sifting through literary works and identifying the radicalizing insights of numerous writers—alive and dead, radical and conservative; Kakfa and Eliot, as well as Dreiser and Malraux.

PR stayed out of the Popular Front and was aligned with, but never formally allied to, the Trotskyists. When the Nazi-Soviet Pact of 1939 destroyed the Popular Front, the editors reiterated their position of supporting a "third force," radical and uncompromised. In 1941 Macdonald and Greenberg published an essay disassociating themselves from American war efforts, seeing them ending with capitalism strengthened. Rahv, however, attacked this "morally absolutist" position and, revising his earlier thinking, called for support of American actions.

The war debate split the *PR* editorial board, leading to Macdonald's resignation. By 1945, new intellectual concerns moved the magazine and its contributors: a renewed focus on American culture; newly emerging considerations of Freud, Sartre, and Jewish culture; and the emergence of a liberal anticommunist position to replace the radical anti-Stalinist arguments of the later 1930s. New editors, including Schwartz and William Barrett, joined as well.

During the 1950s, *PR* became one of the leading journals of postwar culture. The famous symposium "Our Country and Our Culture" demonstrated a new harmonious relationship between American society and the once-radical, now liberal intellectuals. Phillips served on the board of the anticommunist American Committee for Cultural Freedom.

In the 1960s, *PR* moved to Rutgers University. Rahv, in Boston, grew increasingly alienated from *PR*. While Phillips exhibited interest in the counterculture, Rahv disdained it. He resigned in 1969. Staying as editor, Phillips oversaw the magazine's transfer to Boston University in the 1970s and its move back to the political center and, in recent times, toward neoconservatism. *See also*: Communist Party; *Dissent*; Farrell, James T.; Hook, Sidney; Howe, Irving; John Reed Clubs; Shapiro, Meyer

—*Alexander Bloom*

REFERENCES

Bloom, Alexander. *Prodigal Sons: The New York Intellectuals and Their World*. New York: Oxford University Press, 1986.

Cooney, Terry A. *The Rise of the New York Intellectuals: Partisan Review and Its Circle*. Madison: University of Wisconsin Press, 1986.

Gilbert, James B. *Writers and Partisans: A History of Literary Radicalism in America*. New York: Wiley & Sons, 1969.

Phillips, William. *A Partisan View: Five Decades of the Literary Life*. New York: Stein & Day, 1983.

Wald, Alan M. *The New York Intellectuals: The Rise and Decline of the Anti-Stalinist Left from the 1930s to the 1980s*. Chapel Hill: University of North Carolina Press, 1987.

Party Organizer

Very much like its Socialist Party predecessor, the *Party Builder* (1911–14), the Communist *Party Organizer* was intended not as a general-circulation tabloid but rather a nuts-and-bolts organizing bulletin for the dedicated activist. Like the *Party Builder*, it frequently found itself in the conceptual trap of exhortation and confidence-building to the detriment of realistic tactical appraisal and useful lines of action. Relative to the rhetorical level of the public Communist press, on the other hand, the *Party Organizer* remained sober and thoughtful.

Published from 1927, the *Party Organizer* aimed its efforts at the efficiency of organization. Instructions on the ways and means of holding meetings, getting out pertinent leaflets, starting local grievance-oriented labor groups, and above all raising money and selling Party literature, could all be found in abundance. Not even from these straightforward aims, however, could inner Party conflicts be entirely excluded: one chief goal in further integrating the activists into the movement was to lessen the influence of the officially dissolved (but informally still influential) foreign-language groups. But in the *Party Organizer*, one also found collective self-criticisms unthinkable for public consumption.

By the early 1930s, such emphases as work in small industrial towns, and among blacks, suggested the disapora of especially young Party activists from the ethnic city neighborhoods to the outlands and even physically dangerous districts. Soon after, the general shift of the CP into the industrial union movement reemphasized a basic tension in the paper and in the organization: how to maintain a parity of movement building and party building. Clearly, by the later 1930s, the former had been achieved at the expense of the latter, and local contributors understandably bewailed the lag in *Daily Worker* or Party-pamphlet distribution even at times of high industrial mobilization. The compromise formula arrived at, to emphasize both simultaneously (mass work for the masses, and selective literature and recruitment for the promising minority), exhausted activists and actually propelled many union officeholders away from Party meetings that took up too much of their precious organizing (or rest) time. The fluctuation of Party membership, a subject of continual scrutiny (but not successful resolution of the problems), weighed heavily even as membership grew toward its peacetime peak of 65,000. For a nation with a working class the size of America's, this seemed undeniably small.

The dissolution of the *Party Organizer* in 1937, sometimes later regretted by Party veterans, followed the logic of the Popular Front. The Party factions within unions had competed with the larger Left blocs controlled by progressive union leaders themselves, and had become the source of complaint from some of the Party's most prestigious allies. On the other hand, without the factions and the *Party Organizer*, the Communists had nowhere to retreat beyond the decline and ultimate collapse of its public labor and political leadership. As the Party ceased to be a Bolshevik organization of the old time, it lost the need for the *Party Organizer*, but never found an adequate substitute. *See also*: Communist Party, *Daily Worker*

—Paul Buhle

REFERENCES

Alperin, Robert Jay. "Organization in the Communist Party, USA, 1931–1938." Ph.D. diss., Northwestern University, 1959.

Passaic Textile Strike of 1926

This momentous action lasted for an entire year and tied up all six of the woolen and worsted mills and a number of other textile mills in the Passaic, New Jersey, area. At its peak, more than 20,000 workers were involved. Begun in January 1926 as a protest against a 10-percent wage cut at the Botany

Linocut by Ned Hilton

Company, mass picketing was used so extensively and so effectively that the Forstmann & Huffman Company, which had not slashed wages, was forced to close down.

Though Passaic's work force was primarily composed of Slavic workers, a group of Hungarian employees at the Botany mill sparked the walkout and supplied much of the internal leadership. Most notably, the Passaic strike became the first mass walkout in the United States to be led by the Communist Party. Since the strike came at a time when the Party (over the objections of dissidents) still hoped to work within the AFL, strikers joined a United

Front Committee, which disclaimed any intention of being a dual union. Albert Weisbord, a Party member who had only recently graduated from Harvard Law School, directed the strike and earned tremendous admiration from textile workers who dubbed him "Jecusko," meaning "Little Jesus."

As in the Sacco and Vanzetti defense effort, liberals and radicals cooperated in giving support to the Passaic strikers. Elizabeth Gurley Flynn, Rabbi Stephen Wise, Norman Thomas, Mother Bloor, and many others spoke in Passaic; unions such as the Amalgamated Clothing Workers and the Brotherhood of Locomotive Engineers made contributions; Representative Victor Berger and Senator Robert LaFollette, Jr., called for congressional investigations; and the American Civil Liberties Union provided legal defense. The strike received national publicity and the various Passaic Relief Committees raised over $500,000. In Passaic itself, the CP took the lead. Party members organized the numerous mass demonstrations, arranged legal and medical help for those who suffered arrests and beatings, held special meetings for women workers, published a weekly newspaper, and produced a motion picture about the strike.

Weisbord hoped to spread the strike to the neighboring city of Paterson and to Lawrence, Massachusetts, but he failed to accomplish this goal. Despite this disappointment, strikers remained firm through the summer. At this point, the CP, uncertain about how to handle the Passaic situation, decided to hand the strike over to an AFL union, the United Textile Workers. The UTW assumed direction of the work stoppage on the condition that Weisbord be removed from the leadership. After the UTW took over in September 1926, relief funds dried up and the strikers' morale began to drop. Nevertheless, the strike dragged on until the UTW negotiated separate settlements between November 1926 and February 1927. Though the strikers had succeeded in stopping the cuts, they failed to gain union recognition, which had been their primary goal. Tensions between the UTW and the Passaic Workers persisted until 1928, when the UTW expelled the Passaic local for having supported the Communist-led New Bedford, Massachusetts, textile strike of that year.

Coming in the midst of "Coolidge prosperity," the Passaic textile strike revived the Left's hopes that a militant labor movement could once again emerge. From the CP perspective, the strike showed the folly of trying to reform the AFL and gave ammunition to those who favored a dual union strategy. In this sense, the strike served as a preview of other textile battles in New England and in the South between 1928 and 1932. *See also*: Communist Party, Textile Workers, Trade Union Unity League

—David J. Goldberg

REFERENCES

Goldberg, David J. *A Tale of Three Cities: Labor Protest and Organization in Paterson, Passaic, and Lawrence, 1916–1921*. New Brunswick: Rutgers University Press, 1989.

Murphy, Paul L., ed. *The Passaic Textile Strike of 1926*. Belmont, Calif.: Wadsworth Publishing Co., 1974.

Siegal, Morton. "The Passaic Textile Strike of 1926." Ph.D. diss., Columbia University, 1952.

Weisbord, Albert. *Passaic Reviewed*. San Francisco: Germinal Press, 1976.

Weisbord, Vera Buch. *A Radical Life*. Bloomington: Indiana University Press, 1977.

PATERSON, NEW JERSEY, ANARCHISM

On July 15, 1895, an Italian-language anarchist newspaper, *La Questione Sociale*, was launched in Paterson, New Jersey. Sponsored by an affinity group called The Right to Existence, it found its readers and constituents largely among skilled silk weavers and dyers brought to the Paterson mills as cheap labor. While anarchists (many of German and French-Canadian origin) were active in the "Silk City" before 1895—in particular in the strike of 1894—it was the Italian group whose activities inaugurated the period of greatest anarchist influence in Paterson.

The influence of Errico Malatesta, the distinguished protégé of Mikhail Bakunin, was decisive in the formation of the paper. He had previously founded two other papers of the same name, in Florence (1883–84) and Buenos Aires (1885).

In 1895, exiled by governmental responses to the *attentats* of individualist anarchists (like Sante Caserio's assassination of French president Carnot), a small group of anarchist émigrés met in London, among them Malatesta and his friend Pietro Gori—a twenty-nine-year-old lawyer, playwright, poet, and orator who had achieved distinction in the legal defense of anarchists in Italy.

At this time, Francesco Saverio Merlino, editor of *Il Grido degli Oppressi*, published from Bleecker Street, Manhattan, invited Gori to New York on a speaking tour. Malatesta urged him to accept. Once there, Merlino, Gori, and Pedro Esteve—the Catalan anarchist printer, intellectual, and friend of Malatesta from the days of the Barcelona uprising of 1892—resolved to launch the Paterson paper. Esteve, who combined editorial skill with technical ability, provided important supportive links to other ethnic communities, like the Yiddish—through Emma Goldman.

Gori's speaking tour to Italian communities ranging from Barre, Vermont, to San Francisco, and the articles he contributed to the new journal as editor in chief, along with the managing editorship of Esteve, put *La Questione Sociale* on a sound basis with a circulation of about 3,000 by 1896. Max Nettlau, writing in 1924, ranked it, along with *L'Anarchie* of Paris and *Freedom* of London, as among the seventeen most influential anarchist newspapers in the world by 1900.

The Right to Existence group in Paterson was composed of approximately a hundred anarchists, who were predominantly of the Bakuninist-Malatesta "communal anarchist" tradition. Rejecting the authoritarianism of government and the state, they nevertheless accepted the possibility of communal organization on a voluntary, consensual basis if organized "from the ground up." They were called the "*organizzatori*" as opposed to anarchists of the extreme "Max Stirner" type, who were termed "*antiorganizzatori*."

As organizzatori, they worked actively to foster a class-conscious worker's union movement in Paterson whose aims would ultimately be revolutionary. One of their leaders was Antonio Guabello, who led a successful strike of the Industrial Workers of the World against the Victoria Silk Mill in 1905. Ernestina Cravella, a bilingual worker in the Paragon Mill, served as their spokesperson to the English-speaking press. A multilingual Tyrolean, Francis Widmar, served as the group's business manager and fundraiser.

In contrast to the situation with local socialist organizations, women like Cravella played an active role in the leadership of the group. Esteve's companion, Maria Roda, for example, a friend of Emma Goldman and a feminist, was effective in fostering propaganda groups among millworkers—many of whom were women—as early as 1897. She linked these efforts with those of Louise Reville in Paris (1900), who formed an international group around the periodical *Feminist Action*.

The group's educational efforts included public meetings featuring such speakers as John Turner of Britain, Johann Most, Emma Goldman, and Peter Kropotkin himself (November 17, 1897). Writers like Kropotkin and Elisee Reclus contributed articles. The group founded a press that published Italian-language editions of anarchist classics—along with original work by Malatesta and other distinguished Italians.

All of this was thrown into turmoil by the events that occurred after Gori's resignation due to illness in 1896. The successor chosen in 1898 to succeed him as editor in chief was Giuseppe Ciancabilla, a twenty-eight-year-old writer of brilliance who had personally been recruited to anarchism by Malatesta in Ancona, Italy. But Malatesta—by 1898 imprisoned on the island of Lampedusa—and the group did not realize that Ciancabilla, while in Parisian exile, had gravitated to an extreme individualist position—assuming the nom de plume of "Atomo."

As editor, he found himself diametrically opposed to the group and to the dismayed Esteve. An ideological war filled the pages of *La Questione Sociale* through the summer of 1899. Control was dramatically recaptured by the group, however, when Malatesta effected a daring escape from Lampedusa on May 9, 1899, and appeared in Paterson to confront

Ciancabilla personally. Ousted from the editorship, Ciancabilla moved his office to West Hoboken (now Union City), where he gathered his supporters and started to publish *L'Aurora*, an individualist paper. One of these supporters was Gaetano Bresci, weaver in Paterson, but resident in West Hoboken. Bresci was to travel back to Italy in 1900 where, on July 29, he would assassinate King Umberto.

By that time, Malatesta had returned to Europe, having placed the paper in the hands of Esteve. When the storm of reprisals broke on anarchists everywhere in the aftermath, the Right to Existence group, as the most articulate, visible, and well-established organization in the region, bore the brunt of hostile Establishment action. Ciancabilla moved west, where he died as the editor of the individualist newspaper *La Protesta Humana*, on September 11, 1904, at age thirty-three.

Weathering the storm, the group resolved to emphasize American workers' issues, giving less coverage to events in Europe. A disastrous winter in 1901–02, in which fire and flood contributed to destitution in the millworkers' neighborhoods, led to mill closings and layoffs at the very time that living conditions became most desperate. The silk-dyers' strike of 1902 was the result, with the group deeply involved with the Italian workers.

Meanwhile Luigi Galleani had been recruited as editor in chief of *La Questione Sociale*. A Genoese lawyer, forty-one, recently escaped from the penal island of Pantelleria, he spoke French and Italian with equal fluency. And the strike committee had to organize itself by language: Italian, German, Dutch, French, and English being widely spoken by the strikers. Anarchists were strongest among the Italian- and German-speaking groups.

As the strike dragged on from April to July of 1902, the moderate leadership of Paul Breen and James McGrath of the AFL failed to cope effectively with management's strategy of subcontracting dyeing operations to non-striking mills in Pennsylvania. The Paterson weavers failed to join the strike. These factors proved fatal. The dyers were ready to grasp at straws by mid-June.

It was at this point that Galleani combined forces with two anarchist colleagues who came upon the strike-ridden Paterson scene: Rudolph Grossman, an Austrian, and William McQueen, a Scotch disciple of William Morris. The three—covering the languages spoken by the strikers—addressed a meeting of 8,000 on June 17. The subject: an exhortation to promote a general strike.

The speeches were fiery—especially Galleani's—and the frustrated and anguished strikers burst out of the meeting, violently damaging mill property. People were injured by pistol and shotgun fire—including Galleani. Martial law was declared in the city from June 21 to July 2. The strike was smashed, the union fragmented. First Galleani, then Grossman fled to avoid prosecution. McQueen remained to face charges of inciting to riot. Convicted, he languished in prison until 1907 when, pardoned over Theodore Roosevelt's objections, he returned to England, health shattered, to die in 1909.

It took Esteve three years to restore the paper to solvency after the 1902 fiasco. Finally, it went under for the last time in March, 1908—a victim of the anti-"red" campaign of that year. President Roosevelt and reform Republican mayor McBride cooperated to remove the paper's mailing privileges—under obscenity statutes!

The high-water mark of anarchism in the city had passed. By the time of the Great Silk Strike of 1913—the IWW's apogee—the socialist movement was in the ascendency, and had absorbed many of the erstwhile members of the Right to Existence group. *See also*: Anarchism; Anarcho-Syndicalism; Galleani, Luigi; Italian Americans; Paterson Strike of 1913; Textile Workers Unions

—*George W. Carey*

REFERENCES

Carey, George W. "The Vessel, the Deed and the Idea: Anarchists in Paterson, 1895–1908." *Antipode* 10–11 (1979).

Paterson Strike of 1913

A major struggle for the American Left, this strike by 25,000 silk workers shut down the 300 silk mills and dye houses in Paterson for almost five months. From the beginning, the strikers focused on issues of workers' control.

Strike poster

During the strike, they successfully overcame differences of nationality, craft, and gender; their democratic self-organization served as a school in self-management.

Unlike most textile strikes, including the 1912 strike in Lawrence, Massachusetts, the Paterson strike did not begin as a defensive battle against a wage cut. The broad-silk weavers called the strike on February 25 as a way of blocking an increase in loom assignments from two to four. As skilled workers, broad-silk weavers had fought since the 1880s for control over the rate of production. Responding to their strike call, the ribbon weavers and unskilled dyers' helpers joined the 1913 strike, making it the biggest in Paterson history.

Many of the silk workers had brought militant traditions of struggle with them from European textile centers; in Paterson they had welded their traditions together. The Industrial Workers of the World organizers whom they invited to help them in 1913—Elizabeth Gurley Flynn, Carlo Tresca, and Bill Haywood—added some traditions of their own. Flynn held successful weekly meetings for women only. With IWW encouragement, Italian and Jewish women like Carrie Golzio and Hannah Silverman joined the traditional local leadership of male weavers (Adolph Lessig, Louis Magnet, Evald Koettgen). IWW organizers stressed that the active role played by rank-and-file silk strikers in the management of their strike was training for the democratic management of industry and society. This revolutionary vision of workers' control reached its fullest expression in the "Pageant of the Paterson Strike" performed by over a thousand workers in Madison Square Garden on June 7. The event was conceived by John Reed and supported by the IWW, the Socialist Party, Greenwich Village intellectuals, and a social circle associated with heiress Mabel Dodge.

The Pageant was a propaganda success but failed to generate strike funds or decisive political support. Lacking the means to feed their families, the strikers were eventually defeated. Although they had shut down Paterson, beaten off an AFL attempt to undercut the strike, and nonviolently overcome a police offensive against them, they had been unable to extend the strike to annexes of the Paterson mills in Pennsylvania. Paterson manufacturers, victorious but frightened, held back the four-loom system for another decade. Strike supporters were torn apart as a result of the defeat, and the IWW never recovered in the East. Historical interpretations have been dominated by Flynn's version, which blamed the defeat on the Socialists, the Villagers, the ribbon weavers, the Pageant, and (in effect) Haywood. The creative implications of the Paterson strike, for the Left, remain largely unexplored. *See also*: Flynn, Elizabeth Gurley; Industrial Workers of the World; Italian Americans; *Masses*; Reed, John; Socialist Party; Tresca, Carlo

—Steve Golin

REFERENCES

Golin, Steve. *The Fragile Bridge: Paterson Silk Strike, 1913*. Philadelphia: Temple University Press, 1988.

Kornbluh, Joyce L., ed. *Rebel Voices: An I.W.W. Anthology*. Ann Arbor: University of Michigan, 1964.

Scranton, Philip B., ed. *Silk City: Studies on the Paterson Silk Industry, 1860–1940*. Newark: New Jersey Historical Society, 1985.

Tripp, Anne Huber. *The I.W.W. and the Paterson Silk Strike of 1913*. Urbana: University of Illinois Press, 1987.

PATTERSON, LOUISE THOMPSON (*b.* 1901)

As an educator, supporter of black culture, and early civil rights activist in Harlem, Louise Thompson's membership in the Communist Party created an indispensable bridge between black artists and Popular Front cultural politics. Born in Chicago but raised in several predominantly white, often racist communities in the West, she settled with her family in Oakland, California, in 1919. Although she earned a degree in economics from the University of California at Berkeley in 1923, racism limited her career opportunities and she eventually made her way back to the Midwest, where she briefly initiated graduate work at the University of Chicago. Giving up school, as well as a lucrative position at a black-owned Chicago firm, Thompson headed South to take a teaching job in Pine Bluff, Arkansas, in 1925, and a year later accepted a faculty position at Hampton Institute in Virginia. Because she openly supported a student strike at Hampton in 1927, the administration pressured her to resign, after which she headed to New York to accept an Urban League fellowship to study at the New York School for Social Work.

Unimpressed with social-work paternalism as a means to improve the lives of poor blacks, she discontinued her education in 1930 and turned to New York's Congregational Educational Society (CES), a liberal organization interested in the problems of race relations and labor. Simultaneously, she became a prominent figure in black cultural circles, serving as editorial secretary for Langston Hughes and Zora Neale Hurston, and offering her spacious apartment as a meeting place for black artists and intellectuals. Her involvement in social problems and cultural politics, compounded by the Depression, the Scottsboro case, and the growing strength of the CP in Harlem, radicalized Thompson. She and sculptor Augusta Savage formed a left-wing social club called the Vanguard, out of which developed a branch of the Friends of the Soviet Union (FOSU). Soon thereafter Thompson attended classes at the Workers' School, moving deeper into the Party's inner circle.

As secretary of the Harlem chapter of FOSU, she became principal organizer of a group of black artists invited to the Soviet Union in 1932 to make a film about Afro-American life. Although the project was abandoned, she returned to New York with a deeper appreciation of socialism and a greater affinity for Communist politics. In 1933 she left CES and served as assistant national secretary of the National Committee for the Defense of Political Prisoners (NCDPP), through which she was officially asked to join the CP. A year later she accepted a full-time position in the International Workers Order (IWO) and continued to organize cultural and political events on behalf of the CP in Harlem and elsewhere (including Alabama, where in 1934 she spent a night in a Birmingham jail). As black artists joined the Works Progress Administration in the late 1930s, Thompson was a critical liaison linking black popular culture and Harlem's literati with Communist Popular Front politics. In 1938, for example, she and Langston Hughes organized the IWO-sponsored "Harlem Suitcase Theatre," which performed a number of works by black playwrights.

In 1940 Louise Thompson married longtime friend and veteran Party leader William L. Patterson—who more than a decade earlier had suggested she read Marx and look seriously at events in the USSR. Soon afterward she joined "Pat" in Chicago and continued her work nationally and locally. Among other things, she served as national recording secretary of the IWO and helped establish a black community center on Chicago's South Side. Following World War II she was among the founders and leading activists of the Civil Rights Congress (CRC), and in the 1950s joined such luminaries as Charlotta Bass, Shirley Graham, and Alice Childress in forming the Sojourners for Truth and Justice, a black women's auxiliary of the CRC. *See also*: Civil Rights Congress; Communist Party; Hughes, Langston; Patterson, William L.

—Robin D. G. Kelley

REFERENCES

Horne, Gerald. *Communist Front?: The Civil Rights Congress, 1946–1956*. Rutherford, NJ: Fairleigh-Dickinson Press, 1988.

Naison, Mark. *Communists in Harlem During the Depression*. Urbana: University of Illinois Press, 1983.

Patterson, Louise. Interview by Ruth Prago, November 16, 1981 (transcribed), Oral History of the American Left, Tamiment Library, New York University.

Patterson, William L. *The Man Who Cried Genocide: An Autobiography*. New York: International Publishers, 1971.

Rampersad, Arnold. *The Life of Langston Hughes: I, Too, Sing America, Volume I: 1902–1941*. New York: Oxford, 1986.

PATTERSON, WILLIAM L. (1891–1980)

One of the most prominent African-American Left leaders, Patterson made his name as a legal defender of minority rights, Communist journalist, and teacher.

Born in San Francisco, the son of a mother who had been born into slavery in Virginia and of a father from St. Vincent, West Indies, Patterson attended the University of California (suspended for a time for refusing participation in ROTC) and went on to receive a law degree from Hastings College in 1919. After an attempt to emigrate to Liberia, he moved to New York as a practicing lawyer.

Patterson first became prominent as an African-American defender of Sacco and Vanzetti in the 1920s, and was arrested several times on picket lines. Soon a leader of the International Labor Defense (ILD), he abandoned his youthful conviction that the salvation of the African-American people lay in returning to Africa, and joined the Communist Party in 1927.

Returning to New York City after the Sacco-Vanzetti defense work in Boston had ended, Patterson plunged into the Harlem Renaissance. Paul Robeson and Dr. W. E. B. DuBois were among his closest associates. During this period he made his first of many visits to the Soviet Union, where he attended the University of the Toiling People of the Far East until 1931.

Back in the United States during the 1930s, Patterson became Party organizer for Pittsburgh and Harlem, then returned to legal defense as his mainstay. As executive secretary of the ILD, he played a central role in the seventeen-year defense of the "Scottsboro Boys." By 1938 he relocated to Chicago, becoming an associate editor of the *Midwest Daily Record* and a Party organizer for the heavily African-American Chicago South Side.

Patterson returned to national prominence at the end of the 1940s as national executive secretary of the Civil Rights Congress. In 1951 he led a Paris delegation to the United Nations, while Paul Robeson led a delegation in New York, to charge the U.S. government, under the 1948 UN resolution, with officially sanctioning genocidal treatment of African Americans. During this period, he also became a prominent advocate for the integration of professional baseball, and met with team owners and the commissioner of baseball to urge that step.

In 1958, Patterson became editor of the *Sunday Worker*, and remained a prolific journalist and political leader until his death. *See also*: Civil Rights Congress; Communist Party; International Labor Defense; Patterson, Louise Thompson; Sacco-Vanzetti Case

—*Maurice Jackson*

REFERENCES

Horne, Gerald. *"Communist Front?" The Civil Rights Congress, 1946–1954*. Rutherford, N.J.: Fairleigh-Dickinson Press, 1988.

"Humanity's Finest Son." *Daily World*, March 15, 1980.

Patterson, William L. *The Man Who Charged Genocide*. New York: International Publishers, 1971.

PEACE MOVEMENTS

A product of U.S. radicalism long before the appearance of the modern Left, peace movements have intersected with that Left in a continually changing pattern. Sometimes, Left organizations and, especially, leading Left figures have reshaped peace efforts. Far more often, mass-based peace activities have reshaped the prospects of the Left.

Peace activities began in the early nineteenth century, an outgrowth of religious and

"Federal Death Note" leaflet issued by anti-war protesters, 1970

utopian sentiments rooted in a contemporary perfectionism. During the rich social movements of the 1840s–1850s, peace figured regularly with woman's rights, abolitionism, and temperance as a subject of public discussion. The Civil War wrought havoc with popular faith in mediation and nonresistance, but organizations such as the American Peace Union revived afterward, and with them a respectable sentiment for benevolent internationalism.

Neither the immigrant- nor native-based Left, however, had much interaction with these movements beyond a few individuals (mostly prominent women reformers such as Frances Willard) until the U.S. imperial expansion of the 1890s. Anti-imperialism (so described for the first time) drew upon a circle of distinguished intellectuals centered in Boston, many of them likewise touched by Edward Bellamy's *Looking Backward* and by an imported version of British Fabian Socialism. Ernest H. Crosby (1856–1907), a Tolstoyan socialist, was the most prolific of radical agitators on war, with many essays, three volumes of poetry, and a satirical novel, *Captain Jinks, Hero* (1902), to his credit. His assault, in particular, upon the U.S. invasion of the Philippines and Cuba, was a literary high-point of Left antiwar (and antiracist) sentiment for decades to come. Political socialists, for their part, were generally content to denounce the U.S. actions (a prominent section of Jewish socialists, led by Abraham Cahan, endorsed the U.S. invasion of Cuba as a return slap at the Spain of the Inquisition) as the inevitable fruit of capitalism.

The Socialist Party raised the question of prospective world war almost to an obsessive level after 1910. Socialists intuited, correctly, that the ideological sources of their support would be corrupted by pseudo-patriotic militarization and that opponents of war would be fiercely repressed. They tapped into an indigenous isolationist sentiment and an educated pacifist constituency in putting forward arguments before and during World War I. Divided, ultimately defeated and crushed, they had by 1919 nevertheless conducted the most important radical antiwar movement until the 1960s.

To be sure, socialists were caught off guard by the endorsement of war bills by their European comrades. They had believed, naively, that socialist parliamentarians would never agree to armed conflict, and that rank-and-file socialists would not fight the wars. Still, they regained a sense of political balance by conducting vigorous propaganda against the "Preparedness" craze symbolically led by former president Theodore Roosevelt. Socialists reacted as if to a dress rehearsal of world war when, confronted with the U.S. invasion of Mexico, they bitterly attacked the imperialistic motives and bloody practices of the invaders—to the chagrin of conservatives who called for their repression.

In 1916 journalist Allan Benson won the

party's presidential nomination on the strength of a propagandistic antiwar series in the *Appeal to Reason*. Woodrow Wilson's own campaign claim, "He Kept Us Out of War," dealt Benson and the SP a severe setback. However, in March 1917 an emergency convention in St. Louis reaffirmed absolute opposition, including "continuous, active, and public" agitation against conscription. For the first time, significant numbers of intellectuals and trade union leaders defected from the party in favor of Woodrow Wilson and Samuel Gompers. A handful of former socialists went so far as to join government propaganda agencies and semivigilante "loyalty legions." A section of the Left, particularly those drawn to the Bolshevik Revolution later that year, argued that the "St. Louis Manifesto" was insufficiently militant, too pacifistic, or even pro-German.

As the only important social movement opposed to the war, the SP became a focus for activity. Petitions, marches, and street speaking were especially successful where socialists had long-standing political support: specific ethnic neighborhoods or districts (Scandinavian or German, Jewish, and many Eastern European) and a scattering of predominantly native-born areas with high labor or agrarian radicalism (Seattle and sections of Oklahoma). The Espionage Act of 1917 enabled the government to move against socialist publications and individuals, crippling the movement of native-born socialists too exposed and geographically dispersed to evade repression. Many immigrant socialists, on the other hand, found new support in their communities (and also new demands for specific policies suited to the national constituency's aspirations for their particular homeland).

Until riven by Communist and anticommunist factions, the party often did quite well in local elections, sometimes winning but more often raising vote totals over previous years. In New York City, Morris Hillquit ran an especially strong race for mayor on an antiwar platform. New rounds of indictments, along with the organizational schism of 1919, dashed Socialist hopes of rising to major-party status on the antiwar position.

But socialists also joined with pacifists and liberals in a number of other important peace movements. The most popular by far, the People's Council of America for Peace and Democracy formed in 1917 as a coalition of labor-farmer, Left, and pacifist forces. Among its prominent participants, Sidney Hillman and members of his fast-growing, Left-leaning Amalgamated Clothing Workers offered a new chapter to what would later be called "popular front" activities. Among other groups, the Women's Peace Party (later the U.S. branch of the Woman's International League for Peace and Freedom), the Fellowship of Reconciliation, and the National Civil Liberties Bureau (later the ACLU) all had active socialists in their leaderships and ranks.

Younger pacifists, usually religious-trained intellectuals, became socialists as they engaged in militant antiwar work. Kirby Page, Devere Allen, Norman Thomas, and A. J. Muste among many others found common ground in the magazine the *World Tomorrow*, and in conscientious objection to war. The SP supported COs, even as it paid a heavy price for resisting war-patriotism. When the party had dwindled, by the middle 1920s, to flagging support among older ethnics and college-trained intellectuals, that tradition gave it a special attraction otherwise absent. Within the YMCAs and liberal churches, the by-then widespread public disillusionment with war-making found institutional support. In the Fellowship of Reconciliation, where many of these individuals found a political home, socialist inclinations predominated, though without forcing opinions upon the liberal-religious following. The example of Mahatma Gandhi and his philosophy, popularized by the *World Tomorrow*, impressed many as a useful counterpart to socialism or antidote to the socialist philosophy's class-war sentiment.

The Communist Party in the period up to the middle 1930s added a note of militant anti-imperialism, a view hardly popular outside the Party's ranks but explained regularly in publications. More than the Socialists—due to particular Russian fears—Communists campaigned about the war danger in the Far East provoked by Japan's first moves against Nationalist China. Sometimes Communists, Socialists, and religious activists could join together, as in the public protest to the U.S. invasion of Nicaragua in 1926. More often, in these years, Communist sectarianism erected barriers against cooperation with such strident antiwar spokespersons as Socialist leader Norman Thomas.

During the middle to later 1930s, Communist- and Socialist-oriented student movements led massive campus demonstrations avowing nonparticipation in any future U.S. war. At some colleges and universities, such as the University of Wisconsin, administrators broadly shared student sentiments (or adroitly co-opted them), declaring "Peace Assembly" days. At others, students faced punishment and expulsion for their activities. The most formidable difficulty of the combined American Student Union was, however, internal. Communists (and many students of particular ethnic backgrounds with relatives threatened by Naziism) favored some kind of "collective security"; Socialists, with strong if short-lived support in mainstream religious institutions, leaned toward pacifism and a leftist isolationism.

The same strains limited the appeal of an otherwise exceptionally strong Communist-led group, the American League Against War and Fascism, with spotty but sometimes ardent support from ethnic and religious groupings, and with a student affiliate overlapping the ASU. At crucial moments, such as the Italian invasion of Ethiopia or the Spanish Civil War, pacifism and principles of noninvolvement seemed to give way. The SP itself, seriously diminished by the withdrawal of older ethnic groups, exerted less political pressure as it grew more militantly opposed to war. Such important independent peace leaders as A. J. Muste, the emerging public face of the Fellowship of Reconciliation, operated almost outside the existing Left networks.

The Hitler-Stalin Pact provoked a complex division on peace issues. Among unpolitical, American-born trade unionists, instinctively isolationist, support of Communist policies probably reached an apex. Among most liberal (and especially Jewish) intellectuals, support fell drastically. Socialists, led by Norman Thomas, joined a Keep America Out of War Congress, quickly eclipsed however by the conservative-led American First Committee. Trotskyists, for the first time active in antiwar propaganda, conducted a lively campaign among blacks and workers against America's involvement.

Far more than in WW I, U.S. entry (and the German invasion of Russia) brought thorough government repression of peace activities. Exceptions remained. While Communists in almost every case supported mobilization as a priority over labor or individual rights, the SP (like the now-small Industrial Workers of the World) supported the COs, who individually and collectively grew more important in several prisons as military conflict wore on. The Workers Party faction of the Trotskyist movement, although primarily economistic in its appeal to industrial war workers, put forward a militant refusal to accept the logic of war as defined by the major powers. An "Imperialist War fought under democratic slogans," the conflict permitted the growth of the leviathan state and the preparation for future, even worse wars—so ran the shrewd logic of this position. Toward the end of the war and shortly afterward, prominent spokespersons of this position, such as Dwight Macdonald and his *Politics* magazine, appeared increasingly prominent.

Until the height of the McCarthy years, the most visible peace campaigning could be found in the Progressive Party milieux. A significant bloc of New Deal supporters at first rejected the Cold War confrontationism of the Truman administration and its international equation of "freedom" with freedom of American commerce. Many ethnics, especially Greek, southern Slavs, and Chinese, viewed the fate of the homeland as entrusted to Communist-linked coalitions opposed to now U.S.-backed collaborators with fascism. Henry Wallace, Franklin Roosevelt's third-term vice president, seemingly moved to the Left to meet these views, and his challenge to Truman appeared to gain a wide public reception. His campaign for the presidency in 1948 was waged on the issue of the Cold War, but in a political climate of increasingly successful Red Scare tactics and the removal of Communist labor leaders from the CIO mainstream (or their defection to the Truman camp, with the same broad political results). What remained of the Left in 1949 hitched itself to the peace issue, carrying this perspective into the unpopular Korean War, but could not break out of Cold War isolation. At any rate, and in the face of growing revelations about Eastern Europe and Russia under Stalin's rule, "peace" lost much ground as a credible Left issue, especially among anticommunist socialists.

Pacifists, strongly tinged with anarchist sentiments, exerted considerable influence within this relative vacuum. Imprisoned by the hundreds during WW II, they had forged new links in the years afterward, especially on the East and West coasts. Pacifica Radio, in the Bay Area, brought together anarcho-pacifists with a friendly milieu of progressives. A series of literary-political publications, mostly from the West Coast but including Dwight Macdonald's *Politics*, initiated a new wave of cultural expression culminating in the more pacifist-minded works of the Beat Generation. In later years, poet-publisher-bookstore owner Lawrence Ferlinghetti would play an important role as an impresario of peace sentiments among rebellious bohemians. Meanwhile, groups of former prisoners of conscience formed a number of new peace groups including the Committee for Nonviolent Action (CNVA) and Peacemakers. Early and late they and such allies as the Catholic Worker group dramatized their sentiments with demonstrations at atomic weapons facilities.

The civil rights movement, with its seeming proof of nonviolence's efficacy and public appeal, provided the spark to turn a small and sometimes ingrown tendency into a major movement. Meanwhile, the virtual collapse of the CP with its hegemony over peace issues made possible anarcho-pacifists' breakthrough as Left peace leaders. The U.S. nuclear tests in the Pacific had alerted the public, for the first time, to the "fallout" issue. The pacifist Fellowship of Reconciliation (FOR) circulated a petition against testing, with Norman Thomas and Lewis Mumford among the signers.

Meanwhile, peace had begun to gain a respectability unimaginable at the height of the Cold War. The Albert Einstein-Bertrand Russell appeal of July 1955 united prominent scientists worldwide to call for measures of survival. Peace research among social scientists, with pacifist Kenneth Boulding as its leading figure, heralded the formation of many institutes and research organizations, some with radical pacifist connections. That same year, the National Committee for a Sane Nuclear Policy (social-democratic psychologist Erich Fromm supplied the acronym SANE) formed and published its first of many advertisements in the *New York Times*, calling for an end to nuclear testing. By 1958, SANE could claim more than a hundred chapters and some 25,000 members, ranging from distinguished liberals to socialists. While CNVA pressed direct action, the WILPF and FOR arranged press conferences and academic conventions, gathered signatures, and located an interested public.

Popular direct action such as the resistance of 2,000 New Yorkers in 1960 to the annual Civil Defense Drill, matched spreading campus actions. The Student Peace Union, founded in 1959 (and staffed at the national office level, to a large extent, by members of the Young People's Socialist League), announced a position independent of the two power blocs, conducting marches and rallies, and gathering signatures. Local progressive student groups, their leaders containing future New Left luminaries, echoed the call. The folk music revival, dating from the late 1950s and operating mostly on campuses, added considerable cultural ballast to stentorian peacenik exhortations. Mainstreamed in Bob Dylan's early work, it rapidly achieved cult status among youthful self-styled noncomformists.

At an intellectual level, *Liberation* magazine, founded in 1956, brought pacifist positions and a broad spectrum of non-Marxist, Left perspectives—from utopianism to critiques of Cold War culture—into the mainstream of a vaguely reorganizing Left. Anarcho-pacifist intellectuals such as David Dellinger and Paul Goodman helped create the image of the post-Leninist radical thinker, just as dedicated as previous Old Left cadre but also more playful and existential.

The "Ban the Bomb" peace movement, buoyed by a sense of détente, fell short of influencing national policy and, over the 1960s, lost many of its early ties to liberalism. In 1960 congressional critics of SANE, then at the height of its influence, had challenged it to demonstrate its anticommunist purity. SANE did so by dropping Left staff members and changing membership rules to weed out "totalitarians." A "peace delegation" grew in Congress, meanwhile, but only incrementally. The experience of the civil rights movement—largely unprotected by Kennedy officials in the South from the threats of the organized Right—once more proved instructive.

Ratification of the 1963 Test Ban Treaty, ending for the moment nuclear tests in the atmosphere, eclipsed the peace movement. But the Vietnam War soon picked up the pieces. Radical pacifists and SP veterans, including Norman Thomas, led the first anti-Vietnam War protest in New York City, in 1964. Johnson's rapid escalation of the war revived activity on campus. By April 1965, Students for a Democratic Society led a Washington, D.C., rally of 20,000, the largest peace manifestation in that city's history to that point. The Vietnam Day Committee in Berkeley, growing out of the free-speech movement, rallied nearly half that number.

From the standpoint of the traditional Left, a period of deep isolation rather suddenly eased. The campus teach-in movement of 1965 not only ridiculed official views but also brought hitherto unpopular views, and publications, to the attention of students by the tens of thousands. Two coalitions, in bringing together radical pacifists with Communists, Trotskyists, and Socialists, marked an unprecedented unity in the name of common antiwar cause (and party opportunity). The National Coordinating Committee to End the War in Vietnam promoted a low-level renewal of the factional conflict that pitted Left against Left, this time tactically—the Communists (not large in number, but connected and influential) putting forward the demand for U.S.-Vietnamese negotiations, and the Trotskyists (generally more active in local events) the demand for immediate withdrawal. Proliferation of antiwar demonstrations and sentiment tended to resolve this conflict in favor of a New Left style closer to Trotskyist positions but distant from the associated Leninist internal decision-making. On the other hand, the New York Fifth Avenue Parade Committee, founded in 1965 as a coalition of groups with Communists and Trotskyists most prominent (along with the radical pacifists) worked generally in accord over the next eventful years.

The sudden swelling of the peace movement and radicalization of its participants, especially visible on the campuses, created, more than any other influence, the largest U.S. radical movement since the 1930s. Far more than in the mid-1930s or the brief anti-Cold War tendency of the late 1940s, "peace" indeed tended to be equated with social transformation. Twenty years of Cold War military buildup had forged a vast infrastructure—economic, political, and military—that yielded to careful analysis the essential meaning of the current system. The inclusion of well-paid, white industrial workers (especially those working in war production) and the exclusion of minorities from the benefits of the consumer society seemingly validated the view of a radicalism joined to the "counterculture" on one side and to "Black Power" militants on the other.

The further escalation of the war tended to shunt aside pacifism. The assassination of the Rev. Martin Luther King, Jr., in 1968, removed the single leader who—increasingly close to articulating a sort of Christian Socialism—could have made peace sentiments the dominating spirit of the moment. Robert Kennedy's death, and the fiasco of the Chicago Democratic convention nominating Cold War hard-liner Hubert Humphrey against a backdrop of police-and-peace-demonstrator street battles, meanwhile closed off the liberal option.

And yet the peace demonstration remained the dominant form of the social movement, antiwar propaganda the dominant form of radical education. A succession of coalitions and events, then, preoccupied Left agitation. Decisions about tactics (ranging from whether to allow public draft-card burning to whether placards should be regulated) became at times overinflated symbols of differences, at other times the careful calculations for reaching an ever-broader public. The Spring Mobilization Committee of 1967, assembled at a time when U.S. troop involvement in Vietnam numbered nearly a half-million, itself rallied a half-million demonstrators (including 400,000 in New York City), the largest march of its kind ever held in the United States, and marked by tens of thousands from Harlem's all-black contingent. A handful of traditionally progressive unions (mostly locals such as District 65-RWDSU, but also the International Longshoremen's and Warehousemen's Union, and the United Electrical Workers) lent support, but the crowds were mostly students and young people. Later coalitions and marches largely followed these lines, even while greater numbers of unionists were joined by Vietnam Veteran GIs and others who, better than students, presented a "mainstream" anti-war picture to the media. Women's Strike for Peace, a grassroots organization with a background in the Old Left, perhaps exemplified the merger of peace and traditional women's issues.

Not surprisingly, the Federal Bureau of Investigation, local "Red Squads" and for a time the Central Intelligence Agency, undertook the most massive campaign of anti-Left intervention since the McCarthy Era. Enormous energy was devoted, from roughly 1965 to the early 1970s, to collecting information on campus and community dissidents through informants, mail checks, phonetaps (often blatantly illegal) and photographs of crowds. Between various law-enforcement and intelligence-gathering agencies, files upon perhaps a million and a half Americans were assembled. Agents of various kinds operated with virtually unchecked freedom to infiltrate and disrupt organizations, often through provocateurs' insistence upon an ultra-Left, especially violent, response to government outrages. Police violence accelerated against black radicals in 1967–70, making peace-oriented strategies for change increasingly unpalatable. To this government intervention, in no small degree, could be traced the precipitation of factional clashes and internecine warfare which devastated the New Left. Armed government assaults against peace demonstrators, most notoriously at Kent State University in 1970, had far more public emotional impact but less destructive influence upon the Left.

To old-line pacifist groups and sections of the Old Left, went the laurels of staying with the peace movement after the War began to wind down. Major New Left groups (most prominently SDS) fragmented and all but disappeared in any organizational sense. Later court cases would reveal an especially massive government campaign against the Socialist Workers Party, involving hundreds of agents, office break-ins, and other "dirty tricks" (the phrase coined in the 1970s for the Watergate burglary). But like the CPUSA, whose long-time allies in various movements also had a stronger influence in the wake of New Left collapse, the Trotskyist mainstream could withstand political shocks with considerable tenacity. In the last few years before US withdrawal, such new initiatives as the Indochina Peace Campaign of Jane Fonda and Tom Hayden highlighted the increasingly orchestrated character of the protest.

Even before the US withdrawal from Vietnam, some outlines of the future radical peace movement could be discerned. The failure of Alliance for Progress programs and the CIA-arranged overthrow of Salvador Allende of Chile with the wave of bloody suppression following that event swept in considerable sections of the Chilean Catholic clergy, and turned Latin American Catholics in large numbers toward the Left. Their sympathizers, sometimes strategically located within the US Catholic Church, eased away from long-standing Cold War positions to criticism of the existing regimes and of Washington's blatant manipulations. The covert and overt US support of "death squads" in Latin America provided American religious radicals their first important radical martyrs since Martin Luther King, Jr. The Salvadorean killing of three American nuns and the assassination of Archbishop Romero stirred especially wide criticism, and launched a peace initiative with radical overtones.

The participation of many ministers, priests and laypersons in the Sanctuary movement—and US government persecution of them—dramatized the changing situation for peace tendencies. A majority of Americans queried regularly registered opposition to US intervention. Despite generational and other difficulties, wide and varied sections of the US Left managed to play an important role in the anti-Contra Aid and other support campaigns. At the local level, nominally non-political movements, such as Sister Cities, had taken the place, more or less, of the 1920s Soviet Russia Relief campaign, or the ethnic Left working class support for homeland survival. Specific campaigns, such as Witness for Peace, brought thousands of Americans to view first-hand the toll taken by American-directed intervention. "Peace" as a cry for justice had revived, in a remarkable diversity of American milieux, an almost vanished sense of internationalism. The reality of Latin American Catholicism meanwhile virtually banished aggressive atheism as a public Left trait, and seemingly legitimized a religious radicalism of diverse qualities.

The Nuclear Freeze movement, peaking in 1981–82, had similarly popular credentials and ambiguous radical connections. Representing a rejuvenation of the mainstream type of protest characteristic of the 1960s, the Freeze touched communities large and small with the hope of disarmament and brought more than a million people into Manhattan's streets in June, 1982. The largest US demonstration of any kind to that point, it drew upon wide circles of respectables, most notably in the religious and entertainment communities. Perhaps most spectacularly among the protest's wide-ranging participants, Left community arts and protest arts tendencies such as New York's Political Arts Documentation/Distribution (PADD) expressed a graphics creativity for peace not seen since the 1930s if ever. Like the early "Ban the Bomb" movement, however, the Freeze did not succeed in influencing national political policy, and fell into disarray. By the mid-1980s, it had been all but captured and then robbed of meaning by centrist Democratic politicians. The merging of SANE and Freeze, in 1986, also exemplified the victory of professionalism over grassroots enthusiasm within Left-connected anti-war work—at least for the time being.

After the Freeze, small group acts of collective disobedience, and large-scale protests against US policy in Latin America marked the peace movement. Sustained peace "encampments" sometimes highlighted New Age-influenced feminist tendencies related to gender essentialism and directed against the patriarchal world order. Meanwhile, Leftish electoral bids, notably Jesse Jackson's 1988 presidential nomination run, espoused peace and disarmament issues. At the fringes of mass movements, but increasingly important at the end of the 1980s, Jewish radicals (and liberals) of many varieties joined to urge Middle East negotiations and peaceful acceptance of Palestinian self-identity rather than escalating violence and territorial expropriations. *See also*: The Beats and the New Left; Civil Rights Movement; Dellinger, David; Macdonald, Dwight; Pacificism; Rustin, Bayard; Thomas, Norman

—*Paul Buhle*

REFERENCES

Chatfield, Charles. *For Peace and Justice: Pacifism in America, 1914–41*. Knoxville: University of Tennessee Press, 1971.

Halsted, Fred. *Out Now! A Participant's Account of the American Movement Against the Vietnam War*. New York: Monad Press, 1978.

Swarthmore College Peace Collection, Swarthmore, Pennsylvania.

Van Gosse, "'The North American Front': Central American Solidarity in the Reagan Era," and John Trinkl, "Struggles for Disarmament in the USA." In Mike Davis and Michael Sprinker, eds., *Reshaping the American Left: Popular Struggles in the 1980s* London: Verso, 1989.

Wittner, Lawrence. *Rebels Against War: The American Peace Movement, 1933–1983*. Philadelphia: Temple University Press, 1984.

Peekskill Riots

When the Harlem chapter of the Civil Rights Congress announced in July 1949 that Paul Robeson would headline a benefit concert for them that August in Peekskill, New York, the Junior Chamber of Commerce of that city vehemently condemned the concert as Communist inspired and called for demonstrations to stop it. The concert, actually scheduled for Lakeland Acres, a few miles north of Peekskill, was to be the fourth in an annual series of Robeson concerts given at various sites in the vicinity.

But the August 27 concert never occurred. With Cold War hysteria, anticommunism, and racial hatred fanned to a fever pitch, veterans' forces and vigilantes—brandishing billy clubs, brass knuckles, and rocks—brutally assaulted a group of women and children who had arrived early for the concert. A display of books and pamphlets were burned, cars were overturned, and only after thirteen people were seriously injured did the police intervene. Robeson never made it to the picnic grounds.

Deeply angered by the incident, the black community held a large public meeting at Harlem's Golden Gate Ballroom and let it be known that "Harlem will fight back." Later, to an overflow crowd outside the Golden Gate, Communist leader Benjamin J. Davis, Jr., declared, "Let them touch a hair of Paul Robeson's head and they'll pay a price they never calculated." Another concert was planned and Robeson agreed to participate.

More than 20,000 people attended the September 4 concert and Robeson, guarded by a phalanx of trade unionists, performed magnificently. When the concert ended, the riot began. For several miles along the roads leading from the grounds, concertgoers were forced to run a gauntlet of veterans and vigilantes who pelted them with rocks and hurled large stones through the windshields of their cars and buses. At least 140 persons were injured and innumerable cars were wrecked.

In the wake of the violence there was widespread outrage. More than 300 people went to Albany to meet with the governor and to voice their indignation. But Governor Thomas Dewey gave them no hearing, blaming the "Communist groups" for provoking the incident. Robeson and twenty-six other plaintiffs filed a civil suit for over $2 million against Westchester County and two veterans' groups. After three years of litigation, the federal court dismissed the case and all charges against the defendants.

As Dr. Charles Wright noted in his summary of the riots: "The Peekskill affair accelerated many events that were already in progress and made many others possible that seemed only probable before. . . . Republican Senator Joseph R. McCarthy of Wisconsin was already testing the anticommunist line with which he would strangle the nation with brief and terrifying success." Author Howard Fast considers the riots the violent prelude to the anticommunism and racism that would mark the fifties—it was "the first great open manifestation of American fascism." *See also:* McCarthyism; Robeson, Paul

—Herb Boyd

REFERENCES

Fast, Howard. *Peekskill: USA. A Personal Experience.* New York: Civil Rights Congress, 1951.

Shapiro, Herbert. *White Violence and Black Response—From Reconstruction to Montgomery.* Amherst: University of Massachusetts Press, 1988.

Wright, Dr. Charles. "Paul Robeson at Peekskill." In *Paul Robeson: The Great Forerunner,* by the editors of *Freedomways.* New York: Dodd, Mead, 1965.

PEOPLE'S WORLD

From its first issue on January 1, 1938, until its last on May 31, 1986, the *People's World* (known popularly as the *PW*) reported labor and radical news to a milieu within and beyond the Communist Party of the West Coast.

Succeeding the more narrow *Western Worker,* the *PW* brought together Communists from California, Oregon, and Washington in a united front of sorts with progressive unionists, especially of the longshore and seafaring trades, and with prominent liberal supporters from Los Angeles to Seattle. Early on, the paper came to be known for its lively style, fashioned by *Daily Worker* veteran Al Richmond, and dramatized by the extremely popular columnist Mike Quin. A reflection of the West Coast Communist movement—less restricted to insular ethnic milieux and more integral to multiracial milieux than its East Coast equivalent—the *PW* achieved an easy acceptability in union and intellectual circles rare for radicals after 1920. In its years as a daily (1939–49), it had a circulation in the tens of thousands.

The *PW* suffered as the rest of the Communist movement, from McCarthyism and from internal woes of the 1950s–1960s. It succeeded to an extraordinary extent in maintaining (or reestablishing) ties after the worst of the repression, reemerging with prestigious supporters especially among movements for racial equality. More than any other Communist publication, certainly, the *PW* effected an accommodation with the changing political moods of the 1960s. Progressive Democratic Party candidates for local Bay Area and congressional offices, some of them elected, found in the *PW* a valuable source of support, and reciprocated in public gestures.

In 1968 editor Al Richmond left the *PW* after the Soviet invasion of Czechoslovakia. Veteran black journalist Carl Bloice took the editorial reins, and the *PW* continued to provide important coverage of current events (most notably, César Chávez's United Farm Workers crusade, as seen by reporter Sam Kushner). The "united front" character of the paper diminished, however, and the CP remained virtually alone in its support and staffing of the paper. In 1986 the *PW* merged with the *Daily World* to form the *People's Daily World*, which, despite retention of several prominent *PW* writers, more nearly resembled the New York than the California version of Left journalism. *See also*: California, Communist Party, *Daily Worker*

—*Paul Richards*

REFERENCES
Richmond, Al. *A Long View from the Left*. Boston: Beacon Press, 1971.

Pesotta, Rose (1896–1965)

A lifelong anarchist, Pesotta (originally Peisotaya), served as the only woman on the general executive board of the International Ladies Garment Workers Union from 1933 to 1944. Frustrated by the male-dominated leadership, Pesotta poured her energies into her role as general organizer and worked directly and creatively among the 300,000 members, 85 percent of whom were women.

Pesotta was born in the Ukraine, where her parents supported the resistance movement against the Czarist government. In 1913 she decided to follow her older sister to the *Goldene Mdeeni*, the American Land of Gold, and, like thousands of other Jewish teenage women, joined the ranks of New York's shirtwaist makers. Pesotta joined Local 25, which had emerged from the strike of 1909–10 the vital center of the ILGWU, and participated in its innovative educational and recreational programs at Unity House in the nearby Pocono Mountains. By the early 1920s Pesotta had been elected to Local 25's executive board. In 1922 she attended Bryn Mawr College's summer school for working women, and a year later she applied to Brookwood Labor College (Katonah, New York). From these experiences, Pesotta firmed her commitment to the principles of workers' education and applied her lessons directly in her organizing efforts.

Pesotta became active in the Sacco-Vanzetti defense case in 1922 and was arrested in a demonstration protesting their execution in 1927. During this period she was also involved in the International Anarchist Group in New York and attended anarchist conferences throughout the 1920s. Between 1925 and 1929 she served as general secretary of the publication *Road to Freedom* and wrote for the journal until it folded in 1932. Like her friend Emma Goldman, she remained a staunch anticommunist until her death.

The New Deal sanction of collective bargaining inaugurated a decade of trade union organizing for Pesotta. She conducted organizing compaigns in Los Angeles, San Francisco, Puerto Rico, Seattle, Atlantic City, Milwaukee, and Buffalo. In 1937, during the sit-down strikes, she left the garment industry to organize the women's auxiliaries of rubber workers in Akron, Ohio, and auto workers in Flint, Michigan. She returned to her own union in the late 1930s to head very difficult campaigns in Montreal, Cleveland, Boston, and the Mohawk Valley of New York.

Pesotta worked closely with local women leaders in the ILGWU and seemed to possess a remarkable ability to speak to many ethnic groups. Her sincere respect for their labor, her regard for needlework as a craft rather than unskilled trade, undoubtedly provided a bridge between them. When she quit the itinerant life of the organizer, she returned quite happily, it seems, to her trade. She wrote *Bread Upon the Waters* (1945), memoirs of her years with the ILGWU, and another autobiography, *Days of Our Lives* (1958). *See also*: Anarchism, International Ladies Garment Workers Union, Sacco-Vanzetti Case

—*Mari Jo Buhle*

REFERENCES

Kessler-Harris, Alice. "Organizing the Unorganizable: Three Jewish Women and Their Union." In *Class, Sex, and the Woman Worker*, edited by Milton Cantor and Bruce Laurie. Westport: Greenwood Press, 1977.

Rose Pesotta Papers, New York Public Library.

Schofield, Ann. Introduction to *Bread Upon the Waters*, by Rose Pesotta. Ithaca: ILR Press, 1987.

Petersen, Arnold (1885–1976)

Born in Denmark, Petersen was the dominant figure of the (American) Socialist Labor Party after Daniel DeLeon. He joined the SLP in 1908 and served as its national secretary from February 1914 until his resignation in May 1969.

He was completely devoted to DeLeon's program and wrote numerous pamphlets about DeLeon and DeLeonism. Trained as an accountant, he assumed his post with the party in a state of near-bankruptcy and was largely responsible for its relative stability for many years. He opposed unity with the Socialist Party, and during his tenure the SLP refused to work with other groups, characterizing them as reformist. He was also opposed to violence, contending that revolutionary change could occur peaceably in the United States through electoral victory and support from a revolutionary union.

Critics contended that he acted undemocratically and was hostile toward new tactics. Under his administration, there were numerous splits and expulsions. Yet the party's membership shrank mainly from attrition by aging. *See also*: Socialist Labor Party

—*Ben Perry*

REFERENCES

"A Political Rebel Looks Back to '08." *New York Times*, March 8, 1964.

Philosophy

The importation of Marxism to the United States through the immigrant socialist press brought philosophy into Left discussions in the 1870s–1890s. Editors, joined by lecturers and autodidact workers, succeeded in introducing a radical philosophical and political outlook, at least to their constituents, into a terrain dominated by rationalism, empiricism, utopianism, and soon, pragmatism and logical empiricism. In effect, they prepared socialist thought for further development in later decades.

Prior to 1920, Marxism proper itself was not, however, the overpowering influence that it would become for radicals under Communism's Left hegemony. Radical German-American intellectuals, before the 1880s, provided their constituents a mixture of ideas drawing upon German romanticism, and on freethought, anarchist, and socialist doctrines. On the one hand, they like other ethnic socialists were dedicated to disproving theology with "scientific" examination of natural and social conditions. On the other hand, they espoused a militant idealism of the eternal struggle for justice, now realized in the proletarian struggle. At the high point of German influence, the middle 1880s, "natural rights" arguments against all class societies tended to dominate revolutionary socialist discourse. Marxist materialism ruled in the disappointing aftermath, but never without reservations.

Jewish socialists and anarchists conducted a spirited philosophical debate in Yiddish on many of these points, in their newspapers and journals. A deep strain of anti-Marxist philosophy persisted especially among Jewish anarchists, whose greatest intellectual figure, Rudolf Rocker, devoted his chief talents to a disproof of historical materialism. Jewish socialists in many varieties (but notably socialist-Zionists) transmuted historic Jewish doctrines of suffering and redemption into messianic versions of materialist socialism. As with the German Americans, what little could be discerned about Marxist philosophy, through *Capital* and other works, did not suffice and had to be supplemented with other ideas at hand.

With the coming of English-language socialism, Marxism was infused with scientific analogies, notably in the widespread use of Engels's *Socialism, Utopian and Scientific.* Daniel DeLeon preached this doctrine with special fervor, and Walter Thomas Mills's widely used socialist textbook, *The Struggle for Existence* (1901) became a Socialist Party study-group standard for the further simplification of Engels's notions. Nevertheless, *Anti-Dühring* achieved its first translation at the hands of Austin Lewis, who criticized Engels's notions of dialectics as reductive and inadequate. The Charles H. Kerr Company and its popular monthly, the *International Socialist Review,* militantly promoted as revolutionary favorites of the hour philosophers Joseph Dietzgen and Antonio Labriola: the first as articulator of a dialectical materialism that ordinary people could embrace in their daily lives; the second as continuator of the Hegelian tradition within Marxism.

With Debsian Socialism's disintegration, a spirited eclecticism passed. More important, the leadership of Communists coincided, in the 1920s–1930s, with a significant diminution of the autodidact tradition. Lenin's and Stalin's works, particularly the former's *Materialism and Empirio-Criticism,* came to be considered Marxist philosophy par excellence just as the habits of self-learning fell to film, radio, and popular culture with the general disappearance of a diverse Left press. Philosophical rumination, once the domain of the ruminating self-taught intellectual, became an academic science.

Sidney Hook's *Toward An Understanding of Karl Marx* (1933) and *From Hegel to Marx* (1935), reintroduced once-familiar themes of mechanical materialism's limitations, but added to them new revelations about the themes of alienation and praxis in the still-unknown "young Marx." Spokesman of an anti-Soviet Marxism, albeit decreasingly Marxist in tone, Hook tried to subsume Marxism into Deweyian pragmatism, before rejecting it altogether in the 1940s. His sometime allies, among non-Stalinist socialists of the *Modern Quarterly* and the *Partisan Review,* followed much the same course. Max Eastman's pamphlet, *The Last Stand of Dialectical Materialism* (1935), was the outstanding popular (or vulgar) version of the challenge. James Burnham, cofounder of the Left-philosophical journal *Symposium* in the early 1930s, closed out the era with a blistering attack upon dialectics as a hinderance to Trotskyism (which he would, in turn, renounce a few years later, en route to conservatism). The Popular Front–oriented *Science & Society* meanwhile attempted, without great success, to maintain the faith in Russian-style socialism's scientific claims.

Another, more sophisticated and ultimately more influential strain of Marxism emerged in the 1930s–1940s from German exiles and a small group of Trotskyist thinkers. The so-called Frankfurt School developed a "critical theory" of society that provided significant contributions eventually destined to help shape the New Left philosophical approach. C. L. R. James, Raya Dunayevskaya, Grace Lee, and their "Johnson-Forest Tendency" fostered the translation of sections from Marx's *1844 Economic-Philosophical Manuscripts* and urged a rethinking of Marxism in light of Hegel and the young Marx's contributions.

By the 1960s many diverse theoretical and political tendencies emerged in the United States, organized respectively around journals and political organizations such as the Students for a Democratic Society. SDS's formal perspective on U.S. society and its use of empire owed more to C. Wright Mills and William Appleman Williams than to Marx, but many in the New Left turned to various currents of Marxism then circulating. Structuralism, most notably developed by Althusser, found its champion and an intellectual coterie among the readers of *New Left Review* from the middle 1960s onward. A revived Hegelianism reached a younger generation of mostly academic readers via *Telos,* the sole philosophical journal attached to the New Left, and the unique proponent of radicalized phenomenology (principally via the Italian philosopher Enzo Paci and his Eastern European counterparts) en route to a Middle European melange of radicalism and neo-liberalism. *Radical America* reintroduced C. L. R. James as champion of a dialectics liberated from Stalinism and intellectual neocolonialism.

A rising interest in Marxism within the universities from the 1960s onward prompted a Left philosophical revival taking stride just as the New Left proper had disappeared. While a linguistic-oriented analytic philosophy was still hegemonic, universities began hiring more Marxist philosophers who taught Marxist-oriented courses, and major university presses began publishing numerous books on Marxist theory. Marxist philosophy itself underwent dramatic changes. In addition to German currents of a mostly Hegelian Marxism, other imports (from France in particular) were transmuted in attempts to synthesize Marxism with such theories as structuralism, poststructuralism and deconstruction. By the later 1970s, an "analytic Marxism" flourished as an effort to apply techniques of Anglo-American philosophy and game theory to a critical analysis of Marxism. At the same time, feminists proposed a synthesis of Marxism and feminism, while liberation theologians proposed a parallel synthesis of Marxist philosophy with biblical readings and hermeneutics. Fresh attempts to demolish Marxism came from many directions, but especially the "New French Philosophers" and poststructuralists such as Jean Baudrillard. Yet neither new attempts to work out syntheses nor post-Marxist efforts to develop new philosophical perspectives have achieved widespread acceptance. Despite Marxism's evident limitations, no new philosophical theory or synthesis provided a compelling successor. *See also*: Dunayevskaya, Raya; Hook, Sidney; James, C. L. R.

—Steven Best, Paul Buhle, Douglas Kellner

REFERENCES
Buhle, Paul. *Marxism in the USA*. London: Verso, 1987.

Photography

American photography has been enhanced by contributions by photographers who were committed to leftist causes and by photographers who although not particularly politically active contributed work of political significance. In the early days of American photography contributions were made to progressive causes by people who were not especially politically Left in their lives or work. An example of this is the work of Jacob Riis, which documented the inadequate living conditions of New York City's poor. Although he was much more involved with writing and political reform work than with photography, Riis's photographs, which he used in lantern slide-shows and in his book *How the Other Half Lives: Studies Among the Tenements of New York* (1890), contributed to the improvement of the housing laws in New York City.

Lewis Hine very consciously used the camera for political purposes. In his 1909 speech "Social Photography: How the Camera May Help in the Social Uplift," he argued that photography was an important weapon in the fight against social injustice. He felt that the condensed meaning in a photograph and the belief most people have in the honesty of the medium made photographs powerful "levers." He felt that "the picture is a symbol that brings one immediately into close touch with reality. . . . In fact, it is often more effective than the reality would have been, because, in the picture, the nonessential and conflicting interests have been eliminated. The picture is the language of all nationalities and all ages." Working as the staff photographer for the National Child Labor Committee, he used photography to document the miserable working conditions that children were forced to endure. He was also known for his moving photographs of immigrants, his documentary work on life in Pittsburgh, and for his inspiring photographs of workers, particularly his series on the construction of the Empire State Building.

An important documentary project with serious political implications was that done by the Farm Security Administration photographers under the direction of Roy E. Stryker. Although there is debate about the extent to which this work was put to overly reformist uses, there is no disagreement about what an extraordinary achievement it was. The photographers in this federal project—John Collier, Jack Delano, Walker Evans, Theo Jung, Dorothea Lange, Russell Lee, Carl Mydans,

Arthur Rothstein, Ben Shahn, and Marion Post Walcott—were very successful in portraying and documenting the lives of the people suffering the terrible deprivations brought on or exacerbated by the Depression, particularly in rural areas. Their photographs of the conditions that poor and working-class people lived in helped motivate people to work for social justice or at least to have some sympathy for people suffering from the deteriorating economic situation. Certainly their work resulted in a huge archive of photographs that illuminate a part of life in the thirties.

A very different philosophy motivated the Photo League, which was founded by Sid Grossman and Sol Libsohn in 1936. It grew out of the radical Film and Photo League, and the people who founded it and many who joined it later shared the belief that photography could and should be used to further the struggle for peace, freedom, and justice. In the late '30s the Photo League was known for its documentary projects and its school, which taught photography to many who would go on to be excellent photographers. Its programs of exhibitions and its lecture series attracted some of the most important photographers in the world, including Ansel Adams, Berenice Abbott, Margaret Bourke-White, Manuel Alvarez Bravo, Henri Cartier-Bresson, Harold Corsini, Morris Engel, Robert Frank, Lewis Hine (whose work they saved for posterity), Leo Hurwitz, Jerome Liebling, Elizabeth McCausland, Jack Manning, Lisette Model, Paul Strand, Roy Stryker, Weegee, Dan Weiner, and Edward Weston. Many of these people also lectured to the students at the school and contributed to *Photo Notes*, a newsletter that contained articles, reprints from other newspapers and magazines, book reviews, and analyses of exhibitions.

The work that came out of the Photo League was important and impressive. Documentary projects that were completed and shown included Sid Grossman and Sol Libsohn's *Chelsea Document* and Walter Rosenblum's *Pitt Street*. The Feature Group, led by Aaron Siskind, produced a number of important projects such as *Portrait of a Tenement* (1936), *Dead End: The Bowery* (1937–38), *Park Avenue: North and South* (1937), and *The Catholic Worker Movement: St. Joseph's Home* (1939–40). Their most famous and most successful project was *The Harlem Document*, which was undertaken to be a book. Much of this work was exhibited and published in magazines and some of it was exhibited in New York City in 1988.

The League succeeded in supporting a socially oriented, humanistic photography that documented the complexity and contradictions of American society in the '30s and '40s. Unfortunately the organization was a victim of the Red Scare after World War II. Harassed by the FBI and listed by the U.S. attorney general as a Communist-front group in 1947, the League closed its doors in 1951. Many of its old members maintained their social commitments and continued to document life as they saw it. A new generation of photographers and critics rediscovered their work in the 1980s and made it available to the public.

In the postwar years there were photographers who consciously worked to use photography for socially useful purposes, but there were no successful attempts to organize anything like the League. One of the new photographers was Milton Rogovin, who has worked from 1958 to the present on what he calls "the forgotten ones." His photographs of gospel services and of workers in Buffalo show a strong political consciousness. Now eighty years old, he is at work at a documentary project on the life of coal miners. He has photographed miners in Chile, Appalachia, France, Scotland, Spain, and China.

In the '60s there were many photographers who attempted to document the movements to change the country and for a few years in the late '60s and early '70s Liberation News Service attempted to set up an alternative photo service that could provide the many countercultural newspapers and magazines with relevant and useful photographs. But it died with the atrophying of the movements that supported it.

In the years that followed, there were few successful attempts to organize photographers politically or for photographers to work together in politically oriented groups. Occasionally a photographer succeeded in getting politically motivated work out into the world, but it was rare and frequently the audience was very limited. During the Vietnam War, a number of photographs were published that had an effect on the North American public. Malcolm Browne's 1963 photograph of a Buddhist monk burning himself to death in protest against the corrupt Diem regime, Eddie Adams's photograph of the Saigon police chief shooting a prisoner in the head, Nick Ut's photograph of a naked child, Kim Phuc, running down a road after a napalm attack, and Ron Haeberle's famous photograph from the My Lai massacre all had political repercussions though the photographers described themselves as not taking political stands.

Eugene Smith also was not a political activist nor does his writing show a high degree of political consciousness, though he did join the Photo League after WW II and served as its president. His politics could probably be described as liberal or humanistic. Yet he produced one of the few good political books in the '70s. An important photojournalist who worked with *Life*, he went with his wife, Aileen, to the small Japanese city of Minimata. The people who lived in the fishing villages near Minimata were suffering in great numbers from mercury poisoning from the wastes being dumped into the Shiranui Sea by the Chelso Chemical Company. For years, Smith photographed the results of this environmental disaster. He not only photographed the dumping of the chemicals but the tragic results of the chemical companies' utter disregard for the lives of their workers and neighbors. He photographed the deformities and diseases that resulted and the terrible pain they brought to the people of Minimata. He also photographed the struggle to bring the company to account, including the demonstrations, the violence of the company guards, and finally the court trials that resulted. In the process of the struggle, he was badly beaten by the guards and sustained injuries to his head that affected his eye.

In the late '70s and into the '80s a new generation of photographers whose political consciousness could be traced to the Vietnam War protests and countercultural movements began to produce photographic work that was consciously politically oriented. Susan Meiselas's work on Nicaragua, Roland L. Freeman's work on black life in the South, Steve Cagen's work on Nicaragua and industrial collapse in the Midwest, Fred Lonidier's work on health of workers, Allan Sekula's work on schools, workers, and boundaries, Diane Neumaier's work on sexism and racism, Builder Levy's work on miners, Connie Hatch's work about gentrification in California and about gender roles, Ken Light's work on migrant workers and undocumented workers, Earl Dotter and George Cohen's separate works on union members, Mel Rosenthal's work on the South Bronx, a land-rescue community in Puerto Rico, and on refugees in the United States all reveal conscious political stances and point to the vitality of the movement to use photography as a tool for social change.

In 1986 progressive photographers and graphic artists in New York set up Impact Visuals, a cooperative whose purpose was to provide alternative media with affordable visual images regarding issues of political importance. The cooperative quickly grew to 200 members throughout the nation and established contacts with like-minded organizations in other nations. It continues to focus on the radical, community-use, nonprofit, and issue-oriented press, but has gradually begun to serve the commercial press at commercial rates as a means of subsidizing low-cost service to its primary constituency. In this sense Impact Visuals was a renewed effort in the tradition pioneered by the Photo League and Liberation News Service. *See also*: Liberation News Service, Radical Filmmaking—the 1930s

—*Mel Rosenthal*

REFERENCES

Rosenblum, Naomi. *A World History of Photography*. New York: Abbeville Press, 1984.

Trachtenberg, Alan. *Classic Essays on Photography*. New Haven: Yale University Press, 1980.

PM

In June 1940, when the achievements of the New Deal and the CIO were part of an immediate political experience, *PM* was launched to give New York City a daily newspaper that would "crusade for those who improve constructively the way men live together" and would "attack those who push other people around." The venture was made possible by Marshall Field III, the Chicago millionaire who was eccentric enough to think a newspaper should not be impartial in matters of economic and social struggle. Ralph Ingersoll resigned as publisher of *Life* to become editor and 11,000 people applied for the 150 available jobs. Although *PM* would average 165,000 daily circulation, the financial break-even point was 225,000. *PM* was sold in 1948 and renamed the *Star*, which became defunct a year later. The *Daily Compass* tried to carry on the *PM-Star* tradition thereafter, but it, too, quickly expired.

Throughout its existence *PM* was frequently Red-baited for employing politically radical reporters, including known members of the Communist Party. The charge that the paper was Communist-dominated was strongly reinforced when James Wechsler resigned a *PM* staff job in 1946. In articles and public appearances Wechsler charged that the Communist faction had intimidated the editors and other reporters on *PM* to such a degree that news stories were distorted and competent staff people felt compelled to leave. Among the evidence he cited for his view was that *PM* had been highly supportive of the USSR. Wechsler's judgments were recycled in many early accounts of *PM*'s history.

Succeeding historians without any personal involvement with *PM*, particularly Anya Schiffrin, have established a different analysis. The Communists and their allies had fought hard for control of the Newspaper Guild at *PM*, and the resulting acrimony may have been construed by some other staff members as an attempted editorial coup. Domination of the Guild unit, which, after all, was through an elective process, had been interpreted as domination of *PM* itself.

Schiffrin has shown that *PM* had a consistent left-liberal policy. It often opposed the CP line, editorially sparred with the *Daily Worker* and *New Masses*, scoffed at zigzags in the CP line, and downplayed or totally ignored many activities of the CP and its front organizations. A more fundamental problem for *PM* than radicals had been that Ingersoll, who had a clear vision for the publication, had left his post to fight in World War II. John R. Lewis, his replacement, did not have Ingersoll's skills. Production problems made *PM* the most expensive of all the New York City dailies and chronic mismanagement resulted in *PM* usually being the last paper to hit the stands. Adding to the price/lateness problem was that rivals had persuaded many newsdealers not to carry the paper at all or to display it poorly.

An underlying financial stress was that Field had decided that *PM* would carry no advertising, a policy that was not altered until the paper was near collapse. While altruistic, the no-advertising policy not only deprived the paper of needed income but of a feature the general public found positive, if not essential. *PM* was an aesthetic challenge to readers as well. The size and number of photos, the use of colored paper, the nature of some features, the general layout and topography, the early use of staples for binding, and other stylistic aspects were highly influenced by newsweekly formats. These innovations seem to have alienated rather than excited readers, who were also put off by the erratic quality of some of the reporting and the unorthodox editorial perspective. As James Aronson commented some years later, what may have been most remarkable about *PM* was that it survived for as long as it did.

The ultimate collapse of *PM* was a product of the changing political tides. From the mid-1930s to the early 1940s liberals had found it natural to think of radicals as having a legitimate and creative role in American society. *PM*'s founders believed a postwar movement to the left was inevitable and would be enriched by a newspaper that, free from the pressure of advertisers, could expose injustice fearlessly. The end of the war brought a much different era than had been anticipated. That Wechsler, a member of the Young Communist League from 1934 to 1937, was prominent in attacking *PM* is reflective of changing liberal attitudes. Wechsler would become a founder of the liberal Americans for Democratic Action in 1947, and by the early 1950s he had established himself as a respectable anticommunist who opposed McCarthyism on the grounds it was the wrong method for attacking a movement all Americans should regard as genuinely evil. *See also*: Communist Party; Hawes, Elizabeth; *National Guardian*

—*Dan Georgakas*

REFERENCES

Aronson, James. *The Press and the Cold War*. Indianapolis: Bobbs-Merrill, 1970.

Belfrage, Cedric, and James Aronson. *Something to Guard—The Stormy Life of the National Guardian, 1948–1967*. New York: Columbia University Press, 1978.

Schiffren, Anya. "We Are Against People Who Push Other People Around: A Study of the Newspaper *PM*." M.A. thesis, Reed College, 1984, available at Tamiment Library, New York University.

POETRY (ENGLISH LANGUAGE), 1870–1930

In the era of printed literature's greatest media importance, poetry occupied a Left status and a popular readership that have almost steadily diminished since. The proliferation of the local press, in English and non-English languages, found and also created an expanding radical audience, in many cases among a first literate generation. Poets occupied an important, sometimes central role in delivering the battle cry of the Left, mourning the tragedy of impoverishment and servitude, and intoning the eternal song of freedom.

English-language American radical poetry had several distinct origins. From Philip Freneau to William Cullen Bryant to John Greenleaf Whittier, many poets have mixed democratic aspirations with melancholy, as if the highest political ideals were themselves transitory or unrealizable in American life. This sentiment found its overwhelming popular and radical expression in the reform agitations of the 1830s–1850s, touched both by utopian socialism and by a growing sense of dread. Militant women, at the center of agitational and popular literary energy, expressed themselves freely in a radical, "spiritualistic," frequently antiracist vein. Some of their leading political figures, such as writer-agitator Elizabeth Oakes Smith, doubled as important popular poets. Indeed, "The Battle Hymn of the Republic," a major creative expression of the Civil War written by reformer Julia Ward Howe, can be seen as a foremost result of this ferment. Intimately related modes of versifying continued well into the early twentieth century, sometimes achieving form in proto-feminism, sometimes in sentimental reflection on the sorrows of the oppressed, sometimes in bold anticipations of the "Good Time Coming" under socialism. Pro-woman suffrage publications, before and after the Civil War, offered much space to poets conjuring woman's role in the new, purified society ahead. Often, the various themes of gender-consciousness, individuation, and a spiritualistic (or proto-surrealist) anticipation of bourgeois standards overwhelmed were mixed together. Thus the extraordinarily popular semiradical poet Ella Wheeler Wilcox, influenced by both gender consciousness and political events, could write, against the background of urban unrest, of her own emotions as being "like Communists," who "hate king Reason for being Royal" and would "fire his castle and burn him there."

A second current, at some points interrelated, stemmed from the venerable labor song-poem and the reformist currents of the English-speaking autodidact (generally skilled) laborer. From the early nineteenth century, in poetry written for music or for publication on special occasions, artisans had sought to distinguish themselves as a virtuous, hard-working, unique sector of American society proud to be performing their tasks without aspiring to wealth or fame. During the rise of national unions and their presses, especially in the post–Civil War period, many more writers made themselves heard. Profoundly influenced by Robert Burns, Shelley, Byron, and Swinburne, they were also enthusiastic about popular poetry—such as "Man with a Hoe," by Edwin Markham (himself an editor of Poe's published works)—that expressed the endurance and bubbling rage of the downtrodden.

Some of these currents flowed directly into the English-language socialist movement of the 1890s. Hard-pressed to maintain their status in the recession, and increasingly convinced that their America had been stolen away, such poets turned to a millenarianism that crystalized around the image of railroad leader Eugene V. Debs. A poet in the American Railway Union's *Railway Times* wrote about Debs's imprisonment following the 1894 strike at Pullman:

> He is coming! he is coming! like a hero to his doom
> Came the toiler's friend from the partial court to the prison tomb
> There was glory on his forehead, there was luster in his eye,
> And he never spoke to workmen, but what they could rely.
> There was color in his visage though the cheeks of all were wan
> And they marveled as they saw him pass, that great and goodly man.

Six years later, even James Whitcomb Riley wrote verse for Debs's first presidential campaign. And a "proletarian literature" of republican pride and dignity found its way into the far-flung socialist press. Meanwhile, many poets had rallied to the Bellamy nationalist movement. The *New Nation* and other Bellamyist periodicals published radical verse by Charlotte Perkins Gilman (collected in her contemporary volume *In This Our World* and used popularly by soapbox speakers for almost two generations), by Stuart Merrill (who was soon to become an important figure of Stéphane Mallarmé's symbolist movement in France) and Voltairine de Cleyre, who by the turn of the century had become America's best-known anarchist poet.

Yet a third current can be found in Walt Whitman's legacy of free expression, the vision of the open road, and love unfettered by law. Whitman's literary executor and for decades his reputation's chief publicist, Horace Traubel (1858–1919), was for many socialists and their sympathizers (including Traubel's own intimate admirers, among them Don Marquis, Helen Keller, Jack London, and Debs himself) the apex of this inspiration.

Traubel's *Conservator,* the premier socialist literary journal, 1890–1919, carried on the business of Whitman popularization through annual meetings and a steady stream of essays. It also sought to reconcile Whitman with William Morris, Debs, and the literary-political developments of the day as the *completion* of Whitman's vision, "the singer ascendant beyond and become a prophet" voicing the "soul of the workman" as the key reconstructive force of the civilization. In Traubel's own poetry, socialism ("the first glow of the earthly paradise which will yet be in the complete possession of man") called out for fulfillment:

> The great city was beleaguered, yet its foe was its own self, a heart within a heart:
> The great city was delivered, yet its walls were taken down, it was made open to the world.
> Nobody reigned, nobody was afraid, the fruit of the land tasted sweet:
> Men suffered but were not unhappy, death came but these men knew the secret of death:
> The children lingered longer in the fields, they picked no flowers,
> Others with equal title and love were to pass this way:
> The farms were not fenced in, the doors were for the wind and rain, not for man.

> The master workman—when will he come?
> We crouch in the wilds of our black cities, we die of gluttony, we die of starvation,
> Yet with one ear, listen.

In the more popular socialist press, these three themes of sentimental-mystical reformism, republican virtue, and socialist predestination mixed willy-nilly. Some of the most beloved writers worked at the strictly agitational level with humor or pathos. H. M. Tichenor, a popular columnist for the *National Rip-Saw* (and editor of his own socialistic free-thought monthly, the *Melting Pot*) gave forth his ironic brand of poetry without formal stanzas:

> The longer I linger the more I discern that this world of ours is a darn queer concern. It's a crime to pick pockets but it's perfectly right to pick a man's wages on Saturday night; for the laws are constructed, wherever I've been, that the workers are made for the grafters to win. . . . If you murder in war your valor is sung; if you privately murder you're doomed to be hung. If a girl sells her virtue she's branded as vile; but the rooster that bought it is met with a smile. If a man tells the truth, then the people get tired; if he tells them a myth, why they say he's inspired.

Further west, in the "red Oklahoma" where Socialist Party influence reached its highest national level, former Populist agitator Tad Cumbie wrote the well-circulated *New Songs of Freedom* for the socialist audiences to sing. To the tune of "Longing for Home," such verses could be heard across the Southwest:

They have given our lands all away
To the railroads and rich men you see,
And force us and children each day
To work for the landlords each day,
Working each day, working each day,
Work for a landlord each day

The poetry of the Industrial Workers of the World struck a new note by its pointed indifference to the work ethic, and by abandonment of the sentimental feminine themes of simple virtue. Wobbly poets sounded the tone, in the lumber camps, hobo "jungles," and agricultural fields, that the society that submerged its inhabitants deserved no respect or loyalty. Instead of the tearful laments and good-natured hopefulness of earlier craft-oriented labor poets, Wobblies sang defiantly of workers' revenge in such apocalyptic lyrics as Covington Hall's "Us Hoboes and Dreamers," and Ralph Chaplin's "When the Leaves Come Out," a paean to class war that Mary Marcy declared was the most popular poem ever published in the *International Socialist Review*. Wobbly poets also reestablished the primacy of satirical verse. In a devastating critique of "Meet Me in St. Looie," a song composed for the bourgeois self-celebration of the St. Louis World Fair, Richard Brazier wrote:

Meet me in the jungles, Louie,
Meet me over there.
Don't tell me the slaves are eating,
Anywhere else but there;
We will each one be a booster
To catch a big, fat rooster;
Meet me in the jungles, Louie,
Meet me over there.

Often prefiguring what would later be called "black humor," satire was also the hallmark of the Wobbly songs of Joe Hill and T-Bone Slim, as well as of Laura Tane's verse portrayals of "women's work," such as this section of her 1920s verse "Economics":

In the motley drippings
Of a hot grease-world
She waits and waits
Upon the Hungry Crowd
***
I saw a shower
Of blossoms fall
From her orchard
Of smiles
When a corpulent beast
Finished his dinner
And left a patch of green
Beneath the sky-white plate.

Arturo Giovannitti, one of the most renowned American poets of the day, editor of IWW-publicizing *Il Proletario* and agitator-hero of the Lawrence, Massachusetts, "Bread and Roses" strike, contributed his famous verse, "The Walker," from his Massachusetts prison cell. (The IWW quickly and frequently thereafter issued it as a booklet.)

In the pages of the *Masses*, its successor the *Liberator*, and a handful of other semibohemian publications linked to radicalism, a new aesthetic began to take hold. Here, what passed for high-aesthetic poetry, always thought to possess transcendent powers, gained a new playfulness and (to a lesser degree) a modernist free-form. It acquired a dignity in and of its own sake, in the writings of a Claude McKay, Max Eastman, or John Reed, better known for other work.

Most noticeably, it took on a more strident, avowedly feminist eagerness for a female sexuality scarcely imagined in sentimental poetry.

Mix prudence with my ashes;
Write caution on my urn;
While life foams and flashes
Burn, bridges, burn.

as Louise Bogan wrote in the *Liberator*. *May Days*, Genevieve Taggard's 1925 anthology, marked by her perceptive introduction, best presents this aspect as well as the larger drift of radical poetry in the era.

The quasi-modernism of the "Chicago" or Midwestern School, and the intended realism of Carl Sandburg among others, proved the major final note for the English-language socialist poetry aesthetic. Successors to an older bohemianism, Chicago realists both iconoclastic and socialistic sought to confront the dirt, chaos, and rampant exploitation in the modern metropolis with unflinching collective self-recognition. Carl Sandburg, the most active socialist of the major poets, offered hymns to industrial reality, with occasional side-glances of sympathy toward radical opponents. Lyricist Vachel Lindsay's "Why I Vote the Socialist Ticket" probably overstated his enthusiasm for socialism, but not his repugnance at American smugness or his veneration for the real American heroes (foremost, Lincoln) now turned into convenient symbols of reactionary ideals. More aggressively innovative expressions of a liberatory modernism—such as Mina Loy's exuberant feminist futurism/dadaism, Samuel Greenberg's Lower East Side surrealism, and Lew Sarrett's wild evocations of the ecological consciousness of Native Americans—remained isolated from the broad Left, and found few followers in the classically oriented English-language literary milieu.

Disparate and inchoate as any fixed trend, socialist poetry disappeared almost as swiftly after 1920 as the publications that had made it available to great numbers of readers. Its main currents belonged to milieus vanishing from the center of American culture. Perhaps Genevieve Taggard's final anthology, *Long View* (1942), best suggests how poorly this mode stood up to the treatment of such later themes as Russia, the Spanish Civil War, and the "Negro people." Individual socialist poets continued to produce some excellent work—Lola Ridge is perhaps the brightest example from the 1920s—but rather as late blooms of a fading tradition than as bards of a living and growing movement. Thus Marcus Graham's outstanding 350-page *Anthology of Revolutionary Poetry* (1929) proved to be a tribute to past glory, not a harbinger of things to come.

See also: de Cleyre, Voltairine; Giovannitti, Arturo; *Liberator*; *Masses*; McKay, Claude; Sandburg, Carl

—*Paul Buhle*

REFERENCES

Buhle, Mari Jo. *Women and the American Left: A Guide to Sources*. Boston: G. K. Hall & Co., 1983.

Duffey, Bernard. *The Chicago Renaissance in American Letters: A Critical History*. E. Lansing: Michigan State University Press, 1956.

Polish Americans

In the mid-1880s émigré intellectuals from Poland established the first Polish socialist societies in the United States. They soon formed several dozen Polish locals of the Socialist Labor Party, which attracted immigrant craftsmen and industrial workers from the Prussian partition, many of whom had had previous contact with socialists in Europe and German anarchists in America. By 1900 experienced organizers from Russian Poland created the Polish Socialist Alliance (*Związek Socjalistów Polskich*), which supported the left wing of the Polish independence movement aiming to reunite Polish territories absorbed into Russian, Prussian, and Austrian empires.

In 1908 the alliance split into a minority that supported Józef Piłsudski's faction in Europe (dedicated to building a secret military organization and terrorist actions against czarist authority) and a majority that stressed mass education and cooperation with the labor movement. The majority faction formed itself into the Polish Section of the Socialist Party and published the *People's Daily* (*Dziennik Ludowy*) at its Chicago headquarters. The most important constituency for both groups came from literate semiskilled and skilled workers with some urban experience before emigration, especially those from the Russian-dominated partition. Many were recruited through the popular education programs of the Peoples' University run by the Polish Section and by leftist activists among miners in the Pennsylvania anthracite region and textile workers in New England. By 1914 the combined membership of both factions was about 10,000. Polish socialists achieved wider influence by holding key positions and organizing locals in the Polish National Alliance, the leading secular fraternal, the Young Men's Alliance (*Związek Młodzieży Polskiej*), and the Falcons (*Związek Sokołów*).

In 1912 both factions agreed to back Piłsudski in the coming war to force the demand for a democratic Polish state onto the international diplomatic agenda; a Left coalition dominated the Committee for National Defense (*Komitet Obrony Narodowej*) created to raise funds and volunteers from

America for the Legions. By 1916 most of the Polish Section was expelled from the antiwar SP. Once the United States entered the war and supported the formation of a Polish army in France, the Polish Left became further isolated—failing to convince the majority of Polish Americans that the new army was a tool of Roman Dmowski's right-wing National Democratic Party. The committee also had problems explaining to U.S. military intelligence the anticzarist nature of Pilsudski's alliance with Germany. In the meantime, a handful of antiwar Poles, tied to Rosa Luxemburg's Social Democracy of the Kingdom of Poland and Lithuania (SDKPiL), took over the shell of the Polish Section of the SP and eventually formed the Polish Bureau of the Communist Party of the United States. In the 1920s the bulk of the old Polish Left, having lost a great deal of its credibility (with Polish Americans and with the American SP) during the war, concentrated on the more exciting task of building the socialist movement in the new Polish state.

In the 1930s Boleslaw ("Billy") Gebert and other members of the Polish Bureau played a leading role in organizing second-generation Polish Americans in the auto, steel, and meatpacking industries into the CIO. Their paper, the *Peoples' Voice* (*Głos Ludowy*), was published in Detroit into the 1970s. Leo Krzycki (chair of the SP's national executive committee and vice president of the Amalgamated Clothing Workers of America on loan to the CIO from 1936) and Stanley Nowak were also key labor organizers who emerged from the Polish Left during this period. In 1942 Gebert, Krzycki, Nowak, and Oskar Lange (the University of Chicago economist) helped found the American Slav Congress, which supported Roosevelt's wartime alliance with the Soviet Union. As in World War I, positions taken by the organized Polish American Left on foreign affairs alienated the majority of Polish Americans—this was especially true after the Yalta agreement of 1945. *See also*: American Slav Congress

—*Mary Cygan*

REFERENCES

Brożek, Andrzej. *Polish Americans, 1854–1939*. Warsaw: Interpress, 1985.

Frančić, Mirosław. *Komitet Obrony Narodowej w Ameryce, 1912–1918*. Wrocław: Ossolineum, 1983.

Gebert, Bolesław. *Z Tykocina za Ocean*. Warsaw: Czytelnik, 1982.

Groniowski, Krzysztof. "Socjalistyczna Emigracja Polska w USA." *Z Pola Walki*, no. 1 (1977).

Nowak, Margaret Collingwood. *Two Who Were There*. Detroit: Wayne State University Press, 1990.

Pamiętniki Emigrantów, Stany Zjednoczone. Warsaw: Książka i Wiedza, 1977.

Wieczerzak, Joseph. "Bishop Francis Hodur and the Socialists." *Polish American Studies* 40 (Fall 1983).

POLITICAL STUDIES

The fate of Left scholarship in political studies has been closely linked to wider social struggles. From the Second World War until the 1960s, with some exceptions, the field was thoroughly conservative in the United States. Most political scientists believed the political system to be fully open and democratic: all groups able to participate freely; government broadly responsive to all interests, not especially committed to any; and there were no deep or cumulative inequalities. Class, gender, and racial cleavages were barely mentioned. Although political scientists noted the low level of public participation by the poor, they took this acquiescence as evidence of apathy and of satisfaction with the system.

The civil rights and antiwar movements of the 1960s stimulated a wave of Left research, mostly outside political science. C. Wright Mills, G. William Domhoff, Seymour Melman, Frances Fox Piven, and Richard A. Cloward, among others, nevertheless addressed political questions. As Marxist critics later noted, many of these scholars accepted, however, the pluralist theoretical framework by focusing on groups rather than classes, and government institutions rather than the state. Their scholarship, while critical, had not been informed by a socialist vision.

By the 1970s, a second wave of scholarship—this time heavily influenced by European Marxism—shifted focus from government to the State, a move later accepted throughout the political science discipline. The term *State* signifies that the political and social order do not cohere naturally but are structured by an agency whose primary activity is to reproduce the existing system. The new focus also included examining how the functioning of American capitalism forged class inequalities within the United States and abroad, as well as dictated (and distorted) political priorities.

Initially, scholars assumed that reproduction of a capitalist economy was quite straightforward. A leading example was Ralph Miliband, a British theorist, who argued in *The State in Capitalist Society* that there was a close link between the economic and political elites within capitalist societies; indeed, at their higher reaches the two groups are close to being one. Soon, however, a number of scholars heavily influenced by Marxism emphasized the difficulties in reproducing liberal democracy. James O'Connor's *The Fiscal Crisis of the State*, and various essays by Samuel Bowles and Herbert Gintis highlighted the uneasy relationship between capitalist production and democratic political institutions. They argued that the State in capitalist democracies is responsible to two constituencies: it obtains its legitimacy from electoral majorities and, in order to gain widespread support, must distribute material and other benefits on a broad basis. The State is also dependent upon capitalists, however, to assure economic growth and prosperity, and in order to gain their cooperation must pursue probusiness policies that conflict with the interests of the majority. The State's attempt to placate both groups simultaneously provides a key to understanding politics in the United States and other capitalist democracies. Many Left scholars therefore studied the ways in which Franklin D. Roosevelt and the Democratic Party organized a cross-class alliance that effectively contained class conflict for several decades after the Second World War. Progrowth "Keynesian coalitions," in which limited struggles for distribution of the fruits of capitalist growth replaced struggles over the legitimacy of capitalism itself, were found throughout the Western world but especially in the United States, where the absence of a major socialist party denied workers representation on a class basis in the political system.

Left scholars proved prescient in arguing that the State would be unable to contain class contradictions indefinitely. Their works provided tools for analyzing economic crisis and political instability of the 1970s–1980s. They were less successful, however, at predicting the rise of the "populist" Right or in developing Left proposals to resolve the crisis. By the 1980s, a diffusion of Left themes within the broader political science discipline coincided with a decline of radical political scholarship.

See also: Mills, C. Wright

—*Mark Kesselman*

REFERENCES

Miliband, Ralph, et al. *Socialist Register*. London: Merlin Press, annual from 1965.

Political Theater of 1960s–1980s

The 1960s' counterculture inspired a political theater that was considerably different from that of the 1930s. Rather than preparing plays, actors, and playwrights to more or less "conquer" Broadway, the new theater, greatly influenced by Antonin Artaud and Bertolt Brecht, generally had disdain for conventional theatrical forms and physical settings. The new works were often revues and open-ended skits performed in other than theatrical settings. Many of the companies became communal troupes that traveled extensively. Scores of these companies existed throughout the United States and a few, such as the Living Theater, Bread and Puppet Theater, and the San Francisco Mime Troupe, had national and even international impact.

The single most influential of the new theater companies was the Living Theater, conceived in 1946 by anarchists Julian Beck and Judith Malina. Originally presenting plays by well-known writers such as Racine, Auden, Cocteau, and Pirandello, the Living Theater slowly moved to introducing plays by new American playwrights, the most notable success being Jack Gelber's *The Connection*. Both Beck and Malina were regular participants in antiwar demonstrations and were occasionally fined and jailed. With the 1960s the Living Theater became a commune that created collective works designed to stimulate audiences to direct action. While remaining highly political in content, the collective's work was increasingly abstract in form. The Living Theater toured for long periods in Europe and Latin America, and members of the collective often split away to form their own groups. The Living Theater's most ambitious later works were *Paradise Now* and *Frankenstein*.

One of the most distinctive groups in the mass demonstrations of the 1960s was the Bread and Puppet Theater. Using puppets and masks ranging in size from hand-held objects to giant twenty-footers, the group begun by Peter Schumann specialized in outdoor events. First appearing at rallies protesting the war in Vietnam, the company was still active in the 1980s in events protesting the nuclear arms race and American interventions in Latin America.

Another 1960s group with staying power is the San Francisco Mime Troupe, which was started by Ronnie Davis in 1959 as a subdivision of the San Francisco Actors Workshop. The group originally played only in public parks. Through the years the troupe has created works that can be played indoors and at other special settings. The style continues to favor broad comedy: the loud voice, the typed character, the exaggerated gesture, audacious costumes, bold makeup, and easily followed stories. The troupe finds comic hyperbole ideal for the conditions it satirizes for a mass audience.

The Pageant Players of New York also chose to perform in public places in the 1960s, mainly in streets and laundromats. Their first play, *Paper Tiger,* was performed at an antiwar rally in 1965. It featured live music, exaggerated costumes, and no speaking roles. The group continued to perform on street corners, in parks, in lofts, inside laundromats, and occasionally in theaters throughout the New Left period. One of the group's hallmarks was its inclusion of live rock-and-roll music whenever possible.

Although New York generated the most theatrical activity, there were production groups in many cities. In Detroit, socialist Edith Carroll Cantor launched the Unstabled Coffeehouse, which presented plays on weekends, launched comedian Lily Tomlin on a career that would take her to national stardom, and spun off the Concept East, a black theater company run by Woodie King. One of the Unstabled productions was *Sitdown '37,* an original play presented to a United Auto Workers audience in Flint on the twenty-fifth anniversary of the sit-down strikes that unionized General Motors. Groups in other cities include the Firehouse Theater, set up in Minneapolis in 1965; the Caravan Theater of Boston, begun in 1965 under the sponsorship of the American Friends Service Committee; the Performance Group of Chicago, founded by Richard Schechner in 1967; and the Om Theater of Boston, begun by Julie Portman in 1966.

All of the groups were racially integrated, but there were also companies set up to showcase the writing, directing, and acting talents of nonwhites. While somewhat more conventional in their choice of plays and settings, these theaters remained innovative in comparison to the nonpolitical theater. Among the most important of the groups was the New York extension of Detroit's Concept East. Director Woodie King eventually became head of the Franklin Street Theater and was responsible for a number of Broadway productions. LeRoi Jones (soon to be Amiri Baraka) and Larry Neal set up black theater groups in Harlem and later in Newark, New Jersey. Playwright Ed Bullins, then minister of culture for the Black Panther Party, set up the Black Troupe in New York City in 1968. The company was short-lived, as had been Theater Black, formed in Cleveland in 1966.

The major non–English language theater of the period was *El Teatro Campesino* (the Farm Workers' Theater), a traveling company established in 1965 by Luis Miguel Valdez in Delano, California, as part of the lettuce boycott campaign orchestrated by the United Farm Workers union led by César Chávez. The productions were primarily aimed at recruiting farm workers in labor camps and in small towns. Plays were also produced for supporters of the union who lived in major cities.

A Spanish connection was also integral to the Gut Theater of East Harlem, which grew out of Enrique Vargas's 1967 work with street gangs. The teenagers created plays based on their own life experiences and in opposition to the war in Vietnam. Much of the work was slapstick in style. One thirty-minute production, *The Bench,* dealt with a Puerto Rican family freshly arrived in New York. The Drama Group of Mobilization for Youth on New York's Lower East Side dealt with similar themes in a like manner.

The single most performed play of the time was Barbara Garson's *MacBird,* a satire on the war in Vietnam. Garson first comprehended the power of public performance during massive rallies in San Francisco. Like many 1960s authors, Garson pursued various forms of writing. In addition to subsequent plays for adults and children, she also wrote nonfiction about office workers.

Among those who practiced more traditional forms of political theater was Buffalo-based Emmuel J. Fried. In the 1930s he had worked in New York with Clifford Odets, Elia Kazan, and other militants in a subsection of the Group Theater. He'd also taken dancing lessons from Martha Graham. Throughout the 1940s and 1950s, Fried was a labor organizer, an activity that brought him to the attention of the House Un-American Activities Committee. He then turned to writing a series of labor plays that have been performed by alternative theaters in most major U.S. cities. His best-known works are *The Dodo Bird* and *Drop Hammer.*

As the radical movement began to wane in the 1970s, many theatrical groups collapsed or began to perform indoors. New groups sprang up to attempt the establishment of permanent radical theaters in major cities. One of the most successful for a time was the Labor Theater, created by Chuck Portz and Bette Craig. The group staged plays about the Industrial Workers of the World, Jack London, black outlaws, and labor education programs. The theater also shaped a feminist revue, *I Just Wanted Someone to Know,* written by Bette Craig and IWW historian Joyce Kornbluh.

A trend that accelerated in the 1980s was that radical directors, actors, and writers began to find employment in conventional radio, film, and television. They did not see this as a retreat from their old ideals so much as an accommodation to a new political climate and another means of trying to reach a mass audience. A handful of groups continued in the nontraditional vein. In addition to groups already cited, Heart of the Beast, a theatrical company in Minneapolis, became the focal point of the May Day parades revived in the Twin Cities in 1974. Combining socialist, environmental, and pagan themes, the parades wind through residential areas before culminating at a public park for a day of outdoor festivities. Radical author Meridel LeSueur acts as grand marshal and upwards of 10,000 people participate annually.

—Dan Georgakas

REFERENCES

Craig, Bette, and Joyce Kornbluh. *I Just Wanted Someone to Know.* Introduction by Barbara Mayer Wertheimer. New York: Smyrna Press, 1981.

Radical Theatre Repertory—1968–1969. New York: Radical Theatre Repertory Inc., 1970.

Popular Culture

An important if little understood element of the Left experience in the United States during the last hundred years, *popular* culture can be defined, quite simply, as culture that is consumed by large numbers of people, "largeness" being relative to activity and milieu. The term itself has been used to describe everything from the cheap novels promoting the virtues of the work ethic that proliferated following the Civil War to the words, phrases, and jingles that enter common parlance via television commercials today. The term should be distinguished from *folk* culture, which refers specifically to nonliterate culture that is laterally bartered by members of a preindustrial society, and from *mass* culture, which is a term of approbrium used to describe cultural items that are tailored by an economic elite to sell the greatest number of units without regard to aesthetic sacrifice.

During the late nineteenth century, American socialist movements consolidated their power in immigrant communities by offering Left alternatives to the dominant Anglocentric culture. Quasi-religious forms, including martyrology, holiday feasting, liturgical music, and iconography assumed revolutionary identities in linguistically and religiously isolated communities struggling to maintain familiar customs against the pressures of hegemonic assimilation. The group or workers' picnic, reputedly launched by German-American freethinkers to circumvent blue laws that closed public houses on Sundays and thus further restricted the precious little free-time allowed by sixty-hour work weeks, brought together families, neighbors, and co-workers in an environment that allowed for beer drinking and general camaraderie, but also often included political speeches or even didactic theatrical pageants. The establishment of ethnic "social clubs" for entertainment, education, and the promotion of organized sports can be seen as institutionalizations of "picnic" culture. The social club phenomenon persists among recently arrived immigrant groups today.

By the turn of the century, radical immigrant movements increasingly expressed themselves in the press. Virtually every ethnic group of size developed at least one inexpensive, widely distributed organ that brought together Old World cultural themes with immediate political, social, and economic causes. Daily newspapers served not only as conduits for news and editorial opinion, but as the cultural patrons of local poets, cartoonists, and fiction writers. Many papers translated popular European and American novelists into the languages of their constituencies. In some ethnic subcultures, notably Italian (but also Finnish), the mockery of religious institutions and personalities provided a mirror alternative to official culture; catechisms were a favored form of parody. In some cases, this kind of ethnic political activism survived into the radio age. In New York, the Yiddish-language radio station was identified by the call letters WEVD (for "Eugene V. Debs").

Mainstream commercial popular culture, which posed a threat to ethnic identity, appeared as a Janus-faced symbol to many immigrants. On the one hand, it was a threatening vessel of characteristically racist xenophobia. But at the same time, an appreciation of popular songs, films, books, plays, and other works seemed essential to finding one's place in the New World. Charlie Chaplin, greatly loved by the immigrant masses, suggested the universal and progressive possibilities of the cinema and of popular culture in general.

Native-born American radicals generally took a much less eclectic approach to popular culture, tending to focus their energies on literary forms. Walt Whitman, in *Democratic Vistas* (1871), stressed the point that the existence of any democracy is absolutely dependent upon the vitality of its popular culture; that is, the medium by which ideas are circulated and discussed among the masses of citizens. But even Whitman used the term "divine literatus" to describe the ideal artist of such a culture. Abolitionists could proudly claim Harriet Beecher Stowe's *Uncle Tom's Cabin* in this respect. Christian utopian socialists, woman suffragists, and agrarian protest movements all produced popular and would-be popular literary works, as did leftish strains of spiritualism and temperance.

Native-born labor traditions, rooted in the republican prerogatives of the skilled worker, fostered the translation of popular songs into socialistic poems, which appeared widely in labor publications. James Whitcomb Riley, the "Hoosier Poet" whose works attracted a vast audience, brought the central themes of republican virtue together with piety in a lyric for the 1900 presidential campaign of his intimate friend:

> 'An there's 'Gene Debs, a man 'at stands
> An' jist holds up in his two hands
> The kindest heart that ever beat
> Betwixt here an' the jedgment seat.

But in neither the immigrant nor the native-born encounters with popular culture did the concept of culture as the locution of mass consciousness—as the expression of a yearning for a better life—emerge on any theoretical or ideological basis. In Europe, quite the opposite was true. Such theoretical argumentation about the role of popular culture in revolutionary consciousness pervaded the prison notebooks of Antonio Gramsci and the theater of Bertolt Brecht. The writings of T. W. Adorno, Max Horkheimer, Herbert Marcuse, and other members of the Frankfurt School group would bring these issues to bear in America only after World War II.

Direct leftist involvement in mainstream American popular culture reached its apogee during the Popular Front era of the mid- and late 1930s. During this period a wide variety of political progressives helped promote a genuine appreciation of Afro-American music (specifically, the blues) and of liberal and Left-leaning elements in film (such as the Warner Bros. films of social conscience). Even sports heroes, such as Joe Louis, were enshrined as Cincinnatus figures. A hostile reaction to the acceptance of these popular forms by highbrow Left intellectuals galvanized in the pages of the *Partisan Review*. The masses, according to this bookish analysis, needed to be uplifted to the great (i.e., European) works, not patronized with such capitalist consumer schlock as untutored music, Hollywood movies, and professional sports. Clement Greenberg's 1939 essay "Avant-garde and Kitsch" rejected the American popular cultural imagination as a nightmare of degradation.

Twenty years later, *Dissent*'s unremitting hostility toward popular culture reaffirmed that nothing essential had changed the minds of the now highly prestigious, liberal-socialist intelligentsia. Among the popular arts, film alone had been allowed to graduate from "degradation" status into the arena of sympathetic discussion, largely because a new bête noire, television, had lifted it out of the cultural basement. Dwight Macdonald, who in 1953 had claimed that it was structurally impossible for Hollywood to produce a worthwhile film, actually became a film critic before the end of the decade. The surrealist-minded film critic Parker Tyler, who shared Macdonald's Trotskyist leanings, was perhaps the single exception to this condescending view (see especially *The Hollywood Hallucination*).

The Communist Party, whose intellectual influence was marginal by the sixties, had traveled a more ambiguous path through the popular culture question. Party members could rightly claim (though they rarely did) that the commercial rise of "folk music," black and white, from the 1940s to the 1960s, owed much to them. Similarly, the Party could take some credit for the introduction to the public-at-large of black artists and of Afro-American cultural themes. Various film directors dated their political sensibilities to specific Communist-linked movements, especially to the early Screen Actors Guild. During the years of the blacklist, such attachments were suspended or secreted. But rarely, even at times of great optimism and openness (such as during the years immediately following WW II) did these personal engagements translate into theoretical explorations of the popular culture issue. Sidney Finkelstein's *Jazz, A People's Culture* (1949), with its clumsy aesthetic formulae, marks what must pass for a high point relative to the low level of theoretical discussion.

Ironically, the popular culture explosion of the postwar era contained many events that proved to be of radical character, though these were rarely recognized as such as they happened. Bebop, an immediate precursor of rock and roll, touched off a black-white youth rebellion whose importance to the civil rights movement remains underestimated. Major league baseball was at long last integrated. Beat Generation poetry and fiction revived the Whitmanian dream of rediscovering, through the celebration of common experience, what Allen Ginsberg called "the lost America of love." The satires of *Mad* struck back at the monochromaticism of television. All of these phenomena, occurring in a virtual vacuum of Left interpretation under the upturned noses of the highbrow intellectuals, contributed greatly to the education of the baby-boom generation (i.e., the social rebels and war resisters of the sixties).

It was not until the late sixties, with the mammoth entertainment industrial complex now firmly established as a factor in the lives of virtually all Americans, that popular culture finally began to win recognition as a fertile field for interpretive study. Even avant-garde creative expression—nonnarrative painting and film, guerrilla theater, acid-rock music, mimeo-press poetry—tapped popular cultural icons for subject matter. "Pop art," as practiced by Andy Warhol and Robert Rauschenberg, for example, was not so much popular art as it was art that offered a critique of popular culture.

Blacklisting, which had been instituted during the birth of television and had thus had a particularly traumatic effect on that medium's development, was finally eclipsed during the early 1970s by the purchasing power of antiwar, antiracist, and profeminist baby boomers. Ring Lardner, Jr.'s *M*A*S*H* was adapted by Larry Gelbart for television into the form of the much maligned medium's most maligned genre: situation comedy. It became one of TV's greatest commercial successes. Norman Lear, a sitcom *auteur* whose didactic dramatic style smacked of Popular Front theater, dominated the ratings during the seventies with a string of politically liberal sitcoms, including *All in the Family, Maude*, and *Good Times*.

Rock and roll, whose very existence was a remarkable historical convergence of black rhythm and blues with poor white southern music, carried an intrinsic progressive polity that peaked during the Vietnam War. The always explicit messages of sexual freedom were joined by calls for draft resistance, racial harmony, and ecological perserverance. Crosby, Stills, Nash, and Young, for example, put out a string of national hits—"Please Come to Chicago," "Four Dead in Ohio," "Woodstock"—that can be seen as a series of virtually instantaneous analytical responses to the immediate issues of the day. With the end of the draft and the war, the rock establishment soon ossified into a formulaic corporate entity. Even so, the emergence of reggae, of Bruce Springsteen, and to a lesser degree, of punk and politicized Afro-pop, all rowed against the otherwise politically apathetic current of the post-Vietnam period, thus underlining the continuing vitality of rebellious culture during an increasingly conservative era.

Theoretical discussion of popular culture has not kept pace with the expansion of interpretive belletristic writing on the subject that has emerged during the 1980s in publications such as the *Village Voice* and small-circulation "fanzines" devoted to individual arts, especially film. The margins of popular culture criticism contain only a sprinkling of Althusserian or Frankfurtite abstraction here, or an occasional disquisition on the revolutionary virtues of a rock and roll band there. This situation is likely to change, however, because of increasing academic activity in the field. As the political children of the sixties gain tenure in the professoriat, the academic legitimacy of popular culture study continues to grow. Though some institutions, notably Bowling Green State University in Ohio, have attempted to formalize popular culture study into a discipline, such work is more often carried out as a subject area in any of a half dozen or more departments and programs, including American studies, semiotics, sociology, anthropology, and in some places, even history or English. Theoretical fermentation and methodological argument is just beginning to result. Feminist analysis is the first radical strain of popular culture criticism to have made anything like a broad impact on academic thinking.

In *Popular Culture and High Culture*, sociologist Herbert Gans makes the point that all people of all classes have aesthetic preferences and yearnings, a point not conceded by conservative critics from José Ortega y Gasset to Hilton Kramer. The general premise underpinning the entire enterprise of popular culture study is an intrinsically progressive and optimistic one: that culture has been and can become more inclusive and democratic. *See also*: *Dissent*; Folk Music; Guthrie, Woody; Hollywood Left; Lardner, Ring, Jr.; Lawson, John Howard; Marcuse, Herbert; *Partisan Review*; Spiritualism

—*David Marc*

REFERENCES

Buhle, Paul, ed. *Popular Culture in America*. Minneapolis: University of Minnesota Press, 1987.

Marc, David. *Demographic Vistas: Television in American Culture*. Philadelphia: University of Pennsylvania Press, 1984.

———. *Comic Visions: Television Comedy and American Culture*. London: Unwin and Hyman, 1989.

POPULAR FRONT

The Seventh Congress of the Communist International, held in Moscow in the summer of 1935, crystalized the line of the Popular Front, although the Comintern and several of its constituent parties had—since the victory of Nazism in Germany and the threat posed in other countries—already been moving in that

direction. The general line of antifascism, defense and extension of the bourgeois democratic system, and collective security against the fascist powers derived from the basic concept that a bourgeois democratic regime was substantially different from a bourgeois fascist one and that fascism itself was not inevitable. Such an outlook was of course considered applicable also to the United States.

The Communist Party of the United States was present at the congress in the speeches not only of the national leaders Earl Browder and William Z. Foster (the former was elected to the congress's presiding committee) but also those of Sam Darcy from California; Gil Green of the youth movement; Benjamin Careathers, a black leader in Pittsburgh active with the unemployed; and Martha Stone, from the Williamsburg area of New York, surely one of the few women present. Due to its Eurocentrism the congress dealt very schematically with the United States despite its leading role in world capitalism and its vigorous presence in the Far East. Nonetheless, the main speech of Comintern secretary Dimitrov stated clearly that a victory of fascism in the United States would profoundly modify the entire international situation since this country was in a different category from "Hungary, Finland, Bulgaria, and Latvia." He indicated a farmer-labor party as the specific form of the mass antifascist Popular Front in the States. It would have a program against the banks, the trusts, the monopolies, and the principal enemies of the people; would struggle for real social legislation, land reform in the South for black and white sharecroppers, abolition of farm debts, and legal equality for blacks; and it would defend the interests of small shopkeepers, artisans, and professionals. For his part, Browder spoke of the absorption by the CP of the country's revolutionary traditions, but he especially concentrated on the relationship between the government, the conflicts within the capitalist class, and the fascist threat. If Browder criticized President Franklin Roosevelt's demagogy and affirmed that his policy had worsened the conditions of the working class, Foster went much further, declaring that the politics of the president gave an impetus to fascism. Directly in opposition to this, Dimitrov, in his concluding speech, gave a decisive push to the evolution of CP policy when he affirmed that it would be a sign of schematism to state that the New Deal was a clear form of the evolution of the bourgeoisie toward fascism; rather, it was the most reactionary forces of monopoly capital now attacking Roosevelt who were stimulating and organizing the fascist threat. Thus was official sanction given by the Comintern for critical support by American Communists of Roosevelt.

For the CPUSA and other communist parties, the Popular Front can be dated from this Congress till the pact between Germany and the Soviet Union in 1939 and the beginning of the war in Europe. In reality, its roots go back further, and the policy itself would be picked up again during the war and the alliance with the Soviet Union and would not disappear even during the Cold War, when the CP would continue to put forward, although in a somewhat different form, a Popular Front strategy of alliances.

Since Browder had assumed dominance in the Party in the beginning of the thirties, the CPUSA had moved away from its sectarianism and toward the masses and an integration into the U.S. political system. Its participation in the strike wave of 1934–35 and in the development of the CIO, its attempt to follow a United Front policy—unity at the base but also with non-Communist organizations—on issues like antifascism and defense of the rights of blacks and the unemployed, as well as its support at the beginning of 1935 for a labor party, can all be legitimately considered steps on this path before the Seventh Congress of the Comintern, even though many of them were probably taken only after consultation with Moscow. Browder himself became the Party's outstanding spokesman and symbol of its Popular Front positions. His desire to enter into the mainstream was naturally aided by the evolution of the Comintern—especially after the Seventh Congress—but also by a noticeable shift in the positions of the New Deal in early 1935. All of this allowed for the encounter—hesitant and polemical at first, more directly supportive as the thirties advanced—of the CPUSA with Roosevelt and the Democratic Party. With respect to the earlier United Front position, the Seventh Congress and the Popular Front line permitted greater flexibility and less concentration on convincing allies of specific Communist positions.

The Farmer-Labor Party and the general political realignment it would have provoked remained for the Communists the main objective until 1938, when its impossibility, due to the lack of interest of both Roosevelt and the CIO, was no longer deniable. Browder then transformed the Popular Front line into what was called the Democratic Front, stating that the regrouping in any case was already taking place with all the progressive forces in Roosevelt's camp, and implying that this had in some way transformed the president's party. The Communist slogan for this Democratic Front was "Jobs, security, democracy, peace" and most programatic elements remained constant: a battle against the domestic fascist threat; extending political democracy and the rights of the working class and raising its material standards; isolation of the fascist powers through collective security; and an alliance with the Soviet Union. As the New Deal ran out of steam in 1937–38, the CP found itself the main force insisting on the Roosevelt coalition's progressive nature. In order to continue to pursue a Popular Front policy, the CP was increasingly forced to reduce its content. If Roosevelt was continually criticized for his hesitations, therefore, ever more attention was paid to what was considered the antifascist nature of his foreign policy.

Despite the absence of a fundamental realignment in the American political scene, the CP did achieve, through this policy, links with many progressive forces, including elements high and low within the Roosevelt administration. Unlike the Popular Front situation in France and Spain, the CPUSA assumed no governmental responsibility and achieved no formal alliance with any other group. Nor was there unity with the Socialist Party, which, moving toward neutralism and influenced by the Trotskyists, grew increasingly hostile to the Soviet Union and opposed to the New Deal in the name of socialism. The CP, however, was extremely active in many Popular Front organizations—some but not all of which it created—among intellectuals, blacks, and the unemployed. The CIO itself was in a sense a Popular Front organization. Particularly important was the umbrella group the American League for Peace and Democracy. All the groups fought for extending the typical New Deal domestic programs and worked for international solidarity in support of those forces—in Spain, Germany, Italy, and China—which were battling against fascism. On a local level—in Washington, Minnesota, Wisconsin, New York, but also in the South as well as in many cities of the industrial midwest—the Party became an important force in politics and the orientation of the masses as it persistently extended its contacts. In these various organizations, many liberals and progressives were impressed by the dedication and capabilities of the CP militants and freely and openly associated with Communists for common causes. In this sense, the Popular Front must be seen as a policy independent of those linked to the Comintern.

The enormous transformation in the CP

line from the years immediately before the proclamation of the Popular Front through the end of the thirties could not but bring gradual, ever deeper changes in Party ideology and organizational structure. Fascism came to be seen no longer—as during the first New Deal—as a threat directly within the government but now as something that came from without, from the leading circles of finance and monopoly capital and from abroad. American revolutionary traditions were defined in an ever broader and less radical way. Party internal education increasingly concentrated on learning about New Deal politics and functioning in trade unions rather than on traditional Marxism-Leninism and the history of Russian Bolshevism. Militant atheism was no longer in vogue, as the CP reached out to all religious groups, especially the Catholics essential for work among the industrial working class. Work in immigrant organizations was reevaluated—had not Dimitrov spoken about being a good Communist *and* a good Bulgarian?—also for its importance in pressing for an antifascist foreign policy. Most significant, the Popular Front in the United States, as in other countries, now meant that the Communists were without a theory of transition, of how their efforts were in some way related to the final goal of socialism, an objective that became as distant historically as the Soviet Union was geographically.

Organizational structure changed markedly as emphasis shifted from the factory and the streets to the electoral arena. Party districts and sections were redesigned to conform to the divisions of electoral districts. Factory units lost importance and shop papers declined. Communist trade union factions were officially abolished. In general, less was required of militants, as the Party tried to function like a "normal" American political grouping. Activity in one of the many Popular Front organizations was now considered in part a substitute for Party activity. All these ideological and organizational developments were evidently steps in the direction of Browder's line after Teheran—a projected class peace within the United States together with the momentous decision to dissolve the Party and form a "political association"—although it is not clear that "necessarily" the transformations of the thirties had to arrive at this conclusion.

The Popular Front policy did lead to a general extension of Party influence: membership rose from 10,000 at the beginning of the thirties to 65,000 at its end, as militants were increasingly American and English-speaking (children of immigrants or having themselves immigrated when very young). Jews came to be increasingly present also due to recruitment from the middle strata. And despite turnover, especially high among blacks, the Party was able to claim a genuine working-class base. Perhaps more important than an increase of membership was the greater acceptability of the Party as it became integrated into the mass New Deal mentality.

Despite these successes, some in the Party were concerned about the CP losing its specific physiognomy. The Foster-Browder contrast was present in only a slightly veiled form much before the dramatic 1944–45 events in the Party. If the Comintern rejected such preoccupations as sectarian, there was, however, much discussion among leaders and cadres about the problem of "hiding the face of the Party,"—that is, situations where Communists, although generally known as such but evidently concerned about endangering acquired positions, neither made a point of their Party membership nor put forward, if they existed, CP positions different from those of the organizations in which they operated. Thus in some trade unions during the Popular Front, CP membership came to be concentrated more among the leadership and the functionaries than the base. Certainly not all legal and semilegal restrictions against Communists had been lifted, but it is probable that such behavior ultimately worked to the disadvantage of CP militants who could be denounced as "subversive" and "clandestine."

The Popular Front policy of the CP may have been positive for the United States, through its strengthening of the elements of progressive democracy present in the New Deal and its opposition to fascist tendencies present in the country. If such a line did not aid in understanding the position of the United States as an imperial power that blocked the development of vast areas of the globe, it did undoubtedly help prepare the country ideologically for its participation in an antifascist war. Evaluating the policy for the Party itself is more complex: the CP advanced in membership and acceptability, but the terrain of this advance would prove to be, during the liberal-McCarthy repression, very shaky indeed. *See also*: Anticommunism; Browder, Earl; Communist Party; *New Masses*; Popular Culture

—*Malcolm Sylvers*

REFERENCES

Klehr, Harvey. *The Heyday of American Communism, The Depression Decade*. New York: Basic Books, 1984.

Stephenson, Anders. "The CPUSA Conception of the Rooseveltian State, 1933–1939." *Radical History Review*, No. 24 (Fall 1980).

Sylvers, Malcolm. "*Party Organizer* and American Communist Mentality in the 1930s." *Storia Nordamericana* 2 (1985).

PORTUGUESE AMERICANS

Although few in overall numbers, Portuguese-American radicals exerted a significant effect on economic and political life in southeastern New England, especially within the textile unions. They reached the apex of their influence just after World War II and declined sharply thereafter.

Before 1924, a quarter-million Portuguese immigrants came to the United States. More than 80 percent came from the islands: the Azores, Madeira, and Cape Verde, which were overcrowded and exhausted peasant economies. These immigrants settled mainly in two areas: California, where they became farm workers and then landowners, and New Bedford and Fall River, Massachusetts, where they formed a majority of the textile workers. As with most other immigrant groups, the Left community was concentrated among the industrial workers, and their leaders came from the more industrialized areas in the homeland; in this case, the Left was concentrated around Fall River and New Bedford and its leaders were from the mainland, especially from Lisbon.

The Portuguese Left in the United States was strongest between WW I and the immediate post–WW II years. The U.S. movement was influenced by politics in Portugal: the alternating Right and Left governments during and after WW I and the dictatorship of Antonio Salazar, who ruled from 1928 to 1968. Many progressive labor leaders came to the United States during the 1920s and played a major role in the 1928 textile strike.

For six months in 1928, 30,000 New Bedford textile workers struck in the only organized opposition against the general wage cuts in New England during the late 1920s. The backbone of the strike was the Portuguese workers who followed the leadership of the Communist Party and other socialist groups. Their goals were progressive, tactics were militant, and organization was democratic. A number of the young Portuguese workers—including Augusto Pinto (deported to Portugal soon after the strike, and who died under mysterious conditions en route to prison in Cape Verde), Eula Figueiredo (also later deported), and Joe Figueiredo—emerged from the strike as leaders of the Left. Despite impressive community support during the strike's early days, it was lost because of general economic conditions, the antagonism of the established, conservative craft unions toward the newer, more progressive industrial unions, and Red-baiting tactics by the mill owners through the newspapers, courts, and government.

The Great Depression immediately followed the strike, and the Portuguese leadership, as with other national groups, split into a Left, which participated in the National Textile Workers Union (NTWU), and a Right, which joined the United Textile Workers (UTW). The two groups united and competed for leadership when the NTWU merged into the UTW in 1934. In the late 1930s and early 1940s, the Textile Workers Union of America (TWUA) under the CIO organized the mills in the area. While the top leaders were the more conservative labor leaders from Fall River, the rank-and-file leaders were Portuguese workers active in the 1928 strike.

The showdown came in 1947 over the anticommunist affidavit provision in the Taft-

Hartley Act. The leadership of the TWUA favored signing, but the Left ran opposing slates in many of the mills and won a few key elections. The top leaders of the national union, seeking a compromise, agreed to replace the anticommunist director of the joint board with a more progressive leader in return for tacit acceptance of the provision. This was the high point of the Left's influence in the TWUA.

While most of the activity of the Portuguese Left was in the labor movement during the 1930s and 1940s, they also did community and political organizing. Just after the 1928 strike, Joe Figueiredo and others formed a Portuguese Alliance of 200 to 500 members, which during the Depression fought evictions, demanded and received food and clothing from government agencies, and organized support for the antifascist forces in Spain. Following WW II, Figueiredo and other CP members within the alliance had a weekly radio program in Fall River. The program continued through 1948 despite FBI pressure on the station manager to cancel it.

The fall during the anticommunist era was rapid and relentless. As with other immigrant groups, the chief weapon used was fear of deportation. Eula Figueiredo, long a leader of the Portuguese Left, was arrested in 1950, harassed for many years, and finally deported as an undesirable alien in 1953 under the McCarran-Walter Act. This had a chilling effect on the Portuguese community.

Recently, fueled by the new immigration since 1965, the Left has revived somewhat within this generally conservative ethnic group. Portuguese fishermen and boat owners, whose leaders had been union organizers in opposition to Salazar, organized an effective tie-up against the fish buyers in 1980, although a fishermen's strike in 1986 against boat owners split the community. *See also*: Antifascism, Communist Party, Popular Front

—*Daniel Georgianna*

REFERENCES

Aaronson, R. H., and D. Georgianna. "Here We Come—Thousands Strong." *Spinner* 2 (1982).

Pap, L. *The Portuguese-Americans*. Boston: Twayne Publishers, 1981.

Santos, M. "Community and Communism: The 1928 New Bedford Textile Strike." *Labor History* 26 (1985).

PREPARTY FORMATIONS

Under Leninist doctrine a vanguard party is necessary to make a successful revolution, but that party cannot be instantly born out of the proletarian brow. Various publishing groups, militant unions, special-interest movements, ethnic federations, and other social forces must become active before a vanguard party is possible. The groups that eventually fuse into the vanguard party are called preparty formations. From their ranks come the creators of the vanguard party, and their leaders will form the initial central committee.

During the 1970s there was a concerted effort by many radical groups with roots in the 1960s to create a new Marxist-Leninist party in the United States. As these efforts floundered, various components of the preparty movement each declared themselves to be the vanguard party and named a central committee. None of the groups was able to rally a significant following, and each was denounced by the other preparty groups as a premature formation. By the 1980s, the new parties had ceased to exist or had dwindled to the size of sects. Half a century before this unsuccessful movement, various groups previously linked to the Socialist Party and the Industrial Workers of the World had struggled with various organizational forms until the Communist Party was created. In retrospect, these can be seen as successful preparty formations. *See also*: Vanguard Party

—*Dan Georgakas*

PROGRESSIVE

A term employed by the Left (among others) with widely varied meanings, "progressive" has mainly signified, since the middle 1940s, those left-of-center and vigorously opposed to the agenda of Cold War liberalism.

The ambiguity of meaning can be traced to the early 1910s and the emergence of the Progressive (or municipal reform) movement into a national force of consequence. The Progressive Party, mostly the creation of a reform-minded WASP middle-class, chose as presidential nominee the imperialist bully Theodore Roosevelt rather than Wisconsin's Progressive Party leader, Robert M. LaFollette. The Progressive Party failed nationally, and at the state level broke apart in wartime, when LaFollette heroically opposed American intervention (Roosevelt, in his last years, continued to advocate military solutions). LaFollette transformed Progressivism when he rallied an ethnic, worker, and farmer constituency in place of the middle class that had deserted him. But a section of Roosevelt supporters (including former socialists) moved in the other direction with the creation of the *New Republic* in 1914, which advocated war participation as a bridge to greater national control of economic and social resources.

The resurrection of the Progressive Party in 1924, mainly as a vehicle for Robert LaFollette's campaign for the presidency, underlined the most radical definition given the term "progressive." Although LaFollette himself insisted that describing him as socialist was a case of confusing "a chestnut horse and a horse chestnut," the Socialist Party hurled itself into the campaign, while Communists later regretted their sectarian nonparticipation. During the same years, the Committee for Progressive Political Action also sought to create a sustained farmer-labor movement on principles (such as opposition to monopoly) that most socialists could endorse as a transition toward a cooperative society. The Committee for Progressive Labor Action, led by A. J. Muste, essentially evolved into a socialist movement, the American Workers Party, in the Depression.

Failure of a national movement to materialize lent the term "progressive" a midwestern or western connotation, without resolving many basic ambiguities (such as the xenophobia and racism of many self-avowed "progressive" political leaders in the West, especially California). Liberal Republicans in particular—fiscally conservative in many ways but personally libertarian and firmly opposed to Eastern-based corporations' monopoly powers—could distinguish themselves as "progressive" rather than Democratic Party–style "liberal." From a Left standpoint, that differentiation was underlined when many self-avowed progressives (including the LaFollettes) took a relatively isolationist position in the later 1930s, and Wisconsin's Progressive Party all but dissolved. In the world of scholarship, "Progressive History," most closely associated with the public intellectual Charles Beard, also seemingly pointed toward an isolationist-minded opposition to the growth of the national State.

The use of the term revived in the early years of the Cold War, for two related reasons. Cold War liberals, determined to jettison Communist supporters from their organizations, had begun to consolidate their ranks during World War II, with the Union for Democratic Action (later, Americans for Democratic Action) excluding and excoriating Communists. Former vice-president and secretary of agriculture Henry Wallace, widely known as a charismatic "progressive," firmly took up the cudgels against the Cold War camp. Responding to his own expulsion from the Cabinet by Harry Truman for his opposition to the new president's aggressive foreign policy ambitions, Wallace addressed an October 1946 meeting in Los Angeles (sponsored by, among others, the Progressive AFL Committee for Political and Legislative Action), declaring that "more than ever before I am a progressive," meaning a true inheritor of the New Deal mantle.

Commentators widely blamed voter apathy in the 1946 elections on Truman's sharp turn to the right on domestic as well as foreign policy. In November 1946, Henry Wallace became editor of the *New Republic*, in order to urge "progressive" policies upon the Democratic Party (or perhaps, as many CIO committees urged, to prepare for a third party). A call for a national organization of progressives had brought 300 participants together in September, urging a broad platform of reforms. Although this led to no organization, it was advance notice of the merger of the New Dealish Independent Citizens Committee of the Arts and the Science and Professions with the National Citizens Political Action Committee into the Progressive Citizens of America at the end of 1946. Henry Wallace and Fiorello LaGuardia addressed the founding convention.

As the ranks of liberals split into two warring camps, "progressive" became synonymous with "Communist sympathizer" (to anticommunists) and with "unreserved New Dealer" (to progressives). The PCA established three divisions, each with its prominent intellectual figures: Youth; Women's; and Art, Science, and Professions. Of these, the Art, Science, and Professions attracted the most interest, no doubt because of its entertainment celebrities, José Ferrer and Lillian Hellman among many others. Its public events, with such figures as Frank Sinatra participating, proved that "progressivism" had wide support despite the virulent campaign against Wallace and détente by the commercial press, and most Democratic and Republican Party regulars.

Henry Wallace's worldwide tours and the publicity leading up to the 1948 presidential campaign underlined the distinction between "liberal" and "progressive," even though neither Left, Center, nor near-Right would concede either term to opponents. Glen Taylor, former factory worker and a cowboy congressman from Idaho, joining Wallace's fight against Trumanism, symbolized the Plains States connection, playing his banjo and singing with his sons on the lecture trail.

The down-home image did little, however, to bring votes to the overwhelmingly Red-baited Wallace and Taylor. More than half their national vote of a half-million came from New York State, under the American Labor Party standard. Outside the East, "progressivism" had been quashed or its erstwhile proponents (such as George McGovern, who abandoned the Progressive Party after attending its first convention) began to distance the word from its 1948 connotations. Only the *Progressive*, formerly *LaFollette's*, managed to survive as a progressive institution, and that due to the Jewish intellectual Morris Rubin, who managed to create a nationwide audience for the now-monthly magazine.

In the East, "progressivism" also faced difficult times. The *New Republic*, abandoning Wallace in the last months of the presidential campaign, had made a choice similar to that made in WW I, for military-linked nationalism as gatekeeper for domestic reform. The *Nation*, which did not support Wallace but nevertheless, under the editorship of Freda Kirchway, opposed the Cold War, sought to redefine "liberal." The *National Guardian*, which emerged out of the Wallace campaign, became de facto the standard-bearer of a "progressivism" newborn.

This newer "progressivism" could be seen in Popular Front veterans who had never been comfortable with open Communist identification (or, perhaps, Communist Party membership either), but who largely shared Popular Front perspectives. Many erstwhile readers of the *Daily Worker* indeed went over to the *Guardian* for their own self-protection from potential harassment. But as the Communist leadership inclined toward a near-suicidal prediction of potentially imminent fascism, "progressive" came to indicate an *alternative* identity to Cold War liberal or Communist.

For those in that identity, ending the Cold War remained the major priority. But Marxism was no longer avowed as the single key to a scientific solution to poverty and exploitation. Nor was climactic class-struggle anticipated in America, even though unions (especially independent Left unions such as the United Electrical Workers) received enthusiastic support. A rather more vague, if no less heartfelt, emphasis on New Dealish measures, and a hope for the evolution of postcapitalist societies, merged into a vision of "progress" in the atomic age. Support for Third World revolutions that encompassed support for the nonaligned movement, and for the People's Republic of China again set progressives off somewhat from an orthodox Soviet-style perspective. In some ways, although without saying so explicitly, progressives had, far more than the CP, recapitulated the religious-based anti-imperialism of the 1920s–1940s, substituting a concept of morality for specific theism.

Tactically, such "progressives" sought to maintain a third-party presence, despite general Communist inclinations toward a submergence in the Democratic Party. Radical New York City congressman Vito Marcantonio, running his last campaign against Communist advice, became the hero of such independent progressives. In 1958 New York progressives (identified, as well, by their connections with *Monthly Review* magazine, and with Corliss Lamont's Emergency Civil Liberties Committee) sought to reestablish a radical party through cooperation with the Trotskyists, something almost unthinkable for Communist regulars. In general, the *Guardian* maintained a sort of milieu—largely but not entirely limited to Eastern cities, Chicago, and a few California sites—for such like-minded people. Its relationship with the CP proper remained ambiguous, in no small measure because individual Communists shared the progressive perspective while remaining in Party ranks. Very likely, a CP turn toward polycentrism and internal democracy, as attempted by *Daily Worker* "revisionists" in 1956, would have re-created Communism very largely in the progressive image.

By the middle 1960s, the surfacing of the term "radical" (long thought to be politically ambiguous, as well as a dangerous identification) submerged "progressive" nomenclature. The *Guardian* itself shortly became "an independent radical newsweekly." Only the *Progressive* magazine, and the remnants of an older generation, held on to the familiar title. Despite—or perhaps because of—the similarity of campaign rhetoric and even personalities, the Democratic Party reformers of 1972 avoided the titles of 1948.

The collapse of the New Left and the lurch of American politics to the Right not only restored "progressive" terminology, but gave it new meaning. In the most obvious and important example, the environmental movement placed itself within the oldest of progressive traditions, Theodore Roosevelt's conservationism. On the intellectual front, the *Nation* became the de facto national organ for progressive thought, and its regular contributors occasionally appeared on national newsmedia programs dedicated to current events. More subtly, former New Left labor activists and their allies working within existing unions identified themselves in the generally forgotten cloak of "labor progressives." In the America of Ronald Reagan, with congressional liberalism pulled increasingly from the "Vietnam syndrome" toward contra aid, "progressivism" in foreign policy largely returned to the anti-imperial standard of Robert M. La Follette. *See also*: Agrarian Radicalism, Progressive Party

—*Paul Buhle*

REFERENCES

Lader, Lawrence. *Power on the Left*. New York: Norton, 1979.

MacDougall, Curtis D. *Gideon's Army*. Three volumes. New York: Marzani and Munsell, 1965.

Progressive Labor Party: see "Antirevisionism"

Progressive Miners of America

The PMA was formed in Gillespie, Illinois, on September 2, 1932, in response to attempts by United Mine Workers of America (UMWA) president John L. Lewis to control Illinois UMWA District 12. The Illinois miners had a long tradition of autonomy and radicalism. Following World War I, the southern Illinois mining area was a center of Labor Party and "Free Tom Mooney" sentiment, and in 1924 Robert La Follette's Progressive presidential campaign ran strongly in the Illinois mining counties. Many Illinois miners also believed that UMWA president Lewis was pursuing the mine owners' interests and not theirs.

The PMA was initially a left-wing organization. Its leadership and its journal, the *Progressive Miner*, urged members to vote for working-class candidates, and speakers such as Norman Thomas came to local union halls. In counties with a PMA majority, the Socialist Party obtained a higher vote than in those areas loyal to the UMWA.

In mid-1933, however, a split developed within the PMA leadership. Less radical leaders were satisfied with their success in five Illinois counties, while left-wingers believed the PMA needed to be national in scope. A number of radical officials were ousted, beginning with the editor of the *Progressive Miner*, Gerry Allard. Radicals again gained control of the union for a short time in 1935, but were soon defeated. Thereafter the PMA became known for its Red-baiting, antiforeign, and anti-Semitic pronouncements.

At this point, the more radical of the PMA founders believed dramatic action was necessary against those PMA leaders who had discarded the union's founding principles. Such an opportunity came in 1937. In response to coal company's acceleration of mechanization of its mines, radicals began a nine-day sitdown strike inside a mine. The action was timed to coincide with a meeting of PMA and AFL officials in Chicago to discuss affiliation. The strikers hoped to prevent affiliation, but were unsuccessful. The AFL assumed control and appointed the PMA president and secretary-treasurer, thereby destroying one of the primary reasons for the establishment of the PMA, the right of district autonomy.

Between 1938 and 1946, the Progressive Miners of America-AFL paralleled the much larger United Mine Workers-CIO. However, when John L. Lewis brought the UMWA back into the AFL in 1946, the PMA became independent and remained so into the start of the 1990s, when it claimed only a few thousand members. *See also*: Thomas, Norman; United Mine Workers

—*Stephane Booth*

REFERENCES

Booth, Stephane Elise. "The Relationship Between Radicalism and Ethnicity in Southern Illinois Coal Fields, 1870–1940." Ph.D. diss., Illinois State University, 1983.

———. "A Coal Mining Activist in the Fields of Southern Illinois: 1932–1938." *Proceedings of the Second Annual Illinois History Symposium*. Springfield: Illinois State Historical Society, 1982.

Hicken, Victor. "Mine Union Radicalism in Macoupin and Montgomery Counties." *Western Illinois Regional Studies* 3 (Fall 1980).

Hudson, Harriet P. *The Progressive Mine Workers of America*. Urbana: University of Illinois Press, 1952.

Jensen, Prosser Daniel. "Coal Towns in Egypt: Portrait of an Illinois Mining Region, 1890–1930." Ph.D. diss., Northwestern University, 1973.

PROGRESSIVE PARTY, 1948

The last major expression of the Popular Front politics of the New Deal period, the Progressive Party was founded in 1948 to oppose the Truman administration's Cold War policies, and the domestic anticommunist, antilabor, and anti–civil liberties campaigns that accompanied those policies. Former vice president Henry Wallace, who had embodied Left New Deal political values for millions by his wartime advocacy of a "Century of the Common Man," based on prolabor and antimonopoly policies in the United States, and U.S.-Soviet cooperation through the United Nations to internationalize New Deal reforms, was the presidential candidate of the party. The Communist Party and its activists in the CIO and other mass movements served as the PP's leading grass-roots organizing force, joining with non-Communists to try to organize mass opposition to the Cold War and to save both the substance and the style of the labor- and social-welfare-oriented New Deal politics that had given the Left in the 1930s and 1940s its greatest influence in U.S. history.

Centering on the presidential election, the PP had hoped to draw millions of working-class and minority voters away from the Democrats, and early polls showed Wallace getting as much as eight million votes (party strategists saw four million as necessary for a successful campaign). However, Truman's shift to a Left New Deal election strategy (deemphasizing the Cold War, identifying with a strong civil rights plank in the Democratic Party platform, and calling for national health insurance, protection for small farmers, proconsumer price controls, and repeal of the anti–trade union Taft-Hartley Act) combined with massive bipartisan Red-baiting against the Progressives to doom their efforts. The PP lived on after 1948 in an atmosphere of mounting repression, running San Francisco labor lawyer Vincent Hallinan and Charlotta Bass, a black activist, for president and vice president on an anti–Korean War platform in 1952 before it finally went out of existence.

However, it was never a real national force after the 1948 campaign, in which its failure to win over significant numbers of New Deal coalition voters from the Democrats served as a signal to right-wing forces in the CIO to purge Communist-led Left unions, and as a signal to the Truman administration and the conservative coalition in Congress to broaden and deepen their anticommunist campaign. This campaign included trials of the CP national leadership and the Hiss and Rosenberg political "espionage" trials, and was followed by the enactment of the McCarran Internal Security Act of 1950. This act established the Subversive Activities Control Board and made provisions for the establishment of political concentration camps.

Internationally, the PP's political failure removed a domestic deterrent to the broadening of the Truman administration's Cold War interventionism into the formation of NATO in 1949, the building of the hydrogen bomb after the Soviets developed an atomic bomb in 1949, and the involvement of U.S. troops in the Korean War (1950–53). Internally, its defeat encouraged many in the New Deal coalition to either follow the redefinition of New Deal politics into Cold War terms represented by the organizations like the Americans for Democratic Action, politicians like Senator Hubert Humphrey, and political intellectuals like Arthur Schlesinger, Jr., or to retreat from political activism in disillusionment, struggling to map out private space and expand personal freedom in new academic or artistic subcultures.

Without underestimating the short-term significance of its defeat, it is important to remember that many stands pioneered by the PP campaign in 1948 would be vindicated in later struggles. Henry Wallace's challenge of segregation in southern campaign meetings, the party's emphasis on women's rights and commitment to functional representation for minorities and women in its organization and conventions, and its calls for direct meetings between the U.S. president and the Soviet premier to settle Cold War conflicts (all of which were condemned at the time as extreme or subversive) were harbingers of later civil rights, women's rights, and peace struggles (in which PP supporters sometimes played important roles).

Also, the PP's attacks on the alliance of Wall Street and the Pentagon was a harbinger of subsequent critiques of a military-industrial complex and a permanent war economy. Finally, as the rise of Senator Joe McCarthy and the subsequent effects of Cold War interventionism in Vietnam and other parts of the world showed, the PP's stand against a "bipartisan" anticommunist national policy as leading to reaction and war was borne out. *See also*: Communist Party; McCarthyism; National Guardian; Robeson, Paul

—*Norman Markowitz*

REFERENCES

MacDougall, Curtis. *Gideon's Army*. 3 vols. New York: Marzani & Munsell, 1965.

Markowitz, Norman D. *The Rise and Fall of the People's Century: Henry A. Wallace and American Liberalism, 1941–1948*. New York: The Free Press, 1973.

Schmidt, Karl M. *Henry A. Wallace: Quixotic Crusade, 1948*. Syracuse: Syracuse University Press, 1960.

Proletarian and Radical Writers—1930s and 1940s

Proletarian writing emerged in the 1930s in association with the Communist movement and was characterized by fervent class consciousness. Working-class characters rather than upper- or middle-class characters were the major focus of interest, the vernacular was the preferred language, and concerns about racial, ethnic, and sexual exploitation were often blended with class issues. A few works directly addressed the experiences of radical activists, but most had themes that were derived from nineteenth-century literature. Among these were coming-of-age and on-the-road novels.

The proletarian movement is usually written of as an American form of the socialist realism advocated by Soviet theorists. While that connection exists, American writers drew on deep national roots. The two most celebrated American stylists of the previous century, Mark Twain and Walt Whitman, had been champions of the vernacular and had written about working-class America. Even such a symbol-rich work as *Moby Dick* had the characteristic American concern for the work process. Precedents for socially committed literature that sought to change society were set by abolitionist poets such as John Greenleaf Whittier and novels such as Harriet

Beecher Stowe's *Uncle Tom's Cabin*. Best-selling socialist authors such as Jack London, Edward Bellamy, and Upton Sinclair had further developed the political novel. Given this tradition, proletarian writers did not feel they were breaking with the American past but fulfilling its egalitarian vision.

Many of the new writers were of the class they wrote about or directly involved in working-class movements. This allowed them to write from "the inside" and bring their readers directly into the mills, homes, and streets of working America. Only a few of the writers were actual members of the Communist Party, but the CP was their political focus. Many were affiliated with various cultural groups such as the John Reed Clubs or the League of American Writers or met in informal groups like the radical screenwriters who gathered in the back room of Larry Edmund's bookshop in Hollywood. Radical writers often worked in projects sponsored by the New Deal and in trade unions. They worked in different genres simultaneously and published in Communist newspapers or in radical magazines such as the *Anvil*, *New Masses*, *New Theater*, *New Theatre and Film*, and *Partisan Review*. While some theorists tried to differentiate the proletarian writer as a specific literary species, the distinction between radical writing in general and specifically proletarian writing remained vague, observed more often in theory than practice. The prestige of the cultural publications of the CP was so high that some of the nation's best-known writers published in them or helped raise funds for them. Such writers included William Saroyan, Ernest Hemingway, Erskine Caldwell, Dorothy Parker, James Agee, and Archibald MacLeish.

A considerable amount of proletarian writing amounted to a class-modified coming-of-age genre. Thomas Bell's *Out of this Furnace* (1941), for example, followed a Slavic steelworker family through titanic duels between Carnegie Steel and the mill workers of Pittsburgh. This novel also dealt with working-class marital relationships, a theme Bell addressed more directly in *All Brides Are Beautiful* (1936) and *Till I Come Back to You* (1943). Another of his novels, *There Comes a Time* (1946), dealt with organizing white-collar bank employees.

Two other well-received novels in a similar vein were Pietro Di Donato's *Christ in Concrete* (1939) and Jack Conroy's *The Disinherited* (1933). Donato's novel, one of the few to describe the price paid in building the great American cities, centers on a thirteen-year-old Italian boy who takes his father's place as a bricklayer after the father is buried alive in a construction accident. Conroy's book, written in the jaunty style found in all of his work, follows the life of a young miner seeking work during the Great Depression. Even better known than these works were James T. Farrell's Studs Lonigan trilogy (1932–34), about the working Irish of Chicago, and Mike Gold's *Jews Without Money* (1936), about the Yiddish culture of New York's Lower East Side. Changes within an entire family, rather than just an individual, were the concern of Josephine Herbst in a trilogy consisting of *The Rope of Gold* (1939), *Pity Is not Enough* (1933), and *The Executioner Waits* (1934). Feminist concerns are coequal with economic themes in Meridel Le Sueur's short story collection *Salute to Spring* (1940). Like other proletarian authors Le Sueur often made a connection between poverty and subsequent criminal behavior, and in her prose style sought to bring a lyrical quality to the vernacular idioms of her humble characters.

Proletarian on-the-road or down-and-out novels were less popular in their time, but have developed something of a cult following with the passage of years. Best remembered now is *Waiting for Nothing* (1935) by Tom Kromer. Written partially while Kromer lived in flophouses, hobo jungles, missions, and freight cars, the novel harrowingly illustrates the day-to-day life of the unemployed and homeless during the Great Depression. Edward Dahlberg's *Bottom Dogs* (1930) is another highly respected novel with a similar approach. Worthy of attention for their literary worth as well as their proletarian perspectives are Edward Newhouse's *You Can't Sleep Here* (a New York Hooverville is the setting, 1934), Nelson Algren's *Somebody in Boots* (the tribulations of a young Texan, 1935), and William Attaway's *Let Me Breathe Thunder* (two migrant laborers ride the rails, 1939). A more surreal and picaresque approach is found in Kenneth Patchen's *The Journal of Albion Moonlight* (1941).

Many radical writers brought the reader directly into the factory and fields and then out into the union halls and picket lines. *Land of Plenty* (1934), by Robert Cantwell, recreates a savage lumber strike in the Pacific Northwest; *The Foundry* (1934), by Albert Halper, presents an in-depth evocation of the assembly-line process; and *To Make My Bread* (1932), by Grace Lumpkin, tackles the legendary Gastonia textile strike. Chester Himes wove racial concerns into two remarkable workplace novels; *If He Hollers, Let Him Go* (1945) concerns the frame-up of a militant African-American shipyard worker during World War II, and *Lonely Crusade* (1947) centers on how racism and anticommunism within the labor movement affect a radical African-American organizer. Another blend of racial and workplace themes is found in William Attaway's *Blood on the Forge* (1941), a tale of three brothers from the black South and their interactions with Slavic workers in a steel plant near Pittsburgh. *Blood on the Forge* was one of the few American novels of its time to directly relate human exploitation to capitalist exploitation of natural resources. In the late 1980s the novel was reissued as part of the Monthly Review Press's Voices of Resistance series, which features outstanding political novels from around the world. Yet another 1930s' novel that addressed racial themes was Grace Lumpkin's *The Sign of Cain* (1935).

The most controversial proletarian novels featured the radical organizer, usually identified as a Communist, as their central character. In addition to work already cited, this focus is found in *Jake Home* (1943), by Ruth McKenney, the story of how a Pennsylvania miner evolves into a Communist activist; *This is Your Day* (1937), by Edward Newhouse, a vivid rendering of the daily life of a young Communist organizing rural workers; and *Underground Stream* (1940), by Albert Maltz, a poignant account of the kidnapping and murder of a Communist auto-union organizer by a fictional Michigan group modeled on Michigan's fascistic Black Legion. Maltz would become one of the "Hollywood Ten" and was involved in important public debates on the role of the writer in the Communist movement. His other novels include *The Cross and the Arrow* (a German foundry worker defies the Nazis, 1944), *The Journey of Simon McKeever* (an aged pipefitter fights for dignity, 1949), *A Long Day in a Short Life* (racial discrimination in a federal prison, 1957), and *A Tale of One January* (WW II refugees, 1966).

Variety of theme and style was also a hallmark of the proletarian poets. John Beecher wrote often of southern areas where radicalism had never been a strong tradition. Sterling A. Brown did brilliant work within the ballad form, while Kenneth Fearing and Walter Lowenfels applied modern techniques to traditional radical themes. Lowenfels, who had been an intimate of Henry Miller in Paris, eventually took a twenty-year hiatus from writing to edit a labor paper, but he returned to literary work in the 1960s. At that time he became a link to New Left writers by editing anthologies of politically engaged poetry. The most widely read of these was *Where Is Vietnam?* (1967).

Perhaps the most ambitious of all the radical poets was Thomas McGrath. His *Letters to an Imaginary Friend* is no less than a radical equivalent to the *Cantos* of Ezra Pound or the *Paterson* of William Carlos Williams. Stretching from the 1930s to the 1980s, the novelistic poem combines fact and fantasy in a blend of style meant to render a universal statement on the human condition through the actuality of the American experience. McGrath's use of the dialog poem, the "found" poem, snatches of lyrics from popular songs, and other techniques were characteristic of the experimental spirit of most of the radical poets.

Stylistic innovation also concerned prose writers such as Nathanael West and John Dos Passos. Using techniques found in surrealism and expressionism, West savaged mass media and the Horatio Alger myth in four short novels (*Miss Lonely Hearts*, 1933; *Day of the Locust*, 1939; *A Cool Million*, 1934; *The Dream Life of Balso Snell*, 1931) that were highly praised by both avant-garde and political critics. John Dos Passos employed Joycean techniques in his epic *USA* trilogy (*The 42nd Parallel*, 1930; *1919*, 1932; *The Big Money*, 1936), generally regarded as the best single radical novel of the period and a major American literary achievement. Dos Passos was highly influenced by the Industrial Workers of the World, and his caution regarding the authoritarianism of the CP led him to adopt increasingly rightist positions, particularly after WW II. In *USA* he created a form that used a journalistic narrative as a base around which was entwined stream-of-consciousness sections, evocations of newspaper headlines and popular songs, poetic portraits of political radicals and reactionaries, and complete short stories, sometimes rendered in an impressionistic style.

Classification of proletarian writing by rigid stylistic, thematic, or chronological criteria is highly misleading as so much of the work is too complex for facile definitions. Zora Neale Hurston's *Their Eyes Were Watching God* (1937); Richard Wright's first two books, *Uncle Tom's Children* (1938) and *Native Son* (1940); and Meridel Le Sueur's various short stories exemplify this difficulty. Even the subgenre of the antimilitary novel produced highly complex works. Outstanding among these was *Johnny Got His Gun* (1939), by Dalton Trumbo, who decries the brutality of war by adopting the viewpoint of a "basket case," a soldier who has lost all his limbs in battle. Mixed themes are also found in Truman Nelson's *The Sin of the Prophet* (an homage to abolitionist Theodore Parker, 1952), Harriet Arnow's *The Dollmaker* (the migration of a hillbilly family to Detroit, 1954), and Budd Schulberg's *What Makes Sammy Run?* (the organizing of the Screen Writers Guild, 1941). Some of these were not published until the 1950s and some became the basis for motion pictures or television programs made even later, indications that the impact of the proletarian tradition did not collapse entirely with the end of the 1930s or even the 1940s.

Some of the writers who came to the United States as refugees from the Nazi threat in Europe became part of the radical current. The most successful of these was Stefan Heym, a refugee from Germany who began to write in English. His best-selling *The Crusaders* (1948) dealt with the American Army fighting in the European theater as if it were a capitalist venture. One of the novel's features is that individuals who appear to be major characters keep getting killed off, as in a real war, yet are replaced by a new cast of characters who recreate class positions in a manner that seems realistic, if not inevitable. During the McCarthy era, Heym wrote *Goldsborough* (1954), a novel of oppressed miners who turn to radical solutions. This was to be the last book he wrote in the United States. Distraught by the rise of McCarthyism, Heym followed the example of Brecht and repatriated to East Berlin, where he forged an uneasy record of writing novels critical of the system from a decidedly Marxist perspective.

An expatriate often overlooked in accounts of American radical writers is the elusive B. Traven, who successfully hid his true identity and national origins for decades. His rationale for doing so was to place all attention on his work, which proved to have enormous popular as well as critical appeal. Most of his novels deal with exploited Indian peasants in Mexico and the horrible working conditions in the jungle lumber camps: *The Government* (1931), *The Carreta* (1935), *March to the Monteria* (1933), *Rebellion of the Hanged* (1938), *The General of the Jungle* 1940). He also wrote about wandering American Wobblies in Mexico (*The Cotton Pickers,* 1929), stranded merchant seamen (*The Death Ship,* 1934), American fortune hunters (*The Treasure of Sierre Madre,* 1927), and American imperialists (*The White Rose,* 1935).

During the war years, the emphasis on class conflict and opposition to militarism, which had been dominant radical themes, gave way to a perceived need to foster national unity in the war against fascism. With the end of the conflict, the old themes were not easily resurrected. The dubious role Communists were acting out in Eastern Europe and a growing awareness of the repressive nature of the Stalinist regime moved many writers away from former commitments, some adopting an openly critical view of the Soviet system, either from a Right or Left perspective. McCarthyism accelerated the ideological disarray. Outright blacklists, as was the case with Hollywood screenwriters, were rare, but graylists were not. Radical editors were driven out of publishing houses, grants were not awarded radical writers, book clubs rarely adopted radical books, radical critics lost their jobs in the review media, and radical professors were ejected from universities. The cultural institutions of the CP collapsed and attempts to create new radical book clubs or literary magazines were unsuccessful.

Writers with radical roots often quit their literary work in despair, but some persevered and a few prospered despite the new political climate. Authors such as Ruth McKenney, Willard Motley, Irwin Shaw, Alfred Hayes, and Howard Fast would find success with work that lacked the old radical bite. Others like Richard Wright and Nelson Algren would move with new intellectual tides of dissent. Wright became identified with the Third World perspective and Algren forged links with the French existentialists and the small-press movement in America while writing novels about drugs, the destitute, and boxers that found a popular audience. A number of the blacklisted Hollywood screenwriters found work as television writers for the series *You Are There* and a few eventually resumed Hollywood careers and scripted important films such as *Spartacus* (1960) and *M*A*S*H* (1970). Tom McGrath stayed viable through regional associations and the alternative press while African Americans such as Langston Hughes and Claude McKay became more identified with racial consciousness rather than class consciousness, a perception they sometimes encouraged. Meridel Le Sueur would fall into anonymity until her work was revived by the woman's movement of the late 1960s, which related to her feminism more than to her socialism. Writers like James T. Farrell who continued to write in the old mold were usually dismissed by reviewers as being out-of-date. A significant rightward drift was also evident. John Dos Passos's *Mid-Century* (1960) was as conservative as *USA* had been radical. Budd Schulberg was typical of former radicals who became concerned with unions and revolutions that had gone wrong (longshoremen in *Waterfront*, 1955; teamsters in *Everything That Moves*, 1980; and Cuba in *Sanctuary V*, 1969).

Most crippling to any radical continuim was that no new wave of leftist writers emerged from the experiences of the war years. For a moment Norman Mailer seemed to be an exception. His *Naked and the Dead* (1948) dealt with an American military that flirted with fascism and his *Barbary Shore* (1951) featured Trotskyists. Mailer worked for the Progressive Party, was involved with the *National Guardian*, and helped finance the *Village Voice;* but his career moved toward ever more sensationalist and individualistic themes, his liberalism often containing elements usually associated with the Right. James Jones, another best-selling new author, included a wonderful homage to the Industrial Workers of the World in *From Here to Eternity* (1951), a sequence dropped from the film version. His work, however, had only dim notions of class conflict that were often enmeshed within a military system with its own set of particulars.

Intellectual disfavor of radical literature became the norm in universities when political scientists declared an end to ideology and English professors adopted a "New Criticism" that devalued writing that was politically committed. Despite the resilience of individual authors and some new standard-bearers in the 1960s, the literary movement that had blossomed in the 1930s was more or less spent by the early 1950s. The next literary rebellion with radical overtones would be that of the Beat writers. Their movement would be more cultural than political, and their hostility to all forms of authoritarianism would extend beyond Stalin to Lenin and Marx. *See also*: Algren, Nelson; American Writers Congress; *Anvil*; Conroy, Jack; Dos Passos, John; Farrell, James T.; Fast, Howard; Gold, Mike; Goodman, Paul; Le Sueur, Meridel; *Mainstream*; McGrath, Tom; McKenney, Ruth; *New Masses*; Olsen, Tillie; *Partisan Review*; John Reed Clubs; Smedly, Agnes

—Dan Georgakas, Ernie Brill

REFERENCES

Brown, Sterling A., Arthur P. Davis, and Ulysses Lee, eds. *The Negro Caravan*. New York: Citadel, 1941.

Conroy, Jack, and Curt Johnson, eds. *Writers in Revolt: The Anvil Anthology, 1933–1940*. New York: Lawrence Hill & Co., 1973.

Maltz, Albert. "What Shall We Ask of Writers?" *New Masses*, February 12, 1946. Responses in *New Masses* by Howard Fast (February 26, 1946), Joseph

North (February 26, 1946), John Howard Lawson (March 19, 1946), and William Z. Foster (April 23, 1946). Responses in the *Daily Worker* by Mike Gold (February 12 and 23, 1946) and Samuel Sillen (February 11–16, 1946).

Nekola, Charlotte and Paula Rabinowitz. *Writing Red: An Anthology of American Women Writers, 1930–1940.* New York: Feminist Press, 1987.

North, Joseph, ed., with Introduction by Maxwell Geismar. *New Masses: An Anthology of the Rebel Thirties.* New York: International Publishers, 1969.

Salzman, Jack, with Barry Wallenstein, eds. *Years of Protest: A Collection of American Writing of the 1930s.* New York: Pegasus, 1967.

Swados, Harvey, ed. *The American Writer and the Great Depression.* New York: Bobbs-Merrill, 1966.

Proletarian Party

This group was the direct descendent of the Socialist Party of Michigan, and especially of the large left-wing group around the Proletarian University in Detroit, headed by shoe-salesman John Keracher and machinist Dennis Batt. One of the most militantly Marxist groups in the national SP, and a vehement supporter of the Bolshevik Revolution in Russia, the Michigan party was the first of many left-wing groups expelled (in May 1919) by the SP national leadership. At an emergency meeting of the expelled party in June, a resolution was passed calling for a new revolutionary party to be formed in Chicago on September 1, and on that date Keracher, Batt, and others from the "Michigan group," together with supporters from other states, took part in founding the Communist Party.

Fundamental disagreements, however, soon made it impossible for the "Michigan group" to remain in the new party. Keracher, Batt, and their comrades were almost the only founders of American Communism who did not believe that proletarian revolution was imminent in the United States. Active trade-unionists—Batt was a central figure in the Detroit Federation of Labor—they opposed the CP's "underground" and antielectoral orientation as well as its dual unionism. They were also critical of the CP's organization as a loose "federation of federations," and called for a centralized, disciplined party. In January 1920, after CPers tried unsuccessfully to take over the Proletarian University by force, the CP leadership charged Keracher et al. with "Menshevism" and expelled them. Six months later, in June, the expelled members and several newcomers founded the Proletarian Party.

Several thousand workers took out cards in the PP over the years (non-wage-earners were prohibited from joining by the party constitution), but its membership seems to have peaked at around 500 in the late 1920s. Although locals were formed in at least thirty-eight cities, from New York to San Francisco, its stronghold remained the industrial Midwest, especially Detroit, Flint, Chicago, Cleveland, Buffalo, and Rochester.

The PP sent a delegate to the third congress of the Communist International (CI) in June 1921, and at its next convention declared its total agreement with the CI and resolved to continue the PP "until the CI is represented in America by a real Communist Party." Despite efforts by CI officials to convince the PP to reenter the "official" CP, the Proletarians stubbornly pursued their own course nation-

ally while uncritically supporting the Third International line on world politics. Not until the mid-1930s, when Keracher and his friends opposed the Popular Front—in the United States as well as in Europe, but above all in Spain during the Revolution—did the PP challenge the authority of the CP of the Soviet Union on international affairs. But then they turned around and endorsed the Hitler-Stalin Pact and supported the USSR's position on World War II.

Largest of the Communist opposition groups for some fifteen years, the PP was the perennial prey of other oppositionists. German-born Marxist economist Paul Mattick was expelled for factionalism in 1931, and the following year a small group of his supporters left the PP to help him form the short-lived United Workers Party. Several PPers joined the Trotskyists; a few became Lovestoneites; a very few—notably Oakley C. Johnson, Stanley Nowak, and Harry M. Wicks—joined or became associated with the CP.

Notwithstanding the PP's vociferous assertions of its Leninist orthodoxy, PP Marxism remained that of the left-wing of the SP during World War I—a naturalistic Marxism that owed more to Engels than to Marx, as far from the Neo-Hegelianism of the Frankfurt School as from the "diamat" of Moscow, and deeply influenced by Charles Darwin, Lewis Henry Morgan, and Joseph Dietzgen. Essentially a socialist educational group rather than a revolutionary political party—its activity consisted almost exclusively of study classes, forums, lectures, and soapboxing—the PP proved to be a good caretaker for Charles H. Kerr's old socialist publishing co-op, which Keracher and other PPers ran from 1928 till the party's demise in 1971.

For a few years during the Great Depression, the alumni of Proletarian U. enjoyed an activist phase that had a real impact on the broader working-class movement. PPers were active in the Briggs Auto Body strike in Detroit, 1933, and later helped lead sit-downs in Flint and elsewhere. In the early days of the United Auto Workers, PP street speakers expounded the ABC's of Marxism to larger and more receptive crowds than ever. And for a small group, the PP provided the UAW with a disproportionately large number of its best organizers, some of whom—such as Emil Mazey and Frank Marquart—became important leaders of the new union. Many other PPers eventually became top officers of other unions—Carl Berreitter of the International Typographical Union, Al Renner of the Restaurant Workers, Samuel Meyers of the Retail Clerks, and many others noted for their militant and often innovative union-organizing strategies.

In all but a few cases, however, the PPers who became union leaders did not remain in the PP. Like all revolutionary sects, the PP suffered a high turnover rate. By 1940 it was no longer a large sect but a small one, and it grew smaller year by year until 1971, when National Secretary Al Wysocki, who for some time had taken care of the party's day-to-day chores, died after a long illness. None of the handful of surviving party stalwarts, all of them in their sixties and seventies, came forward to fill the breach. The PP never merged with any other party, never admitted defeat, never disbanded. Independent to the end, it just faded away. *See also*: Keracher, John

—*Franklin Rosemont*

REFERENCES

Keracher, John. "Ten Years of Communism in America." *The Proletarian* (Chicago), September 1929, November 1929, February 1930, March–April 1930.

Marquart, Frank. *An Auto Worker's Journal: The UAW from Crusade to One-Party Union*. University Park: Pennsylvania State University Press, 1975.

Il Proletario

Founded in 1896 in Pittsburgh by a group of Italian immigrants belonging to the Socialist Labor Party of Pennsylvania, *Il Proletario* became during much of its twenty-five-year existence the most important periodical of the Italian-American Left. The paper might have died in its infancy had it not been for the important personal involvement of some leading Italian socialist émigrés such as Dino Rondani and Giacinto Menotti Serrati. When in 1902 the latter founded the *Federazione Socialista Italiana del Nord America* (FSI), *Il Proletario* became its official organ, and up until the FSI dissolved itself into the Industrial Workers of the World in 1921, the newspaper's existence became intimately tied to the organizational and ideological vicissitudes of the FSI.

Seldom enjoying a stable financial backing, and having often to rely on ad hoc fundraising campaigns, *Il Proletario* managed to survive one financial crisis after another, thus fulfilling its essential role as a source of information for Italian-American activists, and as a forum for political debate. The newspaper's existence was also marked by a shifting political orientation largely due to the constant change of editors and to the different political conjunctures both in the United States and in Italy. Thus, for instance, under Carlo Tresca's editorship *Il Proletario* became a vehicle for the promotion of industrial unionism and of IWW objectives, whereas under Edmondo Rossoni's brief editorship, in 1915, the paper favored Italy's intervention in the war, a position strongly advocated by the revolutionary syndicalist movement in Italy.

The political repression following U.S. intervention in World War I forced *Il Proletario* to suspend publication. The paper sought to circumvent the government's ban by reappearing under different names, until it was allowed to resume publication in early 1920. When in 1921 the FSI was absorbed by the IWW, *Il Proletario's* existence came to an end, as the paper was transformed into an official IWW organ under the name *The Italian Weekly of the Industrial Workers of the World*. *See also*: Giovannitti, Arturo; Industrial Workers of the World; Italian Americans.

—*Bruno Ramirez*

REFERENCES

Cartosio, Bruno. "Italian Workers and Their Press in the United States, 1900–1920," and Elisabetta Vezzosi, "Class, Ethnicity, and Acculturation in Il Proletario: The WWI Years." In *The Press of Labor Migrants in Europe and North America: 1880s to 1930s* edited by Christiane Harzig and Dirk Hoerder. Bremen: University of Bremen, 1985.

Psychoanalysis

The Left movement in the United States never wholly welcomed psychoanalysis, although the bohemian Marxists of the *Masses* and early feminists were intrigued by its possibilities. Most U.S. psychoanalysts rejected leftist ideas outright, and it was only in the writings of Wilhelm Reich and Herbert Marcuse that a more thorough integration of Marx and Freud was attempted.

The first lengthy popular treatments of Freudian ideas were written by leftists, the *Masses* editors Max Eastman and Floyd Dell. Dell, especially, continued to write of psychoanalysis in the *Masses* and later the *Liberator*, and the influence of Freud on Eastman is clearly visible in his *Marx, Lenin and the Science of Revolution*. Edmund Wilson remarked that he had first learned of psychoanalysis through Eastman's popular treatment in *Everybody's Magazine* in 1915. Dell satirized the contradictions he felt in trying to unite both Freudian and Marxist ideas in "A Psycho-Analytic Confession" in the *Liberator* for April 1920.

Freudian and Marxist ideas often mixed and clashed in the salon of Mabel Dodge, where a special evening was devoted to Freud's teachings, just as another night drew Big Bill Haywood, Emma Goldman, and others in a debate on the Industrial Workers of the World. Other participants in the bohemian Left current who were influenced by psychoanalytic ideas were Randolph Bourne, Isadora Duncan, and Rose Pastor Stokes (in the free-motherhood campaign), and Malcolm Cowley, Kenneth Burke, and Matthew Josephson. But the most outspoken and serious radical to welcome the ideas of Freud was Emma Goldman. Emma Goldman attended lectures by Freud in Vienna (1895) as well as at the famous Clark University conference (1909), and she invoked Freudian teachings for their liberating effect on female sexuality.

Still, radical Freudianism was a hybrid for which the U.S. medical establishment had only disdain and dislike, while many on the Left felt the same distaste for Freudianism. The exclusion of lay analysts from the world of psychoanalytic education, the conservatism of the medical establishment, and the specialized nature of medical education served to limit the number of new psychoanalysts who would have the same broad cultural and political backgrounds as their earlier, European counterparts.

Those aspects of psychoanalysis that could be understood as having radical significance were often obscured. Thus, the respected *Freud and the Americans*, by Nathan G. Hale, details the popularizations carried out by Dell and Eastman without ever mentioning that they were leftists or connected with the *Masses* and the *Liberator*. Meanwhile, early socialists like John Spargo used a superficial "Freudian" character typology to characterize the communists as "hysterics."

Other radical voices spoke out against psychoanalysis: Upton Sinclair had never trusted psychoanalysis, and he revealed in a letter to an associate that he had never known it to work. Sidney Hook, in a debate with Max Eastman, called it "the crassest violation of scientific method," and he insisted elsewhere that Freud could never serve Marx's materialism, while Christopher Caudwell agreed with other U.S. and U.K. Marxists that "Freudism can attain to no psychology beyond bourgeois psychology."

But the radical press was not entirely negative. The popularizer of psychoanalysis, Andre Tridon, had earlier written a book on the Industrial Workers of the World, while one member of the latter organization, known only by his card number, wrote about psychoanalysis in the *Industrial Worker* for January 15, 1921. The militant *New Majority*, the journal of the Chicago Federation of Labor, commented favorably on psychoanalysis with some regularity, and the Eastman/Hook debate mentioned above was carried in V. F. Calverton's *The Modern Quarterly*.

Trotsky had commented favorably on Freud's ideas; Philip Rahv and William Phillips began to read Freud seriously at the time their *Partisan Review* severed its connections with the Stalinist Left, and their journal was as open to "Freudo-Marxists" like Nicolas Calas ("On Revolutionary Sadism") as it was to Trotsky's writings. Joseph Freeman, who broke with Stalinism at approximately that time, wrote of how a single sentence of Freud's provided the major and decisive inspiration for his life's work as a writer, although he also noted that the psychoanalytic turn in the writings of the Left bohemians was often the opening of the door for their reentry into bourgeois society.

The desire to understand the mechanisms of the transmission and internalization of repressive institutions reached a high point in the writings of Wilhelm Reich, who arrived in the United States in 1939. While his descent into biological mysticism is well known, his studies *The Mass Psychology of Fascism* and *Dialectical Materialism and Psychoanalysis* are of great interest. Reich had been a pioneer of sexual education in Europe, and he continued to petition Congress in the United States for the sexual rights of the young. He envisioned the possibility of a nonrepressive society, and he thought that psychoanalysis could lift the veil of repression that stood between humanity and sexual freedom, which he conceived of in genital and orgasmic terms.

Russell Jacoby has documented an episode in the history of U.S. Freudian Marxism that shares the fate of Reich's ideas, insofar as their actual propagation failed in the United States. Otto Fenichel was one of a number of European analysts who had participated in leftist movements in Europe before their forced emigration and their arrival in the United States—some associates of Fenichel ended up in England and others in other parts of Europe. Along with Edith Jacobson, Annie Reich, and others, he conducted a secret *rundbriefe*, or circular letter, designed to preserve the radical notions of psychoanalysis they had brought from Europe, when Wilhelm Reich and others had shared their interests. The German exile community on the West Coast maintained a spirited intellectual life, with cross-fertilization from Frankfurt School members Theodore Adorno and Max Horkheimer, and from J. Robert Oppenheimer and others, but in the end, the secrecy of the *rundbriefe*, the fear the analysts had of losing their immigration status, the dispersion of the original group because of Hitler's conquests and the conservatism of the U.S. medical establishment (and its opposition to lay analysis) combined ultimately to hide the radical import of their work.

Freud himself wrote pessimistically about Marxism and materialism, but in a late letter he noted that he had just learned that Marx and Engels did not deny "the influence of ideas and super-ego factors" and that this knowledge invalidated the contrast "between Marxism and psychoanalysis which I had thought to exist." The gap in Freud's teachings left by this remark was filled especially by the work of Herbert Marcuse.

His *Eros and Civilization* may be the most influential Marxist interpretation of Freud in the United States, but it is undeniable that Reich provided a similar inspiration. Marcuse outlined the principles by which a nonrepressive society could come into being, and like Reich he emphasized the dominance of the pleasure principle. Unlike Reich, however, he opposed the latter's idea of an uninhibited genitality with his notion of the libidinized body, which borrowed inspiration from Geza Roheim and Sandor Ferenczi. His theory of surplus repression as the psychic residue of dominance and his notion of the critical role of fantasy both played a significant part in the orientation of Left movements of the 1960s and early 1970s.

In *Psychoanalysis and Feminism*, Juliet Mitchell has emphasized the importance of psychoanalysis as a critique of patriarchy for Marxist feminists, and in doing so, she has rehabilitated the unconscious as a dynamic principle of mental functioning, and sexuality as the axis around which this principle revolves. Further, the writings of Mitchell, Jacqueline Rose, and others expose the essentially sociological outlook of Neo-Freudian feminists who still trace the source of capitalism and patriarchal rule to primarily external events.

But it is precisely the ideas that society is internal and that the family is the locus for the maintenance of repressive social and psychological structures that has separated the Marxist Freudians from the Neo-Freudians who have seen society acting on the individual from the outside instead of from the inside, and who have denied the importance of unconscious mechanisms of internalization. The Marxists also take issue with the psychotherapeutic emphasis often given to Freudian teachings: "Psychoanalysis is a theory of an unfree society that necessitates psychoanalysis as a therapy," Russell Jacoby has written, and the Marxist Freudian impulse insists that the radical import of Freudianism disappears when the theory is collapsed by the therapy.

See also: *The Liberator*; Marcuse, Herbert; *Masses*; *Modern Quarterly*; *Partisan Review*

—*Paul Garon*

REFERENCES

Frosh, Stephen. *The Politics of Psychoanalysis*. New Haven: Yale University Press, 1987.

Hale, Nathan G. *Freud and the Americans: The Beginnings of Psychoanalysis in the United States*. New York: Oxford University Press, 1971.

Jacoby, Russell. *The Repression of Psychoanalysis: Otto Fenichel and the Political Freudians*. New York: Basic Books, 1983.

Robinson, Paul. *The Freudian Left*. New York: Harper and Row, 1969.

PSYCHOLOGY

Both as a profession and a body of knowledge, psychology has influenced the Left. As professionals, usually employed by universities, individual psychologists have championed liberal campaigns such as the opposition to military conscription and McCarthyism. Histories of these causes show prominent examples of such individuals (e.g., James McKeen Cattell, Edward Tolman).

Less widely known are the activist groupings formed by psychologists, beginning during the period of the Popular Front. The Psychologists League, centered in New York City, debated theoretical issues, was a Socialist-Communist caucus within the American Psychological Association (APA), and attempted to organize psychologists of the Works Progress Administration. Initially formed by clinicians at Bellevue Hospital, it attracted a wide membership, published a journal, held public discussions, and marched on May Day under slogans such as "Fascism is the World's Worst Behavior Disorder," and "Don't Be Unconscious, Join Our Ranks." After the Stalin-Hitler Pact the organization split along Socialist-Communist lines, its president resigned and became an ad hoc FBI informer. The league is notable for having combined features of the science-and-society movement with those of rank-and-file groups such as the Social Work Discussion Clubs (publisher of *Social Work Today*) and Physicians Forum.

Longer lasting has been the Society for the Psychological Study of Social Issues (SPSSI), best known for its members' providing the social psychology brief for the plaintiffs in *Brown v. Board of Education*. SPSSI was formed in 1936 by members of the Socialist Party, New America (a Deweyist-Marxist group), and former Christian socialists to sensitize the APA to the issue of psychologists' unemployment. Initially radical in its perspective, SPSSI pioneered the idea of social science research on war, class conflict, and racism. Distrusting the mass media, it mounted its own exhibit on the irrationality of war and laissez-faire capitalism at the 1939 New York World's Fair. Among the early leaders of SPSSI was George W. Hartmann, a pacifist, perennial SP candidate for office, and chairman of the wartime group Peace Now.

In addition to these primarily disciplinary organizations, psychologists collaborated before in the 1930s with other Left professionals, such as the psychiatrist Frankwood Williams. This joint work occurred in groups including the Medical Bureau to Aid Spanish Democracy (in which psychologists formed their own committee), and the National Research League (formerly the Communist Party's Pen and Hammer Clubs, whose director was a psychologist).

Following World War II, clinical psychologists were active with psychiatrists and social workers in the Benjamin Rush Society (1944–53), initially formed in New York to attract radical psychiatrists leaving the military. The society held public debates over the politics of psychoanalysis, followed similar discussions within European CPs, and published a short-lived bulletin. Its members taught psychology and psychiatry at the Jefferson School of Social Science, wrote for the *New Masses* and *Science & Society*, and provided an informal referral service for Communists needing psychological treatment. It disbanded under the combined impact of McCarthyism, the CP's psychotherapy ban, and the antipsychological, pro-Pavlov campaign in the Soviet and European CPs.

Beginning in the Vietnam War era, leftist caucuses were again active within psychology, including Psychologists for a Democratic Society, Psychologists for Social Action, and Behaviorists for Social Action (a group of Marxist-Leninist Skinnerians). Of far greater influence was the New Left antipsychiatry group the Radical Therapy Collective, publishers of *Radical Therapist*.

Independent of these professional groupings, leftists have often appropriated psychological knowledge for their own use. Most familiar has been the incorporation of revisionist personality theories into socialist and communist views of political motivation. Emigré intellectuals whose work has been so used include Erich Fromm, Herbert Marcuse, and Wilhelm Reich. Native-born theorists include J. F. (Junius Flagg) Brown, Francis H. Bartlett, and Dorothy Dinnerstein. Also, exposés of the history of intelligence testing, written by psychologists such as Leon Kamin, have become a recent addition to leftist critiques of modern capitalism, reminiscent of Albert Deutsch's *Shame of the States* (serialized in *PM*).

Major Left organizations have had an ambiguous relationship to psychology, personality theory, and psychotherapy. Before Max Eastman began popularizing Freud in *The Masses*, psychology was one of the many sciences that Left socialists (e.g., Louis Fraina) believed could contribute to a Marxist understanding of nature. Since then, psychological books and trends have been well covered in the press of the CP, SP, and smaller, Trotskyist groups. Left parties have also responded to members' and sympathizers' psychological interests far beyond what can be seen in party platforms and theoretical journals. In the 1920s, for example, the Socialist Rand School was kept afloat financially by ticket sales to its psychology lectures, organized with the assistance of the behaviorist John B. Watson. Later, psychology courses were so popular at the Jefferson School and its sister schools across the country that such offerings were expanded and multiple sections of the introductory course were often run.

Because of its large, often middle-class membership, the CP has had a special relationship to psychology. By the mid-1930s its Workers School was offering lectures on sex and psychology, while the Medical Bureau of the *Daily Worker* provided advice (often misleading) on mental health, marijuana addiction, and related subjects. The Party's official position on the most popular psychological theory, psychoanalysis, was ambiguous until 1950, when all psychodynamic therapy was proscribed for members and a public anti-Freud campaign was begun. Evidence of this campaign's lack of effect includes Victor Navasky's account of the Hollywood leftists who shared a single therapist, who appears to have collaborated with the FBI and the House Un-American Activities Committee.

Most often, Left groups have downplayed psychological explanations of political events; rare attempts at psychological explanations of activists' behavior (e.g., Reuben Osborn's *Marx and Freud*) have been met with hostility.

By contrast, a few small groups with origins in the New Left, such as the National Caucus of Labor Committees, have recently used psychology either to analyze and control members or as part of public organizing. The latter strategy is currently pursued by the New York-based Institute for Social Therapy; in 1988 one of its staff psychologists was the U.S. presidential candidate of the affiliated New Alliance Party. *See also*: Psychoanalysis, Science

—*Benjamin Harris*

REFERENCES

Finison, Lorenz J. "The Psychological Insurgency, 1936–1945." *Journal of Social Issues* 42 (1986).

Harris, Benjamin. "Reviewing Fifty Years of the Psychology of Social Issues." *Journal of Social Issues* 42 (1986).

Haynes, John Earl. "The 'Rank and File Movement' in Private Social Work." *Labor History* 16 (1975).

Navasky, Victor S. *Naming Names*. New York: Viking, 1980.

Public Sector Unions

During the 1960s and 1970s government unions gained collective-bargaining rights for a majority of city, state, and federal workers. This remarkable turnaround in public-sector unionism was based in part on Left-influenced precursor unions of the 1930s. With the assistance of CIO organizers, many with ties to the Communist Party, government workers joined unions in unprecedented numbers during the Great Depression. The largest of these unions was the State, County, and Municipal Workers of America (SCMWA, not to be confused with its AFL rival, AFSCME, the American Federation of State, County, and Municipal Employees). Headed by Abram Flaxer, SCMWA was strongest among New York City welfare workers, hospital workers, and laborers. Elsewhere Communist Party–influenced unions signed up other disfranchised groups, including blacks in the Panama Canal Zone, part-time mail deliverers (in the Postal Workers of America), temporary teachers (in the Teachers Union), and New Deal federal workers (in the United Federal Workers of America). SCMWA and the United Federal Workers combined in 1946 to form the United Public Workers (UPW), claiming more than 100,000 members.

Yet, unlike steel, auto, and rubber-worker unions, none of the CIO public-sector unions gained collective-bargaining rights. Only the Transport Workers Union (TWU) of New York City, organized on the then-privately owned transit system, later signed contracts for public employees when the bus and subway lines were purchased by the city. Communists and other Left sympathizers, who were instrumental in forming the union, were excluded from union leadership as part of the 1948 recognition agreement between TWU president Michael Quill and New York City mayor William O'Dwyer.

In a few isolated cases, strong CIO organizing drives forced city managements to recognize AFL unions as preferable alternatives. In Philadelphia, a 1939 strike was ended by calling in an AFSCME local not involved in the strike to negotiate its conclusion. Thereafter, AFSCME was the sole representative for most Philadelphia employees. In New York City, when a 1941 TWU-financed SCMWA organizing drive succeeded in signing up 25 percent of the sanitation department, Mayor Fiorello LaGuardia ignored calls for a representation election. Instead he pointed out SCMWA's Communist ties and recognized an AFSMCE local specifically created for the purpose. Following a similar pattern, Cincinnati officials granted exclusive bargaining rights to an AFSCME district council in 1960 in order to preempt a potentially powerful United Mine Worker organizing drive.

Otherwise public-sector unions generally, and the UPW in particular, collapsed during the early 1950s. One reason was new state legislation forcing public unions to disavow the right to strike. In doing so, the UPW found it difficult to differentiate its approach from less militant AFL rivals.

Anticommunism finally destroyed the UPW. Coordinated efforts by government officials and CIO leaders caused thousands of accused Communists to lose their jobs. In 1950 the UPW was expelled from the CIO. And in 1951 Flaxer was sentenced to prison for refusing to turn over membership lists to the U.S. Senate Internal Security Subcommittee (the verdict was overturned seven years later by the Supreme Court). By 1952 the UPW was out of business.

During the 1950s UPW organizers were hired by AFSCME split-offs now affiliated with the Teamsters. The New York City AFSCME locals, led by Jerry Wurf, a Norman Thomas–influenced socialist, protested these appointments. But a more successful strategy for Wurf, one that eventually defeated the Teamsters in key elections and enabled Wurf to take over the national union, was affiliation with the civil rights movement. James Farmer and other black leaders worked as District Council 37 organizers in New York, helping to link AFSCME with the growing civil rights movement as well as with historically strong black unions. In 1969 AFSCME signed the first citywide contract, significantly improving pay and in-service upgrading opportunities for its primarily black and female membership. These organizing successes were repeated in other cities; the Rev. Martin Luther King, Jr., was in Memphis to support an AFSCME sanitation strike when he was assassinated in 1968.

The most important independent Left union during the 1960s was New York City's Social Service Employees Union (SSEU). Founded by former UPW members in 1961, SSEU displaced AFSCME as the representative for social workers in 1964. Strong rank-and-file participation and cooperation with the welfare rights movement enabled the union to win unprecedented pay increases, improved caseloads, and, most controversially, higher grants for welfare recipients. SSEU became less effective after 1967, when collective-bargaining rules undercut the power of independent unions. Consequently, in 1971 SSEU rejoined AFSCME.

SSEU served as a model for the Chicago Independent Union of Public Aid Employees (IUPAE), a split-off from the Building Service International Union. Even though IUPAE won sole bargaining rights after a 1966 strike, the union was unable to gain support from welfare recipients and failed to win contract approval by the Cook County Board of Commissioners.

In New York City, SSEU success prompted Left factions in other unions to press for strikes; by 1971, transit workers, teachers, sanitation workers, firefighters, police, and, on the federal level, postal workers, had gone on strike, often serving as a model for militancy in other cities. However, racial conflict (in particular the Ocean-Hill Brownsville school board dispute) and the 1975 fiscal crisis diminished the influence of Left caucuses within New York's public-sector unions.

On the national level, public-sector unions remain on the left wing of the labor movement. AFSCME, in particular, has a strong democratic socialist influence among its staff; the union was an early opponent of the Vietnam War and has been in the forefront of the struggle for comparable worth pay for women. *See also*: Communist Party, Teachers Union, Transport Workers Union

—*Mark Maier*

REFERENCES

Bellush, Jewel, and Bernard Bellush. *Union Power and New York*. New York: Praeger, 1984.

Jones, Ralph T. "City Employee Unions in New York and Chicago." Ph.D. diss., Harvard University, 1972.

Maier, Mark H. *City Unions: Managing Discontent in New York City*. New Brunswick: Rutgers University Press, 1987.

Spero, Sterling. *Government as Employer*. Carbondale: Southern Illinois University Press, 1972.

Puerto Ricans

The interaction between the status of Puerto Ricans as an oppressed minority in the continental United States and Puerto Rico's semicolonial status has guaranteed that from its inception until the present day the Left has found a presence in the Puerto Rican community.

Until the postwar migration, the number of Puerto Rican–born people in the continental United States was limited, numbering only 1,513 in 1910, 11,811 in 1920, and 52,774 in 1930. Migration from Puerto Rico slowed to a trickle during the Great Depression and then was halted during the war years by the cessation of almost all civilian shipping to and from Puerto Rico.

In 1940, 88 percent of the Puerto Ricans lived in New York City and of this number the majority lived in El Barrio. This community expanded from its original center around East 110th and 111th streets between Park and Madison avenues in the East Harlem section of Manhattan before World War I until 1950, when it occupied the area bounded by Third and Fifth avenues from East 96th to 125th streets. El Barrio not only contained the largest number of Puerto Ricans, it also housed the institutions, churches, cultural centers, political clubs, and shopping that attracted Puerto Ricans from throughout the city.

The establishment of an airplane route from San Juan to New York City and the attraction of the postwar economic boom encouraged a vast migration. Between 1946 and 1964 fully one-third of Puerto Rico's population moved to the continental United States. In 1980 two million Puerto Ricans lived in the continental United States while three million lived in Puerto Rico. The Puerto Rican community spread well beyond El Barrio and New York City so that in 1980 slightly less than 50 percent of the Puerto Rican community resided there. The Puerto Ricans are the second largest Hispanic group in the United States, comprising one-sixth of the Hispanic population.

El Barrio grew within Jewish East Harlem, a great center of Socialist Party politics. Before World War I, *La Escuela Francisco Ferrer y Guardia* (Francisco Ferrer School), a community center serving Hispanics influenced by anarchist ideas, flourished. In 1918 the first Puerto Rican section of the SP appeared. Shortly afterward the *Asociación Nacionalista* came into existence. Founded in 1927, *El Centro Obrero Español* (Spanish Workers Center) became a major center of Communist Party influence in the community. El Centro sponsored a newspaper, *La Vida Obrera* (Worker's Life), and took part in successful labor organizing campaigns. El Barrio enthusiastically supported the presidential candidacy of Robert La Follette in 1924 and was also an integral part of the coalition that elected Fiorello LaGuardia East Harlem's congressperson from 1922 to 1932.

Vito Marcantonio's candidacy for Congress from East Harlem in 1934 opened a new phase in El Barrio's political life. The most successful radical politician in the United States, Marcantonio embraced the cause of Puerto Rico and the Puerto Rican people as his own. In June 1936 Marcantonio submitted a bill calling for "genuine independence [for Puerto Rico and the declaration of] responsibility of the United States for the disastrous state of the economy of Puerto Rico and the abysmal poverty of the people." In August he visited the Island and became engaged as co-attorney for Don Pedro Albizu Campos and six other members of the Nationalist Party, who had been arrested for conspiracy to overthrow the U.S. government. Marcantonio's insistence that the Puerto Ricans were "the most exploited victims of a most devastating imperialism" resonated with El Barrio's deepest feelings. Marcantonio served as de facto congressperson for Puerto Rico until his defeat in 1950. In El Barrio he attended to the everyday needs of his constituents and fought against their vilification in the press. They in turn became an essential part of his electoral coalition, for example, providing 66 percent of their vote for Marcantonio even when he was defeated in 1950.

Although it would be impossible to overlook Marcantonio's involvement, leftism in El Barrio existed independently of the radical congressman. After all, it had predated his arrival on scene. When in 1936 the people of El Barrio had the opportunity to vote for Marcantonio on the All People's Party, a Left party associated with the CP, 57 percent of his vote was registered on that line. One of El Barrio's election districts gave 24 percent of its vote to José Santiago, the CP's candidate for state assemblyman, and he received somewhat lower yet impressive votes from El Barrio in general. That same year El Barrio's vote for Franklin Delano Roosevelt and Herbert H. Lehman on the American Labor Party (ALP) line closely approximated the citywide ALP vote, 8.6 percent, a percentage not matched in any other non-Jewish area.

In 1937 in a special election Oscar García Rivera, the Republican-ALP candidate for state assemblyperson for a district including El Barrio won, becoming the first Puerto Rican elected official in the continental United States. In 1938 he won the same office by running solely on the ALP line. El Barrio provided Israel Amter, the CP's at-large candidate for the city council, his third highest vote of any Manhattan assembly district. In the same election Lehman received two to three times as many votes on the ALP line than his citywide average of 15 percent, and Marcantonio swept El Barrio, receiving three ALP votes for every Republican vote. Nearly 30 percent of El Barrio's voters pulled the ALP lever to vote for Roosevelt in 1940 and in 1941 a majority voted for LaGuardia on the ALP line.

After a decrease in El Barrio's support for the ALP during the early war years, the community resumed voting for this Left party in unprecedented numbers. For example, in 1944 in the Ninth Election District in the heart of El Barrio, Roosevelt received 649 votes (322 on the Democratic and 301 on the ALP lines) and Wendell Willkie received 8 votes. Most striking was its support for the entire ALP slate. In 1948 almost two-thirds of its voters supported Marcantonio, running solely on the ALP line, and approximately 50 percent voted for Manuel Medina, the ALP's candidate for state assemblyman. Most significant, Henry Wallace carried El Barrio. In two election districts he received over 50 percent of the vote. In all, he carried all eight of El Barrio's election districts, which represented 27 percent of the election districts he carried in the entire United States.

Despite intensifying political repression, El Barrio continued voting ALP. In 1949, when Marcantonio ran as the ALP mayoral candidate, he carried El Barrio with two-thirds of the vote. Now running for city council, Medina won 73 percent of the vote in some El Barrio election districts. In 1950 El Barrio cast over 60 percent of its vote for the only congressman to vote against the Korean War and support the right of the CP to a legal existence. Citywide, the ALP candidate for Senate, W. E. B. DuBois, received 6.5 percent of the vote; in El Barrio he received approximately 45 percent. In those few elections the ALP contested before its demise in 1954, its totals in El Barrio were always greatly above those elsewhere in the city. It was only in El Barrio, including areas outside Marcantonio's district, that the ALP became the major party.

During this entire period the Left had a felt presence in El Barrio. There were frequent street meetings and demonstrations. One study published in 1938 noted that political "parades and demonstrations . . . have become almost a part of the life of the colony." Many left-wing organizations had headquarters in the Barrio—ALP clubs, organizations advocating independence for Puerto Rico, Workers Alliance headquarters, a CP club, and as many as six Spanish-speaking lodges of the International Workers Order. Jesus Colón, the leader of the Spanish-language section of the IWO, as a youth had migrated from Puerto Rico to New York City, where he became a CP leader and journalist. The relative weakness of the Catholic church and other potential competing organizations gave even greater prominence to the leftist organizations. Their work was amplified by the widespread circulation of leftist Spanish-language press: a daily, *La Voz* (The Voice), from 1937 to 1939; *Los Pueblos Hispaños* (Hispanic peoples), a weekly founded in 1944; and a succeeding weekly, *Liberación*, which emblazoned on its masthead *"Por la libertad de España, Puerto Rico, y demás paises oprimidos* (For the liberty of Spain, Puerto Rico, and other oppressed nations)."

The Puerto Rican community was comprised of recent immigrants who maintained an unprecedented closeness to the land of their birth. This was largely a by-product of their holding American citizenship, which allowed for travel unimpeded by legal constraints. The influence of Island politics predisposed many of these immigrants to leftist parties. The SP had gained great prominence in Puerto Rico. Although it drifted far to the right, it popularized trade unionism and in some general form class politics. In the late thirties, the rise of the Left popularist People's Democratic Party—with its slogan "Bread, Land, Freedom"—had great impact on the Puerto Rican community. Furthermore, the Nationalist Party's weakness in numbers masked its great influence.

Because the United States was the ruling country, Puerto Rican nationalism has been inextricably tied to left-wing currents. In support of a Nationalist uprising on the Island an attempt was made on President Truman's life on November 1, 1950, by NP members Griselio Torresola (who died of gunshot wounds) and Oscar Collazo. On March 2, 1954, Lolita Lebrón, Rafael Cancel Miranda, Andrés Figueroa Cordero, and Irving Flores Rodríguez unfurled the flag of Puerto Rico, shouted "Que viva Puerto Rico Libre" and fired into the chamber of the House of Representatives. The four Nationalists had bought one-way tickets to Washington, D.C. At their trial Lebrón explained: "I came to die not to kill." These Nationalist actions became justifications for intensified police surveillance of progressive political activity of all kinds within the Puerto Rican community. Later campaigns to free these imprisoned Nationalists contributed to reassembling a Left contingent among Puerto Ricans.

The reappearance of the Puerto Rican Left, however, emerged from an unexpected quarter. In 1967 a Puerto Rican street gang in Chicago under the leadership of José ("Cha Cha") Jiménez became politicized. Closely modeling itself after the Black Panthers, the Young Lords started a breakfast program for schoolchildren. The following year it occupied a church where first a day-care center then later a health clinic were founded. Highly visible direct-action tactics gave the Young Lords much publicity and inspired the organization of other chapters.

The New York City Young Lords, which grew out of a radical study group, *La Sociedad Albizu Campos*, followed closely the pattern of the Chicago group. Perhaps because of the highly educated nature of the New York leadership, however, differences increased between the Chicago and New York City organizations. In 1970 the New York City group officially constituted themselves the Young Lords Party. The Young Lords were for the most part not born on the Island. Many spoke English as their first language and reflected the increasingly non-Island-born contingent of the Puerto Rican population, which had grown by 1970 to 43 percent. The Young Lords' generalized radical philosophy—Maoist in style, pro-Cuban, but not openly hostile to the Soviet Union—met with widespread response among the second-generation Puerto Ricans. The ghetto poor responded to the Young Lords—many of whom were high school and college students—by marching in gang-type gear chanting "*Despierta Boriqua. Defiende Lo Tuyo* (Arise Boriqua, Defend what is yours!)." By 1972, the YLP had changed its name to the Organization of Puerto Rican Revolutionary Workers and had become openly Maoist. It soon exhausted itself in competition with the socialist El Comité and other leftist groups for hegemony among radicalized student and community sectors of the Puerto Rican people.

The formation of the Pro-Independence Movement (MPI) in 1959 met with a relatively weak response. Its successor, the Puerto Rican Socialist Party (PSP), founded in 1971, for some time united significant numbers of Island and mainland Puerto Ricans in the same organization. Although largely composed of intellectuals, the PSP had a base in Puerto Rico's trade union movement. Significantly, it produced *Claridad* (Clarity), a weekly paper whose excellence, especially in cultural areas, gave it a wide and lasting audience. However, the PSP's insistence that Puerto Ricans both in the United States and in Puerto Rico were part of the same nation put it at odds with the rest of the Left, which recognized Puerto Rico as a nation and the Puerto Ricans in the United States as an oppressed national minority. By the end of the decade, however, difficulties of creating a political agenda encompassing the needs of both sectors of the Puerto Rican people precipitated a decline in the PSP.

All elements of the Puerto Rican Left combined to defend a threatened closure of Hostos Community College during the New York City financial crisis of 1975–76. Founded in 1968 as the bilingual unit of City University and located in the South Bronx, Hostos had become of enormous symbolic significance to Puerto Ricans and the wider Latino community. The college was named after Eugenio Mariá de Hostos (1839–1903), a famed Puerto Rican educator, writer, and *independentista*. The threat of closure generated committees to save Hostos that launched traditional and direct-action campaigns to keep the school open. These efforts culminated in an occupation of Hostos and a march of thousands from El Barrio to the headquarters of the city's Financial Control Board. The board rescinded its motion of closure and since that time has faced constant community pressure to improve facilities and services at Hostos.

Puerto Rican immigration has been overwhelmingly of rural and urban working people with few representatives of the owning or intellectual elites. Puerto Ricans remain the poorest of all Latino groups and have an average annual income less than half that of non-Latino groups. Puerto Ricans also suffer from an unemployment rate double that of white America and have the lowest rate of home ownership of any ethnic group. In the late 1980s almost a third of all Puerto Ricans were below federal poverty standards, a status perpetuated by continued discrimination. The community remains politically divided between those who wish to retain the present commonwealth relationship and advocates of either statehood or independence. Uniting all sectors in the late 1980s, however, was opposition to the growing movement to amend the U.S. Constitution to make English the official language of the United States, an effort Puerto Ricans interpreted as an insult and threat to their indigenous culture. *See also* American Labor Party; International Workers Order; Marcantonio, Vito

—Gerald Meyer

REFERENCES

Meyer, Gerald. *Vito Marcantonio: American Radical*. Albany: SUNY Press, 1990.

Moore, Joan, and Harry Pachon. *Hispanics in the United States*. Englewood Cliffs, N.J.: Prentice-Hall, 1985.

Vega, Bernardo. *Memorias de Bernardo Vega: Contribución a la historia de la comunidad puertorriqueña en Nueva York*. Río Piedras, PR: Ediciones Huracán, 1977.

Pullman Strike:

see Debs, Eugene V.

Quill, Mike (1905–66)

One of the most colorful personalities in twentieth-century American labor history, Michael J. Quill was chief organizer and long-time president (1936–66) of the Transport Workers Union of America. Born into an ardently nationalist family in the west of Ireland, Quill emerged from the war of independence with England and the subsequent civil war (Quill fought with Irish Republican Army forces against the partition of Ireland) with a fine war record. This made him *persona non grata* in the Irish Free State, but very welcome in nationalist circles in New York, where he emigrated in 1926. Quill joined the *Clan na Gael*, the American affiliate of the IRA, and after a series of odd jobs went to work in the New York subways in 1926. The New York transit workers, at the time, were more than 70 percent foreign (mostly Irish) born.

When Irish socialist James Gralton was deported from Ireland to the United States in 1933, Quill resumed work begun the year before organizing Irish Workers Clubs in New York. He was among the *Clan na Gael* subway workers whom Gralton tutored in socialism and the writings of James Connolly, Ireland's premier socialist theoretician. Connolly's critique of the 1907 Yonkers, New York, trolleymen's strike, in particular, became a blueprint for the embryonic Transport Workers Union.

A nucleus of *Clan na Gael* members began actively organizing subway workers in 1934, at the same time the Communist Party of the United States was attempting independently to organize New York transit workers. After being refused support for their organizing drive by the major Irish-American fraternal organizations—even though Quill was a well-known figure in New York Irish circles, as a popular emcee for Irish *ceili* dances—Quill and his *Clan na Gael* colleagues sought help from the CPUSA. The Party provided salaries, organizers, legal support, an editor, and the wherewithal to start a union newspaper.

The twelve- to fourteen-hour split shifts, meanwhile, and the seven-day work week required of transit workers, provided New York subway workers ample incentive to join the union. Imposing IRA discipline on union organizers, Quill outflanked the employers' elaborate industrial espionage network. (It was estimated at the time that every fifth employee earned an extra dollar a week by reporting back to the company office on co-workers' activities.)

In 1937 and 1938, union-recognition elections were won decisively by the TWU, which affiliated with the CIO. Quill, meantime, had become a New York celebrity. He was elected to the city council, representing the Bronx, in 1937 (and reelected in 1943 and 1945). He made regular broadcasts from the city-owned radio station, WNYC. The newspapers baited him as "Red Mike," while finding him eminently quotable. (An affectionately sarcastic spoof of Quill's career, "The Shamrock and the Sickle," was the main event at the annual New York City Press Club Dinner in 1946.)

In 1948 Quill, who may or may not have ever officially been a member of the CP, broke with Party policy irrevocably over two issues. He insisted on supporting (in accord with CIO policy) Truman, rather than Wallace, for president in 1948, and he refused to oppose a proposed nickel increase in the subway fare (which was slotted to fund, among other things, a healthy increase in transit workers' wages).

Quill's top officials in the union were privately divided over the wisdom of the CP position on these issues, but publicly condemned Quill, who retaliated by deposing them from office. For several years Quill engaged in Red-baiting, and then quietly readmitted to the TWU a number of the Communists he had expelled, who had been instrumental in founding the union.

In 1966, after engaging in decades of ritual, much-publicized battles with respective New York City mayors as contract negotiations came down to the wire—always settling at the last minute without a strike—Quill led New York's transit workers out on strike. The strike began fifteen minutes into Mayor John Lindsay's new administration, lasted thirteen days, and won a 15-percent pay increase. Quill, characteristically, fed the press corps a barrage of quotable quotes, capped by his memorable: "May the Judge drop dead in his black robes." Jailed in the course of the strike, Quill, who had been ailing, collapsed in his jail cell and was dramatically rushed to the hospital. He died three weeks later. *See also*: American Labor Party, Communist Party, Irish Americans

—*Joe Doyle*

REFERENCES

Cronin, Sean. "James Connolly and the Transport Workers Union of America: The Ideological Links with Mike Quill and His Associates." Dublin: Labour History Workshop, 1983.

Freeman, Joshua. *In Transit: The Transportation Workers Union in New York City, 1933–1936*. New York: Oxford University Press, 1989.

Quill, Shirley. *Mike Quill, Himself*. Greenwich, Connecticut: Devin Adair Publishers, 1985.

Transport Workers Union of America. *Moving Ahead: The TWU at 50*. New York: TWU, 1984.

Whittemore, L. H. *The Man Who Ran the Subways*. New York: Holt, Rinehart, Winston, 1968.

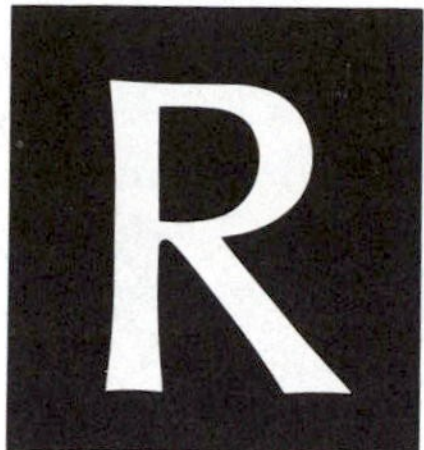

Radical America: *see* History, U.S.

Radical Economics

When Paul Baran, author of *The Political Economy of Growth* (1957) and professor of economics at Stanford University, died of a heart attack in the spring of 1964, he was virtually the only U.S. Marxist economist in the post-McCarthy academy. As one friend of Baran's wrote at the time, "Paul Baran's death . . . almost completely closes the door of the professed open society whose establishment apparently cannot find it possible to tolerate in acadamia or elsewhere any other acknowledged Marxist theoretician."

Just four years after Baran's death, a group of radical economists, many of whom were graduate students at the time, met following the Democratic convention of 1968 and formed the Union for Radical Political Economics (URPE). By the next year the group was distributing to its national membership the *Review of Radical Political Economics,* a journal dedicated to "the development of radical political economic analysis of society and assist individuals and groups working for radical change in American Society." In the wake of the Vietnam War, the civil rights movement, and later the second wave of feminism and the collapse of the postwar boom, the membership of URPE grew to 1,500, and retained more than 1,000 members in the 1980s to become both the oldest and largest disciplinary group of leftists in the academy.

The first task that radical economists set for themselves was to define their relationship to the neoclassical economic paradigm they had rejected. They challenged the neoclassical contention that capitalism is "the best of all possible worlds" and attempted to articulate a socialist alternative. The radical paradigm, based loosely on a class analysis and Marx's method of historical materialism, identified capitalism as a fundamentally irrational system at the root of a wide array of social ills that ranged from inequality and alienation to racism, sexism, and imperialism. The difference between the two paradigms was immediately recognizable, and the work of radical economists was systematically excluded from the leading journals of the economics profession. This exclusion united Left economists who found it increasingly difficult to "pass" as traditional.

The second task for radical economists was to determine their relationship to traditional Marxism. Reading groups on *Capital* acquainted radical economists with traditional Marxism and European Marxist traditions, and the *Monthly Review,* then edited by Paul Sweezy and Leo Huberman, acquainted them with American Marxism outside the academy.

By the mid-1970s, radical political economy had produced a vast and sprawling literature that addressed a variety of topics that included, among others: (1) theories of economic segmentation and poverty, (2) studies of the labor process, (3) economic crisis theory, (4) inquiries into imperialism and dependency, (5) studies of patriarchy and gender and capitalism, (6) contributions to the theory of state, and (7) an investigation of the elements of the method of Marxism and the labor theory of value.

With onset of stagflation in the mid 1970s and "the end of prosperity," radical economists turned to investigating the cause of the "economic crisis." URPE published four "crisis readers" between 1975 and 1987. These readers offered no uniform perspective on the crisis but rather a variety of articles describing the dimensions and causes of the crisis.

More formal inquiries into economic crises dropped their theoretical anchor in either the reworking of Marx's labor theory of value developed by the *Monthly Review* school in the 1950s and 1960s or more directly in the labor theory of value and Marx's *Capital*. *Monopoly Capital* (1966), by Paul Baran and Paul Sweezy, provided the basis of the *Monthly Review* perspective that identified a tendency toward stagnation brought about by monopoly pricing and a lack of demand as the chief law of motion of the postwar U.S. economy. In the 1970s and 1980s Sweezy and Harry Magdoff added a detailed analysis of the mechanisms that monopoly capitalism had at its disposal to attempt to counteract stagnation: wasteful state spending, militarism, and an explosion of corporate, consumer, and government debt.

The competing analysis of "late capitalism" relied more formally on the labor theory of value and located the cause of the crisis not in a lack of demand, but in an endangered profitability at the point of production brought about by a lack of "surplus value" and rising capital costs (or the supply side of the economy). For them, the laws of motion of capitalism described a dynamic but unstable system. These more orthodox theorists argued that Keynesian demand-management policies and state action might temporarily arrest this pattern, but were unable to alter the fundamental character of the crisis of a falling rate of profit.

While the economic crisis debate remained unresolved in the 1980s, other radical economists turned to "rethinking Marxism" and questioning the usefulness of the labor theory of value. Some published obituaries of this theory, labeling it an "embarrassment." Some, inspired by the work of Althusser and Poulantzas, challenged on a more basic level the methodology of Marxism. They argued for a "nonessentialist," or nondeterminist, examination of the structural aspects of capitalism and for a careful delineation of class and nonclass phenomena. Still others applied the mathematical techniques of traditional economics to develop an analytical Marxism that revolves around a reworking of the concept of exploitation divorced from the labor theory of value.

At the same time, North American (and European) Marxist economists launched a study of the social regulation of the capitalist economy. In the United States, these writers identified the social structures of accumulation that supported the "long wave" of expansion called the postwar boom and described the breakdown of those structures in the 1970s and 1980s.

Another group of radical economists, undeterred by these criticisms, devoted their time to compiling a body of empirical work based on Marxian theoretical categories and continued to investigate the cause of economic crises.

U.S. attempts to develop a Marxist theory of the state met with mixed success. Radical economists, however, were able to categorize theories of the state (as either instrumentalist, structuralist, or Hegelian) and to distinguish the legitimization and accumulation effects of state policies. In the 1980s this literature documented the class-war budgets of the Reagan administration and its attack on the welfare state.

More successful was the extension of Marxist perspectives into both the study of the labor process and the segmentation of the labor market. The former was initiated with the question, "What do bosses do?" and ultimately produced a direct application of Marx's own theory of the labor process to the degradation of work in the twentieth century, perhaps best encapsulated in Harry Braverman's *Labor and Monopoly Capital* (1974).

Later Richard Edward's *Contested Terrain* linked the labor process to economic segmentation. Earlier literature had shown how the labor market enforced inequality based on class, racial, and gender differences through a dual labor market that dispensed more privileged jobs through a dominant primary sector and a subordinate secondary sector that handed out poorly paid jobs that offered irregular employment with little chance of advancement.

The same debates that revolved around Marxist crisis theory found their way into literature on imperialism and dependency. This literature forced the recognition of capitalism as a system of accumulation on a world scale and the understanding that the development of the center had produced the underdevelopment of the periphery. At the same time, however, it spawned a series of debates around the nature of the unequal exchange between the center and periphery, the legitimacy of dependency theory, and the nature of Third World social formations.

Perhaps the most profound influence on radical economics and the most serious challenge to the class analytics of Marxist theory came from the study of patriarchy and gender. Initially derived, in part, from Engels's *The Origins of the Family, Private Property, and the State*, this literature examined both the origins of the oppression of women and the likely course of their liberation. Other early writings attempted to fit the study of the role of women in domestic labor and the reproduction of labor power into the traditional Marxist categories. But the initial uniting of Marxism and feminism produced what Heidi Hartmann and Amy Bridges aptly labeled an "unhappy marriage." Focusing on the family as the locus of gender and class, this new socialist-feminist literature studied not only women's role in the reproduction of capitalism and socialism, but also women in the labor market, women's role in the process of Third World development, minority women, and women and socialism. The analysis of gender forced Marxists to broaden their focus on the production of commodities to include also the reproduction of capitalist relations through the family in the private sphere and to regard gender oppression with a centrality that rivaled that of class exploitation.

At the same time that the discipline of political economy was being formalized and rendered academic, radical economists developed a popular political economy dedicated to serving radical movements. The first and perhaps most successful attempt to make this connection was *Dollars and Sense* magazine, which offered "interpretations of current economic events from a socialist perspective." Established in 1973, the magazine gained a readership that grew to about 8,000 by the late 1980s. Later in the 1970s, another group of radical economists formed the Center for Popular Economics, which brought labor activists and other progressives together over the summer for courses in political economy. *See also*: Baran, Paul; *Monthly Review*

—*John A. Miller*

REFERENCES

Attewell, Paul. *Radical Political Economy since the Sixties: A Sociology of Knowledge*. New Brunswick: Rutgers University Press, 1984.

Gintis, Herbert. "The Reemergence of Marxian Economics in America." In *The Left Academy: Marxist Scholarship on American Campuses*, edited by Bertell Ollman and Edward Vernoff. New York: McGraw-Hill, 1982.

Raffish, Rebecca T., and Don L. Ducks. "Red Ink: The First Ten Years of *Dollars and Sense*." *Dollars and Sense* (November 1984).

Resnick, Stephen, and Richard Wolff. *Rethinking Marxism: Essays for Harry Magdoff and Paul Sweezy*. New York: Automedia Inc., 1985.

Sweezy, Paul, and Leo Huberman. "Paul Baran (1910–1964): A Collective Portrait." *Monthly Review* 16, no. 11 (March 1965).

Radical Environmentalism

A direct descendant of the older conservation movement, contemporary environmentalism became conscious of itself as traditional conservationist goals were redefined and expanded in the course of large-scale public-health and workplace-safety struggles in the early 1960s. A specifically left-wing environmentalism—generally known as radical environmentalism or the "ecology movement," influenced by the late '60s New Left, counterculture, and radical American Indian

Emblem of the Earth First! Movement, 1980s

and women's liberation movements—came into prominence in the mid-1970s and early in the next decade was recognized as an important force in the movement.

Conservationism could count an impressive number of poets, artists, and philosophers among its ancestors—including Henry David Thoreau, George Perkins Marsh, and painters John James Audubon, Thomas Cole, and George Catlin—but its beginnings as an organized movement can be credited above all to the indefatigable efforts of the "Yosemite Prophet," John Muir (1838–1914). Born in Scotland, Muir grew up in rural Wisconsin and lived most of his later life in California, much of it in the mountains. A highly original thinker as well as one of America's most inspired and popular writers on nature—his books include *A Thousand Mile Walk to the Gulf*, *Travels in Alaska*, and *The Mountains of California*—he led the successful struggle to protect the Yosemite Valley against mining, lumbering, and other exploitation by having it officially declared a national park in 1889. Three years later he helped cofound the Sierra Club and was elected its first president, an office he held for the rest of his life.

Though influenced to some extent by the esthetic socialism of John Ruskin and the single-tax theories of Henry George, Muir's writings elaborated an indictment of industrial civilization that was almost wholly his own, based on his prolonged and profound experience of the American wilderness. Many of his most revolutionary pronouncements appeared in his journals and remained unpublished until long after his death—those, for example, touching on his rejection of Christianity (because of its supercilious disdain for nature), his militant antianthropocentrism, and his scorn for capitalism, which he called "the gobble-gobble school of economics"—but these fugitive jottings show that Muir was far more radical than the conservation movement he did so much to found. Not too surprisingly, these uncompromising private musings proved to be a powerful inspiration to later radical wilderness activists, especially since the mid-1970s.

In Muir's view, the human experience of the natural beauty of wilderness was the decisive key to solving the ills of society; he regarded mountains and forests as sacred places of freedom, where alone people could learn not only the truths of nature writ large, but also the truth of their own nature, so suppressed and disfigured by the artifices of an acquisitive, exploitative civilization. "Pollution, defilement, squalor," he wrote, "are words that never would have been created had man lived conformably to Nature." The "hope of the world," he was sure, lies in "the great, fresh, unblighted, unredeemed wilderness [where] the galling harness of civilization drops off, and the wounds heal ere we are aware."

The "Muir tradition" of radical conservation—maintained through the years by small bands of devoted amateurs, ardent with the love of wildlife and wilderness for their own sake, independent of human use—contrasts starkly with the conservative, professionalized, much larger and better known wing of the movement, typified by Gifford Pinchot, founder of the U.S. Forest Service and associate of Theodore Roosevelt. Pinchot's concern was not the wonders of nature but the scientific "management of resources." For him, a forest was "a manufacturing plant for the production of wood." The goal of conservation, as he conceived it, was not to save wildlife or wilderness, as such, but rather to save these *crops*, or *commodities*—that is precisely how he saw them—for future exploitation. While Muir boldly challenged anthropocentrism and affirmed the equality of species (he championed especially those animals most feared and hated by modern society, such as wolves and grizzly bears), Pinchot upheld the Western world's traditional notion that man is the "lord of creation" ordained by God to exercise stewardship over the planet and the creatures God made for his use. The task of conservationists, Pinchot argued, was to limit destructive excesses committed by overly rapacious, unscientific industrialists.

The glaring disparity between the two wings of the movement was not perceived by the broad public, and adherents of Muir and Pinchot were able to work together on many issues. The fact that both wings consisted almost entirely of white native-born Anglo-Saxon Protestant males made the movement as a whole vulnerable to the charge of "elitism" frequently leveled at it by opponents on the Right as well as the Left. In John Muir's last great and unsuccessful crusade, to prevent the damming of California's beautiful Hetch-Hetchy Valley, Pinchot took an emphatically pro-dam stand, but even the minor concessions he was willing to make to the Muir forces were too much for Texas congressman Martin Dies, who denounced Pinchot as a "radical." (In the 1930s and 1940s, Dies would head a congressional committee notorious for its persecution of socialists and prolabor radicals.) Notwithstanding Pinchot's demagogic, populist-tinged motto, The Greatest Good for the Greatest Number, his overall view reflected a conservative eastern mugwump Republicanism. After the collapse of the short-lived "Bull Moose" party, Pinchot's closeness to Theodore Roosevelt—who himself, as president, enjoyed a largely undeserved reputation as a champion of conservation—bound the movement to the Republican Party to such an extent that it was not until the New Deal that the Democrats attracted any conservationist following.

Prior to the 1930s, a number of Left writers had attempted to develop a specifically socialist conservationism, or at least a socialist approach to the questions conservationism raised. As early as the 1890s Edward Bellamy, especially in his weekly, the *New Nation*, and in his last book, *Equality* (1897), laid bare the links between the triple exploitation of nature, women, and labor, positing a socialist utopia in which humankind and nature were no longer at odds, and in which the massive restoration of wilderness was a central element. Ernest Thompson Seton, Bellamy-influenced socialist author of best-selling natural-history books for children; "single-taxer" and outdoorsman Dan Beard; Chicago socialist muckraker William Kent, an abolitionist's son and associate of Jane Addams's Hull House; and anarchist novelist J. William Lloyd—to cite four very different figures, widely separated by ideology and temperament—also gave voice to a radical dimension in the conservationist cause, a voice heeded by many in the pre–World War I years, which witnessed the rise of a widespread "back to the land" movement.

The Marxist wing of the socialist movement in those years gave scant attention to this whole question, inhibited as its protagonists were by well-established social-democratic traditions supporting increased productivity and technological progress at all costs. But there were some notable exceptions. Articles urging forest preservation and other conservationist subjects could be found in the popular socialist monthly *Wilshire's*, and elsewhere in the Socialist Party press. Even more significant, *International Socialist Review* editor Algie M. Simons translated a treatise of radical ecology, *Germs of Mind in Plants*, by Austrian biologist Raoul Francé, illustrated by Ralph Chaplin (who, a few years later, would be a leading poet-artist-editor of the Industrial Workers of the World) and published in 1905 by Charles H. Kerr's socialist cooperative in Chicago. This book, which has gone through numerous printings and has remained in print ever since, included a militant preface in which Simons avowed that it was because he was "both a socialist and a nature lover" that he translated it. Kerr also published *The Universal Kinship* and other works by socialist and vegetarian J. Howard Moore, whose conception of "earth-life as a single process . . . every part related and akin to every other part," and whose recognition that "all beings are *ends* [and] no creatures are *means*" make him an important precursor of the environmental ethics of the 1980s.

Conservation issues, however, remained tangential to the broad socialist movement, and not until the 1970s did such concerns figure significantly in any Left party platform. Ironically, the mainstream Marxists—the Socialist Labor Party, SP, Communist Party, and Trotskyists—notwithstanding their voluble opposition to business-union bureaucrats and "robber barons," shared the latter's reified view of wildlife and wilderness to an astonishing degree. It was among the heterodox and libertarian Left, the anarchist movement, and above all the IWW that elements of a radical conservationism developed most freely in earlier years.

The Wobblies, in fact, often exceeded the limits of conservationism as such, and took up the whole gamut of questions later subsumed under the heading "radical environmentalism." The IWW press featured articles protesting the devastation of forests by the lumber industry—"strong conservational action" was demanded by IWW Lumber Workers' Industrial Union 120—but also provided its readers with information on the problem of noise in American cities, on the use of poisons in manufacture (in hatmaking, for example), and other texts on capitalism's destruction and pollution of the planet.

The IWW in its heyday was largely a union of the foreign-born, which may help explain its environmentalist tendency. While upper-class conservationists not infrequently blamed recent immigrants for "ruining" the American landscape, evidence suggests that the adoration of "Mother Nature" expressed, for example, by Italian immigrant anarchist martyr Nicola Sacco in his prison letters, reflected an attitude by no means uncommon among foreign-born radicals. Indeed, immigrant radicals, whose regular activities included picnics in the country and long hikes in the woods, tended to be much more conservation-conscious than their native-born comrades.

However tenuous the links between the socialist and conservation movements, the fact remains that they rose to prominence together during the 1910s and faded together in the 1920s. Significantly, the next major resurgence of militancy within the conservation movement itself—the formation of the Wilderness Society in 1935—was spearheaded by two longtime socialists: Benton MacKaye and Robert Marshall.

MacKaye (1880–1975) was a Connecticut Yankee, the son of actor/playwright Steele MacKaye (who had been a friend of Thoreau's), and a classmate of John Reed's at Harvard, where he went on to teach forestry for a few years before going to work for the U.S. Forest Service. An associate of Oscar Ameringer, "the Mark Twain of American Socialism," MacKaye joined the SP in the heyday of Eugene Debs.

The much younger Bob Marshall (1901–39), of New York, joined the much smaller SP of Norman Thomas, but was even more outspokenly radical than MacKaye, and considered himself a Marxist. Son of a founder/leader of the American Jewish Committee, Marshall, who had a Ph.D. from Johns Hopkins, was one of the first non-WASPs prominent in conservation. Passionately attracted since childhood to "blank places on the map," he was a zealous mountain-climber and an eloquent defender of everything wild against the ravages of capitalist "development." Finding the United States to be "a civilization remote from nature, artificial, dominated by the exploitation of man by man," he affirmed the essential unity of working-class socialism—"production for use and not for profit"—and "the freedom of the wilderness." His best-selling *Arctic Village* (1933) recounted a year's sojourn in a small community in the mountains of Alaska, 200 miles north of Fairbanks, where he found "the most complete liberty one can imagine" and "the happiest folk I had ever encountered." In *The People's Forests*, the first major work of socialist conservationism in the United States, also published in 1933, he called for the socialization of wilderness to assure its protection from the insatiable greed of private industry.

MacKaye and Marshall were two of the four men who conceived the Wilderness Society, and it was they who drew up its "Platform," proclaiming that "the time has come, with the brutalizing pressure of a spreading metropolitan civilization, to recognize the wilderness environment as a serious human need rather than a luxury and a plaything." The first real fusion of socialism and the Muir tradition, the society immediately attracted the most radical-minded conservationists in the country, including Aldo Leopold, whose classic *Sand County Almanac* (1949) would become the most influential conservationist text since Muir. (Although he was generally regarded as "apolitical" by his friends and commentators, it is notable that Leopold voted for Norman Thomas all through the 1930s and 1940s.) Deliberately restricting its membership to unequivocal supporters of wilderness for wilderness's sake—"We want no straddlers," Marshall insisted—the Wilderness Society, and its journal, the *Living Wilderness*, represented the most radical wing of the conservation movement well into the 1970s.

Meanwhile, the radical insurgency of the Depression years affected older conservation groups as well, including the group widely regarded as the oldest: the Audubon Association, which, though its history had in fact been discontinuous, liked to trace its origins back to an earlier New York–based Audubon Society formed in 1886. Feminist Rosalie Edge, a one-time suffragist who became the foremost woman in conservation, led a spirited revolt against the association's corrupt leadership, who had, among other things, rented the group's Louisiana bird sanctuary to hunters and trappers. Largely as a result of her prolonged efforts, assisted by civil libertarian Roger Baldwin, a member of the association's board of directors, the association was substantially reorganized in the mid-1930s (in 1940 it changed its name to the National Audubon Society).

President Franklin Roosevelt's New Deal incorporated elements of conservation, provided jobs for conservationists, and did much to establish conservation as a respectable mainstream current. However, as with all movements for social betterment, conservation invariably declines during wartime, and the movement lapsed into quiescence in the first half of the 1940s. The 1945 publication of Lizzie Marsh Wolfe's Pulitzer Prize–winning biography of John Muir, *Son of the Wilderness*, which led to new editions and collections of Muir's own writings, inspired a notable revival, but not for another decade and a half would a conservation-oriented mass movement emerge, for the first time, in the United States. Rachel Carson's best-selling *Silent Spring* (1962), an exposé of the lethal dangers of pesticides, especially DDT, by a marine zoologist who had been one of the first women to hold an important position in the U.S. Fish and Wildlife Service, provoked enormous controversy in the mass media, and prompted a vast number of related studies—on smog, asbestos poisoning, black-lung disease, cancer-producing substances in food, etc. Never before had so broad a public been confronted by such urgent life-and-death questions of health in a specifically conservationist context. Out of the widespread agitation sparked by Carson's book, bolstered by the already large opposition to nuclear weapons-testing, the environmental movement was born.

From Upton Sinclair and Mary Marcy in the early 1900s to Linus Pauling and Barry Commoner half a century later, socialists had been leading spokespersons of public-health issues, but their efforts had not led to any broad-based ongoing organizations focused on such concerns. In the absence of such a grass-roots movement, the groundswell of popular protest aroused by *Silent Spring* found organizational expression in the existing conservation groups, which were willing to fill the breach. Of course these groups were themselves changed in the process: they grew larger, their outlook broadened and, at least for a time, they tended to become more action-oriented. By implementing the aggressive strategies of David Brower, for example, the Sierra Club, which, during most of its existence, was a narrowly West Coast mountaineering group with a membership of 2,000 or 3,000, became a major social force, national in scope, with a membership well over 100,000 by 1970 and nearly a half-million in the next decade. Wilderness preservation remained its prime focus, but its perspectives were enlarged to include the entire environment, the whole planet; together with the popular wilderness photo-albums by Ansel Adams and Elliot Porter, Sierra Club books took up the problems of overpopulation, air pollution, and nuclear power.

Central to the transformation of old-time conservationism into contemporary environmentalism was the concept of *ecology*, the science of the interrelations of the various components of the natural world. The word had been coined by German biologist Ernst Haeckel in the 1860s, popularized (albeit in a restricted sociological sense) by Robert E. Park and the "Chicago School" of sociology in the 1920s, and used in its current sense by Aldo Leopold and Robert Marshall in the 1920s and 1930s, but did not enter everyday usage until the 1960s, when the emerging environmental movement made it one of its watchwords and even a battle cry.

The new movement's vociferous opposition to what its spokespersons called "corporate greed," and its strong links to the antinuclear and antiwar movements, gave the impression that environmentalism was solidly on the Left. But in fact the alliance between social radicals and environmentalists began uneasily, with considerable mistrust on both sides. Old and New Left ideologists frequently accused environmentalism of being a "bourgeois" fad to divert public attention from other, supposedly more fundamental issues; for many, this charge seemed to be confirmed by President Richard Nixon's adoption of environmentalist rhetoric, and his administration's support of "Earth Day" in 1970, a one-shot day of nationwide environment-related events largely sponsored by Coca-Cola and other multinational corporations that in fact had long-standing anticonservationist policies. Many environmentalists in turn found the Left quarrelsome, sectarian, and indifferent to wildlife/wilderness concerns. Nonetheless, many radicals recognized the revolutionary implications of the ecological critique, and many more environmentalists perceived that the enemies of their movement and of the environment itself were the traditional enemies of the Left. In the larger milieux beyond groups and factions—in the widespread if short-lived "underground" press, for example, and the broad "counterculture"—the New Left and the new environmentalism mingled and to a great extent fused.

All through the 1970s, as professionalization and bureaucratization diluted much of the militancy and impact of the 1960s environmentalist upsurge and steered the movement's energies toward conventional electoral politics and lobbying, new and more radical revivals of the Muir tradition began to emerge. Pointing out that more wilderness was destroyed in the decade following the passage of the 1964 Wilderness Act than in the preceding five decades, and that most of the funds collected by the established environmental groups went to the advertising agencies that conducted their fundraising drives, younger eco-radicals developed a new and specifically environmentalist activism that increasingly expressed itself in civil disobedience and direct action. Even before the end of the 1960s *ecotage* (i.e., sabotage of equipment or property owned by industrial destroyers/polluters of the environment) was recognized as a major problem by industry trade-journals; many tens of thousands of rural billboards were destroyed, for example, by "ecoteurs" who regarded such advertising as a hideous disfigurement of the landscape. For several years the daring exploits of a Chicago-area masked man known only as the Fox repeatedly made headlines nationwide, as when he invaded the executive headquarters of U.S. Steel and poured on the office rug buckets of the same dangerous chemical waste the corporation was dumping into Lake Michigan. Greenpeace, founded in 1971, attained worldwide renown almost overnight as a result of its bold, brave interventions in defense of whales, dolphins, seals, and other species endangered by commercial exploitation. Such dramatic actions fired the imaginations of a broad public, and contributed mightily to the development of a new surge, and a new "style," of environmental radicalism from the mid-'70s on.

Activist first and foremost, the new radical environmentalism appreciably expanded and deepened conservationist theory. Muir, Thoreau, Bob Marshall, Aldo Leopold, and David Brower remained the brightest stars in the new movement's philosophical firmament, but the younger generation also found much to be learned in the works of a wide range of social critics not previously regarded from a conservationist perspective. Many loose ends of American radicalism—including strands of utopianism, anarchism, feminism, the IWW, and heterodox Marxism—have been picked up and developed by proponents of radical ecology. Ralph Borsodi's and Lewis Mumford's critiques of technology and urbanism, dating from the 1920s and 1930s, challenged the centralist assumptions of classical liberalism and Marxism, and stimulated a growing interest in decentralist solutions to social problems. This direction was also pursued, in his later years, by longtime socialist Scott Nearing, who linked his decentralist vision to vegetarianism and a new back-to-the-land movement, as well as by a former Trotskyist, Murray Bookchin, in several works relating ecology to anarchism, starting in the 1960s. Frederick Turner's *Beyond Geography: The Western Spirit Against the Wilderness*, Roderick Nash's *Wilderness and the American Mind*, Barry Lopez's *Of Wolves and Men*, Gary Snyder's *The Old Ways*, Ursula Le Guin's ecotopian novel *Always Coming Home*, and the works of Paul Shepard, Peter Matthiessen, Bill Devall, and the Canadian Farley Mowat are only a few of the most influential recent contributions to radical environmentalist theory.

Perhaps the most representative of the new radical environmentalist groups, and certainly the purest contemporary expression of the Muir tradition, is the movement known as Earth First! (the exclamation point is an essential part of its name), whose motto is No Compromise in Defense of Mother Earth! Founded in the Southwest in 1980, by the end of the decade it had locals all over the United States as well as in many other countries, and had become by far the largest and most influential specifically radical environmentalist group in U.S. history. Not content with demanding the preservation of all existing wilderness, Earth First! calls for the vast *re-creation* of wilderness. Its avowedly extremist orientation and tactics—hammering spikes into trees, for example, as an "immunization against logging"—have sparked heated controversies in the environmental movement and broad Left. Like the old IWW that it has repeatedly acknowledged as its major "philosophical forebear," Earth First!'s decentralized ranks include an impressive number of poets, artists, cartoonists, songwriters, and musicians—its *Li'l Green Song Book*, like its ecotage manual, *Ecodefense*, has gone through many editions—and its direct actions tend to be guerrilla theater strongly marked by humor. Earth First! has also been influenced by Kropotkinian anarchism, by anarchist-inclined novelist Edward Abbey, whose ecotage novel *The Monkey Wrench Gang* (1976) provided the movement with much of its original style, and more recently by the theories of "Deep Ecology" advanced by Norwegian writer Arne Naess, author of studies on Spinoza and Gandhi.

Ideological diversity remains a hallmark not only of Earth First!, but of the whole spectrum of radical environmentalism. New Left, IWW, anarchist, feminist, and even Marxist influences are discernible and, indeed, openly avowed, but so are the very different influences of Taoism, Zen Buddhism, and indigenous (so-called primitive) cultures, as well as a radical poets' countertradition extending from William Blake and Emily Brontë to Robinson Jeffers and Philip Lamantia. These latter influences have helped inspire radical ecology's deepening critique of the values and institutions of Western civilization, which in turn has been a growing influence on social radical thought in recent years, resulting in any number of ideological hybrids. Radical environmentalism today includes many distinct currents—it is a long way from the pragmatic Citizens' Clearing House for Hazardous Waste to Keith Lampe's visionary *Green Hippie*—and such tendencies as bioregionalism, ecofeminism, deep ecology, and antitechnological neo-primitivism, which only a decade ago appeared esoteric, now claim a substantial number of adherents. Notable, too, is the growing trend toward the involvement of organized labor in environmental struggles; the United Farm Workers union, for example, has been in the forefront of antipesticide agitation.

The continuing and, indeed, worsening problems of acid rain, pollution, the greenhouse effect, overpopulation, toxic waste disposal, nuclear power, rainforest destruction, extinction of plant and animal species and other calamities suffice to assure the vitality and growth of radical environmentalism in the coming years. Efforts to import the ideology and style of the European "Green" movement to American shores have thus far met with small success, but cross-pollination between radical ecology and the more traditional forms of American radicalism will doubtless continue, and it does not require a prophet to predict that ecological concerns will be central to the new New Left of the future. *See also*: Animal Rights, Nature Friends, Peace Movements

—Franklin Rosemont

REFERENCES

Devall, Bill. *Simple in Means, Rich in Ends: Practicing Deep Ecology*. Salt Lake City: Peregine Smith, 1988.

Foreman, Dave, and Bill Haywood eds., *Ecodefense: A Field Guide to Monkeywrenching*. Tucson: Nedd Ludd Books, 1987.

Fox, Stephen. *The American Conservation Movement: John Muir and His Legacy*. Madison: University of Wisconsin Press, 1986.

"Radical Environmentalism." Special issue of *Industrial Worker* (May 1988).

Radical Filmmaking—the 1930s

One of the imperatives of the Communist movement as it began to address the problems of the 1930s was to create mass media that would faithfully render its views and experiences. The first major step in this direction was the formation of the Workers' Film and Photo League (FPL) on December 11, 1930. The FPL, an affiliate of the Communist-linked Workers International Relief, absorbed a number of media-oriented groups previously organized by the Communist Party. Its primary agenda was to create motion pictures and still photographs that would advance the cause of the American working class. An adjunct to this mandate was the distribution of radical films made abroad and activities that carried out a radical critique of the Hollywood system.

A score of FPL personalities would remain at the core of radical filmmaking, distribution, and criticism for decades. Among them were Leo Seltzer, David Platt, Leo Hurwitz, and Tom Brandon. The FPL alumni have never been forthcoming about the relationship of their organization to the CP proper, but no one could have been involved with the FPL without realizing the CP was its guardian angel.

The focus of FPL film production was the creation of newsreels. Low production cost and the ability to convey a feeling of immediacy made newsreels an ideal tool for a movement entering its most dynamic decade. FPL members used hand-held cameras with great daring and often plunged into the midst of mass demonstrations to develop a visual style that was a kind of proletarian cinema verité. The most renowned cameraperson was Leo Seltzer, who had a canny way of infiltrating police lines and other adversaries to catch demonstrators approaching class enemies head-on. The work was so all-consuming that the FPL core had virtually no other social, political, or artistic life. Cadre like Seltzer often took up residence in FPL offices.

A point of pride with the FPL was that its newsreels were far more honest in presenting events than were its commercial rivals. One problem with this claim was that some scenes were staged for FPL cameras and some sequences appear in more than one film, so that a demonstration in city X may be shown as having occurred in city Y. Such "cheating" was mainly a matter of economics and in large measure the FPL did, in fact, capture the tenor of the Communist-led class movements of the era.

The FPL had some two dozen branches with a peak membership of nearly one hundred, but only the Detroit, Chicago, Los Angeles, and New York units made films. New York, the creative hub where most of the films were edited and released, also dispatched units to areas of the nation that did not have FPL branches. The scope of FPL interest was wide. Some representatives titles are: *National Hunger March, Harlem Sketches, The Ford Massacre, Chicago May Day, Sheriffed, Workers on the Waterfront, Hillsboro Relief Scandal.* About a dozen newsreels still exist in part or in whole and are available in major film archives.

The photographic component of the organization mainly sold still photos to the radical press. In addition to full-time photographers, a number of filmmakers were active in the unit. After the film division dissolved in the mid-1930s, the Photo League would continue to function and lasted until 1951, when it fell victim to McCarthyism. Among its distinguished members was Lewis Hine, who joined late in his career.

The FPL was enthralled by the film theories of Soviet filmmakers. *Film Front*, the *FPL Bulletin*, and *Experimental Cinema*, journals issued by the FPL or to which its members contributed, published translations of and commentary on the writings of Dziga Vertov and Sergei Eisenstein. The screening of Soviet films such as *Battleship Potemkin* often led to spirited theoretical debates. The dominant FPL view was that the montage theory of Eisenstein was as revolutionary as Marx's dialectic. Among the most innovative FPL initiatives was the establishment of the Harry Alan Potamkin Film School in 1933. This was named after a radical film critic who had died the previous year from a stroke at the age of thirty-one. The school had an enrollment of fifty and there was considerable interaction with the New Dance League and the New Theater League. Such appreciation of film as a major art form was farsighted in a time when film was not so viewed by universities and museums.

Direct action against Hollywood films was as important to the FPL as theory. Boycotts were organized against *Black Fury*, a Warner Bros. film about corrupt unions, and against *No Greater Glory*, a Columbia film glorifying the military. FPL's own screenings took issue with the Hollywood vision of America by frequently pairing a newsreel about the hardships of working-class America with a feature film celebrating social advances in the USSR.

Except for screenings (1932–33) at New York City's Acme Theater, the FPL was never able to regularize commercial sales. Distribution was primarily through a political circuit controlled by the CP. This network included CP meetings, front groups, labor unions, and outdoor screenings in neighborhoods. Two FPL films had the distinction of being used to win court cases involving demonstrations against the police. The FPL deficit had to be covered with funds from Workers International Relief, rental income from foreign films, and donations.

Tensions had always existed within the FPL between individuals like Seltzer, who prized the newsreel form, and those like Hurwitz, who wanted to make fiction films and more complex documentaries. As the CP line shifted to the Popular Front concept, Party publications took FPL films to task for being too humorless, too confrontational, and too crude. The New Film Alliance was created to take over the distribution of foreign films and other activities previously entrusted to the FPL. The schism within FPL ranks led to the formation of Nykino by members who wanted to go beyond the newsreel form. A final blow came with the demise of the Germany-based Workers' International Relief. Although some films released in 1936 and 1937 had begun as FPL projects, by late 1935 the organization had ceased to exist.

Nykino would function for two years before restructuring itself as Frontier Films. During this brief existence Nykino would engender intense theoretical interchanges and produce some interesting films. The filmmakers affiliated with Nykino had particularly close relationships with CP theater groups and hoped to have an impact on cinema comparable to the impact writers like Odets were having on theater.

The most celebrated Nykino work is *Pie in the Sky*, a fourteen-minute satire starring Elia Kazan and Elman Koolish. What there is of a plot involves two tramps in a junkyard mocking all middle-class values. The film has considerable verve, with the tramps taking on organized religion in a manner not seen since the Industrial Workers of the World assaults on the Salvation Army. The zany irreverance of the film is in the same spirit as that which marked the early films of the Newsreel collective some three decades later. But *Pie in the Sky* was the exception among Nykino efforts.

More typically Nykino was *The World Today*, a left-wing version of *The March of Time* format. *The World Today* had its debut on September 22, 1936, in New York City. It was soon packaged with other films and sent to the ten districts of the CP to be used in electoral work. Included in the program was a filmed speech by Earl Browder, a labor cartoon from the *Daily Worker*, and *Millions of Us*, a labor film made independently in Hollywood by American Labor Films.

Two other Nykino films that got some distributions were *Sunnyside* and *Black Legion*. The former aimed to build the alliance of classes by showing middle-class homeowners fighting evictions while the latter dealt with the Michigan-based secret society that preached and practiced violence against Communists, Jews, blacks, Catholics, and trade unionists. As with most Nykino works, no print of *Black Legion* has survived.

The incorporation of Frontier Films in 1937 launched the most vigorous work of the decade. FF would produce four major documentaries and one fiction film: *Heart of Spain* (1937, 30 min.), *China Strikes Back* (1937, 24 min.), *Return to Life* (1938, 45 min.), *People of the Cumberland* (1938, 24 min.), and *Native Land* (1942, 120 min.). The organization also made *United Action Means Victory* (1940, 40 min.) in cooperation with the film department of the United Auto Workers and two films on transportation and ecology made for hire. The hard core of FF consisted of Leo Hurwitz, Paul Strand, Ben Maddow, Sidney Meyers, and Lionel Berman. Among those working on at least one film were Ralph Steiner, Henri Cartier-Bresson, Willard Van Dyke, Earl Robinson, Paul Robeson, Marc Blitzstein, Erskine Caldwell, and Elia Kazan. No women played a major role in any of the productions.

Heart of Spain and *Return to Life*, films about the Spanish Civil War, and *China Strikes Back*, a film featuring the first footage from Maoist Yenan, reflect the FF policy of subordinating any advocacy of socialism to the needs of the Popular Front. The tone is that of good guys versus bad guys with the Communist-supported side being the good guys. *People of the Cumberland* likewises places union and community organizing into a nonthreatening context of folk art revival and mountain populism. Patriotic imagery such as the display of American flags is conspicuous. As a liberal film made by radicals, *People of the Cumberland* fails to express the New Deal zest of films such as Pare Lorentz's *The Plow That Broke the Plains* (1936) and *The River* (1937).

If FF documentaries did not reflect the ideas of Brecht, Stanislavski, Vertov, and Eisenstein, *Native Land* did. Its aim was to create a fiction-documentary poetic form never before seen in American film, a cinematic counterpart to the blend being offered by John Dos Passos in *USA*. The direct inspiration for the film was Leo Huberman's *The Labor Spy Racket* (1937) and the revelations of the La Follette Civil Rights Committee (1936–37). The film involved the cream of FF talent: codirection and editing by Hurwitz; codirection and cinematography by Strand; coscripting by Hurwitz, Maddow, and Strand; music by Blitzstein; singing narration by Robeson; and acting by Howard Da Silva.

The tragedy of *Native Land* was that history would outpace its production process. The film sought to win popular support for workers by presenting them as victims of racism, greed, and police infiltration. These enemies of the working class were also seen as the groups that could become a fascist fifth column in the United States. As the film took shape, the CIO, often using CP cadre as organizers, led millions of workers in often bloody and usually successful strikes for which the victim image was not appropriate. By the time the film was completed, however, the United States was at war and the CP opposed all strike activity in basic industry and any images that weakened patriotic fervor. Having already missed the moment of militant industrial unionism, *Native Land* was judged by the CP to contain images of oppression and class division that were far too strong for a nation at war.

Intended to have launched FF as a major feature film producer, *Native Land* became the organization's swan song. Although it was to earn a measure of fame later, *Native Land* was a financial and political bust. The FF personnel would continue to have individual careers, but the cooperative movement defined by the Film and Photo League, Nykino, and Frontier Films had become history. A quarter century would pass before a new breed of radical filmmakers would attempt to do for their generation what their predecessors had done for the Communist Left of the 1930s. *See also*: Hollywood Left, Photography, Union-Sponsored Radical Films

—*Dan Georgakas*

REFERENCES

Alexander, William. *Film on the Left—American Documentary Film from 1931 to 1942*. Princeton: Princeton University Press, 1981.

Callenback, Ernest. "Native Land." *Film Quarterly* 27, no. 1 (Fall 1973).

Campbell, Russell Drummond. *Radical Cinema in the United States, 1932–1942: The Work of the Film and Photo League, Nykino and Frontier Films*. Ann Arbor: University Microfilms International, 1981.

Experimental Cinema—1930–1934. Reprint of complete editions with introduction by Dr. George Amberg. New York: Arno Press, 1969.

Film Front—December 1934–March 1935. Rochester, N.Y.: Visual Studies Workshop Reprint Book, 1977.

Klein, Michael, and Jill Klein. "Native Land: An Interview with Leo Hurwitz." *Cineaste* 6, no. 3 (1974).

Kline, Herbert, ed. *New Theatre and Film*, 1934–1937. Selections and commentary. Foreword by Arthur Knight. San Diego: Harcourt Brace Jovanovich, 1985.

Radical Novel, 1870–1930

From its emergence as a utopian evocation to its maturation as naturalist epic, the radical novel has expressed central themes of radicalism's "life of the mind." It has also, in its chaotic and shifting form, suggested the difficulty of American intellectuals' search for artistic method.

The radical novel had its tangled roots in the women's literature of the mid-nineteenth century. One side of the critique can be seen in the bizarre allegory *The Salamander: A Legend* (1848), by the prominent abolitionist lecturer Elizabeth Oakes Smith, predicting catastrophe for capitalism, portrayed as using science and technology in the feckless pursuit of profit. The other side is apparent in Caroline Chesebro's *Isa: A Pilgrimage* (1952), about a utopian-minded couple who share a vision of sexual egalitarianism and crusading reformism. During the last thirty years of the nineteenth century, these two sides each found vivid expression.

In the anticipation of moral degradation and disaster, Populist leader Ignatius Donnelly's *Caesar's Column* (1890) was by far the best-selling work, reaching perhaps a total of a half-million copies in the next quarter-century. Here, unchecked economic despotism leads to race suicide and to a vast debacle in which only a minority escape—to found a cooperative colony of settlers somewhere in Africa, with equal rights for women. Jack London's *The Iron Heel* (1911), almost a rewritten version of *Caesar's Column* with racial themes toned down and the urban class struggle seen more carefully, places endless conflict ahead. Socialist science-fiction writer George Allen England's trilogy *Darkness and Dawn* (1916), with a metaphorical treatment of World War I, portrays the total ruin of civilization through some mysterious events, leaving two protagonists to discover a colony where civilization is being reassembled with equal rights and economic egalitarianism.

More realistically intended studies generally portrayed the emerging division of classes in the United States, and sought some kind of resolution of class warfare through cooperative practices. Elizabeth Stuart Phelps's *The Silent Partner* (1871), the best known and probably most effective of these studies, offered a model in women's cross-class cooperation. Helen Campbell's *Mrs. Herndon's Income* (1886) brought an outright socialist into the equation as a sympathetic soul. Most other critics, despite their radical critique, could not go so far. Christian socialist Katherine Pearson Woods, whose *Metzerott, Shoemaker* (1889), suggested how unjust economic conditions, if not remedied, could lead to fanaticism and disaster. Her *Mark of the Beast*, published in an issue of *Lippencott's* in 1890, took a step further in endorsing Christian socialism (but not atheistic, immigrant socialism) as the solution to the woes of the poor and as a moral correction to the excesses of the rich.

The numerous utopian novels of the period drew a more brilliant picture of socialism in operation. Only a few might be described as written by authors familiar with modern socialist principles. Marie Howland, an activist in the American wing of the First International, contributed *Papa's Own Girl* (1874), depicting life in a Fourierist "Social Palace." Henry Allen, a leading participant in the St. Louis "Commune" briefly established by socialists during the 1877 railroad strike, for instance, wrote *A Strange Voyage, A Revision of the Key of Industrial Cooperative Government, An Interesting and Instructive Description of Life on Planet Venus* (1891). Mixing socialism and Swedenborgianism in an improbable plot—a man is invited by a beautiful alien to visit her socialistically organized home planet—it featured gold-lined toilet bowls among other technological innovations. Distributed by a short-lived socialist newspaper network, *Strange Voyage* had a miniscule success compared with that of Edward Bellamy's *Looking Backward* (1889), the most influential socialistic novel worldwide in the nineteenth century. Bellamy's depiction of contemporary poverty versus technological utopia not only inspired a political movement but actually made cooperative society seem *possible* to millions of Americans. His subsequent novel, *Equality* (1897), although analytically clearer in its critique of capitalism and depiction of women's life in a socialist society, failed to retain readers' interest in the continuing tale of *Looking Backward*'s two romantic characters.

Realism, inspired by the grinding poverty of the 1890s and by such foreign models as Emile Zola, made a sudden literary appearance around the turn of the century. A mainstream critic was reported as saying that if Balzac had seen Pittsburgh, he would have exclaimed, "Give me a pen!" Actually, William Dean Howells's novel *A Hazard of New Fortunes* (1894) portrayed an urban setting seething with contradictions, while the short Yiddish fiction of the extended newspaper column (notably by Leon Kobrin) offered a close study of slum conditions. Upton Sinclair's *The Jungle*—serialized in the socialist *Appeal to Reason* and reprinted as a novel in 1906—demonstrated the power and the potential popularity of the genre. Sinclair's depiction of packinghouse life, and unsanitary conditions, had an impact from congressional committees to Socialist Party circles. Of Sinclair's other numerous books, *King Coal* (1917) approached the drama of working-class life, this time amid the Colorado coal strike of 1913–14.

Not many other authors of labor novels approached Sinclair's popular achievement, but at least a few improved upon his often cardboard characterizations and his predictable plots. Arthur Bullard, later a prominent American diplomat, offered in *Comrade Yetta* (1913) a sometimes touching treatment of a young woman radical who helps organize a garment union local, joins the staff of a socialist daily newspaper, and meets the activist love of her life. Ernest Poole's *The Harbor* (1915), which reached the best-seller list of its time, carefully portrays the lives of stokers and dockers who carry along the protagonist in their mighty strike. Leroy Scott's *The Walking Delegate* (1907), virtually alone among labor novels, shows unionists at work in their daily affairs.

Novels of sexual exploitation retouched sentimentalism with socialist coloring and, in a climate of "white slave trade" revelations, briefly had a wide audience. Thus Estelle Baker's *The Rose Door* (1910), popular in socialist ranks, showed women of different classes seduced, deceived, and forced into prostitution. Reginald Kauffman's *House of Bondage* (1910), a nationwide best-seller, fell back upon the plot of the rural refugee trapped by a big-city procurer, but added new insight into the futility of escape from the clutches of business profit and government corruption. Theodore Dreiser's *Sister Carrie* (1903) projected the radical author forward, among his many socialist friends in particular (he allowed a section of his *Idylls of the Poor* to be published in the *New York Call*), as the true-life chronicler of the changing social conditions and mores that caused a "good" woman to act in ostensibly immoral ways.

Novels of personal emancipation, sexual and otherwise, turned this theme around to stress the awakening of women, especially, from the artificial moral restraints a Victorian society had placed upon them. *The Chasm* (1911) by George Cram Cook, converted to socialism and bohemianism by his boyhood friend Floyd Dell, shows a wealthy woman who chooses Marxism (represented by her father's socialist gardener) over Nietzcheanism (represented by her aristocratic husband). Her personal revolt permits the protagonist to choose the proper side. In Susan Glaspell's *The Awakening* (1911), greatly influenced by George Cram Cook, and in Florence Converse's *The Children of Light* (1912), these contradictions are solved less philosophically, as the female protagonists grow into a vision of socialism by extending their vision of sexual emancipation. Charlotte Teller's *The Cage* (1907) likewise interweaves class and gender struggles, but with the twist that the protagonist must educate her ethnic socialist husband to reject the principle of legal marriage as the only legitimate expression of love. In Hutchins Hapgood's *Anarchist Woman* (1909), the problem cannot be solved to the satisfaction of all when a slum woman freed from the limits of her background must finally abandon the anarchist-lover who sought in her development his own Pygmalion-like success.

Perhaps, as Hapgood intimated, individualism more than collectivity held the American future. The best-crafted radical novels of the age came to this rather pessimistic conclusion. Abraham Cahan's *The Rise of David Levinsky* (1917), almost a self-portrait of the successful American businessman who had lost his European soul, exemplifies the archetype. In Jack London's *Martin Eden* (1909), truly a proletarian novel and arguably a spiritual autobiography, neither literary success nor adoring women can ease the psychological pain of the talented proletarian, who can find no home in any existing social class and at last hurls himself into the sea. A young and socialistic Sherwood Anderson, in *Marching Men* (1919), renders the radical leader himself a social-isolate Nietzchean giant who must decide for the masses. In another way, Upton Sinclair's *Jimmie Higgins* (1917)—a pacifist novel that shows the agonizing decline of a young, enthusiastic activist to Army recruit and gibbering madman—has the same moral: socialist politics have failed and, at least in America, only individual credos (none too easy to live) remain. Even *Mooncalf* (1922), Floyd Dell's generally cheery bildungsroman, ends at the same essential perspective.

This sense of alienation had its echo in literary life. Only so long as the older socialist movement remained intact did an intellectual climate exist for common discussion of radical literature and publication of short stories, which served many potential novelists as the site of earliest reception for their work. In the first years of the century, *The Comrade* (1900–05) connected Howells and a range of nineteenth-century literary-reformer types with the young socialist reader. A fairly small-circulation weekly, Horace Traubel's *Conservator* (1890–1919), offered close and sympathetic critiques of Jack London and a range of other writers devoted to Traubel's judgments. For a few years after 1910, the *Coming Nation*, the *Masses*, and to a lesser degree the *Liberator* continued this process, but with diminishing enthusiasm for collective hopes.

By the 1920s, a sense of dread and frequently a repugnance at the state of American life pervade the radical novel. In the Yiddish world, where the novel had only begun to appear and where radicalism remained the prime mood of literateurs, Joseph Opatoshu's *Hibru* (1918) shows middle-class Jewish immigrants smug and arrogant about their material success. Samuel Ornitz's *Haunch, Paunch, and Jowl* (1922), although in English rather than Yiddish, is a similar portrayal of Jewish corruption in America. David Pinski's *The Generations of Noah Eden* (English translation, 1922), shows the Americanized children of a pious and kindly immigrant manufacturer turn to nihilism and self-destruction. Opatoshu's stark novella "Lincherei" (lynchers), published in a 1923 collection, *Race*, sought for the first time in Yiddish to etch the ugliest scenes in American life—hysterically happy southern whites roasting a black man alive for a sexual crime he did not commit. Among the established American writers, Upton Sinclair's *Boston* (1928) sketched out the trial and judicial murder of anarchists Sacco and Vanzetti.

In another sense, the defeat of pre-1920 Left and the export of revolutionary hopes to Russia paralleled the exhaustion of Greenwich Village bohemia in favor of more exotic cultural scenes. Claude McKay's *Home to Harlem* (1929) offered this bohemia "at home," but only to blacks who would remain forever outsiders in America. Waldo Frank's semimystical novels similarly carried their protagonists outside the boundaries of existing American life. Even historical novels about the 1910s American Left, such as Elias Tobenkin's *The Road* (1922) or Max Eastman's *Venture* (1927), seemed to belong to some distant time and place.

This artistic perception posed considerable problems for the Left. The *New Masses*, fostered by Communist supporters, sought in its early years to maintain a balance between bohemian and Marxist sentiments, going over with both feet to a "proletarian literature" that had been demonstrated convincingly, in the form desired, perhaps only by *New Masses* editor Mike Gold himself, in *Jews Without Money* (1922), the ultimate communist bildungsroman. The 1930s bought a temporary and partial fulfillment of this anticipation, but without removing the causes and deeper symptoms of the alienation and sense of unreality that marked the American radical author. Neither did the individual political commitments of literary giants—most prominently Theodore Dreiser, who would lead Left committees and add his name to Communist causes during the 1930s without ever firmly accepting the methods of Marxism or "proletarian literature"—alter the basic difficulty. The proper strategy of literary radicalism remained undetermined. *See also*: Bellamy, Edward; Cahan, Abraham; Campbell, Helen; Frank, Waldo; Gold, Michael; Greenwich Village; Howells, William Dean; London, Jack; McKay, Claude; *The Masses*; Poetry—1870–1930; Sandburg, Carl; *Seven Arts*; Sinclair, Upton; Vorse, Mary Heaton; Winchevsky, Morris; Yiddish Left

—*Paul Buhle*

REFERENCES

Aaron, Daniel. *Writers On the Left*. New York: Harcourt, Brace and World, 1961.

Matthiessen, Francis O. *Theodore Dreiser*. New York: William Sloan Associates, 1951.

Rideout, Walter B. *The Radical Novel in the United States, 1900–1954*. Cambridge: Harvard University Press, 1956.

RADICAL PROFESSIONAL AND ACADEMIC JOURNALS

One of the most lasting expressions of the radicalism of the 1960s is the way in which almost every academic discipline, profession, and major labor and interest group created journals of opinion that voiced the spirit of dissent and social change that informed the movement. In contrast to underground newspapers, which flourished most at the height of the antiwar movement and then either disappeared or were transformed in some way, many of these journals survived, and by the late 1980s were celebrating their twentieth anniversaries with special issues. *Science for the People*, the *Radical Teacher*, the *Insurgent Sociologist*, *Issues in Radical Therapy*, the *Conspiracy*, *Madness Network News*, *Sipapu*, the *Radical Philosopher's Newsjournal*, and *Radical History Review* are just some of the titles that provided an antidote to the official organs of organized disciplines. Nourished by new insights gained from a resurgent Left, academics, professionals, and to a great extent their traditional target groups, students and "clients," designed the landscape of serious periodical literature.

Beginning its twentieth year, *Science for the People* (Boston), reflected on its history: "SftP has been a vehicle for antiwar analysis and activity since its inception. Conceived in the struggle against U.S. involvement in the Vietnam War by an organization then called SESPA—Scientists and Engineers for Social and Political Action—SftP continues to challenge military applications of science and technology." Two aspects of the history of this journal apply to the history of most of these journals. First, the concept of scientists *and* engineers working together in spite of the traditional professional haughtiness of the pure scientist and second, the idea of connectedness—that "professional" life was not something separate and apart from the rest of one's life. The consequences of one's work were a matter of personal moral and political responsibility.

The notion of a holistic approach to one's life may be the most common bond between these academic radicals. The sociologists put it this way: "Radical sociology is whatever radical sociologists do—whether activism, research, teaching, organizing—when, and *only* when, these activities are not divorced from one another." A newsletter put out by the Sociology Liberation Movement/Union of Radical Sociology at Berkeley, the *Insurgent Sociologist* called at first for a radical counter-convention to the 1969 meeting of the American Sociological Association. The *Insurgent Sociologist* quickly broadened its scope to issues outside of academic politics by proposing a five-part agenda: (1) aiding movements of welfare recipients; (2) exposing counterinsurgency research and power structures; (3) exposing and reforming the American sociological establishment; (4) defending teaching jobs of radicals; (5) struggling against bourgeois hegemony and orienting research to the needs of ongoing movements. Eventually the journal changed from a newsletter to a journal, shed its former activist stance, and changed its title to *Critical Sociology* (Department of Sociology, University of Oregon) in the spring of 1988.

As it has done for radicals in the United States for at least a century, the existence of a journal made real for many the existence of a movement. Those who studied religion and who came out of the experience of the Berkeley Free Church asserted that "existing institutions are insufficient to develop a new radical vision or meet the bankruptcy of our liberal society. Presently there does not exist in the United States a radical scholarly journal within the disciplines associated with religion. This explains, in part, why the religious Left remains unfocused and ineffectual." *Radical Religion* was founded in Berkeley in the winter of 1973, just after the radical philosophers of Boston put together the first issue of the *Radical Philosophers' Newsjournal*. The group behind the latter effort "all shared a clear sense of dissatisfaction both with present academic philosophy and with society at large." In common with many radical academics, the philosophers shared an interest in Marx, felt the irrelevancy of mainstream thought in their field—at the time, analytic philosophy—and hoped to make their discipline serve nonacademic purposes. Also in common with other such ventures, the journal served as the basis for discussion groups that sprang up around the country.

Historians in America participated in the movement of the 1960s with at least five major journals, with the last three still publishing in the late 1980s: *Studies on the Left, Marxist Perspectives, Radical America, Socialist Revolution* (now *Socialist Review*), and the *Radical History Review*. The *Radical History Review* began, like the *Insurgent Sociologist*, as a newsletter, the *MARHO Newsletter* (Mid-Atlantic Radical Historians' Organization), first published in 1973 in New York. The editors reflected on the change from an activist newsletter to a scholarly journal this way in 1977: "The growth of the *Review* reflects the emergence of a new generation of Marxist historians in the United States, politically awakened in the 1960s. . . . The collapse of the student based movement of the sixties, and the failure of its strategic vision, left many people on the Left in despair, but inspired in others a mood of introspection, a hunger to analyze the development of a society which seemed so unjust yet resistant to basic change." The *Review* thus became the outlet for a critique of American society based in a Marxist framework. *Socialist Revolution* interested itself in more contemporary problems than the *RHR* did, and also attracted a circle of Left academics beyond the historical profession. In many ways, it continued the work of *Studies on the Left*, which for seven years beginning in 1959 was the precursor of much New Left thought and whose editorial board members resurfaced in many other Left radical journals. According to an obituary written by one of the editors, "*Studies* made its contribution to the thinking of the new radicals in two areas. (1) It identified welfare state liberalism as the political ideology of the large corporation throughout this century, and, therefore, as the dominant political ideology in the United States. (2) It began the process of orienting socialist thought toward the problem of building a post-industrial socialism." *Radical America*, originally an outgrowth of the Radical Education Project of Students for a Democratic Society, was centered in the history department at the University of Wisconsin, which nurtured many of the graduate students who continued to play an active role in Left academic life in the late 1980s. Originally subtitled "An SDS Journal of the History of American Radicalism," it, too, along with *Socialist Review*, broadened its editorial board to include non-historians, and it publishes a mix of contemporary and historical articles.

Radical professional journals in other academic disciplines tended to cluster around area studies, most notably among economists, anthropologists, and political scientists. *NACLA: Report on the Americas* was founded in 1966 as a newsletter, and began *NACLA's Latin American and Empire Report* in 1971 before taking its current form in the mid-seventies. Published by the North American Congress on Latin America, it consistently exposes North American involvement in the political and economic life of Latin America. *MERIP Reports*, the publication of the Middle East Research and Information Project, does the same for the Middle East, and the *Bulletin of Concerned Asian Scholars* for its area. Overall, these radical journals have succeeded in creating and redefining what is possible for academics in the United States, yet these journals and the people who work in them had more direct influence on the general intellectual debate in America than they have had in the world of practical politics. *See also*: African Studies, Anthropology, History (European), History (U.S.), Latin American Studies, North American Congress on Latin America, Sociology

—*Elliott Shore*

RAILROAD STRIKE OF 1877

The first national strike wave with wide socialist participation, and the only occasion for a revolutionary municipal commune-style government, the 1877 "reign of the rabble" invited comparisons with the Paris Commune, still fresh in the public mind, and tested Left theories of labor insurrection. By and large, it found socialists too few in number and too little integrated into U.S. working-class life for a major, sustained reorientation.

Throughout the bitter depression of the 1870s, drastic reductions in wages had set off local labor insurgencies, frequently supported by the community at large, in particular those directed at unpopular railroad giants such as Jay Gould. Armies of unemployed rose to perhaps five million, with soup kitchens providing an inadequate sustenance in major cities. Unions, drastically reduced in strength, played no major role in rallying the discontented. Instead, the more or less spontaneous actions of railroad trainmen resisting repeated wage cuts—first of all in Martinsburg, West Virginia, July 17, then spreading to Baltimore and Pittsburgh by July 20—prompted committees of railroad workers, vaguely connected between cities, to coordinate public response.

In Baltimore and in Pittsburgh, local crowds rioted against the railroad barons by burning freight yards and seizing food and other commerce off the boxcars. In New York, Chicago, and in many other places, strikes spread from trade to trade, encompassing the labor organizations that existed. From railroad line to railroad line, as far west as San Francisco and neglecting only much of New England and the South, the action spread. Socialists provided public oratory, printed strike literature (more in German than in English), gathered the meager financial aid available, and urged strikers to draw the logical conclusions to their instinctive actions. After nearly a week of bloody battles with police and militia (often drawn, purposefully, from out of town), the upsurge generally receded.

The strike in St. Louis and East St. Louis followed a more complex course. The latter, together with St. Louis an important national railroad center, had as its leading official a labor-supported mayor (and indeed, a former "Forty-Eighter" who had briefly involved himself in revolutionary conspiracy before arriving in America and into respectability) determined to keep the peace by turning over the policing of property to the strikers themselves. After a few days, strikers led by young women (possibly members of the Women's Branch of the Workingmen's Party, whose existence had been noted some months before) paraded under banners reading "We Want a Peaceful Revolution," and "We Are Not Slaves, Nor Ever Will Be." No effort was made until the end to challenge their supremacy in the small industrial town.

In St. Louis proper, railroad strikers met under the auspices of the Local WP, which included at least one veteran of the First International, a vigorous group of German-Americans, and a handful of articulate American-born intellectuals. Spreading from trade to trade, the strike found its coordination at WP headquarters. Strikers and their sympathizers meanwhile marched by the thousands, convincing many among the wealthy classes that the insurrection had begun.

Socialists, at the head of the strike's executive committee, declared it to be general in the city. It was described by its outstanding scholar as "one of the first strikes anywhere in the world to paralyze a major industrial city; and without doubt . . . the first general strike of the modern, industrial labor movement in the United States." An especially important moment took place when black deckhands and firemen on steam barges joined the strike; socialists, themselves uneasy about the significance, clearly missed their major opportunity to join hands and make the most of what the New York *Sun* called a "novel feature of the times." Nevertheless, that same day, the red flag rose over many spots in the city. And the executive committee de facto replaced the regular political government for several days.

Revolutionary St. Louis, in the vacuum of a nation successfully repressing the strike, could not survive politically. Regiments of the U.S. Army, freed by the corrupt "Compromise of 1876" from long-term duty in the South defending blacks, marched through St. Louis and East St. Louis, reestablishing bourgeois order. A general arrest of strike leaders followed, notwithstanding a virtual absence of looting or rioting on the lines of Pittsburgh (and notwithstanding frequent journalistic claims of "communist" intent to loot and burn civilization).

In St. Louis, as in many other cities with German-American blue-collar populations, the next few local elections saw a sharp rise of socialist fortunes and the establishment of an English-language socialist press. Both these successes were short-lived. Of the St. Louis Commune's leaders, one went on to become the most noted analytic popularizer of socialism in the American nineteenth century: Laurence Gronlund, whose *Cooperative Commonwealth* (1884), with its Fabian-style argument for state socialism, influenced a precocious generation of American-born socialists. Another St. Louis leader, Albert Currlin, assumed the editorship of the Chicago *Arbeiter Zeitung* after the 1886 arrest of the entire staff. *See also*: Socialist Labor Party

—*Paul Buhle*

REFERENCES

Brecher, Jeremy. *Strike!* San Francisco: Straight Arrow Press, 1972.

Burbank, David. *Rein of the Rabble: The St. Louis General Strike of 1877.* New York: Augustus M. Kelley, 1966.

REVOLUTIONARY ACTION MOVEMENT (RAM): see ARMED STRUGGLE

RAMPARTS MAGAZINE

The preeminent popular journal of the New Left era of the 1960s and early 1970s, *Ramparts*—although plagued with financial problems and a chaotic publishing history—nonetheless managed to print many of the most significant articles of the decade. Most notably, *Ramparts* exposed the Cold War and Vietnam War policies of the U.S. government—insights often sandwiched between colorful ads for Day-Glo posters or psychedelic music. The glossy paper, provocative covers, vivid graphics, and high-profile publicity efforts attracted the attention of the mainstream media, young people just being introduced to the Left, politicians afraid of the Left, and the core activists of Left movements.

Founded in 1962 as a liberal Catholic quarterly, the San Francisco Bay Area–based magazine had 4,000 subscribers in 1964. With the rise of the New Left and the editorship of young, brash, flamboyant, and publicity-seeking Warren Hinckle III, from 1965 to 1968 subscriptions to the now-monthly *Ramparts* soared to perhaps 250,000. Debts and bitterness among *Ramparts'* founders and financial backers also soared out of control. By 1969 paid circulation had fallen to 125,000, and slid gradually to 50,000 when *Ramparts* folded in 1975.

The most influential *Ramparts* stories were often exposés. The ties between Michigan State University academics and South Vietnam's murderous Diem regime, or covert CIA funding and influence on the National Student Association were among the most spectacular. *Ramparts* also carried many dramatic antiwar features, from Tom Hayden and Noam Chomsky's essays to the Rev. Martin Luther King, Jr.'s masterful critique of U.S. foreign policy (he credited his own compulsion to go public on Vietnam to his viewing of *Ramparts'* photo essay about the war's effects on Vietnamese children), to exposure of U.S. intelligence connections with Southeast Asia's drug trade. The first English-language publisher of Che Guevara's diary from Bolivia, *Ramparts* also boosted the Black Panther Party, documented mistreatment of Native Americans, and focused attention on environmental dangers. While in its early days overwhelmingly "male" in style and substance, *Ramparts* began in 1969 to run major feminist features and, soon after, publicized gay liberation.

Ramparts' criticisms of Israeli occupation policies—while balanced by careful support of Israel's existence—provoked the withdrawal of major funder and later *New Republic* owner and aggressive Cold Warrior Martin Peretz. Other *Ramparts* figures shifting rightward included Eldridge Cleaver, David Horowitz (leading *Ramparts* figure for a few years), and Peter Collier. More typically, Robert Scheer, Andrew Kopkind, Alexander Cockburn, James Ridgeway, Derek Shearer, Edward Sorel, and others became leading progressive commentators elsewhere after the magazine's demise.

Financial supporter and editor Adam Hochschild—a leading figure in a split within *Ramparts'* inner circle—went on in 1976 to found *Mother Jones* magazine, which can be viewed as *Ramparts'* most enduring journalistic legacy. Also based in the Bay Area but self-consciously more mainstream and upscale, *Mother Jones* has also featured much dramatic exposé journalism on the environment and other issues. Another notable feature, rooted less in the *Ramparts* experience, has been the leading role of feminist intellectuals on its editorial board and among its writers. Its circulation has reached 200,000. *See also*: New Left

—Robert Shaffer

REFERENCES

Browning, Frank. "The Strange Journey of David Horowitz." *Mother Jones* 12 (May 1987).

Hinckle, Warren. *If You Have a Lemon, Make Lemonade*. New York: Putnam, 1974.

Ridgeway, James. "The *Ramparts* Story: . . . Um, Very Interesting." *New York Times Magazine*, April 20, 1969.

RAND SCHOOL OF SOCIAL SCIENCE

Founded in 1906, the Rand School was the first major workers' school, and it survived the longest. (Ruskin College at Trenton, Missouri, had been founded in 1900 but failed shortly thereafter.) Initially begun as a workers' school under the leadership of the Socialist Party, the Rand School, although it continued to remain committed to a socialist philosophy of education, evolved into an adult-education institution whose offerings were similar to a number of other programs in the city. Its most distinguished administrator, Algernon Lee (1873–1954), a moderate Socialist and member of the New York City Board of Aldermen from 1918 to 1922, headed the school for more than forty years after 1909.

In 1901 a group of socialists including Morris Hillquit, Charles Beard, William Ghent, and George Herron had formed the American Socialist Society (ASS) for the expressed purpose of founding an institution of workers' education. Herron's mother-in-law, Carrie Sherfey Rand, a wealthy widow from Des Moines, Iowa, was a former abolitionist with radical views. Her bequest of the income from $200,000, amounting to $5,000 to $6,000 annually, made it possible to establish the Rand School.

The school opened in the fall of 1906 with ninety students on East Nineteenth Street in Manhattan. Over the next fifty years the school offered courses to working men and women on a variety of cultural and current topics and socialist theory. Teachers included the intellectual leaders of the socialist movement, social pragmatists from the working world and the trade union movement, and such distinguished luminaries as Scott Nearing, Charles Beard, James Harvey Robinson, Stephen Vincent Benet, Bertrand Russell, and John Dewey.

By 1917 the school had outgrown its quarters and purchased a six-story building off Union Square at 7 East Fifteenth Street vacated by the Young Women's Christian Association. The building had an auditorium and spacious classrooms, and its extra space was rented to sympathetic organizations. The "People's House," modeled after a center in Brussels, Belgium, was to become the cultural and educational center for the Socialist movement in New York. The school's educational offerings and programs included a six month full-time residential program, a two-year part-time program for employed workers, a summer session for out-of-towners, a correspondence course, and a labor research department, as well as a library, bookstore, gymnasium, and cafeteria. Courses in the period from 1906 to 1922 pertained to socialist theory, economics, American history, literature, and other traditional subjects.

The antiradical hysteria after World War I subjected the school to a series of police interference and mob attacks. In 1919 the New York State Legislature voted Senator Clayton Lusk (Lusk Committee) $50,000 to investigate "subversive activities." Earlier attacks had included an indictment under the Espionage Act of the ASS and Scott Nearing for his antiwar pamphlet *The Great Madness*, published by the Rand School. The Lusk Committee conducted a raid on the offices, confiscated property, and attempted to close the school by court-ordered injunction. Through a series of court cases the school was able to successfully counter the attacks. Meanwhile the 1919 split in the Socialist Party led to the disappearance of staff and lecturers sympathetic to the Russian Revolution, and the control of the school was left firmly in the hands of the right-wing Socialists. Government harassment disappeared when Al Smith came into gubernatorial office in 1922, and the school was never again subjected to outside interference.

The Rand School entered into a period of expanded course offerings and special educational programs, and student enrollment increased. The curriculum shifted from socialist instruction to a wide range of courses in the areas of trade union policies, education, home economics, music, art, Russian studies, peace education, propaganda and public opinion, psychology, public speaking, and social work. Although it increasingly catered to a large group whose interest was predominantly in liberal education, the administration of the school was committed to offering socialist theory.

Once the Rand trust funds were exhausted the school survived financially through various means, partly supported by the bookstore, Rand School Press, and donations from the Garland Fund and private sources. But the cost of operations perennially exceeded the school's assets. Bertha Howell Mailly, executive secretary from 1912 until her retirement in 1941, is credited with saving the school on many occasions by launching countless fundraising campaigns, including bazaars, dances, and concerts. In 1919 Mailly visited Unity House, a resort owned by a local of the International Ladies Garment Workers Union in Bushkill, Pennsylvania. Learning of an adjacent tract of land for sale, she conceived the idea of extending the Rand School to a workers' summer school and camp. Camp Tamiment, named after an old Indian name for the area, grew to become commercially successful and from 1936 to 1956 provided backing to keep the school afloat. A large part of the camp's success was due to the fact that it had tax-exempt status based on its educational and cultural programs.

By the 1950s the government could no longer overlook what had become one of the largest, most modern, and most profitable resorts in the area. The camp decided that acquiring the title to the school's library would ensure a continued tax exemption. A five-year struggle ensued, during which time the camp systematically withdrew financial support from the school. In 1956 the People's Educational Camp Society (PECS) acquired title and full ownership of the Rand School and the Meyer London Memorial Library and Reading

Room. It dissolved the school and integrated its educational and cultural activities into the Tamiment Institute. After several appeals, in February 1963 the PESC lost its tax case with the IRS. Camp Tamiment was sold, and the library, all that remained of the old Rand School, now renamed the Tamiment Institute Library, was given to New York University Libraries.

During the height of its success between 1910 and 1920, the Rand School enrolled approximately 5,000 students annually. In 1946 13,000 students attended classes and lectures, but shortly thereafter the school suffered a sharp decrease in both enrollment and course offerings.

What remains of the Rand School of significance for the Left is the library. Its extensive collections of socialist and trade union literature, pamphlets, newspapers and periodicals, manuscripts, iconography, and ephemera are open to all. Recent special projects include the Robert F. Wagner Labor Archives, which collects and inventories labor union records, and the Oral History of the American Left. *See also*: Dewey, John; Hillquit, Morris; Labor Education; Socialist Party

—*Dorothy Swanson*

REFERENCES

Cornell, Frederic. "A History of the Rand School of Social Science, 1906 to 1956." Ph.D. diss., Columbia University, 1976.

Rand School of Social Science. Papers. Tamiment Institute Library, New York University.

Schwartz, Rachel Cutler. "The Rand School of Social Science, 1906–1924, a Study of Worker Education in the Socialist Era." Ph.D. diss., SUNY-Buffalo, 1984.

Swanson, Dorothy. *Guide to the Manuscript Collection of the Tamiment Library*. New York: Garland, 1977.

———. "The Tamiment Institute/Ben Josephson Library and Robert F. Wagner Labor Archive at New York University," *Library Quarterly* (April 1989).

RANDOLPH, A. PHILIP (1889–1979)

Asa Philip, the youngest son of an impoverished Florida preacher deeply involved in racial politics, Randolph became the most effective black trade unionist in the United States. In high school, he revealed his flare for political oratory as well as the impeccable dress and diction that led some to think he was a "Cambridge man." Introduced at home to the debates between W. E. B. DuBois and Booker T. Washington, he publicly identified himself with DuBois's vision of "the talented tenth," rejected the accommodationist policies associated with "the Tuskegee Machine," and declared himself a "racial radical" in favor of social equality. These views make Randolph's migration to Harlem in 1911, his rejection of the ministry, and his conversion to socialism seem inevitable. Still, he sympathized with Washington's down-to-earth, matter-of-fact approach to organization, his emphasis on industrial wages as a key to black development, and his separatist approach to achieving equality.

Although he wanted to act, Randolph had more theatrical success in the sectarian debates at City College of New York (1911–17) and as a street orator in Harlem. He organized support for the strikers in Paterson, New Jersey, and Lawrence, Massachusetts, led black opposition to World War I (which DuBois supported), and joined Marcus Garvey, whom he later opposed bitterly, in demands for the Versailles peace negotiations through the International League of Darker Peoples. Garnering 25 percent of the Harlem vote for Socialist Morris Hillquit in 1917, Randolph himself got 200,000 votes as the Socialist Party candidate for state comptroller in 1920. Dubbed "the black Lenin" and "the most dangerous black in America" by Attorney General Mitchell Palmer, Randolph was arrested for antiwar activism, but not prosecuted. He remained a pacifist throughout his life, though he advocated self-defense in response to the "red summer" race riots in 1919 and broke with the SP and Labor's Non-Partisan League over their opposition to World War II.

With his partner, sociologist Chandler Owen, Randolph helped form a number of short-lived political, labor, and community organizations. Their most significant accomplishment was editing the *Messenger*, a magazine that alternately represented Harlem radicals (including Jamaican nationalists), the

Harlem Renaissance (in the early '20s), and, finally, the Pullman porters. In its upbeat combination of culture with politics, its sympathies for the Industrial Workers of the World, its semiofficial status as an organ of the SP, and particularly its opposition to the war, the *Messenger* closely resembled the *Liberator* (later the *New Masses*), though the journals appear to have had little contact.

Because of the SP's inaction on the Negro problem, Randolph withdrew from the party in the early '20s. After a number of false starts with other unions, he accepted an invitation to organize the Brotherhood of Sleeping Car Porters (BSCP) in 1925.

Fighting against Pullman's company union, widespread intimidation, and much of the black press, Randolph built a national organizing committee from current and former porters, including Ashley Totten in New York, Bennie Smith in Detroit, Milton P. Webster from Chicago, C. L. Dellums from Oakland, and E. J. Bradley of St. Louis. His strategy was to use clandestine organizing and public and governmental pressure to force Pullman to recognize the union and improve working conditions, issues he felt were as important as wages.

When the BSCP failed to carry out a threatened strike in 1926, membership plummeted by almost 90 percent and, soon after, labor historians Sterling Spero and Abram Harris announced the union had collapsed. However, in 1935, largely due to New Deal labor legislation Randolph helped to write, the BSCP won the first nationwide election under the new Labor Relations Board, eight to one. Pullman signed its first union contract in 1937, reducing working hours from 400 to 240 a month, and union membership jumped to nearly 15,000.

Randolph remained an independent socialist within and outside the official labor movement. Ironically, the AFL recognized the BSCP only after the Pullman success. Gompers blamed blacks for union racism (a position echoed by Randolph's colleague Bayard Rustin in the 1960s); and the railway unions, so radical in other respects, steadfastly opposed including blacks. Randolph fought unsuccessfully against the color barriers in the AFL throughout the '30s and, as late as 1961, he was personally censured by the AFL-CIO executive council (which included David Dubinsky, Joe Curran, and James Carey) for "causing the gap that has developed between organized labor and the Negro community." Randolph was a constant critic of Communist influence in the labor movement. Despite this, he headed several important United Front organizations, including the 1.2-million-member National Negro Congress.

Randolph's national prominence grew when, in response to his threat to bring 100,000 Negroes to Washington in 1941, Roosevelt issued Executive Order 8802, ending segregation in defense industries. In 1947, this time by threatening a national campaign of civil disobedience against the draft, Randolph helped evoke Truman's Executive Order 9981, ending discrimination in the military.

As the elder stateman for an activist (and separatist) approach to civil rights during the '60s, Randolph was frequently asked to mediate disputes between warring factions. He helped bring the Rev. Martin Luther King, Jr., into the 1957 Prayer Pilgrimage to Washington, supported the Youth Marches for Integrated Schools (1957–58) and helped, along with Rustin and the A. Philip Randolph Institute, to initiate and coordinate the 1963 March on Washington. Randolph (and the institute) were harshly criticized for supporting the United Federation of Teachers during the 1968 teachers' strike and for their negative views of the riots, black power, black capitalism, and black anti-Semitism. Despite this, however, Randolph remains the only American socialist to have achieved prominence in both the black and trade union communities. *See also*: Civil Rights Movement, Socialist Party

—*Evan Stark*

REFERENCES

Anderson, Jervis. *A. Philip Randolph: A Biographical Portrait*. New York: Harcourt Brace Jovanovich, 1973.

Harris, William H. *Keeping the Faith: A. Philip Randolph, Milton P. Webster, and the Brotherhood of Sleeping Car Porters, 1925–37*. Urbana: University of Illinois, 1977.

Wilson, Joseph F. *Tearing Down the Color Bar: A Documentary History and Analysis of the Brotherhood of Sleeping Car Porters*. New York: Columbia University Press, 1989.

Rapp-Coudert Inquiry

Significant as a rehearsal for McCarthyism, this anticommunist inquiry and purge of 1940–41 was undertaken by the New York State Legislature at the time of the Nazi-Soviet Pact. This was not a period when significant numbers abandoned the American Communist Party but rather when alliances between liberals and Communists weakened, leaving Communists vulnerable to attack by several branches of the governmental apparatus. The target of Rapp-Coudert was the New York City schools, reputed to be hotbeds of leftist agitation. The upstate, antimetropolis component of this attack was personally represented by the small-town Genesee County politician Herbert Rapp. The sophisticated New York City component was represented by the well-connected Manhattan lawyer Frederic R. Coudert, Jr. The Coudert thrust prevailed: the schools were investigated and purged, but no assault was made on the school budgets, so that Communists were in effect sacrificial victims for school systems.

The inquiry into Communism at the high school and elementary school levels in New York City was postponed while the municipal colleges—Queens, Hunter, and Brooklyn colleges, and that locus classicus of collegiate radicalism of the 1930s, City College of New York (CCNY)—were slated to be the initial targets of investigation. Faculty and staff informers were found on all campuses, mostly disaffected former Communists, such as Brooklyn College English professor Bernard Greganier and CCNY history instructor Martin Canning. On the basis of their testimony, the Rapp-Coudert Committee subpoenaed dozens of municipal college faculty members for private and then public hearings, the results of which made front-page news in the New York City dailies.

In a manner that would later become institutionalized in the postwar McCarthy period, the governmental authorities merely identified Communists, leaving the task of disciplining them to their employers—in this case the New York City Board of Higher Education. In BHE trials, the suspected Communists were charged with "conduct unbecoming a teacher" for hiding their political affiliation, although the BHE made it clear that they would also fire those who admitted Party membership. This happened in the case of CCNY Party leader and English instructor Morris Schappes, who also served a prison term for perjury. At CCNY more than a dozen faculty and staff members were dismissed, while at the other municipal colleges, smaller groups were fired.

The Rapp-Coudert inquiry was abruptly halted when the Germans invaded the Soviet Union in mid-1941, but after World War II the purge of Communists picked up where it had left off. During the 1950s several more accused Communists were dismissed or resigned at Brooklyn College, while the Feinberg Law brought high school and elementary school teachers into a similar position.

The Rapp-Coudert Committee left an enduring legacy. Its research became the foundation for many of the McCarthy-era purges. Several committee staff members and friendly witnesses, such as Robert Morris and Martin Canning, resurfaced in later federal anticommunist investigating committees, and the precedent of Rapp-Coudert became part of the American anticommunist tradition. In the early 1980s the municipal colleges formally apologized to the surviving dismissed teachers and staff members but offered no financial remuneration for the careers blighted by the Rapp-Coudert purge. *See also*: Communist Party, McCarthyism

—*Marv Gettleman*

REFERENCES

Published and unpublished (the latter in New York State Archives, Albany) reports of the Rapp-Coudert Committee.

Board of Higher Education trial transcripts. Board of Higher Education Archives, New York City.

Chamberlain, Lawrence H. *Loyalty and Legislative Action*. Ithaca: Cornell University Press, 1951.

Gettleman, Marvin E. "Anti-Communist Purges on Campus." *In These Times*, March 10–16, 1982.

Iversen, Robert W. *Communists and the Schools*. New York: Harcourt Brace, 1959.

Schrecker, Ellen W. *No Ivory Tower: McCarthyism and the Universities*. New York: Oxford University Press, 1986.

REALIGNMENT

While various political currents on the Left, including the Communist Party, have held similar strategies, the policy known as "realignment" came out of the Shachtmanite tendency and refers to making the Democratic Party, in effect, a European-style social democratic party.

Like the Socialist Workers Party, both the Workers Party (1940–49) and the Independent Socialist League (1949–58), led by Max Shachtman, had denounced the Democratic Party as a capitalist party and urged workers and minorities to form their own labor party. Reluctantly, however, the Shachtmanites began to realize that the labor movement, including its rank-and-file and minority members, identified the Democratic Party as their own. Shachtman and his followers did not change their assessment of the Democratic Party and believed that labor was mistaken in trusting mainstream moderate-to-liberal Democrats to represent its interests. But so long as labor—which the ISL saw as the only mass movement capable of building a socialist society—allied itself with the Democratic Party, the small socialist movement had no choice but to aid the labor movement in attempting to make the Democratic Party truly its own. In this way, labor might form a de facto labor party within the Democratic Party, or if faced with a clear betrayal of workers' interests, it might begin an independent working-class party of its own.

In 1958, when they entered the Socialist Party, the Shachtmanites began to promote the policy of realignment. They envisioned the fall of city machines through development of a mass labor movement and a welfare state. They identified a key political task in expelling the southern racists from the Democratic Party. Once these two goals were met—according to realignment theory—labor, minorities, and middle-class progressives could form a coalition to take control of the Democratic Party, with the labor movement at its center. This perspective eventually came to dominate virtually all remaining socialist groups. *See also*: Shachtman, Max; Workers Party

—David Hacker

REFERENCES

Isserman, Maurice. *If I Had A Hammer: The Death of the Old Left and the Birth of the New Left*. New York: Basic Books, 1987.

RED DIAPER BABY

This name has been used to label children of communist or socialist parents.

In the 1920s, children of southern California Communist Party members used the phrase to refer derisively to their peers who acted as if birthright alone, not activism or theoretical knowledge, provided revolutionary credentials. In the early years of the New Left, the term was used to identify those who followed the Old Left, particularly the CP. In the mid-1960s, the right-wing John Birch Society published a list of "red diaper babies" who were entering the University of California at Berkeley. This attempt at intimidation failed; the students used the list to create a support network.

A series of annual conferences begun in 1982 provided the first public discussion and collectively generated documentation of the

From *New Pioneer*, October, 1932

"red diaper" experience. By the mid-1980s, the phrase had begun to appear in mainstream media, primarily in reviews of books and films about the American Left.

Shared values, worldview, and childhood experiences form a core "red diaper" experience. For example, red diaper babies describe growing up with a sense of difference, both specialness and fear; feeling part of an international community and yet isolated from the mainstream of their own country. Imbued with the dignity of cooperation, many red diaper babies describe conflicts over upward mobility and continuing efforts to balance personal contentment with political effectiveness. As adults, red diaper babies may or may not be political activists. Within families, siblings often differ in type and degree of activism and impact of the "red diaper" experience on their lives. *See also*: Yiddish Left

—*Linn Shapiro*

REFERENCES

Chernin, Kim. *In My Mother's House*, New Haven: Ticknor and Fields, 1983.

Gornick, Vivian. *The Romance of American Communism*, New York: Basic Books, 1977.

Kaplan, Judy, and Linn Shapiro, eds. *Red Diaper Babies: Children of the Left*. Washington, D.C.: Red Diaper Productions, 1985.

Meeropol, Robert, and Michael Meeropol. *We Are Your Sons: The Legacy of Ethel and Julius Rosenberg*. 2d. ed. Urbana: University of Illinois Press, 1987.

"Red Scare"

The Palmer Raids and the "Red Scare" of the World War I era marked the most brutal, if not necessarily the most extensive and intensive government and private persecution of radicals in U.S. history.

Radical opposition to the war, and specifically American entry into the conflict, precipitated or permitted a wide-ranging legal and extralegal vigilantism. In the process, repression of labor, the labor or radical press, immigrant social and cultural institutions, and a range of other dissenting elements spread in a pattern. The federal government's marshalling of opinion, igniting war hysteria, guided the outcome.

The Espionage Act, passed in 1917, set one precedent by identifying treason or disloyalty with any effort to stir distrust in the nation's military machine. The Sedition Act, passed the following year, added to the dossier of punishable activity a whole range of acts heretofore considered merely unpatriotic. Other measures, directed at aliens, added a new set of provisos to the existing legislation on exclusion (or more to the point, deportation) of any alien anarchist, essentially subjecting immigrant radicals to guilt by association.

In part, the repressive legislation aimed specifically at the Industrial Workers of the World, which had been careful to pose its main opposition to capitalism in general rather than to the war in particular. The eagerness of western businessmen and conservative interests to rid themselves of Wobbly influence precipitated the War Department directives of 1917 to local Army officials to protect public utilities and repress active sedition. In Washington and Montana, troops raided Wobbly headquarters, broke up meetings, took members hostage without charges, patrolled freight cars for migrant activists, and watched local industry to prevent any labor agitation. By 1920–21, the War Department had likewise intervened widely with federal troops in Arizona and Montana copper camps, notwithstanding the end of the war.

Meanwhile, in 1917 the government had raided IWW headquarters in Chicago and across the nation, confiscating organizational records, office equipment, even buttons, stickers, and leaflets, purportedly for the purpose of demonstrating Wobbly criminality under the Selective Service and Espionage Acts. Encouraging state officials to similar acts, the federal government in effect sponsored wide-scale arrests and long prison sentences in Minnesota, California, and other states.

Regulations adopted in 1918 permitting the postmaster to prevent delivery of a publication or incoming mail to dangerous individuals opened a field day for a different style of prosecution. At his discretion, Postmaster Albert S. Burleson first confiscated selected issues of many Socialist publications, and then suspended their second-class mailing permits on the basis of missed issues. Rural Socialist papers, almost entirely dependent upon the mails, suffered the most from this measure, not more than 10 percent of the 1916 rural papers surviving by 1920. Their intellectual lifeline gone, most rural Socialist branches—with leaders facing potential indictment for antiwar agitation—folded. For those Socialist papers that survived, a heavy price had been paid. A number of the most prominent, such as the *Appeal to Reason* or the *Jewish Daily Forward*, had muted their positions on the war, or (in the case of the *Appeal*, renamed *New Appeal*) actually shifted to a pro-Wilson policy until the war's end.

The immigrant Left papers, which could reach most of their readers on a newsstand basis, survived the best. But even here, the government intervened with peculiar veniality. The publications most fractious *within* the Left, bent on a sectarian course of dividing radical forces, often mysteriously survived the censor's efforts. Those inclined to unified action toward some particular goal, whether strike support or antiwar activism, often suffered the most intensive persecution, such as repeated raiding and destruction of presses, attempts to deport large numbers of followers, and jailings without benefit of habeus corpus. The ferociously antiwar Italian immigrant supporters of Luigi Galleani and his anarchist paper, *Cronoca Sovversiva*, were deported wholesale in perhaps the most intensive case of selective repression.

Other manifestations of police-state action multiplied. In a few recorded cases, the government and its vigilante allies resorted to murder. The vigilante lynching and castration of IWW organizer Frank Little was one such case. In another, following a series of explosions on Wall Street, Galleani's chief assistant, brought in for questioning by the New York authorities, reportedly leaped out a window to his death. Far more often, the government proposed long jail sentences on a variety of charges ranging from sedition to "criminal syndicalism." The mass trial of IWW activists in Chicago in 1917, was only the most spectacular of many cases intended to place the radical and labor movements on the defensive, preoccupied with fighting for members' freedom rather than social transformation. Socialists who had long enjoyed a relative freedom of speech and assembly at the local level found themselves unable to use public places or even their own halls for meetings. State conventions (as in South Dakota) were broken up by troopers, speakers were banned on such bizarre grounds as local health ordinances, and in a number of cases agitators were beaten, kidnapped, tarred and feathered by vigilantes.

Continual government raids on offices, purportedly in search of "evidence," completed the strategy. Some newspapers were raided repeatedly, while most faced the crisis of physical damage, stolen mailing lists and other records. In some cases, as that of the monthly magazine *International Socialist Review*, the damage wrought by raiding officers made continuation virtually impossible, eclipsing several of America's most prestigious dissenting publications.

These highly dubious procedures also created an unprecedented category of "political prisoners," heretofore limited to a relative few linked (actually or spuriously) to such violent acts as the *Los Angeles Times* bombing, but now expanded to include hundreds of victims prosecuted for their beliefs. The most notorious of these convicted criminals, Eugene V. Debs, ran for president in 1920 from his federal prison cell.

The Palmer Raids, following real and/or orchestrated bomb threats in January 1920, and deportation of a few thousand radical aliens, climaxed the government show of force. In part frustrated legally in its effort to deport large numbers, in part eager to respond to the temptation offered by avowedly pro-Bolshevik radicals, the Justice Department under A. Mitchell Palmer and the vastly expanded Bureau of Investigation (its "alien radical" division run by the promising young functionary J. Edgar Hoover) ran roughshod over legal niceties. Hoover's division had sent hundreds of its agents into radical organizations, often posing as ultraradicals inciting factional warfare. Now it prepared a massive dragnet with the arrest of 10,000 persons. A procedure historically famous in legal circles for the virtual absence of due process, the indiscriminate grounds for arrest, brutality, threats, and extorted confessions, the manner of the raids drew wide complaints from Congress and the press.

The Immigration Act of 1920, written in large part to correct gaps in the legal persecution of Palmer Raid victims, made aliens punishable for the first time simply for possessing literature or indicating support and sympathy rather than for carrying out teachings in some specific fashion. This most extreme act would rarely be brought into use. With the war ended and most radical-led labor initiatives defeated, the political will faded. Criminal syndicalism laws, enacted mostly by states, addressed specific threats perceived to profitable production; along with the National Guard, reconstituted state-by-state on a peacetime basis with the encouragement of the federal government, states had all the forces they needed to continue a pattern of repression into the 1920s and beyond. *See also*: Haymarket Affair, McCarthyism.

—Paul Buhle

REFERENCES

Murray, Robert K. *Red Scare: A Study in National Hysteria. 1919–1920*. Minneapolis: University of Minnesota Press, 1955.

Preston, William, Jr. *Aliens and Dissenters: Federal Suppression of Radicals, 1903–1933*. Cambridge: Harvard University Press, 1963.

Weinstein, James. *The Decline of Socialism in America, 1912–1925*. New York: Monthly Review Press, 1967.

REED, JOHN (1887–1920)

Born in Portland, Oregon, Reed had a privileged childhood, and an even more privileged education in preparatory school and Harvard. Generally regarded as a playboy, Reed did not join the Socialist Club, whose president was Walter Lippmann. He settled in New York in 1910, became a contributor to the *Masses*, and turned into a symbol of the new freedom as understood in Greenwich Village. In 1913 Reed visited the strike of silk workers in Paterson, New Jersey. Moved by what he saw, he helped organize the "Strike Pageant" in Madison Square Garden with Bill Haywood, leader of the Industrial Workers of the World. In 1914 he traveled with the guerrilla forces of Pancho Villa. *Insurgent Mexico* (1914) was impressionistic and patchily written, but it impressed contemporaries as a new and vivid kind of war reporting. When the war broke out in Europe, Reed denounced it as "The Traders' War." He was sent to Europe in 1914 and 1915 for the *Metropolitan*, but his *The War in Eastern Europe* (1916) lacked the personal involvement of his first book. American entry into the war in 1917, and the revolution in Russia, transformed Reed's life. He arrived in Petrograd in time to witness the Bolshevik seizure of power in October. Although he spoke little Russian, Reed followed events closely, and collected documents that he brought back to the United States in April 1918. He quickly wrote *Ten Days That Shook the World* (1919), the first major account of the revolution to appear in America.

In political life, he achieved far less distinction. In August 1919, Reed and other irregular delegates were expelled from the Socialist Party convention in Chicago. The two competing left-wing parties, the Communist Party and Reed's Communist Labor Party, eventually merged in 1920 into the United Communist Party. By then Reed had returned to Russia for the Second Congress of the Communist International, where his opposition to Zinoviev on the question of trying to work within the AFL was defeated. Guilty of the "infantile disorder" of left-wing communism, Reed passionately argued that the industrial unionism of the Industrial Workers of the World was the only viable model for revolutionary action in America. He contracted typhus at a conference in Baku and died, exhausted and frustrated, on October 17, 1920. He was buried in the wall of the Kremlin. *See also*: Greenwich Village, *Liberator*, *Masses*

—Eric Homberger

REFERENCES

Homberger, Eric. *American Writers and Radical Politics, 1900–39: Equivocal Commitments*. London: Macmillan (per p 1548), 1986.

Rosenstone, Robert A. *Romantic Revolutionary: A Biography of John Reed*. New York: Knopf, 1975.

John Reed Clubs

Founded in New York in November 1929 by the editorial board of the *New Masses*, the clubs were educational and agitational in purpose. They were modeled on literary studios for worker-correspondents created by the Proletcult in the Soviet Union, which Mike Gold and Joseph Freeman had seen during visits earlier in the decade. The shift in Comintern policy into the Third Period in 1928 made the American Left take the class war into every aspect of culture. With a slogan ("Art Is a Class Weapon") designed to emphasize the clubs' opposition to aesthetic doctrines of art for art's sake, the clubs offered an alternative to the "lost generation" and the postwar voices of disillusionment. The JRCs were militant, energetic, and highly political. Branches soon formed in the larger American cities, as well as in smaller towns like Carmel, California, and Kalamazoo, Michigan. By 1934 there were more than thirty clubs, with a reported membership of 1,200. A journal, the *JRC Bulletin*, was published by the national headquarters; regional and national conventions were held; and JRCs for artists were created. The leaders of the JRC were generally members of the Communist Party, though the role of the Party was sometimes disguised. The executive committee of the national organization included Joseph Freeman, Whittaker Chambers, and the artists Louis Lozowick and William Gropper.

The full range of club activities constitutes a legacy of radical cultural practice that the American Left, or the CP, has rarely approached since. Consider the Chicago JRC in 1931. Club members made posters for demonstrations and parades in the city. Murals in the Peoples Auditorium were painted; dramatic material and scenery was provided for the Blue Blouses, a youth drama group; demonstrations were organized on high school and university campuses to win support for the International War Day on August 1; the program for the John Reed Memorial Day held at the Peoples Auditorium was written by members, and consisted of songs, dances, music, a mass chant of an antiwar poem, and a talk on Reed by the former Wobbly Ralph Chaplin. A proletarian art exhibit, including work by Ivan Albright and Mitchell Siporin, and photographs from the JRC Film and Photo Group, was held in the summer. In December, a JRC Ball was held in Chicago to raise money for activities in 1932. The inner life of the JRC was less impressive: Party manipulation, ideological rows, and sectarianism were the order of the day. The New York JRC could call upon a wider range of literary talent (an impressive series of lectures was given by Kenneth Burke, Edward Dahlberg, Horace Gregory, Granville Hicks, John Howard Lawson, and Philip Rahv), but even here the Chicago JRC could boast of the discovery of Richard Wright.

The JRC sent a joint delegation with the *New Masses* in 1930 to the Kharkov Congress of the International Union of Revolutionary Writers. The delegation, which included Mike Gold and William Gropper, was divided along sectarian lines, with younger members seeking to block the affiliation of individuals like Upton Sinclair to the IURW. They called for stricter discipline and adherence, especially in the pages of the *New Masses*, to the rigorous demands of proletarian literature. The problem of relations with non-Party sympathizers was never solved by the JRC, and remained a source of conflict. Alexander Trachtenberg, director of International Publishers and the link between the Party's central committee and the JRC, opposed sectarianism at the JRC convention in 1934, and when it became obvious that the club was unable to keep step with the evolution of Comintern policy toward a Popular Front, the JRC was quietly dissolved and Party efforts were directed toward the League of American Writers. Isolated cities retained active clubs into the next decade, but the journals, from the modest mimeographed *Proletcult* (Portland and Seattle) and *Red Spark* (Cleveland) to the prestigious and elegantly printed *Partisan Review*, edited by Rahv and William Phillips, nearly all died. The loss to American letters was not severe: it takes longer than five years to change a culture. But when the *Partisan Review* was reborn as an anti-Stalinist journal of the Left in 1936, the erosion of Party influence on the American intellectual Left had begun in earnest. *See also*: Conroy, Jack; National Writers Congress; Gold, Mike; New Masses; Partisan Review; Wright, Richard

—*Eric Homberger*

REFERENCES

Aaron, Daniel. *Writers on the Left*. New York: Harcourt, Brace, and World, 1961.

Homberger, Eric. *American Writers and Radical Politics, 1900–39: Equivocal Commitments*. London: Macmillan, 1986.

REGROUPMENT

Following the Khruschev revelations of 1956, several leaders of the Socialist Workers Party concluded that former Communists and parts of the Communist Party periphery might be interested in exploring the ideas of Leon Trotsky and of the opposition to Stalinism that the SWP embodied. A reorganized and broader Left than any presently in existence, some disaffiliated radicals outside the SWP hoped, might take root. The result, "regroupment," took place on three fronts.

Major effort went into an electoral campaign by the Independent Socialist Party in New York State in 1958, which allowed an unprecedented cooperation of Trotskyists and former supporters of the Popular, and United, fronts. The state ticket included Jack McManus, editor of the *National Guardian*, as gubernatorial candidate; Annette T. Rubinstein, longtime Marxist educator and political aide of radical New York City congressman Vito Marcantonio, for lieutenant-governor; and civil rights fighter Captain Hugh Mulzac, First Amendment defendant, for senator. Successful in gaining ballot status and in bringing together former adversaries, the ISP gained neither the permanent ballot status nor the widespread support required to continue.

A second effort, the formation of a new, independent socialist youth organization, took shape in the character of the Young Socialist Alliance. Intended to foster discussion among young people of various tendencies on issues of civil rights, electoral action, and the buildup of war threats in Indochina, it soon narrowed into an SWP junior organization.

The final test of Regroupment came with the Cuban Revolution. The SWP devoted great effort and much of its limited resources to help a united front form around the Fair Play for Cuba Committee (FPCC). At first rather successful, especially on selected campuses, the FPCC suffered from factionalism within and the U.S. government pressure (following the Bay of Pigs invasion) from without.

Ultimately, regroupment efforts failed, as the New Left took its own shape largely independent of older organizations. However, in collaboration with the Marxist Educational Collective, Arthur Felberbaum (1935–79), who had been active in the YSA regroupment effort, established in 1973 the New York Marxist School. The most memorable result of regroupment perspectives, the school continues as an open forum in both special event and classroom format for a variety of political tendencies on the Left, and fosters open discussion on issues of concern to the Left in general. *See also*: Cuban Revolution, *National Guardian*, Socialist Workers Party, Trotskyism

—*Nora R. Wainer*

REITZEL, ROBERT (1848–98)

Perhaps the most prestigious German-American literary stylist of his age, Reitzel was editor of *Der arme Teufel* (1884–1902), a German-language weekly for culture, politics, and critique of religion that sympathized with anarchism. Reitzel became well-known because of his campaign to save the lives of the Haymarket anarchists and for his fiery speech at their graveside.

Reitzel was born in the German revolutionary year, and his democratically inclined mother named him after the murdered "Forty-Eighter" revolutionary Robert Blum. Forced by his conservative father to study theology, the twenty-year-old Reitzel refused and found himself sent penniless to America. He wandered around begging and half-starved until a German minister took him in and gave him a place with a German church in Washington. Awakened by his readings of early socialist philosophy critical of religion, he quarreled with the church synod, founded a "free-thought congregation," and became an atheist, socialist, and soon a popular speaker among the German-speaking American Left. The halls were full when the charismatic Reitzel attacked religious fanaticism, Puritanism, militarism, nationalism, and anti-Semitism. As an advocate of free love and equality of the sexes, he foreshadowed the revolutionary sexual emancipation movements of the twentieth century, and he was also an early advocate of homosexual rights. This cultural revolutionary was a friend of the anarchists Johann Most, Benjamin Tucker, John Henry Mackay and Alexander Berkman. He thought highest of Emma Goldman, who for her part was fascinated by his bohemian personality. Politically, Reitzel tended toward the social wing of anarchism, and his moral critique connected him to the individualistic anarchists, though he claimed independence from all political groups. He held a lifelong admiration for political assassins. For him, they were slayers of tyrants after the manner of German classicism, like Schiller's William Tell.

In the nineties, Reitzel's *Der arme Teufel* became an influential forum for European culture. On a trip to Europe, he met the German naturalists whose group, called "the young ones," had been expelled from the Social Democratic Party and who had gone over to Nietzsche's doctrine of the overman. Reitzel imported Nietzsche's Zarathustra cult into the United States, but he also gave space to critics of irrationalism. He died of tuberculosis of the bone, the illness that killed his favorite writer, Heinrich Heine. *See also*: Anarchism, Haymarket Affair

—*Ulrike Heider, translated by Carol Poore*

REFERENCES

Heider, Ulrike. *Der arme Teufel. Robert Reitzel—Vom Vormärz zum Haymarket*. Bühl-Moos: Elster Verlag, 1986.

RENT STRIKES, NEW YORK CITY

One of the most important political expressions of women radicals and of interracial activism, rent strikes have intermittently provided the Left with a firm neighborhood base of popular support.

Protests against miserable conditions and high rents extend back, at least, to mobilization on the Lower East Side against the sudden

Bank Night

increase of rents by 20–30 percent in the early years of the century. In 1904 several hundred residents announced their refusal to pay, convoked mass meetings, and picketed homes of landlords. Working from the principles of labor solidarity, they formed tenant unions building to building and developed an intense agitation in the immediate neighborhoods. Soon, the male leadership of the United Hebrew Trades, Workmen's Circle, and other organizations formed the New York Rent Protective Association, which soon failed because of internal political differences. Nevertheless, tenants obtained considerable redress, and a sense of empowerment. A 1908 rent strike, directly coordinated by a branch of the Socialist Party, spread from Manhattan to Brooklyn, Harlem, and Newark, as Jewish teamsters refused to move tenants forcibly from their apartments. Once more, however, no organization remained in place to defend gains made. Attacked in the commercial press for leading the second strike, the Socialists failed to incorporate a tenant strategy into their political arsenal.

During the war years, a slowdown in construction and a growing demand for apartments once more provoked a crisis in which socialists and predominantly Jewish unions helped build widespread organizations in the Bronx, Brooklyn, and Manhattan, forcing minor improvements or rescinded rent increases. Socialist efforts reached an especially high level in the Bronx and in Brownsville, both already radicalized by labor militance and by news from abroad. The Socialist *Call* provided much coverage, and the Party offered not only its halls for rent-strike activity, but also some of its finest lawyers for fighting individual cases. Widespread hatred of "rent profiteers" raising their prices increased sympathy, if not necessarily voting totals, for the Socialists. The "Red Scare," the split and disintegration of the Socialist movement, and the legislative approval of rudimentary rent-control laws ultimately detached Socialist influence and dampened the mass activity required to bring effective laws and enforcement. Preoccupied with internal and shop struggles, the young Communist movement made little effort to recoup Socialist neighborhood losses.

Rent-strike activity returned with fervor, and became a specifically Communist issue, with the Depression. As early as 1928, black Communists had begun to protest the effects of the impending disappearance of legal protection for the residents of Harlem. The Harlem Tenants League, with Communist Richard Moore as president, conducted intense protests, accompanied by a series of journalistic exposés of real conditions in the *Daily Worker*. Handicapped by a shortage of Harlem members, Communists failed to pull off the Harlem-wide rent strike they hailed, but their agitation nevertheless stirred residents to consider the possibilities.

The economic crash introduced an element of desperation that Communists almost immediately seized upon as harbinger of revolutionary sentiment. The Left-led Unemployed Councils encouraged eviction resistance with wide success, helping hundreds of families in New York, Chicago, and elsewhere to move furniture back into apartments. Rent strikes, demanding more neighborhood discipline and entailing greater risks, at first began slowly. The Great Rent Strike War of 1932, opening in the Bronx near the Left-inhabited Allerton Avenue "Coops," pitted police against crowds of tenants seeking broad reductions in rent. Women, reputedly the most militant, led the hand-to-hand resistance against officers and horses, and more important, directed the apartment-by-apartment organization of renters. Landlords combined to crush these strikes, but the movement for rent reductions spread to Brownsville, Williamsburg, Boro Park, and other locations where East European Jews had gathered.

By late 1932 and 1933, a much-matured Communist cadre made rent strikes a component of the wider unemployed struggle. Here, most notably in Crotona Park, women's self-mobilization reached new levels and wide victories over landlords were scored. Major legal decisions made rent-resistance more dangerous, with even picketing ruled unlawful. Communists shifted the target, in part, to the home relief bureaus, where impoverished tenants sat-in until they received action (with actual redress made possible by federal funds to local government).

A movement of greater sophistication and less open Communist leadership engaged Harlem and Knickerbocker Village in the middle 1930s, and a citywide tenants council formed in 1936. Clearly a Popular Front mechanism, the council worked comfortably with liberals and abandoned revolutionary rhetoric. Adding affiliates, gaining sophisticated legal assistance, and carefully coordinating legal protest, the organization was held together mostly by unemployed professionals (and Communist militants) rather than slum dwellers. It successfully urged a limited rent-control law, which passed in 1939, but lacking financial resources, did not succeed in establishing a stable infrastructure for itself.

During World War II, tenant organizing gave way to war work and, for male cadre, to military service. Replaced by a United Tenants League, the citywide experiment nevertheless led to successfully pressuring the Office of Price Administration (OPA) into declaring wartime rent controls across New York. Adam Clayton Powell, Jr., popular minister with Communist leanings, organized a People's Committee with wide support in Harlem to this end. American Labor Party clubs in many neighborhoods, following Vito Marcantonio's

East Harlem Club example, created tenant clinics generally staffed by women, for the same purpose. Ironically, OPA rulings badly weakened the UTL by removing the center of action from the neighborhood as such to courts and government offices.

In the immediate aftermath of World War II, with labor conflict abounding, neighborhood actions frequently led by ALP clubs focused on the need to retain OPA guidelines. The Republican Congress, over considerable national protest, abolished most OPA ceilings and rent mobilizations proliferated, generally in such traditional Left-influenced neighborhoods as Williamsburg but especially in the Bronx. Marcantonio and the ALP, by embracing the issue and making it their own also in many ways weakened its independent status—a matter of decisive importance when the Left turned its full attention to the 1948 Progressive Party campaign.

By 1949, both the Left and rent-agitation lost substantial ground. Prosperity and suburbanization removed cadre and eased the housing crisis. Communists already faced with McCarthyism and political demoralization lost their crucial roots in the Lower East Side and other working-class Jewish districts, a strength not made up in new black and Puerto Rican neighborhoods, where cadre remained relatively few. Flagging ALP clubs emphasized community service, and Communists still in the field urged antidiscrimination legislation and a Save Our Homes committee (directed by longtime Communist housing activist Elizabeth Barker), as liberals from the American Jewish Committee and other groups created their own, notably anticommunist, open-housing lobby.

The collapse of the existing Left did not diminish protest entirely. Neighborhood committees pitted themselves against Robert Moses's redevelopment plans (such as a four-lane highway through Washington Square), with the partial support of liberal housing experts such as Jane Jacobs, the *Village Voice*, and Eleanor Roosevelt. Radicalism resurfaced in such sites as Cooper Union, led in part by erstwhile social worker Staughton Lynd, and the Met Council, led by 1930s–1940s activist Jane Benedict.

Civil rights activity established a new political context for the Left. Former ALP Harlem activist Jesse Gray, master of the dramatic publicity event, organized a Harlem Tenants Council and Committee Council on Housing, with a dramatic strike (with little lasting organizational influence) in 1963. Gray sparked the Congress on Racial Equality (CORE) and a series of radical-led neighborhood committees in various organizing drives. The overpowering strength of landlords—willing to abandon or torch their property rather than lose profits—proved insurmountable, and various government agencies operated to fill the gaps. As in other cities, subsequent efforts at tenants' unions had only limited success and offered little visibility for a badly declining Left. Perhaps the desperation of rioters in the Lower East Side of 1988, their placards showing upended cocktail glasses ("The Party's Over"—for yuppie neighborhood in-migrants) marked the latest phase of radicalism, militant but disorganized. *See also*: American Labor Party, Communist Party

—Paul Buhle, Mark Naison

REFERENCES

Lawson, Ronald, ed. *The Tenant Movement in New York City, 1904–1984.* New Brunswick: Rutgers University Press, 1986.

Revolutionary Communist Party: see "Anti-revisionism" (Maoism)

Rivera, Diego (Murals)

Mexican Diego Rivera (1886–1957) made a tremendous impact on the mural movement north of the Rio Grande through murals he created in the United States in the 1930s and the controversy and personal contacts they generated. The enduring controversies about his work and the nature of the work also made him an exemplary figure for the revived mural movement of the 1960s. Although his murals cover thousands of square feet in his native Mexico, Rivera is best remembered in the United States for a work he never completed—*Man at the Crossroads,* made for

Rockefeller Center in New York City (1933). Originally intended as the artistic focal point of the vast office complex, the mural was covered with a canvas, then destroyed, when Rivera refused to remove a prominent and positive portrait of Lenin. The incident became and remains a major cause célèbre in the history of modern art.

The Rockefeller Center mural was not his first in the Untied States, nor was it to be his last. Rivera had done *Allegory of California* for the Luncheon Club of the Pacific Stock Exchange (1930). This was followed by the *Making of a Fresco* at the San Franscisco Art Institute (1930); his major U.S. achievement, *Detroit Industry*, at the Detroit Institute of Arts (1933); a series of twenty-one fresco panels, *Portrait of America*, at the New Workers School in New York City (1933); and *Pan-American Unity*, at the City College of San Francisco (1940). The Detroit murals were threatened with destruction when first completed and again during the McCarthy era, but were saved by the intervention of the Ford family, which had commissioned the work. Only a few panels of the *Portrait of America* series remain, surviving in museum and private collections. *See also*: Mural Movement in the United States

—*Eric Breitbart*

REFERENCES

Diego Rivera. Detroit: Detroit Institute of Arts, 1986.

Favela, Ramon. *The Early Life and Times of Diego Rivera*. Berkeley: University of California Press, 1989.

Wolfe, Bertram. *The Fabulous Life of Diego Rivera*. New York: Stein and Day, 1963.

Rivkin, B. (1883–1945)

The leading anarchist theorist of literature in the United States was born Baruch-Abraham Weinrebe in Latvia. He emigrated to America in 1911, and as Rivkin soon established himself in the pages of the *Freie Arbeter Shtimme* among other journals. The most trenchent and sympathetic critic of *di yunge*—the new literary lights of the Yiddish world—Rivkin saw in their work the highest cultural and spiritual expression of *Yiddishkayt*, the culmination of a millennium of Jewish culture. In his key work, *Di Grunt Tendentsin fun Yiddishe Literatur* (Basic Tendencies of Yiddish Literature, 1947), Rivkin formulated a theory of the Yiddish language as mental homeland within the diaspora, an abstract conception of Jewish socialism. Under the probable influence of his contemporary, Mikhail Bakhtin, Rivkin also advanced a conception of Jewish holidays as "spectacle," the periodical re-creation of a moment out of time. In all, he struggled to free Left cultural discussion from the confinements of realism and, like the German Marxist theologian, Ernst Bloch, to formulate a "philosophy of hope" in an era of despair. While leaning toward anarcho-Zionism, Rivkin remained to the end of his life hopeful for a Jewish cultural renewal within the Soviet Union. *See also*: Anarchism, Yiddish Left

—*Paul Buhle*

REFERENCES

B. Rivkin, Lebn un Shaf. Chicago: Farlag L. M. Shtein, 1953.

Robeson, Paul Leroy (1898–1976)

The extraordinarily multitalented Robeson was the first world-famous singer and actor to become a political activist during his peak performing years. Robeson's father, a runaway slave who became a minister in Princeton, New Jersey, exerted a strong influence on the young Robeson, instilling in him a quiet dignity, a love for African-American culture, and an all-embracing humanism.

An outstanding scholar-athlete at Rutgers University in 1915–19, Robeson went on to become one of the world's leading concert singers, stage actors, and film stars in the 1920s, 1930s and 1940s. During the period 1927–39, when he was based in London, his artistic growth led him to study world cultures and to support social and political movements. He sang concerts to benefit trade unions, especially the Welsh coal-miners' union, and he came to see the connection between the struggles of the British working class and those of the oppressed colonial peoples. Robeson was introduced to socialist ideas through his friendship with George Bernard Shaw and his acquaintanceship with several leaders of the British Labour Party. As a result, Robeson studied the classic Marxist writings and became attracted to the basic premises of communism.

In the early 1930s Robeson met many African students in London and developed a deep appreciation of the close links between the African and African-American cultures, learning several African languages. He also met Jawaharlal Pandit Nehru of India, with whom he formed a lasting friendship. Prompted by the desire to extend his artistic range, Robeson studied many other languages and cultures throughout the 1930s and 1940s, mastering Russian, Chinese, Hebrew, and most European languages. This focus on the centrality of culture went hand-in-hand with Robeson's increasing radicalism—a duality that continued for the remainder of his career.

Robeson responded to the rise of German fascism by becoming one of the world's leading antifascists. Invited to the Soviet Union in 1934 by Soviet filmmaker Sergei Eisenstein, Robeson was almost assaulted by Nazi storm troopers in Berlin as he changed trains on his way to Moscow. In the USSR he was deeply impressed by the lack of racial prejudice and by flourishing diverse cultures in the Soviet republics. These experiences and the communist leadership of the worldwide antifascist and anticolonialist struggles were the basis of his unwavering support for the Soviet people in their attempts to build socialism. The fact that Robeson viewed the Soviet Union and the world communist movement as reliable allies of the colonial liberation movements led him to form a close alliance with Communists despite his private misgivings about the Stalinist purges of 1936–38 and his disagreement with the Communist Left's exaggerated emphasis on class priorities over "nationalist" priorities in the Third World.

In 1938 Robeson demonstrated his commitment to the fight against fascism by going to Spain to sing and speak in support of the Spanish Republic in its civil war against General Francisco Franco's fascist rebellion. The profound effect this experience had on Robeson's radicalization was reflected in his dramatic statement at that time: "The artist must elect to fight for freedom or for slavery. I have made my choice; I had no alternative." By 1939, Robeson was a key figure symbolizing on a world scale the unity of the antifascist and anticolonial struggles.

In the fall of 1939 Robeson returned from England to the United States, where he continued his highly successful concert and theater career while simultaneously becoming a leader of the civil rights movement and a spokesman for left-wing causes. He was the first major performing artist to refuse to perform for segregated audiences and to lead voter registration campaigns in the Deep South. Robeson also played an important role in support of the union-organizing drive of the CIO in the early 1940s, and in bringing black workers into the unions.

In 1946 Robeson challenged President Harry S Truman's refusal to sponsor legislation against lynching by telling him that in the absence of federal protection blacks would exercise their right of armed self-defense. An opponent of the Cold War from its inception, Robeson attended a world peace conference in Paris in 1949 and expressed the view that black Americans should not fight an aggressive war against the Soviet Union on behalf of their own oppressors. In the wake of those remarks, the U.S. government and the media launched an attack of unprecedented ferocity against Robeson that lasted for nine years.

Robeson's passport was revoked in 1950 and was not restored until 1958. Inquiries under the Freedom of Information Act reveal that the Federal Bureau of Investigation, the Central Intelligence Agency, the Department of State, and numerous other U.S. government agencies compiled tens of thousands of documents on Robeson and illegally harassed him over a period of more than twenty years. Robeson was also blacklisted in the entertainment industry and prevented from appearing in professional engagements until 1957. Despite this persecution, Robeson continued to sing and speak in black churches and in the halls of the few surviving left-wing trade unions. He also wrote a book titled *Here I Stand* in collaboration with the black writer and journalist Lloyd L. Brown in which he outlined the program and strategy subsequently adopted by the civil rights movement and foretold the advent of the movement for economic justice.

During the anticommunist witch-hunts of the late 1940s and the 1950s, Robeson defended the rights of Communists and defied congressional committees when they compelled him to testify before them. Although he was not a member of the Communist Party, he refused on constitutional grounds to answer any questions concerning Party membership or affiliation.

Robeson remained publicly neutral concerning the USSR-China rift that began in the late 1950s, maintaining his cordial relations with both countries, and expressed no opinion about Nikita Khrushchev's "secret speech" in 1956 denouncing Stalin's crimes. However, Robeson's political attitude on these issues was conveyed indirectly by his personal friendship with Khrushchev and his enthusiastic support of Khrushchev's domestic and foreign-policy reforms.

In 1958 Robeson's passport was restored on the basis of a Supreme Court decision, and he traveled abroad for five years to reestablish his artistic career. After a successful comeback, Robeson became ill with circulatory disease, and in 1963 he returned to the United States to retire. Contrary to the claims of the media, Robeson was not disillusioned or embittered. As he put it in 1973, three years before his death from a stroke: "Though ill health has compelled my retirement, you can be sure that in my heart I go on singing." Drawing upon lyrics he had made world famous, he continued, "'I must keep laughing instead of crying, I must keep fighting until I'm dying, and Ol' Man River, he just keeps rolling along.'"

—*Paul Robeson Jr.*

REFERENCES

Duberman, Martin. *Paul Robeson*. New York: Alfred A. Knopf, 1989.

Robeson, Paul. *Here I Stand*. Boston: Beacon Press, 1972. (Originally published by Othello Associates, 1958.)

Robeson, Susan. *The Whole World in His Hands*. New York: Citadel Press, 1981.

ROBINSON, EARL (b. 1910)

In the late 1930s and 1940s, no composer was as successful as Earl Robinson in disseminating the values of the United Front to the American public. In songs such as "Joe Hill," "Abe Lincoln," and "The House I Live In," and in cantatas such as *Ballad for Americans* and *The Lonesome Train*, Robinson communicated his perception of America as a great multiethnic nation whose democratic promise had yet to be fulfilled. In these works, for which he is chiefly known, he drew on the revolutionary traditions of 1776 and the Civil War to make the idea of radical change an acceptable modern notion.

Born in Seattle, Robinson attended the University of Washington as a music major. He went to New York in 1934 and joined the Workers Laboratory Theater and the Composers Collective. He wrote revolutionary songs, and sang them to guitar accompaniment, in street-theater productions and on picket lines. He further studied composition with Aaron Copland and Hanns Eisler, adopting a straightforward folk-based style unencumbered by a surfeit of twentieth-century dissonance.

Robinson wrote the music to John Howard Lawson's play *Processional* (1938) and to *Sing for Your Supper* (1939), both Federal Theater Project productions. He based cantatas on the words of Carl Sandburg, Franklin D. Roosevelt, and William O. Douglas. In the '40s he wrote film scores to *A Walk in the Sun, The Roosevelt Story*, and *The House I Live In*, which won an Academy Award. Blacklisted in the 1950s, he taught music at a New York high school. Other works for the stage include: *Sandhog* (1954), from a Theodore Dreiser story; *One Foot in America* (1962), based on two Yuri Suhl books; and *David of Sassoun* (1978), on Armenian legends. Individual songs that became popular were the antiracist "Free and Equal Blues," "Black and White," and "Hurry Sundown."

In the 1970s, Robinson adopted a New Age outlook, adding to his Old Left consciousness such new subjects as American Indians, ecology, reincarnation, gay liberation, and radical theology. *To the Northwest Indians* (1974), an orchestra piece with narration;

Listen for the Dolphin (1981) and *Song of Atlantis* (1983), both stage works; and the cantatas *A Natural Human, I Been Thinkin' About J. C.*, and *A Concert for Francis* (*of the Saint Variety*), all from the mid-1980s, exemplify these later concerns.

Though mostly drawn to composition with texts, Robinson also wrote concertos for banjo and piano, band pieces, and orchestral works. Either by himself or with vocal ensembles he has recorded his own material and many American folk songs. As a one-man performer of his songs he has become an almost legendary figure in Left and folk-music circles. *See also*: Blitzstein, Marc; Composers Collective; Workers Laboratory Theater

—*Eric A. Gordon*

REFERENCES

Denisoff, R. Serge. *Great Day Coming: Folk Music and the American Left*. Baltimore: Penguin, 1973.

"Earl Robinson." *The New Grove Dictionary of Music*. New York: Groves Dictionary of Music, 1986.

Lieberman, Robbie. *People's Songs, American Communism, and the Politics of Culture, 1930–50*. Urbana: University of Illinois Press, 1988.

ROCKER, RUDOLF (1873–1958)

The leading anarchist intellectual of later decades in the immigrant milieus, and easily the most distinguished essayist in Yiddish anarchist circles, Rocker was also the only gentile intellectual to become a leader of Jewish anarchists.

Growing up an orphan in Mainz, Germany, he ran away from his Catholic orphanage several times, eventually to become an itinerant bookbinder. A self-educated anarchist, he became active in German circles and fled to Paris in 1892, just ahead of the police. From there he went on to London's East End, where he completed his transition to "Yiddish" intellectual, to serve the largest available anarchist audience. He joined Morris Winchevsky at the *Arbeter Fraint* and eventually (after a brief and unsuccessful immigration to America in 1898) took over the paper as a center of working-class anarchist Jewish sentiment. Arrested in wartime, Rocker was forcibly returned to Germany, where in the Weimar years he wrote his major study, *Nationalism and Culture*. After Hitler's rise to power, Rocker and his wife, activist Milly Witcop, made their way to the United States.

He found anarchism faded, but still holding on to its most treasured possession, the weekly *Freie Arbeter Shtimme*, which had no notable intellectual leadership since the departure of Sh. Yanofsky to the mainstream labor press. Rocker suited the later phase of the *FAS* perfectly. It had moved from agitation to rumination, a mixture of historical introspection, anarchist interpretation of world events, and generalized free thought. He directed its last great public political effort, international relief to Spanish anarchists from the United States, with agitational tours and financial appeals. Rocker became the premier public figure known to outsiders (especially after the deaths of Emma Goldman and Carlo Tresca), the brilliant mind whose essays proved the veracity of anarchist analysis, the tireless speaker at banquets, and the lecturer whose road trips could bring large audiences to anarchist events.

Not surprisingly, remaining sections of Yiddish anarchists, often by this time affiliates of the Workmen's Circle, put their energies into the Rocker Publications Committee, founded in Los Angeles to make Rocker's work available. Perhaps no other section of the radical movement (not excepting, even, the Communist adulation of Stalin or Trotskyist movement of Trotsky) placed so much emphasis on the personality as well as ideas of its leader. He was, as English-language sympathizers observed, a last figure of the Enlightenment in his singular belief in freedom. His *Pioneers of American Freedom* (1949) hailed individualist anarchists and collectivists as part of a tradition of resistance against the tyrannies of the state and its overdetermining technological counterpart. *See also*: Anarchism, Yiddish Left

—*Paul Buhle*

REFERENCES

Konstan, P. [Ahrne Thorn]. "Rudolf Rocker—der Eybik Yunger Kempfer." *Freie Arbeter Shtimme*, April 10, 1953. [This anniversary issue features several other essays on Rocker.]

Reichert, William O. *Partisans of Freedom: A Study in American Anarchism*. Bowling Green, Ohio: Bowling Green Popular Press, 1966.

Rocker, Rudolf. *In Shturem*. London: London Group "Freie Arbetershtimme," 1952.

ROSENBERG CASE

The Rosenberg-Sobell "atom spy" case is one of the most famous political trials in American history. The defendants were left-wingers and in 1950, when they were arrested, the United States was already well into the period of Cold War anticommunist hysteria. Moreover, both the public and the establishment were still shaken by the recent news that the Soviet Union had tested its first A-bomb, ending the American monopoly. With the outbreak of the Korean War that summer, widespread civil defense preparations for a Soviet atomic bomb attack heightened fears.

On February 2, 1950, British physicist Klaus Fuchs, who had worked in America on the A-bomb project during World War II, was arrested in England as a Soviet spy. Fuchs confessed, said his Communist sympathies had motivated him, and received a fourteen-year sentence.

On May 23, front-page headlines announced an FBI triumph: Harry Gold, a thirty-nine-year-old Philadelphia chemist, had confessed he was Fuchs's American accomplice. On June 16, David Greenglass, an ex-GI, was arrested for giving A-bomb data to Gold while stationed at Los Alamos during the war. Greenglass, a twenty-eight-year-old New York City machinist, was described as a former member of the Young Communist League.

Julius Rosenberg, brother-in-law of Greenglass and his former partner in a small Manhattan machine shop, was arrested on July 17. Rosenberg, a thirty-two-year-old engineer who had been fired from a government job on allegations of Communist Party membership, ridiculed the spy charges and insisted on his innocence. On August 11, Ethel Rosenberg, Julius's wife and David Greenglass's sister, was also arrested; she was said to have been "affiliated with Communist activities." Finally on August 18 Morton Sobell, a City College of New York (CCNY) classmate of Julius's, was arrested in Texas after, it later was disclosed, being kidnapped in Mexico City by Mexican secret police in collusion with FBI agents.

The trial of Julius Rosenberg, Ethel Rosenberg, and Morton Sobell for conspiracy to commit espionage opened March 6, 1951, in Manhattan's federal courthouse and lasted only fourteen trial days. In his opening statement, U.S. Attorney Irving Saypol told the jury: "Sobell and Julius Rosenberg, classmates together in college, dedicated themselves to the cause of Communism. . . . This love of Communism and the Soviet Union soon led them into a Soviet espionage ring." Saypol declared that through Ethel's brother, David Greenglass, the Rosenbergs had stolen "this one weapon that might well hold the key to the survival of this nation and means the peace of the world, the atomic bomb."

The principal prosecution witness, David Greenglass, who had pleaded guilty, was questioned by assistant prosecutor Roy M. Cohn. Corroborated by his wife, Ruth, who had not been indicted, David testified that in 1944 and 1945 he had prepared sketches and written information on the Los Alamos atom bomb project for Julius Rosenberg. In the key espionage episode of the trial, the Greenglasses related that Julius Rosenberg had cut a Jello box side in two and given one half to Ruth and that some months later Harry Gold had appeared at their Albuquerque apartment, identifying himself with the other half of the box and a password with the name "Julius." Gold claimed that he had obtained the password and box half from Anatoli Yakovlev, a former Soviet vice-consul who had left the United States years before. Another witness, Max Elitcher, a CCNY classmate of Julius's, said that over a four-year period the latter had tried, unsuccessfully, to recruit him as a spy and had mentioned that Sobell was "also helping." Elizabeth Bentley, a then widely known self-confessed spy, appeared as an "expert" witness on Communism and also told of phone calls from a man she knew only as "Julius." The Rosenbergs denied all spy charges and refused to discuss their political affiliations. Sobell did not testify but pleaded not guilty. All three were convicted.

Sentencing the Rosenbergs to death, Judge Irving R. Kaufman said their "conduct in putting into the hands of the Russians the A-bomb" had already caused "the Communist aggression in Korea, with the resultant casualties exceeding 50,000 and who knows but that millions more of innocent people may pay the price of your treason."

Sobell was sentenced to thirty years for alleged nonatomic espionage. David Greenglass received fifteen years. The mass media was monolithic in its unquestioning acceptance of the government's case. The Communist *Daily Worker* deplored the sentences, but the Party initially stayed aloof from the affair.

In August 1951 the *National Guardian* began a series of seven articles on the trial by William A. Reuben that posed the question: "Is This the Dreyfus Case of Cold-War America?" Soon after, the National Committee to Secure Justice in the Rosenberg Case was organized.

The committee published the trial record and many who read it noted aspects that aroused their doubts: References to the defendants' left-wing politics permeated the proceedings. The espionage evidence consisted of alleged conversations that were essentially irrefutable. No documentary proof of espionage was introduced. The case against Ethel rested on the claim that she urged Ruth to ask David for information and typed David's handwritten notes on the atom bomb. David, a machinist with no scientific training, was said by the judge to have provided information that had "altered the course of history." Max Elitcher testified under threat of a perjury indictment (for falsely denying CP membership under oath).

In the United States, clemency advocates were largely leftists, though some liberals lent important support. Both Albert Einstein and Harold Urey made public statements and 2,300 clergy endorsed an appeal. The Rosenbergs' prison correspondence was published. Abroad, particularly in Western Europe, the campaign enlisted a wide spectrum of political opinion, with those requesting clemency ranging from Jean-Paul Sartre and Pablo Picasso to the pope and the president of France.

The Supreme Court declined to review the case and Judge Kaufman refused to modify his death sentence unless the Rosenbergs confessed and named others. On January 9, 1953, the Rosenbergs appealed to President Truman for clemency, insisting on their innocence. Truman did not act on the appeal and incoming President Eisenhower denied it.

In early June 1953, with the scheduled executions only weeks away, an emissary from Attorney General Herbert Brownell, Jr., visited the Rosenbergs and urged them to confess in return for clemency. They refused, calling their case "the most monstrous frame-up in the history of our country." Their attorney, Emanuel Bloch, filed an appeal claiming newly discovered evidence, but the courts denied it in record time. Rejecting Bloch's application for a stay by a vote of five to four, the Supreme Court recessed for the summer. But Justice William O. Douglas granted a stay based on a new legal point raised by an outside attorney, Fyke Farmer. Chief Justice Fred M. Vinson, at the request of the attorney general, ordered the vacationing Supreme Court justices to reconvene in an extraordinary special term. On June 19 the judges vacated the Douglas stay by a vote of six to three, and President Eisenhower denied a final clemency plea, declaring that "by immeasurably increasing the chances of atomic war, the Rosenbergs may have condemned to death tens of millions of innocent people all over the world." In Paris, London, and other major cities demonstrators protested; thousands gathered in Manhattan near Union Square. That evening, the Rosenbergs were executed in the Sing Sing electric chair.

The American Left did not permit the case to die. Sobell had been sent to the notorious Alcatraz Penitentiary in an effort to break him. With his wife, Helen Sobell, as its leader, a Committee to Secure Justice for Morton Sobell carried on a long campaign that gained worldwide support. Barred from the mass media, the Left fought the battle for public opinion by publishing its own books: William A. Reuben, *The Atom Spy Hoax* (Action Books, 1955); John Wexley, *The Judgment of Julius and Ethel Rosenberg* (Cameron and Kahn, 1955); Malcolm P. Sharp, with an introduction by Harold C. Urey, *Was Justice Done?* (Monthly Review Press, 1956). However, these books were ignored by mainstream reviewers.

A breakthrough in this wall of unofficial censorship came in 1965, when a book arguing that the Rosenbergs were innocent was issued by a major commercial publisher, Doubleday. *Invitation to an Inquest*, by Walter and Miriam Schneir was widely reviewed and discussed in the mass media. The book charged that the FBI had forged a hotel card, misrepresented other evidence, and encouraged witnesses to create perjured testimony. It documented Harry Gold's background as a habitual liar and an accomplished fantasist. Major discoveries were pretrial statements and recorded interviews of Gold by his attorneys that contained numerous discrepancies from his Rosenberg trial testimony. Most important, the material showed that such key details as the Jello box and "Julius" password were missing from Gold's early account. Commented *Newsweek*: "The Rosenbergs lie in an unquiet grave."

Over the next few years, the case was the subject of a play, *Inquest* (1969–70), by Donald Freed, and a TV documentary, "The Unquiet Death of Julius and Ethel Rosenberg," produced by Alvin H. Goldstein and published as a book (1975). Sobell, released in 1969 after serving more than eighteen years, wrote his account, *On Doing Time* (Scribner's, 1975).

In 1974 the sons of the Rosenbergs, Robert and Michael Meeropol (adoptive name), entered the fight to vindicate their parents and later authored a book, *We Are Your Sons*. Under the newly strengthened Freedom of Information Act, they requested FBI and other government files. Support came from the Fund for Open Information and Accountability (FOIA) and the National Committee to Reopen the Rosenberg Case (NCRRC). The ensuing suit, led by attorney Marshall Perlin, has lasted fourteen years. At present, hundreds of thousands of pages of once-secret files have been released, though many are heavily censored and thousands more are still being withheld.

Findings: Judge Kaufman engaged in improper ex parte communications about the case with both prosecutors and the FBI; documents revealing this collusion appear in *The Kaufman Papers* (NCRRC). Ethel Rosenberg was arrested to "serve as a lever" to make Julius talk; the crucial typing evidence against her was concocted by David and Ruth Greenglass only a few days before the trial. The damning "Julius" password was created out of whole cloth at a prison meeting between Gold and David Greenglass arranged by the FBI seven months after their arrests.

On June 23, 1979, the *New Republic* ran a widely publicized piece, "The Hidden Rosenberg Case," by Sol Stern and Ronald Radosh, which asserted that "Julius was a spy" and "Ethel was framed." Subsequently, a book by Radosh and Joyce Milton, *The Rosenberg File* (Holt, Rinehart and Winston, 1983), revised this split decision, alleging that Ethel was Julius's "accomplice." The book, which deplores the death penalty but is critical of the Rosenbergs themselves (they "were not admirable people"), concludes that Julius was "the coordinator of an extensive espionage operation." It was embraced as definitive by both conservative and liberal critics and even by one on the Left (James Weinstein, editor of *In These Times*).

But the conclusions of Radosh and Milton rest largely on their belief that Julius Rosenberg confessed his espionage exploits and named the members of his spy ring to a prison informer—a thief, pimp, and con man named Jerome Tartakow. Aside from the improbability of this premise, the book suffers from sloppy scholarship and numerous factual errors, according to historians who studied its documentation. In October 1983, when Radosh, Milton, and Stern and the Schneirs appeared at New York's Town Hall in a debate jointly sponsored by the *Nation* and the *New Republic*, the event received national mass media coverage.

As of the late 1980s, the court case against the Rosenbergs and Sobell had been discredited. Those who believed in guilt, however, looked beyond the trial to postulate a large Rosenberg spy ring. They cited as proof reports from the informer Tartakow; FBI hints of secret evidence; and "suspicious" incidents, especially the recent discovery that two friends of Julius's lived and worked in the Soviet Union for decades under assumed names. Unresolved questions on both sides of the affair remain. Meanwhile, the Rosenbergs' own writings show them as remarkably sane, courageous, and politically committed people. *See also*: Communist Party, FBI, Alger Hiss Case, McCarthyism

—*Walter Schneir, Miriam Schneir*

REFERENCES

"Were the Rosenbergs Framed?" Transcript of a public debate held October 20, 1983, at Town Hall, New York City (Nation Institute, print or tape).

Markowitz, Gerald E. "How Not to Write History: A Critique of Radosh and Milton's *The Rosenberg File*." *Science and Society* 48 (Spring 1984).

Meeropol, Robert, and Michael Meeropol. *We Are Your Sons*. 2d ed. Urbana: University of Illinois Press, 1986.

Pessen, Edward. "The Rosenberg Case Revisited: A Critical Essay on a Recent Scholarly Examination." *New York History* 65 (January 1984).

Schneir, Walter, and Miriam Schneir. *Invitation to an Inquest*. With three new chapters. New York: Pantheon, 1983.

———. "The Other 'Julius': The Story the 'Red Spy Queen' Didn't Tell." *Nation*, June 25, 1983.

Ruskin Colony

A "Cooperative Village" first located in 1894 in Ruskin, Tennessee, near Tennessee City, this was one of the most highly publicized of the utopian communities of the 1890s and one of the centers of J. A. Wayland's socialist journalism empire.

Ruskin Colony was conceived by Wayland (1854–1912), an Indiana native who, after a successful career as proprietor of country newspapers in Indiana and Missouri and success in job printing and real estate speculation, became a socialist in Colorado in the 1880s. Wayland then began a career as America's premier socialist journalist. He aspired to convince Americans of the advantages of socialism. His first paper, the *Coming Nation*, was started at Greenburg, Indiana, in 1893 and grew quickly to 25,000 subscribers. Wayland hit upon a scheme to prove to his fellow citizens the viability of socialism by using the paper as the main industry in a socialized town. He moved the paper and some of its employees to Western Tennessee and accepted members who paid $500 to join the Ruskin Cooperative Association. Wayland wrangled with the cooperators and was thrown out after one year. The members took over operation of the paper, moved the colony to a better site several miles away, built some small cottage industry, and thrived for a while on the constant influx of new members and new capital. The *Coming Nation* was edited after Wayland by A. S. Edwards, then by Herbert Casson, and it and the Ruskin Colony started to fail in 1899. An attempt to save it was made by amalgamation with another group in a move to Ware County, Georgia, where the colony disbanded in 1901. *See also*: *Appeal to Reason*, Utopianism

—*Elliott Shore*

REFERENCES

Broom, Isaac. *The Last Days of the Ruskin Cooperative Association*. Chicago: Charles H. Kerr, 1902.

Shore, Elliott. *Talkin' Socialism*. Lawrence: University Press of Kansas, 1988.

Russian Americans

Russian immigrants, among all Eastern European groups settled in the United States, stand out in their persistent, enveloping relationship with their homeland. This predilection, and the central importance of Russian events to Left politics, permitted Russian-American leaders a moment of significance far exceeding their own political skills or experience. Ties with the Russian homeland, along with government repression and changing immigration patterns, also guaranteed the early collapse of the Russian-American Left into a political nonentity.

Statistics detailing the size of the Russian immigrant population vary enormously according to definitions of the group. Treating only the major sector of immigrants, namely Russian-language speakers with adherence to Russian Orthodoxy (or to a dissident sect, i.e., the Dukhobors) and fidelity to Russian culture, the figure may be estimated at several hundred thousand arriving in America from 1880 through 1955. During the first decades of the twentieth century, more than 90 percent were unskilled or semiskilled laborers and their families. They concentrated primarily in the industrial cities of New York, Pennsylvania, Illinois, New Jersey, Connecticut, and Massachusetts, adjacent to coal mines, iron and steel mills, slaughterhouses, and the meat-packing industry. A sizable group migrated to agricultural colonies. The minority of professionals, students, and the "intelligentsia" settled in New York City and found employment in the garment industry. In all, illiteracy was high, nearly 40 percent in 1917. The postrevolutionary immigration of military officers, Orthodox churchmen, aristocrats, and intellectuals were far more literate and did not enter the unskilled labor market. In addition, a significant number of Russian immigrants, perhaps nearly half of all immigrants, returned to their homeland during the 1920s–1930s.

Left-wing activity from its beginnings featured a cosmopolitan intelligentsia with a reputation for enthusiastic revolutionary attitudes and condescension toward the ordinary Russian-American worker. *Znamia*, the first of the socialist publications, appeared in New York City in 1889, and the next year a Russian Social Democratic Society was formed. Events in Russia tended to dominate concerns, from protests against czarist outrages to particular political quarrels among the Russian immigrants. As with other Eastern European nationalities, the Russian Revolution of 1905 played a crystalizing role. Newly arriving Russian radicals reshaped and expanded group activities though activists themselves often remained only a few years in the United States. In 1906 a group of young professional revolutionaries conducted a palace coup within the small social democratic organization, establishing new chapters in a scattering of eastern cities. These small groups of Russian socialists formed the nuclei of the future Russian federation of the American Socialist Party. The only attempt to establish a national press failed when the *Russian-American Worker* (1908) proved far too theoretical for its intended audience.

The syndicalistic, anarchistic, or merely economistic immigrant radicals had vastly more success. Allying themselves with the Industrial Workers of the World through the Union of Russian Workers (*Soiuz Russkikh Robochikh*), they accumulated up to 10,000 members by the 1910s. Establishing numerous workers' clubs and libraries as well as an employment service of sorts, they maintained 200 branches and several newspapers.

In 1909 a Russian Federation became affiliated with the SP, attaining a membership of 500 by 1913. The Russian socialist press organ, *Novyi Mir*, founded in 1911, was at first edited by Russian revolutionary veteran Lev Deutch, a student of Plekhanov and avowed supporter of the Second International. With some success, the Russian Socialists urged improvement of working conditions, support of strikes, and the flourishing of educational and recreational activities. The lure of "dancing till dawn" for causes such as political prisoners in Siberia created great community "spectacles," especially in the New York area. Picnics and other social events, often held in conjunction with the Jewish, Ukrainian, or Finnish Socialist Federations, drew fairly widely upon a nonradical, proletarian public. In 1917 *Novyi Mir* had engaged the talents of two promising intellectuals, N. I. Bukharin and Lev Trotsky, destined to change Russian (but not American or Russian-American) history. Until the Russian Revolution broke out, these two remained within the socialist mainstream of fervently antiwar essays and lectures published and sponsored by the Russian Federation.

The October 1917 Russian Revolution precipitated a second palace coup within the Russian émigré Left. Inspired by events in the homeland, the Bolshevik supporters seized *Novyi Mir* and its allied institutions. Bukharin (by then editor of *Novyi Mir*) and Trotsky toured the country rallying immigrant support for the Bolsheviks. Membership in the federation rose from 5,000 in 1915 to 12,000 in 1919, with a majority joining after 1917. Simultaneously, the Bolshevik-dominated federation began expressing displeasure with the SP. Despite the SP's bold antiwar position, critics assailed "bourgeois" tendencies. Even as early as 1917, Russian-American Left leaders began calling for a split. In 1919 *Novyi Mir* endorsed the formation of the Communist Party of America. Its current leaders (following the exodus of Bukharin and Trotsky) became, almost overnight, foremost hard-line Bolshevik supporters and inveterate factionalists within the American Left. By 1919, a substantial group of Communist supporters broke ranks with the

Communist Party of America to support the more American-based Communist Labor Party. The next year, *Novyi Mir* was suppressed by government action, reappearing in 1926.

The Palmer Raids and continuous government repression during the 1920s fell with unmatched severity upon Russian-American radicals. The Union of Russian Workers, despite retaining its nonpartisan status among radicals, felt the same pressure as Bolsheviks. Russian workers were arrested in their homes, at work, at political clubs, even while attending church services. In short, nearly the entire membership of the CP section was placed behind bars. As many as 5,000 individuals found themselves on Ellis Island, destined for deportation. Remaining Russian émigré Communists, reinforced in their belief in an "underground" movement, lost what little remained of political continuity within the Russian-American community at large.

The Russian-American Left reemerged at a unique disadvantage. Bereft of leaders, either deported or gone home willingly, confronted with new "White Guard" immigrants numbering in the tens of thousands, Russian radicals had few resources for left-wing politics. Through broad organizations such as Friends of the Soviet Union, however, they helped raise several million dollars for Soviet agricultural and industrial communes, also training thousands of Russian-American workers for return as skilled craftsmen. Russian "agents," no doubt the most active and effective agents ever utilized by the Russian government in the United States, searched for individuals willing to work as laborers, mechanics, and farmers on Russian communes.

To the degree possible, the Russian-American Left also focused upon the internal life of the remaining immigrant communities. The Party effort at "Bolshevization," in the middle 1920s, had little apparent effect. Russian-Americans remained loyal to the Left to the degree that they remained self-conscious of their immigrant status. By 1935, *Novyi Mir* had shifted from being the official Russian organ of the Communist movement to a "daily workers' paper." The establishment of children's schools, under the auspices of the International Workers Order, had become a priority by the 1930s. The parent IWO affiliate, the Russian National Mutual Aid Society (RNOV), achieved maximum support within the community at this time, reporting a membership of 25,000. Through these institutions, Russian Americans conducted a vigorous antifascist campaign directed in no small part against the Russian-American Right. RNOV also cooperated in efforts to aid Russian immigrant workers in a scattering of trades, notably the International Longshore Union, Carpenters, International Ladies Garment Workers Union, Fur Workers, United Mine Workers, and Amalgamated Clothing Workers. After a final burst of energy during the Second World War, the Russian-American Left fell victim one final time to conservative immigration, generalized Cold War sentiments, and associated repression. *See also*: Anarchism, Communist Party, Socialist Party

—*Maria Woroby*

REFERENCES

Draper, Theodore. *Roots of American Communism*. New York: Viking, 1957.

Elmer, Ya. *Russkie Rabochie v Amerike*. Philadelphia: RNOV, 1935.

Okuntsov, Ivan. *Russkaia Emigratsiia v Severnoi i Iuzhnoi Amerike*. Buenos Aires: Sembrador, 1967.

Rustin, Bayard (1910–87)

A major African-American civil rights leader who worked behind the scenes, primarily in managerial and counseling capacities, Rustin began his career as a radical exponent of nonviolent resistance to social injustice and war. But from the mid-1960s onward, he moved to increasingly conservative views. At the time of his death, for example, he was chairman of the Social Democrats USA, an anticommunist group primarily supported by conservative labor leaders, and he was executive committee chairman of Freedom House, a neoconservative institution. Rustin's major sinecure, however, was as cochairman of the A. Philip Randolph Institute, a prestigious educational, civil rights, and labor organization.

Rustin was the son of West Indian immigrants and had close family members associated with the Quakers and the NAACP. After taking courses at universities but never receiving a degree, Rustin left his native Pennsylvania for New York City. Attracted by the antiracist activitism of the Communist Party, he joined the Young Communist League in 1936 and two years later he was a YCL organizer on the campus of City College of New York, where he took classes. His major concerns were racial segregation in the U.S. military and the antiwar movement. When the Nazi invasion of the USSR led the CP to abandon its antiwar line and to desist agitating about segregation in the military, Rustin resigned from the YCL. He soon became a youth organizer for A. Philip Randolph's March On Washington.

Rustin's relationship with Randolph would be decisive over the long term, but he severely criticized Randolph when the march was called off following President Franklin Roosevelt's executive order banning racial discrimination in war production. Rustin now joined the staff of the Fellowship of Reconciliation (FOR), through which he was to engage in active civil disobedience for more than a decade. In 1942 he was arrested by Tennessee police for refusing to move to the rear of a segregated interstate bus, and in 1943 he received a two-and-a-half-year term for draft resistance. While in prison in Lewisburg, Pennsylvania, he honed his singing talents and learned to play guitar and lute. While a member of the YCL, he had helped support himself by singing in nightclubs and in the years to come his melodious singing would become familiar to many civil rights activists.

In April 1947 Rustin organized the Journey of Reconciliation, a FOR project to test the Supreme Court ruling prohibiting segregation on interstate buses. This was the first "Freedom Ride" and set the precedent for the more famous Freedom Rides of 1961. In Chapel Hill, North Carolina, Rustin was arrested and sent to work on a chain gang. His articles about that experience were a catalyst in the eventual abolition of that state's chaingang system.

A year after the Freedom Ride, Rustin was working with A. Philip Randolph in the League of Nonviolent Civil Disobedience Against Military Segregation. This addressed an old wound by attempting to pressure President Harry Truman to strictly enforce and then expand FDR's earlier executive order. That same year Rustin traveled to India, where his pacifism was enhanced by a first-hand experience of the accomplishments and nuances of the Gandhian doctrine of nonviolent resistance. Yet another achievement was his role in creating the Committee to Support South African Resistance, later to become the influential American Committee on Africa.

Rustin was named executive director of the War Resister's League in 1953. Two years later with the Rev. Glen Smiley of the FOR staff, Rustin became an adviser to the Rev. Martin Luther King, Jr., first during the Montgomery Bus Boycott and then in the launching of the Southern Christian Leadership Conference (SCLC). Rustin also served as organizer of King's successful legal defense when King was charged with income tax evasion. Their working relationship was temporarily suspended in 1960. The circumstances were that SCLC, in cooperation with A. Philip Randolph's forces, planned to disrupt the national conventions of both political parties. King was informed that if the preparations continued, Rustin's YCL membership and his homosexuality would be used to tar King's movement. King himself would be accused of having a homosexual relationship with his aide. Rustin voluntarily resigned before King came to a decision on what to do. The demonstrations were abandoned.

As the concept for a new March on Washington began to take shape in 1962, King again turned to Rustin. This time King and Randolph had the courage to resist Red-baiting and homophobia. Rustin's organizational skills were instrumental in bringing more than a quarter-million people to the Lincoln Memorial on August 28, 1963. In a move that indicated future behavior, Rustin persuaded the administration to cooperate with a march it had originally opposed. Rustin considered this a triumph, but his critics felt he had allowed the protest to be co-opted.

In 1963 Rustin also became head of the A. Philip Randolph Institute, primarily funded by the AFL-CIO, and he used his position to advance the view that future African-American progress was dependent on alliances with organized labor, churches, and liberals. He soon assailed the Black Power movement and other tendencies he felt fostered racial divisions. His search for coalitions led him to oppose nearly every tactic advanced by radicals, including King's Poor People's Campaign and affirmative action. In 1983 he would oppose the Jobless March on Washington.

Rustin's foreign policy views were even more conservative and contradictory. He condemned most national liberation movements because of their Russian or Chinese support and their violent means, but he did not condemn the American war in Vietnam. He vociferously demanded human rights reforms in the USSR, but was an avid supporter of Israel, despite Israel's treatment of Palestinians, its invasion of Lebanon, and its military aid to the Union of South Africa. Detractors charged that Rustin had been consciously or unconsciously "bought off" by Cold War liberals. By the time of his death, his influence on activists concerned about American policies in Latin America and Asia and his influence on African-American radicals was virtually nonexistent.

Judgment on his mixed political legacy was further complicated by sexual politics. Although his sexual orientation had been a political issue at a crucial time in his career, Rustin did not publicly acknowledge his homosexuality until the last year of his life. Gay activists sympathized with his decision to avoid the issue prior to the gay liberation movement but were disappointed that he did not openly embrace and assist their movement in the 1970s and 1980s. *See also*: Civil Rights; Pacifism; Randolph, A. Philip

—*Dan Georgakas*

REFERENCES

Boyd, Herb. "Bayard Rustin: A Mixed Legacy." Obituary. *Guardian*, September 9, 1987.

Rustin, Bayard. *Down the Line: The Collected Writings of Bayard Rustin*. Chicago: Quadrangle, 1971.

———. *Strategies for Freedom*. New York: Columbia University Press, 1976.

Viorst, Milton. *Fire in the Streets: America in the 1960s*. New York: Simon & Schuster, 1979.

RUTHENBERG, CHARLES E. (1882–1927)

Socialist leader and a founder of the Communist movement, Ruthenberg spent his early years in Cleveland, completing his schooling at age fourteen. Working in business, he became an expert bookkeeper and sales manager until signing on full-time with the Socialist Party in 1917. Ruthenberg first became enamored with the urban reformism of Tom Johnson's "individual initiative." Early in 1908, he borrowed Marx's *Capital* from the Cleveland Public Library; the next year he joined the Socialist Party, and by 1910 became recording secretary of the Cleveland central committee.

Ruthenberg first ran for governor in 1912, a year when Ohio led all other states in total Socialist votes. A delegate to the party's national convention at Indianapolis, he supported the Left on all controversial questions. He thereby became at once a pronounced master of organization and an ardent figure of the left wing. Bitterly opposing American entry into war, and remaining at the helm of political leadership, Ruthenberg became the "most arrested" radical figure of the nation. Taken by federal authorities for antiwar pronouncements in 1917, he was placed under arrest three years later under Ohio's criminal syndicalism laws, then seized by authorities in New York State, and again by federal officials in Michigan in 1922.

Meantime, Ruthenberg had become a major convert to Leninism, a leading spirit in the division of the socialist movement, and the general secretary of the Communist Party, a position he held until his death. It would be fair to say that, as a major participant in the factional contests of the 1920s, Ruthenberg urgently sought to place the young Communist movement on solid organizational and political footing. He would have doubtless remained a foremost figure but for his sudden death in March 1927, of peritonitis. At Ruthenberg's request, his ashes were interred in the Kremlin wall. *See also*: Communist Party, Socialist Party

—*Arthur Zipser*

REFERENCES

Johnson, Oakley. *The Day Is Coming: Life of Charles E. Ruthenberg*. New York: International Publishers, 1957.

S

Sacco-Vanzetti Case

At 3:00 P.M. on April 15, 1920, a paymaster and his guard were carrying a factory payroll of $15,776 through the main street of South Braintree, Massachusetts, a small industrial town south of Boston. Two men standing by a fence suddenly pulled out guns and fired on them. The gunmen snatched up the cash boxes dropped by the mortally wounded pair and jumped into a waiting automobile. The bandit gang, numbering four or five in all, sped away, eluding their pursuers. At first this brutal murder and robbery, not uncommon in post–World War I America, aroused only local interest.

Three weeks later, on the evening of May 5, 1920, two Italians, Nicola Sacco and Bartolomeo Vanzetti, fell into a police trap that had been set for a suspect in the Braintree crime. Although originally not under suspicion, both men were carrying guns at the time of their arrest and when questioned by the authorities they lied. As a result they were held and eventually indicted for the South Braintree crimes. Vanzetti was also charged with an earlier holdup attempt that had taken place on December 24, 1919, in the nearby town of Bridgewater. These events were to mark the beginning of twentieth-century America's most notorious political trial.

Contrary to the usual practice of Massachusetts courts, Vanzetti was tried first in the summer of 1920 on the lesser of the two charges, the failed Bridgewater robbery. Despite a strong alibi supported by many witnesses, Vanzetti was found guilty. Most of Vanzetti's witnesses were Italians who spoke English poorly, and their trial testimony, given largely in translation, failed to convince the American jury. Vanzetti's case had also been seriously damaged when he, for fear of revealing his radical activities, did not take the stand in his own defense.

For a first criminal offense in which no one was hurt, Vanzetti received a sentence that was much harsher than usual, ten to fifteen years. This signaled to the two men and their supporters a hostile bias on the part of the authorities that was political in nature and pointed to the need for a new defense strategy in the Braintree trial.

On the advice of the anarchist militant and editor Carlo Tresca, a new legal counsel was brought in—Fred H. Moore, the well-known socialist lawyer from the West. He had collaborated in many labor and Industrial Workers of the World trials and was especially noted for his important role in the celebrated Ettor-Giovannitti case, which came out of the 1912 Lawrence, Massachusetts, textile strike.

The arrest of Sacco and Vanzetti had coincided with the period of the most intense political repression in American history, the "Red Scare" 1919–20. The police trap they had fallen into had been set for a comrade of theirs, suspected primarily because he was a foreign-born radical. While neither Sacco nor

Vanzetti had any previous criminal record, they were long recognized by the authorities and their communities as anarchist militants who had been extensively involved in labor strikes, political agitation, and antiwar propaganda and who had had several serious confrontations with the law. They were also known to be dedicated supporters of Luigi Galleani's Italian-language journal *Cronaca Sovversiva*, the most influential anarchist journal in America, feared by the authorities for its militancy and its acceptance of revolutionary violence. *Cronaca*, because of its uncompromising antiwar stance, had been forced to halt publication immediately upon the entry of the U.S. government into World War I in 1917; its editors were arrested and at war's end deported to Italy, in 1919. During this period the government's acts of repression, often illegal, were met in turn by the anarchists' attempts to incite social revolution, and at times by retaliatory violence; the authorities and *Cronaca* were pitted against each other in a bitter social struggle just short of open warfare. A former editor of *Cronaca* was strongly suspected of having blown himself up during an *attentat* on Attorney General Palmer's home in Washington, D.C. on June 2, 1919, an act that led Congress to vote funds for antiradical investigations and launch the career of J. Edgar Hoover as the director of the General Intelligence Division in the Department of Justice. The Sacco-Vanzetti case would become one of his first major responsibilities. In 1920, as the Italian anarchist movement was trying to regroup, Andrea Salsedo, a comrade of Sacco and Vanzetti, was detained and, while in custody of the Department of Justice, hurled to his death. On the night of their arrest, authorities found in Sacco's pocket a draft of a handbill for an anarchist meeting that featured Vanzetti as the main speaker. In this treacherous atmosphere, when initial questioning by the police focused on their radical activities and not on the specifics of the Braintree crime, the two men lied in response. These falsehoods created a "consciousness of guilt" in the minds of the authorities, but the implications of that phrase soon became a central issue in the Sacco-Vanzetti case: Did the lies of the two men signify criminal involvement in the Braintree murder and robbery, as the authorities claimed, or did they signify an understandable attempt to conceal their radicalism and protect their friends during a time of national hysteria concerning foreign-born radicals, as their supporters were to claim?

Their new lawyer, Moore, completely changed the nature of the legal strategy. He decided it was no longer possible to defend Sacco and Vanzetti solely against the criminal charges of murder and robbery. Instead he would have them frankly acknowledge their anarchism in court, try to establish that their arrest and prosecution stemmed from their radical activities, and dispute the prosecution's insistence that only hard, nonpolitical evidence had implicated the two men in common crimes. Moore would try to expose the prosecution's hidden motive: its desire to aid the federal and military authorities in suppressing the Italian anarchist movement to which Sacco and Vanzetti belonged.

Moore's defense of the two men soon became so openly and energetically political that its scope quickly transcended its local roots. He organized public meetings, solicited the support of labor unions, contacted international organizations, initiated new investigations, and distributed tens of thousands of defense pamphlets throughout the United States and the world. Much to the chagrin of some anarchist comrades, Moore would even enlist the aid of the Italian government in the defense of Sacco and Vanzetti, who were still, nominally at least, Italian citizens. Moore's aggressive strategy transformed a little known case into an international cause célèbre.

After a hard-fought trial of six weeks, during which the themes of patriotism and radicalism were often sharply contrasted by the prosecution and the defense, the jury found Sacco and Vanzetti guilty of robbery and murder on July 14, 1921. This verdict marked, however, only the beginning of a lengthy legal struggle to save the two men. It extended until 1927, during which time the defense made many separate motions, appeals, and petitions to both state and federal courts in an attempt to gain a new trial.

Presented in these motions were evidence of perjury by prosecution witnesses, of illegal activities by the police and the federal authorities, a confession to the Braintree crimes by convicted bank robber Celestino Madeiros, and powerful evidence that identified the gang involved in the Braintree affair as the notorious Morelli Gang. All were ruled on and rejected by Judge Webster Thayer, the same judge who earlier had so severely sentenced Vanzetti. Judge Thayer would even rule on a motion accusing *himself* of judicial prejudice. His conduct—or misconduct—during the trials and the appeals became another of the controversial issues surrounding the case, but it, too, would prove insufficient to bring about a new trial.

From the beginning, Moore's strategy of politicizing the trial in tradition-bound Massachusetts had been controversial and confrontational. His manner of utilizing mass media was quite modern and effective, but it required enormous sums of money, which he spent too freely in the eyes of many of the anarchist comrades of Sacco and Vanzetti, who had to raise most of it painstakingly from working people, twenty-five and fifty cents at a time. Moore's efforts came to be questioned even by the two defendants, when he, contrary to anarchist ideals, offered a large reward to find the real criminals. As a result, in 1924 he was replaced by a respected Boston lawyer, William Thompson, who assumed control of the legal defense for the last three years of the case. Thompson, a Brahmin who wanted to defend the reputation of Massachusetts law as well as the two men, had no particular sympathy for the ideas of the two men, but he later came to admire them deeply as individuals.

Thompson's defense no longer emphasized the political, but these aspects of the case, once they had been set into motion, could not be stopped and continued to gain momentum. Throughout America liberals and well-meaning people of every sort, troubled and outraged by the injustice of the legal process, joined the more politically radical anarchists, socialists, and communists in protesting the verdict against Sacco and Vanzetti. Felix Frankfurter, then a law professor at Harvard, who did more than any individual to rally "respectable" opinion behind the two men, saw the case as a test of the rule of law itself. Ranged against the defenders of Sacco and Vanzetti were conservatives and patriots who wanted to defend the honor of American justice and to uphold law and order. Many of them came to see these protests as an attack upon the "American way of life" on behalf of two common criminals.

On April 9, 1927, after all recourse in the Massachusetts courts had failed, Sacco and Vanzetti were sentenced to death. By then the dignity and the words of the two men had turned them into powerful symbols of social justice for many throughout the world. Public agitation on their behalf by radicals, workers, immigrants, and Italians had become international in scope, and many demonstrations in the world's great cities—Paris, London, Mexico City, Buenos Aires—protested the unfairness of their trial. This great public pressure, combined with influential behind-the-scenes interventions, finally persuaded the governor of Massachusetts, Alvan T. Fuller, to consider the question of executive clemency for the two men. He appointed an advisory committee, the "Lowell Committee," so-called because its most prominent member was A. Lawrence Lowell, president of Harvard University. The committee, in a decision that was notorious for its loose thinking, concluded that the trial and judicial process had been just "on the whole" and that clemency was not warranted. It only fueled controversy over the fate of the two men, and Harvard, because of Lowell's role, became stigmatized, in the words of one of its alumni, as "Hangman's House." "Not every wop has the switch to the electric chair thrown by the president of Harvard."

Sacco and Vanzetti were executed on August 23, 1927, a date that became a watershed in twentieth-century American history. It became the last of a long train of events that had driven any sense of utopian vision out of American life. The workings of American democracy now seemed to many Americans as flawed and unjust as many of the older societies of the world, no longer embodying any bright ideal, but once again serving the interests of the rich and the powerful. American intellectuals were powerfully moved by the case. In his epochal masterpiece, *USA*, John Dos Passos raged in his Camera Eye, "All right you have won . . . America our nation has been beaten by strangers who have turned our language inside out . . . they have built the electric chair and hired the executioner to throw the switch . . . all right we are two nations . . . ," while Edmund Wilson cooly observed that the Sacco-Vanzetti case "revealed the whole anatomy of American life with all its classes, professions, and points of view and all their relations, and it raised almost every fundamental question of our political and social system."

Up to the present, most writers have focused their attention on the legal, social, and cultural dimensions of the Sacco-Vanzetti case. The legal dimension, in particular, has been rather exhaustively considered, and its two major issues—the fairness of the trial and the innocence or guilt of the two men—still dominates most of the literature about the case.

Earlier opinion almost unanimously felt that the two men were innocent and had been unjustly executed, but later revisionist points of view emerged: some totally, if implausibly, defending the verdict as correct; others more plausibly arguing that, based on new ballistics tests and words by Carlo Tresca and Fred Moore, Sacco was guilty, Vanzetti innocent. No single account nor any ballistics test has been able to put all doubts about innocence or guilt completely to rest, despite the two most recent books that have claimed to have done so, while arriving at almost directly opposite conclusions.

Surprisingly, although the Sacco-Vanzetti case is considered the political case par excellence, few accounts have taken the politics of the two men—their anarchism—very seriously and fewer still are knowledgeable about it. As in all great political trials, the figures of Sacco and Vanzetti have been transformed into passionate symbols, symbols that are often rather facile and far from the truth—philosophical anarchists, common criminals, working-class martyrs, dirty wops, communist agitators, dago Christs, "the good shoemaker and the poor fishpeddler." They allow too easily the essence of the case to be overlooked or misunderstood. A full and accurate account of the political dimension—and, in particular, the anarchist dimension—still remains to be written. The importance of the Sacco-Vanzetti case remains not only because it called into question some of the fundamental assumptions of American society, but because it calls into question some of the fundamental assumptions of American history.

—*Robert D'Attilio*

REFERENCES

The Sacco-Vanzetti Case: Transcript of the Record of the Trial of Nicola Sacco and Bartolomeo Vanzetti in the Courts of Massachusetts and Subsequent Proceedings, 1920–7. 5 vols. with supplemental volume. Mamaroneck, N.Y.: P. P. Appel, 1969.

D'Attilio, Robert, and Jane Manthorn, eds. *Sacco-Vanzetti: Developments and Reconsiderations, 1979.* Boston: Boston Public Library, 1979.

Ehrmann, Herbert B. *The Case That Will Not Die.* Boston: Beacon Press, 1969.

Aldino Felicani Sacco-Vanzetti Collection. Boston Public Library.

Sacco-Vanzetti Case Papers. Harvard Law Library.

H. B. Ehrmann Papers. Harvard Law Library.

Department of Justice/FBI Sacco-Vanzetti Papers. National Archives, Washington, D.C.

Massachusetts State Police Sacco-Vanzetti Files. Massachusetts State Archives.

Sailors' Union of the Pacific

The roots of the SUP go back to 1885 when the Coast Seaman's Union was organized under the leadership of such militant socialists as Burnette G. Haskell and Sigismund Danielwicz. Burnette headed a radical grouping in the West calling itself the International Workingmen's Association, named after the defunct First International; and Danielwicz had distinguished himself as an uncompromising yet unsuccessful foe of the anti-Asian racism which afflicted the West Coast labor movement, extending later into the SUP. In the late 1880s leadership of the union was taken over by the vigorous, practical-minded Andrew Furuseth, who engineered an 1891 merger which formed the SUP and went on to create a larger federation called the International Seamen's Union (ISU), affiliated with the AFL. While embracing the narrow "pure-and-simple" trade unionism which dominated the AFL, Furuseth persistently lobbied "progressive" politicians—and in the context of rising labor militancy in the early 1900s—secured the passage of the 1915 Seamen's Act which greatly improved conditions of maritime workers. During the 1920s, however, his orientation proved less effective, and radical dissidents, including members of the IWW and CP, began to challenge ISU leadership.

By the 1930s the ISU was disintegrating in the face of the Depression and the challenge of radicals. In the SUP, Harry Lundeberg, a Norwegian-born syndicalist, assumed leadership, while Australian-born syndicalist Harry Bridges took leadership of the Westcoast Longshoremen. Both played important roles in the West Coast maritime strike of 1934, Bridges in San Francisco, and Lundeberg in Seattle. When the Maritime Federation of the Pacific was created in 1935, Lundeberg was elected to head it. He and Bridges soon came into conflict. While Bridges maintained close ties with the CP and Roosevelt's New Deal, Lundeberg felt this compromised the interests of workers in general and his own membership in particular. In 1937 when the CIO franchise on the West Coast went to Bridges' union and on the East Coast to the National Maritime Union (NMU) in which CP influence was also strong, Lundeberg led the SUP back into the AFL.

An important role was played in the SUP and its allied organization, the Marine Firemen's Union (8,000 and 7,000 members respectively) by a small group of Trotskyist militants who were sharply critical of the reformist orientation of the CP during its Popular Front and pro-Roosevelt period. This was most evident when a dispute arose in 1936–37 over the Copeland Act. This legislation required every seaman to carry a Continuous Discharge Book, a record of employment which cited length of employment with previous shipowners, reasons for discharge from such employment, record of conduct from time of hiring to moment of discharge—all of which earned it the nickname of "the fink book." Only Lundeberg and his allies were prepared to fight uncompromisingly, if unsuccessfully against this Roosevelt-backed legislation, which was militantly opposed in a tough strike spearheaded by the SUP over the objections of the CP, Bridges, and others in the labor movement committed to an alliance with Roosevelt.

Among the Trotskyists who played a prominent role during the 1930s and 1940s were Tom Kerry (later a central leader of the SWP), Joseph Hansen (a future secretary to Leon Trotsky), Frank Lovell (later SWP trade union director), and Barney Mayes (who left the Trotskyist movement after 1938 to find a position in the labor bureaucracy). Active in a later period was Stan Weir, a member of the Workers Party and eventual founder of Singlejack Books, an effort to bring low-cost radical literature to workers in format that would slip into workclothes easily. Lundeberg noted that he was "not a Trotskyite, or any other sort of political emancipator, and never will be" but that Trotskyists such as Tom Kerry were "sincere . . . capable" and would "work day and night" for the union cause. Trotskyists also played an important role in the first of the postwar national maritime strikes in 1946, particularly in the spectacular Oakland general strike, which won back much ground lost during the enforced "no-strike" period of World War II.

Lundeberg adapted completely to the rising tide of Cold War anticommunism which swept the country and the labor movement in the late 1940s just as he had demonstrated a willingness to accommodate racism among his supporters. Such positions put the Trotskyists on a collision course with their erstwhile ally. In 1949–50 Lundeberg and his loyalists, working in collusion with the government and shipowners, saw to it that Trotskyists were expelled from the union, blacklisted, and driven out of the industry. The Seafarer's International Union, with which the SUP became associated in the AFL, developed a widely used Loyalty oath in which prospective members had to swear that they were not members "of the Communist Party, the IWW, or any Trotskyite group." Years later Trotskyist veterans of the SUP argued that the union's dwindling influence and membership was an indication that the deradicalization fostered by

Lundeberg was a recipe for failure. *See also*: Trotskyism

Paul Le Blanc

REFERENCES

Kerry, Tom. *Workers, Bosses, and Bureaucrats.* New York: Pathfinder, 1980.

Lang, Frederick J. [Frank Lovell]. *Maritime, A Historical Sketch and a Workers' Program.* New York: Pioneer, 1943.

Saxton, Alexander. *The Indispensable Enemy: Labor and the Anti-Chinese Movement in California.* Berkeley: University of California Press, 1971.

Schwartz, Stephen. *Brotherhood of the Sea: A History of the Sailors' Union of the Pacific.* New Brunswick: Transaction, 1986.

Weir, Stan. "The Informal Work Group." In *Rank and File, Personal Histories by Working-Class Organizers*, edited by Alice and Staughton Lynd. Boston: Beacon, 1973.

St. John, Vincent (1876–1929)

Nicknamed the Saint by his fellow workers, Vincent St. John helped guide the Industrial Workers of the World through its near demise in 1906–7 to become general secretary-treasurer (1909–15). Born in Newport, Kentucky to Irish-Dutch parents, St. John spent his teens drifting from job to job. Finally settling in Victor, Colorado, he joined the Western Federation of Miners and worked as a hard-rock miner. He was elected president of the WFM's Telluride local in 1901, and led the bitter strikes in Telluride, Leadville, and San Juan. Blacklisted and harassed by state officials, he was arrested and implicated in the murder of Idaho governor Frank Steunenberg. St. John was among the WFM militants instrumental in establishing the IWW in 1905. Along with William E. Trautmann, he led the antipolitical prosyndicalist faction that sought to commit the IWW to revolutionary industrial unionism. At the IWW's second convention, St. John helped wrest control from President Charles Sherman and was elected to the IWW's general executive board as a representative of the WFM. In 1907 he became a formal member of the IWW and served as assistant secretary and general organizer (1907–8). In 1909 he was elected general secretary-treasurer and provided key strategy and strike leadership during the IWW's critical years. St. John authored *The IWW, Its History, Structure and Method (1912)*, which became the IWW's most widely circulated pamphlet. He resigned as general secretary in 1915 to prospect and manage a small mining operation in Arizona. St. John was arrested in the federal government's mass roundup of IWWs in 1917 and spent several years in the federal penitentiary at Leavenworth, Kansas, although he had been inactive in the IWW since 1915. After his release, St. John resumed prospecting until ill health forced him to move to San Francisco. *See also*: Industrial Workers of the World, Western Federation of Mine/Mine, Mill and Smelter Workers

—Sal Salerno

REFERENCES

Dubofsky, Melvyn. *We Shall Be All: A History of the Industrial Workers of the World.* Chicago: Quadrangle, 1969.

The Industrial Worker, June 29, 1929.

Salt of the Earth: see Union-Sponsored Radical Films

San Francisco General Strike

This action of July 16–19, 1934, was an epic moment in the history of the American working class. Although authorized by the city's conservative labor leadership, it was first and foremost an act of rank-and-file solidarity that galvanized more than 100,000 workers in San Francisco and Alameda counties in support of longshoremen and seamen who had struck the entire West Coast. Denounced by local politicians and the press as a Communist-led insurrection, it was accompanied by widespread police and vigilante violence and derided in some quarters as a major defeat for organized labor. But in its aftermath the marine workers won a great victory and the cause of unionism was dramatically enhanced.

The events in San Francisco were part of a larger wave of class conflict that crested in 1934. The year's major strikes were characterized by raw class conflict pitting strikers and their supporters against police, national guardsmen, and, sometimes, vigilantes and "citizens' armies." Political parties of the Left played a major role in several of these upheavals. The Communist Party was particularly active in the West Coast maritime strikes, placing its newspaper, legal apparatus, and human resources at the disposal of the strikers. But it would be easy to exaggerate the Party's role. It was only one factor among many contributing to the extraordinary determination of the maritime strikers, whom one observer described as "redder than any Communist I ever saw."

The general strike had its roots in the struggle of marine workers to rebuild unions such as the International Longshoremen's Association (ILA) and the Sailors' Union of the Pacific, which had been crushed after World War I by the employers' open-shop offensive. In the summer of 1933, responding in part to New Deal legislation that sanctioned the right to organize and engage in collective bargaining, San Francisco dockworkers enthusiastically welcomed the reappearance of the ILA. Led by an outspoken Australian named Harry Bridges, a number of veteran longshoremen with close ties to the CP played a vital role in the union's renaissance and won recognition as the bona fide leaders of the San Francisco local. When the shipowners refused to make any meaningful concessions to the ILA's demand for union-controlled hiring halls and the closed shop, the longshoremen walked out on May 9, 1934. Reluctantly, the conservative leadership of the AFL seamen's unions joined the strike. In another critical development, teamsters rejected their officials' counsel and refused to handle scab cargo. Within a week every port on the West Coast except Los Angeles was shut down tight.

After nearly two months, San Francisco's most powerful employers convinced the city administration that it was time to break the deadlock by force. On July 3, and again on July 5 ("Bloody Thursday"), police attempted to escort truckloads of cargo through massive picket lines on the waterfront. In the face of the sadistic violence and superior firepower of their adversaries, the strikers displayed "insane courage." With two men dead (both shot in the back by police) and downtown San Francisco transformed into a war zone, the governor of California called in the National Guard, and the picketers were driven from the waterfront. But then came the most dramatic moment in what had already been an extraordinary drama. Responding to the maritime unions' call to honor the martyrs of Bloody Thursday, 15,000 to 20,000 people turned out to participate in a massive funeral march. It was, said the *San Francisco Chronicle,* "a stupendous and reverent procession that astounded the city." In its wake the clamor for a citywide walkout became deafening.

Initially, the conservative labor leadership opposed such a move but felt helpless in the face of rank-and-file pressure. At the crucial moment, however, they were able to seize control of a movement they could no longer suppress. When delegates to the San Francisco Labor Council voted overwhelmingly for a general strike, the council's top officials simply appointed themselves to the strike strategy committee and then used their position to prevent the walkout from becoming an all-out war between labor and capital. After watching the strategy committee send streetcarmen back to work and allow all of the city's restaurants to reopen, a marine union spokesman complained that "our general strike seems to be dissolving under our feet. . . . The conservatives, having all the voting power, seem to be attempting to force us back to work immediately."

In this regard, the conservatives had plenty of help. Typographical workers voted not to join the strike, which allowed newspapers to continue publication. The press kept up a steady barrage of accusations that the strike was a Communist plot to starve the city into submission. Police and vigilantes launched a concerted campaign of terror aimed particularly at Communists and other "alien" elements. Homes, offices, and union halls were ransacked; hundreds were arrested on trumped-up charges. Fearing an imminent backlash against all of organized labor, the Labor Council leadership desperately sought to end the walkout. On the fourth day, delegates voted to terminate the general strike immediately.

For a moment it appeared that the supreme act of labor solidarity had given way to division and demoralization. The maritime strikers accepted arbitration and returned to work at the end of July; other unionists braced for a new open-shop offensive. But militant labor quickly regained its momentum, led again by the marine workers, who took the strike back to the job and turned the world of waterfront labor relations upside down. In October, a presidentially-appointed National Longshoremen's Board met several of the dockworkers' crucial demands, and the men continued to build on that foundation. The seamen won an equally impressive victory. And the example of the marine workers proved contagious. Indeed, it triggered a wave of organizing and ferment among a generation of workers on the West Coast.

In the final analysis, then, the general strike had a dual character. Forced upon the union leadership by an avalanche of class feeling at the grass roots, it was quickly reduced by Labor Council officials to a limited gesture of sympathy, designed more to minimize organized labor's losses than to see the maritime strike through to victory. However, because of the marine workers' stunning triumph, the general strike became a powerful symbol of the solidarity that fueled the forward march of labor in the 1930s. *See also*: Bridges, Harry; California; Communist Party; International Longshoremen's and Warehousemen's Union

—*Bruce Nelson*

REFERENCES

Bernstein, Irving. *Turbulent Years: A History of the American Worker, 1933–1941*. Boston: Houghton Mifflin, 1970.

Kimeldorf, Howard. *Reds or Rackets? The Making of Radical and Conservative Unions on the Waterfront*. Berkeley: University of California Press, 1988.

Larrowe, Charles P. *Harry Bridges: The Rise and Fall of Radical Labor in the United States*. New York: Lawrence Hill, 1972.

Nelson, Bruce. *Workers on the Waterfront: Seamen, Longshoremen, and Unionism in the 1930s*. Urbana: University of Illinois Press, 1988.

Quin, Mike. *The Big Strike*. Olema, Calif.: Olema Publishing Co., 1949.

Selvin, David F. *Sky Full of Storm: A Brief History of California Labor*. San Francisco: California Historical Society, 1975.

SANDBURG, CARL (1878–1967)

Born in Galesburg, Illinois, Sandburg was the son of Swedish immigrants. He left school at thirteen and worked at various jobs to help the family income. At nineteen he hoboed out to the West and worked in wheat fields and hotels. Back in Galesburg, he took a job as driver for a farmer's milk wagon, and later as a painter. During the Spanish-American War, Sandburg served in the Sixth Illinois Volunteers. He worked his way through Lombard College, selling stereoscopic pictures (sets creating a three dimensional effect) for Underwood and Underwood during vacation with classmate Frederick Dickinson.

Philip Green Wright published Sandburg's first book of poems, *In Reckless Ecstasy*, through his Asgard Press in November 1904. During this period he worked for some time for the fire department. Some of his articles on labor were published as "Inklings and Idlings" under the pseudonym of Crimson in the *Galesburg Evening Mail*. He also wrote for the *Galesburg Labor News* and sent poems and articles to *Tomorrow*, a Chicago magazine. He joined the *Lyceumite* (a trade journal of the International Lyceum and Chautauqua Assocation) as advertising manager in December 1906. When a combine of trusts bought the magazine, he lost his job. In the interim he had given several lectures on Walt Whitman and in July had spoken at the Socialist symposium in the Roycroft Chapel in East Aurora, New York.

Sandburg was active in Wisconsin Social-Democratic Party politics from late 1907 until 1912. In December 1907, as Charles A. Sandburg, he became an effective Party organizer for the Lake Shore and Fox River Valley districts, where he was a popular and charismatic orator. In 1908 he married Lilian Steichen, Phi Beta Kappa graduate of the University of Chicago, who had been teaching in Princeton, Illinois. She was a Socialist intellectual who joined in his work as a Party volunteer. Sandburg was a delegate to state and national Socialist conventions in 1908, and he campaigned with Eugene Debs on the Red Special tour of Wisconsin, introducing the candidate in Appleton, where he lived.

From June 1909 until the fall of 1912 the Sandburgs lived in Milwaukee. In the fall and winter of 1909, Sandburg spoke in forty-five different Wisconsin cities for the Anti-Tuberculosis Society. During the spring of 1910 he campaigned actively for Emil Seidel and the Social-Democratic ticket and was later given the post of private secretary to Milwaukee's first Socialist mayor. He held his office for eight months, and then resigned, because the Party felt he would be more useful as editor of the *Social-Democratic Herald*. Sandburg's city hall experience gave him a working knowledge of municipal politics and greater visibility in the Wisconsin Social-Democratic movement. He wrote widely reprinted Socialist and labor tracts such as *Labor and Politics* and *You and Your Job* for Socialist and general periodicals, including Victor Berger's *Social-Democratic Herald*, the *Milwaukee Leader*, *Wilshire's Magazine*, and *La Follette's Weekly*.

In the fall of 1912, when Sandburg was on the *Milwaukee Leader* and still virtually unknown as a poet, he moved his family to Chicago to join the staff of the Socialist *Chicago Evening World*, which had expanded to 600,000 circulation in the wake of a pressman's strike that had closed down most of the other Chicago newspapers. When the *World* folded, he went to the *Day Book*, a liberal and adless Scripps paper.

A group of Sandburg's Chicago poems were published in the March 1914 issue of *Poetry*, a new magazine founded and edited by Harriet Monroe. Sandburg let his membership in the Socialist Party lapse, but still advocated the reforms of socialism. Some selections of *Chicago Poems* (1916) reflect this social idealism. He wrote articles at this time for various magazines, including *International Socialist Review* and *Reedy's Mirror*. *Cornhuskers* came out in 1918, launching him as a major poet. Later that year he went to Sweden to report on the war for the Newspaper Enterprise Association. When *Smoke and Steel* (1920) appeared, his work was written of as greatly improved. His literary reputation was enhanced by the publication of *Slabs of the Sunburnt West* and *Rootabaga Stories* in 1922.

He was working then on *Abraham Lincoln: The Prairie Years* (1926); his collection of American folk songs, published in 1927; and a short biography of Edward Steichen, which included some of his master prints. In 1928 *Good Morning America* was published, the title poem chosen by Harvard as the Phi Beta Kappa poem of the year. *Mary Lincoln: Wife and Widow* came out early in the 1930s, and *The People, Yes* followed in 1936. *Abraham Lincoln: The War Years* was published in 1939 and was awarded the 1940 Pulitzer Prize for history. Sandburg joined with Dorothy Parker and Helen Keller that year to help the American Rescue Ship Mission transport Spanish refugees from France to Mexico to save them from Hitler and Franco.

Sandburg's long novel *Remembrance Rock* came out in 1948, after he had moved from Michigan to Flat Rock, North Carolina. In 1951 he received another Pulitzer Prize for his *Complete Poems*. Sandburg wrote an autobiography of his youth in Galesburg, *Always the Young Strangers* (1952), and a biography of Oliver Barrett, *Lincoln Collector* (1954), and worked on the second part of his autobiography in the late 1950s. His last book of poetry, *Honey and Salt*, came out in 1963. During this period he had denounced McCarthyism as "un-American." Carl Sandburg died in July 1967 at the age of eighty-nine. *See also*: Poetry

—*Margaret Sandburg*

REFERENCES

Callahan, North. *Carl Sandburg, Lincoln of Our Literature, a Biography*. New York: New York University, 1970.

Crowder, Richard. *Carl Sandburg*. New York: Twayne Publishers, 1964.

Sandburg, Margaret, ed. *The Poet and the Dream Girl*. Urbana: University of Illinois Press, 1987.

SANDERS, BERNARD: see

MUNICIPAL SOCIALISM

SANGER, MARGARET (1879–1966)

One of eleven children of an Irish family, Margaret Higgins was born in Corning, New York. While her mother remained loyal to Catholicism, her father was a follower of free-thinker Robert Ingersoll and single-taxer Henry George. Margaret attended college, supported financially by her two older sisters, and worked as a schoolteacher before attending nursing school. At first it seemed that her medical training might be in vain, because she was pressured into leaving school and getting married by William Sanger in 1902, giving birth to her first child in 1903. Sanger, an architect and aspiring artist, moved his family to suburban Westchester, where they had two more children while he commuted to New York. After eight years of restlessness with housewifery and isolation, Margaret insisted that they move back to Manhattan, and she began working as a visiting nurse on the Lower East Side. She also joined the Industrial Workers of the World and did support work for the strikes in Paterson, New Jersey, and Lawrence, Massachusetts. In this network she learned from Emma Goldman that issues concerning women's bodies and health might be understood politically. She spoke and wrote on health issues such as venereal disease and in 1912 began a series of articles on sexual issues in the *Call*. The fact that she received a great deal of enthusiastic response from poor women convinced her that these issues were politically vital. The censorship of one of her columns by the U.S. Post Office in 1913 only brought her more publicity. In 1914 she published several issues of the *Woman Rebel*, a feminist newspaper that discussed sexual issues, and then *Family Limitation*, a pamphlet—intended for mass distribution—containing actual instructions about contraception. Fleeing from arrest, she spent a year in Europe in 1914–15, during which time she learned from Havelock Ellis and Dutch feminist physician Aletta Jacobs.

Upon her return to the United States she was able to crystallize a massive but short-lived radical birth-control movement (approximately 1916–18). But Sanger's reaction to this mass energy was somewhat negative, perhaps because of her sense that it was no longer hers. She soon began to estrange herself from her former left-wing friends. Instead she courted professionals—particularly doctors and academic eugenicists. In 1921 she established the American Birth Control League, a national, professionally dominated lobbying group, to become Planned Parenthood in 1942. Very much in need of recognition, Sanger consistently promoted a view of birth control as something she had invented, and for which her leadership was irreplaceable and indivisible. Yet she was never timid: until the mid-1920s she kept her birth-control clinics operating by smuggling European diaphragms into the United States. Her professional legal strategy was victorious. Contraception was legalized by many states between the 1920s and 1960s, but legalized as a medical device requiring a doctor's prescription. In 1937 the American Medical Association recognized contraception as a legitimate medical service. After World War II, population-control fears renewed support for promoting contraception, and Sanger was instrumental in getting funding for research into hormonal contraception. *See also*: Birth Control; Goldman, Emma; *Woman Rebel*

—*Linda Gordon*

REFERENCES

Gordon, Linda. *Woman's Body, Woman's Right: A Social History of Birth Control in America*. New York: Viking/Penguin, 1976.

———. "The Politics of Birth Control, 1920–40: The Impact of Professionals." *International Journal of Health Issues* 5 (Fall 1975); reprinted in *The Cultural Crisis of Modern Medicine*, edited by John Ehrenreich. New York: Monthly Review Press, 1978.

Reed, James. *From Private Vice to Public Virtue: The Birth Control Movement and American Society Since 1830*. Princeton: Princeton University Press, 1978.

Scales, Junius Irving (b. 1920)

Scales was born into a wealthy southern family with a distinguished history. After an early tutorial education, in 1936 he entered the University of North Carolina, where he soon became a member, then state chairman of the American Student Union. He joined the Communist Party in March 1939, and the following year he attended the national Party training school. He became an organizer in the textile and hosiery industries. After Pearl Harbor, he volunteered for the Army and served four years while being harassed by the FBI and Army intelligence. He returned to Chapel Hill in 1946 and was active in veterans' affairs and the Southern Conference for Human Welfare. He was also vice president of the Southern Negro Youth Congress, its only elected white official. As district chair of the CP in the Carolinas, he held many public meetings.

Soon named to the Southern Regional Committee of the CP, Scales became responsible for activities in Virginia, Tennessee, and northern Mississippi. He shifted to the "underground" methods of operation adopted by the CP to resist oppression, but was arrested in 1954 under the Smith Act. His six-year sentence was reversed by the Supreme Court in 1957. Although he had resigned from the CP, Scales was again tried and this conviction was upheld by a five-to-four decision in the Supreme Court. He served fifteen months in Lewisburg Penitentiary until released by a presidential commutation that followed an international protest movement. Upon his release, Scales became a union proofreader, a job he held until his retirement twenty-five years later. *See also*: Communist Party

—*Richard Nickson*

REFERENCES

Scales, Junius Irving, and Richard Nickson. *Cause at Heart: A Former Communist Remembers*. Athens: University of Georgia Press, 1987.

Schapiro, Meyer (b. 1904)

An enormously gifted scholar trained as a medievalist but with wide-ranging interests that transcend the boundaries of traditional specializations, Schapiro was born in Lithuania and raised in Brooklyn, where he studied painting with John Sloan at the Hebrew Educational Society. Graduating from Columbia College in 1924 with honors in philosophy and art history, Schapiro went on to write a groundbreaking doctoral dissertation on the sculptural decoration of the Romanesque monastery at Moissac. As a teacher at Columbia and the New School for Social Research, Schapiro offered courses in Byzantine, early Christian, and medieval art and art-historical theory, and pioneered the study of modern art—a field not accorded much academic respectability during the 1930s and 1940s. An amateur artist of some skill, he has throughout his career kept in close touch with artists and has often played a crucial role in furthering artistic careers, perhaps most notably in the case of the abstract expressionists.

A lifelong socialist—he joined the Brownsville Young Peoples Socialist League in 1916—Schapiro became more intensely interested in Marxism during the Depression, when he became actively involved with the Left and helped found the American Artists Congress. During the 1930s Schapiro wrote three lengthy articles (on Romanesque and Mozarabic art at Silos, on the nature of abstract art, and on Courbet and popular imagery) that probe the social determinants of artistic production. Like the best Marxist cultural studies of the 1930s (e.g., those of Walter Benjamin), these articles are idiosyncratic, exemplifying a creative adaptation of Marxist ideas and methods to specific historical problems.

Since the 1930s, Schapiro has concentrated less on the social bases of art, and his work has reflected an interest in psychology, philosophy, and semiotics. Yet unlike many of his former colleagues in the anti-Stalinist Left, Schapiro has never repudiated Marxism or socialism and has consistently encouraged Marxist approaches to art history. In a well-known essay on style published in 1953, Schapiro reviewed major explanatory theories and, after demonstrating their strengths and weaknesses, concluded that an undogmatic Marxism held out a possibility of a general theory.

As an American Marxist working in the usually elite and conservative field of art history, Schapiro was in many ways a unique figure. Although he deeply influenced several generations of artists and art historians, almost none of his students have pursued Marxist approaches. It was not until the 1970s that a U.S. school of Marxist art history began to develop. This school initially looked to European scholarship for inspiration; at times highly critical of Schapiro, it has only recently begun to acknowledge the richness and profundity of his scholarship. *See also*: *Partisan Review*

—*Alan Wallach*

REFERENCES

Epstein, Helen. "Meyer Schapiro: 'A Passion to Know and Make Known.'" *Art News* 82 (May and June 1983).

Schapiro, Meyer. *Modern Art*. New York: Braziller, 1977–78.

———. "Style." In *Anthropology Today*, edited by A. L. Kroeber. Chicago: University of Chicago Press, 1953.

Social Research, Special Issue. 45 (Spring 1978).

Wallach, Allan. "Marxism and Art History." In *The Left Academy*, edited by Bertell Ollman and Edward Vernoff. New York: Praeger, 1984.

SCIENCE

The Left view of science, changing enormously with time and place, has proved one of the most difficult if least openly contended philosophical issues of socialism. Within it lay concealed political fault lines that cut across many more obvious differences among radicals and between radicals and U.S. society.

Science in the late nineteenth century had an almost magical lure for socialists as well as others. Spiritualists, often inclined toward socialism, viewed the telegraph key, for instance, as a great potential boon to links with the "Other Side." Utopian literary works depicted a world where machines did much of the labor and freed humanity for cultured pursuits. Immigrant socialists looked to science for leverage against religious obscurantism, and hoped (with Engels) that scientists themselves would naturally favor the social system most suited to their aspirations. Popular scientific explanations, as in the nonsocialist press, took up considerable space in the socialist press.

The new Socialist Party at first seemed to adopt similarly optimistic views. The Charles H. Kerr Company published its "Library of Science for Workers," beginning in 1904, a mostly German series of cheaply priced, popular explanations. They made extensive efforts to fit certain notions of science, specifically mental cognition, into a context where the writings of a Joseph Dietzgen made almost cosmic sense of socialist inevitability. Arthur Morrow Lewis, one of the party's most popular lecturers, drew great crowds with his lectures analogizing events in the physical world and events in society as coeval proof of a sort of Marxist Darwinism. For Lewis as for many self-taught working-class intellectuals through the 1920s, Herbert Spencer's writing supplied the bridge, rendering society an organism whose whole outlived individual parts. Adopting a historical sociology, he sought to demonstrate that progress through human history, and progress in thought, could be demonstrated by the acute observer.

The inherent element of passive confidence in this view, and indeed the entire view itself, was shaken by the outbreak of war in Europe, and even more by the seeming inevitability of U.S. participation. The technologies of destruction, focusing scientific energy upon mass murder of civilian as well as military populations, exposed the barbaric uses of science and the evidently nonutopian future ahead for mankind. A concomitant modernism among intellectuals, especially socialist intellectuals, broke from scientific determinism in the other direction, toward a neo-romanticism that scorned nineteenth-century evolutionary assumptions. Einstein's discovery of $E=mc^2$, by breaking with almost all fixed beliefs in the nature of the universe, may be said to have rendered the older assumptions in some sense scientifically moot. Or so it seemed to many intellectual rebels of the later 1910s and 1920s.

The emergence of the Soviet Union (alongside the growth of fascism) in the 1920s and the world depression of the 1930s effected an unprecedented alliance of many scientists and the Left. These progressive scientists thought the promise of real knowledge, endangered by the dark specter of fascism, might be realized in societies rationally organized. Only the persecutory fury of the Cold War, and disillusionment with the Soviet Union, broke the back of this remarkable rapprochement.

The 1920s–1940s leftish tendency had only small groups of survivors in the 1950s and early 1960s, the most pronounced around the *Bulletin of Atomic Scientists* and its supportive Federation of American Scientists. They questioned atomic testing, and the entire strategic perspective of defensible war fought with megaweapons. With the emergence of SANE and the "Ban the Bomb" movement of 1960–62, a handful of scientists lobbied Congress and voiced their opposition in the press to the development of new, destabilizing weapons systems. At the meetings of the American Society of Microbiology, itself linked with the biological-warfare testing of the U.S. government, they protested complicity.

The Vietnam War proved, as in so many areas, to be a watershed. The U.S. government uses of science in that war—from the extraordinary human torture meeted out by napalm to the biological warfare of Agent Orange against a million acres of Vietnamese countryside to the "Electronic Battlefield" of apparently perfected technological devastation—became a major issue in the public mind. Soon, Nobel Laureates and a legion of scientists signed public protests, once again assuming a leading position among academics, although this time lacking illusions of "scientific socialism" as an alternative in practice somewhere across the globe.

In 1969 the student strike movement hit the scientific field directly, as researchers conducted a one-day stoppage protesting the misuse of scientific knowledge for war purposes. The Scientists and Engineers for Social and Political Action (SESPA) formed out of meetings at the American Physical Society, creating a nucleus for what would later become Science for the People. Meanwhile, as in the 1910s–1920s, philosophers, literary figures, conservationists, and others raised serious questions about the assumptions of science and the fate of the planet.

Mostly younger scientists created the "radical science movement," really a loose-knit series of groups and tendencies, of which the Boston-based Science for the People has been the largest and best organized. Younger scientists in particular have engaged, during the 1970s–1980s, in a wide variety of fields. Their roles in providing technical aid to noncapitalist developing countries; in supplying and interpreting data for consumer, environmental, and other anticorporate organizations; and their efforts to encourage responsibility of fellow scientists, such as those who work in weapons laboratories or accept funding for "Star Wars" projects, have all been vital contributions. In a handful of cases, ongoing organizations have presented their own scientific agendas. Computer Professionals for Peace and the Committee for Social Responsibility in Engineering among others have repeatedly challenged the format and contents of the national associations at the regular meetings. Science for the People has gained a special prominence by insisting on women's issues within the scientific community. Only a few scientists have emerged as major public allies of the Left. Stephen Jay Gould, popular analyst of evolutionism among other issues, is perhaps the most formidable example of a supportive presence at Left events and for Left causes.

Meanwhile, widespread skepticism toward scientific solutions to such problems as the technological devastation of wildlife and various threats to the biosphere has renewed a neo-romantic (or "pagan") resistance even to progressive scientific claims. A radical science, now very much in evolution, has been heavily influenced by the predilection for challenging fundamental assumptions and seeking new premises for the uses of knowledge. Anne Fausto-Sterling's challenging works on science and gender, and Richard Levins and Richard Lewontin's studies of scientific assumptions, highlight a recent radical approach. *See also*: Scientists, 1920–50

—*Paul Buhle*

REFERENCES

Beckwith, Jon. "The Radical Science Movement in the United States." *Monthly Review* 37 (July–August 1986).

Fausto-Sterling, Anne. *Myths of Gender: Biological Theories About Women and Men*. New York: Basic Books, 1985.

Levins, Richard, and Richard Lewontin. *Dialectical Biology*. Cambridge: Harvard University Press, 1985.

Science & Society

An interdisciplinary quarterly journal of Marxist thought and analysis, *Science & Society* is now the oldest continuing Marxist publication in the English language. Although its circulation, ranging around 3,000, has never been large, it is widely known and read, and is found on the shelves of more than 1,000 college and university libraries in the U.S. and abroad.

Science & Society, founded in 1936, quickly gathered a prestigious board of editors, associates, and contributors from across academic life, including J. D. Bernal, Joseph Needham, Louis B. Boudin, Ralph Bunche, E. Franklin Frazier, Robert Morse Lovett, Broadus Mitchell, Paul Sweezy, Margaret Schlauch, Edwin Berry Burgum, J. B. S. Haldane, Dirk Struik, and Granville Hicks. It published a number of essays (such as Herbert Aptheker's studies of slavery) destined to become, in book form, classics of the Left.

Beginning in the early 1940s and intensifying by the end of that decade and into the next, *Science & Society* suffered from the severe repression of U.S. intellectual life. Many of its writers and editors were blacklisted. Some notable contributors developed political reservations and dropped away. On the other hand, two of the journal's primary contributors developed from the early 1940s a critical approach to "Lysenkoism," the official Russian approach toward aspects of scientific theory. During the later 1950s, *Science & Society* felt the shock waves of the Twentieth Congress revelations, and the journal more openly and regularly reflected on the broad changes in Marxist thinking now required.

During the 1960s, *Science & Society*'s unique role offered a forum for many new issues raised and also a ballast of fundamental Marxist theory. By the 1970s, it drew upon a new generation of accomplished scholars from schools large and small, reaching its apex of postrepression days. New theoretical concerns, including Althusserianism, feminism, and dependency theory, were probed and deeper examinations of Marxist political economy undertaken. The 1980s, highlighted by the journal's fiftieth anniversary and a banner celebratory issue, produced penetrating polemics on several key theoretical questions—notably, a new stage in a long-continuing discussion of social transitions, an intense debate on the labor theory of value, and a lively series on the direction of the U.S. economy in the world.

The major accomplishment of *Science & Society* has been the legitimation of Marxist theory within scholarly discourse, both on campuses and in Left political circles. Partly because of—and partly in spite of—its multidisciplinary character, the journal has sustained a stability rare in the Left. *See also*: Aptheker, Herbert; Boudin, Louis B.; Communist Party; Foner, Philip; Hicks, Granville

—*David Goldway*

REFERENCES

Goldway, David. "Fifty Years of *Science & Society*." *Science & Society* 50 (Fall 1986).

SCIENTISTS, 1920–50

American scientists did not engage in significant left-wing political activity until the tail end of the 1930s. Although noteworthy individuals like General Electric research director Charles Steinmetz and psychologist and publisher James McKeen Cattell acted at times on their socialist beliefs prior to World War I, such efforts were at best sporadic and isolated. During the 1920s, even such meager radical activity subsided as scientists strengthened their ties to business and increasing numbers pursued careers in the rapidly proliferating industrial research laboratories. Few dared publicly challenge the dominant conservative ethos at a time when the scientific establishment actively supported Herbert Hoover and career advancement depended on the blessings of an elite who considered unorthodox political views prima facie evidence of untrustworthiness in all judgments, science included. As science advanced, bolstered by corporate and philanthropic funding, scientists received much of the credit for the technologically based industrial prosperity of the 1920s. Confident about the future, scientific spokesmen proclaimed that good science necessarily translated into social progress, and trusted enlightened capitalists to continue making that possible.

During the 1930s, a combination of factors converged to overturn the conservatism that prevailed at the start of the decade. Serious unemployment and sharply reduced research funding eroded scientists' 1920s optimism. On top of this, scientists suddenly found themselves being blamed for the technological unemployment popularly believed to have caused the Depression. Critics, including Secretary of Agriculture Henry Wallace, upbraided them for their political conservatism and social irresponsibility. Such public opprobrium challenged their self-conception as society's benefactors and inspired a number of scientists to reevaluate the facile equation of science and progress. Their exclusion from 1930s relief programs and antagonism to the New Deal's "recovery through scarcity" approach also helped catalyze their political reeducation.

International political developments further heightened scientists' awareness of the socioeconomic and political dimensions of scientific research. Beginning early in the decade, newly radicalized British scientists exerted considerable influence on their American colleagues. Eminent British scientists became spokesmen for the British Association of Scientific Workers (BASW) and articulated the view, commonly associated with crystallographer J. D. Bernal, that capitalism contradicted the ethos of science and inevitably frustrated realization of its liberating potential.

As the decade progressed, American scientists' political views were also influenced by the growing perception of the Soviet Union as a land committed to a rational program of social and economic development based on science and technology. Believing that the Soviets had escaped the ravages of capitalist economic collapse during the 1930s, leading American scientists, including physicist Karl Compton, the chairman of President Roosevelt's Science Advisory Board and president of MIT, contrasted Soviet beneficence toward science with the niggardly attitude expressed by American governmental, philanthropic, and corporate leaders and applauded the demonstrable progress made by Soviet science.

Nazi Germany served as a model of a fundamentally different sort. Thousands of German scientists escaped to the United States and Europe, bringing shocking tales of intellectual and political tyranny. This reinforced American scientists' growing awareness of the subordination of science to politics and alerted them to the dangers of repression at home, as well as abroad. Uncertain of their status in the United States, most of these émigrés kept a low political profile until the 1940s.

Under the combined weight of these factors, signs of a leftward shift in the political attitudes of the scientific community became evident shortly past middecade. In a widely reported public address in mid-1936, American Association for the Advancement of Science (AAAS) president E. G. Conklin, a Princeton biologist, attacked the New Deal and called for "democratic socialism." Conklin collaborated with other AAAS leaders to inaugurate a series of "Science and Society" symposia at semiannual association meetings beginning in December 1937.

The movement gained further momentum throughout 1938, peaking with three major events in December—the formation of the Lincoln's Birthday Committee for Democracy and Intellectual Freedom (LBCDIF), the formation of the American Association of Scientific Workers, and the election of Harvard physiologist Walter B. Cannon to the presidency of the AAAS, in an election in which all five top vote-getters were identified with the science and society movement and three were recognized leaders of the scientific Left.

Cannon's election to head science's leading membership organization, with more than 19,000 members and 750,000 affiliates, reflected the new strength of the scientific Left. Widely regarded as one of America's premier scientists, Cannon, a socialist and militant antifascist, had been American science's most visible leftist in recent years. Closely linked to Pavlov, whose initial enmity to the Soviet government had been overcome by the government's munificent support for physiological research, Cannon delivered the keynote address at the International Congress of Physiology in Leningrad in 1935, an extraordinary event attended by some 200 American scientists. Cannon remained the Soviet Union's most vocal supporter among American scientists. In 1937 he seriously weighed an offer to chair the American Russian Institute. Cannon had also spearheaded the scientists' antifascist movement as chairman of the Medical Bureau to Aid Spanish Democracy. The examples set by Cannon and fellow leftist A. J. Carlson of the University of Chicago, who between them totally dominated American physiology for years, contributed to the radicalization of a remarkable number of physiologists during this period.

The LBCDIF represented the culmination of many years of progressive efforts on the part of America's leading anthropologist, Franz Boas. Boas had spent much of his long career employing science in the fight against racism. In the mid-1930s, he collaborated with other Columbia University faculty members, including sociologist Robert Lynd, Nobel Prize-winning chemist Harold Urey, engineer Walter Rautenstrauch, geneticist L. C. Dunn, and zoologist Selig Hecht, in supporting the Spanish Republic, exposing the unscientific nature of Nazi propaganda and impeding the efforts of reactionary forces in the United States.

In December 1938, Boas released a "Manifesto on the Freedom of Science," signed by 1,284 scientists and college presidents, which condemned Nazi racism and persecution of scientists and teachers and urged a stronger defense of democracy and intellectual freedom in the United States. From these signers, he extracted a core group of nationally prominent scientific progressives who turned Lincoln's Birthday into a day of national demonstrations for democracy and intellectual freedom. Building on the successful mobilization of thousands of scientists and educators in twenty-six cities across the country, Boas and his collaborators decided to turn the LBCDIF into a permanent antifascist organization, the American Committee for Democracy and Intellectual Freedom (ACDIF). Cannon, Urey, Dunn, Carlson, anthropologist Ruth Benedict, astronomer Harlow Shapley, Henry Sigerist, the world's preeminent medical historian, pathologist John Peters, mathematician Dirk Struik, and physicist Arthur Holly Compton joined other nationally prominent scientists to form a steering committee. Boas remained as national chairman and classicist Moses I. Finkelstein (M. I. Finley) served as secretary.

In the following months, the ACDIF carried its antifascist message to high schools and colleges, launching a campaign to expose racist ideology in school textbooks, mobilizing the educational community against reactionary legislation, exposing the efforts of the New York State Chamber of Commerce to curtail public education beyond the point of literacy and fan anti-immigrant sentiment, turning spring commencement and Columbus Day into demonstrations for democracy as part of an ongoing effort to highlight the nation's progressive legacy, and generally resisting mounting incursions against civil liberties.

December 1938 also witnessed the formation of the American Association of Scientific Workers (AASW), a more explicitly radical organization with close ties to the BASW. The AASW's distinguished list of national sponsors included physiologists Cannon, Carlson, A. C. Ivy, and Ralph Gerard, pathologist Thomas Addis, physicists J. Robert Oppenheimer, A. Compton, and K. Compton, chemist Urey, geneticist H. J. Muller, anthropologist Boas, physician and historian Sigerist, mechanical engineer Rautenstrauch, and astronomer Shapley. Despite a significant national following among scientists, the association had a membership concentrated in the nation's intellectual and scientific centers—the Boston-Cambridge area, New York, Philadelphia, Chicago, and Berkeley. Conceived as a "unifying body for all progressive-minded scientists," the AASW sought to apply science and the scientific method in restructuring American society. Like the ACDIF, the AASW fought against fascism abroad and defended civil liberties at home, exposing the Nazi destruction of German science and conducting a boycott of German scientific materials. Also alert to capitalism's frustration of science's potential in the United States, AASW branches supported expanded funding for scientific research, socialized medicine, science popularization, consumer education, and upgraded science education in the public schools. While concrete efforts were undertaken to implement some of these programs, for the most part the AASW remained more of an educational than an activist organization.

Despite the advent of war in Europe, both

the ACDIF and AASW grew steadily in membership and influence until each was sandbagged by the introduction of antiwar resolutions in late 1939 and early 1940. The resolutions, which clearly echoed the new post–Nazi-Soviet Pact Comintern line in their subordination of antifascism to neutralism, staunchly opposed American entry into the war. Despite the implicit renunciation of both organizations' vehement antifascism, the resolutions garnered substantial support. The ACDIF ultimately dropped the resolution in hopes of avoiding an open rift. The AASW, however, pursued the initiative, presenting a petition signed by more than 500 scientists to President Roosevelt. The episode shattered the erstwhile harmony of the 180-member Boston-Cambridge branch. In June, several prominent members of the branch resigned in protest of alleged Communist domination. Subsequent testimony indicates that the charge was not entirely unfounded, as several physicists, chemists, and mathematicians from MIT and Harvard later admitted having been Communist Party members, including former AASW national coordinator W. T. Martin, an MIT mathematician. Although few actually defected, the AASW never regained its lost momentum. Nor could the ACDIF's circumspection protect it from a debilitating onslaught of Red-baiting by Sidney Hook and John Dewey of the Committee for Cultural Freedom, who alleged Communist domination. Capitalizing on mistrust engendered by the Nazi-Soviet Pact, the CCF managed to arrest ACDIF momentum in late 1939 by driving a wedge between liberals and radicals and dissuading financial backers. Although the ACDIF continued functioning during the war and the AASW persevered through the 1950s, neither again approached its initial promise or influence.

Wartime developments forced a profound transformation in the scientists' postwar political agenda, as nuclear issues overshadowed all others in their import and immediacy. Late in the war, Manhattan Project scientists at Chicago's Metallurgical Laboratory had prefigured future concerns in their futile attempt to block surprise military use of the bomb against the Japanese and demand that U.S. officials share the bomb secret with the Soviets in hopes of averting a postwar arms race. Subsequently feeling responsible for the devastation of Hiroshima and Nagasaki and aware how short-lived America's nuclear monopoly would likely be, atomic scientists mounted a campaign for international control of nuclear weapons and civilian control of nuclear research in the United States. To coordinate this effort, Manhattan Project scientists launched the Federation of Atomic Scientists, which was soon broadened into the Federation of American Scientists (FAS). Hundreds of scientists participated in lobbying and educational efforts in Washington and elsewhere around the country, contributing significantly to the defeat of the May-Johnson bill, which would have imposed military control over atomic energy and stringent secrecy provisions. With the support of liberal and left-wing scientists, the McMahon bill (the Atomic Energy Act of 1946) was passed, establishing a civilian Atomic Energy Commission, but compromising on security-related issues. Although many left-wing scientists participated in this effort, the FAS deliberately strove to work within the system and disavowed radical intentions, even rejecting organized participation by the AASW.

Many viewed the scientists' other chief priority, gaining international control of atomic energy, as part of a broader effort to improve relations with the Soviet Union and halt the arms race. Once-warm relations between American and Soviet scientists had cooled in the late 1930s, as the "Lysenko controversy" and resulting purges cut the Soviets off from the world scientific community. Wartime exigencies rekindled closer relations. In November 1943, the science panel of the Congress of American-Soviet Friendship met in New York to commemorate the tenth anniversary of U.S. recognition of the Soviet Union and established a permanent Science Committee of the National Council of American-Soviet Friendship. With Cannon as an honorary co-chairman and L. C. Dunn as chairman, left-wing scientists played a prominent role in Science Committee efforts to strengthen ties between Soviet and American scientists. Changing its name to the American-Soviet

Science Society in 1945, the organization continued to promote collaboration between the United States and the Soviet Union during the postwar period. MIT mathematician Dirk Struik served as chairman of the Massachusetts Council of American-Soviet Friendship.

Left-wing scientists also took a strong hand in shaping America's postwar science policy. During the war, the AASW worked with Senator Harley Kilgore (D-W.Va.) on drafting legislation for a government science agency, predicated on the belief that scientists should be accountable to the public, with research addressing social needs and its results and applications being made freely available. Following the war, Harlow Shapley and Harold Urey formed a Committee for a National Science Foundation, which mobilized support for a watered-down version of the Kilgore bill. Although Shapley and Urey exerted some influence over the final shape of the National Science Foundation established in 1950, their more democratic approach was largely superseded by the elitist version proposed by Vannevar Bush.

Left-wing scientists attempted to influence many of these developments through their participation in the Independent Citizens Committee of the Arts, Sciences, and Professions (ICCASP), which had been formed during the 1944 presidential campaign. Among the Committee's leaders were Albert Einstein, Peters, Rautenstrauch, Shapley, and Ernst Boas. The Science and Technology Division took active stands on a variety of issues, including full employment, the shape of a postwar science policy, international control and peaceful use of atomic energy, and opposition to oppressive postwar security measures. In late 1946, the ICCASP merged with the National Citizens Political Action Committee to form the Political Action Committee, one of whose divisions developed into the National Council of the Arts, Sciences, and Professions (NCASP), chaired by Shapley, who, along with other members, actively supported Henry Wallace's 1948 presidential bid.

Postwar security investigations of scientists began in 1947, when HUAC initiated its probe of the atomic scientists. One of the first targets was physicist Edward U. Condon, head of the National Bureau of Standards. Condon, a former LBCDIFer and a recently outspoken proponent of closer relations between the United States and the Soviet Union, had served as technical adviser to Senator McMahon. In subsequent years, thousands of scientists were among the many citizens probed by congressional committees and government loyalty programs and hundreds lost jobs and security clearances. In 1950 Senator Joseph McCarthy charged that the AASW and the American-Soviet Science Society represented the Communists' two principal efforts to mobilize scientists. The ACDIF was also branded a "Communist Front."

While such charges lacked merit, a good number of scientists did join the CP, especially during the 1940s. Ellen Schrecker, in fact, estimates that close to half the academic Communists were scientists, showing how remarkable a transformation had occurred in scientists' political attitudes in less than two decades. *See also*: Progressive, Science

—*Peter J. Kuznick*

REFERENCES

Hodes, Elizabeth. "Precedents for Social Responsibility Among Scientists: The American Association of Scientific Workers and the Federation of American Scientists." Ph.D. diss., University of California, Santa Barbara, 1983.

Kuznick, Peter J. *Beyond the Laboratory: Scientists as Political Activists in 1930s America*. Chicago and London: University of Chicago Press, 1987.

Smith, Alice Kimball. *A Peril and a Hope: The Scientists' Movement in America: 1945–47*. Chicago: University of Chicago Press, 1965.

SCOTTSBORO CASE

The International Labor Defense's (ILD) involvement in the Scottsboro case, more than any other event, crystallized black support for the Communist Party in the 1930s. Accused of raping two white women (Ruby Bates and Victoria Price) on a freight train near Paint Rock, Alabama, nine young black men (Charlie Weems, Ozie Powell, Clarence Norris, Olen Montgomery, Willie Roberson, Haywood Patterson, Andy and Roy Wright, Eugene Williams), ages thirteen to twenty-one, were arrested on March 25, 1931, tried without adequate counsel, and hastily convicted

Cartoon by Jacob Burck from *The Daily Worker*

on the basis of shallow evidence. All but Roy Wright were sentenced to death. Already in the midst of a mass antilynching campaign begun a year earlier, the ILD gained the confidence of the defendants and their parents, initiated a legal and political campaign for their freedom, and in the process waged a vicious battle for control over the case with the NAACP, who accused the Communists of using the young men for propaganda purposes.

The Scottsboro case was not simply an isolated instance of injustice, the Communists argued, but represented a common manifestation of national oppression and class rule in the South. Maintaining that a fair and impartial trial was impossible, the Party and its auxiliaries publicized the case widely in order to apply mass pressure on the Alabama justice system. Protests erupted throughout the country and as far away as Paris, Moscow, and South Africa, and the governor of Alabama was bombarded with telegrams, postcards, and letters demanding the immediate release of the "Scottsboro Boys." Through Scottsboro and other related cases, black and white Communists gained entrance into churches, lodges, and clubs in the African-American community, and eventually the ILD was regarded by some as a welcome addition to the panoply of "racial defense" organizations. Moreover, although the "Scottsboro Boys" apparently never directly identified with the Party's goals, they became cultural symbols on the Left, the subject of poems, songs, plays, and short stories that were published, circulated, and performed throughout the world.

The ILD waged a more conventional struggle in the courts as well. Its lawyers secured a new trial on appeal by arguing that the defendants were denied the right of counsel. For the new Scottsboro trials, which opened on March 27, 1933, the ILD had retained renowned criminal lawyer Samuel Leibowitz. More significant, a month before the trial date Ruby Bates repudiated the rape charge. Yet, despite new evidence and a brilliant defense, the all-white jury still found the Scottsboro defendants guilty—a verdict that seemed to buttress the Communists' interpretation of justice under capitalism and augmented the ILD's popularity in the black community. In fact, pressure from black militants and some sympathetic clergy and middle-class spokesmen compelled the virulently anticommunist NAACP secretary, Walter White, to develop a working relationship with the ILD in the spring of 1933. Several months later, however, in an unprecedented decision, Alabama circuit Judge James E. Horton overturned the March 1933 verdict and ordered a new trial.

Following a number of incredibly foolish legal and ethical mistakes (including an attempt to bribe Victoria Price), star lawyer Samuel Leibowitz bolted the ILD, which began to lose its prestige in the mid-1930s. With support of conservative black leaders, white liberals, and clergymen, Leibowitz founded the American Scottsboro Committee (ASC) in 1934. However, hostilities between the two bodies were slightly mitigated a year later when the ILD turned to the coalition-building politics of the Popular Front. In a tenuous alliance the ILD, ASC, NAACP, and ACLU, formed the Scottsboro Defense Committee, which opted for a more reformist, legally oriented campaign in lieu of mass tactics. After failing to win the defendants' release in a 1936 trial, the SDC agreed to a strange plea bargain in 1937 whereby four defendants were released and the remaining five endured lengthy prison sentences—the last defendant was not freed until 1950.

Although the ILD did not win the defendants' unconditional release, its campaign to "Free the Scottsboro Boys" had tremendous legal and political implications during the early 1930s. For example, in one of the ILD's many appeals, a 1935 U.S. Supreme Court ruled that the defendant's constitutional rights were violated because blacks were systematically excluded from the jury rolls—a landmark opinion that spurred a battle to include African Americans on the jury rolls. Moreover, the realization that limited mass interracial action was possible challenged traditional liberalism and the politics of racial accommodation; the often scorned tactics of "mass pressure" would eventually be a precedent for civil rights activity two decades later. *See also*: Communist Party; Patterson, William; Herndon Case; International Labor Defense

—*Robin D. G. Kelley*

REFERENCES

Carter, Dan T. *Scottsboro: A Tragedy of the American South*. 2d ed. Baton Rouge: Louisiana State University Press, 1984.

Martin, Charles H. "The International Labor Defense and Black America." *Labor History* 26 (Spring 1985).

Murray, Hugh T., Jr. "The NAACP versus the Communist Party: The Scottsboro Rape Case, 1931–1932." *Phylon* 28 (1967).

Scudder, Vida Dutton (1861–1954)

Born in India of missionary parents, Scudder attended Smith College and Oxford, where John Ruskin taught her to look unblinkingly at the injustices of modern civilization. An avowed socialist, she modeled her life on the conviction that Christians should support and foment radical social change. Scudder's center of gravity remained her Anglican (Episcopalian) faith, and she served her church by acting as an agent provocateur for Christian socialism. At age ninety she was still insisting in her final published work, *My Quest for Reality* (1952), that Christians dare not obfuscate reality with euphemisms.

For Scudder, two forces persisted in constant tension within history—continuity and revolution. "Did either prevail, excluding the other, Christianity would, I think, lose all dynamic power; the Church, which is a profound though partly hidden fact in Western civilization, would either fade into a formal relic or lose all general communal importance to be reckoned with. Would you like me to substitute the word 'Progress' for 'Revolution'? I stubbornly refuse."

A teacher at Wellesley for forty-one years, Scudder was central to the College Settlements Association, providing urban service similar to Jane Addams's Hull House. Author of a score of books on socialism, literature, and religion, Vida Scudder was a founder in 1919 and prime mover of the Church League for Industrial Democracy (CLID). Following World War II, she feared that the middle class would support anti-Left repression. Consequently, she worked at bringing together in CLID a broad-based coalition of middle-class liberals and socialists who would work at civil liberties and industrial reform, under the slogan, "Industrial Democracy." CLID fought the reality that the industrial system was "of, by, and for its owners" and worked toward a society that substituted "fraternal cooperation for mastery in industrial life."

During the 1920s Scudder and William B. Spofford, Episcopal priest-editor of the *Witness* magazine, who became executive director of CLID, focused the league's organizational efforts around three areas: civil liberties, church education about social justice in the workplace, and corporate responsibility. At the same time, CLID attempted to learn from and support secular movements. This thrust continued until the 1950s, when Spofford was summoned before the McCarthy Committee.

In her later years, Scudder believed that minority groups, driven by Christian impulse, would spark future social change. With this progression, CLID served as a bridge from the Social Gospel movement to the 1960s option of empowerment, which saw the direct participation in and funding of secular movements by church groups. Scudder's autobiography, *On Journey*, (1937) and her later book, *My Quest for Reality*, capsulate her experiences. *See also*: Christian Socialism

—*Mary Lou Suhor*

REFERENCES

Donovan, Mary Sudman. *A Different Call: Women's Ministries in the Episcopal Church*. Philadelphia: Morehouse, 1986.

Greathouse, Gordon. "The Church League for Industrial Democracy." In *Which Side Are We On?* Vol. II, *Christian Commitment for the '80s*. Oakland: Interreligious Task Force for Social Analysis, 1980.

Frederick, Peter J. *Knights of the Golden Rule: The Intellectual as Christian Social Reformers in the 1890s*. Lexington: University of Kentucky Press, 1976.

The Seattle General Strike of 1919

By 1918, Seattle's labor movement had attained a degree of solidarity, militancy, and radicalism unrivaled on a citywide basis anywhere in the United States. Radical groups, notably the Industrial Workers of the World, played a powerful ideological role that affected the movement as a whole.

On January 21, 1919, shipyard workers struck to protest the denial of a wage hike that had been promised them once the war was over. Convinced that the shipyard strike was the opening battle against the open-shop offensive of the employers, overwhelming majorities in each of the more than one hundred constituent unions of the Central Labor Council voted to "shut it down" in solidarity with the shipyard workers.

In order to avoid hardship, and to intimidate the federal government and the "Eastern capitalists" who were seen by many to be the root of the problem, workers quickly decided they would have not only to close down the city, they would have to reopen it under labor's management. Under the direction of a largely rank-and-file "Committee of 300" and a fifteen-person executive committee, plans were made for individual unions to carry out necessary tasks such as feeding the populace and policing the city. It was this decision to run the city that made the general strike one of the most radical events in U.S. labor history.

From February 6 through February 11, labor indeed ran the city. Eventually however, confusion over whom the strike was aimed at, combined with intense pressure from national officers of the AFL (who were horrified at this "Bolshevik" action just when the AFL was attaining respectability), forced the Committee of 300 to declare the strike over at noon of February 11. Workers returned to their jobs, "not feeling defeated but quite reasonably successful, glad they had struck, equally glad to call it off," as the official General Strike History Committee later noted.

In the aftermath of this living demonstration of the feasibility of workers' control, the future of radical unionism in Seattle looked bright. A number of workers' cooperatives opened; the circulation of the *Union Record*, labor's first daily newspaper, mushroomed; a newly organized Farmer-Labor Party replaced the Democrats as the second largest party in the Puget Sound area; and a number of militant demonstrations took place, including the refusal of longshoremen to load weapons for delivery to the forces fighting against the Russian Revolution.

But with the closing of the shipyards in mid-1919 (since the wartime need for ships had ended), Seattle was plunged into a depression perhaps twice as deep as anywhere else in the economically troubled country. Many of the cooperatives went under—as did many capitalist enterprises—and the resulting high unemployment led to job competition and political fissures among workers.

Although some accounts judge the general strike a "failure," the truth is more complex. The shipyard strike was certainly lost, and the shipyards themselves closed soon after. Yet despite the severe depression, wages and working conditions in Seattle remained relatively favorable, arguably because the general strike served as a warning to employers. The strike also remained a cultural legacy to the Seattle labor movement through the dark days of the '20s; ironically, its militancy may have helped Dave Beck and other union organizers sell business unionism to the employers as an alternative to dealing with radicals.

The strike had greater implications as well. It has been cited as a factor in the Winnipeg general strike several months later, and in encouraging the creation of the American Communist Party. Most important, it was the first great radical event that tied unionists in the United States to the worldwide post–World War I radical wave. *See also*: Communist Party, General Strike, Industrial Workers of the World, Socialist Party

—*Rob Rosenthal*

REFERENCES

Friedheim, Robert L. *The Seattle General Strike*. Seattle: University of Washington Press, 1964.

O'Connor, Harvey. *Revolution in Seattle*. New York: Monthly Review Press, 1964.

Root and Branch. *The Rise of the Workers' Movements*. Greenwich: Fawcett, 1975.

Strong, Anna Louise. *I Change Worlds*. New York: Garden City Publishing, 1937.

Second International

A federation of mostly European socialist parties and socialistically inclined labor unions, the Second International was decidedly more substantial than its predecessor and less fractured by internal disputes. For most American socialists, its dominating German Social Democracy remained the ideal in strength and rigorous internal self-organization to emulate as far as possible. Its generally biannual congresses, invariably held in Europe, offered opportunities for American delegates to meet the famous and sometimes to offer their own opinions on international affairs. Only rarely, however, did congress resolutions directly affect the conduct of U.S. socialists at home.

A Marxist-led International Workers' Congress held in Paris during July 1889 inaugurated the movement and all but precluded anarchist participation. (Turned back several times, they abandoned efforts at inclusion.) The rise of socialist parliamentary fortunes, trade union activity, and consolidation of political movements long dominated perceptions of and by the Second International. Among other noteworthy efforts, the International established May Day (first celebrated in Chicago, 1886) as the official international workers' holiday. More generally, it established the idea of socialism as a historic force of great consequence rather than a mere terroristic threat to society. Little noticed by the impressionable Americans, and many others, the consolidating Second International also represented a bureaucratic drift into electoralism and institution-building as an accommodation to the apparent stability of capitalism. This drift, culminating in member parties' votes for war credits at the outbreak of the

European conflict, meant the end of the International in 1914.

European leaders, following Engels's sentiments in the latter's final years, expressed little enthusiasm for the Socialist Labor Party of the 1890s. For its part, the financially strapped SLP sent no delegates, allowing itself to be represented, however ambivalently, by the German Social Democrats. On the other hand, the support of the American Federation of Labor for socialism, much desired by Engels (and by Frederich Sorge, reduced to being the mere American correspondent of *Neue Zeit*), appeared after 1896 further away than ever. Samuel Gompers, who avowed his training by First Internationalists, had broken with socialist ideas altogether and planted himself squarely in the American two-party tradition—with a strong inclination toward exclusion of newer immigrants, women, and other (e.g., black or Asian) potential competitors to organized craft workers.

Naturally, then, Second International luminaries warmly greeted the appearance of the Socialist Party of America, however heterodox its approach to questions such as the private ownership of farms. They faced the dilemma, however, of two competing American parties, and as in other such cases, sought for years to mediate a merger between the two organizations, an effort pursued with special vigor when the young Industrial Workers of the World gave many activists of the two parties a common cause. The task proved, however, impossible.

SLP leader Daniel DeLeon had by then become an intractable revolutionary critic of parliamentarism within the International. However small his own forces, his views coincided with those of Luxemburg, Lenin, and others protesting the "revisionist" trends toward complete reformism, toward apologies for colonialism as beneficial for the colonized, and toward restriction of immigration as unfavorable to organized workers. DeLeon's *Flashlights of the Amsterdam Conference* (1906), the only substantial document produced by an American on the course of the International, took this tack throughout. Yet in the main course of relations, American delegates looked to their more successful European brethren with something bordering on awe, and understandably admired the influence and theoretical sophistication of their betters.

In at least one respect, the International had a pronounced influence in reinforcing a tendency of American socialism. The 1907 Stuttgart conference adopted a resolution encouraging socialists everywhere to "strenuously" agitate for woman suffrage. Viewing this as an official endorsement, socialist women successfully pressed for the devotion of greater party resources to the ongoing struggle for suffrage, and the broadening of party support for an annual Woman's Day celebration among other special propaganda efforts. Another element in the 1907 resolution, proscribing collaboration of socialists with bourgeois suffrage elements, could not be so carefully followed in the American context, and proved divisive to women's efforts.

By 1910, the SP's own Left added its voice to the International as William D. Haywood gained election to the Copenhagen delegation. When Victor Berger favored a clause in the resolution presented by the Germans, vetoing the call for a general strike in case of war, Haywood bitterly (and unsuccessfully) opposed him. Likewise, Haywood took the floor to excoriate the AFL and to hail industrial unionism, while Berger and Hillquit defended the labor mainstream. Personal rivalry and factional sparring continued (most notably, over Kate Richards O'Hare's election to the International Secretariat, to which the SP's moderate wing adamantly objected) until the outbreak of war rendered the International impotent.

After the war, even Victor Berger opposed U.S. socialist support of a reconvened Second International. A number of the neutral member parties attempted, in wartime, to reestablish contact, and in 1919 formed a skeletal organization with its first congress the following year. Left socialists in 1921 launched an International Working Union of Socialist Parties, known popularly as the "two and a half" international, in an effort to reunify nonrevisionist Socialist and Communist movements. Two years later, the socialist groups merged into the Labor and Socialist International, which drew the interest particularly of European refugees within the badly shrunken American SP, but lacked the authority to coordinate international opinion even among the amenable parties. It had little effect in the United States and effectively went out of existence in 1940. The revived Socialist International, founded in 1951, consists of social democratic parties, most prominently the European. The U.S. socialist representatives have, in recent decades, been fractured into the Democratic Socialists of America, the tiny Social Democrats USA (essentially a foreign-policy arm of the AFL-CIO chiefs), and the Jewish Bund. The International has occasionally played a positive role in supporting Third World sister parties, encouraging the peace process in the Middle East, and in urging negotiations rather than U.S. military actions in Latin America. *See also*: DeLeon, Daniel; International Woman's Day; May Day; Socialist Party

—Paul Buhle

REFERENCES

Buhle, Mari Jo. *Women and American Socialism.* Urbana: University of Illinois Press, 1981.

DeLeon, Daniel. *Flashlights on the Amsterdam Conference.* New York: New York Labor News Co., 1906.

Miller, Sally M. *Victor Berger and the Promise of Constructive Socialism, 1910–1920.* Westport: Greenwood Press, 1973.

SEEGER, CHARLES (1886–1979)

In a career that spanned the period from his graduation from Harvard in 1909 until his death seventy years later, Seeger established himself as a composer and conductor, musicologist, advocate of the modernist musical aesthetic, and political activist. As the chairman of the music department at the University of California at Berkeley, Seeger offered one of the country's first courses on American musicology. He also introduced the field of ethnomusicology to the New School for Social Research in 1932. It was Seeger's interest in the serious study of folk music that contributed to his development as a composer on the Left in the 1930s, even though he found many American songs to be "complacent, melancholy, defeatist." Writing in the *Daily Worker* as Carl Sands, Seeger advocated the performance of traditional songs that expressed "vigorous resistance" to oppression. As a member of the Composers' Collective (1933–36), Seeger wrote workers' rounds that contributed to that spirit of resistance.

Seeger's commitment to ethnomusicology led to his encouragement of fieldwork in North and Latin America. He served as a musical adviser to the New Deal's Resettlement Administration (1935–38) and was the deputy director of the Works Progress Administration's Federal Music Project (1938–41). In both positions, he supervised the collection and cataloging of music used by Americans in many regions of the country. In addition, he headed the music division of the Pan-American Union (1941–53). His writings on music stressed the importance of observing the acts of musical creation and performance in their historical and social context. He urged a consideration of music beyond the composer-centered Western tradition and contributed to the emergence of folk music as a legitimate area for academic study. The work of his children—Peggy, Mike, and Pete—in collecting and performing folk music has contributed to the popularization of music from a variety of ethnic and working-class sources. *See also*: Folk Music

—Barbara L. Tischler

REFERENCES

Cowell, Henry. *American Composers on American Music.* Stanford: Stanford University Press, 1933, 1962.

Dunaway, D. K. "Charles Seeger and Carl Sands; the Composers' Collective Years." *Ethnomusicology* 26/2 (1980).

SEEGER, PETE (b. 1919)

Musician, singer, songwriter, folklorist, labor activist, environmentalist, and peace advocate, Seeger was born in Patterson, New York, son of Charles and Constance Seeger, whose families traced their ancestry back to the Mayflower. Seeger grew up in an unusually politicized environment. His father, Charles, had been a music professor at the University of California at Berkeley, where his pacifism won him so many enemies that he quit teaching in the fall of 1918.

At thirteen, Pete Seeger became a subscriber to the *New Masses*. His heroes were Lincoln Steffens and Mike Gold, and he aspired to a career in journalism. In 1936 he heard the five-string banjo for the first time at the Folk Song and Dance Festival in Asheville, North Carolina, and his life was changed forever.

Seeger spent two unhappy years at Harvard and left before final exams in the spring of 1938. He made his way to New York, where he eventually landed a job with the Archives of American Folk Music. Seeger spent 1939 and 1940 seeking out legendary folk-song figures such as the blues singer Leadbelly and labor militant Aunt Molly Jackson. By 1940 he had become quite an accomplished musician, thanks in no small part to his enormous self-discipline and Puritan rectitude.

On March 3, 1940, a date folklorist Alan Lomax once said could be celebrated as the beginning of modern folk music, Seeger met Woody Guthrie at a "Grapes of Wrath" migrant-worker benefit concert. In 1940 the duo helped form the Almanac Singers, a loosely organized musical collective that included Lee Hays, Millard Lampell, Sis Cunningham, Sonny Terry, Brownie McGhee, and others.

The Almanac Singers initially recorded labor songs like "The Talking Union Blues," which they created as an organizing song for the CIO. The Almanacs also recorded pacifist tunes like "The Ballad of October 16," in retrospect an embarrassingly shrill attack on Eleanor and Franklin Roosevelt and the effort to prepare for the war against fascism.

With the entry of the United States into World War II and the creation of the U.S.-Soviet alliance, the Almanacs suddenly attained respectability. They appeared on a coast-to-coast radio broadcast, the William Morris Advertising Agency offered to help with publicity, and the group was invited to sing in some of New York's poshest nightclubs. The allure of success posed a problem for Seeger and the Almanacs that has been a particularly nettlesome one for him and artists on the Left: What concessions can or should an artist make to a mass audience without loss of artistic integrity and political radicalism?

By the time Seeger was drafted in 1942, however, critics had called attention to the Almanacs' ties, and the FBI had already begun to fill what is no doubt a very fat file on the tall, skinny balladeer. While on his first leave from the Army, Seeger also married Tashi Ohta, who virtually all of their friends agree played a crucial role in organizing Seeger's career and managing his finances.

Seeger was apparently not entangled in the sectarian squabbling that contributed to the Communist Party's weakness at the end of WW II. He had joined the Party in 1942 and would depart about 1950, but like many artists within the Party orbit, he was often viewed as unreliable.

But regardless of Seeger's feelings about the Party, it didn't take him very long to realize that amidst the paranoia and reaction of the Cold War, the union movement had no interest in associating itself with singing radicals. In 1948 Seeger accompanied Progressive Party presidential candidate Henry Wallace as he toured the South, an experience that seemed particularly depressing and alienating. Soon the People's Songs collective Seeger had established in 1945 fell apart. On September 4, 1949, Seeger's car was attacked and his wife and three-year-old son were slightly injured by shattered glass at the infamous Peekskill, New York, riot.

Seeger's creativity has always seemed nurtured by adversity. Amid the siegelike climate of the late '40s, he and Lee Hays co-wrote "If I Had a Hammer," one of the most optimistic paeans to the possibilities of constructive social change. By 1950 Hays and Seeger, along with Fred Hellerman and Ronnie Gilbert, formed the Weavers and enjoyed instant success with highly sweetened versions of "Goodnight Irene" and other folk tunes.

Just as quickly as the Weavers topped the charts, however, their career was torpedoed by blacklisting, Red-baiting, and numerous cancellations of their performances at the last minute. Seeger spent the fifties defining and nurturing his own audience. He still performed occasionally with the Weavers, but he mainly supported his family with appearances on the college circuit and at Left summer camps. He also recorded five to six albums per year for Folkways Records.

In 1955 Seeger was subpoenaed by the House Un-American Activities Committee and became one of the few witnesses called that year who didn't invoke the Fifth Amendment. In a dramatic appearance before the committee, Seeger claimed that to discuss his political views and associates violated his First Amendment rights.

The following year, which saw Seeger compose "Where Have All the Flowers Gone?," Seeger, Arthur Miller, and six others were indicted for contempt of Congress by an overwhelming vote in the House of Representatives. In 1961 he was found guilty of contempt and on April 2 he was sentenced to ten years in prison. The following year his ordeal ended when the case was dismissed on a technicality.

Seeger had cultivated a folk music revival in the 1950s, and the movement gathered momentum from 1958 into the early 1960s. ABC decided to cash in on the craze with a weekly television show, *Hootenanny*, but enthusiasm for the program waned when it was discovered that Seeger had been blacklisted and would not be permitted to appear.

Pete Seeger spent a considerable amount of time in the South during the civil rights marches of the 1960s. It was his variation of an old spiritual, which Seeger called "We Shall Overcome," that has become an anthem of the crusade for equality in America.

The Vietnam War deeply and personally offended Seeger, who used his network television return on the *Smothers Brothers Comedy Hour* to air a scathing attack on Lyndon Johnson's war policies, "Waist Deep in the Big Muddy." The song was cut by network censors, but Seeger made a second appearance on the program and sang the song without interruption.

Like many Old Leftists, Seeger was not entirely comfortable with the cultural radicalism of the 1960s. He disliked the generational tensions fostered by the movement (he once recorded a song called "Be Kind to Parents") and repeatedly advised young radicals to avoid divisions along generational lines.

Amidst the mud and despair of Resurrection City, an effort by the Rev. Martin Luther King, Jr.'s followers to carry out his dream of establishing a poor people's community in Washington and focusing the nation's attention on the problems of the poor, Seeger began to question the validity of his activism. In the 1970s and 1980s he continued to perform benefits for causes too diverse to list, but increasingly Seeger focused his attention on environmental issues.

When Pete Seeger and his friends launched the sloop *Clearwater* into the Hudson River in 1969, he was in effect fulfilling a lifelong love of the outdoors and a longstanding desire to do something to clean up the environment polluted by irresponsible corporate and public water usage.

Pete Seeger has become a highly visible and much beloved figure in American life. He has issued some one hundred records, written and collaborated on numerous radical songbooks, articles, and technical manuals on playing the banjo. Fifty years after the Popular Front, Seeger is one of the last links with the optimistic and expansive culture of Depression-era America. *see also*: Folk Music; Guthrie, Woody; *Sing Out*!

—*Richard Taskin*

REFERENCES

Dunaway, David King. *How Can I Keep From Singing: Pete Seeger*. New York: McGraw-Hill, 1983.

Seeger, Pete. *The Incompleat Folksinger*. Edited by Jo Metcalf Schwartz. New York: Simon & Schuster, 1972.

THE *SEVEN ARTS*

Both a magazine (1916–17) and a coterie, if not a small movement, of Left-leaning intellectuals and artists, the *Seven Arts* crystalized in New York City in the period marked by the First World War. Edited by James Oppenheim, Van Wyck Brooks, and Waldo Frank, the review published in its brief life such legendary figures as journalist John Reed, poet Carl Sandburg, novelists John Dos Passos and Theodore Dreiser, and essayist Randolph Bourne, along with many other notable names including Sherwood Anderson, D. H. Lawrence, and Romain Rolland. It featured many of the same authors as the older, but more colorful *Masses*. Culture critic Lewis Mumford was one of a few members of the group who did not appear in the magazine because of its early demise. Though vaguely "highbrow" in its tone, the *Seven Arts* was consciously radical in overall intention, designed to function as an evolving manifesto for a new American society. The main editor, James Oppenheim (1882–1932), was a Whitmanesque poet whose strident verse expressed the spirit of the periodical, which intended to go beyond mere commentary and reflection by inaugurating a "communism of genius" to inspire and educate the nation to set aside the limitations of commercial civilization and culture.

Beneath the editorial posture was a collective desire to promote a national cultural renaissance as an alternative to the militaristic nationalism being drummed up by the advocates of U.S. entry into WW I. When Woodrow Wilson declared war on the central powers in April 1917, the *Seven Arts* was opening its pages to Randolph Bourne (1886–1918), an outspoken critic of the war who had been cut off by most journals because of his stand.

Bourne's ensuing essays against the war, published from June through October 1917, covered the question from several perspectives, trying to capture the atmosphere of silent opposition by youth as well as the ins and outs of official prowar strategies and rationalizations. His own deep oppositionism is the strongest motif in the unique series, which ended in the last issue of the *Seven Arts* with "Twilight of Idols." Here he indicted the failure of instrumental pragmatism as a guide in the crisis and argued for intensified defiance on the part of like-minded "malcontents." Bourne called for a bold new movement armed with an ultracritical spirit that would lead the younger generation along paths yet uncharted, but certainly envisioned in the dreams of revolutionaries and radical reformers. In a writing that was quite spare of political rhetoric or axioms, his challenge was strikingly direct.

Bourne's controversial articles, a risky gambit on the part of the editors, brought pressure on the magazine's patron, who abruptly withdrew vital financial backing. The demise of the *Seven Arts* thus repeated within weeks the patriotic suppression of the *Masses*. With the collective effort curtailed, the Seven Arts group turned to work on individual projects. Bourne continued his investigation of the war mentality on a more generic level in his unfinished work, "The State," which was interrupted by his death in December 1918.

Waldo Frank and Van Wyck Brooks came together again in 1926 on the editorial board of the *New Masses*, dedicated to Left culture and politics. With them on the board was Lewis Mumford, who linked with remnants of the Seven Arts circle in 1921 and was close to its leading figures thereafter. Numerous veterans of the *Seven Arts* and the *Masses* joined these editors. In 1935 many enlisted in the new League of American Writers, which grew out of the U.S. Communist John Reed Clubs. Waldo Frank was the league's chairman until he split with the Stalinists over the stormy issue of the Moscow purge trials. Mumford and Brooks also withdrew. Later, in 1940, Frank and Mumford resigned in succession from the *New Republic* because of that journal's shyness about war against the Axis. They tried abortively to start, with the help of protestant theologian Reinhold Niebuhr, a new magazine that was to focus on the world crisis from a Left perspective.

In his individual work Lewis Mumford turned out to be the most prophetic of the group after Bourne, and perhaps the most influential. His criticism of urban civilization, expressed in more than a score of books, anticipated and helped form the radical environmental movement of the 1970s and 1980s, whose base seems destined to grow well into the nineties. His new importance for social theory is best indicated in his discovery (or interpretation) of "the megamachine," which was his term for massed and regimented human labor considered as the archetypal true machine. With such a vision latent in him in the thirties it is no surprise that he could not join in the defense of Stalin's grim vision.

More activist, although not a Communist Party member, was Waldo Frank (1889–1967), who for a time gave open support to Communist initiatives and strove to remain in the forefront of intellectual radicalism through the twenties, thirties, and beyond. An unorthodox Judaic mystic, Frank was also prophetic in a way in his plunge into *Latin Amer-*

ica in the twenties and thirties, meeting Trotsky in Mexico, being assaulted by fascist thugs in Buenos Aires, seeing the sister continent as a lecturer and informal representative of the U.S. Left. Frank also traveled in Republican Spain and other parts of Europe and wrote books about his far-flung observations, his last about Cuba after a visit with Fidel Castro in 1960.

Though his *America's Coming of Age* (1915) was one of the starting points for the socialistic philosophy of the *Seven Arts*, Van Wyck Brooks (1886–1963) was never as visible politically as a John Reed or a Waldo Frank. His deliberate concentration was on literary criticism, especially in the relatively remote field of "classical American literature," where his involvement was so intense that it led to periods of instability and a mental breakdown. Brooks' great contribution to literary criticism, an area of culture that seems peculiarly vulnerable to reactionary turns, was his insistence on a literature rooted in the common essence of human life and reflecting democratic and socialistic values. He stood against the petty formalism introduced by the so-called new critics and, by extension, against the more convoluted formalism of their structuralist and deconstructionist successors.

As a writer on American music and modern art, Paul Rosenfeld (1890–1946) occupied an even more esoteric position than Brooks. He best represents the apolitical strain in the Seven Arts philosophy. A critic of capitalist society and its culture, he was utopian enough to forgo encouragment for the Left's ranks in the thirties because their program did not include radical aesthetic demands. The grain of truth in this position can be granted; it was shared by nearly all of the Seven Arts circle, who felt that a certain poetic temperature not attainable through politics was necessary to fuse the crude and fragmented American masses into a coherent society equal to the awesome potential of twentieth-century civilization. *See also*: Frank, Waldo

—*Joseph Jablonski*

REFERENCES

Aaron, Daniel. *Writers on the Left*. New York: Harcourt, Brace & World, 1961.

Brooks, Van Wyck. *An Autobiography*. New York: Dutton, 1965.

Frank, Waldo. *Memoirs of Waldo Frank*. Amherst: University of Massachusetts Press, 1973.

Hansen, Olaf. ed. *The Radical Will*. New York: Urizen Books, 1977.

Mumford, Lewis. *Findings and Keepings, Analects for an Autobiography*. New York: Harcourt Brace Jovanovich, 1975.

Rosenfeld, Paul. *Port of New York*. Reprint. Urbana: University of Illinois Press, 1966.

The Seven Arts. Edited by James Oppenheim et al. New York (November 1916–October 1917). New York: AMS reprint, 1954.

Shachtman, Max (1904–72)

A teenage enthusiast of the Russian Revolution, a Trotskyist leader, and finally an opponent of U.S. withdrawal from Vietnam, Shachtman journeyed over five decades from one extreme to the other of the U.S. Left. Along the way he trained generations of young followers in Marxism, winning lasting devotion from some and causing bitter disillusionment in others.

A Jew born in Warsaw in 1904, Shachtman came with his mother to New York the next year. He learned socialism from his garment-worker father, his East Harlem neighbors (who nearly elected Socialist Morris Hillquit to Congress in 1916), and his history teacher at DeWitt Clinton High School. He dropped out of City College and spent his time cheering the most radical speakers at "Trotsky Square" (110th Street and Fifth Avenue), hoping someone would recruit him. When he was seventeen he joined the Workers (Communist) Party.

Soon he moved to Chicago and began organizing Southern Illinois miners. In 1925 Party leader Jim Cannon, whose midwestern Wobbly radicalism and impressive oratory Shachtman admired and imitated, made him editor of *Labor Defender*. He made it the U.S. Left's first photographic magazine. As *Labor Defender* editor he fought to save anarchists Nicola Sacco and Bartolomeo Vanzetti from execution, speaking at street-corner meetings that were broken up again and again by police. He supported Cannon in the Communist factional warfare of the 1920s.

Cannon won Shachtman over to Trotskyism in 1928. From a minor Communist leader Shachtman became a major Trotskyist leader. He edited the Trotskyists' newspaper, the *Militant*, and their journal, the *New International*, and founded Pioneer Publishers to publish Trotsky's works. He was Trotsky's admiring and trusted "commissar for foreign affairs," arranging Trotsky's moves from Turkey to France and Norway to Mexico and representing him at European conferences. When the first congress of the Fourth International met in a village outside Paris in 1938, Shachtman presided.

Shachtman's antagonism toward Stalin's regime deepened when he helped expose the 1936–38 Moscow Trials. When the Soviet Union invaded Poland he rejected Trotsky's call to defend the Soviet Union. The Trotskyists split. Shachtman decided that the USSR was a new class society, "bureaucratic collectivism." He opposed the Second World War, calling for Hitler's defeat by resistance movements instead of Allied troops. He attended the United Auto Workers' 1944 convention, convinced its Rank and File Caucus to stand fast against the no-strike pledge, and was vindicated when the convention voted it down.

After the war Shachtman's horror at the spread of Stalinism in eastern Europe and his support for United Auto Workers president Walter Reuther pulled him away from the Fourth International. He called for a rethinking of Marxism as profound as Lenin's. He supported driving Communists from the CIO, urged his followers to back labor candidates in Democratic primaries, and refused to condemn the Bay of Pigs invasion. He also left his first wife and New York City, moving with his second wife to a Long Island suburb. He joined the Socialist Party in 1958 and found new allies among top AFL-CIO officials as well as civil rights organizers like Bayard Rustin.

By 1965 Shachtman felt that his dream of a realigned, labor-based liberal party emerging from the Democratic Party was coming true. But before his realigned party was born it was torn apart by the Vietnam War. Shachtman predicted often that the Vietnam issue would go away soon. For five years he kept his small band of followers in line behind a vague call for negotiations. But while the New Left influenced some Socialists it repelled him. He clung to his allies among hawkish AFL-CIO officials. When he spoke out against U.S. withdrawal from Vietnam in 1970, his old supporters Michael Harrington and Irving Howe denounced him. His distaste for George McGovern's presidential campaign was splitting apart the SP when he died in 1972.

Shachtman captivated his followers with his slashing wit and irony, awed them with his knowledge of Marxist theory, and swept them up in his fierce emotional loyalties. Admiration turned into intense feelings of betrayal among those who recoiled from his politics. Shachtman felt betrayed in his turn by the many followers who he felt had deserted him. His last years were filled with bitterness at these deserters, whom he blamed for his repeated failures to win a mass following for socialism. But his final resolve to support the "goddamn Democrats" was tempered by nostalgic, even sentimental warmth toward those he had worked with in the 1930s to create the anti-Stalinist Left. *See also*: Socialist Party, Socialist Workers Party, Trotskyism, Workers Party

—*Peter Drucker*

REFERENCES

Max Shachtman Papers. Tamiment Library, New York University.

Wald, Alan. *The New York Intellectuals*. Chapel Hill: University of North Carolina Press, 1987.

Share Croppers Union

A predominantly black underground organization of sharecroppers, tenant farmers, and agricultural laborers, the Share Croppers Union (SCU) was the largest Communist-led mass organization in the Deep South. Founded in Alabama in the spring of 1931, the organization was first initiated by black tenant farmers in Tallapoosa County. Ralph and Tommy Gray gathered together a small group of black tenant farmers and sharecroppers and requested assistance from the Communist Party in Birmingham. Mack Coad, an illiterate black steelworker originally from Charleston, South Carolina, was dispatched from Birmingham on behalf of the CP and became the first secretary of the "Croppers and Farm Workers Union" (CFWU). Based mainly in Tallapoosa and Lee counties, Alabama, under Coad's leadership the union built up an estimated membership of 800 within a two-month period.

In July 1931, the union faced its first in a series of violent confrontations with local authorities. A shootout between union members and the local sheriff at Camp Hill, Alabama, left Ralph Gray dead and forced many union and nonunion tenant farmers into hiding. Mack Coad was forced to flee Alabama for the time being, but the union regrouped under the leadership of YCL activist Eula Gray, Tommy Gray's teenage daughter. Once the union was reconstructed, it adopted the name Share Croppers Union.

By the summer of 1932, the reconstituted SCU claimed 600 members and a new secretary was appointed. Al Murphy, a black Birmingham Communist originally from McRae, Georgia, transformed the SCU into a secret, underground organization. SCU militants were armed for self-defense and met under the auspices of "Bible meetings" and "Sewing Clubs." Under Murphy's leadership, the union spread into the "black belt" counties of Alabama and into a few areas on the Georgia-Alabama border.

In December 1932, another shootout occurred near Reeltown, Alabama (not far from Camp Hill), which resulted in the deaths of SCU members Clifford James, John McMullen, and Milo Bentley, and the wounding of several others. The confrontation erupted when SCU members tried to resist the seizure of James's livestock by local authorities who were acting on behalf of James's debtor. Following a wave of arrests and beatings, five SCU members were convicted and jailed for assault with a deadly weapon.

Faced with large-scale evictions resulting from New Deal acreage reduction policies, sharecroppers flocked to the union. Its growth was by no means hindered by the gun battle. By June 1933, Murphy claimed nearly 2,000 members, and by the fall of 1934 the official figures skyrocketed to 8,000. Although most of those who joined the union were victims of mass evictions, the SCU led a series of strikes by cotton pickers in Tallapoosa, Montgomery, and Lee counties. Nevertheless, by 1934 the SCU had failed to recruit a single white member. The Party attempted to form an all-white Tenants League, but the effort proved to be a dismal failure.

Murphy, who left Alabama in the winter of 1934, was replaced by Clyde Johnson (alias Thomas Burke and Al Jackson), a white Communist originally from Minnesota who had had considerable experience as an organizer in Birmingham, Atlanta, and Rome (Georgia). Partially reflecting the new outlook of the Popular Front, Johnson made an effort to bring the SCU out of its underground existence and transform it into a legitimate agricultural labor union. He founded and edited the SCU's first newspaper, the *Union Leader*, and created an executive committee that elected Hosie Hart, a black Communist from Tallapoosa County, as president. Johnson attempted to establish a merger with the newly formed, Socialist-led Southern Tenant Farmers Union, but the leadership of the STFU, particularly H. L. Mitchell and J. R. Butler, rejected the idea, claiming that the SCU was merely a Communist front.

Throughout 1935, despite the union's push for a legal status in the black belt, SCU activists faced severe repression during a cotton choppers' strike in the spring and a cotton pickers' strike between August and September. In Lowndes and Dallas counties, in particular, dozens of strikers were jailed and beaten, and at least six people were killed.

In 1936 the SCU, claiming between 10,000 and 12,000 members, spread into Louisiana and Mississippi. It opened its first public headquarters in New Orleans and, in an attempt to transform the SCU into a trade union, officially abandoned its underground structure. However, the SCU failed to deter the rapid process of proletarianization occurring in the cotton South—a manifestation of mass evictions and the mechanization of agriculture. Johnson continued to make overtures toward the STFU throughout 1936, but all efforts to combine the two unions failed. Thus, with support from Communist rural experts, particularly Donald Henderson, Johnson chose to liquidate the SCU as an autonomous body. All sharecroppers and tenant farmers were transferred into the ranks of the National Farmers Union, and the SCU's agricultural wage laborers were told to join the AFL-affiliated Agricultural Workers Union. The latter soon transferred into the United Cannery, Agricultural, Packing, and Allied Workers of America (UCAPAWA) in 1937.

Failing to solve the problems created by the New Deal and the mechanization of agriculture in the cotton South, the Party's decision to divide the organization "by tenure" in 1937 marked the end of the Share Croppers Union. Nevertheless, a few SCU locals in Alabama and Louisiana chose not to affiliate with any other organization and maintained an autonomous existence well into World War II. *See also*: Agrarian Radicalism; Birmingham; Communist Party; Mitchell, H. L.; Southern Tenant Farmers Union; *Southern Worker*

—*Robin D. G. Kelley*

REFERENCES

Beecher, John. "The Share Croppers' Union in Alabama." *Social Forces* 13 (October 1934).

Dyson, Lowell K. *Red Harvest: The Communist Party and American Farmers*. Lincoln: University of Nebraska Press, 1982.

Kelley, Robin D. G. "Hammer n' Hoe: *Alabama Communists During the Depression*. Chapel Hill: University of North Carolina Press, 1990.

Rosengarten, Theodore. *All God's Dangers: The Life of Nate Shaw* [*Ned Cobb*]. New York: Knopf, 1974.

Shirtwaist Makers Strike, 1909–10

Known as the "Uprising of 20,000," the general strike of New York shirtwaist makers rallied sectors of the entire community. The male leadership of the International Ladies Garment Workers Union was at first thrown off guard by the unanticipated militancy of these teenage immigrant girls but eventually seized the opportunity to put the union on firm ground. The New York Women's Trade Union League (WTUL) enjoyed its finest hour in assisting the young garment workers. Radicals of various kinds envisioned the birth of the modern proletariat and rushed forward to educate the strikers in the principles of socialism.

The strike began on November 22, 1909, at a mass meeting of shirtwaist makers in Cooper Union. After listening to a round of speeches, the young Socialist Clara Lemlich rose from the floor to address the assembly in Yiddish: "I have listened to all the speakers, and I have no further patience for talk. I am one who feels and suffers from the things pictured. I move we go on strike." The audience of 3,000 responded enthusiastically and voted to strike. Preceded by a series of small walkouts, all spontaneous protests over the grueling subcontracting system, the Cooper Union meeting thus marked the beginning of a general strike. More than 15,000 workers walked out the next morning, and within a few days their numbers topped 20,000. With nearly three-quarters of its workers on strike, the shirtwaist industry virtually shut down.

Officers of ILGWU Local 25, the shirtwaist makers' union, were unprepared to oversee a strike of this magnitude, and the responsibility fell to the WTUL, which had already begun to organize in the garment industry, and to women of the New York City Socialist Party. These women shared the work of managing the twenty halls headquartering strikers, organizing picket lines, coordinating publicity, raising funds, staging parades, bailing out jailed picketers, allotting strike benefits, and signing women into the union. Both the WTUL and Socialist women pledged to support the strikers' central demand, union recognition and the closed shop.

Despite their common loyalty to the spirit of the strike, the WTUL and Socialist women came into bitter conflict during its course and gradually hardened the line between reformist and radical strategies. The WTUL hoped to broaden its base of support by rallying women outside the labor movement, particularly those affiliated with the growing movement for woman suffrage. They won several wealthy women to their cause, notably Alva Belmont, a prominent suffragist and multimillionaire, and Anne Morgan, daughter of the financier J. P. Morgan. Whereas Belmont interpreted the strike as a stage for suffrage agitation, Morgan sought to bar Socialists in public meetings and accused them of taking advantage of the situation "to teach their fanatical doctrines." In response, the Socialists who were members of the WTUL called upon the leadership to discipline Belmont and Morgan.

When the league failed to defend Socialists, several resigned and began to issue salvos against the well-to-do suffragists. Theresa Malkiel published a fictional "autobiography," *Diary of a Shirtwaist Striker* (1910), which appeared first as a serial in the *New York Call*. Malkiel, a principal target of Morgan's attacks, worked ceaselessly throughout the strike. She led a vigorous campaign within the SP to limit cooperation with mainstream activists, especially suffragists, whom she now identified as "class enemies." Outside New York and Chicago, however, Socialist women continued to honor their historic relationship with the woman suffrage movement.

While the ranks of Socialist women split over Malkiel's absolute dictum, the party itself gained several prominent trade unionists, including Rose Schneiderman and Leonora O'Reilly, and Socialists moved into the most influential positions in Local 25, ILGWU. When the strike ended without the closed-job agreement in February 1910, Socialist women blamed their former allies, the WTUL, and pledged to keep close to their own organization in all future agitations. Unlike any previous event, the shirtwaist makers' strike served to highlight the limits as well as benefits of cross-class ventures. *See also*: International Ladies Garment Workers Union; Malkiel, Theresa; Socialist Party

—*Mari Jo Buhle*

REFERENCES

Buhle, Mari Jo. *Women and American Socialism, 1870–1920*. Urbana: University of Illinois Press, 1981.

Dye, Nancy Schrom. *As Sisters and As Equals: Feminism, Unionism, and the Women's Trade Union League of New York*. Columbia: University of Missouri Press, 1980.

Schofield, Ann. "The Uprising of the 20,000: The Making of a Labor Legend." In *A Needle, A Bobbin, A Strike: Women Needleworkers in America*, edited by Joan M. Jensen and Sue Davidson. Philadelphia: Temple University Press, 1984.

Tax, Meredith. *The Rising of the Women: Feminist Solidarity and Class Conflict, 1880–1917*. New York: Monthly Review Press, 1980.

Shoe Workers

One of the earliest unions to embrace socialist doctrines, and one of the rare socialistic Irish-dominated unions, the Boot and Shoe Workers Union reflected the strength of the nineteenth-century socialist movement.

Shoemaking, one of the earliest industries organized on a substantial scale, had seen a durable labor institution, the Knights of St. Crispin, and a republican radicalism of sorts, for decades before the appearance of the socialist movement. From the mid-nineteenth century onward, shoe workers also faced a specific, potentially radicalizing condition of accelerated mechanization. Shoe workers formed the largest single segment of the Knights of Labor in Massachusetts. But with the failure of the Knights to consolidate their position, three distinct shoe workers' organizations remained in the field. Successful consolidation took place amid an 1890s boomlet of socialistic sympathies in the labor movement. James F. Carey, later a Socialist state legislator, was among the leaders of the new Boot and Shoe Workers formed in Boston in April 1895, as was Carlton Beals, later a Socialist city marshall of Brockton.

From a political standpoint, the shoe workers provided the most important consolidated constituency for the strong Massachusetts urban socialist movement of the 1890s. As shoe workers had since the 1870s turned toward plans of cooperation to offset the emerging factory system, so shoemakers of the 1890s turned toward socialism in hopes of reducing or reversing the swift decline of conditions and wages.

Socialist influence within the B&SWU faded amid mass unemployment and an internecine conflict with the Socialist Labor Party. The SLP's Socialist Trades and Labor Alliance, unable to woo the B&SWU from the AFL, established a dual union, the General Council of Shoe Workers, both unsuccessful in its own right and destructive in its sectarian approach. At a high point of the controversy, Daniel DeLeon himself publicly debated shoe workers' leaders.

Abandoning the SLP, these leaders attempted for a time to guide a socialist union within the labor mainstream. Joining with the Social Democratic Party in Massachusetts, they helped greatly to rally support to elect John C. Chase, former shoe-worker, mayor of Haverhill, Carey and Louis Scates to the state legislature, and Carey repeatedly as city councilman in Haverhill. During this period, Massachusetts gave the socialist movement a higher vote than did any other state.

Shortly after 1900, many shoe workers joined with others in abandonment of the socialist movement, one of the Socialist Party's first major defeats and the eclipse of New England as a center of Socialist strength. The Catholic church rallied enormous energies against Socialism, as it later would against Communism, especially among Irish and French-Canadian, later also Italian workers. (Attempts by Socialists to field "labor priests" proved a failure, in the face of hierarchical opposition.) After 1903, the SP had passed its Massachusetts peak, and the Boot & Shoe Workers leaders had accepted capitalism (indeed, a number of them eventually took business positions) and Democratic candidates vaguely committed to labor sympathies.

A more conservative, dues-conscious, and undemocratic internal regime followed in the B&SWU, prompting the Industrial Workers of the World and militant socialists to contest for power outside and within the union. Denied victory for elected leadership of the union in 1907, rebels established a radical-led United Shoe Workers of America in 1909, primarily among the highly skilled lasters. In time, the differences between the two organizations lessened, the two weak unions barely surviving the 1920s to grow modestly in the 1930s and the early 1940s. In the postwar period, Communist officers were quickly purged, and the union fell into a decline that runaway shops greatly exacerbated. *See also*: British Americans

—*Paul Buhle*

REFERENCES

Davis, Horace. *Shoes, the Workers, and the Industry*. New York: International Publishers, 1940.

Laslett, John. *Labor and the Left: A Study of Socialist and Radical Influences in the American Labor Movement, 1881–1924*. New York: Basic Books, 1970.

Siegmeister, Elie (b. 1909)

Called a "composer with a conscience," Siegmeister has labored throughout his career to synthesize a modernist compositional bent with a strong desire to compose American music for the American people. As a student at Columbia College, where he earned a B.A. in 1927, Siegmeister studied composition with Seth Bingham and counterpoint with Wallingford Riegger. Between 1927 and 1931, he studied in France with Nadia Boulanger, absorbing valuable lessons from her on compositional technique while feeling ever more dissatisfied with her abstract approach to music's relationship to its audience.

On his return to New York, Siegmeister was a member of the Young Composers Group, which featured meetings and mutual criticism and one performance at the New School for Social Research on January 15, 1933. From 1933 to 1936, Siegmeister was active in the Composers Collective, to which he contributed ideas on the relationship between music and its political and social context as well as several compositions. "Strange Funeral in Braddock" (1933) with a text by Mike Gold, tells the story of Jan Clepak, a Bohemian steelworker who is buried in a vat of liquid metal because of unsafe working conditions. The modernist style of this song conveys the pain and anger of Clepak's family and co-workers, but it was composed for listening rather than audience participation. In contrast, "The Scottsboro Boys Shall Not Die," published by the Collective in its first *Workers Song Book*, is easy to sing while also conveying a sharp political message about racial justice and the evils of lynching. Siegmeister also composed workers' rounds intended for inexperienced performers of the collective's songbooks.

In 1939 Siegmeister founded the American Ballad Singers, a group that performed folk music at a time when the complex American musical heritage was being discovered in the music of immigrants, African Americans, cowboys, and band workers. He conducted this group until 1946. Many of Siegmeister's orchestral compositions from the early 1930s until the late 1940s, including "American Holiday" (1933), "Abraham Lincoln Walks at Midnight" (1937), "Ozark Set" (1943), "Prairie Legend" (1944), and "Sunday in Brooklyn" (1946), reveal an interest in American settings and folk and popular music. In an effort to make folk music more accessible, Siegmeister published *A Treasury of American Folk Song* in 1940. His *Music Lover's Handbook*, first published in 1943, offers many expressions of his philosophy that music and the life of ordinary people must be naturally integrated in order to express an American identity and also be good music. He noted that "Art with a capital *A* is a menace: music must relate to life."

Siegmeister continued to write music with politically conscious themes and texts long after other composers who participated in the activities of various groups on the Left and who used folk and popular music in their compositions for the concert hall shifted to other styles and aesthetic principles. His later works that demonstrate this commitment include the cantata "I Have a Dream" (1967) and "Cantata for FDR" (1981). Siegmeister helped to organize the May 24, 1968, concert presented by "Composers and Musicians for Peace." He taught at Hofstra University from 1949 to 1976, serving as the school's composer-in-residence during the last ten years of that period. *See also*: Composers Collective, Scottsboro Case

—*Barbara L. Tischler*

REFERENCES

Mandel, Alan. "Elie Siegmeister." In *The New Grove Dictionary of American Music*. Edited by Stanley Sadie and H. Wiley Hitchcock. London: Macmillan, 1986.

Oja, Carol J. "Composer with a Conscience: Elie Siegmeister in Profile." *American Music* 6, no. 2 (Summer 1988).

Siegmeister, Elie, ed. *The New Music Lover's Handbook*. Irvington-on-Hudson, N.Y.: Harvey House, 1973.

Simkins, Modjeska Monteith (b. 1899)

In the same year Walter Hines Page wrote a friend that he would rather be "an imp in Hades than a Negro in South Carolina," Simkins was born in South Carolina. Part of the brown bourgeoisie (father a businessman and mother a teacher) of the state capital, Columbia, Simkins received her A.B. degree at Benedict College. She taught school until 1930, when she married Andrew Whitfield Simkins, grandson of a Reconstruction black leader. Since state law prohibited married women from teaching, Modjeska Simkins became involved in civil reform activities. She directed the South Carolina Tuberculosis Association for African-Americans, various social projects, became involved with New Deal agencies, and during the 1930s began focusing on civil rights for blacks. In 1941 she was elected secretary of the newly founded South Carolina Conference for the NAACP.

She worked for the equalization of salaries between white and black teachers, for the abolition of the white primary system, and for the desegregation of South Carolina public schools (including the Clarendon County case that resulted in the Supreme Court's declaring segregated schools unconstitutional). As a spokesperson for African Americans in South Carolina, Simkins became involved in a number of national organizations. In 1946 she became the South Carolina liaison to the Civil Rights Congress (formed when the International Labor Defense and the National Federation for Constitutional Liberties merged) and served on the Resolutions and the Continuations committees. She was the South Carolina liaison to and on the national advisory board of the United Negro and Allied Veterans of America. In 1947 she joined the Southern Conference for Human Welfare and served on their board of representatives and helped produce several reports for the group. That same year she became active in supporting the Southern Negro Youth Conference. In the 1949 "Freedom Caravan from the Fighting South," she campaigned in Harlem for reelection of councilman Benjamin Davis on the Communist Party ticket. In 1951 she became active with the American Peace Crusade. She was an initial sponsor of the group and held several offices and participated as a delegate at different meetings. She also worked in the Southern Regional Council and the Southern Conference Educational Fund. Her name regularly appeared on petitions and letters in the *Daily Worker*, the *Daily People's World*, and the *Worker*.

Always outspoken, Simkins had a deep involvement in civil rights, which increasingly led her to Left movements. She was dismissed as state secretary of the NAACP in 1957 because a number of organizations that Simkins worked with were accused of being Communist fronts. She remained in the NAACP, but accepted a public relations position at the Victory Savings Bank. During her unsuccessful runs for the Columbia City Council (1966) and the State House of Representatives (1968), she was smeared with red paint for associations with groups the House Un-American Activities Committee (the committee had a two-page list on Simkins's affiliations) had declared "Communist fronts" and subversive organizations. For the next two decades, Simkins's civic and reform activities centered around local projects. Most notably, she served as the public relations director of the Richland County Citizens Committee, an organization that encouraged direct political action on the part of the African-American population and sponsored programs to desegregate the city's public schools, to integrate and improve the state mental hospital, and to desegregate the city's recreational facilities. In 1988 she helped bring a victorious voting rights suit against Richland County. *See also*: Civil Rights, Civil Rights Congress, *Daily Worker*, Southern Negro Youth Conference

—*Orville Vernon Burton*

REFERENCES

Modjeska Monteith Simkins Papers, University of South Carolina Library.

Aba-Mecha, Barbara Woods. "Black Woman Activist in Twentieth Century South Carolina: Modjeska Monteith Simkins." Ph.D. diss., Emory University, 1978.

Sinclair, Upton (1878–1968)

The greatest socialist writer of the age, Sinclair poured into novels, plays, and essays his intense hatred for capitalism. He found a readership for denunciations of the many wrongs of American life, and presented an interpretation of society in terms of class struggle, which makes his wide audience all the more interesting. Highbrow readers have often been uncomfortable at the limitations of his work as literature, and laughed at his pre-Freudian view of individual psychology. "In so far as Mr. Sinclair's books show us anything real," wrote Van Wyck Brooks in 1921, "they show us the utter helplessness, the benightedness, the ignorance, the *naiveté* of the American proletarian movement." But such views fail to account for the power of the novels, their widespread influence, and Sinclair's energy and socialist fervor.

He was born in Baltimore, and attended City College in New York. His literary career began in the popular fiction and journalism of the turn of the century. He wrote hackwork in the genres of commercial writing, turning out jokes, stories, sketches, serials, romances, and five-cent novels for adolescents. It was poorly paid, exploitative work that gave Sinclair an understanding of the way the poor were trapped. What he learned about plotting and characterization for a mass readership stayed with him when, in 1902, he was freed by the financial support of the Rev. George D. Herron to write his first serious novel, *Manassas*. His exposure to the Christian socialism of Herron, and the influence of William Morris and his American disciples who published the *Comrade*, came as a revelation. The conversion experience remained central to Sinclair's radicalism. In his most important novels he sought to portray how the conversion to socialism might come about.

In 1904 he spent seven weeks in the stockyards of Chicago investigating conditions in the meatpacking industry. The novel he produced, *The Jungle* (1906), which was serialized in the *Appeal to Reason*, was in the best tradition of muckraking journalism. Jack London called it "the *Uncle Tom's Cabin* of wage slavery." Despite the efforts of the meatpacking industry to discredit his novel, it made a substantial contribution to the campaign to regulate and inspect conditions. A disillusioned Sinclair remarked that he had aimed at the public heart and by accident hit the stomach.

Sinclair joined the Socialist Party in 1904, helped found the Inter-Collegiate Socialist Society, and used some of the profits from *The*

Jungle to found the Helicon Hall Home Colony in Englewood, New Jersey. He remained a convinced socialist long after many of his contemporaries had made their compromises with American capitalism. But he was without millennial expectations and shared the perspective of the right-wing leadership of the party, who believed that the future of the movement lay in patient electoral work, party propaganda, and a cautious cultivation of Samuel Gompers and the AFL. (In *The Industrial Republic*, 1907, he argued for a socialism that made no pretensions at changing business methods, or the moral and intellectual inclinations of his countrymen.) Although he broke with the party in 1917 and went on to publish a war novel (*Jimmie Higgins*), he soon repented his enthusiasm for Woodrow Wilson and in polemical books such as *The Brass Check* (1919), *The Goose Step* (1923), and *Mammonart* (1925), did much to stir up trouble for the establishment. He had an incomparable instinct for the scandals and oppressions of the day. In novels like *King Coal* (1917) and *Oil* (1927) he showed how a journalistic persistence and a flair for exciting narrative could dramatize important contemporary issues from a socialist point of view.

In the early 1930s there was much ambivalence toward Sinclair within the Communist Party. Granville Hicks in *The Great Tradition* (1933) was curtly impatient with Sinclair's free-floating (i.e., non-Party) socialism, and hostile toward his literary achievement. When Sinclair created a political action group, End Poverty in California (EPIC), which won control of the machinery of the Democratic Party in 1934, Communists bitterly opposed his candidacy. Although supported by a broad coalition of the unemployed, trade unionists, and progressives, he was narrowly defeated for governor in 1934.

After the EPIC campaign, Sinclair grew less politically active, but maintained his extraordinary literary output. Beginning in 1939, he wrote a series of eleven "Lanny Budd" novels describing American history through the life of his protagonist. *From Dragon's Teeth*, third in the series, won the Pulitzer Prize in 1943. Other works notably lionized Franklin Roosevelt. The last in the series, *Return of Lanny Budd*, dramatized Sinclair's vision of postwar democratic struggles against the Communists worldwide. Sinclair had, in his way, become almost respectable. He was widely praised in the mainstream media, and translated into forty languages. And yet he remained, in his own eyes, a socialist and visionary late into his old age. *See also*: Radical Novels, 1870–1930

—*Eric Homberger*

REFERENCES

Harris, Leon. *Upton Sinclair: American Rebel*. New York: Crowell, 1975.

Homberger, Eric. *American Writers and Radical Politics, 1900–39: Equivocal Commitments*. London: Macmillan, 1986.

Sing Out!/Broadside

Built on the groundwork laid by *People's Songs*, *Sing Out!* began monthly publication in May 1950. Like its predecessor, *Sing Out!* sought to foster a general revival in folk music and topical songs and create a progressive song movement, spearheaded by a singing labor movement. Many of the same individuals were involved in *Sing Out!*, and many newer singers, composers, and folklorists, like Sis Cunningham, Gordon Friesen, Malvina Reynolds, and others found space for their endeavors within its pages. *Sing Out!* retained and expanded on *People's Songs*' commitment to diverse musical cultures and Pete Seeger remained one of its driving forces. The unexpected commercial success of the Weavers (Seeger, Lee Hays, Ronnie Gilbert, and Fred Hellerman) provided folk music with an audience far broader than previously imagined and laid the foundation for the folk revival of the mid- to late 1950s and early 1960s. After the first few years of financial uncertainty, *Sing Out!* managed to find a national audience of 15,000 and influenced the establishment of similar magazines in England, continental Europe, Australia, New Zealand, and Japan. *Sing Out!* continued into the 1980s to give lyrics and inspiration to popular struggles of the times.

Broadside, a "sibling" of *Sing Out!*, also grew out of this tradition. A crudely mimeographed bulletin foreshadowing the 1960s underground press, it began publication in February 1962, issued "about twice a month," and served as "The National Topical Song Magazine." Although Seeger acted in an advisory capacity, and Sis Cunningham served as editor, *Broadside* was the project of a younger generation of singers and writers interested in topical songs in which "the 'commercial musical world' had little or no interest." *Broadside*'s existence paralleled the emergence of a whole school of talented topical songwriters like Phil Ochs, Bob Dylan, Gil Turner, Ernie Marrs, Pete La Farge, Ana Perez, Nina Simone, Eric Anderson, Dick Farina, Tom Paxton, and Len Chandler among others. While *People's Songs*, and to a lesser extent *Sing Out!*, derived their inspiration from organized labor, *Broadside* found its voice in the civil rights movement and the emergent New Left. It issued special reports, articles, and songs by civil rights activists like Charles Sherrod, Bernice Reagon, and Julius Lester. Political, but in a highly undoctrinaire New Left style, *Broadside*, until its demise in 1970, sowed the seeds of the popular song revolution of that era. *See also*: Folk Music; Seeger, Pete

—*Robert Macieski*

REFERENCES

Seeger, Pete. *The Incompleat Folksinger*. New York: Simon and Schuster, 1972.

Shelton, Robert. *No Direction Home: The Life and Music of Bob Dylan*. New York: Ballantine Books, 1986.

Sing Out! 1, no. 3 (July 1950).

SIT-DOWN STRIKES

Workers remain in their workplace in these strikes, which are also known as sit-in or stay-in strikes. They can range from a quick

Strike graphic, 1937
Drawing by Herb Kruckman

strike in a single department while a particular grievance is negotiated with management to plantwide, companywide, and even nationwide occupation of factories, offices, and stores. An example of the last was the French general strike of 1968 in which ten million French workers occupied virtually all the factories of France and came close to bringing down the DeGaulle government.

Examples of sit-down strikes can be found in preindustrial societies, although they are rare. Some occurred in the nineteenth century, with the first one reported in the United States among brewery workers in Cincinnati in 1884. Major factory occupations took place in Italy just after World War I. Sit-down strikes reached their peak, however, in the 1930s. The first major one to give the technique prominence was at the Goodyear Tire and Rubber Company in Akron, Ohio, in February and March of 1936, part of the organizing drive of the then-new CIO. In May and June of 1936 there were major sit-down strikes in France, following the election of a People's Front coalition government. French unions were not involved in these strikes until well after they had begun and the French Communist Party tried to prevent them to avoid damaging the People's Front government. In December 1936 and well into the winter of 1937, the most influential of these strikes in the United States took place at a series of General Motors facilities, centering in Flint, Michigan. This strike achieved the recognition of the United Auto Workers as bargaining agent for GM workers and set the pattern for a wave of sit-down strikes all over the United States in factories, offices, stores, and other settings.

There is a significant element of spontaneity in sit-down strikes because union leaders tend to be very uneasy about the inherent challenge to private property contained in the taking over of production facilities and, while they may be forced to support such strikes, rarely initiate them. Local union leaders, however, may be very much involved in organizing and sustaining such strikes.

Sit-down strikes have the advantage to workers of preventing scabbing or the continuing of normal or partial operation by employers; they offer protection from attack by police forces or vigilantes; and they hold the property of employers hostage in negotiations over demands or grievances. They are usually illegal, and in the United States, after the wave of sit-down strikes in the 1930s, were made illegal everywhere by direct statute.

There are possible extensions of the sit-down strike that can lead to further challenges to existing societies. In Japan, at the end of WW II, Tokyo bus drivers went on strike by staying on their jobs and running the buses. They simply did not collect fares, thus not alienating the bus-riding public. At the other extreme, the workers of Hungary in 1956 occupied the factories and took over their management through workers' councils, achieving the beginning of a social revolution.

It would seem that sit-down strikes offer too many advantages to workers to disappear entirely from the arsenal of working-class weapons. *See also*: Industrial Workers of the World, United Auto Workers

—*Martin Glaberman*

REFERENCES

Fine, Sidney. *Sit-down: The General Motors Strike of 1936–1937.* Ann Arbor: University of Michigan Press, 1969.

Slovenian Americans

Approximately 200,000 Slovenians came to the United States from the Austro-Hungarian Empire between 1880 and the end of World War I. They came from what is now Slovenia in the northernmost section of Yugoslavia, and from the adjacent territories of the Yugoslav-Austria and Yugoslav-Italian borders. Although Slovenians possessed a higher educational level than surrounding peoples, Slovenian immigrants found themselves overwhelmingly employed in manual labor. A majority settled in the mining regions of the midwest and northwest, as well as in industrial cities such as Cleveland, Pittsburgh and Chicago where they commonly worked in steel, iron and automobile industries.

Due to their language skills, education and ability to combine effectively with other Slavic groups, Slovenian Americans played a disproportionate role in American socialist movements, unions, and socialistically-inclined fraternal organizations. They formed the Slovenian Socialist Federation and later helped form the Croatian and Serbian Socialist Federation. They took a leading role in the Yugoslav Socialist Federation, with Slovenian, Croatian and Serbian branches, founded in 1909 and surviving into the 1950s. *Proletarec* (The proletariat), organ of the Slovenian Socialist Federation, and *Ameriski druzinski Koledar* (Slovenian American family almanac) were published in Chicago for decades. The Slovene National Benefit Society (SNPJ), founded in 1904, not only provided its membership with life and accident insurance, but also with social and ethnic camaraderie and with a press, *Prosveta*, in which its readers could learn about socialist ideas. Its most famed editors, novelist-critic Ivan Molek and Joze Zavertnik, influenced community thought widely.

To the left of the Socialist Party, Slovenians played a major role in the "South Slavonian Federation" of the Socialist Labor Party (SLP), in which Croatians and Serbians also participated, with their own press and calendar. Slovenian SLPer Frank Petrovich was, indeed, perhaps the most important public personality of the post-De Leon SLP. Although of marginal importance to the outside world, the South Slavonian Federation (and its organ, *Radnika Borba*) supplied funds to maintain the SLP's public presence until the federation's demise in the 1960s. Slovenians, unlike the Croatians, never participated significantly either in the Communist Party or its fraternal International Workers Order.

The source of Slovenians' unique alignment within the Left can be traced to national sentiments dramatized by the world wars. The Slovenian faction did not follow the line of the Socialist Party against involvement in the war. Together with liberals, they helped form a Slovenian and later a Yugoslav–Republican Alliance (*Hugoslvansko republicansko Zdrunznje*), an organization that supported the idea of Yugoslavia as a federated republic. Slovenian/socialist leader from Austro-Hungary, Etbin Kristan—caught in the United States, by the outbreak of European fighting, while on a lecture tour—became leader of the organization. The Slovenian socialists rejoined the Socialist Party after the war, and remained one of its faithful (if aging and gradually diminishing) sections, until leaving the Party again, once more to favor war participation, in 1941.

Slovenians, as many other South Slavs, widely favored Tito-partisans, notwithstanding the partisans' Communist affiliations. They formed the powerful Slovenian American National Council with Etbin Kristan as president and Louis Adamic as honorary president. The council in turn helped form the United Committee of South Slavic Americans under Adamic's presidency. A vital part of the American Slav Congress, they opposed the emerging Cold War as unnecessary and harmful to the new Yugoslavia. In their last major political act, South Slav socialists (and SNPJ loyalists) avidly supported Henry Wallace's campaign for the presidency on the Progressive Party ticket.

Unlike the fraternal societies associated with the International Workers Order, the SNPJ escaped the worst of the McCarthy era repression, and has remained a vital community presence with insurance benefits and an ambitious cultural program. Outsurviving its founders by several generations, the SNPJ retains some 50,000 members. Its *Prosveta*, by this time a liberal/social democratic weekly with Slovenian and English language sections, has continued to take strong stands on labor and social issues, especially favoring a detente which would benefit Yugoslav-American relations. *See also*: American Slav Congress, Croatian Americans, Socialist Labor Party

—*Matjaz Klemencic*

REFERENCES

Klemencic, Matjaz. *Ameriski Slovenci in Nob v Jugoslaviji*. Maribor: Zalozbva Obzorja, 1987.

SNPJ Papers, Immigration History Research Center, University of Minnesota.

SMEDLEY, AGNES (*1892–1950*)

An American radical, a feminist, and an internationalist, Smedley achieved distinction as a novelist and foreign correspondent.

Born into a Missouri tenant farmer family, growing up in a succession of Colorado mining camps near the site of the Ludlow massacre, Smedley devoted her life to publicizing and supporting what she saw as the most hopeful and humane forces within the Indian and Chinese independence and revolutionary movements, while waging a fiercely independent lifelong struggle for the equality of women and her own autonomy.

Her autobiographical novel *Daughter of Earth* (1929) is an early feminist classic. However, it was her writing and speaking about and on behalf of independence and liberation movements in India in the 1920s and in China from 1929 until her death in 1950 that left the deepest impression on American and foreign readers during her lifetime.

Smedley was among the first foreign correspondents to report from Communist headquarters in Yenan in 1937. Subsequently, as the only woman war correspondent at the front in the China theater, she traveled with Communist Eighth Route Army forces reporting from behind Japanese lines. Her posthumously published (auto) biography of General Zhu De (old spelling: Chu Teh), *The Great Road: The Life and Times of Chu Teh* (1956) and her reportage from the front, *Battle Hymn of China* (1984)—derived from her experiences in wartime China. Both are major works that express her conviction that the Chinese Communist Party was the single force capable of bringing national independence, democracy, and social justice to China. She died in England in 1950 in the midst of a campaign to brand her as a Communist and a spy. *See also*: Asian Studies

—*Mark Seldon*

REFERENCES

Mackinnon, Janice, and Stephen Mackinnon. *Agnes Smedley: The Life and Times of an American Radical*. Berkeley: University of California Press, 1988.

Smedley, Agnes. *Portraits of Chinese Women in Revolution*. Edited by Jan Mackinnon and Steve Mackinnon. New York: Feminist Press, 1976.

SMITH ACT TRIAL, 1943

Adopted by the U.S. Congress in 1940, the Smith Act made it a crime to teach, advocate, or encourage the overthrow of the U.S. government. It was first used against Trotskyists who were members of the Socialist Workers Party and of Minneapolis Teamsters Local 544. As the United States was preparing for World War II, the Trotskyists refused to refrain from denouncing what they saw as imperialist war aims of the U.S. government. At the same time, they were a powerful force in the Minneapolis Teamsters Union and were locked in a fierce dispute with conservative Teamster president Daniel J. Tobin, a key national labor supporter of Franklin D. Roosevelt.

Of the twenty-eight who were arrested in 1941, eighteen were brought to trial in Minneapolis Federal Court in 1943. Among the defendants were SWP national secretary James P. Cannon; SWP national labor secretary Farrell Dobbs; SWP attorney Albert Goldman, editor of the SWP's weekly *Militant* Felix Morrow, SWP Minnesota organizers Grace Carlson and Oscar Coover, and such leaders and activists in Teamsters Local 544 as V. R. Dunne and Karl Skoglund.

The Communist Party, which considered the Trotskyists pro-Nazi "fifth columnists," supported the Smith Act prosecution, although the very same law would be turned against the CP a few years later. Many others associated with left-wing and liberal causes, however, opposed the trial. Hundreds of local unions throughout the country and several national unions also came out in support of the defendants.

Far from disavowing or blurring their revolutionary ideas, the defendants utilized the trial to proclaim, defend, and explain them. James P. Cannon's trial testimony and Albert Goldman's concluding speech were published in large quantities by the SWP as popular socialist educational tools.

The defendants were convicted and served twelve- to eighteen-month prison sentences during 1944–45. *See also*: Socialist Workers Party, Trotskyism

—*Paul LeBlanc*

REFERENCES

Cannon, James P. *Letters from Prison*. New York: Merit Publishers, 1968.

———. *Socialism on Trial*. New York: Pathfinder Press, 1973.

Dobbs, Farrell. *Teamster Bureaucracy*. New York: Monad Press, 1977.

Farrell, James T. et al. *Who Are the 18 Prisoners in the Minneapolis Labor Case?* New York: Civil Rights Defense Committee, 1944.

Socialist Workers Party. *Why We Are in Prison: Farewell Speeches of the 18 SWP and 544-CIO Minneapolis Prisoners.* New York: Pioneer Publishers, 1944.

Snow, Edgar (1905–72)

Born in Kansas City, Missouri, and educated at the Missouri School of Journalism, Snow rose from his midwestern background to international fame as an intrepid journalist. After graduating from college, he made his way to Shanghai, China, at the age of twenty-two, and traveled by railroad to much of the rest of the country, which was in a chronic state of turmoil due to conflicts among warlords, the Kuomintang, and the young Communist movement. Snow reported on the situation in China for a number of newspapers and journals.

After several years of teaching in Peking, Snow made his way to far western China's Yenan province, where Mao Tse-tung had established a stronghold. In Yenan Snow obtained the confidence of Mao and other leaders, who had just survived the epic long march of several thousand miles from southern China. Snow's account of this, *Red Star over China* (1937), was the first by any Western journalist, and brought the remarkable story of China's Communist movement to world attention.

Snow also covered events in Burma, India, and Indochina, as well as the Soviet Union during World War II, and published some eleven books during his lifetime. His honest, straightforward, and plain-speaking style gained him the confidence of leaders as diverse as Franklin Delano Roosevelt and Gandhi, and his books enjoyed a quite wide circulation.

In his later years, Snow lived in Switzerland, and after his death the Edgar Snow Collection and Visiting Professorship was established at the University of Missouri-Kansas City. *See also*: Asian Studies

—*Fred Whitehead*

REFERENCES

Hamilton, John Maxwell. *Edgar Snow: A Biography.* Bloomington: University of Indiana Press, 1989.

Snow, Edgar. *Journey to the Beginning.* New York: Random House, 1958.

Snow, Lois Wheeler. *Edgar Snow's China.* New York: Random House, 1981.

Socialist Feminism

In the mid-1960s, women activists in the civil rights and New Left movements began to apply radical visions of freedom and equality to their own lives. The women's liberation movement that resulted, passionate and iconclastic, conceptualized feminism in ways that went well beyond earlier feminist movements. Participants developed diverse views of women's liberation, among them socialist feminism. By 1970, socialist feminism had consolidated into a distinct trend within the modern women's movement.

Socialist feminists hoped to meld a materialist analysis of class domination with the best insights of radical feminism—its searing critique of male domination, its insistence that the personal is political, its creative development of nonhierarchical structures, its strategy of organizational autonomy, and its commitment to free sexual choice and expression. Their goal was a collectivist transformation of society that would be simultaneously feminist and socialist. Within the women's movement, socialist feminists sought to develop a feminist practice and theory that could address the needs of the majority of women—be they working-class, poor, black, brown, or red. Socialist feminists considered themselves part of the Left as well as of the women's movement, and many were active in Left organizations. Within the Left, they proposed that progressive individuals and groups pay careful and consistent attention to the special issues of women. Socialist feminists thus attempted to chart a path linking the claims of two quite different social movements. Not surprisingly, they frequently found themselves condemned as "bourgeois individualists" by leftists, and scorned as "male-identified politicos" by radical feminists. Nonetheless, they persisted in their efforts to develop an approach that would integrate the aspirations of the women's liberation movement and the Left.

Socialist feminists emphasized the qualitatively distinct character of the collective experience of diverse groups, and they sought to respect the specificity of each. In particular, they rejected the traditional liberal feminist goal of individual assimilation into the mainstream. They also rejected traditional Left analyses that subsumed issues of racism and sexism within the class struggle, or postponed women's liberation until after the socialist revolution, when all problems would somehow be automatically resolved. The questions socialist feminism posed to and for the Left thus converged, to some extent, with those long posed by the black movement within the United States, and by national liberation movements around the world.

Most American socialist feminists hardly differentiated between Marxist and non-Marxist socialisms, in this way reflecting the weakness of Left traditions in the United States. As the socialist-feminist movement evolved, disagreements concerning the relevance and interpretation of Marx, Marxism, and the Left tradition arose, but it is nonetheless not possible to demarcate some Marxist-feminist trend distinct from socialist feminism. Socialist feminists generally agreed that Marx and Engels paid serious attention to the so-called woman question, and assumed that a historical and materialist approach is necessary. At the same time they argued that the socialist tradition did not provide adequate theoretical or historical accounts of women's situation, much less practical guidance in the struggle for women's liberation. They differed, often widely, on the interpretation of these inadequacies as well as on just which of the tradition's elements remain useful and how more adequate analyses and practice should be developed.

Socialist feminism took a variety of organizational forms. Small socialist-feminist collectives worked with poor and working-class women in factories and communities, seeking to raise consciousness while fighting for maternity benefits and child care or staffing battered women's shelters. Socialist feminists joined or formed women's health collectives that critiqued profit-making health care and developed self-help alternatives. Consciousness-raising groups, which were a central focus of the women's liberation movement, provided an exhilarating opportunity for leftist women to think politically on their own. Citywide socialist-feminist women's unions initiated campaigns for reproductive rights and against sterilization abuse. A national network of study groups pledged to dissolve the tensions between its members' Marxism and their feminism. Many socialist feminists also participated in the broader women's and mass movements of the time; they became active in local feminist groupings, in national organizations such as the National Organization for Women (NOW), the National Abortion Rights Action League, and the Coalition of Labor Union Women, and in antiwar, antinuclear, environmental, electoral, and other progressive campaigns. In the legal and policy arenas, socialist-feminist lawyers and activists worked to develop strategies that would go beyond the narrow individualism of traditional liberal feminism. Socialist-feminist scholars played a leading role in the development of women's studies in colleges and universities.

Some socialist feminists chose to work within Left organizations. One group, the New American Movement, described itself from the start as socialist-feminist, and others attempted to deal consistently with issues of women's liberation. But most Left organizations retained a traditional skepticism toward feminism, even in its newly elaborated socialist-feminist variant. Left groups were especially nervous about socialist feminism's critique of relations in the so-called private sphere, its views on the family, its commitment to the organizational autonomy of the women's movement, and its endorsement of gay rights and a freer sexuality. Feminists who were members of such organizations often paid the heavy price of isolation from the socialist-feminist community without being compensated by support for their efforts from within the group.

Socialist-feminist organizations were generally small and short-lived, never able to consolidate the resources and stability of mainstream feminist groups such as NOW. By the late 1970s, the double assault of economic recession and political reaction had taken its toll. Some socialist feminists concluded that their movement had died, but many argued that although weakened it survived in altered form. All agreed that the gap between socialist-feminist practical and theoretical activities had widened. Socialist-feminist activists were continuing to participate in women's organizations, progressive campaigns, and the Left, but now largely without the support of the vibrant socialist-feminist intellectual culture that had earlier been an integral element of socialist feminism as a movement. Socialist-feminist theorists, increasingly settled in academia, pursued research agendas that were less and less determined by practical questions of social change. A new generation of feminists had come of age that had never experienced the organic personal connections between activists and theorists that had been an everyday experience in the women's liberation movement.

From the start, socialist feminists sought to develop a theoretical foundation that would underpin their myriad practical activities. First in the form of papers, pamphlets, and articles in movement newspapers or magazines, then increasingly as books and scholarly articles, socialist-feminist theoretical work burgeoned. One of the main questions socialist-feminist theorists addressed concerned the sources of women's subordination. Women's activities in the family household constituted, they suggested, the material basis of female oppression. Early socialist-feminist theorists used traditional Marxist categories to examine this "domestic labor." What came to be called the domestic labor debate was heavily criticized, however, as narrow and abstruse. Many proposed that women's experience might better be understood through the concept of patriarchy, imported from radical feminism. By the late 1970s, the predominant view among socialist feminists was that women are trapped within two coordinate systems of oppression, capitalism and patriarchy. In turn, this approach was censured for its simplistic dualism, and for its tendency to leave the analysis of capitalism to an unreconstructed traditional Marxist analysis.

The attempt to generate an integrated Marxist-feminist theoretical framework for the analysis of capitalist patriarchy produced a great deal of frustration among socialist feminists. American efforts to develop socialist-feminist theory were hampered by isolation from the renaissance of Marxist thought that had been flourishing in Europe since the early 1960s, and by a general impatience with theory; in addition, the repressive rightward political shifts of the post-Vietnam era quickly undercut the previous decade's radical optimism. In the more realistic mood of the late 1970s, socialist feminists recognized that the ambiguities of women's experience required a more subtle analytical approach. Many rejected the conceptual frameworks that had led to what they now saw as an "unhappy marriage of Marxism and feminism." They turned instead to historically rooted empirical studies, to more eclectic approaches to theory, or to new philosophical orientations that challenged conventional assumptions about the objectivity and certainty of knowledge. Those socialist feminists who retained the goal of developing a Marxist-feminist theoretical synthesis undertook the task with a more sophisticated awareness of its multitiered complexity.

By the early eighties, socialist feminists were addressing a broad range of concerns: the material basis for and history of women's subordination; the specificity of sexism as opposed to racism or class subordination; the diversity among women, flowing especially from differences of class, race, and ethnicity, but also from distinctions of age, ability, and sexual preference; the relationship between Marxism and feminism; the role of families in societal reproduction; the place of women workers in the economy; the situation of women in socialist societies; the politics of women's liberation; the interplay of sexuality, consciousness, and ideology; the construction, reproduction, and representation of gendered subjectivity. In addition, numerous socialist feminists found themselves with fairly secure positions in academia, where their work adapted itself to disciplinary boundaries.

Socialist-feminist scholars participated in the feminist critique of the traditional academic disciplines, and in the development of new perspectives and methods, often cutting across the disciplines.

Because socialist feminism was a movement committed to social transformation, research on the politics of women's liberation was especially significant. Socialist feminists analyzed the concept of equality, both examining its origins in liberal political theory and affirming its radical potential. They investigated women's activism in earlier social movements, thereby placing contemporary feminist politics in historical context. Socialist-feminist studies of women in Third World countries emphasized the dangers of projecting Western concepts of the politics of women's liberation onto societies with sharply distinct histories and realities. The question of women's liberation in socialist societies was a matter of great interest and debate among socialist feminists, for socialist societies provide an opportunity to examine the relationship between feminism and socialism as it develops in actual historical processes. Socialist feminists offered a diversity of views on both the obstacles to and the prospects for women's liberation in socialist societies.

Despite its commitment to a feminist analysis that includes all women, socialist feminism was a mostly white and predominantly middle-class movement. Black and other Third World women generally remained at a distance from organized feminism, even in its socialist-feminist variant, as did working-class and poor women. At the same time, a practical version of feminism took hold at the grass-roots level among women in poor, working-class, black, and Third World communities throughout the United States. Although often refusing to call themselves feminists, unprecedented numbers of these women, self-respecting and independent, were active on behalf of themselves and their communities. They joined unions, fought for daycare, sued their employers for sex discrimination and sexual harassment, enrolled in college, and formed such organizations as the Association of Black Single Mothers, Mothers for Adequate Welfare, Mothers of East Los Angeles, and the National Congress of Neighborhood Women. Strong, motivated, and persevering, such women embodied in their activism the socialist-feminist analysis of women's subordination as rooted in an integrated system of sex, class, and race oppression.

In the 1980s, the grass-roots activism of poor, working-class, black, and Third World women was complemented by the emergence of networks of progressive feminists of color committed to developing theoretical as well as practical work around their concerns. Moving somewhat independently of organized feminism, black and Latina feminists established research centers, founded publications, and became skilled activists within their professional associations. For example, the Center for Research on Women at Memphis State University has assembled a faculty of black, Latina, Native-American, Asian-American, and white social scientists interested in women of color, poor women, and women of the South. The center supports collaborative research on the intersections of race, culture, gender, and class; publishes newsletters, bibliographies, and a working-paper series; runs speaker programs, curriculum workshops, and summer training institutes; and maintains a computerized information clearinghouse.

Through their activities over more than two decades, socialist-feminist organizations and individuals have had a profound and enduring influence. Within the Left, questions of gender subordination are generally taken more seriously than in the past. Fewer Left organizations dismiss socialist feminism as mere bourgeois individualism, although their assimilation of socialist-feminist analysis may be limited. Some Left periodicals—for example, *Radical America, Socialist Review, Radical History Review,* and the *Review of Radical Political Economics*—assume socialist-feminist perspectives in their editorial policies and regularly publish important socialist-feminist analyses. Within the mainstream women's movement, issues of class and race are often addressed as a matter of course. NOW, for example, transcends its liberal individualist origins by conducting campaigns that oppose economic inequalities among women. Such national feminist publications as *off our backs,*

New Directions for Women, Feminist Studies, and *Signs* frequently reflect socialist-feminist politics. Socialist-feminist perspectives and concerns have spread well beyond their origins in the women's liberation movement. Socialist feminism has not only contributed importantly to efforts on behalf of all women, it has in many ways set the terms of a new feminist discourse. *See also*: New American Movement, *off our backs, Women: A Journal of Liberation,* Women's Liberation, Women's Liberation Unions

—*Lise Vogel*

REFERENCES

Altbach, Edith Hoshino, ed. *From Feminism to Liberation*. Rev. ed. Cambridge, Mass.: Schenkman Publishing Company, 1980.

Eisenstein, Zillah, ed. *Capitalist Patriarchy and the Case for Socialist Feminism*. New York: Monthly Review Press, 1979.

Evans, Sara. *Personal Politics: The Roots of Women's Liberation in the Civil Rights Movement and the New Left*. New York: Knopf, 1979.

Sargent, Lydia, ed. *Women and Revolution: A Discussion of the Unhappy Marriage of Marxism and Feminism*. Boston: South End Press, 1981.

"Socialist-Feminism Today." Series in *Socialist Review*, nos. 73–79, January–February 1984 to January–February 1985.

Vogel, Lise. "Feminist Scholarship: The Impact of Marxism." In *The Left Academy: Marxist Scholarship on American Campuses*, vol. 3, edited by Bertell Ollman and Edward Vernoff. New York: Praeger, 1986.

Sheet music sold to raise funds for the SLP, 1897

SOCIALIST LABOR PARTY

The first major party of American socialism, the SLP has remained in the field to the present, a tiny remnant of late-nineteenth-century political styles. Its history suggests, first, the overwhelming impact of immigrants on American socialism and, second, the power of a single charismatic personality on a Left political movement.

The SLP, founded in 1877 to succeed a one-year experiment, the Workingmen's Party, represented with its earliest breath the curious amalgamation of socialist forces. Heir to the internecine divisions of American socialists, it notably did not include prominent figures in the First International sections linked to Karl Marx and to certain craft unions. Neither did it include many of the American reformers excluded from the First International by the avowed Marxists. Some would return, and other American reformers, including a sprinkling of African Americans, would join the SLP in times of peak interest, such as the late 1870s, the middle 1880s, and the mid-1890s. In general, the native-born (and especially women reformers, unable or unwilling to attend meetings held in taverns) found the SLP socially and culturally unaccommodating.

The SLP seemed instead to promote the hopes of a new type of multiethnic, immigrant working-class coalition. Perennially weak at the national center, it set down hardy roots locally, where even former national leaders of European socialism, relocated to the United States, took their considerable energies. Drawing immediately on the excitement of the 1877 railroad strike—in which small numbers had done yeoman agitation—and the establishment of a German-American socialist daily press in such cities as Philadelphia,

Chicago, and New York (where the dailies founded would endure) and Cincinnati and St. Louis (where only weeklies would survive), SLPers nurtured their gains. Around the dailies or weeklies grew an abundance of social institutions, including clubs, theaters, and socialist-linked taverns. With only a few thousand members at its core, the SLP could rightly claim a following of perhaps five times that size.

For several years after its founding, the SLP enjoyed a brief vigor in electoral socialism, its local sections electing a handful of local and a few scattered state officials. At the peak of this development, the elections of 1878–79, the SLP elected an Illinois state senator, three representatives, and four Chicago city councilmen on a reform platform similar to that of "municipal socialism" decades later. Characteristically, the party itself garnered few short-term and virtually no long-term benefits from this success. Interest in socialism grew rapidly, but party membership did not. By 1880–81, when the protest vote had receded, several socialist candidates were "counted out" through ballot-stuffing and at least one elected candidate was expelled from the SLP for voting inconsistently with socialist principles. The boom had ended. At a national level, a hotly contested decision to support the Greenback Labor Party in 1880s proved doubly damaging when many socialists, refusing to compromise themselves, broke with the SLP and the Greenbackers went down to ignominous defeat.

The SLP record in unionism was rather more complex. The International Labor Union, a child in part of former First Internationalists who had given up party for labor activity but who still retained a strong commitment to socialism, experienced brief success in agitation among textile workers in 1877–79, and quietly expired. The Federated Order of Trades and Labor Unions was founded in 1881 largely by German socialists (party members and otherwise) and such former socialist protégés as Samuel Gompers. Almost immediately, the political nonpartisanship of the FOTLU (which would change its name to the American Federation of Labor in 1885) set off a minor explosion, as did its inclination to achieve labor market stability through limitation of the work force. The ardently socialist Progressive Cigarmakers, established in competition to Gompers' Cigarmakers International Union, looked upon the withdrawal of socialist political commitment as a step toward union conservatism. At a local level, socialists operated best, creating and staffing locals in a variety of trades, striving to work within the existing central labor councils where possible, and establishing new ones where corruption and conservatism reigned supreme.

The SLP could also boast of real intellectual accomplishments, if few organizing results, in the Americanization of socialism. The most famous English-language work of analytical socialist exposition, *The Cooperative Commonwealth* (1884), was written by a Danish immigrant, Laurence Gronlund, who had played an important role in the 1877 St. Louis "commune" established during the national railroad strike. Gronlund, no dogmatic Marxist, assailed capitalism's destructive competitiveness, waste, and cruelty, and looked forward to socialism as an advanced form of state control. Hardly a best-seller, *The Cooperative Commonwealth* acquired readership as a popularization after Edward Bellamy's utopian *Looking Backward* had expanded the market for socialist ideas. The second and more lasting accomplishment, by C. Osborne Ward—First Internationalist and sometime SLP member, civil servant and brother of famed sociologist Frank Lester Ward—was the ponderous two-volume *The Ancient Lowly* (1879). Ward energetically detailed the evidence of a proletariat of sorts in pre-Christian days, tracing its rituals and trade organizations, and detailing his thesis that these laboring poor had been the basis for Christianity's triumph (betrayed by the Church's turn toward power over the Roman state). A classic on the scale of contemporary texts by European socialists Karl Kautsky, Eduard Bernstein, or E. B. Bax on the medieval origins of the modern proletariat, *The Ancient Lowly* has remained a tribute to a peculiarly American Christian socialism.

Despite these formidable efforts, the SLP itself did not prosper in the 1880s. Failure at electoral socialism propelled many energetic militants toward "revolutionary socialism," a predecessor to the later ideas and practices of the Industrial Workers of the World (IWW). Unburdened of faith and patience in slow educational efforts, they led protest activity in a variety of spots, notably Chicago, Denver, and San Francisco, until the crushing blows of repression following the Haymarket Affair virtually eradicated this current. The SLP itself meanwhile dwindled down to a mere nominal affiliation of local union-linked socialists and their press. As old-timers later recalled, they suffered a characteristic identity crisis, unable to cast themselves as political party, pressure group, or education entity.

Most of the links the SLP early obtained with American-born labor reformers and Irish nationalist labor militants had been as good as lost since. This weakness proved catastrophic. As Frederick Engels complained, the SLP found itself utterly unable to encompass the political excitement of the mid-1880s. Socialists in the SLP and outside participated to the fullest in the "eight-hour" movement, led in many cities by German-dominated trades. But they found cooperation with the predominantly American-Irish, temperance-oriented Knights of Labor extremely difficult. New York socialist participation in the 1886 Henry George mayoral campaign brought new energy, but also ended in a sharp disillusionment and internal division.

At a low point, the SLP weakened further. In 1889 the national executive committee, dominated by the *New Yorker Volkszeitung*, expelled the editor of the party's national weekly, *Der Sozialist*, and shut down the press, declaring sharp criticism of unions to be treason. As this action revealed, the local organization and above all its union connections—especially in New York—continued to count for more than any other factor. SLP loyalists had, in effect, come to accept their tactical isolation and sought to live within it, much as the "American Exceptionalism" wing of the Communist movement avowed during the later 1920s.

The SLP members had their reasons, based in the continued success of their own intimate institutions. As activists in the brewery union among others, as fraternal organizers of an impressive insurance, health, and recreational network, as educators of their own ranks, the German immigrants managed their limited resources well. As socialists they already came to regard themselves as *alte genossen*, "old heads" bloodied from repeated thumps against the stone walls of bourgeois American reality. But their acceptance of insularity did nothing to change socialism's "foreign" image in the United States, and furthermore made the capture of the SLP by would-be Americanizers all the easier a few years later.

The early 1890s brought increasing support from local trades councils and their growing press, and the mass emergence of an entirely new constituency, Eastern European Jews. By the mid-1890s, the SLP could call a dozen papers its own, including a new array of Yiddish publications and the first lasting "orthodox" English-language socialist newspaper, the *People*. Opportunity opened, and the party ran its first serious presidential campaign, gaining more than 21,000 votes for its candidate, Simon Wing, in five states. Meanwhile, under Americanized intellectual Daniel DeLeon's firm hand, the *People* and the SLP set out on a path to create a socialist propaganda presence and a socialist labor federation.

Both strategies fell short, for want of resources and because other radical or socialist ideas of the time, from Populism to Eugene Debs's Social Democratic Party, gained more attention. The *People*, with its arch "scientific" tone and its bitter scorn for non-SLP radicals, offered a case in point. Taking the editorship in 1892, DeLeon, deeply admired by his faithful readers, introduced a quasi-anthropological framework (with considerable debt to Lewis Henry Morgan) to explain socialism as the next step of civilization. A handful of his public speeches, reprinted in the *People* as a guide to modern socialist principles, became overnight SLP classics. But DeLeon devoted as much attention to abuse of the Populists—after 1895 the AFL, the followers of Eugene Debs, and various SLP dissidents—as to the exposition of socialism. In his belief, the end of capitalism drew near, and *only* the lures offered by false leaders and sham working-class organizations prevented the SLP from leading the revolutionary column. As it threw critics overboard, it could rightly claim a temporary upward spiral of votes: 40,000 for the presidential ticket in 1896, and a combined local tally of more than 80,000 in 1898.

To skeptics, the advances seemed small, indeed, relative to the political opportunities in this worst of U.S. depressions, with manifestations like the Pullman strike, the Homestead strike, and the "industrial armies" of relief on all sides. Membership never exceeded 5,000. The *People*, too dry for public taste, seemed moreover increasingly shrill and simply unrealistic. To those just learning about socialism, from former Populists and Bellamy Nationalists to craft workers, the *Coming Nation* and local socialistic papers of central trades federations were vastly more acceptable. To a scattering of new immigrant formations—Italian, Russian, Hungarian, and others—the SLP offered few benefits in return for adhesion.

Such criticisms, especially when directed at DeLeon, only reinforced loyalists' determination. Belittled where not scorned, the SLP made one final, glorious effort to establish a labor-political hegemony within the Left. DeLeon's lieutenants seized control of Knights of Labor District Assembly 49, where New York socialists had long been active, and projected a coalition aimed at taking national leadership of the failing Knights of Labor. Actually promised the editorship of the Knights' journal (for Lucien Sanial, the most distinguished of party intellectuals other than DeLeon), the SLP was outvoted at the Knights' 1894 convention and DeLeon himself excluded as a "lawyer." DeLeon led a split, and next year called upon socialists in the AFL (still smarting at Gompers' exclusion of SLP delegate Lucien Sanial from the 1890 national convention, and sufficiently powerful to vote Gompers out of office in 1894, from whence he quickly returned) to likewise abandon their organization. The result, the Socialist Trades and Labor Alliance, was purportedly to organize the unorganized, but actually to give outright socialist leadership to a labor movement growing out of the ruins of the AFL (badly weakened by the depression) and the Knights.

This scheme had historical roots in the splits that German Americans had led from numerous local trades councils of the 1880s–1890s, including that of New York. But it had little chance of success. Among German-American socialists, especially outside New York, the defections from the SLP were many, because the ST&LA could not provide even the limited benefits the AFL offered. Among the Jews, second most important constituency, anarchists joined conservatives to support the existing unions. With a split in Jewish ranks, and a new Jewish non-SLP daily paper, the *Forverts*, posed against the SLP's dry *Abendblott*, the SLP could not recover.

The factional brawls of the next few years exceeded in scope and destruction any thus far in the U.S. Left. Expulsions and defections took the place of agitation. Socialists of various union factions broke each others' strikes. In 1899 the *Volkszeitung* leaders, who had sniped at DeLeon but remained in the organization, helped lead much of the remaining Jewish group, and others, in a fistfight over control of the national office. In essence half the remaining movement of perhaps 5,000 split, each side claiming to be the "true" SLP. The anti-DeLeonists, known as the "Kangaroos" (so named by DeLeon for the kangaroo courts of the lawless western frontier towns), negotiated furiously for two years with Debs's followers until settling upon unity in the new Socialist Party. The SLP, for its part, eliminated all the "immediate demands" from its platform, leaving only the demand for socialism.

Beset by a continuation of small-scale rebellions, little actually remained of the SLP but its *Daily People* (created at great sacrifice in 1900) and scattered foreign-language press, its book arm, the New York Labor News Company (which would specialize in publishing editions of DeLeon's speeches, but also bring out many early translated European Socialist classics), and its claim to more revolutionary virtue than the SP. These were not inconsiderable resources, and despite being numerically overshadowed by the SP and repeatedly divided by further defections, the SLP held on. Its Yiddish press, for instance, was edited by David Pinski, later famed novelist (and Labor Zionist), and its Jewish labor activist leader was Joseph Schlossberg, future Amalgamated

Clothing Workers luminary. The SLP appealed, naturally, to the unreconstructed and uncompromised revolutionary socialist who believed ardently in political education via the soapbox and the press. This approach had a special appeal, at the turn of the century and for decades after, to the working-class autodidact who instinctively mistrusted the generally middle-class leadership of other radical organizations. Among certain ethnic groups (Bulgarians and South Slavs especially) these images had a special resonance.

The SLP enjoyed one final fling at public acclaim. By endorsing the IWW at the latter's foundation in 1905, by providing the new movement both intellectual formulations (articulated brilliantly by DeLeon) and daily publicity denied by the SP press, the SLP made up some lost ground. DeLeon's address, reprinted as a pamphlet, *Preamble to the IWW* (often reprinted later as *The Socialist Reconstruction of Society*), was widely regarded as the most influential statement of industrial society's postpolitical future. Even Debs, however cautiously, echoed a tone of respect toward his frequent adversary, more faithful to the industrial union vision than were Debs's fellow SP leaders.

By cautiously agreeing at first to the Socialist International's appeal for socialist "unity," the SLP made itself appear for a moment to be a foundation stone for a different kind of political movement growing out of the IWW. The early IWW had no luck, however, and its failure dragged down the participants. Moreover, SLP leaders themselves, too accustomed to rigid discipline, drew back from the real likelihood of fusion with the SP. The SLP expectations fell apart, one by one. Internal struggles within the IWW found DeLeon ceaselessly but hopelessly maneuvering for a labor movement in the SLP image, wedded to political education and party-building. Once more excluded at the 1908 IWW convention, DeLeon reconciled himself to the formation of an alternative "Detroit IWW," which managed a few local branches (mostly extensions of SLP locals). The *People* retained a devoted readership, but the SLP had permanently narrowed.

As such, it stabilized at 4,000 or 5,000 members, divided by halves into the English- and immigrant-language organizations. Under the stern hand of Swedish immigrant national secretary Arnold Peterson—personally named as successor by the dying Daniel DeLeon—the SLP survived one last major crisis, involving the defection of some leading members to the Communist movements (a move facilitated by Lenin's praise of DeLeon). Thereafter, growing older with its loyal cadre, the party remained essentially the same, decade after decade. Party life revolved around the distribution of socialist leaflets and the *Weekly People* (in addition to the foreign-language press, for those members), local study-classes organized around "the classics" (Marx, Engels, and DeLeon), and the collection of signatures to obtain ballot status. Its presidential vote, in twelve to twenty-three states, ranged from 15,000 to 50,000, depending mostly on the other "protest parties" that managed to gain ballot strength. Ironically, the SLP reached its all-time-high vote of 53,831 in 1972, although its candidate, Louis Fisher, was able to qualify in the fewest number of states since 1892.

Over the decades, chafing at Petersen's rather authoritarian leadership and the party's apparent status, a multitude of factions spun off, taking with them never more than a few locals. The most notable, the Industrial Union Party centered in Pennsylvania during the 1930s, published the lively *Labor Power*, and just prior to the establishment of the CIO enjoyed some influence among furniture workers. One of the most recent, the 1970s–1980s secession from a St. Louis local, to date publishes the journal *Workers Democracy*. Meanwhile, in the SLP, second-generation members filled some of the gaps left by attrition or division, and a thin strata of fresh recruits—such as erstwhile cabdriver and later *Weekly People* editor and perennial presidential candidate Eric Hass (1905–80)—came forward. The organization grew ever more isolated, save perhaps during the depressed 1930s; but its aggressive socialist propaganda reached many thousands of working people and younger intellectuals with the *idea* of socialism.

By the 1960s, remaining energy waned seriously. The language federations, bulwark of the party treasury, folded their press and their political-fraternal activities. The SLP experienced new and more painful losses as Arnold Petersen died and the New Left passed across the political horizon. Attempting even a measure of adaptation (such as the virtually unprecedented willingness to march with other radical groups), the organization set off a loyalist rebellion. Ultimately, the *People*, removed in the 1970s from New York to Palo Alto, California, appeared semimonthly. Party membership shrunk to a few hundred. Even then, a flicker remained of the old movement: the only Left newspaper that gloried in its reprints of the editorials of a turn-of-the-century intellectual and held out pure socialism as the single solution for humankind's many woes.

—*Paul Buhle*

REFERENCES

Daniel DeLeon: The Man and His Work. New York: New York Labor News, 1918.

Seretan, L. Glen. *Daniel DeLeon: The Odyssey of an American Marxist*. Cambridge: Harvard University Press, 1979.

The Socialist Labor Party, 1890–1930. New York: New York Labor News, 1931.

Socialist Labor Party Papers, State Historical Society of Wisconsin.

Cartoon by Ryan Walker

SOCIALIST PARTY

Founded in 1901 and attaining its apex in the 1910s, the Socialist Party more than any other Left organization in U.S. history impressed its ideas upon the mainstream and propounded a credible, popular vision of socialism. In its failures and its final collapse, it mirrored most of the fundamental weaknesses of the American Left.

The immediate origins of the SP can be found in the 1880s and 1890s, with the rise of labor and social protests and the inability of the mostly immigrant socialists to create a large or durable organization. Eugene Debs, allying his followers from the American Railway Union and Social Democracy of America with dissidents from the Socialist Labor Party, both negotiated the merger and ran for the presidency on a unified ticket in 1900. His own characteristic milieu of native-born skilled workers, lower-middle-class veterans of social protest, and a volatile tenant-farmer population in the Southwest dominated the public tone of the SP in the early years. German, Jewish, and a handful of other immigrant groups, strong in selected neighborhoods and unions, eagerly shared the dream of "Americanizing" the socialist movement.

Popular agitation and education supplied the means to reach the masses, with the Socialist press the key mechanism. By 1912–13, more than 300 periodicals, mostly weeklies but with many dailies and monthlies, were in circulation. The *Jewish Daily Forward*, reaching 200,000 by the close of the 1910s, was the Yiddish circulation leader in the world. *The Appeal to Reason*, peaking at three quarters of a million (and in some special weeks, reaching more than a million) was for a time the most widely circulated political weekly in the United States. Although no clear estimate can be made, a combined circulation figure would run to several million. Most of these had an intense regional or local audience of party members and sympathizers expectant of a swift rise in socialist ranks.

The strength of the Socialist press lay, above all, in its variety and adaptation. Unlike the SLP *Daily People*, which presumed to offer a single position for all socialists to follow, SP papers assumed (sometimes in a very insular way) the inevitability of different tastes for different constituencies. One might note, for example, the extraordinary strength of the Hallettsville (Texas) *Rebel*, supported by 25,000 readers among the district's tenant farmers and followed by supporters of the Mexican Revolution; or again the monthly *National Rip-Saw* from St. Louis, with its 150,000 readers spread across the South and Southwest. In the single district of Chicago, influence was exerted by a dozen or more papers (the Slovakian *Rovnost Ludu* had a readership of almost 10,000, the Slovenian *Proletarec* reached more than 4,000, the Bohemian *Spraredelust* claimed 12,000, and the *Christian Socialist* had nearly 20,000). Many central labor councils such as Cleveland's, with the *Cleveland Citizen*, and a few important national unions such as the brewery workers and western miners, with *Brauer Zeitung* and *Miners Magazine*, respectively, proudly sponsored Socialist loyalties. So widely scattered was this press that Arkansas, Iowa, Kansas, Missouri, Texas, Pennsylvania, and Oklahoma each had more than a dozen papers, often with small circulations of less than a thousand but an intense, semirural following.

In that age, public and especially street-corner (or "soapbox") lectures also offered a major arena for attracting political attention. Hundreds of traveling lecturers, often paid through a percentage on sales of pamphlets, toured each possible constituency in a fashion that the abolition, woman suffrage, temperance, and popular movements had long since made successful. To that, Socialists added a religious-populist favorite, the tent meeting, stretching over days of education and entertainment in rural southwestern locations.

If Socialists praised the agitator, however, they offered little solace and less support to the weighty thinker so prestigious in European socialism. Such a figure as Ernest Untermann, translator of *Capital*'s first volume, had to make do with popularizations for American readers, while sending his more original work for publication to Germany. Untermann's favorite U.S. publication, *International Socialist Review*, jettisoned its theoretically oriented format entirely in 1908 and became a popular magazine, leaving a vacuum never truly filled. The Left's intellectual creation, the *New Review*, did no better, folding after a brave start in 1913–17. Only in the Yiddish monthly *Zukunft* did the theoretically-minded (at that, often restricted to literary or Jewish topics) have anything like free range to explore deeper questions of socialist philosophy.

In the absence of such a discussion, internal differences hinted at a youthful exuberance but also a deep uncertainty over the problems America held for socialist ideas. From an empirical standpoint, the party did not attract the native-born, urban, eastern or midwestern worker in any significant proportion. Frequently Irish and tied to the Democratic Party (or at any rate Catholic, and successfully repelled from socialism by the clergy's denunciations and warnings), this worker also often enjoyed great material advantages over the unskilled, recently immigrated worker. Exceptions could readily be found. Where ethnic factors (such as German descent) nurtured a socialistic leaning, or where a one-industry town minimized the middle class, or again where Socialists had organized and maintained control over central unions, the SP could exert an exceptional force. Even here, however, defeat—often to a fusion ticket of cooperating Republicans and Democrats—often followed on the heels of a victory.

Disputes often centered on solving this problem of reaching the "real American worker," or of finding alternative constituencies. On the "Right," longtime activists in the AFL, occasionally quite successful (as in Milwaukee) in building a local political machine, stressed the party's respectability. Indeed, such Socialists urged support of the AFL's demand for immigration restriction, and acquiesced in its combination of open racism and general denigration of the unskilled worker. On the "Left," a variety of militants and intellectuals insisted on the presentation of the full Socialist program, and believed the goal could be reached by mobilizing the mass of workers, preferably through radical industrial unions. The formation of the Industrial Workers of the World, in 1905, galvanized both sides of the dispute. Jockeying on the IWW and other issues continued until the climactic division of 1919.

By no means could all differences be so characterized, however. On the crucial issue of a farm program—whether land would be "nationalized" or returned to the poor farmer—the rural and urban divisions proved far more important, with "scientific" socialists unable to grasp the unpopularity of state land ownership. On women's rights and specifically the support of the woman suffrage movement, the "Left" frequently disdained such petty reforms as voting requirements while sections of the "Right" found themselves comfortable with suffrage activists. Among youth groups, both community (Young People's Socialist League) and campus (Intercollegiate Socialist Society), "Right" and "Left" likewise shared encouragement and criticisms. On blacks and their status in the United States, few Socialist voices could be heard before 1915. But the "Left," unwilling to make compromising qualifications for any special status of worker, offered what appeared to be empty promises of egalitarian futures.

The rise of the mass strikes among the unskilled, along with a sharp reversal of electoral successes, set the stage for more fundamental antagonisms within the movement. For a moment it seemed that the IWW would succeed in mobilizing large sections of eastern and southern European workers across the East and Midwest, thus revolutionizing the SP. At the party convention of 1912—the banner year, with nearly a million votes for Debs, and the election of hundreds of local officials—William D. Haywood faced removal from the national executive committee (to which he had been elected by the party at large) for advocating sabotage, a practice widely (but only sub rosa) engaged in by workers of many kinds. Provoked by the "Right," Haywood turned from the party. Many of its younger industrial militants abandoned the organization with him (a few hundred were also removed, through purges of membership rolls, mostly in certain foreign-language groups). Far more devastating, local elected officials in power lacked the ability or opportunity to truly transform political life—in a few cases, so much losing interest in Socialism that the SP local expelled them while they remained in office. In this calamity, membership fell to scarcely more than half its 1912 level of some 100,000.

Two other issues at the same pivotal convention raised question marks over the SP's future. A handful of leading Socialist intellectuals, including historian-editor A. M. Simons, greeted a relative leftward shift within the AFL by proposing Socialist support for a labor party. Not many others could agree to the abandonment of party independence, especially on such a weak reed. But this tendency hinted defections to the Right mirroring those to the Left. Second, the party leadership reluctantly agreed to officially charter the growing foreign-language socialist groups into associative federations. This issue, unlike the Haywood matter, had no "Left" or "Right" tilt despite the heavily immigrant character of the later Communist movement. Taken with other developments, it suggested that the Socialists' infrastructure had begun to give way.

The growth of the foreign-language section to some 40 percent of a diminished party by 1916 signaled the consolidation of the changes. While strong local branches, which were organized around election campaigns, arose and rapidly dwindled, specific new immigrant groups integrated the socialist faith and political practice into the logics of their developing communities. Czechs, Finns, Slovenes, Hungarians, Lithuanians, and others, despite their own internal conflicts, revived the Socialist movement in various cities and industrial settlements.

The outbreak of war in Europe underlined the importance of international issues to these constituents in particular. Many felt the aspirations of their relatives in oppressed nations; all, it is safe to say, feared for the worst and sought to gather resources to send back home; in more than a few cases, they also supplied the radical pamphlets and other publications through which the Old World struggle would reorient itself to new realities.

Over the next half-dozen years, the problems of connecting class and national struggles became steadily more complex. But in almost every case, Socialists came to a position of new importance within the crisis-ridden communities desperately seeking dynamic leadership.

For the first time, black socialists also became an estimable factor, albeit almost entirely in northern cities rather than in the rural South, and despite being offered no special encouragement by the Party. Around Pullman car organizer A. Philip Randolph and his group's stylish monthly, the *Messenger*, a Harlem group formed. Aroused by a handful of black Socialists elsewhere as well, and touched by incipient black nationalism, an urban race movement of both intellectuals and workers began to show promise.

The economics of these communities also favored a rapid Socialist growth. Wartime conditions both shut off new immigration to the United States—tightening job markets perceptibly—and prompted an American economic boom following the 1913–14 recession. The IWW, which had hoped to lead these very largely unskilled, mass-production ranks, had been driven to the West by major defeats, and would soon face an unprecedented government-and-business repression. Burgeoning industrial unionism flowed, especially from the U.S. entry into the war, into the existing AFL unions or into newly organized and radical-leaning bodies such as the Amalgamated Clothing Workers. "Practical" unionism with a radical edge emphasized the importance of radical politics, and despite all official party reluctance, the federations became the main recipients of fresh energies.

The party's English-language sector meanwhile suffered serious blows as a result of the war. Woodrow Wilson's appeal for a peace presidency drove socialist electoral talleys far down. European socialist (especially German Socialist) failure to vote against war credits had a devastating effect on morale. Important intellectuals, both Right and Left, defected to patriotism. Repression of the Socialist press fell particularly hard upon the rural papers, which needed second-class mailing permits to survive, and upon rural and small-town constituencies, which now faced severe pressure from the spreading reactionary patriotism. The party's 1917 St. Louis convention mandated an essentially pacifist antiwar program, and party activists—"Right" as well as "Left"—urgently pushed their appeals for a cessation of the fighting. They were quite literally the only major movement in U.S. society to stand adamant against the war currents.

Rising antiwar sentiment, by 1918 or so, began to reward courage and hard work. Deprived of some constituencies, Socialists began to gain others (most especially, but not only, among the victimized nationalities, such as German Americans). Local electoral strongholds returned in some cases, and in others appeared for the first time. This new burst of electoral enthusiasm brought new Socialists to office in Wisconsin, Illinois, Ohio, Indiana, Pennsylvania, New Jersey, New York, Minnesota, Kentucky, and elsewhere. It peaked in 1917 in Ohio, where Socialists received up to 50 percent of the vote in large industrial cities where they had strength; in Chicago, where they received a third of the municipal vote; and in New York.

A second-place finish that year for Morris Hillquit, New York City mayoral hopeful, was viewed not only as an antiwar but also a virtual Socialist mandate. The People's Council for Peace and Democracy, which might be described as the American Left's first Popular Front–style mobilization, drew pacifist and radical labor leaders behind a unified antiwar and antirepression appeal, and gained much popular attention. Meanwhile, key Socialist-led unions such as the Amalgamated Clothing Workers (whose president, Sidney Hillman, also headed the People's Council) quickly consolidated their grip on industries through careful use of government-based mediations. Even among such weakly represented groups as Italians, Socialist support and (less commonly) membership began to grow significantly. The future of the Socialist movement, now more than 50 percent immigrant, might have been seen as a bright one.

The Russian October Revolution, the failure of the revolution in Europe, and the appearance of the Third International meant Socialist division and the loss of precious political opportunities. A Moscow-mandated split in socialist parties took place via growing challenges over war issues (the emerging immigrant-dominated Left demanded not pacifism but "direct action") and control of the party. Right-leaning functionaries, mostly from the older immigrant groups or at least older generation of immigrants and native-born, had watched the steady demographic change of the movement with unease. Still gripping party mechanisms, they set aside a national executive committee election that would have given pro-Bolsheviks an outright majority. Thereafter, one Communist faction withdrew immediately, and another awaited the 1919 convention, denouncing the expulsions of branches, state party sections, and entire foreign-language federations.

Ironically, as with the war issue, the Socialist "Right" for the most part had often taken very "Left" positions on the Russian Revolution, while future American Communist leaders did not entirely see its blessings. All this mattered little when the break took place. Amid massive repression, an organization of more than 100,000 members divided into two or three parts, which altogether could manage no more than 40,000 members two years later. The bulk of the Socialist movement had simply faded away; and while the immigrant groups recovered a portion of this loss, the English-language sector disappeared into farmer-labor movements or simply grew quiescent.

The SP often remained larger than the Communist movement, on the membership rolls, through the early 1930s. But its strength lay mainly in older members, a few local political machines (notably, Milwaukee), ethnic groups (mainly Slovenians) with special reasons for resisting the Soviet Union's appeal, and a handful of unions centered in the garment trades. Between Left-leaning youth and the progressive unions, a handful of Socialists effected an important link through the slick monthly *Labor Age*, and earnestly supported the Brookwood Labor College's activities. Likewise, the Rand School, launched in the 1910s, continued to have a formidable public presence in New York. Christian pacifism also drew a talented group of younger Socialists. But temporary revivals in Socialist activities seemed to end in disappointment.

Most of all, the Socialists exhibited the tiredness of senior radicals who had lost confidence in their mission, and who at times (as in the garment trades and the pages of the weekly *New Leader*) seemed more intent on attacking Communists than in ending capitalism. Well placed in the leadership of the "Jewish unions," and concentrated in the United Hebrew Trades, they had had enough revolutions for the foreseeable future, and yearned for stability. Communists, exuberant in their near-fanatical optimism for world revolution, attracted potential radical activists and intellectuals (including important leaders of the Socialists' reorganized Young People's Socialist League) with their dynamism. The major burst of Socialist energy poured into the Robert M. LaFollette 1924 Progressive campaign added little to the tarnished luster of the party and left further discouragement in its wake.

Norman Thomas almost single-handedly revived the SP. In 1928, the year of his first presidential campaign, membership stood at a staggering low of 8,000. Thomas generated news with his public addresses, and he appealed forcefully to religious and academic liberals such as John Dewey and Paul Douglas, with whom he formed the League for Independent Political Action. As he attracted a respectable if not especially impressive vote, and as the United States entered the Depression, Socialist fortunes improved and membership doubled by 1932.

In retrospect, this was the high point of the SP revival. Thomas's 1932 presidential campaign, which gained 800,000 votes, agitated campus politics on a scale hitherto unprecedented, and reached a wide diversity of Americans (including many almost but not quite willing to vote for him). Adulation bordering upon the hero-worship previously reserved for Eugene Debs surrounded the former Presbyterian minister in his perpetual speaking tours, banquets, and radio addresses. Due in no small part to the extreme Communist sectarianism, a Socialist youth movement of considerable proportions grew from campus to community, and the Socialist presence within the labor movement waxed strong once more. In Wisconsin, in Reading, Pennsylvania, and in a scattering of other cities, local Socialist electoral campaigns took on new life. Certain ethnic groups, notably Jews and Finns, gained fresh energies from returnees, activists disillusioned with Communist practices but still dedicated to socialist ideals. The political activities of other groups, such as Slovenes, resumed to a degree after a long concentration on fraternal institution-building. Chiefly through the Southern Tenant Farmers Union, the Socialists made new ties in the South.

At this apex of expectation, the SP once more fell to external and internal foes. The most formidable of these, the New Deal, dragged leading Socialist unionists into support for Franklin Roosevelt's 1936 reelection campaign, a contradiction that Socialists (unlike Communists) could not tolerate. Even before then, several of Thomas's most promising supporters had defected to Fiorello LaGuardia's mayoral campaign in New York, and Upton Sinclair had seemingly shown another way forward by garnering nearly 900,000 votes on the Democratic ticket in the 1934 gubernatorial race in California. Meanwhile, the generational struggle within the party had begun in earnest with a 1934 showdown of the Old Guard (from the garment unions) against the "Militants" (a heterogenous force of young Socialists, Milwaukeeans, and others eager to upset the New York Socialist veterans' monopoly on leadership). The Militants, electing Milwaukeean and Amalgamated Clothing Workers leader Leo Krzycki party chair, achieved a narrow and pyrrhic victory. Disaster for the Socialists lay straight ahead.

Thomas's 1936 campaign, winning less than half the votes of 1932, offered a dour guide to Socialist troubles. After the party's May convention of that year, the Old Guard withdrew in a bloc, forming the Social Democratic Federation, which threw itself immediately into the American Labor Party and indirect support for Roosevelt's reelection. Along with the Old Guard went several of the party's most precious institutional resources: the Rand School, the *New Leader*, and New York radio station WEVD. Thomas sought to run a campaign that left open the door both for activity in state farmer-labor parties and in the SP. (The next year, Thomas himself would withdraw from the New York mayoral race, leaving the path clear for his supporters to turn to LaGuardia's fusion ticket.)

Such maneuvers could not make up for the losses and the party's internal bleeding. With the leftward tilt of the New Deal in 1936 and the subsequent rise of the CIO, promising young socialists either went to Washington as brain-trust bureaucrats or plunged wholly into labor activities. Despite wide Socialist youth activity on the campuses in particular, the Communist Party, now entering its Popular Front phase, tended to recruit the most promising activists in college and youth movements, or alternatively to capture control of organizations and discourage dissenters. Socialists might publish a respectable weekly (the *Socialist Call*) and organize effectively to help the Flint, Michigan, sit-down strike, but they gained few members for their efforts. Meanwhile the Trotskyist movement entered the SP *en bloc* in 1936 and, after nearly two years of bitter factional fighting, withdrew (or was expelled) with the cream of the recent YPSL crop. Other than scattered municipal support and a pacifist remnant, little remained behind Norman Thomas, who by 1938 indeed called for a turn from electoralism to educational efforts.

It was also notable, albeit as a side issue, how little theoretical effort could be seen in Socialist publications, even relative to the modest intellectual work carried on by contemporary Left groups. Haim Kantorovich, a relatively recent refugee intellectual, conducted the *American Socialist Quarterly* for a few years, with the participation of David P. Berenberg and a small circle of others. They turned their eyes largely to the contemporary European socialists' leftish fringes, and to a vague mulling of the issues of socialism and democracy. Harry W. Laidler, one-man intellectual whirlwind of the League for Industrial Democracy, meanwhile produced volume after volume advocating a British-style nationalization. But perhaps the most notable effort, by Christian socialists in the *World Tomorrow* and after its close in 1934 in their separate books and pamphlets, stood the furthest from traditional Marxism and the Second International. Norman Thomas's best efforts, scarcely theoretical but full of intelligent and humane argument, took place within this last context.

Under Thomas's leadership, this much-reduced organization (by the later 1930s, under 10,000 members) played its most notable role in antiwar propaganda. Socialists organized the Keep America Out of War Congress in 1938. While adamantly hostile to fascism, Thomas accurately predicted the decline of radical prospects following U.S. entry, the erosion of civil liberties, and a world reshaped under the totalitarian image. His warnings, above all of "armament economics," a permanent war economy ruled by the military-industrial complex, proved sadly prescient, as did his complaints against an all-too-compliant and corrupted liberalism. Thomas had anticipated, perhaps better than anyone else, the future effects of the Cold War on all political discourse. By 1941 only a small portion of the SP remained with him to support (but critically) the war against fascism, and to carry on much-needed work on behalf of conscientious objectors and others newly imprisoned.

From that decline, the party could not recover. But it remained doggedly alive, running Norman Thomas through 1948, denouncing both Stalinism and the denouement of American liberalism in the Democratic Party's broad shift to the right. Waiting (but without any early hopes) for the inevitable disillusionment with Communism and capitalism, the SP drifted. The formerly Trotskyist Independent Socialist League of a few hundred members—many of whom had been expelled by the SP in 1938—rejoined the party in 1957, now merged also with the returned Social Democratic Federation. A few thousand, mostly aged, members, confronted the vacuum left by the sorely weakened CP and the newer hopes raised by civil rights and disarmament movements.

By this time, the liberal wing of the Democratic Party and the liberal wing of the existing labor leadership offered the lodestars. "Realignment" of the two-party political system through influence on the Democrats and labor became the all-consuming strategy. Much rested, it was believed, upon the initiatives of well-placed individuals. Michael Harrington, whose *The Other America* (1960) inspired the War on Poverty, offered the model policy-analyst for Democratic Party liberals. Former Trotskyist leader Max Shachtman, ever closer in influence and views to the top leadership of the AFL-CIO, drafted out influential position papers for labor. YPSL luminaries guided the Student Peace Union's meteoric rise to antibomb militancy in the early 1960s, and remained active in Young Democratic and Campus Americans for Democratic Action (CADA) chapters thereafter. Directors of the Student League for Industrial Democracy (SLID), campus connection of the SP since the 1930s, aided the modest rebirth of the movement on a few 1950s campuses and supplied resources for its conversion into the Students for a Democratic Society in 1963—a move later bitterly regretted as opening doors for the New Left.

Faced with the New Left, the SP in general moved swiftly right. Socialist leaders tended (although not uniformly) to support U.S. military posture when the alternative looked suspiciously Communist. They also forcefully opposed "Black Power," and denounced public criticism of Israeli policies. Bayard Rustin, the most prominent black SP leader, thus broke with the Rev. Martin Luther King, Jr.'s avowed opposition to the Vietnam War. By the close of the 1960s, a flagging YPSL viewed itself as the centrist alternative to the booming, radicalized SDS.

Once more the party fractured. The most conservative faction, closely linked to the upper echelons of the labor movement, broke away in 1972 to form Social Democrats USA (SDUSA), whose strident anticommunism, opposition to affirmative action, and unwavering support of Israel have been its most notable features. Several of its youth notables emerged in the 1980s as staff aides to UN Ambassador Jeane Kirkpatrick, or leaders of the hard-line anticommunist National Endowment for Democracy. A second wing, led by Michael Harrington, in 1972 formed the Democratic Socialist Organizing Committee, which a decade later merged with the New American Movement to form the Democratic

Socialists of America. This latter group's ecumenical socialism, its support by the few outspoken radical labor leaders, such as the Machinists' William Winpisinger, and its sometimes lively branch activity—membership hovered at about 5,000—seemed most in keeping with the SP of yore. Its determined activity within the Democratic Party, however, marked the great shift taken in the historic socialist movement, even when (as in DSA's fervent 1988 support for Jesse Jackson) socialists represented the militant left edge of liberalism.

A stubborn group of loyalists kept the SP franchise alive, although just barely, into the 1970s–1980s. Its final major presidential campaign, in 1976, ran former Milwaukee mayor Frank Zeidler and gained votes mostly from that city. The emergence of the Citizen's Party in 1980 fairly well submerged this effort, although the SP maintained its national campaigns with such notables as peace activist David McReynolds in the titular leadership. Outside a very few locations, the SP at the end of the 1980s seemed to have lost its raison d'être, and yet the continued election of an occasional local candidate demonstrated the loyalty that the SP might still command under the proper circumstances. *See also*: Ameringer, Oscar; *Appeal to Reason*; Armenian Americans; Berger, Victor; Blatch, Harriot Stanton; Bohemian Americans; Boudin, Louis; Christian Socialism; *Cleveland Citizen*; Debs, Eugene V.; Farmer-Labor Party; Harrington, Michael; Haywood, William D.; Hughan, Jesse Wallace; Hungarian Americans; Intercollegiate Socialist Society; *International Socialist Review*; Konikow, Antoinette; Laidler, Harry W.; Lawrence Strike; Lilienthal, Meta Stern; Lithuanian Americans; London, Jack; London, Meyer; Lore, Ludwig; Lowe, Caroline A.; Malkiel, Theresa S.; Maurer, James Hudson; Mitchell, H. L.; Municipal Socialism; O'Hare, Kate Richards; Peace Movements; Polish Americans; Rand School; Randolph, A. Philip; Rustin, Bayard; Sandburg, Carl; Sanger, Margaret; Scudder, Vida D.; Socialist Sunday Schools; Southern Tenant Farmers Union; Stokes, Rose Pastor; Student Movements of the 1930s; Student Peace Union; Thomas, Norman; Ukrainian Americans; Union Square; United Brewery Workers; United Cloth Hat and Capmakers; United Mine Workers; Walling, William English; Wilshire, H Gaylord; Winchevsky, Morris; Woman's National Committee; Woman's National Socialist Union; Workers Education; Workmen's Circle; Yiddish Left; Young, Art; Young People's Socialist League

—*Paul Buhle*

REFERENCES

Bell, Daniel. "The Background and Development of Marxian Socialism in the United States," In *Socialism and American Life, I*, edited by Donald Drew Egbert and Stow Persons. Princeton: Princeton University Press, 1952.

Buhle, Paul. *Marxism in the US: Remapping the American Left*. London: Verso, 1987.

Kipnis, Ira. *The American Socialist Movement: 1897–1912*. New York: Columbia University Press, 1952.

Warren, Frank A. *An Alternative Vision: The Socialist Party in the 1930s*. Bloomington: University of Indiana Press, 1974.

Weinstein, James. *The Decline of Socialism in America, 1912–1925*. New York: Monthly Review Press, 1967.

Socialist Party Papers, Duke University.

Socialist Sunday Schools

Sunday schools for working-class children were established by American radicals before the twentieth century, notably by German and Finnish immigrant groups. However, the more extensive Socialist Sunday School (SSS) movement was organized primarily by grass-roots supporters of the Socialist Party of America during the 1900–1920 period. These children's schools were English-speaking, eschewed any ethnic identification, and sought to foster an understanding of and allegiance to working-class interests and basic socialist tenets among the next generation of laborers.

At least one hundred Socialist Sunday schools (sometimes referred to by other names, such as the Children's Socialist Lyceum in Los Angeles) were organized in sixty-four cities and towns in twenty states. Prominent ones were located in New York City (which had fourteen schools in 1912), Rochester, Hartford, Newark, Buffalo (two in 1918), Philadelphia (two in 1912), Washington, D.C., Pittsburgh (two in 1916), Cleveland (three in 1912), Chicago (eight in 1919), Milwaukee (three in 1915), and Los Angeles. Schools varied from a handful of students in one class, as in the case of the Newport, Kentucky, school, to 1,000 students in dozens of classes at the school that met at the Brownsville Labor Lyceum in Brooklyn. The average enrollment was probably less than 100 students. Most schools existed for several years, although there were schools opening and closing in the same year and others that lasted for more than a half-dozen years (e.g., the East Side Socialist School in Manhattan, Williamsburg and Brownsville schools in Brooklyn, Rochester Socialist Sunday School, and International Socialist Sunday School in Milwaukee). The two-hour morning school sessions consisted of age-divided classes and general assembly times (with announcements, recitations, songs, and remarks by visitors).

Socialist Sunday School teaching focused primarily on the nature of working-class life and class conflict, the character of the capitalist system and how it results in serious social problems (such as poverty, crime, and unhealthy living and working conditions), and the value of cooperative industrial and personal relations. The schools were intended to counteract the overly individualistic, competitive, nationalistic, militaristic, and anti-working class themes that seemed to be prevalent in public schools and other aspects of capitalist culture (e.g., the press, mass entertainment, and the church). They were never expected to provide a complete socialist education for youth, only a more formal, systematic one (albeit only two hours a week) than could be gotten at home, at rallies, in youth clubs, and so forth. While some staff members (many of whom had no formal pedagogical training) tended to rely too heavily on the adaptation of adult-oriented reading materials for lessons, the SSS movement as a whole did include a variety of teaching methods and materials, including lecture outlines, question-and-answer discussion formats, socialist and nonsocialist children's readers and magazines, games, role-playing activities, field trips, guest speakers, songs, plays, and pageants.

The first Socialist Sunday schools were initiated soon after the organization of the SP in 1901. For example, the San Jose school was established by members of the local Socialist women's club in 1902, and schools in Chicago, Boston, and Omaha were organized in 1903. A slow but continuous expansion occurred during the first two decades of the century, with a national organization, intercity conferences, and more supportive party initiatives in general taking place by 1918. All of these efforts came to an abrupt halt, however, when the SP split apart in 1919–20. A few schools continued in existence during the 1920s, and about a dozen schools were reorganized in New York City in the 1930s when the party experienced a resurgence. But gone were any prospects for a national movement and the optimistic spirit that had marked the earlier phase of these radical educational experiments. By the end of 1936, when the party experienced another serious split in its ranks, there were no Socialist Sunday schools left in existence in the United States. *See also*: Yiddish Schools

—Kenneth Teitelbaum

REFERENCES

Buhle, Mari Jo. *Women and American Socialism, 1870–1920*. Urbana: University of Illinois Press, 1981.

Teitelbaum, Kenneth. "Contestation and Curriculum: The Efforts of American Socialists, 1900–1920." In *The Curriculum: Problems, Politics, and Possibilities*, edited by Landon E. Beyer and Michael W. Apple. New York: State University of New York Press, 1988.

———. "Outside the Selective Tradition: Socialist Curriculum for Children in the United States, 1900–1920." In *The Formation of School Subjects: The Struggle for Creating an American Institution*, edited by Thomas F. Popkewitz. Philadelphia: Falmer Press, 1987.

Teitelbaum, Kenneth, and William J. Reese. "American Socialist Pedagogy and Experimentation in the Progressive Era: The Socialist Sunday School. *History of Education Quarterly* 23 (Winter 1983).

Socialist Trades & Labor Alliance

The first national effort to launch an explicitly socialist labor federation in the United States, the ST&LA foreshadowed the Industrial Workers of the World and the Communist

Trade Union Unity League in some of its ideals and many of its difficulties.

"Dual unionism" already had a venerable history in the United States by the 1890s. The Knights of Labor, formed in 1869, and the American Federation of Labor, founded twelve years later, operated by the early 1880s in sharp competition to each other. At the local level, in the same period, socialistic German-based trades in many cities broke with conservative (and often corrupt) local federations to found independent citywide labor bodies. Several outright radical unions, notably the Progressive Cigar Makers, fiercely disputed the AFL's political caution and its unaggressive approach toward unskilled workers in particular.

By the early 1890s, a decline of the AFL and near-collapse of the now-small Knights of Labor had become marked. After an unsuccessful effort to exert influence on the latter (in 1894, socialist editor Lucien Sanial had been promised editorship of the Knights' organ, but the offer had been rescinded), District 49, in combination with the New York Central Labor Federation (the more radical of two competing New York bodies), the Brooklyn Socialist Labor Federation, the United Hebrew Trades, and the Newark Central Labor Federation, then formed the nucleus of the Socialist Trades & Labor Alliance.

Fired by the expectation that American capitalism—mired in an unprecedented depression—had entered its final crisis, the ST&LA set out to mobilize the working class. At first it seemed to receive promising signals in particular from New England, where the newly organized Boot & Shoe Workers Union and the National Union of Textile Workers joined the new federation. In a few sectors of the desperately impoverished needles trade, militants led strikes of the most exploited workers, women and the young. The ST&LA promised an industrial unionism, issued over 200 charters, and enrolled between 15,000 and 30,000 members. However, the ST&LA did not draw from the AFL—despite intense internal sparring against AFL president Samuel Gompers—either the existing industrial unions (such as brewery, coal- or metal-mining) or socialistic-minded (likewise brewery, and the machinists or American Railway Union) trades. In effect, the ST&LA had been limited to bodies where Socialist Labor Party members played central roles.

As such, the ST&LA could neither effect an industrial union movement nor successfully resist the overpowering strength of the AFL. Indeed, by 1896 the SLP had itself begun to disintegrate from the withdrawal of the craft-oriented dissidents and their considerable local resources. Soon, internal conflicts shook the organization. When the ST&LA removed its general secretary for printing advertisements of Democratic and Republican politicians, the Central Labor Federation withdrew and the labor alliance entered upon a steady decline. By the turn of the century, it had dwindled to a virtual paper organization.

Ironically, other unionists had already embarked upon a parallel course, via the Western Federation of Miners, the Western Labor Union, and (as it was renamed in 1902) the American Labor Union. ST&LA activists joined with them and others in the formation of the IWW in 1905. While many Socialist Party delegates complained that the ST&LA dominated the founding convention, the ST&LA's fourteen delegates were the fewest of the "big five" labor organizations present. As labor historian Paul Brissenden wrote, the ST&LA's only domination was its "supremacy of ideas." The "political clause" in the Party's preamble, which advocated political as well as economic organization of workers, had been drafted (and was to be widely popularized) by Daniel DeLeon. Its extraction in 1908 marked the end of the SLP influence in that organization, and the renewal of the ST&LA influence, in a sense, through the "Detroit IWW" faction. *See also*: DeLeon, Daniel; Industrial Workers of the World; Shoe workers; Socialist Labor Party

—Don Fitz

REFERENCES

Brissenden, Paul. *The IWW: A Study of American Syndicalism*. New York: Columbia University Press, 1919.

Daniel DeLeon: The Man and His Work. New York: New York Labor News, 1919.

Herreshoff, David. *The Origins of American Marxism*. Detroit: Wayne State University Press, 1967.

Socialist Woman/ Progressive Woman

Published to educate women in the principles of socialism and to encourage them to join the Socialist Party, the *Socialist Woman* (1907–9) appeared monthly under the editorship of Josephine Conger-Kaneko, with the assistance of her husband, Japanese socialist Kiichi Kaneko. Renamed *Progressive Woman* in 1909, ostensibly to reach a broader audience, the magazine resembled the *Appeal to Reason* in style and tone. Conger-Kaneko, born in Centralia, Missouri, had previously edited a column entitled "Hints to the *Appeal*'s Wise Woman" and continued to share, although intermittently, office space and printing facilities with the parent publication. Aspiring to reach a national audience, Conger-Kaneko never departed politically from her original and most loyal readership, radical women in the Midwest and in California. Her journalism captured a political sensibility rooted in late-nineteenth-century reform movements, ranging from suffrage and temperance to social purity, and lacked the seeming sophistication of a materialist analysis of the "woman question." Although Conger-Kaneko had studied scientific socialism with Ernest Untermann at Ruskin College, she maintained a sentimental, almost mystical view of womanhood. The *Progressive Woman* stressed the limitations that capitalism had imposed on women in fulfilling their major roles within the home and for the preservation of the family.

The magazine served as the voice of women's organizational autonomy within the SP. Conger-Kaneko believed that women demanded a special agitational message as well as political space distant from domineering men. When the SP established the Woman's National Committee (WNC), Conger-Kaneko nevertheless accepted the decision and made her publication its unofficial organ.

During the peak period of the WNC, which supplied plenty of copy, the *Progressive Woman* achieved a subscription high of 3,000 and a total circulation of 18,000 for special issues. Alongside regular features, Conger-Kaneko ran large samples of letters from subscribers and inadvertently supplied future historians with information about rank-and-file women from the distant outreaches of Socialist organization. WNC organizers forwarded summaries of their meetings with local women's committees across the country, reported on their involvements in strikes and in state suffrage campaigns, and tested propaganda in the magazine's columns. The *Progressive Woman* also ran monthly lesson plans for local women's committees and thereby publicized socialist primers on the woman question. Conger-Kaneko edited special issues on woman suffrage, child labor, and prostitution and regularly featured on the front cover a photograph of a prominent Socialist woman.

In 1911 the *Progressive Woman* ran into a series of technical and financial difficulties that foreshadowed its demise. Publishing from the SP national office in Chicago, Conger-Kaneko managed for another year before asking the WNC to take on the magazine's financial obligations. The SP's well-established policy against a party-owned press mitigated against this move, and a party subcommittee arranged instead to fund the *Progressive Woman* through a joint-stock company. Income proved insufficient to support the publication at the same time that the new chair of the WNC, Winnie Branstetter, charged the *Progressive Woman*'s editorial staff with ultraleftism.

In 1912 Conger-Kaneko ended the Socialist women's magazine and resumed, with the assistance of her managing editor, Barnett Braverman, publication under the title of a popular socialist newspaper of the 1890s, the *Coming Nation*. A general-interest magazine, the *Coming Nation* ran until July 1913. In its final number, Conger-Kaneko left a long, bitter statement summarizing her experiences as a Socialist editor and crafting a revealing history of the demise of the SP's singular women's magazine. *See also*: Women's National Committee

—*Mari Jo Buhle*

REFERENCES

Buhle, Mari Jo. "*Socialist Woman, Progressive Woman, Coming Nation*." In *The American Radical Press, 1880–1960, II*, edited by Joseph R. Conlin. Westport: Greenwood Press, 1974.

Socialist Workers Party

While never having more than 2,000 members, the SWP has sometimes enjoyed an influence far beyond its numbers in the labor and radical movements. For most of its history it has strongly identified with the revolutionary Marxist, Bolshevik-Leninist perspectives of Leon Trotsky. In the 1980s it has chosen to stress an affinity with the orientation of Fidel Castro's Communist Party of Cuba.

The SWP traces its roots to the early Communist movement of the United States. In 1928 prominent CPers—James P. Cannon, Max Shachtman, Martin Abern, Rose Karsner, Arne Swabeck, Karl Skoglund, V. R. Dunne, Antoinette Konikow, and others—were expelled for "Trotskyism" and went on to organize the Communist League of America, with about one hundred members when founded in 1929. The organization published the weekly *Militant*, a theoretical magazine called *New International* (later renamed *Fourth International* and then *International Socialist Review*), and numerous books and pamphlets by Trotsky and others. Opposing what they considered the bureaucratic-conservative degeneration of the workers' state in the USSR under Joseph Stalin—and the consequent Stalinization of the world Communist movement— the Trotskyists stressed the principles of workers' democracy and revolutionary internationalism as essential aspects of the socialist struggle. They exercised a substantial influence among many leading intellectuals (especially through vigorous opposition to the Stalinist purges of 1936–38). At the same time, the Trotskyists concentrated special attention both in the unemployed movement and among unionizing industrial workers during the Depression years of the 1930s. In 1934 they led the Minneapolis workers to victory during the militant Teamsters' strikes of that city. They played a significant role in other unions—among auto and maritime workers, for example, in the 1930s and 1940s. Some of the SWP's future leaders (such as Farrell Dobbs, Tom Kerry, Joe Hansen, George Breitman, and others) were recruited and developed in this period.

A series of mergers, splits, and fusions led up to the formation of the SWP in 1938, by which time the Trotskyist ranks had swelled to about 1,200. In 1934 the Communist League of America merged with A. J. Muste's American Workers Party to form the Workers Party of the United States. In 1936 this organization went into the Socialist Party of America, led by Norman Thomas, but the Trotskyists and many newly won supporters were soon expelled for challenging the SP's moderate leadership. The 1938 founding of the SWP coincided with the creation of the Fourth International, a worldwide organization of Trotskyists. The SWP was one of the largest components of this international organization, continuing to play an influential consultative role when forced to formally disaffiliate by the Voorhis Act. Another piece of restrictive legislation, the Smith Act, was used first against the Trotskyists, imprisoning eighteen leaders of the SWP and of the Minneapolis Teamsters because of their refusal to refrain from criticizing what they considered imperialist war aims of the U.S. government during World War II. The strategy that Trotskyists advocated for defeating fascism was a working-class united front—independent of the capitalists—that would combine democratic and transitional (socialist-oriented) demands.

Despite wartime repression, the SWP made gains during the 1940s, playing an especially aggressive role in the postwar strike waves. By 1945 it had a membership of 1,500. The Cold War, anticommunist witch-hunts, and the 1950s economic prosperity took a heavy toll, reducing the party to no more than 400 aging veterans by 1959. Yet their authority among U.S. radicals increased when the 1956 Khrushchev revelations vindicated their long-standing condemnation of Stalin's crimes. The anticolonial revolutions generated renewed interest in Trotsky's theory of permanent revolution, and the trajectory of the Cuban Revolution—hailed by SWPers, who helped to form Fair Play for Cuba Committees—also caused many to take a closer look at Trotskyist perspectives. Further, as one New Left veteran (never in the SWP milieu) has reminisced: "In the 1950s and early 1960s when not much was happening on the Left as such, the SWP's local Militant Labor Forums, where they existed, often reached out to young people; and individual SWPers often conducted themselves with a dignity that made an impression on youngsters."

The rise of the black liberation movement in the United States contributed to a new radicalization; by championing and publicizing the ideas of Malcolm X, the SWP further increased its influence—though Afro-American membership never exceeded 7 percent, out of a membership of about 1,200 by the late 1970s. The student and youth radicalization, and especially the mass movement against the U.S. war in Vietnam, brought many recruits into the SWP and its youth group, the Young Socialist Alliance (founded in 1960). The SWP played a central role in the National Mobilization Committee to End the War in Vietnam and in the National Peace Action Coalition, responsible for drawing hundreds of thousands into active opposition to the war. SWPers and YSAers also played a role in women's liberation efforts (and to a lesser extent in gay rights activities). In this period female membership rose to about 40 percent, with significant numbers of women playing leadership roles. Influence was also exerted in the Chicano and Puerto Rican communities. In many areas the SWP became known for running vigorous and sometimes innovative socialist election campaigns to introduce the public to socialist ideas and to dramatize the need for political independence from the procapitalist Democratic and Republican parties.

Over the years many frictions resulted in groupings and individuals leaving the SWP. Among the best known splits were those led by Max Shachtman in 1940 and Bert Cochran in 1953 (representing about 500 and 200 members, respectively). The Shachtmanites viewed the USSR as a "bureaucratic-collectivist" society no less reactionary than capitalism (some later decided it was even more reactionary than capitalism), whereas the SWP majority insisted that the nationalized, planned economy of the USSR represented a working-class gain worth defending from both Western imperialism and Stalinist bureaucrats. The Cochranites believed the classical Trotskyist analysis and party-building perspectives had become outdated in the face of the Cold War confrontation and anticommunist repression, and they viewed the SWP majority as "sectarian" defenders of "sterile orthodoxies."

Many writers and intellectuals in and around the Trotskyist movement during the 1930s later went on to become influential moderate socialist, liberal, and even conservative ideological and cultural figures. Among ex-members who remained on the left end of the political spectrum, continuing to have an influence on the broader radical movement, were A. J. Muste, Harry Braverman, C. L. R. James, Raya Dunayevskaya, Sidney Lens, Hal Draper, Staughton Lynd, and Murray Weiss. Among the revolutionary veterans who continued to make significant contributions from within the the SWP were George Novack, Joseph Hansen, George Breitman, Art Preis, Frank Lovell, Fred Halstead, Paul Siegel, and Evelyn Reed.

By the early 1970s a transition was made to a new leadership team of 1960s recruits headed by Jack Barnes, a former economics student from Carlton College whose predecessors as SWP national secretary had been class-struggle veterans James P. Cannon and Farrell Dobbs. Perhaps a lack of confidence caused the new leadership to impose an increasingly tight internal regime. This lack of confidence was undoubtedly intensified by the failure of a "proletarianization" effort (in which a majority of the members got industrial jobs) to yield hoped-for gains in the late 1970s. In the early 1980s—as the new SWP leadership put forward a far-reaching critique of Trotsky's theory of permanent revolution—about 200 veteran members were driven out for resisting the abandonment of major aspects of the SWP program. Many more drifted away in demoralization, though the SWP remained one of the major organizations of the American Left, with perhaps 700 members. One of its contributions in the 1970s and 1980s was a successful lawsuit against the U.S. government, publicizing many years of vicious and illegal harassment by the FBI and other government agencies. *See also*: Breitman, George; Cannon, James P.; Dobbs, Farrell; Dunayevskaya, Raya; Fourth International; Konikow, Antoinette; Muste, A. J.; Peace Movements; Shachtman, Max; Smith Act Trial, 1943; Trotskyism

—Paul Le Blanc

REFERENCES

Breitman, George, ed. *The Founding of the Socialist Workers Party*. New York: Monad Press, 1982.

Cannon, James P. *The History of American Trotskyism*. New York: Pathfinder Press, 1972.

Halstead, Fred. *Out Now! A Participant's Account of the American Movement Against the Vietnam War*. New York: Monad Press, 1978.

Le Blanc, Paul. *Trotskyism in America, The First Fifty Years*. New York: Fourth Internationalist Tendency, 1987.

Wald, Alan. *The New York Intellectuals, The Rise and Decline of the Anti-Stalinist Left, From the 1930s to the 1980s*. Chapel Hill: University of North Carolina Press, 1987.

SOCIALIST ZIONISM

This movement, and the larger Labor Zionist movement of which it can be considered a part, played a unique role within North American Jewish radicalism. Linked to both anarchist-utopian and Marxist-nationalist tendencies within the Yiddish-speaking community, it sought to resolve the dilemmas of modern Jewry through socialist activism and active Jewish self-defense in the Diaspora, the territorial concentration of the Jewish people, and the development of a sovereign Jewish polity in the ancestral homeland of the Jewish people, *Eretz Yisrael* (the land of Israel). Long a small but significant force in the United States, it retains its status as a primary advocate of humanistic Jewish values, culture, tradition, and education, a just society, Arab-Jewish rapproachment in the Middle East, and peace and active cooperation between the state of Israel and its neighbors.

The formation of Socialist Zionism goes back to the first years of the twentieth century in Eastern and Central Europe. In contrast to other Left trends within Jewish communities, including Bundists and, later, Communists, the Socialist Zionists believed that while socialist theory was important, valuable, and generally correct, the problems of anti-Semitism, social dislocation, and Jewish vulnerability required a particularistic, i.e., Zionist, solution.

Local groups of *Poalei Tzion* (Workers of Zion) developed through Russia and Eastern Europe, and the American branch of the movement can be traced back to 1903. Its weekly Yiddish-language organ, *Der Yiddisher Kempfer* (The Jewish fighter, 1907–present), was widely read in the Jewish community, and rapidly became known for its high literary quality and its emphatic political views. The American *Poalei Tzion* established its own mutual aid society, the *Yiddisher Nationaler Arbeter Farband* (Jewish National Workers Association), which operated in overlapping circles with the socialistic Workmen's Circle. Other innovations included national-radical day schools, which promoted Yiddish-language teaching of Jewish and international literature, and secular Jewish education—a model later taken over, with marked political modifications, by the Workmen's Circle and by the Communist-related International Workers Order schools.

In 1913 another Left-Zionist movement, *Hashomer Hatzair* (The young guard), developed in Europe, drawing on currents as diverse as the German *Wandervogel*, the British Boy Scouts, and Marxist-Leninism. A totally youth-led and youth-oriented movement, *Hashomer Hatzair* shunned Yiddish for Hebrew and stressed *aliya* (literally "going up" to *Eretz Yisrael*). In 1923 immigrants to the United States launched branches, which deprecated formal higher education for internal "movement" education and collective self-development. Like other elements of Socialist Zionism, they were closely tied to their "world units," which led their organizational bases in Europe, later in Israel.

Three major international figures on the Jewish Left lent their talents to the Socialist Zionist cause in the United States. Ber Borokhov (1881–1917), the most rigorous of the Russian Labor Zionist intellectuals, had been founder of the Zionist Socialist Workers Union. He stressed that the extremely distorted class-structure of the Jewish people through their dispersion necessitated a radical change; Jews should strive for control of their own economic infrastructure, through participating in all strata of a state's economy, liberating the Jewish people both nationally and for a final class-emancipation to follow in the worldwide socialist struggle. Nachman Syrkin (1868–1924), another "founding father" in Europe, was a less doctrinaire socialist, holding that a cooperative mass settlement of the Jewish proletariat in *Eretz Yisrael,* with cooperative enterprises and trade unionism would lay the socialist foundations for a new, free Jewish society. Chaim Zhitlovsky (1865–1943), a sweeping figure on the lecture podium and regarded by many as the greatest Yiddish popularist of ideas in his time, moved from a "Diaspora nationalist" perspective to one of the *Poalei Tzion* and offered his pen to Labor Zionism.

During and after the First World War, Labor Zionism swung Right, then apparently Left, then Right again in a desperate effort to effect a solution for the suffering European Jewish masses. David Ben-Gurion, foremost *Poalei Tzion* leader during his American years, led Labor Zionism into official support for WW I against the antiwar sentiments of many Jewish Zionists and nearly all Jewish socialists. By attempting to place his movement at the service of the West, with its commitments to national recognition (and its neocolonial interests), Ben-Gurion, and others, hoped that the Balfour Declaration would usher in a Jewish state. In disappointment (and in recognition of Russian Left-Labor Zionist support of the Bolshevik Revolution), he turned momentarily toward the new Soviet regime for support, a plan he abandoned in the 1920s. Only a small section of the movement, "Left *Poalei Tzion,*" called for participation in the Third International.

At this time, American Labor Zionism began to go through major demographic and political changes. For a brief period, 1917–21, Labor Zionists published a daily paper (one of four Yiddish dailies in North America at the time) and waxed strong. Important socialist labor leaders—notably former SLP activist and Amalgamated Clothing Worker leader Joseph Schlossberg—embraced the Zionist cause and established it firmly within the Jewish trades. During the 1920s, however, Labor Zionism also became steadily less a working-class and more a transclass movement, especially among younger (i.e., American native-born) members.

As part of this drift, once-fervent opposition against Zionist revisionism—long attacked for its worship of militarism, its chauvinism, and its overt antagonism to socialistic values—eased to a degree as the movements found common ground in the struggle to ease the plight of European Jewry and support for Jewish settlement in *Eretz Yisrael.* This turn mirrored the move of the Israeli labor movement to shift the focus from "class" to "nation," and a broad drift within American Jewry from socialist to liberal circles. Many of the original *Poalei* Zionists remained within the Socialist Party. They felt a mutual hostility with Jewish Communists and with the rest of Jewish Social Democracy. A majority of the *Poalei* Zionists in time drifted out of Socialist political activism, even while often retaining their ethical commitments in their "movement activities." Labor Zionism—noted especially in the 1930s–1940s for the English-language publications *Pioneer Woman* (by the Women's Labor Zionist Organization) and *Jewish Frontier*—supported liberal and labor causes, but in a general sense its socialist commitment waned, and its approach has been marred at times by an obsessive anticommunism. The Labor Zionist youth movement that has its roots in *Poalei Tzion, Habonim* (The builders), retained stronger connections with older socialist ideas, and prepared its members for settlement in the labor sector of *Eretz Yisrael.*

By contrast, *Hashomer Hatzair* had always, until the Khrushchev revelations of 1956, held a position of critical support toward the Soviet Union, regarding the Bolshevik Revolution as a struggle for a new world order complementary to that of Socialist Zionist struggle against Jewish life in *Galut* (exile). Even on the eve of World War II, *Hashomer Hatzair* continued to call for the creation of a binational Jewish-Arab state in "mandatory Palestine." After 1947, with the palpable impossibility of that solution, it continued to insist upon amity between the Jews and the Palestinian Arabs, joint victims of a tragic conflict "between two peoples, one returning to its homeland and another already living for many years on that same land." By 1936, *Hashomer Hatzair* had reached its maximum size of 3,000 in the United States and Canada. With the approach of the war, the movement became rent with dissension over the proper response. A Trotskyist-influenced faction insisted on "revolutionary defeatism," i.e., no support for the coming world war; the majority insisting on "fighting fascism within and without" (a position that emerged dominant with the news of Nazi atrocities and attempted genocide).

With the conclusion of the war, and the realization of the massive tragedy inflicted upon the world Jewish community, Socialist Zionists along with Labor Zionists supported or participated in the underground immigration of Jews from war-torn Europe to mandatory Palestine, and the smuggling of arms to Jewish defense forces.

In 1947 *Hashomer Hatzair* created an affiliated "adult organization," the Progressive Zionist League (PZL), and a less ideologically based support organization, Americans for Progressive Israel (API). The Socialist Zionists journal *Israel Horizons* (1952–present) began publication under the stewardship of former *PM* foreign editor and European correspondent Richard Yaffe.

With the foundation of the state of Israel, a number of Socialist Zionists and Labor Zionists themselves immigrated to Israel, many to live on *kibbutzim* of the Kibbutz Artzi Federation, affiliated with Mapam (United Workers Party), or the Ihud, affiliated with the Mapai (Israeli Labor Party). The drain on leadership seriously affected *Hashomer Hatzair*, as did its principled opposition to the Korean War. Attacks upon it spread through mainstream Jewish organizations, not excluding the Labor Zionists, and its was subjected to FBI investigations and harassment.

In the late 1960s and early 1970s, a resurgence of Jewish progressive activism brought campus activity and a revival of interest in the writings of Borokhov, Syrkin, and other Socialist Zionist pioneers. In recent years, Socialist Zionists, specifically API and *Israel Horizons*, have joined hands with other progressive Jewish organizations such as New Jewish Agenda, the Progressive Zionist Caucus, the International Jewish Peace Union, and the Jewish Peace Fellowship, in opposition to the rightward drift of Israeli politics, the invasion of Lebanon, and the continued occupation of the West Bank.

—*Arieh Lebowitz*

REFERENCES

Arian, Charles L. "Zionism, Socialism, and the Kinship of Peoples: *Hashomer Hatzair* in North America." Ph.D. diss., Hebrew Union College, 1986.

Shpizman, Laib. *Geshikhte fun der tsyonistisher arbeter bavegung in Tsofen Amerike*. Vol. 1. New York: Farlag "Yiddisher Kempfer," 1955.

SOCIOLOGY

During the 1919 Palmer Raids, a Russian sociology student was arrested at a Communist cell meeting in Chicago. Explaining his presence to the deportation judge, the young Louis Wirth answered simply "Fieldwork, your honor."

Sociology's appeal to radicals lay in its substantive concerns with "sin and society," in ecological methods such as the survey that gave left-wing intellectuals direct access to oppressed groups, and in its self-image as a scientific instrument of rational reconstruction. Radical sociologists not merely accommodated positivism; they helped establish its dominance.

At the same time, sociology pacified Marxism by integrating elements of conflict and contradiction into the dominant structural-functionalism. By savaging challenges to the status quo, radicals confronted constraints on funding, repression or exclusion from elite universities, the insulation of theory and writing from common parlance, subspecializations beholden to existing institutional practices, and old boys (and girls) who defended the profession.

To exploit "the supressed underculture of sociology," radicals were active "outside" the profession, accommodated mainstream paradigms, created radical enclaves, and organized to democratize the field.

Albion Small committed the first sociology department (1892) to shift from "ameliorating to preventing" social problems by linking study at the University of Chicago to the reform work of Jane Addams (whose Hull House was founded in 1889), Edith Abbott, Mary van Kleeck, Mary E. Richmond, and Jessica Peixotto. But sociology quickly forgot the female activists. Following Small, Robert Park and W. I. Thomas muckraked the 1919 riots, local corruption, and U.S. imperialism. As a result, Thomas was framed on a morals charge and fired, continuing to write under a pseudonym.

Conservative William Graham Sumner was almost fired from Yale in 1898 when he attacked plutocracy and imperialism. E. A. Ross was fired from Stanford in 1900 for attacking the railroad monopoly and Chinese immigration. Like Thorstein Veblen, his chauvinism and racialist analysis mixed with critical support for the Bolshevik Revolution.

Marxist sociologist Jerome Davis was appointed to a chair in practical philanthropy at Yale in 1924. Scorned by the sociology department, Davis coauthored an important text (1927) with original sections on occupational disease, "industrial autocracy," and "economic reconstruction." Davis was active in Popular Front organizations like the Teachers' Union, to which other Communist academics belonged. Fired by Yale, he became head of the newly founded Eastern Sociological Society (1937–38) and the American Federation of Teachers (1936–39). Davis invoked the Fifth Amendment before the McCarran Committee in 1952.

Many graduate students joined the Communist Party in the Depression. Some, like Robert Bellah and Sigmund Diamond, became mainstream sociologists; a few, like Bernhard Stern, continued to espouse Marxist views and some who remained Party members were later fired from southern black schools for civil rights activism.

Sociology abandoned activism before McCarthyism. Charles Ellwood and Veblen emphasized class struggle, but believed Marxism meant promoting sociology as a "science." William Ogburn took his cultural-lag theory from Marx, but felt responsible only for making new knowledge available. This was the Party view during the Popular Front disseminated by Merton and Stern in *Science & Society* (founded in 1936). At Columbia, Robert Lynd recruited C. Wright Mills to defend empiricism. Even Lynd's "Knowledge for What?" takes an instrumental approach to learning, like "concrete" sociology in the Soviet Union during the Stalin years, and anticipates Merton's translation of Marx into the anemic "propositions" of structural functionalism.

Relatively few sociologists were targeted by McCarthyism. Harvard Dean McGeorge Bundy made Robert Bellah undergo a psychiatric exam when he refused to give names, and fired Sigmund Diamond, who was quickly hired by Columbia. Left-wing faculty quit or were fired during loyalty oath controversies at state universities in Washington, California, Ohio, and Florida. Bernhard Stern, a Marxist sociologist of health at Columbia and a founder of *Science & Society*, was the only untenured academic who kept his job despite refusing to cooperate with a congressional committee. Characteristically, Stern claimed to have left the Party, doubting that scholarship and Communism could mix.

The disavowal of Marxism during the late '40s and '50s is documented in *The Academic Mind* (1958), written by the Austrian social democrat Paul Lazarsfeld and Walter Thielens. Critical sociology was sustained by radical enclaves at the New School for Social Research, Brandeis, Columbia, Harvard, and at the Institute for Social Research, which moved to Columbia after 1934. The institute's independent endowment permitted an interdisciplinary atmosphere where the best historical, philosophical, and economic currents of European sociology mixed with the more psychological/biological orientation of the Americans.

The institute's focus on the cultural and psychological barriers to Marxism combined with the skepticism of Adorno, Horkheimer, and Marcuse toward "instrumental reason," in order to generate a critique of conformity and mass culture. The institute's greatest impact was on empirical sociology, however. Starting from the assumption that voting and buying soap were equivalent behaviors, Lazarsfeld linked critical theory and "administrative sociology." From the early interview studies of Weimar workers by Erich Fromm and Lazarsfeld (1930) through the unpublished contract studies of anti-Semitism among American workers to the "authoritarian personality profile," institute sociologists provided the theoretical context for typologies and case-studies lacking in the "Chicago school" and gave a psychoanalytic dimension to applied sociology, without which market research is unthinkable.

Enclaves of radical sociologists in the '60s proved more ephemeral. At Washington University in St. Louis, divisions between "activists" and "theoreticians" led to a purge. At Berkeley, the radical criminology program was dismantled in 1976. At Stanford, Gerald McWorter (Adul Alkalimat), Robert G. Newby, and Ron Bailey briefly formed the African Liberation Support Committee, while Wayne State sociologist Martin Glaberman had introduced Marx (and C. L. R. James) to founders of the League of Revolutionary Black Workers. At Michigan, sociologists Todd Gitlin, Richard Flacks, and Bob Ross were among the authors of the *Port Huron Statement* (1962) and *America and the New Era* (1963), and Gitlin and Ross traded graduate school for grass-roots organizing. Brandeis provided sabbaticals in sociology to leaders of the Student Nonviolent Coordinating Committee and initiated a program in "action sociology" that ended abruptly when the student car sent to "study" a threatened "stall-in" by CORE at the New York World's Fair found it was the only vehicle to block traffic.

When Jay Shulman (CCNY), Marlene Dixon (Chicago), Paul Nyden (Pittsburgh), Howard Erlich (Iowa), David Colfax (University of Connecticut), and other sociologists were fired during the '60s, activists sought to "radicalize" the American Sociological Association (ASA), finally electing Alfred McLung Lee its president (1975–76). Lee was linked to activist alternatives in the ASA, including the Society for the Psychological Study of Social Issues (1936); the Institute for Propaganda Analysis, which targeted Allied and Fascist propaganda during the war; the Society for the Study of Social Problems (SSSP), founded at Roosevelt College in Chicago in 1951; and the Association for Humanist Sociology (AHS), founded at Miami University, Oxford, Ohio, in 1976.

The 1967 ASA convention passed an antiwar resolution that failed a mail ballot. During the 1968 Columbia sit-ins against the Institute for Defense Analysis, graduate students Al Szymanski and Carol Brown started the sociology liberation movement (motto: Knowledge for Whom?). That year, Richard Flacks and Martin Nicolaus responded to a keynote address at the ASA convention by HEW secretary Wilbur Cohen. Subsequent antiwar protests included a memorial for Ho Chi Minh and the presentation of a huge plastic penis painted red, white, and blue at the annual business meeting in 1971.

Although Columbia's chapter collapsed, from 1968 to 1972 the SLM coordinated the activities of regional groups like the East Coast Conference of Socialist Sociologists (originally the East Coast Union of Radical Sociologists), the Western Union of Radical Sociologists, and the Union of Radical American Social Scientists. Regional meetings of the SLM ceased by 1976 and the "Invisible Socialist Sociology Newsletter" bemoaned the lack of "socialist social relations." The next year, the radical caucus gave way to an official "Marxist" section of the ASA, which continues to sponsor didactic sessions.

The *Insurgent Sociologist* (now *Critical Sociology*) first appeared as a counterconvention call in 1969. Its purpose was "to destroy the power structure of the profession, eliminate the power elite that controls the profession through its undemocratic structure, and redefine sociology to correspond to social reality." Published at Douglass College as the newletter of the Union of Radical Sociologists and the SLM until 1971, *IS* then moved to the University of Oregon under Al Syzmanski's editorship, which is now shared with collectives in other cities. Another radical magazine, *Crime and Social Justice* (1974), was started by the Union of Radical Criminologists at Berkeley, (1973).

Within the discipline, as illustrated by the studies of social class by Erik Olin Wright, the tendency is for Marxists to accommodate, incorporate, and reform dominant methodologies, including structural functionalism. Marxist sociologists have contributed to the study of Latin America (Maurice Zeitlin, Jim Petras, Gunder Frank), political sociology (James O'Connor, Robert Alford), the labor process (Stanley Aronowitz, Michael Burroway), and the welfare state (Fred Block, Theda Skotcpol). Still, with the exception of small radical enclaves at SUNY-Binghamton, CUNY, U. C. Santa Cruz, Berkeley, and Rutgers, mainstream sociology continues to ignore or to disparage Marxism, the one systematic theory sociology has to offer. *See also*: Criminology, Radical Professional Journals

—*Evan Stark*

REFERENCES

Critical Sociology (Special Twentieth-Anniversary Issue, "Sociology Liberation Movement") 15 (Summer 1988).

SOLEDAD BROTHERS: see ARMED STRUGGLE; DAVIS, ANGELA

SOLIDARITY, LATIN AMERICAN 1960s–1980s

In the 1980s, solidarity with the peoples of Central America became a key rallying point for a new kind of popular movement in the United States. This development had its own trajectory, and was in no simple sense a revival of anti–Vietnam War organizing. Its political touchstone was, of course, the reservoir of post-Indochina antiinterventionism (however passive or isolationist), which cuts deep into almost all strata in the United States, but its organizing principle was an instinctual solidarity—a commitment to stand with the people, often at some risk. The origins of this solidarity lay in events of the 1960s and 1970s: the Cuban Revolution, the Alliance for Progress and Vatican II–inspired emigration of thousands of North American missionaries and volunteers into the hemisphere's poorest countries, and the seizure of power by U.S.-sponsored dictatorships from the Tierra del Fuego to the Caribbean.

Cuba's triumph placed armed struggle against North American hegemony on the table, with permanent consequences. An ecumenical "hands off Cuba" movement grew up around the Fair Play for Cuba Committee in 1960–61, helping to spark the New Left. Many young activists and new committees joined this proto-solidarity campaign of mass delegations, rallies, speakers' tours, and newspaper appeals before the Cuban missile crisis and various Congressional committees ended matters. Much less visibly, over the decade marked by the coup in Brazil (1964), the invasion of the Dominican Republic (1965), the Green Beret–led counterinsurgency in Guatemala (1966 on), election of the *Unidad Popular* in Chile (1970), and the "dirty war" in Argentina (1974 on), the return of North American faith people from Latin America led to a "conscientization" at the bases of the Catholic church and mainstream Protestant denominations that proved impervious to Cold War logic, spawning the informal intrainstitutional networks of activists central to the movement of the 1970s and 1980s. Meanwhile, Vietnam and the struggle for the rights of African Americans radicalized thousands of people across the United States, generating a large but inchoate and quarrelsome movement unified solely by its commitment to "antiimperialism." Awareness of revolution and repression in Latin America grew rapidly, culminating in the Venceremos Brigades that, coming directly from the ruins of Students for a Democratic Society, sent thousands to do agricultural work in Cuba in the early '70s.

For many different kinds of people, General Pinochet's 1973 coup in Chile was only the most egregious example of full-blown imperialism in the Americas. The fall of Salvador Allende catalyzed antiwar veterans of all stripes, the reviving Communist Party, returned church and lay volunteers, and anti-interventionist McGovern Democrats. The substantial Chile solidarity movement of the '70s also reflected the deep divisions of the Chilean exile movement, which played into political animosities in the United States (e.g., the broad network around the CP-organized National Chile Center versus its smaller, more militant rival, Non-Intervention in Chile—NICH). Similar problems affected the other major effort of the time, the Puerto Rico Solidarity Committee. Very successful campaigns were implemented—against "torture ships" visiting U.S. ports, to free prisoners throughout the hemisphere, for a "Bicentennial Without Colonies," huge concert tours—but coordinated organizing for Chile and Puerto Rico had subsided dramatically by the end of the decade.

In these same years, a faith-based "human rights" community had diffused across the United States in the wake of Vietnam and Chile. Exemplified by the Ecumenical Program for Inter-American Communication and Action (1968), the Washington Office on Latin America (1974), the Coalition for a New Foreign and Military Policy (1975), and offices within the National Council of Churches and the U.S. Catholic Conference, this Washington, D.C.–based informal network dedicated itself, with considerable success, to ending congressional support for the regimes of Latin America's Southern Cone. The presidency of Jimmy Carter became the apogee of such organizing, as activists worked in tandem with some elements of the administration to undercut Somoza and, however briefly, to extend highly conditioned aid to "Nicaragua Libre."

In 1978–79 virtually all the diffuse strands of solidarity and anti-interventionism described above coalesced, summoned by urgent Nicaraguan appeals. In February 1979, the National Network in Solidarity with the Nicaraguan People (later the Nicaragua Network) was formed by local and national Latin America committees, task forces, and human rights groups, with the endorsement of Senator Edward Kennedy and several liberal unions and religious orders. A rapid mobilization across the country encouraged the United States to hasten Somoza's demise and built support for the first successful revolution since Cuba. Simultaneously, Salvadoran exiles in San Francisco, Los Angeles, and elsewhere began organizing systematically among North Americans. In 1980, with Nicaraguan triumph apparently assured, the faith-based networks, peace groups, and self-conscious "solidarity activists" all turned to the bloody confrontation in El Salvador, as pervasive death-squad terror (symbolized by the murders of Archbishop Oscar Romero and four U.S. churchwomen) also radicalized anew larger numbers of church and laypeople.

In October 1980, East and West coast conferences created the Committee in Solidarity with the People of El Salvador (CISPES), which was fueled by an early flood of hundreds of committees; over the next decade CISPES built a distinctive national organization via its close relationship with the Salvadoran community, planned grass-roots expansion, and a systematic program. Faith activists linked up nationally through the Religious Task Force on El Salvador, based in Catholic women's orders, and the Inter-Religious Task Force on El Salvador and Central America, oriented toward the Protestant churches. In the early '80s this very visible movement concentrated almost entirely on blocking intervention in El Salvador in a groundswell of local protest and education, while low-key support for Nicaraguan reconstruction continued on a much-reduced scale. Meanwhile a loose framework for Guatemala solidarity was established in 1980 (the Network in Solidarity with the People of Guatemala and other groups) out of a small but well-established base of churchpeople and scholars, though the absence of awareness and activism around the Guatemalan holocaust was to remain an obvious weakness of solidarity organizing for the next decade.

After the successful "demonstration election" in El Salvador in March 1982, the militance of the movement abated and organizing took on a more regional character as the contra war against Nicaragua heated up. Coffee harvest brigades and the faith-based Witness for Peace program brought thousands of North Americans to Nicaragua, leading to the Pledge of Resistance campaign, a local and national effort that committed tens of thousands to civil disobedience in the event of a major escalation. Meanwhile, a different sort of grass-roots network developed around the plight of Salvadorans and Guatemalans: the Sanctuary Movement, which between 1982 and 1985 committed 400 local congregations to illegally sheltering refugees, provoking major governmental infiltration and prosecution.

The public focus of the Central America movement in Reagan's second term was Nicaragua (following the election of Jose Napoleon Duarte in El Salvador), with dozens of sister-city projects, intense legislative battles, and the "Quest for Peace" campaign that matched U.S. aid to the contras in goods and services to Nicaragua. By 1987–88, an unprecedented commitment from the church and labor hierarchies, impelled by massive if decentralized grass-roots organizing, had convinced the Democratic Party leadership to press its own ambiguous policy of nonintervention as the Iran-contra scandal broke open.

Meanwhile, Salvadoran solidarity groups, the best-organized sector of the movement (and most independent from the vagaries of press and congressional concern), played a crucial role from 1985 on, providing support to the new popular movement in El Salvador. CISPES, and faith-based and labor activists literally "accompanied" this movement throughout the country, funded it, and held back the Salvadoran government's security forces through intensive human rights pressure from the United States.

At the end of the '80s, Nicaragua had survived at enormous cost, and the solidarity movement had done much to limit the proxy war and provide material support, though the Sandinistas were effectively "demonized" in mainstream political discourse here. The largest military commitment of the United States since Vietnam had meanwhile run aground in El Salvador, and consolidated organizing by North Americans had become an integral part of the Salvadoran people's struggle. None of the wars in Central America had reached any final closure, but a maturing and largely united movement had put down deep roots in the United States. *See also*: El Congreso, Cuban Americans, Latin American Studies, New Left, Newsreel and Post-New Left Radical Filmmaking

—*Van Gosse*

REFERENCES

Crittenden, Ann. *Sanctuary*. New York: Weidenfeld & Nicolson, 1988.

Gosse, Van. "'The North American Front:' Central American Solidarity in the Reagan Era." *Reshaping the U.S. Left: Popular Struggles in the 1980s*. Vol. 3, *The Year Left*. Edited by Michael Sprinker and Mike Davis. London: Verso, 1988.

Levinson, Sandra, and Carol Brightman, eds. *Venceremos Brigade*. New York: Simon & Schuster, 1971.

Melville, Thomas, and Marjorie Melville. *Whose Heaven? Whose Earth?* New York: Knopf, 1971.

Schoultz, Lars. *Human Rights and United States Policy Toward Latin America*. Princeton: Princeton University Press, 1981.

SORGE, FRIEDRICH: see GERMAN AMERICANS, INTERNATIONAL WORKINGMEN'S ASSOCIATION

SOUTHERN CONFERENCE EDUCATIONAL FUND

Established in 1946 in New Orleans to eradicate segregation in the South, the first interracial organization publicly so committed in that region, SCEF enlisted the support of the most independent-minded, radical spirits among white and black southerners. Aubrey W. Williams, the New Deal Left-liberal former head of the National Youth Administration (NYA), was the first president of SCEF and remained so nearly until his death in the mid-sixties. Through Williams, Mrs. Eleanor Roosevelt was SCEF's link to the national liberal movement. That was decisive in sustaining SCEF against the McCarthyite witch-hunting of arch-segregationists like Georgia governor Herman P. Talmadge and Mississippi senator James O. Eastland from the Right, and the Red-baiting tactics of Cold War liberals on the moderate Left, Arthur Schlesinger, Jr.'s "vital center," who did what they could to isolate SCEF in the fifties.

Despite this, SCEF enlisted white southerners into the struggle to implement President Harry S Truman's civil rights proposals of 1948, and kept them engaged through the fallow years before the 1954 *Brown* decision sparked a grass-roots movement among southern blacks. SCEF then worked alongside the Rev. Martin Luther King, Jr., the Southern Christian Leadership Conference, and other black southerners to make desegregation the living law of the land. The indefatigable Jim Dombrowski, Christian socialist and early associate of the Highlander Folk School, as executive director of SCEF was indispensable in keeping the organization alive and vigorous through these embattled times.

In its final, and in some ways most action-oriented period of the 1960s, SCEF carved out an original role bridging the older Left with the young militants of the New Left, which made the South the most creative theater for radical social movements in the years 1960–65. SCEF raised funds, publicized the southern struggle, and brought northern activists to the aid of the Student Nonviolent Coordinating Committee from 1960 to 1963, when that lively group was regarded as somewhat of a nuisance by established civil rights organizations. Anne and Carl Braden, independent white socialists and directors of SCEF in its last phase, maintained its older alliances while nourishing the newer ones with younger blacks in the South. Carl's pungent pen and ubiquitous presence was too much for the Red-hunting zealots of the House Un-American Activities Committee. Eventually they saddled him with a ten-month prison term for well-deserved contempt of that committee in 1961, making him one of the last victims of the domestic Cold War.

Before the legislative victories of the Kennedy-Johnson years, SCEF had its office ransacked and its files carted off by Senator Eastland's investigators working in collusion with Louisiana authorities in 1963. SCEF retaliated successfully, arguing for federal court intervention in state cases involving federal civil rights violations, a critical legal precedent that benefited the entire civil rights movement. Along with much of the civil rights movement, however, SCEF was a victim, in a sense, of success. The passage of the civil rights acts of 1964 and 1965 that dismantled legal segregation forced these organizations to search for a new raison d'être. Community organizing, the anti–Vietnam War movement, interracial working-class organizing in the Deep South and Appalachia, support of black nationalism—none succeeded in melding black and white activists together with that overriding sense of purpose of the earlier anti–Jim Crow cause. SCEF self-destructed by 1975, when infighting among black nationalists and white ultraleftists who had entered its ranks in the early 1970s destroyed its effectiveness, something that segregationists and anticommunist liberals had failed to do. It was another dispiriting example of the American Left's endemic inability to sustain itself as a continuous, organized presence on the American scene. *See also*: Braden, Carl and Anne; Civil Rights; Dombrowski, James; Highlander School; Southern Negro Youth Conference; Student Nonviolent Coordinating Committee

—*Irwin Klibaner*

REFERENCES

Klibaner, Irwin. *Conscience of a Troubled South: The Southern Conference Educational Fund, 1946–66*. New York: Carlson, 1989.

———. "The Travail of Southern Radicals: The Southern Conference Educational Fund, 1946–1976." *Journal of Southern History* 49 (May 1983).

Salmond, John A. "The Great Southern Commie Hunt: Aubrey Williams, the Southern Conference Educational Fund, and the Internal Security Subcommittee." *South Atlantic Quarterly*, 77 (Autumn 1978).

Southern Exposure

Launched in 1973, this quarterly is the organ of the Institute for Southern Studies. Black and white southern civil-rights and antiwar activists founded the institute in 1970 to contribute information, ideas, and historical understanding to struggles for long-term, fundamental change. The magazine also serves the Institute's goals of building effective grassroots organizations and nourishing communication among the diverse southern cultural groups. *Southern Exposure*'s first three issues, *The Military and the South, Land and Energy*, and *No More Moanin': Voices of Southern Struggle*, all reflected institute research projects. Other special issues and institute projects have included southern religion, music, black writing, women, sports, civil rights history, working women, the Ku Klux Klan, health care, and electoral politics. *See also*: Civil Rights

—*Marc S. Miller*

REFERENCES

Institute for Southern Studies. *Encyclopedia of Southern Life and Change: 10th Anniversary Special Issue of Southern Exposure*. (1983).

Southern Negro Youth Congress

A predominantly black middle-class youth organization, the Communist-led SNYC was one of the most significant precursors of the modern civil rights movement. Although SNYC chapters were located throughout the South, its organizational centers remained in Birmingham, Richmond, Atlanta, and New Orleans.

SNYC was conceived of at the first National Negro Congress in 1936. Party members and NNC supporters agreed that black youth constituted the most potent political force in the South. Communists Ed Strong, then national youth chairman of the NNC, Chris Alston, and James E. Jackson laid the foundations for a regionwide conference devoted to the problems of southern youth. Appropriately convened on the birthday of Frederick Douglass, the first All-Southern Negro Youth Conference drew more than 500 delegates to Richmond, Virginia, in February 1937. Rallying around an antiracist, militant program for social change, the participants included church groups, fraternal bodies, and a wide array of political organizations. Several SNYC activists proved their commitment to organized labor by remaining in Richmond and assisting in the organization of tobacco workers in the CIO.

Two more highly successful conferences were held in Chattanooga and Birmingham in 1938 and 1939, respectively. In addition to reemphasizing their commitment to black labor in the South, SNYC activists adopted the slogan, "Freedom, Equality, and Opportunity." SNYC's program basically called for an end to discrimination, demanded job security, and it fought against regional wage differentials. Its specific aims were reduced to supporting various forms of New Deal legislation, an antilynching bill, and miscellaneous bills intended to improve the conditions of the unemployed. Nonetheless, SNYC was still in the process of consolidation and thus basically failed to develop a program of direct action by 1939.

The events at the third conference were significant, however, since the delegates agreed to move SNYC's headquarters from Richmond to Birmingham—the industrial center of the South. Only months after the 1939 conference, SNYC began to build a strong cadre of leadership consisting of James E. Jackson, his future wife, Esther Cooper, Ed and Augusta Strong, Herman Long, Ethel Goodman, and Thelma Dale. They were soon joined by Communists Louis and Dorothy Burnham. With an able body of leaders, SNYC activists were now in a position to establish a plan for direct action. By the fourth annual conference in New Orleans in 1940, it was decided to initiate a massive Right to Vote campaign, including voter registration and education throughout the South, and to engage in a resolute battle against police brutality, particularly in Birmingham and Memphis. By May 1941, SNYC published its first edition of *Cavalcade: The March of Southern Youth*, an attractive tabloid that served as the organ of the nascent organization.

Most of SNYC's active work before 1941 was concentrated in Birmingham and New Orleans. In addition to setting up rural committees in the Alabama "black belt" and in the Louisiana countryside under the leadership of Ethel Goodman and Clinton Clark, respectively, SNYC activists joined the NAACP and the Communist-led Southern Committee for People's Rights in the fight for individual civil liberties. Perhaps the most prominent case was the defense of Nora Wilson, a black Alabama domestic worker convicted of assaulting her boss with intent to kill.

The development of a radical cultural tradition was also an essential part of its program. Reflective of the Popular Front's leniency with respect to black artistic expression, young black artists from all over the country participated in SNYC activities. In 1939 Birmingham hosted the first all-black visual arts exhibit in the South, organized under the auspices of SNYC. Poets such as Owen Dodson, Eugene B. Williams, and Waring Cuney published their works regularly in the *Cavalcade*. More significant, SNYC activists combined political activity with stage performances of plays by radical black playwrights such as Langston Hughes, Owen Dodson, and Randolph Edmond. Led by Pernell Collins and Thomas Richardson, "People's Theaters" were established in Richmond, Birmingham, and New Orleans, and this work was supplemented by the "Caravan Puppeteers," a roving puppet show that performed plays in the rural black belt.

During World War II, through organizations such as the Citizen's Committee for Army Welfare, it fought against racial discrimination in the U.S. armed forces. SNYC's active support of the war effort did not lead to an abandonment of workers' struggles, the fight against police brutality, or voter education. In 1941, under the leadership of Bertha Boozer, the Atlanta chapter of SNYC attempted to organize black domestic workers, provided critical support in a strike of garbage collectors, and attempted to organize a boycott of stores refusing to hire African Americans. SNYC leaders called on the War Department to issue a statement against the treatment meted out to black soldiers in the South, and even went as far as requesting the department's participation in SNYC's "Victory Mobilization Day." Its new slogan, "Fight Fascism Abroad and K-K-K-ism at Home," served as the unifying theme for the Fifth All-Southern Negro Youth Congress, held at Tuskegee Institute in 1942. The sixth congress, held in Atlanta, Georgia, in 1944, reemphasized SNYC's struggle for constitutional liberties. Among the participants was the Rev. Martin Luther King, Sr., pastor of Ebenezer Baptist Church in Atlanta.

Immediately after the war, the central issues for SNYC were peace and civil rights. In 1946 SNYC held its seventh annual conference in Columbia, South Carolina, at which W. E. B. DuBois gave his famous "Behold the Land" speech. DuBois's comments set the tone for both the conference and the future plans of its organizers. A new militancy was expressed, demanding full civil rights, an immediate end to segregation, solidarity with Third World anticolonial movements, and the complete destruction of nuclear weapons. James Jackson even suggested a nationwide general strike of black workers.

Although the Columbia conference was a success, SNYC faced considerable difficulty in the years to come due to postwar anticommunist sentiments. Red-baiting and repression reached a climax by the eighth, and final, conference in 1948. SNYC delegates planned to meet in Birmingham, but Public Safety Commissioner Eugene "Bull" Connor harassed several black ministers and political activists weeks before the intended conference. The Rev. Herbert Oliver, the only Birmingham religious leader who refused to submit to the city's intimidation, allowed SNYC to use his church as a meetingplace. Nevertheless, because the delegates violated the city's segregation ordinance, several people were arrested, including Idaho senator Glenn Taylor.

SNYC's confrontation with the city of Birmingham in 1948 was the coup de grace in its destruction. Most of its middle-class supporters were sensitive to charges of Communism, and it failed to develop new leadership from the ranks of younger members. After 1948, most of its leadership body chose to either work full-time in the Communist Party or actively support the campaign of Progressive Henry Wallace. Some chapters continued their activity on a local level for a short while, but in most cases, a substantial portion of its membership went on to become activists in the post-1954 civil rights campaigns.

—Robin D. G. Kelley

REFERENCES

Cavalcade. Schomburg Center for Research on Black Culture, New York Public Library.

Kelley, Robin D. G. *Hammer n' Hoe: Alabama Communists During the Depression*. Chapel Hill: University of North Carolina Press, 1990.

"Southern Negro Youth Congress—Forum," February 6, 1984. In *Oral History of the American Left*, Tamiment Institute, New York University.

Strong, Augusta. "Southern Youth's Proud Heritage." *Freedomways* 4/1 (1964).

Southern Tenant Farmers Union

In the summer of 1934, a remarkable interracial protest movement arose among the sharecroppers and tenant farmers of eastern Arkansas—the Southern Tenant Farmers Union. Battered by the Depression and by New Deal crop reduction programs that led to massive evictions from the land, black and white sharecroppers joined together to try to gain economic security from a collapsing plantation system. Aided by local and national leaders of the Socialist Party, they tried to lobby the federal government to win a share of crop reduction payments and to resist planter efforts to drive them from the land. The union, often led by black and white

Seal of the STFU, drawn by Janet Fraser, 1937

fundamentalist ministers, spread quickly throughout the region. In 1935 it organized a cotton choppers' strike to raise wages for day laborers; it sent members to lobby in Washington, and it maintained interracial solidarity in the face of fierce planter repression. By 1936, the organization claimed more than 25,000 members in Arkansas, Missouri, Oklahoma, Tennessee, and Texas, and had won national recognition for dramatizing the plight of sharecroppers under the New Deal.

However, external and internal pressures prevented the union from consolidating its gains. First of all, planter terror—murders, beatings, arrests—made it impossible for the union to maintain headquarters "in the field." After 1936, its organizers had to operate from the relative safety of Memphis. Second, Socialist-Communist conflict frayed the union's solidarity. When the CIO formed a new agricultural affiliate, the United Cannery, Agricultural, and Allied Workers of America (UCAPAWA), the STFU felt compelled to affiliate; its impoverished membership needed labor support. Unfortunately, the president of UCAPAWA was a Communist ex-professor, Donald Henderson, who regarded the STFU as a utopian agrarian movement rather than a legitimate trade union. Upon affiliation, Henderson flooded the STFU with paperwork and dues requests, demoralizing its membership and panicking its leadership, who regarded Henderson's actions as a Communist plot to take over the union. By 1938, the STFU's Socialist leaders were trying to leave the CIO, or to win a separate affiliation, while Communists in the union were trying to win control of the organization. In 1939, amid a famous protest demonstration by evicted sharecroppers in Missouri, the STFU resolved to leave UCAPAWA. In turn, Henderson sought to persuade rebellious locals to remain in the CIO. By the time the faction fight ended, Henderson had enlisted a few topflight organizers (Rev. Claude Williams and Rev. Owen Whitfield), but few members, while the STFU had lost two-thirds of its locals. UCAPAWA thereupon left the agricultural field, concentrating on food-processing workers, who were covered by the NLRB (and could therefore win federally supervised bargaining elections) while the STFU evolved into a lobbying group for sharecroppers and rural workers. The collapse of the plantation system, and the displacement of its work force, continued apace, unaffected by either organization. But for a brief moment, the STFU had given voice to the poorest of the South's people, demonstrating that blacks and whites could be united around common goals even in the heartland of Jim Crow. *See also*: Mitchell, H. L.; Migratory Agricultural Workers, Share Croppers Union

—*Mark Naison*

REFERENCES

Mitchell, H. L. *Mean Things Happening in This Land: The Life and Times of H. L. Mitchell*. Montclair, N.J.: Allanheld, Osmun, 1979.

SOUTHERN WORKER *AND THE COMMUNIST PRESS IN THE SOUTH*

The idea to publish the *Southern Worker*, the first southern-based Communist tabloid, was proposed in the early part of 1930. Although the *Daily Worker* ran a few disparate articles on the South, a regionally based weekly was seen as a necessity by the Communists since conditions in the South were fundamentally different from those in the rest of the United States. In the spring of 1930, the Communist Party central committee asked James S. Allen (Sol Auerbach), who was cur-

rently editor of the *Labor Defender* (the journal of the International Labor Defense), to launch a weekly newspaper in the South. Although the paper was datelined Birmingham, it was actually launched in Chattanooga since the repression was seemingly greater in Birmingham.

The first issue of the *Southern Worker*, selling for two cents a copy, appeared on August 16, 1930. Three thousand copies were printed and distributed throughout Tennessee, Alabama, Georgia, and the Carolinas. In its first issue, the *Southern Worker* professed to be "neither a 'white' paper, nor a 'Negro' paper. It is a paper of and for both the white and black workers and farmers. It recognizes only one division, the bosses against the workers and the workers against the bosses." The only way to achieve the demands of the working class, the statement continued, was through proletarian revolution. Surprisingly, the editorial statement made no mention of the party's position on self-determination in the "black belt," and it contained very little discussion regarding the specific struggles of Afro-Americans.

Notwithstanding the paper's "credo," most of its columns were devoted to the problems of black sharecroppers and workers in the South. During the early 1930s, the *Southern Worker* published numerous letters from black sharecroppers describing the dismal conditions on most Alabama plantations and in the coal and ore mines of Jefferson County. Although its official circulation was never great, this did not reflect its actual readership. A single copy was often passed from person to person, and in some cases was read aloud to a group of illiterate and semiliterate working people. Articles dealing with Africa and the Caribbean were particularly appealing to black southerners.

Allen and his wife, Isabelle, left the South in the fall of 1931. The editorship of the *Southern Worker* was taken over briefly by Harry Wicks, who also used the name James Allen, but he was soon replaced by Elizabeth Lawson. Lawson, using the name Jim Mallory, maintained publication well into 1932, but it was eventually suspended until May 20, 1933. Between 1933 and November 1936, the *Southern Worker* was published out of Birmingham, appearing irregularly on the average of once a month.

During the fall of 1936, the *Southern Worker* was changed to a small-magazine format under the editorship of Rob Hall, the Party's district organizer in Alabama. Reflecting the Party's Popular Front policies, the newspaper now carried articles directed toward southern liberals, including a regular column entitled "From the Churches." In September 1937, delegates at the first open All-Southern Communist Party Conference in Birmingham agreed to abolish the *Southern Worker* and replace it with "an adequate southern Party organ." Hence, in November 1937 appeared the first issue of the *New South*, a monthly newsmagazine carrying sophisticated political tracts dealing with mainstream southern politics, suffrage, southern liberals, and occasional pieces on southern history. Local news items and letters from workers and sharecroppers were discontinued. And after the first two issues, reference to the CP was removed from its masthead and replaced with "Journal of Progressive Opinion."

In 1939 the *New South* ceased publication, apparently in response to the Party's rapid loss of liberal support due to the Nazi-Soviet Pact. Although no official Communist publication replaced the *New South*, Alabama Communist and leading liberal Joseph

Gelders personally established his own left-wing newspaper in Birmingham, which practically served as the Party's organ. Gelders's idea came to fruition when left-wing philanthropist Dan Gillmor provided the necessary funds to launch the Birmingham-based tabloid. Its first issue appearing on January 25, 1940, Gelders's *Southern News Almanac* was geared toward organized and unorganized labor, poor farmers, and African Americans across class lines. While slightly more sophisticated, it was in many ways reminiscent of the *Southern Worker*, although it never stated an affiliation with the CP.

Gelders also solicited his own staff—a matrix of Communists and non-Communist labor supporters. The original editorial staff consisted of George Londa, Quentin P. Gore, and Sam Hall—three experienced journalists sympathetic to the southern Left and the labor movement. In addition to covering the activities of the southern labor movement in great detail, the *Southern News Almanac* devoted substantial space to the peace movement, civil rights issues, and police brutality in the Birmingham area. Unlike the early issues of the *Southern Worker*, the *Almanac* contained weekly religious columns directed at a working-class audience from radical ministers such as the Reverend Fred E. Maxey and Don West.

The *Southern News Almanac* was short-lived, however. It apparently ceased publication in November 1941. *See also*: Birmingham; Share Croppers Union; West, Don

—*Robin D. G. Kelley*

REFERENCES

Allen, James S. "Communism in the Deep South—The Opening, 1930–1931: A Political Memoir." Unpublished manuscript, 1984.

Kelley, Robin D. G. *Hammer n' Hoe: Alabama Communists During the Depression*. Chapel Hill: University of North Carolina Press, 1990.

SOZIAL-REVOLUTIONÄRE CLUBS

Along with groups oriented mainly toward electoral participation or union activity, another trend developed in German-American radicalism after the national railroad strike of 1877. It centered in Chicago and has been loosely termed "anarchist" though these immigrants called themselves *sozial-revolutionär*. Disillusioned by the decline in votes suffered by the *Sozialistische Arbeiter-Partei* (Socialist Labor Party, SLP) after 1878 and by attempts of corrupt politicians in Chicago to prevent legally elected socialists from assuming office, many members of the SLP began to question their party's policy of participating in electoral politics. The other source of dissension within the party, which led to the development of a separate Social-Revolutionary movement, was differences of opinion over the use of force in the labor movement, as embodied in the armed socialist organizations, the *Lehr- und Wehrvereine*. In 1880 the first *Sozial-Revolutionärer Club* was formed in New York City when a group of party members withdrew from the SLP over the question of force. By 1883 membership in the SLP had dwindled to 1,500, while in 1885, at their peak, the Social-Revolutionaries numbered around 7,000.

The ideological direction of these clubs was marked by their international ties, and in particular, by the influence of German anarchism. The German-American Social-Revolutionaries were affiliated with the International Working People's Association (IWPA), also known as the "Anarchist" or "Black" International, which had been revived in 1881 at a congress in London. In 1882 the most influential German anarchist of the time, Johann Most, arrived in the United States, immediately began issuing his paper, *Freiheit* (Freedom), in New York, and embarked on speaking tours that won many new members for local clubs of Social Revolutionaries. Most, who had been a Social Democratic deputy in the *Reichstag*, had turned in exile after the passage of the Anti-Socialist Laws (1878) toward communist anarchism and the "propaganda of the deed." The high point of his influence on German-American radicalism was 1882–3, when the Social Revolutionary groups were expanding, but in general, his extreme standpoint was attractive to only a few radical German immigrants.

In 1883 the Social Revolutionaries held a national congress in Pittsburgh and issued their program as the *Pittsburgh Manifesto*, "to the Workingmen of America." Written by Most along with the future Haymarket martyrs Albert Parsons and August Spies among others, this statement of principles was no different from that of the socialists in its analysis of capital, surplus value, crises, and the exploitation of workers, but it incorporated the views of the London Conference with respect to force, viewing its utilization as unavoidable in the revolutionary movement to establish a new social order. Also, while the delegates unanimously rejected participation in elections, a resolution introduced by representatives of the IWPA from Chicago was passed—though opposed by Most and his supporters—that called for taking part in trade union organizing. This proposal reflected the actual connections between the IWPA and the German working class in Chicago, for the IWPA was quite influential there within the Central Labor Union, a central federation representing about 12,000 workers in 1885 and composed of unions with a high percentage of foreign-born members with radical leanings. The manifesto of the Black International in the United States as it was welded together in Pittsburgh was, therefore, a nonsynthesized program for revolutionary action that reflected uncertainty and disagreement over the strategy and ultimate goals of socialism and anarchism and invested local sections with full autonomy. The only centralization deemed necessary was the creation of a National Information Bureau in Chicago and the designation of certain newspapers, including the Chicago *Arbeiter-Zeitung* (Workers' newspaper), *Fackel* (Torch), *Vorbote* (Herald), and *Alarm* (English) and Most's *Freiheit* as official publications.

Seen in the larger context of the contemporary U.S. labor movement, the Social Revolutionaries represented one of the most radical tendencies within the waves of strikes that culminated in the national strike for the eight-hour day on May 1, 1886. In Chicago, members of the IWPA and its press played crucial roles in the organizing effort after some debate over its revolutionary potential. As a result of violence surrounding this strike and the bomb that killed several Chicago police at the Haymarket gathering on May 4, the German Social Revolutionaries were singled out by police for especially severe harassment. The *Arbeiter-Zeitung* was raided and shut down briefly, and six of the eight men who were finally charged with conspiracy and murder were German "anarchists." Although it was never proved who threw the fatal bomb, four of these men were hanged on November 11, 1887, one had committed suicide before then, and three spent years in prison before Illinois governor John Altgeld pardoned them in 1893, stating that all eight had been victims of a biased jury. The reaction of the press and public opinion to the bombing was to call indiscriminately for the suppression of all varieties of radicalism and to vilify their adherents as foreigners, particularly Germans, who were spreading alien doctrines and importing class warfare to the United States.

After 1886, then, the Social Revolutionary movement was dead as an organized political force. However, the Germans who had participated in the movement of 1886 were still quite active publicly throughout the next decade. The papers issued by the Haymarket martyrs increased their circulation under editors such as Joseph Dietzgen and Max Baginski and continued to provide a forum for the German labor movement in Chicago. The Pioneer Aid and Support Association of Chicago, which had been created to assist the families of the executed and imprisoned men, was a unifying center for progressive unions and various clubs and associations of workers, sponsoring large demonstrations every November 11 and benefits attended by thousands. Finally, the larger labor movement in Chicago remained highly visible through attempts at independent political action and intensive trade union organizing, and Germans continued their participation. *See also*: Black International; German Americans; Haymarket Affair; Most, Johann; Spies, August

—*Carol Poore*

REFERENCES

Ashbaugh, Carolyn. *Lucy Parsons, American Revolutionary*. Chicago: Charles H. Kerr, 1976.

David, Henry. *The History of the Haymarket Affair*. New York: Farrar & Rinehart, 1936.

Nelson, Bruce C. *Beyond the Martyrs: A Social History of Chicago's Anarchists, 1870–1900.* New Brunswick: Rutgers University Press, 1988.

Rocker, Rudolf. *Johann Most.* Berlin: Verlag "Der Syndikalist," 1924.

Spies, August. *Reminiscenzen.* Chicago: Christine Spies, 1888.

Sozialistischer Turnerbund

With the arrival of those Germans who had been forced to leave their country after the defeat of the 1848 revolution, the Turner movement grew rapidly within the German-American communities around the United States. The first *Turngemeinde* (Turners club) was organized in Cincinnati in late 1848, and it was followed rapidly by the formation of numerous others, including the *Sozial-demokratische Turngemeinde* (Social-democratic Turners club) of Baltimore in 1849 and the *Sozialistischer Ternverein* (Socialist Turners league) of New York in 1850, whose membership drew largely from exiled "Forty-Eighters." In October 1851, the first general *Turnfest* (Turners festival) was held in Philadelphia, and an umbrella organization was formed to unite the local groups, called the *Sozialistischer Turnerbund* (Socialist Turners league). This society published a journal, the *Turnzeitung* (Turners newspaper), from November 15, 1851, until April 16, 1861, when so many Turners joined the Union Army that the organization disbanded for the duration of the Civil War. In its first number, the *Turnzeitung* reported that twenty-two local groups with a total of 1,072 members belonged to the *Turnerbund*. Upon its reorganization in 1865, the designation "socialist" was dropped from the official title of the society, and it was known from then on as the *Nordamerikanischer Turnerbund*. However, gymnastics continued to be a popular pastime of German-American workers throughout the history of German-American socialism, and workers' Turner societies were an important part of the socialist subculture that existed as an alternative to other groups in cities with a sizable German immigrant population.

In the context of the political configuration of 1848, the term "socialist" did not designate a solely working-class or proletarian outlook, but applied to those sectors who hoped to establish a republican democracy in Germany. This was the goal of most Forty-Eighters who came to the United States and of those who participated in the Turner societies, such as Friedrich Hecker, Karl Heinzen, Adolf Douai, Gustav Struve, and Joseph Weydemeyer. The *Turnerbund* viewed its purpose as that of furthering the physical and mental development of its members, and the freedom, prosperity, and education of all social classes. The *Turnerbund* was affiliated with the *Demokratischer Turnerbund* in Germany, and many German-American Turners still had hopes in the early 1850s of returning to Germany and fighting again (this time victoriously) in another revolution. However, as these dreams faded, Turners became more involved in American issues, taking principled stands against the Nativism and Know-Nothingism directed against immigrants, against Puritanism and temperance, and against slavery. After about 1853, the *Turnerbund* placed a decreasing emphasis on socialist principles, and allied itself with the antislavery Free Soil Party. At its 1855 convention in Buffalo, the *Turnerbund* declared its opposition to slavery, and particularly to the extension of slavery into free states. After the Civil War, the German Turner movement lost its more radical tendencies and concentrated primarily on *körperliches* (physical) rather than *geistiges Turnen* (intellectual exercises). However, the Turners still joined together with groups of *Freidenker* (Freethinker) at times to oppose manifestations of Puritanism and temperance and prohibition. *See also*: Freidenker Movement, Germans, Socialist Labor Party

—*Carol Poore*

REFERENCES

Learned, M. D. *The German-American Turner Lyric. Reprint from the 10th Report of the Society for the History of the Germans in Maryland.* Baltimore: Schneidereith, 1897.

Schlüter, Hermann. *Die Anfänge der deutschen Arbeiterbewegung in Amerika.* Stuttgart: Dietz Nachfolger, 1907.

Cover of pamphlet published by Anarchist Federation of America, 1937

Spanish Civil War: *see* Abraham Lincoln Brigade, American Committee to Aid Spanish Democracy, Spanish Revolution of 1936

Spanish Revolution Of 1936

When Franco's fascist troops invaded Spain in July 1936 with the purpose of overthrowing the young and unstable Republic, the Spanish working class responded by making a revolution that went much further toward realizing the classless and stateless ideal of proletarian socialism than any preceding popular revolt. Spontaneously and almost overnight, workers seized factories and other workplaces; land was collectivized; workers' militias were formed throughout the country; the church—age-old enemy of all working-class radicalism and indeed, openly profascist—was dismantled, and its property confiscated; established political institutions disintegrated or were taken over by workers' committees.

In a decade of cataclysmic worldwide depression and spreading fascism, the revolution in Spain signaled a message of renewed hope to the scattered forces of working-class emancipation throughout the globe, not least in the United States. As elsewhere, actual support for the revolution came only from groups far to the left of the traditional social-democratic and Communist parties and was channeled through various like-minded tendencies in Spain itself.

Supporting the workers' revolution were Spain's largest unions, the anarcho-syndicalist *Confederación Nacional del Trabajo* (National Confederation of Labor: CNT) and its rival, the *Union Generale de Trabajadores* (General Union of Workers: UGT), largely led by the Socialist Party (then in a markedly Left phase), as well as such revolutionary groups as the Iberian Anarchist Federation, the independent Workers Party of Marxist Unity (POUM), and a small nucleus of Trotskyists. The Spanish Communist Party, however, and many socialists, maintained that Spain was not historically ripe for an anticapitalist revolution and openly declared themselves for the bourgeois republic. After Franco secured military assistance from Hitler's Germany and Mussolini's Italy, the CP, which, in the early days of the revolution, had been a small sect, rapidly became a major power in the land as Stalin's Russia sent numerous military officers and political advisers, as well as some military aid, to shield the fragile remnant of the republican government from both fascists and the revolutionary Left. While the CP viewed Spain's civil war as a struggle between fascism and democracy, more radical leftists argued that workers' revolution was the only sure way of defeating fascism.

The anarchist movement in the United States in the 1930s was not large, but it quickly mounted a nationwide campaign in defense of workers' Spain that vastly exceeded its numerical energies. The CNT's U.S. representative, Spanish-born Maximiliano Olay—veteran of anarchist labor struggles in Cuba and among immigrant cigar-makers in Tampa, Florida, and for many years a leading figure of Chicago's Free Society Group—moved to New York and opened an office for propaganda on lower Fifth Avenue. At his instigation, the various U.S. Jewish, Russian, Spanish, and Italian anarchist federations and groups, as well as English-language groups such as the New York *Vanguard* group and several branches of the Industrial Workers of the World, formed the ad hoc United Libertarian Organizations to produce a paper of news and information titled *Spanish Revolution*. (Though not actually affiliated, the Gillespie, Illinois, branch of the Progressive Miners of America wholeheartedly supported the effort through a sizable monthly assessment of its members.) Besides publishing *Spanish Revolution*, the United Libertarian Organizations held mass meetings in many cities and raised thousands of dollars for their embattled comrades in Spain. The ULO's constituent groups also promoted the revolution in their own papers, and issued separate publications of their own. The Yiddish-language weekly *Freie Arbeter Shtimme* brought out an English translation of Rudolf Rocker's pamphlet *The Truth About Spain*. The Italian-language *L'Adunata dei Refrattari* carried important communications from Spain by the renowned anarchist theorist Camillo Berneri. The IWW's weekly *Industrial Worker* and *One Big Union Monthly* featured reports by Pat Read and other Wobblies in the Spanish trenches.

In many countries the social-democratic parties opposed the revolution, but in the United States the SP, large sections of which had moved sharply to the left—a development hastened by the influx of a disciplined and energetic group of Trotskyists—took up the banner of the workers' revolution and even organized and funded a substantial military unit, the Debs Column, to fight in Spain. Ernest Erber, a leader of the Young People's Socialist League, joined the editorial staff of the POUM's paper, *La Batalla*. The Friends of Workers' Spain in Chicago existed primarily to promote English-language POUM publications throughout the American labor movement.

Also oriented toward the POUM, though not without sometimes severe criticisms of its policies, were Hugo Oehler's Revolutionary Workers League, B. J. Field's League for a Revolutionary Party, and Albert Weisbord's Communist League of Struggle. Oehler's oft-reprinted pamphlet *Barricades in Barcelona* remains an important eyewitness account of the workers' "May Days" revolt of 1937. Weisbord went to Spain as correspondent for the *Nation*, and issued a "Special Spanish Issue" of his own mimeographed journal, *Class Struggle*, in September 1937. The Trotskyists, inside the SP but still producing publications of their own, issued many polemics by Trotsky and others. Other small Marxist groups, including the Proletarian Party and the Lovestoneites, also defended the revolution in Spain and devoted much space to it in their press.

When fascism emerged triumphant in Spain in 1939, many Spanish revolutionaries sought political asylum in the United States. By far the largest group rallied round *España Libre*, a broad-based bilingual paper devoted to news of struggles in Spain as well as of the widely scattered exile community. Produced in New York by the Confederated Spanish Societies, *España Libre* continued to appear monthly until the death of Franco in 1975.

The first U.S. study of the Spanish Revolution was Trotskyist Felix Morrow's pamphlet *Civil War in Spain* (September 1936), followed a little over a year later by his full-length *Revolution and Counter-Revolution in Spain*. American radicals, especially anarchists, have written prodigiously on the subject ever since. Noam Chomsky's essay "Objectivity and Liberal Scholarship" in his *American Power and the New Mandarins* ((1969), Sam Dolgoff's anthology *The Anarchist Collectives* (1974), and David Porter's *Vision on Fire: Emma Goldman on the Spanish Revolution* (1983) are among the more influential works that have emphasized the revolutionary nature of the struggle in Spain. *See also*: Abraham Lincoln Brigade, American Committee to Aid Spanish Democracy

—*Franklin Rosemont*

REFERENCES

Blackwell, Russell, "*Spanish Revolution* (United Libertarian Organizations), *Spanish Revolution* (Workers' Party of Marxist Unification)." In *The American Radical Press, II* edited by Joseph Conlin. Westport: Greenwood, 1974.

Bolloten, Burnett. *The Spanish Revolution*. Chapel Hill: University of North Carolina Press, 1979.

Low, Mary, and Juan Breà. *Red Spanish Notebook.* San Francisco: City Lights Books, 1981.

Richards, Vernon. *Lessons of the Spanish Revolution.* London: Freedom Press, 1983.

Revolutionary History, Summer 1988.

SPARGO, JOHN (1876–1966)

One of the most prominent socialist writers and speakers before World War I, Spargo had the ability to present complex intellectual issues simply. He affiliated himself with the "Right" wing of the Socialist Party, espousing a sophisticated version of a consumer-and-worker democracy. And yet while stridently anti-Left, he vigorously opposed racism, xenophobia, and indifference to women's issues within the socialist movement.

A British granite-cutter by background, Spargo became a union official and member of the executive committee of the Social Democratic Federation, educating himself in part through extension courses at Oxford and Cambridge. He emigrated to the U.S. in 1901, and five years later wrote the best-selling exposé of slum life, *The Bitter Cry of Children.* His *Socialism* (1906) was widely considered the best textbook popularization of the early movement. *The Spiritual Significance of Modern Socialism* (1907) put forward a bridge to religiously inclined socialist sympathizers. *Karl Marx: His Life and Work* (1910), the first full-length U.S. biographical treatment, depicted the founder of scientific socialism as sentimental, but above all a pragmatic tactician.

Spargo was often the center of political controversy in the socialist movement. While supporting the woman suffrage movement and suggesting a positive attitude toward blacks, he ardently objected to the strongly held view within socialism's conservative wing that immigration restriction would be necessary to protect American labor (and win over the AFL to socialist ideas). He strongly attacked the Industrial Workers of the World, holding that the Wobblies' use of the term *sabotage* and its advocacy of the general strike were inflammatory, inviting employer and state repression. He sought the decentralization of power, calling for each industry and trade to be governed by boards of producing workers and "accredited representatives of society as a whole," and advocating a mixed economy of state enterprises, privately held small business, and worker-owned cooperatives. With the U.S. entry into WW I, Spargo appealed to delegates for a prowar policy. Defeated, he abandoned the SP, became antisocialist, and eventually opposed the New Deal. He also founded, in 1927, the Bennington (Vermont) Museum, an important historical and art repository, devoting most of his remaining years to its development. *See also*: Socialist Party

—Robert Asher

REFERENCES

John Spargo Papers. Special Collections, University of Vermont Library.

SPIES, AUGUST (1855–87)

Leading American spokesperson for revolutionary socialism, a role that contributed to his execution after being framed on charges of conspiring in the 1886 Haymarket bombing, Spies, a German, was born in Landeck and emigrated to the United States at age seventeen. He settled in Chicago, where, by 1876, he had his own upholstery shop. Radicalized by reading socialist literature and witnessing the 1877 mass strike in Chicago, Spies became an active member of the Socialist Labor Party, on whose ticket he frequently ran for office. In 1880 he became manager of the socialist *Arbeiter-Zeitung* newspaper. Spies moved away from political socialism in the early 1880s and gradually adopted anarcho-syndicalist positions. He presided at the opening of the 1881 Chicago Congress, which established the Revolutionary Socialistic Party. In 1883 he was a delegate to the Pittsburgh Congress, which established the anarchist International Working People's Association.

His words just before his execution are among the most famous ever spoken by an American radical: "There will come a time when our silence will be more powerful than the voices you strangle today." *See also*: Black International, Haymarket Affair, Sozial-Revolutionäre Clubs

—David Roediger

REFERENCES
Avrich, Paul. *The Haymarket Tragedy*. Princeton: Princeton University Press, 1984.

Foner, Philip S., ed. *Autobiographies of the Haymarket Martyrs*. New York: Monad Press, 1969.

SPIRITUALISM

The general term given to the widespread social and theological movement of the mid-nineteenth century, spiritualism also consolidated and expressed the utopian, pre-Marxist phase of U.S. radicalism. An important factor in the breakup of the First International's U.S. section, it retained an influence within the native-born Left into the early twentieth century.

Spiritualism had deep historical roots. Utopian socialism, or communitarianism, by far the predominant form and ideology of U.S. socialism until the 1870s, continued the Reformation's dual pursuit of true egalitarianism and untainted holiness. Many communitarian ideas (and a number of leading activists, such as Robert Dale Owen) passed directly from utopian experiments into the spiritualist movement, which sprang up with a rash of seancelike spirit "appearances" in 1848–50. Over the next decade, more than a hundred periodicals devoted to spiritualism spread the word, intellectuals (including an occasional congressman) declared their adherence, and spiritualist congregations approached the overall size of a respectable Protestant denomination. Contemporary reform movements such as woman's rights, abolitionism, temperance, and peace (and more quietly, free love) shared constituencies with spiritualism.

Very quickly, a particularly leftward trend within the movement pronounced its version "philosophical spiritualism" (as differentiated from mere seance-oriented "phenomenal spiritualism"). Andrew Jackson Davis (1826–1910), perhaps the leading American devotee of Immanuel Swedenborg, advocated in many of his volumes drastic reforms to restrain financial manipulation and return democracy to the mass of citizens. "The Pantarch," Stephen Pearl Andrews (1812–1886), became the practicing metaphysical theorist—and perhaps political ghostwriter—for Victoria Woodhull. Through Woodhull and her paper, *Woodhull & Claflin's*, spiritualism reached even into the First International (Marx and his U.S. supporters scoffed at the belief, but other European-based officials adopted a more tolerant view). Woodhull, president of the American Spiritualist Association, served as public symbol for the potential synthesis of the two doctrines. Other spiritualist figures—journalistic spokespersons, practitioners, and poetry or fiction writers, often the same individuals—continued to affirm the centrality of radical reform or socialism to spiritualist expectations for a New World ahead. As late as 1879, a less controversial president of the American Spiritualist Association asserted, in the semiofficial *Banner of Light*, that "if spiritualism has been under a cloud because of its connection with freeloveism, it is destined to pass under a still darker cloud—but that one has a golden lining. This cloud is called SOCIALISM," predicting further that "spiritual-

PSYCHOSOPHY

In Six Parts.

PART I.

THE SOUL IN HUMAN EMBODIMENTS.

MRS. CORA L. V. RICHMOND.

Title-page, 1915

ism . . . will spring up unbidden in the very center of the socialistic camp."

Philosophical spiritualism, in all, offered a philosophy or cosmology akin to the untheoretical socialism of native-born Americans unable to act comfortably within the immigrant-dominated Socialist Labor Party of the later nineteenth century. Spiritualist newspapers from the 1850s–1880s argued for women's equality, better treatment of blacks and Native Americans, abolition of capital punishment, and the long-range enactment of a cooperative order. At a deeper level yet, spiritualists suggested a psychic ecology—the oneness of all matter, living and formerly living—in a grand scheme. Universal consciousness would in this view eclipse class society and racial or gender discrimination. In many subtle ways, such spiritualist doctrines would find their way into the native-born ranks of the Socialist Party, through elders active in movements since the 1840s and through the indirect influence of familiar doctrines.

In general, the spreading faith in materialistic science (and the exposure of numerous individual seance frauds) diminished the appeal of spiritualism in the final decades of the century. In an odd way, however, resistance against this public confidence in bourgeois society prompted a radical-mystical turn of mind within reform-minded sections of the Yankee middle classes in the 1880s–1890s. Andrew Jackson Davis's writings were widely reprinted in the *Coming Nation,* the most popular socialist paper of the day. Bellamy Nationalists set out their actual cooperative colonizing in league with radical Theosophists. Even in the ferociously orthodox SLP, the leading lecturer on the "Bible question," Peter E. Burrowes (who had sojourned through nearly a dozen religions, and at the time of his death set about creating a chess game that would illustrate the workings of the universe), proclaimed in his "Gospel of the Cosmos" a great mystic vision of socialism as climax to mankind's age-old spiritual yearning.

The Kautskyian scientific emphasis of Second International doctrine dampened any formal association of the new SP with the spiritualist heritage. Yet in the pages of a number of popular publications—the *Comrade,* Horace Traubel's *The Conservator,* and the *Socialist Spirit* among others—variants of spiritualism found a new home. A sprinkling of homespun, especially elderly women Yankee radicals continued to argue their doctrines in SP ranks. In Iowa, for instance, "New Thought" believers (mostly aged Yankee reformers) who published the leading Iowa Socialist newspaper claimed to make spiritual contact with others of the same inclination. But spiritualism's greatest impact was upon socialist literature. Jack London, whose mother was a medium, wrote spiritualist ("mind-travel") fiction, and other science-fiction authors, including the highly popular George Allen England and Nathaniel Hawthorne's nephew, Julian Hawthorne, gave their cosmic adventures a socialistic-spiritualist twist. The First World War, virtually destroying the entire milieu for spiritualistic socialism, also produced a last apotheosis of pronouncements of faith's ultimate victory over the gore and cruelty of battle. Anticipating his own death (it would occur in 1919), Traubel—known as the "Socialist Walt Whitman"—depicted his spirit watching over the transformation, and added words of praise and condemnation, in his lyric "I'll Hear It All from Somewhere."

The next radical generation's disapproval of theistic beliefs largely eradicated the memory of their importance, and restricted spiritualistic doctrine for decades into personal credos such as Upton Sinclair's *Mental Radio* (1930). Only in the later 1960s and after, with a return of utopianism, feminist theology, and a nature-centered religiosity, did the themes of spiritualism find sympathetic listeners around the Left. In the hippie movement, for instance, a reverence for Native American wisdom (epitomizing a nature religion) returned from nineteenth-century obscurity into a phenomenon of mass culture. New Left campus and community activists tended to ignore such developments, despite widespread admiration for the Rev. Martin Luther King, Jr.'s religious commitments, but in the New Left collapse the themes of spirituality grew still stronger. By the 1980s, a sometimes radical Jungian feminism became a major topic of well-selling religious studies. *Gnosis* magazine, edited by a longtime activist and editor of *Anarchy Comics*, Jay Kinney, popularized research in mystic traditions. Ecological and animal rights' movements unknowingly renewed spiritualist themes of the sacredness of wilderness and its eons-long inhabitants. Phenomenal spiritualism (seances) never returned to radical fashion, but philosophical spiritualism received a vindication that Marxists had never predicted.

—*Paul Buhle*

REFERENCES

Buhle, Paul. *Marxism in the USA: Remapping the American Left*. London: Verso, 1987.

Moore, R. Lawrence. *In Search of White Crows*. New York: Oxford University Press, 1977.

Stern, Madeleine. *The Pantarch: A Biography of Stephen Pearl Andrews*. Austin: University of Texas Press, 1968.

State, County, Municipal Workers of America: see Public Service Unions

Stelton (N.J.) Colony: see Utopianism

Stokes, Rose Pastor (1879–1933)

Socialist and, later, Communist, Stokes actively campaigned for women's rights, including fair labor conditions and equal wages, suffrage, and birth control. Born in Augustow, Russian Poland, she spent her early childhood in London and immigrated with her family in 1890 to the United States. Settling in Cleveland, she helped to support her six younger siblings by working alternately in cigar and shirtwaist factories. Her co-workers introduced her to socialism and she began reading about the class struggle. The poetry of Edwin Markham and especially Morris Rosenfeld encouraged her to try her hand at visionary verse. In 1903 an offer of an editorial post on *Jewish Daily News and Jewish Gazette* took the aspiring young writer to New York, where she joined a circle of reformers. Assigned to interview the wealthy settlement worker J. G. Phelps Stokes, Rose Pastor married him in 1905 and became, according to the tabloids, "Cinderella of the Sweatshops" and, later, allegedly the inspiration for Anzia Yezierska's *Salome of the Tenements* (1922). In 1906 she and her husband again attracted attention when they joined the Socialist Party.

While Phelps Stokes served as president of the Intercollegiate Socialist Society between 1907 and 1917, Rose Pastor Stokes lectured and wrote for the socialist press. She took part in several important strikes, including the shirtwaist makers in 1909–10, hotel and waiters in 1912, and garment workers in 1913. She was very active in the birth control movement and was arrested in 1916 for attempting to distribute informational leaflets at a rally in Carnegie Hall. A poet and journalist, Stokes also wrote a play about the sexual double standard, *The Woman Who Wouldn't* (1916). With her husband, Stokes resigned from the SP in 1917 in disagreement over its stand against U.S. involvement in World War I. She soon changed her mind, however, and left her husband over his continued support of the U.S. war effort. Having returned to the SP, Stokes was indicted in 1918 under the Espionage Act for writing a newspaper article on war profiteers. Convicted and sentenced to ten years in prison, she won an overturn on appeal in 1921.

Rose Pastor Stokes became a founding member of the Communist Party in 1919 and again in 1920 faced prosecution for her radicalism. An early member of the central committee of the CPUSA and reporter for the newly founded Negro Commission, she attended the fourth congress of the Communist International in Moscow in 1922.

A seasoned agitator for women's rights, Stokes disavowed feminism in the 1920s. Although she advised the Comintern to establish women's committees, she interpreted their role as purely functional, to spread propaganda among working-class women. She refused to admit a "separate women's problem" and became a rigid interpreter of Third Period policy.

Divorced from Phelps Stokes in 1925, she married Isaac Romaine (V. J. Jerome), a CP cultural functionary in 1927. Rose Pastor

Stokes remained active until her health failed. She died of breast cancer, which her friends attributed to a blow she received from a police club. *See also*: Birth Control, Communist Party, Socialist Party

—*Mari Jo Buhle*

REFERENCES

Neidle, Cecyle S. *America's Immigrant Women: Their Contribution to the Development of a Nation from 1609 to the Present*. Boston: Hippocrene Books, 1975.

Renshaw, Patrick. "Rose of the World: The Pastor-Stokes Marriage and the American Left, 1905–1925." *New York History* 6 (October 1981).

Stokes, Rose Pastor. Papers. Yale University Library and Tamiment Institute Library, New York University.

Stone, I. F. (1907–1989)

Born in Philadelphia and educated at the University of Pennsylvania. I. F. Stone began his long career as a journalist at age fourteen when he launched his own monthly, *Progress*. Later that year he got his first newspaper job with a county weekly. He soon moved to a position with a Camden, New Jersey, newspaper and then to various newspapers located in Philadelphia. As an editorial writer for the New York *Post* (1933–39), he was a strong advocate for the New Deal. In 1938 he began an association with the *Nation* and served as its Washington correspondent from 1940 to 1946. During a partly overlapping period (1942–52), he wrote for various liberal New York newspapers: the *Star, PM*, and the *Daily Compass*.

Stone reached his greatest influence with *I. F. Stone's Weekly* (1953–71). This four-page newsletter, which featured Stone's meticulous reading of government documents, became a major resource for other journalists, scholars, and then the general public. The *Weekly*, which reached a circulation of 70,000, was a virtual one-person Left crusade. From opposition to McCarthy and Hoover in the 1950s to opposition to the war in Vietnam, Stone was an independent Left voice heard by his entire profession.

Stone also authored a number of books. The most sensational was *The Hidden History of the Korean War* (1952), which argued that South Korea bore as much if not more responsibility than North Korea for the civil war that rent the peninsula. When the burden of maintaining a weekly publication grew too much for him, Stone retired from journalism to take up his old love of classical literature. In 1988 he published *The Trial of Socrates*, which drew heavily on original Greek texts. In a letter soliciting funds for the unsuccessful 1988 congressional campaign of Burlington, Vermont, socialist mayor Bernie Sanders, Stone not only reaffirmed his identification with the Left but reminded all that he had been a member of the executive committee of the Socialist Party in New Jersey before he was old enough to vote. *See also*: Peace Movements

—*Dan Georgakas*

REFERENCES

Aronson, James. *The Press and the Cold War*. New York: Bobbs-Merrill, 1970.

Stone, I. F. *In a Time of Torment*. New York: Vintage Books, 1968.

Stonewall Riots

Several nights of rioting began early in the morning of June 28, 1969, at the Stonewall Inn, a gay bar in New York's Greenwich Village, in response to a police raid. Such raids on gay bars were common, but the spontaneous rebellion that followed this one was a new response to such tactics. Ejected patrons congregated on the street outside the bar. As police loaded arrestees into paddy wagons, stones, bottles, and trash cans were thrown, small fires were set, and chants were started by a crowd police said included about 400 but which observers estimated at closer to 2,000. In the days immediately following the raid, as moderate homophile groups and New Left activists tried to organize this new, unharnessed gay militancy, the Gay Liberation Front was born. GLF represented for the first time a specifically radical and specifically gay point of view, and continued for the next five years to be in the forefront of the movement for gay rights, and to spawn other organizations that became important in gay politics. *See also*: Gay Liberation

—*Jill Raymond*

REFERENCES
Marotta, Toby. *The Politics of Homosexuality*. Boston: Houghton Mifflin, 1981.

STUDENT MOVEMENTS—1930s

Student organizing was one of the American Left's most successful areas of political activity during the Great Depression. Under the leadership of Communist and Socialist undergraduates, the campus activists of the 1930s built the first mass student protest movement in American history. During its peak years, from spring 1936 to spring 1939, the movement mobilized at least 500,000 collegians (about half of the American student body) in annual one-hour strikes against war. The movement also organized students on behalf of an extensive reform agenda, which included federal aid to education, government job programs for youth, abolition of compulsory ROTC, academic freedom, racial equality, and collective bargaining rights.

The emergence of this protest movement on the nation's campuses represented a major shift in American student politics. During the prosperous 1920s the undergraduate population—overwhelmingly middle class and affluent—had endorsed conservative Republican presidential candidates by an even larger majority than had the general electorate. But this collegiate conservatism eroded steadily as a consequence of the Great Depression. Undergraduates in the early 1930s faced hard times, with the collapse of the job market, and the exhaustion of student loan funds and parental financial support. In 1932 and 1933 even the student body itself began to diminish because of the sinking economy; some 80,000 youths who in more prosperous times would have attended college were in these years unable to enroll. The economic crisis and its growing impact on campus led students to start questioning both the logic and value of American capitalism.

Capitalism's loss was the student Left's

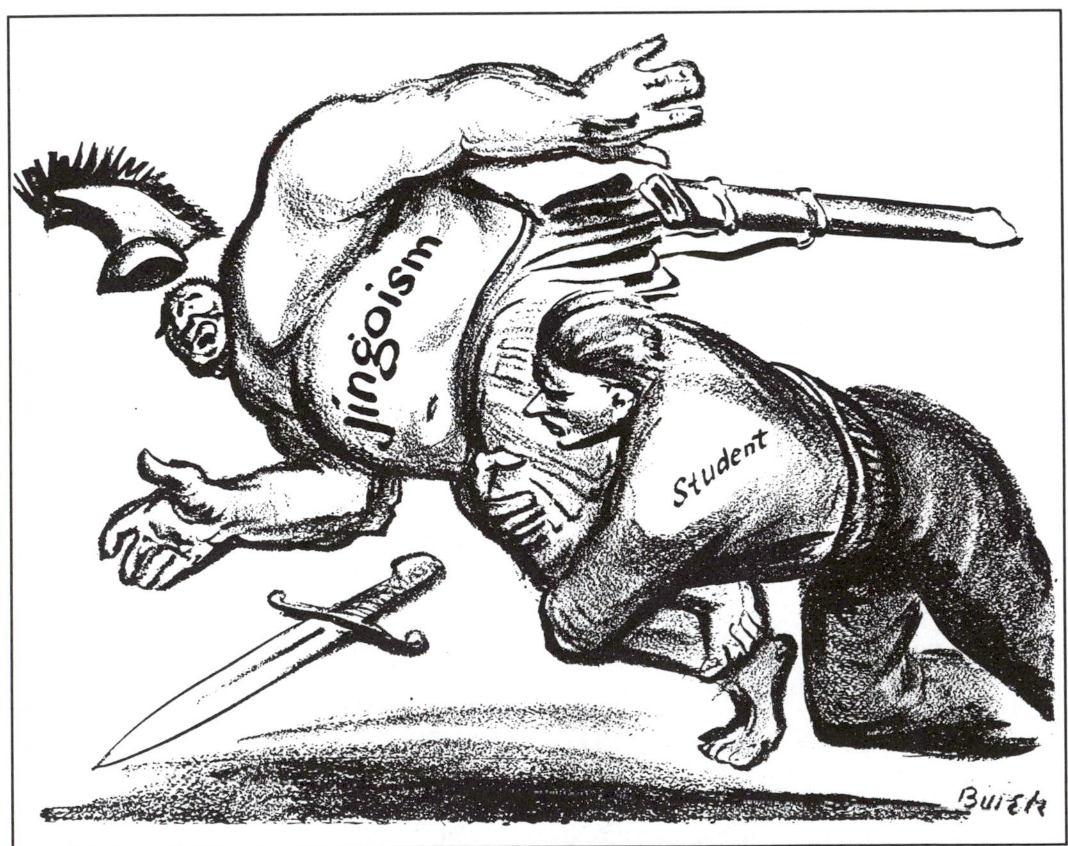

Cartoon by Jacob Burck from *The Daily Worker*, c. 1935

gain. Prior to the Depression, student radicalism had been in a moribund state. During the 1920s the entire American student Left had been confined to a single national organization, the Socialist-led League for Industrial Democracy (the LID, a direct descendant of the Intercollegiate Socialist Society, founded in 1905 by Upton Sinclair); it had only about 2,000 members out of a student population of over a million, and was demoralized because of the 1920s undergraduates' indifference and hostility to the Left. By the early 1930s, however, the Depression had increased the Left's prestige on campus because the economic crisis seemed to bear out the radicals' critique of American capitalism. Many collegians seeking to comprehend the economic crisis found that the Left alone was able to explain the Depression and offer alternatives to the faltering capitalist system. In this changed political atmosphere, the LID not only began to grow, but also for the first time faced competition from the Left, with the emergence in 1931 of the Communist-led National Student League.

The founding of the NSL changed the political style of student radicalism. The NSL prodded the campus Left to become more militant and action-oriented. Where the pre-Depression LID had focused primarily on education and the formation of study groups to discuss radical ideas, the NSL emphasized agitation and the building of a mass student protest movement. The NSL argued that students could be radicalized most effectively not through abstract discussions, but through political organizing drives focusing on issues of concern to the student body. Under the NSL's influence the LID also began to sound more radical. The campus LID emphasized its interest in building a militant student protest movement by changing its name to the *Student* League For Industrial Democracy (SLID) and by temporarily renaming its national magazine (the *LID News Bulletin*) *Revolt*.

This more militant approach to student organizing paid off politically as the NSL obtained an unprecedented degree of press attention in its early campaigns. The first action of the 1930s campus Left to make national headlines was the NSL-sponsored student delegation to the Kentucky's strike-torn coal region in March 1932. Kentucky police and vigilantes assaulted the delegation to prevent it from bringing food and clothing to the impoverished miners, and to halt its investigation of alleged coal company and police brutalization of the strikers. This assault kept the delegation from reaching the Harlan miners, but it also provoked indignation on campus: more than 3,000 students nationwide sent letters and telegrams of protest. The publicity surrounding this incident helped provoke a Senate investigation of conditions in the coal region. This was regarded as a significant victory by the NSL because it seemed to prove that students could assist workers victimized by the Depression and have some national political impact.

Within a few weeks of the Harlan delegation the student Left was again attracting national attention. This time the issue was free speech. Columbia University had expelled student newspaper editor Reed Harris because he repeatedly criticized the campus administration and supported the new student activism. The NSL led a student strike and free speech campaign on behalf of Harris, which won his reinstatement. The stream of good news continued for the student Left through autumn 1932 as the LID and the Young People's Socialist League ran a national campus campaign on behalf of Socialist presidential candidate Norman Thomas. This campaign helped spread the organizational presence of student radicalism across the country, and—according to college straw polls—won Thomas the endorsement of 18 percent of the student body, a far higher level of support than he was able to obtain from the general electorate.

Soon after the economic crisis breathed life into the student Left, the rising crisis in international relations gave campus radicalism an even greater boost. Observing Hitler's ascension to power in 1933, Japan's invasion of Manchuria, and Mussolini's belligerent fascism, American students became increasingly worried that a new world war was in the making. These anxieties were compounded by the widespread disillusionment with the First World War. Influenced by the revisionist scholarship on the causes of the Great War, antiwar novels and movies, and by the Nye Committee investigation, many students were convinced that the United States had gone to war in 1917 to serve plutocracy rather than democracy; they believed that Wilson's lofty rhetoric had hidden the fact that America had entered the war to safeguard the profit margins of bankers and munitions makers. A strong antiwar mood took root on campus, as students grew determined to prevent the United States from again being misled into a bloody foreign crusade.

This antiwar atmosphere enabled the student Left to make rapid progress in building a national campus peace movement. The building process began in December 1932, with the NSL-sponsored Chicago Antiwar Conference, a relatively nonsectarian affair that brought Communist, Socialist, pacifist, and liberal student activists together around a common antiwar program—advocating campus peace demonstrations and anti-ROTC campaigns. These antiwar activists received aid from their British counterparts in 1933, when students at Oxford University made headlines on both sides of the Atlantic by endorsing a pacifist pledge refusing to fight "for King and country." Recognizing an exciting protest tactic when they saw one, student activists in the United States adopted an Americanized version of the Oxford Pledge, in which students declared that they would "refuse to support the government of the United States in any war it might undertake." By autumn 1933 this pledge had been taken by students at antiwar conferences across the United States, and a national poll found 39 percent of the American student body endorsing the pledge (with an additional 33 percent saying that they would take up arms only if the United States was invaded).

At a time when the adult Left was still weakened by bitter sectarian rivalries, the student Left was pioneering a more cooperative and effective approach to political organizing. The NSL and SLID worked together on antiwar campaigns. As early as 1933 the NSL had proposed a merger with the SLID. Though the SLID turned down this offer, the two groups jointly sponsored the first national strike against war in April 1934. This strike consisted of a one-hour boycott of classes, and antiwar demonstrations; it was held on the anniversary of U.S. entry into WW I. The strike day was selected to emphasize the students' desire to prevent a repetition of the interventionism of 1917. The strike drew some 25,000 students, which though only a minority of the national student body, nonetheless drew great press attention because the antiwar walkout was to that point the largest student protest in American history.

The student strike mushroomed into an annual mass protest, as the NSL and SLID extended their Popular Front style of antiwar organizing beyond the Left to religious and liberal groups. In 1935 the NSL and SLID convinced the National Council of Methodist Youth, the Interseminary Movement, and regional branches of the National Student Federation and campus YW and YMCAs to act as cosponsors of the second annual strike against war. This broader sponsorship expanded the peace walkout. Some 175,000 students participated in the 1935 strike. The success of their joint antiwar efforts drew the NSL and SLID closer together, and as the danger of international fascism grew, so did their unity: the two groups merged into the American Student Union (ASU) in December 1935. Strengthened by this merger, the campus antiwar strike of 1936 drew an estimated 500,000 student participants. The ASU soon became the largest student activist organization in the nation's history, with some 20,000 members.

As student peace agitation grew more effective so did the movement's drive to aid youth who had been victimized by the Depression. Having originated the idea of federal student aid in the Hoover years, the student movement during the mid-1930s used its national federation and lobby, the American Youth Congress (founded in 1934), to champion job programs for low-income students and unemployed youth. The Youth Congress initially advocated passage of its own aid bill, the American Youth Act, which would have gone much further than the New Deal in assisting needy youth. Though this bill never passed, the Youth Congress proved so effective in making the case for federal student aid that the Roosevelt administration repeatedly enlisted the Youth Congress' support in staving off Republican efforts to cut the National Youth Administration's aid programs. The movement's activism on behalf of domestic reform also included free speech fights on many campuses, support work for the CIO's blue-collar organizing, the establishment of campus cooperatives and student labor unions, and campaigns against racial segregation in college area stores, services, recreational facilities, athletic teams, and in university admissions. Black Communist veterans of the student movement went on to establish a regional civil rights group, the Southern Negro Youth Congress (founded in 1937), which battled Jim Crow below the Mason-Dixon line.

The student movement's unity cracked in the late 1930s as a result of shifts in both the international situation and the Comintern line. During the Spanish Civil War, liberal and Communist students watched in horror as the neutrality legislation that the student movement had endorsed in the early 1930s was used by the Roosevelt administration to embargo the Spanish Republic—paving the way for the fascist triumph there; they concluded that isolationism and the Oxford Pledge would be useless against fascist aggression. Thus the ASU dropped the Oxford Pledge and embraced collective security in winter 1937, but in the process alienated pacifist, isolationist, Trotskyist, and left-wing socialist students. These alienated groups founded their own national organization, the Youth Committee Against War (YCAW), which clung to the Oxford Pledge and isolationism. This split was not fatal because most of the student population shifted with the ASU away from isolationism—leaving the YCAW with less than 1,000 members. But the ASU was now left without a socialist faction to offset Communist influence.

The consequences of this loss were not immediately apparent, since in both 1938 and the first half of 1939 the ASU's Communist and liberal students were united on a Popular Front antifascist platform. During this period the student movement became even larger and more attractive to liberals because the ASU, in line with the Communist Party's shift rightward, grew more pro-Roosevelt—supporting both the president's domestic reform programs and his "quarantine the aggressor" foreign policy, on the grounds that such support bolstered antifascist unity.

The negative impact of Communist dominance in the ASU became evident after the signing of the Nazi-Soviet Pact in August 1939. Following the new Comintern line, the Communists drove Popular Front liberals out of the ASU's leadership, and forced the organization to drop its militant antifascism in favor of an isolationist "Yanks Are Not Coming" position. This flip-flop and the ASU's refusal to criticize the Soviet invasion of Finland alienated most students, and led to the collapse of both the ASU and the student movement in 1940–41. *See also*: League for Industrial Democracy, Peace Movements, YPSL (Young People's Socialist League)

—Robert Cohen

REFERENCES

Cohen, Robert. "Revolt of the Depression Generation: America's First Mass Student Protest Movement, 1929–1940." Ph.D. diss., University of California at Berkeley, 1987.

Draper, Hal. "The Student Movement of the Thirties: A Political History." In *As We Saw the Thirties*, edited by Rita Simon. Urbana: University of Illinois Press, 1969.

Eagan, Eileen. *Class, Culture and the Classroom: The Student Peace Movement of the 1930s*. Philadelphia: Temple University Press, 1982.

Peterson, Patti. "The Young Socialist Movement in America from 1905 to 1940: A Study of the Young People's Socialist League." Ph.D. diss., University of Wisconsin, 1974.

Phelps, Marianne Beth. "The Response of Higher Education to Student Activism, 1933–1938." Ph.D. diss., George Washington University, 1980.

Rawick, George. "The New Deal and Youth: The Civilian Conservation Corps, the National Youth Administration and the American Youth Congress." Ph.D. diss., University of Wisconsin, 1957.

Student Nonviolent Coordinating Committee

SNCC—pronounced snick—was formed in the spring of 1960 by mostly black college students who were involved in the lunch-counter sit-ins then sweeping the South. They met in Raleigh, North Carolina, at the initiative of Ella Baker, a middle-aged black woman, a veteran of NAACP struggles since the 1930s, who from this time would give intellectual guidance and spiritual inspiration to the young people in SNCC.

Advocating nonviolent direct action, SNCC quickly became the militant thrusting point of the civil rights movement. Using a tiny office in Atlanta as headquarters and paid ten dollars a week, several dozen SNCC "field secretaries" moved out into the Deep South, embedded themselves in the black communities, lived in ramshackle "Freedom Houses," gained the confidence of local blacks, enlisted the aid of local youngsters, and began the dangerous work of challenging racial segregation in every form.

They reorganized the "Freedom Rides" in the spring of 1961, after the Congress of Racial Equality encountered bus-burnings and brutal beatings, and ended up beaten themselves, and jailed. They organized local people to demonstrate against segregation in Albany, Georgia, to register voters in Selma, Alabama, and Hattiesburg, Mississippi, and all over the Deep South. In the summer of 1964, they invited more than 1,000 northern students to come to Mississippi to help with voter registration, teach in "Freedom Schools," and bring racism to national attention. That summer, three SNCC people (two white, one black) were murdered in Neshoba County, Mississippi, and that August, black Mississippians were rebuffed by the Democratic Party at its national convention, which agreed to recognize only the white voting delegation.

SNCC, based on its own bitter experience with federal inaction in the face of white violence, was certainly the most angry and the most independent of civil rights groups in the South. Speaking to the huge biracial March on Washington in the summer of 1963, SNCC leader John Lewis, in the face of censorship by other black leaders, insisted on criticizing the Kennedy administration for its failure to defend black rights.

It would be wrong, in understanding SNCC, to ignore the heritage of older American radical movements. A few of its field secretaries, educated in the North, had some contact with radical ideas. Ella Baker came out of the Left struggles of the thirties and forties, and was also influenced by the socialist, anti-imperialist thinking of W. E. B. DuBois. There was also some impact from the Southern radical tradition: the Southern Conference Education Fund, and the Highlander Folk School. But SNCC was not consciously ideological; its militancy, its spontaneous radicalism, was shaped mostly by its immediate experience in the southern struggle, its closeness to the black poor, its perception that the government, national as well as local, was tied to powerful political and economic interests, and could not be trusted.

When the southern movement had achieved its immediate aims—the right to vote, the end of legal segregation, a new black consciousness, and a new white perception of blacks as refusing to accept the old order—it lost direction and momentum. It was up against the stone wall of the American system. The recognition that racism, while legally eliminated, was deeply embedded in the institutions of the country, especially in those economic arrangements that created a class of poor, and that this class would be largely black, led to more bitterness, more militancy. The cry of "Black Power," arising in 1965–66, meant different things to different people but signaled the frustration of a movement that was at once victorious and unfulfilled.

In this climate, SNCC quickly disintegrated, its people scattered and uncertain, some joining new groups, others still battling, though isolated. But it had affected the thinking of countless people, black and white, and played a pioneering role in creating the climate of the sixties. Its hostility to government (SNCC people were among the first draft resisters), its early raising of the issue (by young SNCC women in the Atlanta office) of sexual equality, its suspicion of centralized authority, and its closeness to grass-roots feelings, all prefigured the great movements of the sixties, against the Vietnam War, for gender equality, and the independent radicalism that came to be called the New Left. *See also*: Civil Rights, New Left

—*Howard Zinn*

REFERENCES
Carson, Claybourne. *In Struggle: SNCC and the Black Awakening of the 1960s.* Cambridge: Harvard University Press, 1981.

Zinn, Howard. *Student Nonviolent Coordinating Committee: The New Abolitionists.* Boston: Beacon Press, 1964.

Students for a Democratic Society

SDS was the most visible and important political organization of the 1960s and the organized expression of the broad movement for social change that exploded in that decade. From its start in 1960 as a tiny offshoot of a long-standing socialist group to its demise amid factionalism and violence in 1970, it was the cutting edge of that decade's progress from protest and reform to resistance and rebellion.

As a formal organization SDS grew from a few young people sleeping around their mimeograph machines and surviving on a diet of peanut butter and rhetoric, to at one point (1968) a national organization with a budget of perhaps $125,000, some 350 official chapters, and the claimed allegiance of 100,000 adherents. But it was as an informal force, nurturing and giving voice to both the political revival known as the New Left and the social disaffection known as the counterculture, that SDS made its most important mark.

SDS was in effect the intellectual headwaters of the New Left, through which both students and the young intelligentsia in and around the academy put forth a variety of challenging new ideas. Its major political document was the *Port Huron Statement,* adopted at a meeting in Port Huron, Michigan, June 11–15, 1962, which first enunciated the alienation of the college generation and introduced the concept of participatory democracy ("that the individual share in those social decisions determining the quality and direction of his life" and "decision-making of basic social consequence be carried on by public groups"). Other concepts, too, emerged under the SDS aegis, including that of the new working class (academics, intellectuals, and the "information society"), university complicity and the role of academics in

Cartoon by Lisa Lyons *Independent Socialist,* Berkeley, California, April 1968

support of the liberal state, and student power, concerning the rights and standing of college students on their campuses.

SDS was the source of energy, as well, for many of the activities that marked the 1960s. It was SDS that provided the core of white participants in the early civil rights protests; the original activists (formed as SDS's Economic Research and Action Project) that began the organization of the poor and made poverty a national issue; the women who were instrumental in the ideas and early actions of the women's movement; the shock troops, organizational finesse, protest techniques (including the teach-in), and many of the leaders of the antiwar and antidraft movement; and the bulk of the activists in the sweeping and tumultuous demonstrations and strikes directed against university administrations (approximately 2,000 in all in every state from coast to coast from 1965 to 1970), including the notable actions at Berkeley, Chicago, Harvard, Wisconsin, Cornell, San Francisco State, and Columbia.

SDS came to an end in an acrimonious split between a faction of national officers called Weatherman and a disciplined subgroup from the neo-Maoist Progressive Labor Party, which erupted at the June 1969 SDS National Convention. Thereafter it quickly lost adherents and influence, reducing itself to a small core devoted to violence and revolution and giving up overground politics in the spring of 1970, following the accidental explosion of its bombs in a townhouse in Greenwich Village (March 6, 1970).

The impact of SDS during the decade was marked, and included a role in the deposition of a president, the defection of the American public that ended the war in Vietnam, the sweeping reforms in campus life and governance at virtually every university, and the political awakening—called "radicalizing"—of a substantial minority of that generation. Its legacy for later generations was the revival and expansion of the Left in America and the development of a homegrown American political perspective, many of whose adherents still play fundamental roles in U.S. political, academic, journalistic, and intellectual circles. *See also*: "Antirevisionism", Armed Struggle, New Left, Participatory Democracy

—*Kirkpatrick Sale*

REFERENCES

Gitlin, Todd. *The Sixties: Years of Hope, Days of Rage*. New York: Bantam, 1987.

Miller, James. *"Democracy In the Streets."* New York: Simon & Schuster, 1987.

Potter, Paul. *A Name for Ourselves*. Boston: Little, Brown, 1971.

Sale, Kirkpatrick. *SDS*. New York: Random House, 1973.

U.S. House of Representatives, "Investigations of Students for a Democratic Society," Committee on Internal Security, Parts 1-A-7-B, 1969.

Studies on the Left

Like graduate students poised between college and profession, *Studies on the Left* occupied a precarious, unstable, but intellectually exciting position. Begun in the fall of 1959 at the University of Wisconsin by graduate students in English and history, the journal stood with one leg in the old progressive camp, a distinguished tradition of historical revisionism born with Frederick Jackson Turner, Charles Beard, and maintained by neo-progressives in the history department at Wisconsin. Also in the balance of influence was the old Communist Party Left, a tradition viewed by the editors as a relevant, but very uncomfortable heritage. The editors—graduate students, James Weinstein, Martin Sklar, Saul Landau, Helen Kramer, Eleanor Hakim, and others—called for a "radicalism of disclosure," which meant intellectual work with a political purpose.

Influenced by historian William Appleman Williams and sociologists Hans Gerth and C. Wright Mills, the journal published some of the best young American historians, sociologists, economists, and literary critics, and helped launch a revisionism that profoundly altered the historical profession in particular. Choosing as their beginning point the turn of the century, *Studies* authors reevaluated the modern reform tradition born in that era. Progressives became "corporate liberals." In the post–World War II era, reformers were known as Cold War liberals.

The uneasy relationship between *Studies* and the Old Left was gradually dissipated as a younger generation of radicals challenged the premises of the "radicalism of disclosure" that seemed to exist without an activist politics. After the journal moved from Madison to New York in 1963, the problems of relevance and activism became more acute. New editors Tom Hayden and Staughton Lynd pushed the journal hard in the direction of the growing New Left movement. *Studies* responded in two ways. It became a bimonthly after 1965, instead of a quarterly, and featured a regular, large section devoted to "the Movements." The last issue appeared in March–April 1967. The journal was now committed to working for socialism, but its relationship to various New Left organizations remained ambiguous.

Some of the original editors launched a sequel beginning in 1970 and called *Socialist Revolution*. Actively committed to building a socialist movement, the new journal resolved some of the disputes *Studies* had with both Old and New Left. But the new journal did not have the impact of *Studies*, which provided an oasis in the intellectually parched early 1960s. *See also*: History, U.S.; New Left

—*James B. Gilbert*

REFERENCES

Weinstein, James, and David Eakins, eds. *For a New America*: Essays in History and Politics from *Studies on the Left*, 1959–1967.

Student Peace Union

For a short period in 1960 and 1961, the SPU was the largest campus organization on the Left in the United States. With more than 3,000 members in over 100 campus chapters concentrated in the Midwest but with outposts throughout the country, the SPU focused attention on nuclear testing, disarmament, and foreign policy questions. Established at a time when American students were beginning to take an interest in political issues and while many of its leaders were involved in such groups as the Young Peoples Socialist League (YPSL) and in the pacifist movement, SPU was a broad-based "issue" organization. Its earliest concern was with nuclear testing. Later, the organization was involved with foreign policy questions, and was one of the first groups to focus on the growing conflict in Vietnam. SPU membership peaked in 1962 at 3,500 national members, but its influence was much larger, since many nonmembers identified with the SPU. Among the SPU major activities were several marches on Washington, D.C., including one in 1962 that was the largest political demonstration in Washington since the 1930s. SPU emphasized its campus chapters and focused attention on campus-based discussions and activities as well as national activities.

The SPU leadership was a combination of peace-oriented students including many pacifists associated with the Fellowship of Reconciliation and the American Friends Service Committee (both of which lent support to the SPU) and socialists associated with the YPSL. SPU took a strong "Third Camp" position, criticizing the foreign policies of both the United States and the Soviet Union. This unique combination permitted the SPU to gain strength at many colleges that were not traditionally involved in campus politics in the Midwest and South such as Grinnell, North Central, Lake Forest, and many others as well as the more traditionally active schools.

By 1964, the SPU dissolved itself, feeling that campus activism had gone in other directions and that its leadership was inadequate to the task. The growing SDS, with its multissue orientation, and the civil rights movement were both more potent forces on campus at the time. Nonetheless, the SPU can be seen as an important transition between the apathy of the 1950s and the New Left. Its leadership, to some extent tied to some of the ideas of the Old Left, nonetheless proved that an independent campus-based organization could be successful in mobilizing large numbers of students and in focusing attention on key national issues. *See also*: New Left, Peace Movements

—*Philip G. Altbach*

REFERENCES

Altbach, Philip G. *Student Politics in America: A Historical Analysis*. New York: McGraw-Hill, 1974.

Isserman, Maurice. *If I Had A Hammer . . . The Death of the Old Left and the Birth of the New Left*. New York: Basic Books, 1987.

Metzenberg, Howard. "Student Peace Union, Five Years Before the New Left." Senior Honors Thesis, Oberlin College, 1978.

Vickers, George. *The Formation of the New Left: The Early Years*. Lexington, Mass.: Lexington Books, 1975.

Sugar, Maurice (1891–1974)

The interrelationship between socialist politics and mass struggle was the crux of the career of Detroit labor lawyer and activist Maurice Sugar. Born in Brimley, Michigan, an Upper Peninsula lumber town where his Lithuanian-Jewish immigrant parents ran the general store, he saw class conflict between lumberjacks and the paper mills' bosses as a way of life, and the working class as the main force for change.

Sugar was a conscious Marxist who followed the faction fighting of the nascent

Communist movement of the 1920s, but he remained an independent Marxist for most of his political life. He first gained national attention for his legal efforts on behalf of the CIO sit-down strikers and the industrial union drives of the 1930s. He was also a writer of union songs in the 1930s. His two most famous were "Sit Down" and "The Soup Song."

Sugar believed the function of a Marxist was to build mass movements, and that much "theoretical" debate was really jousting for position by untested "leaders." During his tenure in the legal department, the UAW grew from a handful of members to an organization representing 700,000 workers. In addition to his trade union work, Sugar used his private legal practice to redefine the law on behalf of industrial workers and others discriminated against by the system. He had a Gramscian-type position in which he thought it correct to struggle within the existing law and culture of capitalism while working for socialist change. He always attempted to relate the legal struggle to the overall class struggle, and in the 1930s he believed the immediate task was to build industrial unions.

Another tactical priority was his view that the struggle of the workplace should be linked to the struggles in the community. In Detroit this often meant taking part in the black movement. Sugar defended many blacks throughout the 1920s and 1930s and sought black support in two unsuccessful bids for local office. He was a vital part of a Left culture that helped to shape many of the black leaders of the 1970s and 1980s, among them Detroit's Mayor Coleman Young and Congressman George Crockett.

Despite his political sophistication and organizational independence, Sugar was driven from his UAW post by Walter Reuther's purge of the Left. When the battle for control of the union first broke out after World War II, Sugar believed the anti-Reuther faction would prevail when the rank and file were mobilized. He underestimated the impact of the Cold War and the power of Red-baiting. The struggle between factions was as fierce as a civil war, and the losers were vanquished from the union. For Sugar this meant the end of his political life, and the end of his legal activism. He retired to live in rural Michigan until his death. *See also*: United Auto Workers

—*Jim Jacobs*

REFERENCES

Johnson, Christopher H. *Maurice Sugar: Law, Labor and the Left in Detroit 1912–1950*. Detroit: Wayne State University, 1988.

Sugar, Maurice. *The Ford Hunger March*. Berkeley: Meiklejohn Civil Liberties Institute, 1980.

Summer Camps

Immigrant radicals arriving in the United States early in the twentieth century developed institutions to nurture values brought from Eastern Europe and to ease adjustment to new circumstances. Summer camps for adults and children were one such institution.

In the summer of 1923, young trade unionists affiliated with the International Ladies Garment Workers Union rented land in Beacon, New York, and established the cooperative Camp Nitgadegit. (In the 1930s, other camps calling themselves Nitgadegit were begun in the Washington, D.C., area and in the Midwest.) Although the Yiddish term meant "No need to worry" and the camp was well-attended, a bitter struggle inside the ILGWU engendered by the Russian Revolution led to a split in the union and in the camp. Political differences between socialists and those aligning with the newly formed Communist Party became apparent in disputes over governance. For example, should anyone having the ten dollars required to buy into the cooperative become an equal partner in decision-making or should adherence to certain political principles be required? After one season, a group left to begin Unity Camp.

In 1927, Unity, which called itself "the first proletarian summer colony" and which would become the first interracial adult camp in the United States, purchased a permanent site in Wingdale, New York. In the late 1930s, returning Spanish Civil War veterans were given jobs and the opportunity for rehabilitation at Unity. During World War II, local residents joined with campers and staff to raise funds for the war effort. A vibrant cultural program attracted guests from more traditional resorts. Cold War harassment—including a 1955 investigation to uncover "Communists' use of summer camps to indoctrinate and disaffect American youth . . ."—and internal disputes over camp policy on such issues as "white chauvinism"—with camp management often taking a position different from that of the CP—resulted in declining attendance. From 1958 to 1963, the children's camp Calumet and Webatuck operated on the site.

Camp Kinderland, founded in 1923 by Jewish progressives active in the Yiddish Nonpartisan Shules, was also a target of the 1955 investigation. In 1930 the camp became part of the Jewish section of the International Workers Order. Despite intermittent efforts to lessen the emphasis on Jewish culture, the tradition of "progressive Yiddishkeit," with its focus on working-class Jewish history and values, was always reaffirmed. In 1971 the original site in Hopewell Junction, New York, was sold and Camp Lakeland, the adult component begun on adjoining property in the early 1930s, was closed. Kinderland moved to its current home in Massachusetts, where it remains the oldest Left-oriented Jewish camp in the United States.

Other efforts to provide progressive recreational experiences for children were WOCHICA (Workers Children's Camp), which operated at the Wingdale site during the late 1920s and early 1930s, the Socialist Party's Pioneer Youth of America which ran a summer camp during the late 1920s and early 1930s, and the Highlander Folk School's Junior Union Camp, 1940–1944. *See also*: Yiddish Left

—*Linn Shapiro*

REFERENCES

Beck, John P. "Highlander's Junior Union Camps, 1940–1944: Workers' Children and Working Class Culture." Paper presented at the Fourth Southern Labor Studies Conference, 1982.

Shapiro, Linn. "Camp Unity: An Experiment in Socialist Living," unpub. mss.

Suller, Elsie. "Camp Kinderland Celebrates." *Jewish Currents* 33 (May 1979).

———. "*Kinderland.*" Anniversary journal. 1979.

SURREALISM

Successor to a long tradition of European avant-gardes, surrealism developed its own

Arsenal/Surrealist Subversion, 1989

radical critique of "bourgeois-Christian civilization" and allied itself with the revolutionary workers' movement internationally in the 1920s. After scattered beginnings, surrealism asserted itself in the United States during the 1960s–1980s as an important radical intellectual-cultural current.

In its first *Manifesto* (1924), the movement's leading theorist, poet André Breton, defined surrealism as "pure psychic automatism, by which it is intended to express, verbally, in writing or by other means, the real functioning of thought." Drawing initially on Freud and poets such as Lautréamont, Rimbaud, and Jarry, Breton and his comrades conceived of the "surrealist revolution" as the realization of poetry in everyday life; recognizing their affinities with Marx's project of proletarian emancipation, they joined the French Communist Party in 1927. Their ideas rebuffed by Party leaders, surrealists became early Left critics of Stalinism.

Although international surrealism centered in the diverse Paris group until the 1950s, surrealist groups were active in many other countries in Europe as well as in South America and Japan. Inspired by Hegel (Lenin's notes on this philosopher appeared first in French in the surrealists' journal) and drawn to the various phases of antibourgeois revolt, surrealists felt especially close to the art and struggles of Third World peoples. Aimé Césaire's *Return to My Native Land* and the "jazz poems" of Ted Joans are among the best known documentations of the reciprocal influences.

Several exhibitions of surrealist painting took place in New York and other cities in the 1930s, but the movement exerted very little influence in the United States until World War II. The short-lived International Federation of Independent Revolutionary Artists (FIARI) —inaugurated by a manifesto Breton coauthored with Leon Trotsky on a visit to Mexico in 1938, and which was published in *Partisan Review*—failed to establish a U.S. section. Two years later the war brought Breton, Max Ernst, Yves Tanguy, Kurt Seligmann, Leonora Carrington, Roberto Matta, Nicolas Calas, and many others to New York, although total abstinence from political activity was a condition of asylum. Nevertheless, these artists and new U.S. friends organized an International Surrealist Exhibition in New York in 1942, and brought out three issues of a lavish, bilingual surrealist journal whose name, *VVV*, reflected the popular expectation of victory over more than the Nazis and Japanese. *VVV* introduced painter Gerome Kamrowski, photographer Clarence John Laughlin, and poet Philip Lamantia, who, at age fifteen, was welcomed into the movement by Breton as "a voice that rises once in a hundred years." *VVV* also initiated the surrealist examination of the movement's American forerunners, including horror writers H. P. Lovecraft and Clark Ashton Smith, and "anesthetic" philosopher Benjamin Paul Blood. In lengthy visits to Canada, the western United States, and the West Indies, Breton developed views on Native American culture, Fourierist utopianism, and New World natural phenomena that would play a key role in later surrealist activity, especially in the United States. But when Breton and the other exiles returned to Paris in 1945, the New York group fell apart.

A generation later, in 1966, the first U.S. surrealist group was formed in Chicago by half a dozen young activists in the Industrial Workers of the World (IWW), who ran the union's Solidarity Bookshop. Poets Franklin and Penelope Rosemont, who visited Breton and took part in surrealist activity in Paris for several months in 1966, played a central role in these and later activities. The first sustained U.S. surrealist-oriented publication, the *Rebel Worker* (1964–67), a mimeographed journal of the Chicago IWW branch, spanned the gap between homegrown U.S. radicalism and the avant-garde tradition, the libertarian wing of the Old Left, and the radical spirit of the later 1960s. Its seven issues contained lively texts on bureaucracy, (mis)education, youth culture, anarchism, Wobbly history, and of course surrealism. Among the *Rebel Worker* pamphlets was a thirty-eight-page anthology, *Surrealism & Revolution* (1966), edited by Franklin Rosemont, who would go on to produce *What Is Surrealism? Selected Writings of André Breton* (1978), a 600-page compendium with an introduction situating Breton and surrealism in the revolutionary currents of the twentieth century.

The first U.S. surrealist group show at Chicago's Gallery Bugs Bunny in 1968 featured works by seven artists, including Franklin Rosemont, Penelope Rosemont, and sculptor/cartoonist Robert Green—all contributors to the *Rebel Worker*—as well as newcomer Paul Garon, whose surrealist studies of black music (*Blues and the Poetic Spirit*, 1976) established him as an important force in the movement.

The following decade brought many new recruits, most notably poet/theorist Joseph Jablonski, collagist/poet Debra Taub, dancer/choreographer Alice Farley, graphic artist/musicologist Hal Rammel, and three "veterans" from *VVV*: Kamrowski, Laughlin, and Lamantia, America's most influential surrealist poet. On May Day, 1976, the huge World Surrealist Exhibition opened in Chicago, with some 600 works by nearly 150 artists from thirty-one countries.

Indeed, throughout the 1970s the surrealist group vastly expanded its activity in many directions. Activists from the start, surrealists held many provocative demonstrations that more than once brought them to the attention of the national media and the local police. In 1970 the group produced a special surrealist issue of the Students for a Democratic Society journal *Radical America*—and later several *Radical America* pamphlets in a "Surrealist Research & Development Monograph Series"—with the pregnant insight that U.S. radicalism and popular culture had been full of objectively surrealist manifestations, from Krazy Kat and Bugs Bunny comics to the blues of Peetie Wheatstraw and Memphis Minnie to the work of obscure autodidact painters and sculptors. That discovery also permeated a 1979 *Cultural Correspondence* anthology, reprinted in book form as *Surrealism and Its Popular Accomplices*, as well as *Free Spirits: Annals of the Insurgent Imagination* (1982), published by City Lights, whose codirector, Nancy Joyce Peters, had become one of American surrealism's leading figures. Along with surrealist games, poetry, theory, polemic, social criticism, and correspondence with Herbert Marcuse, the irregular journal *Arsenal/Surrealist Subversion* (1970–present), one of the most elegantly produced publications of the contemporary U.S. Left, has also pursued the exploration of America's hidden presurrealist heritage.

Taken together, this collective effort has added a new dimension to the understanding of American radicalism, both of its own origins and of the domain of potentially revolutionary practice. Taking fields of close examination in chronological order for a moment, surrealists and their allies have decisively reinterpreted the origins of American utopianism in the radical reformation and its important U.S. offshoots; provided much thoughtful appreciation of Native American life; drawn attention to numerous significant but neglected nineteenth- and twentieth-century thinkers usually regarded as "cranks," including feminist Mary MacLane and Benjamin Paul Blood; established new ground in the study of Edward Bellamy, the most important American socialist writer of the nineteenth century; celebrated African-American music from blues to "free jazz"; studied the shifts in American vernacular ("slang"); analyzed crime and horror drama from the literary pulps of the 1850s to the radio mystery shows and *film noir* of the 1930s and after; broadly reassessed the cultural contributions of the IWW; devoted much loving analysis to newspaper comics as well as to film animation and its master, Tex Avery, as major contributions to world culture; reinterpreted the achievements of the most popular of feminist figures, Isadora Duncan, and modern dance generally; related the radical ecological consciousness of such writers as Thoreau and John Muir to the contemporary "practice of poetry"; and deepened our appreciation of such exemplars of popular culture as Spike Jones, "Lord" Buckley, Ernie Kovacs, and Carl Barks.

By the close of the 1980s, the surrealists' writings on these topics equaled the intellectual depth and probity of any organized Left tendency, small or large. More than that, they have served as provocations for an entirely different approach to the many questions of revolutionary transformation.

—*David Roediger*

REFERENCES

Arsenal/Surrealist Subversion. Chicago: Black Swan Press, 1989.

Biro, Adam, and René Passeron. *Dictionnaire géneral du surréalisme*. Paris: Presses Universitaires de France, 1982.

Rosemont, Franklin, ed. *Surrealism and Its Popular Accomplices*. San Francisco: City Lights Press, 1981.

———, ed. *What Is Surrealism? Selected Writings of André Breton*. New York: Pathfinder Press, 1978.

Swados, Harvey (1920–1972)

Novelist, short-story writer, critic, and journalist, Swados left a small but unique mark on radical literary culture. Born in Buffalo, New York, he was influenced by his sister, Felice, also a novelist, to join the Young Communist League while still in high school. In 1940, at the time he was a senior at the University of Michigan, Swados was converted to Trotskyism and subsequently joined Max Shachtman's Workers Party.

Although he drifted away from the WP in 1942, Swados maintained an independent radical stance for the rest of his life. He was profoundly affected by his youthful work experiences in aircraft factories and, later, in an auto plant, as well as by two years in the merchant marine during World War II. In 1962 a collection of essays called *A Radical's America* promoted a vision of socialism decidedly to the left of liberalism and independent of all existing states. In his last years he was a militant opponent of the Vietnam War.

Several of Swados's novels are of special interest to issues and episodes in the history of American radicalism. *On the Line* (1957) describes the lives of nine assembly-line workers to dramatize the effects of the work process under capitalism. *Standing Fast* (1971) chronicles the radicalization and deradicalization of members of his generation, drawing primarily upon WP history. The posthumously published *Celebration* (1974) presents the diary of the ninety-year-old Samuel Lumen, whose life telescopes many of the ambiguities of the twentieth-century radical intellectual.

These books are noteworthy for their painful honesty and highly developed sense of craft, but weak in communicating the ideas animating the left-wing movements he depicts. Swados's novels and short stories are also remarkable for their autonomy from the fashions of the times in which he wrote. *See also*: New Left Literature, Trotskyism, Workers Party

—*Alan Wald*

REFERENCES

Howe, Irving. "On Harvey Swados." *Massachusetts Review* 24, no. 3 (Fall 1983).

Wald, Alan M. *The New York Intellectuals: The Rise and Decline of the Anti-Stalinist Left from the 1930s to the 1980s*. Chapel Hill: University of North Carolina Press, 1987.

Sweezy, Paul: see Monthly Review

Symbionese Liberation Army: see Armed Struggle

Syndicalist League of North America

Launched in Chicago in September 1912, the SLNA represented the purest organizational form of syndicalism in American labor history. The key figure in the organization was William Z. Foster, who laid out the league's theoretical position and strategies in the pamphlet *Syndicalism* (1912), which he coauthored with Earl C. Ford. Like the Industrial Workers of the World, the league emphasized shop-floor organization and economic struggle to the exclusion of electoral politics, which it saw as an impediment to change. The new syndicalist society would not be based on industrial unions, however, as the IWW claimed, but rather on natural production units already characteristic of large-scale industry. The other major contrast between the two organizations was strategic and important. While the IWW embraced the "dual union" approach, Foster and his league adherents argued vociferously for the strategy of "boring from within" the mainstream unions, an approach Foster had observed among the French syndicalists. Once the working class was fully organized and the labor movement won over to a revolutionary perspective, the means of production would be expropriated through a massive general strike.

The league found its natural constituency among working-class anarchists and those IWW activists who rejected dual unionism. At its height, the SLNA had about a dozen branches located in western and midwestern cities and a membership of perhaps 2,000. League activists joined mainstream American Federation of Labor and Railroad Brotherhood unions and led important organizing drives and strike movements in St. Louis, Kansas City, and in Chicago, where the league maintained its headquarters. Two lively papers, the *Agitator* (later the *Syndicalist*) and the *Toiler* carried the SLNA's message. Launched in a period of IWW activity and growth among immigrant mass-production and lumber workers, the league never achieved a mass following, and it faded out of existence in the course of 1914.

The SLNA is significant, however. It polemicized against the strategy of dual unionism and popularized the notion of boring from within, an approach the Communists and other radicals later used to win a base within the labor movement. The league's other important legacy to the radical labor movement was a cadre of activists with considerable experience and important contacts in local midwestern labor movements. Foster, James Cannon, Jack Johnstone, and others later played important roles in building the Communist Party and providing it with roots in the trade union movement. *See also*: Foster, William Z.

—*James R. Barrett*

REFERENCES

Foner, Philip S. *History of the Labor Movement in the United States*. Vol. 4. *The Industrial Workers of the World, 1905–1917*. New York: International Publishers, 1965.

Foster, William Z. *From Bryan to Stalin*. New York: International Publishers, 1937.

T

Taft-Hartley Loyalty Oath

The major anti–trade union legislation of the postwar years was the Labor Management Act of 1947, which is better known as the Taft-Hartley Act. Its provisions made it difficult for unions to organize aggressively or carry on militant activities. For the Communist-oriented Left, Section 9 (h) contained a poison pill. This section denied any union the right to use the National Labor Relations Board (NLRB) unless each of its officers filed an affidavit that he or she was (1) not a member of the Communist Party, (2) not affiliated with the CP, and (3) did not believe in, was not a member of, or a supporter of any organization that believed in or taught the overthrow of the U.S. government "by force or by any illegal or unconstitutional methods." What this meant was that any union with an elected or appointed Communist officer could not use the NLRB to gain certification as a collective bargaining unit even if the majority of workers voted for it and that any certified union that did not meet the act's provisions could be decertified.

Anti-Communist poster

Many justifications were advanced for Section 9 (h) by its advocates, but what their reasoning boiled down to was that the elimination of domestic Communists from the trade union movement was an essential ingredient of a larger anticommunist crusade. The authors of the act stated that the Communists must be purged to prevent "political strikes," with the implication that such strikes might be ordered from abroad with the aim of weakening the defenses and economy of the United States. Trade unionists who were hostile to or uncomfortable with their CP colleagues justified their support of Section 9 (h) as necessary to keep their unions from being manipulated by outside organizations with independent political agendas, irrespective of the source of those agendas. The sincerity of such sentiments was suspect as other ideological groups, such as various right-wing organizations, were not singled out for punishment. Nor, for that matter, was the Socialist Party.

As soon as Taft-Hartley was introduced, trade unionists spoke out against it in no uncertain terms. They were joined by allies ranging from religious leaders to FDR's third-term vice president, Henry Wallace. Ben Gold, the Communist leader of the Fur and Leather Workers Union, urged the CIO leadership to take dramatic action by calling for a one-day strike or even a five-hour strike before Congress voted, but his counsel was not taken. After the bill was passed, President Truman vetoed it on the grounds the act violated the principles of the New Deal, but his veto was overridden. John L. Lewis, president of the United Mine Workers, then affiliated with the AFL, considered the law "fascistic." At the 1949 AFL national convention, Lewis said the act would be rendered inoperative if all trade unionists refused to comply with its anticommunist affidavit process. His views did not carry, and the UMW soon left the AFL.

The timidity of the AFL leaders would soon find its counterpart in the more militant CIO. Although conventional trade unionists despised the Taft-Hartley Act, many were willing to live with it while opportunistically using the affidavit clause to oust ideological rivals. Such leaders felt that reformers and other non-Communists in alliance with the CP could be neutralized or intimidated into shifting sides. The room for maneuvering was enormous. Jurisdictional raids could be made on any international or local that did not comply. Even if officers submitted affidavits, government informers could charge the officers were lying. Should a trade unionist resign from the CP in order to fulfill the law's requirements, it could be charged that the individual remained a secret member or still adhered to the Party line.

Legal challenges to Section 9 (h) were soon forthcoming. In 1948 Victor Rabinowitz, representing the American Communications Association (ACA), an international CIO union, and the Wholesale and Warehouse Workers Local 65 in New York, a local whose international officers had complied, filed suit that the act illegally abridged rights guaranteed by the First and Fifth amendments. A similar suit was filed by the Steel Workers Union when Inland Steel refused to bargain on pensions with a union whose officials had not filed affidavits.

Union attorneys thought they had a decent chance to win over the Supreme Court to their view, but fate played a heavy hand against them. Two justices the attorneys had counted on to support them died unexpectedly, Justice Frank Murphy in July 1949 and Justice Wiley B. Rutledge in September. Making matters worse was that Justice William O. Douglas, an outstanding liberal, fell from a horse in a mountain area of his home state of Washington just a few days before the argument was heard and could not participate. Justice Tom Clark, appointed to replace Murphy, disqualified himself because he had been attorney general when the law was before Congress, and Justice Sherman Minton, the successor to Rutledge, was not appointed until after the case was heard. The truncated Court upheld the Law 5–1 in *American Communications Association, CIO* v. *Douds*. Justice Hugo Black filed the lone dissenting opinion.

Even as the legal challenges moved through the courts, labor's house was falling apart. The relatively small Fur and Leather Workers Union suffered thirty raids on its locals within a single year. The United Electrical, Radio, and Machine Workers (UE); the Mine, Mill & Smelters; and other larger unions that did not comply were hit even harder. Union after union was rent with internal debate on whether to comply or not. But the trend was unmistakable. From 1947 to 1951, 232,000 non-Communist affidavits were filed.

The profoundly disruptive impact of the affidavits issue on radicalism within the trade unions is indicated by a minor incident that did not even involve the CP. In the late 1930s the Industrial Workers of the World had gained representation in some twenty industrial plants in Cleveland and it had maintained that representation through the war years. If the IWW trade unions did not comply with

Taft-Hartley, the IWW would be decertified; but if they did comply, they would violate IWW principles. Expediency won out over ideology, and in the resulting organizational furor, the IWW lost its last foothold in basic industry.

By May 1949, CIO compliance with Taft-Hartley was in high gear. The executive board, which had previously included known Communists, now banned Communists not only from the board itself but from holding office in any CIO union. The board further tightened the screws by dismissing officers who did not endorse board decisions. Among these decisions were the required approval of the Marshall Plan and disavowal of the Progressive Party. Unions that resisted these litmus measures were expelled. Between November 1949 and August 1950, the CIO kicked out ten unions: the UE; the Farm Equipment Workers; the Mine, Mill & Smelters; the United Office and Professional Workers; the United Public Workers; the American Communications Association; the International Longshoremen's and Warehousemen's Union (including the Fishermen and Allied Workers, which had affiliated with ILWU); the National Union of Marine Cooks and Stewards; and the Food, Tobacco, Agricultural & Allied Workers Union. The International Fur and Leather Workers Union withdrew before it, too, could be expelled. The combined membership of these unions came to nearly a million workers. Two of the unions had been among the eight unions expelled by the AFL in 1935 and a third, the UE, had joined them in the formation of the original CIO. These founding CIO unions, still under the same basic leadership as in the 1930s, were suddenly deemed unacceptable by the very movement they had inaugurated.

The pattern that emerged after explusion was one of constant organizational and individual harassment. Some cities denied public housing to anyone who would not sign non-Communist oaths and some states suspended unemployment compensation to employees of the CP. Various federal agencies used similar measures against individuals until challenged in court by cases that often dragged on for years. The irony in many of these situations was that the benefits denied had often been originally championed by movements led or influenced by the CP.

Within the labor movement itself, the bloodletting was relentless. Complying unions raided expelled unions at every opportunity as the government moved to decertify or charged perjury or insincerity when some trade unionists withdrew from the CP to adhere to the law. In major unions such as the United Auto Workers where there was a considerable CP presence, there was a purge of Communists and their allies. The labor press took a strong anticommunist posture that became a hallmark of the AFL-CIO merger of 1955. More significant than any single conflict in this cataclysmic era was the fact that such traditional goals of labor as organizing the unorganized and advancing the gains of those already organized were severely blunted.

Labor's attempts to have Taft-Hartley repealed failed again and again, but the affidavit proviso came under fire. Understanding that Section 9 (h) was poorly phrased, Congress clarified its intent with the Communist Control Act of 1954. The need to file affidavits was done away with. The new act simply made it a crime to be a member of the CP and simultaneously hold office in a labor union or to hold office within five years of resigning from the CP. The five-year clause was obviously aimed at those who had resigned from the CP to avoid decertification of their unions. Attorneys immediately pointed out the act's legal shortcomings. It created punishments for beliefs rather than for crimes, it punished without due process, and it created penalties for membership in what was still a legal political organization. Despite these unconstitutional aspects, a clear challenge to the act did not develop until the end of the decade.

The person who finally took on the Communist Control Act was Archie Brown, a man who had joined the CP in 1929 and the Longshoremen's Union in 1936. Running as an avowed Communist, Brown was elected to the executive board of Local 10 of the Longshoremen's Union in 1959, 1960, and 1961. He was also very active in an anti–House Un-American Activities Campaign centered in San Francisco. In 1961 he was arrested for violation of the Communist Control Act. His case moved to the Supreme Court with speed. Fourteen years after Section 9 (h) of the original Taft-Hartley Act had been found constitutional, the successor Communist Control Act was struck down by a 5–4 decision written by Chief Justice Earl Warren. The Court held the act was a violation of the right of trial by jury in that it allowed Congress to convict and punish citizens in advance or absence of trial by jury.

Civil libertarians of all persuasions rejoiced at the decision. Remaining state and federal laws of like nature gradually fell into disuse under the assault of legal and political challenges. In fact, however, the original intent of the Taft-Hartley Act had been achieved. The tremendous trade union momentum that had been generated by the great organizing drives of the 1930s had been checked and then reversed; and radical influence within the labor movement had been largely exorcised. Whether judged by bread-and-butter measures such as the percentage of work force organized and gains in real wages or by a more abstract criterion of political influence, the trade union movement declined steadily after passage of Taft-Hartley. This deterioration was partly masked by the relative prosperity of the 1950s and 1960s, but was clearly evident by the 1970s. With the election of the aggressively anti–trade union Reagan administration of the 1980s, organized labor had reached a postwar nadir. *See also*: Federal Bureau of Investigation, McCarthyism

—*Dan Georgakas*

REFERENCES

Ginger, Ann Fagan and David Christiano, eds. *The Cold War Against Labor*. 2 vols. Berkeley: The Meiklejohn Institute, 1987.

T-Bone Slim (1880s–1942)

Born Matt Valentine Huhta in the 1880s, this legendary member of the Industrial Workers of the World—songwriter, humorist, and pamphleteer—was of Finnish descent and lived for many years in the Finnish community of Ashtabula, Ohio. Little is known of his life. After his marriage ended he took to the road, and hoboed from one end of the continent to the other for years. He worked as a logger, logging-camp cook, construction-worker, harvest-hand, and from the early 1930s until his death in 1942, as a barge captain on the Hudson River in New York. Although he was not a public speaker, never held union office, and may not even have held job delegate's credentials, he is still remembered by IWW old-timers as a good organizer, largely because of his exceptional abilities as a writer.

T-Bone's first contribution to the IWW press appears to have been in 1920. His songs—"The Popular Wobbly," "Mysteries of a Hobo's Life," and "I'm Too Old to Be a Scab"—quickly became some of the most popular lyrics in the IWW songbook and, like his "Lumberjack's Prayer" (a poem printed on wallet-size cards), were known by heart to many thousands of migrant workers. His pamphlet *Starving Amidst Too Much*, a black-humor critique of the food industry, was published by the IWW's Foodstuff Workers Industrial Union 460 in 1922. For two decades his columns in the weekly *Industrial Worker* and *Industrial Solidarity*, and his occasional pieces in the monthly *Industrial Pioneer* as well as in less-well-known Wobbly papers such as the *General Construction Workers Bulletin*, were the best-read features of the IWW press.

The most popular IWW writer, T-Bone Slim was also one of the most prolific. Humor, frequently outrageous, always playful, is the hallmark of all that he wrote, and it enabled him to express the IWW outlook in original and appealing ways. Many of his zany neologisms ("civilinsanity," "perhapsbyterian") were once part of the everyday argot of America's hobo jungles, and one of them—"Brisbanality," after Arthur Brisbane, top columnist for the antilabor Hearst newspaper chain—was included by H. L. Mencken in his *American Language*. Some of T-Bone's Wobbly definitions ("Tear gas: the most effective agent used by employers to persuade their employees that the interests of capital and labor are identical"), are as good as anything in Ambrose Bierce. Some of his aphorisms ("Wherever you find injustice, the proper form of politeness is attack") are as forceful as they are funny.

In recent years T-Bone's songs have been recorded by such renowned folksingers as Joe Glazer, Pete Seeger, Utah Phillips, and Faith

Petric. It is only a matter of time before the IWW's greatest "man of letters" gains wider recognition as an important figure in the history of American humor. *See also*: Humor, Industrial Workers of the World

—*Franklin Rosemont*

REFERENCES

Rosemont, Franklin, ed. *Juice Is Stranger than Friction: Selected Writings of T-Bone Slim*. Chicago: Kerr, 1990.

Teachers Union

One of the earliest Left unions among professionals, the TU was also one of the most internally divided. Originally an AFL union founded by New York City school teachers in 1916, it had close links with the Socialist Party, and suffered severe attacks during the 1919–20 Red Scare. The union was also hard put in early years to overcome the major organizing obstacle posed by widespread belief (encouraged by boards of education) that teachers, as "professionals," required no unionization.

The TU first experienced rapid growth during the Depression, developing strong locals in such cities as Philadelphia, Chicago, Boston, and Atlanta, especially among the underpaid and heavily exploited substitute teachers. College faculty also joined the TU, forming in New York City an independent College Teachers Local. New York City remained the union's primary center, with about 40 percent of its total membership.

The TU rapidly became a factional arena for competing sections of the Left. Many of the new teachers who swelled TU membership, especially in New York, were either Communists or Lovestoneites—both hostile to the long-established leadership of the Socialists. Alarmed but unable to manage a mass expulsion, the old leaders (aided by George Counts of Teachers College, and John Dewey of Columbia) seceded to form the Teachers Guild. With the support of AFL president William Green, and in the atmosphere of the Rapp-Coudert persecutions, the Teachers Guild effected the ouster of the TU from the AFL in 1941.

Ironically, the TU split from the AFL and affiliation with the CIO temporarily solidified Left leadership in the TU. Bella Dodd (1904–69), an Italian immigrant and member of the Hunter College faculty, emerged as one of the rare outstanding Communist women labor luminaries. But as in so many other unions, Left leadership could not survive the onslaught of the Cold War and the competition from mainstream unions. Dodd herself, who openly criticized Communist involvement in the 1948 Progressive Party campaign of Henry Wallace as divisive and tactically hopeless, found herself expelled from the Party in 1949, and she converted to a conservative Catholicism (under the guidance of Monsignor Fulton Sheen). Although a purged TU remained alive, it lost members and prestige to the old Teachers Guild, renamed the American Federation of Teachers. Recognizing in 1964 that hopes of challenging the AFT could never be realized, the TU formally disbanded.

Before and after its ouster from the AFL, the TU pioneered the development of antiracist curricula and teaching materials about blacks and other minority populations, especially in such urban school districts as New York and Philadelphia. This pedagogy, originating largely in the antiracist convictions of Communist teachers, foreshadowed Black History Month. This remained the finest legacy of the TU. *See also*: Communist Party, Rapp-Coudert Inquiry

—*Marv Gettleman*

REFERENCES

Dodd, Bella. *School for Darkness*. New York: P. J. Kennedy & Sons, 1954.

Iverson, Robert W. *The Communists and the Schools*. New York: Harcourt, Brace, 1959.

Teachers Union Papers, Cornell University Library.

Zitron, Celia L. *The New York City Teachers Union, 1916–1964: A Story of Educational and Social Commitment*. New York: Humanities, 1968.

Tendencies

A political tendency within a radical organization refers to members who generally vote the same way on most issues or take their orientation from the same individual or group of individuals. A tendency that persists over a long period of time may evolve into a faction that strives to take power in the organization.

A tendency is just as likely to dissolve as events unfold or differences with other members are overcome. *See also*: Factions

—*Dan Georgakas*

Textile Workers Unions

At least four radical textile unions fielded efforts to organize the unorganized across New England and the South from the 1870s to the 1930s. Although ultimately unsuccessful, they provided both a background for the success of the Textile Workers Union of America and an avenue for radical activism, especially in New England.

Building on a New England tradition of philanthropic and gender-conscious appeals for "hours legislation," and on a mixed tradition of sporadic labor upsurge and tenuous craft organization, radicals began to mobilize textile operatives during the 1870s. In the wake of the 1877 railroad strike and reorganization of the immigrant-based socialist movement, a prominent group of socialists and labor reformers created the International Labor Union in the "Little Lancashire" of Fall River, Massachusetts. Founded on a spinners' union, the ILU conducted a notable relief effort for a major Fall River strike, and essentially joined with strikers in local activities, 1878–80. Its president, George McNeill, was perhaps the most prominent Christian Socialist–inclined labor leader of the age; its secretary, Carl Speyer, was a German-American follower of Marx. The ILU's weekly paper, the *Labor Standard*, began as a New York socialist paper and transferred to Fall River under the editorship of J. P. McDonnell, one of the most prominent Irish figures in the First International's U.S. branches. For a moment, the ILU seemed capable of sweeping through New England to western New York and the South; the *Labor Standard* served an important role in elementary communications. Employer strength proved too great, American-born labor leaders turned to hours legislation, and the ILU did not survive to benefit from the return of textile militancy during the 1880s.

The Knights of Labor, growing out of a secret labor society and some aggressive efforts in the Philadelphia area, emerged as a major force in textiles during 1883–85. Predominantly Irish among textile workers in particular, the Knights offered no obvious opening to the mostly German-American Marxists. On a local and regional basis, however, socialist branches reorganized around the growing enthusiasm for the Knights. So long as momentum was sustained (i.e., until May Day, 1886), socialists could join with others in calling for strikes where necessary, workers' control of productive processes, and the substitution of a cooperative society for the existing competitive one. In some places, labor reformers and Christian Socialists even founded "socialistic" day-care centers as an adjunct to the Knights. Local Knights leaders, themselves sometimes veteran Irish-American craft unionists with a Christian Socialist bent, led the broadening of the socialist movement here and there into a transethnic organization.

The retreat of the Knights' leadership into timidity, and its unwillingness to support the Haymarket victims, both reduced the organization to a shell in textile towns and bitterly alienated socialists from the remnant. Socialist sympathies and hopes for industrial unionism (rather than the craft unions of spinners and other trades, mostly ineffectual, surviving in the mills) spawned continuing support campaigns for textile strikes, and the formation of the National Union of Textile Workers in 1894. The NUTW, based in Providence, Rhode Island, had as its president socialist James P. Reid and as its national affiliation the Socialist Trades and Labor Alliance, dominated by the Socialist Labor Party. Strongest in the industrial valleys south of Providence, the NUTW could not survive the deepening depression and the internal strife among socialists. The NUTW folded into the AFL's small and cautious affiliate, the United Textile Workers.

Radicalism revived among textile workers with the Industrial Workers of the World. Strong among sections of Italian Americans in particular, the IWW held "free speech" fights in textile towns and directed many strikes in 1912–13. Dominating public attention, the strikes in Lawrence, Massachusetts, and Paterson, New Jersey, pointed to the hopes and the limits of radical organization. As before, the strike wave revived flagging socialist activity and caused the creation of new branches, although once again often of limited duration. Among local leaders, James P. Reid of Providence especially tied the fate of the socialist movement to that of the Wobblies. By the time wartime prosperity had brought a renewal of militancy, after widespread repression, the IWW had been effectively destroyed as a mass movement. Textile strikers operated temporary organizations of their own, often under "One Big Union" slogans of the IWW.

The Amalgamated Textile Workers Union, founded in 1920 and led by the Rev. A. J. Muste, temporarily filled the leadership gap. Undertaking to coordinate and lead where possible the postwar strikes against reductions of wages and lengthening of hours, the ATWU —modeled after the vastly successful Amalgamated Clothing Workers—was overtly militant and covertly radical. Despite considerable success in several strikes, the ATU faded with the "American Plan" rollback of unionism. Once more the United Textile Workers, small in size and conservative by inclination (despite the participation of some scattered local socialist activists), ruled the field unchallenged.

The Communist Party-dominated Trade Union Unity League established the Providence-based National Textile Workers Union in 1929, with James P. Reid as president. Like its radical predecessors, it had few financial resources and tended to join in or support existing strikes rather than lead labor struggles for union recognition. Its most prominent activist, Anne Burlak, was known as the Red Flame, for her fiery oratory. She led some of the most militant strikes in 1931–32, and was elected national secretary of the NTWU at age twenty-one, the only American woman to hold such a high union post. She carried on NTWU organizing work in New England, South Carolina, Georgia, and New Jersey.

During the "textile general strike" of 1934, the NTWU merged with the United Textile Workers, grown somewhat more militant from the pressure of a grass-roots militancy. The failure of the UTW to take maximum advantage of the strike encouraged the formation of the Textile Workers Organizing Committee, and the industrial union, the Textile Workers Union of America (TWUA). Although former NTWU leaders maintained a low profile around the TWUA, Communists played an important role in a number of branches, until purged for the most part from their leadership positions during the Cold War. The United Textile Workers, whose New England leader, Tom Gorman, had ironically been among the strongest mid-1930s proponents of an independent labor party, operated as the more conservative and craft-conscious alternative, gradually disappearing as mills closed. The TWUA, for its part, later merged with the Amalgamated Clothing Workers to form the ACTWU, one of the most progressive labor bodies in the United States. *See also*: British Americans, Industrial Workers of the World, Portuguese Americans, Socialist Labor Party

—*Paul Buhle*

REFERENCES

Buhle, Paul. "Italian-American Radicals and the Labor Movement, 1905–1930," and "The Knights of Labor in Rhode Island." *Radical History Review* #17 (Spring 1978).

Kelly, Richard. *Nine Lives for Labor*. New York: Praeger, 1956.

McNeill, George E., ed. *The Labor Movement: The Problem of Today*. Boston: A. M. Bridgman, 1887.

Third International (Comintern)

Sustained over decades by Russian direction, the Third International marked the climax and eclipse of international revolutionary coordination. Its influence on the U.S. Left differed considerably from era to era, and changed with the shift of views among other national parties even while reserving for Russian leaders the final political authority.

The formation of the Third International, in 1919, sent out a ringing call to labor militants but mainly to Left socialists to prepare for a new movement. For the initial period, until at least 1921, however, the course of the Left followed activists' inclinations and socialist inner-party dynamics more than any Comintern program. Due to the presence in Moscow of a former Socialist Labor Party leader, Boris Reinstein, the Comintern first issued its call to the SLP and its tiny unionist organization, the Workers International Industrial Union, in addition to the Socialist Party Left and the Industrial Workers of the World. Meanwhile, an official agency of the Russian government was established in New York, headed by Ludwig C. A. K. Martens, with a staff of some thirty-five. This agency, a source of influence separate from the American political Left proper, carried on its own intrigues in the factional brawls of competing Communist entities.

The major effort of the Comintern in the early period was to unify the American Communists, against their own inclination toward feuding and splintering. It insisted on more open participation in strike movements and more public activity, even as the Palmer Raids drove the Communist movement semiunderground, and it sought to centralize the American Communists by limiting the autonomy of the Language Federation groups. It suceeded in some of these aims, unification and intervention within the AFL of the early 1920s; but its "Bolshevization" effort drove away many ethnic activists, precipitating the virtual destruction of several groups and placing impediments between activists and their communities. The Comintern also, especially after 1928, insisted on the importance of the "Negro question" for the American Left. This final point, along with the stress on combating imperialism, was the most lasting and positive of Comintern contributions.

On the negative side, the Comintern's own factional fights at the highest levels in the 1920s caused a perpetual crisis within American Communism. Comintern "reps," representatives sent throughout the 1920s to guide the Americans, proved themselves inveterate factionalists more determined to secure their own positions than the fate of the American Left for its own sake. "John Pepper" (Joseph Pogeny), arriving in 1922 from Moscow, immediately gained a leading role in the Left, articulating best the Communist argument for a labor party, then guiding a series of factions that shared his antipathy for Trotsky. His special protégé, Jay Lovestone, followed Pepper's predilection for intrigue, ultimately serving as a key coordinator of U.S. intelligence agency cooperation with the AFL-CIO. Pogeny himself, returning to Russia at the close of the 1920s, disappeared in the late 1930s Stalinist purges.

Americans traveling to Moscow, at first attempted to defend prewar Left views against Russian leaders, but reconciled themselves for the most part by the middle '20s to seeking Comintern approval for their particular perspectives. In 1927 future American Trotskyist leader James Cannon brought back Trotsky's statements from Moscow, touching off a round of expulsions. In 1928 Jay Lovestone and his followers actually broke with the now-entrenched Stalin leadership in a desperate attempt to protest the effect of the Comintern's wide shift to the Left on American Communism; once again, expulsions followed, with the loss of another important outpost of Communist labor influence.

More subtly, the Comintern made the American Left dependent in two important institutional ways. It subsidized activities of the Communist Party of the United States, perhaps to 10 percent of Party expenses. (A far smaller sum, one should note, than U.S. funds sent to the Soviet Union for famine relief and other purposes). It also created American cadres through training at the Lenin School in Moscow, or other schools, often for several years.

The early Depression reemphasized American Communist reliance on the Comintern, despite the modest growth of Party numbers and of influence (particularly notable among intellectuals). The forced march of revolutionary rhetoric, espoused by William Z. Foster and others, portrayed American "soviets" as the future. The Seventh Congress, in 1935, marked a decisive turning point. Americans, joined by leading figures from other parties, argued that their own success in mass activity, alongside the dangers raised by the victories of fascism, had instituted a new era. Communists would hitherto make claims on behalf of a democracy that elements of the bourgeoisie no longer sought to defend. This line, formulated by the Bulgarian Georgi Dimitroff and others, permitted American Communists to abandon their insurrectionary posture and to enter alliances with a broad spectrum of liberal political movements, not excluding the New Deal itself.

This period came to an end, in a sense, with the Hitler-Stalin Pact of 1939, placing the Comintern in the awkward position of repudiating its members' closest allies. After the invasion of Russia, the Comintern closed its history with a reaffirmation of the anti-fascist position. The Comintern formally dissolved in 1943. This ended the appearance of fraternal parties always acting in concert, but the American Party, like most other Communist parties, retained its ideological dependence on Soviet thinking. *See also*: Communist Party, "Lovestoneites," Trotskyism

—*Paul Buhle*

REFERENCES

Draper, Theodore. *American Communism and Soviet Russia*. New York: Viking, 1960.

THOMAS, NORMAN (1884–1968)

The most noted leader of the U.S. socialist movement after Eugene V. Debs, Thomas was a frequent candidate for the presidency and, in later years, widely regarded as the "conscience of America."

Born into a family of clergymen—his father, grandfather, and great-grandfather were Presbyterian pastors—Thomas graduated from Princeton and was ordained at Union Theological Seminary in 1911. Influenced by the Social Gospel and his own ministry experience in the slums, he became a Christian socialist and antiwar pacifist. Editing the *World Tomorrow*, journal of the Fellowship of Reconciliation, Thomas also worked with anticonscription organizations and the forerunner of the American Civil Liberties Union to support the rights of conscientious objectors. He entered the Socialist Party in 1918, avowing his libertarian commitments, and left the clergy. During the early 1920s he became associate editor of the *Nation* and editor of the short-lived Socialist daily *New York Leader*. In 1924 he entered the race for governor of New York and became a perennial socialist candidate. During the 1920s, Thomas also emerged as a major public spokesman for civil liberties and labor rights. Intervening in the Passaic, New Jersey, silk strike of 1926, he characteristically held a mass meeting in defense of strikers, and was locked up for a "riot law" later declared illegal.

As a political candidate, Thomas won increasing respect within the liberal (and sometimes conservative) mainstream. His 1928 campaign for the presidency did little to revive the membership of a flagging SP, but he drew numerous intellectuals into the Thomas for President clubs. His 1925 and 1929 mayorality campaigns in New York dramatized his attack on corruption, and inspired support among ministers, rabbis, and professors. His 1932 presidential campaign had a particularly dramatic effect on college students, on some of whose campuses a majority favored Thomas. He received 884,781 votes, far less than many socialists expected, but nearly the number Debs had received in 1912, and vastly more than any radical candidate would receive again in the next half-century.

The New Deal, many conservatives and liberals believed, carried out the Socialist program (Thomas retorted that it had been carried out "on a stretcher"). Many Socialist intellectuals and labor leaders soon defected to the Democratic Party. Thomas declined to oppose Fiorello LaGuardia's progressive campaign for New York's mayor, himself joining the city's Charter Revision Commission. By 1936, when Thomas polled less than 200,000 votes in his bid for the presidency, the grandest electoral hopes of the Socialists had passed.

Thomas struggled meanwhile to hold together a SP disintegrating into internal quarrels. Leader of the "Militant" faction, he opposed, successively, the conservative Old Guard wing of aging garment trades Socialists; ultraradicals, who mostly passed over into Communist movements; Trotskyists, whose entry he had encouraged in 1936, only to see paralyzing factional disaster; and finally those within the Party who resisted Thomas's basically antiwar approach (until 1942) toward the impending world war. Due in no small part to Thomas's efforts, the SP emerged as a fighting organization with a solid weekly press (the *Socialist Call*), and aggressive if scattered activism in labor, student movements, civil liberties, race issues, and resistance to the militarization of American society.

Thomas himself continued to crusade, above all in civil liberties, on national and international scales. He became a selfless public figure who would defend even those (such as Communist Party leader Earl Browder, in 1940) bitterly opposed to him. Thomas appealed to presidents and dictators, sometimes successfully, for the safety of imprisoned political leaders. Fearlessly, he invaded Jersey City, challenging Mayor Frank ("I am the law") Hague to arrest him. He faced vigilantes in Arkansas, sustaining arrest and beatings for his support of tenant farmers. During the Second World War, he appealed for justice to Japanese Americans, for the continuance of civil liberties and the advance of civil rights in wartime.

His presidential poll diminished from the 1930s (116,796 in 1940, 80,518 in 1944, and 140,260 in 1948), Thomas turned after 1948 to supporting Democratic presidential candidates. Yet he did not endorse the "better dead than red" policies of the Cold War. He upheld the principles of peaceful coexistence, while generally condemning violations of freedom on both sides. In ripe old age, Thomas helped to found SANE (Committee for a Sane Nuclear Policy), and spoke out against the Vietnam War.

The Rev. Martin Luther King, Jr., perhaps the only twentieth-century American (along with Debs) with equivalent moral credentials, sent a taped message to Thomas as King flew to Norway to accept the Nobel Peace Prize: "I can think of no man who has done more than you to inspire the vision of a society free of injustice and exploitation. . . . Your example has ennobled and dignified the fight for freedom, and all that we hear of the Great Society seems only an echo of your prophetic eloquence." Thomas suffered a stroke after returning home from delivering his final speech, for peace in Vietnam. From his hospital bed he dictated a testament to the SP convention that began, "Not for a minute do we need to assume that the human race is irrevocably damned . . ." *See also*: Peace Movements, Socialist Party

—*Harry Fleischman*

REFERENCES

Fleischman, Harry. *Norman Thomas: A Biography, 1884–1968*. New York: Norton, 1969.

Johnpoll, Bernard K. *Pacifist's Progress: Norman Thomas and the Decline of American Socialism*. Chicago: Quadrangle, 1970.

Norman Thomas Collection, New York Public Library.

Swanberg, W. A. *Norman Thomas: The Last Idealist*. New York: Scribner's, 1976.

TOVERITAR/NAISTEN VIIRI

Beginning in July 1911, *Toveritar* (Female comrade) was published as "the only Finnish women's journal in America" by the Finnish Socialist Federation (*Suomalainen Sosialistijärestö*) in Astoria, Oregon. The newspaper ceased publication in June 1978 in Superior, Wisconsin, where it had been published by Työmies (Worker) Society under the title *Naisten Viiri* (Women's banner) but appeared for a short time as a section in the society's other weekly, *Työmies-Teenpain* (Worker-forward). *Toveritar* was conceived in the years preceding the first edition by socialist Finnish women who wished to improve the oppressed condition of immigrant women living in the United States and Canada. During a discussion of women's role in socialism at the 1906 founding meeting of the Finnish Socialist Federation in Hibbing, Minnesota, three women delegates argued that, indeed, women in America suffer just as men of the working class and in addition are denied the right to vote. To address this and many other problems they experience both as women and as immigrants, the delegates argued, women need their own newspaper.

Established in 1909 with a circulation of 3,000, *Toveritar* was published by *Toveri* (Comrade). The weekly remained in Astoria until 1930 and reached a peak of 10,000 regular subscribers in 1925, surpassing *Toveri*. Its annual Women's Day issue reached 15,000 American and Canadian women. In 1930, *Toveritar* was moved to Superior, Wisconsin, and its name was changed to *Työlaisnainen* (Working woman). In 1936 the name was changed to *Naisten Viiri*. After 1919, it reflected generally the views of the Communist Party.

The paper's expressed purpose was to awaken women to the world around them, to show them that they were exploited and denied full human rights, and to teach them how to improve their lives both collectively and individually. Throughout its existence, the newspaper remained loyal to the labor movement. The editors encouraged working women to contribute writings and thereby opened doors to literary careers for many of them. The paper sought to inspire women to organize, to work together for the common good, for peace and for education of their young. It urged them to participate in elections, to vote for *their* candidates, and always to fight for their rights as women and members of the working class.

Helmi Mattson, a Finnish immigrant woman, served as perhaps the most successful and best-known editor of the paper. Mattson's literary skills and insight into immigrant life made possible *Toveritar*'s popularity in the 1920s and 1930s. She is the most prolific and versatile of women Left authors in the United States, publishing novels, plays, poetry, and essays, most of which first saw print in the paper. *Aavikon Vaeltajat* (Desert wanderers), given away as a premium for new subscriptions in 1928, developed the story of a Finnish-American woman's sojourn through politics and personal life. She also documented the rich history of Finnish-American Left theater. Her autobiography was serialized, after her 1974 death, in *Naisten Viiri*. *See also*: Finnish Americans

—*Velma Doby*

REFERENCES

Karvonen, Hilja J. "Three Proponents of Women's Rights in the Finnish-American Labor Movement from 1910 to 1930: Selma Jokela McCone, Maiju Nurmi and Helmi Mattson." In *For the Common Good: Finnish Immigrants and the Radical Response to Industrial America*, edited by Michael Karni and Douglas Ollila, Jr. Superior, Wis.: Tyomies Society, 1977.

The Helmi Mattson Reader [Working title]. St. Paul: Immigration History Research Center, scheduled for 1990.

TRACHTENBERG, ALEXANDER: *see* INTERNATIONAL PUBLISHERS

TRADE UNION EDUCATIONAL LEAGUE

Formed in Chicago in November 1920 to coordinate the activities of left-wing militants within various unions, the TUEL constituted the most important radical opposition group within the American labor movement until its dissolution in 1929. William Z. Foster, a former syndicalist who joined the Communist Party in 1921 and directed its trade union activity, was the league's driving force. While the league was never formally affiliated with the CP and included many non-Communists in its ranks, it generally adhered to the industrial policies of the Party and, in effect, acted as its trade union body.

The TUEL's program called for industrial over craft organization through amalgamation of trades within the same industry; formation of a labor party; organization of the unorganized; a shop delegate system to ensure rank-and-file control of unions; unemployment insurance; support for the Russian Revolution; and eventually the establishment of a workers' republic. Foster and his colleagues hoped to create progressive blocs in each of the major unions. These groups would push for the TUEL's program within their respective industries and in this way help to win the labor movement over to the revolutionary struggle.

By firmly rejecting the common left-wing strategy of dual unionism, while advocating a militant policy within the mainstream unions, the league scored some notable successes in its early years. Foster established an important alliance with John Fitzpatrick, charismatic president of the progressive Chicago Federation of Labor and the key figure in the labor party movement of the early twenties, and also with Alexander Howat, leader of an insurgent movement within the United Mine Workers of America. A TUEL railroad conference held at Chicago in 1922 drew hundreds of delegates from the many disparate unions in that industry, and hundreds of state federations, city labor councils, and local unions passed resolutions supporting the league's amalgamation plan. Activists were elected to local office in the carpenters, machinists, and other unions, and league adherents won con-

Linoleum cut by William Siegel

trol of both the Ladies Garment Workers Union and the Fur and Leather Workers Union.

The TUEL led important strikes in the textile industry at Passaic, New Jersey, in the New York City garment industry in 1926, and in 1928 at the cotton mills in New Bedford, Massachusetts. The organization and its activists were under attack throughout the twenties, however, from the national AFL leadership and conservative machines in the various unions. The conflict was most severe during the mid-twenties in precisely those unions, notably the Mine Workers and the needle trades, where the Left opposition was strongest.

The TUEL's decline derived from two divergent forces: the Profintern—the international communist labor organization in Moscow—and the conservative leadership of various American unions. The latter set the stage for the formation of separate, revolutionary unions by expelling not only the Communists but thousands of other activists. Such expulsions in many unions during the mid-1920s provided a mass base for and a deep sense of bitterness upon which the TUEL's successor, the Trade Union Unity League (TUUL), was able to build a federation of dual revolutionary unions during the late 1920s and early 1930s. There is little doubt, however, that much of the inspiration for this new initiative came from the Comintern's declaration in 1928 of a new strategic line—class against class—to meet what it saw as the revolutionary challenge of this era. The main rationale for the TUEL—to win the mainstream unions to a revolutionary program—was abandoned as hopeless, and the TUEL gave way to the TUUL. *See also*: Communist Party, International Ladies Garment Workers Union, Trade Union Unity League

—*James R. Barrett*

REFERENCES

Cochran, Bert. *Labor and Communism: The Conflict that Shaped American Unions.* Princeton: Princeton University Press, 1977.

Kopald, Sylvia. *Rebellion in the Labor Unions.* New York: Boni & Liveright, 1924.

Saposs, David. *Left-Wing Unionism*. New York: Russell & Russell, 1926.

Schneider, David. *The Workers' (Communist) Party and American Trade Unions*. Baltimore: Johns Hopkins University Press, 1928.

TRADE UNION UNITY LEAGUE

Established in Cleveland in August 1929 as the American section of the Red International of Labor Unions, the Trade Union Unity League (TUUL) functioned as the industrial arm of the Communist Party during the early years of the Great Depression. The League replaced the Trade Union Educational League (TUEL), founded in 1920 by William Z. Foster. The TUEL was a rank-and-file opposition group designed to "bore from within" mainstream labor organizations and win them over to a revolutionary program. In contrast, the TUUL aimed to build a revolutionary labor movement through the establishment of dual unions. Its program called for a militant "class against class" line and mass strikes rather than labor/management cooperation; organization of the unorganized; the seven-hour day and five-day week; world trade union unity; full equality for black workers; social insurance; and "the overthrow of the present system of capitalist ownership and exploitation and the establishment of a Soviet system."

The TUUL's formation is most often explained in terms of the Comintern's shift from a United Front to a more sectarian line in the course of 1928. The latter held that capitalism was entering a new era offering tremendous potential for revolutionary movements. At this historical moment it was essential for Communists to abandon movements dominated by "reactionaries" and "social fascists" and to develop their own revolutionary labor organizations.

While the TUUL undoubtedly owed its creation in part to such formulations, practical considerations seemed also to dictate this shift. By the beginning of 1929, long before the league's foundation, separate "red unions" had already been created in coal mining, textiles, and the needle trades, where wholesale expulsions of rank-and-file radicals during the late 1920s created a mass base for the revolutionary unions. Communists were also able to build a viable industrial union in the giant New York hotel and restaurant industry. In addition, smaller TUUL unions or leagues were active in auto, electrical manufacturing, meat-packing, steel, tobacco manufacturing, shoe and leather, furniture, the maritime trades, and several other industries. The TUUL's National Textile Workers Union led strikes in Gastonia, North Carolina, Paterson, New Jersey, Lawrence, Massachusetts, and Allentown, Pennsylvania, while the Cannery and Agricultural Workers Industrial Union led a desperate strike of vegetable field laborers in the Imperial Valley of California. In mining, the Communists forged a brief alliance with insurgent elements in the United Mine Workers of America under the banner of the Save the Union movement and waged violent strikes in the western Pennsylvania and Kentucky coalfields during 1931. TUUL membership fluctuated wildly, often in relation to the many strikes the organization led, but it seems clear that the league never represented more than a tiny fraction of organized labor in one of labor's weakest eras.

It would be a mistake, however, to conclude from the TUUL's small size that it had little significance. Its activists organized the Unemployed Councils, the bases for a giant unemployed movement in the early 1930s, and its greatest importance may lie in the groundwork it set for the industrial union movement of the late 1930s. As the Communist line shifted once again during 1934 and the TUUL was dissolved in favor of Popular Front cooperation with other unionists, thousands of experienced Communist activists assumed key roles in the movement that created the giant CIO and unionized American basic industry by the end of World War II. *See also*: Communist Party, International Ladies Garment Workers Union, National Miners Unions, Textile Workers Unions, Trade Union Educational League

—*James R. Barrett*

REFERENCES

Cochran, Bert. *Labor and Communism: The Conflict that Shaped the American Unions*. Princeton: Princeton University Press, 1977.

Klehr, Harvey. *The Heyday of American Communism: The Depression Decade*. New York: Basic Books, 1984.

TRESCA, CARLO (1879–1943)

For three decades Tresca was a free-lance revolutionary paladin among Italian radicals in the United States. His political views had taken shape in his native Abruzzi, where he embraced socialism with the fiery militancy that characterized his entire career. As branch secretary of the Italian Railroad Workers Union and editor of the newspaper *Il Germe* (The seed) at age twenty-two, Tresca was a thorn in the side of the local religious, political, and economic elite. Rather than serve a prison term stemming from his activities, Tresca immigrated to the United States in 1904.

He settled in Philadelphia, where he assumed the editorship of *Il Proletario* (The proletarian), the official organ of the Italian Socialist Federation, and he was instrumental in orienting the majority ISF current to syndicalism. Becoming increasingly anarchistic in his own views, Tresca resigned his editorship in 1906 and began publishing his own newspaper, *La Plebe* (The plebs). Two years later he transferred *La Plebe* to Pittsburgh, where he brought revolutionary ideas to the struggles of Italian coal-mine and mill workers in western Pennsylvania. His opposition included the clergy, Italian consular officials, and mafiosi as well as the capitalist owners of mines and mills and their allies in the Pennsylvania government. His opposition retaliated with heavy fines, imprisonment, and an assassination attempt, but Tresca was not intimidated.

Tresca entered the mainstream of American radicalism and labor in 1912, when the Industrial Workers of the World (IWW) invited him to Lawrence, Massachusetts, to help lead the Italian workers during the campaign to free strike leaders Joseph Ettor and Arturo Giovannitti, who had been falsely accused of murder. Tresca soon became known as the Bull of Lawrence and after the victory in Lawrence was active in the Little Falls, New York, textile workers' strike (1912), the New York hotel workers' strike (1913), the Paterson, New Jersey, silk workers' strike (1913), and the

IL MARTELLO
Published Twice a Month by the "Martello Group"
PRIMO MAGGIO 1936

Mesabi Range, Minnesota, strike of miners (1916). While organizing in the Mesabi Range, Tresca narrowly escaped a lynching and was charged with murder. An agreement in which some IWWs pleaded guilty to government charges was negotiated between the Minnesota authorities and Elizabeth Gurley Flynn (Tresca's comrade and lover since 1912). Ettor was also involved in the arrangement by which Tresca was released. Big Bill Haywood, the official leader of the IWW, was enraged by the terms of the negotiations, which included some guilty pleas; and the association of Tresca, Ettor, and Flynn with the IWW quickly withered.

In 1917, when the entire first-, second-, and third-tier leadership of the IWW was indicted by the federal government, Tresca again defied Haywood. With Ettor, Flynn, and a handful of others, he had had his case severed from the mass trial that would take place in Chicago, thereby escaping the long prison terms and huge fines that were to be the fate of those who followed Haywood's strategy. Tresca did not escape other persecution. Even after the federal charges against him were dropped, *L'Avvenire* (The future), the newspaper Tresca had published in New York since 1913, was suppressed and its successor *Il Martello* (The hammer) was repeatedly confiscated.

The Justice Department kept Tresca under constant surveillance throughout 1919 and 1920, hoping to gather evidence for a deportation. Tresca skillfully avoided running afoul of the law while always remaining a source of assistance for comrades less fortunate in this respect. During this period Tresca became involved in the Sacco-Vanzetti case. He was responsible for bringing the controversial IWW lawyer Fred Moore into the case and helped generate considerable publicity and financial support for the doomed anarchists.

By the time Sacco and Vanzetti were executed, Tresca had become preoccupied with the struggle against fascism. Tresca became the major figure among Italians in America who tried to thwart Mussolini's efforts to organize Italian immigrants into a support group devoted to his fascist principles. In *Il Martello,* Tresca excoriated Mussolini as the arch-traitor of the working class and he attacked the House of Savoy for its cowardly complicity in the fascist takeover.

Tresca's antifascist activities were carefully monitored in Rome. Fearful that opposition from Italians in America would jeopardize his standing with the U.S. government and lending institutions, Mussolini was determined to silence the voices of his transatlantic opponents. In 1923 the Italian ambassador officially requested that the State Department suppress *Il Martello* as the source that was "spreading poison among all the Italian workmen in this country." Federal authorities complied by prosecuting Tresca for sending "obscene matter" through the mails. The excuse for this was a two-line advertisement for a book on birth control. Convicted and sentenced to serve a year and a day—a felony charge that qualified him for deportation—Tresca spent four months in the Atlanta Federal Penitentiary in 1925 before public outcry over the transparent persecution forced President Calvin Coolidge to commute the sentence to time served.

Failing to rid themselves of Tresca by legal means, the fascists resorted to violence. There was an unsuccessful attempt to kill him and other antifascists with a bomb during a rally in 1926. Faced with constant physical attacks, the antifascists responded with daggers and pistols as well as mass demonstrations and street fights. By the end of the decade, pro-Mussolini militants could only hold public demonstrations under police protection. While unable to undermine American business support for Il Duce's regime or prevent the takeover of Italian-American newspapers, radio stations, cultural institutions, and other important vehicles that influenced the Italian community, Tresca and the antifascists did succeed in derailing Mussolini's grandiose plan for the fascistization of Italian America.

By the 1930s Tresca had added the Communists to his list of totalitarian foes. In contrast to anarchists like Malatesta, Goldman, Berkman, and Kropotkin, who had opposed the Bolsheviks early in the course of the revolutionary process, Tresca had given grudging support. He reasoned that a socialist state was preferable to a capitalist state. Throughout the 1920s Tresca regarded the Communists as useful allies in the fight against fascism, and he collaborated with them in such organizations as the Italian Antifascist Alliance of North America. When the Stalinists crushed the anarchist movement in Catalonia and Aragon during the Spanish Civil War, Tresca became an implacable foe of Stalinism. He subsequently served on the John Dewey Commission, which declared Trotsky "not guilty" of the charges presented at the Moscow Purge Trials. Once Tresca took such positions, the Communists conducted a campaign of character assassination aimed at destroying his influence in the antifascist movement.

After Pearl Harbor, Tresca obstructed both the Communists and former fascists from infiltrating the Mazzini Society, the leading organization of Italian antifascists in the United States. He also kept them out of the Italian-American Victory Council, organized by the Office of War Information in 1942 to be an agency through which American policy toward postwar Italy might be influenced. The obstacle that Tresca presented was removed on the night of July 11, 1943, when an assassin shot him to death in a New York street.

Many of Tresca's comrades believed that his murder had been ordered by Generoso Pope, the ex-fascist publisher of *Il Progresso Italo-Americano,* as Tresca had attacked him relentlessly throughout the 1930s and early 1940s. Another suspect was Vittorio Vidali, an agent of the Third International, whom Tresca had accused of murdering anarchist and Trotskyist leaders in Spain during the civil war. The most plausible theory, however, is that Tresca was killed at the order of an Italian underworld figure named Frank Garofalo, whose motives might have been more personal than political. Although the actual triggerman has been identified as a member of the Mafia, the Tresca murder remains officially unsolved. *See also*: Anarcho-syndicalism, Industrial Workers of the World, Italian Americans

—*Nunzio Pernicone*

REFERENCES

Gallagher, Dorothy. *All the Right Enemies.* New Brunswick: Rutgers University Press, 1988.

Pernicone, Nunzio. "Carlo Tresca and the Sacco-Vanzetti Case." *Journal of American History* 66 (December 1979).

TROTSKYISM

American Trotskyism was founded with the expulsion of James P. Cannon, Max Shachtman, and Martin Abern from the Communist Party on October 27, 1928. The three had been leaders of a faction aligned with William Z. Foster. The group viewed itself as a Left opposition to official Communism and devoted most of its energy, particularly in its early years, to a critique of the Soviet Union. The Trotskyists held that the Soviet Union had degenerated by becoming bureaucratized under the leadership of Joseph Stalin. They favored a return to the original Leninist regime, which they believed was more internally democratic and internationally revolutionary. Therefore Trotskyism developed very much in this country as it did in other countries, i.e., in a reactive fashion with Soviet Communism.

American Trotskyists, like their "Stalinist" competitors, sought to replicate on American soil a revolution modeled on the Soviet one. They believed this required the construction of a vanguard party that adhered to the correct policies. The combination of a tightly organized and disciplined party with a belief that adherence to the correct line was the key to eventual revolutionary success encouraged a process of fracturing and splits. The mainstream Communists were able to partially counter this tendency by combining the authority of the Soviet Union with an undemocratic internal regime. Most Trotskyist groups were more democratic and paid the price in splits.

American Trotskyism did have some positive features over its sister parties in Europe and elsewhere, which led it to become the largest and best organized Trotskyist group during Trotsky's lifetime. Cannon and his supporters had led a section of the American CP relatively attuned to American political conditions and with some experience in the American labor movement. James P. Cannon was a pragmatic American and an excellent organizer. This organization and leadership contrasted sharply with the typically small and badly run bands of feuding intellectuals in Europe.

Between 1928 and 1933 the American Trotskyists were extremely weak, with little more than 200 members. Activity consisted largely in publishing and distributing their paper, the *Militant,* for the most part unsuccessfully, to CP-related circles. Factionally ridden, they were all but paralyzed by internal tension on a leadership level between Cannon and Shachtman. They suffered minor but painful splits with groups led by Albert Weisbord, a former Young People's Socialist League leader who briefly rose to fame as Communist field marshall in the Gastonia, North Carolina strike and who continued to direct a minute group for decades after, and B. J. Field, who had achieved his own fame as Trotskyist strategist of a New York restaurant strike.

During 1933 the Trotskyists began to influence working-class politics in the United States with a very effective campaign in favor of a united front against the rise of fascism in Germany. The official Communists had refused to cooperate with the Social Democrats. After 1934 the "Stalinists" adopted the Popular Front policy and the American Trotskyists criticized the official Communists from the left, particularly their support of the Democratic Party and their more conservative policies in the labor movement.

With the workers' victory in the Minneapolis Teamster strike in 1934, the Trotskyists developed a small but vital labor base. At about the same time, the Trotskyist critique of Russian autocracy brought over a number of intellectuals, including an important group around the journal *Partisan Review*.

Between 1934 and 1938 the American Trotskyists went through a process of fusion and entry that contributed to the movement's growth and political impact, though producing splits and wounds among fellow members of the non-CP Left. In 1934 the Trotskyists fused with the American Workers Party, led by A. J. Muste, a group that had distinguished itself in the Toledo Auto-Lite strike. In 1936 the group entered en bloc the Socialist Party, whose conservative wing had departed. An opposition faction around Hugo Oehler opposed the entry and split away to form its own movement with a number of notable organizers and intellectuals, including Sidney Lens. The main body of Trotskyists converted several hundred Socialist youth before their expulsion from the SP in 1938 and the founding of the Socialist Workers Party (SWP) as the premier organization of the Fourth International.

Meanwhile, in 1937, Leon Trotsky arrived in Mexico. The American Trotskyists quickly established a special relationship with their exiled leader, providing the bulk of his secretaries, guards, and funds, and establishing a close practical-theoretical collaboration. American Trotskyist intellectuals, led by George Novack, organized a commission of inquiry into the Moscow Trials and convinced the philosopher John Dewey to head it. The commission's hearings played an important role in efforts to counter Communist versions of the judicial murders. The assassination of Trotsky by a Comintern agent on August 20, 1940, was a deep personal as well as political trauma for U.S. Trotskyism. Many cadres remaining in the movement for twenty or more years sustained themselves through memories of the "Old Man," memories often more vivid than Trotskyism's contemporary activities.

In all, the period of collaboration with Trotsky between 1937 and 1940 had been most productive. Trotskyists developed most of the ideas that have had their impact within the American labor movement, such as advocacy of a shorter work week to counter unemployment, automatic wage escalators to offset inflation, support of rank-and-file democracy in an increasingly bureaucratized labor movement, and promotion of an independent labor-based political party. Actual Trotskyist recruitment of workers and influence within the trade unions was significant but minor when compared with that of the CP in the same period.

Lesser progress was made in recruitment or even understanding of racial minorities and women. Trotsky had urged upon his American supporters a nationalist class policy and aggressive orientation toward blacks. C. L. R. James (J. R. Johnson) interpreted this view in the press but it was scarcely adopted in practice. Unlike the Communist movement, which had a nominal approach to women, including a press and a small apparatus, American Trotskyists produced little more than an occasional essay urging their participation.

In 1940 the Trotskyists split almost in half over the "Russian question." A group led by Max Shachtman, which included most other prominent intellectuals and most of the youth, developed a new theory of the Soviet Union as a bureaucratic collectivist class society. They refused to defend the Soviet Union and evolved a "Third Camp" perspective of opposition to both Washington and Moscow. Cannon's faction included most blue-collar workers and a scattering of intellectuals and adhered faithfully to Trotsky's view of that society as a "degenerated workers' state" still worthy of defense in a conflict with imperialism. The division separated most intellectuals from most workers, with the result that Shachtman's WP maintained a lively but isolated intellectual life while Cannon's SWP maintained an orthodox though stifling internal life with working-class participation. During World War II Dwight Macdonald left Shachtman and published a lively maverick libertarian-pacifist journal, *Politics*. The Smith Act prosecutions of the SWP leaders and Minneapolis Teamster militants soon threw important Trotskyists in prison, which assisted the union bureaucracy in isolating radicals.

Trotsky and both branches of his followers believed that the war would be followed by a revolutionary wave in which leadership could be seized away from Communists and Social Democrats. The combination of successful revolutions led by the "counterrevolutionary Stalinists" (such as in China and Yugoslavia) with prosperity and conservatism in the industrialized countries was most demoralizing. Cannon sought to defy reality with predictions of an imminent revolution, while Shachtman developed frightening visions of a new class system sweeping the world. The confusion led to myriad new splits and recombinations, with an SWP group led by Felix Morrow and Albert Goldman joining the WP, while the WP "Johnson-Forest" group, led by C. L. R. James and Raya Dunayevskaya, joined the SWP. More important, both groups lost the bulk of their membership as prosperity and McCarthyism took a toll on the Left as a whole.

During the 1950s and 1960s the general drift of the Shachtman tendency (the WP, Independent Socialist League, Young Socialist League) was rightward. At first it maintained a course independent of Stalinism and capitalism, advocating a "Third Camp." However, in time, the bulk of the group supported the American camp in the Cold War, abandoned their vanguardism, and evolved into social democrats. Irving Howe dropped out of the group and in 1952 launched the journal *Dissent*, which maintained a position of critical support for America's foreign policy objectives while defending the victims of McCarthyism. In 1958 Shachtman led his group of little more than 200 members into the SP, where in 1972 they became the leadership of the small, aging, hawkish, anti-New Left Social Democrats/USA. Michael Harrington led a wing of former Shachtmanites that maintained a more critical attitude toward American foreign policy, the Democratic Socialist Organizing Committee (later merged with the New American Movement to form the Democratic Socialists of America), which eventually achieved a membership of several thousand. Hal Draper, longtime editor of Shachtman's lively tabloid *Labor Action*, led the majority of the youth out of the SP in 1964 to form the Independent Socialist Clubs (later called International Socialists and gaining a couple of hundred labor-oriented student supporters), which adhered to a more radical but rather syndicalist version of the Shachtmanite variety of Trotskyism.

The SWP had dwindled down by the 1950s to less than 400 members who were hard-pressed to maintain a weekly paper and a quarterly journal. The James-Dunayevskaya group left in 1951 with a few dozen adherents, published a workerist paper, *Correspondence*, for a few years, and divided again into Dunayeskaya's *News & Letters* and James's Facing Reality groups (the latter disintegrating but a remnant led by James Boggs and Grace Lee Boggs, called the National Organization for an American Revolution, surviving), both Detroit based and working-class spontaneitists. A faction emerged in the SWP in 1953 around Bert Cochran, Harry Braverman, and George Clarke that was supported by the bulk of its autoworkers. It included both worker elements seeking a more American and less sectarian political existence and intellectuals impressed with Communist achievements in China and Yugoslavia. Cochran and Braverman, after their expulsion, produced their own lively monthly, the *American Socialist*, which they abandoned in 1960 with Braverman moving on to Monthly Review Press. Sam Marcy led a group of several dozen, largely from the Buffalo area, out of the SWP in 1960, that supported the Russian invasion of Hungary, and called itself the Workers World Party. The Marcy group developed some strength in the late 1960s through the organization of the ultramilitant Youth Against War and Fascism.

Trotskyism's revival came with the radical upsurge of the 1960s. A new youth organization, the Young Socialist Alliance, was founded in 1959 through the assistance of former Shachtmanite youth led by Tim Wohlforth, Shane Mage, and James Robertson. These leaders and others, like Peter Camejo, with the support of party intellectuals George Breitman, George Novack, and Murry Weiss, recruited mostly radicalized students who rejected New Left leadership. The SWP drew much interest to a revived and more widely circulated *Militant*, which popularized support for Fidel Castro and the Cuban Revolution as well as for Malcolm X and black nationalism. But it mainly applied lessons from the 1930s–1940s labor movement to the new antiwar movement, building in a relatively nonsectarian fashion the mass marches of the later 1960s and early 1970s.

All existing Trotskyist groups grew in the aftermath of the collapse of Students for a Democratic Society in 1969, drawing those to the left of the official Communists who rejected Maoism and were attracted to a critical view of Communist-dominated societies and to a rigorous Marxist intellectual life. By 1977 the SWP had more than 1,500 members, more than at the time of its founding convention in 1938, but nearly all of them graduates of the student radicalization. Little progress had been made in recruitment among blacks and even less in the Chicano community. Trade union work had been largely ignored. Others attempted to rebuild Trotskyism in a more traditional manner stressing orthodoxy, vanguard building, and the labor movement. James Robertson had split from the SWP in 1963 and built the Spartacist League into a group of 200 or so members, while Tim Wohlforth left the SWP in 1964 and built the Workers League into a group of about the same size. Both groups opposed the SWP's identification with the Castro leadership of Cuba. The Seattle SWP branch, led by Dick Frazer and Clara Kay, strongly oriented toward civil rights and subsequent black struggles, left the SWP in 1964 to form the Freedom Socialist Party, which eventually grew under Kay's leadership, changing its orientation to the feminist movement. All-told there were about 3,000 Trotskyists in one group or another by the mid-1970s. As with the SWP proper, this was a historic high point.

Thereafter, Trotskyism of all varieties suffered. The number of grouplets had doubled, while combined membership had shrunk by half. The SWP remains the largest Trotskyist group, with the only significant press, the *Militant*, and apparatus, but with its veterans of the 1930s–1940s virtually all dead, resigned, retired, or expelled. Small groups split away in the 1980s, forming the Fourth International Tendency (George Breitman, Frank Lovell), which orients toward reforming the SWP; Socialist Action (Nat Weinstein, Jeff Mackler), which competes with the SWP; and Solidarity. The latter organization was formed through a fusion of former SWPers, and descendants of the Independent Socialists; it publishes the lively journal *Against the Current* and helps maintain the Teamsters for a Democratic Union and the monthly *Labor Notes*. Other groups have clung to existence if not real life.

American Trotskyism has, in sum, been a minority trend within an American Left that has been itself a minority movement. It has also had its moments of vitality and made some lasting contributions, both practical and theoretical. In the 1930s, when the CP dominated the Left, Trotskyism represented a lonely and persecuted (if sometimes internally self-punishing) voice of democratic conscience. Within the labor movement it has contributed to the defense of rank-and-file democracy. While generally a movement of organizers and activists rather than theoreticians and thinkers, it has made efforts to grapple with some of the problems facing the American labor movement. It has hindered itself, even while bolstering its own faith, by the self-imposed vanguardist concept of party organization. This concept, rigidly applied, has forced Trotskyism to fluctuate between permitting a democratic internal life, which encouraged fracturing, or suppressing internal democracy—mimicking the worst side of its Communist rivals—and becoming intellectually ossified. *See also*: Breitman, George; Cannon, James P.; Dobbs, Farrell; Dunayevskaya, Raya; Fourth International; Harrington, Michael; Howe, Irving; James, C. L. R.; Macdonald, Dwight; Minneapolis Truckers Strike; Oehler, Hugo; *Partisan Review*; Shachtman, Max; Socialist Workers Party; Workers Party

—*Tim Wohlforth*

REFERENCES

Cannon, James P. *The History of American Trotskyism*. New York: Pathfinder Press, 1944.

Deutscher, Isaac. *The Prophet Outcast*. New York: Oxford University Press, 1963.

Dobbs, Farrell. *Teamster Rebellion*. New York: Pathfinder Press, 1973.

Draper, Theodore. *American Communism and Soviet Russia*. New York: Viking, 1960.

Myers, Constance. *The Prophet's Army: Trotskyists in America, 1928–1941*. Westport: Greenwood Press, 1977.

Wald, Alan M. *The New York Intellectuals*. Chapel Hill: University of North Carolina Press, 1987.

Wohlforth, Tim. *The Struggle for Marxism in the United States*. New York: Workers League, 1971.

TUCKER, BENJAMIN R. (1854–1939)

An individualist anarchist, Tucker was a man of intellect rather than of action, focusing on the development of his ideas and on the publication of books and journals, especially the journal *Liberty* (1881–1908). Introduced to anarchism, labor reform, and free love by Ezra Heywood in Massachusetts, Tucker was particularly influenced by two individualist anarchists, Josiah Warren and William B. Greene. Tucker summarized his philosophy in this manner: "The Anarchists are simply unterrified Jeffersonian Democrats. They believe that 'the best government is that which governs least,' and that which governs least is no government at all." Besides publishing the writings of the leading individualist anarchists and many other radicals, *Liberty* was probably the earliest American magazine to publish Nietzsche and George Bernard Shaw. Besides *Liberty*, Tucker operated an ambitious book-publishing program, often printing books first serialized in the journal. He translated into English and published the principal works, including *What is Property?*, of Pierre Joseph Proudhon, the first writer in any language to describe himself as an anarchist. He also translated and published Bakunin's *God and the State*, Chernyshevsky's *What Is To Be Done?*, and Tolstoy's *The Kreutzer Sonata*. He published Max Stirner's *The Ego and His Own*, as well as works by Oscar Wilde, Herbert Spencer, Emile Zola, John Henry Mackay, and many others. After a disastrous fire in New York City in 1908 destroyed his warehouse and Unique Book Shop, Tucker left the United States for France, where he lived for the remainder of his life. *See also*: Anarchism, Free Love

—*Martin Blatt*

REFERENCES

Coughlin, Michael, Charles Hamilton, Mark Sullivan, eds. *Benjamin R. Tucker and the Champions of Liberty: A Centenary Anthology*. St. Paul: Coughlin Publications, 1987.

Liberty, 1881–1908, a hardcover reprint of the full run, with an introduction by Herbert Gutman. Westport: Greenwood, 1970.

McElroy, Wendy, ed. *Liberty, 1881–1908: A Comprehensive Index*. St. Paul: Coughlin Publications, 1982.

Martin, James J. *Men Against the State: The Expositors of Individualist Anarchism in America, 1827–1908*. Colorado Springs: Myles Publishers, 1970.

Reichert, William O. *Partisans of Freedom: A Study in American Anarchism*. Bowling Green: Bowling Green University Popular Press, 1970.

"UE": The United Electrical, Radio and Machine Workers of America

Chartered by the CIO in 1935–36, the UE, formed as a merger of three distinct union organizations, bringing together workers concentrated in General Electric, Westinghouse, RCA, Philco, and Delco manufacturing plants.

General Electric workers in particular had a rich history of union organization and contact with the Left. In Schenectady, where thousands worked, machinists had led GE operatives in 1918–19 strikes and political support for the municipal socialist government. There and elsewhere, industrial union ideas survived conservative times chiefly through members of radical, often foreign-language Left groups. By the mid-1930s, Al Coultard, a veteran socialist and skilled worker, headed the union in Lynn, Massachusetts. Julius Emspak, a toolmaker and college graduate, became the key strategist. Progressives and Communists cooperated widely in organizing drives on GE and Westinghouse.

A second branch of UE, machinist locals formerly in the TUUL's Metalworkers Industrial Union (affiliated with the Trade Union Unity League) and later in the machinists union, was led into the UE by radical James Matles. The third branch, a largely young, female work-force at radio and home-appliance shops, had little experience in unionism or radicalism. Temporarily an AFL "federal labor union," the radio workers later abandoned an inequitable arrangement within the largely male, craft-oriented International Brotherhood of Electrical Workers, and joined pragmatically with the emerging UE. James Carey, their leader, was a Catholic anticommunist. To assure unity, the merger made Carey president of the new union, Emspak the secretary-treasurer, and Matles the director of organization.

From the beginning, Left individuals and ethnic groups played a major role in UE, quickly one of the "big three" CIO unions. Italians and, especially, Hungarian workers lent their support to progressive leaders. Aggressive efforts to organize women, who made up a large portion of the electrical union, brought successful, militant unionism and an egalitarian approach toward more equalized wage structures (between men and women, but also between employed and unemployed union members), ideas hitherto unknown in mainstream American unionism.

Already by 1940, factional unrest stirred the union. Avowed anticommunists, led by charismatic Father Owen Rice, launched a public attack on the leadership of a Pittsburgh Westinghouse local. At the national level, union leadership was also contested. A. J. Fitzgerald, the young, newly elected president of Lynn GE Local 201, defeated James Carey for the presidency of the UE. Carey, who went on to become secretary-treasurer of the CIO, used his new position in assaulting alleged Communist domination. This dispute, and the formation of hostile "rank and file" and "progressive" caucuses in the same Pittsburgh plant, foreshadowed the eventual split in the union.

The end of the war brought the first national strike against GE and Westinghouse, in 1946. The union reached a peak membership of approximately 650,000. Successful in its industrial struggle, the UE unwittingly evoked a new strategy from GE in particular, the call for separation of union membership from its leaders. Throughout the late 1940s, major U.S. publications such as the *Saturday Evening Post, American Mercury*, and *Look* "exposed" the dangers of "red" leadership in East Pittsburgh, and the House Un-American Activities Committee held hearings on supposed Communist infiltration just as union elections approached. FBI informants "surfaced" to add more scandal.

The announced 1949 expulsion of the UE from the CIO, and the formation of a competing IUE under James Carey, partly accomplished the companies' goal. The UE had flatly refused to comply with the Taft-Hartley Act, until forced by law to do so, further refused to fire staff and officers due to political beliefs, and attacked the Cold War by supporting Henry Wallace's 1948 Progressive Party campaign. The IUE, with the support of public officials up to President Truman, appealed to nativism, religious fears, and defense-industry self-interest.

Withdrawing from the CIO before its expulsion, the UE gradually lost members until reaching a low of 100,000 in the mid-1960s, when raiding ceased, and 80,000 after multiple plant shutdowns in the 1970s–1980s. Nevertheless, the UE remained a moral beacon of the union movement, its *UE News* (long featuring cartoonist Fred Wright, and in recent years Gary Huck) the most progressive major union newspaper. The UE assumed new significance during the 1960s, as one of the few unions to support the antiwar movement; it prepared the way for a number of unions to oppose U.S. engagement in Central America in the 1980s. Today the UE continues to provide important leadership in many areas, and cooperates with the IUE among other internationals in coordinated bargaining. *See also*: Communist Party, Hungarian Americans, Taft-Hartley Loyalty Oath

—Frank Emspak

REFERENCES

Emspak, Frank. "The Break-Up of the Congress of Industrial Organizations (CIO), 1945–1950." Ph.D. diss., University of Wisconsin, 1972.

Matles, James, and James Higgins. *Them and Us: Struggle of a Rank-and-File Union*. Englewood Cliffs: Prentice Hall, 1974.

Schatz, Ronald W. *The Electrical Workers: A History of Labor at General Electric and Westinghouse, 1923–60*. Urbana: University of Illinois Press, 1983.

Ukrainian Americans

The Ukrainian immigrant Left, strongly but ambivalently linked to political events in Russia and Austria-Hungary, had a forceful if foreshortened role in the ethnic working-class community.

Like numerous other Eastern European groups, Ukrainians had never achieved political independence in their homeland. Not until the end of the nineteenth century did the population at large accept a common designation, easing out the "Ruthenian" cognomen given Ukrainian subjects of the Austro-Hungarian empire and retained for decades by American immigration records. Ethnocultural revival and the worsening condition of the peasantry prompted mass immigration to the United States, numbering (according to varying estimates) approximately 500,000 individuals.

Mostly of peasant origin, Ukrainian immigrants clustered in districts of anthracite coal mining, iron and steel production, meat processing, and auto making, with a minority female work-force in textiles and light manufacturing. Swept up in the drives for unionization of underpaid and dangerous work, Ukrainians took part in numerous violent labor incidents. Left organizations took shape against this background, along with religious institutions and fraternal or cultural associations. Socialists and, later, Communists organized with the dual purpose of emancipating labor and attaining the homeland's national independence.

Ukrainian socialists in the homeland, seeking to extend their support network, began to dispatch agitators and propaganda to America after the turn of the century. In the years following the Russian Revolution of 1905, they found a ready welcome in the *besida*, or public meeting, re-created in the new land. Squabbling over homeland politics and other issues, however, prevented Ukrainian socialists from establishing themselves on a national basis until the outbreak of war in Europe increased membership and consolidated socialist influence in the immigrant community. In 1915 immigrant Ukrainian socialists affiliated twenty locals, numbering approximately 1,000 members, with the Socialist Party. Shortly, this membership doubled, with Michigan emerging as a major center of activity. The Ukrainian Federation organ, *Robitnyk*, daily from 1917, took an extreme Left position within the Ukrainian community, urging antiwar militance and welcoming the Bolshevik Revolution unreservedly. This position, with events in Eastern Europe, fixed the lines of conflict among Ukrainian immigrants, with rival immigrant Social Democrats in the Ukrainian Workingmen's Association denouncing left-wing Ukrainian supporters in the association's organ, the *Narodna Volia* (People's will). The same revolutionary posture also ensured a government attack on *Robitnyk* with three raids culminating in the 1918 destruction of some 19,000 internal documents.

Robitnyk soon reemerged and led a strengthened organization of some 6,000–7,000 from the SP to the CP. Meanwhile, fraternal and educational activities blossomed, including "Ukrainian Workers Schools" and women's organizations, libraries, choirs, and temperance efforts. Just as Ukrainian Communists moved to consolidate their position, government repression struck once more, with destruction of the press, jailing and deportation of leading members.

As a result of these experiences, Ukrainian Communists learned a measure of caution. *Ukrainskyi Shchodennyi Visti* (The Ukrainian daily news), which began in 1920 and continues weekly to the present, never designated itself as a Communist publication. Although adhering to Moscow-aligned policies, the press concerned itself overwhelmingly with practical immigrant problems. Increasing this inward direction, the Ukrainian Left allied itself with the *Soiuz Ukrainskykh Robitnychykh Orhanizatsii*, or Union of Ukrainian Workers (SURO), founded in 1923, rather than the Ukrainian Federation of the Communist Party. As such, it operated freely within the immigrant community. With considerable success, the Ukrainian Left made the argument that a Communist homeland state was superior to no unified country. It also successfully urged more participation in the movement for industrial unions, and in a cultural effort to train the second generation in Ukrainian customs and language.

During the heyday of Communist influence, this practical approach to immigrant problems, and an undaunted devotion to the Ukrainian Soviet Republic, nearly overcame the distrust of immigrants generated by reports of widespread homeland starvation. Ukrainian immigrant Left activities within the community flourished in a host of unions including the furriers, Boot and Shoe Workers, United Mine Workers, and (notably in the New York area) restaurant workers' organizations. By the later 1930s, Communists became especially strident in their denunciations of right-wing Ukrainian nationalists, somewhat accurately depicted as allied with fascist movements. Left Ukrainians also constituted a vital section of the International Workers Order, whose Ukrainian members (along with SURO) in 1936 launched a highly successful "Ukrainian National Association" representing organization with some 20,000 radical and nonradical members against war and fascism.

Between the time of the Moscow Trials and the advent of World War II, SURO membership and activities plummeted. By 1940, SURO ceased to function, while the Left-supported "League of American Ukrainians" numbered scarcely more than 1,000 members. Unlike other Eastern European Communists, the Ukrainian Left failed to rebound significantly during the Second World War. The resurgence of right-wing nationalism among a new generation of notably nonproletarian immigrants, general mistrust of the Soviet Union, and, finally, Khrushchev's revelations at the Twentieth Soviet Congress in 1956 virtually eradicated Communist support. Remaining public activities of the Ukrainian-American Left tended to be largely cultural in nature. A rival immigrant movement, Ukrainian-American Social Democrats, centering organizationally in Scranton, Pennsylvania, and publishing *Narodnia Volya* (1911–present), has exerted considerably less influence, but survived on a narrower gauge, shifting increasingly toward the center of a rightward-turning immigrant public. *See also*: Communist Party

—*Maria Woroby*

REFERENCES

Kuropas, Myron. "The Making of the Ukrainian American, 1884–1939: A Study of Ethno-National Education." Ph.D. diss., University of Chicago, 1974.

Nastisivskyi, M. *Ukrainska Imigratsia v Spoluchenykh Derzhavakh*. New York: Union of Ukrainian Labor Organizations, 1934.

©1984 Michael Roman

Underground Comix

Called "underground" because of their links with the "underground newspapers" of the late 1960s, and spelled "comix" to distinguish them from mainstream comic books, these works have generally celebrated artistic freedom and individual expression, and have nurtured a spirit of rebellion. The comix have also been a vehicle for the occasional expression of socialist, libertarian, proto-Green, feminist, and anarchist sentiments. These have been conveyed through parody or satire, and sometimes promoted directly.

The generation of cartoonists that created underground comix had been deeply impressed in the early 1950s by the craft and irreverence of EC comic books such as *Vault of Horror* and *MAD*. Most of EC's titles were swept away in 1954, when a popular movement against comic book violence led to a collapse of the comic book industry. Many children received their earliest lesson in censorship when their parents burned or discarded their comic book collections. Some of the most prolific and accomplished underground cartoonists saw their work as a conscious attempt to revive the interrupted EC tradition.

The two most popular underground cartoonists have been Robert Crumb, creator of *Zap* and *Mr. Natural*, and Gilbert Shelton, creator of *The Fabulous Furry Freak Brothers*. Their work secured a niche for underground comix in the "head shops," which became the primary distribution outlets for the comix. Both Crumb and Shelton frequently introduced political themes into their topical and humorous comix. Since they were not bound by the self-censorship code of the mainstream comics, they were free to depict counterculture outlaws as heroes and police as villains, and they did so frequently.

In addition to Crumb and Shelton, several other underground cartoonists were openly political. Skip Williamson edited *Conspiracy Capers* (1969) to raise money for the legal defense of the Chicago Eight. Spain Rodriguez, a Marxist, created "Trashman: Agent of the Sixth International," an urban guerrilla, ironic hero. Greg Irons drew nuclear war and ecological disasters as contemporary horror comics, often for Ron Turner's *Slow Death* series

(1970–79). Guy Colwell, inspired by underground comix while jailed for draft resistance, created *Inner City Romance* (1972–79), which dramatized prison and ghetto life.

Appalled at the misogyny in many early underground comix, some women cartoonists responded by creating their own titles, such as *Wimmin's Comix* (1972–) and *Tits and Clits* (1973–). Women involved in the early underground comix period included Trina Robbins, who worked to resurrect the Fiction House rather than EC tradition, Sharon Rudahl, Joyce Farmer, and "Chin Lyvely."

In 1973, five years after Crumb's *Zap #1* and Shelton's *Feds n' Heads*, the underground comix market collapsed. A combination of rising printing costs, tightening obscenity laws, and a glut of inferior material on the racks all combined to break the comix's momentum. The comix publishers—mainly Ron Turner, Denis Kitchen, and Fred Todd—persevered, preventing the comix from disappearing as a passing fad.

The postcrash period of underground comix saw a rising interest in educational and political themes. In addition to the series mentioned above, these have included Harvey Pekar's autobiographical *American Splendor* comics about working-class life in Cleveland (1976–); Leonard Rifas's "EduComics," beginning with *All-Atomic Comics* (1976) about nuclear power's hazards; Larry Gonick's *Cartoon History of the Universe* (1978–); *Gay Comix* (1980–), founded by Howard Cruse; and *World War 3 Illustrated* (1980–), in which founding coeditors Peter Kuper and Seth Tobocman updated the underground aesthetic with an infusion of revolutionary, punk-edged graphics. Art Spiegelman's *RAW* (1980–), primarily a magazine dedicated to promoting cartooning as a form of art, serialized *Maus*, Spiegelman's highly personal cartoon history of Nazi oppression. Several of the above series were anthologized by commercial book publishers. The zenith of political underground comix to date has been *Anarchy Comics* (1978), a series edited by Jay Kinney and Paul Mavrides.

Underground comix kicked life back into what had become a timid and moribund medium. They remain a messy, thrilling demonstration of what freedom of the press looks like in practice. *See also*: New Left

—*Leonard Rifas*

REFERENCES

Davidson, Steef. *The Penguin Book of Political Comics*. Harmondsworth, England: Penguin, 1976, 1982.

Estren, Mark James. *A History of Underground Comics*. San Francisco: Straight Arrow Books, 1974.

Kennedy, Jay. *The Official Underground and Newave Comix Price Guide*. Cambridge: Boatner Norton Press, 1982.

UNDERGROUND PRESS

This phenomenon flourished in the United States between 1967 and 1973 as a proliferation of predominantly tabloid newspapers devoted to the local application of political and cultural movements that swept the nation during that period. Because the production of these newspapers was conducted from public offices, this press was in no way "underground" in the sense of the prerevolutionary press in the Soviet Union or the Jewish anti-Nazi press in occupied Eastern Europe before World War II. At its most millenarian, the underground press of the 1960s did attempt to anticipate postrevolutionary forms of journalism, but by and large "underground"

From *Helix* (Seattle, Washington), late 1960s

referred merely to the evolving youth culture, whose habits, ideas, art, and slang were, in 1967, still unexpressed in the mass media of the day. It was "underground" merely in the bohemian sense.

The underground press movement reflected the regional styles and concerns of U.S. youth whose experience came to be defined with increasing intensity in this period by a debilitating neocolonial war on the one hand and on the other a growing drug use with its accompanying interest in esoterica and the delegitimizing literatures of all world traditions. Both poles in this collective experience were characterized by a powerful sense of alienation from and rejection of U.S. social institutions, and each tendency found its definitions in its own cluster of underground newspapers. Most of the antiwar papers were to be found in smaller university cities in what came to be called the "archipelago" of campuses that had strong antiwar movements. Papers in the larger cities, meanwhile, whose readership was usually more diffuse, tended to emphasize cultural, personal, and drug-related questions with one degree or another of political news and agitation added in.

Of the latter, the most prominent was the *Los Angeles Free Press*, which formed the bridge between the bohemian origins of the underground press in the 1950s and the larger phenomenon of the 1960s. The *East Village Other, Chicago Seed, San Francisco Oracle*, and *Milwaukee Kaleidoscope* were examples of that development. Examples of the more "political" papers, i.e., those that arose more or less sui generis, without being attached to any organization of the Old or New Left, include the *Fifth Estate* (Detroit), *Berkeley Barb*, and *Connections* (Madison).

There were also the papers that were little more than idiosyncratic—in Boston, Mel Lyman's *Avatar* advanced a kind of Stalinist spiritualism—and there were personal literary productions like Cleveland poet d. a. levy's *Buddhist Third-Class Junk Mail Oracle*, and Robert Head and Darlene Fife's paper in New Orleans, *Nola Express*. Others tried to mediate between the political and cultural tendencies, including the Madison edition of *Kaleidoscope, Georgia Straight* (Vancouver), the *Great Speckled Bird* (Atlanta), and *Open City* (Los Angeles).

For most of its years the underground press survived on a combination of unpaid labor, chiliastic energy, psychotropic stimulants, and the certain sense that its journalists were recording the unfolding of a great social movement whose meaning could not be expressed by other journalists working in more established media. By the same token, the underground press collapsed from a combination of physical exhaustion, an ignorance of the skills required to survive over the long haul in the marketplace, and a sense that the historical moment had passed. As later amply documented, the FBI and local "Red Squads," which had harassed the underground press from its earliest days, hastened and made more complete its precipitous decline.

In fact, only a handful of publications retained their identity as "underground" rather than "alternative" newspapers after the famous convention of the Underground Press Syndicate in 1973 in Boulder at which this symbolic change in appelation was overwhelmingly endorsed by delegates. At that moment, the well capitalized, profitable, liberal weekly free tabloids that dominate most big-city markets today, the so-called alternative press, were realized in vitro.

It is perhaps too soon to evaluate what the underground press accomplished during the 1967–73 period, although it is clear by now that it was the expropriation of a generation under duress and inflamed with imaginative energy of a communications technology that had already been eclipsed by the electronic age. The techniques of small-scale photo-offset print reproduction were suddenly made accessible to virtually anyone. In other words, the underground press arose in part because by 1967 capital as such was no longer required to enter the medium. If it was already an outdated technology, the overriding sensibility of those who appropriated it most successfully for political and cultural ends belonged to the electronic media, whose images were brought to bear in a great variety of experiments in print and whose best results were to become the graphic clichés of the 1980s. *See also*: New Left

—*Dave Wagner*

REFERENCES

Gitlin, Todd. *The Whole World Is Watching*. Berkeley: University of California, 1980.

Lewis, Roger. *Outlaws of America, the Underground Press and its Context: Notes on a Cultural Revolution*. London: Pelican, 1972.

Peck, Abe. *Uncovering the Sixties: The Life & Times of the Underground Press*. New York: Pantheon, 1985.

Rips, Geoffrey. "The Campaign Against the Underground Press." In *The Campaign Against the Underground Press*, edited by Anne Janowitz and Nancy J. Peters. San Francisco: City Lights Books, 1981.

UNEMPLOYED COUNCILS: see *UNEMPLOYED MOVEMENTS*

Emblem of the Workers' Alliance of America, 1930s

UNEMPLOYED MOVEMENTS OF THE 1930s

"When you looked out on the scene of misery and desperation during the depression," A. J. Muste later recalled of the 1930s, "you saw that it was the radicals, the left-wingers, the people who had adopted some form of Marxian philosophy, who were *doing something* about the situation, who were banding people together for action, who were putting up a fight." Muste's recollections are borne out by the history of the unemployed movements of the Great Depression era; while many people talked about the problems of the jobless, it was radicals—particularly Communists, Socialists, and Musteites—who actually mobilized the out-of-work for social and political action.

The Communists were the first in the field. Even before the Wall Street crash, American Communists aggressively sought out the jobless on breadlines, outside factory gates, in relief offices, and in working-class neighborhoods. The coming of mass unemployment in 1930 accelerated their efforts and dramatically increased their ability to mobilize discontent into highly visible protests. On March 6, 1930, which the Communists dubbed International Unemployment Day, hundreds of thousands of jobless workers marched through the streets of the nation's major cities. The size of the demonstrations surprised even radicals and awakened many Americans to the existence of mass unemployment and large-scale unrest.

In the summer of 1930, the Communist Party brought this burgeoning unemployment movement together into a national organization, the Unemployed Councils of the USA. Despite the existence of a national office, the Unemployed Councils remained a largely local and decentralized movement rooted in particular local communities. The strength of these councils rested, in fact, on their ability to resolve specific grievances of concern to the jobless in those communities: to force concessions from local relief authorities or to block police from carrying out evictions. Struggles against evictions, for example, mounted as the Depression deepened in 1931 and 1932. When Chicago blacks received eviction notices, "it was not unusual," according to sociologists Horace Cayton and St. Clair Drake, "for a mother to shout to the children, 'Run quick and find the Reds!'"

The local, ad-hoc character of the Unemployed Councils was both a strength and a weakness. Jobless workers might mobilize around specific grievances or demonstrations but then drift away when the issue was resolved or they returned to work. CP members often dominated the formal membership of the councils and official Party policy sometimes conflicted with the localism and the "bread and butter" focus of the councils. Many jobless workers did not see the reason why councils should participate in demonstrations against the "imperialist war danger" or hold up placards calling for "Defense of the Chinese Soviets" or denouncing the Socialists and Musteites as "social fascists." Ultimately, the CP agreed. In late 1930, it shifted the Unemployed Councils toward more direct work among the unemployed and away from revolutionary sloganeering. Locally, councils would represent the jobless in their dealings with relief authorities; nationally, they would work for federal relief and unemployment insurance.

The primary national activities centered around petition drives for unemployment insurance and two national "hunger marches" in December of 1931 and 1932. Herbert Benjamin, an energetic Communist organizer, became the national leader in 1931 and remained with the unemployed movement for most of the decade. Despite Benjamin's able leadership, the councils remained a largely local movement, particularly before 1933.

While Communist organizers confronted the Depression with aggressive organizing of the jobless, Socialists initially responded with inertia. At the beginning of the 1930s, Socialist activity on behalf of the unemployed emphasized traditional Socialist propagandizing and disdained direct organization of the out of work. Only with the entrance into the Socialist Party of a newer generation of young (and often college-educated and native-born) members did the Socialists begin to abandon their passive approach to the unemployed question.

Many of these young, activist Socialists also belonged to the League for Industrial Democracy (LID), an SP offshoot. Under LID leadership, the Chicago Workers Committee on Unemployment organized 25,000 jobless in sixty locals by mid-1932. Inspired by this successful model, Baltimore LID members built the People's Unemployment League, which was surprisingly successful at interracial organizing given its border state location.

The LID's success as well as the growing power of younger activists within the SP, the fear of Communist domination of the unemployed, and the deteriorating economic situation finally persuaded the SP's national executive committee to endorse direct organization of the jobless in February 1932. Although the SP's national office provided some guidance to party branches interested in organizing the jobless, the success or failure of most efforts (as was true among the Unemployed Councils) rested largely on local initiative. In 1935, however, Socialist activists, under the leadership of David Lasser, launched a national organization of the unemployed—the Workers Alliance of America.

The LID and Socialist unemployed groups used many of the same techniques as the Communist unemployed councils: acting as grievance representatives at relief stations, fighting evictions, and holding demonstrations and parades to urge higher relief appropriations. In general, however, Socialists tended to use confrontations and disruptions less than Communists. They often tried to intercede with relief authorities to get money for a family threatened with eviction rather than trying to block it bodily. This moderation gave the Socialist groups a certain respectability that the Communists lacked. "We were not a pariah organization," one leader of the Baltimore People's Unemployment League recalled.

The third major radical movement of the unemployed, which was led by the followers of A. J. Muste, differed in organizing methods and constituency from the Communist and Socialist groups. The Musteites were mostly graduates of Brookwood Labor College, where Muste presided in the 1920s, and adherents of the Conference on Progressive Labor Action, which aspired to be an independent working-class movement competitive with both the AFL and the traditional left-wing political parties. Carl Branin, a Musteite and a Seattle labor editor, was one of the founders of the Seattle Unemployed Citizens League. The UCL began as a "self-help" cooperative, whose members obtained food and fuel through barter and exchange of labor. This "Republic of the Penniless" was typical of the more than 330 self-help groups (with more than 300,000 members) that sprung up among the unemployed, particularly during the worst years of the Depression. It was more unusual in the overtly political turn that it took after self help proved to be only a very partial solution to the problems of the jobless. It took control of the city's relief apparatus, successfully backed candidates for mayor and county commissioner, blocked evictions, and illegally restored terminated electric and gas services.

The success of the UCL inspired imitation among Musteites in other parts of the country. They began building groups around self help and then pushing them toward political militancy. With remarkable success, they mobilized the unemployed in the small industrial and mining towns of Ohio, the steel mills of Pittsburgh, the coalfields of eastern Pennsylvania and West Virginia, and the textile mills of North Carolina. The acceptance that the Musteites won outside the primary centers of American radicalism owed, in part, to what they called their "American approach"—their identification of the Unemployed Leagues (as their groups came to be known) with patriotic symbols and slogans. It equally owed to their explicit focus on the immediate and concrete needs of the jobless and their willingness to work with self-help organizations, which other radicals disdained as "collective picking in garbage cans."

But this willingness to embrace self help and patriotism did not always lead the Unemployed Leagues to an outcome desired by the Musteites. Some groups remained focused solely on their crop picking, and, in the disdainful words of onetime Musteite Louis Budenz, "Potatoes became the opium of the people." At other times, the Musteites' patriotism and seeming conservatism was taken more seriously than they had perhaps intended. At the first national convention of the Leagues in Columbus, Ohio, on July 4, 1933, the Musteites faced a revolt from a "Stars and Stripes" faction, which was unhappy over the mingling of black and white delegates as well as the failure to open the convention with a prayer and the singing of the National Anthem.

The 1933 national convention represented the high point of the Unemployed Leagues, which gradually declined over the next few years because of the changing political climate (particularly the emergence of the New Deal) and the shifting of the interests and energies of the Musteites away from the organizing of the unemployed as they created first the American Workers Party and then (in alliance with the Trotskyists) the Workers Party. These shifts also embroiled the Musteites in a crippling factionalism and sectarianism that alienated many rank-and-file members of the Unemployed Leagues. Nevertheless, the leagues remained an active force in agitating for the needs and rights of the jobless in particular localities. Probably their most notable success came in the 1934 Toledo Auto-Lite strike, where the Lucas County Unemployed Leagues helped win the strike through mass picketing.

The beginning of the New Deal in 1933 and particularly the inauguration of the Works Progress Administration (WPA) in 1935 transformed the climate in which the radical unemployed movements operated. Many jobless workers began to see the federal government (personified by the charismatic figure of Franklin Roosevelt) as their friend and benefactor. But the federal government also became the focus of jobless protests, since it was now the primary source of relief funds and jobs. At the same time that New Deal liberalism and reformism eroded some of the constituency for the unemployed movement, changes within the Left finally made it possible for the three different unemployed groups to unite in a single organization. The rise of fascism in Europe and the emergence of the Popular Front had made Communists much more willing—indeed eager—to unite with the non-Communist left. At the same time, Trotskyists within the leadership of the WP, which now subsumed the Musteite movement, sought entrance into the SP in line with worldwide Trotskyist policy. Consequently, in April 1936 the Unemployed Leagues and the Unemployed Councils merged with the Workers Alliance, which was retained as the name of the new national group.

After 1936, the Workers Alliance focused much of its attention on Washington, where it became a relatively effective lobbying organization for national relief and unemployment insurance measures. Politically, it operated as a kind of left-wing of New Deal liberalism and it developed a close relationship with New Deal relief officials. On the local level, the Workers Alliance served largely as a bargaining agent for relief recipients and WPA workers. Large demonstrations and eviction protests occasionally flared up, but more often the alliance quietly carried out its trade union–like functions. The alliance faded with the coming of the war and the end of mass unemployment.

The legacy of the unemployed movement lies partially in the ways that it concretely improved the lot of the jobless: resolving individual relief grievances, winning higher levels of local relief, establishing more equitable and less degrading relief practices, stopping evictions, fighting WPA cuts, limiting the exploitation of WPA workers. More generally, it helped to refute the still prevalent notion that the jobless were "responsible" for their problems and to establish governmental responsibility for relief and unemployment insurance. Perhaps most important, the unemployed movement raised the political and social consciousness of the thousands of workers who passed through its ranks and learned the power of organization as a political and economic weapon. Veterans of the unemployed movement went on to play crucial roles in other political and social struggles, particularly the campaign for industrial unionism in the late 1930s and early 1940s. Although the unemployed movement of the Depression era never attracted more than a minority of the jobless to its banners, it was the most powerful such movement in U.S. history. It serves, moreover, as a significant example of a locally based, grass-roots movement under radical leadership that worked creatively and militantly to meet the concrete, immediate needs of the unemployed. *See also*: Communist Party; League for Industrial Democracy; Muste, A. J.; Socialist Party

—*Roy Rosenzweig*

REFERENCES

Leab, Daniel J. "'United We Eat': The Creation and Organization of the Unemployed Councils in 1930." *Labor History* 8 (Fall 1967).

Piven, Frances Fox, and Richard A. Cloward. *Poor People's Movements*. New York: Pantheon, 1977.

Rosenzweig, Roy. "Organizing the Unemployed: The Early Years of the Great Depression, 1929–1933." *Radical America* 10 (July–August, 1976).

———. "Radicals and the Jobless: The Musteites and the Unemployed Leagues, 1932–1936." *Labor History* 16 (Winter 1975).

———. "'Socialism in Our Time': The Socialist Party and the Unemployed, 1932–1936." *Labor History* 20 (Fall 1979).

UNION OF PUBLIC WORKERS:

see PUBLIC SERVICE UNIONS

UNION OF RUSSIAN WORKERS:

see RUSSIAN AMERICANS

UNION REFORM/LABOR SUPPORT

The aim of varied radicals since the inception of the modern Left—but defined in a bewildering and contradictory number of ways—union reform took on new salience in the post-1960 era of heightened labor bureaucracy and new youthful radical energies. For many among a New Left generation after the decline of the student movement, union reform became a riveting cause; for their successor generations, labor offered one of the few arenas for youthful idealism and an often harsh introduction into the real world.

By 1959, ten years of congressional investigation into labor racketeering brought the Labor-Management Reporting and Disclosure Act. Scattered union reformers faced overwhelming official opposition, but a network symptomized in the publication *Union Democracy in Action* began to cohere. While the New Left proper conducted its activities on campus, often contemptuous of labor traditions, small groups of individual younger radicals joined others in mounting challenges among various unions. In 1970 Jock Yablonsky's leadership of the Miners for Democracy, and his murder at the hands of henchmen for United Mine Workers leaders, dramatized the changing situation: union democracy had become a life-and-death issue.

Here, the New Left diaspora found amenable currents for significant reform campaigns. Some groups, tied to Marxist-Leninist organizations of older or newer vintage, sought to "colonize" and recruit followers, with little apparent effect. Others published independent local newspapers, sometimes aided by established union reformers, around which they built popular if generally short-lived alliances. Groups of both types tended to dissipate after a few years, but individuals within them, now disaffiliated from any particular radical entity, remained vocal and credible advocates from within union ranks. *Labor Notes*, a Detroit monthly whose lineal predecessors led mostly back to the 1940s Workers Party, became a forum and loose organizational center for shared labor-reform research and information. Teamsters for a Democratic Union, closely allied with *Labor Notes*, proved the most popular and the most durable of the nationally organized union caucuses. The United Steelworkers reform campaign led by Edward Sadlowski, although short-lived, galvanized much of this energy.

By the later 1970s, the Community-Labor Energy Coalition, pieced together by Democratic Socialists of America (DSA) labor figures such as IAM president William Winpisinger among others, sought to respond to the "energy crisis" by spawning a proliferation of local labor-consumer groups. In many cities, now-aging and long disaffiliated former New Leftists around labor (not infrequently business agents for white-collar, service, and health care trades) helped lead the creation of new labor-support entities. Continuing deindustrialization actually heightened assorted efforts at community coalitions, as around Pittsburgh and Youngstown, Ohio. Of local groups with staying power, the *Mill Hunk Herald* gathering and the Mon Valley coalition of Pittsburgh-area activists were outstanding, especially in the democratic production of their occasional magazine and in their good-spirited cultural experimentations in blue-collar life generally. In the long run, the lessening of strikes and the increased sense of job insecurity tended to dampen such coalitions, but not before the Solidarity Day March in Washington, in 1982, had rallied a half-million union workers and their friends against Reaganomics.

Radicals now renewed a strategy familiar to the pre-1920 socialist movements of passing resolutions—this time against U.S. military involvement in Latin America and especially against AFL-CIO entanglement in that effort. Several major unions (such as the International Association of Machinists, Screen Actors Guild, Amalgamated Clothing and Textile Workers Union, and American Federation of Government Employees) recorded themselves as being in opposition to the AFL-CIO leadership on such questions. A landmark if only partial victory—support suspended for U.S. policy on Nicaragua in 1987—marked how far labor had come since the nearly solid AFL-CIO official support of the Vietnam engagement less than twenty years earlier. Ironically, radical reformers often found themselves at odds ideologically with erstwhile socialists become Cold War changelings: Max Shachtman until his death in 1972, and teachers' leader Albert Shanker since, figures whose malign foreign policy influence carried even to the ranks of the ostensibly non- (or anti-) political union reformers.

Three struggles marked particular high points of intervention during the later 1980s. The P-9 meat-cutters of Austin, Minnesota, launched an unprecedented network of activists into action across all geographic, demographic, and racial lines. The Watsonville, California, strike of frozen-food workers, mainly Mexican-American women, first against the company and briefly against the Teamster local itself, drew upon Left support groups with traditions stretching back to the 1930s and continuous through the Teamsters for a Democratic Union. Los Angeles GM-Van Nuys, the only remaining auto plant in the area, had been the site of Maoist and Communist-oriented activists' efforts in the 1970s, so that the community effort to keep the plant open and the work force mobilized against worsening conditions was played out in an often politicized framework. (The presence of former New Left community organizer Eric Mann as industrial activist-writer added an especially public voice to the latter.) Taken together, these three strikes demonstrated the overwhelming indifference of top labor leadership to the desperate quality of the defensive battle, and on the other side, the possibilities of Left-aided solidarity to draw the line successfully.

From the early 1970s to the late 1980s, something had changed fundamentally in radicals' union reform efforts. Several generations of younger activists had come to engage in styles of struggle that strongly resembled other reform movements of the period: they made no sustained effort to interject any political line; and they stayed generally close to the issues of corruption, democracy, and effective unionism, sometimes linked to ending the corrupt links AFL-CIO officialdom had made with the CIA foreign policy apparatus, and to ending labor's participation in destructive environmental acts. The older utopian expressions of a belief in a future "workers' state" or "socialism" had gone by the board, replaced for the moment by the seemingly no less utopian desires to halt the erosion of manufacturing flight and the steady deterioration of working people's conditions. *See also*: International Brotherhood of Teamsters

—*Paul Buhle*

REFERENCES

Bardacke, Frank. "Watsonville: A Mexican Community on Strike." In *The Year Left, 3: Reshaping the U.S. Left, Popular Struggles in the 1980s*, edited by Mike Davis and Michael Sprinker. London: Verso, 1988.

Mann, Eric. *Taking On General Motors: A Case Study of the UAW Campaign to Keep GM Van Nuys Open*. Los Angeles: UCLA Institute of Industrial Relations, 1988.

Moody, Kim. *An Injury to All: The Decline of U.S. Labor*. London: Verso, 1988.

Union-Sponsored Radical Films

Immediately following World War II, radicals attempted to revive the ambience of the New Deal coalition by making films with and for industrial unions. One of the most important collectives was Union Films, which produced a series of films in cooperation with the United Electrical, Radio, and Machine Workers of America (UE) for distribution throughout the CIO. Carl Marzani, who had joined the Communist Party shortly after fighting in the Spanish Civil War and had been a CP section organizer until his resignation from the Party in 1942, was the major figure in Union Films. His goal was to create a network of union-hall film centers, a library of working-class films, a book club, and a slick labor magazine on the model of *Life*.

The working-class cultural offensive envisioned by Marzani was to be truncated by Cold War politics, but between 1946 and 1950 Union Films produced seven black-and-white documentaries: *Deadline for Action* (1946, 40 min.), *The Great Swindle* (1949, 22 min.), *Industry's Disinherited* (1949, 21 min.), *Our Union* (1949, 22 min.), *Men Against Money* (1949, 25 min.), *The Fishermen* (1950, 20 min.), and *Solidarity* (1950, 11 min.). Marzani scripted/directed most of these, including *Deadline* and *Swindle*. *Deadline* was the first American film to place major responsibility for the Cold War on the United States, while *Swindle* explained the relationship between wages, prices, profits, and monopoly control of key sectors of the American economy. One animated sequence in *Swindle* depicted capitalism as a world-devouring octopus, and as in all Union Film productions the representatives of capital were treated in a rude and negative manner reminiscent of images popularized by the Industrial Workers of the World. *Our Union* and *Solidarity* attacked the Taft-Hartley Act, *Men* dealt with a UE strike in Lynn, Massachusetts, *Industry's Disinherited* probed the problems of aging workers, and *The Fishermen* showed how antitrust laws were used to attack the International Fishermen's Union.

Deadline for Action won the approval of Philip Murray and Alex Kroll of the CIO and got a tremendous sendoff in *CIO News*. Thereafter, as the CIO began to swing to the right, most of the films were shown only by expelled left-wing unions. Marzani was jailed for political activity for approximately a year beginning in March 1949. During his absence, the city of New York harassed Union Films with zoning violation fines and other restrictions. Under such pressures and the accelerating assault upon the UE itself, Union Films folded.

After emerging from prison, Marzani persisted in trying to implement his larger vision.

He worked on publications for the UE and was editor of *UE Steward*, a leadership magazine, until 1954. At that time he established the Liberty Book Club with Angus Cameron, a radical editor previously employed by major publishers. One of the first books released was *Labor's Untold Story*, published for the UE and reflecting its views. The Liberty Book Club offered members eight books for a ten-dollar yearly membership. The venture's name eventually changed to Cameron Associates and when Cameron left became Marzani and Munsell. The various imprints produced the first book on the Rosenberg case, the first exposé of FBI informers, and one of the first books on armed black resistance in the civil rights movement. The ventures also published novels and other writing by Ring Lardner, Jr., Alvah Bessie, Abe Polonsky, and Albert Maltz. Five or more pamphlets a year were published and addressed issues such as the Bay of Pigs, the war in Vietnam, and the Warren Commission Report. Publishing activities ended in 1969 when a fire destroyed the Marzani and Munsell offices, which housed all the company's books, mailing lists, and records. The publishers had not been able to secure insurance.

A revival of the filmmaking tradition Marzani hoped to bring to a mass audience occurred in the early 1950s when *Salt of the Earth* was filmed with the cooperation of the International Union of Mine, Mill and Smelter Workers. Based on a 1951–52 strike by predominantly Mexican-American zinc miners in Silver City, New Mexico, the film used the actual strikers for virtually every leading role. The major exception was Rosaura Revolutas, a Mexican film star who played the female lead. Professional actors such as Will Geer played supporting roles depicting management and the police. The filmmakers—director Herbert Biberman, writer Michael Wilson, producer Paul Jarrico, and less well known technicians—were on the Hollywood blacklist. They have since stated that *Salt of the Earth* was the kind of film they would have made in Hollywood, had they been allowed to express their political views.

No American film has ever faced the harassment endured by *Salt of the Earth*. Vigilante groups shot into the cars of the filmmakers and beat up some of the crew, and Revolutas was intimidated by immigration officials, who ultimately deported her as an illegal alien before the film was completed. Congressman Don Jackson (California) and Hearst columnist Victor Riesel charged the film was just a cover so that "Communists" could get near the atomic testing grounds at Los Alamos. Various film processors and technicians refused to work on the film, and when the film was finally ready for distribution, numerous groups and individuals emerged to accuse anyone who wished to see or screen the film of being a Communist or a Communist dupe. Roy Brewer, the anticommunist head of the AFL Hollywood Film Council, pledged that projectionists and other professionals who were members of his union would not show the film and would do anything in their power to keep it off the screen. The American Legion undertook a campaign that was directly responsible for the film being kept out of several locations. Pickets and FBI agents were present at the few sites where the film got a showing.

Given such an environment it is amazing that the film was completed and that it managed to get sporadic screenings in ten cities. The net result of the persecution, of course, was that the film was a financial loss and the chance for further radical feature filmmaking had been killed in the cradle. The film, however, was to prove remarkably viable. Sixteen-millimeter prints were made and *Salt of the Earth* began to acquire legendary stature. In the late 1960s the New Left filmmakers claimed *Salt* as part of their patrimony and activists began to screen it. During the 1970s, the film moved more solidly into the educational film market, being shown in filmmaking classes, history classes, and contexts in which the blacklist period was being examined. Books began to appear on how the film was made and in 1984 the film *A Crime to Fit the Punishment* examined the making, suppression, and impact of *Salt of the Earth*. By decade's end, the film was recognized as one of the finest radical films ever made in the United States and a film honored by nonpolitical as well as political critics.

The basis of *Salt of the Earth*'s fame lies exactly in its political sensibilities. The most obvious level of the film is that of the conflict between the Mine-Mill trade unionists and a sheriff totally under the control of the company. Naive critics thought the film simplistic in its portrayals. If anything, the film was relatively mild in depicting a decades-old struggle in which company lawlessness was the rule. What stands out even more strongly than the class struggles are related themes of sexual and ethnic repression. The striking miners are forced to deal with their own oppression of their wives in order to win the strike, and the strike leader is the worst culprit. This intraclass struggle along a sexual dynamic would have considerable poignancy for post-1960s radicals facing sexism as a major political issue. That the miners were mainly Mexican Americans underscored a basic reality about the West not visible in most Hollywood films. Another layer of ethnic reality is provided by the circumstance that both the union organizer who counsels the miners and the sheriff who leads the fight against them are Anglos.

The filmmakers have written that they had to reshape their original concept for a labor film and had to rewrite many scenes in order to satisfy the objectives of the miners with whom they were working. Even with their anemic budget and the constant harassment, the filmmakers were able to bring sophisticated cinematic techniques to a story taken directly from life and filmed on real-life scenes of battle. In that sense *Salt of the Earth* realized to a large degree the ambition voiced by radicals since at least the time of the Film and Photo League to make films for, by, and with the working class.

The financial and political debacle that immediately accompanied the release of *Salt of the Earth* discouraged any further union ventures into radical filmmaking. A full ten years would pass before there was any effort in the direction indicated by the UE and Mine-Mill projects. This new initiative, *The Inheritance* (1964), was undertaken by the Amalgamated Clothing Workers on the occasion of the union's fiftieth anniversary. Composed mainly of old newsreels and still photos, *The Inheritance* traces the history of labor from 1900 through to the Rev. Martin Luther King, Jr.'s March on Washington, with the history of the Amalgamated as a unifying core. The film's tone is set by its opening lines: "Today is born of yesterday. And there is no birth without pain." Class conflict is underlined by scenes of bloody encounters between police and workers. These include newsreel segments showing the on-camera murder of Communist pickets in a steel strike and the carnage at the Memorial Day Massacre in Chicago. The film also includes clips of Norman Thomas and other leftists, although they are not usually identified by name. Capitalist values are ridiculed by clever and often humorous editing. Partly due to the need to reach the increasing number of black and Hispanic workers in the industry the Amalgamated represents, racism is addressed in no uncertain terms. The film is far more timid ideologically. The socialist aspects of the Amalgamated's history are downplayed and there is no rendering of Sidney Hillman's complex relationship with the CP, the Socialist Party, and the American Labor Party.

The power of *The Inheritance* derives from its graphic and unequivocal support of rank-and-file militancy and its dramatic assertion that for the immigrant worker, the United States was "half-nightmare/half-dream." Original music for the film was created by George Kleinsinger and contains a chorus repeated several times: "Freedom doesn't come like a bird on a wing./Doesn't come like the summer's rain./Freedom, freedom is a hard won thing and/Every generation has to win it again." Other labor oriented songs feature Pete Seeger, Judy Collins, Tom Paxton, the Almanac Singers, and other musicians associated with left-wing causes. The film has a narration by Hollywood actor Robert Ryan written by Millard Lampell, who was on the Hollywood blacklist. Lampell had been writing scripts under assumed names and had had television scripts produced through the kind of process satirized in Woody Allen's *The Front*. His official rehabilitation came in 1965, when he won an Emmy Award for the television drama *Eagle in a Cage*.

Despite the film's radical subtext and its use of blacklisted talent, *The Inheritance* received good reviews in the conventional press. Finding wide acceptance among labor educators as well, the film was soon established as a classic of its kind. *The Inheritance* also won cinematic awards, including First Prize at the prestigious Mannheim Festival in Germany. The Amalgamated, however, did not undertake new projects of like nature and no other union came forward to follow its lead. Unions generally settled for films that lauded their own organization or that could be used for technical training.

When a new generation of radical filmmakers began to emerge in the 1970s, labor unions were not prepared to risk their respectability through direct sponsorship. They increasingly thought it safer economically and politically simply to give grants to filmmakers who had raised funds from other sources as well. The most noteworthy undertaking of this sort was funding by the United Mine Workers toward the costs of *Harlan County-USA* (1976), a film that won an Academy Award in the category of Feature Documentary and had a modest theatrical release. The film's radicalism was more in its situational aspects and implied rather than ideological and overt. Trade unions were also willing to use some specifically radical films such as *Union Maids* (1976), *With Babies and Banners* (1978), and *The Wobblies* (1981) in educational programs, but most remained reluctant to show or financially contribute to films in which Communists were openly depicted in a positive manner. *See also*: Hollywood Blacklist, Independent Radical Films—1960s–1980s, Radical Filmmaking—1930s

—*Dan Georgakas*

REFERENCES

Biberman, Herbert. *Salt of the Earth: The Story of a Film*. New York: Zoetrope-Beacon Press, 1987.

The Cinema Guild Film and Video Catalog, 1988. Notes on Union Films handled by Cinema Guild.

Crowdus, Gary, and Lenny Rubenstein. "Union Films—An Interview with Carl Marzani." *Cineaste* 7, no. 2 (1976).

Miller, Tom. "Salt of the Earth Revisited." *Cineaste* 13, no. 3 (1984).

Navitsky, Victor. *Naming Names*. New York: Viking Press, 1980.

Salt of the Earth. New York: Feminist Press, 1978.

Union Square, New York

During the first four decades of the twentieth century, New York's Union Square district became both a center and a symbol of American radicalism. Bounded at the north and south by Seventeenth and Fourteenth streets, to the east and west by Broadway and Fourth Avenue, the neighborhood offered low rents, inexpensive commerce (street vendors and later Klein's and Ohrbach's discount stores), and entertainment (turn-of-the-century nickelodeons, followed by burlesques and taxi-dance halls), which attracted the immigrant population from the Lower East Side along with artists and writers from Greenwich Village—many of whom contributed to the radical character of the neighborhood by making the working or protesting crowds assembled there the subject of writings and paintings.

A fashionable district in the nineteenth century—home of the original Brentano's bookstore, Tiffany's jewelry store, and the first Academy of Music—the neighborhood changed dramatically as expensive commerce and entertainment moved north. From 1900 to approximately 1920, former residences became sweatshops for the garment industry. The tree-lined Union Square Park, once a private retreat for the well-to-do, served as a contested gathering place and protest center for anarchists, socialists, and members of the Industrial Workers of the World. These groups rallied at annual May Day events and frequent Saturday afternoon meetings. Around Union Square, IWW members gained recruits from among the unemployed and itinerant workers who walked north by day from the Bowery's cheap lodgings to congregate in the park. In an ongoing struggle to use the streets and the park to organize for free speech, they often fought against repressive police measures that produced violent responses. At the height of the 1914–15 economic crisis, the New York press accused the IWW of inciting "the worst elements of the city to plunder" and praised the police, who routinely broke up meetings by clubbing the participants. Only when the Free Speech League denounced police terror did city authorities finally grant the IWW permission to use Union Square for its meetings.

Following a period of relative calm after World War I, with the increasingly tense national and international political climate of the late 1920s, protesters renewed May Day activities, unemployment demonstrations, and protests against police brutality. Conflict resulting from the August 1927 execution of Sacco and Vanzetti began when police injured several of the 5,000 sympathizers who had gathered in the park for an all-night vigil. In 1929, 5,000 Communists staged the first May Day rally in Union Square since 1916. Eighteen days later, when 300 Communist Party members displayed a sign from the windows of the CP headquarters reading "Down with Walker's Police Brutality," police entered the building without a warrant, arresting twenty-seven demonstrators, including nine children. The largest (35,000) and most violent unemployment demonstration erupted on March 30, 1930. By the end of the day, 100 were injured and news accounts across the political spectrum condemned the zealousness with which plainclothes police "pummeled" the victims with their nightsticks.

Such violence galvanized the public against police interference, and city officials once again guaranteed the right to free assembly in Union Square. Though May Day rallies grew substantially in numbers throughout the Depression, they remained peaceful, and continued to reflect the changing political climate. The year 1935 was the last in which Socialists and Communists marched in separate parades; 1936 brought a united demonstration against the threat of fascism—the "quietest parade in years," leading police to set aside their nightsticks. The 1937 parade stressed aid to Spain as its theme.

During the years of greatest political agitation in the early 1930s, many radical organizations achieved high visibility around Union Square. From 1928 until 1930 the block of buildings from 24 to 30 Union Square East housed the offices of the CP, the *Daily Worker*, the Polish, Jewish, and Hungarian dailies; the Workers' Bookstore and School; the Young Communist League of America; and the Cooperative Cafeteria, where Communist organizers gathered. The *New Masses* was located across the square at 39 Union Square West, while the John Reed Club made frequent moves throughout the decade; from 65 West Fifteenth Street in the early 1930s to 131 West Fourteenth Street by the mid-1930s. The Debs auditorium, site of frequent Socialist meetings, lay just off the square at 5 East Fourteenth Street.

Regular Union Square protests, initiated by numerous radical organizations, assumed many forms—from huge May Day celebrations to labor pickets of stores failing to unionize, to talks by lonely soapbox orators whose right to free speech made chroniclers equate Union Square with London's Hyde Park. May Day parades at Union Square peaked in the 1930s, although they have continued sporadically with smaller attendance. While leftist artists like William Gropper drew Union Square rallies in cartoons for the *New Masses*, most mainstream artists avoided depicting protests. Members of the Fourteenth Street School of artists—Kenneth Miller, Reginald Marsh, Isabel Bishop, and Raphael Soyer—painted neighborhood shopping crowds, working women, and unemployed men in ways that expressed a sympathetic awareness of lower-class life. But as leftist artist Philip Evergood pointed out, Marsh painted "classical" bums in acceptable picturesque scenes, as opposed to Evergood's own bands of angry unemployed men. Albert Halper's 1933 Literary Guild novel *Union Square* drew criticism from leftist writers for failing to outline a program for social change.

Even as Union Square gained acceptance as a center for radicalism, municipal leaders and local store owners, concerned about the effects of demonstrations on business, sponsored patriotic events and organizations designed to rid Union Square of its Communist reputation and "cleanse its atmosphere." The Veterans of Foreign Wars were permitted to hold annual May Day activities immediately after Communist rallies. In April 1932, local businesses staged an elaborate Union Square Centennial featuring a civic pageant with colonial costumes and an Americanization meeting. In his letter of support for the event, President Herbert Hoover praised the neighborhood as a center of "industry, finance, and commerce." Noticeably absent was any mention of the park as a center of free speech, assembly, and the fight for social betterment, which decades of radical voices had struggled to achieve. *See also*: Communist Party, Lower East Side, May Day

—Ellen Wiley Todd

REFERENCES

Union Square/Fourteenth Street Archives. Museum of the City of New York.

Photographic Views of New York. The New York Public Library. Microfiche Collection.

Todd, Ellen Wiley. "Gender, Occupation, and Class in Paintings by the Fourteenth Street School, 1925–1940." Ph.D. diss., Stanford University, 1987.

The WPA Guide to New York City: The Federal Writers' Project Guide to 1930s New York. New York: Pantheon Books, 1939, 1982.

UNITED AUTOMOBILE WORKERS

Until the period of the Cold War, the history of autoworkers and their unions was interwoven with the history of the American Left. Even though Socialists, Communists, members of the Industrial Workers of the World, and other radicals constituted only a tiny minority of autoworkers at any time, the Left exercised considerable influence in the industry and was involved in nearly every organizing and strike effort in the preunion period and in many of the key struggles in the early years of the United Automobile Workers Union (UAW).

Though the AFL chartered the International Union of Carriage and Wagon Workers in 1891, it never seriously attempted to organize the autoworkers and even expelled the Union of Carriage and Wagon Workers in 1918 after it added "automobile" to its name and began organizing autoworkers on an industrial basis. The seeds of unionism in the auto industry were sown first by Wobblies, Socialists, and Communists. The IWW, which had several hundred Detroit autoworkers as members before World War I, helped lead the first organized strike by autoworkers, a week-

Cover by Williams Sanderson

long walkout by 6,000 Studebaker workers in 1913 that may have contributed to Ford's decision to initiate the "five-dollar day."

After WW I, William Logan and other socialists led the Carriage, Wagon, and Automobile Workers Union. Largely due to the labor shortage after the war, the Auto Workers Union briefly enjoyed a membership of 40,000 and led several strikes in body shops. The Auto Workers Union remained the only union in the industry through the early 1930s, and though its membership never exceeded 3,000, it laid the groundwork for the successful organization of the industry by introducing the idea of industrial unionism to thousands of workers, including many of those who later organized the UAW.

In 1926 Communist autoworkers won the leadership of the Auto Workers Union, and they eventually affiliated the union with the Trade Union Unity League (TUUL). Under the leadership of Communists Phil Raymond and William Goetz, the union held shop-gate meetings and circulated a regular newspaper that exposed conditions in the plants, and promoted the idea of industrial unionism and the need to unite all workers regardless of skill, race, age, or sex. The union also aided scores of spontaneous strikes, including the most important strike in the pre-UAW period—the strike of some 12,000 Briggs Manufacturing workers against wage cuts in early 1933.

In the first years of the Depression, the campaigns for relief and against evictions of the Communist-initiated Unemployed Councils gave many autoworkers their first sense of organization and collective struggle. On March 6, 1930, a Communist-sponsored unemployment demonstration brought more than 50,000 people into the streets of Detroit and thousands into the streets of such other auto centers as Toledo, Flint, and Pontiac. On March 7, 1932, in what became known as the Ford Massacre, Ford private guards and police fired upon a Communist-led Hunger March outside the Ford plant and killed four workers and wounded fifty others.

The Communists and their progressive allies made their most important contribution to the creation of the UAW in the years between 1933 and 1941. After the passage of the National Industrial Recovery Act and the AFL's start of an organizing drive in the auto industry in 1933, the Communists and their allies in Detroit, Cleveland, and Toledo organized the AFL's most successful federal labor unions, and spearheaded a rank-and-file movement among autoworkers that eventually forced the AFL to charter the UAW in 1935. The leader of the rank-and-file movement and vice president of the new UAW was Wyndham Mortimer, the organizer of the White Motor local in Cleveland. Outside the AFL, Communists and other leftists organized thousands of tool and die makers, most of whom merged with the newly formed UAW.

The key turning point in the establishment of the UAW as well as the CIO generally was the victory of the UAW in the forty-four-day sit-down strike against General Motors in 1936–37. While many factors produced this victory, not the least was a united front that joined in common struggle a variety of leftists and nonleftists, including the Trotskyist Genora Johnson, leader of the Women's Emergency Brigade, the conservative Socialist and CIO representative Adolph Germer, and the socialist Reuther brothers. Key credit, however, must go to the Communists and their supporters. They provided the strategic and ideological direction by their insistence that successful organization required the unity of all workers, an industrial form of organization, and bold strike action, and they provided leaders at every front of the struggle—the early organizational work and strategic planning of Mortimer and Robert Travis, the publicity work of Henry Kraus, the legal help of Lee Pressman and Maurice Sugar, the shop leadership of Walter Moore and Bud Simon, and organization of the strike kitchen by Dorothy Kraus and Margaret Anderson.

While the UAW soon succeeded in organizing most of the industry, except for Ford, the unity that had prevailed during the GM sit-down strike quickly dissolved into bitter factional fights. At the center of this fight was a struggle between the union's president, Homer Martin—who had surrounded himself with members of a small group called the Communist Party Opposition—and Wyndham

Mortimer and the Communists. This fight lasted until 1939, when Martin was defeated, and the nonpolitical R. J. Thomas was elected president.

Though these factional fights as well as the general growth of the union diluted the influence of the Left in the UAW, individual leftists nonetheless still played important roles in the organization of such shops as Ford, Allis Chalmers, Vultee, and North American. At Ford in particular, the National Negro Congress and the fraternal organizations connected with the CP played a crucial role in penetrating the Ford terror to recruit union members among the largely black and Eastern European work force.

Even though Communist membership in the auto industry peaked during the years of WW II, its influence in the union declined. During the so-called national defense period, several leading left-wingers, including Mortimer, were dismissed for leading strikes in defense industries. During the war itself, the Communists support for the war blended with that of the mainstream leaders of the UAW and CIO. As inflation and the workers' unsolved grievances increased, the Workers Party—a small Trotskyist group that opposed the union's wartime no-strike pledge—enjoyed a brief popularity among many autoworkers.

After the war, the Left in the UAW was the first to experience the devastation of the Cold War. In 1946 Walter Reuther fashioned a Center-Right coalition that defeated the Left-Center coalition that had led the union since 1939. Aided by congressional investigations and a media Red Scare, Reuther drove Communists and other leftists from the UAW and became the first CIO leader to comply with the anticommunist affidavit provisions of the Taft-Hartley Act.

While the organized Left virtually disappeared in the union during Reuther's reign, echoes of the radical origins of the union could nonetheless be discerned in the collective bargaining breakthroughs that the UAW made in the 1950s and 1960s, in the union's support for civil rights legislation, and in its opposition to the war in Vietnam. Echoes of the early radicalism could also be heard in the voices of black autoworkers, who fought for better treatment and a greater voice through such groups as the Dodge Revolutionary Union Movement in the late 1960s and early 1970s and in the rank-and-file protests against bargaining concessions and worker-management cooperation schemes in the 1980s. *See also*: Communist Party; League of Revolutionary Black Workers; Sugar, Maurice; Trade Union Unity League; Trotskyism

—*Roger Keeran*

REFERENCES

Keeran, Roger. *The Communist Party and the Auto Workers Unions*. Bloomington: Indiana University Press, 1980.

Kraus, Henry. *The Many and the Few*. Urbana: University of Illinois Press, 1985.

Mortimer, Wyndham. *Organize! My Life as a Union Man*. Boston: Beacon Paperback, 1972.

Peterson, Joyce Shaw. *American Automobile Workers, 1900–1933*. Albany: State University of New York Press, 1987.

UNITED BREWERY WORKERS

The earliest industrial union outside extractive labor, the Brewery Workers Union (as it was known through much of its organizational life) epitomized the rise and decline of Germanic influence on American socialism.

In Germany, beer making had by the later nineteenth century evolved through centuries of handicraft to modern production, with a widespread loss of artisanal standards, and the successful creation of unions. In the United States too late for guild practices, beer making went through its greatest shift with the widescale midcentury abandonment of English-style ale for the aged German hops-flavored lager. By the 1880s–1890s, large manufacturers such as Budweiser had begun to dominate the trade through advertising, price-fixing, and economies of scale. The sheer numbers of local breweries, however, proliferated due to rising demands of the industrial classes, especially immigrants.

Unionization first entered brewing through the cooperation of German immigrants with nonsocialist workers in organizing workers and in promoting boycotts of non-union beer. Long hours, unhealthy conditions, and the brutality of employers contributed to the miserable status of workers, reinforced through beer given them in place of decent wages. Industrial unionism demanded cooperation from workers in a variety of trades, but promised the possibility of victory. Actually, unionization took hold in many places as a modus vivendi between consumers, laborers, and persistently paternalistic owners. Nevertheless, conditions improved considerably in those mostly northeastern districts successfully unionized by the 1890s.

The brewery workers' role in the new socialist movement was considerable. For a time, they designated the *New Yorker Volkszeitung* their official organ and helped that paper considerably throughout its life. Later, the *Brauer Zeitung* was in effect a socialist paper of the trade, loyally endorsing candidates and with perhaps even greater enthusiasm reporting the progress of socialism in Europe. Within the Socialist Labor Party and the Socialist Party, they also facilitated the radicalization of non-German brewery workers (notably Irish) in daily contact with them, together providing a membership base for many socialist locals. As a considerable side benefit, unionization facilitated beer advertising in Socialist papers, a staple of newspaper income. In Milwaukee, where all these factors operated, brewery workers provided a virtual army of municipal Socialist support. (In retrospect, even the study of the union's evolution had a socialist value: Hermann Schlüter's *Brewing Industry and the Brewery Workers' Movement in America* was one of the earliest Marxist attempts in the English language to compile the social history of one segment of the American working class.)

The brewery workers operated with considerably more caution in the economic field. Led by good socialists, they repeatedly toyed with the idea of dual-union federations, but cleaved to the mainstream. One dissident section of the brewery workers provided Daniel DeLeon's largest bloc in the Socialist Trades and Labor Alliance following, for a time. Almost a decade later, *Brauer Zeitung* editor William E. Trautmann articulated syndicalist-like visions of radical industrial unionism that the Industrial Workers of the World soon took over. Trautmann, unable to lead the brewery workers into the IWW, departed to become a national executive of that organization (and after the 1908 split, of the SLP's "Detroit IWW"). The brewery workers' leaders, practical-minded but also idealistic, contented themselves with the hope that the AFL could be transformed by brewers, miners, and others. Something at least could be said for socialist brewery leaders' rhetoric, and occasional initiatives at organizing black workers along with white, rare in that day. Its New Orleans representative (and editor of an English-language paper, the *Labor World*, sponsored by brewery workers), socialist agitator-philosopher-literary-comedian Oscar Ameringer, undertook multiracial strike leadership in turn-of-the-century New Orleans.

The dilution of German-born membership, but even more the propsect of prohibition, diminished the union's socialist temperament as it grew to its peak of more than 100,000 members. Ambivalent socialist attitudes on temperance threw the brewery workers toward Democratic Party "wets," and toward the political lobbying associations of brewery manufacturers. The *Brauer Zeitung* opposed the war and supported the Russian Revolution, but for the first time, in 1920, the union failed to endorse the SP candidate, Eugene Debs. With the passage of the Volstead Act in 1919, beer brewing and for all intents and purposes the union, too, had become a minor factor. Save for local inclinations (as in post-Prohibition Milwaukee), little socialism remained in the various brewery-related merged bodies, first with assorted food-workers and later as a unit within the Teamsters. *See also*: German Americans, *New Yorker Volkszeitung*, Socialist Labor Party, Socialist Party

—*Paul Buhle*

REFERENCES

Ameringer, Oscar. *If You Don't Weaken: The Autobiography of Oscar Ameringer*. New ed. Norman: University of Oklahoma Press, 1983.

Laslett, John M. *Labor and the Left: A Study of Socialist and Radical Influences in the American Labor Movement, 1881–1924*. New York: Basic Books, 1970.

Schlüter, Hermann. *The Brewing Industry and the Brewery Workers Movement in America*. Cincinnati: Brewery Workers Union of America, 1910.

UNITED FARM EQUIPMENT AND METAL WORKERS

The United Farm Equipment and Metal Workers Union (FE) was the first union to organize the International Harvester corporation. Originally an offshoot of the Steel Workers Organizing Committee of the CIO, the FE secured recognition at Harvester's Tractor Works plant in Chicago in 1938. The union brought most of the remainder of the company's agricultural implement plants under contract in 1941. Several of the FE's original organizers were members of the Communist Party, and some of the union's leaders retained an association with the Party throughout the FE's existence. The union's two top officers emerged out of Harvester's Chicago plants: Grant Oakes, the FE's longtime president, was a skilled mechanic at Tractor Works; Gerald Fielde, who became secretary-treasurer, had worked at neighboring McCormick Works. The FE went on to organize other farm-implement plants, largely in the Midwest, and claimed to represent 80,000 workers in the mid-1940s. The union's membership, however, was depleted through raids launched on FE locals by the United Auto Workers (UAW). In 1949 the FE was expelled from the CIO on charges of "Communist domination"; shortly before the CIO's action, the FE had entered into a loosely structured merger with the United Electrical Workers (UE). After a long strike against Harvester in 1952, the FE lost most of the contract clauses that had bolstered the union's strength. In 1955 the FE left the UE and merged with the UAW.

Though the FE's battle with the UAW and with the CIO was seemingly based on questions of jurisdiction and Communist infiltration, larger questions concerning the direction of the labor movement were at the heart of the conflict. The policies pursued by the FE ran counter to the philosophy of labor statesmanship that became predominant in the CIO during the postwar era. Rather than moving to limit shop-floor activity, the FE leadership defended the right to strike between contracts; FE members freely exercised that right, walking out at Harvester 639 times between 1948 and 1951. Harvester's piecework system engendered a high grievance rate, and the FE moved to win these disputes, if possible, at the local level. The FE's Harvester contracts provided for a large number of shop stewards and the union zealously guarded the clause guaranteeing stewards' freedom of movement through the plants. In collective bargaining, the FE's leaders fought to retain one-year contracts, and they opposed both the productivity and the cost-of-living pay increases championed by Walter Reuther in the 1948 UAW-General Motors agreement.

The FE's ideology found expression in politics as well. In 1948, many in the union, from the local to the national level, participated in the Progressive Party campaign; Grant Oakes was the party's candidate for governor of Illinois. These positions drew charges of Communist control from the FE's opponents, particularly the UAW. At International Harvester, however, the FE rank and file was unshaken by the anticommunist campaign. The UAW did not gain representation at any of the ten Harvester plants originally organized by the FE, which comprised the bulk of the membership, until 1954. The decision, the next year, to merge with the UAW was adopted as another Harvester strike loomed and the FE leadership feared for the union's continued existence.

—*Toni Gilpin*

REFERENCES

Gilpin, Toni. "Left By Themselves: A History of the United Farm Equipment and Metal Workers of America, 1938–1955." Senior thesis, Lake Forest College, Lake Forest, Illinois, 1981.

———. "Labor Statesmanship v. Rank and File Unionism: Competing Models of Trade Unionism in Cold War America." Paper presented to the Newberry Library Chicago Area Labor History Group, Chicago, Illinois, February 20, 1987.

Ozanne, Robert. *A Century of Labor-Management Relations at McCormick and International Harvester.* Madison: University of Wisconsin Press, 1967.

Rosswurm, Steven and Toni Gilpin. "The FBI and the Farm Equipment Workers: FBI Surveillance Records as a Source for CIO Union History." *Labor History* 27 (Fall 1986).

UNITED MINE WORKERS

Founded in Columbus, Ohio, in 1890, the UMW, after winning major strikes in 1897 and 1902, grew rapidly, reaching 300,000 members by 1905. It was then the largest union within the AFL. From its earliest days the UMW was organized on an industrial basis, encompassing not only miners with diverse skills but also other workers of different occupations associated with the mines. Radical influences were strong during the first three decades of the union's existence. Socialist-minded colliers from the British Isles brought with them traditions of political activism and artisanal independence as well as ideas of economic democracy that they had practiced in their cooperative stores. These immigrants came to occupy many positions of leadership at the local and district levels of the union. In 1894 delegates of the UMW annual convention endorsed calls for governmental control of mines, railroads, telegraph systems, and other means of production. After 1900, Eugene Debs's Socialist Party attracted a significant minority of UMW members, notably in Illinois, the largest district within the organization. The majority of miners, however, even those whose sympathies lay with the Socialists, rejected third-party politics for fear of alienating friends in the two major parties from whom they might expect at least occasional support. Similarly, few miners in this early period favored anything that could be considered dual unionism, whether it was the Industrial Workers of the World or a new revolutionary union proposed by Debs.

In 1916 there were widespread defections of socialists to Woodrow Wilson, popular because of the enactment of several pieces of labor legislation during his first term. When Wilson led the nation into war in 1917, most miners readily followed. Such patriotic enthusiasm turned to disillusionment and anger when the government refused to cancel a wartime wage freeze after the November 1918 armistice, in spite of runaway inflation and brazen profiteering. In response, the 1919 UMW convention passed resolutions demanding "nationalization and democratic control of the mines" and the formation of a national labor party.

This revival of radicalism coincided, unfortunately for the radicals, with the ascendancy to power of John L. Lewis, who became UMW president in 1920. Lewis had fought the older generation of socialists in his home state of Illinois and he was no friend of the younger native-born militants who came to the fore in the 1919 insurgency. Over the next dozen years Lewis used his considerable abilities and increasingly dictatorial powers to squash one dissident movement after another. Whether it was the Labor Party of 1920, the Progressive International Committee of 1923, the Save the Union movement of 1926, the National Miners Union formed by the Communist Party in 1928, the Reorganized United Mine Workers Union of 1930, or the Progressive Mine Workers of 1932, Lewis was never bested. In putting down these rebellions he was assisted by probusiness politicians and coal industry operators who preferred the UMW's new brand of business unionism to any kind of rank-and-file democracy espoused by Lewis's critics.

Lewis built a despotic union machine in the 1920s, but he could not prevent the precipitous decline of the UMW, the result of a sick coal industry, the successes of open-shop producers, and continued fighting among the miners. By 1932 fewer than 100,000 miners paid their dues, a drop of more than 400,000 from its 1919 peak. Thus, the UMW's turnabout in the 1930s is more remarkable given its immediate past. In this reversal of fortunes the Left played a conspicuous role, albeit subordinate to Lewis. Adolph Germer, John Brophy, and others who had earlier been purged were now invited back to assume key organizing tasks. The UMW not only regained all that it had lost in the way of members and influence; it also made invaluable contributions toward the birth of the CIO and a revitalized labor movement.

During World War II and the early postwar years the UMW continued to be a major if isolated force, resisting the growing power of the national-security state and winning important concessions through highly publicized strikes. Its autocratic leadership, however, remained the union's most defining characteristic. Lewis retired in 1960, a Christ-like figure to many miners who admired his defiant stance in behalf of the union while overlooking or excusing his excesses as necessary in light of the opposition. In the 1960s the UMW sank further into corruption and tyranny, reaching the depths in 1969 when Lewis's hand-picked successor, Tony Boyle, ordered the murder of his presidential rival, Jock Yablonski, along with his wife and daughter. Only then did an organization, Miners for Democracy, come into being committed to reform. Allied with groups such as the Black Lung Association, the MFD in 1972 elected its candidate, Arnold Miller, as the new head of the union. In the next few years several changes were made that helped restore democratic rights to the members. Miller, however, proved to be a frail and ineffective leader. Heart problems led to his resignation in 1979. He was replaced by Sam Church, a Boyle loyalist who had been elevated to the vice presidency after Miller grew distrustful of the reformers in his office. In 1982 Church was defeated in the presidential election by Richard Trumka, a young and urbane lawyer with only a few years experience in the mines. Trumka appeared to have some of Lewis's charisma and ambition. Whether he or any future leader could resurrect the UMW or help forge a resurgent labor movement remained to be seen. *See also*: Jones, "Mother" Mary; Progressive Mine Workers; Trade Union Educational League

—*Ralph Stone*

REFERENCES

Dofoksky, Melvyn and Warren Van Tine. *John L. Lewis: A Biography*. New York: Quadrangle, 1977.

Laslett, John. *Labor and the Left*. New York: Basic Books, 1970.

Singer, Alan. "Which Side Are You On?: Ideological Conflict in the United Mine Workers of America, 1919–1928." Ph.D. diss., Rutgers University, 1982.

Zieger, Robert H. *John L. Lewis, Labor Leader*. Boston: Twayne, 1988.

United Office and Professional Workers of America

Inspired by the industrial unionism of the early CIO, dissident organizers from the AFL's Bookkeepers, Stenographers, and Accountants Union locals requested a charter in 1937 to form the United Office and Professional Workers of America. After thirteen years of increasing success in organizing white-collar workers, the UOPWA was hounded out of the CIO in the 1950 purge of Left unions. While many UOPWA organizers were members of the Communist Party, the union attracted support from urban clerical workers, white-collar professionals, and independent leftists. Membership reached 43,000 workers by 1943.

Along with the United Federal Workers and the State County and Municipal Workers of America, the UOPWA was given a CIO mandate to organize what most leftists saw as a problematical segment of the labor force, the "white collars." Never quite certain whether to view these as potential right-wing sympathizers or as workers with legitimate grievances, the CIO leadership, in any case, found it impossible to make office-work organizing a real concern of industrial unionism. UOPWA's influence was narrowly circumscribed when it was ordered to stay away from office workers falling under the jurisdiction of other industrial unions, which continued, in the 1930s and 1940s, to ignore clerks or to bargain away their interests. The UOPWA was left with paperwork industries, some of which, particularly insurance and banking, had virtually no history of union membership, and were managed by interests dead set against unionization. Nonetheless, UOPWA successfully organized a wide variety of white-collar workers, including direct-mail assembly-line workers, credit-house clearing workers, male insurance agents, book editors, Arthur Murray dance instructors, and thousands of female and male clericals, particularly in New York, Philadelphia, and Chicago.

The organizing of UOPWA's constituency raised important conceptual problems, problems the "workerism" ideology of the Left, focused as it was on male workers in heavy industry and manufacturing, seemed incapable of rethinking. While the union repeatedly challenged racial discrimination, its leaders were unable to confront divisions based on gender and professional elitism, which often happened to combine. Women clerical workers were sometimes patronized, dismissed as incapable of being dedicated unionists, and given almost no professional organizing leadership. Nonetheless, women rose to positions of leadership in some locals, particularly New York's Local 16, and a series of important victories after World War II indicated that wide-ranging office-worker unionism was a real possibility. This optimistic future was ended abruptly in the Taft-Hartley purges of the late 1940s, when the UOPWA leadership refused to sign loyalty oaths; the union was expelled from the CIO and quickly expired. It would be two decades before an industrial unionist approach to white-collar organizing would again appear in the labor movement. *See also*: Federal Bureau of Investigation, Taft-Hartley Loyalty Oath

—*Sharon Hartman Strom*

REFERENCES

McColloch, Mark. *White Collar Workers in Transition: The Boom Years, 1940–1970.* Westport: Greenwood, 1983.

Strom, Sharon Hartman. "'We're No Kitty Foyles': Organizing Office Workers for the Congress of Industrial Organizations, 1937–1950." In *Women, Work and Protest: A Century of U.S. Women's Labor History*, edited by Ruth Milkman. Boston and London: Routledge & Kegan Paul, 1985.

Sturmthal, A. F., ed. *White Collar Trade Unions: Contemporary Developments in Industrialized Societies*. Urbana: University of Illinois Press, 1966.

UTOPIANISM

An age-old longing for a society based on harmony and happiness, often merging with the modern ideals of material growth and personal fulfillment, utopianism has played a fundamental role in the development of modern American society and culture. It has also profoundly influenced oppositional or alternative theory and practice during eras of prospective change. In turn, waves of utopianism have often been followed by institutional submergence or ideological displacement into personal salvation, consumerism, and/or nationalist rituals such as war and imperial adventures.

Prior to 1870, utopianism tended to be defined by the perfectionist thought of the premodern world. "West" on the compass of radical reformation was the direction of human salvation, and many European religious perfectionists established outposts in the New World. Secularization and the beginnings of industrialism added new components. The three modes of utopianism—political, communal, and literary/popular culture—resonated with the millennial passions of Protestant America in the early nineteenth century. Broad reform tendencies such as abolitionism and woman's rights raised ideological challenges containing a religious-utopian premise of sin and salvation. Utopian communes, even in the secular form of Fourierism and Owenism, attempted to escape from corrupt society. An element in the ideological ascension of laissez-faire, utopianism represented a desire to find alternative ways of reconstituting a moral universe in which one could be true to one's own nature. Despite the advocacy of such leading intellectuals as Frances Wright and Horace Greeley, such personal perfectionism did not seriously threaten rising capitalism.

Toward the end of the century, however, the material hardships and moral corruption imposed by monopoly capitalism returned utopianism to public concern. Literary utopias flourished, with hundreds of authors assaying the possibilities of future, better societies, sometimes displaced to undiscovered lands, or even to distant planets. Among them, Edward Bellamy's *Looking Backward* was not only by far the best-selling, but also the most emblematic. While criticizing the profound inequalities of contemporary life, most utopian authors were, like Bellamy, unwilling or unable to conceptualize the future without some form of political or intellectual elite. Their own commitment to an ideology of Christian Socialism or Populism could not overcome their fears about the conflicts that emerged in the contest between capital and labor. Such middle-class utopianism looked to the state as an active instrument in balancing class forces and in facilitating progress and prosperity.

Meanwhile, a number of working class–based socialist movements of the 1880s–1890s viewed utopian communalism as an opportunity to challenge state power through example. Eugene V. Debs's followers, many from the defunct American Railway Union, thus saw in the short-lived Brotherhood of the Cooperative Commonwealth a vehicle to translate utopianism into a vanguard movement for workers' independence and self-development somewhere in the West. Like most other such experiments of the time—the single-tax colony at Fair Hope, the socialist Ruskin cooperative in Tennessee, and the anarchist communities at Home and Equality on the Puget Sound in Washington, and a number of contemporary immigrant socialist experiments—the Brotherhood faded to the political margins. These nevertheless provided important experiences in social change, and helped create a leadership for the mass-based Socialist Party to follow, in which the utopian journalism of a J. A. Wayland and the act of creating colonies gave way to creating socialist propaganda, waging strikes, and seeking political power.

What little utopianism existed in the era of Debsian Socialism usually served the purpose of groups seeking to escape particular environments (such as the Stelton, New Jersey, Colony of mostly removed New York anarchists) or to deal with the collapse of the Socialist movement (such as the Llano, Louisiana, colony led by former West Coast Socialist luminary Job Harriman). Utopianism resumed during the 1930s in a different and much less radical guise, chiefly under the auspices of the New Deal. Drawing in part from the back-to-the-land sentiments of communalists such as Ralph Borsodi, the Jersey Homesteads, for instance, sought to create a cooperative environment for displaced urban workers. Other New Deal communal projects extended the role of the state in the pursuit of deurbanization and welfare capitalism. Even non–New Deal utopian communities of the 1930s, like the anarchist Sunrise Colony in Michigan (composed of a number of veterans from Stelton), became ensnared in various New Deal agencies. In several other instances, however, utopian longings reflected nostalgic yearnings for the closed communities advocated by such right-wing political and religious fundamentalists as Dr. Francis E. Townsend and Father Charles Coughlin.

The utopian content of working-class and black struggles tended to be translated into unions and Left parties, as outlined ideologically in the "proletarian literature" movement with its icons of class. Dystopian fears in such works as Sinclair Lewis's *It Can't Happen Here*, and more subtly in the hard-boiled detective and *film noir* genres, suggested utopianism turned on its head, into the ideologies of the total society against the individual, a condition obvious in fascism, Stalinism, and the mass culture of welfare capitalism.

The 1960s returned utopianism to central concern and gave it the new tasks of challenging the legitimacy not only of the state, but also of materialism and "progress." This was, to a considerable extent, a "children's crusade." Countercultural activities of the young received the theoretical blessing of social critics such as Paul Goodman and Herbert Marcuse, in the search for liberation from the repressiveness of subtly repressive institutions and of bourgeois daily life. The political call for participatory democracy appealed to many of the same utopian desires as the search for new cultural life-styles, the musical taste for Jimi Hendrix and the Doors, or the literary taste for Samuel R. Delany, Marge Piercy, and Ursula LeGuin.

For a brief moment in history, communal experiments flourished once more. Reflecting a split between political activism and cultural retreat, burned-out radicals tried to "get back to the Garden" (as a song lyric from the Woodstock Festival put it) with self-conscious social experiments in the rural areas of Vermont, New Mexico, California, and Oregon. The more widespread "hippie communes," scattered mostly across the western states, offered a generally vague sense of escape from industrialism. In the cities, many young people established more-or-less collective living styles, replicating in some ways the vanishing extended families of their ancestors. Few communes of any kind survived the tests of time and change. *See also*: Bellamy, Edward; Debs, Eugene V.; Ruskin Colony; Spiritualism

—*Francis Shor*

REFERENCES

Barkin, Michael. "Communal Societies and Cyclical Phenomena." *Communal Societies* 4 (1984).

LeWarne, Charles Pierce. *Utopias On Puget Sound, 1885–1915*. Seattle: University of Washington, 1975.

Roemer, Kenneth M. *America as Utopia*. New York: Burt Franklin & Co., 1981.

Shor, Francis. "The Utopian Project in a Communal Experiment of the 1930s, the Sunrise Colony in Historical and Comparative Perspective." *Communal Studies* 7 (1987).

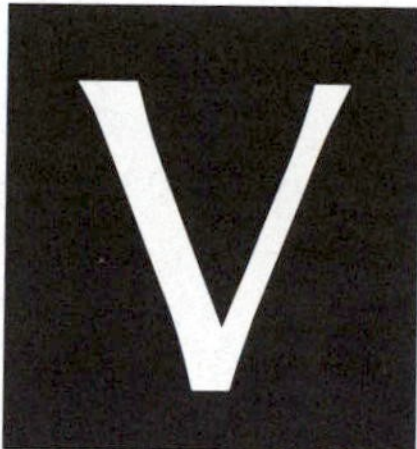

Vanguard Party

A significant variation of Marxist thought was created when V. I. Lenin introduced the concept that revolutionary success is dependent upon a political party composed of professional revolutionaries. This party is to act as the general staff of the revolution and has been compared with the locomotive that harnesses "revolutionary steam." Vanguardists believe that without their intervention, workers and other potential revolutionary social forces will fail to achieve their ends due to inexperience, poor organization, lack of skills, and theoretical underdevelopment.

The vanguard party is organized on a modified military model under a schema termed democratic centralism. Each of the lower bodies of the organization elects representatives to the higher bodies until a central-committee level is reached. The central committee is expected to gather information from all the party units and make final decisions. These decisions comprise the party line and all members are expected to carry out the party line whether they personally agree with it or not. Party members accept this discipline under the assumption that if they had all the information available to the leadership, they would see the wisdom of the decisions made. Rank-and-file members also understand that specific units or fronts may have to be sacrificed in order to save a larger unit or more important position. The process of changing a party line differs from one party to another and is often a point of contention. The guiding principle, however, is that the struggle to change the line must be kept within the party. When the party line shifts, all the members shift their public positions accordingly. On occasion, a 100-percent turnabout in party line gives a poor impression to outsiders, who may judge party members to have slavish loyalty to their organization. Leninists are willing to risk this judgment because they believe uniform adherence to the party line is essential to maximize the vanguard party's impact.

The historical experience of the vanguard party has been that the central committee usually creates an executive that so controls the party apparatus that the organization is far more authoritarian or centralized than democratic. Important posts come to be filled by appointment from above rather than election from below. Critics of the vanguard concept believe the centralizing tendency is inherent in its structure and its underlying elitist notion of revolutionary leadership. They point out that even the smallest vanguard parties usually develop authoritarianism to the point where a cult of personality surrounds the leader. Advocates of the vanguard party concede that maintaining democratic norms within the party is a constant struggle but argue that the experience of authoritarianism in the first period of socialism has made them more sensitive to the needs for democratic safeguards at all levels of party life.

Vanguard parties generally have secret and open members. Secret members are thought necessary because of government repression and volatile public opinion. Open members carry on the official work of the party and give it its public face. The mix of secret and open members depends on the historical conditions of the moment. Communication between members occurs at regularized local meetings augmented by occasional regional and national gatherings and through exposure to party publications. The party press includes a mass newspaper to communicate the party line to the general public, an internal party organ for members only, and a theoretical journal for party and nonparty intellectuals. Larger parties develop youth and arts publications and, depending on circumstances, publications aimed at specific ethnic and racial groups. Frequently there are party schools or workshops to develop the skills of members.

Party work is carried on in identifiable party units, front organizations, special interest groups, and organizations controlled by others. Party organizations are openly identified as linked to the party even though they may accept nonparty participants. A front group is deliberately created by the party as a vehicle for working with nonparty people. Fronts are not expected to become part of the formal party or to adhere to the entire party line. They generally focus on a single issue with broad appeal, such as initiatives against war, civil rights programs, or defense of political prisoners. Fronts are different from groups such as a trade unions or civic groups that party members join and simply try to influence.

Recruitment of new members is a goal of all party work but it is not necessarily a high priority. Vanguardists believe that not all persons can accept the discipline of party life even though they may agree with most of the party's positions. These and other individuals willing to work with the party on a regular basis are termed sympathizers or fellow travelers. A party may prefer that an individual remain outside the formal organization in order to minimize the risk of Red-baiting. Performing artists and other persons who are dependent on the goodwill of the general public may be actively discouraged from becoming members.

The Leninist party is fundamentally different from the socialist mass party, which operates as a parliamentary group and makes no greater demands on its members than its capitalist counterparts. One form or another of vanguard organization has been adopted by the Communist Party and the various Trotskyist and Maoist organizations in the United States. They may be collectively referred to as Marxist-Leninist organizations. *See also*: "Anti-revisionism (Maoism)," Communist Party, Factions, Preparty Formations, Socialist Workers Party

—Dan Georgakas

REFERENCES

Le Blanc, Paul. *Lenin and the Revolutionary Party.* Atlantic Highlands, NJ: Humanities Press, 1990.

VORSE, MARY HEATON (1874–1966)

Feminist, foreign correspondent, popular author of women's fiction, Vorse was also one of the nation's leading labor journalists during the first half of this century. Vorse's knowledgeable reports appeared in middle-class journals and major newspapers, as well as in leftist publications and in dispatches and broadsides distributed by the labor press. Unlike most labor reporters of her time, she emphasized the crucial contribution of women to labor advance. Her writing also helped to convince many Americans of the need for industrial labor organization.

Born into a well-off New England family, Vorse was determined to escape domesticity and to pursue a career. By 1910, she had won a national reputation as a writer of women's popular fiction. As an editor of the *Masses*, a charter member of the Liberal Club and the Heterodoxy Club, and a founder of the Provincetown Players, Vorse was a key member of the group of intellectuals and radicals centered in pre–World War I Greenwich Village. Her experience in the suffrage movement and as a delegate to the women's peace conference held at The Hague in 1915 determined her feminist vision. Twice widowed, Vorse functioned for most of her life as a single mother responsible for the support of her three children. Her desperate struggle to balance the demands of motherhood with those of her profession is a major theme of her life.

Vorse began her career as a labor reporter during the 1912 textile strike in Lawrence, Massachusetts. She continued publicity work with the Industrial Workers of the World in the 1914 New York City unemployed movement and at the 1916 mining strike on the Mesabi Range in Minnesota. After reporting the war in Europe, Vorse served as activist and publicist in the 1919 national steel strike and for the Amalgamated Clothing Workers during 1920. As publicity director of the 1926 Passaic, New Jersey, textile strike, she developed the revolutionary publicity tactics that set the pattern for the successful techniques that marked the labor uprisings of the next decade. Vorse was a firstcomer to the southern labor wars, at Gastonia, North Carolina, in 1929, and in "Bloody Harlan County," Kentucky, in 1931, where she was expelled from the state by night riders. During the 1930s, Vorse reported CIO battles across the nation, Hitler's rise to power, and the scenes of Stalin's Soviet Union. She covered the lives of American factory workers during WW II and postwar reconstruction in Europe. Her last big story to win national attention was her 1952 exposé of crime in the waterfront unions.

Vorse became skeptical of the Communist promise while in Hungary in 1919, and in Moscow in 1921 and 1933. Her disillusionment came much earlier than many of her leftist or liberal friends, and her popularity fell victim to her premature cognizance. She also stumbled at the place where many liberals and democratic socialists turned right. She refused to publicly bait the Communist rank and file during the witch-hunts of the fifties, and she denounced U.S. prosecution of the Cold War as a threat to human survival in the nuclear age.

Vorse spent fifty-four years in active battle for libertarian socialism, feminism, and world peace, a union of ideas far too radical for most of her peers to consider. At a time when the Communists knew her to be unreliable and unreasonable, the federal spy-hunters harassed her for more than forty years, maintaining surveillance of her activities until at least 1956, when she was eighty-two years old. *See also*: Industrial Workers of the World, *Masses*, Passaic Strike

—*Dee Garrison*

REFERENCES

Garrison, Dee. *Mary Heaton Vorse: The Life of an American Insurgent*. Philadelphia: Temple University Press, 1989.

Garrison, Dee, ed. *Rebel Pen: The Writings of Mary Heaton Vorse*. New York: Monthly Review Press, 1985.

Vorse, Mary Heaton. Papers. Archives of Labor History and Urban Affairs, Walter Reuther Library, Wayne State University, Detroit, Michigan.

———. *A Footnote to Folly*. New York: Farrar & Rinehart, 1935.

Wages for Housework

Both a feminist campaign and a distinct and influential theory of the 1970s women's liberation movement, Wages for Housework arose out of the reprinting of the 1953 Selma James essay "A Woman's Place" together with a new essay by Mariarosa dalla Costa, "Women and the Subversion of the Community." The economic meaning of housework in women's lives and the nature of female oppression connected with the housewife role had been explored in feminist literature prior to the publication of James's and dalla Costa's polemic; indeed, the findings of the 1970 Chase Manhattan Bank study "What's a Wife Worth?" (which had calculated the dollar value of the almost one hundred hours a week that the average housewife spends on performing household tasks as being about $13,500) were well known. What was new and dynamic about the James/dalla Costa thesis was its Marxist framework and its revolutionary perspective.

Published at a time when many Marxists were looking for a way to understand women's oppression in terms of the capitalist system, the "Wages for Housework" essays focused on the material nature of unpaid household labor. James and dalla Costa argued that *all* women are housewives and producers of surplus value. In the workplace of the home, it is the woman who performs the reproductive labor necessary to keep the wage earners of the working-class family fed, clothed, and ready for another day of toil in the capitalist marketplace. And when women work outside the home for wages, they are expected to fulfill their "natural" housewife roles along with the tasks of the job. Thus, the waitress must not only serve food but must do it with a smile, making the restaurant patron's dinner comfortable and "homey."

Wages for Housework castigated traditional Marxism for underrating women's unpaid labor and its crucial value to capitalist production. Liberal feminists' advocacy of economic independence through a career and a paycheck was likewise criticized. Wages for Housework argued that the working-class woman is the "slave of the wage slave" and must be encouraged to struggle against more work in the family as well as outside the home.

But Wages for Housework was more than a debate about women's economic status and destiny. Throughout the 1970s the Campaign for Wages for Housework fomented this analysis throughout the Left and feminist movements, providing a vital theoretical link between socialism and feminism while advocating autonomous and class-conscious women's activism. Issues that were especially important to the campaign usually pivoted on the invisible labor of women. The campaign wholeheartedly involved itself in the welfare-rights movement, the struggle for abortion rights and against forced sterilizations, and in women workers' demands for higher wages and shorter hours. The campaign strongly championed the rights of prostitutes to make a decent living and was the only feminist group to analyze the sex industry in terms of its material rather than moral conditions.

A widely reprinted broadside by the campaign declared, "The women of the world are serving notice. We clean your homes and factories. We raise the next generation of workers for you. . . . We have sweated while you have grown rich. Now we want back the wealth we have produced. We want it in cash, retroactive and immediately. And we want all of it."

International in its appeal, the Campaign for Wages for Housework organized during the mid-1970's in Italy, West Germany, England, and Canada. In the United States there were active chapters in Philadelphia, New York City, San Francisco, and Los Angeles. *See also*: Socialist Feminism, Women's Liberation

—*Miriam Frank*

REFERENCES

dalla Costa, Mariarosa. *The Power of Women and the Subversion of the Community*. Bristol, England: Falling Wall Press, 1973.

Grimstad, Kirsten, and Susan Rennie. *The New Woman's Survival Sourcebook*. New York: Knopf, 1975.

Vogel, Lise. *Marxism and the Oppression of Women*. New Brunswick: Rutgers University Press, 1984.

WALLACE, HENRY: see
PROGRESSIVE PARTY

WALLERSTEIN, IMMANUEL (b. 1930)

A theoretician of international stature, Wallerstein developed a synthetic Neo-Marxist paradigm for historical social science known as the world-systems perspective. Through his institution-building, his teaching, and his voluminous publications, most notably *The Modern World-System* (Vol. 1, 1974; II, 1980; III, 1989), he introduced and/or disseminated a number of terms and concepts that quickly gained considerable currency: *core, periphery*, and *semiperiphery; world empire* and *world-economy; commodity chains; hegemonic cycles*.

Born in New York City, educated and first employed at Columbia University, Wallerstein began his academic career as a sociologist of French West Africa. He early showed a gift for synthesis in his *Africa: The Politics of Independence* (1961), a structural but not explicitly Marxian account of the contradictions of colonialism and of the nationalist movements it inevitably spawned. A radical voice in a predominantly liberal environment, Wallerstein was honored with the presidency of the African Studies Association just as he was coming to find it necessary to move to a global level of analysis in order to comprehend the patterns of change in postindependence Africa.

The conservative aftermath of the 1968 student uprising at Columbia prompted Wallerstein to join the faculty at McGill University in Montreal; in 1976 he moved to a distinguished professorship at the State University of New York, Binghamton, where he rejoined his longtime collaborator Terence K. Hopkins, founded a research institute (the Fernand Braudel Center), and established a journal (*Review*). With a notable faculty and a steady stream of visiting Marxists and activist intellectuals from around the world. Binghamton became a major center for research and training in Neo-Marxist social science—probably the most cosmopolitan such center in U.S. history. Research groups, many of them international, focused on such diverse topics as southern Africa, the Ottoman Empire, long cycles in world-economic history, labor movements, households, and semiperipheral countries.

Four main intellectual sources fed Wallerstein's synthesis. From Marxism came a vision of capitalism arising out of the contradictions of feudalism and self-destructing via class struggles. From continental historical economics, particularly Max Weber and Karl Polanyi, came conceptions of modern national states as protectors of citizen privilege vis-à-vis outsiders, and of reciprocity, redistribution, and markets (minisystems, world-empires, and world-economies in Wallerstein's terminology) as the only possible bases—and hence the three historically existing types—of social organization. From the *Annales* school of French historiography came the emphasis on long-term structural persistence, as for example the tripartite core/semi periphery/periphery pattern of post-sixteenth-century capitalism, which Wallerstein sees extending into the twenty-first century. Finally, from the dependency theory and Third World revolutionism of the 1960s came the core/periphery understanding itself, with its corollary that working-class and Marxist movements in the core (industrialized) countries were not (could not have been?) the vanguard of world socialist revolution.

Beyond his insistence on a radical holism, i.e., the primacy of the world-economy as a unit of analysis, Wallerstein's most important theoretical contribution to his own synthesis is probably that of the semiperiphery. This refers to a shifting set of countries asserted to be intermediate between core and periphery on a number of dimensions (economic/technical capacity, state power, standard of living) and to stabilize world capitalism by deflecting peripheral opposition away from the core. His most important empirical argument dated the transition from feudalism to capitalism in the sixteenth century and characterized it largely in terms of market expansion. This involved him in the revived debate over the transition; by the logic of his position, he later came to question the received liberal and Marxist wisdom about the industrial and French revolutions, and to engage in numerous historiographic controversies. *See also*: African Studies, Sociology

—*Walter L. Goldfrank*

REFERENCES

Wallerstein, Immanuel. *The Capitalist World Economy*. Cambridge: Cambridge University Press, 1979.

WALLING, WILLIAM ENGLISH (1877–1936)

One of the few serious and innovative theoretical minds American socialism has produced, Walling was born into a wealthy family. His grandfather had been the Democratic nominee for vice president in 1880. As a youth, Walling committed himself to working on behalf of people who were less privileged than he and worked as a factory inspector and a settlement house resident on the Lower East Side of New York, and helped to found the Women's Trade Union League, which was dedicated to organizing female factory workers into unions. After reporting on a race riot in East St. Louis, he became one of the principal organizers of the NAACP, along with W. E. B. DuBois. Although he had by then become a socialist, he disagreed with some of his comrades by insisting that racial bigotry and discrimination needed to be fought right away instead of waiting for socialism to abolish all forms of discrimination, as they hoped it would. Walling was aware too of the racist attitudes of some American socialists themselves, such as Congressman Victor Berger.

Walling visited Russia during the 1905 revolution and was converted to socialism after meeting and talking with many radical activists. He published one of the few books in English on the thwarted revolution, becoming the first American to write about Lenin in a nationally circulated magazine. He soon gravitated to the left wing within the American Socialist Party, published articles in the *Masses*, the leading journal of the bohemian Left, and began to publish major works of socialist theory. After examining the latest trends in the international movement, he attempted to integrate the ideas of pragmatists like John Dewey. He came to the conclusion that the way toward real socialism was fraught with dangers, primarily coming from the likely development of an oppressive governmental structure. Although the coming social orders, which Walling referred to as state capitalism and state socialism, would carry out reforms, develop a welfare state, and eventually nationalize industry, they would only further the interests of the middle class and a relatively privileged portion of the working class. True socialism would come about only when the unprivileged were able to express their will and organize a democratic socialism from below, overturning organs of state control and finally abolishing all class distinctions whatsoever.

After leaving the SP because of its opposition to American participation in World War I, Walling eventually lost his own belief in a socialist future but became an advocate for what he then saw to be the democratic values of the

AFL and actively supported it as a publicist and consultant. *See also*: Philosophy, Socialist Party

—Jack Stuart

REFERENCES

Walling, William E. *Progressivism and After*. New York: Macmillan, 1914.

William English Walling: A Symposium. New York: Stackpole and Sons, 1938.

Washington Commonwealth Federation

Though it survived for only a decade, the WCF was one of the most active and broad-based left-wing movements in U.S. history. A coalition of socialists, advocates of Upton Sinclair's "production for use" proposals, old-age pension supporters, apostles of "technocracy," and labor activists, the WCF sought, with limited success, to win control of the Washington State Democratic Party.

The federation began in 1934 as "the Commonwealth Builders, Inc." Its founders were middle-class socialists who favored electoral action with the goal of a "cooperative commonwealth"—government-owned large-scale industry and banking, producer- and consumer-owned cooperatives, and small private businesses and farms. Such a vision found fertile soil in Depression-era Washington, especially among labor activists engaged in bitter dock and timber strikes, and among the unemployed.

By 1935, the Commonwealth Builders had won support from many key labor and farm organizations. In October of that year, Commonwealth Builders, Inc. officially became known as the Washington Commonwealth Federation. Its members rejected appeals to form a new party like Minnesota's Farmer-Labor Party and, instead, sought political power as left-wing Democrats.

Radical rhetoric was the WCF hallmark at first. The organization championed "production for use and abolition of the profit system." But after a major setback in the 1936 state election, its tone became decidedly more moderate. Concrete reform proposals led to a rapid growth in membership and some key political victories. The WCF became a force to be reckoned with, though Postmaster General Farley's rumored toast to "the forty-seven states and the Soviet of Washington" was far off the mark—WCF legislators were always a minority in Washington politics.

When the American Communist Party abandoned Third period sectarianism for the Popular Front strategy in 1935, Party members in Washington State saw their major political task as building and influencing the WCF. Initially rebuffed, CP members were permitted to join the federation in 1936. Their organizing skills brought them quickly into key leadership positions.

Early euphoria about WCF prospects turned sour by 1938. Internal splits (between AFL and CIO unions, for example) and Red-baiting badly weakened the federation. CP influence proved powerful, resulting in WCF flip-flops on foreign affairs. After the Hitler-Stalin Pact of 1939, federation newspapers denounced Franklin Roosevelt as a warmonger. From that time until Pearl Harbor, the WCF grew increasingly isolated politically, with sizable defections from its ranks.

Then, during World War II, the organization made a dramatic comeback, winning many legislative seats and sending its leader, Hugh De Lacy, to the U.S. Congress. In that period, Washington State enacted model social and civil rights legislation, and the WCF invented a popular contribution to Left political culture, the hootenany, a folk-song fundraiser.

By 1945, the WCF had become the most important single influence in state Democratic Party politics and, in the minds of its leaders, was no longer needed. The federation was dissolved as a contribution to Democratic Party unity. Its members looked forward confidently to the future.

But the future had other ideas. In the Cold War period, the top leadership of the WCF came under attack as Communists or fellow travelers and the federation's hard-won social programs were dismantled. *See also*: Popular Front

—John de Graaf

REFERENCES
Acena, Albert Anthony. "The Washington Commonwealth Federation: Reform Politics and the Popular Front." Ph.D. diss., University of Washington, 1975.

WAYLAND, J. A.: see APPEAL TO REASON, RUSKIN COLONY

WEATHERMAN: see ARMED STRUGGLE, STUDENTS FOR A DEMOCRATIC SOCIETY

WEST, DON (*b.* 1906)

A poet and activist Christian minister, West's roots go back to his birth as the son of a mountaineer in north Georgia. His family later became sharecroppers, and these experiences established West's sense of loyalty to the common people of the South. In his school years he was expelled for leading a student protest. At Vanderbilt University he encountered the theology of the Social Gospel, met such figures as Alva Taylor and Claude Williams, and received his divinity degree.

After studying in the folk schools of Denmark, West returned to the South just in time for the Depression. Along with Myles Horton he founded the Highlander Folk School at Monteagle, Tennessee, in 1933. He published a first book of poetry, *Crab-Grass* (1931), and was active with the Angelo Herndon case in Atlanta. He experienced a number of "close calls," trials and actual beatings by police and vigilantes in Georgia and Kentucky.

In the 1940s West became a schoolteacher and published *Clods of Southern Earth* (1946), which enjoyed a large circulation for a volume of poetry, especially because of its distribution through the CIO. The advent of the McCarthy period meant that West lost his teaching position at Oglethorpe University, and he again became a farmer. In 1957 West was an uncooperative witness before the House Un-American Activities Committee, and the next year his house and extensive library were burned down by the Ku Klux Klan. Steadfastly refusing to give up, West and his artist wife, Constance, founded the Appalachian South Folklife Center in Pipestem, West Virginia, in 1966.

Don West has played a significant role in rescuing the proud heritage of southern abolitionists, labor organizers, and civil rights activists. Reflecting these traditions, his poetry frequently uses a rhyming style that many poets have rejected. One of his best and most typical stanzas is from the poem "Southern Nights": "Mine shanties in Harlan/Hide their ugliness/Till spluttering lights/Gleam like spikes of gold/Half hammered into the mountainside." His other books include *The Road Is Rocky* (1951), *O Mountaineers!* (1974), and a reader of his work *In a Land of Plenty* (1982).
See also: Highlander Folk School

—*Fred Whitehead*

WESTERN FEDERATION OF MINERS/MILL, MINE, AND SMELTER WORKERS

A legendary radical labor movement of the West, the Western Federation of Miners (WFM) was in its early years an important section of the Industrial Workers of the World and later one of the least typical "red" unions in the CIO. Midwifed by U.S. Army bayonets in prison camps (or "bullpens") in Idaho, the union was marked in its various phases by federal intervention, rank-and-file agitation, hardrock miners' demands for safer working conditions with improved pay, and exemplary interracial relations.

The WFM grew out of the 1892 defeat of Coeur d'Alene, Idaho, miners who were resisting massive wage reductions. Officially founded the next year in Butte, Montana, the new union avowed to defend miners from the misuse of new technology, which increased rock dust and silicosis. The WFM, influenced by socialists such as Eugene V. Debs and by the need for solidarity, supported the formation of the American Labor Union, an effort of scattered workers in Western states to create a more democratic, industrial alternative to the craft-oriented American Federation of Labor. In 1905, the WFM joined the Industrial Workers of the World as its metal mining branch—a decision unpopular in Butte, where many miners viewed the IWW as a divisive political rather than industrial organization. Controversy and splits over this move foreshadowed later difficulties faced by the union over its political orientation.

Political infighting and the reluctance of other major unions to join the IWW prompted the WFM to withdraw from the movement in 1907. The actual organization of miners, now split between WFM and IWW, weakened as a result. The WFM nevertheless remained in its own way a radical organization, its influential *Miners Magazine* widely regarded as a socialistic organ.

The First World War and the process of electrification greatly increased the demand for copper. WFM locals in Michigan and Arizona struggled to maintain working conditions and to raise wages as the cost of living soared. Mine owners and the U.S. government fought back. In the bloody 1913 Calumet Copper Strike, casualties included eighty-nine children killed in a Christmas Day fire (an event later memorialized by Woody Guthrie). In Arizona, WFM and IWW members and supporters were deported at gunpoint and left in the desert without water. Repression and worsening conditions destroyed the Butte Miners Union the following year and prompted the rise of IWW organizing activities, in the course of which IWW organizer Frank Little was lynched. Persistent federal intervention, antisubversive legislation, and miners' rage inspired former Pinkerton detective Dashiell Hammett's *Red Harvest*.

In 1916 the WFM formally became the International Mine, Mill and Smelters Union (IMMSU), thereby recognizing the jurisdiction of the metalliferous mining industrial of the American Federation of Labor. Surviving further factionalism and the lean years of the 1920s, the IMMSU developed afresh during the New Deal and expanded its organizing activities into the East and South. Nonwestern locals were, however, to be a source of opposition to the union leadership.

Southern locals, sites of key victories in civil rights and pay standards, were able to capitalize upon traditions of regional coalminers, federal government neutrality, and the expanding economy of the Second World War. The northeastern advance, essentially a majority of the union's die-casting division (which had amalgamated a formerly independent union into the IUMMSU in 1934), sharply raised the issue of Communist influence within the international. Charges of corruption surrounding the otherwise democratic and hard-working union president, Reid Robinson, weakened the IUMMSU within the CIO. The passage of the Taft-Hartley Act (IUMMSU leaders refused to sign loyalty oaths and refused a referendum on the question) permitted internal opponents, often well-organized, such as the Association of Catholic Trade Unionists and its supportive Catholic clergy, to accelerate secession movements. Neither the resignations of Reid Robinson nor of his successor, admitted Communist Maurice Travis, prevented the union's expulsion from the CIO in 1950. By that time, the union was practically limited to Western miners, who remained largely unshaken by the "red" charges. In the 1960s, however, the weakening union suffered extensive raids from the United Steelworkers and the United Auto Workers. At a 1967 membership of 46,000—just slightly higher than its total thirty year earlier—the IUMMSU merged into the Steelworkers Union.

The IUMMSU is often cited for its pioneer policies in race relations and in women's involvement. During the 1940s, the union won a lawsuit to end the copper companies' custom of keeping separate payrolls for Anglo-American males, paying all others less. In the South, union policies of integration in workforce and leadership were decried as proof of communistic domination. In one of the best-known labor conflicts of the 1950s, the wives of mainly Chicano miners in Boyard, New Mexico, picketed in place of their husbands, who were forbidden to do so by injunction, and added new demands for their own welfare. This conflict was dramatized in the film *Salt of the Earth*. *See also*: Industrial Workers of the World, Union-Sponsored Radical Films

—*Bob Greene*

REFERENCES

Jensen, Vernon H. *Heritage of Conflict*. Ithaca: Cornell University Press, 1950.

———. *Non-Ferrous Metals Industrial Unionism, 1932–1954.* Ithaca: Cornell University Press, 1974.

Lingenfelter, Richard. *The Hardrock Miners.* Berkeley: University of California Press, 1974.

WFM-IMMSU Records. Western Historical Collections, Norlin Library, University of Colorado.

Wildcat Strikes

Essentially strikes that are illegal under union constitutions or labor-management agreements, wildcats can also be illegal under statute law.

They can range from small departmental walkouts to major companywide or industrywide strikes. They tend to be shorter than legal strikes. Sometimes this is because small strikes center around specific grievances that are quickly settled or quickly lost. In the case of larger strikes, because they are outside the normal union bargaining procedure, there is usually no negotiating team to represent the workers. One aspect of these strikes is that very often they are not intended to win specific demands but to make a point—against a union policy, against a new contract, or against a management practice. Although such strikes are not necessarily won, they are not, therefore, necessarily lost—they have forced union leaders or company managements to pay for whatever it is that the workers reject or resent.

Wildcat strikes indicate a rejection of union procedures. They have taken place for almost as long as there have been unions. The largest wave of wildcat strikes in the United States took place during World War II when virtually all unions adopted a no-strike pledge for the duration of the war. In 1943, 1944, and during the first nine months of 1945, about two million workers were involved in strikes each year, representing about 7 percent of the labor force. These were overwhelmingly wildcat strikes.

During WW II in the United States the Left was divided in its attitude toward wildcat strikes. After the German invasion of the Soviet Union, the Communist Party opposed all wildcats, whether related to defense production or not. The two wings of Trotskyism, the Socialist Workers Party and the Workers Party, opposed the role of the United States in the war and supported wildcat strikes. That support did not always include helping to organize or lead such strikes if that would threaten the position of party members in the plants.

Although wildcat strikes violate union contracts and constitutions, they are often supported, and even organized, by local union officers. An example was a strike of Chrysler plants in the Detroit area in 1943 that was organized by local union presidents. More often, however, committeemen or other local union officers risk being fired or penalized with other forms of discipline if they are involved in organizing or supporting wildcat strikes.

In 1955 there was a national wave of wildcats in the auto industry just after the signing of a new agreement between Ford and the United Auto Workers. These strikes, at GM, Ford, and Chrysler plants, did not relate directly to the new Ford agreement but to the fact that the grievance procedure under the old contracts had left thousands of grievances unresolved and to the erosion of working conditions in the plants. In the late 1950s, wildcats at Chrysler and other plants were common, as workers resisted the introduction of automation and the attending speedup. Local managements and union officials tried with varying success to use these strikes to get rid of militant committeemen and rank-and-file workers.

Wildcat strikes reflect the growing alienation that workers feel in relation to unions that historically become more and more bureaucratic. They also reflect the fact that unions increasingly play the role of disciplining workers in production.

Because wildcat strikes are uncontrolled by the usual institutional restraints that are placed on workers by unions, companies, and governments, they can on occasion explode into massive social struggles such as factory occupations, general strikes, and the like. *See also*: United Auto Workers

—*Martin Glaberman*

REFERENCES

Glaberman, Martin. *Wartime Strikes.* Detroit: Bewick Editions, 1980.

WILLARD, FRANCES (1839–1898)

Widely known as "Woman of the Century, " and a strategist and public spokeswoman for the most powerful women's organization in the world, Willard has been less remembered as a vocal Fabian socialist. Born outside Rochester, New York, to a cabinetmaker and farmer, she descended from a long line of Yankee rural folk. Her parents had both enrolled at liberal Oberlin College before moving west to care more properly for young Frances, who had contracted tuberculosis. Reared in the Wisconsin Territory, Willard grew up a tomboy and daughter of a legislator, yearning for more education. She graduated from the North Western Female College in Evanston, Illinois, in 1859, and retained Evanston as a home for most of the rest of her life. She taught and administered at the Genesee Wesleyan Seminary in Lima, New York, became president of the new Evanston College for Ladies, then dean of women and professor of English and art at Northwestern University, which absorbed the college. After friction with Northwestern's president (her former fiancé), she resigned her position in 1874, personally adrift. At this point, the new statewide women's temperance movement of Illinois asked her to become their chairperson, and she readily assented, becoming the corresponding secretary to the newly founded Woman's Christian Temperance Union.

She immediately indicated that temperance, per se, was but one of her broader reform interests, in which she hoped the WCTU would become involved. Resigning from her national position, she threw herself into woman suffrage work, and undertook a mass-petition temperance campaign in Illinois, which became the national model for such efforts. By 1879, the WCTU had named her its national president, a position she retained the rest of her life. From this power base, she became an important contemporary personality and an outstanding presence on the lecture circuit. In 1889 she published an enormously popular autobiography, *Glimpses of Fifty Years*. As her strategy pamphlet, *Do Everything* (1895), indicated, she urged engagement in every reform arena relevant to women's lives, frequently directing that engagement personally.

By this means, she became involved in radical causes. In the late 1880s, drawn to Knights of Labor leader Terrence Powderly and to the cause of labor more generally, she avowed warm support of the Knights. In 1892, at the People's Party's famed St. Louis convention, Willard sought unsuccessfully to combine with Powderly and others to effect a coalition of reformers and radicals in a single antimonopoly movement. (Temperance, along with other issues, proved too divisive.) She had already converted to socialistic ideas through the reading of Edward Bellamy's novel *Looking Backward*.

Bellamy had shown, Willard insisted, how the transformation of society could be conducted, and the cooperative order instituted peacefully, through women's decisive participation. Within the WCTU, she frequently evoked Bellamy's views as the answer to the "labor question," and urged members to join Bellamy's Nationalist Clubs, arguing that "in each Christian there exists a socialist; and in every socialist a Christian."

Troubled by her defeat at St. Louis and the collapse of Populism into the "silver question" in 1896, Willard spent little of her remaining life in the United States. In England, sojourning with a wealthy patron, she joined the Fabian Society. Returning for the WCTU national conventions of 1893 and 1894, she urged Fabian principles of socialism upon the WCTU membership. Over this and other issues, dissidents rose up in the WCTU to challenge her, but members loyally returned her to the presidency. In these last years, she frequently stated that, had she her life to live over, she would have devoted it to socialism rather than temperance. Her health collapsed, and she died in New York in 1898. Her body was moved to Chicago, where a crowd of 20,000 filed past her casket.

Her influence, however, had only begun to affect American socialist women. She had demonstrated by her life and commitment that women had a central role to play in the coming of socialism, and that to do so they had to organize among themselves according to the prevailing moral principles. Socialist women in the rural Midwest, Plains States, and Southwest regarded Willard as their particular avatar. Orators regularly addressed the "woman question" in Willardian tones, asserting that only socialism could bring woman into full equality and meanwhile protect the home. Hundreds or perhaps thousands of erstwhile WCTU members and a handful of leading women agitators, most notably Lena Morrow Lewis and Iowa temperance leader Marion Howard Dunham, moved over from WCTU to socialist agitation. In a broader sense, the format of women's meetings owed much to Willard's influence: the parlor setting, the stress upon women's self-advancement through gender-conscious education, the sentimental evocation of motherhood in the rhetoric.

For their part, socialist publications tirelessly reiterated that (as one headline went) FRANCES WILLARD PREACHED THE "DEBS DOCTRINE." Her photo appeared regularly on magazine covers, especially of the *Socialist Woman,* and in combined photos of socialist women leaders used frequently by local newspapers. Josephine Conger, editor of the *Socialist Woman/Progressive Woman,* urged Willard's example on her readership with notable frequency. Debs himself, emotionally close to Willard's view of home and family, averred to her as a socialist prophet until the end of his life. Thereafter, her memory expunged from the Left pantheon by Communists and claimed for conservatives by the WCTU, Frances Willard disappeared as a radical idol, destined to be rediscovered only by the newer feminist historians. *See also*: Woman's National Socialist Union, *Socialist Woman/Progressive Woman*

—*Mari Jo Buhle*

REFERENCES

Bordin, Ruth. *Woman and Temperance: The Quest for Power and Liberty, 1873–1900.* Philadelphia: Temple University Press, 1981.

———. *Frances Willard: A Biography.* Chapel Hill: University of North Carolina Press, 1986.

Buhle, Mari Jo. *Women and American Socialism, 1870–1920.* Urbana: University of Illinois, 1981.

Gordon, Anna. *The Beautiful Life of Frances Willard.* Chicago: Women's Christian Temperance Union, 1898.

Williams, Claude (1893–1977)

A pioneer in liberation theology, Williams devoted himself to a career of social activism that spanned from the early 1930s until his death. Born in western Tennessee, Williams underwent a transition from a bible-thumping evangelist to an advocate of socialism and racial justice under the guidance of Dr. Alva Taylor of Vanderbilt University. He first attracted public attention for his work with miners in Paris, Arkansas, a small company town at the foot of the Ozarks. His work in organizing unemployed councils and support for a miners' union got him expelled from his parish, but Williams discovered that religion could be a powerful tool in mobilizing previously conservative southern workers. Williams had developed biblical metaphors for class struggle and trade unionism, crystallized in charts and sermons, that he strongly felt were applicable throughout the South.

Williams next tried his approach with black and white sharecroppers of eastern Arkansas who faced eviction and impoverishment as a result of the Depression and government crop-reduction programs. As an organizer for the Southern Tenant Farmers' Union, Williams discovered that Protestant fundamentalism represented an important cultural link between black and white workers that could be employed to unite them in struggle. After being driven out of eastern Arkansas by local planters, Williams assumed a position as director of Commonwealth Labor College in Mena, Arkansas, where he rallied support for the STFU among students and faculty.

Williams's career in the STFU was cut short by conflict with Socialist leaders of the union over his Communist Party ties and his links to the CIO. In 1939 Williams left the union, along with several black ministers who had been key local leaders. He thereupon formed the "People's Institute of Applied Religion," an organization designed to train black and white lay preachers as organizers for the CIO. Armed with bible charts, Williams supporters played an important role in CIO organizing drives in Memphis and Winston-Salem.

In 1942 Williams's work attracted the attention of the Detroit Presbytery, who brought him to that city to help defuse tensions between black and white southerners working in defense plants. Williams sent shop preachers into the factories to counteract the oratory of right-wing evangelists affiliated with the Ku Klux Klan and Gerald L. K. Smith. Williams refused to concede the terrain of fundamentalism to the religious Right; he was convinced that the "scriptural heritage of the people" could be given a progressive slant.

When the war ended, Williams moved to Birmingham, Alabama, where he hoped to aid in a renewed southern organizing drive of the CIO. But the growing atmosphere of anticommunism, coupled with segregationist agitation, made it difficult for him to make ties with the local labor movement. Williams moved his headquarters twenty-five miles south to Fungo Hollow, where he hoped to hold interracial "people's institutes" outside the purview of Birmingham authorities. But the rise of the Klu Klux Klan and White Citizens Councils made it difficult to conduct open political work. Throughout the 1950s and 1960s, Williams endured cross burnings, beatings, and fires set on his land. By the early 1960s, civil rights activism had created a new audience for Williams's message. He put his bible charts and sermons in the service of a voter-registration campaign among blacks in Bessemer, Alabama. He helped train some ministers and students for work in Mississippi. By the late '60s, as segregation finally crumbled, Williams's home became a center of discussion for black and white activists from all over Alabama. The work of black ministers like the Rev. Martin Luther King, Jr., confirmed the approach that Williams had long advocated—finding a message in Protestant evangelism that could mobilize black people in a struggle for racial justice and working people of both races in their quest for a better life.

—Mark D. Naison

REFERENCES

Dunbar, Anthony P. *Against the Grain: Southern Radicals and Prophets, 1929–1959.* Charlottesville: University of Virginia Press, 1981.

Naison, Mark D. "Claude and Joyce Williams: Pilgrims of Justice." *Southern Exposure* 1 (Winter 1974).

Williams, William Appleman:

see Cold War, Revisionism

Wilshire, H. Gaylord (1861–1927)

According to a recent historian, Wilshire "stands out as one of the oddest characters in a movement where eccentricity was entirely normal." A contemporary called him the "P. T. Barnum of American socialism." A real-estate speculator—Wilshire Boulevard in Los Angeles is named for him—publisher, and socialist, Wilshire was born into some wealth; he liked to dress like a dandy and exploit his superficial resemblance to George Bernard Shaw. He knew the leading literary and radical figures in London and New York. He became a billboard magnate and used his billboards to promote his own socialist candidacy as well as his magazines. At one point Wilshire sold gold stock to promote himself, his magazine, and socialism; he promoted health foods, miracle cures, Maxim Gorky's ill-fated American tour, and recordings of famous socialist orators,

some of which he faked himself. Above all, Wilshire promoted Wilshire and *Wilshire's magazine*.

Born in Cincinnati, the son of a wealthy businessman, and educated at Harvard, Wilshire twice ran on Socialist tickets in the early 1890s and then spent four years in England, where he met the radical elite. Returning to southern California in the late 1890s, he began publication of the *Challenge* in support of his attempt to secure the SDP nomination for California's Sixth Congressional District, which he won though he lost the race. Wilshire used the first person singular to glorify himself and his one basic idea, the motto for his publication: Let the Nation Own the Trusts. It was a powerful slogan because it was between 1899 and 1901 that the consolidation of American industry took place, the time when great combinations like U.S. Steel were born. Wilshire used his message, self-promotion in the form of publishing countless letters of praise, and the depth of his pocketbook to reach more than 100,000 readers in the first decade of the twentieth century. *See also*: Socialist Party

—*Elliott Shore*

REFERENCES

Quint, Howard. "Gaylord Wilshire and Socialism's First Congressional Campaign." *Pacific Historical Review* 26 (November 1957).

Reynolds, Robert D., Jr. "The Millionaire Socialists: J. G. Phelps and his Circle of Friends." Ph.D. diss., University of South Carolina, 1974.

Shore, Elliott. *Talkin' Socialism: J. A. Wayland and the Role of the Press in American Radicalism, 1840–1912*. Lawrence: University of Kansas Press, 1988.

WINCHEVSKY, MORRIS (1856–1932)

"Zeyde" (grandfather) of the Yiddish socialist press, outstanding early poet, humorist, and cultural organizer, Winchevsky was perhaps the first immigrant radical to place ethno-cultural pluralism at the center of the socialist worldview.

Grandson of a martyred rabbi who resisted Russian political domination over Poland, Winchevsky grew up in the literary shadow of the midcentury Russian critics Nekrasov and Pisarev. Politically active in Koenigsberg, Germany, he avoided arrest by removing to London's East End, where he established in 1881 the *Poylishe Yidl* (Polish Jew) and its more important successor, the openly socialist *Arbeter Fraint* (Worker's friend). The *Fraint*, at once class-conscious, literary, and keenly self-conscious to the Jewish condition, set the pace for ghetto papers to come. In 1894 Winchevsky immigrated to New York, then Boston, where he published the first heretical cultural sheet within the American socialist movement, *Der Emes* (Truth). Precipitating Jewish unrest at Daniel DeLeon's domineering and assimilation-minded leadership, Winchevsky helped piece together the *Jewish Daily Forward*.

As a journalist, Winchevsky was widely beloved for his alter ego, *di Meshuginer Filosofer*, the "crazy philosopher," who pronounced hilariously sad truths for an imprisoned world. As a poet, he followed the German "Forty-Eighters" in a rhythmic paean to struggle, adding a strongly Jewish content to class themes. As a political figure, he remained restless with moderate socialism, including the Socialist Party, and generally at odds with the vulgar Americanizing of the *Forward's* Abe Cahan. Late in life, he became a founder of the Communist *Freiheit*, which rapidly grew too orthodox for his tastes. He himself had long since become a kind of nostalgic figure in the ghetto, his poetry no longer taken seriously on aesthetic grounds and his worldview old-fashioned, but his moral stature grown by decades of tireless effort. In 1928 the *Freiheit* brought out a six-volume *Verk un Leben*, including a full-scale biography by Kalmon Marmor and a full (if by no means comprehensive) selection of his writings. *See also*: Socialist Labor Party, Tsukunft, Yiddish Left

—*Paul Buhle*

REFERENCES

Marmor, Kalmon. *Morris Vinchefsky, Zayn Lebn un Shafn*. New York: Freiheit Ferlag, 1928.

WINSTON, HENRY (1911–1986)

A leading African-American Communist, Winston pioneered the U.S. anti-imperialist movement in aid to African nations struggling for independence, and for decades played a central role in the organizational life of the Communist Party of the United States.

The son of a sawmill laborer and steelworker relocated from Hattiesburg, Mississippi, to Kansas City, Missouri, Winston was compelled by family economics to leave high school. His political activities began at age nineteen, in Kansas City, where he led the city's Unemployment Council. Over the next few years, he helped organize similar councils in a number of African-American communities, including Harlem and Cleveland. After joining the Young Communist League and the CPUSA, he rose quickly through the ranks of both, due to his outstanding organizational skills. By 1936, he became the YCL's national organizational secretary and a member of the CPUSA's central committee. He was also active in the Scottsboro case and in support of Republican Spain.

During the Second World War, Winston helped enlist more than 15,000 Communists into the armed forces. His own European tour of duty ended with an honorable discharge, despite government discrimination against Communists. Afterward, he was elected national organization secretary of the CPUSA, then faced the emergence of the Cold War. Sentenced in 1947 to jail for five years under the Smith Act, Winston exhausted his appeals and, by decision of the Party, along with three other leaders went "underground." After five years, it was decided that Winston should surrender. He was sentenced to three additional years in the federal penetentiary in Terre Haute, Indiana.

During his prison term, Winston developed a brain tumor that prison officials refused to treat until too late to save his sight. An international campaign for his freedom, including among its supporters Eleanor Roosevelt, Norman Thomas, A. Philip Randolph, and Reinhold Niebuhr, brought a 1961 commutation of his sentence by the new Kennedy administration. (Fidel Castro had offered to exchange him for a Bay of Pigs prisoner.)

In 1966 Winston was voted Party chairman, in which capacity he played an instrumental role in defending Angela Davis from government persecution, and in rallying Communist opposition to the Vietnam War. As an international figure, Winston became friends with many African leaders, including Amilcar Cabral and Kwame Nkrumah. In his major works, *Strategy for a Black Agenda* and *Class, Race, and Black Liberation*, Winston polemicized against theories of race separation, back-to-Africa movements, and black capitalism. He also directed the CPUSA's adoption of a ban on male supremacy. At age sixty-five, Winston received the Order of the October Revolution from the USSR. He died in Moscow, and his ashes were placed in a vault at the Waldheim cemetery in Chicago, with those of other famous American socialists, communists, and labor radicals. *See also*: Communist Party, Young Communist League

—*Maurice Jackson*

REFERENCES

Jackson, Maurice. "He Kept His Eyes on the Prize." *People's Daily World*, February 19, 1987.

The "Woman Question"

Since its inception, the American Left has defined itself principally in relation to the working class, the designated agent of revolutionary change. The role of women within the movement has been, consequently, problematical. Women historically have worked for wages in fewer numbers than men, and their jobs, mainly in low-paying manufacturing and service sectors, have not matched the image of proletarian work as established by the male leadership. Only in 1920 did women gain the right to vote, and therefore women had no direct role in electoral campaigns until relatively recently in the history of the Left. The reality of women's oppression or subordination has nevertheless repeatedly challenged Left theorists and strategists to wrestle with matters defined by gender as well as class. This discussion has been known as the "woman question."

Although this discussion generally dates to abolitionists' confrontation with women's controversial role in the antislavery movement, the Left became intimately involved during the decades after the Civil War. At this time an independent and mass woman's movement took shape and presented socialist and reformist organizations alike with a demand for recognition. German-American socialists responded most forcefully to *Die Frauenfrage* and experimented with the first organizations designed to address women's special concerns. The most important theoretical work on the woman question appeared in Germany in 1879, August Bebel's *Die Frau und der Sozialismus*. Translated by Daniel DeLeon as *Woman Under Socialism* and published in the United States in 1904, Bebel's text supplied the American Left with its standard "answer" through the 1930s.

Bebel opened his text by acknowledging that "woman and workingmen have, since [days of] old, had this in common—oppression." He then constructed a grand historical framework to trace women's distinct role in social production from ancient times to the consolidation of capitalism in the nineteenth century and to relate each historical stage to the intensification of their oppression. While he regretted the pull of women into the waged labor force under modern industry for its impact on family life, he nevertheless looked optimistically upon this development. The trend in social life, Bebel wrote, "is not to banish woman back to the house and hearth as our 'domestic life' fanatics prescribe . . . but is to lead woman out of the narrow sphere of strictly domestic life to a full participation in the public life of the people." As the material conditions of industrial capitalism forced women into wage labor, they, like male workers, could ready themselves for class war and the socialist reconstruction of society. Bebel not only juxtaposed the sufferings of the working class and women across history but explained how women would attain freedom only insofar as they struggled to overthrow capitalism.

Bebel's parallel construction of the oppression of women and workers did not settle the matter. Because women bear a special relation to what Marx and Engels had termed the "reproduction of labor power," that is, the bearing and raising of children as well as the maintenance of the household, their roles as wage-earners never correspond to those of men. When women work for wages they earn less than men, and as an expanding sector of the labor market, women concentrate into a small number of low-paying occupations. Equally important, waged work does not significantly alter women's responsibilities for the family and household. For these reasons, the persistent Left emphasis on social production as the site of revolutionary consciousness and proletarian agency displaces women and their concerns and ensures their questionable status within the movement and its theoretical formulations. *See also*: Socialist Feminism

—*Mari Jo Buhle*

REFERENCES

Eisenstein, Zillah, ed. *Capitalist Patriarchy and the Case for Socialist Feminism*. New York: Monthly Review Press, 1978.

Kuhn, Annette, and Annemarie Wolpe. *Feminism and Materialism: Women and Modes of Production*. Boston: Routledge and Kegan Paul, 1978.

Vogel, Lise. *Marxism and the Oppression of Women*. New Brunswick: Rutgers University Press, 1984.

Woman Rebel

This short-lived anarchist journal is notable because of the editorship of birth-control advocate Margaret Sanger. Produced monthly from March through October, 1914, this eight-page newspaper addressed working-class women in the name of labor militancy, free love, and anticlericalism. In Sanger's opinion, *Woman Rebel* was "red and flaming," and its motto, No Gods, No Masters, complemented its advocacy of direct action.

Sanger reprinted the preamble to the constitution of the Industrial Workers of the World and essays by feminist writers Olive Schreiner, Ellen Key, Helen Keller, and Emma Goldman. Sanger's editorials, which included promotion of birth control, were ultraleftist and occasionally struck out at "bourgeois feminists." In the July issue she published an essay, "In Defense of Assassination," by Herbert A. Thorpe, for which the U.S. Post Office rescinded her mailing privileges. Sanger was then indicted the following month for violating the Comstock Postal Act of 1873. The newspaper folded when Sanger, hoping to avoid arrest, sought exile abroad. *See also*: Anarchism; Sanger, Margaret

—*Mari Jo Buhle*

REFERENCES

Baskin, Alex, ed. *Woman Rebel*. Reprint. New York: Archives of Social History, 1976.

Kennedy, David M. *Birth Control in America: The Career of Margaret Sanger*. New Haven: Yale University Press, 1970.

Woman's National Committee

The WNC represented women and their concerns within the Socialist Party. At the 1907 meeting of the Second International in Stuttgart, Germany, delegates adopted a resolution calling upon Socialists to campaign for woman suffrage but only within their own organizations. The American party responded immediately by appointing its first national lecturer on women's issues. In May 1909 the party's national convention created a special committee "to care for and manage the work of organization among women" and provided funds to maintain a woman organizer in the field.

The establishment of the WNC marked an important event in the history of socialist women because its clear position within the SP signaled the end of autonomous women's organizations. Although women continued to organize separately, they did so as committees within the regularly constituted Socialist locals.

The WNC coordinated several aspects of women's affairs. Two outstanding organizers, Anna A. Maley and Caroline Lowe, chaired the committee during its most active years and made the WNC a valuable educational service to rank-and-file women. They produced and distributed scores of leaflets focused on women's issues and drew up a more extensive curriculum for study. The WNC endorsed the campaign for woman suffrage and sponsored lectures by the party's most popular speakers. The WNC advised local women's committees on conducting strike-support work and on reaching out to immigrant women. Through its work, the role of women within the Socialist movement gained recognition along the lines established by the Second International.

From *Appeal to Reason*, September 6, 1903

As the party endured a bout of intense factionalism around 1912, the national executive committee of the SP ceased its financial support and the leadership of the WNC fell into disarray. By this time, local women's committees had been established in at least fifteen states, and women's membership remained steady. The final chairperson of the WNC, Winnie Branstetter, nevertheless orchestrated its demise, and in June 1915 the national executive committee, after polling its members, officially abolished the WNC. Although most women accepted this decision without formal protest, a few interpreted the event as an affirmation of their own suspicion that the WNC had been little more than an attempt by the party leadership to bring women under their control. After 1915 Socialist women lacked coordination at the national level as well as a distinctive voice within the larger movement. *See also*: Progressive Woman, Socialist Party, Woman's National Socialist Union

—*Mari Jo Buhle*

REFERENCES

Buhle, Mari Jo. *Women and American Socialism, 1870–1920*. Urbana: University of Illinois Press, 1981.

Dancis, Bruce. "Socialism and Women in the United States, 1900–1917." *Socialist Revolution* 6 (January–March 1976).

Miller, Sally. "Women in the Party Bureaucracy: Subservient Functionaries." In *Flawed Liberation: Socialism and Feminism*, edited by Sally Miller. Westport: Greenwood Press, 1981.

WOMAN'S NATIONAL SOCIALIST UNION

Organized independently of the Socialist Party, the WNSU formed in 1901 to rally women to the cause of Socialism. Initiated primarily by California women with roots in Bellamy Nationalism and the Woman's Christian Temperance Union, the WNSU agreed upon a distinct strategy for women's emancipation while allying with the struggle to overthrow capitalism. Although the SP at its founding convention included in its platform a commitment to "equal civil and political rights for men and women," the WNSU acted on the belief that women could achieve only second-class status in locals officiated by men. For both practical and theoretical reasons, they insisted on autonomy.

Although the WNSU failed to make organizational headway outside California and Kansas, its leaders managed to hold a special meeting prior to the SP's national convention in 1904. Delegates to this first national meeting of socialist women discussed the role of women within the larger movement and the wisdom of separate organizations. Several delegates from the New York area criticized the WNSU for its potential role in discouraging women from joining regular party locals and thereby weakening the movement. The party press echoed this opinion, and the WNSU lingered for a few years as a regional network of California clubs. *See also*: Socialist Party, Woman's National Committee

—*Mari Jo Buhle*

REFERENCES

Buhle, Mari Jo. *Women and American Socialism, 1870–1920*. Urbana: University of Illinois Press, 1981.

WOMEN: A JOURNAL OF LIBERATION

This journal first appeared in fall 1969 and continued publishing, more or less regularly, until 1982. Along with *off our backs, Up from Under*, and *Aphra, Women: A Journal* represented the first wave of periodicals to accompany the revival of feminism in the late 1960s. Ideologically, it identified itself with the women's liberation movement, as opposed to the women's rights perspective of the National Organization for Women (NOW): "the word 'liberation' . . . implies a deep consciousness of the significance of our struggle: women are asking for nothing less than the total transformation of the world." (from vol. 2, no. 1, 1970). At a less elevated level of rhetoric, the difference between radical and liberal was not so great; *Women: A Journal* defined its goal for women as greater choice, its target as predetermined social roles. *Women: A Jour-*

nal did not distinguish between what was later called "radical," or "cultural," and "socialist" feminism, but embraced both in its understanding of the tasks of women's liberation. Thus, early issues included articles about both sexuality and class, lifestyle and imperialism. Issues were organized around a thematic focus in a deliberate effort to parallel the consciousness-raising focus of early women's liberation. Early themes included women's history, the family, and women workers under capitalism.

Women: A Journal was published in Baltimore, but served a larger audience. (It estimated its readership in 1970 was 15,000). Inasmuch as the early women's liberation movement was largely local in structure, with almost no national existence, the *Journal* played a crucial role in circulating news and writings between cities. Important articles identified with particular localities—for instance, Roxanne Dunbar's article on poor white women, first published by *No More Fun and Games* in Boston—received a national audience in *Women: A Journal*. Brief reports on women's liberation activities around the United States played a similar function; there, readers learned about the Miss America protest in Atlantic City, abortion activism in Lansing, and what the Redstockings were doing in New York City.

A subscribers' survey in vol. 3, no. 1, 1972, provides information on who read *Women: A Journal*. Subscribers were well-educated but ill-paid (most had some graduate education, most earned under $10,000 a year), presumably white women. Despite the *Journal's* emphasis on communal and other alternative lifestyles, the largest group of subscribers (one-third) lived in nuclear families, which seemed cause for self-criticism ("It seems that we're all fairly conservative in this area, after all").

In keeping with the relentlessly antihierarchical character of the early women's liberation movement, *Women: A Journal* was published by a collective, albeit of changing membership. Pride of authorship was discouraged. Rotating tasks among collective members, distributing rather than consolidating skills, was the rule, even the pride of the publishing collective. By 1980 the magazine appeared more irregularly, and wider swings in ideological focus between issues suggest a lack of continuity in the collective. A further sign of the decline of *Women: A Journal* was the appearance, by 1981, of a single editor and other attempts at professionalization, including a rather formal market research study of the magazine's readership. The last two issues appeared in 1981 (Peace and War) and 1982 (Bodies). *See also*: Socialist Feminism, Women's Liberation

—*Ellen Carol DuBois*

WOMEN STRIKE FOR PEACE

This grass-roots, participatory movement of American women was born on November 1, 1961, as a radioactive cloud from a series of Russian atomic tests was passing over American cities and the United States was threatening its own resumption of atmospheric testing after a three-year moratorium. Worried about the effect of nuclear fallout on the health of children born and unborn, and fearful that the escalation of the nuclear arms race could lead to human extinction by accident or design, tens of thousands of women, in sixty communities from coast to coast, walked out of their kitchens and off their jobs in a unprecedented day-long women's strike for peace. This one-day action was the largest national women's peace protest of the twentieth century.

In the process of transforming the strike into a national woman's peace movement with one hundred locals, ten regional offices, and a network of contacts in Europe, Asia, and Latin America, the women of WSP developed an innovative and feminine political style. It was characterized by an antihierarchical, loosely structured, nonorganizational format, and spontaneous direct action at the grass-roots level. WSP created a nonideological, maternal rhetoric that served the movement well. At a time when peace dissenters were characterized by the political establishment and the media as either "commies" or "kooks," the image projected by WSP of respectable, yet militant, middle-class mothers wearing white gloves and flowered hats while picketing for nuclear disarmament helped to legitimize the movement's radical critique of the Cold War. By stressing the way in which the men in power were undermining mothers' capacity to carry out their assigned role of life preservation and moral guardianship, WSP was able to gain support for confrontations with such sacrosanct military institutions as the Pentagon and NATO, and to win sympathy for its defiance of the House Committee on Un-American Activities (HUAC), which summoned the one-year-old movement to a hearing in December 1962.

WSP had, from its inception, rejected political screening and the exclusion of Communists and former Communists from the movement as a manifestation of outdated Cold War thinking. It is not surprising, then, that WSP did not cower before HUAC. Instead, it challenged the committee's monopoly on Americanism, declaring that, "with the fate of humanity resting on a push-button, the quest for peace has become the highest form of patriotism." When the chairman of the committee asked Dagmar Wilson, one of the five founders of WSP and its acknowledged spokesperson, "Would you permit Communist Party members to occupy leading posts in Women Strike for Peace," she answered, knowing that she spoke for most WSP women:

> Well, my dear sir, I have absolutely no way of controlling, do not desire to control, who wishes to join the demonstrations and the efforts that the women strikers have made for peace. In fact, I would also like to go even further. I would like to say that unless everybody in the whole world joins us in this fight, then God help us.

To the follow-up question, "Would you knowingly permit or welcome Nazis or Fascists," Wilson replied, "If we could only get them on our side." The HUAC hearings on WSP did much to discredit the committee in late 1962. For the first time, headlines critical of the committee were featured on front pages of newspapers across the country. PEACE GALS MAKE RED HUNTERS LOOK SILLY, REDHUNTERS DECAPITATED, PEACE LADIES TANGLE WITH BAFFLED CONGRESS, and IT'S LADIES DAY AT THE CAPITOL: HOOTS, HOWLS, AND CHARM were typical.

At its peak, in 1963, WSP estimated that it had a following of from 100,000 to 500,000. But this was a figure that could neither be verified nor refuted as there never was an official membership list or dues-paying structure. WSP's most successful campaign was for the Test Ban Treaty of 1963, which the women supported as the first limited step toward nuclear disarmament. The movement then turned its attention to nuclear proliferation. In May 1964 WSP organized a NATO Women's Peace Force demonstration at The Hague, Holland. There, women from the NATO countries, including 800 from West Germany, picketed a NATO meeting to draw attention to the dangers of a proposed multilateral nuclear fleet, which would have placed the fingers of German submarine commanders on nuclear triggers. WSP made headlines across Europe as one of its representatives, Ava Helen Pauling, was barred from entering Holland for the demonstration, while the former Nazi general who had been involved in the bombing of Rotterdam was welcomed as a NATO official. While WSP never built a mass movement in opposition to the multilateral nuclear fleet at home or abroad, it mobilized opinion makers in every NATO country. The United States eventually abandoned the plan for a NATO nuclear fleet.

By the end of 1964, WSP was diverted from antinuclear organizing by the escalating war in Vietnam. For the remainder of the decade and until the United States withdrew from Vietnam, WSP was an active part of the antiwar coalition. Refusing to accept the government's characterization of the people of Vietnam as their enemy, WSPers made several trips to Hanoi, and arranged three conferences with the leading women of North Vietnam and the National Liberation Front of the South around the slogan "Not Our Sons, Not Your Sons, Not Their Sons." WSP also played a significant role in the antidraft movement, reaching across race and class lines to counsel more than 100,000 young men on their legal rights under the selective service system. The movement developed a statement of complicity with resisters, which offered not only moral but financial support. WSP women appeared regularly at induction lines, providing adult support to young men who refused to cross the line, and sat in at the trials of resisters to show the judges that "the women are watching." In 1970 WSP was instrumental in electing its own national legislative chairperson, Bella Abzug, to the House of Representatives. Bella ran as a WSP leader, and found that it was her long antiwar record that won her the election.

Most of the women who participated in WSP came from liberal to Left political backgrounds, having been pacifists, Quakers, anarchists, Socialists, or Communists in the years before World War II. Even those who blamed the United States for the Cold War exhibited a postnuclear sensibility that rejected all ideological and abstract justifications for nuclear brinkmanship. The women were powerfully attracted to A. J. Muste's formulation of a "Third Camp" position that rejected both superpowers' disregard for human rights and human life. "No Tests—East or West" was one of WSP's most widely used slogans in the campaign for the Nuclear Test Ban Treaty of 1963.

I. F. Stone, the independent radical journalist, proclaimed in 1970 that he knew of no antiwar or radical organization of any kind that had been as flexible and intelligent in its tactics, and as free from stereotypes and sectarianism in its strategy as WSP. He was, of course, blind to WSP's political use of sex-role stereotypes. WSP built its movement on female culture. The participants were comfortable campaigning to save the children, but they had not yet learned to demand anything for themselves. Because its key women were socialized in the decades after the first wave of feminism, and before the second, WSP had neither the consciousness, the understanding, nor the language with which to connect women's secondary status in the family and the economy with their exclusion from political power.

What WSP did accomplish in the early 1960s was to bring progressive women into the arena of international affairs, from which they had been barred for over a decade by McCarthyism and the feminine mystique. WSP helped to transform the image of the concerned mother from private to public, and from passive to militant. As women in the United States have done many times in the past, WSP used traditional domestic ideology to turn it on its ear, to extend women's influence from the nursery to the body politic. *See also*: Peace Movements

—*Amy Swerdlow*

REFERENCES

Swerdlow, Amy. "Ladies Day at the Capitol: Women Strike for Peace vs. HUAC." *Feminist Studies* 8 (Fall 1982).

WOMEN'S LIBERATION

Historically, many men and women on the Left have dismissed feminism as a bourgeois reform movement merely seeking to secure women's rights within an otherwise unchanged political-economic structure. American feminists, however, have frequently offered a powerful general critique of their culture and society. As an oppositional movement, American feminism has not only helped redress women's grievances, but has also challenged unarticulated assumptions about men and women's proper economic, social, and cultural place in American society. In this way, feminists have played a central historical role in addressing the problems accompanying changes in family life and shifting gender relations.

The "first wave" of feminism had its roots in the abolitionist movement of the nineteenth century. As they fought to end slavery, female activists found themselves ridiculed and even prohibited from public speaking. Their growing awareness of their subordinate legal and social status led to the woman's rights movement. Convened by Elizabeth Cady Stanton and Lucretia Mott, the first woman's rights conference gathered in 1848 at Seneca Falls, New York. It passed an extraordinary document modeled on the Declaration of Independence, "The Declaration of Sentiments," which described women's social, economic, and cultural grievances and called for woman suffrage. After the Civil War, these women suffered a bitter disappointment when the Fourteenth and Fifteenth amendments, which conferred the rights and duties of citizens upon newly freed slaves, excluded women. Told to be patient, that it was the "Negro's hour," American women responded by establishing organizations to secure the vote for themselves. It took four generations of women to obtain suffrage. By the time the Nineteenth Amendment (commonly called the Susan B. Anthony Amendment) was ratified, the American woman's rights movement had narrowed into a single-issue campaign.

The word *Feministe* originated in France in the 1880s, spread across the Channel to England by the 1890s, and made its way across the Atlantic by 1910. In 1912 a small group of twenty-five New York women formed Heterodoxy, a prototypical consciousness-raising group that required each member "not to be orthodox" in her opinion. To these young adventurous women, *Feminism*—which they always capitalized—promised self-fulfillment, encouraged erotic satisfaction, and demanded of its participants radical criticism of the culture at large. Such a radical and expressive definition of feminism appealed to bohemians of Greenwich Village, but failed to capture many followers.

Between 1920 and the emergence of feminism's "second wave," in the 1960s, American feminism was represented largely by the National Woman's Party (NWP), a tactically militant though politically conservative offshoot of the suffrage movement, founded by Alice Paul in 1916. Convinced that suffrage by itself would not improve women's status, Paul drafted the Equal Rights Amendment, which would have declared unconstitutional discrimination on the grounds of sex. A single-issue organization, the NWP kept the ERA alive by persistently lobbying both political parties, but it failed to ally with the civil rights or labor movements. Politically isolated, the NWP narrowed into a small, elite band of Paul's followers who frequently expressed flagrant racist, anti-Semitic, and Red-baiting sentiments.

The contradictions and frustrations faced by many women during the 1950s and early 1960s in effect set the agenda for the second wave of feminism. While the media painted a roseate portrait of suburban motherhood and the happy nuclear family, the preconditions for a new feminist movement were in the making. Popular culture scorned the working woman, but an expanding service sector, coupled with families' desire for a second income to maintain a middle-class standard of living, drew growing numbers of married middle-class mothers into the paid labor force. A high divorce rate and a revolution in birth-control technology pitted traditional attitudes of sexual restraint against a growing sexual liberalism. As women's life-span expanded, the problem of the "empty nest" became more serious. The growing enrollment of female students in colleges and universities created a generation of young women with elevated expectations and a heightened sense of entitlement.

During the 1950s and early 1960s, McCarthyism effectively silenced any dissent or even the frank recognition of the many problems that accompanied women's growing sexual and economic independence. Housewives, as Betty Friedan revealed in her best-selling 1963 exposé, *The Feminine Mystique*, suffered profound despair, interminable boredom, and unbearable isolation as a result of living exclusively as wives and mothers. Most housewives, however, blamed themselves for their unhappiness. Friedan dubbed their discontent "the problem that has no name." Working women encountered wage discrimination, sexual harassment, the absence of child care, and unequal pay in a sex-segregated labor force. The sexual revolution, at first celebrated by many young women as an expression of individual emancipation (as well as an act of generational defiance), also created new opportunities for the sexual exploitation of women. New contraceptives increased women's sexual freedom, but when they failed, they had to confront the reality that abortion remained illegal. Some women resented the objectification of their bodies to promote consumerism, the new permissiveness toward pornography, and the unaltered economic situation that made prostitution a profitable means of survival. Stripped of their traditional sexual veto—by which women had traditionally extracted promises of male financial support and emotional commitment—some women began to regard the sexual revolution of the 1960s as a male-defined proposition.

The 1960s ushered in a new progressive spirit that legitimized women's questioning of authority and of social and cultural traditions. The civil rights movement successfully ended legal desegregation, the antiwar movement questioned the arrogance of the American efort to contain communism by destroying Vietnam, and Third World countries all over the globe waged liberation movements against dictatorships and foreign domination. From these movements, women learned the power of direct action, absorbed the idea of "participatory democracy," and witnessed how self-determination could lead to independence.

In the wake of such social change, two generations of women pressed against the limits of male liberalism and radicalism. In 1961 Esther Peterson successfully pushed President John F. Kennedy to establish the President's Commission on the Status of Women. The commission's findings, published as *American Women* in 1963, documented women's economic and social subordination but offered only timid recommendations that generally ignored working women's basic needs. In 1963 the U.S. Congress passed the Equal Pay Act, which required equal pay for equal work. Symbolically important, the Equal Pay Act never addressed the reality that most women and men work in separate labor forces with separate pay scales. Title VII of the 1964 Civil Rights Act illegalized sex discrimination in employment practices, but the Equal Employment Opportunity Commission had little intention of enforcing it. Besides, the act exempted educational and governmental agencies. At the third annual meeting of the National Conference of State Commissions on Women, in 1966, a group of women fed up with federal government's unwillingness to enforce its own laws founded the National Organization for Women. Among the founders were Betty Friedan, Aileen Hernandez, Pauli Murray, and two dozen fairly influential women. Organized as a national organization with local chapters, NOW became the most visible and broadly based feminist civil rights organization in the United States. Its goal was "to take action to bring women into full participation in the mainstream of American society *now*, exercising all the privileges and responsibilities thereof in truly equal partnership with men." Although NOW eventually embraced many of the more radical goals of the women's liberation movement—such as reproductive rights and the rights of lesbians—it generally concentrated on challenging legal discrimination, improving women's education opportunities, and advancing women's formal equality. Most of NOW's work reflected the liberal feminist belief that government must protect the individual's innate rights to freedom and equal opportunity. NOW therefore worked hard for the ratification of the Equal Rights Amendment. In the 1980s, NOW entered mainstream politics, endorsed national candidates, and became closely associated with liberal feminism's effort to secure equal rights for women. NOW was instrumental in ending sex-segregated want-ads, enforcing Title VII through successful class-action suits, and publicizing women's problems through national task forces.

During the late sixties, another distinct branch of feminism simultaneously emerged in the United States. These were usually younger women, veterans of other movements, who sought radical change and subjected all authority—especially men's—to close scrutiny. Their experiences in the Student Nonviolent Coordinating Committee, Students for a Democratic Society, and other New Left groups enhanced their sense of personal independence, increased their confidence, and taught them valuable organizing and speaking skills. At the same time, the supposed egalitarianism of these groups frequently collided with young men's automatic assumption of leadership and decision-making. Often relegated to menial chores, sometimes treated as interchangeable sexual objects on young men's revolving beds, women in the New Left—like female abolitionists a century earlier—began questioning their subordinate status within a movement ostensibly dedicated to participatory democracy and nonhierarchical relations.

The ridicule that greeted their concerns angered many New Left women and fueled their difficult but eventual decision to create an autonomous women's liberation movement. As early as 1964, Casey Hayden and Mary King anonymously tried to raise the issue of women's subordination within SNCC, only to elicit Stokely Carmichael's joking but symbolic retort that "the only position for women in SNCC is prone." At the SDS conventions of 1965 and 1966, at the National Conference for New Politics in Chicago in 1967, at the 1969 Counter-Inaugural demonstration in Washington, D.C., New Left women repeatedly witnessed their radical "brothers" ridicule their feminist concerns. First in Chicago, then in New York and in Washington, D.C., women in the New Left gathered in small groups to discuss their shared confusion and resentments. At first, they simply called themselves "radical" women to distinguish themselves from the liberal feminists of NOW. Then, to identify themselves with Third World and black liberation movements, they began describing themselves as the "women's liberation movement."

Unlike NOW, the women's liberation movement was allergic to bureacratic and hierarchical organization, indeed, even to leadership itself. In style as well as substance, the early women's liberation movement inherited some of the greatest strengths—as well as weaknesses—from the radical men they had ostensibly left. From the early civil rights movement they inherited the certainty that "separate but equal" would never guarantee equality. From the subsequent Black Power movement, they adopted the belief that women required some degree of separatism to assert their power. From the counterculture, which they often criticized for trying to keep women "barefoot and pregnant," they retained the moral imperative of living as though the future had already replaced the present. From the late New Left—in the midst of its own self-destruction—they inherited an apocalyptic utopianism that shunned structure and leadership, romanticized "participatory democracy" and the need for consensus, avoided alliances with "establishment" groups, spoke a garbled revolutionary rhetoric, glamorized vanguardism, and demanded moral absolutism, ideological purity, and "correct politics."

Between 1968 and 1970, women's liberation groups sprouted rapidly across the country. Sometimes an umbrella group coordinated the formation of new groups, but many thrived in isolation. Newsletters and journals—including the *Voice of Women's Liberation* in Chicago, *It Ain't Me Babe* in Berkeley, California, *off our backs* in Washington, D.C., and *No More Fun and Games* in Boston—speeded the rapid transmission of new activities and ideas.

Seeking radical change, women's liberationists shunned established reformist efforts in favor of educating themselves and society about the pervasive sexual inequality that conventional wisdom assumed to be "natural." Kathie Sarachild, an early activist in New York Radical Women, coined the phrase "consciousness-raising" to describe the process by which women discovered the truth of their situation. Within the safe confines of a "consciousness-raising group," women began unmasking the world around them as they discussed childhood experiences, mother-daughter relationships, marriage, sexual experiences, stereotypes of femininity, and body images, among other issues. By sharing individual problems, members soon recognized the commonality of their female experiences, and the power relations hidden in their personal and public lives. Unlike group therapy, consciousness-raising was not intended to adapt the individual to society, but to galvanize each woman to change society.

An important contribution of the women's liberation movement was its grounding of political theory in women's concrete life experiences. In *Notes from the Second Year* (1970), Carol Hanisch popularized the idea that "the personal is political." This slogan, which soon became central to the women's liberation movement, broke down the false dichotomy between "personal" and "political," and forced women—and some men—to recognize that power relations were just as operative in the bedroom or kitchen as in public life.

Feminist writings—at first printed as pamphlets—quickly made their way across the country, deepening women's understanding of "the personal is political" and accelerating the "consciousness-raising" that was transforming women's perceptions of their lives.

Ann Koedt's "The Myth of the Vaginal Orgasm" questioned the Freudian assumption that intercourse was required for female sexual satisfaction, and left open the possibility that, with clitoral stimulation, women could achieve sexual satisfaction with or without men. Naomi Weisstein, a veteran of other 1960s movements, a founding member of the Chicago women's liberation movement and the Chicago Women's Liberation Rock Band (1970–73), used her training as an experimental psychologist to argue in "Kinder, Kirche, Küche as Scientific Law: Psychology Constructs the Female" that psychology had created and rationalized an artificial ideal of femininity. Pat Mainardi's "The Politics of Housework" disputed the premise that women should bear exclusive responsibility for housework by sardonically repeating the arguments men typically used to avoid sharing domestic work.

To educate the public, early women's liberationists engaged in "zap" actions, essentially street theater. In January 1968, at the Jeanette Rankin Peace Brigade march in Washington, D.C.—the first all-women's anti-Vietnam War peace demonstration—a group of New York radical feminists staged a "Burial of Traditional Womanhood" to dramatize the fact that they were protesting the war as independent women, rather than as mothers or wives of men. Later that year, New York radical feminists gained national attention when they staged an even more theatrical protest at the Miss America contest in Atlantic City. Protesting the use of women as sexual objects to promote consumerism, they crowned a sheep to parody women being treated like meat and threw into a large "freedom trashcan" objects of "female torture"—bras, cosmetics, hair spray, girdles, copies of *Ladies Home Journal*. Later, the press invented the myth that feminists had burned their bras. There were other famous demonstrations. Women's liberationists invaded bridal fairs to protest the legal inequalities in the marriage contract; they staged sit-downs at famous women's magazines to protest the trivialization of women's concerns; dressed as witches, they hexed Wall Street and companies that exploited the poor. The most significant, broad-gauged event took place on August 26, 1970. Sponsored by a coalition of NOW and women's liberation groups, the national Women's Strike for Equality commemorated the fiftieth anniversary of woman suffrage by staging rallies and marches across the country. In New York, some 20,000 women marched down Fifth Avenue, calling for the three preconditions of women's liberation: twenty-four-hour child-care centers, abortion on demand, and equal opportunity in education and employment.

At its best, "the personal is political" breathed new life into American radical politics by legitimizing the analysis of hidden exploitation and by giving "women's issues" political prominence. It drew public attention to the thousands of deaths that resulted from illegal abortions, dramatized how the lack of child care prevented women from entering public life as equals with men, and revealed the astonishing prevalence of unsatisfactory sex and "faked orgasms" that remained a well-guarded secret in the midst of the sexual revolution. During the 1970s, it permitted feminists to "name" the many hidden injuries women suffered in silence: rape, sexual harassment, wife battering, and forced sexual slavery.

As political theory, however, "the personal is political" had drawbacks. If theory was based on women's experiences, then the political program that emerged from a largely white middle-class movement was hardly applicable to women of other races, classes, and cultures. Even worse, defining the personal as political frequently led to the position that how one lived was a political end in itself. In the name of "the personal is political," too many women were judged traitors for living with men, bearing children, pursuing a professional career, or even dressing "incorrectly." Many highly skilled women who assumed authentic leadership were trashed by a movement that feared domination by "male styles."

Critics noted that women's liberationists seemed particularly hostile toward marriage, men, and children—and they weren't entirely wrong. Many movement participants were refugees from the 1950s, a decade that vilified female independence and insisted that women's anatomy was their destiny. The immediate past conjured up images of claustrophobic marriages, coercive motherhood, and constrained chastity. A terror of being trapped—again, or for the very first time—drove activists to search for alternatives to the traditional nuclear families they remembered from the 1950s. As the movement matured, hostility gave way to sophisticated critiques of the institution of marriage, the institution of motherhood, and the impossible burden of raising children alone without help from either men or the government.

From the beginning, radical women theorized about the origins of women's oppression and sought remedies for it. Reacting against the biological determinism of the 1950s, as well as that decade's glorification of women's moral superiority as mothers, early writers emphasized the fundamental similarity of the sexes and sought to eliminate—or at least diminish—sexual difference. Kate Millett's famous *Sexual Politics* (1970), a book that attacked the misogyny of American culture, called for "the annihilation of sex roles." Shulamith Firestone's *The Dialectic of Sex* (1970) viewed women's oppression as rooted in their biological difference, and argued that test-tube babies might make women equal to men. By the mid-1970s, Carolyn Heilbrun, in *Toward a Recognition of Androgyny* (1973), and others were exploring the possibility of combining the best of both masculine and feminine characteristics.

But by the late 1970s, many feminists writers had begun the search for a "woman-centered" definition of female experience. The women's health movement—popularized by early pamphlet versions of the book *Our Bodies, Our Selves* (1971)—redefined birth, menstruation, and menopause as normal processes and helped reverse women's negative feelings toward their bodies. Writers such as Susan Griffin, Mary Daly, and Adrienne Rich began exploring—and celebrating—women's values and experiences. Carol Gilligan's *In a Different Voice* (1982) even argued that women possess a distinct morality. A "woman-centered perspective" helped women to reclaim their "difference" as a valuable asset, rather than as a liability. But claims of women's special nature and natural superiority sometimes came perilously close to agreeing with the Freudian determinism of the 1950s, the sociobiologists of the 1970s, and the Christian antifeminists of the 1980s. How to define woman's nature—when men still remained the frame of reference—was and remains a problem that haunts feminist debates over social policy and litigation.

Many of the splits that destroyed the movement's unity originated in women's differing political assessments of the causes of and solutions to women's subordination. Women in NOW, for example, believed that legal reforms would substantively improve women's status in the United States. Early radical feminists argued that women's oppression was the root of all systems of oppression and that women together could revolutionize society. The slogan "Sisterhood is Powerful," coined by Kathie Sarachild in 1968, best expressed this point of view. Between 1970 and 1972, a "gay/straight split" caused profound ruptures in the movement. Lesbians insisted the movement treat their sexual preference as a legitimate political issue and some argued that lesbians constituted the political vanguard of the women's movement. During the 1970s large numbers of lesbian-feminists created a separatist woman's culture politically based in a growing network of women's centers, rape crisis centers, battered women's shelters, and culturally expressed in feminist bookstores, coffeehouses, and music festivals. Separatists believed that only a woman's culture could fundamentally challenge the "compulsory heterosexuality" of patriarchal culture. By the later 1970s, feminists further splintered into groups that promoted spirituality (womanspirit and goddess worship), ecology (ecofeminism), and specifically anti-masculinist antiwar and antinuclear campaigns.

In the earliest years of the movement, feminists who remained most closely yoked to the Left were derided as "male identified" "politicos" by radical feminists. Later, they described themselves as socialist-feminists or Marxist-feminists. Like radical feminists, socialist-feminists believed that radical change, not merely reform, was necessary to free women. Some leftist feminists accepted the traditional Marxist belief that women's liberation would be achieved after the overthrow of capitalism, the elimination of private property, and the establishment of a socialist society. Noting women's grim position in socialist countries, however, others argued that patriarchy and capitalism both oppressed women. Two short pamphlets in the late 1960s—Margaret Benston's "The Political Economy of Women's Liberation" and Juliet Mitchell's "Women: The Longest Revolution"—were among the first attempts to synthesize the insights of radical feminism with the class analysis of Marxism. One writer called the effort an "unhappy marriage." Still, autonomous socialist-feminist groups formed in dozens of cities. In the late 1960s, the Boston organization Bread and Roses early defined itself as a socialist-feminist group, and throughout the 1970s socialist-feminists formed women's unions, attempting—mostly unsuccessfully—to organize working women. In 1975 a national socialist-feminist conference in Yellow Springs, Ohio, drew more than 2,000 women.

Still, socialist-feminism had a minimal impact on American feminism as a whole. Its highly sophisticated and often jargon-ridden rhetoric limited its ability to appeal to ordinary women. Expressed in abstract language, socialist-feminist writings rarely embodied the emotional appeal of radical feminist descriptions of women's concrete suffering. Americans' instinctive fear of collectivist solutions and deeply rooted anticommunism, moreover, left socialist-feminism a largely self-referential and marginalized group. Its greatest impact was in the universities and colleges, where socialist-feminists had a disproportionate influence as faculty members. Their prolific feminist scholarship reinvigorated many feminist issues and analyses with a class and racial dimension and helped keep alive the early women's liberation belief that there can be no individual solution to women's problems.

Neither radical feminism nor socialist-feminism had the power to determine how feminism became translated into mainstream culture. By the end of the 1970s, liberal feminists and the media had helped integrate feminism into an American liberal tradition that emphasized individual rights and individual solutions to social problems. In a sudden media blitz during 1970, the national media dramatically turned a small movement into a household cliché and at the same time created fraudulent celebrities, discredited participants as hysterical man-haters or lesbians, and distorted ideas. As the women's liberation movement intersected with the human potential movement, feminism became redefined as a process of individual self-realization. Women's magazines helped women cope with their new responsibilities by teaching assertiveness, dressing for success, stress management, and other privatized techniques.

By 1980, it was clear that the more emancipatory ideas of the women's movement—those that had proposed the transformation of the private sphere—had been excluded from the new image of the "superwoman." Women's entry into the labor force had not been followed by a commensurate reorganization of public institutions ("flextime," child-care, or paid parental leave), or in the home. Women's lives broadened, but often at the cost of sheer exhaustion as they worked—without help—a "double shift" as both a paid worker and an unpaid housewife. The result, as so many noticed in the 1980s, was a new prescriptive role: the myth that a woman can "have it all" and, moreover, do it all, but by herself. Family problems continued to be defined as women's issues. The fantasy of the superwoman obscured the stubborn persistence of a sex-segregated labor market and the fact that, while substantial numbers of middle-class women had moved into the professions, a growing number of women, especially after divorce, had slid into poverty.

In 1980, too, the press repeatedly pronounced the movement dead. Feminists had to admit that their movement was on the defensive. The Equal Rights Amendment, passed by Congress in 1972, met stiff opposition from the New Right and was granted a five-year extension to obtain ratification. By 1982, the ERA still failed to win ratification, and was successfully defeated by right-wing propaganda and poor organization and tactics on the part of its proponents.

Pundits described a new "postfeminist" era, implying feminism had already achieved its goals. It had not; nor was it obsolete. The movement had already spread deeper into mainstream culture and society than most people realized. Across the nation, feminist scholars challenged the paradigms and canons of virtually every academic discipline. During the 1970s, organizations of black, Chicana, and working women created their own feminist organizations. During the UN's Decade for Women (1975–85), networks of feminists gradually transcended cultural and ideological tensions to create a new global feminist movement. At the U.S.-government-sponsored National Conference on Women at Houston in 1977, American women—representing all classes, regions, religions, and political and sexual persuasions—managed to agree on a national agenda of women's needs that incorporated some of the radical visions of the early woman's liberation movement. In national politics, the New Right's introduction of "family politics" onto the national agenda curiously testified to feminism's success in making private issues a matter of public debate. Much more remained to be done. But at least feminists of all political persuasions could claim the not immodest victory of having made gender a salient issue in every aspect of American social, economic, cultural, and political life. *See also*: Socialist Feminism, *Women: A Journal of Liberation*

—*Ruth Rosen*

REFERENCES

Carden, Maren Lockwood. *The New Feminist Movement*. New York: Russell Sage Foundation, 1974.

Evans, Sara. *Personal Politics: The Roots of Women's Liberation in the Civil Rights Movement and the New Left*. New York: Vintage, 1980.

Freeman, Jo. *The Politics of Women's Liberation*. New York: Longman, 1975.

WOMEN'S LIBERATION UNIONS

Between 1969 and 1975 upwards of twenty women's unions were founded across the country to express a radical vision of women's liberation. As the term gained currency in the early 1970s, most of these women's unions became explicitly "socialist-feminist" organizations and constituted one of the major institutional vehicles for socialist-feminist politics during the decade.

Unlike many Left organizations, the women's unions were not located only on the east and west coasts; midwestern and industrial heartland cities had them as well. Although the membership was concentrated among women in their twenties, it included working women as well as students. The first wave of founders frequently came out of organizing experience in the civil rights movement, the antiwar movement, community organizing, and Students for a Democratic Society. Within a few years, however, membership expanded beyond this base, drawing in women for whom the women's union and women's liberation was their first political experience. A substantial portion of women's union members were lesbian or bisexual, and the women's unions prided themselves on good relations between lesbian and straight members.

The organizational structure of the women's unions varied. The San Francisco Women's Union adopted perhaps the most democratic-centralist structure; the Chicago Women's Liberation Union (CWLU) typified the umbrella structure of most of the unions, with project work-groups, a steering committee, and membership meetings. True to their roots in the women's movement, the women's unions took issues of process and internal democracy very seriously. Many of them produced newsletters, which are available in the Special Collections at Northwestern University Library.

Most women's unions tried to select projects that expressed their vision of socialist-feminist politics, which meant an emphasis on anti–Vietnam War agitation, working and working-class women, sexuality/abortion/women's health, prisoner support work, and coalition work with Third World solidarity groups or people of color. Many sponsored successful International Women's Day celebrations. Some unions, notably the Berkeley-Oakland Women's Union, took the development of socialist-feminist theory as a serious task; others such as the CWLU were more project-oriented. The women's unions, in collaboration with the New American Movement, organized a national conference on socialist-feminism held in Yellow Springs, Ohio, in the summer of 1975 and attended by more than 1,600 women.

The women's unions could not sustain themselves following the collapse of the Left in the mid-1970s. The national conference, which appeared to mark the takeoff point for socialist-feminism, actually revealed the cleavages within it. The women's unions' actual base was almost exclusively white and heavily middle-class, despite calls for outreach to women of color and working-class women. Some unions collapsed under the pressure from long-term members and from Maoist groups to suspend what they perceived as mindless activity in favor of study and the development of theory. These critics did not see in socialist-feminist theory an adequate strategy for socialist revolution. Other members, now more rooted in their workplaces and communities, wanted to become more involved in mainstream political activity. They felt the call for more study to be a drain in the direction of more mindless theorizing. Almost all of the women's unions had dissolved by 1977.

As concrete achievements, the women's unions provided a generation of women activists with organizing and speaking skills that many have gone on to put to other uses—personal, professional, and political. Former women's union members are found in significant numbers in trade unions, the women's health movement, local and state government, community organizations, and educational institutions. As autonomous but not separatist women's organizations, they made visible the politics of women's liberation and forced the Left to take those politics seriously. *See also*: Socialist Feminism, Women's Liberation

—*Margaret Strobel*

REFERENCES

Hansen, Karen. "The Women's Unions and the Search for a Political Identity." *Socialist Review*, 86 (March–April 1986).

"The National Conference on Socialist Feminism." *Socialist Revolution*, 26 (October–December 1975).

Popkin, Ann. "The Personal Is Political: The Women's Liberation Movement." In *They Should Have Served That Cup of Coffee*, edited by Dick Custer. Boston: South End Press, 1979.

"The 'Principles of Unity' of the Berkeley-Oakland Women's Union." *Socialist Revolution* 19 (January–March 1974).

Red Apple Collective. "Socialist-Feminist Women's Unions, Past and Present." *Socialist Review*, 38 (March–April 1978).

Women's Studies

"Women's Studies is not simply the study of women," the Hunter College Women's Studies Collective explained, "It is the study of women which places women's own experiences in the center of the process. It examines the world and the human beings who inhabit it with questions, analyses, and theories built directly on women's experiences." As an academic field, women's studies developed alongside not only the women's liberation movement but the civil rights, antiwar, and student movements of the late 1960s. The emerging interdisciplinary field therefore gathered young faculty and graduate students who viewed scholarly work as incontestably political and antiestablishment. Although the field soon widened to encompass many perspectives, its pioneering scholars represented the radical sector of the academy.

By 1970 women's studies courses, mainly in the liberal arts, were taught on college campuses, and within a few years the numbers grew at such a rate that the first undergraduate majors were established. By the decade's end, programs in women's studies totaled approximately 350. Specialized journals appeared, such as *Feminist Studies, Women's Studies, Signs, Frontiers*, and the *Women's Studies Newsletter*. The National Women's Studies Association formed in 1977, and by the early 1980s its annual meetings drew between 1,000 and 2,000 participants. The major professional organizations, such as the American Psychological Association, Modern Languages Association, and American Historical Association, housed feminist or women's caucuses by the mid-1980s.

Although feminist scholars began in the late 1960s by criticizing the male bias of contemporary disciplinary literature, a sizable sector turned to study the origins and nature of women's oppression and asked questions concerning women's historical agency. Drawing on older works, such as Simone de Beauvoir's *The Second Sex* (1949), Mary Ritter Beard's *Woman as Force in History* (1946), or Friedrich Engels's *The Origin of the Family, Private Property, and the State* (1884), they came upon an earlier scholarly tradition influenced by historical materialism. Feminist anthropologists, sociologists, and historians in particular centered their initial analyses on the sexual division of labor in its specific cultural and historic forms as a guide to understanding the status of women and the relations between the sexes.

A groundbreaking contribution was Margaret Benston's essay "The Political Economy of Women's Liberation," which appeared in *Monthly Review* in 1969. Employing Marxist terminology, Benston analyzed women's oppression as a function of their particular place in capitalist production, namely their assignment to the production of use-value in the home. Because the value of domestic work remains unrecognized in a capitalist economy, she argued, women carry the stigma of their distance from commodity production. Although Benston's specific analysis suffered a series of criticisms, her demonstration of the connections between women, the family, and the larger society inspired other scholars to make the study of political economy an important facet of their work.

This framework stood out in the early scholarship in the field of anthropology and especially so in the work of Michelle Rosaldo. Although Rosaldo discarded Engels's dictum that women's subordination occurred only with the institution of private property in favor of a theory of universal female subordination, she nevertheless took a materialist approach. Rosaldo studied social and cultural organization as a function of the sexual division of labor and reasoned that women's reproductive function and responsibility led to a "differentiation of domestic and public spheres of activity." Women's oppression and agency depended, in Rosaldo's analysis, on the degree of "sexual asymmetry."

The concept of distinct "spheres," structural divisions by private and public, showed itself prominently in early feminist scholarship in the field of history. In the influential essay "The Social Relations of the Sexes: Methodological Implications of Women's History," published in 1976, Joan Kelly (1928–82) speculated that when the differentiation between family and society was minimal, women's status more nearly approximated that of men; when there was a sharp break between the private and public spheres, sexual inequality increased. The historical scholarship of the early 1970s incorporated this line of argument, which generated in turn a major subfield, women's labor history. Shop-floor studies in trades with high rates of female participation, analyses of women's role in specific strikes and unions, and new perspective on the significance of women's domestic labor, all highlighted a challenge made by women scholars to traditional as well as Left labor historiography.

Feminist scholars, Rosaldo and Kelly among the most articulate, did not, however, simply transpose the materially determinist frameworks of earlier generations onto their own work. They insisted that sex, class, and race were co-equally integral and interactive concepts.

Outside the social sciences, the influence of the Left has been more circuitous. Feminist literary criticism began in the late 1960s by criticizing the canon for its virtual exclusion of women writers and exposing the misogynist handling of female characters by male authors. Scholars proceeded to uncover a lost tradition of women writers, the Feminist Press under Florence Howe's leadership in the 1970s playing the leading role in reprinting primary sources.

By the mid-1980s an entirely different approach had taken over the field. In a loose combination of Marxism, psychoanalysis, and deconstruction, many scholars proposed new lines of interpretation. The historical materialist approach yielded to theories of representation that highlighted the ambiguity of the text in light of the triumph and subsequent fragmentation of Western thought. *See also*: Socialist Feminism

—*Mari Jo Buhle*

REFERENCES

DuBois, Ellen Carol, Gail Paradise Kelly, Elizabeth Lapovsky Kennedy, Carolyn W. Korsmeyer, and Lillian S. Robinson. *Feminist Scholarship: Kindling in the Groves of Academe*. Urbana: University of Illinois Press, 1985.

Hunter College Women's Studies Collective. *Women's Realities, Women's Choices: An Introduction to Women's Studies*. New York: Oxford University Press, 1983.

WOODHULL, VICTORIA: *see* WOODHULL AND CLAFLIN'S WEEKLY

WOODHULL AND CLAFLIN'S WEEKLY

This journal appeared in New York City from May 14, 1870, until June 10, 1876 (with an interruption from June 22 to December 28, 1872), under the masthead "Upward and Onward," which changed to the bolder "Progress! Free Thought! Untrammelled Lives!" Published and edited by two sisters, Tennessee Claflin and Victoria Claflin Woodhull, with the active collaboration of the anarchist philosopher Stephen Pearl Andrews, it reflected their views and promoted Woodhull's career. Inspired by socialist, libertarian, and utopian ideas, the *Weekly* advocated a comprehensive program of universal justice, women's rights, world government, and free love, tinged with spiritualism.

After Woodhull's experience on Wall Street as a stockbroker, the *Weekly* launched a muckraking campaign and denounced speculation for "cheating, swindling rich, middle, and laboring classes . . ."

At the same time, the *Weekly* orchestrated Woodhull's political career based on her commitment to woman suffrage and to the First International Workingmen's Association. On November 19, 1870, the *Weekly* launched her candidacy for the presidency of the United States and published her "Memorial," in which she argued that, as citizens of the United States, women were enfranchised according to the Fourteenth and Fifteenth Amendments of the Constitution. The National Woman Suffrage Association (NWSA) welcomed this new strategy. Meanwhile, in 1871 the *Weekly* reported Woodhull's triumph at the NWSA convention in Washington, followed by her call to revolution, the "Great Secession Speech."

In April 1872 the *Weekly* published a manifesto, endorsed by the NWSA leaders, calling a convention to form the new People's Party "based on human rights," with Woodhull for president. But Susan B. Anthony refused this association, thus terminating their collaboration and Woodhull's political venture. The *Weekly* supported women in other ways by attacking the current impractical fashions, deploring the harassment of prostitutes, and advocating employment and higher wages for women.

On December 30, 1871, the *Weekly* published the *Communist Manifesto* for the first time in English. Thereafter it promoted the views of the American sections of the First International, announced meetings, and reported events such as the celebration of the Paris Commune on March 30, 1872. When Section 12 (a faction within the American movement) came under fire by the International for not toeing the party line on the class-struggle issue and promoting women's rights and "social freedom," the *Weekly* published discussions, resolutions, and William West's report of the Congress in The Hague in September 1872 confirming the expulsion of Section 12.

Free love was a dominant theme in the *Weekly*. Woodhull and Andrews criticized marriage as enslaving women and constraining individual feeling and freedom. The *Weekly* reported her sensational speech on social (read "sexual") freedom (November 21, 1871) and the mounting insinuations against the Rev. Henry Ward Beecher. The special issue of November 2, 1872, contained two explosive articles: the first revealed Beecher's sexual affair with the wife of Theodore Tilton, a religious and political associate of Beecher; the second described the debauches of a broker, Luther C. Challis, and led to the Claflin sisters' arrest under the Comstock laws, that prohibited sending obscenity through the mail. Nevertheless, the *Weekly* continued discussing free love, reporting the Beecher-Tilton trial, Woodhull's lectures, and spiritualist meetings. Leaning more and more toward conservatism and mysticism, in 1875 the *Weekly* prophesied the advent of the Apocalypse and proclaimed its allegiance to the Bible. The new message preached the sanctity of the human body, the holiness of the family, and the redeeming mission of women. *See also*: International Workingmen's Association ("First International")

—*Françoise Basch*

REFERENCES

Basch, Françoise. *Mariage, amour libre et politique: deux rebelles américaines au dix-neuvième siècle.* Paris: à paraître au Mercure de France, 1988.

Sachs, Emanie. *The Terrible Siren, Victoria Woodhull.* New York: Harpers Brothers, 1928.

Stern, Madeline, ed. *The Victoria Woodhull Reader.* Weston, Mass.: M & S Press, 1974.

Woodworkers of Chicago

Chicago's phenomenal growth attracted workers of all nationalities to the expansive construction industry. Hence no one national group numerically dominated the largely foreign-born building carpenters, although the top union leadership was usually Anglo-Irish. Germans and Scandinavians, in contrast, predominated in Chicago's large furniture industry until its decline in the early twentieth century.

Chicago's woodworkers were particularly prominent in trade union organization and Left political activity in the second half of the nineteenth century. In the early 1870s Chicago's German cabinetmakers led the movement for a national furniture workers' union, and their local received the number *one* in recognition of their efforts; a descendant of this local still exists. Like their international union, Chicago's furniture workers were among the earliest advocates of industrial unionism. During the great railroad strikes of 1877, a meeting of Chicago furniture workers in the Bohemian Turner Hall was attacked by the police in one of the most violent and controversial occurrences in the Chicago upheaval.

Chicago's building carpenters were slower to organize stable unions, in part because of the deeper and more numerous ethnic divisions among them; but by the early 1890s they had created the strongest interethnic union in Chicago. After a huge strike in 1890, they won higher wages, union recognition, and the eight-hour day, victories that put them at the forefront of the Chicago labor movement.

Although it is easier to trace Chicago's woodworkers as unionists than as participants in Left political activity, recent work has found that woodworkers were prominent in the founding of Chicago's socialist German-language labor press in the mid-1870s and well represented in the constituency of Chicago's anarchist movement. Carpenters made up the largest skilled occupational group among the members of the International Working Peoples Association, while cabinetmakers ranked fourth. Carpenters were also significantly involved in independent labor political movements in 1886–87, 1894, and 1919.

Furniture workers formed an important constituency for the Left when the industry was marked by rapid mechanization within production units that nonetheless still utilized large numbers of craft workers in specialized departments. Construction carpenters also felt the impact of mechanization through the production of standardized, prefabricated building parts. Ethnically diverse and well organized, Chicago's building carpenters have been able to maintain an enviable tradition of controlling their industry from the late nineteenth century up to the present, although, with significant exceptions in the late nineteenth and early twentieth centuries, their politics have been confined to the Democratic Party. *See also*: Black International, Haymarket Affair

—*John B. Jentz*

REFERENCES

Jentz, John B. "Artisan Culture and the Organization of Chicago's German Workers in the Gilded Age, 1860 to 1890." *Amerika-Studien* 29, no. 2 (1984).

———. "Skilled Workers and Industrialization: Chicago's German Cabinetmakers and Machinists, 1880–1900." In *German Workers in Industrial Chicago, 1850–1910: A Comparative Perspective*, edited by Hartmut Keil and John B. Jentz. DeKalb: Northern Illinois University Press, 1983.

Nelson, Bruce C. "Culture and Conspiracy: A Social History of Chicago Anarchism, 1870–1900." Ph.D. diss., Northern Illinois University, 1986.

Schneirov, Richard, and Thomas J. Suhrbur. *Union Brotherhood, Union Town: A History of the Carpenters' Union of Chicago, 1863 to 1987*. Carbondale: Southern Illinois University Press, 1988.

Shurbur, Thomas J. "Ethnicity and the Formation of the Chicago Carpenters Union: 1855–1890." Keil and Jentz, *German Workers*.

Workers Alliance of America: see Unemployed Movements, 1930s

Workers (Communist) Party: see Communist Party

Workers' Control

This phrase connotes the goal of producers to reduce the degree of employee subjugation and if possible to control their own procedures by various means ranging from subtle day-to-day maneuvers to negotiated contracts to mass direct action. "Workers' control" has frequently implied "production for use" rather than for profit, a distinction that has impelled advocates toward socialist alliances.

The desire for control of production, rooted deeply in the substantial real autonomy of the nineteenth-century craftsmen, took on radical dimensions with the pattern of strikes to enforce union recognition and union rules during the later 1880s and the 1890s. Sympathy strikes joined workers separated by geography and by trade, prompting a variety of class-consciousness central to many crafts or industrial districts organized or influenced by socialists. Defeats, economic depression, and the increasing regularization of union chain-of-command diminished such sympathy strikes by the mid-1890s, but hardly eradicated a deeper desire for participation in workplace decisions. Nor did it nullify the dream of a better world with clean, democratic factories, a vision shared by turn-of-the-century socialists.

The rise of the Industrial Workers of the World introduced new dimensions to "workers' control." The movement's philosophers, drawing alike on Marxism, European syndicalism, and American labor experience, concretized the rather dreamy concepts of American socialist intellectuals, articulating the vision of a society in which the coercive political state had been replaced wholly by a functional cooperation of producers' collectives. Described by Daniel DeLeon as a new phase in civilization, the concept had a compelling attraction to labor visionaries and to many workers. Wobbly strikes of 1909–17, continually raised philosophical questions of workers' control through propagandistic stress upon workers' creation of all use value.

Defeat of the IWW drive shifted the dimensions of "workers' control" back toward such practical matters as contracts, shop stewards, and in some cases toward the highly skilled work-force minority. Somewhat different varieties of "workers' control," then, took shape along the leftward edges of the mainstream labor movement. Both accelerating Taylorization and the rising urges of workers in favorable conditions for strikes prompted newly popular sentiments. The open-shop drive against machinists, for instance, brought protracted sympathy strikes at great collective sacrifice, and the election of international officers close to the Socialist Party. Local coalitions of assorted SPers, SLPers, and IWWs, such as those gathered around the Westinghouse Electric plant near Pittsburgh, helped lead the organization of unique independent unions stressing class solidarity and demanding various improvements. The Amalgamated Clothing Workers, a radically inclined new union born of strikes and mass mobilization, promoted at the end of the 1910s a widespread sense of unionists gaining as much from the reshaping of production as they could gain from employers' wage packets. "Control strikes," which reached a peak in 1916–20, introduced the phrase "workers' control" to wide usage for the first time by frequency of demands for nonwage issues.

The working-class Left that might have emerged under these banners—revealing its potential most clearly in the Seattle general strike of 1919—had no clear political counterpart. The SP's electoral orientation, shifted largely to antiwar activism, had little room for industrial demands as such. The party's largely foreign-born Left, although frequently close to participants in the contemporary strikes, formulated its proto-Communist programs largely on the basis of developments in the Soviet Union (and only briefly in the shape of the "soviets," workers' councils proper, rather than the Bolshevik Party). Left socialist magazines such as the *International Socialist Review* that had encouraged discussion of industrial issues fell by the wayside, repressed and destroyed. Left caucuses established within unions such as the International Ladies Garment Workers Union mixed their industrial programs with the demands of the emerging Communist movement, substantially obscuring the workers' control issue.

Again, a series of new formations and stirrings within existing unions had the most telling effect during the early 1920s. The One Big Union, founded in Calgary, Canada, in 1919, stemmed from AFL machinists and others who believed in "abolition of the present system of production for profit and the substitution therefore of production for use." With a following in Canada and the U.S. Northwest, the OBU reached its apex in the Winnipeg general strike of 1919 and declined thereafter. In a parallel development, United Mine Workers District 2 leaders, joined by railroad brotherhood workers, campaigned for government ownership (with labor participation in management) of the railway system, and a strategy to mine and sell coal through a council of workers, technicians, and consumers. These plans collapsed together with a failed collaboration of the two sectors.

Nevertheless, Communists and their allies in many ways subsequently carried on important elements of historic "workers' control" sympathies. Using the Russian model of workers' (or government) supervision over finances but not necessarily production, they did not necessarily grasp at first the character of American workers' impulses. The Trade Union Educational League and the Trade Union Unity League, respectively, nevertheless defended the autonomy of existing locals to formulate such demands, and put forward new demands on behalf of the unskilled industrial workers. The first, conducting a backstairs struggle against conservatism and the "American Plan," encouraged a discussion of resistance to Taylorization and the further bureaucratization of labor decision-making. Labor colleges and the socialistic monthly *Labor Age* continued this discussion, as did the IWW's *Industrial Pioneer* and the Amalgamated Clothing Workers' *Advance*, among labor intellectuals. The second, prompting the publication of "shop papers" addressing the particular, immediate woes of local situations, foreshadowed the rise of the CIO.

Demands for workers' control were expressed in a wide variety of ways during the upsurge of industrial unionism, often but by no means always related to Communists, Socialists, and other radicals. City general strikes, as in San Francisco and Minneapolis in 1934, reflected a coordinated desire for labor influence (over the hiring hall, for instance) and perhaps control of the urban-industrial space. The demands of electrical workers for a sharing of unemployment's burdens (and also a more equitable ratio of male and female pay), for instance, and the widespread practice of direct action on the shop floor in the young CIO unions all gave "workers' control" new scope. Concerned most with unionization and international issues, Left groups only obliquely addressed the issue of control.

The wide bureaucratization during and following World War II eclipsed many of the radical programs, but above all removed most union officials from democratic controls. Elements of the Left, albeit hamstrung by the Cold War mood, struggled unsuccessfully to make political issues of the increasing reluctance to correct grievances rather than referring them to some protracted and uncertain process. At the same time, the new possibilities of consumerism available also reduced the significance of workers' control issues in the eyes of many workers themselves.

Nevertheless, workers' control as a response to accelerated mechanization returned sharply with automation and the "wildcat strikes" of the 1950s. A badly reduced Left played little role in these movements, although some saw in them proof of class resiliency. With the rise of Black Power at the end of the 1960s, industrial demands (mixed with race complaints, as against the forms of speed-up labeled "niggermation") prompted radical union challenges over control issues (especially in Detroit, home of the League of Revolutionary Black Workers) among others. A few years later, insurgent movements popped up here and there (Lordstown, Ohio, site of the most sophisticated automobile automation in the world, offered one striking example), ardently supported by sections of the New Left. But these generally faded with their successful isolation from any wider union reform current.

Deindustrialization, with the accompanying massive reduction in existing work-force and union membership, seemingly quieted the urgings for workers' control. Yet sub rosa movements of various kinds, influenced by the Left or not, continued to pose the question. Left-oriented caucuses, such as the Teamsters for a Democratic Union, continued to raise issues apart from wages, posing questions of truly satisfying labor against so-called quality-work-life programs. The scattered sectors of successful union organizing (such as at Yale University or Harvard University) frequently gathered their support from workers most concerned with questions of dignity, job status, and the like. "Workers' control," virtually absent as a slogan, remained an idea behind resilient labor idealism. *See also*: Amalgamated Clothing Workers of America, Anarcho-Syndicalism, Council Communism, Detroit IWW, General Strike, Industrial Workers of the World, Knights of Labor, Seattle General Strike, Wildcat Strikes

—*Paul Buhle*

REFERENCES

James, C. L. R. *State Capitalism and World Revolution*. Chicago: Charles H. Kerr, 1986.

Montgomery, David. *The Fall of the House of Labor: The Workplace, the State, and American Labor Activism, 1865–1925*. Cambridge: Cambridge University Press, 1987.

———. *Workers Control in America: Studies in the History of Work, Technology, and Labor Struggles*. Cambridge: Cambridge University Press, 1979.

Moody, Kim. *An Injury to All: The Decline of American Unionism*. London: Verso, 1988.

Workers Defense League

The WDL was formed in 1936, in effect a nonpartisan alternative to the Communist-dominated International Labor Defense, to coordinate legal and financial resources and organize publicly to defend the rights of endangered workers. It has been historically associated with the Socialist movement. Before its formation, Norman Thomas—destined to be the most important public figure of the WDL for several decades—had organized ad hoc defense committees for labor, unemployed, and civil rights movements during the early 1930s. The WDL had been shaped by such experiences as the general strike in Terre Haute, Indiana, and the reign of military law that followed; the murder by the Ku Klux Klan of a leader of the unemployed in Tampa, Florida (where Thomas helped force the convictions of police who doubled as Klansmen); and the Arkansas cotton choppers' strike of 1936.

That year, Thomas headed a WDL organizing committee that included David L. Clendenin, the Rev. Aron S. Gilmartin, and attorneys Max Delson and Francis Heisler, among others. The new organization won three rapid, important southern victories. First came the conviction of a sheriff (who was also a plantation owner in Arkansas), guilty of holding farm workers in virtual slavery. The WDL exposed forced labor in Broward County, Florida, where a sheriff falsely arrested black workers, charged exorbitant fines, and rented them as day laborers to farm growers until their fines were paid. And the WDL helped the racially integrated Southern Tenant Farmers Union win better pay, housing, and working conditions for thousands of poor tenant farmers and sharecroppers. In 1937 Norman Thomas defied Mayor Frank (known, in his own words as, "I Am the Law") Hague of Jersey City, New Jersey, who had barred CIO organizers from town. Stoned, rotten-egged, and run out of town, Thomas and the WDL nevertheless opened Jersey City to unionists.

Among many later activities, the WDL was the first group during World War II to protest the internment of Japanese Americans. It won a change in the military's policies concerning less-than-honorable discharges, and helped desegregate the armed forces. It forced reform of the nation's Industrial Personnel Security Program, under which employers had used Cold War tensions to fire union activists as "security risks." In 1948 the WDL created an international Commission of Inquiry into Forced Labor in the Communist countries, southern Africa, and the U.S. South. That inquiry, with the backing of the AFL, led to a UN Commission on Forced Labor.

By the 1960s, the WDL Apprenticeship Program to train minority youth to pass apprenticeship tests in the building trades evolved into the Recruitment and Training Program, Inc. More than 30,000 young minority men and women throughout the country won union membership and well-paid skilled trades jobs. In recent years, the WDL has, among other work, publicized the return of debt peonage to agricultural workers, and helped form committees to aid the unemployed and the homeless. *See also*: Socialist Party; Thomas, Norman

—*Harry Fleischman*

REFERENCES

Workers Defense League Files, Reuther Library, Wayne State University.

Workers Defense League Golden Anniversary Journal, December 1986.

The
MODERN
SCHOOL
A MONTHLY MAGAZINE DEVOTED TO LIBERTARIAN IDEAS IN EDUCATION
Quarterly Number
JANUARY · FEBRUARY · MARCH
Published by
THE FERRER MODERN SCHOOL, Stelton, New Jersey
25c.

Cover by Rockwell Kent, 1910s

WORKERS' EDUCATION

Beginning around 1918, several dozen "labor colleges" were established across the United States by progressive unionists and pro-labor intellectuals. A kindred movement in England, developing since the establishment of Ruskin College at Oxford in 1899, was to some extent the inspiration of workers' education in America. So were the various socialist schools—from the People's College of Fort Scott, Kansas, to the Work People's College in Duluth, Minnesota, to the Rand School in New York—which never grew large, and which had been raided by federal and local authorities in wartime. Perhaps most important, however, was the labor turbulence and hopes of 1918–20, with the emergence of what many called the "new unionism," democratic and socially conscious. One of the major publicists of the newer labor education, Arthur Gleason, called it "training in the science of reconstruction."

U.S. labor colleges fell generally into three categories. Programs of evening classes sponsored by central labor councils and the needle trades unions educated the most students by far. In New York, for example, the "Workers' University" sponsored by the International Ladies Garment Workers Union met in public school buildings on evenings and weekends. In other cities, while some programs were ephemeral, schools such as the Boston Trade Union College and the Philadelphia Labor College were well established. Summer schools aimed primarily toward women marked a second type, including the

Bryn Mawr Summer School for Women Workers in Industry, the Barnard Summer School, and the University of Wisconsin Summer School. Third were the residential labor schools, such as Brookwood in Katonah, New York, and Commonwealth College in Mena, Arkansas.

The founders and leaders of these programs included many radicals eager to move beyond the narrow parameters of Socialist and Communist parties proper. Brookwood, for example, was launched by socialist and pacifist opponents of World War I, and proponents of farmer-labor politics following the war. Commonwealth College was founded in 1923 by Kate Richards O'Hare and other southwestern socialists who had moved to the New Llano utopian colony in Louisiana (relocated to Arkansas) seeking a new life. Explicitly class-conscious, workers' education aimed (in Selig Perlman's words) to "educate the worker, not as an individual but as a member of his social class." Consideration of radical possibilities naturally entered into classroom discourse, introduced either by instructors or students. Labor movement and academic supporters of the workers' education institutions sought to maintain a balance between this sometimes radical content and a moderate image intended to minimize public controversy and maintain support.

The rightward shift of the AFL made this compromise ultimately untenable. In 1928 the AFL charged Brookwood with teaching communism and ordered all AFL affiliates to withhold further support. In 1934 the trustees of Bryn Mawr College drove the summer school off campus amid charges that radical instructors were using the program to supply pickets to nearby strikes. Commonwealth College, which grew more action-oriented and shifted from a Socialist to Communist tilt, was closed after continued harassment by state and local authorities. Even the Works Education Bureau, founded in 1921 as an umbrella organization for the movement, sharply divided between those critical of conservative AFL policies and loyal adherents of the AFL leadership, which dominated the WEB.

By the later 1930s, many of the labor colleges went into decline or disappeared due to political or financial problems. Encompassed into the New Deal via the Federal Emergency Relief Administration (later the Works Progress Administration) as a workers' education division for the instruction of labor-education teachers, a handful of labor education veterans continued their work. This experiment ended with WW II. Subsequent efforts at revival with congressional support failed, due in part to conservative and corporate hostility. The "labor education" that continued, mostly through union education departments and university-based extension programs, stressed leadership training and disregarded radical ideas or alternatives.

"Workers' education" has survived, as a name, in Workers' Education Local 189, an organization of several hundred founded at Brookwood in 1922. Originally affiliated with the American Federation of Teachers, Local 189 was forced out in 1976 as a result of its criticisms of AFT leadership. Local 189 members, along with many others, have been instructors in the new wave of "labor colleges" that reappeared during the 1970s–1980s as credit programs within mainstream institutions offering degrees in labor studies. These programs vary widely. But the presence of New Left, antiwar, and (albeit to a considerably lesser degree) feminist movement veterans, and the curriculum combining social science, unionism, writing and speaking skills, harken back in modest fashion to the historic workers' education movement. *See also*: Muste, A. J.; Rand School

—*Jon Bloom*

REFERENCES

Brameld, Theodore. *Workers' Education in the United States*. New York: Harper & Brothers, 1941.

Gleason, Arthur. *Workers' Education*. New York: Bureau of Industrial Research, 1921.

Workers Laboratory Theater—Theater of Action

The leader of a workers' theater movement during the 1930s, WLT/TOA was characterized by an agitprop style intended to educate working-class audiences about left-wing issues.

Founded in 1929 by several young theater enthusiasts in New York City, it was inspired by German and Soviet traveling political theater troupes and cultural efforts by the Communist Party's John Reed Clubs and the *New Masses*. It performed short, original, highly stylized political sketches for political rallies, strikes, Unemployed Councils, and other organizing efforts associated with the CP.

As a mobile theater able to bring social drama to working-class audiences without previous theatrical exposure, it presented skits that blended elements of symbolism, realism, vaudeville, dance, music, and mass chant into strident Marxist indictments of capitalism, racism, fascism, and the bourgeois state. Characters were portrayed as caricatures in cartoonlike renditions of politicians, factory owners, corrupt union officials, and newspaper editors.

In 1931, responding to growing interest from other workers' theater groups and the desire to create a national network, the Workers Lab (now merged with a German workers' theater troupe, the *Prolet Buhne*) put out the first issue of *Workers Theater*. Later that year, a national workers' theater conference drew 130 organizations representing artists in theater, film, dance, and literature, including Hallie Flanagan, who several years later would direct the New Deal's Federal Theater Project. By 1933, an estimated 250 workers' theater groups existed as part of a national League of Workers' Theaters. In 1934 *Workers' Theater* was renamed *New Theater*, achieving a monthly circulation of 10,000, with Jimmy Durante, Burgess Meredith, and Groucho Marx among its subscribers.

By 1932, the Workers Lab had a studio loft on the Lower East Side. Its core was a full-time "Shock Troupe" of twelve to eighteen members, with an Evening Troupe of 100. Putting their socialist beliefs into practice, the Shock Troupe lived together communally, sharing the meager funds they earned from union and worker fraternal-order bookings. Daily classes were held in acting, movement, voice, current affairs, and Marxist theory. In 1933 they had a repertory of twenty sketches, performed two or three times daily, reaching an estimated 100,000 workers during that year.

"Newsboy" (1933) was their most successful and well-known production. Adapted from a poem by CP cultural official V. J. Jerome, the twenty-minute, montagelike sketch contrasted headlines of the daily press with scenes from Depression life as seen through the eyes of a newsboy. Fast-paced realistic vignettes, dance movement, and mass chants were integrated into what was reviewed as the first application of Eisenstein's film theories to American theater. "Newsboy" quickly became a standard of workers' theater groups nationwide. Among theater professionals, the Workers Lab was recognized for advancing agitprop to a higher dramatic standard.

In 1934 the Workers Lab changed its name to the Theater of Action, marking a growing theatrical sophistication. TOA's prestige was confirmed by the steady stream of artists and intellectuals visiting their loft, including Moss Hart, Bertolt Brecht, Kurt Weil, Orson Welles, and John Howard Lawson. It now had a "younger brother" relationship with the Group Theater, with members Elia Kazan, Sandy Meisner, Lou Leveritt, and Bobby Lewis teaching TOA classes.

While continuing their regular performances for left-wing functions with a repertory of eighty sketches, TOA produced several full-length plays. In 1935 *The Young Go First*, codirected by Elia Kazan and Al Saxe, was their first and last attempt at a Broadway production. It closed after six weeks. TOA seemed unable to transform its mobile, political style into effective proscenium form. Six years of performing for next to nothing also prompted a desire to seek more established theatrical careers.

In 1936 TOA was incorporated into the WPA's Federal Theater Project as the One-Act Experimental Theater, lasting one season. Many of its members then worked in various FTP productions, e.g., Nick Ray stage-managed the Living Newspapers; Al Saxe was assistant director for *One-Third of a Nation*. On a larger level, in terms of affecting mainstream culture, the Workers Lab/Theater of Action influenced a whole generation of young artists and intellectuals who would continue producing works of social significance in theater, film, and television. *See also*: Federal Theater Project; Lawson, John Howard

—*Joel Saxe*

REFERENCES

Goldstein, Malcolm. *The Political Stage: American Drama and Theater of the Great Depression*. New York: Oxford University Press, 1974.

Himelstein, Morgan. *Drama Was a Weapon: The Left-Wing Theater in New York, 1929–1941*. New Brunswick: Rutgers University Press, 1963.

McConachie, Bruce A., and Daniel Friedman, eds. *Theater for Working Class Audiences in the United States, 1830–1980*. Westport: Greenwood Press, 1985.

Samuel, Raphael, Ewan MacColl, and Stuart Cosgrove. *Theaters of the Left, 1880–1935, Workers' Theater in Britain and America*. London: Routledge and Kegan Paul, 1985.

Williams, Jay. *Stage Left*. New York: Scribners, 1974.

WORKERS PARTY

The WP was founded in 1940 as a result of the first major split in the American Trotskyist movement, then constituted as the Socialist Workers Party. Within the SWP a minority had coalesced around the leadership of James Burnham, Martin Abern, and Max Shachtman that had increasing doubts as to whether the Soviet Union was still some form of workers' state, even a "degenerated" one as proclaimed by the party's majority. The issue was whether revolutionary socialists should continue to give their political support to the Soviet Union and use that country as even a deeply flawed model for socialist transformation. The Soviet Union's attack on Finland, which followed its occupation of eastern Poland and the Baltic states in the wake of the Nazi-Soviet Pact of 1939, brought matters to a head. The minority was now confronted by what it viewed as Soviet imperialism, a phenomenon not expected from a workers' state. After insisting on expanded freedom to express its factional views, the minority was expelled.

James Burnham, a professor of philosophy, had taken the lead in suggesting that the Soviet Union had become a new form of class society, dominated by a bureaucratic ruling class. After he completed his brief sojourn in the newly founded WP, its intellectual leadership clearly shifted to Max Shachtman and before long the group came to be known as the Shachtmanites. Its theoretical basis was developed in the pages of the *New International*, the journal that the minority had taken with it from the SWP. While still identifying with Lenin and the Bolshevik Revolution, Shachtman argued that Stalin had carried out a completely successful counterrevolution.

The WP defined its politics largely on its position on the "Russian question." Labeling the Soviet Union an example of bureaucratic collectivism, it argued that a nationalized economy alone did not constitute socialism, because the entire apparatus of the state was controlled by the privileged Soviet bureaucrats, not the working class. The economic transformation carried out under Stalin's five-year plans was compared with capitalism's period of primary accumulation, except that the Soviet version was more brutal and murderous in its execution. Thus bureaucratic collectivism was not a form of socialism but an alternative form of development to capitalism.

Rejecting both capitalism and bureaucratic collectivism, the WP declared its independence of the leaders of the two systems in its slogan, "Neither Washington nor Moscow," and called for the formation of a revolutionary "Third Camp." It refused to support the United States or its allies during World War II, considering it to be a struggle among rival imperialisms. Although strongly opposed to Nazism and fascism, the party supported only indigenous resistance movements in Europe and not the governments of Great Britain and the United States, which it expected to take fascist turns themselves under the impact of the war. The "no-strike pledge," supported by much of U.S. labor and eventually the Communist Party to further the war effort, was scornfully rejected as part of the erosion of workers' rights and democracy expected by the party during wartime.

Membership in the WP generally ran in the low hundreds, the bulk of them intellectuals rather than workers, a large proportion from New York. Among its better-known members or supporters were such writers as Saul Bellow, Harvey Swados, Dwight Macdonald, James T. Farrell, and Irving Howe, who edited its newspaper, *Labor Action*. Many of its members answered the call to take factory jobs and become active in local unions. By 1949, recognizing that it was not really functioning as a party, but as a "socialist propaganda group," its name was changed to the Independent Socialist League. As such it became the first group to be granted a hearing and subsequent removal from the attorney general's list of subversive organizations.

Calling itself an advocate of democratic socialism, the ISL strongly identified itself with the anti-Stalinist upheavals in East Berlin in 1953 and Hungary in 1956 and sought to take advantage of the upheaval in the CP caused by the revelations in Nikita Khrushchev's denunciation of Stalin at the Twentieth Congress of the Soviet CP. Despite this, as well as its efforts in support of the burgeoning civil rights movement, the ISL remained a small, isolated sect and continued to lose members, such as the group led by Irving Howe that later began to publish *Dissent*. To overcome its isolation, the leadership of the ISL developed a perspective for merger into the Socialist Party and the creation of a broad, revitalized "Debsian" socialist movement.

After the merger was achieved in 1958, Shachtman proposed a political reorientation toward working within the existing Democratic Party and the ultimate carrying out of a "realignment" of the major parties, so that the Democrats would become truly the party of labor, liberals, minorities, and the Left. Under the leadership of Hal Draper, former editor of *Labor Action*, a vocal group opposed this policy and reaffirmed the traditional ISL support for the formation of a labor party independent of the Democrats.

Shachtman's anticommunism ultimately led to his support for U.S. military involvement in Vietnam. Subsequently the labor-party faction left to form the Independent Socialist Clubs, later the International Socialists, which continued to support the idea of the Third Camp. Another group, under the leadership of writer Michael Harrington, while supporting realignment broke with Shachtman over Vietnam and formed the Democratic Socialist Organizing Committee, later Democratic Socialists of America. The remainder of the SP reorganized as Social Democrats USA.

The WP and its progeny are most notable for sharpening the discussions on the nature and dynamics of Soviet society and for training a number of future leaders of the labor and civil rights movements. *See also*: Dunayevskaya, Raya; Harrington, Michael; Howe, Irving; *New International*, James, C. L. R.; Realignment; Shachtman, Max; Trotskyism, YPSL

—*Jack Stuart*

REFERENCES

Howe, Irving. *A Margin of Hope*. New York: Harcourt Brace, 1982.

Isserman, Maurice. *If I Had a Hammer*. New York: Basic Books, 1987.

Wald, Alan M. *The New York Intellectuals*. Chapel Hill: University of North Carolina Press, 1987.

Workers Party of the United States: see American Workers Party

Workers Schools

Four years after the founding of the US Communist Party, and after some of the initial factional tensions had subsided, the CPUSA began to develop its educational/propaganda program, including a Party press and Party-run schools. In this, the CP was merely continuing similar efforts carried out by the Socialist Party, most notably at the Rand School of Social Science in New York City. Communist Workers Schools sprang up in several cities around the country where there were a sufficient number of militants, especially in New York City, where a Workers School opened on University Place near Union Square in October 1923 and later moved to Party headquarters on East Fourteenth Street.

Its teaching staff and administrators were drawn from the ranks of Party professionals and intellectuals. The New York Workers School's first co-directors—until the expulsion of the Lovestonite faction—were Bertram D. Wolfe and Ben Davidson. Afterward, the school was administered by a politically orthodox New York pharmacist named Abraham Markoff, and after Markoff died in the late 1930s the position devolved upon former top Party leader William Weinstone.

The Workers School's aims were stated in the initial promotional brochure of 1923, and were revised and restated regularly:

> The Workers School has been founded for the purpose of advancing true proletarian education, and of training workers for effective leadership in the American Labor Movement.

A year later, the school's educational aims were spelled out in greater detail, and it is clear that this was intended to be no ivory tower:

> Courses [at the Workers School] are designed to give workers that knowledge of revolutionary theory and tactics, and labor history, which is essential for militant activity in the struggle against capitalism.

Later in the decade when the Party adopted its grim "third period" outlook Workers School publications and courses spelled out the educational implications:

> Workers education as given in the Workers School renders permanent the class knowledge of the working class, puts it on a broader and deeper basis and projects it forward as an instrument by means of which the American labor movement might cope more effectively with the growing power of the American ruling class.

School publications proudly noted that school members, students, faculty, and adminstrators actively participated in the struggles of the day: "the fight for Sacco and Vanzetti, the Hands-Off-China Campaign, Passaic Relief, etc." It was obvious that the Workers School and its successors aimed at avoiding "the academic approach." Political advocacy was a regular component of the pedagogical process. The school's teaching, as one brochure put it, "is permeated with the live issues of the day, with the practical activity of the American people, with history in the making." As with the later Jefferson School of Social Science, this was an expression of the Marxian principle of the unity of theory and action; if the evils of capitalism and imperialism were studied in class, it made perfect *educational* sense to join teacher and fellow students in the next anti-imperialist demonstration, or to march alongside them in the May Day parade.

The school trained not only already signed-up Party members, it also functioned as a recruiting mechanism for potential Party activists. The students were mostly proletarian, many foreign-born, drawn from New York's factories and shops—especially shoe, jewelry, and food preparation industries, the building trades, retailing, and especially the needle trades. In time, satellite centers would appear in the Bronx, Harlem, Brooklyn, and in New Jersey industrial towns as well.

Except for a few day sessions for workers on the night shift, classes were held in the evenings, after regular working hours. The core course was "Fundamentals of Communism," which covered such basic concepts as class struggle, dialectic, and the necessity of revolution. The texts were penny pamphlets like Moissaye Olgin's *ABC of Communism*, or Lenin's *State and Revolution*. In addition there were, once Workers School enrollments had risen into the thousands, a variety of other courses and special lectures, some conducted by top Party leaders, such as Alexander Bittelman (Tactics of the Third International), General Secretary Earl Browder (The Chinese Revolution), Cochairman William Z. Foster (Trade Union Problems), etc. Harvey O'Connor, Sender Garlin, and Whittaker Chambers taught journalism; historian Arthur Calhoun offered American labor history; Scott Nearing did contemporary Europe; Bertram Wolfe offered a course on "the American Mind"; writer Michael Gold conducted a seminar on "proletarian writing"; and several staff members expounded on aspects of Marxian economic theory. The Workers School, reflecting the CP's antiracism, developed (under the leadership of writer/teacher Elizabeth Lawson) courses and readings giving an authentic and usable history of black Americans intended both to appeal to black workers and to combat prejudice among whites.

Teachers' pay at the Workers School, which came out of tuition fees, was $12 a week for what a later generation would call a "teaching load" of ten to fifteen two-hour classes a week. Student tuition was $3.50 per twelve-session, one-evening-a-week course, payable in installments. Twice-weekly English courses were $6 a term. A special tuition deal was available: any trade union, working-class fraternal organization, or foreign-language association, on payment of $25, could send a representative to take four courses each term for a whole year.

The content of the readings, courses, and lectures was predictably bounded by the standard Party line of the period—whether the "third period" belief in the imminence of revolutionary struggle, or the later Popular Front conceptions of acceptable collaboration with "progressive" sections of the bourgeoisie. The Soviet Union was of course considered the sacred bulwark of progressive forces everywhere, and even a model for an eventual socialist United States, although the impact of this belief on day-to-day Party work has probably been exaggerated in the standard non- and anticommunist literature. In 1943 the Workers School, after two decades of continuous operation, merged with the Party's Jefferson School of Social Science. *See also*: Jefferson School, Jewish Workers University

—*Marv Gettleman*

REFERENCES

Workers School catalogues and brochures. New York Public Library Annex.

WORKERS WORLD PARTY: see TROTSKYISM

WORKING WOMAN/WOMAN TODAY

These magazines were the voices of the National Women's Department of the Communist Party of the United States, and their women writers were the key group articulating a Communist position on women's rights.

Working Woman grew from the 1920s organ of New York's United Council of Working Class Women. In 1929 it began national publication as an obscure monthly, its readership confined to the Party's hard core of ethnic clubs and women's auxiliaries in the industrial belt. Though as fiercely militant and worker-oriented as the rest of the Party press at that point, *Working Woman*, edited by Women's Department head Anna Damon, was the one Party text in which the worker's world was not a wholly masculine space. Short stories and readers' letters sounded notes of contradiction and identity beyond the war of class against class. Other than photos of Soviet flyers and female strikers, it had no visual embellishment to its rough newsprint columns.

In the early 1930s, as the CPUSA shifted away from workerism and toward neighborhood and family-centered resistance, *Working Woman* vividly chronicled women in bread and meat boycotts, miners' strikes, and the struggle to save the "Scottsboro boys," wherein the firsthand experience of black women was a major theme. In 1934 the publication adopted a more modern and attractive magazine format as Margaret Cowl became secretary of the Women's Department and editor.

As a magazine, *Working Woman* blended an appeal to women as housekeepers (its "Household Corner" column) and young single workers (its regular "Fashion Letter") with an aggressive defense of women's equal role in the labor movement versus husbands and anyone else who would keep them at home. Graphically it approximated the boldness of a good leaflet; for example, the July 1935 cover drawing of massed placards called for "Free Birth Control Clinics," "Equal Pay for Equal Work," "Fight Against War and Fascism," "Reduce Meat Prices," and "Free Milk for Workers' Children."

Woman Today replaced *Working Woman* in March 1936 with a dramatic art-deco look. This change signified the Party's attempt to forge an alliance with radicalized middle-class and intellectual sectors, including feminists. Lasting only until 1938, it championed women's "democratic rights," under assault internationally by fascism, in the name of New Deal progressivism "for a better world." By contrast to the class-conscious wisecracking of *Working Woman*, *Woman Today* was cosmopolitan and even literary, with an impressive list of non-Party contributors and sponsors (Mary Van Kleeck, Freda Kirchwey, and Josephine Herbst, among others). *See also*: Communist Party, Rent Strikes

—*Van Gosse*

REFERENCES

Cowl, Margaret. "Women's Struggles for Equality." *Political Affairs* 53 (May 1974).

Dixler, Elsa Jane. "The Communist Party and the Woman Question, 1929–41." Ph.D. diss., Yale University, 1974.

Shaffer, Robert. "Women and the Communist Party, USA, 1930–40." *Socialist Review* 45 (May–June 1979).

WORKINGMEN'S PARTY OF THE UNITED STATES

The first nationwide socialist organization in the United States, the WPUS was formed in July 1876 through a merger of several groupings, including the North American remnants of Karl Marx's First International. The organization included many immigrant and native-born labor radicals, including Adolph Douai, Samuel Gompers, Laurence Gronlund, J. P. McDonnell, P. J. McGuire, Thomas J. Morgan, Albert and Lucy Parsons, George Schilling, Friedrich Sorge, Adolph Strasser, Philip Van Patten, and Otto Weydemeyer, as well as the first known African-American socialist Peter H. Clark. It published the Chicago *Vorbote* (Herald), the New York *Arbeiter-Stimme* (Labor's voice), and the English-language weekly *Labor Standard* (edited by J. P. McDonnell, a former Irish Fenian and secretary to Karl Marx in the International Workingmen's Association).

During its brief existence, the WPUS doubled its membership to 7,000, largely but not exclusively German Americans, the bulk of whom appear to have been skilled craft workers. They were pioneers in trade unionism, socialist electoral work, agitation for the eight-hour workday, and the dissemination and popularization of Marxism and socialist ideas in the United States. When the spontaneous upsurge of mass strikes and working-class street actions swept the country in 1877, WPUS militants played a prominent role—particularly in St. Louis, but also in Chicago and other cities.

The WPUS favored working-class unity transcending racial and ethnic divisions. Yet there is evidence of prejudice among some members in California toward imported Chinese laborers and in Missouri toward black workers. Nor was there an appreciation in the organization of the catastrophe wrought by the Republican Party's final betrayal of Reconstruction and black rights in the South. There were also differences over whether women workers should be organized or instead driven back to their "rightful place" in the home, so as not to compete with male labor.

The most salient division, however, revolved around electoral activity. The party initially adopted a position favoring independent labor-socialist electoral campaigns only after a trade union movement was securely established. In the wake of the 1877 labor upsurge, however, many WPUS sections ran candidates—with some initial successes (e.g., Chicago, Cincinnati). This resulted in a split by October 1877, with a sizable minority (led by such people as Sorge, Strasser, McDonnell, Weydemeyer, and Gompers) leaving the organization to concentrate on trade union work; many of these were later centrally involved in establishing the AFL. The majority of the WPUS transformed the organization into the Socialist Labor Party, which remained a vital force for socialism and labor action until it was split by new differences in the early 1880s. *See also*: 1877 Railroad Strikes, Socialist Labor Party

—*Paul Le Blanc*

REFERENCES

Commons, John R., et al. *History of Labor in the United States*. Vol. 2. New York: Macmillan, 1918.

Foner, Philip S. *The Great Labor Uprising of 1877*. New York: Monad Press, 1977.

———. *The Workingmen's Party of the United States, a History of the First Marxist Party in the Americas*. Minneapolis: MEP Publications, 1984.

Kaufman, Stuart Bruce. *Samuel Gompers and the Origins of the American Federation of Labor*. Westport: Greenwood Press, 1973.

Sorge, Friedrich A. *Labor Movement in the United States*. Westport: Greenwood Press, 1977.

WORKMEN'S CIRCLE

The roots of the Workmen's Circle (Yiddish: *Arbeter ring*), the Jewish Labor fraternal order, go back to 1892, when a group of Jewish immigrant workers met on New York's Lower East Side to found a new mutual-aid society. The new society was to differ from other such groups by its devotion to the cause of the working class and the absence of quasi-masonic or religious ritual. Despite the opposition of many socialist and anarchist intellectuals, who feared that the Workmen's Circle would draw attention away from the weak trade union and political movements, many radical workers joined the new association. By 1899 branches had been organized in Harlem and in Williamsburg, Brooklyn.

The three branches, joined by another in Brooklyn, reorganized the Workmen's Circle into a national fraternal order in 1900. The order grew rapidly, particularly between 1906 and 1910, when it expanded from 6,776 members of 38,866. During this time, the arrival of many veterans of the failed Russian Revolution of 1905 contributed to the order's growth. The new arrivals, most notably followers of the Jewish Labor Bund, successfully pushed for increased support for Yiddish cultural expression, over the objections of the more "cosmopolitan" old guard. Between 1910 and 1920, the Workmen's Circle developed a broad cultural and educational program that included lectures, publications, theater groups, choruses, and orchestras.

One of the most significant new initiatives by the Workmen's Circle was the establishment of a system of secular Jewish schools for children. The first schools opened in 1917, following a resolution passed by the 1916 convention. They aimed to acquaint the children with the Yiddish language and literature, instruct them in Jewish history, and cultivate in them an affinity for the socialist ideals of their parents.

The split between the Socialists and Communists tested the organization severely during the 1920s. The Workmen's Circle's early attitude toward the Soviet Union was one of critical support. Starting in 1922, however, the order's conventions also regularly adopted resolutions calling for the liberation of socialist political prisoners in the USSR. Confrontations between "left" and "right" became increasingly acrimonious throughout the 1920s, echoing clashes within the garment unions and other branches of the Jewish labor movement. The Communists and their allies were finally expelled in 1929.

The depression and the rise of fascism in Europe provided the context for the order's development in the 1930s. The Workmen's Circle participated in the decade's anti-Nazi boycotts and protests, raised money for the republican struggle in Spain, and formed the backbone of the Jewish Labor Committee, formed in 1934 to aid Jewish labor organizations in Europe and Jewish socialist refugees from fascism. In 1932 the order continued its traditional support for the Socialist Party, but by 1936 many members had come to support the New Deal as the implementation of much of the Socialist program. In 1940 concern for the fate of the Jews under Nazi rule led the order to repudiate the SP's pacifist stance and endorse Roosevelt for the first time.

Severe restrictions placed on immigration following World War I eliminated the order's most important source of new members. Membership reached its peak in 1925 at nearly 85,000, but declined slowly thereafter. The average age of members, on the other hand, grew steadily from 28.3 years in 1911 to 55.03 in 1951. American-born, English-speaking Jews made up an increasingly large proportion of the membership, especially after WW II.

Since WW II, the Workmen's Circle has further deemphasized its adherence to socialism, although it has continued to support a liberal conception of state-supported social programs, maintained ties to the mainstream of the labor movement, and participated in the early years of the civil rights movement. Increasingly, however, it has devoted its energies to aiding the state of Israel politically and materially, defending Jewish rights in the Soviet Union and elsewhere, and providing secular Jewish education and cultural activities.

The benefits provided by the Workmen's Circle to its members have always been central to the order's existence. The first convention in 1901 established a series of sick and death benefits, and in later years the order provided its members with an extensive insurance program and low-cost health care. Although the shifting needs of the membership have led to changes in the kinds of services provided (the order's sanitarium for tubercular patients was closed in 1955, four years after the New York branches opened their home for the aged), the benefits offered by the order continued to attract middle-class American-born Jews to the Workmen's Circle toward the end of the twentieth century. *See also*: Jewish Labor Bund, Socialist Party, Yiddish Left, Yiddish Schools

—Daniel Soyer

REFERENCES

Epstein, Melech. *Jewish Labor in USA: An Industrial, Political, and Cultural History of the Jewish Labor Movement*. 2 vols. New York, 1950–1953. Reprint. New York: Ktav Publishing House, 1969.

Hertz, J. S. *50 yor arbeter-ring in yidishn lebn*. New York: National Executive Committee of the Workmen's Circle, 1950.

Shapiro, Judah J. *The Friendly Society: A History of the Workmen's Circle*. New York: Media Judaica, 1970.

Zakhs, A. S. *Di geshikhte fun arbayter ring*. 2 vols. New York: National Executive Committee of the Workmen's Circle, 1925.

World Socialist Party

The WSP is the U.S. companion party of the Socialist Party of Great Britain (SPGB), which was formed in 1904 by a group of antireformist Marxists who had broken with H. M. Hyndman's Social Democratic Federation. During World War I, SPGB members Moses Baritz and Adolph Kohn came to the United States to avoid conscription, and they established a following in Detroit. In 1916 some of their supporters founded the SP of the United States, but changed its name to Workers' Socialist Party a few months later when they found that the name Socialist Party had been copyrighted by the SP of America. The new party at first existed only in Detroit, and from 1919 to 1922 took the name Detroit Socialist Educational Society.

WSP locals have existed off and on in several U.S. cities, including New York, San Francisco, and Los Angeles. But its real stronghold, and the only city where it can be said to have had an enduring influence, was Boston, where the tireless I. Rab conducted Marxist study classes and lively forums almost nightly from the early 1930s through the late 1940s, and more or less weekly for many years thereafter. In the 1970s the Boston WSP local had a regular program on radio.

In 1939 the WSP started publication of *The Western Socialist* ("Journal of Scientific Socialism in the Western Hemisphere"). The name World Socialist Party was adopted in 1947 to avoid confusion with the Trotskyist Socialist Workers Party.

Tractarians and debaters rather than activists, the WSP persists today as a very small educational group, pamphleteering and leafleting for what it regards as the only truly and purely Marxian socialism. *See also*: Proletarian Party

—Franklin Rosemont

REFERENCES

Jerome, W. "A Brief History of the World Socialist Party." *The Western Socialist* 33, no. 252 (1966).

The World Tomorrow

Published from 1921 to 1934, this monthly popularized and epitomized a particular Christian Socialist view tied to the struggles for peace and social justice, and closely allied to the Socialist Party.

The *World Tomorrow* had its immediate roots in the pacifism arising among young Christian Socialists during World War I. Devere Allen (1891–1955), leader of a pacifist group in Oberlin, Ohio, articulated a philosophy of nonviolent action and a vision of an international peace movement. Editor of the pacifist *Young Democracy*, 1918–21, he turned to the newly founded *World Tomorrow*, becoming its managing editor, which he remained for nearly all the magazine's span. Joined and aided by other leading members of the Fellowship for Reconciliation, Allen guided the magazine on an independent, militant course.

Kirby Page (1890–1957), an ordained minister in the Disciples of Christ and briefly a pastor in Brooklyn, added an important voice to the *World Tomorrow*. Sherwood Eddy (1871–1963), who had become a worldwide leader in the overseas work of the YMCA before WW I, took on Page as his personal secretary during the war, becoming himself more radically inclined, and lending Page powerful institutional support for Christian Socialist views. Eddy established the Sherwood Eddy Seminars for pastors and others, leading many trips abroad and gaining wide access to world leaders. While Gandhi and his movement understandably impressed most deeply Christian visitors (and *World Tomorrow* writers), Russia and China became powerful contrasting examples in the fate of the nonindustrial world. Page, joining the *World Tomorrow* as editor in 1926, related these international experiences to the domestic problems of the United States.

The ascendence of Norman Thomas to leadership of the SP gave these Christian Socialists and the *World Tomorrow* a special importance. The reduced SP, as a critic wrote, attracted YMCA workers more readily than industrial workers, and if it faltered as a class-struggle mechanism, it soared as an organ of moral critique. Mirroring the rise of ministers and Christian laymen in many SP locals, Allen himself ran for the state senate in Connecticut and served at the upper levels of SP councils. He and Page toured almost continuously and wrote a plethora of socialist pamphlets and books, including devotional texts used by Christian Socialists and others in their daily meditations.

The Depression heightened the importance of these activities, but also produced overwhelming pressures on the Thomas leadership of the SP and on the *World Tomorrow*. The magazine survived only by a year Allen's own 1933 departure from it, to establish No Frontiers News Service, a pacifist news source of great importance to the labor, religious, rural, and small-town press. Later renamed the Worldwide Press, it served a vital, religious liberal and crypto-radical milieu until Allen's death. Meanwhile, the approach of WW II once more heightened pacifist issues in and around the SP, especially just before but also during the war (when the SP and the Fellowship of Reconciliation embraced the newer generations of radical pacifists, such as David Dellinger, James Farmer, and Bayard Rustin). Toward the end of their lives, and contrary to the hardening Cold War positions of many ethnic socialists, the milieu that had grown up around the *World Tomorrow* remained faithful to the antiwar vision. In that sense, they also pioneered the nonviolence of the civil rights movement, and the antiwar sentiment around the New Left, as well as the liberation theology movement that emerged in the 1970s–1980s. *See also*: Christian Socialism, Pacifism, Peace Movements, Socialist Party

—*Paul Buhle*

REFERENCES

Chatfield, C. Charles. *Devere Allen: Life and Writings*. New York: Garland, 1976.

Chatfield, Charles, and Charles DeBendetti, eds. *Kirby Page and the Social Gospel: An Anthology*. New York: Garland, 1976.

Wortis, Rose (1886–1958)

Born in the village of Krasilov, in czarist Russia, Wortis arrived in Brooklyn, New York, in 1900. She immediately went to work in a blouse factory at three dollars a week but also attended school at night. Living in the Williamsburg section, she soon became involved in the very active Socialist Party until the split over the question of U.S. entry into World War I. She then became a charter member of the Communist Party of the United States. At the same time, she became active in Local 22 of the International Ladies Garment Workers Union. She became proficient in speaking and writing and became a leader of the rank-and-file movement to democratize the union. She was found on picket lines wherever workers were struggling for better conditions, particularly in the textile industry. She wrote articles for the *Daily Worker*, the *Communist*, and *Labor Unity*.

When the Trade Union Unity League was organized in 1929, attended by 690 delegates, representing about 70,000 members, Wortis was elected secretary. The TUUL was an outgrowth of the Trade Union Educational League (TUEL) organized in 1920 to work within the AFL to make it more progressive. TUUL emphasized the organization of the unorganized into industrial, revolutionary industrial unions and organized left-wingers in the old unions on the principle of class struggle. In later years, she was an elected official in the complaints department of Local 22, ILGWU.

See *also*: Communist Party, International Ladies Garment Workers Union, Trade Union Unity League

—*Rose Lewis*

Wright, Fred (1907–84)

The leading labor-Left cartoonist of the 1940s–1970s, Wright was the most universally reprinted artist after Art Young. As labor caricature, his work heralded the abandonment of the symbolic proletarian muscular giant in favor of a workaday Joe (or Jane) fighting back against inflation, automation, and employer attacks.

Wright was born in Derby, England, descendant of many generations of wheelwrights. Emigrating to America with his family, he first learned drawing from his grandfather, an amateur artist and a striper in automobile factories. In his late teens, Fred became a professional saxophone player, in resorts and in New York "clip joints." During the late 1920s, still interested in drawing, he attended classes at the New York Art Students League, where he first met radicals. The Depression truly radicalized him, and on board ship—where he had gone to work as a musician—he came into close contact with organizers of the National Maritime Union. Wright drew his first published labor cartoon in 1936, and began drawing regularly for the first time in the NMU organ, the *Pilot*, and then for an Army base newspaper during World War II. He returned afterward as a staff artist of the *Pilot*, and his work was widely reprinted in the labor press—until the rightward-turning NMU chiefs insisted that he draw Communists as rats.

Tempted to return to a musician's life, Wright chose instead to join *UE News*. There he came into his own. His Art Young–type philosophical approach to the difficulties of modern existence transcended socialist and class clichés without, however, losing the basic points of unfairness and exploitation. Over the years, he believed, his style became simpler, with more frequent use of old gags in new dress. His weekly cartoons filled several anthologies, the largest, *So Long, Partner!* (1975). He was more widely reprinted in Europe—especially beloved in Italy and England—than any U.S. labor-radical artist since Young. He contributed a campaign satire *Goldwater Coloring Book* (1964), several experiments with early animated films, and labor's first series of anti–Vietnam War cartoons of the 1960s. At his death, he was at work on a cartoon history of the industrial revolution. *See also*: Humor, "UE"

—*Paul Buhle*

REFERENCES

"U.E. Mourns Fred Wright," *UE News*. January 14, 1985.

Wright, Fred. Interview. Oral History of the American Left, Tamiment Library, New York University.

Wright, Richard (1908–60)

Born in Natchez, Mississippi, Wright became the most famous black writer in the world after publication of his first novel, *Native Son* (1940). A Book-of-the-Month-Club selection, it sold 250,000 copies in three weeks. Wright's grandparents had been slaves. His grandfather, Richard Wilson, had been the property of John Charles Alexander of Woodville, Mississippi, until he escaped during the Civil War. His grandmother, Margaret Bolden Wilson, was the daughter of a man of Irish-Scottish ancestry and a slave. Wright's mother, Ella Wilson, a country schoolteacher, married an illiterate sharecropper, Nathan Wright, who deserted his family for a woman he met in a saloon.

Wright completed school to the eighth grade. Years later, he commented that his being deprived of anything but a grammar school education had, perhaps, saved him from the pernicious influences of two southern cultural traditions: Christianity, which stresses submissiveness; and philanthropy, which purchases silence. He moved to Chicago in 1927, and to earn a living worked as a bellhop, porter, insurance agent, delivery man in a delicatessen, and postal clerk.

Wright joined the Communist Party in 1932, and a few years later the Party sent him to New York City to take charge of the Harlem bureau of the *Daily Worker*. Conflicts between the Party line and Wright's view of black life began almost immediately. The Party attacked his *Uncle Tom's Children* (1938) as an unrealistic portrayal of southern black life. *Native Son* (1940) alarmed the Communists because of its realistic view of how society drove a black youngster to embrace criminality and his portrayal of the ineffectuality of a CP solution. The Party was also fearful that the murder of a white woman, although accidental and without sexual innuendo, would reinforce popular misconceptions about black lust. Yet some of his most memorable journalism, notably on Joe Louis's triumph over Max Schmelling, was published in the *Daily Worker* sports columns. Allegations of a warped mentality and muddled thinking, along with demands that he submit to Communist discipline, thoroughly alienated Wright. He stopped working for the Party in 1941, but did not formally resign until 1944.

In *Black Boy* (1945), an underlying theme in *Uncle Tom's Children* that continuous conflict between black and white and between black and black was inevitable under present circumstances, was reemphasized. The difficulty blacks have living as civilized beings in a society that denies their humanity, and the probability of violence as the only solution to social deadlock, continued as a major preoccupation to the end of Wright's life. In chapters of *Black Boy*, unpublished until 1944 (then by Constance Webb in private circulation), he suggested that Americans will have to learn how to live as civilized humans "by marching down history's bloody road."

Although henceforth Wright was hostile toward organizations that claimed to be leaders in social change, he remained staunchly revolutionary. While alienated from the dominant Left, Wright was battered by the government Right. His *12 Million Black Voices: A Folk History of the Negro in the United States (1941)*, a book of photographs illustrating three centuries of black experience, brought him to the attention of the War Department and the FBI. For the rest of his life, he was harassed by one or another of America's security organizations.

He moved to Paris in July 1947 hoping to escape the pressures inherent in life as a black man in the United States. Living in exile, Wright wrote increasingly about alienation and the descent into a personal hell. He became a close friend of Jean Paul Sartre, who was fascinated by this American's understanding of existentialism. Wright also had considerable influence on Jean Genet, advising him during his work on *The Blacks*. In his Paris diary Wright predicted that "the next great area of discovery in the Negro will be the dark landscape of his own mind." He became a major, acknowledged influence on succeeding generations of black writers, including Ralph Ellison, James Baldwin, Chester Himes, and one of his biographers, John A. Williams. He also produced serious nonfictional works—*Bandung Conference* (1956), a report on the efforts of Third World leaders to establish the non-Western political-cultural-economic agenda and *White Man, Listen!* (1957), a final plea for understanding. Wright died suddenly in Paris in 1960. He was fifty-two years old. *See also*: Civil Rights, Communist Party, *Daily Worker*

—*Constance Webb*

REFERENCES

Baldwin, James. *The Price of the Ticket*. New York: St. Martin's Marek, 1985.

Bennet, Lerone, Jr., *Confrontation: Black and White*. Chicago: Johnson Publishing Co., 1965.

Cayton, Horace. *Long Old Road*. New York: Trident Press, 1965.

Fabre, Michel. *The Unfinished Quest of Richard Wright*. New York: William Morrow, 1973.

Gayle, Addison. *Richard Wright, Ordeal of a Native Son*. New York: Doubleday, 1983.

Walter, Margaret. *Daemonic Genius*. New York: Warner Books, 1989.

Webb, Constance. *Richard Wright: A Biography*. New York: G. P. Putnam's Sons, 1968.

Wright, Richard. "I Tried to Be a Communist." *Atlantic Monthly* 184 (August–September 1944).

Ybor City

Presently part of Tampa, Florida, this was a planned community begun in 1885 by cigar industrialist Vicente Martinez Ybor. The cigar industry provided the context for the community's initial radical orientation. Cuban and Spanish cigar workers brought to Florida a well-developed proletarian consciousness and a firm commitment to leftist political and labor ideologies. Joined soon by Sicilian immigrants, many of whom had belonged to socialist-led workers' leagues (*fasci dei lavoratori*) in the 1890s, "Latin" immigrants fashioned a radical culture of unusual complexity, durability, and diversity.

By the twentieth century, Ybor City possessed a full spectrum of radical debating clubs, political groups, reading societies, consumer cooperatives, and newspapers. Adherents of virtually every leftist viewpoint could be found in the community, including right- and left-wing socialists, centrists, revolutionary and IWW (Industrial Workers of the World) syndicalists, and pacifistic and "propaganda of the deed" anarchists. The strength and pervasiveness of radical ideologies could be measured in part by the weakness of organized religion, which struggled for decades to acquire membership and respect. Ybor City quickly integrated itself into a worldwide network of radical settlements, becoming a regular stop on the propaganda tours of various luminaries and maintaining close links with outside events and personalities.

Nowhere was the radical presence more in evidence than in the cigar industry itself. All large factories possessed readers (*lectores*) who read to workers during the day. Drawing from the works of leftist masters, proletarian novels, and labor tracts, readers were critical elements in the politicization of workers.

Ybor City's militant cigar unions emerged from this environment. Socialists such as Giovanni Vaccaro and anarchists such as Pedro Esteve and Alfonso Coniglio played important leadership roles in organizing workers and directing them in industrywide strikes. Major walkouts occurred in 1899, 1901, 1910, 1920, and 1931, with numerous smaller confrontations taking place in other years. The radical presence—in unions, factories, and the general community—contributed to the strength of employer and native hostility, which often took the form of vigilantism, nativism, and violence. Defeat in the ten-month 1920 strike, the shocks of Red Scare repression, and the collapse of the 1931 strike (led by the Communist Tobacco Worker's International Union), seriously eroded the labor position and community standing of the leftists. Anticommunist drives of the 1950s continued the deterioration.

Even after radical decline, Ybor City manifested a leftist orientation, as seen in such aspects as support for antifascism, labor unionism, and left-of-center politics. Few post-Castro Cuban émigrés chose Tampa for settlement, further testimony of the enduring image and makeup of the community. *See also*: Anarchism, Cubans, Italian Americans

—*George E. Pozzetta*

REFERENCES

Mormino, Gary R., and George E. Pozzetta. *The Immigrant World of Ybor City: Italians and Their Latin Neighbors in Tampa, 1885–1985*. Urbana: University of Illinois Press, 1987.

Perez, Louis A., Jr. "Reminiscences of a Lector: Cuban Cigar Workers in Tampa." *Florida Historical Quarterly* 53 (April 1975).

Pozzetta, George E. "An Immigrant Library: The Tampa Italian Club Collection," *Ex Libris* 1 (1978).

Yiddish Left

As differentiated from the broader but more diffuse Jewish Left, Left Yiddishists have occupied a special niche with their fusion of linguistic, cultural, and political commitments. *Yiddishkayt*, literally "Yiddishness," has been a wild card on the Left, unaccounted for by Marxist theories but vital in its successful and unsuccessful applications to the situation of the immigrant Jewish working class in its most influential eras.

A Yiddishist discourse arrived in the 1890s Left unbidden and even unwilled. Rooted in a half-millennium or so of European history, Yiddish (a derivation of Middle High German, with varying elements of Slavic and Hebrew) served as the profane or daily language of *shtetl*, which is to say village Jews in the Pale. Disapproved by "cultured" (Russian or German, middle-class) Jews who hoped to educate the masses out of a "mongrel" language, Yiddish nevertheless grew up into a miniliterature with the spread of books and literacy at the end of the nineteenth century. The foremost writers—I. L. Peretz and Sholom Aleichem paramount among them—preached a doctrine of ethical uplift, but also a folkish communalism that verged on socialism.

Yiddish came to America with the half-million Jewish immigrants from the middle 1880s, but especially from the early 1890s on. Yiddish-language socialist periodicals appeared almost immediately, often written and edited by intellectuals who had little knowledge of Yiddish before their own immigration. A handful of them would remain important intellectual and political figures of the Jewish Left for decades. Foremost among them was an anarchistic-minded early immigrant from Eastern Europe named Abraham Cahan, who was reputedly the first to hold a U.S. radical political meeting in Yiddish, in 1884. Two years earlier the first labor leaflet in Yiddish had been issued, warning immigrants against strikebreaking. The formation of the United Hebrew Trades in 1888 formally announced the emergence of the Eastern European Jew (in contrast to the generally middle-class German Jew) as a force in the New York labor movement.

At the same time, a precocious poetic outburst in Yiddish gave the impoverished Jewish immigrants lyrics for the struggle. David Edelstadt (1866–92), an early fatality to the "*proletarishe krank*" (workers' disease, i.e., tuberculosis), wrote verses in his short life that would be sung for generations by Yiddish choruses. Fellow anarchist Joseph Bovshover (1872–1915), who wrote a famous elegy to the dead Edelstadt, penned poetic denunciations of the rich, of religion, and of the stupidity of bourgeois life—before going mad himself.

Edelstadt and Bovshover both failed in one important respect, as Yiddish and *Yiddishkayt* emerged as an issue, if only covertly, in the fierce competition of the early 1890s between anarchists and socialists. By now Cahan, a leading editor of the weekly *Arbeter Zeitung* (Workers press), had begun to assemble a literary repertoire of poets, prose artists, and semiskilled journalists who could appeal to the Jewish proletarian community (which included sizable numbers of petty merchants, salesmen, and other non-wage laborers) at large. The anarchist *Freie Arbeter Shtimme* (Free voice of labor) of Edelstadt and Bovshover, its prose a mere didacticism offset by a little poetry, offered no serious competition. Nor did the anarchists compromise with the religious sentiments of the immigrant majority, mocking the holy days while the *Arbeter Zeitung* explained socialist ideas in religious phraseology.

Determinedly adapting to America as well as to their immediate audience, Cahan and his fellow early socialists nevertheless nearly all believed in an assimilation that would eradi-

Marx, The Modern Liberator

cate Yiddish. They therefore found themselves in the anomalous position of constructing a presumably doomed sensibility. In this curious way, they came to promote cultural figures with deeper Yiddishist sentiments. Two key individuals, both poets, became deeply beloved in the Lower East Side ghetto. Morris Rosenfeld, the master "Teardrop Millionaire" (so named for an ability to raise emotion in his readers), appealed in virtual Zionist tones for the emancipation of the historically downtrodden Jew. With no Zion in sight (as literary critic B. Rivkin later argued), Yiddish with a messianic socialist content itself became a sort of realm of imagined liberation—a mental homeland. Morris Winchevsky, the "zeyde" (grandfather) of Yiddish socialist journalism, relocated from London to New York in 1894 and soon thereafter roused a rebellion of Yiddish socialists from the political and cultural tyranny of Socialist Labor Party leadership.

The *Jewish Daily Forward*, chief product of the split, evolved after a few years into Cahan's own brilliant journalistic expression. Upholding the cause of socialism and of labor (especially Jewish labor), the *Forward* rapidly became an example of *gele* (yellow) journalism to match any in the contemporary New York press. By the mid-1910s, it had reached a circulation of a quarter-million, larger than any socialist paper other than the *Appeal to Reason*, and by far the most circulated Jewish paper in the world.

Utterly sensationalistic, the *Forward* was known for its gruesome accounts of murders and its directives on immigrant etiquette as much as its sociological investigation of neighborhood life. And in its quasi-assimilationist manner, it evolved a prose increasingly interlaced with English words and phrases. The paper fairly invented, at least for Yiddish, the one-column short story, often brilliant socialist-realist vignettes from daily life by writers such as Z. Libin, capmaker by trade, or Leon Kobrin, known as the Zola of the ghetto.

In strengths and weaknesses, the *Forward* fairly represented the mentality of the 1880s–1890s immigrants who had risen to the leadership of the labor and journalistic ghetto spheres. Socialists of a Bundist turn, they had learned that socialism was likely to be very far away, and they had learned to make an institutional accommodation to the realities of the transition. They viewed competitors, especially newcomers or those to the left of themselves, with great suspicion. The *Forward* notably savaged Cahan's personal enemies, or ignored them and thereby banished them to a corner of Jewish life. "Cahan edits the Yiddish press," as the saying went, suggested the weight of his personal domination of cultural and political life.

Yiddish theater, heavily influenced by socialist themes, offered another important realm of cultural self-definition. Its very creation, at the dawn of the 1890s, had been shaped by political motives. As it rapidly grew commercially viable, socialist giants arose side by side with schlockmeisters. For twenty years Jakob Gordin, a heavy moralist, uplifted the Yiddish theater and created roles that the outstanding actors and actresses could fill out, to great public approval. Socialist ideas took on new graphic guises and (as Gordin in his own numerous literary essays suggested) escaped the abstractions through which they were too often interpreted.

By 1910, the newer immigrants, "1905ers"—who had in many cases experienced the contemporary Russian uprising and the accompanying *pogroms* firsthand—began to assert themselves across American Jewish life. In their Europe, Yiddish had gained a greater dignity and literary artfulness, and Jewish identity (for bad reasons as well as good) seemed less an option and more a finality. Over a decade or so, they transformed Left institutional life in several important ways.

In large numbers, they entered the major fraternal institution, the *Arbeter Ring*/Workmen's Circle, and there began to insist (against the inclinations of the older Jewish immigrants) upon a program of Yiddish language day-schools. By the late 1910s, this program became a centerpiece of radical Jewish activities. Their most artistic-minded members (known as *di Yunge*, the youth) issued a veritable literary manifesto of Yiddish as capable of high artistic, undidactic possibility. Although virtually banned from the *Forward*, they began their own small-scale publishing, and infiltrated the other presses, including the anarchist *Freie Arbeter Shtimme*. Their ranks, cultural and political enthusiasts, fed rebellion from the Jewish socialist establishment. Perhaps the *Yunge*'s chief organizer, David Ignatov, anthologizer and organizer, provided its ultimate fictional expression in his three-volume *Euf Veite Vegn* (Horizons, 1930–32), in which a protagonist wanders through American life, discovering its wonders and horrors, and seeking finally a socialism with a spiritual quality lacking in the secular Left.

The Leftward edge of *di Yunge* made the Yiddish "revolution of the word" a call for political-economic revolution as well. They shared the rage of young Jewish radicals against the institutional conservatism of Jewish labor leaders who considered themselves cautious socialists. They expressed their special resentment at assimilationism, as a fatal break with a thousand years of cultural tradition and willful abandonment of a tongue equal to the finest literary possibilities. In their *Yiddishkayt*, they also offered an alternative to the undercurrent of Hebracism (predominantly conservative or Zionist in implication) as well as the overwhelming fact of Americanization. The Russian Revolution, opening up the promise of an institutionalized, socialist Yiddish renaissance, evoked their enthusiasm. Moshe Leib Halpern, one of the most enraged and talented of the younger poets, gladly dedicated himself to the new hopes stirred by Russia. H. Leiveck, another of the famed circle, wrote stunning proletarian dramas in the 1920s. Even the less political, such as aestheticist Mani Leib, could for a time be sufficiently entranced by such Left (and ostensibly non-Jewish) causes as the Sacco-Vanzetti case to write stirring social lyrics. Such figures provoked great pride among Yiddishists at large, and during the era of their radical commitment, also provoked a gnawing uneasiness among the powerfully situated Jewish critics of Bolshevism.

The *Yunge* rebellion, in one sense, led directly to the founding of the Yiddish Communist daily newspaper in 1922, *Morgen Freiheit*. Perhaps the most aesthetically successful of the new Communist dailies, its early columns included a handful of the outstanding *Yunge*, poets and dramaturges, and its supporters included many of the outstanding Yiddish pedagogues and fraternal activists. During the 1920s their circles established the Jewish Folk Chorus, with its outstanding leader, Jacob Shaffer, and Camp Kinderland, a largely Yiddish-inclined summer center. After a split in the Workmen's Circle, Yiddish Communists created their own International Workers Order (IWO) schools as well.

No one author so well symbolized the long-term shift of individual writers and artists toward the Yiddishist Left as did Moshe Nadir (1885–1943). Known as the "bad boy" or the "great cynic" of Yiddish literature in the 1910s, Nadir wrote comic sketches and aesthete-erotic verses, mocking the self-seriousness of Jewish political and social life. After the Russian Revolution, he swung to the Left and he remained with the *Freiheit* almost to the end of his life, faithful to designated political positions and (to a lesser degree) favored aesthetic modes. Notwithstanding his notoriously bohemian personal life, the *Freiheit* and its associated institutions made him an idol with an intense following for his voluminous output—poetry, feuilletons, travelogues, and children's books running to nearly fifteen volumes. For his part, Nadir usually carried the "party line" fairly lightly and in his own peculiar fashion. The 1920s found him honestly enraged at xenophobic American capitalism, the Depression sorrowful at the human waste and hopeful for the Soviet experiment, and the later 1930s thankful for American cultural pluralism. With the Hitler-Stalin Pact, Nadir lost heart, and died a broken man.

The *Freiheit* never remotely rivaled the *Forward* in circulation, peaking at no more than 10,000. But its readers regarded it almost as a sacred organ for the mission of socialism and *Yiddishkayt*. It suffered terribly as a result of Communist-style "proletarian literature," which drove away some of its notable writers (although a few, including the fine novelist Isaac Raboi, adapted themselves remarkably to it), and the Palestinian uprising of 1929, whose welcoming by the Communist Party drove away others. A core of talented enthusiasts always remained, strongly influencing Yiddish art, theater, music, even puppet shows (the modernist Zuni Maud created, with writer Yosel Kotler, a Modikot puppet troupe that toured widely) and above all, literature. At the *Freiheit* itself and to a lesser degree at *Der Hammer*, its monthly sister cultural publication (a sort of Jewish *New Masses*, fine prose flourished almost regardless of shifting political line and, at times, a vulgar general approach to cultural questions. The *Freiheit*'s own publishing company brought out many volumes of centrally important Yiddish literature, including extensive collections of work by Winchevsky.

In the Popular Front era, this approach reached its maximum influence. The *Yiddishe Kultur Farband* (YKUF) was founded in 1937, an international body to consolidate and further Yiddish efforts. A distinguished journal, *Yiddishe Kultur*, and a scholarly publishing company demonstrated the Left Yiddishists' seriousness even as the Hitler-Stalin Pact drove out many allies. When the details of the Holocaust began to become known, the leaders of the YKUF demanded and received a greater measure of autonomy within the IWO Yiddish schools, but also a commitment that Communists had never previously made, to a multilinguistic American society.

This commitment arrived too late, both for Yiddish and for the Left. The Cold War and Stalin's attack on Soviet *Yiddishkayt* uprooted and ultimately discredited, to a large degree, Left Yiddish institutions just as they had reestablished themselves in the years following the war. The number of IWO schools rapidly shrank (as they did in the Workmen's Circle milieu, for nonpolitical reasons as well: suburbanization and assimilation made the schools both impractical to organize and less desirable). The U.S. government destroyed the IWO, although the Jewish clubs and societies maintained an insular existence.

In the same years, the creation of Israel detracted seriously from Yiddish concerns. The Poale, or Labor, Zionists, ardent in their own Yiddish literary pursuits even if less determined about the language's ultimate destiny, had been since the 1920s a small milieu increasingly focused solely on the Middle East. The sabotage of Yiddish presses by "revisionist" Hebraists, and the official adoption of Hebrew as the sole official language of the new land, shut off Yiddish as a less-than-desirable element of the past.

At this juncture, Yiddish began to acquire a scholarly life that deemphasized but did not by any means neglect its socialist connections. The YKUF, especially under the leadership of Kalmon Marmor and, later, Nakhman Meisel, published outstanding historical studies of Yiddish literature (in Yiddish), and comprehensive anthologies. No other American radical literature, until the 1970s–1980s, received nearly such close critical attention, notwithstanding the shrinking number of Yiddish writers and readers. *Amerike in Yiddishe Vort* (America in Yiddish Word), edited by Meisel, provided 500 quarto pages of poetry and prose, an unparalleled bit of Left-literary scholarship. In English, Irving Howe began his efforts at cultural recuperation via translation and explanation of context. Slanted against the Communist Left, they had nevertheless a great importance in reaching a Jewish audience with the historical validity of the Yiddish experience.

The step-by-step departure of the *Freiheit* from the Communist milieu encouraged this development, and made the paper a pantheon of Left *Yiddishkayt* until its demise in September 1988. By that time its editor, Paul Novick, on hand since its founding sixty-six years earlier, had become the most distinguished senior figure of Yiddish journalism in the world, his own writing long a beacon on independent socialistic *Yiddishkayt*.

Among socialists, and the smaller allied scatterings of Bundists and Labor Zionists, a modest Yiddish revival also took place during the 1970s–1980s. The *Forward*, down to 25,000 circulation, had become in old age a champion of Yiddish language circles and even paid close attention to Yiddish in the hated Soviet Union. It also offered, along with fervent denunciations of Communists and other perceived opponents of Israel, strident criticisms of Israeli warmaking in Lebanon and brutality in the West Bank. Unlike the later generation's roughly neoliberal Jewish publications, it kept somewhat of a radical edge. Its editors, most former editors at the *Freiheit*, had not entirely left behind the socialism of their youth.

At the end of the 1980s, *Yiddish Kultur*, edited by erstwhile Left pedagogue Itche Goldberg, remained one of two finest Yiddish literary publications in the world (the other, published in Israel, had no socialistic political inclination). The *Forward* offered a double-page of "pearls from Yiddish poetry," mostly of long-vanished radical writers. And in Amherst, Massachusetts, a young project of radical connections, the National Yiddish Book Center, had embarked on the difficult project of cultural renewal. *See also*: ARTEF; Cahan, Abraham; Freie *Arbeter Shtimme*; Jewish Labor Bund; Olgin, Moissaye; Socialist Zionism; Tsukunft; Workmen's Circle, *Zukunft*

—*Paul Buhle*

REFERENCES

Buhle, Paul. "Jews and American Communism: The Cultural Question." *Radical History Review* 23 (Spring 1980).

Epstein, Melech. *Jewish Labor in the USA*. 2 vols. New York: Trade Union Sponsoring Committee, 1950.

Howe, Irving. *World of Our Fathers*. New York: Simon & Schuster, 1976.

Maisel, Nachman, ed. *Amerike in Yiddishe Vort*. New York: Yiddishe Kultur Farband, 1953.

Yiddish Schools

East European Jewish immigrants created Yiddish children's schools in the early twentieth century as an extension of their *veltlikhkayt* (secularism). Responding to the challenges of modernization by transforming Judaism and Jewishness, Diaspora-oriented Jewish secularists believed that modern Jewish life was not dependent upon religion or a territory, but upon the autonomy of Jewish communal institutions and the creation of a secular culture. School activists hoped that the creation of a nonreligious Jewish educational system would ensure the perpetuation of a progressive Jewish nation in the diaspora. Yiddish, the everyday language of the Jewish masses, was at the center of their ideology.

Of the five school movements (the Jewish National Workers Alliance, the Sholem Aleichem Folk Institute, the Workmen's Circle [WC], the International Workers Order [IWO], and the Left Poale Zion that existed in the United States and Canada), only the WC (founded in 1918) and the IWO (founded in 1926) were actively committed to a radical political agenda. They creatively fused either Socialism or Communism with Diaspora nationalism, and were known as the *linke shules* (left-wing schools). Providing supplementary afternoon and weekend education for thousands of children from kindergarten through high school, the *shules* of the WC and the IWO flourished in the 1930s, sponsoring publishing houses, summer camps, and a Jewish Teachers Seminary. By 1935 more than half of all Jewish children who received a Yiddish education attended the schools of the WC and IWO.

The curricula of the two left-wing Yiddish school movements, in particular the mix between nationalism and internationalism, evolved over time. In the late teens and early 1920s—encouraged by the success of the Russian revolution—the WC schools emphasized socialism. Classes stressed the history of the international working class and capitalist exploitation. The children's Yiddish readers highlighted the lives of important socialist figures such as Karl Marx and Jean Jaures. Marching in the annual May Day parade was a highlight of the school year. Holiday celebration was limited to Passover, Purim, and Chanukah, holidays that could be given a universal, socialist, and secular interpretation.

The IWO schools emerged out of the bitter ideological feuds between the Socialist and Communist Left in the 1920s, which permanently divided politics and the unions into two hostile camps. In 1926 a group of *shule* activists seceded from the WC, creating the "Nonpartisan Jewish Workers Children's Schools," which in 1930 officially merged with the Communist Party's International Workers Order. From 1926 till 1933 (the "Third Period") the "Nonpartisan/IWO" schools taught a curriculum of "national-nihilism" in which few positive symbols of Jewishness appeared. Proletarian culture and activism was paramount. The school's magazine contained articles on Soviet life, Spanish Republicans, and American strikers. Children regularly joined their teachers on picket lines.

Hitler's election in 1933, the growth of fascist anti-Semitism in Europe, and the effect of assimilation on the schoolchildren challenged activists in both movements to reevaluate the weight given to the national element in their curricula. By the end of the decade, WC and IWO school textbooks and magazines had become increasingly sensitive to anti-Semitism and Jewish culture.

Yet, important differences distinguished the two movements. Changes in the WC *shules'* curriculum were due as much to an internal concern for the perpetuation of Jewish culture as to the external threats of anti-Semitism. WC activists had already created pedagogical materials in the late 1920s that affirmed the uniqueness of Jewish history and the Jewish people. And by the mid-1930s a new biography series included Rashi (1040–1105), a medieval figure of traditional piety and learning. Socialism was still central to the schools' curriculum, but cultural self-preservation became their highest priority.

CP policy informed the curricular changes in the IWO schools. During the Popular Front (1936–39) when the Soviet Union made efforts to cultivate political support from among its national minorities, IWO activists put a new emphasis on the teaching of Jewish history. They taught Yiddish as an end in itself (not only as a means to further Jewish proletarian culture) through the works of the Soviet Yiddish writers (e.g., Leib Kvitko, Peretz Markish, and David Bergelson). The Hitler-Stalin Pact in 1939 forced *shule* activists to vitiate their commitment to Jewish culture. But by 1942, Hitler again the enemy of the Soviet Union, the national element resurfaced to become an essential component in the IWO curriculum. (Their allegiance to the IWO notwithstanding, some teachers resisted Party doctrine when it contravened their own consciences, such as refusing to keep the schools open on Yom Kippur.)

The devastation of European Jewry during World War II, the linguistic acculturation of the immigrants' American-born grandchildren, and the upward mobility of the Jewish community portended the end of the left-wing Yiddish schools by the 1950s. Yet at their peak they enriched the American Left, embodying a vision of political radicalism in which national and international aspirations coexisted in a taut, but creative, tension. *See also*: Socialist Sunday Schools, Yiddish Left

—*Nancy Sinkoff*

REFERENCES

Buhle, Paul. "Jews and American Communism: The Cultural Question." *Radical History Review* 23 (Spring 1980).

Dubnow, Simon. *Nationalism and History*. Edited by Koppel Pinson. New York: Atheneum, 1970.

Frankel, Jonathan. *Prophecy and Politics: Socialism, Nationalism, & the Russian Jews, 1862–1917*. New York: Cambridge University Press, 1981.

Garfinkle, Harry. "Ideological Elements in the Development of the American Yiddish School Movement," Ph.D. diss., Columbia University, 1954.

Liebman, Arthur. *Jews and the Left*. New York: John Wiley & Sons, 1979.

Sinkoff, Nancy B. "Learning To Be Free: Socialist and Communist Yiddish Education in the 1930s." Bachelor's thesis, Harvard-Radcliffe College, 1982.

Yiddishe Kempfer: see Socialist Zionism

Yiddishe Kultur Farband: see Yiddish Left

Yippies

A highly self-conscious creation by Vietnam War protesters in the late 1960s, the "Yippie" phenomenon was never a formally organized party or structured movement. Rather, the term labeled an amorphous group led by antiwar organizers that politicized the countercultural figure of the hippie. The name of the group (and its variations, including "Youth International Party") was created by Abbie Hoffman, Jerry Rubin, and others following the October 1967 March on the Pentagon. Specifically, Yippies were invented to attract media attention and to gain publicity for antiwar rallies planned to coincide with the 1968 Democratic National Convention in Chicago. A Yippie, it was said, was any hippie who was going to Chicago to protest the war. The Yippie phenomenon successfully demonstrated the political content of cultural rebellion.

Yippie war protest was characterized by carnivalesque techniques of burlesque, clowning, and ridicule. As such, it posed a set of problems to the New Left and to formal antiwar efforts, such as the National Mobilization Committee to End the War in Vietnam. On the one hand, the bizarre tactics of Yippies attracted media attention considered crucial to war protest; on the other hand, the anarchic and unstructured nature of Yippie activity made it impossible for the Left to organize and control the group. The nonsense that characterized Yippie protest clashed with the hardheaded seriousness of the antiwar Left.

The name created after the Pentagon March successfully labeled a practice that had been growing in popularity during antiwar rallies. The huge, immovable, and intransigent government machinery responsible for perpetuating the war in Vietnam led many Americans to react with laughter and liberating playfulness. Yippie responses to authoritarianism resembled western European medieval carnival practices. These carnivals were officially tolerated, popular releases held in seasons of church feasts, during which the lower strata of society would mock, ridicule, and figuratively turn upside down the rigid economic and political structures of their society. The rise of modern state capitalism made the destructive potential of such seasonal outbursts intolerable, and the promise of participatory democracy made them irrelevant, and so gradually, through suppression and degeneration, seasonal carnival practices disappeared. Vestiges would nonetheless surface in authoritarian social contexts; for example, American colonial Puritans would report the need to suppress activities such as Maypole dancing in seventeenth-century New England.

Frolic and playfulness were characteristic of many antiwar rallies in this period. At the Pentagon in October 1967 Hoffman led an "exorcism" of demons from the building, surrounding it with young people chanting and singing songs. The juxtaposition of such activities with the armed National Guard troops there to protect government buildings presented a clear package for consumption by print and television news media. Yippie strategists were conscious of the need to present antiwar messages in contexts that the various media would find novel and thus newsworthy. In particular, as television relies heavily on the juxtaposition of images, Yippie protest would often present images of radical contradistinction, such as placing flowers in National Guard gun-barrels. Such practices, however, clashed with the antiwar program of the New Left, and pointed to irreconcilable differences between the two strategies. If anything, Yippie tactics pointed to the absurdity of politicking in the liberal sense of the word and argued the closed and totalitarian nature of the American state. Whereas the Left stood for political praxis, Yippies testified to a sense of political insignificance and exhaustion on the part of many Americans in this period.

Yippie carnival tactics were highly visible in the "Festival of Life" held outside the 1968 Democratic National Convention in Chicago, and in the absurdist behavior presented by the Yippie component of the Chicago Conspiracy Trial defense in 1969–70. Visual and verbal playfulness were hallmarks of the group's strategy. At Chicago, Yippies nominated a live pig ("Pigasus") as their presidential candidate; in court, their witnesses sang songs from the stand and Yippie defendants mocked judicial structures of decorum. Although speakers Hoffman and Rubin insisted that the group was apolitical, it was, in fact, more a politicization of countercultural temperament than a distinct political program. It was a coalescence of the era's antiauthoritarianism, and through its carnival strategy it was highly conscious of the unwritten rules of social decorum and civil behavior that undergird modern democratic society.

Although the public phase of the Yippie phenomenon ended after the Chicago Conspiracy Trial, an organization calling itself by the same name continues to exist and to publish protest material and "underground" news. *See also*: New Left, Underground Press

—*Joseph R. Urgo*

REFERENCES

Urgo, Joseph R. "Comedic Impulses and Societal Propriety: The Yippie Carnival." *Studies in Popular Culture* 10:1 (1987).

The New Yippie Book Collective. *Blacklisted News, Secret History . . . From Chicago, '68, to 1984*. New York: Bleecker, 1983.

YOUNG, ART (1866–1943)

This leading socialist cartoonist and humorist of the early twentieth century, Young believed the best political cartoons were those that directly attacked the capitalist system.

Young was raised in Monroe, Wisconsin, and at age seventeen moved to Chicago. From 1884 to 1887 he worked for the *Daily Mail* and the *Daily News*. During that time he created the definitive sketches of the Haymarket anarchists.

After studying art in New York and Paris for eight years, Young returned to Chicago and worked for the *Inter-Ocean* newspaper with Thomas Nast. In late 1895 he returned to

The Religion of the Press
(See Editorial)

Art Young for *Good Morning*, 1920

New York and drew political cartoons of a Republican and later reformist nature.

His socialist period began around 1910 after he became active with Greenwich Village radicals. His most famous work appeared in the magazines *Life, Puck,* the *Masses,* the *Liberator,* the *Metropolitan,* and his own radical humor magazine, *Good Morning.*

In the words of historian Richard Fitzgerald, Young died a "pre–World War I latitudinarian socialist." In 1934 Young wrote optimistically of his socialism: " . . . I don't know the meaning of 'dialectical materialism.' . . . All I know is . . . the cause of the workers is right and rule of Capitalism is wrong, and right will win." *See also*: Humor, *Masses*

—*Mike Konopacki*

REFERENCES

Beffel, John Nicholas, ed. *Art Young: His Life and Times.* New York: Sheridan House, 1939.

Fitzgerald, Richard. *Art and Politics: Cartoonists of the "Masses" and "Liberator."* Westport: Greenwood, 1973.

Young, Art. *On My Way: Being the Book of Art Young in Text and Pictures.* New York: Livewright, 1928.

Young Communist League (and Successors)

The YCL, Labor Youth League, DuBois Clubs, Young Workers Liberation League, and (most recently) renamed Young Communist League have operated as the youth wing of the Communist Party. In more successful times, they have reached considerable numbers of youth beyond ordinary Left circles, and exerted a nearly independent force within the social movements of the day. In most times, they have provided a youth corps of future Party activists and leaders, made up in large part—especially in recent decades—of Communists' descendants.

In April 1922, as the Communist movement prepared to come "aboveground" from its persecuted and insular existence, the Young Communist League formed secretly in Bethel, Connecticut; the next month, a "legal convention" was held for the new Young Workers League. As a document of the latter declared, the new movement sought to play its role "by participating in the struggle of the working-class youth for a better chance to live . . . stressing the most vital issues that confront the youth." The two organizations merged a few years later into the YCL, with the same intent and essentially the same membership, its leaders generally drawn from prominent young members of the CP proper.

The 1920s proved both a difficult and a fascinating time for the YCL. More than the adult movement, largely made up of stable, ethnic community members (such as Finns and Lithuanians) not greatly involved in the frantic factionalism of the period, the YCL was riven by efforts to follow the trends and bitter arguments of the day. At its best, the YCL/YWL recruited thousands of young, largely second-generation ethnic radicals—children of socialists or friends of socialists' children—in urban areas, especially Jewish neighborhoods. These young recruits exhibited enormous energy, determination, and—in many threatening situations—great courage. From Chicago, New York, and smaller towns they ventured out to strike scenes in textile towns or coal patches where Communists had influence, aided logistics, distributed the *Daily Worker,* and attempted to organize YCL/YWL branches (in many cases, these formed only to dissolve not long afterward). In 1925, the YWL claimed a membership of 4,000 and a readership of its lively semimonthly organ, the *Young Worker,* considerably higher.

It is doubtful that the YCL/YWL reached a figure much higher before the Depression. In many places, younger Communists "assigned" to the YCL had also multiple other duties (such as work in non-English language circles, or Negro-oriented movements, or peace movements, etc.) that prevented them from serious youth engagement. However, they learned the internal logic of the Party as few else could. Among the later national leaders produced by the YCL/YWL could be counted Jack Stachel, John Williamson, Sam Darcy, Harry Haywood, Pat Toohey, Carl Winter, and Gil Green. They also managed, in the *Young Worker,* to produce at times a fine account of working and living conditions as seen by rebellious, even alienated lower-class youth. Second-generation immigrants, they used the YCL as a mechanism to grow out of their particular ethnic communities, and to seek to establish themselves in the English-speaking majority culture. Holding views distant from those in "American" culture, including the English-speaking working class, the YCLers necessarily formed their own subgroup, whose intensity—and fervent expectation—overcame the sense of collective isolation, but at a cost.

In the early years of the Depression, that cost became more evident. While the YCL blossomed to perhaps 10,000 members, it developed at first little of the momentum anticipated in an obvious social crisis. The *Young Communist* remained a junior version of adult Communist publications rather than a paper aimed successfully at American youth. Sectarian rancor prevented YCL members from reaching out to liberals and socialists who were also beginning, at the local level, to wrestle with the severe problems of mass poverty and lack of community organization. As in the 1920s, YCLers could be found in mass struggles—such as the Harlan County, Kentucky, mine-workers' mobilization of 1932—but largely by virtue of being sent in from the outside. Outstanding individual YCLers, in any case, often abandoned youth activity as such to travel to a factory sector where unionization seemed possible. Outside the ethnic neighborhoods of major eastern and midwestern cities, that shift meant nominal YCL activity.

Nevertheless, the YCL registered some major successes. Within the Trade Union Unity League organizations, youth sections were formed, through YCL prodding, to articulate the special problems of young workers. In 1932 the YCL launched its earliest efforts to build a broad antifascist youth front, a project that gained steam over the decade. In neighborhood situations of strength, the approach differed in important ways. YCLers began to participate in immediate struggles, and to draw practical conclusions. At first engaged (with other Communists) in direct-action marches on city hall and other such dramatic (but frequently bloody, and generally unsuccessful) tactics, they turned increasingly to lower profile work among their own unpoliticized peers. Here, the leadership of 1920s YCL veterans, most of all Gil Green, became crucial. Somewhat anticipating the Popular Front, YCLers in many circumstances eased their personal isolation, abandoned the strident calls for a "Soviet America," and began effective mass work on immediate issues at hand.

The turn toward the Popular Front, in 1934–35, made far more effective action possible. The YCL operated, for the duration of the 1930s, at the historical peak of its influence. Its new publication, *Champion of Youth* (later, *Champion Youth Monthly*), achieved a respectability that earlier YCLers could only have fantasized, with a much-sharpened format, a wide circulation on campuses, and contributors that included Sinclair Lewis, Robert Morse Lovett, sportswriter John R. Tunis, and City College of New York basketball coach Nat Holman.

Ironically, at no point did the YCL receive as much institutional competition from other CP units equally eager for youth and student participation. The National Student League, founded in 1931 and merged with the Student League for Industrial Democracy in 1935, occupied a far more public arena. Youth sections of the International Workers Order, especially among the more ethnically identified teens, also usurped what otherwise might have been (and had been in the 1920s) YCL terrain. The fast-rising labor movement spirited more young people away. Yet the YCL found its niche around and through these and other mass organizations of the Left and of the broader American society. In substantially Jewish, lower-class neighborhoods especially, the YCL was able to establish clubhouses with a nonpolitical, cultural appeal to school friends and others outside the Left networks. At its peak, the New York YCL alone had perhaps 12,000 members, with clubs of 200–500 in such districts as the Lower East Side, Williamsburg, Brownsville, Yorkville, Harlem, and the South Bronx.

Within Left-oriented mass-affiliated organizations, such as the American League Against War and Fascism, the Southern Negro Youth Congress, or the American Youth Congress, the YCL placed and trained its members in organizing skills and directed their political orientation on specific issues. In sports activities (YCLers tilted toward the Brooklyn Dodgers) and music (YCLers tended to love swing), even more perhaps than in the Popular Front politics of the day, the YCL effected an Americanization more organic than any other section of the Communist movement. The admiration YCLers stirred from the likes of Eleanor Roosevelt, who took up the American Youth Act sponsored by the YCL, seemed to demonstrate this achievement. In all, the YCL seemingly represented, for that optimistic moment, the generation that would make the American Left into a movement of millions. Perhaps the World Assembly of Youth Against Fascism, in Poughkeepsie, New York, in 1937, and the Madison Square Garden Swing Concert of 1939, sponsored by the YCL, equally symbolized in their own distinct ways the possibilities ahead.

YCLers had succeeded even more grandly, perhaps, outside the Left orbits proper. Hundreds if not thousands entered industry for the industrial union drive, and many achieved union leadership at the local level during the crucial years. In a scattering of sites, such as New York's District 65, the "Fur Floor Boys" of the Furriers Union, the United Electrical Workers, and the Ford River Rouge Plant in Dearborn, YCLers outnumbered CP members. Their special approach to young workers distinguished their efforts. On the international front, a majority of the 3,200 American Communists who volunteered for the Abraham Lincoln Brigade were YCLers, leaving behind many enthusiastic supporters for whom that war was a peak of activity.

Despite these impressive efforts, the YCL organization had not reached far beyond the older ethnic limits of the Left, or sunk in its roots deeply. With the succession of the Hitler-Stalin Pact, the brief but telling Red-Scare, and the national mobilization following the Pearl Harbor attack, the YCL lost its immediate prospects, the bulk of its active members, and even the tone of its periodicals. The 1943 dissolution of the CP also dissolved the YCL, into American Youth for Democracy, but unlike the parent group, it did not reestablish itself as such in 1945. Party youth sections grew but did not especially flourish, and what youth activity took place in the immediate postwar years centered around the revival of fraternal movements such as the powerful Jewish People's Fraternal Order, friendship work with the Soviet Union (the American section of the World Federation of Democratic Youth), coalitions joined to the broader liberal movement and Henry Wallace's Progressive Party campaign for the presidency (American Youth for Democracy, succeeded by the short-lived Young Progressives of America).

The Labor Youth League, founded in 1949 on the morrow of the disappointing Wallace vote, had a timbre distinctly different from its predecessors. It aimed itself along familiar lines, with special emphasis on the Cold War crisis, racism, and the war in Korea. It reestablished *Challenge* as a monthly publication, pressed the government for the eighteen-year-old vote, more money for school building programs, a higher minimum wage, and similar issues intended to gather support from working-class youth. It sponsored and drew close to a journal intended to have more popular appeal, *New Foundations,* with a format revised in 1951 to feature cultural discussions. Given the period, the LYL carried on a remarkable array of agitation. But times had changed, a fact reflected most evidently in the GI Bill, which opened up college education to the working class for the first time. The LYL gained its basic constituency from college-bound, generally upwardly mobile intellectuals more theoretical-minded and more theoretically open-minded than their predecessors. Claiming up to 200 chapters and 5,000 members, the LYL sometimes—especially after appearances in 1953–54 before the Subversive Activities Control Board—operated as a semi-secret organization. (On large and liberal campuses such as the University of Wisconsin, it might have "open" and "secret" members.) It did not grow to a mass movement so much as train its activists for intellectual, social, cultural, and organizational contributions to the civil rights, antiwar, and other movements in later decades. Former members loomed especially large in campus life of the 1960s, as senior advisers to the New Left.

The CP dissolved the LYL in 1957, amid the internal upheavals of the Twentieth Soviet Congress. In the aftermath, a few branches of the LYL retained their name, but for the most part, new groups such as the Progressive Youth Organizing Committee, Teens Ahead, or Burning Issues grew up on the local level, sometimes successfully attaching themselves to civil rights and other current movements. In 1965, drawing initially upon local initiatives on the West Coast, the DuBois Clubs were formed. (Richard Nixon would charge, with unintended hilarity, that the name's similarity to "The Boys Clubs" had been intended to confuse youth.) Never more than a small number within the massive political mobilization of the time, the DuBois Clubs were distinguished by their multiracial composition and their earnestness. Often raised within the Left, their members had organizing skills especially useful in a variety of campus and community movements. But persistently overshadowed, they dissolved in 1971.

The Young Workers Liberation League, founded that year, represented an effort to recombine campus and community activities in a broader public movement, successor to a collapsing New Left. To a certain extent, the YWLL succeeded in recruiting disappointed New Left veterans and other young people. It hesitantly embraced such new causes as women's liberation (not, however, gay liberation), retaining heavy stress upon racial equality and class issues. Despite activity in a broad spectrum of contemporary movements, however, the YWLL reached no more than a few thousand membership, and dissolved in 1984. The newly reorganized Young Communist League, in effect the YWLL under a different name, made a more ambitious beginning, including a fresh magazine, *Dynamic*, and enjoyed a series of small victories such as electing a student body co-president at a prominent eastern school. *See also*: Communist Party, Student Movements—1930s

—Paul Buhle

REFERENCES

Glaberman, Martin, and George P. Rawick. "'Champion of Youth' and 'Champion of Labor Monthly.'" In *The American Radical Press, 1880–1960, I*, edited by Joseph Conlin. Westport: Greenwood Press, 1974.

Highlights of a Fighting History: Sixty Years of the Communist Party USA. New York: International Publishers, 1979.

Klehr, Harvey. *The Heyday of American Communism: The Depression Decade*. New York: Basic Books, 1984.

Reminiscences of former LYL members. In *History & the New Left: Madison, Wisconsin, 1950–1970*, edited by Paul Buhle. Philadelphia: Temple University Press, 1989.

Young People's Socialist League

Long known as "Yipsel," the YPSL represented youth and, often, an organized Left within the Socialist Party. Unlike the Young Communist League, it could never be viewed as merely a youth expression of the adult movement, but was seen rather as a radical youth movement in which the SP played a generally supportive, avuncular role.

The youth movement, restricted in the nineteenth century socialist organizations to fraternal and cultural auxiliaries, grew up in the early years of the SP through a number of individual groups (some with names such as the Athenian Literary Society, or the Social Science Study Club) created by SP locals to attract young people mainly through recreational programs. The Young Socialist League of Chicago, perhaps the best known, occupied a floor of the *Chicago Daily Socialist* building and claimed 300 members. By the 1912 apex of the Party, the convention officially gave its stamp of approval to such experiments and promised to aid them. Following the logic of the nineteenth-century ethnic movement, the Women's Department was given initial responsibility for building a socialist youth bloc.

By 1915 a coherent national organization had been established, with an age limit established at fifteen to thirty years. YPSL national secretary William F. Kruse claimed a membership of 5,000 in 147 cities, the *Young Socialists' Magazine* with a circulation of 10,000, and a special YPSL number of the *American Socialist* running to 90,000. With the coming of World War I, YPSL fell under government repression,

Kruse received a twenty-year sentence and other leaders varying amounts for opposition to American involvement in the war. In 1919, their membership reported at 10,000, Yipsels voted in convention to join the Communist movement—itself on the verge of debilitating internal division. The first golden age of the movement had come to an end.

By the early 1920s, the YPSL had successfully reorganized under the leadership of former Harvard student Albert Weisbord. While Weisbord himself defected to the Communist movement in 1924, the Yipsels carried on a vigorous campaign in Robert LaFollette's 1924 Progressive Party presidential bid. The decline of the SP thereafter deprived the YPSL of finances and momentum. In 1929 it began to revive in force. The organization reappeared as a national movement in 1932, as part of the dynamic Norman Thomas presidential campaign. By the following year, it began publication of the *Challenge*, and embarked on an ambitious series of campaigns around the labor and unemployed movements.

With an exceptionally strong following in Greater New York of several thousand and ardent branches in Chicago, Philadelphia, Boston, Pittsburgh, Milwaukee, and elsewhere, the movement became a major player in SP affairs. Indeed, the often aging, foreign-born, and geographically scattered adult movement depended on the YPSL (along with its campus sister organization, the Student League for Industrial Democracy) for serious, organized political competition to the Communist Party. This circumstance gave the political favorites of Yipsels—the leftish "Militants" around Norman Thomas rather than the "Old Guard" around the Rand School, the *New Leader*, and the garment trades—an important factional advantage. It also heightened the internal conflict in the SP, resulting in the 1936 departure of the Old Guard with its major institutions. The YPSL overwhelmingly opposed any support of potential imperialist wars, even those against the likes of Hitler, and it shunned electoral alliances with the Democrats. Naturally, then, Yipsels early suspended their cooperation with their Young Communist opposite numbers in the student movement when the CP entered its Popular Front mode.

From an SP viewpoint, YPSL had only avoided the frying pan for the fire. Drawn to the Trotskyists, who had joined the Socialists in 1936 intent upon building internal caucuses and "capturing" members, the YPSL came to be looked upon, in large part, as a now-disloyal element. Denied credentials to the 1937 convention—in some cases expelled from "reorganized" Socialist locals—the several hundred Trotskyist-minded Yipsels formed the "YPSL (Fourth International)," which itself dissipated with the war and further splits in the Trotskyist movement. In any case, the overwhelming popularity of Franklin Roosevelt, the growing antifascist sentiment, and the growing influence of the CP limited the appeal of any socialist youth movement uncompromised on liberal capitalism and the war. A second golden age, brief but furious, had nearly closed on the movement.

Many young socialists, organized and unorganized, simply gave their full attention to the CIO and the labor movement generally. YPSL served, in the long run, as a school for labor leadership—without, however, itself taking much benefit from this estimable contribution. Meanwhile, the remnants of the YPSL remained a mainstay of the now-floundering, but determined, SP. Working mainly with pacifist and church groups to oppose U.S. involvement in world war, it helped organize the Youth Committee Against War, and the youth section of the Keep America Out of War Congress, in which Norman Thomas was a leading figure. Briefly, despite the renewed threats of government repression, the movement caught fire. The invasion of Pearl Harbor dampened such energies and the national mobilization effectively dispersed YPSL personnel.

Maintaining a tenuous existence for another decade, YPSL suffered one final prominent defection in 1953 when its foremost spokesman, Michael Harrington, led a noteworthy group into the Young Socialist League of the Independent Socialist League (formerly the Workers Party, whose predecessors had drawn another generation of YPSLs into Trotskyism sixteen years earlier). The YSL, a lively discussion circle on several campuses of the 1950s, returned *en bloc* to the SP alongside the bulk of the Independent Socialist League for the 1958 merger. With figures such as Harrington, Bayard Rustin, David McReynolds, and Bogdan Denitch, the reconstituted YPSL took on new life.

Although hardly numerous, YPSL of the late 1950s and early 1960s essentially provided leadership—sometimes openly and sometimes less than openly—to the emerging "movement," from civil rights to the Student Peace Union. Here and there, they could also be found to be the leading personnel of the campus Young Democrats, or of the youth wing of the Americans for Democratic Action. Despite such widespread influence, YPSL never regained a wide membership, perhaps because its style of maneuver did little to encourage mass enrollment.

The birth of Students for a Democratic Society in 1962, out of the Student League for Industrial Democracy, placed YPSL in the awkward position of loyal youth wing to the Old Left—similar, in a certain generational respect, to the Communists' and orthodox Trotskyists' own youth movements. SDS, and many local movements under a variety of names, rapidly outstripped YPSL, whose leaders increasingly made a reputation for their hard-line Cold War positions. While SDS urged "immediate withdrawal" from Vietnam, YPSL launched its major late-1960s campaign as "Negotiations Now," a move seen by most student activists as backhanded support for further U.S. occupation. It attracted comparatively little following.

YPSL virtually ceased activity in 1972, with the departure of Michael Harrington and his followers from the SP to the Democratic Socialist Organizing Committee. Remaining a part of the rightward-leaning Social Democrats, USA, YPSL officially disbanded in 1977. Meanwhile DSOC, and its successor, Democratic Socialists of America, included among their leadership rolls many former YPSL luminaries. DSA Youth appeared, more than any other existing movement in the 1980s, to be the lineal successor to the YPSL of yore. *See also*: Socialist Party, Student Movements of the 1930s, Trotskyism

—*Paul Buhle*

REFERENCES

Peterson, Patti. "The Young Socialist Movement in America from 1905–1940: A Study of the Young People's Socialist Movement." Ph.D. diss., University of Wisconsin, 1974.

Young Pioneers of America

The YPA, the children's organization of the Communist Party of the United States, was founded to provide "proletarian education" for working-class children between the ages of seven and fourteen. Its membership consisted mainly of children from Communist families.

The Young Pioneers was organized in 1923 as the Junior Section of the Young Workers League, which was the youth section of the Workers Party. When the "legal" WP and the "clandestine" CP merged in 1926, the Young Pioneers became the designated children's organization of the CP. The YPA retained this form until 1934, when it faded away and its role was taken over by the Junior Section of the International Workers Order (IWO), the Communist-led federation of ethnically based fraternal benefit societies. YPA publications included the *Young Comrade* (1924–26), the *Young Pioneer* (1926–31), and the *New Pioneer* (1931–34, taken over by IWO Juniors, 1934–38).

The Young Pioneers of America drew upon the traditions of socialist and anarchist educational programs for children in the United States and were influenced by the development of Young Pioneers organizations in Germany and the Soviet Union.

The Young Pioneers had three functions within the Communist movement: developing Communist education for its membership; organizing working-class children into political campaigns; and providing the political leadership for more broadly based children's groups within the Communist orbit.

Communist-influenced organizations often had separate children's sections in which Young Pioneers were expected to play a role similar to that of CP members in adult organizations. Such was the case with the Young Liberators of the International Labor Defense. During the 1926 silk strike in Paterson, New Jersey, the 1929 textile strike in Gastonia, North Carolina, and the 1929 strikes led by the National Miners Union, the YPA mobilized workers' children in association with the Trade Union Unity League (TUUL).

The Pioneers were strongest among children in the Jewish working-class communities of New York and the Finnish agricultural and mining communities of the Midwest. Young Pioneer meetings involved discussions of current events and planning political campaigns. Readings were drawn from a series of Communist children's books. The YPA campaigned against child labor, "bourgeois, reactionary" children's organizations like the Boy Scouts, and patriotic propaganda in the schools. They fought for integrated swimming pools and free lunches for children of the unemployed. They also sponsored summer camps, often in association with other Communist-affiliated organizations.

The YPA emphasized class identities to the exclusion of ethnicity, which they viewed as nationalist and reactionary. This created a tension between the YPA and Communist parents of immigrant backgrounds who wanted to transmit their ethnic heritage to their children. This narrow understanding of culture was transformed later in the 1930s when the ethnically organized IWO Juniors replaced the Young Pioneers as the Communist children's organization during the period of the Popular Front. *See also*: Young Communist League

—Paul C. Mishler

REFERENCES

Mishler, Paul C. "The Littlest Proletariat: American Communists and Their Children, 1922–1950," Ph.D. diss., Boston University, 1988.

Teitelbaum, Kenneth, and William Reese. "American Socialist Pedagogy and Experimentation in the Progressive Era: The Socialist Sunday School." *History of Education Quarterly* 23, no. 4 Winter 1983.

U.S. Congress. House. Special Committee to Investigate Communist Activities. *Investigation of Communist Propaganda*. 71st Congress. 2d Sess., 1930. Vol. 1, pt. 3.

YOUTH AGAINST WAR AND FASCISM: see TROTSKYISM

ZEIDLER, FRANK: see MILWAUKEE, MUNICIPAL SOCIALISM

DI ZUKUNFT

Founded in 1890, the Yiddish-language *Di Zukunft* (The future) is the longest-surviving Left periodical in the United States (the Socialist Labor Party's tabloid, the *People*, founded in 1891, stands second). In its heyday, it was by far the most circulated journal, and the closest U.S. relative to European social democratic theoretical publications.

Di Zukunft began life as the monthly organ of the SLP's Yiddish-language sections. In some respects, it greatly resembled the popularizing literary-scientific German-American socialist tabloids published either as separate weeklies or as weekend supplements to the daily press. *Di Zukunft* sought to uplift readers with elementary explanations of astronomy, sound waves, or the technical components of poetry. Like the other papers, it carried lavish tributes to historical, political, and intellectual figures, especially to recently deceased heroes such as British socialist Renaissance man William Morris. From almost the earliest days, however, *Di Zukunft* permitted a level of serious controversy rare outside the space-restricted letters columns of the SLP press. The journal's editors, leading luminaries of Yiddish ghetto socialism, including B. Feigenbaum, Philip Krantz, and Abraham Cahan, seemed already themselves too large for the confinement of Daniel DeLeon's political leadership.

Breaking with DeLeon, *Di Zukunft* barely survived the fractured politics and economic hard times of the late 1890s and the first years of the twentieth century. A succession of editors, including Morris Winchevsky, rode herd over a rambunctious group of ghetto writers who, for a variety of reasons, had chosen not to transfer their intellectual energies into English. Like the *International Socialist Review* of Chicago, *Di Zukunft* did not especially prosper in circulation with the early upswing of the Socialist Party. More Jews than other American socialists interested themselves in theory, but not so many as in a counterpart European movement. Nor, perhaps most important, did publication in *Di Zukunft* confer the prestige and dignity of similar activity in the German *Neue Zeit*, its inevitable model. Still, page-for-page, *Di Zukunft* had more theoretical discussion—and far more literary-cultural discussion—that any other U.S. publication, particularly after the *ISR* converted to a popular format in 1908.

The ascendancy of Abraham Liessin (1872–1938) to the editor's chair in 1902 changed the publication's entire relation with the Jewish community. A melodramatic poet and leading Yiddish-language socialist in Minsk, Liessin, soon after his arrival in the U.S., had become a sort of cultural organizer and intellectual-political magus. Working out a shrewd arrangement on all sides, Liessin managed to obtain the financial backing of

Abraham Cahan without overt editorial limitations, and the warm support of Jewish unions and the Left community leaders for his project of making *Di Zukunft* more popular and more political.

With an enlarged format and an ardent monthly editorial on the pressing political questions of the day, *Di Zukunft* gained a new visibility in the ghetto. Liessin became a guide to the perplexed immigrant seeking a balance of socialist and ethnic aspirations through the confused and difficult wartime era. Indeed, Liessin's articulation of political identity made him and *Di Zukunft* important to the evolving philosophy of the Jewish Bund across Europe. The Russian Revolution challenged Liessin's particular faith, and the postwar attraction of Russia greatly diminished *Di Zukunft*'s audience, but not nearly as much as the loss of faith in democratic socialism and the tendency to assimilation. Doggedly loyal to his position, Liessin continued his policies, slowly accepting the inevitability of Jewish socialism's marginality. His death might have killed less institutionally rooted publications. *Di Zukunft* has continued with a succession of editors and, over the years, a more single-minded literary approach to the preservation of vanishing *Yiddishkayt*. In the background of cultural discussion, however, remains a strong sense of Jewish history and a hope for the social transformation of class society at large.

See also: Yiddish Left

—*Paul Buhle*

REFERENCES

Feyn, Yoni. "Di Antviklung fun 'A Probe'." *Di Zukunft* 95 (January–April, 1988).

Rogoff, Harry. "Abraham Liessin." In *Nine Yiddish Writers*. New York: The Forward, 1931.

Special issue on A. Liessin. *Di Zukunft* 24 (April 1919).

Index of Names

Subject Index